MANUAL OF
Orchids

THE NEW **ROYAL HORTICULTURAL SOCIETY** DICTIONARY

MANUAL OF
Orchids

Consultant Editor JOYCE STEWART
Series Editor MARK GRIFFITHS

TIMBER PRESS
Portland, Oregon

Derived from
The New Royal Horticultural Society Dictionary of Gardening
Editor in Chief Anthony Huxley
Editor Mark Griffiths, Managing Editor Margot Levy
in four volumes, 1992.

First published 1995 by Macmillan Reference Books
a division of Macmillan Publishers Limited
25 Eccleston Place, London SW1W 9NF
and Basingstoke

Associated companies around the world

First published in North America in 1995 by
Timber Press, Inc.
The Haseltine Building
133 S.W. Second Avenue, Suite 450
Portland, Oregon 97204, U.S.A.

ISBN 0-88192-334-6

Printed and bound in Great Britain by
Butler & Tanner Ltd, Frome and London

Contents

Preface

Orchids are unlike any other plants, and not even like each other. Blanched, below ground, there grows in Australia a plant which, if exhumed, might be thought to combine the looks of an artichoke heart and a witchetty grub. Passing its entire life just beneath the surface, it needs neither the free air for its pollinators, nor light for food. In Southeast Asia and Polynesia grow distant relations of this buried bloom. Their cane-like stems, taller than a man, form great clumps lodged in trees and decked with metre-long sprays of leopard-spotted flowers. Across Europe, small, terrestrial herbs have evolved as masters of deceit. Mimicking female insects in outline, texture, colour and scent, their flowers lure the males of the species into false acts of procreation that result in the spilling of a thousand seeds. In the forests of Madagascar, a plant can be found whose starry white flowers bear a nectar-filled spur over 30cm long designed to woo a single species of Cyrano-like moth. Elsewhere, natural selection has wrought adaptations so ingenious as to make its random basis seem scarcely plausible – flowers with mobile parts, honey scents and carrion odours, explosive pollen, pollinator prisons, pitstops and pitfalls. Some orchids impersonate not insects but wholly unrelated *plants*, whose pollinators they casually poach without so much as a promise of nectar. Such variety is by no means confined to the business of reproduction. There are epiphytes, lithophytes, saprophytes and terrestrials, diminutive herbs, robust semi-succulents and vigorous climbers, species with no leaves, species so small that they can colonize others' leaves and some with leaves so beautiful that they have been held in the lore of their native lands to be the tattered remnants of the saris of fleeing wood nymphs.

Nothing if not paradoxical, orchids outnumber almost all other families of flowering plants in terms of taxa, yet they have a reputation for rarity that is largely deserved. They have taken root on almost every surface and feature of the landscape, yet are more adversely affected by environmental change than any of their neighbours. More often than not, 'success' for these most advanced and showy plants will depend on the lowliest of micro-organisms. No other plants produce viable seed in greater quantity, and no other seed is less likely to germinate. In the last century, a sum equivalent to five under-gardeners' annual wages was paid for a single specimen – no plants are more highly prized, yet only one among twenty thousand species has true economic value. Orchids have achieved a higher profile and exercised more horticultural talents and resources than any other group of plants, but they remain, perhaps, the least commonly grown and least easy to perceive as belonging to mainstream gardening.

In view of which, it is hardly surprising that orchids should have taken a root-hold on culture as well as horticulture. The tubers of *Ophrys* and *Orchis* were esteemed in Ancient Greece and Medieval England as fertility emblems and a source of aphrodisiacs. The spotted leaves of *Dactylorhiza* were said to have been marked by blood falling from the Cross. The 'long purples' that accompanied Ophelia's decline and demise were orchids. More recently, they have become synonymous in the general consciousness with adventure, with a type of decadent opulence, and with sex. Orchids set the scene in *The Big Sleep* and solved the crime *In the Heat of the Night*. What was for Proust the perfect symbol of Odette's sensuality was also the thing denied Miss Blandish. The equatorial regions of the *Boy's Own Magazine* were festooned with orchids blue, black and man-eating [sic], variously to be sought for science or escaped by feats of derring-do. In her *Notes for an*

Herbarium, (*Pour un Herbier*, 1948), Colette tells the tale of a 19th-century big-game hunter with a taste for killing jaguars. One day, having sought his quarry in vain, our hunter rests beside a tree. In its branches he spies an orchid, 'one that resembled a bird, a crab, a butterfly, an evil charm, a sexual organ – maybe, even, a flower'. The hunter lays down his rifle and climbs high into the tree to 'bag' this bewitching bloom. Armed with only the orchid, he then returns to the forest floor and comes face-to-face with a magnificent jaguar. The cat looks the hunter up and down, and continues serenely on its way. Not long after this incident, Colette tells us, the hunter resolves to abandon his rifle altogether, becoming a botanist instead. The conclusion of this Damascene tale captures the orchid's mystique and allure:

> I would love to know whether the hunter converted out of gratitude toward the merciful jaguar, or whether the orchid – whose spell is more powerful than that of any other game – had cast him forever into those regions where a man, caught between two dangers, never fails to choose the greater.

Carl Theodor Hartweg chose the greater danger. Within one month of arriving in Mexico to begin his 1836 collecting trip, he had discovered 65 new species of orchid. Four years later, he was active in Guatemala, where he found a further 140 species.

Hartweg's enterprise was sponsored by what would later become the Royal Horticultural Society. Newly arrived in London, his discoveries fell under the gaze of one of the Society's greatest luminaries, the orchidologist John Lindley, remembered to this day in the names of so many orchid species, and in that of the Society's library. Lindley's devotion to Orchidaceae was shared by other gardening 'greats' active within the Royal Horticultural Society – for example, those unrivalled orchid growers the Veitch family. By the time of the Great War, Messrs. Veitch were responsible for the introduction of 232 orchid species, the first orchid hybrids and publication of the seminal *Veitch's Manual of Orchidaceous Plants*. James Veitch (1815–1869) is commemorated in one of the Society's highest honours. Elected in 1885, Sir Trevor Lawrence was one of the Royal Horticultural Society's most distinguished Presidents. The caption of his Spy portrait in *Vanity Fair* may be general enough (it reads, simply, 'Horticulture'), but he is pictured clutching the blooms of *Laelia tenebrosa* – orchids, close to his heart and to the heart of the Society over which he presided for 28 years. Through the work of its committees and publications, the Society's commitment to orchids has, if anything, deepened since the great age of collecting. It is only appropriate that, of all the projects to grow out of *The New Royal Horticultural Society Dictionary of Gardening*, a manual of orchids should be foremost.

The genus-by-genus accounts in this Manual are largely drawn from the Dictionary, where species-coverage and nomenclature were adjudicated by Joyce Stewart, Dr Phillip Cribb and Dr Alec Pridgeon. Their great labour is, again, gratefully acknowledged here. Among the many who deserve thanks for their hard work in compiling descriptions, Isobyl La Croix (on the orchids of Africa) and Mollie Pottinger (*Paphiopedilum*) made particularly important contributions. The accounts of intergeneric hybrids, grexes and cultivars were written by Joyce Stewart. As Consultant Editor, she has also written the Introduction to this volume and proved the perfect referee for the remainder of the text, ever generous with her time and vast expertise. Warmest thanks are also due to Dr Brent Elliott and his colleagues at the Lindley Library, and to the Keeper and Librarian of the Royal Botanic Gardens, Kew.

Kew's long association with orchids is nowhere more evident than in the thousands of illustrations produced by Walter Hood Fitch under the aegis of the Hookers. Around 1869, Fitch said of these plants:

> Perhaps there are no flowers more varied in size, form and colour than those of the orchids, and, I think I may add, more difficult to sketch … Indeed, they almost seem to have been created to puzzle botanists or to test the artist's abilities, and consequently they are all the

more worthy of a skilful pencil in endeavouring to do justice to them ... It is impossible to lay down rules for sketching these protean plants, but if the structure is not correctly rendered in a drawing, it is worse than useless, as no colouring will redeem it.

In drawing the plates for this Manual, the artists' abilities have been tested and their pencils (or pens) found so skilful that no colouring is needed. Thanks are due especially to Camilla Speight, who prepared all the new artwork, apart from a few efforts of my own, and to those artists whose contributions to the *New Royal Horticultural Society Dictionary of Gardening* are reproduced here – Christine Hart-Davies (*Dactylorhiza*; *Ophrys*; *Orchis*), Margaret Stevens (*Paphiopedilum*), and Susanna Stuart-Smith (*Cattleya*). It remains to thank Mick Card and, as ever, Margot Levy.

Mark Griffiths   London 1995

Introduction

The orchids have been described as the 'royal family' of the Plant Kingdom. In many respects orchids are special, intriguing, and different from other flowering plants. They are not difficult to grow, but each has its own unique requirements. Vegetatively they are mostly small perennials, herbaceous, very varied, but not conspicuous. It is their elegant and often exciting flowers which make them instantly recognizable.

The Orchidaceae is the largest family of all the monocotyledons, with *c* 900 genera and more than 20,000 species. The Compositae (daisy family) contains *circa* 1550 genera and 25,000 species and is often cited as the largest family of all the flowering plants. Nearly 100,000 artificial orchid hybrids have been registered and this total is being added to by new crosses every day. In 1994 alone, over 3,000 new crosses were registered at the Royal Horticultural Society, the applications coming from many different parts of the world.

Wild orchids flourish in undisturbed places wherever conditions are suitable for plant life. Seven species have been recorded within the Arctic Circle and fifty are known in the British Isles. But it is in the tropical and subtropical regions of the world that the majority of species is found. The mountains of Central and South America, parts of the Himalaya range, and the montane areas of Borneo and Madagascar are particularly rich. In these and other areas, the mosaic of hills and valleys covered with forest, bush or grassland provides many niches for orchid plants.

More than half the known species grow as epiphytes, clinging to the bark of trees and shrubs and obtaining all the minerals they need from nutrients dissolved in the rain water that percolates their roots. Some have become adapted to life on rocks or cliffs or in rock crevices and are known as lithophytes. Others, the terrestrials, grow in the earth, like the vast majority of plants. A few are saprophytic: lacking chlorophyll, they have rhizomes or tubers underground, living in an intimate association with mycorrhizal fungi, and they only put up an aerial stem for a short flowering season. The Australian genus *Rhizanthella* is not only saprophytic, but spends its entire life below the soil surface.

In many regions where orchid species are prolific, the climate has a regular alternation of wet and dry seasons which imposes a particular kind of stress on plants. Orchids are adapted to seasonal habits of growth, flowering and resting, and many have specialized vegetative features to help them survive drought. Swollen stems called pseudobulbs contain stored moisture that becomes available during long dry periods. The pseudobulbs may become very shrivelled but swell up again when the rains return. Succulent leaves not only conserve moisture, but have developed special photosynthetic techniques enabling them to keep their stomata closed during the heat of the day, and open for gas exchange and moisture loss at night when temperatures are lower. Aerial roots have a thick layer of specialized cells called velamen on their outer surface which helps to absorb moisture from dew, mists and clouds. Being white and filled with air when dry, this layer also protects the inner part of the root from intense heat and light on hot sunny days. Many orchids produce their flowers after a prolonged 'rest' when there is little or no growth because temperatures are too low or there is too little moisture, or not enough light. Hence the late winter and spring months are the best time of year to see a wide variety of orchids in flower.

There is tremendous diversity in the shape, colour, size and fragrance of orchid flowers, yet almost all are alike in their basic form. Six colourful parts, three sepals surrounding three petals, enclose the rather solid central column in every flower. The sepals and petals (tepals) may be similar to each other but most often the dorsal sepal is different from the two lateral ones in size, shape and sometimes colour. Similarly, the petals may be larger or smaller than the sepals, and one of the petals is modified to form a lip, often larger than the rest of the flower. The lip is usually a landing platform for a visiting insect-pollinator. As a rule the lip is on the lower side of the flower because the inferior ovary is twisted through 180° so that the flower is 'resupinate'. In some flowers, however, the ovary is twisted through 360°, while in others it is not twisted at all, and in both of these types the lip is on the upper side of the flower, often protruding between the two enlarged lateral sepals. Such flowers are termed 'non-resupinate'. The slipper orchids depart from the general pattern of the orchid flower in having the lateral sepals fused in a synsepal behind the pouch-like lip. Many orchids in the Subtribe Pleurothallidinae also exhibit fused sepals in varying degrees.

In most orchids there is a single stamen and stigma united in the central column; only the slipper orchids have two stamens, one on each side of the lower surface of the column. Within the stamen all the pollen grains cohere in 1–8 mealy or waxy masses called pollinia. Each of these can be transported to another flower, either alone or altogether, by becoming attached to a visiting insect or bird which is prospecting for some kind of reward.

Part of the mystique of the orchid flower in the mind of many plant-lovers lies in its special adaptations for pollination and its relationship with the pollinator. The shape, colour, size, scent and flowering period seem to be specifically related to a particular creature, usually an insect. Sometimes there is a promise of food in yellow floury cells on the surface, drink such as nectar or alcohol in a long nectary or swollen cells, or the sight of a suitable place to lay eggs in the dark, meaty-looking surface of a flower with a putrid smell. Most strange of all is the deceit practised by bee orchids in Europe and other species in Australia in deluding the insect by their suggestions of sex. Not only do the flowers resemble the female of the species in question in shape, colour and hairiness, but they also produce volatile chemicals very similar to insect pheromones as an added lure. All this happens two or three weeks before the female insects are on the wing so the males cannot resist the flower's attraction. In making repeated visits to several flowers the insects carry pollen from one to another.

If pollination is successful, thousands of seeds will be produced in each orchid fruit or capsule. These are very small and light and easily dispersed by air currents to new sites. There they usually germinate only if they become infected with a symbiotic fungus which forms a mycorrhizal association with the young protocorm and developing roots of the tiny seedling.

Thus orchids face two challenges in their normal life cycle – pollination and germination. The success of both depends on another organism in the immediate environment, an insect and a fungus. Perhaps this dependence explains why orchids are uncommon or rare plants in general but abundant in suitable places. They also face great perils today because so many natural habitats are being destroyed or changed. Where all the trees are felled, the site for epiphytes has gone. When swamps are drained and pastures are treated with chemical fertilizers, the fungi disappear. The production of field and plantation crops deprives insects of their food plants, so that even where a few orchid plants might still survive, there will be no insects to pollinate them. The collection of wild plants for horticulture has also had a deleterious effect on wild populations over the last two hundred years, but is now very carefully controlled. At the same time, methods have been developed to propagate orchids in the glasshouse and laboratory, and both species and man-made hybrids are now available from many reputable growers. There is great interest in growing a wide variety of orchids and there are more growers worldwide than ever before. Thus horticulture plays a role in the conservation of orchids as well as other rare plants.

Orchid Culture

Orchids have been grown under glass in temperate regions for more than two hundred years and are not difficult to maintain if the correct environmental conditions are provided. A major problem in small glasshouses is the excessively high temperatures that can develop in summer, so much more shading is required for orchids than is used for most other glasshouse plants.

Orchids which are not frost-hardy originate from subtropical and tropical parts of the world and, depending on their altitudinal range in nature, are usually designated 'warm', 'intermediate' or 'cool' in their growing requirements. Briefly, each can be defined by the minimum night temperature to be provided during the winter months. If three or four separate houses (or compartments in a large glasshouse) are available, each with different night temperatures, a wide range of orchids can be grown. Where only one glasshouse is available, it is necessary to select those orchids which grow under similar conditions and which are suitable for the degree of warmth that can be provided in winter.

'Warm-growing' orchids are those which occur in the wild at sea level or low altitudes in tropical regions, and hybrids derived from these wild species. They grow and flower best where there is a minimum night temperature of c20–24°C/68–75°F throughout the year. *Phalaenopsis* species and hybrids, *Vanda* and many other vandaceous orchids including the larger angraecums, catasetums, a few paphiopedilums and some of the larger dendrobiums do best under this regime.

'Intermediate-growing' orchids are those from moderate altitudes where the minimum night temperature falls to 15–20°C/58–60°F during the winter months but may be slightly higher during the summer. A wide range of orchids can be grown under glass if these conditions are reproduced, including cattleyas and their relatives and hybrids with laelias, brassavolas, oncidiums, brassias, some coelogynes, many paphiopedilums, dendrobiums and bulbophyllums.

'Cool-growing' orchids are those from medium or high altitudes in the tropics. They grow and flower best where the minimum night temperature drops to c10–13°C/50–55°F during the winter months or even lower for short periods. Slightly higher minimum temperatures are beneficial during the summer. Many kinds of orchids tolerate these temperatures or flourish under them, including cymbidiums, paphiopedilums of montane origin, coelogynes from higher altitudes, masdevallias, odontoglossums and their hybrids, many central American and Andean species including lycastes, laelias, oncidiums and maxillarias, New Guinea and Australian species and many epiphytes from eastern Africa.

These three cultural categories are not always hard and fast. Some orchids will adapt, growing equally well in intermediate as they would in warm conditions and *vice versa*. Likewise 'cool' and 'intermediate' plants may grow happily side-by-side. Although it is best to follow these general divisions, there is scope for experimentation with orchids, especially where space is limited.

Some of these orchids can be grown as house plants in a suitable windowsill, or under artificial light in specialized growth rooms or cabinets.

Orchids of temperate origin do not thrive in heated glasshouses and are usually treated as alpines. They can also be grown in pots in unheated conservatories or as garden plants.

Glasshouse orchids

Some *Paphiopedilum* and *Cymbidium* species and hybrids are grown for cut flower production in glasshouse beds, but most orchids are grown in containers placed on the staging or suspended from the walls or special framework within the glasshouse. Clay or plastic pots are used most frequently, but baskets made of wire or wooden slats are usually used for some of the more robust epiphytes, for plants with a pendulous habit, and for *Stanhopea, Acineta* and *Dracula* whose flowers grow downwards.

In choosing a pot, the need for perfect drainage should be borne in mind. It is usually necessary to enlarge the drainage holes with a hammer or hole saw even if a very loose compost is used. While orchids can be grown with a mixture of other tropical plants, they are usually kept separate as this makes the control of glasshouse pests easier. In either case, it is very important to pay careful attention to hygiene, removing dead leaves and faded blooms regularly as well as unsightly moss and other weeds, and to ensure the correct environmental conditions are maintained (see below under Orchid House).

Composts

For orchids, compost has the dual function of supporting the plant in its container and providing the roots with a medium which is well aerated yet moisture-retentive. It is seldom replaced more than once a year, and often at longer intervals, so it must decompose slowly. Composts in use today are usually mixtures of natural materials, such as pieces of pine or fir bark, coarse grit, coir, fibrous peat, chopped dried leaves or sphagnum, and inert materials like perlite, perlag, pieces of horticultural-grade charcoal and sometimes pieces of polystyrene. Individual growers have favourite mixes best suited to their own glasshouses and different watering regimes. A mix containing large particles with large spaces between them will need watering more frequently than a close mix with particles of small size.

Many growers add bone meal, dried blood or hoof and horn meal to these mixtures when plants are potted. Others prefer a compost which is completely inert so that they can supply known quantities of liquid fertilizer to the plants as a dilute feed on a regular basis throughout the growing season. In commercial nurseries both the watering and feeding are usually computer-controlled.

Two tried and tested compost mixes are given below, but each can be modified to suit individual orchids. Wherever possible, an alternative to fibrous peat should be sought.

Basic epiphyte mix: 3 parts washed bark chips, medium grade; 1 part coarse perlag; 1 part charcoal, horticultural grade; 1 part fibrous peat or coir or broken leaves or chopped sphagnum.

Basic mix for terrestrial orchids: 3 parts fibrous peat or coir; 2 parts coarse perlite; 2 parts coarse grit; 1 part charcoal, horticultural grade.

A fairly new medium for orchid growing is made up of water-repellent rockwool mixed with perlite. In effect it provides a substrate very similar to that of the mossy branches of trees in tropical forests, with a surface of springy, wet, air bubbles surrounding the plant roots. A carefully controlled system of watering and feeding is obviously necessary with this medium, a different system from that undertaken with conventional composts. It may not be convenient to use both rockwool and other composts for plants in a mixed collection, but for odontoglossums and their allies, paphiopedilums and many orchids in the pleurothallid alliance it is proving more successful than most other composts. On the commercial scale where it is used very successfully, the provision of water and nutrients to plants grown in this and similar mixtures is usually computer-controlled.

Potting

Choosing the right size of pot is the first essential when potting an orchid. Its roots need to have ample space within the container, allowing enough space for at least one year's growth. Nonetheless, few plants are so intolerant of overpotting as orchids. Trying to save time by putting plants of small or medium size in a large pot is usually detrimental because too much compost can cause poor drainage. Weak roots need to be restricted and the base of the plant kept dry until healthy new roots develop. Many orchids do best in rather small pots. To ensure that drainage is efficient the container is often filled one third full with pieces of polystyrene, crock or large stones. The crocks should be packed vertically to ensure perfect drainage. Stones are particularly useful in plastic pots as the extra weight provides stability.

With the exceptions of some hardy terrestrials such as *Ophrys*, which may benefit from the transfer of a little of the old compost when repotting, it is essential to prepare fresh compost for each session of potting or repotting. Before use it is usually necessary to soak pine bark, and peat and other components should be moistened slightly. The synthetic materials such as perlite and rockwool are also more pleasant to use if slightly damp.

The technique of potting is simple. The plant is held in the pot with one hand so that the crown of the plant, the base of the pseudobulbs, or the part of the plant from which the roots emerge is just below the level of the rim. Compost is filled in around the roots with the other hand and gently shaken into the spaces between them by tapping the pot gently on the bench several times. Small plants or those with a poor root system may need to be tied to a stake, a short piece of cane or stiff wire, until they become established.

After potting, the compost is usually watered thoroughly, sometimes on two or three consecutive days, to make sure that the constituents are completely moistened. Newly potted plants are then kept dry for two or three weeks to allow the roots to settle. During this time the plants must be kept in a humid place and misted over frequently to stimulate production of new roots and to make sure that the leaves do not become desiccated.

Repotting

Orchid plants need repotting from time to time. After a good season they may begin to grow over the edge of the pot or root growth may be so good that the whole plant is pushed up out of the pot. An abundance of adventitious and aerial roots is quite normal in many genera, particularly *Phalaenopsis* and members of the *Cattleya* alliance, and many plants flower best if they are undisturbed for many seasons. In some genera, notably *Coelogyne* and *Bulbophyllum*, the pot serves as little more than a focus for cascades of rhizomes, while the vandaceous orchids simply use the pot as an anchor. None of these plants is regularly repotted in the wild! In the glasshouse, however, large plants may need dividing or potting on into a larger container. Plants which have died off in the middle or on one side may need rejuvenating.

The commonest reason for repotting is that the compost has deteriorated. If there is difficulty getting a well grown plant out of the old pot, it is sometimes helpful to leave it in a bucket of water for an hour or two. The saturated plant then slides out easily. Where a plant with thick and adhesive roots has become really fixed to the surface of the pot, a hammer may be needed to break the pot; the roots can then be peeled off carefully. Plants grown in rockwool have the advantage that repotting is required much less frequently, and often the rockwool can be used a second time.

During repotting, the old compost is removed and discarded. Dead roots, which are soft and brown, should be removed carefully, as near as possible to the point where they emerge from the upper parts of the plant. It is a good idea to use sterile tools for this operation in order to avoid the transmission of viruses. Healthy roots will be white and should be damaged as little as possible. They are rather brittle, but if they crack no harm will be done. Without compost and with clean healthy roots, the plant can then be carefully examined for any sign of scale insects, treated if necessary, and divided or reshaped as required. Old leafless pseudobulbs can be removed for propagation before the tidy plant is repotted in a clean pot with fresh compost as described above. The stems of monopodial orchids can be shortened, the denuded base usually being discarded and the free-rooting, leafy top replanted, but if there are plenty of aerial roots and leaves on each section, two or more plants will be made from every elongated one.

Some orchids resent disturbance and take a long time to re-establish after repotting. For some of the larger orchids in the *Vanda* alliance, including *Angraecum* species, repotting is rarely necessary as very coarse bark pieces are used in the compost mix and these take a long time to deteriorate unless the plants are frequently over-watered.

Mounted plants

Many epiphytes also grow well if mounted on slabs of cork oak bark of suitable size or firmly attached to wooden slat rafts or to chunks of tree fern fibre. At first, they must be tied firmly to the surface, usually with coarse nylon thread, plastic tape or copper wire, but new roots will soon grow out and attach themselves to the support. Plants with fine roots or a substantial moisture requirement may benefit from being attached to their mounts within an envelope or against a pad of sphagnum moss mixed with a little orchid compost. Mounted plants on bark or tree fern slabs may not need further attention for many years, apart from regular misting or plunging and a weak liquid feed from time to time. If the plants become loose it may be desirable to transfer them to a fresh mount. Sometimes a thick growth of unwanted moss or slime mould may develop around mounted plants and this may need to be removed from time to time to make sure the roots do not lack air.

Watering and spraying

Most orchid plants need to dry out periodically and many adapt well to a weekly watering regime. A few need watering or misting every day, especially those which are mounted, while others grow best with a long, moist growing season followed by a dry period of several months. The best approach for the new grower is to try to find out as much as possible about the natural habitat of the different kinds of orchids and find ways of imitating the wild environment in the management of the glasshouse. Rainwater is best, but it should be stored in a dark tank in the glasshouse so that it stays clean and is at the right temperature for the plants.

After repotting, plants will need very little water in the pot because their roots are inactive. Swamping them at this stage may damage those roots which remain. During a period of a month or two, the plant's moisture needs can be met by spraying or misting over the leaves, early in the day or, on sunny days, several times during the day. It is best to make sure that moisture does not lodge in leaf axils or the apex of new shoots overnight when temperatures drop, as the recently established plants may be more susceptible to water-borne disease. Misting over the leaves is always a useful exercise on sunny days as it helps to ensure high humidity in the greenhouse and also lowers the leaf temperature.

Once the plants are properly established in their pots or baskets and new root growth is evident, a regular watering regime can begin. On each occasion plants should be heavily and thoroughly watered, so that the compost is really wetted. If a hose is used, it is helpful to fit a water breaker to it, or to use a watering lance with a fine rose. This ensures a gentle flow of water so that the loose compost is not washed out of the pot. The frequency of watering will depend on the size of the pot and the kinds of compost used, as well as on the weather. There is really no substitute for daily inspection of the plants. The need for water can often be assessed by the weight of the pots once one becomes used to handling them. Once or twice a week is a good routine, but daily watering may be necessary in summer. During the winter, watering is usually reduced to once every week or two, and for a few plants water is given only monthly. Some people prefer to water their plants early in the day so that the foliage will have dried off by nightfall when temperatures drop. In the tropical habitats of many orchids, however, storms arise at midday or in the afternoons and the plants are frequently still wet at night. Some growers make a habit of watering their plants in the late afternoon and, provided there is good air movement within the glasshouse to prevent stagnation and inhibit pathogens, many plants grow well under this regime.

Feeding

Because orchid composts are relatively inert, it is very beneficial to feed the plants during their growing season. If they are potted in rockwool this is essential. A dilute liquid fertilizer is the most convenient form to use as it can be applied with watering. Many of the proprietary brands of liquid fertilizer are suitable, but they need to be diluted to quarter or half the strength that is recommended for other pot plants. 'Little and often' is a good maxim, but only when the plant is in active growth. Foliar feeding is sometimes recommended, but uptake through the leaves of many orchids is rather limited.

Many growers prefer to use a high nitrogen fertilizer (30.10.10) early in the summer to encourage maximum growth while temperatures are high and days are long. Once the growths have matured, it is a good idea to change to a fertilizer that will encourage flowering, such as some of those sold for tomato crops, which are high in potash (10.10.30). Other growers prefer to use more natural fertilizers such as chicken manure or a liquid feed prepared from sea-weeds. Great care must be taken to ensure that whatever is used is sufficiently dilute or the orchid roots can be damaged.

Resting

Many terrestrial orchids undergo a long dormant season when their pseudobulbs or tubers wait underground until conditions favourable for growth return. The season may be inimical because it is too hot or too cold but it is nearly always dry. Similarly the epiphytic orchids with pseudobulbs and succulent leaves are structurally adapted to withstand a period of drought. This often coincides with lower temperatures. Except for the species which grow in swamps or in equatorial or cloud forests, where some rain falls in every month, orchids need to dry out and 'rest' at some stage during their normal growth cycle.

In cultivation this need must not be forgotten. It is of no use, and indeed may be harm-ful, to continue to give water and fertilizer to dormant plants. At best it will only produce weak growths that do not flower. The resting period may be only a few weeks. In the Indian *Dendrobium* species, for example, it is recognisable at its start by the withering of leaves and at its end by the development of new shoots. As soon as a new pseudobulb begins to grow, plants should be watered freely again; in the resting season either no water is required or only enough to prevent excessive shrivelling of the pseudobulbs. In many Mexican orchids, especially those at high altitude, the dry season lasts for several of the winter months and plants often flower during this period. The days are short and, with less light and lower temperatures, growth is minimal. Nevertheless, plants must be main-tained in a humid environment, particularly at night, or they will become too desiccated. If the leaves begin to fall or pseudobulbs become wrinkled, a little water can safely be given.

Staking and flowering

Most orchids flower once a year according to the season, although some hybrids flower more frequently. *Odontoglossum* species and hybrids, for example, will flower at ten-month inter-vals under ideal conditions and *Phalaenopsis* hybrids twice a year. Many orchid genera pro-duce long inflorescences bearing many flowers, but most plants of *Paphiopedilum* and *Lycaste* species and hybrids bear flowers singly.

For attractive presentation, whether in the glasshouse or home or on the showbench, nearly all inflorescences need some kind of training. It is best to place a cane of suitable size and length adjacent to each flower spike soon after it appears. A pointed cane or stiff wire can be pushed into the compost, not too close to the side of the pot where active roots could be dam-aged, and not too close to the base of the plant where new roots might be squashed. Indicating the emergence of spikes in this way also prevents accidental damage to them during routine work in the glasshouse. Young flower spikes can be tied to the cane as they develop, starting when they are 10 –15 cm/4–6 in. high.

Orchids which naturally produce arching or pendulous spikes are best trained in their natural shape with stiff wire supports. The support should be kept to a minimum, depending on the length of the spray. Solitary flowers often need only a single tie, just below the pedicel, and multiflowered orchids should have the top tie just below the first flower.

The presentation of flowers and spikes is best when plants are not moved, or even turned around, while the buds are developing, because they often re-orient themselves in relation to the strongest source of light when they have been moved. This can result in bent and twisted rather than gracefully arching spikes.

Cultural problems

Discoloration of leaves can be caused by mineral deficiencies. This problem will disappear when the plants are given sufficient fertilizer. It is well worth giving suspect plants a teaspoon or two of epsom salts (magnesium sulphate), sprinkled on the surface of the compost and watered in, once or twice a month.

Stunted growth may also indicate a lack of nutrients, particularly nitrogen. Lack of flowers or fewer flowers than expected can also be due to an unbalanced fertilizer programme and can indicate a need for a high concentration of potassium or phosphorus in the feeding programme.

Too much fertilizer, especially nitrogen, is likely to promote very long but weak growths and thin leaves. Plants will need extra staking to prevent their breaking should this occur. Too heavy a feeding can also result in loss of leaves. Salts dissolved in the water supply, as well as chemical fertilizers or a build up of excess salts in the potting medium, can cause leaf tip dieback. A generous flushing of the compost with plain water every month or so is very beneficial.

Distortions of the foliage sometimes occur on young growths, particularly in members of the *Oncidium* alliance, and also in hybrids of *Cymbidium* and *Paphiopedilum*. This usually occurs as a result of a severe check, such as dryness or low temperatures, during the early development of the shoot, and can be avoided by greater attention to these details for subsequent growths. It can also be a genetic defect, and, if too unsightly, plants which regularly grow in an ugly way should be abandoned.

Pests and Diseases

Orchids are no more prone to attack by pests and diseases than any other glasshouse plants. Provided their growing conditions are hygenic and buoyant, most plants will never need treatment with sprays or insecticides. A glasshouse should always be kept clean and tidy with benches and pots free from weeds. Dead leaves and dying flowers should be removed regularly. New plants should be inspected very carefully before they are added to a collection – they may be harbouring pests which should be destroyed rather than introduced to a new collection. All insecticides and other chemicals should be used with the greatest care, wearing gloves, and strictly following the makers' instructions. They must only be used in the correct concentration and can be harmful to the plant if applied in bright sunlight or used when temperatures are high.

Pests

Aphids are often a nuisance on young shoots and on flower buds, especially during the winter months. Unless they are very numerous they can usually be gently removed with finger and thumb, or killed off by spraying with soapy water. Malathion is the safest general purpose insecticide for glasshouse use and is effective against aphids and many kinds of scale insects. Mealybugs are more resilient because of their water-resistant outer covering. These sap-sucking insects lurk on the undersides of leaves, under the sheaths on pseudobulbs and stems and within the bracts supporting the flowers. Regular inspection and treatment is the best means of keeping down insect pests. Insecticides such as Malathion are best used as wettable powders rather than as liquids which have xylene as a solvent. There is no danger of foliage burn with wettable powders, but they may leave an unsightly deposit.

Insects which eat parts of orchid plants, especially the flowers, include vine weevils and cockroaches. Both are nocturnal and the best way of dealing with them is to catch them in the act of feeding. Apart from catching pests, it can be a pleasure to be in a glasshouse in the evening – some orchids are powerfully scented then, and others have colours which glow in the dusk and under artificial light. Caterpillars and other insect larvae can be voracious and cause devastation even in a single night. Woodlice are sometimes a problem in bark composts as they feed on decaying plant material and may turn their attention to young roots. They are not easy to eradicate, but can be controlled by careful attention to good hygiene, regular cleaning of the glasshouse and the use of a suitable powder sprinkled around the door and on the floor where they may enter.

Slugs and snails can do considerable damage to buds, flowers and young shoots. The best way to deal with them is to search for them at night with a torch and remove the marauders by hand. Several different kinds of bait are available, usually containing metaldehyde or methiocarb, and these should help to keep the numbers down if used frequently. Some growers swear that beer is the most successful kind of bait for slugs. Mice are also heavy feeders on young buds and shoots.

Red spider mites and several species of false spider mite are probably the worst pests of orchid plants. They are very small and difficult to see, even with a magnifying lens, but the damage they do is readily recognizable. Small pits or tiny silver spots on the lower surface of the leaves are evidence of their presence. Other species make irregularly shaped depressions in the leaf surface which are often yellowish brown in colour. Mites multiply rapidly in warm and dry conditions. This is usually the key to their control. If mites are present in a glasshouse, it means that the environment is not humid enough for orchids. A heavy infestation of mites can be controlled with a miticide such as Kelthane or Pentac. Either of these should be used in cool weather and at least two applications should be made at ten-day intervals in order to ensure that all stages of the mite's life cycle are killed.

Fungus and bacterial diseases

Black or brown spots on leaves and flowers and watery patches in leaf tissue are a sure sign that a pathogen has invaded the plant. Over-watering, careless repotting, direct sunlight on a wet leaf, low temperatures, poor ventilation and stagnant air can all precipitate fungal or bacterial invasion. A number of fungi have been identified as orchid pathogens, particularly in tropical countries. Usually the rot or infection has gone too far for treatment by the time it becomes obvious. The best treatment is to remove the affected tissue and about 1cm (0.5 in.) of adjacent healthy tissue, and disinfect the cut surface with flowers of sulphur, Captan or Physan. Damaged parts should be removed and burned to avoid infecting other plants. Badly affected plants should be removed and discarded to avoid infecting the rest of the collection.

Virus diseases

Several different virus diseases have been identified in cultivated orchids. The symptoms of virus infection are pale patches, often in the form of an irregular mosaic pattern, on the young shoots and leaves. These become brown or black as the plant ages. The most common orchid virus is Cymbidium Mosaic Virus (CyMV) which is particularly common in *Cymbidium* collections but has also been identified, with slightly different symptoms, on other orchids including *Phalaenopsis* species and hybrids, *Angraecum*, amd various members of the *Cattleya* and

Oncidium alliances. It is hardly worth keeping suspect plants, which often grow weakly and flower poorly, as they can contaminate other plants, the virus passed on through insect bites or cutting tools. There is no cure for virus infections in orchid plants at present.

Propagation

Orchids can be increased by division of mature plants, by propagation from dormant buds on 'backbulbs', by taking stem or inflorescence cuttings, and by hand pollinating the plants to obtain seeds.

Divisions and 'backbulbs'

Large plants are easily divided into two or more parts when they are repotted. Sometimes a plant will literally fall apart into several pieces. Other plants have pseudobulbs joined to each other by a tough rhizome which needs to be cut with a sterile knife or secateurs. It is a mistake to make too many divisions in the interests of rapid multiplication of plants as they may then be too small to survive. For most orchids, at least three growths should be retained in each division. *Cattleya* and *Laelia* and their allies need at least one leafy pseudobulb on the back growth, with a prominent dormant bud at its base, to have a chance of success. For *Lycaste* and members of the *Odontoglossum* alliance, two or three pseudobulbs are usually retained per division. Cymbidiums are the easiest to propagate from old leafless pseudobulbs removed from the back (i.e. the oldest, 'spent' part) of the plant. All loose sheaths should be removed and the cut base of each pseudobulb allowed to dry. Then it can be immersed up to one third of its depth in sharp sand or grit and kept moist in a cool corner of the greenhouse. Within two to three months a new shoot will appear above the surface. After a further two or three months the shoot will have its own roots and can be potted up in normal compost, preferably with the old pseudobulb still attached for the first year. New plants propagated in this way may reach flowering size in two or three years.

Cuttings

The pseudobulbs, stems and inflorescence stalks of some orchids make suitable propagating material when they are divided into cuttings. Each section must contain one or more dormant buds. Detached from the rest of the plant and kept in suitably humid surroundings, for example laid on a bed of damp moss or inserted in a pan of moist grit, the buds arising from these sections will form new plantlets. After a few months they can be removed from the old piece of plant and potted up individually. The cane-like stems of *Epidendrum* and *Dendrobium* will often yield new plants in this way. The basal parts of the inflorescence stalks of *Phalaenopsis, Phaius* and *Calanthe* also have a few dormant buds which will each make a new plantlet under appropriate conditions. On many pseudobulbs, dormant buds will occasionally develop little plants, sometimes known as 'keikis', quite spontaneously – often to be seen on the top of *Pleione* pseudobulbs and on *Epidendrum* inflorescences. These can be removed and potted up as soon as they have a few roots to support their independent growth.

Seeds

Orchid seeds are extremely minute. Each consists of only a tiny embryo surrounded by a single layer of protective cells. They are so small that the food reserves in the embryo are inadequate, by themselves, for the early development of the new plant. In nature most orchid seeds begin life in a partnership with a symbiotic fungus. The fungal hyphae, which are present in the soil or on the bark of a host tree, invade the seed and enter the cells of the embryo. The orchid soon begins to digest the fungal tissue and obtain nutrients from it, thus using the fungus as an intermediary in obtaining nutrients from decaying material in the soil.

   In the laboratory this process can be imitated by sowing sterilized seeds with a culture of the fungus on a suitable jelly-like medium called agar with the addition of porridge oats which the fungus can utilize. A simpler method is to use a medium containing all the mineral nutrients, water and sugar that the germinating seed needs and dispense with the fungus. All these techniques must be carried out in sterile conditions - otherwise it is extremely easy for the nutrient medium to become infected with unwanted micro-organisms that develop at the expense of the orchid. The work can be carried out in the kitchen, using a domestic pressure cooker to sterilize the glassware and growing media. A sterile box or even a large polythene bag can be used as a cover for the operation which should be carried out as speedily as possible. However, the technique is more easily successfully performed in a specialized laboratory on a laminar flow bench.

Conical flasks, petri dishes or sterile bottles containing the newly sown seeds are kept under controlled conditions while the embryo grows out through the seedcoat to form, first, a rounded protocorm covered in rhizoids and then a small plantlet. Sometimes the containers need to be kept in the dark for the first few months, but the epiphytic orchids develop green protocorms almost immediately and are kept under artificial light for 12 –16 hours per day. Although the flasks are sealed, the medium becomes too solid through dehydration after a few months, and the plantlets need to be transferred to freshly prepared medium in a new container. These techniques must also be carried out under sterile conditions. Eventually, about six to twelve months after sowing, the plantlets are large enough to be taken out of the flask, washed carefully to remove all traces of agar, and then potted up in a fine compost mix. For their first few weeks in the greenhouse they need special care. Extra warmth and humidity, as can be provided in a small propagating case, is often beneficial.

Different kinds of orchids develop at different rates. Some of the quickest are the *Phalaenopsis* species and hybrids which can grow from seeds to flowering size in as little as 18–20 months. Others take much longer. Four to six years is an average length of time for most orchids.

Meristem propagation

A feature of orchid culture, both commercially and as a hobby, is the high value that is placed on plants which have received awards from the Royal Horticultural Society (RHS), American Orchid Society (AOS) and other award-giving bodies around the world. Many people would like to have divisions of such desirable plants, and the demand makes their price high. The advent in 1960 of techniques for the culture and multiplication of the apical meristem of a young shoot, and the various forms of tissue culture which have been developed since then, have been extremely successful and have made it possible for many people to own and enjoy some of the best plants at the same price that they would have to pay for seedlings. The technique of growing new plants in this way is very similar to propagation from seeds, but, since the starting material is already mature, the protocorms which are obtained by this method develop into new, flowering size plants, much more quickly. Sterilized conditions, containers and plant material are employed, and a warm growth chamber is necessary for the young plants on agar. After they are transferred to a normal orchid compost in the greenhouse they grow very rapidly. This technique is not difficult and modifications of it are carried out today in many parts of the world for a wide range of orchids.

Use of colchicine

The poisonous alkaloid colchicine can be used to change the chromosome constituents in the cells of orchid protocorms. The concentration and duration of the application of the chemical to plantlets in flasks must be carefully and accurately monitored. Colchicine treatment has a pronounced effect on the appearance of the adult plant which will usually have larger leaves and flowers of superior shape, but the plants grow to flowering size more slowly and may have fewer flowers. If colchicine is incorrectly applied, monstrosities may result.

Colchicine has been used successfully with many of the free-flowering *Cymbidium* hybrids, to produce flowers with better form and to promote fertility in some of the more unusual crosses. Recently it has been tried with some of the *Paphiopedilum* protocorms which have also developed into fertile plants with superior flowers.

Hybridization

The first artificial hybrids among the orchids were made in the 1850's at the Veitch nursery in Exeter. The first seedlings that germinated were of the genus *Cattleya*, but the first orchid hybrid to flower was a *Calanthe* in 1856. Following this success, many seed capsules were produced from a wide variety of crosses. Germination of the seeds was not easy, but a few plants of various genera were raised, usually on the compost surrounding the mother plant. Advances were made when the process of symbiotic germination was developed by Bernard and Burgeff at the turn of the century. Thereafter orchid seeds were germinated on an agar medium infected with a mycorrhizal fungus. The greatest discovery, however, was the demonstration by Knudson in 1922 that the fungus could be dispensed with and that orchid seeds would germinate on an entirely artificial medium which combined suitable basic chemicals with agar and a supply of sugar, usually sucrose. This development precipitated an enormous increase in the number and variety of orchid hybrids made, which continues to this day.

Orchid hybrid and cultivar nomenclature

It was decided at an early stage in orchid hybridization that precise records should be kept of crosses made and the fertile hybrids that resulted. From 1871, *Gardeners' Chronicle* published new hybrids and *The Orchid Review* also published new hybrids from its inception in 1893. The most comprehensive listing of orchid hybrids was carried out by Frederick K. Sander and his family, starting in 1901 and culminating, in 1906, in the first issue of *Sander's List of Orchid Hybrids*. Subsequently, at intervals, several volumes of addenda have been published, and orchid hybridists throughout the world are greatly indebted to the Sander family for the initiative taken in providing this invaluable service.

These duties were taken over by The Royal Horticultural Society with effect from 1 January 1961, and in accordance with obligations accepted as International Registration Authority, the Society agreed to publish, from time to time, a list of all registrations accepted after 31 December 1960. In order to maintain continuity, the title *Sander's List of Orchid Hybrids* is retained. A listing of nearly 100,000 orchid hybrids, made and registered up to 1 December 1990, is thus available in the printed volumes and on a compact disk.

The Royal Horticultural Society has carried out the task of International Registrar of Orchid Hybrids in accordance with a set of rules agreed by the International Orchid Commission (IOC) following those of the International Code of Nomenclature for Cultivated Plants (ICNCP). In 1969 the IOC published a *Handbook on Orchid Nomenclature and Registration* (fourth edition, 1993) which outlines the general principles of plant nomenclature, the rules as they affect the nomenclature of wild and cultivated orchids, and the requirements for the registration of orchid hybrids.

Orchid hybrids are distinguished from wild species and from the hybrids in many other groups of plants by a system of naming at two or three levels, for example, in the hybrid *Cattleya* Bow Bells 'White Wings', the name of the **genus** is *Cattleya*, the name of the **grex** is *Cattleya* Bow Bells and the name of the cultivar is *Cattleya* Bow Bells 'White Wings'.

The term **grex** (Latin, 'herd') denotes a group of individual plants of an artificial hybrid all bearing the same grex name. This grex name is applied to all the progeny arising directly from the crossing of the same parents. These parents may be species or themselves hybrids. The cross itself may be made and remade at different times using different individuals, cultivars or colour forms of the parents and regardless of which is used as the seed or pollen parent, but so long as the basic indentity of the parents remains the same, all their hybrid offspring will constitute a grex. Thus all the progeny arising directly from the crossing of *Paphiopedilum callosum* with *Paphiopedilum lawrenceanum* are described by the name *P*.Maudiae. The term grex name used in this way is unique to the orchids and is covered by the term **collective name** in the ICNCP. Thus *Sander's List of Orchid Hybrids* is a register of grex names.

A **cultivar** in orchids is a clone, that is, a genetically similar assemblage of individuals derived originally from a single seedling individual by vegetative propagation. Cultivar epithets are fancy names enclosed in single quotes, e.g. 'White Wings' in the example given above. Strictly, grex and cultivar epithets cannot be used singly. The full name of an individual plant of this hybrid orchid is thus *Cattleya* Bow Bells 'White Wings'. Orchid species can also be given cultivar epithets to distinguish particularly remarkable individual plants, e.g. *Paphiopedilum insigne* 'Harefield Hall'.

Further details and the rules regarding the registration of orchid hybrids can be found in the Handbook referred to above which is available from the Royal Horticultural Society.

Merit Awards

The system of giving awards to particularly meritorious plants was started in England by the Manchester and North of England Orchid Society and followed shortly thereafter by the Royal Horticultural Society. Since 1889 the RHS has had an Orchid Committee which makes recommendations for awards to the Council. The importance of the cultivar epithet in an orchid name becomes apparent, as awards are given to individual plants. Awards are usually abbreviated to just the first letter of each word and the name of the body which makes the Award, e.g. FCC/RHS (First Class Certificate/Royal Horticultural Society), AM/AOS (Award of Merit/American Orchid Society). They are usually written after the orchid name and followed by the year of the award, e.g *Lycaste* Wyld Fire 'Blaze of Tara' AM/RHS 1988.

There are now more than 40 orchid societies and associations giving a variety of awards around the world. A complete list is available in the *Handbook on Orchid Nomenclature and Registration* (see above).

Sources of Plants

Orchid plants are available from a wide range of specialist nurseries who advertise in the horticultural press and specialist magazines such as *The Orchid Review*, the orchid journal of the Royal Horticultural Society, *Die Orchidee*, the official journal of the Deutsche Orchideen-Gesellschaft, the *American Orchid Society Bulletin* and many others. Many hybrids which are now propagated in bulk are also available from garden centres. The British Orchid Growers' Association and the British Orchid Council combine to produce a leaflet annually in which details of the major producers and growers in UK are listed.

Wild orchid plants are specially protected in most countries and should on no account be collected without proper (i.e. officially and scientifically sanctioned) reason and permission. The Convention on International Trade in Endangered Species of Wild Fauna and Flora (CITES) controls the import and export of orchid species through a permit system administered by each of the signatory nations.

Hardy Orchids

A number of orchid genera whose species are amenable to cultivation occur mainly in the mountains of sub-tropical regions and in temperate areas. They may require frost-free conditions or a completely dry period during the cool weather when they are dormant. They are most easily accommodated in a cold frame or unheated glasshouse and can be treated in exactly the same way as many bulbs and alpine plants.

The best-known group of temperate orchids from tropical regions comprises the species and hybrids of the genus *Pleione*. They grow best in shallow pans and need repotting annually into a fine, fast-draining but moisture-retentive compost. Repotting should be carried out in late winter, just as the new flowering shoots begin to emerge. The plants grow well in warm and humid conditions during the summer, but need to be dried off as the leaves turn yellow and fall in the autumn and kept very cool during the winter months.

European orchids, including the genera *Orchis, Ophrys* and *Dactylorhiza*, can also be grown very easily in pots in an alpine house. Similarly, some of the Australian terrestrial genera, particularly the greenhoods, *Pterostylis* species and hybrids, make an attractive display when in flower and need a pronounced dry season once the growth has died back to the tubers below ground. Some of the north American and Asiatic species of *Cypripedium* also respond well to pot culture, but require shadier conditions than other temperate orchids. Some of the Japanese species and hybrids of *Calanthe* are also very tolerant of this treatment and some forms of *Bletilla striata* are widely grown.

When purchasing terrestrial orchids it is important to be sure that they have originated as nursery-propagated plants and have not been taken directly from the wild.

Orchids in the garden

Some very attractive terrestrial genera from the northern temperate areas of the world are completely deciduous during the cold weather. They do not begin their annual cycle of growth until temperatures begin to rise in spring and they flower during late spring or mid-summer, set seeds during the later summer and autumn, and die down again before the first frosts of winter. The genera include some of the species of the genus, *Cypripedium* (Lady's Slipper), and also a number of species of *Dactylorhiza*, both of which can make a spectacular addition to the woodland border and drier regions of the bog garden. The North American *Epipactis gigantea* is an irrepressible and beautiful ornament to any damp, slightly acidic situation, forming large clumps especially beside streams. All these orchids require a humus-rich, moisture-retentive soil, which should not become waterlogged or be allowed to dry out completely. Any good garden loam can be made suitable by the incorporation of peat and decaying leaves into the top 30cm/12 in. of soil. The dormant rhizomes or tuberous roots can be planted in this mixture. Dappled shade, or a position which is sunny for only part of the day, is suitable for several of the species. A few species prefer calcareous soils, including the European *Cypripedium calceolus*, and a suitable niche for this species can be prepared by adding small pieces of chalk or limestone to the prepared site.

Some of the orchids which normally grow in grassland habitats, including species of *Orchis* and *Ophrys*, grow well in lawns in various parts of England. The only special care required is that they should not be mown early in the year, before or immediately after flowering. The plants should also be established while the tubers are dormant, and, because they come into growth rather earlier than the woodland species, it is probably best to introduce the tubers during the autumn. Each should be set in a small cavity lined with sharp sand, at least 5cm/2 in. below the surface of the ground.

The Orchid House

When choosing a glasshouse specifically for orchid growing it is important to bear in mind that small houses are much more difficult to keep cool in summer, without losing some of the essential humidity, than larger ones. The cost of heating a small structure in winter is proportionally greater because of its large surface area. For heat conservation it is wise to choose a 'planthouse' type of structure, with solid walls up to the level of the staging, rather than the 'glass-to-ground' style which is more suitable for tomatoes. Sometimes orchid glasshouses are partially sunk below ground level and this can be very satisfactory in improving heat conservation and maintaining high humidity. For good air movement and ventilation it is desirable to have the eaves as high as possible, at least 2m above ground level, and a pitched roof above the plants so that there is plenty of space for heated air to accumulate and escape through the ventilators.

Size. The minimum size for efficiency in a small orchid house is 3m long (8 ft × 10 ft). If the width can be increased to 3.8m (12 ft), it will be possible to fit in a centre bench, as well as benches along the sides, and many more plants can be accommodated.

Site. Siting a glasshouse for orchid growing in a small garden can present problems. It will need the maximum amount of light possible during the winter months, so should not be shaded by trees or buildings on the south side. Shading the glasshouse by artificial means is much more satisfactory than trying to arrange shading from permanent features of the plot or boundary such as deciduous trees. The orientation of a small orchid house is not important, but for the larger collections a house that is aligned east–west is best. With the longest side of the house facing south, the maximum amount of light will enter during the winter. Similarly a conservatory for orchid growing should be on the south side of the house for maximum winter light and warmth. Connecting electricity, heating appliances and water to a conservatory attached to the house is no problem, and it may be wise to site a free-standing glasshouse as near as possible to a dwelling for the same reason and for ease of access during the winter months.

Structure. Orchid houses have traditionally been built of wood with large panes of horticultural glass. Cedar is the most suitable wood available today as it requires little or no maintenance compared with softwoods which need repainting regularly. Metal houses are now used increasingly, particularly those made of aluminium which do not corrode or rust, and are equally satisfactory.

Several different kinds of glazing materials are currently used successfuly in orchid houses. The most common is horticultural glass in large panes that permit the glazing bars to be spaced at least 60cm (2 ft) apart. Rippled glass is also very suitable but is heavier and more expensive. Its use is therefore limited to strongly built structures. Acrylic panels marketed as Plexiglass are becoming popular, but are more expensive than glass. Constructed in two layers, they provide excellent insulation for the plants but slightly less light than glass. Polyethylene sheeting is not suitable for permanent structures as the material currently available has a relatively short life and the heat loss is much greater than through glass.

Staging. Open staging made of slats of wood or galvanized mesh will promote air circulation around the plants but it should not be too widely spaced or small pots will fall over. It used to be the custom to build a 'moisture staging', a solid framework containing gravel or charcoal, just below the slats on which the plants stand. This system works well: surplus water draining from the plants at each watering ensures that the material remains moist and enhances humidity in the vicinity of the plants. Nonetheless, orchids will grow successfully without this refinement, and the cool-growing ones in particular benefit from a more open type of staging, such as that provided by wire mesh, where there is good air circulation around the pot and plant. A compromise can be struck by placing the plants on strong wire mesh stood on bricks some 15cm/6in. over sheet staging which is covered in damp gravel.

In addition to formal, table-like staging, which can be tiered to make plants easier to reach on wide benches, space must be arranged for mounted plants and epiphytic plants in baskets to hang, so that water will not drip from them on to the plants underneath. A piece of stout mesh hung along one end wall of the house is often a very useful surface for attaching small plants.

Floor. It is helpful to have an earth or gravel-covered floor beneath the benches. Constant evaporation from this surface, and from the ferns and other plants which may grow in it, helps to maintain high humidity. It has the disadvantage that it may provide a home for slugs and other pests and some growers prefer to have a hard surface throughout the house. It is always helpful to have a gravel or concrete path or stepping stones between the benches, but these should have a rough surface so that they do not become slippery as a result of algal growth in the humid conditions.

Environmental factors. In the wild orchids grow in competition with other plants whether in the canopy of trees, among rocks or in open grasslands. A study of the details of their environment will reveal the kind of conditions that are best for them in a glasshouse: shading from direct sunlight, moderate to warm temperatures but not excessively high, good drainage, high relative humidity coupled with good air movement, and plenty of rain water during the growing season. It is not always easy, in a glasshouse, to provide all these features at optimum levels in combination, but it is important to achieve the best possible balance of humidity, light, warm temperatures and air movement for healthy growth and maximum flowering. A glasshouse full of plants is usually a well balanced one, and there are many other plants whose growing requirements are compatible with those of orchids. Begonias, hoyas, columneas, bromeliads, peperomias, ferns and other tropical plants can all find a place in a heated glasshouse and help to provide the right atmosphere for orchids.

Shading. Orchids have a wide range of light requirements. *Ludisia* and some of the paphiopedilums grow in the deepest shade of tropical forests; others, some of the laelias and encyclias, for example, grow naturally in full sunlight. By arranging the plants carefully in relation to each other in the glasshouse their individual needs can be met. But there are also big seasonal differences in the amount of light available in temperate regions. For part of the year it will be necessary to have some means of excluding some of the incident light because it greatly increases the temperature in enclosed glass structures.

This can be achieved in various ways. The simplest method is to apply a coat of temporary glasshouse paint, such as 'Summer Cloud', to the outside of the glass as soon as the days become appreciably longer and brighter. By early summer this may need to be removed and replaced with a thicker coat. The paint ought to be removed in one or two steps during the autumn when more light is again required.

It is also useful to have some form of additional shading over the glass during the brightest summer months. Laths or blinds giving about 50 per cent shade which are raised 20–30 cm (10–12in.) above the glass are ideal. Such shading not only cuts down the amount of light entering the house through the roof but also provides a layer of insulation above the glass, thus helping to keep temperatures inside the house somewhat lower.

A thermal screen material installed inside the house for insulation during winter nights can also be used to provide shading during the summer. This is not so effective in lowering the temperature as shading material on the outside of the house.

Heating and cooling. Many orchids are adaptable to a wide range of temperature conditions within certain minima and maxima. Keeping up the required night time temperatures is often only a problem of expense. It is best achieved by using water filled pipes which are warmed by an outside boiler or electric fan heaters which are stationed so that they do not blow warm air directly on to the plants. Any approved glasshouse heating system can be used, but oil or solid fuel burners must be carefully ventilated as there is always a danger that fumes from the heater will cause bud-drop or premature ageing of the flowers. Conveniently situated glasshouses can be connected to a domestic central heating source.

In many glasshouses, particularly the smaller ones, the main difficulty is not in keeping the house warm enough in winter but in keeping the temperatures down in summer. Some of the cooler growing orchids, masdevallias and odontoglossums, for example, grow poorly if temperatures exceed 25°C (75°F), and all orchids are under stress if the temperature exceeds 32°C

(90°F). These temperatures are easily exceeded inside a small glass structure on a hot summer day. Plenty of ventilation is essential, but opening all the windows and doors can result in a sudden lowering of humidity which is undesirable.

Cooling can be effected by increasing the water content of the air. The well known practice of 'damping down', by spraying water on the benches and floors, both increases the humidity inside the house and lowers the temperature. Misting over the plants can also have a cooling effect on their tissues on a hot day. Some form of shading over the outside of the glass, and continuously running greenhouse fans are also extremely useful, both for their cooling effect and in keeping the air fresh and buoyant. In dry climates an evaporative cooling system can be very effective and sometimes a refrigerative air conditioning unit can be employed.

Ventilation. Anyone who has travelled in tropical countries, especially at medium or higher altitudes where orchids grow, notices how comfortable the atmosphere is – despite the temperature and humidity – because of the constant breeze. The need for constant fresh and moving air in the greenhouse where orchids are grown cannot be stressed too strongly. Ventilators should be open whenever the outside temperatures are warm enough. This can be arranged automatically by a simple device which has thermostatic controls. Fans especially designed for glasshouse use are invaluable. Anyone who has tried to grow orchids without a fan notices an immediate response in the growth of the plants when one is installed.

Insulation. Small glasshouses can be lined with one or more layers of plastic or 'bubble plastic' for all or part of the year. This achieves the same effect as double glazing, which is used in some expensive installations, and is very cost-effective in retaining heat in the house. However, it also reduces the amount of light reaching the plants, and care must be taken that it is kept free of algae and replaced as soon as it becomes discoloured.

Humidity. Most orchids grow where humidity levels are high at night as well as during the day. The optimum relative humidity for most orchids is 65-75 per cent at midday, but for *Phalaenopsis, Vanda* and their relatives it can be higher. Damping down several times a day and in the evening is effective. A more sophisticated system, using a humidistat among the plants to operate an automatic under bench sprayline, is very useful for those who are away from their plants during the day. Sometimes the humidity is more difficult to regulate during the winter months, especially at night when heating systems are working full-time. Damping down last thing at night is a very useful exercise.

Orchids under artificial light

Orchids can be grown without a garden or glasshouse in a special area of the home where extra artificial light can be provided together with enhanced humidity. Sometimes orchids grown in this way are superior to those grown in a glasshouse as they can be provided with the same quality of light for 12 hours or more every day, as in the tropics, instead of having to survive short winter days.

Fluorescent tubes of the 'warm white' variety are the best source of light. They can be erected in banks of four or more over a growing area of trays containing gravel, Hortag, or charcoal on which the plants are set. The leaf surface of the plant needs to be kept 15–45cm (6–18in.) below the lights – nearer will be too hot and further away not light enough. Sometimes a growing area is enclosed in a glass case, or in a recess, where it is much easier to maintain the best humidity levels for orchids. Specially designed plant cases, in modern or traditional style, can be very attractive pieces of furniture and very suitable for paphiopedilums, *Phalaenopsis* and other orchids with low light requirements.

Orchids for the window sill

Many of the tropical orchids which have been cosseted in greenhouses in the past will do equally well in the home on a window sill if a few basic rules are observed. The most important are ensuring that there is enough light for the plants, without too much heat, and also that there is adequate humidity in the immediate surroundings.

During the winter months a south-facing window sill, or a table in the curve of a bay window, is probably the best place in the home for orchids, but this might prove too hot in the summer even when the plants are protected by a sun-filtering curtain. For the summer they are probably best in an east-facing window sill where they will receive the morning sun. A deep window sill is ideal as it can be fitted with a polypropylene tray containing about 2–3cm (1 in.) of gravel, Hortag or some other clean, moisture-retentive material. If the contents of the tray are kept moist but not waterlogged, there will always be a suitably humid atmosphere around the orchid pots placed on top. Frequent misting will raise the humidity still further and is especially beneficial for plants with abundant aerial roots, and for genera like *Masdevallia* which suffer in overheated conditions.

Orchids with 'intermediate' or 'warm' temperature requirements do best in modern, centrally heated homes. Many *Phalaenopsis* and *Paphiopedilum* species and hybrids give pleasure with their long-lasting flowers and a wide variety of species can be grown successfully with patience and understanding.

Classification

Few plant families stand to benefit more by systematic classification than the Orchidaceae. The subfamilies, tribes and subtribes into which this vast family may be divided make its dazzling diversity sensible and accessible to botanists. More important for us, they reveal alliances of genera with features of horticultural importance in common – general appearance, hybrid compatibility and cultural requirements, to name but three.

The synopsis on pages xxx–xxxii is based on Robert L. Dressler's magisterial work, *The Orchids: Natural History and Classification* (1981). In the 1990 edition of his work, Dr. Dressler's researches take him yet further; his revised classification is reproduced here in outline:

     Apostasioideae

     Cypripedioideae

     Spiranthoideae
          Diceratosteleae
          Tropidieae
          Cranichideae

     Orchidoideae
          Diurideae
          Diseae
          Orchideae

     Epidendroideae
      I. Primitive tribes
          Gastrodieae
          Neottieae
          Nervilieae
          Palmorchideae
          Triphoreae
          Vanilleae
      II. Cymbidioid phylad
          Malaxideae
          Calypsoeae
          Cymbidieae
          Maxillarieae (incl. Oncidiinae)
      III. Epidendroid phylad
          Arethuseae
          Coelogyneae
          Epidendreae
          Glomereae (or Old World Epidendreae)
          IIIA. Dendrobioid subclade
             Podochileae
             Dendrobieae
             Vandeae

The 1981 system is retained for the synopsis, however, having gained wide currency among students and growers of orchids.

Synopsis

SUBFAMILY	TRIBE	SUBTRIBE	GENERA INCLUDED IN THIS VOLUME
Apostasioideae			—
Cypripedioideae			*Cypripedium, Paphiopedilum, Phragmipedium, Selenipedium*
Spiranthoideae	Erythrodeae	Tropidiinae	*Corymborkis*
		Goodyerinae	*Anoectochilus, Goodyera, Ludisia Macodes, Zeuxine*
	Cranichideae	Spiranthinae	*Lankesterella, Spiranthes, Stenorrhynchos*
		Pachyplectroninae	—
		Manniellinae	—
		Cranichidinae	—
		Cryptostylidinae	*Cryptostylis*
Orchidoideae	Neottieae	Limodorinae	*Cephalanthera, Epipactis*
		Listerinae	*Listera*
	Diurideae	Chloraeinae	—
		Caladeniinae	*Arthrochilus, Caladenia, Chiloglottis, Cyrtostylis, Drakaea, Elythranthera, Eriochilus, Glossodia, Lyperanthus*
		Pterostylidinae	*Pterostylis*
		Acianthinae	*Acianthus, Corybas*
		Diuridinae	*Calochilus, Diuris, Thelymitra*
		Prasophyllinae	*Microtis, Prasophyllum*
	Orchideae	Orchidinae	*Aceras, Amitostigma, Anacamptis, Barlia, Brachycorythis, Coeloglossum, Comperia, Dactylorhiza, Gymnadenia, Himantoglossum, Nigritella, Ophrys, Orchis, Platanthera, Ponerorchis, Serapias, Stenoglottis*
		Habenariinae	*Bonatea, Cynorkis, Diplomeris, Habenaria, Pecteilis,*
		Huttonaeinae	—
	Diseae	Disinae	*Disa*
		Satyriinae	*Satyrium*
		Coryciinae	*Disperis*
Anomalous tribes	Triphoreae		—
	Wullschlaegelieae		—
Epidendroideae	Vanilleae	Vanillinae	*Vanilla*
		Lecanorchidinae	—
		Palmorchidinae	—
		Pogoniinae	*Cleistes, Pogonia*
	Gastrodieae	Nerviliinae	*Nervilia*
		Gastrodiinae	—
		Rhizanthellinae	—
	Epipogieae		—

SUBFAMILY	TRIBE	SUBTRIBE	GENERA INCLUDED IN THIS VOLUME
Epidendroideae *(continued)*	Arethuseae	Arethusinae	*Arethusa*
		Thuniinae	*Thunia*
		Bletiinae	*Acanthephippium, Ancistrochilus, Arundina, Bletia, Bletilla, Calanthe, Calopogon, Chysis, Coelia, Nephelaphyllum, Phaius, Spathoglottis, Tainia*
		Sobraliinae	*Arpophyllum, Elleanthus, Sobralia*
	Coelogyneae	Coelogyninae	*Coelogyne, Dendrochilum, Otochilus, Panisea, Pholidota, Pleione*
		Adrorhizinae	—
	Malaxideae		*Liparis, Malaxis, Oberonia*
	Cryptarrheneae		—
	Calypsoeae		*Calypso*
	Epidendreae	Eriinae	*Ceratostylis, Eria, Porpax, Trichotosia*
		Podochilinae	—
		Thelasiinae	—
		Glomerinae	—
		Laeliinae	*Barkeria, Brassavola, Broughtonia, Cattleya, Cattleyopsis, Caularthron, Constantia, Dimerandra, Domingoa, Encyclia, Epidendrum, Hagsatera, Hexadesmia, Hexisea, Isabelia, Isochilus, Jacquiniella, Laelia, Laeliopsis, Lanium, Leptotes, Nageliella, Nanodes, Neocogniauxia, Nidema, Oerstedella, Rhyncholaelia, Scaphyglottis, Schomburgkia, Sophronitella, Sophronitis, Tetramicra*
		Meiracylliinae	*Meiracyllium, Neolauchea*
		Pleurothallidinae	*Barbosella, Barbrodria, Dracula, Dresslerella, Dryadella, Lepanthes, Lepanthopsis, Masdevallia, Octomeria, Platystele, Pleurothallis, Porroglossum, Restrepia, Restrepiella, Scaphosepalum, Stelis, Trichosalpinx, Trisetella, Zootrophion*
		Dendrobiinae	*Cadetia, Dendrobium, Diplocaulobium, Epigeneium*
		Bulbophyllinae	*Bulbophyllum, Trias*
		Sunipiinae	*Sunipia*
Vandoideae	Polystachyeae		*Neobenthamia, Polystachya*
	Vandeae	Sarcanthinae	*Acampe, Aerides, Amesiella, Arachnis, Ascocentrum, Ascoglossum, Chiloschista, Cleisostoma, Dimorphorchis, Doritis, Dyakia, Esmeralda, Euanthe, Gastrochilus, Grosourdya, Haraella, Holcoglossum, Kingidium, Luisia, Micropera, Neofinetia, Papilionanthe, Paraphalaenopsis, Phalaenopsis, Plectorrhiza, Pomatocalpa, Renanthera, Rhinerrhiza, Rhynchostylis, Robiquetia, Sarcochilus, Schoenorchis, Sedirea, Seidenfadenia, Smitinandia, Taeniophyllum, Thrixspermum, Trichoglottis, Trudelia, Vanda, Vandopsis*

SUBFAMILY	TRIBE	SUBTRIBE	GENERA INCLUDED IN THIS VOLUME
Vandoideae *(continued)*		Angraecinae	*Aeranthes, Angraecum, Cryptopus, Dendrophylax, Jumellea, Listrostachys, Neobathiea, Oeonia, Oeoniella*
		Aerangidinae	*Aerangis, Ancistrorhynchus, Angraecopsis, Calyptrochilum, Chamaeangis, Cribbia, Cyrtorchis, Diaphananthe, Eurychone, Microterangis, Mystacidium, Plectrelminthus, Podangis, Rangaeris, Solenangis, Summerhayesia, Tridactyle, Ypsilopus*
	Maxillarieae	Corallorhizinae	*Govenia*
		Zygopetalinae	*Acacallis, Aganisia, Batemannia, Bollea, Chaubardia, Chaubardiella, Chondrorhyncha, Cochleanthes, Huntleya, Kefersteinia, Koellensteinia, Mendoncella, Neogardneria, Otostylis, Pabstia, Pescatorea, Promenaea, Stenia, Warrea, Warreella, Zygopetalum, Zygosepalum*
		Bifrenariinae	*Bifrenaria, Teuscheria, Xylobium*
		Lycastinae	*Anguloa, Lycaste, Neomoorea*
		Maxillariinae	*Cryptocentrum, Cyrtidiorchis, Maxillaria, Mormolyca, Scuticaria, Trigonidium*
		Dichaeinae	*Dichaea*
		Telipogoninae	*Telipogon, Trichoceros*
		Ornithocephalinae	*Dipteranthus, Ornithocephalus, Zygostates*
	Cymbidieae	Cyrtopodiinae	*Ansellia, Bromheadia, Cymbidiella, Cymbidium, Cyrtopodium, Dipodium, Eriopsis, Eulophia, Eulophiella, Galeandra, Geodorum, Grammangis, Grammatophyllum, Graphorkis, Grobya, Oeceoclades*
		Genyorchidinae	—
		Thecostelinae	—
		Acriopsidinae	*Acriopsis*
		Catasetinae	*Catasetum, Clowesia, Cycnoches, Dressleria, Mormodes*
		Stanhopeinae	*Acineta, Cirrhaea, Coeliopsis, Coryanthes, Embreea, Gongora, Houlletia, Kegeliella, Lacaena, Lueddemannia, Paphinia, Peristeria, Polycycnis, Sievekingia, Stanhopea*
		Pachyphyllinae	—
		Oncidiinae	*Ada, Aspasia, Brassia, Capanemia, Cischweinfia, Cochlioda, Comparettia, Cuitlauzina, Erycina, Gomesa, Ionopsis, Lemboglossum, Leochilus, Leucohyle, Lockhartia, Macradenia, Mexicoa, Miltonia, Miltoniopsis, Notylia, Odontoglossum, Oncidium, Ornithophora, Osmoglossum, Otoglossum, Palumbina, Papperitzia, Psychopsis, Rodriguezia, Rodrigueziella, Rossioglossum, Sigmatostalix, Solenidium, Symphyglossum, Ticoglossum, Tolumnia, Trichocentrum, Trichopilia, Warmingia*

List of Genera

Illustrated genera are marked with an asterisk (*).

Acacallis
Acampe
Acanthephippium
Aceras
Acianthus
Acineta*
Acriopsis
Ada
Aerangis*
Aeranthes
Aerides*
Aganisia
× Alexanderara
× Aliceara
Amblostoma
Amesiella
Amitostigma
Anacamptis
Ancistrochilus
Ancistrorhynchus
Angraecopsis
Angraecum*
Anguloa*
× Angulocaste
Anoectochilus*
Ansellia
Arachnis*
× Aranda
Arethusa
Arpophyllum
Arthrochilus
Arundina
× Ascocenda
Ascocentrum
× Ascofinetia
Ascoglossum
× Asconopsis
Aspasia

Barbosella
Barbrodria
Barkeria*
Barlia
Batemannia
Bifrenaria*
Bletia*
Bletilla
Bollea*
Bonatea
Brachycorythis
Brassavola*
Brassia*
× Brassocattleya
× Brassoepidendrum
× Brassolaeliocattleya
Bromheadia
Broughtonia
Bulbophyllum*

Cadetia
Caladenia*
Calanthe*
Calochilus
Calopogon
Calypso*
Calyptrochilum
Capanemia
Catasetum*
Cattleya*
Cattleyopsis
× Cattleytonia
Caularthron
Cephalanthera
Ceratostylis
Chamaeangis
Chaubardia
Chaubardiella*
Chiloglottis
Chiloschista*
Chondrorhyncha*
× Christieara
Chysis
Cirrhaea
Cischweinfia
Cleisostoma
Cleistes
Clowesia
Cochleanthes*
Cochlioda*
Coelia
Coeliopsis
Coeloglossum
Coelogyne*
Comparettia
Comperia
Constantia
Coryanthes*
Corybas*
Corymborkis
Cribbia
Cryptocentrum
Cryptopus
Cryptostylis
Cuitlauzina*
Cycnoches*
Cymbidiella*
Cymbidium*
Cynorkis
Cypripedium*
Cyrtidiorchis
Cyrtopodium
Cyrtorchis
Cyrtostylis

Dactylorhiza*
Dendrobium*

Dendrochilum*
Dendrophylax
× Dialaelia
Diaphananthe
Dichaea*
Dimerandra
Dimorphorchis*
Diplocaulobium
Diplomeris
Dipodium
Dipteranthus
Disa*
Disperis
Diuris*
Domingoa
× Doritaenopsis
Doritis
Dracula*
Dresslerella
Dressleria
Dryadella
Dyakia

Elleanthus
Elythranthera*
Embreea
Encyclia*
× Epicattleya
Epidendrum*
Epigeneium*
Epipactis
× Epiphronitis
Eria*
Eriochilus
Eriopsis
Erycina
Esmeralda*
Euanthe*
Eulophia*
Eulophiella
Eurychone

Flickingeria

Galeandra
Gastrochilus
Geodorum
Glossodia
Gomesa
Gongora*
Goodyera
Govenia
Grammangis
Grammatophyllum
Graphorkis
Grobya
Grosourdya
Gymnadenia

Habenaria*
Hagsatera
Haraella
Hexadesmia
Hexisea
Himantoglossum
Holcoglossum
Houlletia*
Huntleya*

Ionopsis
Isabelia*
Isochilus

Jacquiniella
Jumellea

Kefersteinia
Kegeliella
Kingidium
Koellensteinia

Lacaena
Laelia*
× Laeliocattleya
Laeliopsis
Lanium
Lankesterella
Lemboglossum*
Leochilus
Lepanthes*
Lepanthopsis
Leptotes
Leucohyle
Liparis
Listera
Listrostachys
Lockhartia
Ludisia*
Lueddemannia
Luisia
Lycaste*
Lyperanthus*

× Maclellanara
Macodes*
Macradenia
Malaxis
Masdevallia*
Maxillaria*
Meiracyllium
Mendoncella
Mexicoa
Micropera
Microterangis
Microtis
Miltonia*

× Miltonidium
Miltoniopsis*
× Mokara
Mormodes*
Mormolyca
Mystacidium

Nageliella*
Nanodes
Neobathiea
Neobenthamia
Neocogniauxia
Neofinetia
Neogardneria
Neolauchea
Neomoorea
Nephelaphyllum
Nervilia
Nidema
Nigritella
Notylia

Oberonia*
Octomeria
× Odontioda
× Odontobrassia
× Odontocidium
Odontoglossum*
× Odontonia
× Odontorettia
Oeceoclades*
Oeonia
Oeoniella
Oerstedella
× Oncidioda
Oncidium*
Ophrys*
× Opsistylis
Orchis*
Ornithocephalus
Ornithophora
Osmoglossum*
Otochilus

Otoglossum*
Otostylis
Pabstia
Palumbina
Panisea
Paphinia
Paphiopedilum*
Papilionanthe*
Papperitzia
Paraphalaenopsis
Pecteilis*
Peristeria
Pescatorea*
Phaius*
Phalaenopsis*
Pholidota*
Phragmipedium*
Platanthera
Platystele
Plectorrhiza
Plectrelminthus
Pleione*
Pleurothallis*
Podangis
Pogonia
Polycycnis
Polystachya
Pomatocalpa
Ponerorchis
Porpax
Porroglossum
× Potinara
Prasophyllum
Promenaea*
Psychopsis*
Pterostylis*

Rangaeris
× Renanopsis
× Renantanda
Renanthera*
× Renanthopsis
Restrepia*
Restrepiella

Rhinerrhiza
Rhyncholaelia*
Rhynchostylis
× Rhynchovanda
Robiquetia
Rodriguezia
Rodriqueziella
Rossioglossum*

Sarcochilus*
× Sarconopsis
Satyrium
Scaphosepalum
Scaphyglottis
Schoenorchis
Schomburgkia
Scuticaria*
Sedirea
Seidenfadenia
Selenipedium
Serapias
Sievekingia
Sigmatostalix
Smitinandia
Sobralia*
Solenangis
Solenidium
× Sophrocattleya
× Sophrolaelia
× Sophrolaeliocattleya
Sophronitella*
Sophronitis*
Spathoglottis
Spiranthes
Stanhopea*
Stelis*
Stenia
Stenoglottis
Stenorrhynchos
× Stewartara
Summerhayesia
Sunipia
Symphyglossum

Taeniophyllum
Tainia
Telipogon*
Tetramicra
Teuscheria
Thelymitra
Thrixspermum
Thunia*
Ticoglossum
Tolumnia*
Trias
Trichocentrum
Trichoceros
Trichoglottis
Trichopilia*
Trichosalpinx
Trichotosia
Tridactyle
Trigonidium
Trisetella
Trudelia*

Vanda*
Vandopsis
Vanilla*
× Vascostylis
× Vuylstekeara

Warmingia
Warrea
Warreella
× Wilsonara

Xylobium

Ypsilopus

Zeuxine
Zootrophion
Zygopetalum*
Zygosepalum
Zygostates

Glossary

abaxial of the surface or part of a lateral organ, turned or facing away from the axis and toward the plant's base; thus the underside of a leaf or perianth segment even when that surface may be uppermost because of the twisting of a stalk, strong incurving of petals or the hanging attitude of a branch or inflorescence; cf. adaxial.

abbreviated shortened.

aberrant unusual or atypical, differing from the normal form.

abortive (of reproductive organs) undeveloped or not perfectly developed, and therefore barren; (of seeds) failing to develop normally.

above (1) pertaining to the adaxial surface of a leaf, petal or sepal; (2) pertaining to the upper portions of a stem, branch or inflorescence.

abrupt of a leaf or perianth segment tip, terminating suddenly without tapering, usually when broadly rounded or squared; 'abruptly acute' refers to parts terminating in this way but tipped with a short sharp point.

abscission, abscissing (abscising) (of leaves, sheaths etc.) a separating or falling away, caused by disintegration of a layer of plant tissues at the base of the organ (e.g., as the result of environmental conditions or pollination leading to hormonal action), with a subsequent development of scar tissue or periderm at the point of abscission.

acaulescent of a plant whose stem is absent or, more usually, appears to be absent, being very short or subterranean.

acicular needle-shaped, and usually rounded rather than flat in cross-section.

acinaciform shaped like a scimitar.

acinose resembling a bunch of grapes, composed of granular bodies tightly packed.

aculeiform prickle-shaped.

acuminate (of leaves and perianth segments) with the tip or, less commonly, the base tapering gradually to a point, usually with somewhat concave sides.

acutangular when stems are sharply angular.

acute (of the tips or bases of leaves or perianth segments) where two almost straight or slightly convex sides converge to terminate in a sharp point, the point shorter and usually broader than in an acuminate leaf tip.

adaxial turned or facing toward the axis and apex, thus the upper, if not always the uppermost surface of an organ, sometimes used interchangeably with ventral.

adherent of parts usually free or separate (i.e. petals) but clinging or held closely together. Such parts are sometimes loosely described as united or, inaccurately, as fused, which is strictly synonymous with coherent. Some authors use this word to describe the fusion of dissimilar parts.

adnate attached by its whole length or surface to the face of an organ.

adpressed (appressed) (of indumentum, leaves, leaf sheaths etc.) used of an organ which lies flat and close to the stem or leaf to which it is attached.

adventitious (adventive) occurring in an unusual location, originating from other than the normal place, applied to buds developing along a stem rather than at leaf axils; to viviparously produced plantlets and to roots that develop not from the radicle and its subdivisions but from another part such as the stem or leaf axil.

aerial used broadly of all plant parts found above ground.

aerial roots roots borne wholly above ground, either adventitiously from the stems or from the basal rooting axis as in many epiphytes.

affixed fixed upon.

afoliate leafless.

ageotropic (apogeotropic) applied to parts that are negatively geotropic, i.e. growing upwards against the influence of gravity, a feature found in the secondary roots of some epiphytic orchids such as *Ansellia* and *Catasetum.*

agglomerate crowded together in a head.

agglutinate glued together, as in the pollen masses of Orchidaceae.

alate winged, usually of stems, petioles and fruits where the main body is furnished with marginal membranous bands.

alliance a group of related genera. The term often relates directly to the more botanical *Subtribe;* thus the pleurothallid alliance consists of those genera in the Subtribe Pleurothallidinae. Less formally but more specifically, the *Odontoglossum alliance* contains the genus *Odontoglossum* and its near relations (allies).

alternate (1) of leaves, branches, pedicels, etc., arranged in two ranks along the stem, rachis, etc., with the insertions of the two ranks not parallel but alternating, thus the antithesis of paired or opposite; (2) of two types of organ or structure, when one is placed in an alternating sequence with another.

amplexicaul (of a leaf base or dilated petiole) enlarged and embracing or clasping the stem.

ampulla an organ shaped like a squat, rounded flask or a bladder.

ampullaceous ampulla-shaped.

anastomosing of veins forming a network, united at their points of contact.

ancipitous with two sharp edges.

androecium the male component of a flower, the stamen or stamens as a whole.

anfractuose (anfractuous) closely or tightly sinous, or spirally twisted.

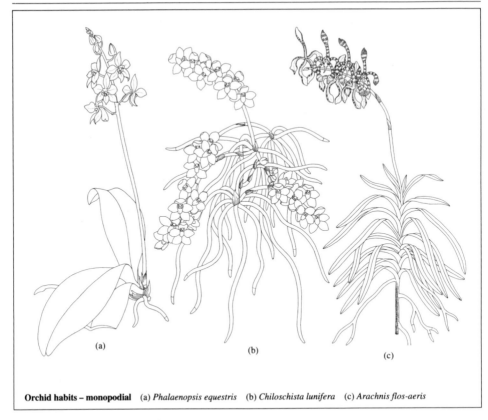

Orchid habits – monopodial   (a) *Phalaenopsis equestris*   (b) *Chiloschista lunifera*   (c) *Arachnis flos-aeris*

angular, angulate with laterally projecting angles, as in longitudinally ridged and angled stems.

annular of organs of parts in a circular arrangement or forming rings.

annulate ring-shaped.

antemarginal lying within, or extending just short of, the margin.

anterior of the surface or part of an organ turned away from or furthest from the axis and projecting forward or toward the base or (in the case of a flower) any subtending bract; close to abaxial but broader in definition, meaning not only 'beneath' but also 'lower' or 'furthest' as in the tip of an organ, cf. posterior.

anther the pollen-bearing portion of the stamen, either sessile or attached to a filament.

anther cap the case enclosing the pollinia.

anther sac a sac-shaped unit containing pollen.

anthesis the expansion or opening of a flower, the period in which the anthers and stigmas become functional, enabling fertilization to take place.

antipetalous opposite to or superposed on a petal, i.e. not alternate.

antisepalous opposite to or superposed on a sepal, i.e. not alternate.

antrorse turned, curved or bent upward or forward, toward the apex; cf. retrorse.

apetalous lacking petals.

apex the growing point of a stem or root; the tip of an organ or structure, most commonly used of a leaf tip.

aphyllous lacking leaves.

apical borne at the apex of an organ, farthest from the point of attachment; pertaining to the apex.

apiculate possessing an apicule.

apicule a short sharp but not rigid point terminating a leaf, bract or perianth segment.

appendage secondary part or process attached to or developed from any larger organ.

appendiculate furnished with appendages.

applanate flattened.

appressed see adpressed.

approximate drawn very closely together, sometimes confused with *proximate*.

arching curved gently downwards, usually of branches, stems, large leaves and inflorescences, usually more freely than *arcuate* and less markedly than *pendent*.

arcuate curved downwards, bow-shaped, usually applied to a smaller, more rigid structure than would be described as arching, e.g. the column of an orchid.

aristate of a leaf apex abruptly terminated in an acicular continuation of the midrib. Otherwise, awned.

aristulate bearing a small awn.

articulate, articulated jointed; possessing distinct nodes or joints, sometimes swollen at their attachment and breaking easily.

arundinaceous reed-like, resembling a cane or reed, as in the stems of *Arundina*.

ascending rising or extending upwards, usually from an oblique or horizontal position, thus differing from erect.

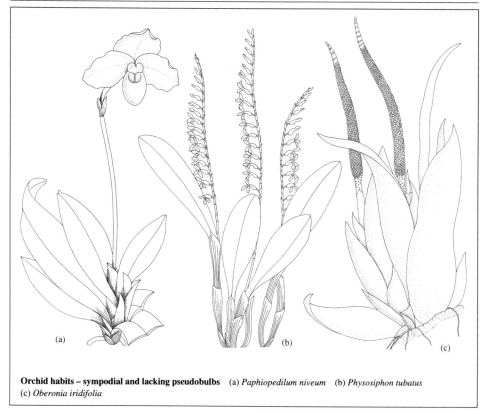

Orchid habits – sympodial and lacking pseudobulbs (a) *Paphiopedilum niveum* (b) *Physosiphon tubatus*
(c) *Oberonia iridifolia*

asperous rough.

asperulous of a very rough surface, possessing short, hard projections or points.

astragaloid dice-shaped.

asymmetric, asymmetrical (1) irregular or unequal in outline or shape, (2) of a flower incapable of being cut in any vertical plane into similar halves.

attenuate (of the apex or base) tapering finely and concavely to a long drawn out point.

auricle an ear-like lobe or outgrowth, often at the base of an organ.

auricled see auriculate.

auriculate possessing two rounded, ear-shaped lobes that project beyond the general outline of the organ.

autogamous self-fertilizing.

awl-shaped narrowly wedge-shaped and tapering finely to a point, subulate.

awn a slender sharp point or bristle-like appendage.

awned see aristate.

axe-shaped dolabriform.

axial relating to the morphological axis.

axil the upper angle between an axis and any off-shoot or lateral organ arising from it, especially a leaf.

axillary situated in, or arising from, or pertaining to an axil.

axis a notional point or line around or along which organs are developed or arranged, whether a stem, stalk or clump; thus the vegetative or growth axis and the floral axis describe the configuration and development of buds and shoots and flowers

respectively, and any stem or point of origination on which they are found.

bacciform berry-shaped.

bacilliform rod- or club-shaped.

backbulb a dormant pseudobulb having completed its growth cycle and been surpassed by a new pseudobulb or the lead growth.

backcross a cross between a hybrid and one of its parent plants.

baculiform rod-like.

barb a hooked semi-rigid hair.

barbate bearded, with hairs in long weak tufts.

barbed of bristles or awns with short, stiff lateral or terminal hairs which are hooked sharply backward or downward.

barbellae short, stiff hairs of the sort found on the lip of *Bulbophyllum barbigerum*.

barbellate furnished with barbellae.

basal at or arising from the base or point of attach-ment of a whole plant or organ, thus basal leaves arise from the rootstock or a very short or buried stem and a basal inflorescence arises from the root-stock or the base of a stem or storage organ.

basifixed (of an organ) attached by its base rather than its back, as an anther joined to its filament by its base.

basipetalous developing from apex to base, as in an inflorescence where the terminal flowers open first, cf. acropetal.

beak a long, pointed, horn-like projection.

beaked furnished with a beak.

beard a tuft or zone of hair.

bearded possessing tufts or zones of indumentum on parts of the surface.

below pertaining to the lower, basal portions of an organ or whole plant, thus 'stems devoid of leaves below'. 'Leaves ciliate below' meaning leaves whose margins are ciliate in the lower half of their margins (not on their undersurface).

beneath pertaining to the abaxial surface of an organ, thus 'leaves tomentose beneath'. See *below*.

biauriculate with two auricles.

bibracteolate with two bracteoles.

bicalcarate with two spurs.

bicallose with two callosities.

bicarinate with two keels.

bicornute two-horned.

bicrenate doubly crenate.

bidentate (1) (of an apex) possessing two teeth; (2) of a margin, with teeth, the teeth themselves toothed.

bifid cleft deeply, forming two points or lobes.

bifoliate having two leaves.

bifoliolate (of a compound leaf) bearing two leaflets.

bifurcate twice forked.

biserial arranged in two rows.

biserrate with a row of double saw-teeth.

bisexual of flowers with both stamens and pistils; of plants with perfect (hermaphrodite) flowers.

bitten see praemorse.

bivalvate having two valves.

blade the thin, expanded part of a leaf or petal, also known as the lamina, excluding the petiole, leaf sheath, or the claw of a perianth segment.

blistered see bullate.

bloom a waxy or pruinose covering.

blunt rounded, as in a leaf or bud tip that is neither finely tapered or pointed nor abruptly cut off. See obtuse, retuse.

boat-shaped see carinate, cymbiform, navicular.

botuliform sausage-shaped.

bract a modified protective leaf associated with the inflorescence (clothing the stalk and subtending the flowers), with buds and with newly emerging shoots and stems.

bracteate possessing or bearing bracts.

bracteolate possessing or bearing bracteoles.

bracteole a secondary or miniature bract.

bristly see echinate, hispid and setose.

brushlike see muscariform.

bulbiform in the shape of, resembling, a bulb.

bulbous (of a stem) swollen at the base.

bullate where the surface of an organ is 'blistered' or puckered (i.e. with many superficial interveinal convexities), as in the tepals of *Huntleya* and the synsepalum of *Masdevallia schroederiana*.

cactiform with succulent stems resembling those of Cactaceae.

caducous abscising very early, soon falling.

caespitose a habit description: tufted, growing in small, dense clumps.

calcarate furnished with a spur.

calceolate slipper-shaped; resembling a round-toed shoe in form.

calcicole a plant dwelling on and favouring calcareous soils.

calciform shaped like a slipper or boot.

calcifuge a plant avoiding and damaged by calcareous soils.

callose (1) bearing callosities; (2) hard and thick in texture.

callosity a leathery or hard isolated thickening of an organ.

callus an isolated thickening of tissue, e.g. the calli (superficial protuberances) on the lips of many orchid flowers.

calyx a collective term for the sepals, whether separate or united, which form the outer whorl of the perianth or floral envelope.

campanulate (of a perianth) bell-shaped.

canaliculate channelled with a long, concave groove, like a gutter.

canescent hoary, or becoming so; densely covered with short, grey-white pubescence.

cano-tomentose indumentum midway between canescent and tomentose.

capillary slender and hair-like; much as filiform, but even more delicate.

capitate (1) arranged in heads; (2) terminating in a knob or somewhat spherical tip.

capitellate (1) minutely head-shaped; (2) clustered in a small, compact, capitate group.

capitiform, capitose see capitate.

capitulum a head of densely clustered and sessile or subsessile flowers on a compressed axis, e.g. *Elleanthus capitatus*.

capsule a dry, dehiscent seed vessel.

carina keel, the midvein of a leaf, petal or sepal, prominent to ridged beneath.

carinate of a leaf, bract or perianth segment, boat-shaped or, more usually, keeled, with a line or ridge along the centre of its dorsal surface.

cartilaginous hard and tough in texture, but flexible.

cassideous helmet-shaped, e.g. the dorsal sepals of *Disperis fanniniae* or the lip of *Catasetum macrocarpum*.

castaneous deep reddish brown or chestnut coloured.

caudate (of a leaf or perianth segment apex) tapering gradually into a long tail-shaped appendage.

caudicle tails of tissue derived from the anther and connected to the pollinia.

caulescent producing a well-developed stem above ground.

cauline attached to or arising from the stem.

cernuous nodding, usually applied to flowers with curved or drooping pedicels attached to a straight or erect inflorescence axis; cf. nutant.

cespitose see caespitose.

channelled (channeled) see canaliculate and sulcate.

chartaceous (of leaf and bract texture) thin and papery.

cilia (*sing.* cilium) fine marginal hairs.

ciliate bearing a marginal fringe of fine hairs.

ciliolate bearing a marginal fringe of minute hairs.

cinereous ashy grey.

cirrhous (cirrose) (of the apex) terminating in a coiled or spiralling continuation of the midrib.

clambering of a vine climbing or growing over obstacles without the support of twining stems or tendrils, e.g. *Vanilla*.

clasping partially or wholly surrounding an organ, as a leaf-base clasps a stem.

clavate shaped like a club or a baseball bat; thickening to the apex from a tapered base.

clavellate a diminutive of clavate; club-shaped, but smaller.

claviform club-shaped.

claw the narrowed petiole-like base of some sepals and petals.

clawed possessing a claw.

cleft of a flat organ (i.e. leaf or perianth segment), cut almost to the middle.

cleistogamous with self-pollination occurring in the closed flower, as sometimes occurs in *Cattleya aurantiaca*.

clinandrium the part of the column containing the anther.

clone the asexually produced offspring of a single parent to which it is genetically identical.

club-shaped gradually thickened upwards from a slender base, clavate.

clypeate shield-shaped.

coarctate crowded together.

cochlear, cochleariform, spoon-shaped.

cochleate coiled like a snail's shell.

coherent of parts usually free or separate fused together, as in a corolla tube. This term is sometimes used to describe the adhesion of similar parts; cf. adherent.

column a feature of orchids where the style and stamens are fused together in a single structure.

column foot a basal platform found in the column of some Orchidaceae, to which the lip is attached.

complanate flattened, compressed.

compound divided into two or more subsidiary parts or orders.

compressed flattened, usually applied to pseudobulbs and other stems and qualified by 'laterally', 'dorsally' and 'ventrally'.

concatenate linked as in a chain, for example the pseudobulbs of *Otochilus*.

conduplicate (of leaves) folded once lengthwise, so that the sides are parallel or applied.

conferted closely packed or crowded.

confluent merging one into the other.

congested crowded.

conglomerate tightly clustered, usually into a ball.

congregate (*adj.*) collected into close proximity.

conic, conical cone-shaped; tapering evenly from base to apex in three dimensions.

connate united, usually applied to similar features when fused in a single structure.

connivent converging, and even coming into contact, but not fused; (of petals) gradually inclining toward the centre of their flower.

conspicuous easily visible to the naked eye, often used to mean enlarged or showy (as in 'conspicuously veined'); cf. prominent.

constipate (*adj.*) crowded or massed together.

constricted abruptly narrowed, contracted.

contiguous in contact, touching but not fused.

continuous an uninterrupted symmetrical arrangement, sometimes used as a synonym of decurrent.

contorted twisted or bent, in aestivation the same as convolute.

contracted narrowed and/or shortened.

convergent see connivent.

convolute rolled or twisted together longitudinally, with the margins overlapping, as leaves or petals in the bud.

coralloid resembling coral in structure, applied to the roots of saprophytes and to the calli of some flowers.

cordate heart-shaped, usually ovate-acute in outline with a rounded base and a deep basal sinus or notch.

coriaceous leathery or tough but smooth and pliable in texture.

cork a protective tissue, usually elastic and spongy in texture and with air-filled outer cells; it replaces epidermis in the older superficial parts of some plants.

corky composed of cork or of a porous, elastic and cork-like texture.

corm a solid, swollen, subterranean, bulb-like stem or stem-base; it is annual, the next year's corm developing from the terminal bud or, in its absence, one of the lateral buds.

corniculate bearing or terminating in a small horn-like protuberance.

corolla the interior perianth whorl; a floral envelope composed of free or fused petals.

corrugate (*adj.*) crumpled or wrinkled but more loosely so than in rugose.

corymb an indeterminate flat-topped or convex inflorescence, where the outer flowers open first; cf. umbel.

corymbose, corymbiform resembling or forming a corymb.

costa a single pronounced midvein or midrib.

costate with a single, pronounced vein, the midrib.

crateriform shaped like a goblet; a concave hemisphere slightly contracted at the base.

crenate scalloped, with shallow, rounded teeth; bicrenate is where the teeth themselves have crenate teeth.

crenulate minutely crenate.

crest an irregular or dentate elevation or ridge.

crispate curled and twisted extremely irregularly, used most often of hairs.

crispy-hairy (of hairs) wavy and curved, in dense short ringlets.

cristate crested or, less commonly, 'crest-like', sometimes used to denote the presence of crests (cristae) (e.g. *Coelogyne cristata*), more often used to describe a closely ruffled margin.

crowded (of leaves) arranged close to each other or gathered toward a stem or branch tip, often in whorled or scattered fashion.

cruciate, cruciform cross-shaped.

crumpled see corrugate.

ctenoid comb-like.

cubiform dice-shaped, cubic.

cucullate furnished with or shaped like a hood.

cucumiform cucumber-like.

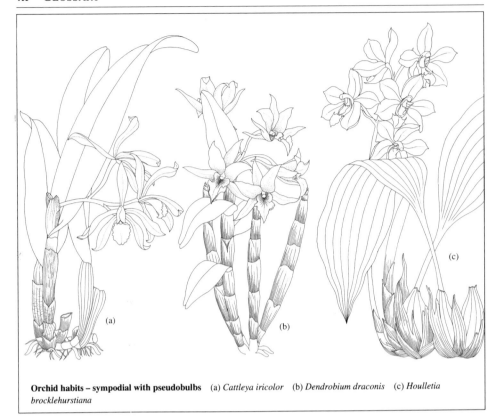

Orchid habits – sympodial with pseudobulbs (a) *Cattleya iricolor* (b) *Dendrobium draconis* (c) *Houlletia brocklehurstiana*

cultrate, cultriform knife-shaped, resembling the blade of a knife.

cuneate, cuneiform inversely triangular, wedge-shaped.

cupreous with the colour and lustre of copper.

cusp a short, stiff, abrupt point.

cusped see cuspidate.

cuspidate (of apices) terminating abruptly in a sharp, inflexible point, or cusp.

cuspidulate minutely cuspidate.

cuticle the outermost skin, multi-layered and waxy tissues composed of the epidermis and containing cutin, fatty acids and cellulose.

cyclic disposed in whorls or circles.

cylindric, cylindrical elongated and virtually circular in cross-section.

cymbiform boat-shaped, attenuated and upturned at both ends with an external dorsal ridge.

cyme a more or less flat-topped and determinate inflorescence, the central or terminal flower opening first.

cymose arranged in or resembling a cyme or bearing cymes.

cymule a small and generally few-flowered cyme.

dactyloid, dactylose fingerlike.

dealbate whitened, covered with a white powder.

deciduous (1) falling off when no longer functional, as non-evergreen leaves, or the petals of many flowers; (2) a plant that sheds its leaves annually, or at certain periods, as opposed to evergreen plants.

declinate bent or curved downward or forward.

decrescent gradually reduced in size.

decumbent of a stem, lying horizontally along the ground, but with the apex ascending and almost erect.

decurrent where the base of a leaf blade extends down and is adnate to the petiole (if any) and the stem.

decurved curved downwards.

decussate of leaves, arranged in opposite pairs with adjacent pairs at right angles to each other, thus forming four longitudinal rows.

deflected bent or turned abruptly downwards.

deflexed bent downward and outwards; cf. reflexed.

deflorate past the flowering state.

defoliate with leaves shed.

deformed disfigured or distorted.

deltoid (deltate) an equilateral triangle attached by the broad end rather than the point; shaped like the Greek letter delta.

dentate toothed, of the margins of leaf blades and other flattened organs, cut with teeth. Strictly, the teeth are shallow and represent two sides of a roughly equilateral triangle, in contrast to serrate (saw-toothed), where the teeth are sharper and curved forwards, or crenate, where the teeth are blunt and rounded. Less precisely, the term is used to cover any type of toothed margin.

dentation the teeth on the margin of an organ.

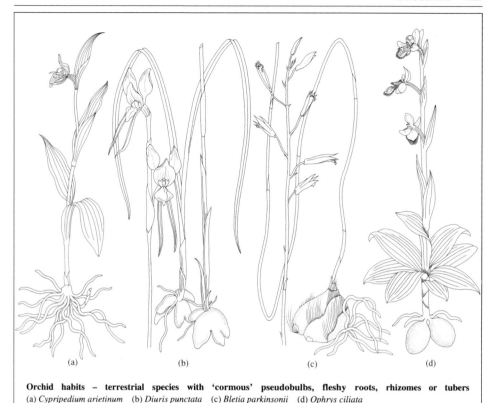

Orchid habits – terrestrial species with 'cormous' pseudobulbs, fleshy roots, rhizomes or tubers
(a) *Cypripedium arietinum*   (b) *Diuris punctata*   (c) *Bletia parkinsonii*   (d) *Ophrys ciliata*

denticulate minutely dentate.

dentiform tooth-shaped.

denudate stripped, made bare.

denuded see naked.

depauperate reduced in stature, number or function as if starved and ill-formed. Species with organs described thus are, however, usually perfectly healthy but adapted to cope with some environmental stress.

dependent hanging downward as a result of its weight, as in a flower- or fruit-laden branch.

deplanate flattened or expanded.

depressed sunken or flattened as if pressed from above.

descending tending gradually downwards.

dichotomous branching regularly by forking repeatedly in two; the two branches of each division are basically equal.

difform dissimilar.

diffuse spreading widely outwards by frequent branching.

digitate 'fingered', with divisions arising from the same point at the apex of a stalk.

digonous two-angled.

dilated, dilating broadened, expanded.

dimorphic, dimorphous occurring in two dissimilar forms or shapes.

dioecious with male and female sporophylls or staminate and pistillate flowers on different plants.

disc, disk the central part of the lip, often elevated and callused or crested.

disciform, discoid circular and flattened.

discoid of leaves, with a round fleshy blade and thickened margins.

dissected cut in any way, a general term applicable to leaf blades or other flattened organs that are incised, lacerate, laciniate, pinnatisect or palmatisect.

distal the part furthest from the axis, thus the tip of a leaf is distal; cf. proximal.

distant (of leaves on a stem, stipes on a rhizome or flowers on a floral axis) widely spaced, synonymous with remote and the antithesis of proximate.

distichous (of leaves) distinctly arranged in two opposite ranks along a stem or branch, as in *Angraecum distichum*.

distinct separate, not connate or in any way united, with similar parts; more generally meaning evident or obvious, easily distinguishable.

divaricate broadly divergent and spreading, a term usually applied to branching patterns where branches spread from 70° to 90° outwards from the main axis.

divergent broadly spreading from the centre.

divided a vague term meaning compound or deeply cut, lobed or cleft.

dolabriform hatchet-shaped.

doleiform barrel-shaped.

dorsal pertaining to the back of an organ, or to the surface turned away from the axis, thus abaxial. A term confused by some authors with its opposite, ventral. In orchids, the **dorsal sepal** is usually the uppermost, standing between the petals. cf. *lateral*; *sepal*; *tepal*.

dorsifixed of an organ attached by its dorsal surface to another.

dorsiventral flattened, and having separate dorsal and ventral surfaces, as most leaves and leaf-blades.

downy see pubescent.

ebracteate without bracts.

ecallose not callused.

eccentric one-sided, off-centre.

echinate covered with many stiff hairs or bristles, or thick, blunt prickles.

eciliate lacking cilia, not ciliate.

eglandular without glands.

eligulate not ligulate; not possessing ligules.

ellipsoid elliptic, but 3-dimensional.

elliptic, elliptical ellipse-shaped; midway between oblong and ovate but with equally rounded or narrowed ends, with two planes of symmetry and widest across the middle.

elongate lengthened, as if stretched or extended.

emarginate (of the apex) shallowly notched, the indentation (sinus) being acute.

embracing clasping by the base.

ensiform sword-shaped, straighter than lorate, and with an acute point.

entire continuous; uninterrupted by divisions or teeth or lobes, thus 'leaves entire' meaning, margins not toothed or lobed.

ephemeral very short-lived, lasting for only one day or less.

epichile the terminal part of a tripartite lip, as found in some Orchidaceae, e.g. *Stanhopea*.

epidermis the outer layer of a periderm.

epilithic growing on rocks.

epiphyllic, epiphyllous positioned on or growing from the leaf, as in an epiphyllous flower or inflorescence.

epiphyte a plant which grows wholly upon another plant, but is not parasitic and does not depend on it for nourishment.

epiphytic growing on other plants without being parasitic.

epruinose lacking a pruinose coating.

equal, equalling said of parts or categories of plants held in comparison where one is the same as the other in length or, less often, number.

equilateral equal-sided.

equitant when conduplicate leaves overlap or stand inside each other in two ranks in a strongly compressed fan, as in *Maxillaria valenzuelana* and *Oberonia*.

erect of habit, organ or arrangement of parts upright, perpendicular to the ground or point of attachment.

erianthous woolly flowered.

erinous prickly, coarsely textured with sharp points.

erose irregularly dentate, as if gnawed or eroded.

erumpent on the point of breaking through, or apparently so.

evergreen (having) foliage that remains green for at least a year, through more than one growing season.

evolute unfolded.

exarate grooved.

exceed, exceeding said of parts or categories of parts held in comparison where one is longer than the other.

excentric one-sided, out of the centre.

excrescence an outgrowth or abnormal development.

excurrent projecting beyond the margin or apex of its organ, as a midvein terminating in a mucro or an awn.

exfoliating peeling off in thin layers, shreds or plates.

explanate spread out, flat.

exserted obviously projecting or extending beyond the organs or parts surrounding it; cf. included.

extrorse turned or facing outwards, abaxial; cf. introrse.

falcate strongly curved sideways, resembling a scythe or sickle.

farina the powdery or mealy coating on the stems, leaves, and sometimes flowers of certain plants.

farinose see farinaceous.

farinose, farinaceous having a mealy, granular texture.

fasciated (of stems or similar axes, 'bundled') where two or more narrow parts grow abnormally together lengthwise in a congested manner; (of one part) flattened and misshapen as if composed of several parts joined in that way.

fascicle a cluster or bundle of flowers, racemes, leaves, stems or roots, almost always independent but appearing to arise from a common point.

fascicled, fasciculate arranged in a fascicle or fascicles.

felted-tomentose tomentose, but more woolly and matted, the hairs curling and closely adpressed to the surface.

ferruginous brown-red, rust-coloured.

fibrillose with thread-like fibres or scales.

fibrous of a thread-like, woody texture.

fiddle-shaped see pandurate.

filament a threadlike or filiform organ, hair or appendage.

filamentous composed of or bearing filaments.

filiferous bearing filiform appendages.

filiform (of leaves, branches etc.) filament-like, i.e. long and very slender, rounded in cross-section.

fimbria a fringe.

fimbriate bordered with a fringe of slender processes, usually derived from the lamina rather than attached as hairs; cf. ciliate.

fissile splitting easily.

fistulose, fistular hollow and cylindrical like a pipe.

flabellate, flabelliform fan-shaped, with a wedge-shaped outline and sometimes conspicuously pleated or nerved.

flaccid weak, limp, floppy, lax etc.

flagellate with whip-like outgrowths.

flagelliform long, tapering, supple, whip-like; for example the leaves of *Brassavola* and *Scuticaria*.

fleshy-rooted used of plants with thick fleshy roots or storage organs.

flexuous (of an axis) zig-zag, bending or curving in alternate and opposite directions.

floccose possessing dense, woolly hairs that fall away easily in tufts.

flocculent, flocculose slightly floccose, woolly.

floriferous bearing flowers freely.

foliaceous resembling a leaf, in appearance or texture.

foliolate bearing leaves. In many of the species descriptions that follow, pseudobulbs are described as 'apically 1/2/3-foliate', meaning they bear however many leaves at their summits, in addition to any leafy sheaths that may embrace them.

fractiflex in intermittent zig-zag lines.

free (strictly of dissimilar parts or organs) separate, not fused or attached to each other; 'distinct' describes the separateness of similar organs.

fringed see fimbriate.

fugacious falling off or withering rapidly; transitory.

funnelform (of a lip) funnel-like, widening gradually upwards and into the spreading limb.

furcate forked, the terminal lobes prong-like.

furfuraceous scurfy, with soft, bran-like scales.

furrowed channelled or grooved lengthwise, a term covering both sulcate and conspicuously striate.

fuscous dusky, blackish-grey.

fused (of parts usually free or separate) joined together to form a continuous surface; cf. coherent.

fusiform spindle-shaped, swollen in the middle and tapering to both ends.

fusoid somewhat fusiform.

FYM farmyard manure, an excellent fertilizer and soil-ameliorant, it is sometimes incorporated into the potting medium of heavy-feeding terrestrials. It should only be used in its most leached, rotted and dried states.

galeate helmet-shaped, hollow and domed.

geminate paired.

gemmiparous bearing vegetative buds.

geniculate bent abruptly, in the form of a flexed knee.

geniculum a knee-like joint or node where an organ or axis is sharply bent.

geophyte a plant, often deciduous and growing with a swollen stem, bulb or tuber below ground, adapted for water storage – usually applied to plants from arid lands.

gibbosity a basal or apical swelling.

gibbous swollen on one side or at the base.

glabrate see glabrescent.

glabrescent (1) nearly glabrous, or becoming glabrous with age; (2) minutely and invisibly pubescent.

glabrous smooth, hairless.

gladiate sword-like.

gland any cell or cells secreting a substance or substances, such as oil, calcium or sugar, e.g. nectaries.

glandular generally, beaing glands; (of hairs) bearing a gland, or gland-like prominence at the tip.

glandular-pubescent either covered with intermixed glands and hairs, or possessing hairs terminated by glands.

glaucescent slightly glaucous.

glaucous coated with a fine bloom, whitish, or blue-green or grey and easily rubbed off.

globose spherical, sometimes used to mean near-spherical.

globular composed of globose forms; sometimes used where *globose* is meant.

globulose diminutive of globose.

glomerate aggregated in one or more dense or compact clusters.

glomerule a cluster of capitula or grouped flowers, strictly subtended by a single involucre.

glutinose, glutinous see viscid.

graminaceous grassy, resembling grass in texture or habit.

granular (of a leaf) composed of granules, or minute knobs or knots; (of its surface) grainy, as if covered by small granules.

grex a group name for all plants derived from the crossing of the same two or more species. It is printed in roman with a capital initial. The grex name may be combined with a cultivar name where a particular clone of that crossing is meant. The cultivar name is printed within quotation marks, e.g. *Paphiopedilum* Maudiae 'The Queen'.

grooved a more general term for striate or sulcate.

gynandrium a structure in which the stamens are adnate to the pistils.

gynandrous with the stamens adnate to the pistils, as in Orchidaceae.

gynodioecious bearing perfect or pistillate flowers on separate plants.

gynostemium a single structure combining androecium and gynoecium, as in the column of Orchidaceae.

gyrate curving in a circular or spiral fashion.

hair an outgrowth of the epidermis, unicellular or comprising a row of cells and conforming to one of several types (i.e. dendritic, stellate, scale-like, peltate, etc.) according to branching, form, grouping and attachment.

hamate hooked at the tip.

hastate arrow-shaped, triangular, with two equal and approximately triangular basal lobes, pointing laterally outward rather than toward the stalk (see sagittate).

head a dense cluster or spike of flowers; a capitulum.

helicoid spirally clustered, in the shape of a spring or a snail-shell.

helminthoid worm-shaped.

herbaceous (1) lacking persistent aerial parts; (2) softly leafy, pertaining to leaves; (3) thin, soft and bright green.

hermaphroditic bisexual, having both pistils and stamens in the same flower.

heterophyllous bearing two or more differnt forms of leaf on the same plant, either contemporaneously or at different times; sometimes used of different leaf forms exhibited by individuals of the same species.

hippocrepiform shaped like a horse-shoe.

hirsute with long hairs, usually rather coarse and distinct.

hirsutullous slightly hirsute.

hirtellous minutely or softly hirsute.

hirtuse see hirsute.

hispid with stiff, bristly hairs, not so distinct or sharp as when setose.

hispidulous minutely hispid.

hoary densely covered with white or grey hairs.

homogamous having hermaphrodite flowers, or flowers of the same sex.

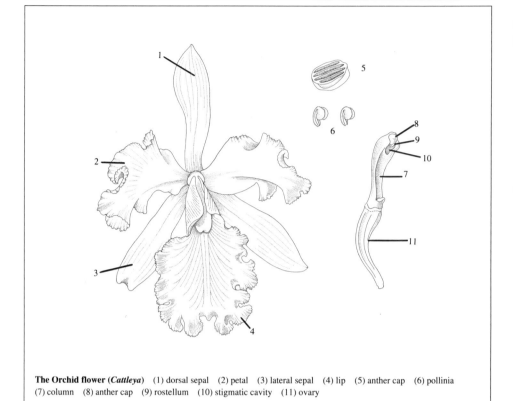

The Orchid flower (*Cattleya*) (1) dorsal sepal (2) petal (3) lateral sepal (4) lip (5) anther cap (6) pollinia (7) column (8) anther cap (9) rostellum (10) stigmatic cavity (11) ovary

hooded cucullate or, more loosely, referring to inarching parts enclosing others in the resulting concavity.

horn appendage shaped like an animal's horn, see cornute.

horny hard and brittle, but with a fine texture and easily cut.

hyaline transparent, translucent, usually applied to the margins of leaves and bracts.

hypochile the lower or basal part of the complex lip of certain orchids, usually swollen or inflated and distinct in form from the mesochile (central portion) and epichile (apical portion).

hypocrateriform see salverform.

imbricate (of organs such as leaves or bracts) overlapping; more strictly applied to such organs when closely overlapping in a regular pattern, sometimes encircling the axis.

immersed embedded and sunken below the surface.

imperfect when certain parts usually present are not developed. Imperfect flowers are unisexual.

impressed sunken into the surface.

incised dissected, but cut deeply and irregularly with the segments joined by broad lamina.

included 'enclosed within'.

incrassate thickened; especially of skin.

incurved bending inwards from without.

indumentum a covering of hair, scurf or scales, most often used in the general sense of 'hair'.

induplicate folded inwards.

indurate hardened and toughened.

inferior beneath.

inflated bladder-like, blown up and swollen, as in the lip of *Cypripedium*; cf. saccate.

inflected bent or flexed.

inflexed bent inwards towards the main axis.

inflorescence the arrangement of flowers and their accessory parts on an axis.

infundibular, infundibuliform funnel-shaped.

inserted attached to or placed upon; *not* the antithesis of exserted.

insertion the point or mode of attachment for a body to its support, a leaf insertion is where the leaf joins the stem forming an axil.

internode the portion of stem between two nodes.

interrupted not continuous; the disturbance of an otherwise symmetrical arrangement.

intricate entangled.

introrse turned or facing inwards, towards the axis or base.

invaginated enclosed in a sheath.

involucral forming an involucre.

involucrate possessing an involucre.

involucre a single, highly conspicuous bract, bract pair, whorl or whorls of bracts or leaves subtending a flower or inflorescence.

involute rolled inward, toward the uppermost side (see revolute).

irregular zygomorphic; asymmetrical.

jointed see articulate.

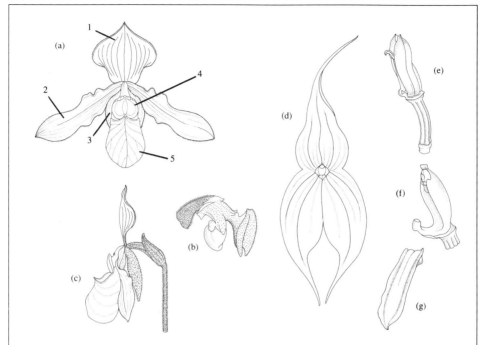

The Orchid flower   (a) *Paphiopedilum* (1) dorsal sepal (2) petal (3) synsepalum (synsepal) formed by fusion of lateral sepals (4) staminode (5) slipper-like lip   (b) dissection showing apex of ovary, pollinia and staminode   (c) side view   (d) *Masdevallia* – flower with fused sepals   (e) dissection with sepals removed revealing small petals, lip and ovary   (f) column with lip   (g) detached.

jugate see paired.

jugum a pair, especially of lobes.

keel a prominent ridge, like the keel of a boat, running longitudinally down the centre of the under-surface of a leaf, petiole, bracts, petal or sepal; also used to describe the ridged crests on the lips of some orchids.

keeled possessing a keel; see also carinate.

keiki a plantlet developing adventitiously on a cane-like stem, a pseudobulb, inflorescence branch, or, very rarely, a root.

kidney-shaped reniform.

knobbed see capitate.

knotted see torulose.

labellum (lip) the enlarged or otherwise distinctive third petal of an orchid, developed as a landing platform for pollinators.

lacerate irregularly, and more or less broadly and shallowly, cut, as if torn.

laciniate irregularly and finely cut, as if slashed.

lacrimiform, lachrymaeform tear-shaped.

lacunose pitted with many deep depressions or holes.

laevigate appearing smoothly polished.

lageniform flask-shaped.

lamella raised ribbon-like developments of tissue on the lips of some orchids, for example the crests on the lips of *Coelogyne*.

lamellate composed of one or more thin, flat scales or plates.

lamina see blade.

lanate woolly, possessing long, densely matted and curling hairs.

lanceolate lance-shaped, narrowly ovate, but 3–6 times as long as broad and with the broadest point below the middle, tapering to a spear-like apex.

lanose woolly, see lanate.

lanuginose as lanate, but with the hairs shorter; somewhat woolly or cottony.

lanulose as lanate, but with extremely short hairs.

lateral on or to the side of an axis or organ. In orchids, the lateral or ventral sepals are usually the lowest of the tepals, held below the petals and either side of the lip. cf. *dorsal sepal*, *tepals*. Lateral lobes are the side lobes of a lip with 3 or more lobes.

lax loose, e.g. of flowers in an inflorescence or a loose arrangement of leaves.

laxpendent hanging loosely.

leathery coriaceous.

lenticular, lenticulate lens-shaped; almost flattened and elliptical, but with both sides convex.

lentiginous minutely dotted, as if with dust.

lepidote, leprous covered with tiny, scurfy, peltate scales.

leprous see lepidote.

ligneous, lignose woody in texture.

ligulate strap-shaped, usually more narrowly so than in lorate.

limb a broadened, flattened part of an organ, extending from a narrower base.

linear slender, elongated, the margins parallel or virtually so.

lineate see striated.

lined see striated.

lingulate resembling a tongue.

lip see labellum.

lithophyte a plant that grows on rocks, deriving nourishment from the atmosphere rather than the soil.

lobe see lobed.

lobed divided into (usually rounded) segments – lobes – separated from adjacent segments by sinuses which reach halfway or less to the middle of the organ (see cleft).

lobulate possessing or bearing lobules.

lobule a small lobe.

lorate strap-shaped.

lunate crescent-shaped.

lyrate more or less pinnately lobed, but with a large, rounded terminal lobe and smaller lateral lobes diminishing in size toward the base of the whole.

maculate blotched by wide, irregular patches of colour.

mamillate, mammillate furnished with nipple-like prominences.

marcescent withered but persisting.

marginal affixed at the edge or margin of an organ.

marginate with a distinct or conspicuous margin or border.

mealy farinose.

median pertaining to the central transverse area of a leaf, thus 'median width', width through midpoint.

membranous [membraneous], membranaceous thin-textured, soft and flexible.

mentum a chin-like, backward extension of the flower, formed by the association of the bases of the lateral sepals with the foot of the column in many orchids and rather like a shorter, blunter spur.

meristem undifferentiated tissue capable of developing into organs or special tissues.

mesochile the middle part of the distinctly tripartite, complex lip of some orchids, such as *Stanhopea*.

midrib the primary vein of a leaf, usually running down its centre as a continuation of the petiole.

midvein see midrib.

moniliform where a cylindrical or terete organ is regularly constricted, giving the appearance of a string of beads or a knotted rope; cf. torulose.

monocot a monocotyledonous plant. The monocots are one of the two primary divisions of the angiosperms, the other being the dicots. They are characterized by the single, not double, cotyledon in the seed, usually the absence of cambium and thus woody tissue and, in many cases, parallel venation. The monocotyledons include Gramineae, Musaceae, Agavaceae, Liliaceae, Amaryllidaceae, Orchidaceae, Araceae, Iridaceae, Bromeliaceae, Palmae, etc.

monoecious with bisexual flowers or both staminate and pistillate flowers present on the same plant; cf. dioecious.

monopodial of a stem or rhizome in which growth continues indefinitely from the apical or terminal bud, and which generally exhibits little or no secondary branching; cf. Sympodial.

monospecific see monotypic.

monotypic having only one component, e.g. a genus with one species. The term is misleading for all genera, no matter how large, are based on a single type; equally, a genus with a single species may be termed monotypic yet contain many distinctive named entities (varieties and cultivars) each of which will have its own type. In such cases, the term monospecific is sometimes preferred.

motile (of hairs, appendages and lobes) capable of movement; the tepal hairs of some *Bulbophyllum* species are motile, as are the hinged lips of others in this genus and in *Dracula*.

mucilage a viscous substance or solution.

mucilaginous slimy.

mucro an abrupt, sharp, terminal spur, spine or tip.

mucronate (of an apex) terminating suddenly with an abrupt spur or spine developed from the midrib.

mucronulate diminutive of mucronate.

multifid as bifid, but cleft more than once, forming many lobes.

multigeneric refers to hybrids with more than two genera involved in their ancestry. Multigeneric hybrid names are formed either by combining the generic names of the parents, as for example in × *Sophrolaeliocattleya*, or by creating a commemorative personal name using the suffix -ara, e.g. × *Potinara* (*Brassavola* × *Cattleya* × *Laelia* × *Sophronitis*).

muricate rough-surfaced, furnished with many short, hard, pointed projections.

muriculate slightly muricate.

muscariform in the shape of a broom or brush.

mycorrhiza (literally 'fungus root') an association of fungal mycelium with the roots of a higher plant, from which the latter may derive some benefit. For orchids, this term often appears in descriptions of the seed germination process where the seed (which lacks the nutritious endosperm found in other flowering plant families) sustains itself at first by deriving carbohydrates and nutrients from a mycorrhizal fungus which infects its embryo.

mycorrhizal a term describing roots which associate with a fungal mycelium, and can derive a benefit, through symbiosis or digestion, from the latter.

myrmecophyte a plant in symbiosis with ants – such plants are myrmecophilous. The best-known orchid myrmecophyte is *Schomburgkia tibicinis*, also known as *Myrmecophila tibicinis*.

navicular, naviculate shaped like a deeply keeled boat.

nectary a gland, often in the form of a protuberance or depression, which secretes and sometimes absorbs nectar.

needle-like see acicular.

nervation see venation.

nerved furnished with ribs or veins.

nervose see nerved.

netted reticulate, net-veined.

nigrescent turning black.

nocturnal opening or active only during the night.

node the point on an axis where one or more leaves, shoots, whorls, branches or flowers are attached.

nodose possessing many closely packed nodes; knobbly.

nodule a small, virtually spherical protuberance.

non-resupinate (of a leaf or flower) inverted by a twisting of the petiole or pedicel – in the case of some orchids (e.g. *Polystachya*) this results in 'upside-down' flowers with the lip uppermost.

nutant nodding, usually applied to a whole inflorescence or stem; cf. cernuous.

obconic, obconical as conic, but with the point of attachment at the narrower end.

obcordate as with cordate, but with the sinus at the apex rather than the base.

obcuneate as cuneate, but with the point of attachment at the broad end.

obhastate as hastate, but with the triangular lobes at the apex.

oblanceolate as with lanceolate, but with the broadest part above the middle, and tapering to the base rather than the apex.

oblate spherical but dorsally and ventrally compressed.

obligate essential, unable to exist without; cf. facultative.

oblique (1) (of the base) with sides of unequal angles and dimensions; (2) (of direction) extending laterally, the margin upwards and the apex pointed horizontally.

oblong essentially linear, about 2–3 times as long as broad, with virtually parallel sides terminating obtusely at both ends.

obovate ovate, but broadest above rather than below the middle, thus narrowest toward the base rather than the apex.

obovoid as ovoid, but broadest below the middle; obovate in cross-section.

obpyramidal inversely pyramidal, tapering from the apex.

obpyriform inversely pear-shaped, thus narrowing toward the base.

obsolescent (of an organ) reduced to the point of being vestigial.

obsolete extinct, or not evident; where an organ is absent, or apparently absent, from its expected location.

obtuse (of apex or base) terminating gradually in a blunt or rounded end.

opposite two organs at the same level, or at the same or parallel nodes, on opposite sides of the axis.

orbicular perfectly circular, or nearly so.

orchid pot a pot, usually clay, its sides pierced with holes to promote air circulation, free drainage and healthy aerial root activity.

osmophore a floral gland producing scent to attract pollinators.

ovary the basal part of a pistil, containing the ovules.

ovate egg-shaped in outline, rounded at both ends but broadest below the middle, and 1.5–2 times as long as it is broad (see elliptic).

ovoid egg-shaped, ovate but 3-dimensional.

paleaceous bearing small, chaffy bracts or scales (paleae); more generally, chaffy in texture.

pandurate fiddle-shaped; rounded at both ends, one end being enlarged, and markedly constricted or indented on both sides in or around the middle. See, for example, the lip of *Coelogyne pandurata*.

panduriform see pandurate.

panicle an indeterminate branched inflorescence, the branches generally racemose or corymbose.

paniculate resembling, or in the form of a panicle.

pannose felt-like in texture, being densely covered in woolly hairs.

papillae small, soft, pimple-like excrescences or protuberances.

papillate, papillose covered with small, soft pimple-like excrescences or protuberances.

papyraceous papery.

parallel where the veins are more or less parallel to the margins, running lengthwise.

parted divided almost to the base into a determinate number of segments; a more general term for, e.g. pinnate, palmate, etc.

partite see parted.

patellate see patelliform.

patelliform orbicular and thick, having a convex lower surface and a concave upper surface.

patent spreading.

pectinate pinnately divided, arranged or marked, the parts or markings being many, slender and long, and close together, like the teeth of a comb.

pedicel the stalk supporting an individual flower or fruit, in Orchidaceae this is often replaced by a stalk-like ovary.

pedicelled, pedicellate growing on a pedicel.

peduncle the stalk of an inflorescence.

peduncled, peduncular, pedunculate borne on or possessing a peduncle.

pellicle a thin, generally non-cellular coat or skin.

pellucid virtually transparent.

peltate of a leaf whose stalk is attached inside its margin rather than at the edge, usually at the centre beneath.

pendent hanging downwards, more markedly than arching or nodding but not as a result of the weight of the part in question or the weakness of its attachment or support (pendulous).

pendulous dependent, but as a result of the weakness of the support, as in a densely flowered weeping raceme.

penicillate brush-shaped, or like a tuft of hairs.

pentangular five-angled.

perfect a bisexual flower or an organ with all its constituent members.

perianth the collective term for the floral envelopes, the corolla and calyx, especially when the two are not clearly differentiated.

perigone the perianth, especially when undifferentiated, or anything surrounding a reproductive structure.

persistent of an organ, neither falling off nor withering.

petal one of the modified leaves of the corolla, generally brightly coloured and often providing a place on which pollinators may alight.

petaloid petal-like in colour, shape and texture.

petiolate, petioled furnished with a petiole.

petiole the leaf stalk.

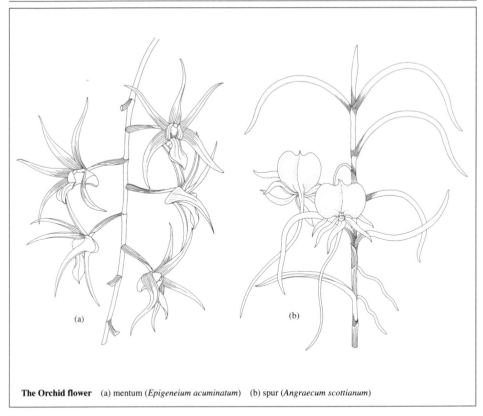

The Orchid flower   (a) mentum (*Epigeneium acuminatum*)   (b) spur (*Angraecum scottianum*)

pilose covered with diffuse, soft, slender hairs.

pilosulous slightly pilose.

pinnatifid pinnately cleft nearly to the midrib in broad divisions.

pinnatipartite see pinnatifid.

pinnatisect deeply and pinnately cut to, or near to, the midrib; the divisions, narrower than when pinnatifid, are themselves not truly distinct segments.

pitcher a tubular or cup-like vessel.

pitcher-shaped campanulate but with a distinct narrowing toward the orifice.

pitted see lacunose.

plane flat; a flat surface.

plantlet a small or secondary plant, developing on a larger plant.

pleated see plicate.

plicate folded lengthwise, pleated, as a closed fan.

plumed see plumose.

plumose feather-like; with long, fine hairs, which themselves have fine secondary hairs.

pollinarium collective term for the pollinia, stipe and viscidium.

pollinium a regular mass of more or less coherent pollen grains.

polygamodioecious (1) a plant that is functionally dioecious but contains some perfect flowers in its inflorescence; (2) a species which has perfect and imperfect flowers on separate individuals.

polygamous bearing both unisexual and bisexual flowers on the same or different plants within the same species.

polymorphic occurring in more than two distinct forms, possessing variety in some morphological feature.

polystichous arranged in many rows.

polytrichous having many hairs.

porrect extending or stretching outward and forward.

posterior at or towards the back or adaxial surface.

praemorse raggedly or irregularly truncated, as if gnawed or bitten.

primordium a tissue or organ in its earliest state, having undergone differentiation and just prior to emergence.

proboscis see beak.

procumbent trailing loosely or lying flat along the surface of the ground, without rooting.

projecting clearly thrust outwards beyond the apical margins.

proliferating producing buds or off-shoots, especially from unusual organs.

proliferous see proliferating.

prominent (usually applied to veins and surface features) clearly visible or palpable, standing out from the surface.

prostrate lying flat on the ground.

protruding exserted.

proximal the part nearest to the axis, thus the base of a leaf is proximal; cf. distal.

proximate close together; see distant.

pruinose thickly frosted with white, rather than blue-grey bloom, usually on a dark ground colour, e.g. garnet or black.

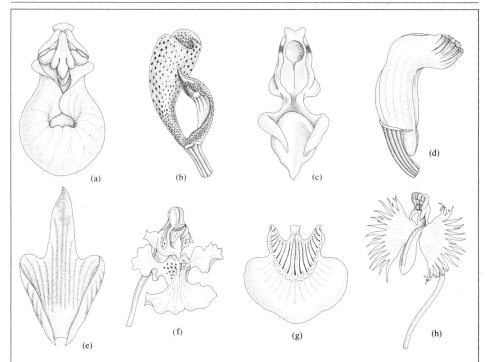

The Orchid flower – lips (a) *Cypripedium fasciculatum* (b) *Mormodes buccinator* (c) *Stanhopea costaricensis* (d) *Phaius flavus* (e) *Sophronitis coccinea* (f) *Oncidium cavendishianum* (g) *Pescatorea cerina* (h) *Pecteilis susannae*

pseudobulb the water-storing thickened 'bulb-like' stems found in many sympodial orchids – predominantly aerial and a feature of epiphytic or lithophytic species, but also in some terrestrials (e.g. *Eulophia, Calanthe*), where they may be buried. Pseudobulbs arise from a rhizome, sometimes so short as to give them the appearance of being clumped. They vary in shape and size from species to species and usually grow actively for only one season, persisting thereafter as backbulbs.

pseudobulbous resembling or pertaining to the pseudobulb.

pseudocopulation a strategy whereby orchid flowers mimic the females of the pollinator species, attracting the males of that species whose frantic but vain sexual activity effects pollination. A ruse most beautifully illustrated by *Ophrys* and *Arthrochilus*.

pseudoterminal of an inflorescence or solitary flower, situated at or close to the stem apex but in fact axillary.

puberulent, puberulous minutely pubescent; covered with minute, soft hairs.

puberulose, puberulous see puberulent.

pubescent generally hairy; more specifically, covered with short, fine, soft hairs.

pulverulent powdery, covered in a fine bloom.

pulvinate possessing a pulvinus; also sometimes used of cushion-like plants.

pulvinus a cushion of enlarged tissue on a stem at the insertion of a stalk.

punctate dotted with minute, translucent impressions, pits or dark spots.

puncticulate minutely punctate.

pungent ending in a rigid and sharp long point.

pustular, pustulate of a surface covered with pustules.

pustule a pimple-like or blister-like eruption.

pustuliform blister-like.

pyramidal conical, but with more angular sides.

pyriform pear-shaped.

quadrangular four-angled.

quadrate more or less square.

quadrilateral four-sided.

raceme an indeterminate, unbranched and, usually, elongate inflorescence composed of pedicelled flowers. The inflorescences of most orchids are strictly *spicate*, the individual flower 'stalks' in fact being ovaries; however, this term tends to be confined to plants with very compact, slender inflorescences (e.g. *Arpophyllum*), whereas the looser flower sprays of – say – *Cymbidium* are described as racemes or said to be racemose. To confuse matters further, growers habitually refer to most multi-flowered orchid inflorescences as 'spikes'.

racemiform of an inflorescence that appears to be a raceme, i.e. slender, simple and with apparently stalked flowers.

racemose of flowers borne in a raceme; of an inflorescence that is a raceme.

rachis (pl. rachises, rachides) the axis of a compound inflorescence, as an extension of the peduncle.

radiate (adj.) spreading outward from a common centre.

radical arising directly from the root, rootstock or root-like stems, usually applied to leaves that are basal rather than cauline.

raft a plaque made of wooden slats, used as foothold for epiphytic orchids.

ramentaceous (on stems or leaves) possessing small, loose, brownish scales.

reclinate see reclining.

reclining tending gradually backwards from the vertical.

reflexed abruptly deflexed at more than a 90° angle.

remontant of a plant that flowers twice or more in a season, in distinct phases.

remote see distant.

reniform kidney-shaped; lunate, but with the concave centre of the shape attached to the base, and the ends obtuse.

repand sinuate, but with less pronounced undulations.

resiniferous see resinous.

resinous containing or exuding resin.

resupinate, resupine inverted by a twisting of 180° of the stalk, this is true of most orchid flowers with the result that the lip is held lowermost; cf. non-resupinate.

reticulate netted, i.e. with a close or open network of anastomosing veins, ribs or colouring, as in the leaves of *Anoectochilus* or the fibrous basal sheaths of *Isabelia*.

reticulation a network of reticulate veins, ribs, colouring or fibres.

retrorse (usually of a minor organ attached to a larger part, e.g. a prickle on a stem, a barb on a leaf or a callus on a lip) turned, curved or bent downwards or backwards, away from the apex; cf. introrse.

retuse (of apices) emarginate, but with a small, rounded sinus, and the adjacent lobes blunt.

revolute of margins, rolled under, i.e. toward the dorsal surface, the antithesis of involute.

rhizomatous producing or possessing rhizomes; rhizome-like.

rhizome a specialized stem, slender or swollen, branching or simple, subterranean or lying close to the soil surface (except in epiphytes), that produces roots and aerial parts (stems, leaves, inflorescences) along its length and at its apex, common to many perennial herbs.

rhomboid (of leaves, tepals etc.) diamond-shaped, angularly oval, the base and apex forming acute angles, and both sides forming obtuse angles.

ribbed possessing one or more prominent veins or nerves.

roridulous covered with small, translucent prominences, giving the appearance of dewdrops.

rosette (of leaves) radiating from a common crown or centre.

rostellum the beak-like tissue separating the anther from the stigma in Orchidaceae.

rostrate see beaked.

rosulate of leaves arranged in a basal rosette or rosettes.

rotund rounded, curved like the arc of a circle.

rudimentary fragmentary, imperfectly developed.

rufescent, rufous reddish-brown.

rugose wrinkled by irregular lines and veins.

rugulose finely rugose.

ruminate (adj.) appearing as if chewed.

saccate bag- or pouch-like, shaped like a round shoe.

sagittate arrow- or spear-shaped, where the equal and approximately triangular basal lobes point downward or toward the stalk or claw; see hastate.

salverform of a whole perianth or a lip with a long, slim tube and an abruptly expanded, flattened limb.

saprophyte a plant deriving nutrition from dead or decayed organic matter and usually lacking chlorophyll. Several orchids are saprophytic, including the Coral Root, the Ghost Orchid, Bird's Nest Orchid, the giant climbing *Galeola* and the subterranean *Rhizanthella*. Because of their highly specialized habitats and fragile symbiotic associations, they rarely survive in cultivation.

saprophytic deriving its nutrition from dissolved or decayed organic matter.

saxicolous growing in or near rocky places, or on rocks.

scaberulous finely or minutely scabrous.

scabrid a little scabrous, or rough.

scabridulous minutely scabrid.

scabrous rough, harsh to the touch because of minute projections, scales, tiny teeth or bristles.

scandent climbing – few orchids are truly climbing; they include *Vanilla* and the saprophyte *Galeola*. Several monopodial orchids produce long, semi-scandent stems, *Papilionanthe*, *Dimorphorchis Aerides* and *Angraecum* among them.

scape an erect, leafless stalk bearing terminal flower or flowers.

scapose producing scapes or borne on a scape.

scarabaeiform beetle-shaped.

scariose see scarious.

scarious thin, dry and shrivelled; consisting of more or less translucent tissue.

scarred bearing scars where bodies have fallen off, e.g. leaf scars on stems.

scurfy covered with tiny bran-like scales, or scale-like particles.

scutate shaped like a shield or buckler; with a concrete centre surrounded by an elevated margin.

scutelliform shaped like a small shield.

sectile (of pollinia) gathered loosely in 'packets'.

secund (of flowers, leaves) where all the parts are borne along one side of the axis, or appear to be arranged in this way because of twists in their stalks.

semiterete a semi-cylindrical form, terete on one side, but flattened on the other, as some petioles.

sepal one of the members of the outer floral envelope, enclosing and protecting the inner floral parts prior to anthesis, the segments composing the calyx, sometimes leafy, sometimes bract- or scale-like, sometimes petaloid. Sepals when described as such are usually free; they may, however, be wholly or partially fused in a calyx tube, a sepaline cup or a synsepalum. See also *dorsal*, *lateral*, *tepal*.

sepaline pertaining to the sepals.

sepaloid sepal-like.

sericeous silky, covered with fine, soft, adpressed hairs.

serrate essentially dentate, but with apically directed teeth resembling those of a saw; biserrate is when the teeth are themselves serrate. (See dentate.)

serrulate minutely or finely serrate.

sessile stalkless.

seta a bristle, or bristle-shaped organ.

setaceous either bearing bristles, or bristle-like.

setiform bristle-shaped.

setose covered with sharply pointed bristles.

setulose finely or minutely setose.

sharp-pointed see acute, mucronate and pungent.

sheath a tubular structure surrounding an organ or part; most often, the basal part of a leaf surrounding the stem, either inrolled as a tube, or strongly conduplicate and therefore distinct from the leaf blade.

sheathing where the tubular, convolute or conduplicate base of a leaf or spathe invests and surrounds the stem or other parts.

sigmoid, sigmoidal S-shaped, curving in one direction and then the other, for example the column of *Cycnoches*, or the lip apex in *Cirrhaea dependens*.

simple not compound; not divided into secondary units, thus in one part or unbranched.

sinuate (of the outline of a margin) wavy, alternatively concave and convex. (See undulate.)

sinus the indentation or space between two divisions, e.g. between lobes.

solitary used either of a single flower which constitutes a whole inflorescence, or a single flower in an axil (but perhaps in a much larger overall inflorescence).

spathaceous furnished with a spathe.

spathe a conspicuous leaf or bract subtending an inflorescence.

spatheole a small or secondary spathe.

spathiform spathe-shaped.

spathulate, spatulate spatula-shaped, essentially oblong, but attenuated at the base and rounded at the apex.

speculum a 'mirror', the iridescent blue patch found on the lips of some *Ophrys*.

spicate spike-like, or borne in a spikelike inflorescence.

spiciform spike-shaped.

spiculate furnished with fine, fleshy points.

spike an indeterminate inflorescence bearing sessile flowers on an unbranched axis; but see also raceme.

spikelet a small spike, forming one part of a compound spicate inflorescence.

spinescent (1) bearing or capable of developing spines; (2) terminating in, or modified to, a spine-like tip.

spinose bearing spines.

spinule a small spine.

spinulose bearing small or sparsely distributed spines.

spur a tubular or sac-like basal extension of the perianth, generally projecting backwards and containing nectar – a feature found in many orchids but nowhere more famously than in *Angraecum sesquipedale*, the spurs of which may be 35cm long

and are adapted to receive the proboscis of a single species of moth; cf. mentum.

spurred furnished with a spur or spurs.

squamate, squamose, squamous covered with scales.

squamulose covered or furnished with small scales.

squarrose rough or hostile as a result of the outward projection of scales or bracts with reflexed tips perpendicular to the axis; also used of parts spreading at right angles from a common axis.

stalk a general term for the stem-like support of any organ.

stamen the male floral organ, bearing an anther, generally on a filament, and producing pollen.

staminal attached to or relating to the stamen.

staminate of the male, a unisexual, male flower, bearing stamens and no functional pistils.

staminodal relating to a staminode.

staminode a sterile stamen or stamen-like structure. In many plant families, this can be an attractive, petal-like feature giving rise to 'double' flowers. In Orchidaceae, the term is used only in relation to the slipper orchids. *Paphiopedilum*, for example, carries a fleshy, shield-like staminode on its short column, standing between and covering the 2 fertile stamens.

stellate star-like.

stigma the apical unit of a pistil which receives the pollen and normally differs in texture from the rest of the style.

stigmatic attached or relating to the stigma.

stipe a stalk connecting pollinia and viscidium.

stipitate provided with a small stalk or stalk-like base.

stramineous straw-like, in colour, texture or shape.

striate striped with fine longitudinal lines, grooves or ridges.

strict erect and straight.

strigose covered with sharp, stiff, adpressed hairs.

strigulose minutely or finely strigose.

striolated gently or obscurely striated.

style the elongated and narrow part of the pistil between the ovary and stigma; absent if the stigma is sessile.

subimbricate somewhat overlapping.

subopposite more or less opposite, but with one leaf or leaflet of a pair slightly above or below its partner.

subsessile with a partial or minute stalk.

subtend (*verb*) of a bract, bracteole, spathe, leaf, etc., to be inserted directly below a different organ or structure, often sheathing or enclosing it.

subterranean, subterraneous underground, i.e. not aerial.

subulate awl-shaped, tapering from a narrow base to a fine, sharp point.

succulent thickly cellular and fleshy, a plant with roots, stems or leaves with this quality.

sulcate lined with deep longitudinal grooves or channels, often confined to parts possessing a single deep gulley, i.e. some petioles.

sympodial a form of growth in which the terminal bud dies or terminates in an inflorescence, and growth is continued by successive secondary axes growing from lateral buds; cf. monopodial.

synflorescence a 'compound' inflorescence strictly composed of a terminal inflorescence and lateral inflorescences; e.g. *Epidendrum porphyreum.*

synsepalum (synsepal) a discrete structure formed by the fusion of two or more sepals – in *Masdevallia* all three sepals are fused in varying degrees, forming a cup – or shield-like unit. In *Paphiopedilum* and most *Cypripedium*, only the lateral sepals are fused, forming a single bract-like organ behind the lip.

teeth marginal lobes, usually relatively small, regularly disposed and with the sides tapering toward their apex, thus differing from broad lobes or very narrow divisions; see dentate, serrate.

tentacle a sensitive glandular hair.

tepal usually a unit of an undifferentiated perianth, which cannot be distinguished as a sepal or petal, as might be found with the 'petals' of a tulip. In orchids, however (for which the term was coined), it is applied to the sepals and petals viewed collectively but *excluding* the labellum, despite the lips being a modified third petal. Thus 'tepals narrow, red; lip showy, yellow' means 'petals and sepals narrow, red; lip showy, yellow'.

terete cylindrical and smoothly circular in cross-section, as in the leaves of *Luisia* and *Papilionanthe.*

terminal at the tip or apex of a stem, the summit of an axis.

terrestrial growing in the soil; a land plant.

tessellated chequered, marked with a grid of small squares, for example, the tepals of *Vanda tessellata.*

tetragonal, tetragonous four-angled; e.g. the pseudobulbs of *Dendrobium tetragonum.*

tetrapterous four-winged.

threadlike see filiform.

throat the orifice of the tubular part of a lip.

tomentose with densely woolly, short, rigid hairs, perceptible to the touch.

tomentulose slightly tomentose.

tomentum a tomentose pubescence.

toothed possessing teeth, usually used of margins, often interchangeably with dentate or, qualified, as saw-toothed or bluntly toothed.

tortuous irregularly bent and turned in many directions.

torulose of a cylindrical, ellipsoid or terete body, swollen and constricted at intervals but less markedly and regularly so than moniliform.

trailing (of stems) prostrate but not rooting.

trapeziform asymmetrical and four-sided, as a trapezium.

tri- prefix denoting three.

trichome a unbranched, hair-like outgrowth of the epidermis, often glandular-tipped.

trichotomous branching regularly by dividing regularly into three.

tridactylate with 3 narrow, finger-like lobes, for example, the lips of the appropriately named genus *Tridactyle.*

tridentate when the teeth of a margin have teeth which are themselves toothed or when an organ terminates in 3 distinct teeth.

tridenticulate finely or minutely tridentate.

trifid as bifid, but twice cleft into three lobe-like divisions.

trifoliate three-leaved.

trifurcate with three branches or forked in three.

trigonal three-angled.

trigonous a solid body which is triangular but obtusely angled in cross-section.

trilobed having three lobes, as in the lips of many orchids.

trimorphic as polymorphic, or dimorphic, but occurring in three distinct forms.

trinervate three-nerved.

tripartite divided almost to the base in three segments.

tripterous three-winged.

triquetrous triangular in cross-section.

trisulcate with three grooves or furrows.

trullate, trulliform trowel-shaped.

truncate where the organ is abruptly terminated as if cut cleanly straight across, perpendicular to the midrib.

tuber a swollen, generally subterranean stem, branch or root used for storage; cf. tuberoid.

tubercle a small, warty, conical to spherical excrescence.

tubercular, tuberculose see tuberculate.

tuberculate, tubercled covered with small, blunt, warty excrescences.

tuberiferous bearing tubers.

tuberoid a swollen subterranean storage organ like a tuber but composed of both stem and root tissues. (Strictly, a tuber consists of only one type of tissue.) Tuberoids are common features of deciduous terrestrial orchids. The term tends to be used interchangeably with 'tuber'.

tuberous bearing tubers, or resembling a tuber.

tumid see turgid.

turbinate top-shaped; inversely conical, but contracted near the apex.

turgid more or less swollen or inflated, sometimes by fluid contents.

umbel a flat-topped inflorescence like a corymb, but with all the pedicels (rays) radiating from the same point at the apex of the main axis, best illustrated in Orchidaceae by *Bulbophyllum* spp.

umbellate borne in or furnished with an umbel; resembling an umbel.

umbelliform in the form of or resembling an umbel.

umbilicate with a more or less central depression, like a navel.

umbonate bossed; orbicular, with a point projecting from the centre.

umbraculiferous shaped like a parasol.

unarmed devoid of spines, prickles or other sharp points.

uncinate (of hairs) hooked, where the tips are acutely deflexed, or where the sides are denticulate, or bear minute, retrorse barbs.

undifferentiated of parts or tissues with no apparent characters to distinguish them — e.g. the units of an undifferentiated perianth, where sepals and petals resemble each other so closely as to be indistinguishable; cf. tepal.

undulate wavy, but of the margin's surface rather than outline (see sinuate).

unguiculate of petals and sepals, bearing a basal claw.

unifoliate bearing a single leaf.

uniform of one type only (by contrast with dimorphous or polymorphic).

unilateral one-sided; borne or arranged on one side only.

unisexual either staminate or pistillate; with flowers of one sex only.

united of parts usually free or separate held closely or clinging together so as to be scarcely distinguishable or wholly fused forming a single whole. The term covers both adherent and coherent.

urceolate (of a perianth) urn-shaped; globose to subcylindrical but with a considerable constriction at or below the mouth. Viewed from the side, the flowers of *Acanthephippium* are strongly urceolate.

vaginate possessing or enclosed by a sheath.

valvate (1) describing parts with touching but not overlapping margins; (2) opening by or pertaining to valves.

variegated marked irregularly with various colours.

vein an externally visible strand of vascular tissues.

velamen corky epidermis of aerial roots in some epiphytes, through which atmospheric moisture is absorbed.

velutinous velvety, coated with fine soft hairs, more densely so than in tomentose and giving the appearance and texture of velvet.

venation the arrangement or disposition of veins on the surface of an organ.

venose possessing veins.

ventral attached or relating to the inner or adaxial surface or part of an organ; sometimes wrongly applied to the undersurface.

ventricose unequally swollen; inflated on one side in a more pronounced manner than if gibbous.

vermiculate worm-shaped, with a pattern of impressed, close, wavy lines.

verrucose warty.

verruculose finely verrucose.

verticil a ring or whorl of three or more parts at one node.

verticillaster a false whorl where opposite cymes, being almost sessile, appear to surround the stem in a whorl.

verticillate forming or appearing to form a whorl.

vesicle a small, bladder-like sac or cavity, filled with fluid or air.

vesicular of, possessing, or composed of vesicles.

vestigial of a part or organ which was functional and fully developed in ancestral forms, but is now reduced and obsolete.

villous with shaggy pubescence.

virgate long, slim and straight, like a rod or wand.

viscid covered in a sticky or gelatinous exudation.

viscidium the viscid area of the rostellum to which the pollinia attach.

viviparous with buds which become plantlets while still attached to the parent plant.

whorl when three or more organs are arranged in a circle at one node or near one another around the same axis.

wing a thin, flat, often membranous extension or appendage or an organ.

woolly see lanate, lanuginose and tomentose.

xerophyte a plant adapted to survival in an arid habitat.

xerophytic adapted to withstand drought.

zygomorphic bilaterally symmetrical, having only one plane of symmetry by which it can be divided into two equal halves.

Temperature Conversion

$$°C = 5/9 \, (°F - 32) \qquad °F = 9/5 \, °C + 32$$

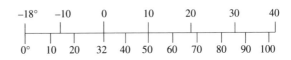

Celsius	−18°	−10	0	10	20	30	40
Fahrenheit	0° 10 20	32 40	50 60	70	80	90	100

Conversions of Measurements

Length			
	1 millimetre	=	0.0394 inch
	1 centimetre	=	0.3937 inch
	1 metre	=	1.0936 yards
	1 kilometre	=	0.6214 miles

Range of Average Annual Minimum Temperature for each Climatic Zone

Zone	°F	°C
1	< −50	< −45.5
2	−50 to −40	−45.5 to −40.1
3	−40 to −30	−40.0 to −34.5
4	−30 to −20	−34.4 to −28.8
5	−20 to −10	−28.8 to −23.4
6	−10 to 0	−23.3 to −17.8
7	0 to +10	−17.7 to −12.3
8	+10 to +20	−12.2 to −6.7
9	+20 to +30	−6.6 to −1.2
10	+30 to +40	−1.1 to +4.4
11	> +40	> +4.4

Abbreviations

c	circa (before a date or measurement)	N	North (e.g. N America)
C	Central (e.g. C Asia)	pet.	petal(s)
cv.	cultivar	pubesc.	pubescent
cvs	cultivars	rhiz.	rhizome
diam.	diameter	S	South (e.g. S America)
E	East (e.g. E Indies)	seg.	segment(s)
fl.	flower	sep.	sepal(s)
fld.	flowered	sp.	species
fls	flowers	spp.	species (plural)
f.	forma	ssp.	subspecies
infl.	inflorescence	sspp.	subspecies (plural)
lf	leaf	var.	variety
lvs	leaves	W	West (e.g. W Indies)
mts	mountains		

Orchids

A to Z

Acacallis Lindl. (From Gk Akakallis, the lover of Apollo.) 1 species, an epiphyte. Rhizome creeping, slender. Pseudobulbs to 5cm, ovoid, lustrous green, compressed, unifoliate or bifoliate at apex. Leaves to 20cm, erect, coriaceous, oblong-lanceolate, short-stalked. Inflorescence a basal raceme, erect or arching, surpassing leaves, loosely-few to several-flowered; flowers showy, fragrant; sepals and petals subsimilar, to 4×2.5cm, blue-mauve, interior flushed lavender-pink, elliptic, apex acute or apiculate, slightly concave above; lip to 2.5×3cm, gold-bronze to red-purple, centre blue-violet, unguiculate, reniform, apex rounded, apiculate, concave, margin undulate; callus yellow-orange, fleshy, erect; column with a long slender foot, erect, apex with 2 subquadrate wings, streaked red-mauve. Brazil, Venezuela, Colombia.

CULTIVATION   This epiphyte has a strongly ascending habit and striking 'blue' flowers. It succeeds best attached to bark or rafts on pads of sphagnum, palm, or tree fern fibre. Suspend in a moist, warm atmosphere (min. 15°C/60°F) in dappled sunlight, misting daily when in growth. Propagate by divisions of not fewer than two pseudobulbs.

A.cyanea Lindl. (*Aganisia coerulea* Rchb. f.).

Acampe Lindl. (From Gk *akampes*, rigid, referring to the flowers.) Some 13 species of monopodial epiphytes and lithophytes. Stems robust. Roots thick. Leaves 2-ranked, alternate, fleshy, ligulate, coriaceous, recurved, basally articulated to a leaf sheath. Inflorescence axillary, few- to many-flowered, dense, subcapitate or cylindric; flowers waxy, fragrant; sepals and petals spreading, lateral sepals fused to the lip; lip projecting from column base, entire or trilobed, saccate or spurred, often with raised calli or pubescence descending into the spur, or on inflated base. Indo-Malaya, Africa.

CULTIVATION   Robust *Vanda*-like plants producing relatively small spotted flowers, often in compact racemes or crowded heads. Grow in baskets or orchid pots of an extremely open bark-based medium in full sunlight and intermediate or warm conditions. Mist daily, reducing supplies during the flowering period. Plants grow vigorously, producing many stout aerial roots, and may require regeneration by removing denuded lower portions of the stem.

A.dentata Lindl. See *A.ochracea.*
A.multiflora (Lindl.) Lindl. See *A.rigida.*

A.ochracea (Lindl.) Hochr. (*A.dentata* Lindl.).
Stems to 60cm. Lvs arching. Panicle lax, many-fld, to 30cm; fls successional, fragrant, yellow-white; sep. and pet. blotched brown; lip white streaked dull purple or maroon, basally saccate. India.

A.papillosa (Lindl.) Lindl.
Stems to 90cm, ultimately scandent, branched. Lvs 7.5–15cm, oblong-ligulate. Umbel to 2.5cm, many-fld; fls to 1.8cm diam., yellow blotched brown, lip white or cream, fragrant;

sep. oblong or oblong-elliptic, obtuse; pet. similar; lip with midlobe ovate, lateral lobes triangular, basally saccate, pubesc., papillose above. Himalaya, India to Burma.

A.praemorsa (Roxb.) Blatter & McCann. See *A.rigida.*

A.rigida (Buch.-Ham. ex Sm.) P. Hunt (*A.multiflora* (Lindl.) Lindl.; *A.praemorsa* (Roxb.) Blatter & McCann).
Stems very tall. Lvs 15–45cm coriaceous, ligulate. Infl. 5–20cm, racemose, many-fld, shortly branching; sep. and pet. obovate-elliptic, rounded, yellow, spotted or marked red-brown to crimson; lip white, with midlobe ovate, lateral lobes erect, rounded, callus ridged, pubesc., fleshy. Asia, E Africa.

Acanthephippium Bl. (From Gk *akantha*, thorn, and *ephippion*, saddle, referring to the shape of the lip.) Some 15 species of terrestrials. Pseudobulbs large, ovoid to subconical, fleshy, flushed mauve, grooved with age, apically trifoliate. Leaves large, plicate, elliptic to oblong-lanceolate, tapering to a stalk, falling within 2 seasons. Inflorescence a lateral raceme; peduncle short, stout; sepals connate, forming an urn-shaped tube surrounding the petals and lip; petals free, spathulate, narrower than sepals; lip trilobed, saddle-shaped, lateral lobes erect, hinged at column base, spur present or absent. Asia to Fiji.

CULTIVATION   Terrestrials with curious, waxy, cup-like flowers, suitable for shaded positions in the intermediate house. They require a perfectly drained sandy medium rich in leafmould and garden compost and plentiful supplies of water and food when in growth. Resentful of frequent repotting.

A.bicolor Lindl.
Pseudobulbs to 5cm. Lvs to 30×10cm. Raceme erect, to 6-fld; bracts prominent; fls fragrant, waxy, pale yellow, streaked red-brown; lip lemon yellow. Indochina.

A.javanicum Bl.
Pseudobulbs to 25cm. Lvs to 60×20cm. Racemes to 25cm and over, from central nodes of pseudobulb, few-fld; fls fragrant, campanulate, dull yellow, streaked and dappled pink or rose-purple, the lip pale yellow and white with mid-lobe tipped purple, lateral lobes dotted red; sep. to 4.5cm; pet. slightly protruding between sep. at tube aperture; lip deeply trilobed, almost obscured by sep., midlobe convex, recurved, lateral lobes oblong, erect, apically truncate and dilated. Malaysia.

A.mantinianum Lindl. & Cogn.
Pseudobulbs to 5cm, dark purple. Lvs to 30×13cm, deeply

plicate, fleshy, tinged purple below. Racemes to 25cm, to 5-fld; fls to 5cm, fragrant, fleshy, yellow, striped dull red-brown; lip pale yellow to vivid gold. Philippines.

A.striatum Lindl.
Pseudobulbs 14–20cm, initially with violet-lined sheaths. Racemes 2–3-fld, erect; fls fragrant, to 3.25cm, white or cream-yellow, tinged dull red; sep. and pet. oblong, acute, almost equal, lip midlobe recurved, triangular, acute, lateral lobes triangular-falcate, disc with red-purple calli. N India.

A.sylhetense Lindl.
Resembles *A.bicolor*, but more robust . Fls to 5cm, thick, waxy, long-lasting, cream to dull yellow, spotted and streaked dull purple; sep. and pet. oblong-lanceolate; lip midlobe ligulate, lateral lobes small, fleshy, disc with 3 fringed calli. Himalaya.

Aceras R. Br. (From Gk *a*-, without, and *keras*, horn; referring to the spurless lips on its flowers.) 1 species, terrestrial. Tubers not lobed. Stems 10–60cm glabrous, leafy; basal sheaths papery, white or brown. Leaves 5–12×1.5–2.5cm, oblong-lanceolate to ovate-elliptic, obtuse to acute, reduced toward summit of stem. Flowers crowded in spikes, to 3cm long; dorsal sepal and petals valvate, incurved, forming hood, olive green tinted red at margins; lip spurless, decurved, trilobed, lateral lobes slender, midlobe cleft. Summer. W & C Europe.

CULTIVATION   See Introduction: Hardy Orchids.

A.anthropophorum (L.) Ait. f. MAN ORCHID.

Acianthus R. Br. (From Gk *akis*, point, and *anthos*, flower.) Some 20 species of terrestrials. Tubers globose. Leaf solitary, ovate, cordate, entire or, rarely, dissected, held above basal sheath or slightly higher, encircling scape. Inflorescence a scapose raceme; flowers loosely spiralling, subtended by bracts; dorsal sepal incurved or erect, concave, ovate to lanceolate, often tapering to a slender point, lateral sepals narrow, spreading or ascending; petals equalling or smaller than dorsal sepal, lanceolate to linear, spreading or deflexed; lip entire, spreading, with 2 calli at base or dotted with tubercles; column incurved. Australia, New Zealand, Solomon Is., New Caledonia.

CULTIVATION   Bizarre terrestrials with slender stems of bug-like flowers, suited to cultivation in pans of extremely gritty, slightly acid loam-based medium in the alpine and cool house. Give full sunlight, water copiously when in growth; impose a marked dry dormancy of a month or so after flowering. Tubers require cleaning and repotting every second season, at which point they can be divided. On perfectly drained, dry soils and with some protection from wind and damp, these intriguing plants can be grown outside in Zone 8.

A.brunonis F. Muell. See *A.fornicatus*.

A.caudatus R. Br. MAYFLY ORCHID.
Flowering stems slender, glabrous, to 22cm. Lf to 4cm, ovate-cordate, purple beneath. Pedicels short; fls 1–9, malodorous, violet or maroon to black; dorsal sep. to 3.5cm, slightly incurved, tapering to a long filamentous tip, as do lateral sepals, margins slightly revolute, equal or exceeding laterals; pet. to 5mm, lanceolate, falcate, spreading or reflexed; lip mauve-rose to dark violet, rounded and involute at base, lanceolate, acute toward tip with glandular apical portion; column to 4mm. Late summer–mid autumn. C & SE Australia.

A.exsertus R. Br. MOSQUITO ORCHID. Flowering stems glabrous, slender, to 21cm. Lf to 4.5cm, ovate-cordate or bilobed, sessile, dark green above, purple beneath. Pedicels short; fls 3–20, translucent pale green to green tinted red or mauve, the lip a darker purple-red, the anther bright yellow-white; dorsal sep. ovate-acuminate, incurved, concave, 5–8mm, lateral sep. to 9mm, narrowly subulate, spreading,

tips acute or with swollen, club-shaped appendages; pet. 2–5mm, lanceolate; lip to 6mm, ovate-lanceolate to 6mm, basally concave, glabrous or glandular, calli comma-shaped, apex thicker with many minute glands; column to 4mm. Spring–summer. Temperate Australia.

A.fornicatus R. Br. (*A.brunonis* F. Muell.). PIXIE CAPS.
Flowering stems to 30cm. Lf cordate, 2.5–5cm, basal or clasping stem with broad auricles, entire to sinuate or 3-lobed. Fls 4–14; dorsal sep. 5–12mm, green flushed or spotted violet-pink, ovate-lanceolate, erect, concave, tapering, point filiform to 6mm, lateral, sep. 4–9mm, incurved or decurved, linear; pet. green marked purple, lanceolate; lip shorter than sep., forward-pointing, ovate-acute to broadly lanceolate, concave at base with 2 short, mauve calli, central region smooth, green, grooved, margins fringed, reflexed, with peripheral row of maroon papillae. Late spring–early autumn. E Australia.

A.reniformis (R. Br.) Schltr. See *Cyrtostylis reniformis*.

Acineta Lindl. (From Gk *akinetos*, immobile, referring to the lip which is fused to the column.) Some 15 species of epiphytes and lithophytes. Pseudobulbs clustered, ovoid to cylindrical, glossy olive green, laterally compressed, finely wrinkled, grooved or ridged, basally sheathed. Leaves 2–4, 30–60cm, terminal, thick, glabrous, plicate or ribbed, narrow-elliptic to oblanceolate, acute, stalked. Inflorescence to 70cm, basal, pendulous, racemose; floral bracts large, lanceolate, spreading or sheathing pedicels; flowers to 6cm diam., clustered, thick, waxy, nodding, fragrant, ivory to golden yellow or maroon, marked oxblood above; sepals broadly lanceolate, acute, incurved, concave above; petals thinner than sepals; lip fleshy, rigid, basally concave or subsaccate, midlobe short, narrow-oblong to rhombic, disc with prominent calli, lateral lobes erect, rounded, larger than midlobe; column thick, pubescent. Spring–summer. Tropical America.

CULTIVATION   As for *Stanhopea*, but with a shorter resting period and heavier shade when in growth; as with that genus, flower spikes may require guidance if they are not to become buried (if grown in pots) or trapped by slats in baskets.

A.barkeri (Batem.) Lindl. (*Peristeria barkeri* Batem.).
Infl. to 50cm; bracts shining bronze-green; fls to 12, to 4.5cm diam., cupped, spice-scented, ochre to golden yellow; pet. basally flecked or spotted blood-red above; lip deeper yellow, mottled red to maroon, midlobe slender, rectangular, apically notched or dolabriform, concave above, keeled beneath, disc prominent, fleshy, lateral lobes incurved, broadly reniform; column cream-white, narrowly winged at apex. Mexico.

A.chrysantha (Morr.) Lindl. & Paxt. (*A.densa* Lindl. & Paxt.; *A.warscewiczii* Klotzsch).
Infl. to 70cm; bracts papery; fls to 20, clustered in apical half of raceme, to 6cm diam., very fleshy, cup-like, vanilla-scented, long-lived; pet. yellow, concave, lateral sep. abruptly acute, dorsal sep. obtuse; pet. yellow, flecked blood-red at base and margins, narrower and thinner than sep.; lip golden, mottled and spotted red to maroon, basally saccate and appearing bluntly spurred, midlobe short, fleshy, square to

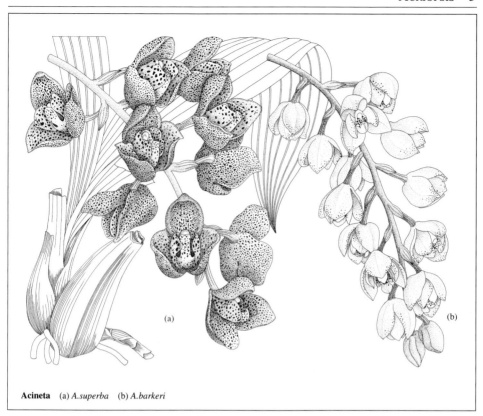

Acineta   (a) *A.superba*   (b) *A.barkeri*

rhombic, disc prominently callused, winged, toothed, lateral lobes erect, rounded, clasping column; column narrowly winged. Guatemala, Costa Rica, Panama.

A.densa Lindl. & Paxt. See *A.chrysantha.*

A.erythroxantha Rchb. f.
Infl. to 45cm, axis slightly scurfy; bracts somewhat inflated, olive green, flushed mauve; sep. thick, dull gold, dorsal sep. to 4cm, concave, lateral sep. to 5cm, more spreading, oblanceolate, fuzzy at tips beneath; pet. golden, basally spotted dark maroon above, to 3.6cm, narrower than sep. with thin margins; lip to 4×2cm, basally saccate, ivory flushed maroon, spotted dark red, midlobe waxy, yellow, callus 2-ridged, glossy blood-red with a retrorse, russet plate, lateral lobes yellow, spotted red near callus; column ivory, finely pubesc. above, woolly beneath. Venezuela, Colombia.

A.superba (HBK) Rchb. f.
Fls to 8cm diam., fleshy, cupped and not opening fully, muskily perfumed, colour variable – golden yellow to ochre, finely spotted maroon or yellow-bronze throughout and heavily mottled oxblood to chocolate; lip very fleshy, midlobe blunt, narrowly carinate, callus fleshy, 2-ridged, ridges divergent, lateral lobes erect, obcuneate; column thick, pubesc., apical wings hooding clinandrium. Panama to Peru. Europe

A.warscewiczii Klotzsch. See *A.chrysantha.*

Acriopsis Reinw. ex Bl. (From Gk *akris*, locust, and *opsis*, resembling.) Some 5 species of small epiphytes. Pseudobulbs crowded, ovoid to subpyriform, sheathed, apically 2–4-leaved. Leaves linear, stalked. Raceme or panicle basal, many-flowered; bracts triangular, membranous, acute; flowers twisted; dorsal sepal lanceolate, apically incurved, lateral sepals fused, situated behind the lip; petals oblong to obovate, shorter or equalling sepals; lip forming a tube with column base, trilobed or entire, basally tubular, apically keeled, glabrous or pubescent. SE Asia to Solomon Is.

CULTIVATION   See *Bulbophyllum.*

A.densiflora Lindl.
Pseudobulbs 1.5–2.5cm. Lvs narrow-oblong, obtuse. Infl. simple, erect; fls dark purple, lip edged white; dorsal sep. 3-veined, acute, lateral sep. 4–5-nerved; lip trilobed, narrowing basally, deflexed, midlobe broadly spathulate, lateral lobes oblong to triangular. Borneo, Sumatra.

A.javanica Reinw. ex Bl. (*Spathoglottis trivalvis* Wallich; *A.picta* Lindl.).
Pseudobulbs ridged, 1.3–6cm, apically bifoliate or trifoliate. Lvs to 18cm, linear, tapering basally. Infl. to 55cm, ascending from rhiz., basally sheathed; dorsal sep. concave, 3-nerved, pale yellow, sometimes striped purple, lateral sep. apically

obtuse, 2–6-nerved; pet. oblong to ovate, spreading, white or cream, apical blotch or stripe purple; lip narrowing basally, keeled, lateral lobes spreading, midlobe notched, crimson-purple, edged white; column dark purple-brown, hood pale. Sumatra to New Guinea.

A.picta Lindl. See *A.javanica.*

Ada Lindl. (Named after the queen of Caria in Asia Minor.) 15 species of epiphytes and lithophytes. Rhizomes short, bracteate. Pseudobulbs narrow-ovoid, laterally compressed, sheathed with leaflike bracts. Leaves 1–2, apical, glabrous, dark green, flexible, linear-lanceolate to ligulate, acute, base folded and petiole-like. Inflorescence to 50cm, racemose, lateral, arching, bracteate; flowers semi-tubular, nodding; sepals free, subequal, linear-lanceolate, acute, strongly forward-pointing, tips recurved, dorsal sepal erect, lateral sepals downcurved; petals smaller than sepals; lip entire, narrow-lanceolate or pandurate, acuminate, recurved, callus 2-ridged; column short, subterete, basally inflated with a depression containing base of callus. Winter–spring. Colombian Andes, New Grenada.

CULTIVATION   As for cool-growing *Odontoglossum.* Reduce water supply once growths are developed; increase on appearance of flower spike. Afford shade from direct sunlight and a moist, cool, buoyant atmosphere.

A.aurantiaca Lindl.
Pseudobulbs to 10cm. Lvs ligulate, to 30cm. Infl. to 30cm; fls to 18, to 2.5cm, scarlet, dark to bright orange or cinnabar red. Colombian Andes. A variable species. Closely related are the white-lipped *A.lehmannii* Rolfe from NW Colombia and the red-flowered *A.bennettorum* Dodson, from Peru.

Aerangis Rchb. f. (From Gk *aer,* air, and *angos,* vessel.) About 50 species of monopodial epiphytes and lithophytes. Stems short or elongated and woody; roots numerous, arising from lower part of stem. Leaves in 2 rows, leathery or fleshy, unequally bilobed at apex, often oblanceolate. Racemes axillary, long or short, few- to many-flowered; flowers white, sometimes tinged with green, yellow or salmon-pink, usually in 2 ranks with the spurs hanging below; sepals and petals free, spreading or reflexed, rarely cup-shaped, similar, usually lanceolate, acute; lip entire, often similar to petals, with long or short spur; column short and stout or long and slender; pollinia 2. Mainland Africa, Madagascar and Mascarene Is.; 1 species Sri Lanka.

CULTIVATION   Cool, intermediate or warm-growing (min. winter temperature 10–20°C/50–68°F), they require semi-shaded, humid to buoyant conditions. They succeed best on vertically hung rafts, cork mounts or fibre slabs, and attached, initially, to a pad of chopped moss and garden compost. After flowering, reduce water and temperatures, moving plants (in cool temperate climates) to higher positions in the greenhouse to receive maximum winter sunlight. The flowers are usually white, sometimes with red, yellow or green tints; they are nocturnally fragrant, long-spurred and exceptionally graceful – as with so many angraecoid orchids, the lines and shapes in this genus are remarkable, although the colour is basically the same. One notable exception is *A.luteoalba* var. *rhodosticta,* a tiny plant with disproportionately large, rounded ivory flowers, each with a vivid orange-red column. The miniature species are excellent growing-case plants. Under such conditions, do not allow water to lodge in the leaf axils.

A.apiculatum Hook. See *A.biloba.*

A.appendiculata (De Wild.) Schltr.
Stem short; roots grey, to 5mm diam. Lvs 3–4, to 8×3cm, dark green, leathery or fleshy, obovate, obtusely or subacutely unequally bilobed at apex. Racemes pendent, to 15cm, laxly to 10-fld; fls white; pedicel and ovary 10–15mm; sep. 5–8mm, elliptic or obovate, dorsal sep. erect or arched over column, lateral sep. reflexed; pet. similar, spreading; lip 7–8×3–4mm, elliptic-oblong, slightly apiculate; spur 4–6cm, slender, slightly incurved; column short, to 2mm. Zambia, Malawi, Zimbabwe, Mozambique.

A.arachnopus (Rchb. f.) Schltr. (*Angraecum arachnopus* Rchb. f.).
Stem to 12cm. Lvs 5–7,. 7–20×2–5.5cm, oblanceolate, unequally and obtusely bilobed at apex. Racemes pendent, 30–60cm, laxly to 15-fld; fls white, sometimes tinged with pink; pedicel and ovary 3–4cm; sep. 14–18×3mm, spreading, linear-lanceolate, acuminate; pet. similar but shorter and reflexed; lip 12–14×3–4mm, oblong-lanceolate, acuminate, deflexed, the margins reflexed; spur 6–7cm, incurved; column slender. W Africa to Zaire.

A.articulata (Rchb. f.) Schltr. (*Angraecum articulatum* Rchb. f.; *A.descendens* Rchb. f.).
Stem to 30cm, sometimes branched. Lvs 12–15×4–5cm, very dark green, slightly unequally bilobed at apex, the lobes rounded. Raceme pendent, 15–25cm, to 18-fld; fls white, scented; ovary and pedicel to 2cm; sep. and pet. 12–20×4–5mm, spreading, elliptic, acute; lip 12–20×5mm, oblong, acute; spur 10–20cm; column short and stout, anth. cap with pronounced beak or point in centre. Winter. Madagascar.

A.biloba (Lindl.) Schltr. (*Angraecum bilobum* Lindl.; *A.apiculatum* Hook.).
Stem to 20cm, usually less. Lvs 4–10, distichous, to 18cm, 3–6cm wide near apex, obovate with acutely or obtusely bilobed apex, dark green dotted with black, with noticeable reticulate venation. Raceme pendent, 10–40cm, 8–20-fld; fls white; pedicel and spur often tinged pink; pedicel and ovary 2–3cm; sep. and pet. 12–25mm, spreading, narrowly lanceolate, acute; lip 15–25×6–8mm, deflexed, oblanceolate, cuspidate; spur usually 5–6cm, straight or incurved; column stout, 5–6mm. W Africa.

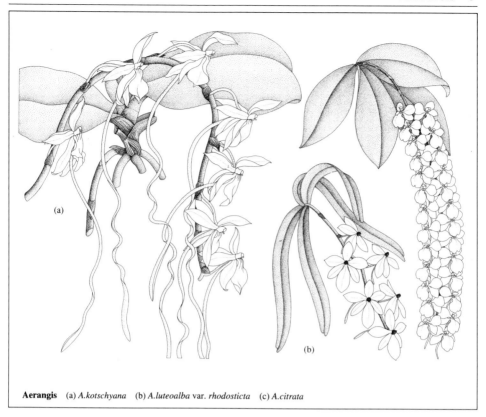

Aerangis (a) *A.kotschyana* (b) *A.luteoalba* var. *rhodosticta* (c) *A.citrata*

A.brachycarpa (A. Rich.) Dur. & Schinz.
Stem to 20cm, usually less; roots grey, 5–6mm diam. Lvs 4–12, to 25cm, 2–6cm wide near apex, obovate, acutely or obtusely unequally bilobed at apex, fleshy or leathery, dark green often dotted with black. Racemes arching or pendent, to 40cm, 2–12-fld; fls white; pet. and spur sometimes tinged pink; pedicel and ovary 3.5–7cm; sep. and pet. 20–45×4–8mm, narrowly lanceolate, acuminate, dorsal sep. erect, lateral sep. and pet. reflexed; lip 20–45×5–10mm, deflexed, lanceolate, acuminate; spur 12–20cm, straight or slightly incurved; column slender, 6–8mm. Ethiopia, Kenya, Uganda, Tanzania, Zambia, Angola.

A.calantha (Schltr.) Schltr.
Stem to 3cm; roots grey, 1–1.5mm diam. Lvs 2–6, 3–8cm×4–8mm, linear or falcate, unevenly and acutely bilobed at apex, dark green with some black dots. Racemes spreading or pendent, to 11cm, 2–8-fld; fls white, the spur and pedicel and ovary often tinged pink; pedicel and ovary 12–17mm; sep. 7–12×2–3.5mm, oblong-lanceolate, subacute, dorsal sep. erect, lateral sep. curving forwards; pet. similar but slightly shorter and narrower, spreading or slightly reflexed; lip 7–10×2–3.5mm, oblong-lanceolate, apiculate; spur 2.5–4cm, slender, with the tip often curved forwards like a hook; column stout, to 2mm. Ghana, Central African Republic, Cameroun, Equatorial Guinea, Zaire, Uganda, Tanzania, Angola.

A.calligera (Rchb. f.) Garay. See *A.ellisii*.

A.citrata (Thouars) Schltr. (*Angraecum citratum* Thouars).
Stem short, to 6cm; roots fine, almost wiry, 1.5–2.5mm diam. Lvs 9–12×2.5–3.5cm, elliptic, acutely and unequally bilobed at apex, dark green, thin-textured. Raceme to 25cm; fls 12–18, all in the same plane, pale yellow to creamy white, 15–18mm diam.; pedicel and ovary 6–8mm; dorsal sep. 5×4mm, arching over column, broadly ovate, obtuse, lateral

sep. 9×4mm, ovate, obtuse; pet. 10×8mm, broadly ovate; lip 8–10×7–10mm, broadly obovate or suborbicular, emarginate at apex; spur 3cm, enlarged and rounded at apex. Madagascar.

A.clavigera H. Perrier. See *A.macrocentra*.

A.confusa J. Stewart.
Stem to 10cm; roots grey, 2–3mm diam. Lvs 5–24× 1.5–5.5cm, oblanceolate or obovate, acutely or obtusely bilobed at apex, dark green. Racemes spreading or pendent, to 20cm; fls white, often tinged pink; pedicel and ovary 2–6cm; sep. 15–25mm, lanceolate, acuminate, the dorsal sep. arching over column, lateral sep. spreading; pet. 15–22×3–5mm, reflexed, lanceolate, acuminate; lip similar to pet. but wider, deflexed, margins recurved; spur 4–6cm, slender, tapering or slightly enlarged at apex; column 6–8mm. Kenya, Tanzania.

A.coriacea Summerh.
Stem woody, to 10cm; roots stout, grey, to 5mm diam. Lvs distichous, to 22×2–4.5cm, ligulate or obovate-ligulate, unequally bilobed at apex, the lobes rounded, fleshy, deep green with darker reticulate venation. Racemes arching, to 40cm, 4–22-fld; fls white, the spur and base of sep. and pet. tinged rose-pink or green; pedicel and ovary 2–3cm; dorsal sep. 13–20×7–10mm, erect, lanceolate-elliptic, lateral sep. and pet. similar but narrower, reflexed, oblanceolate, the margins recurved; lip 14–18×6–10mm, deflexed, lanceolate with recurved margins, the apex acute and reflexed; spur 11–17cm, pendent, curving, slender but slightly enlarged and flattened at the apex; column stout, 4mm. Kenya, Tanzania.

A.cryptodon (Rchb. f.) Schltr. (*Angraecum cryptodon* Rchb. f.).
Stems short. Lvs fleshy, dark green, 9–15×2.5–3.5cm, oblong, obtusely bilobed at apex. Racemes arching, 30–40cm, 8–20-fld; sep. and spur tinged with reddish-pink; sep. and pet. about 18mm, lanceolate, acuminate, the dorsal sep. erect, the

others reflexed; lip 14×6.5mm, obovate, acuminate, with 2 teeth in the mouth of the spur; spur 10–14cm, pendent, curved, dilated in lower half; apex of column with 2 denticulate wings standing above anth. Madagascar.

A.curnowiana (Rchb. f.) Schltr.
Stem very short; roots grey, finely verrucose, to 6mm diam. Lvs 3–4×1–2cm, obovate, unequally bilobed at apex, the lobes acute or rounded, leathery, grey-green with a brown margin. Racemes 7–8cm, 1–2-fld; fls white; sep. and pet. spreading, sep. and spur sometimes tinged with pink-brown; pedicel and ovary 5.5–7cm; sep. 18–20×4–5mm, lanceolate, acute; pet. similar but slightly shorter and narrower; lip 22×8mm, ovate, acute; spur 10–13cm, slender, curved, forming a circle in bud. Madagascar.

A.decaryana H. Perrier.
Stem very short; roots stout, 5mm diam. Lvs 6–7, 9–10×2–2.5cm, oblanceolate, apex unequally bilobed, grey-green, the margin undulate and pink-brown. Racemes pendent, to 40cm, to 20-fld; fls fragrant, white, the spur tinged with brown; pedicel and ovary 18–20mm; dorsal sep. 9–20×4mm, lanceolate, acute, arching over column, lateral sep. and pet. slightly longer, strongly reflexed; lip 20×4mm, deflexed, lanceolate, acute, the margins recurved; spur 6–12cm, pendent, straight, slender. Madagascar.

A.distincta Joyce Stewart & I.F. la Croix.
Stem woody, to 15cm but usually shorter; roots 3mm diam. Lvs 3–12, distichous, 4–16×1.5–5cm, narrowly triangular, apex deeply bilobed, lobes acute or subacute, dark green, leathery with longitudinal ridges, sometimes spotted black. Racemes to 27cm, pendent, 2–5-fld; fls white, the extremities usually tinged salmon-pink; pedicel and ovary 4–6cm; sep. and pet. narrowly lanceolate, acuminate, dorsal sep. 25–50×7–9mm, erect or arching over column, lateral sep. 35–65×5–7mm, reflexed, pet. 25–45×5–6mm, always shorter than lateral sep., spreading or reflexed; lip 27–45mm, 9mm wide towards base, abruptly constricted at about halfway to a long, slender acumen; spur 13–23cm, pendent, straight; column 5–7mm. Malawi.

A.ellisii (Rchb. f.) Schltr. (*A.calligera* (Rchb. f.) Garay; *Angraecum buyssonii* Godef.-Leb.; *Angraecum calligerum* Rchb. f.).
Stem to 80cm, branched, eventually pendent; roots numerous, to 6mm diam. Lvs 13–15×3–4cm, thick and fleshy, widely spaced along stem. Racemes to 40cm, 13–17-fld; fls white, fragrant; pedicel and ovary 5cm; sep. and pet. 15–22×6mm, ovate, acute, all reflexed; lip deflexed, similar but with the margins upcurved toward apex; spur 11–18cm, slender, pendent, straight; column sometimes hairy on upper or lower surface or both. Madagascar. var. **grandiflora** Joyce Stewart. Differs in fls larger, sep. and pet. 18–30mm and spur 18–27cm.

A.fastuosa (Rchb. f.) Schltr. (*Angraecum fastuosum* Rchb. f.).
A variable species. Stem very short; roots fine, 1mm diam. Lvs 4–6, 4–8×2–4cm, oblong, fleshy, the apex with rounded lobes. Racemes 2–6cm, 1–6-fld; fls glistening white, the tip of spur green, not opening widely; pedicel and ovary 2cm; sep. and pet. 20–30×10mm, oblong, obtuse; lip slightly longer and variable in width; spur 6–8cm, sometimes coiled; column short and stout. Madagascar.

A.fuscata (Rchb. f.) Schltr. (*A.umbonata* Schltr.; *Angraecum fuscatum* Rchb. f.).
Stem short. Lvs 4–5, 6–8×2–3cm, fleshy, dark, glossy green, elliptic or obovate. Racemes 3–4-fld; fls white, sep. and pet. tinged pink or green; pedicel and ovary 3cm; dorsal sep. 28–30×3–4mm, lanceolate, acuminate, lateral sep. and pet. shorter and narrower; lip 30×6–7mm, lanceolate, acuminate, somewhat V-shaped; spur to 9cm, pendent, tapering from a funnel-shaped mouth. Madagascar.

A.gracillima (Kränzl.) J.C. Arends & J.Stewart.
Stem pendulous, to 8cm; roots 3mm diam. Lvs 6–14, 11–24×2.5–6cm, distichous, leathery, narrowly falcate-obo-

vate, unequally bilobed at apex. Raceme to 75cm, pendent, 7–12-fld, the rachis flexuous; fls white, the lip and upper half of sep. and pet. tinged rusty red, spur and ovary light brown; pedicel 5–10mm; ovary 50–60mm, sigmoid; sep. and pet. narrowly elliptic, acuminate, the margins reflexed in the basal half, sep. 35–50×3–6mm, spreading, pet. 35–45×3–4mm, slightly reflexed; lip 35–45×4–6mm; spur 18–25cm, pendent, slender, inflated at apex to a spoon-shaped pouch 15×3mm; column 30–37mm, slender. Cameroun, Gabon.

A.hyaloides (Rchb. f.) Schltr. (*Angraecum hyaloides* Rchb. f.).
Stem very short, sometimes branched; roots 2–2.5mm diam. Lvs 2–8, set close together, 5–7×1.5–2cm, elliptic, unequally bilobed at apex, coriaceous, dark, glossy green. Racemes more or less erect, 5–7cm, 6–20-fld; fls glistening white, somewhat cup-shaped; sep. 6–8×1.5mm, lanceolate, acute; pet. similar but slightly wider; lip 8×2mm; spur very short, 5–12mm, inflated at apex. Madagascar.

A.kirkii (Rchb. f.) Schltr. (*Angraecum kirkii* Rchb. f.).
Stem short, to 5cm; roots numerous, 1–2mm diam., pale grey. Lvs 2–7, set close together, to 15×3cm, oblanceolate or linear-lanceolate, widest at apex which is deeply bilobed, the lobes acute or rounded, dark grey-green, leathery. Racemes horizontal or pendent, to 17cm, 2–6-fld; fls white, spur tinged pink; pedicel and ovary to 25mm; dorsal sep. erect, 18–25×5–7mm, ovate-lanceolate, acuminate, lateral sep. spreading, 22–28×4–6mm, lanceolate, acuminate; pet. 16–20×5–6mm, oblanceolate, acuminate, usually spreading, occasionally slightly reflexed; lip 16–20×7–8mm, oblong, apiculate or acuminate; spur 6–7.5cm, pendent, somewhat incurved, slender but slightly swollen in lower half, narrowing again to apex; column 4mm. Kenya, Tanzania, Mozambique.

A.kotschyana (Rchb. f.) Schltr. (*Angraecum kotschyanum* Rchb. f.).
Stem stout, to 20cm but often less; roots numerous, to 9mm diam. Lvs 3–20, set close together, 6–30×2–8cm, distichous, leathery, obovate, the apex unequally bilobed. Racemes arching or pendent, to 45cm, 8–20-fld; fls white, usually tinged with salmon-pink in centre, spur and ovary salmon-pink; pedicel and ovary 2–3cm; sep. 20–30×7–10mm, lanceolate, apiculate, dorsal sep. erect or arching over column, lateral sep. spreading; pet. similar but shorter, strongly reflexed; lip 15–25×8–23mm with 2 crests in mouth of spur, deflexed, pandurate, apiculate, the margins reflexed towards tip; spur 13–24cm with a spiral twist in lower half, slender but inflated and flattened in apical third; column stout, 3–6mm. Widespread in tropical Africa.

A.luteoalba (Kränzl.) Schltr.
Stem short, to 3cm; roots numerous, slender. Lvs 2–3, to 15cm×6–15mm, linear-ligulate or linear-oblong, apex unequally bilobed, the lobes rounded, dark green. Racemes arching or pendent, to 35cm, 25-fld, the fls all arranged in the same plane; fls white, cream or yellow-white, all parts spreading; pedicel and ovary 10–20mm; sep. 10–15×3–7mm, oblanceolate, acute; pet. similar but wider; lip 15–20×7–15mm, obovate or rhomboid; spur 2–4cm, incurved, slender but thickened in apical half; column stout, 2–3mm. Zaire, Uganda. var. **rhodosticta** (Kränzl.) J. Stewart (*Angraecum rhodostictum* Kränzl.). Column bright red. Central African Republic, Cameroun, Zaire, Ethiopia, Uganda, Kenya, Tanzania.

A.macrocentra (Schltr.) Schltr. (*A.clavigera* H. Perrier).
Robust but short-stemmed plants; roots 3mm diam., often flattened. Lvs to 20×3.5cm, lanceolate-falcate, glossy, often blue- or grey-green but sometimes dark green. Racemes pendent, to 30cm, 12–30-fld, the fls borne in 2 rows on short projections from rachis; fls white, the spur, pedicel and ovary tinged pink; pedicel and ovary 2cm, decurved so that fls are drooping; dorsal sep. 8–10×3–4mm, oblong, obtuse, lateral sep. and pet. similar but narrower, all parts reflexed; lip 8–10×4–7mm, lanceolate or oblong, apiculate; spur 5.5–6cm, inflated at apex. Madagascar.

A.modesta (Hook. f.) Schltr. (*Angraecum modestum* Hook. f.; *Angraecum sanderianum* Rchb. f.).
Stem to 15cm but often much shorter. Lvs 2–4, to 12.5×3cm, obovate, unequally bilobed at apex, fleshy-coriaceous. Racemes to 30cm, more or less pendent, 6–15-fld, the fls well spaced out, often with apical flower opening first and larger than others; fls white, not opening wide; ovary and pedicel 8–10mm; sep. and pet. about 12mm, lanceolate, subacute or obtuse; lip slightly larger and acuminate; spur 4–7cm, very slender; column 2–3mm, the anth.-cap with a beak or point in the centre. Madagascar; Comoros Is.

A.mooreana (Rolfe ex Sander) Cribb & Joyce Stewart (*Angraecum mooreanum* Rolfe ex Sander).
Short-stemmed. Lvs 8–12×2.5–4cm, oblong, apex obtusely bilobed. Racemes pendent, to 18cm, 5–18-fld; peduncle and rachis wiry; fls white or pale pink; dorsal sep. 6–9×1–2mm, lanceolate, always smaller than other perianth parts, lateral sep. 10–13×2–3mm, pet. slightly smaller; lip 8–13×3–8mm, obovate, acute, flat or reflexed; spur 7–9cm, slender; column slender, 5–8mm. Madagascar; Comoros Is.

A.mystacidii (Rchb. f.) Schltr. (*Angraecum mystacidii* Rchb. f.).
Stem short, to 4cm; roots numerous, grey, 4–5mm diam. Lvs 2–8, distichous, 4–23× 1–5cm, oblanceolate or obovate, equally or unequally bilobed, the lobes acute or obtuse, dark olive green, leathery, occasionally fleshy. Racemes arching or pendent, to 20cm, 3–25-fld; fls white, often tinged with salmon-pink in centre, spur, pedicel and ovary salmon pink; pedicel and ovary 15–20mm; sep. 7–14×2–5mm, oblong, apiculate, dorsal sep. erect or arching over column, lateral sep. deflexed; pet. similar but usually strongly reflexed; lip deflexed, 7–14×3–8mm, oblong, acute; spur 6–8cm, incurved, slightly inflated in apical third; column stout, 2–4mm. Tanzania, Malawi, Mozambique, Zambia, Zimbabwe, Swaziland, S Africa.

A.pallidiflora H. Perrier (*A.seegeri* Sengh.).
Stem very short. Lvs 3–6, lying in the same plane and forming a fan, 3–7×1–2cm, base conduplicate, petiole-like. Raceme to 20cm, 7–9-fld; fls yellow-green, star-shaped; pedicel and ovary 1cm; sep. 8×2mm, lanceolate, acute; pet. similar but narrower; lip 9×2mm; spur very short, 2–2.5cm. Madagascar.

A.punctata J. Stewart.
Small; stems 1–2cm; roots grey, verrucose, flattened against substrate. Lvs 2–4, 2–3.5cm×6–12mm, elliptic or oblong, dull grey-green with minute silver dots, apex acutely bilobed. Fls solitary, white sometimes tinged with green or brown, lip white; pedicel and ovary 2.5–3.5cm; sep. 14–20×3–4mm, lanceolate, acuminate; pet. shorter and narrower; pet. 16–22×7–9mm, ovate, acuminate; spur 10–12cm, pendent, flexuous, slender from a funnel-shaped mouth; column short and stout, 3mm. Madagascar.

A.seegeri Sengh. See *A.pallidiflora*.

A.somalensis (Schltr.) Schltr. (*Angraecum somalense* Schltr.).
Stem short, erect; roots numerous, grey, 5–7mm diam. Lvs 2–6, distichous, 2–11×1.5–3.5cm, oblong or obovate, apex unequally bilobed, the lobes rounded, fleshy or leathery, grey-green with darker reticulate veins, sometimes tinged with red-purple. Racemes to 20cm, 2–17-fld; fls white, sometimes tinged salmon-pink; pedicel and ovary 1.5–2cm; sep. 8–14×3–6mm, the dorsal sep. arching over column, ovate, apiculate, slightly shorter and wider than laterals, lateral sep. reflexed, oblong, apiculate; pet. 8–11×3–5mm, spreading, oblong, apiculate; lip 9–13×4–7mm, oblong, apiculate; spur 10–15cm, pendent, straight or slightly incurved, sometimes slightly inflated in apical half; column stout, to 4mm. Ethiopia, Tanzania, Malawi, S Africa.

A.stylosa (Rolfe) Schltr. (*Angraecum stylosum* Rolfe).
Stem short. Lvs 3–4, variable in size and shape, 6.5–17×4–5cm, fleshy, glossy grey-green, usually edged red. Racemes arching or pendent, to 60cm, 9–15-fld; fls white, sometimes tinged pink or brown; pedicel and ovary 2.5–4cm; dorsal sep. arching over column, 18–20×7–8mm, oblanceolate, acute, lateral sep. 20–24×6–8mm, reflexed; pet. similar to dorsal sep. but reflexed; lip about 20×8mm, oblong; spur 10–15cm, slender; column 8–9mm. Madagascar.

A.thomsonii (Rolfe) Schltr.
Stem woody, elongated, 10–100cm; roots numerous, pale grey, to 9mm diam., arising from lower part of stem. Lvs 8–20, distichous, 8–28×1.5–4.5cm, ligulate, apex unequally bilobed, the lobes obtuse, dark green, leathery or fleshy. Racemes arching, to 30cm, 4–10-fld; fls in 2 rows, white; pedicel and ovary 3–6cm; sep. 22–32×5–9mm, lanceolate-elliptic, dorsal sep. erect, cuspidate, lateral sep. reflexed, acuminate; pet. 20–25×6–8mm, reflexed, lanceolate-elliptic, acute; lip 20–25×7–8mm, elliptic-lanceolate, acuminate; spur 10–15cm, pendent, flexuous, flattened and enlarged towards the apex; column 6–8mm. Uganda, Kenya, Tanzania.

A.ugandensis Summerh.
Stem to 20cm but usually less; roots 3–4mm diam., green-grey. Lvs 4–12, distichous, 5–15×1–2cm, oblanceolate, apex unequally bilobed, the lobes rounded, leathery, dark green with black dots. Racemes pendent, to 15cm; fls white, often tinged with green; sep. 6–12×3–4mm, oblong-lanceolate, apiculate, dorsal sep. erect, lateral sep. often somewhat reflexed; pet. 6–10×3mm, reflexed, oblong-lanceolate, acute; lip 6–10×3–5mm, oblong, acute; spur straight, 1–2.5cm; column 2mm. Zaire, Burundi, Uganda, Kenya.

A.umbonata Schltr. See *A.fuscata*.

A.verdickii (De Wild.) Schltr.
Stem to 6cm, usually less; roots numerous, long, 6–9mm diam. Leaves 2–6, 5–20×2–5cm, oblong-ligulate or oblanceolate, acutely bilobed at apex, fleshy, grey-green sometimes tinged purple, margin often undulate. Racemes to 40cm, 4–15-fld; fls white, very sweetly scented; pedicel and ovary 2–3.5cm; sep. 11–22×3–8mm, reflexed, ovate or oblong, apiculate, dorsal sep. arching over column, lateral sep. spreading or deflexed, slightly longer and narrower than dorsal sep.; pet. 12–21×3.5–8mm, reflexed, obovate-oblong, apiculate; lip 11–20×5–9mm, oblong-obovate with 2 ridges in mouth of spur; spur 12–20cm, slightly curving, slender but thickened in apical third; column 3–5mm. Zaire, Tanzania, Zambia, Malawi, Mozambique, Zimbabwe, Angola, S Africa.

Aeranthes Lindl. (From Gk *aer*, air, and *anthos*, flower.) Over 40 monopodial epiphytes. Stems short; roots slender. Leaves fleshy or leathery. Inflorescences simple or branched, single- to many-flowered, usually pendent with a wiry peduncle; flowers green, green-white or rarely pure white, sometimes membranous and semi-translucent; dorsal sepal and petals free, lateral sepals adnate to column foot; lip entire, set in front of the mouth of the spur; column short or fairly long; pollinia, stipites and viscidia 2. Madagascar, Mascarene Is., Comoros Is., with 2 species on mainland Africa.

CULTIVATION Given intermediate or warm conditions (min. winter temperature 18°C/64°F), they will thrive in exactly the same regime as *Aerangis*. These species are valued for the sheer fascination of the flowers – usually solitary, translucent, tessellated lime-green and with long-tipped tepals.

A.arachnites Lindl.
Stem to 8cm, often less. Lvs 20–30×2–2.5cm, ligulate, apex unevenly bilobed, pale green, leathery. Racemes 20–40cm, few-fld; fls pale green; pedicel and ovary 2cm; dorsal sep. 3cm long, 0.8cm wide at base, tapering abruptly to a long acumen, lateral sep. similar but 1.2cm wide at base; pet. like dorsal sep. but 2cm long; lip 3–3.3×1.2cm, oblong, truncate; spur 0.8cm, bulbous at tip. Réunion.

A.caudata Rolfe.
Differs from *A.ramosa* in smaller, paler fls. Stem to 15cm. Lvs 20–30×2–3.5cm, ligulate, somewhat undulate. Raceme to 100cm, 3–8-fld; fls green; pedicel and ovary 12–14mm; sep. 10–12cm long, 1cm wide at base, tapering abruptly to a long, slender acumen; pet. 5–6cm, of similar shape but with a shorter acumen; lip 5cm long, 2cm wide at base, narrowing abruptly to acumen; spur 1cm, slender. Comoros Is., Madagascar.

A.grandiflora Lindl.
Stem to 10cm, often less. Lvs 15–30×3–4cm, ligulate, articulated at base, apex unequally bilobed, light green, leathery, often undulate. Racemes pendent, to about 50cm, few-fld; peduncle completely covered by sheaths which are longer than the internodes; fls cream to yellow-green; pedicel and ovary 8–10cm; sep. and pet. ovate at base, tapering abruptly to a long acumen, sep. 5–6×1.5cm, pet. about 1cm shorter; lip 5cm long, the base 2cm wide, obovate with a few bristles, narrowing abruptly to a long acumen, but shorter than that of sep.; spur 1.5cm, swollen at apex, glabrous inside. Madagascar.

A.henrici Schltr.
Robust; stems to 15cm but often less. Lvs 4–8, to 23×5cm, ligulate, leathery, often undulate. Racemes pendent, 12–40cm, 5–6-fld.; fls white with a green lip, very large; pedicel and ovary 4–6cm; sep. 11cm, lanceolate, long-acuminate; pet. similar but 9cm; lip fringed, 10cm long, 3–4cm wide at the base, narrowing abruptly to a tongue-like projection, truncate at apex but with a hair-like acumen at the tip; spur 16cm, filiform; column 0.8cm. Madagascar.

A.peyrotii Bosser.
Stem to 10cm. Lvs 35–40×1–1.5cm, linear, pendent. Panicle 30–50cm, bearing fls over a 2–3-year period but with only 1 fl. open at a time; fls bright green; sep. 4–4.5×1cm, lanceolate, acuminate; pet. 3.5×0.5cm; lip 3×1cm, ovate, caudate; spur 1cm, straight or slightly curved, clavate at tip. Madagascar.

A.ramosa Rolfe. Stem very short. Lvs 5–6, more or less equitant, to 28×6cm, leathery, oblong, obtusely bilobed at apex. Infl. pendent, simple or branched. 20–100cm, hanging far below plant, few or several-fld; fls dark olive green, spur white; pedicel and ovary 2cm; dorsal sep. 4×1.5cm, ovate-lanceolate, long-acuminate, lateral sep. longer and wider at base; pet. like dorsal sep. but shorter; lip 4×2cm, obovate, cuspidate, auriculate at base; spur 1.5cm, swollen at apex; column very short. Madagascar.

A.imerinensis H. Perrier. See *A.caudata*.

Aerides Lour. (From Gk *aer*, air, due to the apparent ability of these orchids to thrive on air.) 40 species of monopodial epiphytes. Stems erect, usually simple. Leaves alternate in 2 opposite ranks, strap-shaped, bases sheathing stem. Racemes axillary, arching; flowers fragrant; sepals and petals spreading, broad, lateral sepals fused to column foot; lip entire or trilobed, the lobes often erect and overlapping, boss-like, base spurred and forward-projecting. Tropical & E Asia, W Malaysia.

CULTIVATION Handsome epiphytes for the cool or intermediate house. They bear showy, moth-like flowers in arching racemes, usually crystalline white and variously tinted rose or purple. Grow in baskets or shallow pots in a very open bark-base medium; otherwise, as for *Vanda*.

A.affinis Lindl. See *A.multiflora*.
A.ampullacea Roxb. See *Ascocentrum ampullacea*.
A.arachnites Sw. See *Arachnis flos-aeris*.
A.calceolaris Buch.-Ham. ex Sm. See *Gastrochilus calceolaris*.

A.crassifolia Parish ex Burb.
Lvs oblong-ligulate, to 20cm, rigid, thick, olive green, bilobed at apex. Fls to 50 per raceme, magenta to amethyst, tips darkest, base white; lip midlobe deep purple, ovate, broad, often emarginate, lateral lip lobes crescent-shaped. Burma, Laos, Thailand.

A.crispa Lindl. (*A.lindleyana* Wight).
Lvs ligulate, coriaceous, 15–22.5cm, apex retuse or bifid, sinus mucronulate. Raceme pendent; fls many, white suffused rose-purple; sep. and pet. ovate to obovate, acute; lip midlobe ovate, broad, margin fringed, base bidentate, lateral lobes small, erect, ovate, obtuse; spur horn-shaped, weakly incurved. India.

A.expansa Rchb. f. See *A.falcata*.

A.falcata Lindl. (*A.expansa* Rchb. f.).
Similar to *A.crassifolia*. Lvs somewhat glaucous above, often streaked dark green or oxblood beneath, coriaceous, 15–20×3–4cm. Racemes equalling or exceeding lvs, lax; fls many, 2.5–4cm diam., white, blotched violet, lip midlobe violet, spur green; sep. and pet. ovate-oblong, obtuse, lateral sep. broader than dorsal sep., pet. narrower; lip midlobe ovate-obovate, dentate; spur forward-pointing. SE Asia.

A.falcata var. *houlletiana* (Rchb. f.) Veitch. See *A.houlletiana*.
A.fieldingii B.S. Williams. See *A.rosea*.

A.flabellata Rolfe ex Downie.
Stem to 13cm, upper portion densely leafy. Lvs lorate, curved, keeled, apex bilobed, 7–10×1.3–1.5cm. Infl. 6–13cm, lax; fls. maroon, lip white, blotched purple; dorsal sep. and pet. ovate, broad, to 0.8×0.5cm, apex truncate, lateral sep. cordate, broad, subacute; lip claw channelled, midlobe from front of spur, flabelliform, fringed, lateral lobes oblong, rounded. Burma, China, Thailand.

Aerides and Sedirea   (a) *Sedirea japonica*   (b) *Aerides odorata*   (c) *Aerides multiflora*   (d) *Aerides quinquevulnera*

A.houlletiana Rchb. f. (*A.falcata* var. *houlletiana* (Rchb. f.) Veitch).
Lvs ligulate, apex bilobed. Racemes dense; fls large, fleshy, yellow-brown, marked purple, lip cream with a central magenta or umber blotch; dorsal sep. oblong, obtuse, lateral sep. broader; lip midlobe subrhombic, fimbriate, lateral lobes broad, curving, callus grooved near spur aperture; spur conical, laterally compressed. Thailand, Vietnam, Cambodia.

A.japonica Lind. & Rchb. f. See *Sedirea japonica*.
A.jarckiana Schltr. See *A.quinquevulnera*.

A.kraibiensis Seidenf.
Stems small, tufted, 8–10cm. Lvs closely distichous, conduplicate, apex broad, pointed. Infl. to 5.5cm; fls 12–15; dorsal sep. purple, edged violet, lateral sep. white edged purple; pet. deep purple, lip paler, disc darker; dorsal sep. ovate, rounded, 0.7×0.6cm, lateral sep. suborbicular, 0.8×0.8cm; pet. 0.8×0.6cm, obovate, rounded; lip weakly trilobed, lobes rounded; spur to 2mm. Thailand.

A.lawrenciae Rchb. f.
Lvs 20–30×4–5cm. Infl. dense, to 30cm; fls to 4cm diam., typically white with a conspicuous purple-pink blotch on each segment; dorsal sep. white, apical blotch violet-red, lip midlobe deep violet, with 2 red, longitudinal streaks, spur green; dorsal sep. cuneate, oblong, obtuse, lateral sep. broader; pet. cuneate to ligulate, obtuse; lip cream, midlobe ligulate, minutely dentate, obtuse; spur conic, incurved, green; callus within trilobed. Philippines.

A.lindleyana Wight. See *A.crispa*.
A.lobbii hort. ex Lem. See *A.multiflora*.

A.maculosa Lindl.
Stem 4–6cm. Lvs ligulate, weakly curved, 15–20×3–4.5cm, apical lobes rounded. Infl. usually branched, to 40cm, lax; fls many, white suffused rose, spotted purple, tipped bright rose or amethyst, lip amethyst, margin paler, claw and auricles white, streaked purple, spur tipped green; sep. elliptic-oblong, to 1.5×0.5cm; pet. similar, shorter; lip trilobed, claw short, tubercles at base 2, white, midlobe ovate to ovate-oblong, margins undulate, obtuse or retuse, lateral lobes minutely lobed; spur slender, incurved. India.

A.mitrata Rchb. f. See *Seidenfadenia mitrata*.

A.multiflora Roxb. (*A.lobbii* hort. ex Lem.; *A.affinis* Lindl.).
Stem 10–25cm, stout. Lvs many, ligulate, closely distichous, channels and keels prominent, 15–35×1.5–2cm, apex bilobed. Infl. rarely branched, 15–30cm, pendulous, crowded; fls many, 2–3.5cm diam., fragrant, rose-purple or white, occasionally spotted dark amethyst at tips, lip pale amethyst; sep. and pet. oblong, orbicular or elliptic-oblong, rounded; lip abruptly bent, convex, margins recurved, midlobe cordate or hastate-ovate, rounded, weakly convex above, callus fleshy, incurved, bilobed; spur forward-pointing compressed, straight. Himalaya, India to Thailand, Indochina.

A.odorata Lour.
To 1m. Stem stout, pendent, branching, 10–30cm. Lvs oblong-ligulate, fleshy, 15–30cm, pale green, apical lobes rounded. Infl. to 3, pendent; fls to 30, highly fragrant, purple to pure white, often spotted and tipped purple, spur tipped green or yellow; dorsal sep. oblong, obtuse, 1.2×0.8cm, lateral sep. triangular-lanceolate, narrow, exceeding dorsal; pet. oblong, narrow, obtuse, 1.2×0.7cm; lip nearly enveloping column, midlobe oblong-lanceolate, incurved, entire to erose, lateral lobes subcuneate to subquadrate, margins entire or dentate, disc keeled near nectary, appendages 2, near the mouth; spur horn-shaped, strongly incurved. India, SE Asia, Java to Philippines.

A.paniculata Ker-Gawl. See *Cleisostoma paniculatum*.

A.quinquevulnera Lindl. (*A.jarckiana* Schltr.).
Stems 20–40cm. Lvs lorate, 20–35×3–4cm, apex bilobed. Infl. 20–40cm; fls many, fragrant, waxy, to 2cm diam., white spotted purple-red, particularly at apex of sep. and pet. where the colour becomes virtually solid, lip midlobe dark purple, lateral lobes white, faintly spotted purple, spur green; sep. elliptic to suborbicular, obtuse, dorsal sep. concave, lateral sep. oblique; lip midlobe oblong-linear, sharply incurved, lateral lobes broad, rounded, fused with midlobe almost to the apex, infolded, overlapping covering spur; spur narrow, conic. Philippines.

A.racemifera Lindl. See *Cleisostoma racemiferum*.

A.rosea Lodd. ex Lindl. & Paxt.
Stem 10–25cm, stout. Lvs ligulate, keeled beneath, deeply grooved, 15–35×2.5–4.5cm, apex bilobed. Infl. dense, rarely branched at base, 45–60cm+; fls many, to 4cm diam.; dorsal sep. and pet. amethyst, suffused white, base sometimes white, spotted purple, lateral sep. white with pale purple apical spot, lip amethyst, speckled white; dorsal sep. and pet. obovate, obtuse, lateral sep. elliptic, broad, 1.2–2×0.7cm; lip deltoid, slender-acuminate, 1.6×1cm, midlobe sagittate, acute, lateral lobes incurved over spur aperture; spur funnel-shaped. India, N Vietnam, S China.

A.vandarum Rchb. f. See *Papilionanthe vandarum*.
A.williamsii Warner. See *A.rosea*.

Aganisia Lindl. (From Gk *aganos*, desirable.) 2 species of small epiphytes allied to *Zygopetalum*. Spring–summer.

CULTIVATION   Mount on rafts or fern slabs, or pot in shallow pans in a compost suitable for *Masdevallia*. Afford shady, humid, warm conditions. Water frequently, allowing the compost to become slightly dry between waterings.

A.brachystalix (Rchb. f.) Rolfe. See *Otostylis brachystalix*.
A.coerulea Rchb. f. See *Acacallis cyanea*.
A.ionoptera (Lind. & Rchb. f.) Nichols. See *Koellensteinia ionoptera*.
A.kellneriana (Rchb. f.) Benth. See *Koellensteinia kellneriana*.
A.lepida Lind. & Rchb. f. See *Otostylis lepida*.

A.pulchella Lindl. Rhiz. creeping, closely bracteate. Pseudobulbs remote, ovoid, to 2.5cm, olive green. Lvs terminal, solitary, to 12cm, narrow-oblong to lanceolate, acute, basally narrowed to a stalk. Infl. to 12cm, racemose, erect to arching; fls to 8, to 4cm across, sometimes scented; sep. and pet. subequal, ovate-oblong, acute, white; lip entire, basally rounded, concave, white spotted red, apical portion spreading, ovate, white, disc yellow with golden-glandular lamella at base. Guyana, N Brazil.

A.tricolor (Lindl.) Bois. See *Warrea warreana*.

× **Alexanderara** (*Brassia* × *Cochlioda* × *Odontoglossum* × *Oncidium*). Intergeneric hybrids with four different genera in their ancestry. Plants consist of a group of compressed pseudobulbs, often large, growing from a basal rhizome, each with one or two leaves at its apex and two or more leaf-like sheaths arising at its base. Inflorescences arise in the axils of these sheaths and may be simple or branched. Flowers usually with long narrow sepals and petals, lip large or small depending on the ancestry, often conspicuously marked in a variety of colours.

CULTIVATION   Tolerant of warmer conditions than other members of the *Odontoglossum* alliance.

×A. St.Ouen 'Trinity'.
Large branching spikes of small to medium, well-shaped fls;
fls yellow-green heavily overlaid with dark brown, coalescing
spots, lip oblong, bright clear yellow with brown spots surrounding the yellow crest.

× **Aliceara** (*Brassia* × *Miltonia* × *Oncidium*). Trigeneric hybrid. Plants consist of a group of compressed pseudobulbs growing from a basal rhizome, each with one or two leaves at its apex and two or more leaf-like sheaths arising at its base. Inflorescences arise in the axils of these sheaths and may be simple or branched. Flowers with long narrow sepals and petals, conspicuously marked in a variety of colours, lip large. Tolerant of intermediate conditions.

×A.Maury Island 'Fantasy'.
Long sprays of many fls; fls basically yellow with brown
spots on sep. and pet., lip larger than the rest of the fl., chestnut brown with darker spots, each spot outlined in yellow.

Amblostoma Scheidw. (From Gk *amblos*, blunt, and *stoma*, mouth; referring to the form of the lip.) 9 epiphytes or lithophytes allied to *Epidendrum*. Pseudobulbs slender, clustered, narrow-ellipsoid or cylindric. Leaves thin, linear-lanceolate, subterminal. Inflorescence terminal, erect, dense, racemose or paniculate; flowers small, delicate; sepals and petals subequal, spreading; lip trilobed, midlobe smaller than lateral lobes. Summer. Brazilian Andes.

CULTIVATION   As for *Encyclia fragrans* alliance.

A.tridactylon (Lindl.) Rchb. f. (*Epidendrum tridactylon*
Lindl.)
Pseudobulbs slender, to 20cm, olive green. Lvs to 25cm. Infl.
to 15cm; fls to 1.25cm diam., green to ivory. Brazil.

Amesiella Garay (For Prof. Oakes Ames (1874–1950), founder of the Orchid Herbarium at Harvard University.) 1 species, a short-stemmed, monopodial epiphyte. Stems 3–6cm. Roots fleshy. Leaves 2.5–5cm, elliptic-oblong, obtuse, fleshy, 2-ranked along stem. Racemes axillary, few-flowered; flowers disproportionately large, white; peduncle fleshy, winged; bracts winged, triangular, fleshy; dorsal sepal to 2.2cm, elliptic, basally cuneate, lateral sepals similar; petals broadly spathulate, obtuse; lip trilobed, lobes oblong, midlobe apically rounded, spur slender. Philippines.

CULTIVATION   As for the smaller *Aerangis* species.

A.philippinensis (Ames) Garay (*Angraecum philippinense* Ames).

Amitostigma Schltr. (Gk *a*, not, *mitos*, thread and stigma, i.e. not *Mitostigma*.) Some 15 species of small terrestrials. Stems erect. Leaves 1–4, linear to lanceolate. Racemes with few to many rose-purple to white flowers; sepals free, oblong to ovate; petals similar, forming a hood; lip trilobed, spur short. India, E Asia.

CULTIVATION   See Introduction: Hardy Orchids.

A.keiskei (Maxim.) Schltr.
Stems 5–15cm. Lvs 3–7cm, oblong, basally sheathing. Fls
pale maroon; dorsal sep. elliptic; pet. ovate, oblique,
incurved, margins speckled red; lip 3-lobed, with 2 broken
parallel lines of purple blotches at base, midlobe apically
cleft. Summer. Japan.

Anacamptis Rich. (From Gk *anakampto*, to bend back, referring to the flowers' spur.) 1 species, a deciduous terrestrial. Tubers globose or ovoid. Stems to 75cm, usually shorter, slender, glabrous; basal sheaths green-white to brown. Basal leaves to 20×2cm in a loose rosette, lanceolate, glabrous, light green, withering before flowers; stem leaves narrower, emerging rolled, becoming reduced as bracts toward apex of stem. Inflorescence a crowded, pyramidal spike to 8cm; bracts exceeding ovaries; flowers pink, rose or mauve, rarely white, with musky odour; sepals and petals to 8×3mm, incurved except spreading laterals; lip to 9×10mm, lobes 3, to 4mm, oblong, obtuse, callus of ridges from base of lip to spur; spur 1cm, descending. Summer. Europe, N Africa.

CULTIVATION   See Introduction: Hardy Orchids.

A.pyramidalis (L.) Rich. PYRAMID ORCHID.

Ancistrochilus Rolfe. (From Gk *ankistron*, hook, and *cheilos*, lip, referring to the shape of the lip.) 2 species of epiphytes. Pseudobulbs clustered, globose to pyriform, bearing 1–2 apical leaves. Leaves plicate, membranous, lanceolate, acuminate. Raceme basal, arching, 1–5-flowered; flowers white to rose-pink or purple; sepals spreading, pubescent beneath, oblanceolate, acute; petals similar but smaller; lip trilobed, subsaccate at base, lateral lobes erect on either side of column, midlobe with apex tapering, recurved like a hook; column clavate, pubescent. W Africa to Uganda.

CULTIVATION   Minimum winter temperature 13°C/55°F. Pot in a medium-grade bark mix with additional leafmould. Protect from full sunlight and draughts. Water freely until completion of pseudobulbs, thereafter reduce watering to promote flower production. Do not allow pseudobulbs to shrivel. Feed fortnightly when in growth. Repot annually after flowering. Propagate by division. Easily raised from seed.

A.rothschildianus O'Brien.
Pseudobulbs to 5.5cm diam., subglobose, conical or pyriform. Lvs to 40x7cm. Racemes 1–2, to 20cm, 2–5-fld; sep. 2–3x1cm, elliptic to lanceolate, pale or deep rose-pink or mauve; pet. spreading, slightly narrower than sep.; lip to 1.7cm, pink or purple, midlobe darker and recurved, lateral lobes erect, oblong, rounded; column 17mm, arched. W Africa to Uganda.

A.thomsonianus (Rchb. f.) Rolfe.
Pseudobulbs to 2.5cm diam., squat, pyriform. Lvs to 20x3cm. Racemes 1–2, erect or arching, 2–3-fld; sep. to 4.5cm, oblong-lanceolate, acuminate, white, green at base; lateral lobes of lip to 1cm, erect, oblong, obtuse, green with brown marks, midlobe 16–25mm, rosey purple, linear, acuminate, recurved; column 15mm, slender. Nigeria, Cameroun.

Ancistrorhynchus Finet. (From Gk *ankistron*, hook, and *rhynchos*, snout, referring to the shape of the rostellum.) 13 species of epiphytes. Stems short and thick. Leaves imbricate, suberect, spreading or recurved, linear, ligulate or lanceolate, unequally bilobed at apex. Racemes arising from axils of lower leaves, almost sessile, usually short and densely flowered, occasionally lax and few-flowered; flowers usually white, sometimes with green or yellow markings; sepals and petals similar; lip entire or trilobed, ovate, oblong or orbicular; spur straight or sigmoid, constricted in middle and swollen at apex, shorter than ovary; pollinia 2; stipites 2, or one divided in upper half; rostellum first projecting downwards, parallel to column, then sharply reflexed, forming a hook. Tropical Africa, reaching southern limit in Malawi.

CULTIVATION   As for *Angraecum*.

A.capitatus (Lindl.) Summerh.
Lvs 17–44×1.5–3cm, linear-lanceolate, acutely bilobed at apex, sharply dentate below the apex on either side. Raceme short and dense; fls white or pale rose with yellow patches on inside of lip; sep. and pet. 3.5–6mm, ovate, obtuse; lip entire, 4.5–5.5×3.5–5mm, oblong, always longer than broad; spur 7–11mm, straight or slightly curved. Sierra Leone to Uganda.

A.cephalotes (Rchb. f.) Summerh.
Lvs 7–35×1–2cm, linear or ligulate, entire. Racemes short and dense; fls fragrant, white with green or yellow blotches on lip; sep. and pet. 4–7mm, ovate, obtuse; lip 4–7×4–9mm, suborbicular, obscurely trilobed, lobes rounded; spur 6–10mm. W Africa.

A.clandestinus (Lindl.) Schltr. Lvs to 180×3.5cm, linear, stiff and leathery, very unequally bilobed at apex, the longer lobe to 7cm, the other very short or sometimes absent, so that apex seems entire. Racemes to 4cm, fairly densely fld; fls white, with green marks in throat; sep. and pet. 3–5.5mm, ovate, obtuse; lip 5–7.5mm, trilobed, midlobe undulate; spur sigmoid, swollen at apex. W Africa to Zaire.

A.ovatus Summerh. Stem to 20cm; roots 1–2mm diam. Lvs 7–20×0.5–1.5cm, linear-ligulate, unequally bilobed at apex. Raceme 1–2×1–2cm, densely many-fld; bracts scarious, as long as fls; fls white; sep. and pet. 3–4.5×1.5–2mm, elliptic, rounded at apex; lip 3–4.5×2.5–3.5mm, entire, concave, broadly ovate, apex rounded, edge slightly undulate; spur 4.5–6mm, inflated in apical third. Congo, Zaire, Uganda.

A.refractus (Kränzl.) Summerh. Stems short; roots numerous; plants often pendulous when older. Lvs about 8, forming fan, 7–33×1cm, dark green, thick-textured, erect or spreading when young. Racemes 2-fld; fls shining white; dorsal sep. 10×4mm, lanceolate, obtuse, lateral sep. 13×4mm, oblong, obtuse; pet. 13×4mm, lanceolate, obtuse; lip 17×7mm, oblong, concave; spur 17mm, narrowing from a wide base, then expanding again to a swollen apex, somewhat S-shaped. Tanzania.

A.serratus Summerh. Stem elongated, branched, densely leafy above, covered with sheaths below. Lvs distichous, imbricate, 5–11cm×7–10mm, ligulate, V-shaped in cross-section, unequally bilobed at apex, the lobes irregularly serrate. Racemes very short, more or less capitate, 1cm, several- to many-fld; fls white; pedicel and ovary 3.5–4mm; sep. 3–3.5×1–1.5mm, oblong-elliptic; pet. 3×1mm, obliquely oblanceolate; lip 2.5×4mm, obscurely trilobed, enfolding column, transversely elliptic, shortly apiculate; spur 4–4.5mm, almost straight, wide-mouthed and inflated at apex, constricted in middle. Nigeria, Cameroun.

Angraecopsis Kränzl. (From *Angraecum* and Gk *opsis*, resemblance.) About 16 species of monopodial epiphytes. Stems short, woody; roots usually fine. Leaves distichous, linear, ligulate or oblanceolate, often falcate, coriaceous or somewhat fleshy. Inflorescence racemose, axillary, few- to many-flowered, often pendent; flowers small, white, green-white or yellow-green; lateral sepals often longer than dorsal sepal and petals; lip usually trilobed, rarely entire, spurred, without a callus; column short; pollinia 2, stipites 2, viscidium usually 2, rarely 1. Tropical Africa, Madagascar, Mascarene Is., Comoros Is.

CULTIVATION   See *Angraecum.*

A.amaniensis Summerh.
Dwarf, almost stemless; roots numerous, grey-green. Lvs 2–4, to 40×7mm, elliptic, blue-green, rather fleshy. Raceme to 7cm, densely 10–20-fld; fls sweetly scented, yellow-green or green-white; dorsal sep. 5×1.5mm, elliptic, erect, lateral sep. 7×1.5mm, spreading, falcate; pet. 4×1mm, triangular; lip 7×2mm, lanceolate, with small, tooth-like lobes at base; spur 9mm, slender, slightly incurved. Kenya, Tanzania, Malawi, Zambia, Zimbabwe.

A.boutonii (Rchb. f.) H. Perrier. See *Microterangis boutonii.*

A.gracillima (Rolfe) Summerh. (*Mystacidium gracillimum* Rolfe).
Stem 1–7cm, pendent. Lvs linear, curved, lying in one plane. Raceme 4–16cm, few- to several-fld; fls white, usually tinged with orange at base of perianth parts; pedicel and ovary 15–25mm; dorsal sep. 2–3×1.5mm, ovate, obtuse, lateral sep. 7–9×1.5mm, spathulate, deflexed; pet. 2–5×2.5–5.5mm, triangular, joined to lateral sep. at base; lip 5–6×2–2.5mm, trilobed towards base, lateral lobes about 1.5mm, reflexed, midlobe about 4.5mm; spur slender, more or less straight, about 4cm. Kenya, Uganda, Zambia.

A.parviflora (Thouars) Schltr.
Stems short; roots fine. Lvs 3–5, to 25×1.5cm, pendent, dark green, slightly fleshy, falcate to ligulate, acutely and unevenly bilobed, lying in same plane. Raceme pendent, 6–10cm, densely 10–15-fld; peduncle slender and wiry; fls green-white, turning creamy yellow with age; dorsal sep. 1–2×1mm, erect, ovate, lateral sep. 4mm long, less than 1mm wide, deflexed, oblique; pet. 1.5–2×1mm, triangular; lip 4mm, trilobed near base, midlobe 3×1mm, lateral lobes shorter and narrower, spreading and slightly upward curving; spur 8mm, incurved, slender but swollen at apex. W Africa, Tanzania, Malawi, Zimbabwe, Mozambique, Madagascar, Mascarene Is.

A.tenerrima Kränzl.
Stem 1–4cm, rarely longer, pendent. Lvs 6–20×1.5–2cm, linear to oblanceolate, curved, unequally bilobed at apex, dark green, lying in one plane. Raceme 7.5–20cm, laxly 3–7-fld; fls white, apex of spur green; pedicel and ovary 2–3cm; dorsal sep. about 3×1.5mm, elliptic, obtuse, lateral sep. 8.5–11.5×2–2.5mm, spathulate; pet. 3–3.5×4–5mm, triangular, acute, joined at base to lateral sep.; lip 9–9.5× 6.5–8mm, trilobed, all lobes 4–5mm; spur 5–6mm, slender from a fairly wide mouth. Tanzania.

Angraecum Bory. (Latinized form of Malay *anggrek* or *angurek*, used for all orchids with aerial roots.) 100–150 species of epiphytes. Stems long or short; leaves almost always leathery, linear or ligulate, articulated to the sheath, bilobed at apex. Racemes axillary, 1- to many-flowered; flowers white, green or yellow-green; sepals and petals free, usually spreading, similar; lip spurred, entire, shell- or boat-shaped, usually very concave, the base more or less encircling the column; column without column foot; rostellum short, deeply cleft. Tropical and S Africa, Indian Ocean Is.

CULTIVATION   A genus of spectacular orchids, characterized, as a whole, by the cool contrast of deep green foliage and nocturnally scented white or ivory blooms. There is, however, great diversity of form and size – from the dwarf creeping *A.distichum* to the robust *A.eburneum* (one of the most popular species with arching racemes of upside-down lime and white flowers) to the celebrated *A.sesquipedale*, with flowers like great waxy stars, tailed with foot-long spurs adapted to attract a single pollinator species with a very long proboscis.

They are mostly warm-growing epiphytes suited to culture in orchid pots or baskets filled with coarse-grade bark mix. Water freely throughout the year, syringing daily and fertilizing fortnightly when growth is most active (the majority of roots in most spp. will be aerial). Suspend in an airy position in semi-shade and high humidity (minimum temp. 18°C/65°F). Offsets are sometimes produced by the more robust species (usually when the apical meristem has been damaged). These can be detached and rooted. Most are increased by seed sown *in vitro.*

A.Alabaster (*A.eburneum* × *A.Veitchii*)
Robust, to 120cm. Lvs about 10 pairs, to 30×5cm, distichous, ligulate. Racemes erect, 10–12-fld; fls 11–12cm diam., white; sep. and pet. usually tinged green, 65–67×14–17mm, lanceolate, acute, the dorsal sep. erect, lateral sep. and pet. spreading; lip 60×53mm, obovate, narrowing abruptly to an acumen; spur 12–15cm, slender, horizontal or somewhat upturned. Winter. Garden origin.

A.arachnites Schltr.
Stems branched, to 30cm, slightly flattened. Lvs numerous, to 20×4mm, distichous, oblong, dark green. Infl. 1-fld, arising along stem between lf sheaths; fls pale green with white lip; sep. and pet. filiform, sep. 4.5–5.5cm, pet. 3.5cm; lip shell-shaped with a long acumen, the basal part 1.5×1cm, the acumen 1.5cm long; spur 10–11cm, very slender, straight or flexuous. Madagascar.

A.arachnopus Rchb. f. See *Aerangis arachnopus.*
A.arcuatum Lindl. See *Cyrtorchis arcuata.*

A.articulatum Rchb. f. See *Aerangis articulata.*

A.bicallosum H. Perrier.
Stem to 15cm, slightly flattened; old sheaths 4–5mm, transversely wrinkled; roots smooth. Lvs 15–25×8–11mm, broadly elliptic, deeply and obtusely bilobed at apex. Infl. 1-fld; sep. and pet. and spur light yellow-russet, lip white, sep. 30×6mm, lanceolate, acute, pet. similar but 4mm wide; lip 30×15mm, broadly ovate, acute, with a prominent callus on either side of the mouth of the spur; spur 12cm, tapering from a mouth 3mm wide; column 4mm. Summer. Madagascar.

A.bidens Sw. See *Diaphananthe bidens.*
A.bilobum Lindl. See *Aerangis biloba.*

A.birrimense Rolfe.
Stem fairly long. Lvs 7–14×1.5–3.5cm, ligulate, unequally bilobed at apex. Infl. 2–3-fld; fls pale green, the lip white with a green centre; sep. and pet. 3–5.5cm, lanceolate, acute; lip 2.5–3.5cm long and wide, more or less orbicular, long-apiculate; spur less than 5cm, almost straight, conical at base,

narrow in middle and swollen and fusiform towards apex. W Africa.

A.boutonii Rchb. f. See *Microterangis boutonii.*
A.brongniartianum Rchb. f. See *A.eburneum* ssp. *superbum.*
A.buyssonii Godef.-Leb. See *Aerangis ellisii.*

A.calceolus Thouars.
Stem very short. Lvs 3–10, to 20cm×18mm, narrowly lanceolate or ligulate. Infl. to 15cm, slightly shorter than lvs, racemose or sometimes paniculate with 1–3 short branches, laxly several-fld; fls pale green; sep. 8×3mm, lanceolate, acute; pet. slightly shorter and narrower; lip to 10×5mm, the basal part ovate-lanceolate, concave, the apex long-acuminate; spur 12–15mm, slightly bulbous at apex. Summer. Indian Ocean Is.; Mozambique.

A.calligerum Rchb. f. See *Aerangis ellisii.*
A.capense (L. f.) Lindl. See *Mystacidium capense.*
A.caudatum Lindl. See *Plectrelminthus caudatus.*
A.chaillauanum Hook. f. See *Cyrtorchis chaillauana.*
A.christyanum Rchb. f. See *Calyptrochilum christyanum.*
A.citratum (Thouars). See *Aerangis citrata.*
A.comorense Kränzl. See *A.eburneum.*

A.compactum Schltr.
Stem short and stout, lengthening with age; old sheaths large, flattened, transversely wrinkled with a dorsal keel. Lvs 5–6, to 10×3cm, spreading or recurved, thick and leathery, Infl. piercing the lf sheaths, 1–3-fld; fls white; peduncle 8–10mm, covered by sheaths; pedicel and ovary 6cm, pedicel flattened, ovary 3-winged; sep. 20×10mm, oblong; pet. similar but slightly broader; lip 25mm long, 12–20mm wide when flattened, boat-shaped, the apex rounded with a short apiculus; spur 12–13cm, slender, tapering from a wide (10mm) mouth, at first parallel to ovary, later bent sharply forwards. Summer. Madagascar.

A.conchiferum Lindl.
Stem to 30cm, usually pendent; sheaths dotted with black; roots grey, verrucose, 3–4mm diam. Lvs 40–50×7mm, narrowly ligulate or linear, dark green, distichous. Infl. 1–2-fld, borne along stem opposite lf axils; fls white; sep. and pet. 25×3mm, narrowly lanceolate, acute; lip c13×13mm, shell-shaped, apiculate; spur 4–5cm, straight, tapering. Kenya, Tanzania, Malawi, Zimbabwe, S Africa.

A.cryptodon Rchb. f. See *Aerangis cryptodon.*

A.cultriforme Summerh.
Stem to 20cm; roots 1–2mm diam. Lvs several, borne towards apex of stem, c40×7mm, distichous, falcate, deeply, unequally and acutely bilobed at apex, dull olive green, often tinged with bronze. Infl. 1-fld, often arising from the same node in successive years; fls straw-orange; dorsal sep. 11–20×2–3mm, lanceolate, acute, lateral sep. oblique and slightly shorter and wider; pet. 10–15×1.5–3mm, curved linear-lanceolate; lip 8.5–15× 4.5–6mm, boat-shaped, with a central keel along the lower half of the upper surface; spur 15–26mm, slender but inflated in apical third; column 1–2mm. Kenya, Tanzania, Malawi, Zambia, Zimbabwe, S Africa.

A.dasycarpum Schltr.
Stems to 10cm, densely leafy; roots pubesc. Lvs 7–10×4–7mm, oblong, obtuse, sometimes shortly apiculate, fleshy with a cartilaginous margin. Infl. 1-fld; fls white; peduncle, pedicel and ovary all very short; sep. and pet. 6–7mm, oblong; lip 5–6mm, oblong-ligulate, obtuse, concave, slightly narrowed above the middle; spur 4mm, obtuse, adpressed to the ovary; column very short. Madagascar.

A.dendrobiopsis Schltr.
Stem pendent, 25–60cm, leafy, sometimes branched. Lvs 5–12cm×5–8mm, linear-lanceolate, unequally and acutely bilobed at apex. Racemes 4–12cm, usually 2–4-fld but sometimes 1-fld; fls white, rather fleshy; dorsal sep. 23×7mm, lanceolate, subacuminate, lateral sep. similar but 27mm long and joined together at base; pet. 22×8mm, ovate, subacumi-

nate; lip 18–20×8–13mm, rhomboid, concave, auriculate, narrowing gradually from the base then abruptly constricted to a cylindrical point 5mm long; spur horizontal or erect, 35mm, tapering from a relatively wide (4mm) mouth; column 5mm. Spring. Madagascar.

A.descendens Rchb. f. See *Aerangis articulata.*

A.didieri Baill. ex Finet.
Stem to 15cm, sheaths transversely wrinkled; roots verrucose. Lvs 5–7, to 5×1cm, ligulate, coriaceous, unequally and obtusely bilobed at apex. Infl. 1-fld, sometimes with a rudimentary second fl.; fls white; sep. 22–35×5–7mm, lanceolate, acute; pet. similar but slightly narrower; lip 23–32×12–15mm, elliptic or ovate, acute, very concave; spur 8–15cm, slender. Summer. Madagascar.

A.distichum Lindl.
Stem to 25cm, curved to sprawling, leafy. Lvs distichous, overlapping, bilaterally flattened, 5–11×3–7mm, fleshy, broadly elliptic-oblong, falcate, obtuse, recurved, with a narrow groove extending for halfway along upper surface. Infl. 1-fld; fls white; pedicel and ovary 5mm; bracts 2mm; sep. and pet. 2–3mm, oblong, obtuse, pet. slightly shorter than sep.; lip 2mm, ovate-oblong, obscurely trilobed, lateral lobes broadly rounded, midlobe triangular, acute; spur 5–7mm; column very short. W Africa, Zaire, Uganda, Angola.

A.eburneum Bory (*A.comorense* Kränzl.).
Robust, erect, forming large clumps; roots stout, 4–5mm diam. Lvs 10–15, distichous, 30–40×3–5cm, ligulate, stiff, leathery. Racemes axillary, as long as or longer than the lvs, many-fld; fls 4–6cm diam., scented in evening; sep. green, pet. and lip white; sep. and pet. 30–40mm, lanceolate, acute, sep. 10mm wide, pet. slightly narrower; lip 35×30mm, held uppermost, broadly ovate, concave, with an acumen 10mm long and a median keel in the lower half; spur 6–7cm, tapering from a mouth 5mm wide; column stout, 8mm. Winter. Mascarene Is., Comoros Is., Madagascar, Seychelles. ssp. *giryamae* (Rendle) Cribb & Sengh. Differs in having a broader lip (30–35×40–50mm) and a shorter spur (4–6cm). E Africa. ssp. *superbum* (Thouars) H. Perrier (*A.superbum* Thouars; *A.brongniartianum* Rchb. f.). Differs in having larger, whiter fls; lip 40mm long, including the acumen, 47mm wide, subquadrate, auriculate at base, with suggestion of being trilobed; median keel more prominent. Madagascar. var. *longicalcar* Bosser. Stem to 40cm; roots 5mm diam., lvs to 60×8cm. Raceme to 100cm. Several-fld; sep. and pet. 48–52×9–13mm, lanceolate, acute; lip 50mm long (including 18mm-long acumen), 60–65mm wide; spur 35–40cm. Madagascar. ssp. *xerophilum* H. Perrier. Stem to 35cm; roots 6mm diam. Lvs to 15cm. Fls smaller than in typical form, tepals to 30mm; lip much wider than long, 35mm wide, 20mm long, not including acumen; spur 7–8cm. Summer. Madagascar.

A.eichlerianum Kränzl.
Stem elongated; roots numerous. Lvs to 12×3cm, elliptic or ligulate, unequally and obtusely bilobed at apex. Racemes arising opposite lvs, 2–3-fld; fls green, margin and upper half of lip white; sep. 35–40mm, ovate-lanceolate, acute or acuminate; pet. similar but slightly shorter; lip 35×35mm, subquadrate, the apex abruptly acuminate and recurved; spur 3cm, curved, tapering from a wide mouth to a narrow point in the middle, then swollen and fusiform at apex. Nigeria, Cameroun, Gabon, Congo, Angola.

A.elephantinum Schltr.
Stem 10–15cm, stout, 8mm diam.; roots 4mm diam., grey, somewhat verrucose. Lvs 7.5–12×2–2.5cm, ligulate, leathery, unequally and obtusely bilobed at apex. Infl. 1-fld (occasionally 2-fld), very short; fls white, sep. sometimes tinged with peach; sep. 35–45×10–13mm, ligulate, lateral sep. with a slight dorsal keel; pet. similar but narrower; lip 30–40× 20–25mm, ovate, obtuse, concave, enfolding column at base; spur 11cm, filiform, curved; column short. Winter. Madagascar.

Angraecum (a) *A.distichum* (b) *A.eburneum* (c) *A.sesquipedale* (d) *A.infundibulare*

A.emarginatum Sw. See *Calyptrochilum emarginatum.*

A.equitans Schltr.
Compact, 9–10cm; stem stout, 8–10mm diam., sometimes branched, densely leafy; roots wiry, 1mm diam. Lvs 3–6×1–2cm, fleshy, spreading, curved with a dorsal keel. Raceme 1–3-fld; peduncle very short, covered with sheaths; pedicel and ovary 4cm, ovary 4-angled; fls white, scented; sep. 17–20mm, lateral sep. slightly longer than dorsal sep., narrowly lanceolate with dorsal keel; pet. similar to dorsal sep.; lip 17–20×9–15mm, elliptic, acuminate, concave with a median keel near the base on the upper surface; spur 8–11cm, filiform from a funnel-shaped mouth. Spring–summer. Madagascar.

A.fastuosum Rchb. f. See *Aerangis fastuosa.*

A.florulentum Rchb. f.
Stems 15–30cm×5–6mm, flattened, sinuous, often branched; roots wiry, 1–1.5mm diam., arising at base of stem. Lvs numerous, 4.5–7×1–1.5cm, distichous, narrowly lanceolate, unequally and obtusely bilobed at apex. Racemes short, to 5cm, 2–4-fld; fls white; pedicel and ovary 3–3.5cm, very thin; tepals 20–25×4–8mm, lanceolate, acuminate; lip 23×6mm, very concave; spur 9–10cm, filiform; column short and stout. Comoros Is.

A.fragrans Thouars. See *Jumellea fragrans.*
A.fuscatum Rchb. f. See *Aerangis fuscata.*

A.germinyanum Hook. f.
Stem to 1m, much-branched, somewhat flattened; roots grey-white, c1mm diam. Lvs 3–4×1.5–2cm, distichous, oblong, obtusely bilobed, bright, glossy green. Infl. 1-fld; fls non-resupinate, white, sep. and pet. sometimes tinged amber-yellow; peduncle very short, to 1cm; pedicel and ovary 3cm; tepals more or less filiform, 7–10cm×3–4mm, usually twisted; lip 17–25mm long and wide, shell-shaped, with acumen 20mm; spur 10–13cm; column very short. Madagascar.

A.hamatum Rolfe. See *Cyrtorchis hamata.*
A.hildebrandtii Rchb. f. See *Microterangis hildebrandtii.*

A.humbertii H. Perrier.
To 20cm; stem short and thick; roots numerous, many aerial, 2–3mm diam. Lvs 12–13×1–1.5cm, distichous, linear or ligulate, unequally bilobed at apex, lobes rounded. Racemes to 20cm, 4–8-fld; fls green-white, lip pure white; pedicel and ovary 4–4.5cm; sep. and pet. narrowly lanceolate, long-acuminate, tapering to become almost filiform, dorsal sep. 5cm long, 5mm wide at base, lateral sep. 7cm×7mm, pet. 4cm×4mm; lip 5cm long, including 2cm acumen, 2cm wide, very concave; spur 11–14cm, tapering to become filiform from a mouth 7mm wide; column 4mm. Madagascar.

A.humblotii Rchb. f. See *A.leonis.*
A.hyaloides Rchb. f. See *Aerangis hyaloides.*
A.imbricatum Lindl. See *Calyptrochilum emarginatum.*

A.infundibulare Lindl.
Stems leafy, scrambling, to 1–2m, pendent or horizontal. Lvs 9–11×2–2.5cm, broadly ligulate, unequally bilobed at apex. Infl. pendent, 1-fld; fls green-white, turning ivory with age; sep. and pet. 5–8cm, narrowly lanceolate, acuminate, pet. slightly shorter than sep.; lip 5–8×4–5cm, oblong, apiculate, concave; spur 15–23cm, funnel-shaped for first 5cm, then narrowing abruptly to become cylindrical. Nigeria, Cameroun, Principe, Congo, Zaire, Uganda, Kenya.

A.kirkii Rchb. f. See *Aerangis kirkii.*
A.kotschyanum Rchb. f. See *Aerangis kotschyana.*

A.Lady Lisa (*A.magdalenae* × *A.scottianum*)
Stem erect, to 15cm or more, sometimes branched near base. Lvs in 2 ranks, 12–15cm, dark green, V-shaped in cross-section for about 3cm above the open, sheathing base, then the upper surfaces fused to form a thick, folded lf, sometimes free at apex, folded part 7–9mm wide; lf sheaths transversely wrinkled. Infl. axillary, 1–2-fld; peduncle 7–8cm; fls pure white; sep. and pet. 3–4×1cm, lanceolate; lip uppermost or

held sideways, 3×4cm, orbicular-quadrate, widest toward apex, shortly apiculate; spur 13cm, straight, slender from broadly funnel-shaped base; column 4mm, stout, with large quadrate wings on either side of stigma. Spring–summer. Garden origin.

A.leonis (Rchb. f.) Veitch (*A.humblotii* Rchb. f.).
Stem very short. Lvs usually 4, arranged like a St Andrew's cross, bilaterally flattened, somewhat fleshy, falcate, 5–20×1.5–3.5cm. Racemes 1–2, 7–10cm, arising below lvs, 2–4-fld; fls white, fleshy, scented; pedicel and ovary 3.5–5cm; bracts 3mm; sep. 20–60×5–7mm, lanceolate, acuminate, keeled on the outer surface; pet. similar but slightly wider and less acuminate; lip 22–50×18–35mm, broadly boat-shaped, apiculate; spur 7–15cm, flexuous, very slender from a funnel-shaped mouth 6mm wide; column 4×5mm. Spring. Madagascar, Comoros Is. Plants from the Comoros Is. have fls about twice the size of those from Madagascar.

A.magdalenae Schltr.
Stems short; roots 3–4mm diam. Lvs 6–8, to 30×5cm, distichous, oblong-ligulate, unequally and obtusely bilobed at apex, rather fleshy with many transverse wrinkles. Infl. to 10cm, arising below lvs, 1–2-fld; fls pure white, rather fleshy and broad, to 10cm diam.; pedicel 6–7cm, straight, stout, ovary 2.5–3cm, curved, with 6 grooves; sep. 40–50×18mm, lanceolate, obtuse, lateral sep. somewhat curved; pet. ovate, slightly shorter and wider; lip 5×4–4.5cm, suborbicular to obovate with an acuminate tip folded into a keel; spur 10–11cm, sigmoid, tapering from a wide mouth to become almost filiform; column wider (5–6mm) than high. Spring–autumn. Madagascar.

A.mauritianum (Poir.) Frappier.
Stems 25–40cm, more or less pendent, flattened, branched and sinuous. Lvs numerous, 4.5–6×1–1.5cm, distichous, oblong-lanceolate. Infl. 1-fld; fls pure white; peduncle 12–15mm with 2 short sheaths at base; pedicel and ovary 3–3.5cm; sep. 15–20×4mm, lanceolate, acuminate, dorsal sep. slightly shorter than lateral sep., lateral sep. shortly joined at base; pet. 12×3mm, lanceolate; lip 15×7mm, lanceolate, acute; spur 8cm, somewhat incurved; column 3mm high and of similar width. Mascarene Is.

A.maxillarioides Ridl. See *Jumellea maxillarioides.*

A.mirabile Schltr.
Plant c15cm high; stem stiff, covered with wrinkled, verrucose sheaths. Lvs numerous, 4–5cm long, 2.5mm wide when flattened, narrowly linear but with edges inrolled so as to appear subulate. Infl. usually 1-fld; fls non-resupinate, white, tepals sometimes tinged with yellow; peduncle 4.5–5.5cm, stiff and wiry; pedicel and ovary 2cm; tepals 35mm, lanceolate, acuminate, becoming filiform; lip 30×13mm, shell-shaped with a long acumen; spur 11–12cm, narrowing from a wide mouth to become filiform. Madagascar.

A.modestum Hook. f. See *Aerangis modesta.*
A.mooreanum Rolfe ex Sander. See *Aerangis mooreana.*
A.mystacidii Rchb. f. See *Aerangis mystacidii.*

A.ochraceum (Ridl.) Schltr.
Stem short, several-lvd. Lvs about 10×0.5cm, narrowly linear-lanceolate, unequally bilobed at apex. Infl. to 7.5cm, 1-fld; fls small, ochre-yellow; sep. 4×2mm, narrowly lanceolate, acute; pet. similar but slightly shorter and narrower; lip boat-shaped, acute; spur about 20mm, filiform but slightly inflated at apex. Madagascar.

A.pellucidum Lindl. See *Diaphananthe pellucida.*
A.pertusum Lindl. See *Listrostachys pertusa.*
A.philippinense Ames. See *Amesiella philippinensis.*

A.reygaertii De Wildeman.
Stems elongated, leafy, erect or pendulous. Lvs 10–15×2–3cm, oblong, slightly bilobed at apex. Infl. about 6cm, arising on stem opposite lvs, 1-fld; fls white, the lip green towards base; sep. about 30×5mm, lanceolate, acumi-

nate, dorsal sep. reflexed; pet. 26×4mm, narrowly lanceolate, acute; lip 25×4mm, lanceolate or oblong-lanceolate, acute or acuminate; spur 5–6cm, almost straight; column 4mm. Cameroun, Zaire, Uganda.

A.rhodostictum Kränzl. See *Aerangis luteoalba* var. *rhodosticta*.

A.rothschildianum O'Brien. See *Eurychone rothschildiana*.

A.*rutenbergianum* Kränzl.
4–12cm; roots 1.5–2.5mm diam., rather rough but not verrucose. Lvs 4–12, 2.5–6×0.5–0.7cm, stiff, linear, unequally and obtusely bilobed at apex. Infl. 1-fld; fls 5.5–6cm diam., white, the spur turning green towards apex; peduncle 5–10mm, completely covered with scarious sheaths; pedicel and ovary 2–3cm; sep. 30–37×6–6.5mm, lanceolate, acute; pet. 27–35×3.5mm; lip 25–35×17–18mm, rhomboid-elliptic, apiculate; spur 6–14cm, filiform; column short, wider than high. Summer. Madagascar.

A.sanderianum Rchb. f. See *Aerangis modesta*.

A.*scottianum* Rchb. f.
Slender, to 30cm, erect when young, pendent when old; roots 2mm diam., finely verrucose. Lvs 6–30, 6–10×0.5cm, terete with a groove on upper surface. Racemes axillary, to 10cm, 1–4-fld; fls white; pedicel and ovary 3cm, twisted at apex; sep. 25–27×4mm, ligulate, acute; pet. similar but narrower; lip 2.5–3×4cm, concave, transversely oblong, apiculate, clasping column at base; spur 9–15cm, filiform from a wide mouth, pendent; column short and thick. Spring–autumn. Comoros Is.

A.*sesquipedale* Thouars (*Macroplectron sesquipedale* (Thouars) Pfitzer). COMET ORCHID.
To 120cm, usually unbranched, often forming dense clumps; roots stout, 6–10mm diam. Lvs numerous, 25–40×6–7cm, distichous, ligulate, unequally and obtusely bilobed at apex. Racemes axillary, shorter than lvs, 1–4-fld; fls ivory to pure white, fleshy, to 22cm diam., with a spicy scent at night; sep. and pet. 7–11×2–3.5cm, narrowly ovate, long- acuminate, pet. slightly shorter and wider than sep.; lip 7–9×3.5–4.5cm, pandurate or oblong, with an acumen 2–3cm long, and with a callus on either side of the mouth of the spur; spur 30–35cm, slender, tapering; column 6×10mm. Winter. Madagascar.

A.somalense Schltr. See *Aerangis somalensis*.

A.*sororium* Schltr.
Erect, terrestrial, 60–100cm; stem rarely branched, 10–15mm wide, rather flattened, with numerous lvs on upper quarter of stem. Lvs 20–30×3–4.5cm, distichous, stiff, more or less erect, ligulate, unequally bilobed at apex, lobes rounded. Racemes shorter than lvs, 1–4-fld; fls pure white; pedicel and ovary 4–6.5cm; sep. 50–60×16mm, broadly lanceolate, acute, with prominent dorsal keel, lateral sep. joined at the base and enclosing base of spur; pet. 50–60×20mm with a small auricle at base on inner edge; lip 50–60×30–33mm, broadly ovate with a conical terminal acumen; spur 25–32cm, tapering to an

obtuse apex from a mouth 5mm wide; column 7mm high and wide. Summer–autumn. Madagascar.

A.*striatum* Thouars.
Stem 5–7cm; roots 3–4mm diam. Lvs 20–24×2–3cm, ligulate, leathery, light green, with 9–11 prominent veins. Racemes arising from base of plant, 10–15cm, densely 5–7-fld; fls white, column and spur green; sep. 17–18×7mm; pet. 15×6mm; lip 12×7mm; spur 3–4mm, conical. Mascarene Is. (Réunion).

A.stylosum Rolfe. See *Aerangis stylosa*.

A.superbum Thouars. See *A.eburneum* ssp. *superbum*.

A.*teretifolium* Ridl.
Stem to 40cm, pendent, sometimes branched, 1.5mm diam., leafy, somewhat flexuous, covered with light brown lf sheaths towards base; roots 1–1.5mm diam. Lvs to 11cm×1mm, distichous, terete with a shallow groove along the upper surface, acute, stiff, dark green. Infl. 1-fld; fls green-white to white tinged with pink-brown; peduncle wiry, 3.5–5.5cm; pedicel and ovary 15–16mm; sep. and pet. lanceolate at base, then acuminate-filiform, sometimes reflexed, sep. 30–40×4mm, lateral sep. slightly narrower, pet. 20×3mm; lip 25–30× 7–9mm, boat-shaped, with needle-like acumen; spur 10–13cm. Spring. Madagascar.

A.tridactylites Rolfe. See *Tridactyle tridactylites*.

A.*triquetrum* Thouars.
Stem very short, branching at base. Lvs 5–7, forming a fan, 8–9×1.5cm, ligulate, unequally and obtusely bilobed at apex, somewhat leathery. Infl. 1.5cm, 1-fld, arising at base of stem; fls white; sep. 22–24×9–10mm, broadly lanceolate, acute; pet. 22×6mm, lanceolate, acute; lip 20–22×20–22mm, suborbicular, apiculate; spur 6–7cm, filiform. Réunion.

A.Veitchii. (*A.sesquipedale* × *A.eburneum*.)
Robust, to 1.5m. Lvs several, to 30×5cm, distichous, ligulate. Racemes 6–10-fld; fls 9–12cm diam., green- or ivory-tinted at first, then pure white; tepals 6–7×1.5cm, lanceolate, acute, dorsal sep. erect, lateral sep. and pet. spreading; lip 6–7×4cm, boat-shaped, abruptly narrowed to an acumen about 2cm long; spur slender, c15cm, horizontal or semi-erect. Winter. Garden origin.

A.*vigueri* Schltr.
Stems short; roots 3–4mm diam., densely verrucose, greywhite with golden brown growing tips, arising at base of stem. Lvs 6–14cm×8–12mm, linear-ligulate, unequally bilobed at apex. Infl. 1-fld; fls white, or lip white and sep., pet. and spur tinged with brown, salmon or yellow-gold; peduncle 3–3.5cm, the base covered with scarious sheaths; pedicel short, ovary 3.5–4cm, 3-veined; sep. and pet. 55–85× 5–10mm, linear-ligulate, acuminate; lip 50–70×35–50mm, shell-shaped, with an acumen 15–25mm long; spur 9–13cm, tapering abruptly from a funnel-shaped mouth to become filiform. Spring. Madagascar.

A.wakefieldii Rolfe. See *Solenangis wakefieldii*.

Anguloa (a) *A.brevilabris* (b) *A.clowesii* (c) *A.cliftonii* (d) *A.uniflora*

Anguloa Ruiz & Pav. CRADLE ORCHID; TULIP ORCHID. (For Don Francisco de Angulo (*fl.* 1790), Spanish naturalist.) Some 10 species of terrestrials or epiphytes allied to *Lycaste*. Rhizomes short. Pseudobulbs to 15cm, clustered, cylindric or narrow-ovoid or ellipsoid and laterally compressed, glossy dark green becoming olive green and somewhat wrinkled, losing leaves after one season, with leafy basal sheaths. Leaves 3, to 80×30cm, apical, glabrous, deep green, thin, plicate, strongly ribbed, broadly lanceolate, acuminate, tapering to a grooved stalk. Inflorescence basal, accompanying new growth, a series of solitary flowers on robust, sheathed stalks to 30cm; flowers fleshy, fragrant; sepals and petals waxy to 7cm, rigid, erect, strongly concave, broadly ovate-lanceolate, subequal, cupped and incurved, not opening fully; lip to 5×3cm, fleshy, hinged to column foot and slightly mobile when gently rocked, trilobed, midlobe usually small, retuse, pubescent, callus forked, lateral lobes ovate to triangular, erect; column stout, decurved semi-terete above, concave or flat beneath. Spring–summer. Colombia, Venezuela, Ecuador, Peru.

CULTIVATION   Cool to intermediate (min. winter night temperature 9°C/48°F). *Lycaste*-like with large, cupped-'inflated', waxy blooms. Pot annually into a mixture of 2:2:1:1 coarse bark, leafmould, charcoal and well-rotted FYM, having removed any exhausted backbulbs, dead roots and damaged foliage. Maximize temperatures and humidity during the spring–summer growing season to produce fat pseudobulbs and large leaves in buoyant, brightly lit conditions. Feed and water copiously at this time. Reduce water and allow maximum light once pseudobulbs are set, allowing the medium to dry out for up to a week during the dormant period. When vegetation or flowering activity (these usually simultaneous) is first visible at base of lead pseudobulb, repot and slowly increase water. Propagate by division and back-bulbs.

A.brevilabris Rolfe.
Resembles *A.ruckeri*, but fls smaller, duller yellow within. Colombia.

A.cliftonii Rolfe.
Fls among largest in the genus (to 9×8.5cm), also more 'open', pale dull yellow to ochre marked maroon to blood red, especially toward base of tepals, strongly scented. Colombia.

A.clowesii Lindl.
Fls to 8cm, pure lemon or golden yellow, covered in a fine bloom at base, scented of wintergreen and chocolate. Colombia, Venezuela.

A.eburnea Williams. See *A.uniflora*.

A.ruckeri Lindl.
Fls to 9cm deep; sep. and pet. subequal, elliptic-oblong, olive green to pale bronze beneath, ochre closely spotted blood red above, rarely solid maroon-red or ivory. Colombia.

A.uniflora Ruiz & Pav. (*A.virginalis* Lindl.; *A.eburnea* Williams).
Fls to 10.5cm deep, more open than in other spp., sickly-scented, lasting well; sep. and pet. ivory, flushed rose above, dotted crimson near base, pet. narrower than sep.; lip off-white, mottled chocolate. Throughout genus range.

A.virginalis Lindl. See *A.uniflora*.

× **Angulocaste** (*Anguloa* × *Lycaste*). These intergeneric hybrids resemble both parents in vegetative growth and often become very large plants with huge leaves. The flowers are also somewhat intermediate, borne singly or in pairs on long stems from the base of the pseudobulb. Each flower is somewhat tulip-shaped, the sepals are thick and waxy and much larger than the petals and lip which are usually similar in colour. These plants flourish in intermediate conditions but need fresh air and extra shade in summer. They should be kept dry during the cooler season.

× *A.*Andromeda: this has the largest fls of all, pink with darker freckles.
× *A.*Apollo 'Goldcourt': fls rich yellow with pale red freckles.
× *A.*Aurora: beautiful red and orange fls.
× *A.*Jupiter 'Sunset': fls rich gold, heavily marked with red.
× *A.*Lady Bath: very vigorous plant; fls pure white.
× *A.*Olympus: fls cup-shaped, white or beige often with pink freckles as in the clones 'Mayflower' and 'Magnolia', sometimes yellow as in the clone 'Honey'.

× *A.*Sanderae: rather variable; fls striking white with golden throat to palest pinks.
× *A.*Tudor: very open fls of heavy texture, pale pink with darker pink spots.
× *A.*Wyld Charm: fls luminous clear deep pink.
× *A.*Wyld Delight: free-flowering, fls scented, yellow with fine red spotting.

Anoectochilus and allies (a) *Anoectochilus roxburghii* (b) *Anoectochilus reinwardtii* (c) *Macodes petola* var. *argenteoreticulata* (d) *Ludisia discolor*

Anoectochilus Bl. (From Gk *anoiktos*, open, and *cheilos*, lip, referring to the spreading tip of the lip.) JEWEL ORCHID. Some 25 species of terrestrial, lithophytic or, rarely, epiphytic herbs lacking pseudobulbs. Stems slender, fleshy, rooting at nodes, creeping then ascending. Roots ciliate, adhesive. Leaves alternate on stem, clustering in a loose rosette at apex, petiolate, sheathing stem at base, ovate to elliptic, minutely papillose above, often appearing velvety with silver-white or gold metallic reticulation. Inflorescence an erect terminal raceme; dorsal sepal forming a hood with petals; lip adpressed to column base, contracted, becoming a lobed claw beyond the base. Asia to W Pacific.

CULTIVATION The pride of many Victorian pits and Wardian cases, these exquisite plants were grown (or at least supplied) in far greater numbers than they are today. Those wishing to enjoy their fabled velvety and metallic leaves more often than not resort to their tougher ally, *Ludisia discolor*, widely available and easy to grow. Beautiful foliage orchids for the warm house or growing case (minimum temperature 18°C/65°F). Set the fragile, fleshy rhizomes on a bed of 2:1:1 leafmould, fine-grade bark and charcoal in half-crocked clay pans. Dust with a little green sulphur. Top dress with sphagnum. Keep evenly moist (never saturated, never dry) in humid, shaded conditions. Avoid wetting foliage. Do not trouble to pinch out flower spikes, as is sometimes advised – a plant growing well enough to produce them at all will survive the exertion. Propagate by division, removing sections of rhizome and dressing with sulphur. Unless carefully watered and kept at high temperatures these plants will rot away very quickly.

A.brevilabris Lindl. See *A.sikkimensis*.

A.regalis Bl.
Lvs to 5×3.5cm, to 5 in a loose rosette, subcordate to ovate-acute, velvety, dark emerald green netted gold above, purple-green beneath. Infl. to 20cm; fls to 1.3cm, few, crowded near apex; sep. and pet. green-white; lip white, sparkling, deeply fringed, spur long-cylindric, curved. S India, Sri Lanka.

A.reinwardtii Bl.
Lvs ovate, velvety, black-red above with gold, reticulate venation. Raceme to 15cm, 3–4-fld; peduncle pubesc.; sep. red-brown, oblong, acute, exterior glandular-pubesc.; pet. oblong-falcate, acuminate, white, spur to 7mm, oblong, flattened, pale green. Sumatra, Java.

A.roxburghii (Wallich) Lindl.
Resembles *A.regalis*, distinguished by lvs with central longitudinal zone of gold on lime green ground colour, veins gold suffused red, leaves otherwise chocolate-olive to bronze-black. Fls to 5; sep. and pet. pale buff; lip white with 2 basal calli, fringed, spur with 2 projections. N India.

A.sanderianus hort. See *Macodes sanderiana*.

A.sikkimensis King & Pantl. (*A.brevilabris* Lindl.).
Lvs to 5.25×3.5cm, in a loose rosette, subcordate to broad-elliptic, acute, velvety, maroon to garnet netted pale gold to copper above, matt red-green beneath. Infl. to 18cm; axis pale red, pubesc.; fls 12mm; sep. and pet. green to white; lip white with green teeth, spur green. Sikkim.

Ansellia Lindl. (For John Ansell (*d*1847), English gardener who collected the type specimen on Fernando Po.) 1 species, a robust epiphyte, rarely terrestrial or lithophytic, 50–100cm. Pseudobulbs clustered, 60×2–3cm, cylindric or fusiform (basically cane-like) with several nodes, ridged, yellow or yellow-green, leafy toward apex. Roots of two kinds: stout and clinging to substrate, or fine and erect, all arising at base of plant. Leaves 4–10, borne toward apex of pseudobulb, 15–50×1.5–5cm, oblong-obovate to strap-shaped, ribbed, especially on sheath, dark green. Panicle terminal, laxly many-flowered; flowers 4–5cm diam., usually pale to deep yellow, lightly or heavily blotched with deep maroon or chestnut brown, occasionally unblotched and pale yellow or yellow-green, or densely blotched to wholly chocolate-maroon; sepals 15–35×5–10mm, elliptic-lanceolate; petals similar but slightly shorter and broader; lip to 22mm, trilobed, with 2–3 longitudinal keels down the centre, lateral lobes erect, midlobe orbicular, apiculate; column 10–12mm; pollinia 4, in two pairs. Winter–spring. Tropical & S Africa.

CULTIVATION Epiphytes for the intermediate greenhouse. Pot tightly in well-crocked clay pots containing equal parts coarse bark, leafmould and well-rotted FYM. Place in brightly lit, well-ventilated and humid conditions. Syringe each morning during growth; water and feed freely at this time, reducing the water and allowing still more light as the growth nears completion and the flower spike develops. Propagate by division.

A.africana Lindl. (*A.gigantea* Rchb. f.; *A.nilotica* (Bak.) N.E. Br.). LEOPARD ORCHID.

A.gigantea Rchb. f. See *A.africana.*
A.nilotica (Bak.) N.E. Br. See *A.africana.*

Arachnis Bl. (From Gk *arachnis*, spider, referring to the appearance of the flowers.) SCORPION ORCHID. Some 7 species of monopodial, scrambling epiphytes to 2.5m. Stems thick, robust, becoming bare and hardened at base. Roots thick, adventitious. Leaves strap-shaped, thick, fleshy, basally sheathing stem in 2 ranks, alternate along stem. Inflorescence a raceme, axillary, erect or pendulous, simple or branched; flowers fragrant, fleshy; sepals and petals almost equal, spreading, narrow, widening and decurved apically, appearing clavate, margin revolute; lip articulate, attached to the column base by a short stalk, trilobed, midlobe fleshy, centrally keeled, a single fleshy callus below the apex, lateral lobes erect, rectangular to triangular. SE Asia, W Malaysia.

CULTIVATION Robust *Vanda*-like epiphytes with long branching spikes of brightly banded flowers favoured for cutting and commonly seen in floristry. For the lath-house in Zone 10 or the warm greenhouse. Grow in full sunlight and high humidity. Mist and water moderately throughout the year.

A.flos-aeris (L.) Rchb. f. (*Aerides arachnites* Sw.). Infl. branched or simple, pendent or ascending; fls fragrant, dark green or yellow, horizontally striped or spotted maroon, lip with orange ridges; dorsal sep. erect, linear, all seg. linear-spathulate, broad, falcate; lip 1.5–2cm, midlobe obovate, horizontally spurred, lateral lobes rectangular. Malaysia to Philippines.

A.hookeriana (Rchb. f.) Rchb. f. Infl. to 60cm, simple, erect; sep. and pet. similar, cream, dotted purple; dorsal sep. to 4cm; lip purple or purple-striped, midlobe keeled with apical callus, lateral lobes diverging, recurved. Malaysia.

A.lowii (Lindl.) Rchb. f. See *Dimorphorchis lowii.*

A.Maggie Oei.
Tall plants with long sprays of large spidery fls, yellow with red spots, lip rosy red.

× **Aranda** (*Arachnis* × *Vanda*). The first hybrid × *Aranda* was bred by Prof. Eric Holttum in Singapore and it and many of its progeny and similar crosses laid the foundation for the cut-flower industry of Singapore. Many of the plants are shorter than the *Arachnis* parent and more floriferous. Stems upright with the alternate leaves in two rows, leaves narrowly channelled. Inflorescences axillary, on upright spikes, sometimes branching; flowers star-shaped with narrow sepals and petals and a small lip, usually very brightly coloured. More complex hybrids have been bred from many of these plants, e.g. × *Holttumara* (*Arachnis* × *Renanthera* × *Vanda*) and × *Bokchoonara* (*Arachnis* × *Ascocentrum* × *Phalaenopsis* × *Vanda*), which have brightly coloured flowers of rounder shape than the earlier crosses but maintain their lasting qualities. The flowers are long-lasting on the plant and as cut flowers. The plants need bright light, high humidity and warm temperatures to grow and flower well. They grow extremely well out of doors in the humid tropics but are less easy in the glasshouse.

× A.Baby Teoh: very tall plants; upright spikes of many large fls; fls bright cerise pink with brick red lip, column white and yellow.
× A.Christine: tall plants and free-flowering; fls blue-violet freckled with deep cerise, lip with darker violet midlobe, white at the base with a yellow flash in the throat.
× A.Hilda Galistan 'Suntan': tall plants and very free-flowering on upright spikes; fls bright orange-tan, covered with fine darker spots, lip lilac and white.
× A.How Yee Peng 'Ada': compact plants that are easy to grow with upright spikes; fls lilac-pink with iridescent texture, lip darker.

× A.Majula: tall plants with upright spikes; fls deep yellow with red spots throughout, lip bright cerise pink, column white.
× A.Noorah Alsagoff: tall plants with strong upright infl.; fls brilliant blue-violet with darker lip, column pale pink and yellow.
× A.Singapore: long, upright infl.; fls star-shaped in bright yellow with red markings.
× A.Wendy Scott: long upright infl.; fls long-lasting, blue-violet with darker tessellations, lip darker violet.

Arethusa L. (From Arethusa, the river nymph, referring to the wet habitat of the species.) 2 species of terrestrials. Corms bulb-like, subterranean. Leaves solitary, slender, developing after flower opens. Inflorescence 1 or 2, terminal, slender, erect, 1-flowered; flowers showy; sepals and petals subequal, connivent forming a hood over column; lip reflexed, short-clawed, disc with a coloured, fringed crest; column adherent to lip, widening at apex, anther terminal, operculate, incumbent, bilocular, pollinia 2. Canada, US, Japan

CULTIVATION Charming hardy orchids, denizens of wet acid meadows and mosses in eastern Canada and NE US. They can, with some difficulty, be naturalized in cool, wet, peaty places in the rock or bog garden, or beside streams. Greater success can be assured by planting the corms in a well-crocked pan containing equal parts coir, chopped sphagnum moss, leafmould and charcoal. Stand the pan in a few centimetres of rainwater in a well-lit, unheated greenhouse. When growth commences, the pan can be plunged in the bog garden or on a shallow pond shelf. At the season's end, bring back under cover and reduce water – never allow to dry. Repot every third year. Increase by division.

A.bulbosa L. SWAMP PINK; DRAGON'S MOUTH; BOG ROSE.
Lvs to 23×1cm, grass-like, linear-lanceolate. Fls to 5cm, light to dark rose-purple, fragrant; dorsal sep. to 48×10mm, linear-elliptic to linear-oblong, acute or obtuse, lateral sep. to 46×9mm, broadly oblong-lanceolate, acute; pet. to 42×10mm, linear-lanceolate to linear-oblong, acute or obtuse, recurved; lip to 46mm, usually pale rose-purple, obscurely trilobed, oblong, arching to recurved, spreading, retuse, erose, crest glandular-fringed, yellow, apex purple; column to 35mm, compressed, linear-spathulate. Canada, US.

A.divaricata L. See *Cleistes divaricata*.
A.ophioglossoides L. See *Pogonia ophioglossoides*.

Arpophyllum La Ll. & Lex. (From Gk *harpe*, sickle, and *phyllon*, leaf, describing the falcate leaves of the type species, *A.spicatum*.) BOTTLEBRUSH ORCHID. 5 species of epiphytes, lithophytes or terrestrials. Rhizomes stout, corky, short, branching. Pseudobulbs very slender, narrowly cylindric, laterally compressed, clothed at base with papery sheaths. Leaves solitary, apical, rigid, glabrous, olive to dark green, linear-lanceolate to ligulate, semi-erect, falcate, grooved to conduplicate at base. Inflorescence terminal, an erect, crowded, narrowly cylindric raceme; flowers small, non-resupinate, white flushed rose to flamingo pink, lip often paler; sepals equal, fleshy, ovate-acute to triangular; petals narrower than sepals, thinner in texture; lip shorter than or equalling tepals, entire, basally saccate. Spring–summer. Mexico to Venezuela, W Indies.

CULTIVATION Vigorous, large plants for the cool to intermediate house, producing narrow spikes of crowded pink flowers on slender pseudobulbs topped with rigid, strap-like leaves. Grow as for the *Encyclia fragrans* alliance, but with additional shade in summer and regular watering throughout the year. Plants will only flower well when extremely pot-bound.

A.alpinum Lindl. (*A.medium* Rchb. f.).
Pseudobulbs to 30×1.5cm, enclosed by 3 or more mottled, papery sheaths. Lvs to 60×2.25cm, ligulate, obtuse or subacute, usually conduplicate. Infl. to 15×2.25cm, densely flowered; fls to 1.75cm diam.; tepals magenta; lip white to pale pink or lilac. Mexico, Guatemala, Honduras.

A.cardinale Lind. ex Rchb. f. See *A.giganteum*.

A.giganteum Hartw. ex Lindl. (*A.cardinale* Lind. ex Rchb. f.).
Pseudobulbs to 20×1cm. Lvs to 55×2.5cm, semi-rigid, strap-like, semi-erect to curved. Infl. to 25cm, with flowers crowded in upper third; fls rose pink to magenta, to 2cm diam. Throughout genus range.

A.medium Rchb. f. See *A.alpinum*.

A.spicatum La Ll. & Lex.
Differs from other spp. in stature (to 1.2m), bright rose fls to 1.5cm diam. and darkly glandular-pubesc. ovaries. Throughout genus range.

Arthrochilus F. Muell. (From Gk *arthron*, joint and *cheilos*, lip.) Some 10 species of glabrous, tuberous, terrestrials. Leaves absent or withered at flowering. Racemes few- to many-flowered; flowers non-resupinate; sepals and petals linear, dorsal sepal erect, laterals and petals reflexed or spreading; lip jointed, mobile, lamina slender with insect-like callus, convex, peltate. SE Australia.

CULTIVATION Pot in shallow pans or half pots containing a sandy, open mix low in pH and high in leafmould. Provide an airy, brightly lit position in a frost-free glasshouse. Keep damp and humid when in growth, dry when dormant (the foliage dies back). Repot and resume watering in mid-spring as growth begins.

A.irritabilis F. Muell. (*Spiculaea irritabilis* (F. Muell.) Schltr.; *Drakaea irritabilis* (F. Muell.) Rchb. f.).
Stems 5–37cm, slender. Lvs 3–10cm, 2–5, ovate-oblong to lanceolate, usually basal, light green, midrib prominent. Scape clothed with bracts; raceme lax; bracteoles acute; pedicels short; fls 2–30; dorsal sep. to 14mm, erect or curved forward, following line of column, linear, golden-green flushed or spotted red, lateral sep. narrow-lanceolate to ligulate-acute, pale green, sharply reflexed and decurved; pet. subfiliform, equalling lateral sep.; lip fixed by stalk to basal development of column, claw linear, to 5mm, mauve-green, lamina 7mm, club-shaped, basally swollen, darkly glandular-pubesc., constricting to apex which then expands as a maroon-black, glossy callus. Winter–spring.

Arundina Bl. (From Lat. *arundo*, reed, referring to the reed-like stems.) Some 8 species of clump-forming terrestrials. Stems simple, reed-like, crowded on short rhizome. Leaves narrow-linear, sheathing at base. Inflorescence terminal, single or branched; flowers purple or white; sepals lanceolate, acuminate, spreading; petals similar, broader; lip sessile, enveloping column, tubular. Himalaya to Pacific.

CULTIVATION   As for *Sobralia*.

A.bambusifolia (Roxb.) Lindl. See *A.graminifolia*.

A.chinensis Bl.
Similar to *A.graminifolia* but smaller and more delicate in appearance. Sep. almost linear; pet. broader; lip trilobed, midlobe blotched crimson, lateral lobes rounded. Java, Hong Kong, China.

A.densa Lindl. See *A.graminifolia*.

A.graminifolia (D. Don) Hochr. (*A.speciosa* Bl.; *A.bambusifolia* (Roxb.) Lindl.; *A.densa* Lindl.).
Stems to 2.5m. Lvs to 30cm, linear-lanceolate, narrow, acute, grass-like, 2-ranked. Infl. to 30cm, erect, scapose, bracteate, 2–3 fls opening at a time; fls short-lived, scented, resembling a small *Cattleya*, white, mauve or pale pink, lip usually a deeper purple; sep. to 4cm elliptic-lanceolate, narrow; pet. orbicular-ovate, undulate; lip obscurely trilobed, midlobe almost rectangular, margins irregularly undulate, lateral lobes incurved around the column. Indochina, Thailand, Malaya. May flower in succession throughout the year. Popular in subtropical gardens, becoming naturalized, particularly in Hawaii.

A.speciosa Bl. See *A.graminifolia*.

× **Ascocenda** (*Ascocentrum* × *Vanda*). The first miniature vandas, as these hybrids are often called, were produced in the 1960s. They had many desirable qualities for the orchid grower – tolerant of lower temperatures, dwarf habit, the ability to flower continuously, upright inflorescences of flat, dainty flowers of bright colours. As back crosses to the *Vanda* side of the parentage were continued the flowers became larger but so did the plants and many modern hybrids are quite large. Plants upright with alternate leaves in two rows, deeply channelled with uneven leaf tips. Inflorescences, axillary, upright, many-flowered; flowers round and flat with overlapping sepals and petals and small lip, brightly coloured. A small selection of the many crosses available is given below.

× A.Carolaine: fls large and well spaced, very flat with heavy texture; rose pink with darker red spots, lip golden-orange at the base with brick red front lobe.

× A.Bangkok: lvs quarter-terete, plants easy to grow and often in flower; fls peachy orange with orange red lip.

× A.Bicentennial: strong plants with upright spikes of closely arranged fls; fls deep rose pink with red tessellation.

× A.Bonanza: compact plants with upright spikes of large fls; fls basically orange, with dark red tessellation.

× A.Capricorn: strong plants with many flower spikes; fls yellow to orange with deep chestnut tessellations on lateral sep. and less markings on other sep. and pet., lip brick-red.

× A.David Parker: fls large, brilliant deep pink-purple with darker venation.

× A.Dong Tarn: compact plants that flower early; infl. upright with many fls closely arranged; fls bright red, heavily speckled or marked with deep maroon, lip magenta with yellow side lobes.

× A.Eileen Beauty: small plants with upright spikes of small to medium fls; fls dark red with darker tessellation.

× A.Fiftieth State Beauty: compact plants with upright spikes of nicely arranged medium size fls; fls medium rose red, lip with yellow side lobes, good shape.

× A.Guo Chia Long: fls large, somewhat cup-shaped, pale yellow to deep orange, densely covered with dark brown spots.

× A.Jacob Fuchs: fls large, lime-green with orange lip, excellent shape.

× A.Madame Nok: fls yellow or pale creamy beige with dark red spots, denser towards the apex of sep. and pet. and surrounding column, midlobe of lip deep red.

× A.Meda Arnold: strong-growing small plants; fls lovely deep pink or red with iridescent texture; the clone 'Red Scarlet' is one of the best bred in Thailand.

× A.Medasand: small plants with upright spikes of small fls; fls copper-coloured with bright red tessellation

× A.Mildred Furumizo 'Hisae': strong but compact plants; fls large, well-shaped, white or pale pink but dominated by deep rose tessellations throughout sep. and pet., lip red, white below, with yellow side lobes.

× A.Pak-Chong: fls large, lovely lime green with white column.

× A.Princess Mikasa: fls large, well-shaped, blue with darker blue tessellations.

× A.Su-Fun Beauty: compact plants with upright infl.; fls tightly arranged, medium-size, bright orange.

× A.Suk Samran Beauty: fls medium size, compact, bright petunia pink with darker tessellations.

× A.Sumon Gold: fls large, deep yellow, freckled with small brown spots.

× A.Tan Chai Beng: strong but compact plants; fls deep lilac blue with darker venation.

× A.To Soon: fls large, heavy-textured, rich golden orange.

× A.Udomchai: fls small to medium size, well-shaped, bright orange with darker tessellations on lateral sep.

× A.Wanpen: compact plants with large fls, fls bright yellow with a tinge of green on the lateral sep.

× A.Yip Sum Wah: compact plants with many small, brilliant orange fls.

Ascocentrum Schltr. (From Gk *askos*, bag, and *kentron*, spur, referring to the large spur of the lip.) Some 5 species of monopodial epiphytes, resembling a dwarf *Vanda*. Stems to 30cm, rigid and sheathed by old leaf bases at base. Leaves 2-ranked, alternate, recurved, fleshy, coriaceous, and strap-like or semi-terete, centrally furrowed. Inflorescence an axillary compact spike, erect or spreading; sepals and petals similar; lip trilobed, attached to column base, midlobe strap-like, lateral lobes small, united with column; spur smaller than pedicel, with a small callus near the aperture. Himalaya to Borneo.

CULTIVATION Miniature *Vanda*-like plants for well lit, humid, intermediate to warm conditions. They fare best grown in baskets or mounted on bark and rafts. Small rounded flowers in tones of rose, scarlet and orange are produced in compact spikes.

A.ampullaceum (Roxb.) Schltr. (*Aerides ampullacea* Roxb.).
Stems simple. Lvs to 14cm, many, ligulate, truncate, keeled beneath. Infl. to 8cm; fls to 1.8cm diam., sparkling rose-red; sep. elliptic-obovate, round or obtuse, spreading; pet. similar, longer; lip deflexed, apically rounded, spur horizontal, exceeding lip, inflated at tip. Himalaya, Burma.

A.curvifolium (Lindl.) Schltr. (*Saccolabium curvifolium* Lindl.).
To 25cm. Lvs decurved, apically 2-toothed or ragged. Infl. crowded; fls deep burnt orange to scarlet, lip golden-yellow, column cinnabar-red, spur orange; sep. obovate-oblong, api-cally obtuse or rounded; pet. obovate, obtuse; lip obscurely 3-lobed, truncate, midlobe linear-oblong, lateral lobes triangular, spur horizontal, inflated at tip. Burma, Thailand, Laos.

A.garayi E. Christ (*A.miniatum* (Lindl.) Schltr.).
Lvs strap-like, apically cleft, to 2-toothed. Raceme erect, sub-cylindric, dense; fls brilliant golden-orange; sep. elliptic-obovate, obtuse; pet. similar, shorter; lip ligulate, deflexed, spur cylindric, pendent, curved. Indochina.

A.hendersonianum Rchb. f. See *Dyakia hendersoniana*.
A.miniatum (Lindl.) Schltr. See *A.garayi*.

× **Ascofinetia** (*Ascocentrum* × *Neofinetia*). Miniature plants which have great appeal to hobbyist orchid growers because of the floriferousness and small size. Rather few crosses have been registered as yet. Plants small, upright with curved leaves in two rows. The plants often branch near the base producing clumps of stems which grow well in baskets. Inflorescences axillary, usually several at once. Flowers small, intermediate between the parents. The first and most well known is × *A*.Cherry Blossom, a small plant with many sprays of small pink flowers.

Ascoglossum Schltr. (From Gk *askos*, bag, and *glossa*, tongue, referring to the saccate lip.) Some 2 species of monopodial epiphytes allied to *Renanthera* and *Ascocentrum*. Leaves linear-ligulate, erect, pointed, coriaceous. Inflorescence axillary, branched, nodal, lax; flowers many; sepals pointed, dorsal sepal oblong, obscurely clawed, lateral sepals oblong, oblique, clawed; petals elliptic or oblong, almost equalling dorsal sepal; lip trilobed, midlobe reflexed, oblong or lanceolate, acute, lateral lobes erect, spur saccate, laterally flattened. New Guinea, Solomon Is.

CULTIVATION As for *Vanda*.

A.calopterum (Rchb. f.) Schltr. (*Saccolabium calopterum* Rchb. f.).
Stems to 30cm, robust. Lvs to 18.5cm, closely 2-ranked, cori-aceous. Infl. erect or horizontal, dense; fls pale purple to magenta; dorsal sep. 9–12mm, oblong-lanceolate, lateral sep. clawed; pet. elliptic-lanceolate; lip midlobe linear-lanceolate, reflexed, lateral lobes erect, spur cylindric. New Guinea.

× **Asconopsis** (*Ascocentrum* × *Phalaenopsis*). Plants intermediate between parents, with short stems and tough wide leaves in two rows. Inflorescences upright or spreading, often branching with small attractive flowers. The most successful and widely grown cross is × *A*.Irene Dobkin: plants upright with two rows of alternate leaves and upright flower spikes; flowers pale orange or apricot, round and dainty; many clones have been awarded.

Aspasia Lindl. (For Aspasia, mother of Pericles; from Gk *aspazomai*, I embrace, referring to the way the column is embraced by the base of the lip.) 5 species, epiphytes or lithophytes. Rhizomes creeping, slender, bracteate. Pseudobulbs to 12×5cm, ellipsoid to oblong, laterally compressed, glossy light green, becoming ridged with age, basally produced on a short rhizomatous stalk or foot and sheathed. Leaves to 30×5cm, borne 2 basally, 2 at apex, glabrous, subcoriaceous, lanceolate to ligulate, acute, basally conduplicate and articulate, basal pair sheathing. Inflorescence a lateral raceme, 1 or 2 per pseudobulb, to 25cm, ascending; flowers 1–9, white to olive green marked brown or purple, lip white marked chocolate to rose or lavender with golden centre; sepals spreading, narrowly ovate to lanceolate, acute, concave; petals resembling sepals, often fused to column base; lip entire or obscurely trilobed, base narrow, apex broad, pandurate or reniform, often crenate or undulate, callus fleshy, 2–4-ridged. Summer. Tropical America.

CULTIVATION Largely as for *Brassia*. Impose a short rest (1–2 months) after flowering. *Aspasia* is extremely floriferous if very tightly potted or mounted and allowed to sprawl beyond the confines of its foothold. Fertilize throughout growing period.

A.epidendroides Lindl. (*A.fragrans* Klotzsch).
Pseudobulbs to 12×5cm. Lvs to 30×5cm. Infl. to 25cm; fls to 3.5cm diam., fragrant in high temperatures; sep. yellow-green to bronze, broadly banded chocolate or dull violet; pet. wholly mauve or bronze; lip white, marked purple at centre, disc golden yellow. Guatemala to Colombia.

A.fragrans Klotzsch. See *A.epidendroides*.

A.lunata Lindl.
Pseudobulbs to 6cm, strongly laterally compressed. Lvs to 20cm. Infl. to 9cm; fls 1–3, to 3.5cm diam.; sep. and pet. green, banded and spotted brown; lip white, centrally stained purple. Brazil.

A.principissa Rchb. f.
Resembling *A.epidendroides*, except growths smaller, fls to 6cm diam., sep. and pet. broader, lime to olive green, finely and longitudinally striped brown or ochre, lip ivory, with many very fine rose veins emanating from the yellow disc. Costa Rica, Panama.

A.variegata Lindl.
Resembling *A.principissa*, except fls slightly smaller, fragrant, sep. and pet. green basally banded chocolate or maroon, lip obscurely trilobed, white spotted purple. Costa Rica, Panama.

Barbosella Schltr. (For J. Barbosa-Rodrigues (1842–1909), Brazilian orchidologist.) Some 20 species of diminutive epiphytes. Stems slender, dwarf, tufted, terete, enclosed by a thin, basal sheath. Leaves solitary, apical, ascending or patent, linear to lanceolate, tough and coarse or fleshy, coriaceous, midvein impressed above, apex obtuse or minutely tridentate. Flowers solitary, long-stalked, emerging from a papery bract at leaf insertion; dorsal sepal semi-erect, concave above, lanceolate to ovate, lateral sepals fused, forming a cupped, ovate-acute synsepalum; petals free, narrow-elliptic, often fringed; lip shorter than sepals and petals, trilobed, hinged to column base, midlobe broad, fleshy, lateral lobes erect, thin, pellucid; column stout, concave, hooded or winged. Venezuela, Colombia, Ecuador, Peru.

CULTIVATION   As for *Masdevallia*.

B.australis (Cogn.) Schltr.
Creeping. Fls membranous, showy, held high above leaves; lip oblong, apex forked. S Brazil.

B.cucullata (Lindl.) Schltr. (*Restrepia cucullata* Lindl.; *Pleurothallis angustisegmenta* Schweinf.).
Lvs to 5×0.75cm, fleshy, coarse, apex minutely tridentate. Fls

wholly golden-green to purple, borne on a stalk to 8cm; dorsal sep. to 2×0.2cm, synsepalum to 2×0.6cm; lip to 0.3×0.2cm. Throughout genus range.

B.miersii (Lindl.) Schltr. See *Barbrodria miersii*.

Barbrodria Luer. (For the Brazilian naturalist João Barbosa Rodriguez.) 1 species, an epiphyte closely allied to *Barbosella*. Rhizome elongate, creeping. Pseudobulbs absent. Secondary stems short, enveloped by glabrous sheaths, each bearing a single terminal leaf. Leaves small, fleshy-coriaceous, elliptic. Inflorescence erect, filiform, far exceeding leaves, 1-flowered; dorsal sepal and petals free, lateral sepals connate at base, petals serrulate; lip articulated to column base, recurved below middle, obovate; column short, wings absent, anther terminal, pollinia 4. Brazil.

CULTIVATION   As for *Masdevallia*.

B.miersii (Lindl.) Luer (*Pleurothallis miersii* Lindl.; *Restrepia miersii* (Lindl.) Rchb. f.; *Barbosella miersii* (Lindl.) Schltr.).

Barkeria Knowles & Westc. (For George Barker of Springfield, England, the first to import the type species.) Some 10 species of epiphytes or lithophytes allied to *Epidendrum*. Rhizome short or absent; roots thick, silver-grey to white, freely produced from base of pseudobulbs. Pseudobulbs slender, fusiform to cylindrical, cane-like, enveloped by scarious leaf sheaths. Leaves alternate, linear-lanceolate to broadly ovate, articulated, sessile, stem-clasping, slightly fleshy, rather soft-textured, persisting 1–2 seasons. Inflorescence a long-stalked cylindrical to pyramidal terminal raceme, few- to many-flowered; flowers usually showy, white to rose or deep magenta, pedicellate; sepals and petals subsimilar, free, reflexed or porrect; lip free or adnate to column base, simple, spreading or somewhat reflexed, usually undulate; callus usually carinate, marked yellow or white; column short to elongate, with fleshy, spreading wings, anther terminal, operculate, incumbent, pollinia 4, waxy, compressed. C America.

CULTIVATION   Epiphytes for the cool or intermediate house (minimum winter temperature 10°C/50°F). Repot plants reduced to 1–2 leads and 3–5 old canes, after flowering into small pots or baskets of a very freely draining coarse bark mix. Alternatively mount on rafts. Suspend in a well ventilated, humid, brightly lit position. Water, feed and syringe very freely while the canes are being produced and roots (almost all of them aerial and strongly adhesive) can be seen to be active (i.e. green-tipped). Thereafter give only enough water to prevent leaf-shrivelling and encourage flower formation. The beautiful, pale or vivid pink flowers are normally produced in the depths of winter – at this time, the plants should be kept cool, dry and in bright light.

B.cyclotella Rchb. f.
Closely resembles *B.lindleyana* except smaller in most parts with narrower, purple or red-tinted lvs; infl. shorter; erect; fls smaller, vivid magenta to crimson; lip flattened, obovate to subquadrate, mucronate; disc indistinctly carinate, column shorter. Mexico.

B.elegans Knowles & Westcott.
Fls 2–5 per raceme, each to 6cm diam.; tepals ovate-lanceolate, spreading and held in a horizontal plane, dark rose; lip subquadrate, apex blunt, retuse and usually apiculate, pale rose-white with a large dark crimson blotch toward the apex; column yellow dotted purple-red. Guatemala.

B.lindleyana Batem. ex Lindl. (*Epidendrum lindleyana* (Batem. ex Lindl.) Rchb. f.).
Pseudobulbs to 15cm, fusiform-cylindrical. Lvs to 15×4cm,

linear-lanceolate to oblong-lanceolate, subcoriaceous, acute to acuminate, soft grey-green sometimes flushed rosy-purple. Infl. to 36cm, loosely few- to many-fld; fls to 7.5cm diam., on decurved pedicels, white or lilac to deep purple; sep. to 17–37×5–10mm, linear-lanceolate to elliptic, subacute to acuminate; pet. to 17–37×7–20mm, broadly ovate, obtuse to acuminate, undulate, usually reflexed; lip to 35×25mm, often lined red-purple, ovate-suborbicular to oblong-quadrate, retuse or apiculate, undulate; disc with 3–5 central keels; column to 14mm. Mexico to Costa Rica.

B.skinneri (Batem. ex Lindl.) Paxt. (*Epidendrum skinneri* Batem. ex Lindl.).
Pseudobulbs to 14cm, fusiform-cylindrical, several-lvd. Lvs to 15×2cm, fleshy, elliptic to elliptic-lanceolate, acute to acuminate, pale green. Infl. 15–30cm, erect, few- to many-fld; fls to 4cm diam., long-lived, lilac-purple or rose-purple to

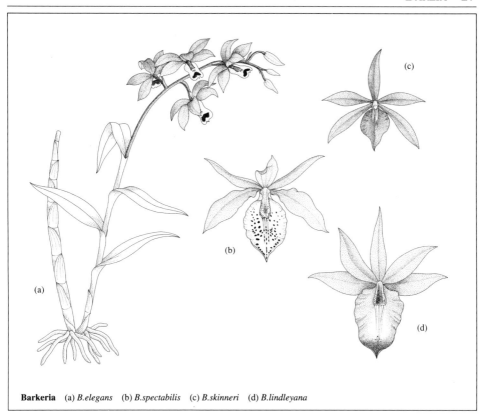

Barkeria   (a) *B.elegans*   (b) *B.spectabilis*   (c) *B.skinneri*   (d) *B.lindleyana*

red-magenta; sep. 18–22×5–8mm, elliptic or elliptic-lanceo-late, acute to acuminate; pet. 18–22×8–10mm, ovate to ellip-tic, acute to acuminate; lip 15–18×1–15mm, adnate to column base, ovate to elliptic, obtuse to acuminate; disc with 3 yel-low, median keels; column to 8mm. Guatemala.

B.spectabilis Batem. ex Lindl. (*Epidendrum spectabile* (Batem. ex Lindl.) Rchb. f.).
Pseudobulbs to 15cm, fusiform-cylindrical, erect. Lvs to 15×4cm, ovate to linear-lanceolate, subcoriaceous, acute to acuminate. Infl. loosely few- to many-fld; fls usually pale lilac; sep. 25–37×7–10mm, linear-lanceolate to elliptic, acute to acuminate; pet. 23–37×8–20mm, ovate-suborbicular to elliptic-lanceolate, obtuse to acuminate, undulate; lip spotted red-purple, 28–35×20–25mm, ovate to elliptic, retuse or apic-ulate, spreading, broadly undulate; disc with 3–5 keels; col-umn to 18mm. S Mexico, Guatemala, El Salvador.

Barlia Parl. (For Jean Baptiste Barla (1817–1896), French botanist at Nice.) 2 species, deciduous terrestrials resembling *Himantoglossum*, from which they differ in having bracts longer than flowers, erect sepals and a shorter lip with a straight, not twisted, central lobe. Tubers ovoid or round. Stems 25–60cm; basal sheaths 2. Basal leaves oblong or elliptic to ovate, fleshy; stem leaves reduced to bracts. Spike 6–23cm, cylindric, dense; flowers fragrant; sepals and petals pale olive tinted brown to purple-violet, interior spotted purple; lip 15–22mm, pale rose dotted or flecked purple, lobes 3, pale green, lateral lobes undulate, central lobe longer than laterals, cleft; spur conical, pointed downwards, containing pubescent nectary. Summer. Mediterranean.

CULTIVATION   See Introduction: Hardy Orchids.

B.robertiana (Lois.) Greuter (*Himantoglossum longibractea-tum* (Bernh.) Schltr.). GIANT ORCHID. (Described above.)

Batemannia Lindl. (For James Bateman (1811–97), orchid collector.) 5 species of epiphytes. Rhizomes short, branching. Pseudobulbs clustered, glabrous, light green, oblong-ovoid, tetragonal, with 2 short-lived basal sheaths. Leaves apical, paired, elliptic-lanceolate, apex acute, base acuminate, semi-rigid, dull olive green, midvein impressed above, keeled below. Inflorescence a basal raceme; floral bracts conspicuous, hooded, lime green; flowers to 5, showy, fragrant, held semi-erect and in one direction; dorsal sepal elliptic-oblong, lateral sepals linear, falcate, inrolled; petals oblong-ovoid, slightly larger than dorsal sepal; lip trilobed, fleshy, erect, adpressed to base of column, midlobe cuneate to square, cleft, decurved, callus 2-ridged, dentate, lateral lobes rounded, erect, tips jagged, recurved. Brazil to Bolivia.

CULTIVATION   As for *Bifrenaria*.

B.colleyi Lindl.
Pseudobulbs to 6cm. Lvs to 20×6cm. Fls to 7.5cm diam., shining with nectar secretion, dorsal sep. and pet. claret to sienna, tinted chocolate, tipped green, lateral sep. claret to rust, edged lime green, lip white stained garnet at base of midlobe, callus maroon.

B.grandiflora (A. Rich.) Rchb. f. See *Mendoncella grandiflora.*
B.meleagris (Lindl.) Rchb. f. See *Huntleya meleagris.*

Bifrenaria Lindl. (From Lat. *bi-*, two, and *frenum*, bridle, referring to the double band by which pollinia are connected.) Some 30 species of epiphytes or terrestrials. Rhizomes thick, long, branching. Pseudobulbs well-spaced on rhizomes, narrow-ovoid to conical, hard, glossy olive green to yellow, often with a black collar at apex, becoming ridged and somewhat laterally compressed. Leaves solitary, apical, short-stalked, broad-elliptic, acuminate, erect, glabrous, coriaceous, with at least 3 veins prominent beneath. Inflorescence short, basal, racemose, semi-erect; flowers 1–5, waxy, fragrant; sepals and petals spreading, oval, obtuse; lip trilobed, midlobe square or rounded, reflexed, undulate or crispate, velvety, callus fleshy, ridged, lateral lobes erect, sheathing column, oblong, resembling midlobe in colour and texture; spur to half length of ovary. Spring. S America.

CULTIVATION   *Bifrenaria* resents disturbance and will fail to flower unless potbound or outgrowing its container. Pot in shallow clay pans or baskets in a coarse bark/charcoal mixture. Grow in intermediate conditions in full sunlight and high humidity. Water and feed copiously while growth is developing. Once pseudobulbs have hardened, remove to a cooler, drier site in bright sunlight and reduce watering to a daily misting during flower development (1–3 months). Avoid wetting flowers. Recommence watering when new growth appears. Propagate by divisions of 3 or more pseudobulbs after flowering.

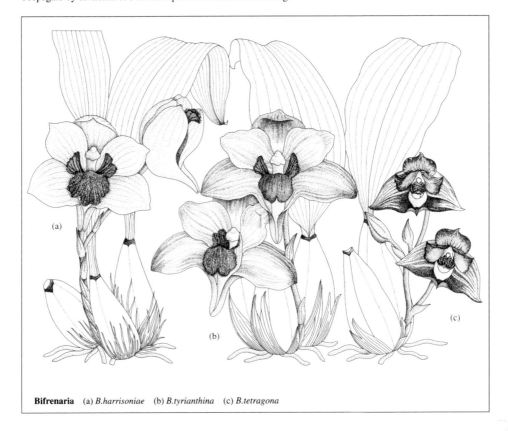

Bifrenaria   (a) *B.harrisoniae*   (b) *B.tyrianthina*   (c) *B.tetragona*

B.atropurpurea (Lodd.) Lindl.
Pseudobulbs to 8cm, ovoid, obscurely tetragonal. Lvs to 25cm. Fls to 5 per infl., to 5.5cm diam., damask purple with a central zone of yellow-cream, lip white or rose. Brazil.

B.aurantiaca Lindl.
Pseudobulbs globose, strongly laterally compressed, obscurely ridged, olive green, finely spotted maroon at base and apex. Lvs to 22×6cm. Infl. axis purple-green; fls to 3, to 4cm diam., golden, marked chocolate above, flushed pink-brown below, margins recurved, lip glossy pink-brown with thick, white pubescence. Guyana, Venezuela, Colombia, Peru, Amazon.

B.harrisoniae (Hook.) Rchb. f.
Pseudobulbs to 9cm, tetragonal, yellow-green with dark collar at apex. Lf to 30×12cm, tough, glossy dark green. Infl. to 7cm, 1–2-fld, usually arising 2 per pseudobulb; fls to 7.5cm diam., very waxy and fragrant, ivory, lip tipped deep rose to garnet or blood red, with darker veins and dense apical pubescence above, disc golden-pubesc. Brazil.

B.inodora Lindl.
Resembles *B.harrisoniae* except fls sometimes unscented, sep. yellow to lime green, acute, far exceeding pet., lip white, ivory or rose flushed claret. Brazil.

B.longicornis Lindl.
Pseudobulbs to 10cm, narrow-ovoid. Lvs to 30×8cm, obscurely plicate, tough. Infl. usually 1 per growth, to 15cm, axis slightly flattened, red-green; fls 2.75cm diam., light bronze or yellow, marked oxblood, lip ivory edged pale rose; lateral sep. basally fused to form pseudospur to 1cm. Venezuela, Guyana, Surinam, Brazil, Colombia, Peru, Amazon.

B.maguirei Schweinf.
Pseudobulbs long-ovoid, to 8cm, clothed with basal sheaths to 15cm. Lvs to 65cm, of which over half is a purple-green petiole. Infl. to 1m, erect, 1–3-fld, clothed with slightly inflated bracts; fls to 12cm diam., fleshy, ochre, flushed pink beneath, margins becoming revolute, lip white, veined dark purple. Venezuela.

B.tetragona (Lindl.) Schltr.
Pseudobulbs markedly tetragonal, ovoid, to 9.5cm. Lvs fleshy, narrow-elliptic, to 36cm. Fls 3–4 per infl., to 5.5cm diam.; tepals broadly ovate-acute, lateral sep. far larger than pet., green streaked or flecked chocolate or maroon, lip suffused violet at base. Brazil.

B.tyrianthina (Loud.) Rchb. f.
Resembles *B.harrisoniae* except more robust in all parts, fls to 8.5cm diam., ivory strongly flushed red-mauve towards tips, lip strongly marked mauve and densely white-pubesc. Brazil.

B.wageneri Rchb. f. See *Teuscheria wageneri*.

Bletia Ruiz & Pav. (Named for Luis Blet (*fl.* 1794), Spanish apothecary, who had a noted botanic garden in Algeciras.) Some 40 species of deciduous terrestrials. Pseudobulbs subterranean, corm-like. Leaves lanceolate, plicate, solitary or to 5 in an extended whorl, arising laterally. Inflorescence an erect, leafless raceme borne laterally or terminally and distinct from vegetative axis; sepals and petals free, showy; lip entire or trilobed. Spring–summer. Florida, W Indies, C America, northern S America.

CULTIVATION Repot 'corms' annually after flowering into a free-draining mixture of leafmould, bark, sharp sand and well rotted farmyard manure. Grow in full sunlight at intermediate temperatures; water and feed liberally. Upon fading of foliage and ripening of 'corms', withhold water to encourage production of flowers. Water sparingly during blooming; increase water supply after repotting. Propagate by division at repotting.

B.campanulata La Ll. & Lex.
Easily recognized by large, campanulate fls; tepals bright rose to magenta, hooding the undulate, white, rose-edged lip. Mexico.

B.catenulata Ruiz & Pav.
Pseudobulbs to 6cm diam., dorsally compressed. Lvs to 6, to 60×8.5cm, linear-lanceolate, petiolate. Infl. to 88cm; fls to 9, to 4.5cm diam., sep. and pet. spreading, rose pink to magenta, lip magenta, margins crispate, paler, lamellae white or ivory. Brazil, Peru.

B.coccinea La Ll. & Lex.
Fls bright orange-red; tepals spreading. Mexico.

B.florida (Salisb.) R. Br. See *B.purpurea*.

B.gracilis Lodd.
Pseudobulbs to 4cm diam., purple-green. Lvs solitary, to 30cm, papery, somewhat purple below. Infl. to 45cm, axis wiry, flushed maroon; fls to 8, to 3.75cm diam., yellow, pale bronze, mauve or magenta, lip green, veined blood-red or violet, flushed pink at base, lime green at apex, disc lamellate. Mexico, Guatemala.

B.hyacinthina (Sm.) R. Br. See *Bletilla striata*.

B.patula Hook.
Pseudobulbs squat, globose, ivory, ringed, to 5cm diam. Lvs to 60cm. Infl. to 90cm; fls to 6, to 6cm diam., slightly pendulous, seldom opening fully, rose madder or deep magenta with to 5 prominent white keels on lip. Cuba, Hispaniola, Puerto Rico.

B.purpurea (Lam.) DC. (*B.florida* (Salisb.) R. Br.; *B.shepherdii* Hook.; *B.verecunda* R. Br.).
Variable sp. Pseudobulbs to 4cm diam., strongly dorsally compressed, developing in chains, often semi-exposed. Lvs to 90×4cm, closely plicate, olive green. Infl. to 1.5m, sometimes branching; fls to 4.5cm diam., rose, magenta, mauve or white, lip darker with yellow-white lamellae; sep. ovate, acute, spreading; pet. similar in shape, incurved, hooding column; lip trilobed, midlobe rectangular, crispate, callus to 6-ridged, lateral lobes subreniform, erect, veined; column arching. Throughout genus range.

B.shepherdii Hook. See *B.purpurea*.
B.striata (Thunb.) Druce. See *Bletilla striata*.
B.verecunda R. Br. See *B.purpurea*.

Bletilla Rchb. f. (Resembles *Bletia*, for Luis Blet (*d. c*1794) Spanish apothecary.) Some 10 species of deciduous terrestrials. Rhizomes short; stem base forms a corm-like pseudobulb. Leaves to 4, apical, linear to obovate-lanceolate, plicate. Raceme terminal, lax; sepals and petals similar; lip trilobed, midlobe recurved, lateral lobes enveloping column, disc callused or papillose. E Asia.

CULTIVATION   Hardy in Zone 7. Plant in early spring, just burying the corm in friable, damp soil enriched with leafmould and never likely to become waterlogged, *Bletilla* will tolerate light shade or full sun, but tends to thrive best in association with hardy ferns, *Arisaema, Trillium*, etc., in other words, in somewhat protected, semi-woodland or acid gardens. Flowering stems may require staking. In harsh winters, protect crowns with bracken or lift and store dry in sawdust. Divide before replacing. Slugs may be a problem. Variegated cultivars are usually grown in the lath or alpine house – they are rather more tender than the type and are valued as bonsai in Japan.

B.hyacinthina Rchb. f. See *B.striata*.

B.striata (Thunb.) Rchb. f. (*Bletia hyacinthina* (Sm.) R. Br.; *B.hyacinthina* (Sm.) Rchb. f.).
Stems to 60cm, erect, basally sheathed. Lvs to 45cm, plicate, oblong-lanceolate, narrow-acuminate. Infl. erect, slender; fls several; sep. and pet. obovate-lanceolate, acute, rose to magenta; lip to 3.5cm, deep magenta, throat white to ivory, midlobe almost rectangular, lateral lobes erect, disc with 5 parallel, frilled, white or mauve calli. Early summer. Japan, China, Tibet. White-flowered forms occur as do some with narrower, longitudinally white-variegated lvs, the latter particularly prized in Japan.

Bollea Rchb. f. (For Carl Bolle (1821–1909), German dendrologist.) 11 species of epiphytes, allied to *Chondrorhyncha, Huntleya* and *Pescatorea*, which they resemble in many respects and from which they are most readily distinguished by the apically enlarged column and extensive calli on the basal half of the lip. Summer. Colombia, Guianas, Venezuela.

CULTIVATION   As for *Huntleya*.

B.coelestis (Rchb. f.) Rchb. f.
Lvs to 30×5cm, to 10, in 2 alternate ranks of a fan-shaped growth, strap-shaped, thin-textured, slightly concave above, pale green, new growths, roots and fls borne in lf axils. Fls to 9cm diam., solitary, on ascending stalk to 16cm, fleshy, waxy, hyacinth-scented, cream, flushed amethyst, opal or deep lilac at base, lip similar with a yellow disc, column violet to blue above, yellow below, spotted red at base; sep. and pet. obovate, acute, spreading or incurved; lip lined with blunt ridges, apex rhombic, strongly recurved. Colombia.

B.hemixantha Rchb. f.
Lvs to 30×4cm in a loose fan, midvein deeply sunken above, keeled beneath. Fls solitary, to 7.5cm diam., shaped as for *B.coelestis*, very short-stalked, ivory at base fading to white, then lemon yellow to ochre in apical half, lip lemon yellow with a golden callus. Venezuela, Colombia.

B.lawrenceana Rchb. f.
Resembles *B.coelestis* except in fl. stalks to 12cm, fls to 8cm diam., sep. and pet. concave, oblanceolate, cream-white blotched violet-purple toward tips, lip lilac, callus violet or claret, column white with violet anth. Colombia.

B.violacea (Lindl.) Rchb. f.
Closely resembles *B.coelestis* except sep. and pet. deep amethyst edged white, lip dark violet, disc yellow, to 13-ridged, column violet. Guianas.

Bollea and allies (a) *Bollea coelestis* (b) *Chondrorhyncha chestertonii* (c) *Pescatorea lehmannii* (d) *Chaubardiella tigrina* (e) *Cochleanthes flabelliformis*

Bonatea Willd. (For Prof. Giuseppe Antonio Bonat (1753–1856), Professor of Botany at the University of Padua.) About 10 species of terrestrials. Roots elongated, fleshy or tuberous. Stem leafy. Raceme terminal, 1- to many-flowered. Flowers green or yellow-green and white; dorsal sepal forming hood with petals, lateral sepals partly joined to lip, lower petal lobes and stigmatic arms; petals bilobed, upper lobe adnate to dorsal sepal, lower lobe adnate at base to lip and stigmatic arm; lip adnate at base to stigmatic arms, lateral sepals and lower petal lobes, free part trilobed, spurred at base, often with a tooth in the mouth of the spur; anther erect, with long anther-canals; pollinia 2, each with a long, slender caudicle and naked viscidium. Mainland Africa, 1 species Yemen.

CULTIVATION   Intriguing terrestrials for the intermediate house, they resemble large and showy *Habenaria* or *Pecteilis* species. Cultivation is as for *Disa* but in a somewhat grittier mixture and drier, brighter conditions.

B.antennifera Rolfe.
Stem to 70cm; tubers cylindrical, 2–2.5cm. Lvs several, to 9×3cm, ovate, acute, sheathing at base. Raceme densely many-fld; fls green and white; pedicel 30mm; ovary 15mm; dorsal sep. 16–18×12mm, ovate, acute, very convex, lateral sep. to 24mm, rolled lengthways; pet. upper lobe 16–18mm, lower lobes 20–25mm, both lobes narrowly linear; lip 40–45mm, joined to stigma for 8mm at base, lobes filiform, midlobe 25–35mm, lateral lobes 20–30mm; spur 30–50mm, slender, swollen at apex; stigmatic arms 15–20mm. Zimbabwe, Mozambique, Southern Africa.

B.cassidea Sonder.
Slender, 25–50cm; stem leafy. Lvs 10–12, 1–4×1–3cm, falcate, acute, sometimes starting to wither at flowering time. Raceme to 20cm, several to many-fld; fls green, the lower pet. lobes and lateral lobes of lip white; pedicel and ovary 2–3cm; sep. 9–12×4–8mm, ovate, acute, dorsal sep. convex, lateral sep. slightly rolled lengthways; pet. upper lobes 10×0.5mm, linear, lower lobes 10–15×3.5–6.5mm, obliquely oblanceolate; lip 16–20mm, claw 8mm, midlobe linear, 10–12mm, lateral lobes 9–15×3.5–7mm, semi-orbicular from a narrow base; spur 11–25mm, slightly swollen in apical half; stigmatic arms 7–9mm. Zimbabwe, S Africa.

B.pulchella Summerh.
Slender, to 25cm; roots fleshy, cylindrical, to 6×2cm. Lvs several in a basal rosette, 5–10×1.5–2.5cm, lanceolate to ovate, acute; stem with 3 sheathing lvs. Raceme 10–12cm, laxly 2–5-fld; fls green and white; pedicel 15mm; ovary 25mm; sep. 11–13×6–8mm, dorsal sep. forming a hood, lateral sep. obliquely ovate; pet. upper lobe 10–12.5×1mm, linear, lower lobes filiform, 40–50mm, less than 1mm wide; lip claw 5mm, midlobe 24–30mm, narrowly linear, lateral lobes 45–55mm, filiform; spur 5.5–7cm; stigmatic arms 8–9.5mm. Mozambique, S Africa.

B.speciosa (L. f.) Willd. (*Habenaria bonatea* L. f.).
Robust, 40–50cm; stem leafy. Lvs to 10×2.5cm, lanceolate to ovate, sheathing at base. Raceme to 15-fld; fls green and white with a slightly spicy scent; sep. 18–22×6–12mm, ovate-acute, dorsal sep. very convex, lateral sep. oblique and inrolled; pet. upper lobe 15–16×2–3mm, lower lobes 20–25×1mm, oblanceolate or linear, slightly curved; lip 25–32mm, claw 10mm, all lobes linear, 20–23×1.5–2mm; spur 3.5–4cm; stigmatic arms 10–16mm. Zimbabwe, S Africa.

B.steudneri (Rchb. f.) T. Dur. & Schinz (*B.ugandae* Summerh.).
Robust, to 1m; roots thick, tuberous, hairy. Stem leafy. Lvs 7–12.5×3–4.5cm, ovate, acute or apiculate, amplexicaul. Raceme fairly laxly 10–20-fld; fls green and white; pedicel and ovary 5–6cm; sep. 22–26×11–16mm, ovate, acute, dorsal sep. very convex, lateral sep. deflexed; pet. upper lobe 20–25mm, lower lobes 55–60mm, all lobes less than 1mm wide, linear becoming filiform; lip claw 20mm, lobes 45–50mm, linear, tapering; spur 10–21cm, slender, swollen toward apex; stigmatic arms 20–30mm, enlarged at tips. Widespread in eastern tropical Africa; Yemen.

B.ugandae Summerh. See **B.steudneri**.

Brachycorythis Lindl. (From Gk *brachys*, short, and *korys*, helmet, referring to the structure of the flower.) Over 30 species of terrestrials and (rarely) epiphytes. Roots fusiform or ellipsoid. Stem leafy, the leaves usually numerous and overlapping, glabrous or pubescent. Raceme terminal, usually many-flowered; flowers usually pink, mauve or purple, occasionally white or yellow, often with darker spots; sepals green, free; petals usually adnate at base to side of column; lip spurred or saccate at base, the apical part entire or lobed; column erect. Tropical & S Africa, tropical Asia.

CULTIVATION   As for *Phaius*.

B.kalbreyeri Rchb. f.
Epiphytic, 15–40cm, usually dying back in resting season; roots thick and fleshy, woolly. Lvs to 15, lanceolate, acute, to 11×2.5cm. Raceme to 17cm, lax; fls to 22 but usually fewer, pale lilac or mauve or almost white, about 5cm diam. with spicy scent; pedicel and ovary 15–25mm; bracts leafy, longer than fls at base of raceme; dorsal sep. 15–16mm, elliptic, subacute, lateral sep. oblique and slightly longer; pet. 10–15mm, broadly ovate, obtuse; lip 15–30mm, trilobed in upper part, midlobe triangular, upcurved, much smaller than the broadly triangular, incurved lateral lobes; spur absent; column stout, 4mm. W Africa, Zaire, E Africa.

B.macrantha (Lindl.) Summerh.
Robust, terrestrial, to 40cm. Lvs to 13×5cm, broadly lanceolate, more or less spreading. Raceme densely to 20-fld; fls green and mauve; pedicel and ovary 10–12mm; bracts to 35mm; sep. and pet. 10mm, oblong, the dorsal sep. forming hood with pet., lateral sep. spreading; lip 20–22mm, blade 15–20mm long and broad, obcordate; spur 7.5–10mm, conical, tapering to an acute apex from a wide mouth. W Africa.

Brassavola   (a) *B.cucullata*   (b) *B.nodosa*   (c) *B.acaulis*   (d) *B.flagellaris*   (e) *B.tuberculata*

Brassavola R. Br. (For A.M. Brasavola (1500–1555), Venetian botanist. His name was spelt with a single 's', the genus takes 2.) Some 30 species of epiphytes and lithophytes allied to *Cattleya*. Rhizomes woody, creeping. Pseudobulbs remote or clustered, narrowly cylindrical, sheathed, dark green or purple. Leaves solitary, apical, more or less terete, fleshy, coriaceous, linear, acute. Flowers solitary or to 7 per raceme, borne at leaf insertion or from rhizomes (*B.acaulis*), showy, often pendulous, white, ivory or green, nocturnally fragrant. Summer or continuously. Mexico, Jamaica, Brazil, Bolivia, Peru.

CULTIVATION Most species are pendulous to some degree and thrive best on rafts against pads of sphagnum and well rotted farmyard manure or in baskets containing a medium suitable for *Cattleya* and lined with sphagnum or *Tillandsia usneoides*. Provide intermediate conditions in bright sunlight. Water while in growth, allowing the medium to dry between drenchings. During this period, apply a weak liquid fertilizer with every third watering. Withhold water for up to a month on completion of pseudobulbs, misting only lightly to avoid excessive shrivelling.

B.acaulis Lindl. & Paxt. (*B.lineata* Hook.).
Pseudobulbs massed, to 15cm. Lvs to 60cm, usually shorter, strongly pendulous, terete, acute, fleshy, dark green flushed red. Infl. shorter than lvs, borne on rhiz.; fls 1–5, waxy, very fragrant, to 8cm diam.; sep. and pet. subequal, slender, nodding to hooded, green, white tinted green, or deep ivory; lip bright white, base tubular, apex expanded and flattened, prominently veined. Guatemala, Costa Rica, Panama.

B.appendiculata A. Rich. See *B.cucullata*.

B.cebolleta Rchb. f.
Closely resembles *B.tuberculata* except fls fewer, to 5cm diam., sep. and pet. ivory to yellow-green, lip pure white. Brazil.

B.cordata Lindl. (*B.subulifolia* Rolfe).
Pseudobulbs to 16cm, terete, jointed, dark green with papery sheaths. Lvs to 45cm, slender, terete, ascending or pendulous. Fls solitary or in sparse racemes to 4.5cm diam., vanilla-scented, resembling those of *B.nodosa*, except smaller and more profusely borne; sep. and pet. lime green to ivory; lip showy, white, enclosing column with a narrow, toothed claw. W Indies, Lesser Antilles, Brazil.

B.cucullata (L.) R. Br. (*B.appendiculata* A. Rich.).
Lvs pendulous, semi-terete, sulcate, glossy dark green, straight or curved, to 25×0.8cm, carried on a slender, petiole-like pseudobulb to 12cm, sheathing bracts papery, ashy grey spotted brown. Peduncles to 20cm, borne at junction of lf and pseudobulb; fls solitary, fragrant, pendulous; sep. and pet. drooping, linear-lanceolate, to 7×0.7cm, dorsal sep. slightly longer and narrower, ivory tipped green; lip to 5.5×2cm, white tinted green at apex, base fringed and often stained red. Mexico, Guatemala, El Salvador, Honduras, Venezuela, W Indies.

B.digbyana Lindl. See *Rhyncholaelia digbyana*.

B.flagellaris Barb. Rodr.
Pseudobulbs very slender, stem-like, to 30cm. Lvs to 45cm, terete, acute, whip-like and pendulous. Infl. lax, 2–9-fld; fls to 6.5cm diam.; sep. and pet. linear, acuminate, outspread, ivory; lip elliptic, apiculate, white or cream stained lime green in throat. Brazil.

B.glauca Lindl. See *Rhyncholaelia glauca*.
B.lineata Hook. See *B.acaulis*.

B.martiana Lindl.
Resembles *B.cucullata* except smaller, fls to 6 on pedicels to 8cm; sep. linear, to 4.8×0.7cm, pale green, slightly revolute; pet. shorter, otherwise similar to sep.; lip to 3×2cm, white flushed pale yellow at throat, basally fringed, apically acute. N Brazil, Guianas, Venezuela, Amazon.

B.nodosa (L.) Lindl. LADY OF THE NIGHT.
Pseudobulbs virtually absent or reduced to a slender, sheathed stem to 15cm. Lf to 18×1cm (usually less), erect or pendent, linear to horn-like, fleshy, sulcate. Infl. to 15cm, bracteate, bearing 3–5 fls; fls to 7.5cm diam., highly scented at night; sep. and pet. pale green, ivory or white, lax, forward-pointing, to 8×0.6cm; lip to 7.5cm, claw slender, green, extending as a green midvein to pure white apex, throat sparsely spotted maroon. May flower throughout the year. Throughout genus range.

B.perrinii Lindl. See *B.tuberculata*.
B.subulifolia Lindl. See *B.cordata*.

B.tuberculata Hook. (*B.perrinii* Lindl.).
Habit resembling *B.flagellaris*. Pseudobulbs very stem-like, to 14cm. Lvs to 25cm, terete, strongly sulcate. Infl. a short raceme; fls 3–6, to 7cm diam., strongly fragrant at night and seldom opening fully; sep. and pet. linear, yellow-ivory or lime green sometimes spotted blood red (*B.perrinii*); lip elliptic, spreading, white often flushed bright green in throat. Brazil.

Brassia R. Br. (For William Brass, 18th-century botanist who collected in Guinea and South Africa.) Some 25 species, mostly epiphytes. Rhizome stout, horizontal to ascending, short or elongate. Pseudobulbs usually remotely spaced on rhizomes, ovoid-subglobose to cylindrical, bases enveloped by several overlapping sheaths, the innermost of which are leaf-like, apices bearing 1–3 leaves. Leaves coriaceous, glabrous, ligulate to oblong-lanceolate, slightly conduplicate. Inflorescence lateral, from base of pseudobulb, a raceme or rarely a panicle, erect to arching, few to many-flowered; flowers sulphur yellow to lime green variously marked white, dark brown or maroon, sometimes muskily scented, usually held horizontally away from axis in 2 distinct and opposite ranks; sepals free, similar, very long and slender, held vertically or starry and spreading, lateral sepals larger than dorsal sepal; petals subsimilar to sepals, shorter; lip shorter than sepals, sessile, simple or obscurely trilobed, spreading, sometimes convex, disc with a longitudinal bilamellate, bicarinate or heavily warted callus at base; column short, stout, erect, footless, wingless, anther terminal, operculate, incumbent, pollinia 2, waxy, pyriform. Tropical Americas.

CULTIVATION   Striking epiphytes for the cool or intermediate house, producing arching sprays of strangely scented, lime, yellow and dark brown-banded flowers with very slender petals and sepals, earning them the name Spider Orchids. Mount on a pad of fibre on a raft or pot in a very open bark mix; allow the rhizome to run freely; most rooting will be aerial. Water and feed copiously when in growth, providing light shade and high temperatures; once the new pseudobulb is complete, reduce water and temperature, ventilating freely and keeping more or less dry. Resume watering once root, flower spike and vegetation activity are visible, usually in late spring. Propagate by division.

B.angusta Lindl. See *B.lawrenceana*.

B.arcuigera Rchb. f. (*B.longissima* (Rchb. f.) Nash).
Pseudobulbs strongly compressed and ancipitous, each bearing a single oblong-lorate leaf. Raceme to 80cm, usually pendulous; sep. to 25cm, very slender, standing erect or (laterals) drooping, tapering to fine points, rich yellow to olive heavily barred red-brown, lip large, triangular-hastate, white to pale primrose, spotted brown at base, callus yellow. Costa Rica to Ecuador.

B.bidens Lindl. (*B.lanceana* var. *viridifolia* Hook.).
Epiphytic or terrestrial. Pseudobulbs to 15×3cm, ellipsoid to oblong, slightly laterally compressed, light green, apex usually bifoliate. Lvs 24–50×3–7cm, oblong to elliptic-oblong or elliptic-oblanceolate, subacute, light green. Raceme, to 90cm, several to many-fld; peduncle terete, light green, erect to arching; tepals yellow-green marked chocolate-brown, sep. to 75×7mm, linear-lanceolate, acuminate; pet. to 6.5×6mm, linear-lanceolate, falcate, acuminate; lip to 4×2.5cm, yellow or yellow-green marked chocolate-brown, obovate-rhombic to oblong-rhombic, interior slightly verrucose, undulate, callus bilamellate, yellow at base; column to 5mm, cream-green, clavate. Venezuela, Peru, Brazil, Guyana.

B.brachiata Lindl. See *B.verrucosa*.

B.caudata (L.) Lindl.
Epiphytic. Pseudobulbs to 15×4cm, linear to elliptic-oblong, laterally compressed, apex bifoliate or trifoliate. Lvs to 35×6cm, ligulate, oblong-elliptic or oblanceolate, acute or obtuse. Raceme, 38–80cm, suberect to arching; fls in 2 ranks; tepals light yellow-green to yellow-orange, often marked red-brown, dorsal sep. to 90×6mm, linear-lanceolate, long-acuminate, lateral sep. to 180×6mm, oblique; pet. to 45×6mm, narrowly lanceolate, long-acuminate; lip to 40×13mm, light yellow to green, base spotted red-brown, oblong-lanceolate to elliptic-obovate, long-acuminate, undulate or crenulate, callus bilamellate, apex dentate, pubesc.; column to 5mm. Mexico to Panama, Florida, W Indies.

B.cochleata Knowles & Westc. See *B.lawrenceana*.

B.elegantula (Rchb. f.) Rchb. f.
Rhiz. short. Pseudobulbs small, ovoid-subglobose to cylindrical. Lvs to 10×1.5cm, linear or ligulate, acute. Raceme to 8cm, loosely few-fld; fls small, spreading; tepals green barred brown, dorsal sep. to 12mm, lanceolate or oblong-lanceolate; lateral sep. falcate, deflexed, pet. similar to dorsal sep., shorter; lip white, lightly spotted purple, oblong to ovate-oblong, acute, apex reflexed, callus with 2 longitudinal, pubesc. keels; column green marked brown. Peru.

B.forgetiana hort. ex Garden.
Pseudobulbs to 12×3cm, ovoid to oblong-ellipsoid, apex uni-foliate or bifoliate. Lvs to 35×7cm, oblong or elliptic-oblong, acute to obtuse, light green. Raceme 20cm, densely many-fld, slightly arching; fls spreading, fragrant; tepals light yellow-green or green-white, barred brown, dorsal sep. to 60×8mm, narrowly lanceolate, long-acuminate, concave, lateral sep. to 65×8mm, linear-lanceolate, long-acuminate, pet. to 37×7mm, obliquely linear-lanceolate, long-acuminate; lip cream-yellow, basally spotted dark brown, to 4.5×2cm, oblong-pandurate, apex rounded, callus white marked bright yellow, bilamellate; column to 6mm, cream. Peru, Venezuela.

B.gireoudiana Rchb. f. & Warsc.
Pseudobulbs to 11×4cm, ovoid-ellipsoid, laterally compressed, apex bifoliate. Lvs to 35×5cm, lanceolate to ligulate, acute. Infl. usually surpassing lvs, arching, many-fld; fls large, showy; tepals yellow-green marked brown at base, sep. elongate, narrowly linear-lanceolate; dorsal sep. to 100×4mm; lateral sep. to 150×5mm; pet. similar to dorsal sep.; lip to 4.5×2.5cm, yellow, finely spotted brown in centre, rhombic, basal portion oblong to subquadrate, apex shortly acuminate or apiculate, callus bicarinate, minutely pubesc. apex bilobulate; column to 5mm. Costa Rica, Panama.

B.guttata Lindl. See *B.maculata*.

B.lanceana Lindl. (*B.pumila* Lindl.).
Pseudobulbs to 12×3.5cm, ovoid-oblong to subconical, laterally compressed, light green, apex bifoliate. Lvs to 34×6cm, oblong to oblanceolate, acute, rigid. Raceme to 35cm, suberect to arching, many-fld, resembling a chorus line; tepals yellow to yellow-green or yellow-brown, marked dark brown-maroon, sep. linear-lanceolate to linear-ligulate, long-acuminate, dorsal sep. to 60×7mm, lateral sep. to 65×7mm, pet. to 30×6mm, lanceolate to linear-lanceolate, falcate, long-acuminate; lip to 35×14mm, cream slightly spotted brown, elliptic-oblong, long-acuminate, undulate, callus white, tipped bright yellow, bilamellate, pilose; column to 9mm, cream. Panama, Colombia, Brazil, Venezuela, Tobago, Guyana, Surinam.

B.lanceana var. *viridifolia* Hook. See *B.bidens*.

B.lawrenceana Lindl. (*B.angusta* Lindl.; *B.cochleata* Knowles & Westc.). SPIDER ORCHID.
Epiphytic. Pseudobulbs to 10×3cm, long-oblong to ovate-oblong, laterally compressed, glossy pale green, apex usually bifoliate. Lvs to 40×6cm, narrowly oblong, elliptic-oblanceolate to narrow elliptic, acute or shortly acuminate. Raceme arcuate to pendent; often surpassing lvs; peduncle light green, slightly compressed; fls thin-textured; tepals pale green or yellow, spotted red-purple at base the margins often inrolled; dorsal sep. to 60×6mm, linear-lanceolate, long-acuminate, twisted, lateral sep. similar, to 70×6mm, pet. to 35×3mm, narrowly lanceolate, falcate, long-acuminate; lip to 45×22mm,

Brassia   (a) *B.arcuigera*   (b) *B.verrucosa*   (c) *B.lanceana*

white to pale green or pale yellow, obovate-pandurate, acute to long-acuminate, apex undulate, lateral margins revolute, callus yellow, bicarinate, pubesc.; column to 8mm, white at base, apex green, clavate. Brazil, Surinam, Venezuela, Guyana.

B.longissima (Rchb. f.) Nash. See *B.arcuigera.*

B.maculata R. Br. (*B.wrayae* Skinner; *B.guttata* Lindl.). Epiphytic or rarely terrestrial. Pseudobulbs to 15×5cm, ovoid to elliptic-oblong, laterally compressed, apex unifoliate or bifoliate. Lvs to 45×6cm, linear-oblong to ligulate, acute or obtuse. Raceme 30–90cm, loosely few to many-fld; peduncle green marked brown-purple; fls to 7cm across, yellow-green marked or spotted purple; sep. to 65×6mm, linear-lanceolate, acuminate, concave beneath or inrolled; lateral sep. oblique, pet. to 35×4mm, linear-lanceolate, falcate strongly upturned, acuminate; lip to 32×25mm, yellow-spotted purple, subpandurate, undulate-crenulate, recurved, apex obtuse to rounded, callus bilamellate, yellow to orange, slightly pubesc.; column to 5mm, bright green flecked brown. W Indies, Guatemala, Honduras, Belize.

B.pumila Lindl. See *B.lanceana.*

B.verrucosa Lindl. (*B.brachiata* Lindl.). SPIDER ORCHID. Epiphytic. Pseudobulbs to 10×4cm, narrow-ovoid to oblong, clustered to widely spaced, laterally compressed, apex 1–3-lvd. Lvs to 45×5cm, elliptic-oblong to oblanceolate or ligulate, acute, arching, bright green, conduplicate at base. Raceme to 75cm, loosely few-fld, held ascending then horizontal to arching, the fls in 2 even, opposite ranks, muskily fragrant; peduncle green to dark purple; tepals sulphur yellow to lime green, base marked or finely spotted red-brown to black, very slender, held in a strong, near-vertical plane; sep. to 120×7mm, linear-lanceolate, acuminate, often inrolled or undulate, pet. to 85×7mm, linear-lanceolate, obfalcate, acuminate; lip to 5×2.5cm, white spotted brick-red or mahogany at base, subpandurate, with prominent green warts which take on a pink tint with age, undulate, recurved, apex acuminate to rounded, callus frilly, bilamellate, white to yellow, pubesc.; column to 7mm, green, finely papillose. Mexico, Guatemala, Venezuela, Honduras.

B.wrayae Skinner. See *B.maculata.*

B.grexes.
B.Edvah Loo: large plants, fls intermediate between the parents, pale green-hued cream with dark spots.
B.Rex: large, robust plants with magnificent fls larger than either of the parents. Many awarded clones.

× **Brassocattleya** (*Brassavola* (and *Rhyncholaelia*) × *Cattleya*). Rather varied plants depending on which species are used in the cross or are present in the background. Crosses using *Brassavola nodosa* make small, compact plants with succulent narrow leaves and the flowers have narrow sepals and petals with a large oval lip. They are very floriferous and easy to grow in cool bright conditions. Crosses with *Rhyncholaelia digbyana* in their ancestry tend to produce much larger plants, with a single large leaf on each pseudobulb and very full flowers with a large lip which has a frilled or ruffled margin. They grow best in intermediate conditions with bright light. Other species of *Brassavola* have also been used as parents producing plants which are somewhat intermediate in habit and flowers between these two types.

× *B.*Binosa 'Lynn': small plants with succulent leaves, fls elegant, long lasting, lime green sep. and pet. with lip pale pink spotted with purple.
× *B.*Daffodil: primary hybrid making compact plants; fls glossy, waxy, in bright butter yellow, long-lasting.
× *B.*Deesse: strong plants with enormous white fls, sometimes pale pink on the back of the sep., pet. and lip frilled, the lip with a little yellow in the centre; the clones 'Charles', 'French Lace' and 'Perfection' have all received awards.
× *B.*Languedoc: large plants; fls large, pastel pink with large frilled lip.
× *B.*Lilliputian Princess 'Cameo': slender plants with succulent lvs and long infl.; fls pastel, beautiful pale pink sep. and pet. and a large primrose lip.
× *B.*Lindleyana: primary hybrid making strong but compact plants; fls creamy white with purple lip, many have splash pet.
× *B.*Maikai: small plants with two thick leaves per pseudobulb; very floriferous with clusters of lavender pink fls, lip oval and spotted.

× *B.*Mount Anderson: large plants; fls large, lovely pastel pink or lavender, excellent shape, large lip with ruffled margin, chartreuse green in the throat.
× *B.*Mount Hood: large plants; excellent fls, very large, pastel shades white, pink and cream, fragrant; many awarded clones and an excellent parent.
× *B.*Pamela Heatherington: large plants; fls very large and excellent shape, lovely clear pink; the clone 'Coronation' has received many awards.
× *B.*Pastoral 'Innocence': strong plants; superb white fls, exceptionally full and flat with large frilly lip, green in the throat.
× *B.*Ria Meyer: compact plants with one or two narrow leaves per pseudobulbs; fls small, in clusters, bright clear yellow to orange.
× *B.*Star Ruby: rather small plants with one succulent narrow leaf per pseudobulb; fls with narrow green sep. and pet. flushed magenta at the margins, lip wide, brilliant magenta purple.

× **Brassoepidendrum** (*Brassavola* (and *Rhyncholaelia*)× *Epidendrum*). Rather few crosses have been made to date and most turn out to be intermediate between the parents. Apart from *Epidendrum pseudepidendrum*, which is a parent of the cultivar listed below, most grexes involve the species of *Epidendrum* which are now classified in *Encyclia*, though currently still treated as *Epidendrum* for the purposes of hybrid registration.

× B.Pseudosa 'Green Glades': striking hybrids of compact growth with large fls; sep. and pet. bright green, lip large, yellow.

× **Brassolaeliocattleya** (*Brassavola* (and *Rhyncholaelia*) × *Cattleya* × *Laelia*). Very many intergeneric crosses have been made involving these three genera. *Brassavola digbyana* (syn. *Rhyncholaelia*) has been used in the majority of crosses. Thus the plants resemble large cattleyas with one or two large leaves per pseudobulb. The flowers are produced in few-flowered inflorescences and are usually large, colourful and with a frilly margin to the conspicuous lip. A huge number of grexes has been registered and a selection of some of the best is given below.

× B.Acapana: large plants with robust leaves and pseudobulbs; fls acid yellow outlined in orange, the huge square lip completely apricot-orange.

× B.Amy Wakasugi: strong plants; large fls of excellent shape, medium lavender with darker lip; many awarded clones.

× B.Ann Miyamoto: strong plants with brilliant yellow fls.

× B.Black Beauty: strong plants; fls very dark lavender with rich purple lip.

× B.Bonus Baby: strong plants; fls striking, very crisp semi-alba types with magenta chevrons of colour in the outer half of the white pet., solid red lip and column.

× B.Bryce Canyon: large plants of the cattleya type; fls large and of excellent shape, brilliant rose magenta, large lip has an orange flush at the base; many awarded clones.

× B.Canyon View: large plants of the cattleya type; superb large fls of excellent shape in brilliant rose magenta, large lip frilled at the margin and slightly darker.

× B.Cardinal Lyranda: cattleya-type plants of medium size; fls 2–6 per infl., brilliant orange red with magenta lip.

× B.Clyde's Melody: large strong plants; lovely lavender fls with strong yellow over basal part of the lip.

× B.Dinsmore: large plants, fls large, lovely pastel pink, orange in the throat of the ruffled lip; the clone 'Perfection' has been highly awarded.

× B.Ermine 'Lines': strong plants; fls nicely shaped, concolor yellows.

× B.Esmeralda: compact plants: wonderful green cattleya with long-lasting fls, lip paler than sep. and pet. but darker in throat; many awarded clones.

× B.Fantasy Maker 'H & R': large plants with clusters of spectacular fls; fls well shaped of the splash pet. type, pale pink with dark magenta tips to the pet., lip large and frilly, edged with magenta throughout, the apical part completely purple; the clone 'Powder Puff' lacks the magenta colouring and is completely creamy pink with a darker pink flush.

× B.Fortune 'Spellbound': large plants; fls large, sep. and pet. clear golden yellow, lip large, full and ruffled, yellow tinged with orange at the margin and with a large orange patch in the centre with gold venation.

× B.Golden Jubilee: compact plants, very floriferous; fls bright golden yellow with darker lip.

× B.Golden Shrine: large plants with beautifully shaped large fls which are completely orange with some magenta streaks towards the margin of the large lip.

× B.Greenwich: strong-growing plants; fls of excellent shape, clear lemon green with purple margin at the apex of the frilled lip; several awarded clones.

× B.Herons Ghyll: large plants with many fls per stem; exceptional large fls of deep lavender with prominent lip of intense colour; the clones 'Nigrescens' and 'Dignity' are widely grown and awarded.

× B.Horizon Flight: large plants; fls in clusters, brilliant apricot overlaid with gold and orange, the large lip magenta in the apical half.

× B.Lemon Magic: compact plants; excellent fls with clear, medium yellow sep. and pet., lip has darker yellow side lobes and paler mid lobe with lavender venation, column bright fuchsia.

× B.Lorraine Malworth: strong plants; fls excellent shape, brilliant yellow with some orange in the base of the lip.

× B.Magnificent Obsession 'New Day': strong growing plants; fls an incredible deep petunia purple with velvety red lip which has two yellow eyes near the base.

× B.Malworth Sunset: strong growing plants; fls medium to large, brilliant orange.

× B.Malworth: strong plants; fls large, of excellent shape, apricot yellow with a darker, pink-bordered lip; the clone 'Orchidglade' has received many awards and is sometimes described as the best yellow of the century.

× B.Melinda Wheeler: medium size plants; fls spectacular, lime green to yellow with the pet. bordered magenta, lip magenta with a yellow blotch on either side.

× B.Mem. Helen Brown 'Sweet Afton': strong, compact plants; fls medium size, pale green, lip rich purple centrally bordered with yellow, white margin; sweetly scented.

× B.Mem. Crispin Rosales: strong plants; fls wonderful dark lavender with velvety lip, excellent shape and proportion; many awarded clones.

× B.Nacouchee: large pink blooms with lovely fragrance, lip pink fringed and with deep chartreuse green throat; several awarded clones.

× B.Norman's Bay 'Low': an early hybrid which has been an important parent in rich lavender breeding; fls of good shape, brilliant lavender and magenta with darker lip; many other awarded clones.

× B.Orange Nugget: strong plants; clusters of bright orange fls, good substance.

× B.Orglade's Gold Touch: very strong plants; fls large, deep yellow, excellent shape with large magenta-red lip.

× B.Pennsylvania Spring: strong plants easy to grow, fls green when opened in low light, becoming mustard yellow, always attractive; several awarded clones.

× B.Pokai Tangerine: compact plants; small inflorescences of bright orange fls of excellent shape.

× B.Ports of Paradise 'Emerald Isle': famous hybrid with pure chartreuse green fls with a wonderful ruffled lip; fragrant.

× B.Puregold: typical cattleya-type plants of medium size; fls large, 2–3 per infl., brilliant yellow with red veining on the lip.

× B.Rattanakosin: strong plants with large fls; fls large, variable, golden shades, some pure yellow with orange flush in throat of ruffled lip, others outlined in orange or scarlet; fragrant and long-lasting.

× *B*.South Ghyll: strong plants; one of the finest of the large lavender cattleyas, fine pet. and deeper coloured large lip; several awarded clones.

× *B*.Toshie Aoki: large plants with most attractive fls; sep. and pet. primrose yellow with a median stripe of purple in the apical half of the sep.; lip large, well-shaped, brilliant magenta purple; several awarded clones.

× *B*.Waikiki Gold: strong plants; fls pale green with bright yellow lip.

× *B*.Waikiki Sunset: strong growing plants; fls deep orange yellow contrasting with magenta and yellow lip.

× *B*.William Stewart: strong plants; large, well-formed yellow fls with same colour lip or with orange red markings, some with pink frilled margin.

× *B*.Xanthette: small, compact growers; fls yellow with burnt orange lip, in clusters; many awarded clones.

× *B*.Yellow Diamond: strong plants; attractive large golden fls with some reddish veining, lip frilled, solid red in front, yellow edged with red near the base.

Bromheadia Lindl. (For Sir E.T.F. Bromhead, Bt. (1789–1855), botanist.) 20 species of terrestrials or epiphytes. Stems slender. Leaves numerous, oblong to lanceolate, held horizontally or laterally compressed in one plane with stem. Raceme terminal or lateral; flowers ephemeral, in long succession, in 2 opposite rows, white or yellow; sepals and petals lanceolate, spreading, petals shorter; lip trilobed, midlobe recurved with papillose centre, lateral lobes erect. Malaysia to Australia.

CULTIVATION   As for *Sobralia*, but with minimum winter temperatures of 18°C/65°F and shade from full sunlight.

B.finlaysoniana (Lindl.) Miq. (*B.palustris* Lindl.).
Terrestrial. Stems to 2m, basally sheathed, densely crowded. Lvs lanceolate, narrow-acuminate, distichous, fleshy, to 6 pairs. Raceme erect, sometimes branched. to over 10cm, sheathed at base; fls variable; pet. wider than sep.; lip mid-lobe rounded, margins minutely dentate, papillae yellow, lateral lobes enveloping column, veined purple. Thailand, Malaysia.

B.palustris Lindl. See *B.finlaysoniana*.

Broughtonia R. Br. (For Arthur Broughton (*d*. 1796), English botanist.) 2 epiphytes allied to *Cattleyopsis* and *Laeliopsis*: *B.sanguinea*, the most frequently cultivated species, is described here. Rhizomes very short, creeping. Pseudobulbs clustered, globose to subcylindric, to 4.75cm, dull green to grey, grooved with age. Leaves to 18cm, paired, rigid, narrow-oblong, abruptly acute, smooth, dark green. Inflorescence to 50cm, terminal, slender, sometimes branching; flowers to 15 in upper quarter of stem, to 2.25cm diam.; sepals slightly incurved, oblong-lanceolate, smaller than petals, brilliant crimson, rarely white or yellow; petals resembling sepals in colour, spreading, broadly elliptic to rhombic; lip broad, rounded, crispate to obscurely dentate, yellow to ivory at base with bright magenta veins. Winter and continuously thereafter. Jamaica.

CULTIVATION   As for smaller *Laelia* spp.; *Broughtonia* is best suited to raft or slab cultivation.

B.coccinea Hook. See *B.sanguinea*.
B.domingensis (Lindl.) Rolfe. See *Laeliopsis domingensis*.

B.sanguinea (Sw.) R. Br. (*B.coccinea* Hook.).

Bulbophyllum Thouars. (From Gk *bylbos* bulb, and *phyllon* leaf, referring to the large, leafy pseudobulb.) (Including *Cirrhopetalum*.) Some 1200 species of epiphytes and lithophytes. Rhizomes variable, creeping or pendent, covered by membranous sheaths. Pseudobulbs sessile, often angular, remote or clustered along the rhizome. Leaves 1 or 2, apical, sessile or petiolate, thin to fleshy, coriaceous. Inflorescences basal, erect or pendent, flowers 1 to many, in umbels, racemes or spikes; dorsal sepal free, lateral sepals often far larger, decurved, fused to the column foot, forming a saccate projection or longer still, hanging vertically and twisted above; petals free, smaller, sometimes vestigial; lip entire to trilobed, fleshy, fringed or pubescent, laxly attached to the column foot. Tropical.

CULTIVATION   A genus not only remarkable for its size but also for its diversity – some are so small that they can only be discerned with a magnifying glass, growing on the leaf surface of another plant; others are large and spectacular. Those species formerly included in *Cirrhopetalum* have umbellate inflorescences on slender, arching stalks arising from fairly small plants. The twisting lateral sepals point downwards and out, making a beautiful circle of the flowers – a dull, blood-red-spotted ochre in *B.guttulatum* and a ghostly mop of ivory in *B.medusae*. Many *Bulbophyllum* spp. have tufts, filaments and appendages on their tepal tips – often the whole inflorescence is designed to shift eerily in the breeze, attracting pollinators (for example *B.putidum*). In *B.falcatum* the peduncle is flattened, like a knife blade, with tiny maroon flowers along its surfaces; in *B.purpureorhachis*, the structure is similar but spirals. The most showy flowers, if bizarre, can be found in *B.lobbii*, *B.leopardinum*, *B.calamarium* and *B.barbigerum*. Some species are exceptionally resilient and free-flowering in cultivation, most notably *B.longiflorum*. All should be grown in small, shallow pots or on fibre rafts or in baskets in dappled sunlight with intermediate conditions and high humidity. Withhold water when not in growth, but mist to prevent shrivelling of pseudobulbs. Propagate by division.

B.ambrosia (Hance) Schltr. (*B.watsonianum* Rchb. f.).
Pseudobulbs ellipsoid, to 5cm. Lvs ligulate, coriaceous, to 15cm. Fls fragrant; sep. white to pale green, lined maroon, dorsal sep. oblong, acute, lateral sep. oblong to round, acute; pet. triangular, lip midlobe ligulate, broad, reflexed, lateral lobes suboblong. Hong Kong, China.

B.antenniferum (Lindl.) Rchb. f. (*B.leysianum* Burb.; *Cirrhopetalum antenniferum* Lindl.).
Pseudobulbs to 3×2cm. Lf lanceolate, coriaceous, to 14×3.5cm; petiole to 3.5cm. Dorsal sep. pale violet, base and apex green, lateral sep. pale green, base dark violet, pet. white, speckled violet, lip pale green, speckled violet, red-hirsute within; dorsal sep. ovate to lanceolate, shortly fringed, lateral sep. lanceolate, falcate; pet. similar, acute. Java, Borneo.

B.auricomum Lindl.
Pseudobulbs ovoid-oblong, to 3.5×2.5cm. Lvs oblong, shed before flowering, to 15×2.5cm. Infl. a drooping raceme to 22cm, fls many, yellow or white marked yellow, fragrant; dorsal sep. lanceolate, elongate, 3-veined, lateral sep. similar, longer; pet. ovate-oblong, ciliate; lip oblong-lanceolate, finely pubesc, column white. India.

B.barbigerum Lindl.
Rhiz. creeping. Pseudobulbs globose to ellipsoid, clustered, to 3×3cm. Lf oblong to elliptic; to 11×3cm. Infl. to 20cm, racemose, spreading or erect; bracts ovate, narrow; fls deep red to burgundy; sep. tinged green, linear-lanceolate, to 1×0.3cm; pet. minute, triangular; lip linear-ligulate, ciliate, with dense, clavate hairs at apex. Summer. W & C Africa.

B.beccarii Rchb. f.
Pseudobulbs angular, distant, to 4×3cm. Lf elliptic, subsessile, unusually long, to 60×40cm. Infl. a pendent raceme, to 20cm; fls malodorous, to 1cm diam., yellow, veined and blotched deep red, lip golden-yellow, streaked red, pet. lanceolate, acute, to 0.5cm; lip cordate-oblong. Borneo.

B.biflorum Teijsm. & Binnend. (*Cirrhopetalum biflorum* (Teijsm. & Binnend.) J.J. Sm.)
Pseudobulbs erect, to 4×1.5cm. Lf lanceolate, obtuse, to 13×3cm. Fls 2 per stem; sep. pale green, streaked red-brown, pet. pale green or white, streaked dark red, lip yellow, speckled red, dorsal sep. oblong, acuminate, lateral sep. very long, linear, upper half tubular, apex club-shaped; lip triangular-ligulate. Java.

B.binnendijkii J.J. Sm. (*Cirrhopetalum leopardinum* Teijsm. & Binnend.).
Pseudobulbs laterally compressed, cylindric, to 17×1.5cm. Lf

oblong, bluntly tapered, to 40×15.5cm; petiole to 6.5cm. Infl. to 20cm, umbellate; fls to 12, pale green, pet. dark violet at base, speckled pale violet near apex, lip densely speckled dark violet, streaked white, sep. oblong to 10×1.5cm, twisted, pet. falcate; lip recurved. Java.

B.calamarium Lindl.
Pseudobulbs ovoid, ridged, sheathed to 4cm. Lvs oblong, coriaceous, to 12.5cm. Infl. a crowded raceme to 30cm; fls dull yellow-ochre, lip purple; sep. lanceolate, spreading; pet. minute, adpressed to column; lip trilobed, base saccate, midlobe linear-lanceolate, weakly pendent, pointed, basal margins shortly fringed, hairs at apex longer, crimson, lateral lobes small, erect, fringed. Africa.

B.careyanum (Hook.) Spreng.
Pseudobulbs remote, spherical to oblong, to 5×2.5cm. Lf solitary, oblong or linear-oblong, to 25×5cm. Infl. to 23cm, a dense cylindric raceme; bracts exceeding or equalling fls; fls orange-yellow or green, spotted or tinged purple or red-brown, lip violet; sep. oblong-ovate; pet. ovate, vestigial; lip base lobed, recurved, to 0.5×0.2cm. Autumn–winter. E Himalaya, Burma, Thailand.

B.cocoinum Batem. ex Lindl.
Pseudobulbs ovoid, angled. Lf solitary, lanceolate to oblong-lanceolate, to 30×3cm. Infl. to 45cm, pendent, fls many, white, green or cream, often suffused purple or pink; sep. lanceolate; pet. oblanceolate, minutely dentate; lip entire or minutely lobed, denticulate or fringed. W Africa.

B.comosum Collett & Hemsl.
Pseudobulbs globose-ovoid. Lvs linear-oblong. Scape to 25cm; sheaths 2–3, raceme deflexed, cylindric, dense, to 6.5cm; fls cream tinged green; sep. subequal, membranous, translucent, subulate to lanceolate, villous, hairs flaccid; pet. small, linear-oblong, obtuse, 1-nerved; lip lanceolate, recurved, stipitate. Burma.

B.cumingii (Lindl.) Rchb. f. (*Cirrhopetalum cumingii* Lindl.)
Rhiz. creeping. Pseudobulbs oblong-ovoid, glossy, to 2×1cm. Lvs oblong-elliptic, coriaceous, 8–14×2.5cm; petioles to 1.5cm, sulcate. Peduncle to 22cm; infl. umbellate; fls deep straw-yellow tinged purple; dorsal sep. concave, slender, filamentous, margin fringed, lateral sep. elliptic, narrow, base free, apex fused; pet. linear-triangular, margin fringed, hairs yellow, apex filamentous; lip ligulate, fleshy. Philippines.

B.cupreum Lindl.
Pseudobulbs subglobose, fleshy, to 2.5cm. Lvs oblong, coria-

ceous. Peduncle to 10cm; raceme lax, to 2.5cm; fls copper-yellow; sep. lanceolate, lateral sep. deflexed, ×2 larger than dorsal; pet. small, subulate; lip trilobed, oblong-ligulate, spur basally inflated, midlobe obtuse, keeled, margins pubesc., lateral lobes short, acute. India.

B.dayanum Rchb. f.
Rhiz. creeping, stout. Pseudobulbs globose to ovoid, channelled. Lf to 10×5cm, oblong, coriaceous, deep green above, purple beneath. Fls to 3, to 2.5cm diam., sep. yellow-green, spotted dark purple, pet. and lip purple, edged green; sep. ovate, fringed, spreading, pubesc.; pet. linear-oblong fringed; lip minute, midlobe oblong, broad, disc longitudinally crested, lateral lobes forming plates, oblong, crenulate. Burma.

B.dearei Rchb. f. (*B.godseffianum* Weathers).
Pseudobulbs clustered or closely spaced, conical, narrow, to 3×1cm. Lf solitary, elliptic-oblong, to 17×5cm. Infl. erect, almost equalling the lvs, fls solitary, dorsal sep. tawny-yellow, spotted red, lateral sep. marked purple, pet. tawny-yellow, venation darker, spotted maroon, lip white mottled purple; dorsal sep. ovate-lanceolate, to 4.5×2cm, lateral sep. lanceolate, falcate, base saccate; pet. linear-lanceolate; lip mobile, apex reflexed, crest U-shaped. Philippines.

B.falcatum (Lindl.) Rchb. f.
Pseudobulbs ovoid to elongate, to 6cm. Lvs 2, oblong-lanceolate, to 16cm. Infl. to 35cm, spicate; rachis purple or green, flattened, strongly undulate; fls very short-stalked, situated along both surfaces, red, purple or green, sometimes marked purple, pet. tipped yellow; dorsal sep. spathulate, apical margins fleshy, lateral sep. falcate; pet. oblong or linear, apex thickened; lip curved, thin, glabrous. Spring–autumn. W Africa.

B.fascinator (Rolfe) Rolfe. See *B.putidum*.

B.fletcherianum Rolfe.
Pseudobulbs oblong, clustered, surface granular, streaked purple, to 5cm. Lvs elliptic or oblong, glaucous, green edged purple, 30–60×4cm. Fls 12–30, fleshy, malodorous, clustered, dorsal sep. claret, speckled white, lateral sep. similar, with fewer spots, pet. claret, lip similar; dorsal sep. lanceolate, broad, to 5cm, lateral sep. narrower, connivent, base saccate, lower margins fused, upper parallel, base almost enclosing lip; pet. triangular, erect; lip ligulate, 2-ridged, apex reflexed. New Guinea.

B.frostii Summerh.
Pseudobulbs to 2cm, ovoid, compressed, clustered. Lvs sessile, elliptic, fleshy, to 3.5×2cm. Peduncle to 2cm; fls purple, lip base pale yellow, median venation faint; sep. irregularly papillose beneath, fringed, dorsal sep. ovate to orbicular, convex, shortly acuminate, lateral sep. oblong-lanceolate, to 2×1cm; pet. oblong, weakly convex, margins jagged, fringed; lip fleshy, sagittate, curved, to 0.5cm. Indo-China.

B.godseffianum Weathers. See *B.dearei*.

B.gracillimum (Rolfe) Rolfe (*Cirrhopetalum gracillimum* Rolfe).
Pseudobulbs ovoid, to 2cm. Lf elliptic, blunt to 12×2.5cm. Peduncle purple, to 30cm; fls crimson, lip violet-purple; sep. and pet. filamentous at apex, fringed, base red, dorsal sep. ovate, forming a hood, lateral sep. fused at base, pet. narrower at base; lip to 2mm. New Guinea, Malaya.

B.graveolens (Bail.) J.J. Sm. (*Cirrhopetalum graveolens* Bail.; *Cirrhopetalum robustum* Rolfe).
Pseudobulbs clustered, ovoid, to 8cm. Lf oblanceolate, to 45×10cm, bright green above, mottled, with darker spots beneath. Fls umbellate, many, sep. yellow green, base streaked or suffused rose, pet. yellow, suffused pale rose, lip crimson; dorsal sep. oblong, concave, cuspidate, lateral sep. linear-oblong, to 5cm; pet. oblong, cuspidate; lip ovate-oblong, fleshy, recurved, central furrow solitary, keels 2; base pubesc. New Guinea.

B.guttulatum (Hook. f.) Balak. (*Cirrhopetalum guttulatum* Hook. f.).
Pseudobulbs ovoid, to 5cm. Peduncle marked purple, 15–25cm; fls umbellate, few, sep. yellow or green, speckled purple, lip pale purple; sep. spreading, dorsal sep. ovate, obtuse, 3-nerved, lateral sep. ovate-lanceolate, to 2.0cm; lip short; column spurs slender. India. cf. *B.umbellatum*.

B.imbricatum Lindl.
Readily distinguished by the remarkable inflorescence – a narrowly cylindrical, tapering spike to 12cm long, closely covered with overlapping, glossy purple-brown, scale-like bracts, the whole resembling an attenuated rattlesnake's tail. Small, dark purple-bronze fls open in succession and resemble flies. W Africa.

B.lasiochilum Par. & Rchb.f. (*Cirrhopetalum breviscapum* Rolfe).
Pseudobulbs to 5cm, ovoid-globose on creeping rhiz. Lvs to 6cm, oblong-obovate. Fls solitary or a few in slender-stalked umbels; dorsal sep. and pet. falcate, glossy maroon; lateral sep. far larger, incurved like a pair of mandibles, dull cream speckled red-brown; lip small, red-brown, horseshoe-shaped with hairy margins. SE Asia.

B.lemniscatum Parish.
Pseudobulbs to 2cm, depressed and agglomerated, tuberculose. Lvs 3–4 from pseudobulb base, elliptic-lanceolate, deciduous, to 5cm. Infl. to 15cm, a pendent spike; fls crowded, overlapping, sep. dark purple, base green, pet. white, with solitary purple streak, lip dark blue-purple; sep. orbicular to ovate, fused towards base, hairs spreading; appendages red-purple, bands white, callus undulate; pet. linear-lanceolate, obtuse; lip ovate, broad, convex, obtuse. Burma.

B.leopardinum Lindl.
Pseudobulbs clustered, ovoid-oblong or ovoid-cylindric, to 5×2cm. Lf solitary, oblong, coriaceous, to 20×6cm; petiole to 7cm. Infl. 1–2cm; fls to 3, globose-campanulate, to 3cm diam., pale yellow-brown or green, densely spotted purple or pink, lip deep purple or crimson; dorsal sep. ovate-lanceolate, lateral sep. ovate, oblique, to 1.5cm; pet. broadly ovate, to 1.5cm; lip ovate, fleshy, decurved, basal auricles minutely dentate, central line bordered by 2 ridges. Spring–summer. E Himalaya to Burma, N Thailand.

B.leysianum Burb. See *B.antenniferum*.

B.lobbii Lindl.
Pseudobulbs ovoid, to 5×3cm, remote pale green with darker reticulation. Infl. to 15cm, speckled; fls solitary, to 10cm diam., colour variable, red-yellow, ochre or pale yellow, veined red or speckled pink and yellow, lined brown; dorsal sep. lanceolate, to 5cm, lateral sep. ovate-lanceolate, falcate, base concave; pet. narrower than sep., spreading; lip ovate, recurved. NE India, SE Asia to Philippines.

B.longiflorum Thouars (*Cirrhopetalum umbellatum* (Forst. f.) Hook. & Arn.).
Pseudobulbs globose to narrow-ovoid, to 4.5×2cm, bluntly tetragonal, on creeping rhiz. Lf to 8cm, lanceolate-oblong, coriaceous. Infl. to 20cm, often shorter, slender-stalked, umbellate; fls to 6 in a semi-circle, opening simultaneously, sep. cream or yellow, dorsal sep. spotted maroon to dark red, lateral sep. spotted, stained or lined pale maroon to red, lip dark red or yellow, suffused dark black-red; dorsal sep. round to elliptic, margins dentate at apex, tip with a fine club-shaped hair, lateral sep. to 5cm, linear-lanceolate, basally twisted and lying closely parallel to each other; pet. oblong to ovate-oblong, apically filamentous and denticulate; lip narrow, triangular, entire, base concave, central ridge weak. Africa, Indonesia, Australia, Fiji. A widespread, free-flowering and popular species. See note under *B.umbellatum*.

B.longiscapum Rolfe.
Pseudobulbs ovoid, to 2.5cm. Lvs linear-oblong, coriaceous, subacute, to 13×3cm. Infl. slender, to 30cm; fls few, solitary, to 2.5cm, pale green, lip red-purple, apex suffused deep yel-

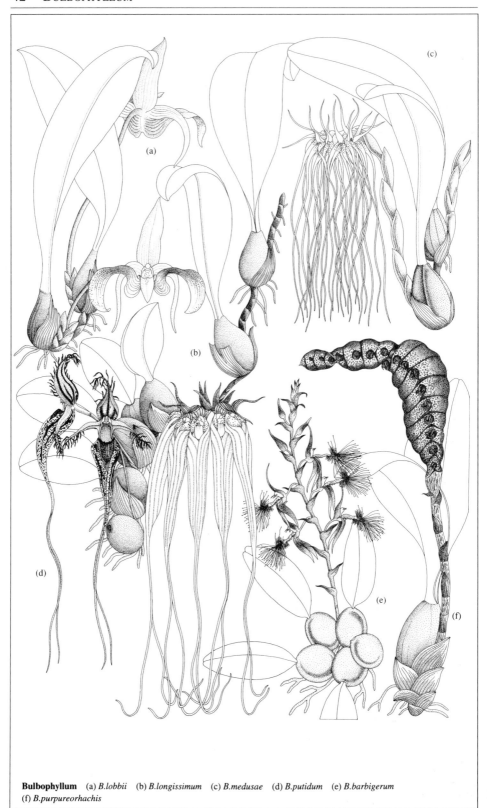

Bulbophyllum   (a) *B.lobbii*   (b) *B.longissimum*   (c) *B.medusae*   (d) *B.putidum*   (e) *B.barbigerum*
(f) *B.purpureorhachis*

low; sep. triangular-lanceolate, acuminate, to 2.5cm; pet. ovate-oblong, minutely dentate, apex bristly; lip broad, elongate, base broad, midlobe keels 2, apex slender, tapering, acute, fleshy, undulate, lateral lobes erect, oblong. Fiji.

B.longissimum (Ridl.) J.J. Sm. (*Cirrhopetalum longissimum* Ridl.).
Pseudobulbs ovoid, sheathed, to 6.5cm. Lvs oblong, coriaceous, subsessile, to 15×4.5cm. Infl. umbellate, curved or pendent, to 20cm; fls white, streaked rose, dorsal sep. with 5, red, longitudinal veins, lateral sep. streaked pink; dorsal sep. oblong-lanceolate, fringed, to 2cm, concave, lateral sep. linear, articulate, to 30cm, apex filamentous; pet. oblong or oblong-lanceolate, fringed; lip ovate-oblong, recurved, fleshy, centre channelled. Borneo, Malaysia.

B.macranthum Lindl.
Pseudobulbs ovoid-elliptic, to 3cm. Lvs oblong, fleshy, to 25×10cm; petiole to 3cm. Fls to 6cm diam., solitary, fleshy, burgundy, fading to dull violet, speckled dark violet; sep. pale green or yellow, edged yellow or green, dorsal sep. oblong, lateral sep. ovate-triangular, to 3cm; pet. oblong-lanceolate, pointed; lip to 0.5cm, basal teeth 2, pointed, midlobe triangular-falcate. Burma.

B.macrobulbon Rolfe.
Pseudobulbs dull olive-green, ovoid, clustered, to 8cm. Lvs oblong, margin and midrib tinged purple, to 33×7cm. Racemes 4–5-fld; fls large, malodorous, yellow-white, lined and blotched purple, pet. base and lip crimson; sep. to 4.5cm, dorsal sep. ovate, erect, concave, lateral sep. ovate, oblique; pet. ovate, subacute, undulate; lip elliptic-oblong, recurved, fleshy, disc papillose, furrowed. New Guinea.

B.mandibulare Rchb. f.
Pseudobulbs narrow-ellipsoid, glaucous, to 5cm. Lvs oblong, acute, to 25cm. Peduncle slender; bracts triangular, concave; sep. bronze, suffused pale green, pet. interior similar, striped purple, lip yellow, marked red-brown; dorsal sep. carinate, lateral sep. ligulate, acute; lip triangular-cordate. Borneo.

B.mastersianum (Rolfe) J.J. Sm. (*Cirrhopetalum mastersianum* Rolfe).
Pseudobulbs ovoid, to 3.5cm. Lvs oblong, coriaceous, to 13×2.5cm. Infl. curved or suberect, umbellate, to 15cm; fls yellow, tinged amber; sep. elliptic-ovate, concave, margin fringed, lateral sep. linear-oblong, fused almost to apex, base narrow; pet. oblong, falcate, finely fringed, to 0.6cm; lip linear-oblong, recurved, fleshy, to 4cm. Malaysia.

B.maximum (Lindl.) Rchb. f.
Pseudobulbs ovoid, narrow, to 10×3cm. Lvs to 3, oblong to linear-lanceolate, coriaceous, to 20×6cm. Infl. to 90cm, many-fld; bracts elliptic to ovate; sep. and pet. yellow or green, usually tipped bright yellow, usually marked purple or brown, lip cream or yellow, spotted purple; dorsal sep. ovate-lanceolate, concave, apex thickened, lateral sep. free, rhombic to ovate; lip fleshy, ovate-oblong, recurved, margins at base deeply and irregularly divided, ridge single, truncate. Africa.

B.medusae (Lindl.) Rchb. f. (*Cirrhopetalum medusae* Lindl.).
Pseudobulbs ovoid, dark brown, to 4cm. Lvs ligulate, fleshy, to 15×1cm. Scape erect or arched; infl. umbellate, a dense head of long, cascading, ivory filaments; fls white or cream, spotted red or yellow; sep. ovate-lanceolate, dorsal sep. caudate, acuminate, lateral sep. flaccid with fine apical filaments to 15cm; pet. ovate-lanceolate; lip ovate, acuminate. Winter. Malay Peninsula, Thailand, Borneo.

B.obrienianum Rolfe.
Pseudobulbs ovoid, sheathed, to 1.5cm. Lvs oblong, subacute, to 2.5cm. Fls solitary; sep. and pet. pale yellow to brown, spotted dark maroon, base pale yellow, lip deep maroon, straw-coloured below; dorsal sep. ovate, obtuse, concave to 2.5cm, lateral sep. similar; pet. ovate, obtuse; lip linear-oblong, fleshy, keels 2, recurved, margin recurved. Himalaya.

B.odoratissimum Lindl.
Pseudobulbs subcylindric, to 2.5cm, spreading. Lf oblong-

lanceolate, to 8×1cm. Fls white, fragrant; sep. lanceolate, almost equal, the apices terete; pet. smaller than sep. ovate; lip oblong-lanceolate, fleshy, central furrow solitary, margins fringed. India, Burma, S China.

B.ornatissimum (Rchb. f.) J.J. Sm. (*Cirrhopetalum ornatissimum* Rchb. f.).
Pseudobulbs ovoid, to 5cm. Lvs linear-oblong, obtuse to 15cm. Fls 3 per scape, straw-yellow, striped and dotted purple; dorsal sep. ovate-lanceolate, fringed, lateral sep. similar, to 10cm, tips filamentous, fringed; pet. subulate to lanceolate, falcate; lip short, oblong, obtuse, recurved. India.

B.pahudii (De Vriese) Rchb. f.
Pseudobulbs oblong, to 11×2cm. Lvs elliptic-oblong, acuminate. Infl. to 15cm; fls 10–12, pale brown-yellow or green, speckled red-brown, dense at base; sep. and pet. linear, apices filamentous. Java.

B.paleaceum (Lindl.) Hook. f. See *Sunipia cirrhata*.

B.patens King ex Hook. f.
Pseudobulbs ellipsoid, remote. Lf elliptic-oblong, fleshy, to 20×7cm; petiole to 2cm. Infl. arched, short; bracts yellow, speckled red, overlapping; sep. white or pale yellow, pet. tinted and spotted maroon, lip purple; dorsal sep. linear-lanceolate, incurved, lateral sep. ovate-lanceolate, decurved, falcate; pet. linear-oblanceolate; lip linear-oblong, fleshy. Malaysia, Thailand, Sumatra, Borneo.

B.picturatum (Lodd.) Rchb. f. (*Cirrhopetalum picturatum* Lodd.).
Pseudobulbs ovoid, angular, dark green, to 65cm. Lvs linear-oblong, obtuse, margins recurved, to 15×4cm. Infl. umbellate, ascending, erect toward apex, to 25.5cm, green, speckled purple; sheaths pale-brown, speckled red; dorsal sep. papillose at apex, dull green spotted crimson, lateral sep. pale green, pet. similar to dorsal sep., lip crimson; dorsal sep. erect, obtuse, hooded, lateral sep. connivent, linear, convex, exterior inflated near base; pet. ovate, rounded; lip ligulate, obtuse. India.

B.pulchrum (N.E. Br.) J.J. Sm.
Pseudobulbs to 2.5cm, slender, oblong. Lvs oblong, base narrow, apex obtuse. Infl. erect, dorsal sep. purple, dotted dark purple, lateral sep. pale yellow, mottled purple, pet. and lip purple; dorsal sep. circular, concave, apex bristled, pointed, lateral sep. linear-lanceolate, obtuse, connate; pet. minute, falcate; lip slender, linear-oblong, recurved to 5cm. Summer. New Guinea.

B.purpureorhachis (De Wildeman) Schltr.
Lvs to 15×6cm, paired, thick, coriaceous. Infl. to 30cm, erect to arching, rachis strongly compressed and spiralling, olive-green to bronze flecked maroon, lanceolate, horizontally ridged at fl. insertions, bearing to 20 small, maroon fls on each surface on a median longitudinal axis. Zaire.

B.putidum (Teijsm. & Binnend.) J.J. Sm. (*B.fascinator* (Rolfe) Rolfe; *Cirrhopetalum fascinator* Rolfe; *Cirrhopetalum putidum* Teijsm. & Binnend.).
Pseudobulbs clustered, ovoid, glossy, to 2cm. Lf sessile, elliptic-oblong, coriaceous, to 5×3cm. Peduncle almost erect, to 10cm; fls solitary; dorsal sep. to 3cm, ovate, green with purple-red filamentous appendages above apex and purple-fringed margins, lateral sep. to 20cm, green striped purple-red, oblong-lanceolate, tapering finely, bases fused, apex free, appendages long; pet. to 2cm, falcate-oblong, purple, fringed; lip ovate-oblong, recurved, channelled, central ridges 2. Malaysia.

B.refractum (Zoll. & Moritzi) Rchb. f. (*Cirrhopetalum refractum* Zoll. & Moritzi).
Pseudobulbs conic, to 2.5cm. Lvs 2, deciduous, lanceolate, to 13cm. Raceme lax, to 40cm; fls to 10, orange-yellow; dorsal sep. ovate, acute, interior sparsely pubesc., lateral sep. linear, sparsely fringed; pet. triangular, subulate, apex long-pubesc.; lip fleshy, sigmoid, base remotely bilobed, rounded, long-pubesc. Himalaya, Java.

B.retusiusculum Rchb. f. (*Cirrhopetalum wallichii* Lindl.).
Pseudobulbs ovoid to 2.5cm. Lvs oblong, obtuse, coriaceous, to 8cm. Fls pale green to yellow, sometimes marked purple, dorsal sep. basally tinged brown, spotted white, lip dull purple; dorsal sep. oblong, truncate, minutely dentate, to 3mm, lateral sep. linear-oblong, connate; lip linear-oblong, recurved. India, Nepal to Malaysia.

B.rothschildianum (O'Brien) J.J. Sm. (*Cirrhopetalum rothschildianum* O'Brien).
Pseudobulbs ovoid, to 4cm. Lvs to 15×2.5. Infl. erect, few-fld, more or less umbellate, green, speckled purple; fls maroon to pink-purple blotched yellow, malodorous; dorsal sep. yellow, lined purple, tipped purple, forming a hood, fringed; pet. resembling dorsal sep.; lateral sep. to 15cm long, tapering finely, twisted inwards; lip triangular, grooved. India.

B.roxburghii (Lindl.) Rchb. (*Cirrhopetalum roxburghii* Lindl.).
Pseudobulbs subglobose. Lvs linear-oblong, to 10cm. Infl. exceeding lvs; dorsal sep. and pet. yellow, striped red, lateral sep. yellow, lip maroon; dorsal sep. ovate, awned, fringed, lateral sep. linear, to 1.7cm, subfalcate, obtuse, ×3–4 size of dorsal sep.; pet. similar to dorsal sep., 3-nerved; lip glabrous. India.

B.rufinum Rchb. f.
Pseudobulbs oblong, to 5cm. Lvs to 25cm, oblanceolate; petiole to 10cm. Infl. decurved; sheaths 2–3; fls erect, green and yellow, veined purple; dorsal sep. ovate, broad, obtuse, lateral sep. oblong, obtuse, concave, 3–5-nerved, fused, projecting from column foot; pet. oblong; lip compressed, base stalked. Himalaya, India.

B.scaberulum (Rolfe) Bolus.
Floral rachis thickened, flattened and blade-like, with a leathery texture and a strong purple tint; fls many in a line along each side of rachis, dull olive to yellow marked purple-red. Africa.

B.suavissimum Rolfe.
Pseudobulbs ovoid-oblong, to 2.5cm. Lvs oblanceolate, narrow, to 10cm. Infl. to 25cm; sheaths 2, membranous; fls pendent, fragrant; sep. and pet. primrose, lip golden; sep. linear-oblong, narrow, 3-nerved; pet. shorter, ovate or ovate-lanceolate, obscurely jagged; lip linear-oblong, sessile, obtuse, recurved. Burma.

B.umbellatum hort. non Lindl. See *B.longiflorum*.

B.umbellatum Lindl. (*Cirrhopetalum maculosum* Lindl.).
Infl. to 30cm, umbellate; fls to 8 per scape, cream to dull ivory overlaid with radiating lines of fine purple-pink spots; lip white, densely marked rose-purple; dorsal sep. to 2.5cm, oblong-ovate, hooded, pet. somewhat shorter, obovate; lateral sep. to 7cm, ovate-lanceolate, spreading and inrolled; lip to1.8cm, tongue-like. Nepal to Taiwan. A popular and beautiful species. Confusion sometimes arises over the name of this plant. *Cirrhopetalum umbellatum* (Forst.) Hook. & Arn. is properly a synonym of *Bulbophyllum longiflorum*. The true *Bulbophyllum umbellatum* described here, being very typically a member of *Bulbophyllum* sect. *Cirrhopetalum*, is sometimes misnamed *C.umbellatum*. It is also close to and possibly synonymous with *B.guttulatum*.

B.uniflorum (Bl.) Hassk.
Pseudobulbs to 10×1.5cm, slender, erect. Lf oblong, to 23×8cm; petiole to 4cm. Infl. borne on rhiz.; peduncle to 9cm; fls 1–2, to 4.5cm diam., dull tan, lip red-brown, apex and exterior yellow, sep. suffused brown-red; dorsal sep. oblong, long-acuminate, to 4×1.5cm, lateral sep. falcate, base ovate, long, subulate; pet. similar, smaller; lip cordate, recurved. Java.

B.vaginatum (Lindl.) Rchb. f. (*Cirrhopetalum vaginatum* Lindl.).
Pseudobulbs ovoid, to 2.5×1cm. Lvs oblong, coriaceous, convex, to 12×2.5cm. Peduncle to 10cm; fls pale straw-yellow, fringed; dorsal sep. ovate, lateral sep. fused at base; pet. elliptic to oblong; lip oblong-triangular. Java.

B.wallichii Rchb. f.
Pseudobulbs conical, clustered, to 2.5cm. Lvs narrow-oblong, to 12×2cm. Fls many, fragrant, pale green, ageing yellow-brown, dotted purple; dorsal sep. lanceolate, fringed, lateral sep. similar, larger; pet. triangular, margins densely fringed; lip oblong, fleshy, hairs purple, glandular, tufted. Himalaya to Burma, Thailand, Indo-China.

B.watsonianum Rchb. f. See *B.ambrosia*.

B.wendlandianum (Kränzl.) U. Dammer (*Cirrhopetalum collettii* Hemsl.).
Broadly resembling a multi-flowered *B.putidum*. Pseudobulbs oblong, to 3cm. Lvs to 14cm, coriaceous, elliptic-oblong to lanceolate. Infl. to 10cm; fls to 6, yellow, the lateral sep. strongly striped purple, lip purple; dorsal sep. boot-shaped, to 1.5cm, with a showy purple-red fringe, apex filamentous, lateral sep. linear-lanceolate, to 15cm; pet. broad, purple-fringed; lip smooth, fleshy, recurved, base sagittate. Burma.

Cadetia Gaudich. (For Cadet de Gassicourt, French chemist.) Some 55 species of epiphytes allied to *Dendrobium* but superficially resembling *Pleurothallis*. Rhizomes short. Pseudobulbs slender, tufted, stem-like. Leaves solitary, terminal, obovate to oblong-elliptic, retuse. Flowers small, solitary or clustered at leaf base; sepals and petals free, similar; lip trilobed, midlobe decurved, pubescent, lateral lobes erect, base fused to the column foot. Papuasia.

CULTIVATION   Intermediate to warm-growing (minimum winter temperature 15°C/60°F). Tie the slender rhizomes to pads of moss and palm fibre, attach to rafts and suspend in dappled shade in very humid conditions. Mist daily and apply a weak foliar feed fortnightly when in active growth. Propagate by division.

C.hispida (A. Rich.) Schltr.
Stems to 10cm, usually far shorter. Lvs to 7.5cm. Fls solitary, white, marked purple; dorsal sep. subovate, almost forming a hood, lateral sep. similar, slightly square, base fused, spurred; pet. equalling sep., oblong-spathulate, narrow, erect; lip keeled, weakly trilobed, midlobe, suborbicular, abruptly acute, lateral lobes minute, obtuse. Solomon Is., New Guinea.

C.taylori (F. Muell.) Schltr.
Stems to 10cm, usually far shorter, cylindric, shallowly furrowed, initially sheathed.   Lf 1.5–5cm. Fls solitary, ephemeral, to 1.2cm diam., white, lip pink and yellow; dorsal sep. oblong, incurved, lateral sep. ovate or oblong, broad, spreading, forming a subcylindric extension with the column foot. NE Australia, New Guinea.

Caladenia R. Br. (From Gk *kalos*, beautiful, and *adenos*, gland, referring to the rows of prominent, often coloured glands set with the disc of the labellum.) Some 70 species of terrestrials. Leaf solitary, oblong or linear-lanceolate, basal, with a papery sheath. Flowers 1–8 in a lax panicle or raceme; dorsal sepal erect, narrow, incurved, forming a hood, lateral sepals similar, spreading or reflexed; petals erect, narrow, reflexed or spreading; lip basally erect, entire or trilobed, the midlobe recurved, with sessile or stalked calli in rows or scattered, margins fringed or dentate. Australia, New Zealand, Malaysia, New Caledonia.

CULTIVATION   In early spring, bury the tubers in pans of equal parts fine grit, silver sand and leafmould or well-rotted garden compost (decayed or dried and broken *Eucalyptus* leaves are sometimes added). Place in full sunlight and freely ventilated conditions in the cool or alpine house. Water sparingly or merely syringe to initiate growth. Once the shoots appear, keep damp by watering from beneath (always with rainwater); do not wet foliage or flowers. Feed fortnightly prior to appearance of flower spikes. Staking of flowers should not be necessary except, perhaps, with *C.dilatata*. After flowering and leaf production, gradually reduce water supplies,allowing the soil to become almost dry by midwinter. Propagate by division. These beautiful ground orchids are best planted in quantity and allowed to increase for a 2–3-year period before repotting.

C.alba R. Br. (*C.carnea* var. *alba* (R. Br.) Benth.). WHITE CALADENIA.
To 30cm. Lf linear, sparsely pubesc. Fls 1–2, to 5cm diam., pink or white, midlobe orange- or yellow-tipped; pet. and sep. similar to those of *C.carnea*, 12–20mm; lip white, trilobed with white or yellow calli in 2 rows, midlobe fringed, undulate, lateral lobes obtuse, tinted purple or crimson. Mid spring–mid autumn. E Australia.

C.caerulea R.Br.
Infl. to 25cm; fls solitary, to 2.5cm diam., cobalt to mauve-blue; dorsal sep. lanceolate, erect, lateral sep. longer and broader, lanceolate-falcate, held in a horizontal, outspread plane below lip; lip erect to porrect, deep lilac marked or tinted amethyst, paler below, stained pale yellow at apex. Australia.

C.cairnsiana F. Muell. ZEBRA ORCHID.
To 30cm. Lf linear, 5–12cm, tinged red. Fls 1–2, pale yellow marked purple or red; sep. and pet. linear-lanceolate, pubesc. beneath, apex often glandular-tipped, dorsal sep. erect, slightly recurved, lateral sep. strongly reflexed, pet. similar; lip erect, clawed, broadly ovate, calli in 2 rows, venation divergent, deep red or purple, with an apical margin of dark calli. Summer–mid autumn. SW Western Australia.

C.carnea R. Br.
Stem slender, 8–20cm. Lf linear, sparsely pubesc. Fls 1–3; pet. and sep. green, glandular-pubesc., brilliant pink above (sometimes white), glabrous; dorsal sep. lanceolate, falcate, incurved or erect, 10–16mm, lateral sep. and pet. similar, spreading, pet. narrower; lip trilobed, basally erect, recurved, to 8mm, with red horizontal broken lines, calli in 2–4 rows, stalked, midlobe lanceolate, fringed or dentate, lateral lobes with obtuse anterior margin. Summer–mid winter. SE Australia, New Zealand, New Caledonia.

C.carnea var.*alba* (R. Br.) Benth. See *C.alba*.

C.deformis R. Br.
To 17cm. Lf linear-lanceolate, 4–10cm. Fl solitary, deep blue, rarely yellow, white or pink; sep. and pet. with minute scattered purple glands, dorsal sep. 12–25mm, elliptic-lanceolate, erect, recurved, lateral sep. lanceolate, falcate, pet. oblong-lanceolate, erect, spreading, equalling sep.; lip to 15mm, trilobed, narrowing basally, and clasping column, calli linear or club-shaped, 4–6 rows, midlobe triangular, fringed with dentate calli, lateral lobes apically dentate. Summer–mid autumn. SE Australia.

C.dilatata R. Br. GREAT COMB; SPIDER ORCHID.
Stems 15–45cm, pubesc. Lf villous, elliptic-lanceolate to oblong, 5–12cm. Fl solitary, to 10cm; dorsal sep. erect, dilated, narrowing to a filamentous or clavate tip, lateral sep. basally deflexed, apically spreading, sometimes crossed; pet. lanceolate, falcate, tapering, 3–4cm; lip mobile, centrally recurved, trilobed, green, maroon and pale yellow, midlobe lanceolate, recurved, margins toothed, tip maroon, lateral lobes erect, entire, anterior margins fringed, calli maroon, base fleshy, tips linear. Summer–winter. SE & SW Australia.

C.discoidea Lindl. BEE ORCHID; DANCING ORCHID.
Stems to 30cm, pubesc. Lf linear-ovate or lanceolate, to 15cm or more. Fls 1–3, yellow-green lined red; sep. to 1cm, dorsal sep. narrow, incurved, concave, erect, lateral sep. lanceolate, falcate; pet. narrower and longer; lip broadly ovate, veined dark red, deeply fringed, calli centrally clustered, oblong or obovate. Summer–mid autumn. SW Western Australia.

C.eminens (Domin.) M.Clements & D.Jones.
Infl. to 60cm; fls solitary, held high above downy foliage; tepals pure white, to 12cm, basically lanceolate but tapering to very fine, long tips, deflexed except for erect dorsal sep.; lip porrect, white fringed in red-pink. W Australia.

C.flava R. Br. COWSLIP ORCHID.
To 30cm. Glandular-pubesc. Lf lanceolate. Fls 2–4, to 4.5cm,

yellow; sep. and pet. ovate-lanceolate, acute dorsal sep. smaller than lateral sep. with a scarlet central line or blotches, pet. smaller; lip to 1cm, claw concave, calli in 2 rows, converging, forming a semicircle, midlobe lanceolate, bordered with 2–3 calli, lateral lobes ovate, abruptly acuminate. Mid summer–mid autumn. SW Western Australia.

C.gemmata Lindl.
10–25cm. Lf ovate or ovate-lanceolate, pubesc., purple beneath, 3–3.5cm; bract solitary, 1.5–2.5cm, in upper stem. Fls 1–2, 4–7cm diam., deep blue or white; sep. and pet. erect, dorsal sep. with recurved tip, elliptic-oblong, basally narrowing; lip ovate, erect and recurved, calli many, small, club-shaped, in horizontal rows covering most of lamina. Mid summer–mid autumn. SW Western Australia.

C.hirta Lindl. SUGAR CANDY ORCHID.
To 30cm. Lf oblong or lanceolate, 5–13cm. Fls 1–3, white and pink or pink; sep. and pet. irregularly acuminate; lip half sep. length, oblong or oblong-lanceolate, basally constricted and erect, fringed, apically recurved, calli in 4–6 regularly spaced rows. Mid summer–mid autumn. SW Western Australia.

C.latifolia R. Br.
To 30cm. Lf pubesc., lanceolate to oblong-lanceolate, 4–10cm. Fls 1–4, white to pink; pet. and sep. glandular-pubesc, spreading, dorsal sep. erect, acute, shorter than laterals, lateral sep. oblong-lanceolate, obtuse; pet. lanceolate; lip deeply trilobed, midlobe blotched pink, lateral lobes oblong, vertically lined pink, entire or serrate, calli in 2 semicircular rows. Autumn–mid winter. SE & SW Australia.

C.lobata Fitzg.
To 45cm. Lf oblong-lanceolate, densely pubesc., basally sheathing; bract midway on stem, to 3cm. Fls 1–2, yellow-green or yellow, streaked red; dorsal sep. clavate, erect, incurved, 6–8cm, lateral sep. basally dilated, sharply upcurved; pet. basally dilated, tapering, becoming filiform; lip to 3cm, clawed, central lobe lanceolate, reflexed, minutely dentate, basally inflated, deep maroon, lateral lobes green, fringed with dark calli in 2 rows, uniting near base. Autumn. SW Western Australia.

C.magniclavata Nicholls.
To 35cm. Lf linear to linear-lanceolate, pubesc., 25–30cm; bract midway on stem. Fls 1–2, 7–8cm diam.; pet. and sep. yellow to yellow-green, striped purple or crimson, lanceolate, basally dilated, apically tapering, tip clavate, yellow with dark glands, dorsal sep. erect, incurved, lanceolate, 4.5–5cm, lateral sep. similar, spreading, pet. shorter and narrower; lip ovate, recurved, yellow, blotched maroon, tipped dark purple, margins fringed, calli in 4 rows. Late summer–early autumn. SW Western Australia.

C.menziesii R. Br.
To 25cm. Lf glabrous or sparsely pubesc. oblong-lanceolate or ovate-lanceolate, 3–9cm. Fls 1–3, white and pink, rarely wholly white; dorsal sep. enveloping column, spathulate-lanceolate, exterior glandular-pubesc., lateral sep. 11–15mm, crescent-shaped, spreading; pet. basally narrowed, clavate, apically glandular, maroon; lip clawed, orbicular-ovate, to 10mm, white, marked pink, entire, calli in 2–4 lines. Summer–autumn. SE Australia.

C.patersonii R. Br.
To 40cm. Lf oblong to linear-lanceolate, pubesc., 10–20cm. Fls 1–4, white or cream, tipped dark purple, rarely crimson, yellow-green, yellow or brown; dorsal sep. erect or incurved, basally dilated, tapering to filiform, lateral sep. and pet. similar, spreading, pet. narrower; lip 1.5–3cm, ovate-lanceolate, clawed, erect, tipped purple or scarlet, margins toothed or serrate, calli L-shaped, in 4–8 rows. Summer–autumn. SE & SW Australia.

C.sericea Lindl.
To 35cm, villous. Lf broad, oblong-lanceolate, 2.5–8cm. Fls blue or mauve; sep. and pet. equal, oblong-lanceolate, dorsal sep. erect, concave; lip to 2cm, base cuneate, tip equally trilobed, calli linear, often fused at base, forming plates, midlobe recurved, fringed with calli, lateral lobes erect, oblong, obtuse, incurved. Mid summer–mid autumn. SW Western Australia.

Calanthe R. Br. (From Gk *kalos*, beautiful, and *anthos*, flower, referring to the showy flowers.) Some 120 species of terrestrials, rarely epiphytes. Pseudobulbs small, corm-like and subterranean or large, exposed and angular-oblong-ellipsoid, usually sheathed by leaf bases. Leaves 2 to several, in a loose basal rosette and sheathing and terminating pseudobulbs, plicate, petiolate, deciduous or evergreen. Inflorescence a lateral raceme, lax to dense; sepals spreading, rarely converging, petals similar, narrow to broad; lip fused to column foot, trilobed, spur usually present, slender, decurved, midlobe often deeply bifid; disc base velvety or lamellate. Tropical and temperate Asia, Polynesia, Madagascar.

CULTIVATION   An important genus in the history of orchid cultivation. *C.*Dominyi and *C.*Veitchii are the first recorded orchid hybrids, produced at the Veitch nursery in the 1850s. All species produce an abundance of spurred flowers in tones from rose to lilac, primrose yellow to bronze, on erect or gracefully arching racemes. *Cc.rosea, rubens, vestita* and Veitchii produce their flowers before the emergence of stout, ribbed leaves, usually in the dead of winter. On completion of pseudobulbs, dry these species thoroughly, placing them in a cool bright place (minimum temperature 10°C/50°F). Once the foliage has withered, root activity ceased and the new bulb become firm, clean and covered in onion-like skin, detach it from withered pseudobulbs, remove dead roots and pot singly into a well-drained mix of leafmould, turfy loam, charcoal, finely composted bark and dried FYM, burying only the very base. Raise heat and humidity to initiate rooting, aiming for temperatures circa 18°C/65°F and high humidity to promote flowering. Racemes should have developed by late winter; they may require support. After flowering, increase temperatures further and water freely as leaves emerge. It is vital to grow these plants fast in warm, humid semi-shade and feed heavily to encourage the largest possible leaves and pseudobulbs; the growth cycle will otherwise be impaired and flowering poor. They are, however, easy plants to handle and were for many years among the most popular winter-flowering display plants.

All other species except *C.discolor* and *C.striata* require warm, humid growing conditions (minimum temperature 15°C/60°F), shade and water throughout the year. Their potting medium needs to be correspondingly more open – as for *Paphiopedilum* but with some additional leafmould. *C.discolor* and *C.striata* are exquisite, small, semi-evergreen species suited to the alpine or cool house or, where some dry winter protection can be provided, sheltered situations in hardiness zone 8, in the bog, woodland or rock garden. Plant in a gritty open mix rich in leafmould; keep damp throughout the year but never wet in winter; protect from full sunlight, strong winds and slugs. Propagate all species by division. Poorly grown (i.e. badly rested) plants of the first group may produce offsets at their pseudobulb apices and bases.

C.alismifolia Lindl.
Pseudobulbs cylindric, narrow, to 5cm. Lvs elliptic to elliptic-ovate, acuminate, to 15cm; petioles slender, sulcate, to 15cm. Infl. to 5cm, raceme minutely pubesc; fls white, to 2cm diam.; sep. elliptic-ovate, tipped green; pet. similar; lip midlobe obovate, bilobulate, lobules broad, minutely crenate, lateral lobes oblong-lanceolate, obtuse; spur cylindric. India.

C.alpina Hook. f.
Pseudobulbs ovoid, subcylindric, 2–2.5cm. Lvs to 17cm, sessile, oblong-elliptic, acuminate. Infl. exceeding lvs, few-fld; fls to 2cm diam., white, tipped green, lip dull red, base and spur pale yellow; sep. ovate-oblong, acuminate; pet. elliptic-lanceolate, to 0.8cm; lip semicircular, margin fringed. India.

C.ceciliae Rchb. f.
Lvs elliptic-oblong, erect, recurved, 33–43×10–16cm; petiole 11–13cm. Infl. to 45cm; fls to 3cm diam. violet becoming suffused orange, lip white, becoming yellow, spur deep violet; sep. and pet. elliptic, sometimes convex above; lip midlobe, subsessile, cuneate, bilobulate, lobes rounded, callus velvety, lateral lobes oblong-ligulate, spreading; spur filiform, acuminate. Malaysia.

C.curculigoides Wallich. See *C.pulchra*.

C.discolor Lindl.
Pseudobulbs small, sheathed by lf bases, to 3cm, 2–4-leaved. Lvs elliptic-lanceolate to obovate-oblong, minutely pubesc. above, narrowed below to a sulcate petiole, 15–25×6cm. Infl. erect, lax, 10–15-fld, 40–50cm; rachis minutely pubesc.; fls 4–5cm diam., maroon, bronze, purple or white, lip pale pink; dorsal sep. elliptic-oblong, acute, 2–2.5×1cm, lateral sep. similar; pet. linear-spathulate, acute; lip base cuneate to flabellate, midlobe obcordate, apex notched, lateral lobes larger than midlobe, oblong-ovate to semi-ovate; disc lamellae 3, raised, extending to the midlobe; spur incurved, minutely pubesc. Japan, Ryuku Is.

C.herbacea Lindl.
Pseudobulbs to 3cm, subfusiform, sheathed. Lvs 15–25×5–10cm, elliptic to elliptic-lanceolate, acuminate; petiole to 15cm. Infl. stout, to 60cm; fls fragrant, brown-green, lip yellow; sep. oblong or oblanceolate, acute; pet. subspathulate, 0.5–1.5cm; lip midlobe with 2 oblong, spreading lobules, lateral lobes elliptic-oblong. Sikkim.

C.masuca (D. Don) Lindl. (*C.versicolor* Lindl.).
Pseudobulbs elongate, conic. Lvs oblong-lanceolate to lanceolate, plicate, acuminate, to 50×15cm. Infl. 10–15cm, dense; fls to 5cm diam., pale lilac, lip intensely violet; sep. and pet. oblong, spreading, acuminate; lip midlobe broad, almost cuneate, lateral lobes linear-oblong, subfalcate, disc crested; spur linear, subspathulate, to 4cm. India.

C.natalensis Rchb. f. See *C.sylvatica*.

C.pulchra Lindl. (*C.curculigoides* Wallich).
Pseudobulbs very small, apparently absent. Lvs linear to lanceolate, broad, to 70×10cm. Scape to 70cm; raceme dense; fls deep orange-yellow, lip orange-red; sep. oblong, subacute; lip subhastate, midlobe subflabellate, lateral lobes small, obtuse; spur short, hooked. India.

C.reflexa Maxim.
Evergreen. Lvs to 35cm, broadly lanceolate. Racemes erect, bracteate, to 15cm, to 30-fld; fls to 2.5cm diam., rose to magenta or white; tepals ovate-acuminate, reflexed; lip deeply 3-lobed, somewhat darker in colour except for yellow-stained base, spur absent. Japan.

C.regnieri Rchb. f. See *C.vestita*.

C.rosea (Lindl.) Benth.
Pseudobulbs elliptic to fusiform. Lvs deciduous, oblong-lanceolate, plicate, glabrous. Infl. erect, emerging before lvs. Fls pale rose, lip paler, becoming white; sep. and pet. oblong-ovate, obtuse; lip oblong, flat, retuse; spur horizontal, obtuse. Burma.

C.rubens Ridl.
Pseudobulbs conic or ovoid, furrowed and angled, 5–15×5cm, silvery. Lvs elliptic, acuminate, to 40×15cm; petiole short. Infl. to 50cm, emerging before lvs; fls pink, rarely white, lip central stripe crimson, exterior pubesc.; sep. elliptic, narrow, acuminate or acute, 1.5–2cm; pet. obovate, obtuse, 1.5×0.8cm; lip base trilobed, 1.5–2cm, midlobe cuneate, with

Calanthe (a) *C.tricarinata* (b) *C.discolor* (c) *C.masuca* (d) *C.vestita* (e) *C.triplicata* (f) *C.striata*

2 oblong, lobules to 1cm, lateral lobes similar to lobules; spur pubesc., slender, pendent, aperture broad, to 2cm. Thailand, N Malaysia.

C.sieboldii Decne. ex Reg. See *C.striata*.

C.striata (Banks) R. Br. (*C.sieboldii* Decne. ex Reg.).
Pseudobulb 2.5–15cm stem-like, emerging from lf sheaths. Lvs elliptic-lanceolate, acute, plicate, 15–25cm; petiole to 20cm. Infl. to 45cm; fls 3.8–6.5cm diam., variable, yellow to bronze, often streaked brown-red; dorsal sep. oblong, spreading, apex recurved, lateral sep. oblong-lanceolate; pet. narrower; lip midlobe cuneate, obcordate, lateral lobes variable, semi-ovate to orbicular; disc lamellate; spur slender, incurved. Japan.

C.sylvatica (Thouars) Lindl. (*C.natalensis* Rchb. f.; *C.volkensii* Rolfe).
Pseudobulbs sheathed by lf bases, small, nodes 2–4. Lvs elliptic-lanceolate, acuminate, narrowed to a petiole, 20–30cm. Infl. to +70cm, erect; fls 2.5–5cm diam., white to lilac, lip white to dark red-purple, callus yellow-orange or white; sep. ovate-lanceolate, acuminate; pet. elliptic-lanceolate, acuminate, smaller than sep.; lip midlobe cuneate to flabellate or obcordate, apex notched, lateral lobes auriculate to oblong, disc with 3 rows of tubercles at the base; spur incurved, sometimes sigmoid, slender. Mascarene Is, Africa.

C.tricarinata Lindl.
Pseudobulbs short, ovoid. Lvs elliptic or lanceolate-elliptic, plicate, acute, 17–30cm. Infl. 30–50cm, lax; fls yellow-green, lip brown-red; sep. and pet. ovate-elliptic, spreading; lip spreading, midlobe obcordate to orbicular, undulate, apex notched, lateral lobes suborbicular, disc 3-ridged, minutely crenate; spur obsolete. India, Japan.

C.triplicata (Willem.) Ames.
To 1m. Pseudobulbs ovoid, 3–6-leaved. Lvs ovate-lanceolate to elliptic-lanceolate, plicate, prominently ribbed, puberulent beneath, 45–60×12cm; petiole long. Infl. congested toward apex, minutely pubesc.; fls white, sep. tipped pale green, callus orange or yellow; sep. elliptic-obovate, oblong, broad or oblanceolate, apex notched; lip midlobe deeply divided, seg. 2, linear-oblong, falcate, recurved, sinus acute, lateral lobes oblong, obtuse, spreading, disc tuberculate; spur slender, curved, 1.5–2cm. SE Asia to Australia, Fiji.

C.versicolor Lindl. See *C.masuca*.

C.vestita Wallich ex Lindl. (*C.regnieri* Rchb. f.).
Pseudobulbs oblong-conical, obscurely tetragonal, 8–12.5cm, striped pale green-green with silvery, onion-skin-like sheath vestiges. Lvs deciduous, lanceolate, broad, 45–60cm, narrowing below to a winged, sulcate petiole, prominently ribbed. Infl. produced before lvs, suberect then nodding; peduncle pubesc.; bracts ovate-lanceolate, acuminate; sep. and pet. white to pale rose, lip white to rose or magenta, callus golden yellow to crimson or violet, spur ivory to green; sep. elliptic-oblong, spreading, apex pointed, 2×0.7cm, oblique; pet. obovate-oblong, obtuse; lip obovate, flat, midlobe obcordate, broad, deeply bifid, lateral lobes oblong, oblique, obtuse, to 1cm; spur curved, slender. Burma, Indochina to Celebes.

C.volkensii Rolfe. See *C.sylvatica*.

C.grexes
C.Baron Schröder: deciduous plants; tall spikes of pink fls in winter.
C.Bryan: deciduous plants; tall spikes of pure white fls in winter.
C.Diana Broughton: deciduous plants; tall spikes of deep rose pink or rosy red fls in winter.
C.Dominyi: evergreen plants; short spikes of muddy lilac fls; the first artificial orchid hybrid to flower in cultivation.
C.Hexham Gem: deciduous plants; tall spikes of dark red fls in winter.
C.Veitchii: deciduous plants; tall spikes of pale pink fls in winter.

Calochilus R.Br. (From Gk *kalos,* beautiful, and *cheilos,* lip, referring to the colourful, hairy lip.) 12 species, herbaceous terrestrials. Leaf solitary, narrow, basal, arising from subterranean tubers. Inflorescence a tall slender spike; dorsal sepal and petals broadly ovate, more or less equal and forming a hood; lateral sepals larger, decurved; lip large, basically triangular-hastate but obscured by a mass of long, fleshy hairs derived from the calli; column short, often with two dark, shining 'eyes' at its base. Autumn–early spring. Australasia.

CULTIVATION   Among the most striking and unusual of ground orchids, with spikes of green and purple flowers with thickly bearded lips and bespectacled columns. Their general culture is as for *Caladenia.*

C.campestris R.Br.
Infl. to 60cm, robust, to 15-fld; fls to 2.5cm diam.; tepals olive green veined purple-red; lip to 3cm, densely covered with long, regularly radiating, fleshy, dark violet hairs derived from a violet-blue, shiny callus; column flanked by two conspicuous shining black eyes. E Australia.

C.robertsonii Benth.
Differs from *C.campestris* in the longer, narrow lip beset with more disorderly hairs of a paler purple-brown; the callus, rather than tongue-like, is composed of bead-like glands and the column 'eyes' are smaller. E Australia, New Zealand.

Calopogon R. Br. (From Gk *kalos*, beautiful, and *pogon*, beard, referring to the coloured beard or crest which adorns the lip.) Some 4 species of terrestrials. Corm subterranean, globose or ellipsoid, usually unifoliate. Leaves basal, grass-like. Inflorescence a terminal, lax raceme, few to several-flowered; flowers often large, showy, white to magenta or crimson; sepals and petals free, spreading; lip obscurely trilobed, lateral lobes minute, midlobe dilated toward apex, apex papillose, centre with numerous beard-like hairs; column free, slightly arching, apex winged, anther terminal, operculate, incumbent, bilocular, pollinia 4, yellow. N America to W Indies.

CULTIVATION   Beautiful terrestrials suited to cultivation in clay pans of damp, slightly acid composted bark and turfy loam in the alpine or cool house, or to sheltered situations in the bog or woodland garden in hardiness zones 7–9.

C.barbatus (Walter) Ames.
Lvs to 18×0.2cm, narrowly linear, long-acuminate. Infl. to 45cm, slender, subcapitate; fls to 3.5cm diam., usually rose-pink, sometimes white, spreading; dorsal sep. to 17×6mm, linear-oblong to elliptic-oblong, acute or apiculate, lateral sep. to 13×7mm, obliquely ovate, acute or apiculate; pet. to 15×5mm, short-clawed, oblong, base rounded, apex obtuse; lip to 13mm, midlobe broadly obovate to suborbicular, rounded, hairs on centre of disc deep rust-red, apical papillae pale lavender; column to 8×7.5mm, broadly winged forming a rounded blade. SE US.

C.pulchellus (Salisb.) R. Br. See *C.tuberosus*.

C.tuberosus (L.) BSP (*C.pulchellus* (Salisb.) R. Br.).
Corm small. Lvs to 50×5cm, linear to linear-lanceolate. Infl. to 46cm, few to many-fld; fls rose to magenta, sometimes white; dorsal sep. to 27×10mm, oblong to elliptic-oblong, acute to apiculate, lateral sep. ovate to ovate-lanceolate, acute; pet. to 24×9mm, short-clawed, oblong-pandurate to oblong-elliptic, obtuse or rounded; lip transversely elliptic-oblong or obreniform to cuneate-flabellate, retuse or rounded, disc 3-veined, bearded; column to 20×9mm, strongly arched, broadly winged forming an obovate blade. Canada, NE US to Florida, Cuba, Bahamas.

Calypso Salisb. (From Gk Calypso, the sea nymph famed for her elusiveness.) 1 terrestrial species. Corm ovoid, sparsely rooting. Stem 10–20cm with basal leaf sheaths. Leaf single, emerging plicate, elliptic-oblong or ovate, venation distinct; petiole short. Flowers solitary, terminal; sepals and petals to 2cm, narrow-lanceolate, widely spreading, often reflexed upwards or twisted, bright rose to magenta; lip to 2.5cm, slipper-shaped and 2-spurred, terminal lobe folded over and outwards with a tuft of crest hairs at its base (i.e. on the rim), basic colour white, striped purple-red behind, apical lobe pure white often with one or two rose blotches, hairs golden or white; column broad, pink. Early spring–midsummer. Scandinavia, Russia, N Asia, N America.

CULTIVATION   For the alpine house, acid pockets in the rockery or for naturalizing in woodland or bog gardens in hardiness zones 6 and over, their diminutive habit (a single leaf far exceeded by a rosy, solitary flower) has great charm. Plant the tubers shallowly in pans of well-drained but consistently damp fibrous mix (neutral to acid, with plenty of leafmould and horticultural charcoal). Grow in full or dappled sunlight. Reduce temperatures and water once foliage withers.

C.bulbosa (L.) Oakes.
As for the genus. var. *americana* (R. Br.) Luer. Lip hairs yellow, apical lobe faintly marked. N America. var. *occidentalis* (Holzing.) Cald. & Tayl. Lip hairs white, apical lobe mottled purple. N America. The typical variety grows in Europe and Asia.

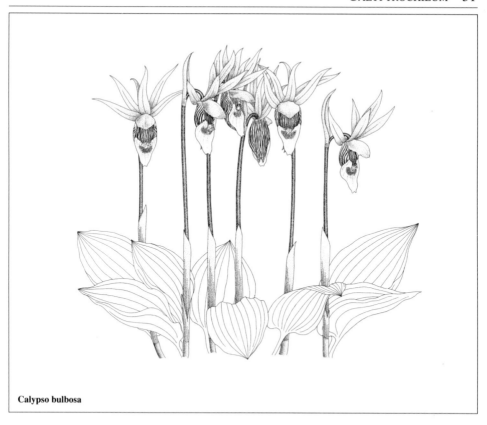

Calypso bulbosa

Calyptrochilum Kränzl. (From Gk *kalyptra*, covering, and *cheilos*, lip.) 2 epiphytes. Stems long, leafy; roots numerous. Leaves oblong, fleshy. Racemes borne along stem, dense, few- to many-flowered; flowers, white; sepals and petals subsimilar; lip trilobed, spurred; column short. Tropical Africa.

CULTIVATION   See *Angraecum*.

C.christyanum (Rchb. f.) Summerh. (*Angraecum christyanum* Rchb. f.).
Robust. Stem elongated, stout, 8mm diam. Lvs numerous, 6–13×1–3cm, distichous, oblong, unequally bilobed at apex, the lobes rounded, fleshy, olive green. Racemes borne on underside of stem, to 4cm, 6–9-fld; rachis flexuous; fls lemon-scented, white, yellow in throat, spur green; sep. and pet. 6–10×4mm, ovate; lip trilobed at base, lateral lobes erect, auriculate, midlobe to 10×8mm, oblong, apiculate; spur 8–10mm, geniculate, globose at tip; column stout, 3mm. Tropical Africa (widespread).

C.emarginatum (Sw.) Schltr. (*Angraecum emarginatum* Sw.; *Angraecum imbricatum* Lindl.).
Stems long, leafy. Lvs 6–17×2.5–5cm, oblong. Racemes axillary, to 5cm, densely fld; fls strongly scented, particularly at night, pet. white, lip yellow or yellow-green; pedicel and ovary 10–12mm; bracts 6–12mm, ovate, acute, overlapping; sep. and pet. 6–10mm, ovate, acute, concave, dorsal sep. keeled; lip 15–17mm, oblong, concave, obscurely trilobed, lateral lobes broadly rounded, midlobe smaller, acute; spur 8mm, sharply incurved, swollen at apex; column very short. W Africa, Zaire, Angola.

Capanemia Barb. Rodr. (For Dr Guillemo Schuch de Capanema, Brazilian naturalist.) Some 15 species of epiphytes. Pseudobulbs small, enveloped by 2 or 3 sheaths, apex unifoliate. Leaves small, fleshy, often linear, terete. Inflorescence a raceme, small, densely few to many-flowered; peduncle filiform; flowers small or minute, usually white or green; sepals and petals subequal, subsimilar, narrow, free or with lateral sepals sometimes slightly connate; lip sessile, simple, disc with 1 or 2 fleshy calli; column short, fleshy, erect, footless, apex biauriculate, pollinia 2, waxy, ovoid-subglobose. Brazil, Paraguay, Argentina.

CULTIVATION Small, white-flowered epiphytes suitable for mounting on bark or rafts in the intermediate house. Syringe daily; plunge actively growing plants in rainwater every second day and give a weak, fortnightly, foliar feed. Suspend in a bright, humid position, protected from full sunlight.

C.micromera Barb. Rodr. (*Quekettia micromera* (Barb. Rodr.) Cogn.).
Pseudobulbs minute, ovoid or obovoid. Lvs to 25×1mm, narrowly linear, subterete, acute. Infl. to 15mm, ascending, 1 to few-fld; fls white; dorsal sep. to 2×1mm, narrowly oblong or oblong-lanceolate, acute or acuminate; lateral sep. larger, spreading, ligulate; pet. to 2.5×1mm, oblong-lanceolate or narrowly obovate, acute; lip to 2.5×1mm, oblong-pandurate, acute, callus yellow, a simple flattened keel; column minute, apex recurved. Brazil.

C.superflua (Rchb. f.) Garay (*Oncidium superfluum* Rchb. f.).
Pseudobulbs small, elongate, attenuate. Lvs to 7×3cm, terete, acute. Infl. to 7cm, erect to pendent, few to many-fld; fls sparkling white with golden yellow disc and a maroon spot at the base of the column; dorsal sep. to 4×2mm, oblong to obovate, incurved, lateral sep. to 5×3mm, oblong, acute or obtuse; pet. to 4×3mm, broadly oblong to elliptic, erect, acute; lip to 6×4mm, broadly spathulate or obcordate to subpandurate, retuse, pubesc. below, disc with 2 oblong, elevated calli; column short, apex lilac. Brazil, Argentina.

Catasetum Rich. ex Kunth. (From Gk *kata*, downward, and Lat. *seta*, bristle, referring to the position of the two horns of the column.) Some 100 species of 'dioecious' epiphytes, lithophytes or terrestrials allied to *Cycnoches* and *Mormodes* (see below). Rhizomes short. Pseudobulbs fleshy, ovoid to fusiform, covered with numerous large sheaths; roots often with many erect secondary rootlets forming dense mats. Leaves alternate in 2 ranks, plicate, strongly veined or ribbed, seldom persisting beyond one season, elliptic-lanceolate to oblanceolate, olive green to grey-green, glabrous to scarious, bases closely enveloping pseudobulbs and remaining after fall of blades, leaving short apical spines. Inflorescence a lateral raceme, erect or pendent; flowers few to many, showy, dimorphic (unisexual) males and females on separate inflorescences, rarely perfect, or occurring together on the same inflorescence; sepals free, spreading or reflexed, fleshy or thin; petals similar to sepals. Male flowers conspicuously coloured; lip fleshy, spreading, sessile, saccate or galeate, margins entire, dentate, crenulate or deeply fimbriate; column erect, footless, 2 antennae at base which eject pollinia explosively when touched; anther terminal, incumbent, opercular, 1-celled or 2 imperfect cells, pollinia 2 or 4, waxy, deeply sulcate. Female flowers appear less frequently on few-flowered racemes; lip fleshy, saccate or galeate, often calciform, margins entire; column short, stout, antennae absent, non-functional anther often present. Summer. C America, S America, W Indies.

At first, ignorance of the unstable dioecy of *Catasetum* led to much confusion. Lindley named two genera, one, *Monachanthus*, described plants bearing female flowers, the other, *Myanthus*, bearing male flowers. Dodson (1962, 1975) split *Catasetum* ; the segregates, *Clowesia* and *Dressleria*, reliably bear bisexual flowers. The production of male or female flowers in *Catasetum* is probably determined by growing conditions: in deteriorating sites, i.e. those in drought-stricken, full sunlight or saturated, deep shade, female flowers are almost invariably produced as an outbreeding mechanism for the endangered population. The same plants will bear male flowers under improved conditions.

CULTIVATION Remarkable epiphytes for the intermediate house. Pot in long clays (crocked to one-third depth) or in baskets in a mix of coarse bark, dried FYM, charcoal and sphagnum moss. Suspend in airy, bright, humid conditions; protect from full sunlight (see note above for possible consequences of stress); water and feed frequently when in growth. The fleshy, curiously shaped flowers are produced either with or on completion of the new growth or, occasionally, when the plant is at rest. Once the pseudobulbs are completed, water only to prevent shrivelling and place in full sunlight.

C.barbatum (Lindl.) Lindl.
Racemes suberect to pendent, to 20-fld, stout, exceeding lvs. Male fls large, membranous; tepals deep green, flecked maroon or violet, margins toothed; sep. to 32×9mm; pet. to 31×7mm; lip pale green marked rose to red, to 20×4mm, oblong, saccate at centre with conical sac on posterior portion, margin lacerate or deeply fimbriate; disc with large conical tooth at base; column cream, pollinia 2, yellow. Female fls smaller than males, similar to males in colour, fleshy; tepals similar, to 24×7mm; lip to 2×1.2cm, deeply saccate with subrotund sac, margins undulate; column thick, fleshy, 11.3cm. Peru, Brazil, Guyana, Colombia, Venezuela, Ecuador.

C.bicolor Klotsch.
Fls in arching racemes; tepals ovate-lanceolate, with margins inrolled, bronze-maroon to chocolate, dorsal sep. and pet. forming an erect narrow hood, lateral sep. strongly divergent;

lip small, saccate, bright lime green with maroon spots. Panama, Colombia, Venezuela.

C.buccinator (Lindl.) Lindl. ex Stein. See *Mormodes buccinator*.

C.bungerothii N.E. Br. See *C.pileatum*.

C.cernuum (Lindl.) Rchb.f.
Fls many in arching racemes; tepals obovate-lanceolate, more or less equal, lime to olive green heavily mottled chocolate to maroon, sometimes solid maroon; lip large, 3-lobed, green spotted brown. Brazil.

C.christyanum Rchb. See *C.saccatum*.

C.dilectum Rchb. f. See *Dressleria dilecta*.

C.discolor (Lindl.) Lindl. (*C.roseo-album* Hook.).
Infl. erect to pendent, to 25-fld; peduncle shiny maroon-brown. Male fls often inverted, to 4cm; sep. to 15×5.5mm,

Catasetum   (a) *C.discolor* (1) var. *fimbriatum* (2) var. *roseo-album* (3) var. *viridiflorum*   (b) *C.macrocarpum*
(c) *C.barbatum*   (d) *C tenebrosum*   (e) *C.saccatum*   (f) *C.pileatum*

pale yellow-green, tinted pink-red or pale pink-cream; lip saccate, flattened, with two lateral fringes, lip exterior and marginal fringe shiny green, tinged red, lip interior pubesc., green tinted red-pink; column white, basal antennae not distinct; anther white, pollinia 2, yellow. Female fls similar to males, except generally larger. Brazil, Venezuela, Colombia, Surinam, Guyana.

C.eburneum Rolfe. See *Dressleria eburnea*.

C.expansum Rchb. f.
Fls many in arching racemes, yellow-white to primrose or golden yellow, sometimes white or green; pet. and dorsal sep. erect, oblong-obovate, overlapping, lateral sep. spreading horizontally, more or less obscured by the broad, flabellate lip; callus fleshy, yellow-orange. Ecuador.

C.fimbriatum (Morr.) Lindl.
Raceme pendent, to 90cm loosely many-fld, variable. Male fls to 5cm diam., fragrant, inverted; tepals to 3.8×1.4cm yellow to olive green flushed rose, spotted or streaked maroon, dorsal sep. and pet. closely erect, lateral sep. descending; lip to 3×4cm, yellow-green, margins tinged pink at base, saccate, anterior recurved, margins erose-fimbriate; column to 2.5cm, white, antennae short, parallel or slightly incurved; anth. white, pollinia 2, yellow. Female fls sometimes on same infl. as male fls, inverted, yellow-green; tepals strongly recurved; lip apiculate, slightly recurved, margins entire. Tropical S America.

C.floribundum Hook. See *C.macrocarpum*.

C.gnomus Lind. & Rchb. f.
3 sexual forms occur, male, female and hermaphrodite; infl. pendent, loosely many-fld; peduncle to 60cm; bracts to 6cm, fleshy; male fls fleshy, to 7cm diam., green, flecked maroon-purple; sep. to 5×1.8cm, fleshy, spreading; pet. to 4.5×1.2cm, almost parallel with column; lip to 2cm, white, flecked purple, green at base, deeply saccate, margins undulate-dentate; antennae to 20cm, one incurved apically, one porrect. Female fls tepals similar to male; lip pale green, pale yellow marginally, deeply saccate, margins dentate. Brazil.

C.integerrimum Hook. (*C.maculatum* Batem. non Kunth).
Resembles *C.maculatum* except fls bear few maroon markings and a more broadly conical lip. Guatemala.

C.macrocarpum Rich. ex Kunth (*C.tridentatum* Hook.; *C.floribundum* Hook.). JUMPING ORCHID.
Infl. erect or arching, to 10-fld; peduncle to 30cm. Male fls yellow-green, variously flecked maroon-purple, fleshy, fragrant; sep. to 4.5×1.4cm, incurved, concave; pet. to 4×2.4cm, concave; lip green-yellow, lateral lobes white, interior deep maroon-purple, fleshy, deeply saccate, apex tridentate, midlobe tongue-shaped; column white, flecked dark maroon, pale green-yellow centrally, rostrate; antennae to 3cm, one strongly decurved, apically, one porrect; anth. pale green, pollinia 2, green. Female fls on same infl. as male fls; sep. yellow-green flecked maroon-purple; lip exterior green, interior yellow, to 3×2.5cm, galeate. Tropical S America, Trinidad.

C.maculatum Kunth (*C.oerstedii* Rchb. f.).
Allied to *C.macrocarpum* and *C.integerrimum*. Infl. arching; peduncle to 40cm, bracts to 1cm; fls green to green-brown, tinted or flecked maroon-purple or red-brown, lip green to yellow, tinged maroon-purple or red-brown, column pale green-cream, flecked maroon. Male fls with sep. to 4.5×1.8cm, concave, incurving over column, margins involute; pet. to 4×1.7cm, incurving over column, margins ciliate; lip to 3.5×2.2cm, fleshy, rigid, obconic, margins fimbriate; column to 3×1.2cm, rostrate; antennae slender, one curved, one porrect. Female fls fleshy; tepals reflexed, to 2×1cm; lip to 3×1.8cm, saccate, broad at apex, margins fimbriate; column short, fleshy. Colombia, Venezuela, Ecuador, Nicaragua, Costa Rica.

C.maculatum Batem. non Kunth. See *C.integerrimum*.

C.microglossum Rolfe.
Infl. pendent, loosely many-fld; peduncles to 65cm. Male fls purple or purple-maroon; pet. and dorsal sep. erect, to 2.5×0.6cm; lateral sep. broader, parallel; lip yellow, saccate with sides erect, reflexed, to 8mm; covered with many toothlike calluses; column to 1.7cm; antennae almost parallel, incurved. Female fls similar to male, lacking antennae, galeate. Peru.

C.oerstedii Rchb. f. See *C.maculatum*.

C.pileatum Rchb. f. (*C.bungerothii* N.E. Br.).
Male infl. pendent, to 40cm, several to many-fld. Male fls to 11cm diam., opening flat, fragrant, usually ivory white, variously tinged yellow-green or yellow-cream, sometimes flecked purple; sep. to 7×1.7cm, incurved; pet. to 7×2.5cm, thin; lip to 5×7cm, transversely oblong to rounded, short-saccate, with a small, triangular sac just below lip insertion, orange-red; column white, to 4cm, rostrate; antennae crossing, one incurved, one porrect. Female fls cream, lip deep yellow to pale yellow, saccate, margins slightly recurved. Venezuela, Colombia, Ecuador, Trinidad, Brazil.

C.roseo-album Hook. See *C.discolor*.
C.roseum (Lindl.) Rchb. f. See *Clowesia rosea*.
C.russellianum Hook. See *Clowesia russelliana*.

C.saccatum Lindl. (*C.christyanum* Rchb.).
Infl. loosely few to many-fld; peduncle to 40cm, erect to pendent; bracts to 1.3cm. Male fls to 10cm diam., spreading or nodding, dull green, tinged and dotted purple-brown or olive-brown; sep. to 65×9mm, concave; pet. to 58×8mm, erect, connivent with dorsal sep.; lip purple-brown, to 3cm, deeply saccate basally, reflexed, anterior trilobed, margins fimbriate; midlobe oblong-ovate, lateral lobes rounded, green; column to 5.5cm, subclavate, long-rostrate at apex; antennae to 1.5cm, one incurved, one porrect. Female fls yellow-green dotted red-brown; sep. to 29×7.5mm; pet. to 2.9×1.2cm; lip to 2.9cm, laterally compressed, deeply saccate, margins decurved, fimbriate; column to 1cm, stout, rostrate at apex. Guyana, Brazil, Peru.

C.sanguineum Lindl.
Variable species. Racemes many-fld, usually green-white spotted or banded maroon, this colour intensifying in the lip and almost solid red-black in the midlobe; tepals ovate-elliptic, held upright (but usually downwards); lip held uppermost, strongly saccate and green below with a 3-lobed, garnet, porrect blade above. Colombia, Venezuela.

C.suave Ames & Schweinf. See *Dressleria suavis*.

C.tabulare Lindl.
Raceme many-fld; tepals lanceolate with inrolled margins, light green blotched maroon to solid maroon, dorsal sep. and pet. forming a hood, lateral sep. strongly divergent; lip obovate lanceolate, apparently entire, navicular, a paler brown-red with a very conspicuous, fleshy, tongue-shaped, raised, cream callus. Colombia.

C.tenebrosum Kränzl.
Raceme many-fld; tepals a rich chocolate-maroon, dorsal sep. and pet. held erect, obovate, lateral sep. obovate-cordate, divergent; lip fleshy, obcordate-orbicular, crenulate, yellow. SE Ecuador.

C.thylaciochilum Lem. See *Clowesia thylaciochila*.
C.tridentatum Hook. See *C.macrocarpum*.

C.trulla Lindl.
Raceme many-fld, arching to pendent; tepals lime to yellow-green, spotted or blotched maroon, dorsal sep. and pet. lanceolate, held erect, lateral sep. longer and strongly divergent with inrolled margins; lip 3-lobed, basically green spotted

maroon, lateral lobes fringed, base saccate, apex with a prominent, tongue-shaped, fleshy, orange thickening. S Brazil.

C.viridiflavum Hook.
Raceme many-fld; tepals yellow-green fading to parchment, dorsal sep. and pet. obovate, held erect (but downwards),

inrolled and becoming rather papery, lateral sep. narrower, divergent; lip held uppermost, glossy, fleshy, helmet-shaped, green to yellow-green with an orange-yellow interior. Guatemala, Panama.

C.warscewiczii Lindl. See *Clowesia warscewiczii.*

Cattleya Lindl. (For William Cattley (*d*1832), English horticulturist.) Some 50 species of epiphytes and lithophytes allied to *Laelia*. Rhizome short or elongate, stout, ring-scarred, often hardening. Pseudobulbs erect, conspicuously stalked, remote or proximate on rhizome, oblong to obovoid to clavate-cylindric and cane-like, usually strongly laterally compressed, becoming fissured after 1 season, enveloped by scarious sheaths. Leaves oblong to broadly obovate, usually coriaceous, borne 1–2 (1–3) at apex of pseudobulb (this distinction, between unifoliate, e.g. *C.labiata*, and bifoliate, e.g. *C.guttata*, is important in identification and determining growing requirements). Inflorescence a terminal raceme, usually enveloped by a thick spathaceous sheath, 1- to several-flowered; flowers usually large, showy, sometimes fragrant; sepals subequal, free, fleshy, spreading; petals usually wider than sepals; lip broadly funnelform, sessile or short-clawed, simple to deeply trilobed, lateral lobes erect, inrolled, clasping column, midlobe often broad, brightly coloured, with a fringed or ruffled margin; column elongate, subterete, arcuate, wingless, footless, anther terminal operculate, incumbent, bilocular, pollinia 4, slightly compressed. Tropical C & S Amer.

CULTIVATION Few orchid genera are so valued and fabled as *Cattleya* and none so extravagantly beautiful. The larger-flowered unifoliates like *C.labiata*, *C.mossiae*, *C.dowiana* and grexes like Bob Betts are the blowsy fragrant blooms held in the popular imagination, at least, to be most typically 'orchids'. They have fascinated collectors, corsage-wearers and commentators as far from the horticultural community as Proust and Nabokov. Among the bifoliate species are found slender-stemmed and smaller-flowered plants with blooms in a dazzling range of colours and texture from magenta, rose and buff to white, purple, green, vermilion and bronze, from the waxy to the glossy to the crystalline and fragile.

All prefer intermediate conditions (with the possible exceptions of *C.aurantiaca* and *C.forbesii* and *C.bowringiana*, which will cope with temperature as low as 5°C/40°F provided they are dry), but may with careful adjustment of the watering regime, be attempted in the cool or warm house. They can also be tried as houseplants – the limiting factors being poor light values and inadequate humidity when in growth.

Pot every one or two years, before growth resumes, in heavily crocked clays or baskets in an open orchid mix (largely coarse bark, with some rockwool, perlite or coconut fibre). In repotting, remove any dead roots and the oldest one or two canes (pseudobulbs), these may be used for propagation, dress the cut rhizome with charcoal or sulphur. Position the rhizome level with the surface of the medium with the leading edge (latest stem) an inch from the pot edge, pinning it down if necessary; firm the medium gently around the roots. Water sparingly at first, increasing quantities once the new growth is plainly visible and new roots are developing at its base. Place in buoyant, humid conditions in full sunlight (although new foliage and flowers may require protection from scorching). Water and feed heavily to promote the fullest possible growth. As this nears completion, a sheath will emerge between the leaves, enclosing the flower buds. Impose a dry rest and lower temperatures. The flowers will break the sheath (they sometimes require assistance and may not even develop until the cane is some two years old), opening, usually, in the winter months, or early spring.

The unifoliate Cattleyas are tougher than the bifoliates and adapt well to cultivation on bark blocks or rafts suspended in the roof of the house and plunged daily in the summer months. No *Cattleya* appreciates regular syringing. It can be injurious to new growths and will certainly mark flowers. Propagate by division or raise from seeds.

C.aclandiae Lindl.
Pseudobulbs 8–12cm, subcylindrical, grooved, apex bifoliate. Lvs 6.75–10×1.75–2.5cm, fleshy, coriaceous, spreading, broadly elliptic, obtuse. Infl. 1 or 2-fld; fls 7–11cm diam., strongly fragrant, waxy, long-lived; sep. 30–50×10–18mm, lime green or sulphur yellow to buff, blotched chocolate or spotted maroon, fleshy, ovate-oblong or elliptic-oblong, obtuse, undulate; pet. 27.5–45×8–18mm, same colour as sep., similar to sep.; lip 35–50×2.5–3.7cm, 3-lobed, lateral lobes rose-purple, suberect, scarcely enveloping column, rounded, undulate, midlobe bright rose-purple veined deep purple, yellow at base, oblong to reniform, emarginate, undulate; column to 25mm, clavate, white or rose-white. N Brazil.

C.alexandrae Lind. & Rolfe. See *C.elongata.*
C.amabilis hort. See *C.intermedia.*
C.amethystina Morr. See *C.intermedia.*

C.amethystoglossa Lind. & Rchb. f. ex Warner (*C.guttata* f. *prinzii* (Rchb. f.) A.D. Hawkes).
Easily distinguished from the closely related and very similar *C.guttata* by its fls, which are white or pale rose spotted dark rose or mauve on sep. and pet.; the lip has white lateral lobes and a magenta midlobe tinted mauve, the throat is usually marked white or pale gold. Brazil.

C.aurantiaca (Batem. ex Lindl.) P.N. Don.
Rhiz. branching freely, producing multiple leads. Pseudobulbs 12–35cm, fusiform-clavate or narrowly cylindrical, becoming fissured with age, often yellow-green, apex 2–3-lvd. Lvs to 18×5.5cm, broadly ovate to elliptic-oblong, retuse, rigidly fleshy, bright, sometimes glossy green. Infl. 6–10cm, few- to many-fld; fls 1.5–4cm diam., orange-yellow to bright vermilion or cinnabar, often streaked and spotted darker red or maroon especially on the lip; sep. 6–27×3–6mm, lanceolate to linear-elliptic, acute;

Cattleya (a) *C.maxima* (b) *C.dormanniana* (c) *C.rex* (d) *C.labiata* (e) *C.walkeriana* (f) *C.mossiae* (flower)
(g) *C.dowiana* (flower) (h) *C.iricolor* (i) *C.percivaliana* column and details showing structure of typical *Cattleya*
flower (i) side view of column; (ii) tip of column showing 3 lobes holding anther cap; (iii) ventral view of column
showing rostellum separating anther cap and stigmatic surface; (iv) pollinia within anther cap; (v) pollinia; (vi) pollinium

pet. somewhat smaller than sep., elliptic-oblanceolate, acute; lip to 15–22×6–10mm, ovate to elliptic-oblong, acute in outline but strongly inrolled-tubular, simple or very shallowly 3-lobed; column to 8mm, terete, slightly arcuate. Guatemala, Honduras, Mexico, El Salvador, Nicaragua. A highly variable species ranging widely in stature and flower colour: pale golden and deep fiery red forms occur and have been hybridized with similarly coloured spp. within *Laelia* (e.g. *Ll. harpophylla, milleri, flava, cinnabarina*). *C.aurantiaca* may bear cleistogamous fls which fail to open fully and being narrow, acute and nodding, give the infl. a rather willowy mien.

C.bicolor Lindl.
Pseudobulbs 14–30cm, slender, cylindrical, grooved, bifoliate. Lvs 8–16×1.2–2.5cm, coriaceous, oblong-lanceolate, obtuse, spreading. Infl. to 20cm, 1- to several-fld; fls to 10cm diam., strongly fragrant, long-lived; sep. 28–46×8–10mm, pale green flushed yellow-brown or copper-brown, oblong to oblong-lanceolate, acute or obtuse, lateral sep. falcate; pet. 30–45×10–16mm, same colour as sep., oblong or obovate, apiculate, usually undulate; lip to 35×17mm, crimson-purple, simple, oblong-cuneate, reflexed, recurved, apex bilobed, crisped; column to 30mm, usually pink. Brazil.

C.bowringiana O'Brien.
Lithophyte. Pseudobulbs 28–45×0.8–1.25cm, densely clustered, narrowly cylindrical to compressed clavate, glaucous blue-green to ashy grey, apex 2–3-lvd, base often swollen. Lvs 8–20×3–6cm, thickly coriaceous, narrowly oblong or elliptic-oblong, obtuse, glaucous blue-green, ultimately dark green. Infl. 9–25cm, few- to many-fld, erect or nodding; fls to 7.5cm diam., rather short-lived, borne very freely; sep. to 2–5×0.5–1cm, rose to magenta with darker veins, narrowly elliptic to oblong, acute; pet. to 5×3cm, same colour as sep., ovate-oblong, obtuse, undulate; lip 2.25–4×1.75–3.5cm, pale rose-purple at base, edged dark purple or garnet, throat blotched white, ovate-oblong, acute, tubular, undulate; column to 12mm. Guatemala, Belize. Forms with fls in different shades of pink and mauve, also white, were once widespread in cultivation.

C.bulbosa Lindl. See *C.walkeriana*.
C.citrina (La Ll. & Lex.) Lindl. See *Encyclia citrina*.

C.deckeri Klotzsch (C.skinneri var. parviflora Hook.).
Pseudobulbs 12–30cm, clustered, laterally compressed, clavate, apex bifoliate. Lvs to 8–15×3–5cm, ovate-oblong. Infl. 6–15cm, few-fld; fls to 5cm diam.; sep. 1.5–2.5×0.6–1cm, pale rose-purple, elliptic-lanceolate, acute or apiculate; pet. slightly broader than sep., ovate-oblong, same colour as sep., acute, undulate; lip deep purple, to 1.75–2.5×1.25–2cm, obscurely 3-lobed, obovate-elliptic, midlobe acute; column to 1cm, apex dilated. Mexico, C America, northern S America, W Indies.

C.dolosa (Rchb. f.) Rchb. f.
Pseudobulbs 9–25×1.25–3cm, fusiform, apex bifoliate. Lvs 8–15×3.75–6.5cm, narrowly elliptic or elliptic-oblong, obtuse or rounded. Infl. to 9cm, usually shorter, 1- to few-fld; fls to 12cm diam., fragrant; sep. 3.5–5×0.75–1.5cm, light to dark rose or lavender, elliptic, slightly recurved; pet. to 4.5×3cm, same colour as sep., oblanceolate, acuminate, undulate, recurved; lip to 4×4.5cm, light rose, base and margins dark rose, transversely obovate, undulate, obscurely 3-lobed, disc yellow; column to 3cm, white tinged lilac. Brazil.

C.dowiana Batem. & Rchb. f. (C.labiata var. dowiana (Batem. & Rchb. f.) Veitch).
Pseudobulbs 12–22cm, clavate-oblong, laterally compressed, channelled, remote and stalked on rhiz., apex unifoliate. Lvs 8–25×3–7cm, coriaceous, oblong, obtuse or rounded. Infl. short, few- to several-fld; fls to 15cm diam., highly fragrant; sep. and pet. rich golden-yellow to pale bronze, pet. sometimes veined rosy purple, sep. 5.5–8.7×1.5–1.7cm, lanceolate or oblong-lanceolate, pet. 6.5–8×3.75–5cm, elliptic or elliptic-oblong, obtuse, strongly undulate-crisped; lip 8–10×

6–7cm, rich velvety crimson-purple with golden-yellow veins and 3 yellow central streaks, oblong, emarginate, obscurely 3-lobed, lateral lobes erect, partly enclosing column, midlobe broadly spreading, strongly undulate and crispate; column to 3.5cm, yellow. Costa Rica, Panama, Colombia.

C.elatior Lindl. See *C.guttata*.

C.eldorado Lind. (C.mcmorlandii Nichols.; C.virginalis Lind. & André).
Pseudobulbs 8–15×1–1.5cm, subcylindrical, compressed, apex unifoliate. Lvs 8.5–24×3–5cm, rigidly coriaceous, oblong, obtuse. Infl. short, 1- to few-fld; fls to 14cm diam.; sep. and pet. pale rose-pink, sep. 5–7×1.75–2.5cm, narrowly elliptic-oblong, acute, lateral sep. deflexed, pet. 5–6.5×3.75–4.5cm, elliptic, subacute to obtuse; lip to 7×5cm, cream-white, throat orange-yellow, margins white, obscurely 3-lobed, midlobe blotched purple in front, apex with a deep mauve spot, emarginate, spreading, erose; column to 3cm. Brazil.

C.elongata Barb. Rodr. (C.alexandrae Lind. & Rolfe).
Pseudobulbs 30–70×1.75–3cm, narrowly cylindrical, bifoliate. Lvs to 8.5–20×6–10cm, narrowly elliptic. Infl. 20–60cm, 2- to several-fld; fls to 8cm diam., slightly fragrant, variable in colour; sep. and pet. copper-brown to purple-brown, sometimes spotted deep purple-brown, sep. 4–6×1.25–2cm, narrowly oblanceolate to linear-oblong, obtuse, reflexed, undulate, pet. similar to sep.; lip to 5×5cm, light to dark magenta or lavender, 3-lobed, lateral lobes acuminate, recurved, midlobe edged pale lavender, clawed, broadly reniform, retuse or emarginate. Brazil.

C.flavida Klotzsch. See *C.luteola*.

C.forbesii Lindl. (C.vestalis Hoffsgg.).
Pseudobulbs 8–25cm, usually diminutive and tufted, compressed narrow-oblong to subcylindrical, grooved with age, bifoliate. Lvs to 15×5cm, coriaceous, oblong or narrowly elliptic, obtuse to rounded. Infl. 4.5–12cm, erect, 1- to few-fld; fls to 11cm diam., waxy, strongly fragrant, long-lived; sep. and pet. 2.7–5×1–1.25cm, olive-green, pale bronze or buff, often tinged purple-brown, similar, oblong-ligulate to linear-lanceolate, subacute, spreading (lateral sep. and pet. falcate); lip to 4.5×3.5cm, somewhat tubular, throat yellow-ochre faintly veined red, lateral lobes rounded, incurved, concealing column, white flushed or veined pale rose or claret, midlobe spreading, rounded, crisped-undulate, dull red or buff edged white. Brazil.

C.gaskelliana Sander.
Pseudobulbs 10–20×1.75–2cm, clavate, compressed, grooved, unifoliate. Lvs 12–23×5–7cm, coriaceous, oblong-elliptic to ovate-elliptic, obtuse. Infl. few-fld; fls to 15cm diam., fragrant, colour variable: sep. and pet. white to pale amethyst, sometimes deep amethyst with a white median band; sep. 6–9×1.25–2cm, oblanceolate, subacute, pet. far broader than sep., ovate to elliptic, obtuse; lip to 8×6cm, crisped, 3-lobed, lateral lobes pale purple, midlobe elliptic-oblong, rose-mauve, throat orange or yellow, with a large white spot on each side, blotched rich purple toward apex. Venezuela. var. *alba* Williams ex Warner & Williams. Fls pure white except yellow blotch extending from lip tube on to midlobe.

C.gigas Lind. & André. See *C.warscewiczii*.

C.granulosa Lindl.
Pseudobulbs 26–50×1.25–2cm, cylindrical, laterally compressed, bifoliate. Lvs to 15–24×5.5–7.5cm, coriaceous, oblong-lanceolate, obtuse. Infl. short, few- to several-fld; fls to 15cm diam., strongly fragrant, long-lived; sep. and pet. green to olive-green, spotted maroon-brown, sep. 5.75–8.5×1.75–2.5cm, usually undulate, acute or obtuse, dorsal sep. elliptic-oblong, lateral sep. falcate, elliptic-lanceolate; pet. slightly shorter but broader than sep., obovate-oblong, obtuse or rounded, undulate, lip yellow-orange spotted orange to crimson, sides and apex white, deeply 3-lobed, lateral lobes triangular-ovate, acute or

obtuse, midlobe clawed, flabellate, crisped-undulate, disc granular-papillose; column to 3cm, clavate. Brazil, Guatemala. var. *buyssoniana* O'Brien. Sep. and pet. pure white, lip rose-pink.

C.granulosa f. *schofieldiana* (Rchb. f.) A.D. Hawkes. See *C.schofieldiana*.

C.guttata Lindl. (*C.elatior* Lindl.).
Pseudobulbs 50–75cm, narrowly elongate-cylindrical, bifoliate. Lvs 10–22cm, tough, coriaceous, broadly lanceolate or elliptic-oblong, obtuse, bright to mid-green, sometimes faintly conduplicate. Infl. to 25cm, several- to many-fld; fls to 10cm diam., usually less, fragrant, waxy; sep. and pet. yellow-green to olive or lime green, spotted to irregularly banded deep purple, maroon or chestnut, sep. 2.5–3.8×0.5–1cm, oblong to oblong-lanceolate, obtuse, lateral sep. falcate, outspread-ascending, pet. to 2.5–3.5×0.8–1.3cm, oblong to oblong-elliptic, obtuse, undulate; lip to 2.8×2.4cm, 3-lobed, lateral lobes white or rose, acute, erect, midlobe rose-purple or bright magenta, obcordate, often undulate, papillose; column triquetrous. Brazil.

C.guttata var. *leopoldii* (Versch. ex Lem.) Rolfe. See *C.leopoldii*.
C.guttata f. *prinzii* (Rchb. f.) A.D. Hawkes. See *C.amethystoglossa*.

C.harrisoniana Batem. ex Lindl. (*C.loddigesii* var. *harrisoniana* (Batem. ex Lindl.) Veitch).
Pseudobulbs 12–30×1.25–1.5cm, subclavate, laterally compressed, distal portion slightly inflated, apex bifoliate. Lvs 7.5–10×3–5cm, narrowly elliptic to obovate. Infl. to 10cm, few-fld; fls unscented; sep. and pet. dark rose to lavender, sep. 4–6.5×1–1.5cm, narrowly lanceolate, acuminate, lateral sep. falcate, pet. slightly shorter and broader than sep., narrowly lanceolate to oblong, undulate; lip pale lavender with darker lavender margins, 3-lobed, midlobe subquadrate, margins crisped and reflexed, disc deep yellow or orange-yellow, carinate, column to 3cm, slightly incurved. Brazil. Differs from the very closely related *C.loddigesii* in its unscented darker fls. var. *alba* Berr. Fls pure white; lip with a yellow, basal blotch.

C.intermedia Graham ex Hook. (*C.amethystina* Morr.; *C.amabilis* hort.).
Pseudobulbs 25–40×1–1.5cm, cylindric, bifoliate. Lvs to 8–15×4.5–7cm, fleshy, spreading, ovate-oblong, obtuse. Infl. to 25cm, few- to several-fld; fls to 12.5cm diam., strongly fragrant, long-lived; sep. and pet. white to pale purple, sometimes spotted purple, sep. 4–6.5×1–1.5cm, reflexed, oblong to oblong-lanceolate, acute or obtuse, lateral sep. falcate, pet. 3.75–5.5×1–1.5cm, oblong to narrowly lanceolate, acute, undulate; lip to 5×4cm, ovate-oblong, 3-lobed, lateral lobes white to pale purple, oblong, rounded, midlobe rich purple, orbicular, crisped-undulate; column to 2.5cm, pale purple, clavate. Brazil, Paraguay, Uruguay. var. *punctatissima* Sander. Closely resembles *C.intermedia* except sep. and pet. finely spotted red.

C.iricolor Rchb. f.
Pseudobulbs 8–12.5cm, clavate, compressed, unifoliate. Lvs 7–30cm, ligulate, emarginate. Infl. to 10cm, few-fld; fls to 7.5cm diam.; sep. and pet. white to cream-white, sep. 3.5–5×0.75–1cm, narrowly elliptic-lanceolate, acute, lateral sep. subfalcate, deflexed, pet. to 3–4×0.75–1cm, subsimilar to sep.; lip to 3.5×3cm, white, central portion orange, striped and suffused purple, obscurely 3-lobed, midlobe acute, reflexed; column to 8cm, white, clavate. Ecuador.

C.jenmanii Rolfe.
Pseudobulbs to 10–18×2.5–4cm, clavate, clustered, compressed, unifoliate. Lvs to 9–20×4.5–7cm, elliptic-oblong, coriaceous, acute. Infl. short, few-fld; sep. and pet. lavender, sep. 5.5–8×1.5–2cm, oblong-lanceolate, pet. twice as broad as sep., ovate; lip to 8×5.5cm, throat yellow to orange or maroon-orange, grading laterally into white or pale lavender,

margins lavender, apex lavender veined and flushed purple; column to 3cm, white. Brazil.

C.labiata Lindl. (*C.lemoiniana* Lindl.).
Pseudobulbs 9–30cm, clavate-oblong, slightly laterally compressed, stalked, grooved with age, unifoliate. Lvs 8–30×3.5–8cm, coriaceous, oblong, obtuse, semi-erect. Infl. short, few-fld; fls to 17cm diam., exceptionally showy, of sparkling texture and a rather loose ruffled and extravagant disposition, sep. and pet. white-rose to bright rose or mauve, sep. 6–8×1.5–2cm, narrowly oblong to lanceolate, acute to obtuse, apex recurved, pet. to 7.5×5.5cm, ovate or elliptic, obtuse, spreading and reflexed toward apex, strongly crisped-undulate; lip very large, ovate-oblong, obscurely 3-lobed, lateral lobes rose, incurved, midlobe deep purple-magenta, margins rose-lilac, with a pale yellow blotch lined red-purple, spreading, deeply emarginate, crisped-undulate; column clavate. Brazil. var. *alba* Lind. & Rodigas. Sep. and pet. pure white; lip pure white, throat sometimes yellow. var. *coerulea* hort. Fls deep lilac to icy opaline blue. cf. *C.mossiae* var. *caerulea*.

C.labiata var. *dowiana* (Batem. & Rchb. f.) Veitch. See *C.dowiana*.
C.labiata var. *lueddemanniana* (Rchb. f.) Rchb. f. See *C.lueddemanniana*.
C.labiata var. *mendelii* (hort.) Rchb. f. See *C.mendelii*.
C.labiata var. *mossiae* (Hook.) Lindl. See *C.mossiae*.
C.labiata var. *percivaliana* Rchb. f. See *C.percivaliana*.
C.labiata var. *warneri* (T. Moore) Veitch. See *C.warneri*.
C.labiata var. *warscewiczii* (Rchb. f.) Rchb. f. See *C.warscewiczii*.

C.lawrenceana Rchb. f.
Pseudobulbs 15–25×1.5–2.5cm, fusiform-subclavate, slightly compressed, often purple-green or red-brown, unifoliate. Lvs 10–25×3.75–6cm, rigidly coriaceous, oblong to oblong-ligulate, obtuse, green, sometimes spotted purple. Infl. to 15cm, usually erect, few- to several-fld; fls to 12.5cm diam.; sep. 4–7×1.5–2cm, white-rose to rose-purple, oblong to narrowly elliptic, acute to obtuse, lateral sep. subfalcate, pet. 4–7×3–4.5cm, same colour as sep., oblong to elliptic or subrhombic, obtuse, undulate; lip to 6×4cm, light rose-purple, white at centre veined purple, apex dark violet, simple, oblong to elliptic, deeply bilobed, revolute; column to 20mm, white. Venezuela, Guyana, N Brazil.

C.lemoiniana Lindl. See *C.labiata*.

C.leopoldii Versch. ex Lem. (*C.guttata* var. *leopoldii* (Versch. ex Lem.) Rolfe). Pseudobulbs 18–30cm, subcylindrical, bifoliate. Lvs 10–12.5×4–5.5cm, coriaceous, oblong-elliptic, obtuse. Infl. to 30cm, few-fld; fls to 11cm diam.; sep. 4–6.5×1.5–2cm, pale rose-lilac, oblong-elliptic, obtuse, lateral sep. falcate, deflexed; pet. to 6×2.5cm, similar in shape and colour to sep., undulate; lip light rose-lilac at base, suborbicular, lateral lobes oblong, dentate in front, midlobe pale amethyst, spreading, crisped, disc white grading to yellow below; column to 3cm, white, clavate. S Brazil.

C.loddigesii Lindl.
Pseudobulbs 18–30cm, slender-cylindrical to narrowly clavate, somewhat compressed, bifoliate. Lvs 8–12.5×3.75–5.5cm, coriaceous, oblong-elliptic to broadly obovate, obtuse. Infl. to 30cm, few-fld; fls to 11cm diam., fragrant, long-lived, waxy; sep. 4–6.5×2–3cm, white tinted pink to pale, sparkling rose-lilac, oblong to oblong-elliptic, obtuse, lateral sep. subfalcate; pet. broader than sep., same colour, obliquely oblong to oblong-elliptic, obtuse, undulate; lip suborbicular, lateral lobes shallow, erect, white to pale rose-lilac, oblong, midlobe pale to rich lilac-rose, subquadrate, the margin recurved, ivory, crisped, like the lip of a shell; column to 3cm, clavate. Brazil, Paraguay. cf. *C.harrisoniana*, from which this sp. differs in its paler, scented fls.

C.loddigesii var. *harrisoniana* (Batem. ex Lindl.) Veitch. See *C.harrisoniana*.

Cattleya (a) *C.loddigesii* (b) *C.bowringiana* (c) *C.aurantiaca* (d) *C.forbesii* (e) *C.aclandiae* (f) *C.skinneri* (flower)

C.lueddemanniana Rchb. f. (*C.labiata* var. *lueddemanniana* (Rchb. f.) Rchb. f.).
Pseudobulbs 18–25cm, cylindrical, compressed, unifoliate. Lvs 12–20×4–5.5cm, coriaceous, erect, oblong, obtuse, often grey-green. Infl. few-fld; fls to 21cm diam., strongly fragrant; sep. narrowly oblong, acute or obtuse, undulate, light to dark lavender, suffused white, dorsal sep. 6–10×2–3cm, laterals to 9×3cm; pet. to 9.5×8cm, of same colour as sep., elliptic, undulate; lip to 9.5×5.5cm, lavender, subrectangular, midlobe suborbicular, crisped, emarginate, with 2 semicircular, pale yellow blotches near margins, irregularly spotted dark lavender; column lavender. Venezuela. var. *alba* hort. ex Godef.-Leb. Sep. and pet. pure white; lip pure white with yellow throat.

C.luteola Lindl. (*C.flavida* Klotzsch).
Pseudobulbs 9–15cm, ovoid to clavate-cylindrical, slightly compressed, grooved with age, unifoliate. Lvs 12–20×3–4cm, elliptic-oblong, obtuse or emarginate, coriaceous. Infl. shorter than lvs, few- to several-fld; fls to 5cm diam., spreading, waxy, long-lived; sep. to 4.5cm, yellow to yellow-green, oblong or narrowly elliptic-oblong, acute, apices often recurved; pet. slightly falcate, otherwise as for sep.; lip to 2.8cm, yellow or yellow-green, often spotted or streaked crimson, obscurely 3-lobed, suborbicular, midlobe crenulate, disc densely pubesc. toward tip; column to 14mm. Brazil, Peru, Ecuador, Bolivia.

C.maxima Lindl.
Pseudobulbs 18–35cm, subcylindrical, clavate toward apex, slightly compressed, grooved with age, unifoliate. Lvs 15–25×5–7.5cm, fleshy-coriaceous, oblong or ligulate-oblong, obtuse or rounded. Infl. to 20cm, erect or arching, few- to many-fld; fls to 12.5cm diam., fragrant, long-lived, spreading; sep. 6–8.5cm, pale lustrous rose to lilac, narrowly elliptic-lanceolate, acute or acuminate; pet. of same colour, wider than sep., ovate-oblong or elliptic-oblong, acute, undulate; lip to 7×4cm, pale pink veined purple, banded yellow across centre, ovate-subquadrate, lateral lobes shallow, angular, midlobe rounded, spreading, undulate; column to 2.5cm, white. Ecuador, Colombia, Peru. var. *alba* Veitch. Sep. and pet. pure white; lip white veined purple.

C.mcmorlandii Nichols. See *C.eldorado*.

C.mendelii hort. (*C.labiata* var. *mendelii* (hort.) Rchb. f.).
Pseudobulbs 12–18×1.5–2cm, cylindrical, grooved, unifoliate. Lvs 15–23×4–6cm, strongly coriaceous, oblong, rounded. Infl. few-fld; fls to 17cm diam., fragrant, long-lived; sep. to 9.5×2.5cm, white, often tinged rose, narrowly elliptic-lanceolate, acute; pet. to 9×6cm, of same colour as sep., ovate to elliptic, subacute to obtuse, minutely denticulate, undulate; lip to 8.5×5cm, oblong, obscurely 3-lobed, lateral lobes white to lilac, midlobe rich purple-crimson, spreading, suborbicular, crisped, distinctly separated from disc, disc bright to dull yellow, often streaked purple; column to 3.5cm, clavate. Colombia.

C.mossiae Hook. (*C.labiata* var. *mossiae* (Hook.) Lindl.).
Pseudobulbs 10–25cm, fusiform, unifoliate, grooved with age. Lvs 12–28×4–4.5cm, oblong to ovate-oblong, rounded, erect or semi-erect, faintly conduplicate toward base. Infl. to 30cm, few-fld; fls to 20cm diam., very showy, fragrant, long-lived, variable in colour; sep. to 8.5×1.5cm, white to rose pink, pale magenta or lilac, narrowly lanceolate, acute; pet. to 8.5×5cm, of same colour as sep., ovate-elliptic, obtuse, strongly undulate, broadly spreading, appearing rather lacy and flaccid, erose; lip to 7×4.5cm, white to rose-lilac, throat with a central yellow-orange band lined deep purple to magenta, apex rich purple, lateral lobes erect, midlobe spreading, rounded, undulate-crisped; column to 3.5cm, clavate. Venezuela. var. *coerulea* hort. Fls a cool orchid 'blue', i.e. deep lilac to washed-out indigo. var. *wageneri* O'Brien. Sep. and pet. pure white; lip similar colour as *C.mossiae*.

C.nobilior Rchb. f.
Pseudobulbs to 7×3cm, ellipsoid, bifoliate. Lvs to 6×4cm, elliptic to elliptic-oblong, usually coriaceous. Infl. to 8cm,

slender, 1- to few-fld; fls to 12cm diam., slightly fragrant; sep. 5.5–7.5×2–2.5cm, rose-lavender, reflexed; pet. of same colour, far wider than sep., broadly elliptic, undulate; lip to 7×6.5cm, rose-lavender, darker toward apex, pandurate, midlobe with a yellow-cream spot, reflexed, undulate; column to 3cm, white tinged pink-lavender. Brazil.

C.percivaliana (Rchb. f.) O'Brien (*C.labiata* var. *percivaliana* Rchb. f.).
Pseudobulbs 8–15×1.5–2cm, subcylindrical, compressed, unifoliate. Lvs to 8–25×3–5cm, rigid, elliptic-oblong, obtuse. Infl. to 25cm, few-fld; fls to 12.5cm diam., with a musty fragrance, short-lived; sep. 4.5–7.5×1.5–2.5cm, lilac-rose, often tinged purple, elliptic or elliptic-oblanceolate, acute, lateral sep. decurved; pet. 4.5–7.5×3.5–6cm, of same colour as sep., ovate to subrhombic, obtuse, undulate, erose; lip maroon veined yellow at base, centre golden-yellow veined maroon, apex deep magenta, broadly elliptic to oblong, truncate. Venezuela. var. *alba* Sander. Sep. and pet. pure white; lip pure white with yellow throat.

C.porphyroglossa Lind. & Rchb. f.
Pseudobulbs to 12–25×1–1.5cm, cylindrical, laterally compressed, bifoliate. Lvs to 10–15×4–5cm, elliptic, coriaceous. Infl. to 10cm, several-fld; fls to 7.5cm diam., strongly fragrant, long-lived; sep. 3.75–5×1–1.5cm, yellow-brown to green, sometimes suffused faint red; oblong-elliptic to elliptic-lanceolate; pet. 3.5–4.5×1.5–2cm, same colour as sep., spathulate to oblanceolate, rounded, undulate; lip to 3.5×3cm, cream-white suffused magenta, veined purple, distinctly 3-lobed, lateral lobes triangular, midlobe short-unguiculate, dentate, disc yellow; column to 1.5cm. Brazil.

C.rex O'Brien.
Pseudobulbs 20–35cm, clavate-cylindrical, slightly compressed, unifoliate. Lvs 20–35×4–6cm, coriaceous, oblong or elliptic-oblong, obtuse. Infl. to 20cm, loosely few- to several-fld; sep. 6–8cm, white or cream-white, usually flushed yellow, narrowly elliptic-lanceolate, subacute; pet. 3 times wider than sep., same colour, elliptic-rhomboid, obtuse, undulate; lip to 8×5cm, deep yellow, throat often marked red-rose or red-brown, obovate to ovate-oblong, entire or obscurely 3-lobed above, undulate-crisped; column to 35mm, clavate. Peru, Colombia.

C.schilleriana Rchb. f.
Pseudobulbs 8–15cm, subcylindrical to clavate, grooved, often tinged red-purple, bifoliate. Lvs 10–15cm, broadly elliptic to elliptic-oblong, dark green above, tinged red-purple below, obtuse, coriaceous, spreading. Infl. 1- or 2-fld; fls waxy, fragrant, long-lived; sep. 4.5–6×1.5–2cm, brown or dark olive-brown to dark green, densely spotted or broken-banded dark maroon; lanceolate-oblong, obtuse, slightly undulate, lateral sep. subfalcate; pet. 4.5–5.5×1.5–2.25cm, same colour as sep., ligulate, obtuse, undulate; lip to 5.5×4cm, white with purple venation or light red-purple with deep magenta venation, central portion yellow, 3-lobed, lateral lobes subacute, apex recurved, midlobe flabellate, fimbriate; column to 3cm, white marked and spotted purple, clavate. Brazil.

C.schofieldiana Rchb. f. (*C.granulosa* f. *schofieldiana* (Rchb. f.) A.D. Hawkes).
Closely resembles *C.granulosa* except pseudobulbs larger. Fls larger; sep. and pet. tawny yellow suffused purple and green, densely spotted purple-crimson, lateral sep. abruptly incurved, pet. broad, rounded markedly narrowing toward base; lip large, lateral lobes white tinged rose, midlobe magenta, with hair-like excrescences. Brazil.

C.schroederae hort.
Closely resembles *C.trianaei* except fls larger, strongly fragrant, white to rose-pink or light purple, pet. strongly crisped, broader, lip with larger midlobe, strongly crisped, disc large, orange. Colombia. var. *alba* Sander. Sep. and pet. pure white; lip pure white, throat yellow.

C.skinneri Batem.
Pseudobulbs 15–35×2–3cm, clavate, slightly compressed,

Cattleya (a) *C.granulosa* (b) *C.amethystoglossa* (c) *C.guttata* (d) *C.bicolor*, lip (e) *C.leopoldii* (f) *C.elongata* (g) *C.porphyroglossa* (h) *C.schilleriana*

bifoliate. Lvs to 12–20×4–6cm, coriaceous, oblong or elliptic-oblong, obtuse. Infl. to 13cm, usually erect, few- to many-fld; fls slightly fragrant; sep. 4.75–6.5×1.5–2cm, rose to bright purple, elliptic-lanceolate or linear-lanceolate, acute or obtuse; pet. to 6.7×3.5cm, same colour as sep., broadly ovate, rounded to apiculate, undulate; lip to 5×3.5cm, throat often white or cream, entire to obscurely 3-lobed, elliptic-oblong, with a small, transverse keel along centre, obtuse or emarginate; column to 1.2cm, clinandrium slightly tridentate. Guatemala, Honduras, Mexico, Costa Rica, Venezuela, Belize.

C.skinneri var. *parviflora* Hook. See *C.deckeri.*
C.superba Schomb. ex Lindl. See *C.violacea.*

C.trianaei Lind. & Rchb. f.
Pseudobulbs 18–30×1.25–2cm, grooved with age, clavate, unifoliate. Lvs 15–28×5–7cm, oblong to elliptic-oblong, apex rounded. Infl. to 30cm, few-fld; fls variable in size and colour; sep. and pet. pure white or rose-white to bronze suffused red or deep purple, sep. 6–8.5×1.5–2cm, oblanceolate, subacute, pet. 6–8.5×4–6cm, ovate-elliptic, obtuse, usually crisped; lip to 8×6cm, ovate-oblong to elliptic, obscurely 3-lobed, lateral lobes similar colour as sep. and pet., midlobe usually rich magenta-crimson, sometimes paler or flecked crimson to magenta, disc usually yellow-orange, sometimes streaked pale purple or white; column to 3.5cm. Colombia.

C.velutina Rchb. f.
Resembles *C.bicolor* and *C.aclandiae* except fls larger; sep. and pet. light orange or yellow-orange, spotted deep purple or brown-purple, oblong, crisped; lip white streaked magenta towards centre, lateral lobes suborbicular, midlobe broadly cordate, disc golden-yellow. Brazil.

C.vestalis Hoffsgg. See *C.forbesii.*

C.violacea (HBK) Rolfe (*C.superba* Schomb. ex Lindl.).
Pseudobulbs 15–30×1.5–2cm, clavate to cylindrical, slightly compressed, grooved with age, often flushed red, bifoliate, sheaths green or violet-green. Lvs 12–16.5×6–8.5cm, coriaceous, elliptic to ovate-suborbicular, obtuse to rounded, recurved, green flushed violet or red-violet. Infl. to 30cm, erect or suberect, few- to several-fld; peduncle terete, usually flushed red; fls to 12.5cm diam., strongly fragrant, long-lived; sep. and pet. rose-purple, sometimes suffused white, dorsal sep. 5.5–7×1cm, narrowly linear-lanceolate, acute, lateral sep. slightly broader, pet. 5–6.5×2–3.5cm, lanceolate-subrhombic, obtuse, slightly undulate; lip to 5.5×5cm, deep violet, marked yellow, basally white, deeply 3-lobed, lateral lobes subovate or triangular, erect, acute to obtuse, midlobe transversely elliptic-oblong, truncate or emarginate, erose; column to 3cm, subclavate, slightly arcuate. Venezuela, Guyana, Brazil, Colombia, Peru. var. *alba* (Rolfe) Fowlie. Fls pure white or faint rose-purple. var. *splendens* (Lem.) Fowlie. Fls larger than species type, darker-coloured.

C.virginalis Lind. & André. See *C.eldorado.*

C.walkeriana Gardn. (*C.bulbosa* Lindl.).
Habit small, tufted. Pseudobulbs 5.5–8×1.25–2cm, fusiform, unifoliate or bifoliate. Lvs 5–10×2–5cm, coriaceous, ovate or elliptic-oblong, rounded. Infl. to 20cm, 1- to few-fld; fls fragrant; sep. 3–5×0.75–1cm, pale pink-lilac to bright rose-purple, lanceolate or oblong-lanceolate, acute; pet. at least twice width of sep., same colour as sep., ovate or elliptic, acute to obtuse, undulate; lip to 4×3cm, pandurate, obscurely 3-lobed, lateral lobes rounded, midlobe often bright magenta-purple, spreading, reniform to suborbicular, emarginate, margin deflexed, disc white or pale yellow streaked purple; column to 2.5cm, clavate. Brazil.

C.warneri T. Moore (*C.labiata* var. *warneri* (T. Moore) Veitch).
Closely resembles *C.labiata* except fls larger, to 20cm diam., strongly fragrant, sep. and pet. pale rose tinged dark

amethyst-rose, lip densely veined purple, margins pale amethyst-rose, disc tawny yellow or orange-yellow, streaked pale lilac or white. Brazil.

C.warscewiczii Rchb. f. (*C.labiata* var. *warscewiczii* (Rchb. f.) Rchb. f.; *C.gigas* Lind. & André).
Pseudobulbs 6–10×1.5–2cm, grooved with age, subcylindrical, unifoliate. Lvs 8–20×2–5cm, coriaceous, oblong, rounded. Infl. to 45cm, few- to several-fld; fls fragrant; sep. and pet. rose, sep. 6.5–10×1.75–2.5cm, narrowly oblanceolate, acute, lateral sep. falcate, pet. 8–9.5×3.75–5cm, ovate-elliptic, obtuse, undulate; lip to 8×5.5cm, carmine, throat blotched yellow, oblong-pandurate, entire to obscurely 3-lobed, midlobe undulate-crisped, reflexed, disc golden-yellow, often lined red-purple; column to 3cm, clavate. Colombia.

C.grexes and cultivars (see also under × *Brassocattleya*, × *Brassolaeliocattleya*, × *Laeliocattleya*, × *Sophrolaeliocattleya* and × *Potinara*, intergeneric hybrids involving *Cattleya* parentage).
C.Angel Bells 'Suzie': beautiful white fls of fine shape and waxy texture.
C.Angelwalker: small plants with pure white, flat fls of great charm; many named and awarded clones.
C.Ariel 'Coerulea': large clusters of fls, lilac-blue with darker colour bordering the lip.
C.Bob Betts 'White Wings': one of the most outstanding white cattleyas, spring flowering, 2–3 large fls of good shape and substance per spike. Many other named clones.
C.Bow Bells 'Purity': fine white with 2–4 fls per spike usually in the autumn.
C.Brabantiae: small plants with flat fls, sep. and pet. pale pink-lilac with many magenta freckles.
C.Chocolate Drop: tall plants with large clusters of small orange red, shiny fls with darker lip.
C.Claesiana: clusters of medium-sized white fls of good substance.
C.Eileen Wilson 'George Kennedy': excellent white-fld cattleya of fine form, pale yellow in the lip, June-flowering.
C.Enid Alba: very large fls with pure white sep. and pet. and deep lavender purple lip with yellow veining in the throat. Many named clones.
C.Guatemalensis: natural hybrid, clusters of small salmon pink fls in spring.
C.Hawaiian Variable: delightful clusters of medium sized fls, sep. pale green with pure white pale. and lip.
C.Henrietta Japhet: robust plants with clusters of medium-sized white fls, easy.
C.Irene Holgium 'Brown Eyes': large rosy lilac fls, lip orange at base and deep magenta, 2–6 fls per spike.
C.Joyce Hannington 'Perfection': a near-perfect white cattleya, large, well-balanced fls with yellow throat.
C.Louise Georgiana: prolific, pure white fls of medium size, flowering twice a year.
C.Mary Ann Barnett 'Exquisita': large and beautiful, white with yellow throat.
C.Nigritian 'King of Kings': most famous of dark lavender cattleyas, clusters of many fls.
C.Orglade's Classic 'Orchidglade': white fls of medium size and excellent shape, several per spike.
C.Portia 'Cannizaroo': one of the largest of the cluster-type cattleyas with huge clusters of lavender fls.
C.Portia Coerulea: one of the best of the 'blue' cattleyas, large clusters of fls in the autumn and early winter.
C.Summer Stars 'Purette': large clusters of pure white fls of medium size and starry shape, easy to grow and flower.
C.Wolteriana: medium-sized fls of bright orange.

Cattleyopsis Lindl. (From Gk *opsis*, appearance, the flowers of this genus resemble those of *Cattleya*.) 3 species of small epiphytes or lithophytes allied to *Broughtonia* and *Laeliopsis*. Pseudobulbs globose to elongate-ovoid, borne on creeping rhizomes. Leaves paired, apical, rigid, leathery, dark green, margins scabrous to serrulate. Inflorescence an apical raceme or panicle of small, vivid pink flowers. Winter. Bahamas, Cuba.

CULTIVATION   As for the smaller *Laelia* spp.

C.lindenii (Lindl.) Cogn.
Pseudobulbs to 6cm, globose to broad-cylindric, dull green, ringed and sheathed. Lvs to 12cm, rigidly coriaceous, dull to glaucous green, very shallowly serrulate. Infl. to 70cm, slender, erect to arching, sometimes branching; fls to 12 in apical quarter, to 5cm diam., sep. and pet. fragile and crystalline in texture, rose, lip showy, rose to crimson or magenta, lined white with a yellow throat. Cuba.

C.ortgiesiana (Rchb. f.) Cogn.
Growth smaller than in *C.lindenii*, infl. taller, to 100cm, fls more spreading, sep. and pet. rose to rose madder or magenta, lip rounded, deep magenta lined a deeper shade again, with white or golden throat. Cuba.

× **Cattleytonia** (*Cattleya* × *Broughtonia*). Compact plants made by crossing the bright rose pink *Broughtonia sanguinea* with a variety of *Cattleya* species, mainly those of the bifoliate section. The resulting grexes are very colourful, the flowers in clusters on long inflorescences, and mostly have excellent shape.

× *C.*Brandi: short, compact plants; clusters of burgundy red fls on tall infl.

× *C.*Hunabu Fairly Flare: compact plants with short pseudobulbs and leaves; fls in clusters on long infl., small but of excellent shape, bright magenta purple.

× *C.*Jamaica Red: compact plants; clusters of deep rosy-magenta fls on tall infl.; several awarded clones.

× *C.*Keith Roth: one of the first of this cross and an excellent parent; fls rosy pink with a brighter lip.

× *C.*Maui Maid 'Lemon Whip': compact plants with long infl.; fls with lemon yellow sep. and pet. and a large white lip.

× *C.*Rosy Jewel: small plants with short pseudobulbs and compact growth; clusters of fls on long infl., brilliant rosy mauve with dark magenta lip; many awarded clones.

× *C.*Why Not: compact plants with tall infl.; fls small, orange red with bright yellow throat; very attractive and many awarded clones. 'Upstart' is one of the best.

Caularthron Raf. (From Gk *kaulos*, stem, and *arthron*, joint.) 2 species of epiphytes allied to *Laelia*. Rhizomes short, sheathed with papery bracts. Pseudobulbs to 25cm, fusiform, elongate-ovoid or cylindric, glossy red-green, covered in bleached, papery bracts, bases hollow and colonized by ants. Leaves to 4, lanceolate to ligulate, to 20×3.5cm, sessile, apical, glossy green, glabrous, semi-rigid, fleshy, midrib sunken above, keeled beneath. Inflorescence to 30cm, terminal, a slender, erect raceme with small bracts; pedicels, twisted, slender; flowers numerous, resembling *Epidendrum* or *Laelia* spp., showy, white flushed rose-pink; sepals and petals free, obovate-elliptic, acuminate, spreading; lip trilobed, midlobe triangular to lanceolate, disc with 2 erect calli, lateral lobes erect with tooth like projections. Winter–spring. C & S America, W Indies.

CULTIVATION   As for the unifoliate *Cattleya* spp., with maximum sun exposure but no prolonged dry rest.

C.bicornutum (Hook.) Raf. (*Epidendrum bicornutum* Hook.; *Diacrium bicornutum* Benth. (Hook.); *Diacrium amazonicum* Schltr.).
Fls white, flushed or delicately veined pink beneath; dorsal sep. to 30×15mm, lateral sep. to 30×13mm; pet. to 28×21mm; lip to 28×12mm, white, calli yellow to tan; column white, spotted purple beneath. Throughout genus range.

C.bilamellatum (Rchb. f.) R.E. Schult. (*Epidendrum bilamellatum* Rchb. f.; *Diacrium bigibberosum* Hemsl.; *Diacrium bilamellatum* (Rchb. f.) Hemsl.; *Diacrium indivisum* Broadway; *Diacrium venezuelanum* Schltr.).

Fls white, fragrant, often cleistogamous; dorsal sep. to 22×10mm, elliptic to rhombic, somewhat fleshy, lateral sep. 22×12mm, elliptic, spreading, keeled beneath; pet. narrower and thinner than sep., midvein slightly prominent above, flushed pink beneath; lip to 20×8mm, white, calli 2, tinted yellow to lime green; column white. Guatemala to Panama, Trinidad, Venezuela, Colombia. A dwarf form occurs in Venezuela, to 20cm, with smaller, rose-pink fls which tend not to be cleistogamous.

Cephalanthera Rich. (From Gk *kephale*, head, and Lat. *anthera*, stamen, referring to the shape of the single stamen.) 12 species of herbaceous terrestrials. Rhizomes creeping; stems erect, leafy. Flowers few on lax terminal spike; sepals and petals hooded; lip constricted midway, basal portion incurved, sheathing base of column, apical portion spreading with longitudinal ridges or callus, spur reduced or absent. Late spring–early summer. Temperate Europe, Asia, N Africa.

CULTIVATION   See Introduction: Hardy Orchids.

C.damasonium (Mill.) Druce (*C.grandiflora* Gray). WHITE HELLEBORINE.
Stem erect to 60cm; basal sheaths 2–3. Lvs 4–10cm, ovate-lanceolate, narrower toward infl. Spike lax, fls to 16, off-white or cream, narrowly campanulate, scarcely opening; lip shorter than sep., golden yellow at base, apical half cordate, recurved, with to 5 golden ridges. N & C Europe, N Africa, USSR.

C.falcata (Thunb.) Bl. (*Epipactis falcata* Thunb.).
Stem 30–80cm, erect; basal sheaths acuminate. Lvs 8–15cm, alternate, broad-lanceolate. Spike 4–12-fld; fls to 1.5cm yellow; lip trilobed, central lobe cordate, lateral triangular; spur short. Japan, Korea, China.

C.floribunda Woron. See *C.kurdica.*
C.grandiflora Gray. See *C.damasonium.*

C.kurdica Bornm. (*C.floribunda* Woron.).
Stem slender, to 70cm. Lvs broad-lanceolate to elliptic, reduced toward summit of stem. Spike to 40cm; fls rose-pink; sep. to 2cm, spreading; lip divided, pale rose at base, lateral lobes broadly triangular, midlobe white, spur to 4mm. Europe, Mediterranean, Asia.

C.longifolia (L.) Fritsch. SWORD-LEAVED HELLEBORINE; WHITE LADY.
Stem to 60cm densely leafy; basal sheaths 2–4, white tipped green. Lvs dark green, linear-lanceolate, plicately ribbed. Spike to 60cm; fls white; pet. and sep. incurved; lip pubesc., golden at base, callus orange, 5–7-ridged. Europe, Mediterranean, Asia.

C.rubra (L.) Rich. RED HELLEBORINE.
Stem 10–60cm, erect, slender, pubesc.; basal sheaths brown. Lvs 3–8, lower lvs oblong-lanceolate to lanceolate, upper lvs linear-lanceolate. Spike lax; fls bright rose-pink or lilac; lip white edged pink, callus yellow, 7–9-ridged, spur reduced or absent. Europe, Mediterranean, Asia.

Ceratostylis Bl. (From Gk *keras*, horn, *stylis*, referring to the fleshy, horn-like column.) Some 60 species of epiphytes. Pseudobulbs clustered, usually small and slender, terete. Leaves 1 per pseudobulb, narrow, linear to terete. Flowers solitary, produced at the base of new growth. Asia, Polynesia.

CULTIVATION   As for *Octomeria.*

C.retisquama Rchb.f. (*C.rubra* Ames).
Habit trailing; rhiz. clothed in persistent brown sheaths; pseudobulbs small. Lvs tough, linear-falcate. Fls small, pale orange to brick red; tepals more or less equal, oblong-obovate; lip very small, beak-like. Philippines.

Chamaeangis Schltr. (From Gk *chamai*, lowly, and *angos*, vessel.) 7 species of epiphytes. Stems short or fairly long. Leaves leathery or fleshy, unequally bilobed at apex. Racemes many-flowered, erect or pendulous, flowers usually borne in opposite pairs or in whorls of 3 or 4; flowers small, green, yellow or salmon; sepals and petals free; lip entire, spurred; pollinia and stipites 2, viscidium single. Tropical Africa, Madagascar, Mascarene Is., Comoros Is.

CULTIVATION   As for *Aerides.*

C.boutonii (Rchb. f.) Garay. See *Microterangis boutonii.*
C.hariotiana (Kränzl.) Schltr. See *Microterangis hariotiana.*
C.hildebrandtii (Rchb. f.) Garay. See *Microterangis hildebrandtii.*

C.odoratissima (Rchb. f.) Schltr.
Robust; stems to 30cm, pendent. Lvs numerous, to 20×2.5cm, distichous, ligulate, often falcate, rather fleshy, unevenly and acutely bilobed at apex. Racemes arising opposite lvs, to 15cm, pendent, densely many-fld; fls 4mm diam., creamy-yellow, turning more yellow with age, scented, arranged in whorls of 4; pedicel and ovary 3mm; sep. 1.5×1.5mm, suborbicular, dorsal sep. erect, lateral sep. spreading; pet. 1×1.5mm, standing forward beside column; lip 1.5–2×1mm, oblong; spur 12mm, slender but slightly inflated at apex, parallel to rachis; column short and stout. W to E Africa, south to Malawi.

C.orientalis Summerh. See *C.sarcophylla.*

C.sarcophylla Schltr. (*C.orientalis* Summerh.).
Stem to 12cm, leafy above and with woody sheaths below. Lvs 8–25cm×7–12mm, spreading or recurved, ligulate, more or less falcate, rather fleshy, V-shaped in cross-section, unequally bilobed at apex. Racemes axillary, to 30cm, erect, spreading or pendent, densely or fairly densely many-fld; fls scented, yellow-brown, ochre or salmon, in pairs or whorls of 4; pedicel and ovary 3–5mm; sep. and pet. recurved, sep. 3–4×1.5–2.5mm, elliptic-ovate, pet. slightly shorter and narrower, triangular-ovate, acute; lip 3–3.5mm×2–3mm, broadly ovate, obtuse, rather fleshy; spur 15–20mm, slender but slightly inflated in apical half; column short and stout. Zaire, E Africa.

C.vesicata (Lindl.) Schltr.
Stems very short. Lvs 15–40×1–3cm, linear or narrowly lanceolate, falcate, fleshy, V-shaped in cross-section, unevenly and acutely bilobed at apex. Racemes to 30cm, pendent, many-fld; fls fleshy, green or yellow-green in opposite pairs or in threes; pedicel and ovary 4mm, bracts 1mm; sep. 1.5–3mm, ovate, apiculate; pet. slightly smaller; lip 1.5–3mm, oblong or lanceolate; spur 4.5–10mm, curved, slender at base and swollen to an ellipsoid sac at apex; column short and stout. W to E Africa.

Chaubardia Rchb.f. (For L.A. Chaubard (1785–1854), French botanist.) 4 species, epiphytes, allied to *Huntleya* and *Chondrorhyncha* but with small pseudobulbs present. S America.

CULTIVATION   As for *Huntleya* .

C.heteroclita (Poepp. & Endl.) Dodson & Bennett (*Huntleya heteroclita* (Poepp. & Endl.) Garay; *Maxillaria heteroclita* Poepp. & Endl.).
Pseudobulbs small, rectangular, flattened, concealed by overlapping leaf sheaths, bearing a single leaf at apex. Lvs to 44×6.5cm, lanceolate to oblanceolate, acute to acuminate, light green, spreading. Fls solitary, produced from leaf axils on ascending stalks to 15cm; tepals glossy dull yellow shaded and streaked chestnut brown, sep. to 4 x 1cm, lanceolate, acuminate, pet. to 4×0.7cm, oblong-lanceolate, acuminate; lip glossy mauve-pink, tongue-like, to 2.4×1.5cm, obscurely 3-lobed, lateral lobes erect, auriculate, midlobe recurved, ovate-rhombic, acuminate; callus prominent, white. Andes (Colombia to Peru). This species has been crossed with *Cochleanthes discolor*, the resulting × *Huntleanthes* grexes have lilac to pink lips.

C.tigrina Garay & Dunst. See *Chaubardiella tigrina.*

Chaubardiella Garay. (Gk *-iella*, resembling, from its resemblance to *Chaubardia*.) 8 species of epiphytes, allied to *Huntleya* and *Chondrorhyncha* and formerly included in *Chaubardia* but lacking pseudobulbs. S America.

CULTIVATION   As for *Huntleya* .

C.tigrina (Garay & Dunst.) Garay (*Chaubardia tigrina* Garay & Dunst.).
Growth tufted. Lvs to 20×3cm in a loose fan, pale green, soft, oblong-lanceolate to strap-shaped, keeled beneath and overlapping below. Fls to 4.5cm diam., solitary, axillary, on short stalks which lie on surface of substrate; tepals broadly lanceolate, acute, fleshy, cream to olive or buff densely and irregularly banded or spotted brown; lip to 1.5×1.2cm, fleshy, shallowly cup-like, markings as for tepals but darker; column bright cream. Surinam to Peru.

Chiloglottis R. Br. (From Gk *cheilos*, lip and *glottis*, glottis.) 15 species of tuberous terrestrials. Tubers subterranean, subglobose. Leaves basal, 2. Scape single-flowered; bract absent; dorsal sepal erect, concave, incurved, basally constricted, lateral sepals terete or narrow-linear; petals lanceolate, falcate; lip oblong-ovate or obovate, entire; calli dark, glossy, insect-like; ovary pedicellate, greatly elongating if fertilized. Australia, New Zealand.

CULTIVATION   Terrestrials for the cool or alpine house.

C.formicifera Fitzg. ANT ORCHID.
To 12cm. Lvs to 5cm, ovate-lanceolate, undulate or entire, tapering to a petiole. Fl. green, marked purple or brown; dorsal sep. 1–1.2cm, lateral sep. linear, spreading, reflexed; pet. transparent, strongly reflexed, acute; lip rhombic, apically recurved, calli numerous, variable, densely massed to form a shiny dark ant-like body, pink to black. Early–mid autumn. SE Australia.

C.gunnii Lindl.
To 4cm. Lvs to 10cm, near-prostrate, ovate to ovate-lanceolate. Fls 1, rarely 2, green, violet or maroon; dorsal sep. oblong, lateral sep. linear, projecting below lip; pet. spreading or incurved; lip ovate, purple, with a prominent slender gland near the base, calli dark red or black, some stalked. Autumn–midwinter. SE Australia, New Zealand.

C.trapeziformis Fitzg.
Lvs dark green, handsome. Fls small, green-brown; dorsal sep. erect, oblanceolate; pet. falcate, strongly reflexed; lateral sep. erect then spreading; lip trapeziform; calli massed in a bug-like body, shiny black. Australia.

C.truncata D. Jones & M. Clements.
Lvs to 6cm, narrow, elliptic, dark green above, paler beneath, undulate. Scape to 10cm, green, fleshy; fl. to 12mm diam., green; sep. erect, lateral sep. apically decurved; pet. retrorse; lip to 8mm, spathulate, erect, oblique, obtuse, calli black, glossy, almost covering lip, gland stalked, erect, notched. Summer–early autumn. C Eastern Australia.

C.valida D.Jones
Fls largest in genus (to 4cm diam.); tepals erect and incurved, red-brown to purple-green, lateral sep. narrower than pet. or dorsel sep.; lip obcordate, green, hinged and easily rocked; calli large, purple-black, stalked. New Zealand, SE Australia.

Chiloschista Lindl. (From Gk *cheilos*, lip, and *schistos*, cleft.) Some 20 species, epiphytes close to *Sarcochilus* but with leaves absent or very reduced. Asia, Australasia.

CULTIVATION   Attractive and intriguing epiphytes for the intermediate house. Unlike many other leafless species (for example *Taeniophyllum*), the flowers are quite showy and the photosynthetic roots require high light levels and favour fairly smooth surfaces. Attach to branches or slabs, position in bright light and high humidity. Syringe daily.

C.lunifera (Rchb. f.) J.J. Sm.
Racemes several, to 10cm, produced from a mass of ghostly grey roots; fls to 2cm diam., to 10 per infl., pure golden yellow or with a brown blotch on each tepal; tepals broadly ovate, more or less equal; lip pouch-like, midlobe incurved, paler than tepals, lateral lobes tinted red-brown. SE Asia. *C.parishii* differs in fls finely spotted brown.

Chondrorhyncha Lindl. (From Gk *chondros*, cartilage, and *rhynchos*, beak, referring to the beak-like rostellum.) Some 35 species of epiphytes allied to *Cochleanthes, Bollea* and *Huntleya*. Pseudobulbs absent. Leaves 2-ranked, in a loose fan, basally overlapping, strap-shaped, keeled beneath. Flowers solitary, stalked, arising from leaf axils or base of leaf fan. Summer. Mexico to Brazil.

CULTIVATION   As for *Huntleya*.

C.aromatica (Rchb. f.) P. Allen. See *Zygopetalum wendlandii*.

C.bicolor Rolfe.
Fls to 5cm diam., pure white except for chocolate spotting around disk; tepals forward-pointing, ovate-lanceolate, pet. not lacerate-fimbriate; lip with strongly incurved lateral margins and acute to acuminate apex, margin not lacerate-fimbriate.

C.chestertonii Rchb. f.
Fls to 7cm diam., fleshy, highly scented, ivory to pale green, lip often lime green to yellow; sep. and pet. lanceolate to elliptic, acute, pet. broader than sep. and deeply fringed and frilled; lip to 3.5cm, rounded, deeply fimbriate, marked redbrown; callus 3-lobed. Colombia.

C.costaricensis (Schltr.) P. Allen. See *Kersteinia costaricensis*.
C.discolor (Lindl.) P. Allen. See *Cochleanthes discolor*.
C.fimbriata (Lind. & Rchb. f.) Rchb. f. See *C.flaveola*.

C.flaveola (Lind. & Rchb. f.) Garay (*C.fimbriata* (Lind. & Rchb. f.) Rchb. f.).
Fls to 7.5cm diam.; sep. and pet. subequal, lemon yellow to golden, pet. larger, deeply fimbriate; lip lemon yellow, banded chocolate near base, deeply fringed. Venezuela, Colombia, Ecuador, Peru.

C.lactea (Rchb. f.) L.O. Williams. See *Kersteinia lactea*.

C.lendyana Rchb. f.
Fls to 5.25cm diam., lemon yellow to ivory tinted yellow; sep. and pet. narrow-elliptic to lanceolate, subequal, somewhat concave above, spreading and strongly recurved; lip rolled-tubular, apex wavy to crispate. Mexico, Guatemala, Costa Rica, Panama.

C.lipscombiae Rolfe. See *Cochleanthes marginata*.
C.lojae (Schltr.) Schweinf. See *Kersteinia lojae*.

C.rosea Lindl.
Fls to 8.5cm diam., sep. and pet. pale green fading to ivory at tips, lip tubular, entire, sap green fading to white at tip beneath, lemon yellow above, basally spotted magenta, shifting to golden yellow at median, then damask pink to white at apex, callus 3-ridged, white spotted pink. Venezuela.

× **Christieara** (*Aerides* × *Ascocentrum* × *Vanda*). Stems upright but dwarf. Leaves alternate in 2 rows, narrowly channelled. Inflorescences axillary, on upright spikes; flowers flat and well-shaped with a small lip, usually very brightly coloured, long-lasting on the plant and as cut flowers. The plants need bright light, high humidity and warm temperatures to grow and flower well. They grow extremely well out of doors in the humid tropics but are less easy in the glasshouse.

× *C.*Malibu Gold 'Richella': tall and floriferous; fls yellow with orange-red lip.

Chysis Lindl. (From Gk *kysis*, melting, a reference to the fused pollinia occurring in autogamous forms.) About 6 species of epiphytes. Rhizomes short, stout. Pseudobulbs clumped, pendent, large, clavate or fusiform, jointed, scarred and clothed with papery sheaths. Leaves apical and alternate along upper half of pseudobulbs, broad-lanceolate, arching, plicate or ribbed, thin-textured or slightly fleshy, falling after one season. Inflorescence basal or nodal in basal quarter of developing pseudobulb, arching, robust, racemose, bracteate; flowers to 10, waxy, fragrant; dorsal sepal free, elliptic, lateral sepals basally fused, held to foot of column, forming a conspicuous chin or mentum; petals resembling sepals, but smaller; lip fleshy, united to base of column, inrolled to tubular, midlobe undulate, cleft, broad, recurved or expanding, disc conspicuously 3–5-ridged, lateral lobes broad, rounded or falcate, hooding column. Summer. Mexico to Peru.

CULTIVATION   Repot as seldom as possible in baskets containing a medium suitable for *Cattleya* but with additional leafmould. Provide intermediate conditions with bright, filtered light, copious supplies of water and monthly feeding while growths are forming. On completion of pseudobulbs, reduce watering to a minimum, impose a cool regime and stop feeding. New growths and flower spikes will form simultaneously: gradually increase temperature and watering during the flowering period.

C.aurea Lindl.
Pseudobulbs to 45cm, narrow-ellipsoid, elongate, sprawling or pendulous. Lvs to 45×5.5cm, oblong-lanceolate, undulate, acuminate, soft, basally conduplicate and sheathing. Infl. to 25cm; fls to 12, to 7.25cm diam., waxy, heavily perfumed, ivory to lemon yellow, lip ivory or white, variably marked oxblood, disc with to 5 velvety, golden ridges. Throughout genus range.

C.bractescens Lindl.
Differs from *C.aurea* chiefly in having more conspicuous floral bracts, to 2.75cm, white to cream tepals and a golden, 5–7-ridged lip. Most frequently cultivated species. Mexico, Belize, Guatemala.

C.laevis Lindl. (*C.tricostata* Schltr.).
Fls to 6.75cm diam., cream or golden at base, peach or rusty orange in apical half, lip pale yellow to peach, fading at centre to ivory, spotted red, with 5–7 ridges, of which only the central 3 are especially prominent and bright white. Mexico to Costa Rica.

C.tricostata Schltr. See *C.laevis*.

Cirrhaea Lindl. (From Lat. *cirrus*, lock of hair, tendril; the rostellum is prolonged like a tendril.) 7 species of epiphytes allied to *Gongora*. Brazil.

CULTIVATION   See *Gongora*.

C.dependens (Lodd.) Rchb. f.
Rhiz. long, creeping. Pseudobulbs clustered, ovoid, to 7cm, dark green to yellow, furrowed and ridged. Lvs solitary, to 30cm, broadly lanceolate, petiolate, dark green, glabrous, thick, obscurely plicate. Infl. a basal raceme to 45cm, strongly pendulous; pedicels to 90° at axis, then abruptly decurved; fls to 25, to 5cm diam., facing outwards, not opening fully, lasting well, lightly scented, hanging upside-down; sep. and pet. subequal, oblanceolate, spreading or forward-pointing, pale green, ochre or sienna, variably mottled or banded blood-red or terracotta; lip trilobed, clawed, similar in colour to sep. or wholly maroon; column white. Summer.

C.loddigesii Lindl.
Differs from *C.dependens* in fls with spreading segments, to 6cm diam., green-white to rusty brown with darker red spotting and a chestnut-banded midlobe to lip. SE Brazil.

C.saccata Lindl.
Fls green to red-brown; differs from both the above in the lip midlobe which is broad and shell-shaped rather than flat and narrow. SE Brazil.

Cischweinfia Dressler & N. Williams. (For the American botanist Charles Schweinfurth, whose name is abbreviated C. Schweinf. in botanical citations.) 7 species of epiphytes. Pseudobulbs small, subtended and terminated by strap-shaped leaves. Inflorescence a short, few-flowered, axillary raceme; tepals more or less equal, spreading, oblong-lanceolate; lip more or less funnel-shaped, entire; column with a hood-like extension over pollinia. S America.

CULTIVATION   Intermediate conditions in dappled sunlight or light shade; high humidity and buoyant atmosphere; very open medium; water and syringe regularly throughout the year.

C.dasyandra (Rchb.f.) Dressler & N. Williams.
Fls to 1.8cm diam.; tepals lime green; lip cream mottled and stained pale purple-pink, not broadly spreading. Costa Rica to Ecuador.

C.rostrata Dressler & N. Williams.
Fls to 2.5cm diam.; tepals pale olive to buff; lip cream, margins veined purple-pink, broadly spreading. Colombia to Ecuador.

Cleisostoma Bl. (From Greek *kleistos,* closed, and *stoma,* mouth, referring to the calli which almost block the spur entrance.) Some 100 species of monopodial epiphytes. Stems erect or pendent. Leaves terete or flat. Inflorescence pendent or erect, simple or branched; flowers many, fleshy, spurred; sepals and petals subequal, spreading; lip trilobed, fused to column base by the basal margins of lateral lobes, callus conspicuous, projecting from the posterior wall of the spur or on anterior wall midlobe at base, midlobe straight, or incurved, triangular, basally barbed, spreading, lateral lobes triangular, erect, spur cylindric or conic, rarely saccate, often divided longitudinally. Nepal to New Guinea.

CULTIVATION   As for *Aerides.*

C.micranthum (Lind.) King & Pantl. See *Smitinandia micrantha.*

C.paniculatum (Ker-Gawl.) Garay (*Aerides paniculata* Ker-Gawl.).
Lvs linear, keeled, to 15cm. Scape axillary; fls to 12, white marked purple; pet. oblong, undulate; lip oblong, turgid, convex, lateral lobes lanceolate, broad, acute. India.

C.racemiferum (Lindl.) Garay (*Sarcanthus pallidus* Lindl.; *Aerides racemifera* Lindl.).
Lvs ligulate, spreading. Panicle branched, many-fld; fls to 8mm diam., violet-black, edged yellow, lip white or yellow; dorsal sep. elliptic, lateral sep. oblique, obtuse; pet. similar, smaller, rounded apically; lip midlobe fleshy, triangular, hollow callus roundly bilobed, lateral lobes triangular, oblique, acuminate, spur incurved, almost cylindric. India, Nepal, Thailand, Burma.

C.siamense Rolfe ex Downie. See *Pomatocalpa siamensis.*
C.spathulatum Bl. See *Robiquetia spathulata.*

Cleistes Rich. ex Lindl. (From Gk *kleistos,* closed, an allusion to the narrowly funnel-shaped corolla.) Some 50 species of terrestrials allied to *Pogonia.* Roots slender, fibrous. Rhizome short. Stems erect, unifoliate. Leaf inserted above middle of stem. Inflorescence a raceme, 1 to 3-flowered; flowers terminal, large, showy, subtended by a large bract; sepals similar, subequal; petals similar to sepals, usually held forward over lip; lip funnelform, simple to trilobed, disc crested; column free, subterete, anther terminal, operculate, incumbent, pollinia 2, finely granular, clinandrium denticulate. N & S America.

CULTIVATION   *C.divaricata* as for *Calypso; C.rosea* as for *Phaius.*

C.divaricata (L.) Ames (*Arethusa divaricata* L.; *Pogonia divaricata* (L.) R. Br.). SPREADING POGONIA; FUNNEL-CREST ROSEBUD ORCHID.
Stems to 75cm. Lvs to 20×2cm, oblong-elliptic to oblong-lanceolate, obtuse to acuminate, glaucous. Fls to 12.5cm diam., fragrant; floral bract to 10×1cm, lanceolate, acuminate; tepals magenta-pink to white and brown, sep. to 65×5mm, linear-lanceolate, acuminate, spreading, pet. to 45×14mm, oblanceolate-spathulate, acute, joined to lip forming a cylindrical tube; lip to 45×20mm, usually pale pink, broadly oblong, obscurely 3-lobed, lateral lobes rounded, involute, midlobe ovate-triangular, revolute, crest marked dark pink, fleshy-papillose; column to 25mm, slender. NE US.

C.rosea Lindl. (*Pogonia rosea* (Lindl.) Rchb. f.).
Stems to 1.5m. Lvs to 12×2.5cm, lanceolate, acute or obtuse. Fls to 10cm diam.; tepals rose, dorsal sep. to 65×8mm, linear-elliptic to elliptic-lanceolate, acute, lateral sep. to 65×11mm, lanceolate to linear-lanceolate, acute, pet. to 65×16mm, elliptic to ovate-elliptic, acuminate; lip to 55×30mm, dark rose, narrowly obovate to broadly oblanceolate, obtuse, with a median lamellate plate, serrulate towards apex. Panama, northern S America.

Clowesia Lindl. (For the Rev. John H. Clowes of Broughton Hall, Manchester, the first to flower the type species.) 6 species of epiphytes. Pseudobulbs fleshy, stout, clustered, ovoid to pyriform, enveloped by several leaf-sheaths when young, several-leaved. Leaves large, plicate, distichous, articulate, deciduous. Inflorescence from base of pseudobulbs, a lateral raceme, pendent, few to several-flowered; flowers bisexual (cf. *Catasetum*); dorsal sepals free, concave, lateral sepals adnate to column, erect; petals similar to lateral sepals, often fringed; lip free from column, fleshy, 3-lobed, saccate or spurred, lateral lobes erect, midlobe reflexed, apex fimbriate or denticulate; column short, with an explosive trigger mechanism that releases the viscidium, anther ventral, imperfectly bilocular, pollinia 2, waxy, sulcate. Mexico to Venezuela.

CULTIVATION   As for *Catasetum*.

C.rosea Lindl. (*Catasetum roseum* (Lindl.) Rchb. f.).
Pseudobulbs to 6×2.5cm, enveloped by grey, overlapping sheaths, 4 to 5-lvd. Lvs to 40×6cm, elliptic-lanceolate, acuminate, flexible. Infl. to 12cm, several-fld; fls to 2.5cm, campanulate, deep rose-pink to light pink; dorsal sep. to 1.7×0.8cm, elliptic, subacute, lateral sep. to 2cm, paler than dorsal sep., slightly connate; pet. to 1.8×1.3cm, elliptic-ovate, acute, erose-lacerate; lip to 2×2cm, gibbous at base, apex recurved, apiculate, obovate, ciliate-fimbriate, lateral lobes small, callus 2-ridged, apex fleshy, ciliate; column to 9mm, green marked yellow at base, apex ciliate. Early winter. Mexico.

C.russelliana (Hook.) Dodson (*Catasetum russellianum* Hook.).
Pseudobulbs to 7×3.5cm, ovoid to elliptic-conical, grey-green, 6 to 8-lvd. Lvs to 40×7cm, oblong-lanceolate to elliptic-obovate, acute or acuminate. Infl. to 35cm, many-fld; fls to 6cm diam., sweetly fragrant; sepals and petals clear-green to white-green, veined dark green; dorsal sep. to 3.5×1.2cm, elliptic-oblong, acute, apiculate, concave, incurved, lateral sep. to 4×1.4cm, obliquely oblong to elliptic-oblong, obtuse-apiculate, pet. to 4×1.8cm, elliptic to ovate-elliptic, acute or apiculate, minutely erose; lip to 4×1.6cm, base green grading to white, saccate below, lamina oblong-obovate to elliptic-obovate, apex rounded or truncate, crisped-dentate, callus central, V-shaped, dentate; column to 20mm, erect. Mexico to Panama and Venezuela.

C.thylaciochila (Lem.) Dodson (*Catasetum thylaciochilum* Lem.).
Pseudobulbs to 10×3cm, with persistent, grey sheaths, several-lvd. Lvs to 40×6cm, elliptic, acuminate, prominently veined. Infl. to 35cm, many-fld; fls yellow-green, veined brown, outspread; sep. to 3.5×0.8cm, similar, lanceolate to oblong-linear; pet. to 3.5×1.2cm, obovate or ovate; lip to 3.5cm, saccate at base, sac to 1cm, lamina to 1.8cm, ovate-triangular; callus 3-ridged, fleshy; column to 11mm, apex rounded, winged. Mexico.

C.warscewiczii (Lindl. & Paxt.) Dodson (*Catasetum warscewiczii* Lindl.).
Pseudobulbs to 9×7cm, narrowly ovoid to oblong, wrinkled with age, 4 to 6-lvd. Lvs to 40×8cm, elliptic-lanceolate or oblong-lanceolate, acute or acuminate. Infl. to 30cm, several-fld; fls showy, fragrant; tepals clear-green or green-white to white veined pale green: sep. ovate or elliptic-ovate, rounded or obtuse, dorsal sep. to 1.2×1cm, concave, lateral sep. to 1.8×1.4cm, oblique, pet. to 1.7×1.3cm, ovate to ovate-suborbicular, concave, obtuse; lip to 1.5×2.5cm, similar colour to tepals, saccate at base, 3-lobed, lateral lobes obtuse, fimbriate, midlobe reflexed, apex strongly fimbriate-lacerate; column to 7mm. Costa Rica, Panama, Colombia, Venezuela, Guyana.

Cochleanthes Raf. (From Gk *kochlos*, shell, and *anthos*, flower, a reference to the shell-like shape of the lip.) 17 species of epiphytes allied to *Chondrorhyncha* and *Huntleya*, which they closely resemble. Pseudobulbs absent. Rhizomes short, produced from basal leaf axils. Leaves gathered in a loose, 2-ranked fan, alternate, basally overlapping, linear-lanceolate, pale green, basally articulate. Flowers solitary, axillary, often pendent on long pedicels; sepals subequal, spreading to reflexed, broadly lanceolate, acuminate; petals thin, spreading, slender, erect; lip entire or obscurely trilobed, concave, often pandurate or extended and spur-like at base, lateral lobes erect, forming a tube and enclosing column if present, callus cusp-shaped, smooth or ridged. Summer. C America.

CULTIVATION   As for *Huntleya*.

C.amazonica (Rchb.f. & Warscz.) R.E. Schult. & Garay.
Fls to 8cm diam.; tepals white, lanceolate, spreading; lip large, funnel-like with 2 large, spreading, lateral lobes and midlobe cleft, thus appearing 4-lobed, margin frilled, white to pale opal, disc veined purple to blue-mauve. Amazonia.

C.discolor (Lindl.) R.E. Schult. & Garay (*Chondrorhyncha discolor* (Lindl.) P. Allen).
Lvs to 20×2.5cm. Peduncle erect, to 10cm; sep. green-white to pale olive, the lateral sep. narrowly lanceolate and strongly reflexed, the dorsal sep. broader, to 3.5×1.8cm, held forward over column with tip curled back; pet. green to ivory, veined and flushed violet above, to 3.5×2cm, held forward over lip with tips rolled back; lip to 4×4cm, funnelform, more or less entire, undulate, pale green strongly suffused deep violet or amethyst; callus pale gold; column white. Cuba, Honduras, Costa Rica, Panama, Venezuela. Has been crossed with *Huntleya* and *Chaubardia* to produce the × *Huntleanthes* grexes.

C.flabelliformis (Sw.) R.E. Schult. & Garay (*Warscewiczella flabelliformis* (Sw.) Cogn.; *Zygopetalum cochleare* Lindl.).
Lvs to 24×5cm. Sep. spreading, ivory to lime green, dorsal sep. to 2.8×1.2cm, lateral sep. slightly larger; pet. similar in colour to sep., to 2.6×0.8cm; lip to 4.5×3.5cm, usually less due to constriction of fleshy callus, broadly flabellate, white suffused rosy-mauve, veined violet, callus deltoid, near base of lip, veined violet, apex ribbed-undulate, not toothed; column white, sparsely streaked violet beneath. Throughout C America.

C.marginata (Rchb. f.) R.E. Schult. & Garay (*Warscewiczella marginata* Rchb. f.; *Chondrorhyncha lipscombiae* Rolfe).
Lvs to 30×5cm. Sep. semi-rigid, pale green ageing ivory or white, dorsal sep. to 3×1.5cm, lateral sep. to 3.5×1.8cm; pet. off-white, weaker than sep., to 3×1.5cm; lip to 4×4cm, white suffused and veined violet at centre, edged rose-purple, callus white, sometimes lightly stained mauve; column white with a violet V-shape at base. Venezuela, Colombia, Ecuador.

Cochlioda Lindl. (From Gk *kochlion*, a little snail, referring to the curiously shaped callus.) 6 species of epiphytes. Rhizomes short, slender, creeping. Pseudobulbs to 7cm, apically unifoliate, ovoid, laterally compressed, wrinkled with age. Leaves to 20cm, strap-shaped, soft, dark green. Inflorescence to 45cm, a slender, arching raceme; sepals and petals spreading, elliptic, tips obtuse, recurved; lip trilobed, lateral lobes rounded, midlobe subcordate, disc 4-ridged. Peru.

CULTIVATION   As for *Lemboglossum*.

C.Floryi (*C.noezliana* × *C.rosea*).
Compact plants with dark green lvs and pseudobulbs: small bright orange fls on long sprays.

C.noezliana (Rchb. f.) Rolfe.
Infl. to 45cm; fls to 4.5cm diam., vivid scarlet; lateral lobes of lip rounded, disc 4-ridged, pubesc. Summer–autumn.

C.rosea (Lindl.) Benth.
Resembles *C.noezliana* except in fls to 3.75cm diam., deep rose madder to crimson; lateral lobes of lip rhombic, midlobe narrow-oblong, exceeding lateral lobes, disc abruptly oblong-callused. Late spring–summer.

C.sanguinea (Rchb. f.) Benth. See *Symphyglossum sanguineum*.

C.vulcanica (Rchb. f.) Benth.
Smaller in all parts than preceding spp. Fls rose to damask pink, the lip with a faded, central region; lip midlobe cordate to ovate, disc coarsely 4-ridged, lateral lobes rounded or square. Late summer–winter.

Cochlioda   (a) *C.rosea*   (b) *C.noezliana*

Coelia Lindl. (From Gk *koilos*, hollow; the pollen masses were mistakenly thought to be concave within.) Some 5 species of epiphytes or terrestrials. Rhizomes short. Pseudobulbs clustered, glossy, olive green, ovoid to ellipsoid. Leaves to 5, carried apically, petiolate, linear-lanceolate, soft, ribbed or plicate. Inflorescence borne basally amid sheaths, a short raceme; flowers fleshy, fragrant, often not opening fully, white, cream or buff, variously marked rose or violet. Summer. Mexico, C America.

CULTIVATION   Pot tightly in an open bark, sphagnum and charcoal mix. Provide light shade in well ventilated, intermediate conditions. Water throughout the year, allowing a partial drying-out between waterings. Apply a weak foliar feed once a fortnight while new growths are forming. Avoid wetting flowers and leaf scorch.

C.baueriana Lindl. See *C.triptera*.

C.bella (Lem.) Rchb. f. (*Bothriochilus bellus* Lem.).
Pseudobulbs to 5cm, globose to squat-ovoid, terminating in a terete stem. Lvs to 50cm, usually shorter, to 4, clustered at apex, narrow-lanceolate, acuminate, plicate, glossy green. Infl. to 12cm, bracteate; fls to 6, to 5.5cm, held upright, sweetly scented, broadly tubular to campanulate, ivory tipped rose or violet, lip midlobe golden to orange. Mexico, Guatemala, Honduras.

C.densiflora Rolfe (*Bothriochilus densiflorus* (Rolfe) Ames & Correll).
Pseudobulbs to 6.25cm. Lvs broader than in *C.bella*. Infl. a packed, short raceme; fls to 1.5cm, spirally arranged, very fragrant, translucent, sparkling white. Guatemala, Honduras.

C.guatemalensis Rchb. f. (*Bothriochilus guatemalensis* (Rchb. f.) L.O. Williams).
Lvs shorter than in other spp., thick, ribbed. Infl. to 18cm, clothed in hooded, conspicuous bracts; fls to 7, to 2cm, white tipped rose, lip centrally thickened. Guatemala.

C.macrostachya Lindl. (*Bothriochilus macrostachyus* (Lindl.) L.O. Williams.
Lvs fleshy, to 80×5cm. Infl. erect, to 60cm, a cylindrical, crowded raceme; fls to 1cm, highly fragrant, white to glistening rose; lip bearing an obscurely bilobed basal sac. Throughout genus range.

C.triptera (Sm.) G. Don ex Steud. (*C.baueriana* Lindl.).
Pseudobulbs subglobose, to 5.25cm, produced as a stalk at apex. Lvs to 4, to 38×4.5cm, usually smaller, arching, narrow-lanceolate, obscurely plicate, tough. Infl. to 16cm, a lax or crowded, bracteate raceme; fls to 1.5cm, never opening fully, fragrant, crystalline white; ovary winged. Mexico, Guatemala, W Indies.

Coeliopsis Rchb. f. (From Gk *opsis*, appearance, denoting this genus's similarity to *Coelia*.) 1 species, an epiphyte. Rhizomes short, creeping. Pseudobulbs elongate-ovoid, to 10cm, olive green to yellow, often rugose. Leaves to 60×8cm, 3–4, borne near apex or sheathing bulb, plicate, prominently ribbed beneath, conduplicate and petiolate at base. Inflorescence a dense basal, capitate raceme, sharply decurved to pendulous, to 8.5cm, stout, sheathed with papery, lanceolate bracts; flowers to 15, to 2.25cm diam., seldom opening fully, waxy, fragrant; sepals equal, ovate, cream, dorsal sepal free, lateral sepals fused at base, forming a blunt 'spur'; petals concave, broadly lanceolate, ivory; lip trilobed, fleshy, white stained gold to orange at base, midlobe truncate-ovate, reflexed, fimbriate, disc not callused, lateral lobes basally fleshy, erect, margins thin, translucent, fimbriate. Summer. Costa Rica, Panama.

CULTIVATION   As for *Coelia*, but plant in baskets to allow for pendent inflorescences.

C.hyacinthosma Rchb. f.

Coeloglossum Hartm. (From Gk *koilos*, hollow, and *glossa*, tongue, describing the lip.) FROG ORCHID. 1 species, a terrestrial. Tubers 2, ovoid or lobed. Stems 6–40cm, basal sheaths brown. Leaves light green, ovate to oblong becoming lanceolate toward stem apex. Spike 2–15cm, lax, cylindric, 5–25-flowered; lower bracts twice flower length; petals and sepals sometimes forming a hood, green to yellow-green, suffused purple, with red margins; lip 6–8mm, linear-oblong, central lobe shorter than laterals, yellow or yellow-brown, spur pale green, short. Late spring–summer. Europe, Asia.

CULTIVATION   See Introduction: Hardy Orchids.

C.viride (L.) Hartm.

Coelogyne Lindl. (From Gk *koilos*, hollow, and *gyne*, woman, referring to the deep stigmatic cavity.) Some 200 species of rhizomatous epiphytes. Pseudobulbs conical, cylindric, ovoid or globose, clustered or remote. Leaves 1–2 per pseudobulb, apical, rarely basal and sheathing, elliptic to lanceolate, sometimes plicate. Inflorescence a terminal raceme, rarely lateral, erect or pendent, 1- to many-flowered; sepals free, often concave; petals free, often flanking the column; lip trilobed, disc keels often spreading to lip midlobe. Indomalaya, Tropical China, W Pacific.

CULTIVATION   A diverse genus that includes species with trusses of lacy, snow-white, fragrant blooms (*C.cristata*), sinister salmon pink solitary flowers (*C.speciosa*), chain-like racemes in shades of topaz and chocolate brown (*C.tomentosa*), erect, delicate white, spicily scented spikes (*C.nitida*) and spectacular emerald green flowers marked with blue-black (*C.pandurata*). All except *C.mayeriana*, *C.pandurata*, *C.speciosa* and *C.*Burfordiense will thrive in the cool or intermediate house in bright, well ventilated conditions. The exceptions require stove temperatures with high humidity and semi-shade. Pot in an open mix, preferably in clay pans or (for pendulous-flowered spp.) baskets. Water and syringe freely when in growth. Impose a dry rest in winter.

C.asperata Lindl.
Pseudobulbs broadly conical, slightly compressed, ribbed, to 15cm. Infl. to 30cm, arching, crowded; bracts ovate, concave; fls cream-white, fragrant, lip lateral lobes veined pale brown, keels deep brown; sep. lanceolate, acute; pet. similar, narrower, 3.5×0.5cm; lip midlobe ovate, deflexed, acute, warty, lateral lobes rounded, erect; disc 2-keeled. Malaysia to New Guinea.

C.barbata Griff.
Pseudobulbs conical to ovoid, clustered, pale green to 10×2.5cm. Lvs 2, oblong-lanceolate, coriaceous, undulate, to 40×5cm, usually smaller. Infl. erect or arched, to 45cm, to 10-fld; fls to 7cm diam., fragrant, white, disc brown; dorsal sep. carinate, lateral sep. subfalcate; pet. linear-lanceolate, acute; lip midlobe triangular, deeply fringed, lateral lobes rounded, disc 3-keeled, fringed from base to apex. India.

C.beccarii Rchb. f.
Pseudobulbs turbinate. Lvs 2, 20–30cm, lanceolate, acuminate. Fls 3, ivory, lip lateral lobes and keels cinnamon; sep. ligulate, acute; pet. linear, acute; midlobe triangular-hastate, acute, margins revolute, lateral lobes triangular; keels lamellate. New Guinea.

C.brachyptera Rchb. f. (*C.virescens* Rolfe).
Pseudobulbs elongate-ovoid, angled, 9–15cm, base sheathed. Lvs 2, elliptic-lanceolate, subacute, plicate, 13–15cm. Infl. to 18cm, to 7-fld; fls green-yellow, lip dotted sepia to black, disc orange; sep. spreading, dorsal sep. ovate-lanceolate, subacute, 3.2–3.8cm, lateral sep. oblong-lanceolate, acute; pet. similar to lateral sep.; lip to 2.5cm, midlobe orbicular, undulate, lateral lobes similar, suborbicular, disc with 3, wavy keels, apex warty. Burma.

C.brunnea Lindl. See *C.fuscescens* var. *brunnea*.

C.Burfordiense. (*C.asperata* × *C.pandurata*)
Racemes dense; fls similar to *C.pandurata*, lime green, lip marked black, fading brown.

C.corymbosa Lindl.
Pseudobulbs ovoid to subrhombic, 2.5–4cm, clustered. Lvs 2, elliptic-lanceolate, suberect, acute, 10–20×2–3.5cm. Infl. erect or pendent, to 20cm, 2–4-fld; fls to 7cm diam., white, lip with 4 yellow blotches bordered orange-red; sep. lanceolate, acute, 2.5–4×1cm; pet. lanceolate, narrow, acute; lip to 3×2cm, midlobe ovate to ovate-lanceolate, acute to acuminate, lateral lobes erose, disc ridges 3, extending to midlobe. Himalaya.

C.cristata Lindl.
Pseudobulbs remote, globose to oblong, to 7.5×4cm. Lvs 2, lanceolate, acuminate, sessile, 15–30×3cm. Infl. pendent, 3–10-fld, 15–30cm; fls to 8cm diam. white, lip white, midlobe plates 2, minutely crenate, yellow, lamellae between lateral lobes golden yellow; sep. elliptic-oblong, narrow, undulate, subacute, to 5×2cm; pet. similar, to 4.5–2cm, acute; lip to 4×3.5cm, midlobe suborbicular, lateral lobes large, rounded, disc extending to midlobe, keels fringed. E

Himalaya. var. **hololeuca** Rchb. f. Pseudobulbs more distinctly spaced than *C.cristata*. Fls pure white. India.

C.cumingii Lindl.
Rhiz. creeping. Pseudobulbs ovate, weakly angled, acuminate. Lvs 2, lanceolate, acuminate. Infl. axillary, 3–5-fld; fls white, lip white or cream stained orange; sep. ovate-lanceolate, spreading; pet. linear-lanceolate, acute or acuminate; lip oblong, broad, midlobe ovate-obovate, obtuse, undulate, crisped, minutely dentate, lateral lobes involute, disc keels 3, crisped, crested. Singapore, Malaysia.

C.dayana Rchb. f.
Pseudobulbs conical, elongate, 10–25cm. Lvs lanceolate, weakly plicate, acute, veins prominent beneath, 30–75×7–10cm. Racemes 4–100cm, 20–30-fld; fls cream to pale brown, lip brown with a white streak, lateral lobes streaked yellow; sep. lanceolate, acute, to 3.5cm; pet. shorter, narrower; lip lateral lobes rounded, crenate, broad, disc 2-ridged, becoming 3-ridged, crispate. Borneo.

C.fimbriata Lindl.
Pseudobulbs remote, ovoid to ellipsoid, 2.5×1cm. Lvs 2, oblong-elliptic, acute, to 10×1.5cm. Infl. to 5cm, 1–3-fld; fls 3–3.5cm diam., pale yellow, lip white or pale yellow, marked brown; sep. lanceolate, acute; pet. linear-filiform, subacute to acute, to 2cm; lip to 2cm, midlobe oblong to subquadrate, obtuse or retuse, lateral lobes oblong-elliptic, obtuse or acute, disc keeled, outer keels undulate, 2, flanked by 2 shorter keels at the midlobe centre. India, Vietnam to Hong Kong.

C.flaccida Lindl.
Pseudobulbs to 12×2.5cm, conical. Lvs 2, lanceolate, acuminate, to 20×3cm; petiole to 4cm. Infl. to 20cm, pendent, to 9-fld; fls to 3.5cm diam., white, lip with yellow central blotch, midlobe base spotted and lateral lobes striped yellow-red; sep. lanceolate, acute, to 2.5–0.5cm; pet. linear, reflexed, subacute; lip midlobe ovate-lanceolate, reflexed, acute, lateral lobes oblong, rounded, erect, disc keels 3, undulate from lip base to midlobe base. E Himalaya.

C.fuliginosa Hook.
Pseudobulbs remote, ellipsoid to fusiform, 5–7.5cm. Lvs 2, lanceolate, membranous to coriaceous, to 15×3cm. Infl. to 4-fld; fls buff to orange-yellow, lip stained or finely streaked chocolate to mahogany; sep. oblong-lanceolate, acute; pet. filiform; lip to 2×1cm, midlobe ovate, margin fringed, lateral lobes oblong, inner margins hirsute, fringed, base keels 3, exterior keels flanked by shorter keels at midlobe. Burma, Java.

C.fuscescens Lindl.
Pseudobulbs clustered along rhiz., narrow-ellipsoid, 8–10×1–2cm. Lvs 2, oblanceolate to oblong-elliptic, acute, to 28×6cm. Infl. erect to suberect; fls 3.5–5cm diam., pale yellow or pale yellow-green, apex flushed brown, lip white marked brown, central stripe pale yellow-green; sep. oblong-lanceolate, acute 3–4×1cm; pet. linear, acute, 2.7–3.5cm; lip elliptic-oblong, narrow, 3–4cm, midlobe ovate to cordate, broad, acute, lateral lobes oblong, narrower than midlobe, disc keels 3, fleshy from lip base to midlobe base. India,

Nepal. var. **brunnea** (Lindl.) Lindl. (*C.brunnea* Lindl.). As *C.fuscescens* except lip marked brown, midlobe acute. Burma, Thailand to Vietnam.

C.huettneriana Rchb. f.
Pseudobulbs narrow-ellipsoid, wrinkled. Lvs oblong-lanceolate. Infl. arched, to 18cm, 8–10-fld; fls white; sep. ovate-lanceolate, acuminate; pet. linear; lip midlobe dentate, lateral lobes rounded, disc keels 3, crisped, ovate, acuminate. Burma.

C.lactea Rchb. f.
Pseudobulbs ovoid-conical, slightly grooved, 6–12×1.5–4cm. Lvs 2, oblong, acute, to 20×3.5cm; petiole fleshy, to 2.5cm. Infl. to 18cm, to 10-fld, horizontal; fls to 4cm diam., cream-white, lip lateral lobes brown; sep. oblong, to 2.5×0.8cm; pet. linear, obtuse or subacute; lip to 2cm, midlobe ovate, acute, lateral lobes shorter, ovate, upcurved, flanking column, disc keels 3, undulate. Burma, Thailand, Laos, Vietnam.

C.lawrenceana Rolfe.
Pseudobulbs ovoid-oblong 5–7×2.5–3cm. Leaves 2, lanceolate, broad, acuminate, 20–27×3.2cm. Scape 17–20cm; fl. solitary, green-yellow to yellow, lip white, apex tinged sulphur, disc mottled pale brown; sep. to 7cm, oblong-lanceolate, spreading, subacute, exterior keeled; pet. linear, acute, spreading; lip base weakly saccate, midlobe ovate, broad, weakly undulate, recurved, apex, obtuse, sometimes notched, lateral lobes oblong, broad, obtuse, erect, disc keels 5, fringed, 2, smaller near base. Vietnam, Malaysia, India.

C.lentiginosa Lindl.
Pseudobulbs ellipsoid, cylindric, narrow or ovoid, 3.5–9.5cm, glossy, pale green becoming yellow. Lvs 2, elliptic to oblanceolate, narrow, arched to suberect, acute, 8–20×1.5–2cm. Infl. erect, 6–16cm, 4–5-fld; fls pale green, lip white, marked dark or red-brown, midlobe broadly fringed orange; sep. and pet. lanceolate, narrow, acute, 1.7–2.2cm; lip weakly arched, 1–8cm, midlobe spreading, base broadly clawed, apex ovate, subacute, lateral lobes oblong, narrow, rounded, keels 3, low, undulate from lip base to midlobe. Burma, Thailand, Vietnam.

C.massangeana Rchb. f. See. *C.tomentosa*.

C.mayeriana Rchb.f.
Very similar to *C.pandurata*, but differs in the oblong, deeply ruffled, not pandurate lip. Malaysia, Indonesia.

C.Mem. W. Micholitz.
Fls large, white, golden orange at base of lip with chestnut hairs.

C.mooreana Rolfe.
Pseudobulbs ovoid, weakly furrowed, bluntly angled, clustered. Lvs linear-oblanceolate, narrow, acute, petiolate, to 40×3.5cm. Fls to 10cm diam., white, lip disc ochre or orange; sep. lanceolate, broad, weakly keeled, acute to acuminate, 5–1.3cm; pet. similar; lip to 4×3cm, midlobe ovate, acute, lateral lobes rounded, broad, erect, enveloping column, disc with 3 fringed lamellae. Vietnam.

C.nitida (Wallich) Lindl. (*C.ochracea* Lindl.; *C.ocellata* Lindl.).
Pseudobulbs ovoid to oblong, 3–8×1.3cm. Lvs 2, elliptic-lanceolate, narrow, acute, 8–23×2–6cm. Infl. to 20cm, erect or pendent, 3–6-fld, terminal, emerging from young shoots; fls sweetly scented, to 4cm diam., white, lip lateral lobes marked yellow, disc yellow edged red; sep. oblong, narrow, subacute to obtuse, to 3.5×0.7cm; pet. oblong-lanceolate, narrow, subacute to obtuse; lip subovate, 1.9×1.6cm, midlobe round to cordate, lateral lobes oblong to rounded, disc 3-keeled at base, 2 outer keels extending to midlobe base. India to Burma and Laos.

C.occulata Hook. f.
Rhiz. stout, sheathed. Pseudobulbs fusiform or ellipsoid, to 4×1.3cm. Lvs 2, lanceolate, coriaceous, to 10×2.5cm. Infl. exceeding lvs, 2–4-fld; fls to 5cm diam., white, lip blotched and streaked yellow; sep. oblanceolate, acute, 3–3.5cm; pet.

similar, narrower; lip to 3.5cm, midlobe oblong, acute, decurved, lateral lobes rounded, margins minutely crenate, disc with 3, crenulate. India.

C.ocellata Lindl. See *C.nitida*.
C.ochracea Lindl. See *C.nitida*.

C.ovalis Lindl.
Pseudobulbs remote, globose to oblong-ellipsoid, 3–6×1.5cm. Lvs 2, narrow-elliptic, acute to acuminate, 9–15×2.5–4cm. Infl. to 8cm, few-fld; fls to 3cm diam., pale tan, lip markings bronze to dark brown; sep. ovate-lanceolate, acute, to 3×1.5cm; pet. linear, acute; lip midlobe ovate, shortly fringed, lateral lobes triangular or oblong, somewhat truncate, fringed, disc 3-keeled at base, outer keels undulate, extending to midlobe. India, Nepal, China to Thailand.

C.pandurata Lindl.
Pseudobulbs remote, oblong to subglobose, laterally compressed, furrowed 7.5–12.5×2–3cm. Lvs elliptic-lanceolate, semi-rigid, 20–45×7cm. Infl. 15–30cm; fls few, 10–13cm diam., fragrant, jade to lime green, mottled or netted dark violet to black on midlobe of lip, sometimes overlaying white, operculum sometimes blue-grey; dorsal sep. larger than lateral sep., exterior keeled, linear-oblong, 3.5–5×1.3cm, acute; pet. clawed, subspathulate, acute, to 4.5×1.2cm; lip to 4cm, pandurate, base cordate, midlobe crispate to undulate, lateral lobes small, recurved, disc lamellae 2, warty on midlobe. Malaysia to Borneo.

C.parishii Hook. f.
Pseudobulbs conic, angled, narrow, yellow-green, 10–15×0.7cm. Lvs 2, elliptic or lanceolate, subacute, to 18×3.5cm. Infl. pendent or erect, 3–5-fld; fls 7–7.5cm diam., green to yellow-green, lip blue-green, blotched dark purple; sep. lanceolate, acute, to 2.3×1.6cm; lip pandurate, 2.3×1.6cm, midlobe broadly clawed, undulate, wider than long, base truncate, lateral lobes auriculate, disc ridges 4, combed, becoming warty. Burma.

C.rochussenii De Vriese.
Pseudobulbs remote, cylindric, narrow, furrowed, to 20cm. Lvs oblanceolate to obovate, acute or acuminate, to 30×11cm; petiole to 6cm. Infl. to 70cm, to 40-fld; fls to 3–7cm diam., fragrant, lemon yellow; sep. lanceolate, narrow, acute, to 2.5×0.5cm; pet. oblanceolate, acute, to 2.5×0.3cm; lip to 3cm, midlobe lanceolate, acuminate, decurved, lateral lobes elliptic, narrow, rounded, disc keels 2, rounded, toothed, outer keel extending to the midlobe, flanked by shorter keels. Malaya, Sumatra to Philippines.

C.rumphii Lindl.
Pseudobulbs oblong, to 10×2–3cm. Lf solitary, lanceolate, erect, obscurely plicate, acuminate, 30–20×5–10cm. Racemes 10–20cm, 4–5-fld; fls pale green, lip white, central blotch orange, midlobe marked brown, lateral lobes dotted brown-red; sep. lanceolate, broad; pet. linear, acute; lip elliptic-oblong, midlobe obcordate, broad, lateral lobes obtuse, rounded, oblique, erect. Malaysia, New Guinea.

C.schilleriana Rchb. f.
Pseudobulbs oblong-pyriform, clustered. Lvs 2, lanceolate, coriaceous, acute. Fls tawny yellow, midlobe blotched and spotted orange, disc orange; sep. lanceolate, patent, acute, to 40cm; pet. linear, pendent; lip forward-pointing, lyrate, midlobe orbicular, margin dentate, undulate, apex bifid, lateral lobes oblong, incurved over the column, disc ridges 3, vertical, several transverse. Burma.

C.speciosa (Bl.) Lindl.
Pseudobulbs ovoid, 2.5–8cm. Lf solitary, elliptic or lanceolate, acute, 10–30×3–10cm. Infl. erect to nodding, 1–3-fld; fls green-yellow to pale salmon pink, lip dark or red-brown, apex white; sep. oblong-lanceolate, acute, to 6×0.9cm; pet. linear, narrow, reflexed, acute, to 5×0.3cm; lip to 5cm, midlobe claw broad, rounded, erose, lateral lobes obtuse, toothed, disc ridges 3, warty with tubular projections. Java, Malaysia to Sumatra. var. **salmonicolor** Rchb. f. As *C.speciosa* except

Coelogyne (a) *C.tomentosa* (b) *C.dayana* (c) *C.cristata*; lip (1) (d) *C.pandurata*; lip (1); lip of *C.parishii* (2)

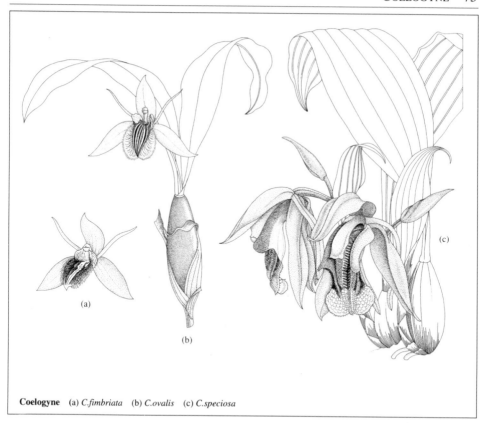

Coelogyne (a) *C.fimbriata* (b) *C.ovalis* (c) *C.speciosa*

pseudobulbs fusiform; lvs undulate; fl. solitary, salmon pink, lip chequered brown.

C.suaveolens Hook. f.
Pseudobulbs conical-ovoid, to 9×3cm. Lvs 2, elliptic-lanceolate, sessile, acuminate, undulate, to 25×6cm. Infl. 15–20cm; fls many, white, keels yellow; sep. oblong-lanceolate, acute, 1.2–1.5cm; pet. oblong-ovate, subacute; lip midlobe ovate or orbicular, broad, lateral lobes rounded, disc ridges 4–6, crenate. India.

C.swaniana Rolfe.
Pseudobulbs ovoid-pyramidal, angled, sides concave, 8–12×4cm. Lvs elliptic-lanceolate, acuminate, undulate, venation prominent beneath, 20–25×6cm. Infl. 20–40cm, many-fld; fls to 5cm diam., white, lip pale brown, margins and lobe tips darker; sep. and pet. oblong-lanceolate, pet. narrower than sep.; lip entire, midlobe orbicular-ovate, obtuse, lateral lobes short, rounded, disc ridges crested, some basal lamellae fringed. Philippines, Borneo.

C.testacea Lindl.
Pseudobulbs oblong-ovoid, compressed, angled, clustered; 7.5–12.5cm. Lvs 2, lanceolate, 23–40cm; long-stalked. Infl. pendent, to 40cm, 8–10-fld; fls to 4cm diam., pale brown, lip lateral lobes dark brown, edged white; sep. and pet. similar, oblong-lanceolate, obtuse, weakly apiculate; lip oblong, broad, recurved, midlobe obtuse, weakly undulate, lateral lobes rounded, short, keels 4, fringed or crested. Malaysia.

C.tomentosa Lindl. (*C.massangeana* Rchb. f.).
Pseudobulbs conical-elongate, angled 5–10×2.5cm. Lvs 1, rarely 2, elliptic-ovate, broad, 10–50×3.5–8cm; petiole long. Infl. pendulous, to 30-fld, lateral, axis flexuous, wiry, to

45cm; fls to 6cm diam., pale yellow, ivory or tan, lip midlobe veined brown and pale yellow, lateral lobes veined yellow or white, brown-maroon or blue-grey with age; sep. oblong-lanceolate, subacute, to 3×0.6cm; pet. oblong-lanceolate, narrow, to 3×0.5cm; lip midlobe oblong, obtuse, pendent, lateral lobes elliptic-oblong, narrow or rounded, erect above column, disc base warty, fringed, 3-keeled, running into the midlobe with 2 outer keels. Malaysia to Java.

C.tomentosa auct. non Lindl. See. *C.velutina.*

C.velutina de Vogel (*C.tomentosa* auct. non Lindl.).
Pseudobulbs ovoid, often narrowly so, to 6×3cm. Lvs lanceolate, rigid, 30–50×2.5–10cm; petiole to 8cm. Infl. 30–45cm; bracts pubesc., persistent; fls numerous, salmon pink or pale orange, lip yellow, lateral lobes streaked brown; sep. oblong, narrow, subacute to acute, 2.5–3.5×0.7cm; pet. oblong-lanceolate, narrow, acute, to 2.5×0.8cm; lip 2.5×1.7cm, midlobe ovate, acute, pendent, lateral lobes rounded, erect, flanking column, shorter than midlobe, disc keels 3, papillose, from base to midlobe, often with a further 2 keels on lateral lobes. Malaysia to Borneo.

C.virescens Rolfe. See *C.brachyptera.*

C.viscosa Rchb. f.
Pseudobulbs narrow-ovoid or fusiform, grooved, glossy, 2.5–4.5cm. Lvs 2, lanceolate, acute, to 30×3cm, base tapering. Infl. erect, 10–15cm, 2–4-fld; fls fragrant, to 4cm diam., white to ivory, lip lateral lobes veined brown, keels brown; sep. ovate-lanceolate, acute, spreading to 3×1cm; pet. linear-lanceolate, reflexed, acuminate; lip midlobe ovate, broad, lateral lobes rounded, keels 3, from lip base to apex. India.

Comparettia Poepp. & Endl. (For Andrea Comparetti (1745–1801), Italian botanist.) 8 species of epiphytes allied to *Ionopsis*. Rhizomes short, creeping. Pseudobulbs small, long-ellipsoid, terete or laterally compressed, sheathed with papery bracts. Leaves solitary, apical, oblong-elliptic, obtuse, coriaceous, erect, folded at base. Inflorescence to 35cm, basal, delicate, arching, sometimes irregularly branched; flowers relatively large, vividly coloured; tepals far smaller than lip, dorsal sepal free, broadly lanceolate, acuminate, lateral sepals fused at base to form a large spur; petals resembling dorsal sepal; lip large, trilobed, wavy, midlobe reniform, apically cleft, callus a basal crest with 2 spur-like projections extending into a large spur, lateral lobes small, erect, rounded, held at base within spur aperture. Winter. Andes, W Indies, Mexico.

CULTIVATION   Mount on rafts or fern slabs dressed with sphagnum, or pot in fine bark or palm fibre in well-drained pans. Provide a shaded site in humid, buoyant, intermediate conditions. Water throughout the year, allowing only a slight drying between waterings; mist regularly in high temperatures; feed while new growths are forming.

C.coccinea Lindl.
Fls to 8, to 2.25cm diam.; sep. and pet. narrow-elliptic, acute, scarlet; lip flattened, rounded, scarlet above, yellow below; spur to 1cm. Brazil.

C.falcata Poepp. & Endl. (*C.rosea* Lindl.).
Fls to 2cm diam., cerise, fading to rose or white at base of seg. Throughout genus range.

C.macroplectron Rchb. & Triana.
Fls to 8, to 4cm diam., white, pale mauve or lilac, spotted purple; spur to 5cm. Colombia.

C.rosea Lindl. See *C.falcata.*

C.speciosa Rchb.f.
Fls to 5cm diam., bright orange-yellow to orange. Ecuador to Peru.

Comperia K. Koch. (Derived from the specific epithet, in honour of Compère, the French botanist who first collected this plant in the Crimea.) 1 species, a terrestrial. Tubers 2, ovoid. Stems to 60cm, erect, basal leaves to 15×15cm, 3–4, oblong or oblong-ovate; sheaths 2–3. Spike broadly cylindric, lax or dense; sepals and petals maroon or green tinted purple, fused, forming a hood; lip broad, deeply trilobed, each lobe narrowing to a long, twisted, maroon filament, central lobe cleft, white or rose veined red with green or maroon filaments. Europe, Middle East.

CULTIVATION   See Introduction: Hardy Orchids.

C.comperiana (Steven) Asch. & Gräbn. (*Orchis comperiana* Steven; *C.taurica* K. Koch; *C.karduchorum* Bornm. & Kränzl.).

C.karduchorum Bornm. & Kränzl. See *C.comperiana.*
C.taurica K. Koch. See *C.comperiana.*

Constantia Barb. Rodr. (For Constanca Barbosa Rodrigues, wife and expedition companion of Joao Barbosa Rodrigues (1842–1909), Brazilian botanist.) 3 species of very dwarf, epiphytes resembling *Sophronitis*, often found on larger herbs, e.g. the branches of *Vellozia*. Pseudobulbs crowded on creeping, massed, branching rhizomes, globose to obpyriform, to 0.5cm. Leaves terminal, paired, to 0.5cm, suborbicular to reniform, retuse or abruptly acute, depressed, bright green, coarse. Inflorescence apical, sessile, solitary; flowers to 0.75cm, excluding ovary; sepals and petals lanceolate to ovate, petals smaller than sepals and forward-pointing; lip 3-lobed, midlobe largest, ovate-rhombic with a prominent, ridged callus. Winter–spring. Brazil.

CULTIVATION   Mount on vertical slabs of fern fibre or closely fissured bark in intermediate conditions. Establish by dressing with damp sphagnum and rooting in warm shade. Thereafter, grow in dappled sunlight in a cooler, airy position and allow to dry slightly between morning mistings.

C.cipoensis Campos Porto & Brade.
Fls creamy white, lip stained deep yellow on callus.

Coryanthes Hook. (From Gk *korys*, helmet, and *anthos*, flower, referring to the helmet-shaped lip.) HELMET ORCHID; BUCKET ORCHID. 30 species of epiphytes or lithophytes. Rhizomes short, stout. Pseudobulbs squat-cylindric, elongate-ovoid or fusiform, glossy dark green to olive, furrowed and ridged with age, sheathed at base by papery grey-brown bracts. Leaves apical, 2–3, broadly lanceolate, acuminate, glabrous, obscurely plicate, prominently veined beneath, basally conduplicate, petiolate. Inflorescence basal, racemose, bracteate, arching to pendulous; flowers waxy, fragrant, short-lived, to 5; sepals broadly elliptic, wing-like, free, membranous and appearing twisted or withered, lateral sepals exceeding dorsal sepal; petals reflexed or replicate, undulate, narrower and shorter than sepals; lip pendent, clawed at base, comprising 3 processes – the hypochile, a basal, concave, saccate 'helmet', from which emerges the slender, tube-like mesochile which expands into the bucket-shaped epichile, the epichile is trilobed, midlobe claw-like, cleft, almost touching column; column stout, terete, arched, winged, with 2 fleshy basal excrescences which secrete fluid into the epichile. Summer. Tropical America. Males of the bee *Eulaema* are drawn to the musky odour of *Coryanthes*. To gather the attar, they palp the column excrescences so vigorously that they fall, exhausted, into the epichile; they can only escape the epichile via the tubular mesochile, where contact forces them to deposit or remove pollinia. The odour and secretion of the disturbed flower are then suppressed for some 18 hours, a possible strategy against self-pollination.

CULTIVATION The Bucket Orchids are unequalled in the Orchidaceae for the strangeness of their flowers (resembling flesh- or leather-coloured bats in flight) and the ingenuity of their pollination mechanism. Their general requirements are as for *Stanhopea* but under intermediate conditions in an acidic and highly fertile medium with copious water throughout the year.

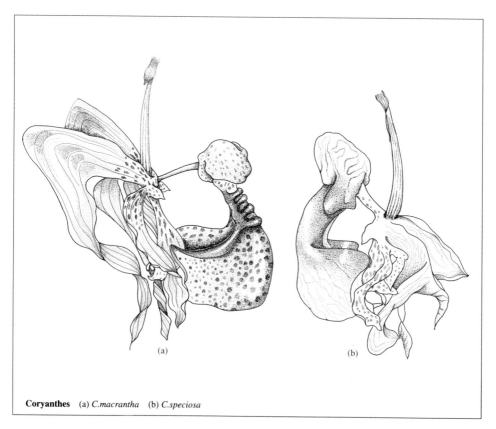

Coryanthes   (a) *C.macrantha*   (b) *C.speciosa*

C.bicalcarata Schltr.
Fls waxy white densely spotted and flecked red-pink. NE Peru.

C.biflora Barb. Rodr.
Dorsal sep. 4×5.5cm, translucent bronze, lateral sep. to 12×8cm, light brown spotted oxblood; pet. to 6×1.5cm, ivory, spotted or ringed blood red; epichile interior waxy, ivory spotted blood red, fading to orange, exterior yellow flushed red. Venezuela, Brazil, Peru.

C.elegantium Lind. & Rchb.f.
Fls ochre to deep red-brown flecked and spotted dark rusty red to oxblood. W Ecuador, Colombia.

C.leucocorys Rolfe
Fls scented of mint; tepals red-grey, rather like rotten beef; hypochile massive, inflated, waxy pure white, epichile damask to deep wine red. NE Peru, SE Ecuador.

C.macrantha (Hook.) Hook.
Widespread and variable. Tepals large, pale buff finely

flecked maroon, margins usually strongly inrolled and folded; lip large, shifting in colour from deep, glossy amber at the small hypochile and the mesochile (which has a series of distinctive ridges), to pale, semi-lucent buff at the epichile. W Indies to Peru.

C.maculata Hook.
Fls variable, to 9cm diam.; sep. and pet. membranous, yellow-ochre spotted purple or maroon, lip yellow spotted oxblood. Panama, Colombia, Venezuela, Guianas, Brazil.

C.speciosa (Hook.) Hook.
Sep. and pet. light bronze, closely spotted oxblood or maroon, epichile ivory within, mottled maroon, exterior ivory or buff, flushed red-purple, interior spotting visible through translucent walls; dorsal sep. to 2×2.5cm, lateral sep. to 6×4cm; pet. to 3.5×0.8cm; lip to 6cm. Guatemala to Peru.

Corybas Salisb. (From the Gk *korybas*, one of a group of priests known for their mad frenzy.) HELMET ORCHID. Some 100 species of herbaceous, terrestrials. Tubers small, globose. Leaf solitary, rounded, reniform, ovate-cordate, lying more or less flat on surface of substrate. Flower solitary, sessile or short pedicelled borne in axil of the leaf and therefore, representing the full height of the plant; dorsal sepal erect, forming a large hood, lateral sepals and petals linear, minute; lip erect, tubular, recurved or denticulate, or protruding, concave, or fringed. Indomalaya, Australia, New Zealand.

CULTIVATION   Pot the very small tubers 3cm deep in pans of gritty acid mix. Keep evenly moist when in growth, dry once leaves have withered. Position in a cool, well ventilated humid house in bright sunlight – the alpine house is usually more successful than any adapted for orchids, although it may be necessary to protect pans with cloches or bell jars should the air become dry when the plants are in growth.

C.aconitiflorus Salisb. (*Corysanthes bicalcarata* R. Br.; *Corysanthes cheesmanii* Hook. f. ex T. Kirk).
Lf thin-textured. Fl. to 4cm; dorsal sep. purple-brown, hooded and deeply concave, lateral sep. minute, linear, to 5mm; lip white, marked purple or red, margins convex, recurved, tubular, narrowing basally, with 2 conical, forward-projecting spurs. Late spring–mid summer. E Australia, Tasmania, New Zealand.

C.diemenicus (Lindl.) Rupp.
Lf to 3cm. Fl. to 2.5cm; dorsal sep. narrow, ovate, concave, green-grey blotched and spotted purple to maroon, lateral sep. and pet. to 2mm; lip with a yellow or white channelled central plate and small basal calli, margins incurved, denticulate. Midsummer–early autumn. C & S Australia, Tasmania.

C.fimbriatus (R. Br.) Rchb. f.
Lf fleshy, to 4cm. Fl. to 3cm, glossy crimson to purple-red;

dorsal sep. basally constricted, transparent, spotted purple-red, tip cuneate, lateral sep. and pet. linear, minute; lip purple to maroon at margins, paler at base and spotted red, tubular becoming decurved, expanded, ovate, with central boss, margins deeply fringed, spurs 2. Mid-spring–late summer. E Australia.

C.pruinosus (R. Cunn.) Rchb. f. (*Corysanthes pruinosa* R. Cunn.).
Lf 2–3cm. Fls to 3cm, grey-green marked deep plum or violet to maroon; dorsal sep. narrow, concave, projecting beyond the lip, lateral sep. and pet. to 2mm, filiform; lip a narrow tube at base, central plate orbicular with purple-red patch, margins fringed with slender teeth,calli many. Mid-spring–midsummer. SE Australia.

Corymborkis Thouars. (From Gk *korymbos*, cluster, referring to the corymb or cluster of flowers.) Some 8 species of terrestrials. Rhizomes short, branching. Aerial stems reed-like, terete, erect, bracteate, leafy, simple. Leaves alternate, ovate to elliptic, often narrow, acute or acuminate, sessile or subsessile. Inflorescence axillary; bracts triangular, keeled; flowers white to green-white or yellow, often fragrant; dorsal sepal fused to column foot; petals broader than sepals; lip keels 2, prominent. Tropical Asia, Australia, S Pacific, 2 spp. in tropical America.

CULTIVATION   See *Phaius*.

C.veratrifolia (Reinw.) Bl.
Stems to 1.5m. Lvs to 20cm, ovate, plicate, margins loosely undulate, base sheathing. Fls to 60 in a pseudoterminal cluster, fragrant, to 2.5cm diam.; sep. and pet. green, linear to oblong-spathulate, dorsal sep. concave, deflexed, to 3×0.3cm,

lateral sep. falcate, divergent or incurved, to 2.5×0.5cm, pet. recurved, margins undulate or crisped; lip white narrow, tubular, base enveloping column, apex expanded, ovate to suborbicular, undulate or crisped. Asia.

Cribbia Sengh. (For Dr P.J. Cribb (*b*1946), Head of the Orchid Herbarium at Kew.) 1 species, an epiphyte. Stem very short; roots fine. Leaves 3–4, 6–16×1–2cm, ligulate or oblanceolate, unequally and obtusely bilobed at apex. Racemes arising from base of plant, equalling or slightly shorter than leaves, laxly few-flowered; flowers green-white or pale green-yellow, fragrant; pedicel and ovary 6mm; bracts 2–5mm; dorsal sepal 4×1.5mm, lanceolate, acute, lateral sepal 6×1mm, falcate; petals 3×1.5mm, ovate, acute; lip entire, 4–6×2–4mm, ovate, acute; spur 4–6mm, straight, tapering from funnel-shaped mouth; pollinia, stipites and viscidia 2; rostellum trilobed, the midlobe longer than the lateral side lobes. W Africa, Sao Tomé, Zaire, Uganda, Kenya.

CULTIVATION   As for *Aerangis*.

C.brachyceras Summerh. (*Rangaeris brachyceras* (Summerh.) Summerh.).

Cryptocentrum Benth. (From Gk *kryptos*, hidden, and *kentron*, spur.) Some 14 species, epiphytes allied to *Maxillaria*, they generally lack pseudobulbs, bearing their leaves in tufts or rosettes. Solitary, scapose flowers arise from the base of the plant with narrow, spreading tepals and a small lip; although well formed, the spur is usually enclosed by the uppermost scape bract. S America.

CULTIVATION   Intermediate-growing; attach to slabs of bark, or to rafts, or plant in small pans of a very open, bark-based mix with additional sphagnum and coir. Postion in light shade and high humidity. Only a short, semi-dry winter rest is necessary.

C.gracillimum Ames & C. Schweinf.
Scapes not exceeding lvs; fls to 2cm diam., uniformly dull olive green to tan, dorsal sep. erect, narrowly lanceolate, margins strongly revolute, lateral sep. longer and narrower, downward-pointing; pet. shorter than sep., margins tightly revolute; lip short, tongue-like. Costa Rica, Panama.

Cryptopus Lindl. (From Gk *kryptos*, hidden, and *pous*, foot, with a hidden stalk.) 3 species, monopodial epiphytes. Stems long, slender, branching, producing long, twisted roots. Leaves tough, 2-ranked. Flowers white, *Angraecum*-like, but with deeply lobed petals and lip. Madagascar, Reunion, Mauritius.

CULTIVATION   As for *Aerangis*, but with high humidity, constant water supplies and deep shade.

C.elatus Lindl.
Infl. to 60cm, racemose, many-fld; tepals creamy white to buff, pet. 4-lobed; lip 4-lobed, sometimes tinted rose-pink. Mauritius, Reunion. The 2 other species, both native to Madagascar, are seldom grown – *C.brachiatus*, with a short, unbranched inflorescence and T-shaped petals and *C.paniculatus* with panicles of flowers each with a 3-lobed lip.

Cryptostylis R. Br. (From Gk *kryptos*, hidden and *stylos*, pillar – the column is enclosed in a sac formed by the lower part of the lip.) Some 20 species of glabrous terrestrials. Leaves few, basal, from buried rhizome, ovate to lanceolate, erect, often marked or conspicuously spotted or veined. Inflorescence an erect raceme arising independently; flowers non-resupinate, green; sepals and petals usually linear, petals shorter; lip entire, concave or convex, margins strongly reflexed, colour variable, calli longitudinally ridged; column appendages lateral. Indomalaya, W Pacific, Taiwan, Australia.

CULTIVATION   Requirements much like those of *Phaius*.

C.arachnites (Bl.) Hassk. (*Zosterostylis arachnites* Bl.).
To 60cm. Lvs to 17cm, 1–4, ovate, acute, pale green with darker reticulate veins; petiole to 15cm, spotted purple. Scape basally sheathed by large bracts; fls crowded; perianth seg. green, sometimes tinted red; dorsal sep. decurved, linear-lanceolate, margin inrolled, lateral sep. spreading; pet. lanceolate, spreading; lip erect, basally concave, maroon, apex paler, velvety, spotted dark red or purple. Summer. Malaysia.

C.leptochila F. Muell. ex Benth.
To 35cm. Lvs to 6cm, ovate, narrowing to form petioles, green above, deep red, brown or purple beneath. Fls to 4cm diam., 9–12; sep. and pet. filiform; lip wide at base, enclosing column, narrowing to linear, fleshy, tip recurved with dark, glossy central lamina, margins sunken, each bearing a line of to 8 stellate calli. Winter–mid spring. SE Australia.

C.longifolia R. Br. See *C.subulata*.

C.subulata (Labill.) Rchb. f. (*C.longifolia* R. Br.).
Stems to 90cm, slender. Lvs 1–4, to 4.5cm, narrow-ovate or oblong, green, sometimes red beneath; petiole 1–9cm. Fls 2–14; sep. and pet. 15–30cm, spreading or deflexed, yellow or green, tapering from apex to base; lip oblong, acute, bright red-brown, margins centrally deflexed or depressed, convex above, rolled back beneath, callus longitudinally ridged, glossy dark purple, terminating in a bilobed projection. Australasia.

Cuitlauzina La Ll. & Lex. (For King Cuitlahuatzin of the Iztapalapae people, who brought rare trees and plants to gardens in W Mexico.) 1 species, an epiphyte or terrestrial allied to and formerly included in *Odontoglossum*; rhizomes short. Pseudobulbs to 15×7cm, ovoid, clustered, compressed, dull or glossy light green, wrinkled with age, apically bifoliate. Leaves to 30×5cm, broadly ligulate, acute or obtuse, coriaceous. Raceme pendulous, crowded, cylindrical, 40–100cm on a long arching peduncle, borne laterally on new growth; flowers to 7.5cm diam., lemon-scented, waxy, long-lived; sepals and petals usually pure white, variously tinged rose or lilac toward base, sepals to 2.5×1.5cm, short-clawed, ovate-oblong, obtuse, undulate, petals slightly longer than sepals, elliptic, obtuse to emarginate, short-clawed, undulate; lip bright or pale mauve-pink with long yellow claw, lamina to 3.5×4cm, reniform, emarginate, callus on claw bilamellate, spotted rose; column with 1 dorsal and 2 lateral wings, lateral wings erose-dentate. Late spring–autumn. Mexico.

CULTIVATION Generally as for *Odontoglossum*; shown to best advantage in baskets or long toms.

C.pendula La Ll. & Lex. (*Odontoglossum pendulum* (La Ll. & Lex.) Batem.; *Odontoglossum citrosmum* Lindl.; *Oncidium citrosmum* (Lindl.) Beer; *Oncidium galeottianum* Drapiez).

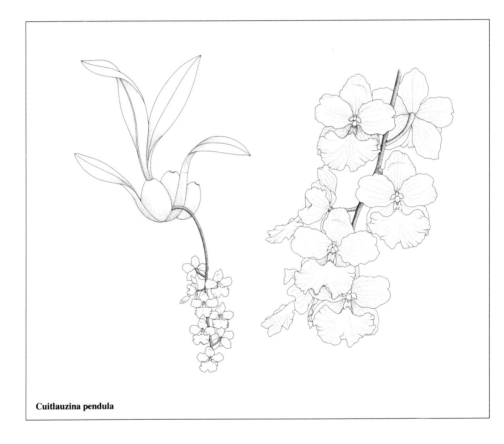

Cuitlauzina pendula

Cycnoches Lindl. (From Gk *kyknos*, swan, and *auchen*, neck, referring to the arching, slender column of the male flowers.) SWAN ORCHID. Some 12 species of epiphytes or terrestrials. Rhizome short. Pseudobulbs elongate, fusiform to conical, thick, fleshy, becoming fissured, enveloped by fibrous sheaths. Leaves membranaceous, plicate, lanceolate, sheathing and auriculate at base, alternate to near-opposite in upper third of pseudobulb and paired at apex, deciduous. Inflorescence a lateral raceme, arching or pendent, few- to many-flowered; flowers often large, showy, unisexual, dimorphic; sepals and petals similar (the petals somewhat broader), fleshy or thin-textured, free, spreading or reflexed; lip held uppermost, fleshy, shortly unguiculate, continuous with column base, ovate-elliptic to suborbicular, spreading, entire or lobed, crested or fringed; disc with a prominent callus; column of staminate flowers elongate, slender, strongly arching, wingless; column of pistillate flowers short, stout, arching, winged; anther terminal, operculate, incumbent, unilocular, pollinia 2, waxy, pyriform. Tropical America. Like its allies in the genus *Catasetum*, *Cycnoches* produces unisexual, dimorphic flowers. The sex of the inflorescence appears to be determined by light intensity (see *Catasetum*) and it is usually the male form (encouraged by poor light and deficient nutrient supply) that is encountered in cultivation. The male flowers are characteristically swan-like, borne on curving pedicels with a 'body' of reflexed sepals and petals and the slender, arching swan's neck of the column. Female flowers tend to be fewer in number, fleshy, spreading, and with a less conspicuous column.

CULTIVATION   As for *Catasetum*.

C.aureum Lindl & Paxt.
Fls to 8cm diam.; tepals yellow to lime green, often spotted red as is the slender column; lip small, pure white, margin crispate with toothed processes. Costa Rica, Panama.

C.barbatum Lindl. See *Polycycnis barbata*.
C.chlorochilon Klotzsch. See *C.ventricosum* var. *chlorochilon*.
C.cucullata Lindl. See *C.loddigesii*.
C.egertonianum Batem. (*C.ventricosum* var. *egertonianum* (Batem.) Hook.).
Pseudobulbs 8–12×1.25–2cm, clustered, subcylindrical, 2- to several-lvd. Lvs 15–21×1.5–3cm, lanceolate, acuminate. Male infl. 40–85cm, many-fld; fls to 6.5cm diam.; sep. and pet. to 3×7cm, thin-textured, pale green to green-tan (rarely yellow or white), sometimes flushed deep purple, spotted purple, lanceolate or linear-lanceolate, acute, sometimes reflexed; lip to 1.5×0.6cm, white to pale green, marked rose-purple, obovate, concave, clawed, disc ovate to suborbicular, bearing several elongate, clavate, rounded processes, column to 3cm, slender, strongly arching, clavate. Female infl. short, 1- to several-fld; fls fleshy; sep. and pet. to 4×1.5cm, green-white, lanceolate, acuminate; lip to 3.5×1.5cm, yellow, fleshy, ovate-lanceolate, acute, column to 1cm, short, stout. Mexico and Guatemala to Colombia, Peru & Brazil.

C.haagii Barb. Rodr.
Fls to 6cm diam.; tepals rich bronze to rusty brown; lip entire, heart-shaped, white to deep rose. Venezuela to Brazil.

C.loddigesii Lindl. (*C.cucullata* Lindl.).
Pseudobulbs 10–25cm, cylindrical, several-lvd. Lvs 20–40×4.5–7cm, oblong-lanceolate, acute to obtuse. Infl. pendent; staminate and pistillate fls subsimilar; sep. and pet. light green-brown, blotched and veined maroon; dorsal sep. 6.5–10×1–1.5cm, narrowly elliptic to linear-elliptic, acuminate, lateral sep. 5–7.5×1–2cm, narrowly elliptic, acute, recurved; pet. 4–6.5×1.5–2.25cm, lanceolate, acuminate; lip to 7×2cm, white to pale pink, sometimes lightly spotted red-brown, convex, lanceolate, acute or acuminate, column maroon, to 8cm, slender, winged, clinandrium green spotted maroon. Venezuela, Colombia, Brazil, Guianas.

C.musciferum Lindl. & Paxt. See *Polycycnis muscifera*.

C.pentadactylon Lindl.
Pseudobulbs to 15×2.5cm, cylindrical to subconical. Lvs 22–30×4.25–5cm, lanceolate-ligulate, long-acuminate. Male infl. 18–25cm, arching to pendent, densely many-fld; fls to 10cm diam., pendent, fragrant; sep. and pet. white to yellow-green, spotted and barred red-brown or chocolate-brown; sep. 3.75–5×0.75–1cm, lanceolate-ligulate, acuminate, reflexed; pet. 3.5–4×0.8–1.5cm, oblong, acute, reflexed; lip white to green, spotted purple or chocolate-brown, fleshy, claw with an erect, arcuate, finger-like process, lamina 4-lobed, tip ligulate to lanceolate, column to 4.5cm, purple, slender, clinandrium yellow-white spotted purple. Female infl. short, 1- to few-fld; fls fleshy, pendent; sep. and pet. yellow-white spotted red-maroon towards base, similar to staminate fls, slightly smaller; lip white, fleshy, claw yellow, lamina ovate-oblong, short-acuminate, disc bicallose, column to 2.5cm, yellow spotted purple, clavate, stout. Brazil.

C.pescatorei Lindl. See *Lueddemannia pescatorei*.

C.ventricosum Batem.
Pseudobulbs 18–30×2–3cm, cylindrical, slightly compressed, several-lvd. Lvs 10–35×4.5–8cm, elliptic-lanceolate to linear-lanceolate, acute to acuminate. Infl. 15–30cm, several-fld; staminate and pistillate fls similar, to 12.5cm diam., fragrant, long-lived; sep. and pet. green; dorsal sep. 4–6×0.75–1.5cm, linear-elliptic, acute to acuminate, lateral sep. obliquely lanceolate; pet. 4–6×1.5–2.5cm, reflexed, elliptic to elliptic-lanceolate, acute to acuminate; lip to 5×2cm, white, ovate or ovate-lanceolate, long-clawed in typical plants, convex, acute to acuminate, callus lunate, rounded, black, column to 3.5cm. Mexico to Panama. var. **chlorochilon** (Klotzsch) Allen (*C.chlorochilon* Klotzsch; *C.chlorochilum* auct.). Fls large, dove-grey to pale green, tepals not reflexed, the lip white, not clawed. cf. *C.warscewiczii*.

C.ventricosum var. **egertonianum** (Batem.) Hook. See *C.egertonianum*.

C.warscewiczii Rchb.f.
Close to *C.ventricosum* and often confused with it and its variety *chlorochilon*. Differs in its broad, spreading, apple-green tepals and the lip, whose claw is neither long nor virtually absent, but of medium length. Costa Rica, Panama.

Cycnoches (a) *C.aureum* (b) *C.loddigesii* (c) *C.egertonianum* (d) *C.ventricosum* (e) *C.ventricosum* var. *chlorochilon*

Cymbidiella Rolfe. (Diminutive of *Cymbidium*, which this genus broadly resembles in habit.) 3 species of large terrestrials or epiphytes with elongated pseudobulbs bearing 8–40 leaves. Leaves distichous, plicate, articulated at the top of the leaf sheath, more or less covering pseudobulb. Inflorescence racemose or paniculate, arising from axils of lower leaves near the base of a mature pseudobulb, many-flowered; flowers large; sepals and petals free or shortly joined to column-foot; lip 3–4-lobed, lacking a spur, with a callus or lamellae toward the base; column with a short foot; pollinia attached by the base to a retractile caudicle. Summer. Madagascar.

CULTIVATION   Striking plants for the intermediate to warm greenhouse (minimum temperature 16°C/60°F). In habitat, they are often found on the trunks of palms and growing in association with large epiphytic ferns – conditions simulated in cultivation by a very open, coarse bark mix or placement on rafts on generous pads of fern fibre, moss and dried FYM. Position in bright humid conditions and water copiously when in growth. On completion of pseudobulbs, reduce water, temperature and humidity and increase light values to promote flowering. Increase by division.

C.falcigera (Rchb. f.) Garay (*C.humblotii* (Rolfe) Rolfe; *Grammangis falcigera* Rchb. f.).
Pseudobulbs large, narrow, clothed with 7–40 distichous lvs. Lvs 25–60×2–3cm, narrowly ligulate or linear-lanceolate, folded. Panicle 80–100cm, many-fld; fls pale green, lip heavily marked with dark purple; dorsal sep. 45×10mm, erect or strongly reflexed, lanceolate, acuminate, thick-textured, lateral sep. of similar size but oblique and falcate; pet. 40×15mm, erect or arching over column, ovate-lanceolate, acute; lip 30×30mm, trilobed, lateral lobes erect beside column, broadly ovate, midlobe quadrate with reflexed, acute apex, the margin undulate, with yellow, bilobed callus towards base extended into 3 verrucose keels; column 10–14mm.

C.flabellata (Thouars) Rolfe.
Pseudobulbs remote, narrow, covered with sheaths, bearing 6–8 lvs. Lvs 20–50×1.5–2cm, linear or narrowly ligulate, acute. Raceme much longer than lvs, peduncle very long, rachis 10–15cm, 10–15-fld; pedicel and ovary 3cm; fls yellow-green, the pet. scattered with red dots, the lip spotted and edged with red; sep. 15–20mm, oblong, subacute; pet. slightly shorter and obtuse; lip 15–20×14–18mm, obovate in outline, trilobed

below middle, lateral lobes erect, small and obtuse, midlobe broadly obovate or flabellate, apex emarginate, almost bilobed, the edge strongly undulate, with 2 lamellae arising at the base; column 8–10mm, column-foot short, 1–3mm.

C.humblotii (Rolfe) Rolfe. See *C.falcigera*.

C.pardalina (Rchb. f.) Garay (*C.rhodocheila* (Rolfe) Rolfe; *Grammangis pardalina* Rchb. f.).
Pseudobulbs 7.5–12cm, oblong-conical, dark purple with age. Lvs 5–10, 65–100cm, ligulate, acute, dark green. Racemes arising from base of mature pseudobulbs, erect, equalling lvs, many-fld; fls 10cm diam., yellow-green or apple-green, with large dark green or purple spots on the pet., lip red with a yellow throat; sep. 37–45×12–14mm, fleshy, oblong-lanceolate, apiculate, concave in the upper half; pet. 35–40×17–20mm, ovate-lanceolate, apiculate, less fleshy than sep., with a dorsal furrow; lip 4×3cm, concave, recurved, 4-lobed, basal lobes 12×12–14mm, fleshy, triangular, apical lobes 20–25×18–20, rounded, thin-textured, undulate; column 10mm.

C.rhodocheila (Rolfe) Rolfe. See *C.pardalina*.

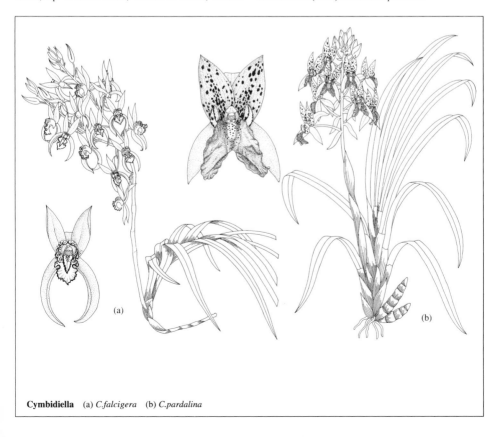

Cymbidiella   (a) *C.falcigera*   (b) *C.pardalina*

Cymbidium Sw. (Diminutive of Gk *kymbe*, boat; a reference to the hollow recess in the lip.) Some 50 species of epiphytes or terrestrials. Pseudobulbs ovoid or spindle-shaped, sometimes absent, clumped or along a short rhizome. Roots thick, white, branching. Leaves persistent, glossy, glabrous, grass-like in the Japanese species, linear, strap-like in the majority, succulent in *C.aloifolium*, oblong-spathulate in *C.devonianum*, few, alternate, 2-ranked, erect to arching, to 8 sheathing pseudobulb and borne 1–3 at apex. Inflorescence racemose, erect, arching or pendulous, borne basally on 1-year-old pseudobulbs, sheathed at base with papery, lanceolate bracts; flowers 1 to many, waxy, to 12cm diam., sepals and petals usually similar, or petals, narrower than sepals, free, spreading or forward-pointing; lip trilobed, fleshy, fused to column base or free, midlobe often recurved, callus usually parallel ridges, often broken, converging or reducing to 2 swellings at the midlobe base, or absent, lateral lobes erect, laxly clasping column. Asia to Australia.

CULTIVATION   The most popular orchid genus, widely cultivated as an orchidist's fancy, a houseplant, and an important florists' crop. The first *Cymbidium* hybrid flowered in 1889 at Veitch's nurseries, a cross between *C.eburneum* and *C.lowianum*, *C.*Eburneo-Lowianum. The great boom in *Cymbidium* breeding did not take place, however, until H.G. Alexander, orchidist at Westonbirt House, crossed Veitch's hybrid with *C.insigne* to produce the grex *C.*Alexanderi and, most notably, its selected cultivar 'Westonbirt'. Since 1911, *C.*'Westonbirt' has been involved in crosses with most of the larger-flowered species. Today, *Cymbidium* grexes and cultivars range from dwarf or miniature to robust plants to 1.75m, from those with arching to those with erect racemes, rounded flowers from 10cm across to more slender blooms to only 5cm across, in colour from white to rose to green to oxblood, brick red, bronze, apricot, yellow, cream, scarlet, peach and any combinations thereof.

Cool-growing (min. temperature 4°C/40°F), they will grow outdoors or under laths in the Mediterranean, Madeira and California, even tolerating a very light frost. Repot only when growth has reached the pot edge (i.e. every 2–3 years). Having removed the most exhausted backbulbs and any dead roots, pot tightly into a well drained mix to which has been added a slow-release fertilizer, i.e. hoof and horn. Cymbidiums are gross feeders. As growth begins, water freely and syringe foliage (giving a weak foliar feed every fortnight), keeping plants in a bright, but not exposed, well-ventilated position. Avoid leaf scorch and excessively high summer temperatures. A sharp contrast between day and night temperatures in summer is often the key to controlling over-luxuriant growth and promoting the development of fat, dark flowering shoots. In cool temperature zones, this is best achieved by placing outdoors in the height of summer. With the onset of autumn, decrease water and temperatures to admit full sunlight. Once the new pseudobulbs have ripened, water only to prevent their shrivelling. Flower spikes will develop over the autumn and winter; they may need staking and training. This regime can be easily adapted to plants grown in the home.

C.aloifolium and *C.devonianum* have strong pendulous flower spikes that may bury themselves in the medium unless carefully guided. These are somewhat unusual species – the first can be treated virtually as a succulent and requires baking in summer; the second, with rather thinner, paddle-shaped leaves, responds well to very cool, buoyant and humid conditions and should never be allowed to remain dry for too long.

Dwarf, grassy species are highly prized in China and Japan, where they have been cultivated for centuries for their solitary, quietly beautiful flowers, elegant habit and – in some cases – their variegated leaves. Such species require a somewhat finer, damper medium (as, say, for the hardy *Calanthe* spp.) and cool shade.

Propagate by divisions of 1–2 growths or backbulbs removed at repotting. On the larger scale, meristem culture is widely used.

Cymbidium is affected by scale insects and slugs. Damaged growths and pseudobulbs will attract fungal rots. Fluctuating temperatures may cause flower bud drop. Cymbidium mosaic virus (CMV) is a major problem, disfiguring foliage, suppressing flower production and spreading quickly to other plants via insect and human vectors. Plants so affected should be destroyed. Any cutting implement should be sterilized between each operation. Overfeeding will cause the virus to express itself more gravely in such infected stock as the grower may decide to maintain. Meristem culture is securing virus-free stocks of many of the finest plants.

C.affine Griff. See *C.mastersii*.

C.aloifolium (L.) Sw.
Pseudobulbs very small, ovoid. Lvs to 60×3cm, ligulate, rigid, erect, curved, emarginate, fleshy, pea green, colouring red in strong sunlight. Scape to 90cm, pendent; fls to 45, to 5.5cm diam., sep. and pet. pale yellow to cream, central stripe maroon-brown, often darkly streaked, dorsal sep. oblong to narrowly ligulate-elliptic, lateral sep. similar, oblique, spreading, pet. narrow-elliptic, forward-pointing; lip cream or white, base yellow, saccate, papillose or pubesc., lobes veined maroon, midlobe ovate, recurved, entire, callus yellow, ridges 2, often broken, lateral lobes erect, forward-pointing, laxly enveloping column. Early spring–summer. India, S China to Java.

C.atropurpureum (Lindl.) Rolfe (*C.pendulum* var. *atropurpureum* Lindl.).
Resembles *C.aloifolium* except fls scented of coconut; sep. maroon or dull yellow-green tinged maroon, dorsal sep. ligulate-elliptic, narrow, margins revolute, lateral sep. similar, fal-

cate, forward-pointing; pet. to 3cm, elliptic, narrow, margins sometimes revolute; lip white, ageing yellow, pubesc. or papillose, midlobe, broadly ovate to rhomboid, apex yellow, blotched maroon, callus ridges 2, sigmoid, lateral lobes tinted maroon beneath. Spring–summer. Thailand, Malaysia to Philippines.

C.bicolor Lindl.
Pseudobulbs ellipsoid, laterally compressed, to 5×2.5cm. Lvs ligulate, thick, coriaceous, apex oblique to unequally bilobed, to 90×3cm. Scape to 72cm, arched or pendent; fls to 26, to 4.5cm diam., fragrant; sep. and pet. pale yellow cream, central stripe maroon-brown, dorsal sep. oblong to oblong-ligulate, narrow, erect, lateral sep. similar, oblique, spreading, pet. elliptic to oblong, narrow, forward-pointing; lip cream or white, base pale yellow, saccate, papillose or pubesc., midlobe elliptic to ovate, base white to yellow, dotted or blotched purple-brown or maroon, apex pointed, strongly recurved, margins cream, often undulate, callus 2-ridged, entire to sigmoid, lateral lobes erect, loosely embracing column, forward-

Cymbidium   (a) *C.insigne*   (b) *C.erythrostylum*   (c) *C.lowianum*   (d) *C.tracyanum*   (e) *C.eburneum*

pointing to recurved, dappled purple-brown or maroon. Spring–summer. Indochina to Malaysia. ssp. *pubescens* (Lindl.) Dupuy & Cribb (*C.pubescens* Lindl.). Lvs narrow, to 45×2cm. Scape pendulous, crowded, to 25cm; pet. spreading, bronze to olive with a central maroon stripe; lip ivory, pubesc. within, midlobe pale gold streaked maroon, tip recurved, callus yellow, ridged, broken, lateral lobes not exceeding column, tips free, acute, yellow, spotted mauve; column purple-maroon above, cream spotted purple below.

C.canaliculatum R. Br.
Pseudobulbs narrow-ellipsoid. Lvs to 65×4cm, stiff, coriaceous, olive green, linear, acute, deeply grooved above. Scapes arching, crowded, often several per pseudobulb; fls variable, to 4cm diam.; sep. and pet. equal, lanceolate to elliptic, abruptly acute, green, brown or maroon beneath, olive green to pale bronze, streaked or spotted maroon or oxblood above; lip ivory, spotted purple or red, minutely pubesc. within, midlobe ovate, acute, sometimes undulate, callus pale green or cream, pubesc., lateral lobes small, forward-pointing; column half length of lip, thick, somewhat incurved. Autumn–winter. Australia. var. *sparkesii* (Rendle) Bail. Fls deep blood red; tepals longer.

C.dayanum Rchb. f.
Pseudobulbs indistinct, strongly compressed-ellipsoid, growth appearing tufted. Lvs to 115×2.5cm, narrow-linear, acute, sheath somewhat inflated near base, midrib prominent beneath. Scape to 35cm; sheaths pink-veined, to 8cm; fls fragrant, to 5cm diam.; sep. and pet. unequal, spreading, oblong-lanceolate to narrow-elliptic, cream or white, central maroon stripe terminating before apex, occasionally tinged burgundy, margin darker at base, maroon to white; lip white, marked maroon, base orange or yellow, midlobe ovate, entire, recurved, minutely papillose and downy, maroon with pale yellow triangular basal stripe, callus ridges 2, parallel, glandular-pubesc., lateral lobes erect, tips forward-pointing, white, minutely papillose, veins and margins maroon. Summer. N India to China, Japan to Sabah.

C.devonianum Lindl. & Paxt. (*C.sikkimense* Hook. f.).
Pseudobulbs very small, ovoid, hidden by lf sheaths. Lvs to 30×6cm, blade oblong to elliptic-spathulate, abruptly acute, coriaceous, dark green, midrib prominent beneath; petiole slender, grooved. Scape pendulous, to 44cm, olive green, spotted or flushed purple; fls to 3.5cm diam.; sep. and pet. spreading, elliptic or (pet.) subrhombic, somewhat revolute, pale bronze to dull green, dappled or lined maroon; lip garnet red, trilobed, papillose, midlobe triangular-ovate, decurved or slightly recurved, maroon with 2 purple basal spots, calli 2 at midlobe base, lateral lobes cream, dappled maroon. Spring–early summer. NE India to N Thailand.

C.eburneum Lindl.
Pseudobulbs ellipsoid to ovoid. Lvs to 60×2cm, ligulate, narrow, pliable. Scape to 36cm; fls to 12cm diam., lilac-scented; sep. and pet. white, often tinged pink, waxy, oblong, acute, dorsal sep. concave, finely tipped, pet. subfalcate; lip ovate, lateral lobes embracing column, rounded, ivory, midlobe white to cream, triangular, margin undulate to crispate, minutely pubesc., centre and base golden yellow often dotted maroon, calli 3, yellow, prominent, velvety. Winter–spring. N India, Nepal, N Burma, China.

C.eburneum var. *parishii* (Rchb. f.) Hook. f. See *C.parishii*.

C.elegans Lindl.
Epiphyte. Pseudobulbs to 7×4cm, ovoid, laterally compressed. Lvs to 80×2cm. Scape slender, to 60cm; fls to 3cm diam., pendent, campanulate, slightly scented; sep. and pet. incurved, obovate, abruptly acute, pale straw yellow to cream, occasionally tinged pale pink, or pale bronze; lip triangular, fused to column base, pale green to cream, rarely with random red spots, midlobe apically bilobed, margin undulate, centre shortly pubesc., callus bright orange-yellow, basal depression cream or brown, pubesc., ridges converging at apex, lateral lobes triangular, erect, clasping the column, for-

ward-pointing. Late autumn–mid winter. N India, Burma, China.

C.ensifolium (L.) Sw.
Pseudobulbs very small, ovoid, often subterranean. Lvs grass-like, tufted, linear, arched, apex sometimes minutely serrate, to 95cm. Scape to 70cm; fls 3–5cm diam., often scented; sep. and pet. spreading, straw yellow to green, lined red or red-brown, pet. wider than sep.; lip green or pale yellow, rarely white, midlobe ovate to triangular, papillose, blotched or spotted red, margins undulate, callus ridges converging at apex forming a tube at midlobe base, lateral lobes rounded, minutely papillose, streaked red, margins red. India, China to Philippines.

C.erythrostylum Rolfe.
Pseudobulbs narrow-ovoid, to 6×2cm. Lvs linear, thin, narrow, arched. Infl. erect or arching, to 60cm; fls to 7, to 11cm diam.; sep. spreading, white; pet. forward-pointing, covering column, white with broken lines of pink near base; lip yellow-white, fused to column base, midlobe triangular, slightly recurved, margin undulate, shortly pubesc., yellow, with deep red veins becoming blotched, broader toward apex, fragmented toward lateral lobes, callus cream, dappled pink, 3–5-ridged, converging, apex trilobed, lateral lobes embracing column, veins downy. Spring–summer. Vietnam.

C.finlaysonianum Lindl.
Pseudobulbs ovoid, small, largely obscured by lf sheaths. Lvs tough, rigid, sword-like, grooved, to 85×6cm, apex shallowly notched. Scape to 140cm, pendent, sheathed; fls to 6cm diam., slightly fragrant; sep. and pet. olive to yellow-green, tinted pink near centre, fleshy, sep. narrow-elliptic, spreading, pet. broader, somewhat incurved; lip white, papillose or sparsely pubesc., midlobe broad-elliptic, undulate, apex notched, triangular, recurved, blotched maroon or spotted red, callus 2-ridged, basal, yellow or claret at base, lateral lobes erect, veined and tinted claret. Summer–autumn. Vietnam, Malaysia, Philippines.

C.floribundum Lindl. (*C.pumilum* Rolfe).
Pseudobulbs ovoid, sheathed, to 2.5cm. Lvs linear, arched, apex subacute, oblique, to 55×2cm. Scape arching, to 40cm; fls crowded, 3–4cm diam.; sep. and pet. rusty brown or green edged yellow-green, oblong, obtuse, sep. spreading, pet. narrower, incurved; lip white, minutely papillose, midlobe ovate, broad, blotched maroon (rarely pink), base yellow, calli 2, bright yellow, ridges converging at apex, lateral lobes obtuse or rounded, erect. Spring–summer. S China, Taiwan.

C.fragrans Salisb. See *C.sinense*.
C.giganteum Wallich ex Lindl. See *C.iridioides*.
C.giganteum var. *lowianum* Rchb. f. See *C.lowianum*.

C.goeringii (Rchb. f.) Rchb. f.
Pseudobulbs small, ovoid. Lvs linear-elliptic, acute, arched, margins often finely toothed, to 80×1cm. Scape erect, basally sheathed; fls to 5cm diam., sometimes fragrant; sep. and pet. green to burnt sienna, tinted red at base, spreading, obovate-elliptic, margins incurved (pet. often wider and strongly forward-pointing); lip entire to trilobed, papillose, midlobe ovate to oblong, recurved, cream marked red, callus tubular at midlobe base, lateral lobes reduced, erect, edged and spotted crimson with large discs of callus. Winter–spring. China, Japan (Ryukyu Is.), Taiwan.

C.grandiflorum Griff. See *C.hookerianum*.

C.hookerianum Rchb. f. (*C.grandiflorum* Griff.).
Pseudobulbs ovoid, elongate, to 6cm. Lvs to 65cm, ligulate, base expanded as corrugated sheath striped paler green. Scape robust, to 70cm, erect, then nodding; fls to 14cm diam., scented; sep. and pet. apple green, base spotted red, rarely tinged red-brown; lip cream, base bright yellow, spotted maroon, edged green, midlobe ovate-cordate, papillose, sometimes sparsely pubesc., callus 2-ridged, pubesc., lateral lobes triangular, margins fringed, short-pubesc. or papillose. Winter–early spring. N India, China.

C.insigne Rolfe (*C.sanderi* O'Brien).
Resembling *C.erythrostylum* in habit. Pseudobulbs ovoid, to 8×5cm. Lvs linear-elliptic, acute, to 100×1.8cm. Scape to 150cm, arched, sheathed; fls to 9cm diam., sparsely arranged; sep. and pet. white or pale pink, midvein and base often spotted red, obovate, spreading (pet. narrower); lip white, fused to column base, papillose, veined and dotted maroon-red, midlobe triangular, entire, undulate, centre and base blotched yellow, central cluster of blotches pubesc., callus 2-ridged, densely pubesc., lateral lobes laxly embracing column, somewhat pubesc. Late autumn–spring. Vietnam, China, Thailand.

C.iridifolium Cunn. See *C.madidum.*

C.iridioides D. Don (*C.giganteum* Wallich ex Lindl.).
Pseudobulbs elongate-ovoid, to 17×6cm. Lvs to 90×4cm, ligulate, acute, keeled, becoming rolled-tubular and yellow-green near base. Scape to 90cm, suberect or horizontal; fls to 10cm diam., remote, scented; sep. and pet. olive green, irregularly striped rusty-red or maroon, margins cream, sep. obovate, concave, forward-pointing, pet. narrower, falcate; lip trilobed, oblong, midlobe pubesc. above, margins reflexed, wavy, ciliate, yellow spotted red, callus pubesc., 2-ridged, lateral lobes triangular, veined like tepals; column white-yellow above, streaked blood-red beneath. Summer. N India, Burma, SW China.

C.lancifolium Hook.
Pseudobulbs narrow-ellipsoid, to 15×1.5cm, clustered. Lvs to 21×3cm, lanceolate-elliptic, apex acute, or rarely serrulate, semi-rigid, narrowing and folded as a 4.5cm stalk. Scape to 35cm, erect; fls to 6, remote, to 5cm diam., fragrant; sep. narrow-oblong, abruptly acute, white to olive green, pet. shorter than sep., white to green with an interrupted claret midvein and scattered spots; lip papillose, midlobe apically decurved, white, banded purple-red at base with 2 purple lines near apex, callus short, 2-ridged, near base, lateral lobes not equalling column, rounded, white, edged and marked red-purple; column green-white streaked maroon. Summer. N India to Japan, W Malaysia to New Guinea.

C.lowianum (Rchb. f.) Rchb. f. (*C.giganteum* var. *lowianum* Rchb. f.).
Resembling *C.iridioides* in habit. Scape to 100cm+, robust, ascending or arching; sep. and pet. olive green to lime green, irregularly and obscurely veined rusty-brown or blood-red, sep. narrow-obovate, incurved or spreading, margins slightly thickened or revolute, pet. narrow-obovate, subfalcate, spreading; lip yellow to white, base orange or bright yellow, spotted red-brown, fused to column, midlobe cordate, short-pubesc. at centre and base, with deep red, velvety, V-shaped marking from tip to apex of lateral lobes, margin jagged, undulate, callus 2-ridged, finely pubesc., apex dilated, lateral lobes triangular, pubesc., obscurely fringed. Late winter–early summer. Burma, China, Thailand. 'Concolor': sep. and pet. pale bronze to lime green; lip white and yellow.

C.madidum Lindl. (*C.iridifolium* Cunn.).
Resembling *C.canaliculatum* in habit except lvs to 90×5cm, softer, not so deeply grooved. Scape pendent; fls to 3cm diam., fleshy, faintly scented; sep. and pet. bronze to brown beneath, yellow-green above; lip minutely pubesc., primrose, with deep yellow stripe and 2 red-brown blotches at base, midlobe large, truncate, callus a central, shining, viscid line, lateral lobes small, erect, acute. Summer–winter. Australia.

C.mastersii Griff. ex Lindl. (*C.affine* Griff.).
Pseudobulbs elongate-ellipsoid. Lvs to 65×2.5cm, ligulate, arched. Scape to 30cm; fl. solitary, to 6cm diam., scented of almonds; sep. and pet. white or tinted pink, oblong-elliptic to narrowly obovate, concave, tips spreading (pet. narrower than sep.); lip white, fused to column base, often spotted and tinged maroon, midlobe to 1.3×1.3cm, ovate, mucronate or rounded, base blotched yellow, minutely pubesc., callus bright yellow. Autumn–winter. N India, Burma, N Thailand.

C.parishii Rchb. f. (*C.eburneum* var. *parishii* (Rchb. f.) Hook. f.).
Resembles *C.eburneum* except in lvs to 45×2.5cm, obscurely striped pale green; fls highly scented; lip broader, disc deeper golden yellow, callus not velvety on midlobe. Summer. Burma.

C.parishii var. *sanderae* Rolfe. See *C.sanderae.*
C.pendulum var. *atropurpureum* Lindl. See *C.atropurpureum.*
C.pubescens Lindl. See *C.bicolor* ssp. *pubescens.*
C.pumilum Rolfe. See *C.floribundum.*

C.sanderae Sander ex Rolfe (*C.parishii* var. *sanderae* Rolfe).
Resembles *C.parishii* except lvs to 50×2.5cm, (to 8cm diam.), sep. and pet. white, flushed pink beneath and spotted purple at base of pet.; lip cream, centre and base blotched yellow, pubesc., margin and lateral lobes marked maroon. Winter–late spring. Vietnam.

C.sanderi O'Brien. See *C.insigne.*
C.sikkimense Hook. f. See *C.devonianum.*

C.sinense (Jackson) Willd. (*C.fragrans* Salisb.).
Pseudobulbs ovoid, to 3×2cm. Lvs narrow-linear, glossy. Scape to 80cm, erect; sheaths overlapping; fls to 5cm diam., scented; sep. yellow veined oxblood, purple-brown, or very dark, dorsal sep. often forward-pointing, concave, pet. paler, often dark-veined; lip cream or pale yellow, papillose or minutely pubesc., midlobe blotched and dotted dark red, oblong, margin undulate or kinked, callus 2-ridged, lateral lobes erect, rounded. Autumn–spring. Burma to Hong Kong, Taiwan, Ryukyu Is.

C.tigrinum Parish ex Hook.
Pseudobulb to 6×3.5cm, ovoid-globose. Lvs to 25×3.5cm, coriaceous, lanceolate, arching. Racemes erect, exceeding lvs; fls to 5cm diam., fragrant; sep. and pet. olive to yellow, faintly lined and spotted purple or red, pet. narrower than sep.; lip white, lined and spotted purple, margins purple, callus 2-ridged, glabrous. Spring–mid summer. Burma, NE India.

C.tracyanum L. Castle.
Resembles *C.iridioides,* except scape to 120cm, densely flowered, fls to 12.5cm diam., tepals with stronger markings, lip cream to yellow, lined brown or maroon, lateral lobes fringed, column green-white to olive green, spotted red. Autumn–summer. China, Burma, Thailand.

C.grexes and cultivars.
C.Alexanderi: fls to 10cm diam., white, cream or pale rose pink.
C.Alexanderi 'Westonbirt': standard size, blush white fls with dense red spotting on the lip, an important ancestor of modern tetraploid plants. There is also a pure white form of great charm, Alexanderi 'Album' which is diploid.
C.Angelica 'Advent': large standard plants with yellow, early-flowering.
C.Annan 'Cooksbridge': miniature with upright spikes of many fls, deep red.
C.Aviemore 'Cooksbridge Delight': miniature with large heads of pastel pink fls which are offset by delicate white lip.
C.Ayres Rock 'Mont Millais': standard fls, deep rosy pink fls of superb shape, mid to late season flowering.
C.Babylon 'Castle Hill': famous tetraploid, of tremendous size and vigour, fls rich pink, handsome spotted lip with pink edge and yellow crests.
C.Balkis: many different clones of standard size, large white and blush white, round flowers with spotted lip and pink column. The clones 'France' and 'Silver Orb' are particularly fine.
C.Beresford 'Jersey Giant': very large plants with large fls, up to 12.5cm diam., vibrant yellow with a bold red band around the lip.
C.Bulbarrow: miniature plants with upright or pendent flower spikes, small green or brown fls with a band of deep velvety red on the lip.

Cymbidium   (a) *C.aloifolium*   (b) *C.atropurpureum*   (c) *C.elegans*   (d) *C.goeringii*   (e) *C.ensifolium*
(f) *C.devonianum*

C.Burgundian 'Chateau': standard size, deep pink with a coppery sheen, with a large deep rose lip.

C.Caithness Ice 'Lewes': standard, fine-shaped green fls with spotted lip.

C.Cariga 'Tetra Canary': standard size, large spikes of brilliant yellow fls with bold red lip. Other fine clones are 'Mont Millais' and 'Bouton d'Or'.

C.Castle of Mey 'Pinkie': miniature plants, fls 5–7.5cm diam., in a delicate shade of shell pink.

C.Clarisse Carlton: standard size fls on large spikes, fls good shape, deep fuchsia pink with a red band on the lip.

C.Dag: miniature with pendent spikes of many small apple green fls. 'Celeste' and 'Lollipop' are good clones.

C.Del Rosa 'The King': famous plants with standard size fls on erect spikes, very large white fls with bright red lip.

C.Earlybird 'Pacific': standard size, beautiful white fls with small, lightly spotted lip.

C.Eburneo-Lowianum: fls to 12.5cm diam., tinted yellow, fragrant; lip midlobe marking V-shaped, purple-crimson.

C.Esmeralda: standard size but narrow fls borne in great abundance on long arching spray, fls clear golden green, lip with a white margin and yellow crest.

C.Featherhill 'Heritage': standard size, dark red fls of excellent form and shape, sep. and pet. outlined in white, lip beautifully marked.

C.Flirtation: miniature with delightful blush rose or pink flowers.

C.Gladys Whitesell 'The Charmer': large plants with miniature fls well-spaced on long arching or pendent spikes; fls cream with very large dark red spots on yellow lip.

C.Gymer 'Cooksbridge': standard-size fls on large plants, fls bright golden yellow with deep crimson marked lip produced late in the season.

C.Hawtescens: large plants with standard-size, tremendous, long-lasting yellow which does not fade, lip marked with red and bordered pale pink.

C.Highland Mist: standard, large white fls with finely marked lip on tall erect spikes. Excellent cut flowers.

C.Kurun: many fine clones of white, blush, pale green, pink, deep pink, salmon-coloured or red fls, early-flowering.

C.Leodogran: miniature with attractive pink fls.

C.Levis Duke 'Bella Vista': standard size fls, one of the best pastel green fls with a slightly spotted, pink-bordered lip.

C.Lillian Stewart: standard size, many fine clones of large fls in various shades of pink.

C.Mavourneen 'Jester': an outstanding apple green-fld plant with red markings on the pet. similar to the lip.

C.Miniatures' Delight 'Stonehurst': miniature plants with long pendent spikes of small, brilliant red fls.

C.Miretta: standard size, many fine clones of deep green fls, each with a large white lip heavily marked with red.

C.Ngaire: standard size plants with fls of medium size, deep rosy red with a white margin to all parts and a broad red band on the lip.

C.Nonna 'Goldilocks': large plants with miniature yellow fls, tall erect or arching spikes bearing 20–30 fls each.

C.Pauwelsii: primary hybrid with narrow, green-brown fls and a broad red band on the lip. The tetraploid form 'Compte de Hemptinne' is a richer colour with broader sep. and pet., an important ancestor of modern hybrids.

C.Rievaulx 'Cooksbridge': standard size, a rich deep pink fl., rather wide, with a large lip beautifully marked in red spots and stripes.

C.Rio Rita 'Radiant': famous breeder, standard-size fls which are a beautiful shade of deep rose with deeper veining on sep. and pet., very attractive crimson lip.

C.Rosanna 'Pinkie': a good cv from a famous cross, standard size, pale pink fls.

C.St. Helier 'Trinity': standard-size, splendid ice green fls with delicate clear white lip; mid- to late flowering.

C.Sensation: standard fls but rather small, brilliant wine-red with a well-marked lip.

C.Showgirl: one of the most famous miniature cymbidiums with many fine clones; fls white, cream, blush, pink or pale green.

C.Thurso 'Mont Millais': standard-size, fine-shaped green fls with delicate pink suffusion and heavily spotted lip, flowering early to mid-season.

C.Tiger Tail: miniature plants with delightful upright spikes of small lemon yellow fls.

C.Vieux Rose 'Del Park': standard-size, famous pink tetraploid with heavily dotted lip, flowering mid-season.

Cynorkis Thouars. (From Gk *kyon*, dog, and *orchis*, testicle – a reference to the shape of the tubers.) 120–130 species of terrestrials, occasionally epiphytes. Tubers 1–2, globose or ovoid. Stem often glandular-hairy. Leaves 1 to several, mostly radical; cauline leaves small and sheath-like. Raceme terminal, lax or dense, 1- to many-flowered; flowers usually pink, mauve or purple, rarely orange or white, often with darker spots; dorsal sepal forming a hood with petals, lateral sepals spreading; lip free, spurred at base, entire or lobed, often much larger than other perianth parts; column short and stout. Mainland Africa, Madagascar, Mascarene Is.

CULTIVATION As for *Disa*.

C.compacta (Rchb. f.) Rolfe.
Terrestrial herb to 20cm; tubers ovate or elongate. Lf 1, basal, to 8cm, ovate-oblong, acute, erect but often becoming horizontal. Raceme to 20cm, glabrous, fairly densely to about 15-fld; fls white with red-purple spots on lip; dorsal sep. 4×2–3mm, erect, ovate, convex, lateral sep. slightly longer, spreading; pet. 4mm, forming hood with dorsal sep.; lip *c*9mm long, 9mm wide across basal lobes, 3–5-lobed, basal lobes much larger than apical lobes, all lobes wider toward apex and rounded; spur 3mm, parallel to ovary. S Africa (Natal).

C.fastigiata Thouars.
Terrestrial, 10–30cm. Lvs 1–2, rarely 3, 6–20×0.5–4cm, narrowly lanceolate or linear-lanceolate. Infl. subcorymbose, few- to many-fld; fls about 3cm including ovary, pale purple-rose with a creamy white lip, glabrous; ovary 18–30mm, bracts shorter; sep. 5–6mm, obtuse; pet. 5×1–1.5mm, narrowly oblong, obtuse; lip 10–15mm, with 4 more or less equal lobes; spur 18–30mm, straight. Madagascar, Mascarene Is.

C.gibbosa Ridl.
Terrestrial, 25–50cm. Lvs 1, occasionally 2, basal,

10–20×3–5.5cm, oblong-lanceolate, clasping the stem at base, often spotted purple. Scape usually glandular-hairy but sometimes glabrous, with 2–3 sheaths; infl. densely 10–40-fld, subcorymbose; rachis very short; fls large, salmon pink or carmine-red; ovary and outside of sep. often glandular; ovary 2–3cm; dorsal sep. 12mm, lateral sep. and pet. 15mm, pet. somewhat narrower; lip trilobed, joined to column at base, lateral lobes slightly emarginate at apex, midlobe deeply bilobed, with a median keel prolonged into an apiculus; spur 2–2.5cm, slender, swollen at apex. Madagascar.

C.kassneriana Kränzl.
Terrestrial, occasionally low-level epiphyte, 15–50cm; tubers ellipsoid. Lvs usually 1, sometimes 2, at base of stem, erect or spreading, to 20×4cm, oblanceolate or elliptic, glabrous, dark, glossy green above, purple below. Stem glandular-hairy, with 1–2 sheathing lvs; raceme laxly or fairly densely to 20-fld; fls pink-purple with dark purple marks; pedicel and ovary 1–2cm, ovary and rachis glandular-hairy; dorsal sep. 5–7mm, erect, ovate, convex, lateral sep. 6–8×4mm, spreading, obliquely ovate, all sep. glandular-hairy on outside; pet.

4.5–7.5mm, lanceolate, forming hood with dorsal sep.; lip 5–10×2.5–5mm, trilobed at about halfway, all lobes almost triangular, midlobe largest; spur 6–9mm, sometimes swollen at apex, parallel to ovary. Widespread in tropical Africa; S Africa (Transvaal).

C.Kewensis (*C.lowiana* × *C.purpurascens*).
Terrestrial, 1-lvd at base. Lf about 30×4cm, lanceolate, arching, bright green. Raceme laxly about 5-fld; sep. and pet. lilac, lip bright lilac-purple with white and purple blotches at base; ovary and pedicel 4–5cm; sep. and pet. about 10mm, pet. slightly shorter and narrower than sep.; lip about 30×25cm, with 4 subequal lobes, all oblanceolate and truncate at apex; spur about 3cm, slender. Spring. Garden origin.

C.kirkii Rolfe.
Terrestrial or lithophytic, 10–50cm; tubers ellipsoid. Stem glabrous, with usually 1 sheathing lf. Lvs 1, occasionally 2, basal, erect or spreading, 4.5–22×2–5.5cm, lanceolate, light green, glabrous. Raceme fairly densely 1–11-fld; rachis glandular-hairy, to 5cm; fls lilac-pink or mauve, lip paler than sep. and pet. but with tips of lobes darker, sometimes yellow at base; pedicel and ovary 2.5–3.5cm, glabrous; dorsal sep. 5×5mm, erect, ovate, convex, lateral sep. spreading, 5–6mm, elliptic; pet.

5×2.5mm, falcate, forming hood with dorsal sep.; lip projecting forwards, 10–20mm, 4-lobed, lobes 4mm wide, oblong or obovate, rounded or truncate at apex; spur 20–30mm, pendent, slender. Tanzania, Malawi, Zimbabwe, Mozambique.

C.lowiana Rchb. f.
Terrestrial, 10–16cm, 1-lvd. Lf 4.5–13×0.5–1.5cm, narrowly linear-lanceolate. Scape slender, 7–12cm, usually 1-fld, rarely 2-fld; fls large, sep. and pet. green, tinged with pink, lip carmine-red with darker median spot; pedicel and ovary 2.5–4.5cm; sep. and pet. 8–10mm; lip 22×27mm, 4-lobed, basal lobes often the largest; spur slender, equalling ovary or slightly longer. Madagascar.

C.purpurascens Thouars.
Lithophytic, rarely epiphytic, 25–50cm. Lf 1, sometimes not developed at flowering time, 20–40×4–10cm, ovate or lanceolate. Scape glabrous with 1 sheath; infl. subcorymbose, densely 10–35-fld; fls large, mauve; ovary and pedicel 3–6cm, with some stalked glands; sep. 10mm long, lateral sep. wider than dorsal sep.; pet. 7–10×2–3mm; lip 18–25mm, narrow and channelled at base, with 4 subequal lobes, the basal pair slightly wider; spur 1.5–4cm. Madagascar, Mascarene Is.

Cypripedium L. (From *Cypros* (Cyprus), the island sacred to Venus, and *pedilon*, slipper, corrupted to *pedium*.) SLIPPER ORCHID; LADY'S SLIPPER ORCHID; MOCCASIN FLOWER. 45 species of herbaceous terrestrials. Rhizomes short, roots fleshy, often ciliate. Stem erect, slender, glabrous or erect, basally sheathed. Leaves 2–4, basal or cauline, spiral or paired, near-opposite, glabrous to downy, prominently veined, usually plicate. Flowers 1–12 in a slender-stalked terminal raceme, subtended or enclosed at first by leafy bracts; petals and dorsal sepal free, outspread to erect, narrow-lanceolate to ovate-acute, lateral sepals usually fused in a synsepalum, held behind lip (but not in *C.arietinum*); lip strongly inflated, saccate with upper margin involute, forming a rim, the aperture filled to varying degrees by staminode. N & C America, Europe, Asia. The name *Cypripedium* formerly included the genera *Paphiopedilum, Phragmipedium* and *Selenipedium* (q.v.); these have long been considered distinct; for this reason, the many names originally combined in *Cypripedium*, but now treated as *Paphiopedilum*, are not listed here.

CULTIVATION Beautiful herbaceous perennials for shady wild, rock, peat and bog gardens, where they grow well in association with ferns and the dwarf bog-loving Ericaceae, slowly forming clumps of growth bearing pleated foliage and exquisite lady's slipper blooms in late spring. The most celebrated are the chocolate and rose moccasin flower, *C.acaule*, the spectacular *C.reginae*, with rounded and inflated blooms in white and pink, and the delicate *C.calceolus* in shades of yellow, maroon and brown. There are also curiosities, like the dwarf *C.debile*, best grown in the alpine house or protected rock gardens, with paired heart-shaped leaves and slender-stalked nodding flowers in green and ruby.

C.acaule, C.arietinum, C.guttatum, C.passerinum and *C.reginae* are fully hardy and should be planted in semi-shade on damp acid soils rich in decayed leaf matter. *C.calceolus* (but not *C.c.* var. *parviflorum*) and *C.montanum* require positions in light shade or sun on a medium of leafmould, peat, turfy loam and crushed limestone. Similar to this group, but not so calcicole, are *C.calceolus* var. *pubescens, C.japonicum* and *C.fasciculatum*. Less hardy are *C.himalaicum* and *C.macranthum*. These demand damp but well-aerated soils rich in organic matter and protected from sunlight and heavy frosts. All appreciate a winter mulch of dead leaves and/or leafmould and garden compost. Propagate by division in early spring, removing part of the rootball with the original soil intact. *Cypripedium* spp. resent any disturbance. They are sometimes affected by slugs and grey moulds.

C.acaule Ait. (*C.humile* Salisb.).
To 40cm. Lvs to 30cm, 2, broad-elliptic, basal, opposite, pale green, puberulous above, silver-green beneath, plicate-ribbed. Fl. solitary; dorsal sep. linear-oblong, finely tapered, falling forward, maroon to chocolate-brown; pet. lanceolate, falcate, shorter than lip; lip very inflated, the rim and apex channelled and swollen, typically deep rose pink. Spring–summer. Eastern N America.

C.album Ait. See *C.reginae*.

C.arietinum R. Br. RAM'S HEAD. Pubesc., to 30cm. Lvs 3–4, elliptic-lanceolate, plicate, to 10cm, spiralling around stem. Fl. solitary; dorsal sep. ovate-lanceolate, green veined purple-brown, lateral sep. to 2cm, free, linear-lanceolate, slightly twisted, incurved around the lip, green to purple; pet. similar; lip shorter than pet., basin-shaped with a blunt, short spur, white veined purple, rim hairy. Late spring–early summer. CE & N US.

C.calceolus L. LADY'S SLIPPER ORCHID.
To 50cm. Lvs 3–4, alternate, elliptic to ovate-oblong, furrowed and prominently veined, sheathing stem at base. Fl. usually solitary; sep. and pet. deep maroon, becoming dark purple-brown (rarely yellow-green), lip. ovate to elliptic-lanceolate, pet. 4–6cm, exceeding lip, linear-lanceolate, acuminate; lip to 3.75cm, strongly inflated, bright yellow sometimes spotted red within. Mid spring–mid summer. Europe, Mediterranean. var. *parviflorum* (Salisb.) Fern. (*C.parviflorum* Salisb.). Fls 1 or 2, small, dorsal sep. 2–4cm, ovate-lanceolate, undulate, red to purple-brown, pet. linear-lanceolate, spiralled; lip golden yellow, spotted purple within. Mid spring–late summer. Eastern N America. var. *pubescens* (Willd.) Correll (*C.pubescens* Willd.). Sep. and pet. yellow-green dotted brown, dorsal sep. to 8cm, ovate-lanceolate, undulate; pet. to 10cm linear-lanceolate, falcate; lip bright yellow. Spring–summer. N America, Japan.

Cypripedium (a) *C.reginae* (b) *C.acaule* (c) *C.debile* (d) *C.calceolus* (e) *C.californicum* (f) *C.margaritaceum* (g) *C.macranthum*

C.californicum A. Gray.
Stems to 120cm. Lvs to 15×6cm, 5–10, pubesc., elliptic-lanceolate, alternate, plicate, sheathing stem. Fls 1–12; tepals yellow-green, dorsal sep. to 2cm elliptic, lateral sep. elliptic, fused almost to apex; pet. to 1.8cm lanceolate, spreading; lip to 1.8cm, white, suffused pink or spotted purple around aperture. Mid spring–mid summer. WC US.

C.debile Rchb.
Stems 5–10cm, glabrous. Lvs to 5cm, ovate cordate, 2, opposite at apex of short stem and subtending slender nodding pedicel, glossy with veins sunken, not plicate. Fl. 1–2cm diam., solitary, pendulous, pale yellow-green marked red basally; dorsal sep. ovate-lanceolate, finely acuminate; pet. narrower, 1–1.5cm; lip to 1cm, inflated, green, paler within and veined maroon to garnet. Spring. Japan, China.

C.fasciculatum Wats.
To 20cm. Lvs 5–12cm, elliptic, plicate, opposite, pubesc. below. Fls to 4, clustered, maroon to green, pendent; dorsal sep. 1.5–2cm, ovate-lanceolate, veined purple-brown; pet. similar to dorsal sep., ovate, acuminate; lip dull yellow-green streaked or dappled purple. Mid spring–mid summer. WC & N US.

C.flavum P. Hunt & Summerh. (*C.luteum* Franch. non Ait.).
To 45cm, erect, brown-pubesc. Lvs 5–23cm, pubesc. Fl. solitary; lateral sep. fully fused; pet. narrower than dorsal sep., clear yellow; lip very inflated, vivid yellow, dotted or blotched purple-brown. Summer. SW China.

C.guttatum Sw.
To 50cm, sparsely pubesc. Lvs 6–12cm, elliptic to elliptic-ovate, blue-green. Fls solitary, white speckled purple; dorsal sep. to 3cm, ovate, concave, lateral sep. shorter, green-white, fused almost to tip; pet. dotted purple, spreading; lip white tinged yellow, spotted lilac. Mid spring–mid summer. USSR, China, Korea, Japan. var. **yatabeanum** (Mak.) Pfitz. (*C.yatabeanum* Mak.). Stem 10–30cm. Lvs 7–15cm, 2, oblong, opposite on stem. Fl. solitary, yellow-green chequered brown; dorsal sep. ovate, incurved; pet. oblong to 2cm. Early summer. Japan.

C.henryi Rolfe.
To 60cm. Lvs 10–18cm, 4–5, ovate-oblong, plicate, acuminate. Fls to 7cm diam., 2–3, green to yellow-green; dorsal sep. 3.5–5cm, ovate, acuminate, incurved; pet. 3.5–4cm, linear, broad, falcate, incurved. Spring. S China.

C.himalaicum Hemsl.
To 30cm. Lvs to 8cm, ovate-elliptic to oblong. Fls to 6cm diam., purple-brown; sep. ovate-oblong, concave, acute; pet. exceeding dorsal sep., spreading; lip pendent, aperture margins crenate, flushed and veined purple. Summer. Himalaya.

C.humile Salisb. See *C.acaule*.

C.irapeanum La Ll. & Lex.
To 150cm, pubesc. Lvs to 15cm, ovate-lanceolate, undulate, bright green. Fls to 12cm diam., bright yellow, 1–8; dorsal sep. 3–6cm, ovate-lanceolate; pet. to 6.5cm, oblique, oblong; lip golden, spotted or blotched red. Summer–early autumn. Mexico.

C.japonicum Thunb.
To 50cm, pubesc. Lvs to 20×20cm, 2, opposite, held well clear of base, fan-shaped, plicate. Fl. solitary; sep. green spotted purple-maroon at base, lateral sep. fused almost to tip; pet. to 6cm, exceeding lip, acuminate; lip rose-pink spotted mauve, very inflated, wrinkled. Early summer. Japan, China.

C.kentuckiense Reed.
Similar to *C.calceolus* except larger. Lvs 5, broad-ovate, apex narrow, twisted. Fl. to 15cm diam., solitary, terminal, white to pale cream or amber. Late spring. US.

C.luteum Franch. non Ait. See *C.flavum*.

C.macranthum Sw.
To 40cm. Lvs 8–20cm, 3–5, oblong, plicate. Fl. solitary, white, veined or stained pale purple-pink; dorsal sep. ovate, pointed, incurved; pet. ovate-lanceolate; lip inflated, white, lined and tinted rose pink. Early summer. USSR, Japan. var. **speciosum** (Rolfe) Koidz. (*C.speciosum* Rolfe). Fl. pale pink, veined magenta. Early summer. USSR, China, Korea. var. **ventricosum** (Sw.) Rchb. f. Fls to 10cm diam., rather pale; lateral sep. not wholly fused, exceeding lip. Lip oblong-saccate. Early summer. Japan.

C.margaritaceum Franch.
To 20cm, usually shorter or stemless. Lvs to 18×18cm, 2, opposite, broad-elliptic, plicate, green spotted purple. Fl. to 5cm diam., held just above or nestling between lvs, solitary, bractless; sep. and pet. ovate, yellow-green spotted purple, exceeding lip; lip inflated, ovoid, outspread, pale yellow, glandular-pubesc., spotted purple. Summer. China.

C.montanum Douglas.
To 70cm. Lvs to 6, ovate-lanceolate, plicate, alternate. Fls 1–3; dorsal sep. 3–6cm, ovate-lanceolate, undulate, suffused, purple, lateral sep. similar, fused almost to the apex; pet. 4–7cm, linear-lanceolate, purple, twisted; lip saccate, basally veined or suffused pink or purple, interior spotted purple. Late spring–summer. W North America.

C.parviflorum Salisb. See *C.calceolus* var. *parviflorum*.

C.passerinum Richardson.
To 35cm. Lvs 5–15cm, ovate-lanceolate, plicate, glandular-pubesc., sheathing stem. Fls solitary; dorsal sep. 1.5–2cm, suborbicular, concave, yellow-green, lateral sep. similar to dorsal, fused, basally concave; pet. to 2cm, linear-oblong, spreading, white; lip to 1.25cm, white sometimes flushed pink, spotted purple within. Summer. W & C North America.

C.pubescens Willd. See *C.calceolus* var. *pubescens*.

C.reginae Walter (*C.album* Ait.).
To 90cm. Lvs 10–25cm, 3–7, ovate-lanceolate, undulate, plicate. Fls to 9cm diam. 1–2, rarely 3–4; dorsal sep. to 4.5cm, broad-elliptic to orbicular, acute, white, lateral sep. fused, obtuse; pet. to 5cm, spreading, oblong, obtuse, white; lip large, inflated, pink mottled white or wholly white. Spring–summer. NE North America. var. **album** Ait. Fls cream to ivory.

C.speciosum Rolfe. See *C.macranthum* var. *speciosum*.

C.tibeticum King & Pantl.
Stem to 30cm. Lvs to 4.5cm broadly ovate or elliptic, minutely pubesc., alternate. Fl. solitary; dorsal sep. tapering apically and basally, lateral sep. fused, lanceolate; pet. elliptic, equalling dorsal sep., green-yellow streaked and dotted maroon; lip inflated, conspicuously veined. Summer. Tibet.

C.yatabeanum Mak. See *C.guttatum* var. *yatabeanum*.

C.yunnanense Franch.
Resembles *C.macranthum* but smaller overall. Lvs elliptic to lanceolate or ovate, acuminate. Fls white, veined pink; pet. lanceolate, acuminate, twisted; lip 2.3–5cm. Summer. China.

Cyrtidiorchis S. Rauschert. 5 species of epiphytes allied to *Maxillaria*. Summer. Venezuela, Colombia, Peru.

CULTIVATION As for high-altitude spp. in *Maxillaria*.

C.rhomboglossum (Lehm. & Kränzl.) S. Rauschert.
Rhiz. creeping or ascending, to 60cm, branching, leafy. Pseudobulbs globose to ovoid, to 4×2.5cm, olive green flushed red-brown, lightly compressed. Lvs 2, terminal, strap-shaped, to 10×2cm, or overlapping on stems, to 8×1.5cm, midvein sulcate above. Fls solitary, insect-like, borne in succession at base of lvs on stems; pedicels sheathed; sepals and petals to 2×0.6cm, fleshy, tangerine to ochre, finely veined chocolate or maroon, edged bronze; lip to 1×0.8cm, sericeous above, pale brown marked maroon with buff and violet-black hairs, midlobe minutely ciliate, disc a band of smooth, bronze calli, lateral lobes spreading or somewhat revolute; column pale brown, terete, downy. Colombia.

Cyrtopodium R. Br. (From Gk *kyrtos*, curved, and *podion*, little foot, referring to the shape of the lip.) Some 30 species of terrestrials or epiphytes. Rhizomes stout, short, sheathed with papery bracts. Pseudobulbs thick, narrow-ellipsoid to cane-like or long-ovoid, usually closely sheathed with bracts and old leaf bases. Leaves in 2 ranks, alternate, linear-lanceolate, arching, borne near apex of pseudobulb, thin, scarious, often somewhat grass-like in texture, ribbed or loosely plicate near base, apex long-acuminate. Inflorescence racemose, erect to arching, exceeding leaves, robust, produced basally with new growth, often branching; flowers showy, fleshy; sepals and petals usually lanceolate, crispate and undulate, reflexed; lip rigid, strongly 3-lobed, crispate and often verrucose. Summer. Brazil, Guyana, Venezuela, W Indies.

CULTIVATION Removing two back bulbs for each lead, repot every 2–3 years in long, perfectly drained, clay pots in a mixture of 2:1:1:1 coarse bark, loam, sharp sand and farmyard manure. Provide full sunlight in intermediate to warm conditions. Water and feed heavily while pseudobulbs are forming, avoid waterlogging; reduce water supply once pseudobulbs are ripened and withhold completely until inflorescence and new lead emerge; recommence watering when spike is some 6cm long.

C.aliciae Lind. & Rolfe.
Resembles *C.punctatum* except in fls smaller (to 2.25cm diam.), lip with reduced midlobe and petals markedly clawed. Brazil, Paraguay.

C.andersonii (Lamb. ex Andrews) R. Br.
Pseudobulbs erect, narrow-ellipsoid to stout, cane-like, to 120×6cm. Lvs deciduous, to 75cm, narrow-lanceolate, olive green, ribbed, falling to leave papery sheaths with coarsely jagged abscission line. Infl. erect, robust, branching, to 2m; fls to 5cm diam., fragrant, fleshy; sep. oblanceolate, crispate, bronze-yellow tinged green; pet. obovate, undulate, reflexed, lemon yellow flushed lime green at apex; lip lemon yellow, disc golden to apricot, ridged. W Indies to Brazil.

C.elegans Hamilt. See *Tetramicra canaliculata*.

C.punctatum (L.) Lindl.
Pseudobulbs to 1m, cane-like. Lvs linear, arching, grassy, to 75cm, falling to leave jagged lf scars. Infl. robust, branching, to 1.75m; bracts conspicuous, undulate, tortuous, lanceolate, olive green to bronze, spotted or splashed blood red to deep chocolate; fls to 4cm diam.; sep. lanceolate, spreading, crispate, undulate, ochre, heavily mottled and spotted maroon, clawed at base; lip triloded, basally clawed, midlobe truncate, crispate or ragged, maroon or amethyst with golden centre, or golden dotted red at apex and on lateral lobes, callus fleshy, irregularly toothed and grooved, lateral lobes reniform, erect, hooding column, burnt sienna. S Florida, W Indies, C & S America to Argentina.

C.virescens Rchb. f. & Warm.
Pseudobulbs ovoid to conical, to 10×4cm, at first sheathed with lf bases, later naked, with conspicuous abscission marks. Lvs to 45cm, linear-lanceolate, acute, deciduous, basally plicate. Infl. to 1.25m, erect, branching; fls to 4.75cm diam., spreading, bronze-green spotted chocolate; lip often oxblood, disc multi-lamellate. Brazil, Paraguay, Uruguay.

Cyrtorchis Schltr. (From Gk *kyrtos*, curved, and *orchis*, orchid, referring to the curved spur.) About 16 species of monopodial epiphytes. Stems long or short; roots usually stout. Leaves fleshy or leathery, unequally bilobed at apex. Inflorescence racemose, arising from stem or among leaves, several to many-flowered; flowers 2-ranked, pure white to ivory, turning apricot with age, often scented, more or less regular in shape, rather similar in all species except for size; sepals and petals free, similar; lip spurred; column short and stout; apex of rostellum bifid; pollinia and stipites 2, viscidium 1. Tropical and S Africa.

CULTIVATION Epiphytes for the intermediate or warm house. Their cultural requirements are close to those of *Aerangis* and *Angraecum*, although they are more tolerant of drier and brighter situations. Mount on rafts suspended vertically in dappled sunlight in buoyant, humid conditions. Plunge and syringe daily and apply a foliar feed weekly when in growth. When the tips of the thick, sprawling aerial roots are no longer active, reduce water to a weekly dousing. The flowers, borne on short horizontal racemes, are crystalline white, long-spurred and beautifully scented; their 2-ranked arrangement is particularly attractive, even in death, when the blooms become a rich topaz.

C.arcuata (Lindl.) Schltr. (*Angraecum arcuatum* Lindl.; *C.sedenii* (Rchb. f.) Schltr.; *Listrostachys sedenii* (Rchb. f.) Schltr.).
Robust, developing long stems with age. Lvs 5–10, to 24×5cm, variable in size and shape but usually oblong or ligulate, fleshy or coriaceous, dark green. Racemes axillary, to 18cm, to 8-fld; pedicel and ovary 2.5–4cm; bracts 12–15mm, ovate, brown and scarious at flowering; all perianth parts lanceolate, acuminate, spreading and somewhat recurved, sep. 28–45×6–8mm, pet. 24–26×4–5mm, lip similar to pet.; spur 3–10.5cm, wide-mouthed, tapering to an acute apex, straight or somewhat S-shaped; column 2–3mm, stout. Tropical & S Africa. 5 subspecies are recognized, differing mainly in size of fl. and length of spur.

C.chailluana (Hook. f.) Schltr. (*Angraecum chailluanum* Hook. f.).
Stem erect, 15–20cm. Lvs numerous, 8–25×2–3.5cm, oblong, coriaceous. Racemes axillary, 15–24cm, many-fld; pedicel and ovary 3–5cm; bracts 10–25mm, broadly ovate, sheathing; all perianth parts triangular-lanceolate, acuminate, recurved, sep. 30–50mm, pet. slightly shorter and narrower than sep.; lip like pet. but slightly broader; spur 9–15cm, tapering to become slender from a conical mouth; column stout, 8mm. Nigeria, Cameroun, Gabon, Zaire, Uganda.

C.crassifolia Schltr.
Stems very short; roots stout, 5mm diam., grey-green, clinging tightly to substrate. Lvs to 6, to 3×1cm, distichous, succulent, folded, glaucous grey-green. Racemes 1–2 from axils of lower leaves, 4cm, to 8-fld; fls most distinctly in double row, not opening wide; pedicel and ovary 10–12mm, slightly arched; bracts 5×4mm, scarious; all perianth parts triangular-lanceolate, acute, slightly recurved at tips, sep. 14×3mm, pet. 10×2mm, lip 10×3mm; spur 1–2cm long, 3mm wide at base, tapering, rather sigmoid; column very short. Zaire, Tanzania, Malawi, Zambia, Zimbabwe, Angola.

C.hamata (Rolfe) Schltr. (*Angraecum hamatum* Rolfe).
Lvs 9–24×1.5–4cm, ligulate. Racemes 5–17cm; fls with green spur; all perianth parts triangular-lanceolate, acuminate, 20–40mm; spur 3.5–5cm, the apex thickened, hooked or almost rolled up. Ghana, Nigeria.

C.monteiroae (Rchb. f.) Schltr. (*Listrostachys monteiroae* Rchb. f.).
Stems 10cm+. Lvs 5–20×1.5–5.5cm, oblong-elliptic or oblanceolate. Racemes to 30cm, many-fld; fls with spur tinged green or orange; pedicel and ovary 12–18mm; bracts 6–8mm, broadly ovate; all perianth parts lanceolate, acuminate, recurved, sep. 10–12mm, pet. slightly shorter, lip 8–10mm; spur 2.5–4.5cm, tapering from a wide mouth; column 2mm, very stout. W Africa, Zaire, Uganda, Angola.

C.praetermissa Summerh.
Stem usually short, but can reach 30cm, woody at base; roots 3–4mm diam. Lvs 8–12, borne towards apex of stem, 6–9×1cm, spreading or recurved, ligulate, dark green, thick-textured, V-shaped in cross-section. Racemes 2–4, arising below lvs, pendent, densely 8–12-fld; fls about 2cm diam., distinctly in 2 rows; all perianth segments triangular-lanceolate, acuminate, recurved, sep. 8×3mm, pet. slightly shorter and narrower, lip 7–8×4mm; spur 3–4cm, tapering from a wide mouth, slightly curved; column very short. Zaire to Uganda, south to Mozambique and S Africa.

Cyrtostylis R. Br. (From Gk *kyrtos*, curved, and *stylis*, column.) 5 species, terrestrials. Stems 5–19cm. Leaf 1.5–4cm, solitary, entire, orbicular-cordate, green. Flowers 1–7 in terminal raceme, red-brown, rarely green; dorsal sepal to 15mm, linear-lanceolate, erect, concave, incurved, lateral sepals and petals spreading, linear; lip to 15mm, broad-oblong, acuminate to obtuse with two dark basal protrusions becoming raised plates along the lamina. Spring–autumn. Australia, New Zealand.

CULTIVATION Terrestrials for the alpine or cool house.

C.reniformis R. Br. (*Acianthus reniformis* (R. Br.) Schltr.).
GNAT ORCHID.

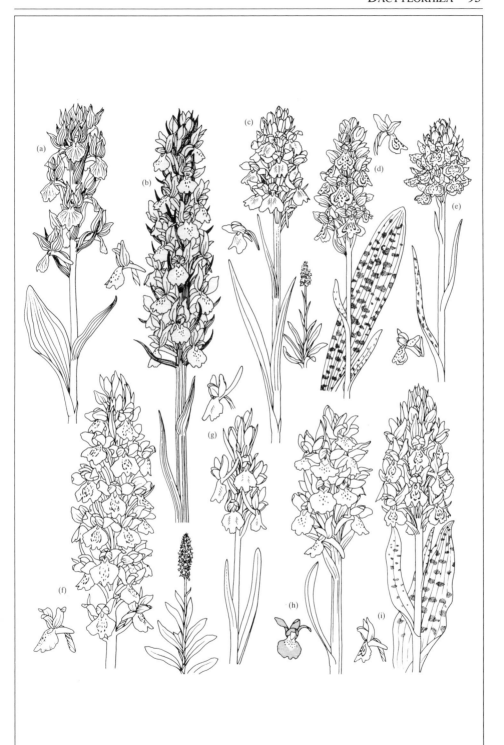

Dactylorhiza (a) *D.aristata* (b) *D.elata*, flower, whole plant (c) *D.foliosa*, flower, whole plant *(d) D.fuchsii*, flower, basal leaf (e) *D.maculata*, flower (f) *D.praetermissa*, flower (g) *D.romana*, flower (h) *D.sambucina*, flower showing colour variation (i) *D.majalis*, flower, basal leaf

Dactylorhiza Necker ex Nevski. (From Gk *daktylos*, finger and *rhiza*, root; referring to its finger-like tubers.) Some 30 species of deciduous terrestrials. Tubers 2–3, flat, lobed, tapering. Leaves linear to lanceolate, glabrous green, sometimes spotted purple. Flowers rose-purple, purple-violet, yellow, rarely white in subcylindric to rounded spikes with leaflike bracts; lateral sepals 2, spreading dorsal sepal, forming a hood with petals; lip entire or trilobed, spurred, minutely pubesc. above, marked with dark lines and dots. Europe, Asia, N America, N Africa.

CULTIVATION   See Introduction: Hardy Orchids.

D.aristata (Fisch.) Soó (*Orchis aristata* Fisch. ex Lindl.). Stem 10–40cm. Lvs 3–4, linear-lanceolate, sometimes spotted purple. Spike dense, fl. colour variable, usually maroon; lip trilobed to 25mm, spotted dark purple, spur to 25mm. Spring–mid summer. Japan, Korea, N America.

D.elata (Poir.) Soó (*Orchis sesquipedaliensis* Willd.; *Orchis elata* Poir.). ROBUST MARSH ORCHID. Stems 30–110cm. Lvs 6–14, linear to ovate-lanceolate, erect, reduced toward infl. Spike lax or dense; fls pink to maroon; lateral sep. reflexed, lanceolate or ovate-lanceolate; lip entire or trilobed, spur and ovary of equal length. Spring–mid summer. Mediterranean.

D.fistulosa (Moench) H. Baumann. See *D.majalis*.

D.foliosa (Sol. ex Lowe) Soó (*Orchis maderensis* Summerh.). MADEIRAN ORCHID. Stems 40–60cm, lvs lanceolate, 4–5. Spike dense; fls pink to light maroon; lateral sep. incurved, twisted; lip trilobed: lateral lobes obtuse, midlobe spreading, lanceolate; spur slender, twice length of ovary. Late spring–early summer. Madeira.

D.fuchsii (Druce) Soó. COMMON SPOTTED ORCHID. Stem 20–60cm. Lvs 7–12, ovate-oblong to lanceolate-elliptic, spotted purple. Fl. colour varies from pale pink to white or mauve spotted or lined deep red or purple; lip deeply trilobed. Late spring–early summer. Europe (calcicole).

D.iberica (Willd.) Soó (*Orchis iberica* Willd.). Stoloniferous. Stems slender, erect, 20–60cm. Lvs linear-lanceolate. Spike ovoid or cylindric, lax, 6–10-fld; fls rose pink, spotted purple or magenta; sep. and pet. form hood; lip flabellate, minutely pubesc., apical portion narrowly triangular, spur narrow, slender, down-curved, marked white at base. Late spring–late summer. Europe, Asia, Middle East.

D.incarnata (L.) Soó (*Orchis incarnata* Soó). EARLY MARSH ORCHID. Tuber 3–5-lobed. Stems 15–80cm. Lvs lanceolate, tips often involute, upper lvs equal or exceeding infl. Spike dense, cylindric; fls pale rose, pink, cream or purple; lip entire or trilobed, revolute, with 1 or 2 inner patterns of red spots. Spring–summer. Mediterranean.

D.latifolia (L.) Soó. See *D.majalis*.

D.maculata (L.) Soó (*Orchis maculata* L.). Stem 15–60cm. Lvs 5–12, linear-lanceolate, ovate or oblong, plain green or spotted. Spike dense; fls white, rose-pink, red or mauve; sep. spreading or incurved; lip trilobed, midlobe shorter, narrower than laterals, marked deep purple, spur cylindric, shorter than or equalling ovary. Mid spring–late summer. Europe (calcifuge).

D.maculata ssp. *fuchsii* (Druce) Hylander. See *D.fuchsii*. **D.maderensis** hort. See *D.foliosa*.

D.majalis (Rchb. f.) P. Hunt & Summerh. (*D.latifolia* (L.) Soó; *D.fistulosa* (Moench) H. Baumann). BROAD-LEAVED MARSH ORCHID. Tubers 2–5-lobed. Stems 20–75cm. Lvs 4–8, ovate-lanceolate, plain green or spotted maroon. Spike dense, ovoid or

cylindric; sep. lilac to magenta, ovate-oblong, spreading, reflexed; lip triloboed, spotted white and streaked purple, lateral lobes broad, midlobe smaller, triangular. Late spring–mid summer. C Europe, W USSR.

D.praetermissa (Druce) Soó (*Orchis praetermissa* Druce). SOUTHERN MARSH ORCHID. Stem 20–70cm. Lvs 5–7, lanceolate, plain green. Spike dense, fls pale garnet; lip 10–14mm, spotted and streaked purple, lobes 3, shallow, equal. Summer. NW Europe, S GB.

D.purpurella (T. & T.A. Stephenson) Soó (*Orchis purpurella* T. & T.A. Stephenson). NORTHERN MARSH ORCHID. Stem to 40cm. Lvs 5–8, lanceolate, often spotted purple toward apex. Fls pale claret to maroon; sep. ovate-oblong to lanceolate; pet. lanceolate-ovate; lip 10–14mm, shallowly trilobed or subentire, with central cluster of purple spots and lines. Mid–late summer. NW Europe, N GB.

D.romana (Sebast. & Mauri) Soó (*D.sulphurea* Franco). Stem 15–35cm; basal sheaths 2–3, brown. Basal lvs to 10, linear to lanceolate. Fls yellow; lateral sep. almost erect, ovate; lip trilobed, midlobe oblong-rectangular, exceeding laterals, spur 12–25mm, cylindric. horizontal to vertical. Spring–summer. SW Europe.

D.saccifera (Brongn.) Soó (*Orchis saccifera* Brongn.). Stems slender, 30–50cm. Lvs 4–5, obovate to elliptic. Spike lax, bracts twice length of fls; fls pink; lateral sep. to 10mm, spreading; lip equally trilobed, spotted deep red, spur 7–13mm, saccate or cylindrical equalling ovary. Late spring–mid summer. Mediterranean.

D.sambucina (L.) Soó (*Orchis sambucina* L.). ELDERFLOWER ORCHID. Tubers slightly lobed. Stem 10–30cm. Lvs obovate to lanceolate, plain green. Bracts exceed ovaries; fls yellow or magenta, rarely bicolour; sep. and pet. forming hood; lip trilobed with minute brown spots, lobes ovate-triangular, short, spur 8–15mm, downward-pointing or horizontal. Early spring–mid summer. Europe.

D.sulphurea (Link) Soó. See *D.romana*. **D.sulphurea** ssp. *pseudosambucina* (Ten.) Franco. See *D.romana*.

D.traunsteineri (Rchb.) Soó (*Orchis traunsteineri* Rchb.). IRISH MARSH ORCHID. Tubers 2–4-lobed. Stems 15–50cm. Lvs 4–7, linear to oblong-lanceolate, almost erect, spotted or plain. Spike cylindric, lax; bracts exceeding ovaries; fls magenta to mauve; sep. oblong-lanceolate; lip trilobed or entire, marked maroon, sometimes deflexed; spur conical. Mid–late summer. N and C Europe, Scandinavia.

Dendrobium Sw. (From Gk *dendron*, a tree, and *bios*, life, referring to the epiphytic habit of most species.) A large and very variable genus of epiphytic or lithophytic, rarely terrestrial herbs; estimates of numbers vary from 900 to over 1400 species. Stems rhizomatous or not, erect or creeping, pseudobulbous or not, from 1cm to 5m long. Leaves 1 to many. Flowers usually showy; petals generally narrower, but sometimes broader than sepals; lip entire or trilobed, joined to column-foot at base, sometimes forming spur or spur-like mentum with lateral sepals; column usually short with column-foot joined to lip and lateral sepals; pollinia 4, in 2 pairs, naked, without caudicles or viscidia. India, China, SE Asia, Japan, Malaysia, Philippines, New Guinea, Pacific Islands, Australia, New Zealand.

CULTIVATION A very large and diversified genus with a correspondingly wide range of requirements. In terms of temperature, they fall roughly into cool-growing types (e.g. *Dd.aggregatum, aphyllum, chrysanthum, cuthbertsonii, densiflorum, engae, fimbriatum, finisterrae, infundibulum, kingianum, nobile, moschatum, subclausum, thyrsiflorum, vexillarius, victoriae-reginae, wardianum*) and intermediate to warm-growing types (e.g. *Dd.atroviolaceum, bigibbum, bracteosum, brymerianum, canaliculatum, crumenatum, cucumerinum, gouldii, leonis, loddigesii, pseudoglomeratum, secundum, smillieae, speciosum, spectabile, stratiotes, strebloceras*).

They should be potted in small clay orchid pots, pans or baskets in a free-draining mixture of coarse bark, leaf mould and perlite. In very humid conditions, they can also be attached to bark slabs, branches or rafts – a practice that suits the strongly pendulous habit of *D.aphyllum*, as it does the dwarf and tufted *D.cuthbertsonii* and the succulent, creeping *Dd.cucumerinum* and *lichenastrum*. Repot every 2–3 years when new growth commences. All species require bright, filtered sunlight throughout the year, although care should be taken to avoid scorch during the summer. The canes of cooler-growing species will fail to ripen adequately unless given maximum light from autumn to mid-spring. The warm-and intermediate-growing species will sometimes grow throughout the year and demand regular, if not frequent, watering during winter. Cool-growing types enter a resting phase in winter and should be watered or misted only to prevent severe shrivelling of the pseudobulbs. When in full growth (mid spring to autumn) all *Dendrobiums* appreciate a weak, fortnightly foliar feed and daily misting. In the home, a bright windowsill is a suitable position, with humidity boosted by misting and trays of damp gravel. *D.nobile* and *D.bigibbum* make excellent houseplants, as does *D.speciosum* (tolerant of brutal neglect, overcrowding and summers passed outdoors on sunny patios). The dwarf, gem-like species from the Pacific Islands are excellent plants for indoor growing cases. *D.cunninghamii* from New Zealand is the southernmost representative of the genus and will thrive in barely frost-free, airy and humid glasshouses. *Dendrobiums* are sometimes troubled by scale insects and slugs. By far the greatest threat is presented by overwatering, soured potting compost and stagnant atmospheres. If too warm and damp, many will produce adventitious plantlets instead of flower buds: these can be detached and grown on. Otherwise propagate by division of canes when repotting (one active growth per division plus at least two spent canes) or by laying sections of canes on damp sphagnum or perlite, having dusted the wounds with charcoal and sulphur. In high temperatures, plantlets will develop on the nodes of these sections.

D.aduncum Wallich ex Lindl.
Stems 40–60cm, slender, cylindrical, branched, pendent. Lvs 7–9×1.5cm, linear-lanceolate, acuminate, deciduous. Racemes about 7cm, 2–5-fld, borne on upper nodes of old stems; fls to 3.5cm diam., pale pink or white with purple anther-cap; tepals 16–20×7–12mm; lip 12–18×10–12mm, clawed at base, rounded, concave, hairy inside, with sharply reflexed apex and shiny central callus. Spring. Burma, Sikkim, Indochina.

D.aemulum R. Br.
Epiphytic, sometimes lithophytic; pseudobulbs to 30×1cm, but often much shorter, linear to oblong, erect, clustered, dark brown, 2–4-lvd at apex. Lvs to 5×3cm, ovate or oblong, leathery. Racemes to 10cm, fairly densely 3–12-fld; fls about 25mm diam., white, occasionally pink-tinged, with yellow ridge on lip; tepals linear, spreading, sep. to 25×3.5mm; pet. to 26×1mm, sometimes recurved; lip 7×5mm, trilobed, lateral lobes erect, clasping column, midlobe deflexed, with undulate yellow ridge. Australia.

D.aggregatum Roxb. See *D.lindleyi*.

D.albosanguineum Lindl.
Pseudobulbs 12–28cm, clustered, cylindrical or club-shaped, covered with white, sheathing bracts. Lvs 10–15×2.5–3cm, linear-lanceolate, pale green. Racemes arising from upper nodes, 5–8cm, 2–3-fld; fls scented, 9cm diam., rather fleshy, cream-white or pale yellow, the lip with 2 purple or crimson spots at base; sep. 40–50×10–13mm, lanceolate, acuminate, lateral sep. slightly longer than dorsal; pet. 50×25mm, elliptical; lip 50×35mm, obovate, edge undulate, apex emarginate; column purple. Burma.

D.amethystoglossum Rchb. f.
Stems cane-like, 50–90cm. Lvs deciduous after 1 season. Racemes pendent, densely 15–20-fld; fls long-lasting, to 30mm diam., white with amethyst-purple lip; sep. and pet. lanceolate, acute; lip more or less trilobed, lateral lobes erect, midlobe acute. Winter. Philippines.

D.anceps Sw.
Stems 30–60cm, about 1cm diam., somewhat flattened. Lvs about 3cm, lanceolate or ovate, fleshy, imbricate, acute. Racemes short, axillary; fls small, green or yellow; tepals about 1cm; lip oblong, wedge-shaped at base, obscurely trilobed, edges crisped. India (Ganges Delta, Sikkim, Assam).

D.anosmum Lindl. (*D.macrophyllum* Lindl.; *D.superbum* Rchb. f.).
Stem 60–120cm, less than 1cm diam., arching or pendent. Lvs 12–18×2.5–3cm, oblong-elliptic, acute, deciduous. Infl. 1–2-fld, arising at nodes; fls scented, pink to purple with purple throat; sep. 40–60×10mm, lanceolate, acuminate; pet. of similar length but twice as wide; lip 40–60×30mm, broadly ovate, acute with a pubesc. disc; column very short. Philippines, Malay Peninsula, Laos, Vietnam, New Guinea.

D.antelope Rchb. f. See *D.bicaudatum*.

D.antennatum Lindl.
Pseudobulbs 15–75×1–1.5cm, somewhat spindle-shaped, clustered. Lvs 4–15×0.5–4cm, distichous, oblong to elliptic, apex unequally and acutely bilobed, leathery or fleshy. Racemes to 35cm, 3–15-fld; fls scented, sep. white, pet. green or yellow-green, lip white with purple veins; pedicel and ovary 2–3.5cm; sep. 15–25×6–7mm, oblong-lanceolate, acute

or acuminate, recurved, dorsal sep. often spirally twisted; pet. 25–50×2–4mm, erect, linear, acute, twisted once or twice; lip 15–23×9–12mm with a callus of 5 longitudinal ridges, trilobed, lateral lobes erect, rounded, midlobe orbicular or ovate; column 5–6mm. New Guinea to Solomon Is. and NE Australia.

D.aphyllum (Roxb.) C. Fisch. (*D.pierardii* (Roxb.) C. Fisch.).
Stems to 90cm, 1cm wide, pendent, leafy. Lvs 5–12×2–3cm, lanceolate or narrowly ovate, acuminate, deciduous. Infl. short, arising at nodes of old stems, 1–3-fld; fls scented, thin-textured, 5cm diam.; tepals white or mauve-pink, lip cream or light yellow, marked with purple towards base; sep. 25–30×6–8mm, oblong-lanceolate, acute; pet. 25×15mm, oblong-elliptic, obtuse; lip 25×25mm, tubular at base then more or less orbicular, obscurely trilobed, pubesc. above, the edge erose; column 9mm. NE India and China, south to Malaya.

D.atroviolaceum Rolfe.
Pseudobulbs to 30×1.5cm, spindle-shaped, 2–4-lvd at apex. Lvs to 13×6cm, oblong, obtusely bilobed at apex, thick-textured, dark green on upper surface, paler below. Racemes short, arising just below apex, 8- to many-fld; fls scented, 7.5cm diam.; tepals primrose-yellow to green-white, spotted with purple, lip green on outside, striped with purple inside, the apex purple; sep. 28–30×13mm, ovate, lateral sep. keeled on outside; pet. of similar length but slightly wider, obovate, acute, edge undulate; lip 20×20mm, trilobed, lateral lobes erect, midlobe broadly ovate, reflexed, with basal callus of 3 ridges. New Guinea.

D.aurantiacum Rchb. f. (*D.chryseum* Rolfe).
Stems 30–60cm, slender, clustered, erect, 3–4-lvd near apex. Lvs 5–8cm long, about 1cm wide, linear-oblong, bilobed at apex. Racemes arising from upper and lower nodes of leafless stems, 1–3-fld; fls 35–40mm diam., golden-yellow to orange, the base of lip sometimes faintly streaked with crimson; sep. to 30×18mm, oblong-lanceolate, acuminate; pet. broader; lip shortly clawed at base then orbicular, about 25mm wide, rather obscurely trilobed, lateral lobes pubesc., enfolding column, margins minutely fringed. India (Bhutan and E Himalaya).

D.aureum Lindl. See *D.heterocarpum*.

D.bellatulum Rolfe.
Pseudobulbs to 10×2cm, ovoid to spindle-shaped, clustered, longitudinally ribbed. Lvs 2–4, 3–5×0.5–1.5cm, ligulate or elliptic, with black hairs. Racemes axillary, 1–3-fld; fls scented, tepals cream-white, lip yellow, lateral lobes vermilion red, disc with 5 red ridges; dorsal sep. 2×1cm, oblong, acute, lateral sep 3×1cm, triangular; pet. 2–2.5×0.8–10cm, obovate, acute; lip 2.5–3cm, trilobed, midlobe reflexed, bilobed, lateral lobes rounded. Burma, Yunnan, Vietnam, Thailand.

D.bensoniae Rchb. f.
Stems to 1m, stout, cylindrical, suberect to pendent. Lvs 5–8cm, linear, bilobed at apex. Racemes arising on leafless stems, short, 1–3-fld; fls about 6cm diam., white or pale yellow, lip yellow with 2 purple spots; sep. linear-oblong, obtuse; pet. larger; lip large, orbicular from a short claw, concave, pubesc. India, Burma.

D.bicaudatum Reinw. ex Lindl. (*D.antelope* Rchb. f.).
Pseudobulbs to 43×1cm, clustered, cane-like, swollen at or below middle, with up to 20 nodes. Lvs 4–10, to 9×2.5cm, lanceolate, unequally bilobed at the apex, thin and leathery. Racemes to 15cm, few-fld; fls green or yellow-green, sometimes flushed with red or brown, lip white or green, purple-veined; pedicel and ovary 15–25mm; dorsal sep. 15–20×4mm, lanceolate, acute, apex recurved, lateral sep. slightly longer and about twice as wide, oblique, curved; pet. 23–50×2–3mm, linear, acute, either not twisted or with 1 twist; lip 15–18×10–15mm, with a callus of 5 fleshy ridges, trilobed, lateral lobes rounded, midlobe 4×10mm, trans-

versely oblong, apiculate, edges incurved; column 4–5mm. N Celebes, Sulu archipelago, Moluccas.

D.bigibbum Lindl. (*D.phalaenopsis* Fitzg.).
Pseudobulbs to over 1m tall and 2cm wide, erect, cane-like but somewhat spindle-shaped. Lvs 3–7, distichous, to 15×3.5cm, lanceolate, dark green, sometimes edge with purple. Racemes arching, to 40cm, 2–20-fld; fls white, lilac-purple, mauve or pink; dorsal sep. to 30×11mm, erect or recurved, lateral sep. spreading, to 25×11mm; pet. to 30×30mm, usually recurved; lip about 25×20mm, trilobed, lateral lobes erect, midlobe decurved with 5 hairy ridges. New Guinea, Australia. ssp. *bigibbum*. Fls relatively small, about 5cm diam., light mauve, often with white patch on lip. ssp. *compactum* (C.T. White) Clements & Jones. Pseudobulbs short and stout, to 25×2mm, spindle-shaped. ssp. *phalaenopsis* (Fitzg.) Clements & Cribb. Fls large, to 7cm diam., usually deep purple, seg. not, or only slightly, recurved. 'Albomarginatum': tepals edged with white. 'Album', 'Hololeucum': fls white.

D.bracteosum Rchb. f.
Pseudobulbs 20–40cm long, cylindrical, clustered, erect or pendent, covered in papery sheaths, with up to 6 lvs. Lvs 4–8×1–2cm, ligulate. Racemes short, densely 3- to several-fld, bracts almost as long as fls; fls scented, waxy, tepals white, pink or purple, lip orange-red; sep. 10–20mm, lanceolate, acuminate; pet. 10–12mm, obovate, acute; lip oblong-elliptic or spathulate, concave, with shiny, fleshy callus. Papua New Guinea, New Ireland.

D.brymerianum Rchb. f.
Pseudobulbs 30–50×1–1.5cm, bulbous at base then spindle-shaped, with up to 6 lvs near apex. Lvs distichous, 10–15×1–2.5cm, oblong or lanceolate acuminate. Racemes to 11cm, borne near apex, 1- to few-fld; fls 5–6cm diam., yellow, the lip with orange laterals lobes; tepals 30×10–12mm, dorsal sep. and pet. ligulate, lateral ovate; lip 50×35mm, clawed at base then ovate, with branched threads to 12mm long around the margin. Burma, Laos, Thailand.

D.bullenianum Rchb. f. (*D.topaziacum* Ames).
Stems 25–60×0.5cm, covered with sheaths. Lvs 7–14×1.5–3cm, oblong, obtusely bilobed at apex, thin-textured. Infl. to 7cm, almost globose, densely many-fld; fls yellow to orange, striped red and purple; dorsal sep. 6×3.5mm, oblong, acute, laterals 18–20×4mm; pet. 6×3mm, oblanceolate, acute; lip subspathulate, 17×5mm, emarginate, with basal callus on claw; column short, anther-cap with 3 teeth. Philippines and W Samoa.

D.canaliculatum R. Br.
Pseudobulbs 3–12×1.5–3cm, spindle-shaped or ovoid, covered when young with sheathing bracts, 2–6-lvd near apex. Lvs to 20×1cm, linear, acute, semi-cylindrical, grooved on upper surface. Racemes 10–40cm, densely many-fld; fls scented, to 25mm diam., tepals yellow or brown, white at base, lip white with purple markings; sep. 7–15×3–4mm, oblong, acute, with 1 twist; pet. 12–18×2–3mm, suberect, linear or spathulate, 0-2-twisted; lip 9–15×8–9mm, trilobed, with 3 longitudinal ridges becoming raised and undulate on midlobe, lateral lobes rounded or truncate, midlobe ovate, acute or apiculate, sometimes recurved. New Guinea, NE Australia.

D.capillipes Rchb. f.
Pseudobulbs 10–15×2cm, clustered, spindle-shaped, leafless at flowering time. Lvs 10–15×1–1.5cm, lanceolate or ligulate, acuminate. Racemes 12–15cm, borne near apex of pseudobulbs, 1–4-fld; fls 3cm diam., yellow, orange in centre; dorsal sep. 15×7–8mm, oblong, acute, laterals similar but up to 23mm long; pet. 15×15mm, oblong-ovate, obtuse; lip 20×25mm, kidney-shaped with a short claw, bilobed, the edge undulate. Burma, China, Thailand.

D.capitisyork M. Clements & D. Jones (*D.tetragonum* var. *giganteum* Gilbert).
Pseudobulbs to 40×1.5cm, almost pendent, cylindrical at base then 4-angled. Lvs 2–4, to 8×4cm, ovate. Racemes to 2cm,

Dendrobium (a) *D.infundibulum* (b) *D.spectabile* (c) *D.fimbriatum*

2–5-fld; fls yellow-green spotted with red, lip white with red lines on lateral lobes; tepals spreading, linear, acuminate; dorsal sep. to 65×5mm, lateral sep. to 60×10mm; pet. to 40×2mm; lip 17–20×12–14mm, curved, trilobed, with basal callus of 3–5-ridges, lateral lobes large, erect, midlobe narrow, long-acuminate. Australia (NE Queensland).

D.cariniferum Rchb. f.
Stems 15–25cm. Lvs 5–8cm, linear-oblong, coriaceous, the sheaths sparsely hairy. Racemes short, 2–3-fld; fls scented, pale buff, the lip with golden-yellow streaks inside, occasionally marked with brick-red; sep. lanceolate, keeled on outside, lateral sep. forming an acute, incurved mentum; pet. somewhat broader, elliptic-oblong, apiculate; lip trilobed, lateral lobes rounded with an undulate edge, midlobe obovate, disc fringed, edge crisped. India, Burma.

D.chrysanthum Wallich ex Lindl.
Stems 1–2m, pendent. Lvs 10–20×1–3.5cm, lanceolate-ovate, acuminate. Infl. short, arising opposite lvs, 1–3-fld; fls scented, golden-yellow, the lip usually with 2 basal chestnut-brown spots; sep. 16–21×8–11mm, oblong, obtuse; pet. 16–20×15–17mm, obovate, obtuse, slightly dentate near apex; lip 22–24×15–24mm, suborbicular, concave, the edge denticulate. E Himalaya to Burma and Thailand.

D.chryseum Rolfe. See *D.aurantiacum*.

D.chrysocrepis Parish & Rchb. f.
Pseudobulbs 15–25cm, somewhat club-shaped. Lvs 5–8cm, lanceolate, acute and unevenly bilobed at apex. Infl. single-fld, borne on leafless stems; fls about 3cm diam., golden yellow, the lip with red-brown hairs on disc.; sep. oblong, subacute, mentum short; pet. broader, obovate; lip hairy, pear-shaped, the edges inrolled. Burma.

D.chrysoglossum auct. See *D.pseudoglomeratum*.

D.chrysotoxum Lindl. (*D.suavissimum* Rchb. f.).
Pseudobulbs 12–30cm, clustered, spindle-shaped or club-shaped, 2–4-lvd near apex. Lvs 10–15×2.5cm, lanceolate or oblong. Racemes to 20cm, arched, pendent, laxly to about 20-fld; fls scented, 4–5cm diam., golden-yellow, the lip orange in centre; sep. 20×7–8mm, oblong, obtuse; pet. 22×15mm, obovate, rounded; lip 20×23mm, densely hairy, edge fringed. Assam, Burma, Thailand, China (Yunnan), Laos.

D.coelogyne Rchb. f. See *Epigeneium coelogyne*.
D.crassinode Benson & Rchb. f. See *D.pendulum*.

D.crepidatum Lindl. & Paxt.
Pseudobulbs 15–50cm, fairly erect to pendent, with several lvs. Lvs 5–12×1–1.5cm, lanceolate, acute. Infl. arising from nodes of leafless stems, 1–3-fld; fls scented, to 4.5cm diam.; tepals white with pink tips, lip white, tip pink or magenta, disc orange; tepals 20×12mm, oblong or ovate, obtuse; lip 25×18–20mm, obovate with a short claw, edge somewhat undulate. Assam, Sikkim, Burma.

D.cretaceum Lindl. See *D.polyanthum*.

D.cruentum Rchb. f.
Pseudobulbs erect, about 30cm high, cylindrical but swollen at base. Lvs oblong, unequally bilobed at apex, deciduous. Infl. 1–2-fld, arising at nodes; fls 3–5cm diam., pale green to cream, lateral lobes, edge of midlobe and crest of lip marked brilliant scarlet to blood red; sep. triangular-ovate, keeled on outside, mentum rounded; pet. linear, acute; lip trilobed, side lobes erect, oblong; midlobe ovate, apiculate, with 3 red ridges. Malay Peninsula.

D.crumenatum Sw.
Stems 60–90cm, robust, branched, spindle-shaped at base. Lvs 4–8×1cm, oblong, obtuse or bilobed, coriaceous. Infl. short, arising on leafless ends of branches, several- to many-fld.; fls scented, about 4cm diam., fls white, lip with primrose yellow disc and sometimes pink-veined; dorsal sep. 25×8mm, ovate-lanceolate, lateral sep. slightly wider, acuminate, forming a conical, acute, incurved mentum equalling them in length; pet. about 20×7mm, linear-oblong; lip 33×14mm,

trilobed, lateral lobes truncate, midlobe suborbicular, edge crisped or fimbriate, disc with 3 crenate ridges. Andaman Is., Sri Lanka, Burma, Thailand, Malaysia, S China.

D.crystallinum Rchb. f.
Pseudobulbs 30–50cm, pendent, cylindrical, furrowed. Lvs 10–15cm, curved-lanceolate, acute. Racemes 1–3-fld; fls 5cm diam., white, the tepals purple-tipped, lip orange, the edge paler; sep. oblong-lanceolate, acute, mentum short; pet. much broader; lip suborbicular from a short claw, somewhat funnel-shaped at base, disc pubesc. Sikkim, Burma.

D.cucumerinum Macleay ex Lindl.
Stems spreading, branched, about 4mm diam., covered with fibrous sheaths. Lvs widely spaced, to 35×12mm, ovate, fleshy, lumpy, borne alternately. Racemes to 5cm, 2–10-fld; fls about 12mm diam., green-white to cream with purple veining towards base of seg., lip with dark red ridges; sep. and pet. twisted, sep. to 20×3mm, lanceolate, dorsal sep. erect, laterals spreading, pet. to 20×1.5mm, linear, erect, the apices sometimes curving down; lip about 14×5mm, with a callus of 3 ridges becoming undulate on midlobe, lateral lobes erect, clasping column, midlobe recurved, edges crisped. Australia.

D.cunninghamii Lindl.
Pseudobulbs slender, 'stem-like' and branching, to 100cm long. Fls paired, small, white with purple-red markings on lateral lobes of lip. New Zealand.

D.cuthbertsonii F. Muell. (*D.sophronites* Schltr.).
Epiphytic, rarely terrestrial, 2–8cm. Pseudobulbs clustered, usually globose or ovoid but sometimes stem-like with short branches, 1–5-lvd. Lvs to 4×1.5cm, linear to elliptic or ovate, closely rugose-papillose above, dark green, often tinged purple below. Infl. 1-fld, usually terminal; fls usually scarlet to brick red, but may be purple, pink, orange, yellow, white or bi-coloured; dorsal sep. 10–20×3–12mm, oblong, obtuse, laterals similar but longer, forming mentum 9–18mm high; pet. 10–20×6–16mm, obovate to suborbicular; lip entire, 12–30×5–15mm, obovate, concave, sometimes with a V- or U-shaped ridge near base. New Guinea.

D.dalhousianum Wallich. See *D.pulchellum*.

D.dearei Rchb. f.
Pseudobulbs 60–90cm long, erect, leafy, the leaf sheaths covered with black hairs. Lvs to 25×5cm, oblong, obtuse. Racemes 6–18-fld; fls 5–6cm diam., white, the lip yellow or lime green at base; ovary winged; sep. 25×8mm, ovate, acuminate, keeled; pet. 25–30×25mm, broadly ovate to orbicular; lip 25mm long, trilobed, lateral lobes very small, midlobe ovate, emarginate, edge crisped. Philippines.

D.delacourii Guillaum.
Pseudobulbs squat, yellow-tinted, leafy, to 60cm. Fls to 10 per scapose, erect raceme; tepals green-white to pale lime green or sulphur-yellow; lip broadly funnel-shaped, conspicuously veined purple-red and deeply fringed. Burma, Thailand, Laos, Vietnam.

D.densiflorum Wallich ex Lindl.
Pseudobulbs 30–50×2cm, erect, clustered, almost 4-angled, 3–5-lvd near apex. Lvs to 16×2.5cm, lanceolate or ovate, acute. Racemes arising near apex of stem, to 26cm, pendent, very densely many-fld; fls scented, yellow, the lip orange at base, column orange-yellow; sep. 20–25mm, ovate-oblong, subacute; pet. 20–25mm, suborbicular with a short basal claw, edge denticulate near base; lip 22×25–28mm, orbicular with a short claw, edge fringed. Nepal, Assam, Sikkim, Burma.

D.devonianum Paxt.
Pseudobulbs 60–100cm, cylindrical, pendent. Lvs 8–10cm, less than 1cm wide, linear-lanceolate, acuminate. Infl. short, 1–2-fld, arising on leafless stems; fls 7–8cm diam., white or pale primrose yellow, sep. and lip purple-tipped; sep. lanceolate, acute, mentum saccate; pet. ovate, ciliate; lip orbicular, base shortly funnel-shaped, edge deeply fringed. India (Bhotan Himalaya, Assam), Burma.

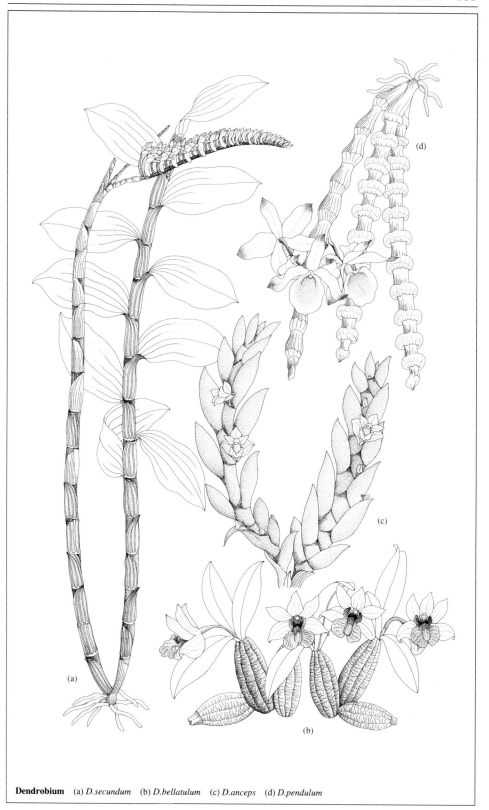

Dendrobium   (a) *D.secundum*   (b) *D.bellatulum*   (c) *D.anceps*   (d) *D.pendulum*

D.discolor Lindl. (*D.undulatum* R. Br.).
Stems to 5m tall, 1–5cm wide, cylindrical but swollen at base and in middle, green or brown, sometimes purple-striped. Lvs distichous, 5–20×3–8cm, elliptical or ovate. Racemes to 60cm, arched, densely 10–80-fld; fls cream, yellow, bronze or brown, often flushed with brown or purple; lip purple-veined, callus white; tepals twisted and crisped, dorsal sep. to 40×6mm, linear-oblong, laterals similar but wider, spreading, pet. to 50×8mm, spathulate, erect but divergent; lip to 25×15mm, trilobed, lateral lobes erect, midlobe recurved, often twisted, ovate, with callus of 5 ridges on basal half. Australia, New Guinea.

D.dixanthum Rchb. f.
Pseudobulbs to 1m, erect, cylindrical, usually 4-lvd. Lvs to 17×1cm, lanceolate to ligulate, acute or acuminate. Racemes borne at nodes of leafless stems, to 5cm, 2–5-fld; fls yellow, striped with red at base of lip; sep. 25–28×10mm, oblong-lanceolate, acute; pet. 23×13mm, oblong, obtuse, the edge finely serrate; lip 25×18–20mm, suborbicular with a short claw, the edge undulate and serrate or fringed. Burma, Thailand, Laos.

D.draconis Rchb. f.
Pseudobulbs 30–45×1–1.5cm, clustered, spindle- or club-shaped, the sheaths with short black hairs. Lvs to 10×2cm, lanceolate or ligulate, acutely bilobed at apex, dark green, leathery. Racemes arising from nodes near apex, 2–5-fld; fls scented, 6–7cm diam., ivory-white with red or orange towards base of lip; sep. 40×10mm, lanceolate, acuminate, the laterals forming a prominent mentum 20mm long; pet. 40×15mm, lanceolate, acuminate; lip 55×20mm, trilobed, lateral lobes small and rounded, midlobe oblong, acute, edge undulate; disc with 3 ridges. Burma, Thailand, Indochina.

D.engae T.M.Reeve.
Broadly similar to *D.spectabile* in habit. Raceme erect, robust; fls 3-18, 5-6cm diam., long-lasting, fragrant; tepals ovate-lanceolate, cool lime green; lip green with lateral lobes veined purple and midlobe spotted purple. Papua, New Guinea.

D.falconeri Hook.
Stems 60–100cm, slender, branched, pendent, rather straggling. Lvs to 10cm, linear-lanceolate, acute. Infl. single-fld; fls 5–11cm diam., rose-pink or white with purple-tipped seg., lip purple and orange; sep. narrowly oblong, acuminate, mentum incurved; pet. ovate-lanceolate; lip with short funnel-shaped base then broadly ovate, acute or acuminate, edges recurved and ciliate. India (Bhotan Himalaya, Assam), Upper Burma.

D.farmeri Paxt.
Pseudobulbs 20–30×2–2.5cm, spindle-shaped but swollen at base, 4-angled. Lvs 8–18×3.5×6cm, ovate-lanceolate, acute or acuminate, leathery. Racemes borne on leafless stems, 20–30cm, pendent, densely many-fld; fls to 5cm diam., white or lilac mauve, lip yellow; sep. 20–25×10–12mm, ovate-oblong; pet. 20–25×20mm, suborbicular; lip 22×22mm, orbicular with a short basal claw, edge finely serrate. Himalaya, Burma, Thailand, Malaya.

D.fimbriatum Hook.
Pseudobulbs to 120cm, spindle-shaped, erect, arched or pendent, leafy. Lvs 8–15×2–3cm, oblong or lanceolate, acute or acuminate, deciduous. Racemes arising from apex of leafless stems, to 18cm, pendent, to 15-fld; fls orange-yellow, lip deeper coloured than tepals; sep. and pet. 25–30×12–18mm, ovate or oblong, the edges finely toothed; lip 25–30×30mm, suborbicular with a short claw, edge fringed. Nepal, Burma, Thailand, India, China, Malaya.

D.finisterrae Schltr.
Pseudobulbs 'stem-like', to 70cm. Lvs 2 at apex. Infl. sparse; fls not opening fully; tepals yellow- white, concave above, their exteriors densely covered with purple-tinted, warty hairs; lip cupped, strongly 3-lobed, green with broken red lines. Papua, New Guinea.

D.forbesii Ridley.
Similar in habit to *D.spectabile*. Highly floriferous. Fls to 8cm diam., snowy white, honey-scented; tepals broadly ovate-lanceolate, somewhat undulate, as is lip, the whole appearing lace-like. New Guinea.

D.formosum Roxb.ex Lindl.
Pseudobulbs to 45×1.5cm, erect, cylindrical, leafy for most of their length. Lvs to 13×3cm, oblong, obtuse, leathery, lf sheaths hairy. Racemes arising at apex and from nodes near apex; fls to 12cm diam., white with yellow lip; sep. 40–60×12–25mm, lanceolate, keeled; pet. to 60×36mm, obovate, edge undulate; lip about 50×40mm, obscurely trilobed, lateral lobes small, erect, midlobe obovate, edge undulate. Nepal to Burma and Thailand.

D.fuscatum Lindl. See *D.gibsonii*.
D.fusiforme (Bail.) Bail. See *D.jonesii*.

D.gibsonii Lindl. (*D.fuscatum* Lindl.).
Stems slender, to almost 1m. Lvs lanceolate, acuminate. Racemes pendent, many-fld; fls to 5cm diam., orange-yellow, the lip with 2 brown blotches; sep. suborbicular, pet. broader; lip suborbicular from a wedge-shaped base, concave, the margins ciliate and rolled back. Sikkim, Assam, Burma.

D.glomeratum auct. See *D.pseudoglomeratum*.

D.gouldii Rchb. f.
Epiphytic or lithophytic; pseudobulbs 90–180cm, cane-like, often somewhat swollen in middle. Lvs to 18×6.5cm, oblong or elliptic, leathery. Racemes 30–70cm, several- to many-fld; fls variable in colour and size, sep. white to yellow, pet. white, yellow, brown or violet, lip white to yellow with purple veining; dorsal sep. 20–25×5–6mm, linear-lanceolate, acute, recurved, laterals slightly wider; pet. 27–40×3–5mm, narrowly spathulate, obtuse, with 1–3 twists; lip 22–24×13–15mm with a callus of 5 ridges, trilobed, lateral lobes rounded, the margins erose, midlobe subspathulate, apiculate, margins erose; column 6–8mm, apex denticulate. Solomon Is., New Ireland, Vanuatu.

D.gracilicaule F. Muell.
Epiphytic or lithophytic; pseudobulbs to 90×1cm, cylindrical, clustered, ribbed, yellow-green, 3–6-lvd at apex. Lvs to 13×4cm, ovate, unequally bilobed at apex. Racemes to 12cm, few- to many-fld; fls about 15mm diam., often drooping, dull green, yellow or orange, blotched with red-brown outside; sep. and pet. spreading, sep. to 10×4mm, oblong, pet. similar but half as wide; lip 8×6mm with callus of 3 ridges, trilobed, lateral lobes erect, midlobe kidney-shaped. Australia. Sometimes considered to be conspecific with *D.macropus* (Endl.) Rchb. f. ex Lindl. from the Pacific Islands.

D.gratiosissimum Rchb. f.
Pseudobulbs to 90cm, swollen at nodes, usually pendent. Lvs 7–10×1–1.5cm, ligulate, bilobed at apex, deciduous. Infl. borne at nodes of leafless stems, 1–3-fld; fls to 7cm diam., white, all parts tipped with purple-pink, the lip orange in centre; sep. 30–35×10mm, lanceolate, acuminate; pet. similar but almost twice as wide; lip 30×25mm, ovate, funnel-shaped at base. Burma, Thailand.

D.harveyanum Rchb. f.
Pseudobulbs 15–25cm, erect, spindle-shaped, 2–3-lvd. Lvs to 11×3cm, ovate-oblong. Infl. arising below lvs, 2–6-fld; fls fragrant, about 5cm diam., bright canary yellow, the lip orange in throat; sep. 18–20×8–9mm, lanceolate, acute, mentum short; pet. 20–30×7mm, elliptic, the edge deeply fringed; lip to 21×25mm, orbicular to reniform, more or less funnel-shaped, margin fringed. Summer. Burma, Thailand, Vietnam.

D.hercoglossum Rchb. f.
Pseudobulbs to 35cm, less than 1cm wide, clustered, cylindrical, almost covered by sheaths. Lvs to 10×1cm, linear-lanceolate, obtusely and unevenly bilobed at apex. Racemes borne on leafy or leafless stems, 2–5-fld; sep. and pet. magenta, lip white, apex magenta; tepals 10–20×5–7mm, lanceolate, acuminate; lip 10–15mm, basal part orbicular, concave, the sides

enfolding column, apical part lanceolate, acuminate, the 2 parts separated by a transverse, fringed keel. Thailand, Indochina.

D.heterocarpum Lindl. (*D.aureum* Lindl.).
Pseudobulbs 40–150cm, clustered, spindle-shaped, erect or pendent. Lvs to 18×2.5cm, oblong-lanceolate, acute or obtuse. Racemes borne at nodes of leafless stems, 2–3-fld; fls scented, to 8cm diam., pale yellow with dark red blotch on lip; sep. to 40mm, oblong-lanceolate, subacute; pet. to 35mm, ovate, acuminate; lip 35×20mm, lanceolate-ovate, folded round column at base, margins finely toothed, apex reflexed. A variable species. Winter. Sri Lanka, India, Burma and West to Philippines.

D.infundibulum Lindl. (*D.jamesianum* Rchb. f.).
Pseudobulbs to 1m long, 1cm wide, erect, leafy, the sheaths with black hairs. Lvs 8.5×2cm, lanceolate or narrowly ovate, slightly bilobed at apex, dark green. Racemes short, few-fld, arising near apex of old stems; fls to 8cm diam., white, lined with orange and red towards base of lip; sep. 30–42×9–13mm, ovate, acute, the mentum 25–30mm long, slender, curved; pet. 35–50×30–40mm, orbicular; lip 32–50×25–35mm, obovate, trilobed, lateral lobes erect, midlobe emarginate, edge undulate and serrate, disc with 5 ridges. Burma, Thailand.

D.jamesianum Rchb. f. See *D.infundibulum*.
D.japonicum Lindl. See *D.moniliforme*.
D.jenkinsii Wallich ex Lindl.
Pseudobulbs 2–3cm, laterally compressed, 1-lvd, forming dense tufts or mats. Racemes pendent, 1–3-fld; fls large, golden yellow; lip entire, almost orbicular, the apex emarginate. Assam.

D.johnsoniae F. Muell.
Pseudobulbs 20–30×1–1.5cm, spindle-shaped, 4–5-lvd toward apex. Lvs to 15×4.5cm, ovate, obtuse. Racemes arising near apex of stem, to 40cm, few- to many-fld; fls 7–12cm diam., white, streaked with purple on lateral lobes of lip and base of column; sep. to 38×10mm, lanceolate, acuminate, lateral sep. slightly longer and wider than dorsal; pet. 40–50×18–30mm, rhombic, acuminate from a narrow claw; lip to 45×30mm, trilobed, with a 2-ridged callus at base, lateral lobes erect, midlobe ovate, acuminate. New Guinea, Bougainville.

D.jonesii Rendle (*D.fusiforme* (Bail.) Bail.; *D.ruppianum* A.D. Hawkes).
Epiphytic or lithophytic; pseudobulbs to 50×4cm, swollen at base then fusiform, dark green-brown, ribbed, 2–7-lvd at apex. Lvs to 15×6cm, ovate, leathery, dark green. Racemes to 40cm, arched, many-fld; fls scented, white or cream turning yellow as they age, the lip white with purple marks; sep. and pet. spreading, linear-lanceolate, acute, sep. to 22×4.5mm, pet. to 22×2mm; lip 8×7mm, curved, trilobed, with a linear orange ridge towards base, lateral lobes crescent-shaped, midlobe oblong, truncate. Australia, New Guinea.

D.kingianum Bidwill ex Lindl.
Lithophytic, forming large clumps; very variable. Pseudobulbs 6–35×1–2cm, narrowly conical, often tinged with red, 2–7-lvd at apex. Lvs to 12×2cm, lanceolate, ovate or obovate. Racemes to 20cm, few- to about 20-fld; fls white, pink, mauve, purple or red, the lip sometimes with darker stripes; sep. to 18×7mm, dorsal sep. erect, laterals spreading; pet. to 15×3mm, erect or incurved; lip about 15×8mm, trilobed, lateral lobes narrow, erect, midlobe recurved, acute. Australia.

D.lasianthera J.J. Sm.
Pseudobulbs to 2.5m, cane-like, leafy in upper half. Lvs about 6×3cm, elliptic, leathery. Racemes to 50cm, several- to many-fld; fls pink or yellow, flushed with purple or maroon; dorsal sep. 25–32×10mm, erect, lanceolate, acute, laterals to 40×13mm, linear, recurved, spirally twisted, mentum conical, about 18mm; pet. 35–45×4–6mm, suberect, narrowly spathulate with 3–4 spiral twists; lip 36–48×18mm, trilobed, with a callus of 3 ridges reaching base of midlobe, lateral lobes

spreading, rounded, midlobe 8×6–8mm, spathulate, apiculate, margins recurved; column about 9mm. New Guinea.

D.lawesii F. Muell.
Pseudobulbs to 45cm, subcylindrical, pendent, covered with maroon leaf sheaths that turn scarious with age. Lvs distichous, 6–7×2cm, ovate-elliptic, thin-textured. Racemes borne on leafless stems, very short, 1–6-fld; fls pendent, white, red, orange, yellow or mauve; dorsal sep. 7–10mm, ovate or oblong, lateral sep. 20×7mm, oblong, forming curved mentum almost 20mm long; pet. similar to dorsal sep.; lip to 15×9mm, spathulate, margin very finely toothed, lower edge rolled in. New Guinea, Bougainville.

D.leonis (Lindl.) Rchb.f.
Pseudobulbs slender, cane-like, to 25cm, usually pendulous. Fls to 1.5cm diam., borne singly or in pairs in profusion toward stem tips, somewhat tubular; tepals cream marked or stained purple-red on exterior; lip blotched purple-red. SE Asia.

D.lichenastrum (F. Muell.) Kranzl.
Dwarf, creeping lithophyte. Pseudobulbs replaced by solitary, succulent leaves arising directly from rhizome, these 1 to 5cm long, ovoid or tusk-like, thick. Fls solitary at base of lf, small, cream to apricot with some red and yellow marking on lip, often sweetly fragrant. NE Australia.

D.lindleyi Steud. (*D.aggregatum* Roxb.).
Pseudobulbs 3–8cm, almost spindle-shaped, clustered, fairly erect, 1-lvd. Lf 5–16×1.5–3cm, oblong, leathery. Racemes 10–30cm, 5–15-fld, often pendent; fls scented, pale golden yellow, the lip orange in the throat; sep. 15×5mm, ligulate, acute; pet. 17×8–10mm, obovate; lip with basal claw then transversely oblong, 22×22mm, apex emarginate, margins undulate. Assam, Burma, S China, Malaya, Indochina.

D.lineale Rolfe.
Pseudobulbs to 3m, clustered, cane-like, leafy in upper two-thirds. Lvs to 14×9cm, elliptic, leathery. Racemes to 75cm, laxly or densely many-fld; sep. and lip white or pale yellow, the lip purple-veined, pet. white, pink, or blue-mauve; sep. recurved, dorsal 18–20×5–6mm, linear, acuminate, laterals of similar length but twice as wide forming conical mentum 8–11mm long; pet. 22–30×4–6mm, erect, spathulate, half twisted or not twisted at all; lip 20–24×15–16mm, trilobed, with callus of 3 keels raised in centre of midlobe, lateral lobes rounded with erose margins, midlobe oblong, apiculate, the margin undulate and erose; column 6mm. New Guinea.

D.linguiforme Sw.
Small, mat-forming epiphytic plant with branched stems about 4mm thick. Lvs arising alternately on stem, to 4×1.5cm, oblong to obovate, fleshy, dark green, furrowed. Racemes to 15cm, to 20-fld; fls white or cream; sep. and pet. linear, acute, sep. to 22×5mm, lateral sep. slightly wider than dorsal, pet. to 20×2mm; lip curved, about 6×4mm, trilobed, with callus of 3 ridges becoming undulate on midlobe lateral lobes small, midlobe ovate, acute, edge undulate. Australia.

D.lituiflorum Lindl.
Pseudobulbs 45–60×0.5cm, reed-like with swollen bases, clustered, pendent. Lvs to 12.5×3.5cm, fleshy, linear-lanceolate. Racemes arising at nodes, 1–5-fld; fls scented, to 10cm diam., white, lilac or purple, lip maroon or purple at base, surrounded by white or yellow; sep. 25–50×10mm, oblong, acute; pet. similar but 15mm wide; lip 25×25mm, trumpet-shaped. NE India, Burma, Thailand.

D.loddigesii Rolfe
Pseudobulbs 10–17×5–7cm, clustered, pendent, cylindrical, with white sheaths. Lvs 4–6×1–2cm, oblong, fleshy. Fls borne single at nodes of leafless stems, 5cm diam., lilac-purple, the lip purple-edge, orange in centre; sep. 20–25×8–9mm, ovate, obtuse; pet. 20×12mm, elliptic; lip 18×15mm, suborbicular with a short claw, margin fringed. Laos, S China.

D.longicornu Wallich. ex Lindl.
Pseudobulbs 15–30×0.5cm, clustered, zigzag, covered with black hairs, leafy near apex. Lvs 7×0.5–2cm, linear-lanceolate, acute, deciduous. Racemes arising near top of leafy stems, short, 1–3-fld; fls fragrant, white, the lip marked with red and yellow; dorsal sep. 15–20×6–7mm, ovate, acute, laterals 40–50×6–7mm, almost triangular, forming mentum 20–30mm long; pet. similar to dorsal sep.; lip trilobed, with branched, fleshy basal callus, lateral lobes erect, rounded, midlobe rounded, fringed in front. Nepal, Sikkim, Burma.

D.lyonii Ames. See *Epigeneium lyonii*.

D.maccarthiae Thwaites.
Pseudobulbs 30–60cm, slender, cylindrical, pendent, leafy near apex. Lvs 4–10×1cm, lanceolate, acuminate, thin-textured. Racemes arising on leafy stems, 5–8cm, pendent, laxly 2–5-fld; fls not opening wide, rose-pink or violet-pink, the lip maroon or purple in centre; sep. 35–45×10mm, lanceolate, acuminate; pet. 40–45×20mm, ovate-oblong, acute; lip 60×30mm, subspathulate, obscurely trilobed, lateral lobes rounded, folded up, midlobe ovate, subacute. Sri Lanka.

D.macranthum A. Rich.
Pseudobulbs to 60×1.5cm, clustered, cane-like, somewhat swollen at base. Lvs 7–12×2.5–4.5cm, oblong or elliptic, leathery, unequally bilobed at apex, the lobes rounded. Racemes to about 30cm, suberect, laxly to about 20-fld; fls yellow, yellow-green or lime green, the lip paler in middle with a lilac callus, purple-veined; dorsal sep. 25–38×5–6mm, linear-lanceolate, acute, laterals recurved, 30–36×7–10mm, oblique, curved, forming narrow, conical mentum 10–12mm long; lip 25–32×12–13mm, trilobed, with callus of 3 ridges, lateral lobes truncate in front with erose margins, midlobe 12–20×7–8mm, linear-lanceolate, acuminate. Santa Cruz Is., Vanuatu, New Caledonia.

D.macrophyllum A. Rich. (*D.veitchianum* Lindl.).
Pseudobulbs clustered, to 50cm, club-shaped or rarely spindle-shaped, 3–7-lvd. Lvs 15–30×3–9cm, oblong, obtuse. Racemes erect, to 40cm, usually densely many-fld; fls yellow or yellow-green with purple spots or stripes on lip and, often, tepals; sep. hairy outside, 20–26mm long, dorsal sep. oblong, laterals obliquely triangular; pet. 18–22mm, oblanceolate, acute, the edge somewhat undulate; lip 10–20×16–27mm, recurved, trilobed, lateral lobes erect, midlobe transversely oblong, apiculate, the margins curved up; ovary hairy. Malaysia to New Guinea, Bougainville, Solomon Is., Fiji, Samoa.

D.macrophyllum Lindl. non A. Rich. See *D.anosmum*.

D.mirbelianum Gaud.
Pseudobulbs to 3m tall, 1.5–3cm diam., cane-like, somewhat swollen toward base. Lvs 8–12.5×2.5–5.5cm, oblong, elliptic or ovate, obtusely bilobed at apex. Racemes to 45cm, few- to many-fld; fls variable in size, yellow-green to olive-brown, the lip with purple-brown veins and a white callus marked with purple; sep. 22–28×6–7mm, linear-lanceolate, dorsal sep. erect, laterals spreading and forming a conical mentum 7–8mm high; pet. 22–50×4–7mm, spathulate, half twisted or not twisted at all; lip 16–35×12–15mm, trilobed, with callus of 5 erose ridges, lateral lobes rounded, erose on margins, midlobe 9–15mm, recurved, ovate, acute, the edges undulate and erose; column 4–5mm, apex denticulate. Moluccas, New Guinea, Bismarck Archipelago, Solomon Is., Australia.

D.mohlianum Rchb. f.
Stems to 50cm, cylindrical, clustered, ribbed, sometimes pendent. Lvs distichous, 6–13×1–2.5cm, lanceolate. Racemes axillary on leafless stems, to 3cm, 4–6-fld; fls orange or red; dorsal sep. 9mm, ovate, laterals 15mm, triangular; pet. similar to dorsal sep; lip 16×10mm, obovate, the apex hooded. Vanuatu, Solomon Is., Fiji, Samoa.

D.moniliforme (L.) Sw. (*D.japonicum* Lindl.).
Pseudobulbs 10–40cm, clustered, pendent, cylindrical or spindle-shaped, purple-brown with grey sheaths, turning yellow with age. Lvs 5–6×1cm, lanceolate, obtuse, deciduous. Infl. arising at nodes of leafless stems, 2-fld; fls scented, white tinged with pink, the base of lip yellow-green with brown spots; sep. and pet. to 30×12mm, lanceolate or ovate; lip 14–28×14mm, trilobed, lateral lobes erect, midlobe ovate, reflexed, the disc with a horizontal line of red dots. Japan, Korea, Taiwan.

D.moorei F. Muell.
Pseudobulbs to 25×1cm erect, cylindrical, clustered, 2–5-lvd near apex. Lvs to 12×3cm, oblong, leathery, dark green. Racemes to 8cm, 2–15-fld; fls white, somewhat drooping and not opening wide; sep. and pet. about 15×2.5mm, lanceolate, acute; lip about 10×5mm, trilobed, lateral side lobes erect, midlobe acute, margins crisped. Australia (Lord Howe Is.).

D.moschatum (Buch.-Ham.) Sw.
Pseudobulbs to 1.5m, cylindrical, erect, arched or pendent, the upper half leafy. Lvs about 15×3.5cm, elliptic or ovate, acute, leathery. Racemes to 20cm, pendent, arising towards apex of old stems, 8–10-fld; fls pale yellow or apricot, veined with light purple, the lip with 2 maroon blotches; sep. 40×15mm, elliptic, obtuse; pet. similar but 20mm wide; lip 25×25mm, hairy, concave-saccate, margins inrolled. Sikkim, Burma, Laos, Thailand.

D.nardoides Schltr.
Pseudobulbs to 25×5mm, ovoid or cylindrical, clustered, 1–4-lvd at apex. Lvs to 60×2mm, linear, channelled, often stiff. Infl. terminal on leafy and leafless stems, 1–2-fld; fls purple-pink, the lip apex scarlet; dorsal sep. 5–10×2–3mm, oblong-lanceolate, acuminate, laterals 10–20×2–3.5mm, oblong-lanceolate, acuminate, forming cylindrical mentum 5–10mm long; pet. 4–9×1–2mm, linear or oblanceolate, acute or apiculate; lip 9–16×1–2mm, narrowly oblanceolate, obscurely trilobed, recurved. E New Guinea.

D.nobile Lindl.
Pseudobulbs 30–50cm tall, erect, clustered, furrowed when old. Lvs distichous, 7–12×1–3cm, ligulate, lasting for 2 years. Infl. arising at nodes of leafy and leafless stems, short, 2–4-fld; fls scented, 6–8cm diam.; sep. and pet. mauve or pink paling to white at base, lip maroon in throat, surrounded by yellow or white; sep. to 40×15mm, lanceolate, acute; pet. 40×25mm, ovate, edge somewhat undulate; lip 45×30mm, obovate, funnel-shaped at base. NE India to China, Laos and Thailand.

D.ochreatum Lindl.
Stems 15–25cm, stout, cylindrical, decumbent. Lvs 10–13cm, ovate-lanceolate, acuminate, unequally subcordate at base. Racemes 2-fld, arising opposite a leaf; fls 7.5cm diam., golden yellow, the disc of lip red; sep. oblong, obtuse; pet. larger; lip funnel-shaped at base then orbicular, concave, pubesc., the edge erose and rolled back. India.

D.palpebrae Lindl.
Pseudobulbs 15–50×1–1.5cm, subcylindrical, clustered, 2–5-lvd near apex. Lvs 7.5–15×1–3cm, lanceolate, acute. Racemes to 10cm, many-fld; fls scented, to 6cm diam.; pink or white, the lip with yellow or orange disc; sep. and pet. elliptic; lip ovate or orbicular with a short claw, concave, the edge ciliate. Sikkim, Burma, Thailand, China.

D.papilio Loher.
Stems thin, grass-like. Lvs linear, channelled to base. Fls large, solitary, fragrant, pendent; sep. and pet. pale rose; lip yellow with purple venation, long-stalked, undulate. Philippines.

D.parishii Rchb. f.
Pseudobulbs to 50×2cm, cylindrical, arching to pendent. Lvs 5–10cm, elliptic, obtuse, bilobed at apex, deciduous. Racemes borne at nodes of leafless pseudobulbs, 2–3-fld; fls rose-purple, white towards base, lip with 2 purple blotches in throat; sep. 30–35×12mm, oblong-lanceolate; pet. 25–30×15–20mm, oblong, acute; lip 20–25×20–23mm, suborbicular with a short claw, obscurely trilobed. Burma, Thailand, Laos, Indochina, S China.

D.pendulum Roxb. (*D.crassinode* Benson & Rchb. f.).
Pseudobulbs 30–60×2.5cm, clustered, furrowed with very prominent, knuckle-like nodes, somewhat pendent. Lvs to 12×2.5cm, lanceolate, acute, deciduous. Infl. arising from nodes of old pseudobulbs, 1–3-fld; fls scented, long-lasting, to 7cm diam., white with purple tips to seg., lip yellow in throat; sep. 20–35×8–12mm, oblong, acute, apex reflexed; pet. 20–30×12–15mm, oblong; lip 20–25×20–25mm, orbicular from a short claw, pubesc. in middle. Assam, Burma, Thailand.

D.phalaenopsis Fitzg. See *D.bigibbum*.

D.pierardii (Roxb.) C. Fisch. See *D.aphyllum*.

D.polyanthum Lindl. (*D.cretaceum* Lindl.).
Pseudobulbs 25–30cm, stout, curved, almost pendent. Lvs 5–8×1.5–2cm, lanceolate, deciduous. Infl. single-fld, borne at nodes of leafless stems; fls 4–5cm diam., white, lip with yellow disc and crimson veins; tepals subequal, linear-oblong, obtuse; mentum conical, obtuse; lip pubesc., funnel-shaped at base then orbicular or ovate, the margin undulate and minutely fringed. India, Andaman Is., Burma, Thailand.

D.polysema Schltr.
Differs from *D.macrophyllum* in duller green tepals more closely hairy beneath and more densely spotted purple-red, and in the lip which is spotted red and has tapering, not rounded, lateral lobes. New Guinea.

D.primulinum Lindl.
Pseudobulbs 30–45×1–1.5cm, cylindrical, more or less erect, prostrate or pendent, covered with white sheaths. Lvs to 10×3cm, oblong, obtusely and unequally bilobed at apex. Infl. arising from nodes, 1–2-fld; fls scented, to 7cm diam., tepals pink, paler towards base, lip pale yellow, red in throat; tepals 28–35×8–10mm, oblong or ovate, obtuse; lip 30–35×50mm, transversely elliptical, funnel-shaped at base. Nepal and Sikkim Himalayas, Burma, Thailand, Vietnam, Malaya, S China.

D.pseudoglomeratum T.M. Reeve & J.J. Wood. (*D.glomeratum* auct.)
Stems slender, to 1m. Fls clustered, 1.25–4cm diam.; tepals bright cerise, oblong-obovate; lip entire with margins slightly inrolled, bright orange. New Guinea.

D.pulchellum Roxb. ex Lindl. (*D.dalhousianum* Wallich).
Pseudobulbs 1–2m, slender, cylindrical, erect, the leaf sheaths striped purple. Lvs 10–15×3mm, oblong, obtuse or acute. Racemes arising on leafy or leafless stems, pendent, 5–12-fld; fls to 8cm diam., pink-buff to cream-yellow, lip white, yellow at base, with 2 maroon blotches; sep. 40–45×20mm, ovate, acute; pet. similar but slightly wider; lip 28×25mm, concave, emarginate; disc with 2 fringed keels. Assam, Burma, Thailand, Malaya, Indochina.

D.purpureum Roxb.
Pseudobulbs to 50cm, subcylindrical but 4-angled and swollen at base, pendent. Lvs to 14×2cm, oblong-lanceolate, dark green. Racemes arising from nodes of leafless stems, short, 10–15-fld; fls rose-purple or white; dorsal sep. 8mm, oblong-lanceolate, laterals 15mm, oblong, forming mentum 6mm long; pet. 7mm, lanceolate; lip 10×5mm, saccate at base, the apex deflexed, erose. Vanuatu, Malaysia, New Guinea, Bougainville, Caroline Is., Fiji.

D.regale Schltr. See *Diplocaulobium regale*.

D.rhodostictum F. Muell. & Kränzl.
Epiphytic or terrestrial; pseudobulbs to 25×1cm, club-shaped, 2–4-lvd near apex. Lvs to 11×2.5cm, lanceolate, acute or obtuse. Racemes arising near apex, erect or arched, few-fld; fls somewhat drooping, white, the edges of lip with purple spots; sep. 18–25×10–11mm, ovate or lanceolate, acute or acuminate; mentum conical, 8–10mm; pet. 30–35×15–25mm, obovate, lip 20–26×18–28mm, broadly obovate, obscurely trilobed in apical half, lateral lobes erect, midlobe small, apiculate; callus of 3 ridges, lobed at base. Papua New Guinea and Solomon Is.

D.ruppianum A.D. Hawkes. See *D.jonesii*.

D.sanderae Rolfe.
Pseudobulbs to 80cm, erect, subcylindrical but thicker in basal half, leafy, the sheaths with black hairs. Lvs 5×1.5–2cm, ovate, bilobed at apex. Racemes about 6cm, 3–4-fld; fls to 7cm diam., white, the base and side lobes of lip streaked with red or purple; sep. 35–40mm, lanceolate, acuminate, mentum slender, to 25mm; pet. 35–38×20–30mm, obovate; lip 42×32mm, trilobed, base tubular, midlobe truncate. Philippines.

D.sanguinolentum Lindl.
Stems 60–100cm, pendent. Lvs 5–20cm, ovate or lanceolate, the underside red. Racemes short, arising on leafless stems, 3–5-fld; fls small, about 25mm diam., yellow, seg. violet-tipped, lip with red blotch; sep. ovate, obtuse, forming short mentum; pet. orbicular to oblong; lip clawed at base, trilobed, lateral lobes rounded, midlobe subquadrate, emarginate. Malaysia.

D.scabrilingue Lindl.
Pseudobulbs to 30×1.5cm, clustered, club-shaped, 4–6-lvd, the sheaths with black hairs. Lvs to 10.5×2cm, ligulate. Infl. very short, arising at nodes, 2-fld; fls scented, cream-white, the mentum green, the lip yellow in centre and marked with red on lateral lobes; sep. 20–22×7–8mm, triangular, acute, forming a conical mentum; pet. 18×7–8mm, lanceolate, acute, slightly reflexed; lip 18×8–9mm, erect, trilobed, with disc of 5–7 ridges. Burma, Thailand.

D.schuetzii Rolfe.
Pseudobulbs 15–40cm, erect, leafy, thicker at base and in apical half. Lvs 8.5×2.5cm, ovate. Racemes short, 3–4-fld; fls scented, to 9.5cm diam., white, the disc green tinged with purple; sep. 30–50mm long, oblong-lanceolate, acuminate; pet. to 55×40mm, suborbicular; lip 40–45mm, trilobed, lateral lobes incurved, forming basal tube, midlobe recurved, 35–40mm wide, obovate, truncate, apiculate. Philippines.

D.sculptum Rchb. f.
Evergreen. Pseudobulbs to 45×1cm. Fls to 5cm diam., produced from top of mature growth, 3 or 4 per spike; lip white with a square orange blotch in centre, base wrinkled. Borneo.

D.secundum (Bl.) Lindl.
Pseudobulbs to 1m long, 2cm diam., erect or almost pendent, spindle-shaped, leafy. Lvs 6–10×3–6cm, oblong, acute. Racemes arising from upper nodes, to 12cm, densely many-fld; fls pink, purple or white, lip orange or yellow towards apex; dorsal sep. 7×4mm, ovate, acute, concave, laterals 15×4mm, forming mentum 10mm long; pet. similar to dorsal sep.; lip spathulate, with transverse keel about halfway along. Burma, Thailand, Indochina, Malaysia, Sumatra, Philippines, Pacific Is.

D.senile Parish & Rchb. f.
Pseudobulbs 5–10cm long, almost club-shaped, 2–3-lvd. Lvs 5–8cm, sickle-shaped, hairy. Infl. 1–2-fld; fls 5cm diam., golden yellow; sep. lanceolate, acute, mentum rounded; pet. similar but broader; lip obscurely trilobed, lateral lobes rounded, midlobe ovate, obtuse, the apex slightly pubesc. Burma.

D.smillieae F. Muell. BOTTLE-BRUSH ORCHID.
Pseudobulbs to 100×3cm, clustered, spindle-shaped, ribbed, leafy. Lvs to 20×4cm, oblong or lanceolate. Racemes erect, to 15cm, densely many-fld; fls waxy-textured, almost tubular, white, cream, green-white or pink, the apex of lip shiny bright green; dorsal sep. 10×4mm, ovate or oblong, obtuse, laterals slightly shorter and wider; pet. to 10×3mm, spathulate, obtuse; lip about 16×4mm, held uppermost, funnel-shaped at base. New Guinea, Australia.

D.sophronites Schltr. See *D.cuthbertsonii*.

D.speciosissimum Rolfe. See *D.spectatissimum*.

D.speciosum Sm. ROCK ORCHID.
A variable epiphytic or lithophytic species; pseudobulbs to 100×6cm, cylindrical or club-shaped, 2–5-lvd at apex. Lvs to 25×8cm, oblong, leathery. Racemes erect or pendent, to

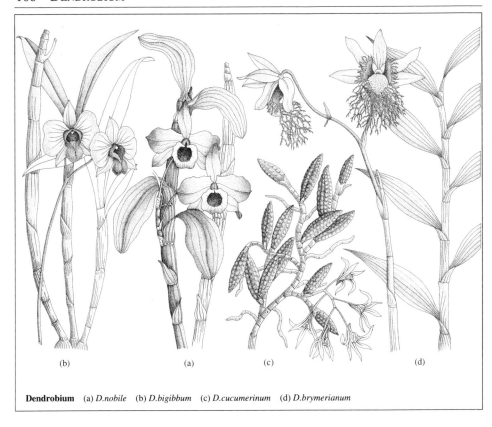

Dendrobium (a) *D.nobile* (b) *D.bigibbum* (c) *D.cucumerinum* (d) *D.brymerianum*

60cm, densely many-fld; fls scented, white, cream or yellow, the lip marked with red or purple; dorsal sep. 20–40×5–10mm, linear, acute, laterals 15–35×4–10mm, curved-linear, obtuse; pet. 15–35×2–5mm, linear, acute; lip to 30×20–40mm, trilobed, midlobe subquadrate or transversely oblong. E Australia.

D.spectabile (Bl.) Miq. (*D.tigrinum* Hemsl.).
Pseudobulbs to 40×1–1.5cm, cane-like but swollen at base, clustered; 4–6-lvd near apex. Lvs to 23×8cm, elliptic, obtuse. Racemes 20–40cm long, few to many-fld; fls yellow or cream, tepals speckled with maroon, lip with maroon lines and white callus, all parts with margins strongly and irregularly crispate-undulate; sep. about 35×5–12mm, recurved, lanceolate, acuminate; laterals wider than the dorsal; mentum about 10mm long, obliquely conical; pet. 40×6mm, linear-lanceolate, acuminate, twisted; lip 40–50×15–25mm, recurved, trilobed, lateral lobes erect, midlobe lanceolate, long-acuminate; callus of 3 ridges. New Guinea, Bougainville, Solomon Is.

D.spectatissimum Rchb. f. (*D.speciosissimum* Rolfe).
Pseudobulbs to 40cm, slender, erect, covered with rather sparse black hairs; lvs also sparsely hairy. Racemes arising near apex of stems, 1–2-fld; fls scented, long-lasting, 7–10cm diam., white with a red and yellow line on lip; sep. lanceolate, keeled on outside; pet. broadly ovate, rounded; lip trilobed, lateral lobes erect. Sabah.

D.stratiotes Rchb. f.
Pseudobulbs to 1m tall, occasionally more, 2cm diam., cane-like or spindle-shaped, somewhat swollen in basal half. Lvs 8–13×2–5cm, ovate or oblong, unequally and acutely bilobed at apex. Racemes borne on stems below lvs, to 30cm, suberect, 4–8-fld; fls white, sep. and pet. green or yellow-green towards apex, lip purple-veined; sep. 30–40×6–12mm, lanceolate, acuminate, edges undulate, the laterals longer than

dorsal; mentum about 15mm high; pet. 50–65×2mm, linear, erect, twisted 2–4-times; lip 32–40×20–25mm, trilobed, lateral lobes oblong, midlobe ovate, acute; callus with 3–5 ridges. Moluccas, New Guinea.

D.strebloceras Rchb. f.
Pseudobulbs to 1.5m tall, 1.5cm diam., cylindrical but slightly swollen in lower half. Lvs to 16×5cm, ovate or lanceolate, fleshy, acutely and unequally bilobed at apex. Racemes to 40cm, laxly 6–8-fld; fls fragrant, sep. and pet. pale yellow or green, tinged with dull purple or dark brown, lip marked with violet; sep. recurved, 23–30×7–8mm, narrowly oblong, acute, margins undulate, the dorsal slightly longer than laterals; mentum 8–10mm; pet. 25–40×4–6mm, linear-spathulate, erect or reflexed, twisted about 3 times; lip 22×15mm, trilobed, lateral lobes erect, midlobe ovate with a long claw, the margins erose; callus of 5 keels. Moluccas.

D.striolatum Rchb.f.
Rhiz. creeping, forming dense masses. Lvs to 6cm, thick, succulent, semi- terete, resembling a Kenyan bean. Raceme short, slender-stemmed, 1-2-fld; fls fragrant; tepals to 1cm, oblong-lanceolate, yellow to green-yellow or ochre with fine brown flecks or stripes, lip white, held uppermost. S. Australia.

D.suavissimum Rchb. f. See *D.chrysotoxum*.

D.subclausum Rolfe.
Pseudobulbs slender and branched or relatively stout, cane-like, sometimes pendulous. Lvs in 2 rows, oblong-lanceolate. Fls in clusters surrounding lengths of previous year's cane, somewhat tubular, waxy, typically scarlet at base becoming bright yellow toward tips of tepals, sometimes wholly yellow (var. *pandanicola*), or orange, or salmon. New Guinea.

D.superbum Rchb. f. See *D.anosmum*.

D.taurinum Lindl.
Pseudobulbs to 1.3m tall, 1–2.5cm diam., cylindrical or spindle-shaped, covered with white sheaths. Lvs to 15×7.5cm, oblong or elliptic, obtusely and unevenly bilobed at apex. Racemes arising near apex, to 60cm, 20–30-fld; sep. yellow-green or green-white, pet. pink or purple paling to white at base, lip white tinged with purple; dorsal sep. recurved, 20–30×7–9mm, triangular, laterals recurved, 30–40× 10–17mm, obliquely lanceolate, forming conical mentum 10–20mm long; pet. 20–30×4mm, suberect, linear-spathulate, twisted no more than once; lip 30–35×18–25mm, trilobed towards apex, lateral lobes very small, midlobe transversely oblong, crisped, disc with 3 keels. Philippines.

D.teretifolium R. Br.
Stems about 4mm diam., zigzag, branched, forming pendent clumps to 3m long. Lvs to 60×1cm, fleshy, terete. Racemes to 10cm, 10–15-fld; fls scented, cream or white, striped with red or purple at base of parts; sep. and pet. spreading, tips often recurved; dorsal sep. to 25×2.5mm, lanceolate, acuminate, laterals similar but slightly longer and broader; pet. to 28×1mm, linear-lanceolate; lip 20×5mm, recurved, trilobed, lateral lobes erect, midlobe ovate, acuminate, the margins undulate; callus of 3 ridges. Australia. 'Aureum': fls yellow.

D.tetragonum Cunn.
Pseudobulbs to 45×1.5cm, more or less pendent, spindle-shaped but 4-angled, 2–5-lvs. Lvs 3–10×1.5–3cm, ovate, acute, dark green, often somewhat twisted. Racemes arising near apex, to 3cm long, 1–5-fld; fls 3–6cm diam., green or yellow-green, sometimes edged with brown, or yellow blotched with purple-red; sep. and pet. spreading; sep. 20–50×3–5mm, lanceolate, long-acuminate; pet. 35×1–2mm, linear-lanceolate, long acuminate; lip 10–14×6–13mm, trilobed, with callus of 3 parallel ridges in basal half, lateral lobes erect, midlobe reflexed. Australia.

D.tetragonum var. *giganteum* Gilbert. See *D.capitisyork*.

D.thyrsiflorum Rchb. f. ex André.
Pseudobulbs 30–50×2cm, erect, clustered, spindle-shaped, slightly grooved, 3–5-lvd near apex. Lvs to 16×2.5cm, ovate, acute. Racemes borne near apex of stem, pendent, to 26cm, densely several- to many-fld; sep. and pet. white or cream, lip golden yellow; sep. and pet. 20–25mm, sep. ovate, pet. orbicular from a short claw, the edge finely toothed; lip clawed at base then orbicular, margin fringed. Nepal, Assam. Sometimes considered conspecific with *D.densiflorum* 'Alboluteum'

D.tigrinum Hemsl. See *D.spectabile*.
D.topaziacum Ames. See *D.bullenianum*.

D.transparens Wallich ex Lindl.
Pseudobulbs 30–60×0.5cm, erect or pendent, cylindrical but swollen at base, dark grey with yellow streaks, 5–7-lvd. Lvs deciduous, 4–11×1.5–2cm, linear-lanceolate, acute, recurved. Racemes 2–3-fld, arising from large, translucent bracts at nodes of old stems; fls fragrant, 3–5cm diam., transparent white, the parts tipped with pink, lip with purple streaks; dorsal sep. about 22×6mm, elliptical, obtuse, laterals 25–30×5–9mm, triangular, acuminate; pet. 10–12×5mm, oblong; lip about 25×15mm, oblong, funnel-shaped at base. NE India, Burma, Nepal.

D.triflorum (Bl.) Lindl. See *Epigeneium triflorum*.

D.trigonopus Rchb. f. (*D.velutinum* Rolfe).
Pseudobulbs 15–20×1cm, clustered, spindle-shaped, shiny brown-purple, 1–3-lvd near apex. Lvs to 10cm, ligulate, the underside and leaf sheaths hairy. Infl. 1–2-fld; fls 5cm diam., golden yellow, lip green-tinged in centre and with red lines on lateral lobes; sep. 25–30×8mm, lanceolate, acute, keeled; pet. about 23×10mm, oblong, acute; lip 13×13mm, trilobed with a basal claw, lateral lobes small, the front edge finely toothed, midlobe oblong, obtuse, edge papillose. Burma, Yunnan, Laos, Thailand.

D.undulatum R. Br. See *D.discolor*.

D.unicum Seidenf.
Pseudobulbs to 25×1cm, subcylindrical, semi-erect or pendulous, 1–5-lvd near apex. Lvs to 6×2cm, lanceolate or elliptic. Racemes axillary, short, to 4-fld; fls bright orange, the lip buff with darker veins; sep. to 30×5mm, lanceolate, the apex hooded, laterals slightly larger than dorsal; pet. to 25×7mm, lanceolate; lip to 30×13mm, elliptic-ovate, entire, with 3 longitudinal ridges reaching apex. Laos, Thailand.

D.veitchianum Lindl. See *D.macrophyllum*.
D.velutinum Rolfe. See *D.trigonopus*.

D.vexillarius J.J. Sm.
Tuft-forming epiphytic or terrestrial plants, usually erect but sometimes pendent; pseudobulbs to 30×1.5cm, often much smaller, ovoid to cylindrical, 2–10-lvd in apical half. Lvs to 16×2cm, linear or elliptic, green or dark purple. Racemes arising on leafy or leafless stems, usually 2–5-fld; fls about 4cm diam., lasting for about 6 months, red, orange, yellow, white, green, blue-green, blue, grey, lilac, purple or pink, the lip dark green, usually red or orange at apex; dorsal sep. to 20×9mm, ovate or elliptic, laterals to 45×13mm, almost triangular, often with crest on midvein on outside, forming conical mentum to 30mm long; pet. to 20×9mm, oblong-obovate; lip 18–39×3–7mm, almost linear, obscurely trilobed. Moluccas, New Guinea, Bismarck Archipelago.

D.victoriae-reginae Loher.
Pseudobulbs 25–60cm long, pendent, branched, cylindrical but swollen at nodes, covered with sheaths. Lvs about 12, 3–8×1–2cm, oblong or lanceolate, acute or acuminate. Racemes very short, arising on old stems, 3–12-fld; fls violet-blue, white towards base of seg., lip with 5 violet lines in throat; sep. 15–18×6mm, oblong; pet. 15×6mm, obovate-oblong; lip 20–35×8–11mm, obovate, somewhat concave, the basal edges shortly toothed and reflexed. Philippines.

D.wardianum Warner.
Pseudobulbs to 120cm long, 1–2cm diam., erect or pendent, cylindrical but thickened at nodes. Lvs 8–15×1.5–2.5cm, oblong-lanceolate, deciduous. Racemes short, arising at nodes of leafless stems, 1–3-fld; fls fragrant, to 10cm diam., white with purple-tipped seg., lip yellow in throat with 2 maroon spots; sep. 40–50×20mm, oblong, obtuse; pet. 45–50× 25–30mm, ovate-oblong; lip 40×30mm, ovate or suborbicular, enfolding column at base. Assam, Burma, Thailand.

D.williamsonii Day & Rchb. f.
Pseudobulbs 30–40×1cm, erect, spindle-shaped, leafy toward apex. Lvs to 10×2cm, lanceolate, velvety, the sheaths with black hairs. Infl. 1–2-fld; fls to 7.5cm diam., fragrant, waxy, cream to pale yellow, lip with large red or brown blotch in centre; column white with red spot below stigma; dorsal sep. 30×6–7mm, laterals to 45×15mm, triangular, acuminate; pet. similar to dorsal sep.; lip 45×25mm, flabellate, trilobed, margins finely toothed or ciliate, veins with long hairs, lateral lobes rounded, hairy, midlobe orbicular, edge crisped. Assam, Burma, Thailand.

D.williamsianum Rchb. f.
Stems to 3m, cane-like, erect. lvs distichous, borne towards apex of stem. Racemes arising near stem apex, erect or arching, 3–10-fld, the fls facing downwards; fls mauve, sep. and pet. purple-veined, lip deep purple, the edge paler; sep. and pet. broadly ovate, rounded at tip; lip more or less orbicular, curving up at the sides. Papua New Guinea.

D.grexes and cultivars.
D.Ainsworthii: an old hybrid of the '*nobile*-type'; fls creamy yellow with purple tips to the sep. and pet. and a deep purple patch in the throat of the lip.
D.Alice Iwanaga: lovely hybrid of the '*formosum* group'; fls large, white with some maroon in the throat of the lip.
D.American Beauty: lovely hybrid of the '*phalaenopsis*-type'; fls deep magenta purple on long spikes, deeper colour in the lip.

*D.*Anne Marie: a fine hybrid of the '*nobile*-type'; fls white or cream with purple tips to all the parts, a deep purple patch surrounded with yellow in the throat.

*D.*Australian Beauty: a complex hybrid with many different species in its background; large canes bearing several infl.; tall spikes with many fls, sep. and pet. narrow, bright yellow, lip magenta.

*D.*Autumn Lace: a floriferous hybrid bred from *D.canaliculatum*; compact plants with many sprays of orange yellow, brown and white fls.

*D.*Banana Royal: a floriferous hybrid bred from *D.canaliculatum*; fls in long sprays, whitetipped in yellow, lip yellow or yellow veined purple.

*D.*Bangkok Fancy: a floriferous hybrid of the '*phalaenopsis*-type'; fls in long arching infl. in combinations of lavender and red-purple colours.

*D.*Betty Ho: a floriferous hybrid of the evergreen type; large yellow fls with brick-red lip.

*D.*Blue Sparkle: a floriferous hybrid bred from *D.canaliculatum*; fls small in long sprays, blue-purple and white.

*D.*Candy Stripe: attractive hybrids of the '*phalaenopsis*-type'; fls pale pink, striped deeper pink.

*D.*Chinsae: a lovely hybrid bred from *D.moniliforme*; fls lemon yellow with golden yellow lip.

*D.*Circe 'Gail': a fine hybrid of the evergreen type; vigorous sprays of deep royal purple fls, starry shape.

*D.*Cybele: a primary hybrid of the '*nobile*-type'; fls cream with purple tips to all the parts, a small deep purple patch in the throat.

*D.*Dale Takiguchi: a fine hybrid of '*phalaenopsis*-type' with pure white fls of good shape and substance.

*D.*Dawn Maree: splendid hybrid of the '*formosum* group'; fls crystal white, the wide lip heavily marked with a large patch of orange scarlet and orange hairs.

*D.*Doreen 'Kodama': one of the finest of the '*phalaenopsis*-type'; pure white fls of excellent shape.

*D.*Ellen: compact plants with evergreen lvs; fls star-shaped, mostly deep pink.

*D.*Fiftieth State: an interesting hybrid of the evergreen type; fls white or pale pink overlaid and veined with soft red, long-lasting.

*D.*Fire Coral: a beautiful hybrid of the '*formosum* group': fls shiny white with a bright red patch on the lower half of the lip.

*D.*Floy Day 'Susan': robust, evergreen plants producing huge sprays of yellow-green fls with brown-red lip.

*D.*Gatton Sunray: a magnificent hybrid, one of the largest of the cultivated dendrobiums; fls large and showy in short trusses in the early summer, yellow-beige with deep purple-brown in the lip.

*D.*Golden Blossom: a fine modern hybrid of the '*nobile*-type'; fls deep golden yellow.

*D.*Hawaiian Gem: a floriferous hybrid of the '*antennatum*-type'; fls white with pretty pink lip.

*D.*Hawaiian King: a splendid hybrid of the '*formosum* group'; fls very large, pure white.

*D.*Hickam Deb: outstanding hybrid of the '*phalaenopsis*-type'; fls deep magenta purple on long spikes.

*D.*Hilda Poxon: compact plants with evergreen lvs; fls star-shaped, various shades of yellow and orange.

*D.*Ise 'Pearl': a delightful hybrid of the '*nobile*-type'; fls glistening white, lip narrow, pale green in the throat.

*D.*Jaquelyn Thomas: well-known hybrid of the evergreen type; fls white with the outer half of all seg. rose pink or purple.

*D.*Kultana: one of the hard-cane, warm-growing hybrids bred from *D.phalaenopsis*; fls blue-purple.

*D.*Lady Fay: a fine hybrid of the '*phalaenopsis*-type'; superb fls in brilliant magenta purple, perfect shape.

*D.*Lady Hamilton: a fine hybrid of the '*phalaenopsis*-type'; lovely fls of fine shape in deep magenta-purple.

*D.*Lisa Sainsbury: small compact plants with evergreen lvs; fls white, nodding, with purple stripes and spots on lip.

*D.*Mary Mak: prolific hybrid of the evergreen type; long infl. with large yellow fls, red lines in the lip.

*D.*New Guinea: a primary hybrid which is more robust and easier to grow than either of its parents; fls pale green, nodding, lip similar but densely striped with purple.

*D.*Orglade's Orbit: a superb modern hybrid of the '*phalaenopsis*-type'; fls very dark magenta purple, darker in the lip, superb shape.

*D.*Peewee: an unusual cross; plants with upright canes and short spikes of star-shaped, purple fls.

*D.*Pixie Princess: a floriferous hybrid bred from *D.canaliculatum*; fls yellow and white with purple lip.

*D.*Plumptonense: a fine old hybrid with wide pet., rose pink fls, paler towards the centre and deep purple in the throat.

*D.*Precious Pearl: a lovely hybrid of the '*formosum* group'; fls creamy white, the lip pale yellow, bright orange towards the base.

*D.*Princess Sharon 'Makaha': a superb hybrid of the '*phalaenopsis*-type'; long, graceful sprays of iridescent burgundy fls, good shape.

*D.*Ram Misra 'Orchidglade's Black Sapphire': most unusual fls of the '*phalaenopsis*-type'; fls black-red with sparkling texture.

*D.*Snow Festival: a strong hybrid of the '*formosum* group'; fls white with large pet. and a very large lip which is deep pink at the base.

*D.*Stardust: a lovely hybrid bred from *D.moniliforme*; fls bright orange, lip with bold stripes.

*D.*Tomie: evergreen type; long graceful sprays of fls in two tones, white flushed pink, with outer half of the pet. and lip deep pink.

*D.*Utopia: a fine hybrid of the '*nobile*-type'; large plants with deep rose pink fls and yellow in the lip; the clone 'Messenger' is particularly fine.

*D.*Wiganiae: a primary hybrid of the '*nobile*-type'; fls white, flushed with light mauve towards the tips of all the parts, a small dark purple patch in the throat.

*D.*Winter Dawn: a lovely hybrid of the '*formosum* group'; fls shiny white, lip deep yellow.

*D.*Yamamoto Hybrids: this term is used to describe a group of modern hybrids bred in Hawaii and developed from the early '*nobile*-type' crosses; there is a wide range of colours available; strong plants with fls of excellent shape and substance.

*D.*Youppadeewan: lovely hybrid of the '*phalaenopsis*-type'; fls white, outlined in magenta, with magenta at base of pet. and most of lip.

*D.*Yukidaruma: one of the modern '*nobile*-type' crosses with large fls of magnificent shape, various colours.

Dendrochilum Bl. (From Gk *dendron*, tree and *cheilos*, lip, referring to the configuration of the lip.) GOLDEN CHAIN ORCHID. (*Platyclinis* Benth.) Some 120 species of epiphytes. Rhizomes creeping. Pseudobulbs ovoid to cylindrical, basally sheathed by thin bracts. Leaves 1–2, borne at pseudobulb apex, tough, lanceolate to elliptic, rolled in bud; petiole slender. Inflorescence racemose, lateral, appearing from heart of emerging growths, slender, long, ascending then markedly decurved and pendulous, chain-like; flowers crowded, 2-ranked, small, fragrant, star-like; dorsal sepal often keeled, lateral sepals fused to base of column; lip oblong, simple or trilobed, mobile, base fleshy, often 2–3-keeled; column apically winged. SE Asia, Malaysia.

CULTIVATION   Epiphytes with slender chains of small flowers. A cool regime, open potting mixture and short winter rest suit them.

D.cobbianum Rchb. f.
Pseudobulbs yellow-green, conical, clustered, to 8×2cm. Lf solitary, oblong-lanceolate, midrib prominent, to 35×6cm. Infl. to 50cm; bracts papery, ovate, to 0.7cm; fls to 1.8cm diam., in 2 spiralling ranks; sep. and pet. dull white; lip yellow to orange, flabellate or cuneate, basal callus nearly oblong. Philippines.

D.filiforme Lindl.
Pseudobulbs ovoid, densely clustered, to 2.5×1cm. Lvs 2, linear-lanceolate, to 18×1cm. Infl. to 45cm, crowded, sharply pendulous, very slender; fls to 100+, to 0.6cm diam., fragrant, pale yellow; dorsal sep. elliptic-oblong, lateral sep. lanceolate; pet. obovate to cuneate; lip faintly trilobed, sometimes golden, 2-ridged. Philippines.

D.glumaceum Lindl.
Pseudobulbs ovoid, clustered, to 4×2cm; bracts faintly flushed pink, lasting only one season. Lf solitary, erect, narrow-elliptic, to 45×4cm. Infl. to 50cm, very slender; fls to

2cm diam., white to ivory, lip pale green; sep. lanceolate; pet. linear to oblong-lanceolate; lip midlobe ovate to orbicular, disc 2-ridged, lateral lobes broad, triangular, falcate. Philippines.

D.longifolium Rchb. f.
Pseudobulbs conical, narrow, pale green, to 8×2cm. Lf usually solitary, lanceolate-elliptic, to 40×7cm. Infl. dense, arched, to 40cm; fls pale green to bronze, tipped chocolate; sep. oblong, narrow, to 0.8×0.4cm; pet. elliptic-oblong, narrow; lip recurved, midlobe obovate-cuneate, lateral lobes triangular, falcate, disc between lateral lobes forms 2 ridges. Malaysia to New Guinea.

D.uncatum Rchb. f.
Resembles a diminutive *D.filiforme*. Pseudobulbs conical, to 4cm. Lvs oblong, tapering to 10×1.5cm; petiole to 2cm. Infl. to 10cm, slender, raceme lax; fls to 0.9cm across; sep. and pet. ivory to yellow-green, narrow-oblong; lip obtuse, bronze to sepia. Philippines.

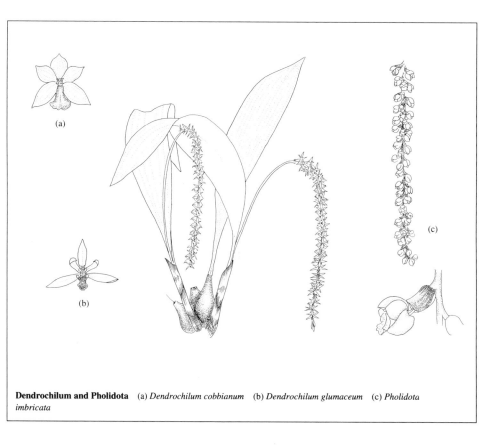

Dendrochilum and Pholidota   (a) *Dendrochilum cobbianum*   (b) *Dendrochilum glumaceum*   (c) *Pholidota imbricata*

Dendrophylax Rchb. f. (From Gk *dendron*, tree, and *phylax*, guard, an allusion to the epiphytic habit.) 5 species, epiphytes lacking leaves and apparent aerial parts. They consist largely of a mass of silver-grey roots, these perform photosynthesis. Flowers usually solitary, slender-stalked and long-spurred, generally similar to *Angraecum*. Carribean region.

CULTIVATION   As for *Chiloschista*.

D.funalis Fawcett.
Fls to 6cm diam.; tepals oblong-oblanceolate, pale green; lip rounded, deeply bilobed, pure white. Jamaica.

× **Dialaelia** (*Caularthron* (*Diacrium*) × *Laelia*). An intergeneric hybrid between *Caularthron* and a variety of *Laelia* species. The most well known is *D.*Snowflake, which has also proved itself a useful parent in further crosses.

× *D.***Snowflake.**
Compact plants with several lvs per pseudobulb; fls in clusters on tall infl., white.

Diaphananthe Schltr. (From Gk *diaphanes*, transparent, and *anthos*, flower.) Over 45 species of epiphytes. Stems long or short; roots numerous, often streaked with white. Inflorescence racemose, usually arching or pendent, arising from old leaf scars; flowers translucent, white, cream, yellow, orange or green; petals often shorter and rounder than sepals; lip spurred, usually as broad as, or broader than long, usually entire but sometimes trilobed at apex, edge often undulate, sometimes with an apiculus at apex and often with a tooth in the mouth of the spur; column fairly short; rostellum beak-like; viscidia 1 or 2. Tropical & S Africa.

CULTIVATION   As for *Angraecum*.

D.bidens (Sw. ex Pers.) Schltr. (*Angraecum bidens* Sw.).
Stem elongated, to 1m or more, scandent; roots stout. Lvs numerous, regularly arranged along stem, 5–14×1.5–4.5cm, oblong-lanceolate or ovate, unequally and acutely bilobed at apex. Racemes 5–18cm, pendent, many-fld; fls salmon pink, yellow-pink, flesh-coloured or white; pedicel and ovary 3–4mm; bracts 1mm; sep. 3–5×2mm, lanceolate, acute; pet. similar but narrower; lip 3.5–5×3.5–5mm, quadrate, the edge undulate, more or less trilobed at apex, midlobe represented by a small apiculus; spur 5–6mm, swollen in middle then tapering to obtuse apex; column 1mm; viscidium 1. W Africa, Central African Republic, Zaire, Uganda, Angola.

D.fragrantissima (Rchb. f.) Schltr.
Stem short but elongating with age; roots fine. Lvs several, to 30×3.5cm, pendent, sword-shaped, apex very unequally bilobed with 1 lobe acute, the other more or less absent, fleshy, folded, dull olive green. Racemes to 35cm, laxly or densely many-fld, the fls arranged in opposite pairs; fls translucent yellow or yellow-green; pedicel and ovary 3mm; sep. 12–14mm, lanceolate, fairly acuminate; pet. similar but shorter and acute; lip 8–10×8mm, quadrate or broadly ovate, lateral margins recurved and undulate, apex apiculate; spur 10mm, swollen in apical half but tapering to an obtuse apex; column 3mm, stout; viscidium 1. Ethiopia, Sudan, Zaire, E Africa to S Africa and Angola.

D.kamerunensis (Schltr.) Schltr.
Stem short, leafy at apex. Lvs 20–50×2–5cm, narrowly oblanceolate, succulent, folded, bilobed at apex. Racemes 10–30cm, several-fld; fls pale green; sep. and pet. 15–20mm; lip 17–19mm, obovate from a narrow base with a tooth-like callus in the mouth of the spur, the front margin denticulate, shortly apiculate at apex; spur 15–16mm, slightly shorter than lip. Cameroun, Uganda, Zambia.

D.pellucida (Lindl.) Schltr. (*Angraecum pellucidum* Lindl.).
Robust, stems pendent, turning up toward apex. Lvs numerous, to 70×8cm, fleshy, distichous, lanceolate. Racemes arising below lvs and in axils of lower lvs, 60–80cm, pendent, many-fld; fls translucent, pearly white often tinged with green or yellow; sep. and pet. 9–11×3mm, lanceolate, acute, pet. ciliate on margins; lip 9–10×10–12mm, quadrate or transversely oblong, margin fimbriate; spur 9–10mm; column short and stout. W Africa to Uganda.

D.pulchella Summerh.
Stem to 10cm, erect or pendent; roots 2–6mm diam., fine or stout. Lvs 5–7, 5–12×1–1.5cm, ligulate, falcate, pale or dark green. Racemes 3–4 arising from base of plant, arching or pendent, to 8cm, laxly or densely 10–12-fld; fls translucent, white or creamy yellow, 15mm diam.; pedicel and ovary 4mm; sep. 8×2–3mm, obovate; pet. 8×4mm, elliptic; lip 10×8mm, oblong, erose on lower margin with tooth in mouth of spur; spur 10mm. Kenya, Tanzania, Malawi, Zambia.

D.rutila (Rchb. f.) Summerh.
Stems to 30cm, pendent; roots fine, 2mm diam., growing tips purple. Lvs numerous, 7–15×0.5–3cm, ligulate or oblanceolate, obtusely and unequally bilobed, dark olive green, sometimes tinged purple. Racemes some 12cm, densely several- to many-fld; fls khaki-purple or occasionally creamy white; pedicel and ovary 3mm, purple; dorsal sep. 2.5–3×2mm, broadly ovate, lateral sep. 3×1mm, spreading, obliquely ovate; pet. 2×2mm, orbicular; lip 2–3×3–4.5mm, fan-shaped; spur 8–12mm, slender, slightly incurved; column 1mm. Tropical Africa (widespread).

D.stolzii Schltr.
Stem 50–60cm, pendent; roots 3mm diam., numerous, many aerial. Lvs numerous, arranged along stem, to 5×2.5cm, distichous, oblong, obtusely bilobed at apex, dark green. Racemes borne along stem, to 4cm, 2–5-fld; fls about 2cm diam., creamy white or green-white, scented, especially in evening; pedicel and ovary 9mm; dorsal sep. 9×3.5–4mm, ovate, lateral sep. narrower and oblique, deflexed; pet. 9×5mm, ovate, apiculate; lip 10×12mm, broadly fan-shaped, with tooth 1mm long in mouth of spur, the lower edge undulate and somewhat erose; spur 18–25mm, slender, slightly incurved; column 2–3mm, slender; viscidia 2. Tanzania, Malawi, Zimbabwe.

D.tenuicalcar Summerh.
Stem 7–16cm, often pendent; roots numerous. Lvs at apex of stem, distichous, 4–5×1–1.5cm, curved oblong-lanceolate, unequally bilobed at apex. Raceme axillary, 10–17mm, 3–4-fld; fls white; pedicel and ovary 8–12mm; bracts very short; dorsal sep. 4.5×3mm, oblong-elliptic, rounded, lateral sep. 5×2.5mm, ligulate, slightly curved, obtuse; pet. 4.5–5×3mm, ovate, acute; lip 7.5×6.5mm with tooth-like callus in mouth of spur, fan-shaped, apex emarginate with apiculus in centre; spur 25mm, slender, slightly incurved. Uganda, Kenya.

D.xanthopollinia (Rchb. f.) Summerh.
Very variable species. Stem very short, or long, to 30cm; roots 3–4mm wide. Lvs 4–8×0.5–2.5cm, in short-stemmed plants fleshy, yellow-green, V-shaped in cross-section, in long-stemmed plants dark green, linear or ligulate, all unequally and obtusely bilobed at apex. Raceme 4–10cm, densely 12- to many-fld; fls translucent creamy yellow, lilac-scented; sep. 3–5mm, oblong, obtuse, lateral sep. slightly longer than dorsal sep.; pet. 2×3mm, rounded; lip 3×5mm, broadly fan-shaped with no tooth in mouth of spur, the lower edge rolled back; spur 5–7mm, inflated in middle. E Africa, Zambia, Zimbabwe, Angola, S Africa.

Dichaea Lindl. (From Gk *diche*, in two parts, referring to the strongly distichous alternate leaf arrangement of all species.) Some 100 species of diminutive, long-stemmed epiphytes or lithophytes. Pseudobulbs absent. Stems leafy, slender, elongated, tufted, sprawling, sometimes branching, rooting nodally, closely sheathed with overlapping leaf bases. Leaves evergreen or semi-deciduous (often persisting only in upper portions of stems, the lower parts becoming naked and scarred), distichous, alternate to opposite, spreading or sharply reflexed in a pinnate configuration, ovate-acute to linear-lanceolate, somewhat chartaceous, olive green to glaucous blue-green, glabrous to hispidulous, midvein sunken, base articulate; leaf bases conspicuous, folded, carinate. Flowers solitary, fleshy, short-stalked, axillary, often fragrant, yellow to ochre, marked red to indigo, proportionately large; sepals and petals spreading to incurved, subequal, free; lip fused to column foot, sessile or clawed, broadly elliptic to sagittate, usually 3-lobed; column erect. Tropical America.

CULTIVATION Cool to intermediate-growing. Plant in baskets or on rafts against a thick pad of moss. Mist daily when in growth; do not expose to full sunlight. The scaly sprawling stems of *D.muricata*, picked out with small lavender flowers, are ideally suited to basket culture in the semi-shaded, humid corners of the greenhouse or growing case.

D.glauca (Sw.) Lindl.
Stems to 60cm, ascending or pendulous. Lvs to 7×1.3cm, at 1–2cm intervals, semi-erect, linear-oblong, apically cusped, carinate beneath, glaucous. Fls borne toward summit of stems, vanilla-scented; sep. and pet. to 10×4mm, grey-white spotted mauve and amber, spreading, basally concave, similar, elliptic to lanceolate, acute; lip to 8×10mm, minutely papillose, more heavily marked than sep. and pet., anchor-shaped with slender, erect lobules; ovary smooth. W Indies, Mexico, Costa Rica, Guatemala.

D.graminoides (Sw.) Lindl.
Stems to 30cm, sprawling, often branching. Lvs 2–4cm×3–6mm, alternate, at 1cm intervals, often of variable size and shape, linear-elliptic, ciliate, sap-green, thin-textured. Fls to 1cm diam., white; lip pandurate; ovary smooth. Guatemala, Colombia.

D.hystricina Rchb. f.
Stems to 30cm, sprawling then ascending. Lvs strongly 2-ranked, ciliate, deciduous. Fls comparatively large, slender-stalked, cream to lime spotted purple-red; lip with 2 prominent calli at base; ovary echinate. W Indies, Guatemala, Ecuador, Venezuela.

D.morrisii Fawcett & Rendle (*D.robusta* Schltr.).
Stems to 10cm, rigid, pendulous. Lvs to 2×1cm, borne closely oblong-elliptic, obtuse, (apiculate at first), olive green, glabrous or coarsely puberulent, tough, papery, strongly articulate, blades sharply reflexed from bases, falling after one season. Sep. to 8×3mm, elliptic, cupped, bronze-green, sometimes off-white; pet. to 7×2.5mm, lanceolate; lip to 8×6mm, white with purple apex, flabellate with lateral lobules often attenuate and incurved; column green-white, sometimes flecked violet; ovary glandular-pubesc. W Indies, Hispaniola, Costa Rica to Bolivia.

D.muricata (Sw.) Lindl.
Stems to 22cm, branching, sprawling. Lvs to 1.2cm, oblong-lanceolate, scabrid to puberulent, olive-green, coarsely papery, reflexed; sheaths grey-green, sometimes spotted dark green. Fls borne in upper axils; sep. to 12×5mm, spreading to incurved, somewhat concave at base, fleshy, elliptic-lanceolate, acuminate, olive-white to orange-buff, spotted or banded oxblood, often verrucose beneath; pet. to 12×4mm, linear-oblong, acuminate, olive-bronze to orange-white, spotted or mottled lavender-mauve; lip to 8×5mm, indigo, fleshy at base, sagittate; ovary echinate. C America.

D.panamensis Lindl.
Distinguished from the closely related *D.graminoides* by its semi-erect, clumped habit, glaucous lvs, green-white fls spotted garnet or violet, and sagittate, not pandurate, lip. Mexico to Peru.

D.pendula (Aubl.) Cogn.
Stems to 50cm clumped in pendulous festoons. Lvs to 4×1cm, papery, soft, olive green, apiculate and minutely serrulate near apex. Sep. 6.5×4mm, fleshy, concave, bronze to yellow, mottled lilac near apex, softly ciliate, verrucose beneath; pet. to 5.6×3mm, otherwise resembling sep.; lip to 5.5×5mm, fleshy, obscurely 3-lobed, cupped, ciliate, lilac mottled indigo; ovary muricate. W Indies, Costa Rica, Venezuela, Colombia, Ecuador.

D.picta Rchb. f.
Stems compact, tufted, to 18cm, erect or sprawling and ascending. Lvs to 15×5mm, olive green, oblong-lanceolate, held at 90° to clasping sheath. Sep. and pet. fleshy, similar, to 6×4mm, bronze-green mottled pink to mauve; lip fleshy, rigid, to 7.5×6mm, white flecked garnet; ovary smooth. Guyana, Venezuela, Trinidad.

D.robusta Schltr. See *D.morrisii.*

D.trulla Rchb. f.
Stems to 50cm, pendulous. Lvs to 8×0.8cm, deep green, soft, glossy, usually glabrous, linear-lanceolate, obscurely carinate beneath. Sep. and pet. to 8.5×4mm, oblong-lanceolate, concave above, pale ochre; lip to 7×7mm, obscurely and broadly hastate, involute, minutely ciliate, green to violet at apex; ovary smooth. Costa Rica, Panama, Venezuela, Colombia, Ecuador, Brazil, Guyana. White-fld forms occur.

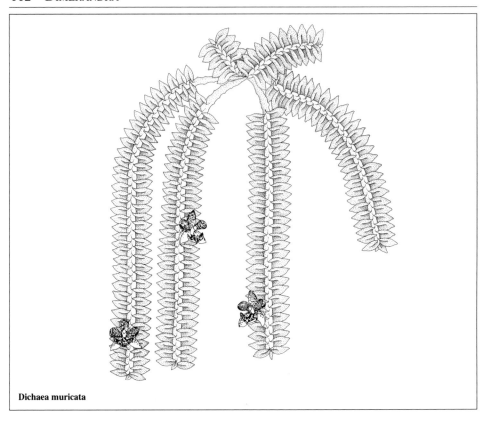

Dichaea muricata

Dimerandra Schltr. (From Gk *dimeres*, bipartite, and *andra*, stamens, from *aner*, man.) 9 species, sympodial epiphytes. Rhizomes short, creeping. Roots thick, silver-grey to white. Pseudobulbs to 35cm, clumped, cane-like, swollen, striated, tapering, jointed at leaf insertions, ultimately only bearing leaves in upper third and sheathed with grey, papery leaf bases near base. Leaves to 12×1cm, alternate, remote, in 2 ranks, ligulate to lanceolate, apex retuse, base clasping and sheathing, semi-rigid, dark green with midvein sunken above. Inflorescence a short terminal raceme; flowers to 3cm diam.; tepals rose madder to magenta, spreading or cupped, sepals elliptic-lanceolate, petals elliptic-obovate; lip obscurely obcordate, dark rose to mauve, marked white at base and on callus; column dark pink. W Indies, C & S America.

CULTIVATION   As for *Epidendrum*.

D.emarginata (G.F.Mey.) Hoehne (*D.stenopetala* (Hook.) Schltr.; *D.rimbachii* (Schltr.) Schltr.; *Epidendrum lamellatum* Westc. ex Lindl.; *Epidendrum stenopetalum* Hook.). Described above.

D.rimbachii (Schltr.) Schltr. See *D.emarginata*. *D.stenopetala* (Hook.) Schltr. See *D.emarginata*.

Dimorphorchis Rolfe. (From *di-*, two, *morphe*, shape and *Orchis*, referring to the difference in shape and colour between flowers on the same spike.) 2 species of monopodial epiphytes. Stems erect or arched. Leaves ligulate, coriaceous. Inflorescence sharply pendent, loosely flowered; flowers large, dimorphic; sepals and petals linear-oblong; lip saccate with a fleshy finger-like projection from a central disc. Borneo.

CULTIVATION   As for *Vanda*.

D.lowii (Lindl.)   Rolfe (*Arachnis lowii* (Lindl.) Rchb. f.; *Vanda lowii* Lindl.).
Stems to 2m, erect or arching. Lvs to 90cm, densely 2-ranked, ligulate, apex unequally bilobed. Infl. to 3m, arching, slender, many-fld; lower fls 2–3, to 7.5cm diam., tawny-yellow, spotted cinnabar-brown, broad, fleshy, upper fls strongly undulate, larger, massively blotched deep red or chocolate, tipped yellow; lip somewhat inflated, with a fleshy yellow appendage.

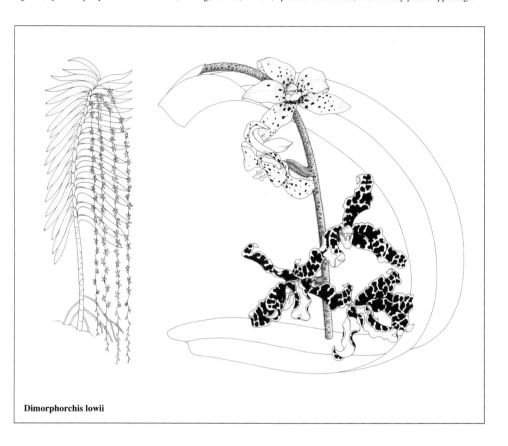

Dimorphorchis lowii

Diplocaulobium (Rchb. f.) Kränzl. (From Gk *diploos*, double, *kaulos*, stem, and *lobion*, lobe, referring to the creeping stems with swollen pseudobulbs.) 100 species of small epiphytes. Pseudobulbs clustered on short rhizome, either grooved, attenuate-pyriform or (in flowering growths) narrow except for swollen, ridged and sheathed base. Leaves solitary, apical. Inflorescence a raceme borne at leaf base from papery sheath, flowers ephemeral, appearing in succession over a long period. Malaysia to W Pacific.

CULTIVATION   Epiphytes suitable for basket or raft cultivation in the intermediate house. Reduce water when at rest; otherwise water and syringe freely. Protect from strong sunlight.

D.regale (Schltr.) A.D. Hawkes (*Dendrobium regale* Schltr.). Lvs oblong-ligulate, obtuse, to 20cm. Fls rose-pink; sep. oblong-ligulate, obtuse, to 4cm, lateral sep. oblique; pet. ellip-tic, oblique, glabrous; lip rhombic, curved, midlobe triangular, keels from lip base 2, divergent, lateral lobes round, obtuse. New Guinea.

Diplomeris D. Don. (From Gk *diploos*, double, and *meris*, part, from the form of the anther.) Some 3 species of terrestrials, often tuberous. Leaves solitary or few, broadly oblong or ensiform, glabrous or pubescent. Inflorescence erect; flowers 1–2; sepals ovate-oblong to lanceolate, subequal, spreading; petals similar, larger; lip clawed, fused to the column base, trilobed or entire, spurred. Himalaya.

CULTIVATION   As for *Disa*.

D.hirsuta (Lindl.) Lindl. Tubers globose or subglobose. Stem short. Lf oblong-elliptic, sessile, solitary, pubesc. or glabrous. Fl. 3.5–4cm diam.; sep. ovate-oblong, white; pet. orbicular-reniform, acute; lip yellow, suborbicular, midlobe acute, lateral lobes rounded, spur to 4.5cm, slender, curved, exterior pubesc.

Dipodium R. Br. (From Gk *di*-, two and *podion*, little foot; referring to the stipes supporting the pollen masses.) Some 22 species of glabrous terrestrials. Stems short, slender, leafless, with reduced bracts, or elongated, scandent, leafy and rooting at nodes, appearing monopodial. Inflorescence erect, axillary; flowers pink to deep red-mauve, often spotted, or yellow to yellow-green, spotted red; petals and sepals free, almost equal; lip trilobed, erect, midlobe longer than lateral lobes, with pubescent line. Malaysia to New Caledonia.

CULTIVATION   Scrambling terrestrials for shaded positions in the warm greenhouse. Pot in a mix of coarse bark, leafmould and sphagnum moss; water and syringe throughout the year; avoid waterlogging.

D.ensifolium F. Muell. Stems elongating to 1m, erect, becoming prostrate, straggling. Lvs 6–20cm, linear, canaliculate, prominently ribbed. Racemes 15–55cm, 1–4; fls rose to mauve, spotted red or deep mauve, column white, lip deep crimson; pet. and sep. 15–18mm, oblong-lanceolate; lip to 15mm, midlobe ovate-oblong with pubesc. line from base to apex, callus with 2 slender pubesc. lines divided by a keel, lateral lobes erect, falcate. Mid autumn–mid winter. NE Australia.

D.hamiltonianum Bail. (*D.punctatum* (Sm.) R. Br.). Rhiz. spreading, subterranean, swollen to tuberous. Stems to 60cm, leafless, dull green-brown spotted red, with overlapping bracts. Peduncles spotted green; fls to 5cm diam., bright yellow to dull yellow-green, spotted or streaked red; sep. 20–30mm, oblong; pet. shorter, narrower; lip to 18mm, lateral lobes 2–3mm, oblong, midlobe 7–9mm, ovate, central pubesc. band wide, from base to apex, callus with 2 centrally fused pubesc. ridges. Late autumn–late winter. SE Australia.

D.pictum (Lindl.) Rchb. f. Stems elongating, scandent, leafy, rooting at nodes. Lvs to 2.5cm, dense, linear-lanceolate, basally overlapping, keeled. Racemes erect from upper lf axils; fls to 2cm, sep. and pet. pale yellow, blotched purple beneath, narrow, oblong-obtuse; lip midlobe obtuse, striped purple at base, white pubesc. at tip. Summer–autumn. Malaysia.

D.punctatum (Sm.) R. Br. See *D.hamiltonianum*.

Dipteranthus Barb. Rodr. (From Gk *dipteros*, two-winged, and *anthos*, flower.) 12 species of dwarf, sympodial epiphytes from S America, of which only 1 species is in general cultivation.

CULTIVATION Grow in baskets or on bark slabs suspended in bright filtered light in the intermediate house. Mist throughout the year. Propagate by division.

D.planifolius (Rchb. f.) Garay (*Ornithocephalus planifolius* Rchb. f.).
Rhiz. slender, creeping. Pseudobulbs to 3mm, ovoid, with papery basal sheaths. Lvs to 4×0.6cm, semi-rigid, linear-oblong to narrow-lanceolate, glabrous, terminal and sheathing, forming a neat fan. Infl. a lateral raceme to 9cm, erect or arching to pendulous, compact or lax, axis glabrous, obscurely rugulose, winged, angled, conspicuously bracteate; fls yellow, white or green; sep. to 4.5×2mm, broadly lanceolate, obtuse, spreading or sharply deflexed and clasping pedicel in types with erect, compact infl.; pet. to 4.2×4mm, broadly ovate, undulate and slightly crisped; lip to 4×1mm, asymmetric, amber to olive, glossy, basally concave and white viscid-pubesc.; column light gold, rounded at base and projecting forward as a narrow, swan-like neck with a rounded concavity containing 4 pollinia and a twisted, displaced rostellum. Venezuela.

Disa Bergius. (Alluding to the mythical Queen Disa of Sweden who came to the King of the Sveas wrapped in a fishing-net: the dorsal sepal of *D.uniflora*, the type species, is net-veined.) About 130 species of terrestrials with ovoid, globose or ellipsoid tubers. Leaves either along flowering stem or on separate sterile shoot with sheathing leaves only on fertile stem. Raceme one to many-flowered; sepals free, the dorsal sepal spurred, usually forming hood, the laterals large, usually spreading; petals smaller, entire or lobed, often lying inside hood; lip usually narrow, not spurred; column short; anther erect, horizontal or reflexed; stigma cushion-like, lying below anther; pollinia 2, each with caudicle and naked viscidium. Tropical and S Africa, with 4 species in Madagascar and Mascarene Is.

CULTIVATION Beautiful terrestrials, much prized as emblematic flowers in their native regions. Grow in the cool glasshouse or conservatory in pans of neutral to acid fibrous mix rich in leafmould; protect from scorching sunlight and avoid watering foliage. Keep plants moist throughout the growing season. Decrease water supplies slightly after flowering. Repot every two years. Propagate by division or seed.

D.aurata (Bol.) Koopowitz (*D.tripetaloides* ssp. *aurata* (Bol.) Lind.).
Differs from *D.tripetaloides* in fls bright golden yellow, lateral sep. 14–16mm; spur 0.5–2.5mm. S Africa (Cape Province).

D.cardinalis Lind.
Slender, 30–60cm, evergreen in the wild, often stoloniferous; tubers about 1.5cm. Lvs 6–10 at base of stem, 5–10cm, suberect, narrowly elliptical, acute; stem lvs sheathing, to 3cm. Raceme to 30cm, 8–40-fld; fls 2.5–3cm diam., bright red; dorsal sep. 10–15×8–10mm, forming a hood 6–8mm deep with conical, obtuse spur 4mm long, lateral sep. 18–28mm, spreading, elliptic with apiculus about 1mm long; pet. 6–7×2mm, entire, lying inside hood; lip 6–7mm, narrowly oblong. S Africa (Cape Province).

D.crassicornis Lindl.
Robust, to 1m. Lvs 3–4, to 40×5cm, erect, narrowly lanceolate, acute; stem lvs sheathing, overlapping, grading into bracts. Raceme 10–30cm, cylindrical, fairly laxly 5–25-fld; fls about 5cm diam., fragrant, white or cream spotted with pink or purple; dorsal sep. 20–40×15–30mm, forming hood 10–15mm deep narrowing to form a cylindric, decurved spur 30–40mm long, slightly inflated at apex, lateral sep. 25–30×10–20mm with apiculi 1mm long, spreading, lanceolate or ovate, acute; pet. 20–30×10–15mm, erect, narrowly ovate, acute or acuminate, either completely included in hood or protruding from it; lip 20–25×4–15mm, horizontal then decurved, elliptic. S Africa (E Cape, Transkei, Natal), Lesotho.

D.grandiflora L. f. See *D.uniflora*.

D.racemosa L. f.
Slender, 30–100cm. Basal lvs 3–10, usually about 10cm long, narrowly lanceolate, acute, grading into sheathlike stem lvs. Raceme laxly 2–12-fld; sep. pale to mid pink with darker veins, pet. and lip white to yellow, the pet. with horizontal purple bars; ovary 10–25mm; bracts of similar length; dorsal sep. 17–24×13–20mm, forming dish-shaped hood 5–8mm deep, spur almost obsolete; lateral sep. 15–25mm with apiculi 1mm long, spreading, oblong or elliptic; pet. 10–15mm, lying inside hood, curving over anth.; lip 10mm, linear. S Africa (Cape Province).

D.sagittalis (L. f.) Sw.
Stem 7–30cm; tubers large, to 6cm. Basal lvs 5–10, to 9cm, elliptical, green at flowering time; stem lvs dry, sheathing. Raceme 2–12cm, laxly or densely few to many-fld; fls white or mauve, the pet. often darker than sep.; ovary 1–2cm, forming angle of about 45° with scape; bracts of similar length, scarious; dorsal sep. 6–13×8–12mm, forming shallow hood, half-moon-shaped toward apex with the lateral extensions reflexed; spur 2–7mm, slender from a conical base; lateral sep. 5–10mm, spreading, oblong, obtuse; pet. 7–12mm, lobed at base then narrowly lanceolate; lip 5–10mm, oblanceolate. S Africa (Cape Province, Transkei, S Natal).

D.tripetaloides (L. f.) N.E. Br.
Slender, 10–60cm, stoloniferous. Basal lvs about 10, to 14cm, spreading, narrowly oblanceolate or elliptic, acute; stem lvs sheathing. Raceme to 25cm but usually less, laxly several-fld.; fls white or pink or bright yellow; ovary 1–2cm; bracts shorter than ovary and enclosing it; dorsal sep. 5–12mm forming hood 3–5mm deep; spur conical, rarely cylindrical; lateral sep. 7–16mm, spreading, broadly obovate to oblong; pet. 4–5mm, narrowly oblong, lying inside hood, the apices curved over anth.; lip 3–4mm, projecting, the apex upward-curving. S Africa (Cape Province).

D.tripetaloides ssp. *aurata* (Bol.) Lind. See *D.aurata*.

D.uniflora Bergius (*D.grandiflora* L. f.).
Stems 15–60cm. Lvs borne along stem, the largest towards the base, to 25cm, lanceolate, acute or acuminate. Raceme usually 1–3-fld, rarely to 10-fld, lateral sep. and lip usually carmine red, the hood orange inside with red veining, pet. light carmine red at base, the blade yellow with red spots; yellow and pink forms also occur; ovary 1.5–4cm; bracts enclosing ovary and slightly longer; dorsal sep. erect, 20–60×15–20mm, forming hood 15mm deep with lower front margins incurved; spur 10–15mm, parallel to ovary, conical, acute, laterally flattened; lateral sep. 35–65mm, spreading forwards, narrowly ovate, acute or acuminate, the apex often reflexed; pet. 20–25mm, narrowly obovate, the apices curved over the anth.; lip 20–25mm, linear, projecting forwards, the apex reflexed. S Africa (Cape Province).

Disa (a) *D.tripetaloides* (b) *D.crassicornis* (c) *D.uniflora*

D.grexes.
D.Betty's Bay: tall plants with bright orange red fls.
D.Diores: tall plants with many fls in various shades of pink, red and orange.
D.Foam: one of the best of the *D.uniflora* hybrids; several fls per stem in bright orange red.
D.Helmut Meyer: small, bright orange red fls on tall spikes; very floriferous.

D.Kewensis: small fls in various shades of pink and orange.
D.Kirstenbosch Pride: tall spikes with many small fls in bright orange red.
D.Langleyensis: tall spikes of pale pink fls.
D.Veitchii: the first of the *Disa* hybrids and remade many times; tall spikes of bright orange red fls.
D.Watsonii: one of the earliest hybrids and remade many times; fls light magenta, spotted, on tall spikes.

Disperis Sw. (From Gk *dis*, twice, and *pera*, wallet or sac, referring to the sac-like spur on each lateral sepal.) 70–80 species of terrestrials and epiphytes. Tubers small. Stems erect, slender, with 1 to few cataphylls at base and 1 to few opposite or alternate leaves, sometimes lacking. Flowers small, usually less than 2cm, solitary or in racemes; dorsal sepal joined to petals forming shallow or elongate, saccate hood, lateral sepals almost always with spur near inner edge; lip much modified and very complex with claw adnate to face of column, usually extended into a straight or reflexed limb bearing a simple or bilobed appendage; column erect; anther loculi parallel; pollinia granular, arranged in double row on edge of flattened caudicles; stigma bilobed. Tropical & S Africa, Mascarene Is., India and east to New Guinea.

CULTIVATION   As for *Disa* but with slightly higher temperatures (i.e. intermediate conditions).

D.capensis (L. f.) Sw.
Stem 15–30cm. Lvs 1–2, alternate, borne on lower half of stem, to 7×1.5cm, lanceolate, acute. Inflorescence 1–2-fld; bracts leafy; fls mainly yellow-green; pet. sometimes rose purple; dorsal sep. to 3cm, lanceolate, long-acuminate, forming a hood with pet., lateral sep. 2.5–3cm, reflexed, narrowly lanceolate, acuminate, with blunt sac 2–3mm long near base; pet. adnate to lower half of dorsal sep.; lip complex, folded back over column, mostly hidden inside hood. Winter. S Africa (Cape Province).

D.fanniniae Harv. GRANNY'S BONNET.
Stem 10–20cm. Lvs 3–4, alternate, to 8×3cm, lanceolate, acute, cordate, amplexicaul, dark glossy green, purple beneath. Raceme several-fld; bracts leafy; fls white, often tinged purple, almost monkshood-like; dorsal sep. forming blunt hood 9–10mm high, lateral sep. 8mm, deflexed, lanceolate, acuminate, with blunt sac about half-way along; pet.

adnate to dorsal sep. along inner margin, with rounded lobe on outer margin, often spotted with green or purple; lip folded back over column and hidden inside hood. S Africa (Transvaal to E Cape).

D.johnstonii Rolfe.
Stem 4–15cm. Lvs 1–3, alternate, 2–3×1.5–2cm, ovate, acute, cordate, amplexicaul, dark green with pale veins above, purple beneath. Raceme 1–5-fld; bracts leafy; dorsal sep. and pet. yellow or mauve, lateral sep. white, sometimes tinged with mauve; pedicel and ovary 10–12mm; dorsal sep. 8–12× 1–2mm, adnate to pet. to form open hood 8–10×7–10mm, lateral sep. 8–14×5–6mm, obliquely semi-orbicular, apiculate, joined to each other for about half their length, each with sac-like spur to 1mm; lip folded back over column, lying inside hood, bearing 2-lobed papillose appendage. Nigeria, Cameroun, Zaire, Tanzania, Malawi, Zambia, Zimbabwe, S Africa (Natal).

Diuris Sm. (From Gk *dis*, double, and *oura*, tail, referring to the pendent lateral sepals.) DOUBLE TAILS. Some 40 species of terrestrial herbs. Tubers subglobose. Stem with several overlapping scales at base. Leaves narrow-lanceolate to linear, grassy, often paired, above them a few sheathing bracts. Raceme tall, erect; flowers solitary or many; petals usually erect and conspicuously clawed; dorsal sepal erect, hooded, clasping the column, lateral sepals long, narrow, strongly decurved, sometimes crossing, spreading; lip equalling or exceeding the dorsal sepal, basally narrow, keeled, trilobed, lateral lobes often reduced. Java, Australia.

CULTIVATION   As for *Disa*.

D.alba R. Br. (*D.punctata* var. *alba* (R. Br.) Ewart & B. Rees).
As *D.punctata* except fls white often tinged or spotted purple, fragrant. E Australia.

D.aurea Sm.
To 60cm. Lvs to 30cm, channelled, ribbed, usually paired. Fls to 35cm diam., to 8; dorsal sep. recurved, ovate, golden spotted or stained brown, lateral sep. bronze-green, often widened at tips and overlapping each other; pet. golden or orange, claws short, spotted brown; lip to 22mm, deflexed, midlobe suborbicular, twice length of lateral lobes, lateral lobes spotted maroon, even, crisped. Australia (NSW).

D.corymbosa Lindl.
To 45cm. Lvs to 20cm, linear, erect or lax, 1–3. Fls 25–75mm diam., 1–8, yellow to red-brown tinted purple; dorsal sep. ovate, broad, incurved, erect at tip, lateral sep. to 25mm, green, deflexed, parallel or crossed; pet. erect, oblique or reflexed, broadly ovate, clawed; lip projecting or obliquely deflexed, midlobe to 10mm, lateral lobes spreading or

recurved, entire, callus ridged, extending to the rear of the midlobe. SW & E Australia.

D.cuneata Fitzg. See *D.punctata* var. *longissima*.

D.lanceolata Lindl. SNAKE ORCHID.
To 40cm. Lvs 3–9, linear-filiform, tufted. Fls to 25mm diam., 1–4, nodding, lemon yellow, exterior with darker markings; dorsal sep. ovate, incurved, often apically recurved, lateral sep. linear, obliquely deflexed; pet. to 20mm, elliptic, claw red-brown, to 5mm; lip deflexed, oblique, midlobe ovate, lateral lobes to 5mm, margins irregularly dentate, callus fleshy, 2-ridged. SE Australia.

D.laxiflora Lindl.
To 25cm. Lvs linear-filiform, erect, 2–4. Fls 1–4, yellow, markings dark brown (especially on lip and pet.); dorsal sep. to 7mm, ovate, lateral sep. decurved or deflexed, brown; pet. 8mm ovate, erect or recurved, claw 4mm; lip deflexed, midlobe flat or folded, flabellate, lateral lobes spreading, margins undulate or entire, callus ridges 2, raised, spreading. SW Australia.

D.longifolia R. Br.
To 45cm. Lvs to 20cm, 2–3, lanceolate or linear. Fls 1–8, purple and mauve, dorsal sep. and lip tinted yellow; dorsal sep. to 12mm, ovate, lateral sep. 18–25mm, linear, tips widened, parallel or crossing each other; pet. ovate or elliptic, clawed, recurved or spreading; lip to 10mm, deep brown suffused yellow or mauve, midlobe cuneate, recurved, lateral lobes oblong-cuneate, spreading or recurved, wavy or entire. SE & SW Australia.

D.maculata Sm.
To 30cm. Lvs 10–24cm, 2–3, linear. Fls 2–8, yellow, spotted dark brown; dorsal sep. ovate, lateral sep. linear, parallel or crossed, green marked dark purple; pet. broadly ovate, yellow, dotted or blotched brown, darker below, claw red-brown; lip 6–7mm, midlobe cuneate, folded, lateral lobes spreading or recurved, equal or shorter than midlobe, callus fleshy, 2-ridged. SE Australia.

D.palustris Lindl.
To 18cm. Lvs 8–10, narrow-linear, twisted, crimson at base. Fls to 20mm diam., 1–4, yellow, blotched dark brown with a spicy fragrance; dorsal sep. ovate, blunt to 8mm, lateral sep. linear, spreading below the lip, green or bronze, 15–18mm; pet. with a purple claw, recurved to 10mm; lip 6–10mm, ovate, forward pointing, lobes oblong, irregularly dentate, interior yellow, exterior blotched brown, callus 2-ridged, fleshy. SE Australia.

D.punctata Sm.
To 60cm. Lvs 2–4, linear, to 25cm. Fls 2–10, purple with darker blotches, rarely yellow or white; dorsal sep. ovate, erect or apically recurved, lateral sep. narrow-linear, pendulous, crossed or curved, to 9cm; pet. elliptic-oblong to 15mm, basal claw darker; lip to 2cm, midlobe flabellate often folded, lateral lobes oblong-falcate, pendulous, spreading, callus 2-ridged. E Australia. var. ***longissima*** Benth. (*D.cuneata* Fitzg.). To 40cm. Lvs linear to filiform, 1–2. Fls 2–6, pale lilac with darker spots and stripes; dorsal sep. ovate, erect, lateral sep. very long, narrow, green; pet. narrow, elliptic, to 12mm, claw to 4mm; lip deflexed, striped purple, midlobe flabellate, broad, to 8mm, lateral lobes upcurved, irregular, callus ridged, expanded apically. SE Australia.

D.punctata var. *alba* (R. Br.) Docker. See *D.alba*.

D.sulphurea R. Br.
To 60cm. Lvs 2–3, linear. Fls 3–7, fragrant, yellow, marked dark brown; dorsal sep. to 22mm, ovate, often recurved, with two central conspicuous dark brown dots, lateral sep. linear, bronze-green, acuminate, parallel or crossed; pet. clawed, elliptic, spreading; lip deflexed, yellow marked dark brown, midlobe rectangular, margins often recurved, lateral lobes recurved, outer margins irregularly dentate, callus a single ridge. C & SE Australia.

D.tricolor Fitzg.
To 40cm. Lvs linear, channelled, to 25cm. Fls 3–6, suffused purple, to 25mm diam.; dorsal sep. ovate, erect, red-dotted, lateral sep. narrow, deflexed, to 30mm, often crossed; pet. elliptic, spreading, basal claw to 7mm; lip oblique, deflexed, midlobe ovate, broad, lateral lobes obtuse, entire, upcurved, callus 2-ridged, curved, fleshy. SE Australia.

Domingoa Schltr. (For the island on which the Dominican Republic is located.) 4 species of epiphytes allied to *Laelia* but superficially resembling *Pleurothallis*. Winter. Cuba, Hispaniola, Puerto Rico.

CULTIVATION As for *Masdevallia* but provide dappled sunlight and warm conditions.

D.hymenodes (Rchb. f.) Schltr.
Pseudobulbs to 3.25cm, very slender, cylindrical, obscurely ridged. Lf to 7×2cm, narrow-obovate to elliptic, acute or obtuse, thin, coarse, deep green. Infl. terminal, to 12.5cm, slender, bracteate, subcorymbose; fls to 2.5cm diam., fragrant; sep. and pet. spreading, broadly lanceolate, acute, translucent, green-white, often faintly lined violet or maroon; lip obovoid, emarginate, cream marked maroon at centre, disc 2-ridged. Cuba, Hispaniola.

× **Doritaenopsis** (*Doritis* × *Phalaenopsis*). The first *Doritaenopsis* hybrids were made in Hawaii in 1923 but it was nearly 40 years before this was followed by the range of hybrids known today. Crossing the hybrids with *Phalaenopsis* parents produces larger flowers in the next generation, while backcrossing to the *Doritis* parent increases the intensity of the colour. The plants are tough, vigorous and free-flowering, intermediate between those of the parents with wide, succulent leaves alternating along a short upright stem. Inflorescence long, erect, with flowers in the upper half or third; flowers white, pink or red, variously dotted or striped, varied in size depending on the breeding. Long lasting. A small selection of well known grexes is listed below.

× *D*.Coral Gleam: tall branching spikes of medium size fls; flowers deep pink.

× *D*.Flame Mountain `Zuma Bay': compact plants with branching spikes; fls deep pink with cerise-red stripes, lip deep raspberry pink.

× *D*.Firecracker: an early hybrid with small, intense, deep cerise pink fls on branching sprays.

× *D*.George Moler: well shaped fls, basically white with narrow stripes of deep pink, lip deep red.

× *D*.Happy Valentine: fls large, pale to deep pink, with darker red or orange lip; the clone 'Zuma Canyon' is particularly fine.

× *D*.Hinacity Glow: large fls, well-shaped, very deep lavender pink with darker lip.

× *D*.Jason Beard: fls well-shaped, beautiful pale pink with red lip.

× *D*.Lady Jewel: finely shaped white fls on tall infl.

× *D*.Orglade's Hot Spot: fls large white with pink-purple lip.

× *D*.Orglade's Latin Tempo: branching spikes of many fls; fls white with deep red stripes throughout, lip deep red.

× *D*.Orglade's Puff: fls large, superb shape, white with gold markings in the lip.

× *D*.Red Coral: an outstanding early hybrid with many deep pink-red fls on tall branching sprays.

Doritis Lindl. (From Gk *dory*, spear, referring to the spear-shaped lip.) 2 species of monopodial epiphytes. Roots thick, flattened. Stems short, leafy. Leaves coriaceous, fleshy, semi-rigid, alternate, 2-ranked, sheathing stem, dark green to red-purple, elliptic to broad-lanceolate. Panicle or raceme lateral; sepals spreading, lateral sepals forming a spur-like projection with column base; lip sessile or clawed, trilobed, fused to column base, lateral lobes erect, disc with a bilobed plate or callus. Indo-Malaya.

CULTIVATION   As for *Phalaenopsis*.

D.pulcherrima Lindl. (*Phalaenopsis pulcherrima* (Lindl.) J.J. Sm.).
Stems to 10cm, usually far shorter. Lvs to 15cm. Infl. 20–60cm simple, erect, often flowering continuously, many-fld; fls deep magenta, with lip midlobe a deeper magenta, lateral lobes red, disc lined white; dorsal sep. narrow, elliptic, lateral sep. oblong, obtuse, connate to column base, spur-like projection to 9mm; pet. obovate, obtuse; lip claw with cal-lused disc, bordered with 2 erect, falcate lobes, midlobe oblong-ovate, lateral lobes oblong, erect.

D.taenialis (Lind.) Hook. f. See *Kingidium taeniale*.
D.wightii (Rchb. f.) Benth. & Hook. f. See *Kingidium delicosum*.

Dracula Luer. (From Lat. *dracula*, a little dragon, referring to the bizarre and sinister flowers of some species.) About 100 species of tufted epiphytic or lithophytic herbs, formerly included in *Masdevallia* but distinguished by their pendulous flowers and floral lips, divided into epichile (blade) and hypochile (claw). The epichile may be saccate, rigidly concave, convex or flat, ribbed or veined, oblong, reniform or spherical. The hypochile is hinged to the column foot. C America, Colombia, Ecuador, Peru.

CULTIVATION   Plant in sphagnum-lined teak baskets to allow for vigorous offsetting and pendulous racemes. Suspend in buoyant, humid, shaded conditions in a minimum temperature of 14°C/57°F. Mist frequently. Otherwise, cultivation as for *Masdevallia*. In many species, the older leaf tips discolour and die back – a problem observed in the wild and seldom affecting the performance of the plant.

D.bella (Rchb. f.) Luer.
Lvs to 18×3cm, lanceolate-spathulate, obtuse, dark green, fleshy, erect, tufted, numerous. Raceme to 20cm, borne at lf base, strongly pendulous; fls solitary, nodding; sep. to 12×2.5cm, triangular, glabrous, buff or dull olive, densely spotted oxblood, each with a dark, slender, pendulous tail to 14cm and basally fused to form a sepaline cup to 5×1.5cm; pet. to 8mm, ivory spotted chocolate or red, pandurate, cleft, papillose, clawed; epichile to 1.5×2cm, reniform, concave, pure white or off-white lined blood-red, hypochile to 5mm, fleshy pink; column to 4mm, squat, maroon. Colombia.

D.benedicti (Rchb.f.) Luer.
Sepaline cup to 2cm diam., almost circular, exterior pale (sometimes near-white), interior a deep, velvety purple-red to black, tails to 3cm; lip small, pale red to white. Colombia.

D.carderi (Rchb.f.) Luer.
Sepaline cup small, deep, densely pubesc. within, white spotted or broadly blotched purple, tails divergent; lip small, concave, neither ridged nor toothed. Colombia.

D.chestertonii (Rchb. f.) Luer.
Lvs to 20cm, lanceolate, dark green, thinly coriaceous. Infl. to 20cm, pendulous, bearing fls singly in succession; sep. to 3×2cm, spreading, ovate, sulphur-green spotted and bordered with violet-blue to grey-black warts, abruptly caudate, the tails to 1.5cm, black, dorsal sep. distinct, lateral sep. fused along central axis; pet. to 5mm, clavate, hooded, cartilaginous, orange spotted black; epichile to 2cm across, broadly reniform, margin involute, the two dilated valves ochre to rust-red and lined with radiating red gills, the whole resembling an upturned mushroom. Colombia.

D.chimaera (Rchb. f.) Luer.
Lvs to 25×5cm, oblong-spathulate, obtuse. Infl. erect, to 55cm; fls to 6, developing successively; sep. to 6cm, spreading and twisting, obscurely triangular, tapering to violet tails some 18cm long, buff to olive-green, flecked and stained maroon or violet-black, coarsely hairy, warty, sepaline cup to 1cm deep, dorsal sep. apparently distinct, inner margins of lateral sep. basally fused for some 3cm; pet. to 6mm, obovate, cream marked violet; epichile to 2cm, pouch-like, cream to fleshy pink, hypochile narrow, buff and orange. Colombia.

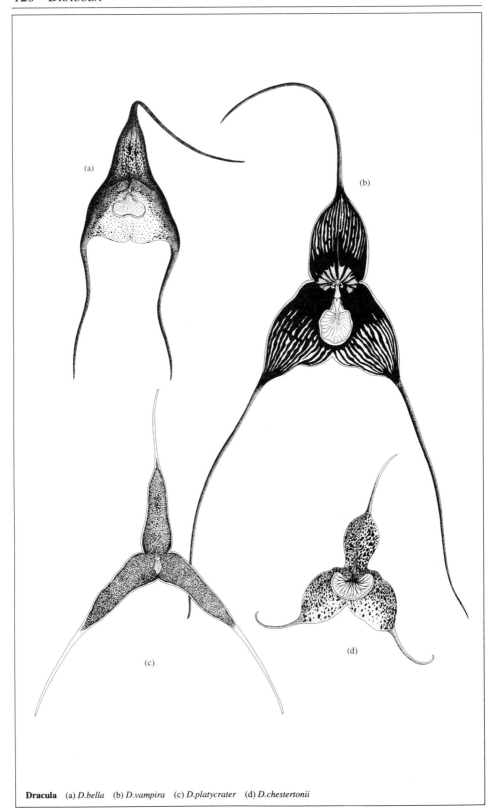

Dracula   (a) *D.bella*   (b) *D.vampira*   (c) *D.platycrater*   (d) *D.chestertonii*

D.cutis-bufonis Luer & Escobar.
Close to *D.chestertonii*, differing in the more prominently warty sepals and the smaller lip, which is loosely hinged, not fixed. Colombia

D.erythrochaete (Rchb. f.) Luer.
Luer. Lvs 8, 23×2–3cm, erect, fleshy, tough, narrow-obovate, subacute. Infl. to 20cm, descending; fls produced singly in succession, nodding; sep. to 6cm, spreading, broadly ovate, fused to form a broad cup to 0.8cm deep, cream to grey-pink, minutely spotted maroon, white-pubesc. above, contracted to maroon tails to 4cm; pet. 3×1.5mm, oblong, pale brown-yellow with an oxblood blotch; epichile to 1cm, orbicular, inrolled, somewhat inflated, fleshy, white or buff with 3 lamellae radiating from the centre within, hypochile to 8mm, deeply grooved with 2 erect, obtuse, basal lobes. Guatemala, Nicaragua, Costa Rica, Panama.

D.felix (Luer) Luer.
Fls small, pale, cup-shaped, produced in abundance, possibly cleistogamous in some cases. Colombia, Ecuador.

D.gigas (Luer & Andreetta) Luer.
Habit large and robust. Scapes ascending to 60cm; fls produced in succession, large, pink. Ecuador.

D.gorgona (Veitch) Luer & Escobar.
Fls large, basically creamy white, the three distinct and divergent sepals densely spotted blood-red or purple-brown in their basal half and at their tips, becoming solid blood red in the long tails, the whole of the interior densely covered in long hairs; lip small, pouch-like, pink; column yellow. Colombia.

D.iricolor (Rchb.f.) Luer & Escobar.
Scapes erect, bearing small, short-tailed lilac fls in succession. Colombia, Ecuador.

D.nycterina (Rchb.f.) Luer.
Resembles a smaller *D.bella* with sep. more evenly mottled, tails more divergent and lip narrower and smaller. Colombia.

D.orientalis Luer & Escobar.
Sep. distinct, ovate, white, densely spotted deep red-brown, minutely pubescent, tails very long, slender, uppermost erect, lowermost downward-pointing; lip small, white, toothed and ridged.E. Colombia.

D.platycrater (Rchb.f.) Luer.
Sep. very distinct, narrow, strongly divergent, oblong-lanceolate with slender tails, white to rose dotted purple-red; lip small, pink, ridged, convex. Colombia.

D.psyche (Luer) Luer.
Fls on erect scapes, small, cupped, white lined and streaked red with red, forward-pointing slender tails, the lowermost often crossing or parallel. Ecuador.

D.robledorum (P. Ortiz) Luer & Escobar.
Fls large, borne in succession on an erect scape; sep. spreading, pubesc., yellow or orange with purple spots merging toward centre, becoming radiating stripes at base of dorsal sep., tails more or less equalling blades. Colombia.

D.simia (Luer) Luer.
Fls large; sep. broad, red-brown, long-tailed, white at base around pet. and column; lip white, ridged. The whole resembling a monkey's face. Ecuador.

D.sodiroi (Scltr.) Luer.
Fls produced several together on an erect raceme, drooping, bell-shaped, orange, sepaline tails more or less equalling blades, downward-pointing. Ecuador.

D.tubeana (Rchb.f) Luer.
Fls large; sep. distinct, broadly ovate, tapering to long, slender tails, chestnut to blood red, white at base except for a bright blood red dot at either side of white column; lip white, concave, reniform, ridged. Ecuador.

D.vampira (Luer) Luer.
Lvs to 25cm, lanceolate-elliptic, subacute, dark green, fleshy, subcoriaceous, erect. Infl. creeping to pendulous, to 45cm; fls to 6, produced singly in succession; sep. to 5cm, ovate, tapering to tails to 10cm, the dorsal sep. largely free, the laterals connate to two-thirds of interior margins, glabrous, yellow-white to sulphur-green densely veined maroon-black with a sulphur-yellow sunburst above column, tails black; pet. to 8mm, white flecked violet; epichile to 2cm, reniform, concave above, white veined pink, hypochile to 0.75cm, grooved, winged. Ecuador.

D.velutina (Rchb.f.) Luer.
Fls small, produced in succession, cup-shaped to expanded, white spotted or suffused purple, hairy within. Colombia.

D.vespertilio (Rchb.f.) Luer.
Close to *D.bella* and *D.nycterina*; differs in large, white, transverse lip which is smooth above. C America to Ecuador.

D.wallisii (Rchb.f.) Luer.
Fls large, variable, with purple spots and long hairs on the inner surface; lip rounded, hinged and capable of movement (thus differing from *D.chimaera*). Colombia.

Dresslerella Luer. (For Robert Dressler, see *Dressleria*.) 8 species, small epiphytes and lithophytes close to *Restrepia*, with leaves oblong-elliptic to oblong-lanceolate, often lying flat and to varying degrees hairy. C & S America, Nicaragua to Peru.

CULTIVATION   As for *Pleurothallis*.

D.pilosissima (Schltr.) Luer.
Lvs densely long-pubesc., papillose. Fls small, solitary, white-hairy, buff and deep garnet. Costa Rica.

D.stellaris Luer & Escobar.
Lvs large. Fls large, fleshy, solitary, not opening fully, dark garnet, white-hairy. Costa Rica, Colombia.

Dressleria Dodson (For Robert Dressler (*b*.1927), orchid taxonomist.) 4 species of epiphytes or lithophytes allied to *Catasetum*. Rhizome short. Roots thick, adhering to substrate, grey-white. Pseudobulbs clumped, fusiform to narrow-cylindric, clothed in first season by sheathing leaf bases, later by their grey, papery remnants. Leaves tough, papery, obscurely plicate, lanceolate-elliptic, acuminate, to 8 borne in 2 alternate ranks on pseudobulb, at first emerging as a lateral fan. Inflorescence erect, racemose or subcapitate, borne from basal nodes of pseudobulb, bracteate; flowers bisexual, fleshy; sepals similar, reflexed, narrow-lanceolate, apiculate; petals reflexed, elliptic-ovate, acute, sometimes strongly involute; lip entire, callused or lacking callus, adnate to column, apical margin often swollen, rigid and involute, basally concave; column short, fleshy, lacking a foot, anther with 2 rounded lateral lobes, apex apiculate. C America to Ecuador.

CULTIVATION   See *Catasetum*.

D.dilecta (Rchb. f.) Dodson (*Catasetum dilectum* Rchb. f.). Infl. subcapitate; fls 5–10, usually non-resupinate; sep. and pet. to 18×5mm, strongly reflexed, tan to cream; lip to 2.5×2.2cm, yellow to ochre, waxy, lustrous, margins translucent. Costa Rica, Nicaragua, Panama, Venezuela, Colombia, Ecuador.

D.eburnea (Rolfe) Dodson (*Catasetum eburneum* Rolfe). Infl. racemose; fls pale green-yellow, non-resupinate; lip to 4cm, lacking callus or rigid, pouched apical margin. Colombia, Ecuador.

D.suavis (Ames & Schweinf.) Dodson (*Catasetum suave* Ames & Schweinf.). Infl. racemose; fls olive-green, ochre or cream; lip to 2cm, adnate to only half of column, with an erect, translucent margin around cavity and callus formed by swelling of sides of cavity. Nicaragua, Costa Rica, Panama.

Dryadella Luer (*Trigonanthe* (Schltr.) Brieger). (Named for the dryads, nymphs of trees and forests.) Some 40 species of dwarf epiphytes or lithophytes formerly included in *Masdevallia*. Stems short, tufted, unifoliate. Leaves thick, linear, erect. Flowers borne singly atop slender stalks produced at leaf bases or in a short, successional raceme; sepals ovate to triangular, acute to caudate, basally connate, the laterals dorsally carinate and transversely callused at base, forming a mentum below the column foot; petals usually rhombic, small, held within sepaline cup; lip unguiculate, basally bilobulate. C & S America.

CULTIVATION   As for *Masdevallia*.

D.aviceps (Rchb. f.) Luer (*D.obrieniana*). Lvs large, broad, purple-tinted. Fls yellow-green spotted purple, sep. with short tails. S Brazil

D.edwallii (Cogn.) Luer. Lvs to 8×1cm, leathery, linear-spathulate, obtuse, dark green. Infl. to 2cm; sep. to 1cm (basally fused for some 3mm), triangular to ovate, caudate (tails to 1cm), spreading or forward-projecting, ochre to golden yellow, spotted or banded oxblood; pet. to 3×4mm, trapeziform, serrulate at apex; lip to 3mm, broadly-ligulate, maroon. Brazil.

D.guatemalensis (Schltr.) Luer. See *D.simula*.
D.obrieniana. See *D.aviceps*.

D.simula (Rchb. f.) Luer (*D.guatemalensis* (Schltr.) Luer). Lvs to 10×1.5cm, erect, linear-oblanceolate, rounded, apex minutely 3-toothed, dark green often flushed purple. Infl. to 1cm; fls solitary; sep. 1.2×0.35cm, ovate-oblong, acuminate, forward-projecting, white marked purple; pet. 0.35×0.3cm, rhombic, white marked maroon; lip to 0.5cm, obscurely 3-lobed to flabellate, biauriculate at base, white to maroon. C America, Colombia.

D.zebrina (Porsch) Luer. Lvs to 5×0.5cm, erect, rigid, linear to narrow-lanceolate, strongly carinate beneath, dark green flushed purple. Infl. to 2cm; sep. to 1cm, adnate-cupped to spreading, caudate, cream densely spotted or banded violet-black to ash-grey; pet. to 0.3cm, cream to maroon; lip to 0.5cm, grey-white. Brazil.

Dyakia Christenson. (For the Dyak aborigines of Borneo.) 1 species, an epiphyte similar to *Ascocentrum* except leaves flat, bilobed, obtuse; lip lateral lobes small, spur bilaterally compressed, callus solitary, prominent; rosetellum S-shaped. To 8cm. Leaves oblong-ligulate, rigid, coriaceous, to 10cm. Racemes dense, ascending; flowers to 2.5cm, sweetly scented, vivid, sparkling rose madder to magenta with a white lip; dorsal sepal elliptic, lateral sepals oblong, cuneate, base fused to the lip base, apex obtuse; lip almost reduced to a spur, midlobe triangular, flat in the upper front of the spur; spur oblong-ligulate, obtuse. Borneo.

CULTIVATION   See *Ascocentrum*.

D.hendersoniana (Rchb. f.) Christenson (*Ascocentrum hendersonianum* Rchb. f.).

Elleanthus Presl (From Gk *eilein*, to shut in, and *anthos*, flower, a reference to the bracts which enclose the flowers.) Some 50 species of epiphytes or terrestrials, lacking pseudobulbs. Rhizomes short. Stems reed-like, simple or branched, erect, leafy, usually tufted, covered by scarious or fibrous sheaths toward apex. Leaves alternate, cauline, plicate, scarious, glaucous, sometimes sparsely hirsute, linear-lanceolate to oblanceolate or elliptic-ovate, acute or acuminate, bases sheathing stem. Inflorescence terminal, erect; flowers in dense bracteate heads or spicate racemes; floral bracts usually exceeding flower, imbricate, sometimes pubescent; sepals free, erect, acute, or apiculate; petals narrower and thinner than sepals; lip attached at base of column, simple or somewhat trilobed, enclosing column, margins entire, dentate or ciliate, basal portion of lip concave with 2 distinct calli; column erect, footless, semi-terete or winged in the middle; anther 2-celled, operculate, slightly incumbent; pollinia 4 in each cell, ovoid, waxy. C America, S America, W Indies.

CULTIVATION   As for *Sobralia*.

E.aurantiacus. (Lindl.) Rchb. f.
To 100cm, stem frequently branched. Lvs to 12×2cm, variable, lanceolate, mucronate, coriaceous. Infl. to 10cm, usually shorter; floral bracts 5–15×3–5mm; fls bright orange, edged red, sep. to 9×3.5mm; pet. to 9×2.5mm; lip to 12mm, orange, simple, shallow-erose to fimbriate, base concave, calli yellow to cream; column white; anth. pale maroon, apex purple; pollinia pale cream. Venezuela, Colombia, Ecuador, Peru.

E.capitatus (R. Br.) Rchb. f.
To 150cm. Lvs to 23×7cm, lanceolate to lanceolate-elliptic, long-acuminate, chartaceous. Infl. to 8.5×6cm, capitate, compact, gummy; sep. pink-white, to 7×2.5mm; pet. pink-white, to 6×1.5mm; lip to 14mm, pink-white, simple, reniform if spread, erose-fimbriate, concave at base, calli white; column white, obtuse tubercle on anterior side; anth. pink; pollinia pink. Summer. Widespread throughout genus range.

E.caravata (Aubl.) Rchb. f.
To 60cm. Lvs to 16×2cm, lanceolate, rigid, gradually attenuate, variably mucronate, subverrucose above. Infl. a dense raceme; fls numerous; sep. to 9×3mm, pale to bright yellow, pubesc. beneath; pet. to 8.5×2.5mm, bright yellow; lip to 1.2×0.8cm, reniform, apex retuse, base gibbous, margin erose-fimbriate, white at base, calli white, subglobose, basal; column white; anth. bright purple. Autumn. Venezuela, Guyana, French Guiana.

E.furfuraceus (Lindl.) Rchb. f.
To 50cm; stem simple or sparsely branched. Lvs to 14×2.5cm, lanceolate or elliptic-lanceolate, sharply long-acuminate. Fls 4–16, magenta, base white; sep. to 8×3.5mm, thickened at acute apex; pet. to 7.5×3.5mm; lip magenta, basally saccate, margin erose to fimbriate, calli white; column white, subclavate; anth. pink; pollinia purple-grey. Summer. Guyana, Venezuela, Colombia, Ecuador, Peru. .

E.linifolius Presl.
To 30cm. Lvs to 10cm×4mm, linear, apex unevenly tridentate or acute, clear green, base strict to arcuate. Infl. compact, to 3.5×1.5mm; floral bracts large, cymbiform, 2-ranked, imbricate, largely concealing flowers; sep. white, tipped pale green, to 3.5×1.5mm; pet. similar; lip to 4mm, obscurely trilobed, margins erose-dentate, base deeply concave, calli 2, basal, ovoid; column very pale green, about 2mm; anth. bright yellow-green; pollinia pale yellow. W Indies, Mexico, C America to Peru.

E.longibracteatus (Lindl. ex Griseb.) Fawcett.
To 90cm, stem simple. Lvs to 20×3cm, lanceolate to elliptic-lanceolate, acuminate. Infl. a spike to 8cm; floral bracts to 3cm; fls cream to pale yellow; sep. to 10mm; pet. to 7mm; lip not exceeding sep., indistinctly trilobed, apical margin dentate-fimbriate, base saccate, containing 2 ovoid calli; column to 6mm, winged on each side. W Indies, Colombia, Ecuador, Bolivia.

E.xanthocomus Rchb. f. ex Hook.
To 30cm, stem simple. Lvs to 17.5×2.5cm, lanceolate to oblong-lanceolate, acuminate. Infl. to 7.5cm; floral bracts yellow, green at apex; fls numerous, bright yellow. Spring. Peru.

Elythranthera (Endl.) A.S. George. (From Gk *elytron*, a cover, and *anthera*, anther; referring to the hood over the anther.) ENAMEL ORCHID. 2 species of tuberous terrestrials. Leaf basal, solitary, lanceolate, glandular-pubescent. Scape erect; flowers pink or purple, 1–4; sepals and petals iridescent, glossy above, spotted beneath, spreading, oblong-lanceolate; lip sessile, membranous, glabrous, recurved or sigmoid with 2 mobile basal calli; column erect, lateral wings forming a hood over anther. Late summer–mid winter. SW West Australia.

CULTIVATION   As for *Disa*, but in a grittier medium with a semi-dry rest in winter.

E.brunonis (Endl.) A.S. George (*Glossodia brunonis* Endl.).
To 30cm, aerial parts glandular-pubesc. Lf 2–8cm, oblong-oblanceolate, green, purple at base. Fls 1–3; sep. and pet. 12–20mm, purple, paler above, blotched deeper purple; dorsal sep. erect, tip recurved; lip white, lanceolate, entire, base marked purple, calli, linear, obtuse, sometimes basally fused.

E.emarginata (Lindl.) A.S. George.
Stems to 30cm, pubesc. Lf 6–10cm, linear-lanceolate to lanceolate, glandular-pubesc.; stem bracts 2. Fls 1–4, rose pink, spotted below; lip linear to narrow oblong, marked rose-purple, obtuse or truncate, emarginate, basal calli linear, clavate, almost covering lip; anth. enclosed by a hooded wing to 1cm.

Elythranthera and other Australian Terrestrials   (a) *Arthrochilus irritabilis*   (b) *Lyperanthus suaveolens*
(c) *Calochilus campestris*   (d) *Caladenia dilatata*   (e) *Pterostylis concinna*   (f) *Diuris maculata*   (g) *Corybas fimbriatus*   (h) *Elythranthera emarginata*

Embreea Dodson. (For Alvin Embree, contemporary orchidologist.) 1 species, an epiphyte very close in general appearance to *Stanhopea*, from which it differs in its 4-angled pseudobulbs each bearing a solitary, grey-green leaf. The flowers are solitary, pendulous and very large; tepals spreading, ovate-lanceolate, grey- or green-white, densely spotted chestnut brown above, more sparsely blotched beneath; lip waxy, complex, grey- or blue-white. closely spotted blood red or chestnut, wings of mesochile T-shaped and incurved, each with a distinctive, fang-shaped horn; column slender below and arching, dilated above with 2 narrow wings, finely spotted red-brown. Colombia, Ecuador.

CULTIVATION   As for *Stanhopea*, but with light shade, excellent air circulation and abundant humidity and moisture throughout the year.

E.rodigasiana (Claes ex Cogn.) Dodson.

Encyclia Hook. (From the Gk *enkyklo*, to encircle, referring to the characteristic of the lateral lobes of the lip which encircle the column.) Some 150 species of epiphytes and lithophytes closely allied to and formerly included in *Epidendrum*. Rhizome short or elongate. Pseudobulbs ovoid, pyriform or fusiform, sometimes slender, 1 to 4-leaved at apex. Leaves oblong to ligulate, fleshy to coriaceous, sessile or short-petiolate. In the following descriptions the leaf number applies to the number of leaves per apex of each pseudobulb – it may happen that pseudobulbs also bear basal, sheathing leaves. Inflorescence a terminal raceme or panicle, few- to many-flowered; flowers showy, sometimes non-resupinate; sepals free, spreading or reflexed, subequal; petals largely similar to sepals; lip simple or trilobed, free or partially adnate to column, sometimes enveloping column; column subterete to triquetrous, subclavate, apex tridentate; anther terminal, incumbent, operculate, pollinia 4, waxy, obovate or elliptic-ovate, compressed. Subtropical and Tropical Americas W Indies.

CULTIVATION   A highly varied genus of epiphytic orchids. *E.fragrans* and its allies should be grown in pans or baskets of very open bark-based mix in cool to intermediate conditions: bright sunlight and a marked dry rest in winter are both essential, although the soft pea-green growths of these species may be easily scorched. These guidelines apply to most other species, with a few exceptions – *E.adenocaula* and *E.hanburyi* and their respective associates require rather more sunlight. *E.pygmaea*, *E.polybulbon* and *E.tripunctata* should be mounted on fibre blocks on pads of moss and kept just moist and in filtered sunlight throughout the year. *E.vitellina* requires cool, buoyant, rather dry conditions in full sunlight and a decided dry winter rest. Culture of the remaining glaucous species, *E.mariae* and *E.citrina*, is complicated further by their pendulous habit (especially strong in *E.citrina*): they must be mounted 'upside-down', suspended in a cool, bright, dry environment. Plunge daily when in growth. Once growths are complete, lower temperatures (to near-freezing if possible) and withold water completely. With lengthening days, start back into growth by raising temperatures slightly and misting roots – this will encourage development of flower spikes for spring blooming.

E.citrina is among the most beautiful of all orchids. Its hanging, leaden-grey growths are in stark contrast with the large, waxen and wonderfully fragrant, lemon-yellow blooms. Its fondness for complete neglect commends it for cool greenhouses, porches and conservatories.

E.adenocaula (La Ll. & Lex.) Schltr. (*Epidendrum adenocaulum* La Ll. & Lex.; *E.nemoralis* (Lindl.) Schltr.; *Epidendrum nemorale* Lindl.).
Pseudobulbs to 8×6cm, ovoid to ovoid-conical, clustered, 1–3-lvd. Lvs to 35×3cm, ligulate, glossy, hard, acute or obtuse. Infl. to 100cm, a panicle, many-fld; peduncle verrucose; fls pale rose-pink to pale purple sometimes streaked dark rose, the lip often paler with dark markings; sep. to 50×7mm, elliptic-lanceolate to elliptic-linear, acute; pet. to 45×8mm, narrowly elliptic to oblanceolate, acute; lip to 4.5cm, trilobed, lateral lobes oblong to oblong-lanceolate, oblique, midlobe to 3cm, suborbicular to ovate-oblong, mucronate, callus elliptic, sulcate; column to 1.5cm, clavate, alate, wings oblong, midtooth triangular. Spring–summer. Mexico.

E.adenocaula var. *kennedyi* (Fowlie & Withner) Hagsater & Gonzalez. See *E.kennedyi*.

E.alata (Batem.) Schltr. (*Epidendrum alatum* Batem.; *Epidendrum longipetalum* Lindl. & Paxt.; *Epidendrum calocheilum* Hook.).
Pseudobulbs to 12×6cm, ovoid-conical or pyriform, 1–3-lvd. Lvs to 55×4cm, linear-lanceolate, acute, tough, somewhat thickened, often flushed red-purple, 1–3-lvd. Infl. to 150cm, usually branching, many-fld; fls pale green or yellow-green marked purple or red-brown, lip usually white veined maroon; sep. to 30×8mm, oblanceolate to elliptic-oblanceolate, obtuse, slightly reflexed; pet. to 28×7mm, oblanceolate-spathulate, obtuse or mucronate; lip to 25mm, 3-lobed, lateral lobes oblong-obovate, apex rounded, clasping column, midlobe orbicular-obovate or transversely subrhombic, retuse, undulate, with numerous verrucose veins; callus ovate, fleshy, sulcate; column to 12mm, clavate, teeth short, triangular, wings quadrate-oblong. Summer. Mexico to Nicaragua.

E.ambigua (Lindl.) Schltr. (*Epidendrum ambiguum* Lindl.; *Epidendrum trachychilum* Lindl.; *E.trachychila* (Lindl.) Schltr.).
Pseudobulbs to 8×4cm, clustered, ovoid-conical, 2–3-lvd. Lvs to 37×3cm, linear-ligulate, acute. Infl. to 80cm, usually a panicle, many-fld; peduncle minutely verrucose; fls to 3.5cm diam., fragrant, cream-yellow or green-yellow, sometimes tinged pale brown, lip cream to straw-yellow spotted and streaked red; sep. to 30×7mm, lanceolate to elliptic-lanceolate, acute; pet. to 28×9mm, clawed, elliptic to elliptic-oblanceolate, acute; lip to 25mm, 3-lobed lateral lobes clasping column at base, oblong, obtuse, midlobe ovate to ovate-oblong, obtuse, undulate-crisped, venation verrucose, callus sulcate, elliptic; column to 12mm, clavate, arcuate, alate, wings oblong, apical teeth short, obtuse. Summer. Honduras, Guatemala, Mexico.

E.aromatica (Batem.) Schltr. (*Epidendrum aromaticum* Batem.; *Epidendrum incumbens* Lindl.).
Pseudobulbs to 8×5cm, conical to subspheric, clustered, often dark purple-brown, 1–2-lvd. Lvs to 30×4cm, linear-ligulate or elliptic-ligulate, acute or obtuse. Infl. to 90cm, a panicle, erect; fls cream, pale yellow or yellow-green, often suffused red-brown, lip cream or yellow veined red-brown; sep. to 20×5mm, oblanceolate to elliptic-oblanceolate, acute to

obtuse; pet. to 18×9mm, obovate to spathulate; lip to 15mm, 3-lobed, lateral lobes spreading, oblong to lanceolate, obtuse, midlobe suborbicular or subrhombic, strongly undulate, verrucose, callus elliptic-obovate, fleshy, sulcate; column to 7mm, arcuate, wings absent, midtooth short, triangular. Mostly spring. Guatemala, Mexico.

E.baculus (Rchb. f.) Dressler & Pollard (*Epidendrum baculus* Rchb. f.; *Epidendrum pentotis* Rchb. f.).
Pseudobulbs to 30×2cm, narrowly cylindrical to fusiform-cylindrical, slightly compressed, usually 2-lvd. Lvs to 30×3cm, linear-elliptic to lanceolate, obtuse to acuminate, bright green, pliable, thinly coriaceous. Infl. to 7cm, erect, 2 to 3-fld; fls large, showy, fragrant, white-cream to pale yellow-green, the lip white or cream longitudinally striped maroon to violet; sep. to 60×8mm, oblong-lanceolate to elliptic-lanceolate, acute; pet. to 40×10mm, elliptic to elliptic-lanceolate, acute or acuminate; lip to 25×16mm simple, ovate-quadrate to ovate-triangular, basally cordate, concave above, abruptly acuminate, callus oblong, thickened, grooved; column to 10mm, stout, spotted purple, midtooth fleshy, triangular. Spring–summer. Mexico, Brazil, Colombia, Nicaragua, Honduras, Guatemala, El Salvador.

E.belizensis (Rchb. f.) Schltr. (*Epidendrum belizense* Rchb. f.; *E.virens* (Lindl. & Paxt.) Schltr.; *Epidendrum virens* Lindl. & Paxt.).
Pseudobulbs to 4.5×2cm, clustered, ovoid-conical, 2-lvd. Lvs to 50×2cm, elliptic-lanceolate to linear, obtuse, coriaceous. Infl. to 90cm, often branched, erect or arching, loosely few to many-fld; fls to 4cm diam., fragrant, long-lived, pale yellow to olive green, the tip white to cream streaked red-brown; sep. to 23×7mm, oblanceolate, obtuse; pet. to 21×7mm, oblanceolate to oblanceolate-spathulate, acute to obtuse; lip to 17mm, 3-lobed, lateral lobes oblong, clasping column, slightly falcate, midlobe suborbicular, obtuse, undulate, veins verrucose, callus obovate-elliptic, sulcate; column to 10mm, clavate, alate, apical teeth short, triangular, obtuse. Spring–summer. Belize, Honduras, Mexico.

E.bicamerata (Rchb. f.) Dressler & Pollard (*Epidendrum bicameratum* Rchb. f.).
Pseudobulbs to 7×3cm, ovoid, clustered, 1–3-lvd. Lvs to 25×3.5cm, elliptic-oblong, broadly acute. Infl. to 40cm, many-fld; fls to 2.5cm diam., fragrant tawny-brown or chestnut-brown; the lip white stained ochre at base and spotted purple on callus; sep. to 14×7mm, obovate-oblong, mucronate; pet. to 12×6mm, obovate, obtuse; lip to 10mm, 3-lobed, lateral lobes subquadrate, midlobe transversely oblong to subreniform; callus large, oblong, sulcate; column to 6mm, teeth subequal, ovate, obtuse. Spring–summer. Mexico.

E.boothiana (Lindl.) Dressler (*Epidendrum boothianum* Lindl.; *Epidendrum bidentatum* Lindl.).
Pseudobulbs to 3.5×2.5cm, suborbicular, laterally compressed, lustrous yellow-green, 1–3-lvd. Lvs to 17×3cm, oblanceolate, acute to obtuse, rigid, slightly twisted. Infl. to 25cm, loosely few-fld; fls showy, yellow blotched deep red-brown, the lip yellow-green marked white; sep. to 14×4mm, elliptic to oblanceolate, acute to subacuminate, slightly revolute; pet. to 13×3mm, linear-oblanceolate, acute to obtuse; lip to 10×7mm, subrhombic or obscurely 3-lobed, lateral lobes obtuse, strongly deflexed, midlobe apex fleshy-thickened, callus fleshy, oblong-quadrate; column to 7mm, green at base, apex white, midtooth surpassing lateral teeth, subglobose. Winter. Florida, Mexico, W Indies, British Honduras.

E.bractescens (Lindl.) Hoehne (*Epidendrum bractescens* Lindl.).
Pseudobulbs to 3.5×2cm, clustered, conical or ovoid-conical, slightly rugose, 2-lvd. Lvs to 27×1cm, ligulate to linear-lanceolate, obtuse to subacute, lustrous. Infl. to 30cm, sometimes branched, few to many-fld; sep. and pet. yellow-brown to brick-red; sep. to 30×5mm, lanceolate to elliptic-lanceolate, acute or acuminate, pet. to 30×5mm, narrowly oblanceolate, acuminate; lip to 25mm, white-yellow with numerous red-

purple veins, deeply 3-lobed, lateral lobes linear or linear-oblong, obtuse, porrect, midlobe clawed, suborbicular-obovate to transversely oblong, retuse, undulate-crenulate, heavily veined, callus oblong, sulcate, pubesc.; column to 11mm, dark green or yellow spotted red, midtooth oblong, wings rounded-triangular. Winter–summer. Mexico, Guatemala, Honduras, British Honduras.

E.brassavolae (Rchb. f.) Dressler (*Epidendrum brassavolae* Rchb. f.).
Pseudobulbs to 20×5cm, ovoid to pyriform or fusiform-ovoid, slightly compressed, 2–3-lvd, widely spaced on rhiz. Lvs to 28×5cm, oblong-elliptic to oblong-lanceolate, obtuse, pale to mid-green, pliable. Infl. to 50cm, erect, few to many-fld; fls large; sep. and pet. green-yellow to olive-tan, spreading, linear-lanceolate, acuminate often revolute, sep. to 55×6mm, pet. to 47×3mm; lip to 45×16mm, rose-purple, cream at base, clawed, ovate-lanceolate to elliptic-oblong, acuminate, with fleshy longitudinal keel; column to 15mm, midtooth spathulate, serrate, lateral teeth triangular. Summer–autumn. C America, Mexico to Panama.

E.bulbosa (Vell.) Pabst (*Epidendrum bulbosum* Vell.; *Epidendrum inversum* Lindl.).
Pseudobulbs to 9×1.5cm, fusiform, lustrous green, 2-lvd. Lvs to 21×2.5cm, coriaceous, ligulate, obtuse. Infl. to 12cm, erect, few-fld; fls to 5cm diam., cream-white, the lip marked purple; sep. to 28×3mm, exceeding pet. narrowly lanceolate, acute to acuminate; lip to 12×6mm, simple, clawed, lanceolate, acuminate, callus 3-keeled; column to 8mm, fleshy, triquetrous. Brazil, Paraguay.

E.calamaria (Lindl.) Pabst (*Epidendrum calamarium* Lindl.).
Pseudobulbs to 5×1cm, fusiform, lustrous green, 2–3-lvd. Lvs to 11×8mm, narrowly oblanceolate to linear-oblanceolate, acute or obtuse. Infl. to 6cm, few-fld; fls to 3cm diam., white-cream to pale yellow-green, the lip streaked purple; sep. to 14×3mm, linear, acute; pet. subequal to sep., oblanceolate or narrowly spathulate, acuminate; lip to 8×6mm, simple, ovate to cordate, acute, callus small, bicarinate; column to 6mm, fleshy, dilated towards apex. Brazil.

E.campylostalix (Rchb. f.) Schltr. (*Epidendrum campylostalix* Rchb. f.).
Pseudobulbs to 12×4cm, ovoid-oblong to ellipsoid, strongly compressed, 1-lvd. Lvs to 30×8cm, subcoriaceous, elliptic to oblong, acute, dark green above. Infl. to 38cm, sometimes branched, erect, loosely few to many-fld; fls showy, spreading, pendent, red-purple lined yellow, grey-green below, lip white spotted red at base; sep. to 25×4mm, linear-lanceolate, acute; pet. to 20×3mm, ensiform to narrowly linear-oblanceolate, acute; lip to 2×1cm, clawed, 3-lobed, lateral lobes suborbicular to oblong, obtuse, midlobe obovate to suborbicular, subapiculate or rounded, callus tricarinate; column to 9mm, red-purple. Guatemala, Panama, Costa Rica.

E.candollei (Lindl.) Schltr. (*Epidendrum candollei* Lindl.).
Pseudobulbs to 8×3.5cm, ovoid-conical to globose, clustered, 1–3-lvd. Lvs to 35×4cm, coriaceous, elliptic-ligulate to narrowly lanceolate, acute or obtuse. Infl. to 90cm, a panicle, loosely many-fld; fls yellow-green or yellow brown to chocolate, the lip white to cream streaked purple; sep. to 20×5mm, oblanceolate to elliptic-oblanceolate, obtuse to subacute; pet. to 18×7mm, obliquely spathulate or cuneate-obovate, rounded or mucronate; lip to 16×15mm, 3-lobed, lateral lobes free, oblong, obtuse, overlapping midlobe, midlobe suborbicular to suborbicular-flabellate, acute to shortly acuminate, veins papillose, callus to 7mm, elliptic-obovate, sulcate, papillose; column to 7mm, arcuate, midtooth short, triangular. Spring–summer. Guatemala, Mexico.

E.ceratistes (Lindl.) Schltr. (*Epidendrum ceratistes* Lindl.).
Pseudobulbs to 7×2.5cm, ovoid to ovoid-pyriform, wrinkled, 2–4-lvd. Lvs to 45×2cm, linear-ligulate, obtuse. Infl. to 1m, branched, suberect to pendent, many-fld; sep. and pet. cream to pale green or green-yellow, sep. to 20×5mm, elliptic to elliptic-lanceolate, acute, slightly recurved, pet. to 18×5mm, oblanceo-

Encyclia   (a) *E.citrina*   (b) *E.pygmaea*   (c) *E.cochleata*   (d) *E.adenocaula*   (e) *E.vitellina*

late-spathulate, acute; lip to 17×13mm, white to yellow-cream, 3-lobed, lateral lobes blotched dark green, clasping column at base, oblong to oblong-lanceolate, obtuse, midlobe lined dark purple, suborbicular to ovate-triangular, acute, callus 4-keeled, lateral keels short, median keels passing onto midlobe; column to 8mm, pale green flushed purple, usually alate, wings triangular, midtooth short, triangular, anth. yellow. Spring–autumn. Venezuela, Colombia, C America, Mexico.

E.chacaoensis (Rchb. f.) Dressler & Pollard (*Epidendrum chacaoense* Rchb. f.).
Pseudobulbs to 10×5cm, ovoid to fusiform, slightly compressed, smooth, pale green, often initially somewhat glaucous, 2–3-lvd. Lvs to 30×5cm, elliptic, obtuse, pale green, pliable. Infl. to 10cm, 2 to 7-fld; fls to 4cm diam., usually non-resupinate, white, cream or green-cream the lip longitudinally striped maroon or purple; sep. to 2.5×1cm, oblong-lanceolate or elliptic, acute, lateral sep. oblique; pet. to 2×1cm, elliptic-lanceolate, acute; lip to 2×2.5cm, adnate to column at base, broadly ovate to suborbicular, subtruncate, concave above, callus oblong-quadrate, pubesc.; column to 12mm, midtooth orbicular-subquadrate.   Spring–summer.   C   America, Venezuela, Colombia.

E.chondylobulbon (Rich. & Gal.) Dressler & Pollard (*Epidendrum chondylobulbon* Rich. & Gal.).
Pseudobulbs to 25×2.5cm, widely spaced on rhiz., slightly compressed, fusiform, 3 to 5-lvd. Lvs to 40×2cm, linear to narrowly linear-lanceolate, acute or subobtuse. Infl. to 13cm, a raceme, few-fld; fls white or yellow-cream, the lip longitudinally marked purple; sep. to 35×6mm, lanceolate, acuminate; pet. to 30×5mm, elliptic-lanceolate, acuminate; lip to 22×11mm, short-clawed, concave, ovate-cordate, long-acuminate, callus oblong, fleshy; column to 6mm, teeth fleshy. Summer–autumn. Mexico, Guatemala, El Salvador.

E.citrina (La Ll. & Lex.) Dressler (*Epidendrum citrinum* (La Ll. & Lex.) Rchb. f.; *Cattleya citrina* (La Ll. & Lex.) Lindl.; *Sobralia citrina* La Ll. & Lax.).
Habit strongly pendulous. Pseudobulbs to 6×3cm, ovoid to conical or fusiform, dotted in papery sheaths, clustered, 2–4-lvd. Lvs to 26×4cm, elliptic-lanceolate, acute or obtuse, pliable, glaucous grey-green. Infl. to 10cm, usually far shorter, 1 or 2-fld, pendulous; fls lemon-yellow to golden, often somewhat glaucous below, the lip a deeper yellow with pale margins and callus and orange-flushed midlobe and veins, highly fragrant, appearing only partially opened; sep. to 6.5×2cm, fleshy, oblong to oblong-elliptic, acute or obtuse; pet. to 6.5×2.5cm, elliptic-oblong to elliptic-obovate, obtuse; lip to 6.5×5cm, obovate-oblong, conspicuously veined, 3-lobed, lateral lobes clasping column; midlobe orange, sub-quadrate, obtuse or retuse, crisped-crenulate, callus fleshy, sulcate, extending onto midlobe; column to 4cm, teeth truncate, midtooth surpassing lateral teeth. Spring–early summer. Mexico.

E.cochleata (L.) Lemée (*Epidendrum cochleatum* L.). COCKLE ORCHID; CLAMSHELL ORCHID. A variable species. Pseudobulbs to 25×4cm, pyriform to ellipsoid, slightly compressed, sometimes stalked, 1–3-lvd. Lvs to 40×5cm, elliptic-lanceolate to linear-lanceolate, acute to acuminate. Infl. to 50cm, erect, few to many-fld; fls non-resupinate, opening in succession and over many seasons, sep. and pet. to 7×0.7cm, yellow-green to lime green marked purple near base, linear-lanceolate, long-acuminate, twisted, reflexed; lip to 2.5×3cm, deep purple to black, white toward base with deep purple veins, concave above, orbicular-cordate, broadly acute or obtuse, callus oblong-rectangular with a central groove; column to 9mm, stout, pale green marked purple-black, midtooth short, blunt. Colombia, Venezuela, Florida, W Indies, C America.

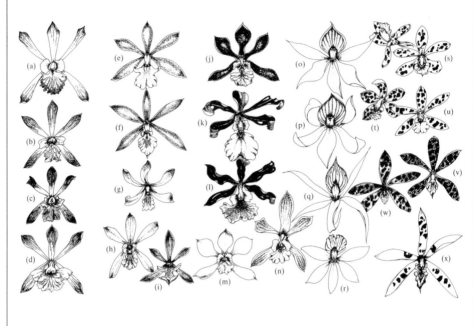

Encyclia   (a) *E.alata*   (b) *E.belizensis*   (c) *E.belizensis* ssp. *parviflora*   (d) *E.adenocarpa*   (e) *E.michuacana*
(f) *E.guatemalensis*   (g) *E.luteorosea*   (h) *E.tampensis*   (i) *E.concolor*   (j) *E.selligera*   (k) *E.cordigera*
(l) *E.hanburyi*   (m) *E.diota*   (n) *E.diota* ssp. *atrorubens*   (o) *E.fragrans*   (p) *E.chacaoensis*   (q) *E.baculus*
(r) *E.radiata*   (s) *E.vespa*   (t) *E.brachiata*   (u) *E.panthera*   (v) *E.boothiana*   (w) *E.boothiana* ssp. *favoris*
(x) *E.prismatocarpa*

E.concolor (La Ll. & Lex.) Schltr. (*Epidendrum concolor* La Ll. & Lex.).
Pseudobulbs to 6×3cm, ovoid to globose, slightly compressed, usually 1-lvd. Lvs to 19×3cm, narrowly lanceolate or elliptic-lanceolate, acute. Infl. to 45cm, sometimes branched, few to many-fld; peduncle slender; fls green-brown, yellow-brown or ochre, the lip white to pale yellow; sep. to 15×5mm, oblanceolate, acute exceeding pet.; lip to 12mm, 3-lobed, lateral lobes obovate-oblong, elongate, midlobe transversely oblong or obcordate, retuse or mucronate; callus fleshy, oblong; column to 5mm, teeth subequal, obtuse. Winter–early summer. Mexico.

E.cordigera (HBK) Dressler (*Epidendrum atropurpureum* auct. non Willd.; *E.doeringii* Hoehne).
Pseudobulbs to 11×8cm, clustered, conical-ovoid, 2-lvd. Lvs to 45×4cm, linear-lanceolate, obtuse or subacute. Infl. to 70cm, few to many-fld; fls brown, purple-brown or purple-green, the lip cream streaked or flushed rose to magenta; sep. to 38×14mm, oblanceolate, obtuse; pet. to 35×15mm, spathulate to spathulate-oblanceolate, undulate; lip to 5cm, 3-lobed, lateral lobes embracing column, oblong or oblong-lanceolate, obtuse, midlobe suborbicular to ovate, emarginate, undulate, veins thickened, callus elliptic, shallowly sulcate; column to 18mm, midtooth oblong, obtuse, wings absent. Mostly spring. C America, Colombia, Venezuela, Mexico.

E.diota (Lindl.) Schltr. (*Epidendrum diotum* Lindl.; *E.insidiosa* (Rchb. f.) Schltr.).
Pseudobulbs to 8×4cm, clustered, ovoid-conical. Lvs to 40×4cm, spreading, linear-ligulate to elliptic-ligulate, acute or obtuse. Infl. to 95cm, a panicle, many-fld; fls to 2.5cm diam., sweet-scented, yellow-brown to cinnamon, often edged yellow, the lip yellow or orange streaked deep brown; sep. to 20×8mm, obovate-spathulate to elliptic-oblanceolate, acute or mucronate; pet. to 16×11mm, ovate to ovate-orbicular; lip to

15mm, fleshy, 3-lobed, lateral lobes pandurate-oblong, clasping column, reflexed, midlobe ovate-cordate to ovate-rhombic, acute, undulate, prominently veined; callus elliptic-obovate, 4-keeled near base, pubesc.; column to 9mm, erect, midtooth short. Spring–early summer. Guatemala, Honduras, Nicaragua, Mexico. Plants with large, fleshy-pink and chestnut marked flowers are sometimes offered as sp. *atrorubens*.

E.doeringii Hoehne. See *E.cordigera*.

E.fragrans (Sw.) Lemée (*Epidendrum fragrans* Sw.).
Pseudobulbs to 13cm, quite widely spaced on rhizome, fusiform to ellipsoid, slightly compressed, 1–2-lvd. Lvs to 30×5cm, oblong-ligulate to elliptic, acute to obtuse, pale green, pliable. Infl. to 17cm, loosely few-fld; fls to 2cm, white, cream or green-white, the lip longitudinally striped violet or maroon, usually non-resupinate, fragrant; sep. to 35×8mm, linear-lanceolate to elliptic-lanceolate, acuminate; pet. to 30×12mm, elliptic to elliptic-lanceolate, acuminate; lip to 2×1.5cm, orbicular-ovate, abruptly acuminate, concave above, callus fleshy, oblong, nervose, column to 7mm, clavate, midtooth rounded. Mostly summer. C America, northern S America, W Indies.

E.ghiesbreghtiana (Rich. & Gal.) Dressler (*Epidendrum ghiesbreghtianum* Rich. & Gal.).
Pseudobulbs to 6×2.5cm, ovoid to ellipsoid, clustered, 2–3-lvd. Lvs to 20×1.5cm, lanceolate to elliptic-ligulate, acute or obtuse. Infl. to 12cm, usually 2-fld; fls pale green striped or spotted brown, the lip white faintly marked mauve at base; sep. to 25×9mm, lanceolate to elliptic-lanceolate, acute; pet. to 22×6mm, elliptic, acute; lip to 27×30mm, simple, suborbicular to subquadrate, obcordate, retuse, callus oblong, produced into 3 fleshy veins; column stout, to 7mm, teeth subequal, obtuse. Winter–spring. Mexico.

E.gravida (Lindl.) Schltr. (*Epidendrum gravidum* Lindl.).
Pseudobulbs to 4×3cm, ovoid-conical, 2–3-lvd. Lvs to

28×2cm, linear-ligulate, acute or obtuse. Infl. to 35cm, sometimes branched, few-fld; erect; olive green to ochre, sep. to 20×4mm, lanceolate or elliptic-lanceolate, acute, pet. to 18×4mm, oblanceolate or elliptic-oblanceolate, acute; lip to 14mm, 3-lobed, lateral lobes green, veined purple, porrect, oblong-lanceolate, midlobe suborbicular to subrhombic, white veined purple, acute, veins prominent, verrucose, callus oblong, deeply sulcate; column to 7mm, white, alate, midtooth triangular. Mostly autumn–winter. C America, Mexico.

E.guatemalensis (Klotzsch) Dressler & Pollard (*Epidendrum guatemalense* Klotzsch).
Pseudobulbs to 5×3.5cm, conical to ovoid, clustered, 2–3-lvd. Lvs to 32×2.5cm, linear-ligulate, acute. Infl. to 60cm, often branched, several to many-fld; peduncle sometimes verrucose; fls green, tinged red-brown or chocolate-brown, the lip white or yellow veined purple; sep. to 17×7mm, obovate-oblanceolate to elliptic, concave, acute or obtuse; pet. to 16×7mm, spathulate or obovate, acute or obtuse; lip to 15mm, 3-lobed, lateral lobes oblong to ovate-oblong, obtuse, clasping column, midlobe suborbicular, acute, undulate, prominently veined, callus bicarinate, distally truncate; column to 9mm, clavate, alate, wings subquadrate, midtooth short, obtuse. Spring–summer. Guatemala, Honduras, El Salvador, Nicaragua, Mexico.

E.guttata (Rich. & Gal.) Schltr. See *E.maculosa.*

E.hanburyi (Lindl.) Schltr. (*Epidendrum hanburyi* Lindl.).
Pseudobulbs to 8×4cm, ovoid-conical, clustered, 1–2-lvd. Lvs to 23×3cm, linear-elliptic to oblong-elliptic, obtuse. Infl. to 1m, sometimes branched, erect, many-fld; fls to 5cm diam., showy, dull purple-brown to yellow-brown streaked purple, the lip white to rose veined purple-red; sep. to 24×9mm, oblanceolate to spathulate, acute; pet. to 23×11mm, obovate to broadly spathulate, obtuse or mucronate; lip to 22mm, 3-lobed, lateral lobes clasping column, slightly spreading, pandurate-oblong, midlobe subreniform to suborbicular, undulate, retuse or obtuse, callus obovate to ovate-rhombic, sulcate, pubesc., 1-keeled; column to 11mm, arcuate, midtooth short, obtuse, triangular. Spring–summer. Mexico.

E.hastata (Lindl.) Dressler & Pollard (*Epidendrum hastatum* Lindl.).
Pseudobulbs to 5×2cm, ovoid to ellipsoid, compressed, clustered, usually 1-lvd. Lvs to 16×2cm, linear-elliptic, acute. Infl. to 25cm, 1- to several-fld; fls purple-brown or green-brown, veined dark purple, the lip pure white; sep. to 18×6mm, elliptic, acute; pet. to 15×4mm, elliptic-oblanceolate, acute; lip to 15×17mm, simple, suborbicular to subquadrate, obtuse, callus rectangular-quadrate, extending into 3 fleshy veins; column to 6mm, teeth subequal, obtuse. Spring. Mexico.

E.insidiosa (Rchb. f.) Schltr. See *E.diota.*

E.kennedyi (Fowlie & Withner) Hagsater (*Epidendrum kennedyi* Fowlie & Withner; *E.adenocaula* var. *kennedyi* (Fowlie & Withner) Hagsater & Gonzalez).
Resembles *E.adenocaula* except fls deeper red, lip with prominent midvein and narrower lateral lobes. Summer. Mexico.

E.kienastii (Rchb. f.) Dressler & Pollard (*Epidendrum kienastii* Rchb. f.).
Pseudobulbs to 11×2cm, narrowly fusiform or cylindrical, 2–3-lvd. Lvs to 15×4cm, oblong-lanceolate to oblong-elliptic, acute. Infl. to 37cm, sometimes branched; fls to 5cm diam., light rose-pink veined dark purple, the lip white to pale rose veined purple; sep. to 25×6mm, lanceolate, acute; pet. to 30×4mm, elliptic-oblanceolate, cuneate at base; lip to 25mm, 3-lobed, lateral lobes cuneate-ligulate, slightly falcate, subacute, apex bidentate, midlobe short-clawed, obovate-oblong, acute, slightly undulate, callus oblong, produced distally into 2 finger-like processes; column to 12mm, sharply arcuate at centre, slender, clavate, midtooth short, obtuse. Spring. Mexico.

E.lancifolia (Pav. ex Lindl.) Dressler & Pollard (*Epidendrum lancifolium* Pav. ex Lindl.; *Epidendrum trulla* Rchb. f.).
Pseudobulbs to 14×5cm, fusiform-ellipsoid or pyriform, compressed, loosely clustered, 2-lvd. Lvs to 27×4cm, elliptic, acute. Infl. to 12cm, several-fld; fls cream or green-white to yellow-white, the lip green or yellow green, streaked or striped purple; sep. to 22×8mm, elliptic to elliptic-lanceolate, acute; pet. to 18×8mm, elliptic, acute; lip to 12×17mm, simple, suborbicular to ovate-triangular, concave, obtuse, callus oblong; column to 8mm, stout, often spotted purple, midtooth short, fleshy, rounded. Summer–autumn. Mexico.

E.livida (Lindl.) Dressler (*Epidendrum lividum* Lindl.; *Epidendrum tesselatum* Batem. ex Lindl.).
Pseudobulbs to 10×2cm, widely spaced on rhiz., compressed, fusiform, pale to light green, 2-lvd. Lvs to 22×2cm, elliptic to elliptic-ligulate, acute or obtuse, light green. Infl. to 15cm, few to several-fld; fls to 1.5cm diam., pale green suffused brown, the lip ivory to pale yellow veined purple; sep. to 11×5mm, oblong-obovate to oblong; pet. to 10×4mm, obovate-lanceolate; lip to 11×6mm, obscurely 3-lobed, lateral lobes obtuse, undulate, midlobe suborbicular to subquadrate, strongly undulate-crisped, callus densely pubesc., with 3 apical longitudinal rows of teeth; column to 6mm, lateral teeth short, midtooth truncate. Flowering throughout year. Mexico to Panama, Venezuela, Colombia.

E.luteorosea (Rich. & Gal.) Dressler & Pollard (*Epidendrum luteoroseum* Rich. & Gal.; *Epidendrum lineare* Ruiz & Pav.).
Pseudobulbs to 7×2.5cm, ovoid-fusiform, 2–3-lvd. Lvs to 28×1m, narrowly linear to elliptic-ligulate, acute. Infl. to 45cm, usually branched, loosely many-fld; fls yellow-green or yellow-brown, tinged brown distally, the lip ivory marked purple-pink; sep. to 12×3mm, elliptic to elliptic-oblanceolate, acute or obtuse; pet. to 12×2mm, spathulate, obtuse; lip to 12×5mm, obcordate to obovate, retuse, callus subquadrate, bicarinate, extending into 5 verrucose veins; column to 5mm, midtooth short, obtuse. Mostly spring–autumn. C America to Venezuela, Peru.

E.maculosa (Ames, Hubb. & Schweinf.) Hoehne (*Epidendrum maculosum* Ames, Hubb. & Schweinf.; *E.guttata* (Rich. & Gal.) Schltr.; *Epidendrum guttatum* Rich. & Gal.).
Pseudobulbs to 12×2.5cm, ovoid-fusiform to ovoid-conical, 2–3-lvd. Lvs to 30×2cm, elliptic to linear-oblong, acute or obtuse. Infl. to 20cm, erect, few to many-fld; fls to 5cm diam., fragrant orange or orange-brown, sometimes spotted red-brown, the lip white spotted purple or maroon; sep. to 7×3cm, obovate to oblanceolate, acute, often verrucose; pet. to 6×3mm, obovate-spathulate to oblanceolate, mucronate; lip to 6.5mm, 3-lobed, lateral lobes obliquely oblong to oblong-rhombic, clasping column, midlobe ovate-oblong, obtuse, 3-nerved, callus obovate, thick, tridentate at front; column to 5mm, teeth fimbriate, subequal. Spring–summer. Mexico.

E.mariae (Ames) Hoehne (*Epidendrum mariae* Ames).
Somewhat similar to *E.citrina* in habit, but not so completely pendulous. Pseudobulbs to 4×3cm, ovoid to squat pyriform, grey-green, clustered, 2–3-lvd, clothed with thin, papery grey sheaths. Lvs to 18×3cm, oblong or oblong-elliptic, acute, glaucous grey-green or olive-green. Infl. to 27cm, usually far shorter, few-fld, arching weakly or pendulous; fls large, showy, lustrous lime-green to olive-green, the lip brilliant white tinted or lined with green; sep. to 44×11mm, fleshy, elliptic to oblanceolate, acute or obtuse; pet. to 43×8mm, oblanceolate, acute; lip to 75×50mm, simple, subpandurate to oblong-elliptic, enveloping column at base, deeply retuse, slightly undulate, callus to 30mm, bilamellate; column to 20mm, teeth subequal, fleshy, truncate. Summer. Mexico.

E.meliosma (Rchb. f.) Schltr. (*Epidendrum meliosmum* Rchb. f.).
Pseudobulbs to 9×7cm, subspherical to ovoid-conical, 1–2-lvd. Lvs to 36×4cm, ligulate to elliptic-ligulate, acute or

obtuse. Infl. to 1m, branched, many-fld; fls yellow to yellow-green streaked and tinged red-brown, the lip cream to yellow veined red-brown; sep. to 18×8mm, oblanceolate, acute or obtuse; pet. subequal to sep., spathulate or oblanceolate, acute or mucronate; lip to 13mm, 3-lobed, lateral lobes clasping column, oblong, obtuse, sometimes connate to midlobe, midlobe elliptic-ovate to rhombic-ovate, acuminate, callus obovate, sulcate, pubesc., 4-keeled at base; column to 7mm, erect or arcuate, midtooth triangular. Spring–summer. Mexico.

E.michuacana (La Ll. & Lex.) Schltr. (*Epidendrum michuacanum* La Ll. & Lex.; *Epidendrum virgatum* Lindl.).
Pseudobulbs to 8×4cm, ovoid to pyriform, clustered, 2–3-lvd. Lvs to 60×6cm, elliptic-lanceolate to ligulate, acute. Infl. to 2m, branched, many-fld; fls red-brown or green-brown, the lip cream or pale yellow, often spotted purple; sep. to 17×5mm, elliptic-lanceolate to oblanceolate, acute; pet. to 15×3mm, linear-oblanceolate; lip to 15mm, 3-lobed, lateral lobes oblong to obovate, obtuse, midlobe suborbicular, triangular-ovate or transversely oblong, callus fleshy, cushion-like, with 3 keels extending to midlobe; column to 7mm, midtooth fleshy, subquadrate. Flowering throughout year. Mexico, Guatemala, Honduras.

E.nemoralis (Lindl.) Schltr. See *E.adenocaula*.

E.microbulbon (Hook.) Schltr. (*Epidendrum microbulbon* Hook.; *E.ovula* (Lindl.) Schltr.; *Epidendrum ovulum* Lindl.).
Pseudobulbs to 4×2.5cm, ovoid-conical, clustered, 1–2-lvd. Lvs to 12×1cm, linear to elliptic-ligulate, acute or obtuse. Infl. to 45cm, sometimes branched, few or many-fld; fls green, veined red-brown, the lip white sometimes spotted red; sep. to 22×4mm, linear-oblanceolate or oblanceolate, acute or obtuse; pet. to 21×3mm, similar to sep.; lip to 19mm, 3-lobed, lateral lobes to 3×2mm, triangular-oblong, obtuse, arching, midlobe to 9×9mm, ovate to suborbicular, cuneate, dentate-undulate, verrucose, callus inconspicuous; column to 8mm, slender, teeth subequal, oblong-triangular, obtuse. Winter–summer. Mexico.

E.ochracea (Lindl.) Dressler (*Epidendrum ochraceum* Lindl.).
Pseudobulbs to 10×1cm, ovoid-cylindrical or narrowly ovoid, 2–3-lvd, widely spaced on rhiz. Lvs to 25×1.5cm, narrowly linear-ligulate or linear-lanceolate, acute. Infl. to 20cm, densely many-fld; fls yellow-brown, the lip white or yellow spotted red; sep. to 12×3mm, elliptic-oblong or obovate-oblong, acute or obtuse; pet. to 10×2mm, obliquely oblanceolate, obtuse; lip to 13×12mm, 3-lobed, lateral lobes suborbicular to subquadrate, upcurved, midlobe quadrate-oblong or triangular-oblong, obtuse or retuse, undulate-crisped, callus oblong-quadrate, sulcate; column to 5mm, teeth subequal, fimbriate. Flowering throughout year. Mexico to Cost Rica.

E.ovula (Lindl.) Schltr. See *E.microbulbon*.

E.panthera (Rchb. f.) Schltr. (*Epidendrum panthera* Rchb. f.; *Epidendrum papyriferum* Schltr.).
Pseudobulbs to 9×1.5cm, widely spaced on rhiz., fusiform to ovoid-fusiform, 2–3-lvd. Lvs to 22×8mm, linear-ligulate, obtuse. Infl. to 22cm, many-fld; fls olive green to yellow-orange blotched and spotted deep red-brown, the lip white to ivory; sep. to 9×3mm, oblanceolate-oblong to elliptic-oblong, acute or obtuse; pet. to 8×3mm, oblanceolate, arcuate, obtuse; lip to 8×4mm, lateral lobes subquadrate, clasping column, midlobe quadrate, undulate, retuse, 3-veined, callus narrow, oblong, sulcate; column to 6mm, teeth subequal, fimbriate. Winter–spring. Guatemala, Mexico.

E.polybulbon (Sw.) Dressler (*Epidendrum polybulbon* Sw.; *Dinema polybulbon* (Sw.) Lindl.).
Pseudobulbs to 20×8mm, widely spaced on rhiz., ovoid to ovoid-cylindrical, usually 2-lvd, Lvs to 8×1cm, ovate-elliptic to elliptic-oblong, obtuse. Infl. a solitary fl., to 3cm, pale yellow flushed brown, the lip yellow-white; sep. to 18×3mm, elliptic-lanceolate to linear-lanceolate, acuminate, spreading;

pet. to 16×2mm, linear to linear-oblanceolate, acute; lip to 18×12mm, short-clawed, adnate to column at base, suborbicular-ovate to cordate, denticulate, undulate; column to 7mm, alate, midtooth obtuse, lateral teeth forming 2 sharp, lanceolate projections, to 3mm. Mostly Autumn–winter. Mexico to Honduras, Cuba, Jamaica. .

E.prismatocarpa (Rchb. f.) Dressler (*Epidendrum prismatocarpum* Rchb. f.).
Pseudobulbs to 30cm, pyriform to cylindrical, bifoliate or trifoliate. Lvs to 37cm. Racemes to 35cm, many-fld, erect; fls to 5cm diam., fragrant; sep. and pet. yellow-green spotted dark purple or black, lanceolate; lip 3-lobed, lilac-purple, yellow-green at base, margins white, midlobe lanceolate, lateral lobes auriculate. Costa Rica to Brazil.

E.pseudopygmaea (Finet) Dressler & Pollard (*Hormidium pseudopygmaeum* Finet).
Resembles *E.pygmaea* except pseudobulbs to 10×1cm, narrowly fusiform, very widely spaced on rhiz. Lvs to 15×1.5cm, narrowly lanceolate. Fls larger, numerous. Winter. C America to Panama, Mexico.

E.pygmaea (Hook.) Dressler (*Epidendrum pygmaeum* Hook.; *Hormidium pygmaeum* (Hook.) Benth. & Hook. f. ex Hemsl.).
Dwarf. Rhiz. creeping, branching, bearing pseudobulbs at 3cm intervals. Pseudobulbs to 10cm, typically far smaller, ovoid, ellipsoid or fusiform, 2-lvd. Lvs to 10×2cm, narrowly ovate to elliptic, apiculate, acute. Fls to 5mm, usually solitary, fleshy, pale green tinged lavender; sep. to 11×4mm, elliptic to oblong-lanceolate, acuminate, lateral sep. shortly connate at base; pet. to 9×2mm, linear, acuminate; lip to 8×8mm, lateral lobes ovate-oblong to suborbicular, slightly erose, midlobe minute, triangular; column to 5mm, fleshy. Tropical Americas. cf. *E.pseudopygmaea*.

E.radiata (Lindl.) Dressler (*Epidendrum radiatum* Lindl.).
Pseudobulbs to 11×3cm, narrowly fusiform to ellipsoid-ovoid, quite widely spaced on rhiz., slightly compressed, strongly grooved, 2–3-lvd. Lvs to 35×3cm, elliptic-lanceolate to linear-lanceolate, obtuse to acuminate, pale green, pliable. Infl. to 24cm, few to many-fld; fls cream or pale green-white, the lip longitudinally striped purple or maroon, fragrant, sometimes non-resupinate; sep. to 22×7mm, elliptic to elliptic-lanceolate, acute; pet. to 23×13mm, broadly elliptic or elliptic-obovate, acute; lip to 15×23mm, triangular-reniform to ovate-cordate, undulate-crenate, callus oblong-quadrate, smooth; column to 11mm, midtooth erose. Spring–summer. Guatemala, Honduras, Mexico.

E.selligera (Lindl.) Schltr. (*Epidendrum selligerum* Batem. ex Lindl.).
Pseudobulbs to 10×5cm, clustered, ovoid, 1–2-lvd. Lvs to 30×4cm, linear-ligulate to elliptic-ligulate, obtuse to acute. Infl. to 1m, usually branched, loosely many-fld; fls fragrant, pale green or green-brown suffused red-brown, the lip white, cream or pink, veined purple; sep. to 24×9mm, spathulate-oblanceolate to elliptic-oblanceolate, acute or obtuse; pet. to 21×9mm, obovate to spathulate, obtuse or mucronate; lip to 22mm, short-clawed, lateral lobes ovate-oblong to triangular-oblong, obtuse, midlobe suborbicular-obovate or ovate, undulate-crisped, callus elliptic, sulcate, bicarinate; column to 13mm, subterete, midtooth, short, oblong-triangular. Winter–spring. Guatemala, Mexico.

E.spondiada (Rchb. f.) Dressler (*Epidendrum spondiadum* Rchb. f.).
Pseudobulbs to 16×1.5cm, cylindrical to narrowly ovoid, clustered, 1-lvd. Lvs to 30×5cm, ligulate to elliptic, obtuse. Infl. to 11cm, few-fld; fls yellow-green, tinged red-purple at tips of pet. and sep., the lip purple-brown edged pale green; sep. to 20×6mm, lanceolate to oblong, acute or acuminate; pet. to 17×6mm, lanceolate to ovate-lanceolate, acute or acuminate; lip to 15×12mm, short-clawed, suborbicular-reniform to cordate, apiculate, lateral lobes obscure, callus produced into 3 thickened veins; column to 5mm,

lateral teeth obtuse or retuse. Winter. Jamaica, Costa Rica, Panama.

E.tampensis (Lindl.) Small (*Epidendrum tampense* Lindl.). Pseudobulbs to 8cm, ovoid to suborbicular, lustrous green, often tinged purple, clustered, 1–3-lvd. Lvs to 42×1.5cm, linear to linear-lanceolate, acute, coriaceous. Infl. to 75cm, sometimes branched, 1- to many-fld; fls to 4cm diam., ochre to olive sometimes flushed rose or garnet, the lip white blotched and veined purple or magenta, fragrant, long-lived, showy; sep. to 20×6mm, oblong to oblong-oblanceolate, obtuse; lip to 18mm, free, lateral lobes erect, porrect, obliquely ovate-oblong, obtuse to rounded, midlobe short-clawed, suborbicular, slightly undulate, callus 3-keeled, median keel apical, short; column to 10mm, alate, wings incurved. Spring–winter. Florida, Bahamas.

E.tenuissima (Ames, Hubb. & Schweinf.) Dressler (*Epidendrum tenuissimum* Ames, Hubb. & Schweinf.). Pseudobulbs to 1.5×1cm, ovoid to ovoid-spherical, clustered, 2–3-lvd. Lvs to 85×4mm, linear, acute to obtuse. Infl. to 15cm, sometimes branched, few to many-fld; fls yellow to yellow-orange; sep. to 13×3mm, oblong-elliptic, acute; pet. to 12×3mm, oblanceolate, acute or obtuse; lip to 13×7mm, simple, obovate, obtuse, veins fleshy, verrucose, callus with 2 short basal keels; column to 6mm, midtooth shorter than lateral teeth, obtuse. Winter–early summer. Mexico.

E.trachychila (Lindl.) Schltr. See *E.ambigua.*

E.tripunctata (Lindl.) Dressler (*Epidendrum tripunctatum* Lindl.; *Epidendrum micropus* Rchb. f.; *Epidendrum diguetii* Ames). Dwarf. Pseudobulbs to 4×2cm, usually far smaller, ovoid to ovoid-ellipsoid, slightly compressed, closely clustered, 2–3-lvd. Lvs to 6–20×0.5–1.5cm, linear-elliptic, acute or obtuse, soft, grassy green. Infl. to 10cm, few-fld; fls pale green to yellow-green, the lip white and the column a distinctive purple with yellow teeth; sep. to 20×5mm, lanceolate or elliptic-lanceolate, acute; pet. to 17×3mm, linear-oblanceolate, acute; lip to 18mm, lateral lobes small, triangular, acute, midlobe suborbicular, subacute or obtuse; callus oblong, pubesc.; column to 8mm, obtuse, midtooth surpassing lateral teeth. Spring–summer. Mexico.

E.tuerckheimii Schltr. (*Epidendrum tuerckheimii* (Schltr.) Ames, Hubb. & Schweinf.). Pseudobulbs to 6×3cm, clustered, ovoid, 2-lvd. Lvs to 40×3.5cm, ligulate to linear-lanceolate, acute to obtuse. Infl. to 70cm, sometimes branched, erect, loosely many-fld; peduncle verrucose; fls green to yellow-brown or bronze; sep. to 30×6mm, lanceolate to elliptic-lanceolate, acute or acuminate, slightly revolute; pet. to 28×5mm, elliptic-oblanceolate, acute to acuminate; lip to 23×10mm, lateral lobes obliquely oblanceolate, obtuse to subtruncate, apically crenate, midlobe clawed, elliptic-oblong to elliptic-obovate, acuminate, undulate-crisped, callus on claw of midlobe, oblong, concave-sulcate, 3-keeled; column to 10mm, clavate, wings triangular, obtuse, apical teeth triangular. Late spring–summer. Mexico, Guatemala to Costa Rica.

E.varicosa (Lindl.) Schltr. (*Epidendrum varicosum* Batem. ex Lindl.; *Epidendrum quadratum* Klotzsch). Pseudobulbs to 20cm, ovoid-fusiform or ovoid-elliptic at base, extending as a slender neck above, 2–3-lvd. Lvs to 30×4.5cm, elliptic-oblong to elliptic-lanceolate, acute or sub-obtuse. Infl. to 60cm, loosely few to many-fld; fls fragrant, green-brown or red-brown, the lip cream to yellow, sometimes tinted green, often spotted red or purple; sep. to 18×6.5mm, obovate-oblanceolate to oblong, acute to obtuse; pet. to 16×7mm, oblanceolate to obovate-spathulate, obtuse, slightly undulate; lip to 15mm, clawed, lateral lobes oblong to triangular-lanceolate, acute or obtuse, often recurved, midlobe transversely oblong or obreniform, retuse, callus fleshy, puberulent, often tridentate; column to 8mm, midtooth subquadrate, lateral teeth short. Mostly winter. Mexico to Panama.

E.venosa (Lindl.) Schltr. (*E.wendlandiana* (Kränzl.) Schltr.; *Epidendrum venosum* Lindl.; *Epidendrum wendlandianum* Kränzl.). Pseudobulbs to 8×2cm, ellipsoid to fusiform, widely spaced on rhiz., 2–3-lvd. Lvs to 22×2cm, narrowly elliptic-oblong to elliptic-ligulate, acute. Infl. to 12cm, few fld; fls pale green or yellow-green, sometimes striped red-brown, the lip snow white veined purple on lateral lobes; sep. to 27×4mm, lanceolate to elliptic-lanceolate, acute or acuminate; pet. subsimilar; lip to 20×14mm, lateral lobes oblong to triangular, midlobe triangular-cordate, callus fleshy, ovate-oblong, pubesc., 3-veined; column to 8mm, teeth obtuse, subequal. Spring–autumn. Mexico.

E.vespa (Vell.) Dressler (*Epidendrum vespa* Vell.; *Epidendrum variegatum* Hook.). Pseudobulbs to 20×5cm, ovoid-fusiform or ellipsoid to cylindric, compressed, usually 2-lvd. Lvs to 40×6cm, elliptic-oblong to linear-oblong, acute to rounded. Infl. to 35cm, erect, loosely few to many-fld; fls to 1.5cm diam., fleshy cream-green or yellow-green, spotted or blotched maroon-purple, the lip white to yellow marked pink; sep. to 15×6mm, ovate to obovate-oblong, obtuse; pet. to 11×4mm, obovate-ligulate or cuneate, obtuse; lip to 8×9mm, simple or obscurely 3-lobed, lamina fleshy, transversely elliptic to ovate-cordate, acute, callus large, fleshy, sulcate, oblong; column to 5mm, stout, usually pale green, midtooth rounded. Mostly spring. Tropical America.

E.virens (Lindl. & Paxt.) Schltr. See *E.belizensis.*

E.vitellina (Lindl.) Dressler (*Epidendrum vitellinum* Lindl.). Pseudobulbs to 6cm, ovoid-conical, clustered, slightly compressed, 1–3-lvd. Lvs to 25×4cm, usually shorter, elliptic-lanceolate to linear-lanceolate, acute to obtuse, grey-green. Infl. to 40cm, rarely branched, fls showy, vermilion to scarlet, the lip orange to yellow; sep. to 22×8mm, elliptic or elliptic-lanceolate, acute to acuminate; pet. wider than sep., broadly elliptic to elliptic-oblong, acute, undulate; lip to 15×5mm, adnate to column at base, elliptic to elliptic-oblong, acute, slightly reflexed, callus oblong, 3-keeled; column to 8mm, midtooth short, subquadrate. Spring–summer. Mexico, Guatemala.

E.wendlandiana (Kränzl.) Schltr. See *E.venosa.*
E.xipheres Rchb. f. See *Epidendrum xipheres.*

× **Epicattleya** (*Epidendrum* × *Cattleya*). A wide range of plants depending on the characters of the parents used; all characterized by brightly coloured flowers that are usually borne in clusters well above the foliage.

× E.Autumn Gold: lovely clusters of bright red fls on tall infl.

× E.Envy: compact plants; fls rich green with creamy white lip; lemon scented.

× E.Lime Sherbet: compact growing plants; fls long lasting and scented, many green fls with contrasting white lip, borne in clusters.

× E.Purple Glory: strong bifoliate plants; numerous medium lavender fls on tall infl.

× E.Rosita: strong compact bifoliate; lovely medium lavender fls, broad segments and full lip with creamy white markings.

Epidendrum L. (From Gk *epi*, upon, and *dendron*, tree, referring to the epiphytic habit of most species.) Some 500 species: the tall cane-growing spp. are often at least initially terrestrial, the smaller caned spp. and pseudobulbous plants are epiphytic and lithophytic. Rhizome absent or conspicuous. Stems long-pseudobulbous or cane-like, erect or clustered, thickened or slender, simple or branched, 1- to many-leaved, the cane-producing spp. rooting freely at nodes. Leaves terete or flattened, solitary or several, distichous or apical on pseudobulbs, sheathing stems, fleshy or coriaceous, variable in shape. Inflorescence terminal, rarely lateral, a raceme, panicle, or subumbellate, erect or pendent, 1- to many-flowered; flowers small to large and showy, sometimes non-resupinate; sepals spreading, subequal, reflexed or subconnivent; petals usually similar to sepals; lip often enclosing column, clawed, lamina entire or trilobed, smooth or callose; column stout or slender, short or elongate, sometimes winged, anther terminal, operculate, incumbent, 2-celled, pollinia 4, waxy, compressed. Tropical Americas. Many species formerly included in *Epidendrum* can now be found described under *Encyclia*. Lip dimensions here refer to the free portion, the lamina or blade, and not to the claw, which is in most species parallel and largely adnate to the column.

CULTIVATION Pseudobulbous species (e.g. *E.ciliare*) should be cultivated as for *Laelia* or *Rhyncholaelia*, potted tightly into an open bark-based mix, grown in cool to intermediate conditions with excellent light and a cool dry winter rest. The tall-growing cane species (e.g. *E.ibaguense*) are amongst the most (literally) flexible of all orchids: in frost-free sunny conditions, they will scramble freely, bearing a profusion of brilliantly coloured flowers throughout the year. Provide a foothold in a bark mix with plenty of well-rotted FYM. For good blooms, syringe and foliar-feed regularly. Propagate by adventitious plantlets.

The smaller cane-type (e.g. *E.pseudepidendrum*) require intermediate conditions, high humidity, dappled sunlight and only a semi-dry winter rest. The magnificent *E.parkinsonianum* should be treated as a large *Brassavola*, but mounted on bark or a raft and suspended in full sunlight where its ruddy succulent leaves will offset perfectly the ghostly white flowers.

E.adenocaulum La Ll. & Lex. See *Encyclia adenocaula*.

E.adolphii Schltr. See *Oerstedella endresii*.

E.alatum Batem. See *Encyclia alata*.

E.aloifolium Batem. See *E.parkinsonianum*.

E altissimum Lehmann & Kranzl.

Fls clustered on long-stalked racemes; sep. to 2cm, linear-oblanceolate, flesh- to dull purple-pink; pet. very slender, flesh pink; lip and column white to candy pink, lateral lobes triangular-ovate, toothed, reflexed, midlobe small, upturned. Colombia, Ecuador.

E.ambiguum Lindl. See *Encyclia ambigua*.

E.amethystinum Rchb.f.

Growths short, neatly tufted, cane-like. Infl. a pendulous, densely flowered raceme; fls to 1.5cm diam., nodding to downward-pointing, thus scarcely appearing open ; tepals deep cerise to rosy mauve, ovate; lip small, paler than tepals. Ecuador.

E.anceps Jacq. (*E.musciferum* Lindl.; *E.fuscatum* Sm.; *E.viridipurpureum* Hook.).

Stems tufted, strongly compressed, erect, leafy. Lvs to 20×4cm, linear-elliptic to oblong, coriaceous, green often flecked purple. Raceme subcapitate, terminal; peduncle elongate, compressed, sheathed; fls to 1.5cm diam.; sep. and pet. green-brown to chocolate, fleshy, glossy, sep. to 9×4mm, obovate to oblong-elliptic, blunt to acuminate, pet. to 8×2mm, linear to linear-oblanceolate, acute to obtuse; lip adnate to column, lamina to 6×8mm, pale green flushed pink, lateral lobes short, rounded to subquadrate, midlobe transversely oblong, apiculate, disc centrally keeled; column to 5mm. Florida, Mexico to Panama, W Indies, northern S America.

E.atropurpureum auct. non Willd. See *Encyclia cordigera*.

E.aromaticum Batem. See *Encyclia aromatica*.

E.avicula Lindl. See *Lanium avicula*.

E.baculus Rchb. f. See *Encyclia baculus*.

E.basilare Klotzsch. See *E.stamfordianum*.

E.belizense Rchb. f. See *Encyclia belizensis*.

E.bicameratum Rchb. f. See *Encyclia bicamerata*.

E.bicornutum Hook. See *Caularthron bicornutum*.

E.bidentatum Lindl. See *Encyclia boothiana*.

E.bilamellatum Rchb. f. See *Caularthron bilamellatum*.

E.boothianum Lindl. See *Encyclia boothiana*.

E.boothii (Lindl.) L.O. Williams. See *Nidema boothii*.

E.bractescens Lindl. See *Encyclia bractescens*.

E.brassavolae Rchb. f. See *Encyclia brassavolae*.

E.bulbosum Vell. See *Encyclia bulbosa*.

E.cajamaracae Schltr. See *E.geminiflorum*.

E.calamarium Lindl. See *Encyclia calamaria*.

E.calanthum Rchb.f.& Warscz.

Very close to *E.ibaguense* in habit. Fls to 2cm diam., usually bright rose or magenta with a yellow crest on lip (white forms occur); tepals oblong-lanceolate; lip comparatively large, basically lunate, margins erose-laciniate. Widespread in S America.

E.calocheilum Hook. See *Encyclia alata*.

E.campylostalix Rchb. f. See *Encyclia campylostalix*.

E.candollei Lindl. See *Encyclia candollei*.

E.caroli Schltr.

Stems clumped, to 9cm, clavate, compressed, keeled. Lvs 2 or more per stem, to 8×2cm, produced toward stem apex, elliptic to oblong, coriaceous. Raceme simple or, rarely, branched, slender, few-fld; fls small; pedicellate ovary to 5mm; sep. and pet. green-brown or purple-brown, sep. to 6×3mm, elliptic to lanceolate, lateral sep. oblique, concave, pet. to 5×2mm, elliptic to linear, oblique, obtuse, finely erose; lip yellow, fleshy, ovate-cordate, to 5×5mm, lateral margins upcurved, disc fleshy, callused; column to 2mm, pale green marked purple. Guatemala.

E.catillus Rchb. f. & Warsc. (*E.vinosum* Schltr.).
Stems to 1m, simple, leafy toward apex. Lvs to 7.5×3.5cm, ovate to oblong-lanceolate, fleshy-coriaceous, dorsally carinate, basally sheathing. Raceme or panicle erect, terminal, loosely or densely few- to many-fld; peduncle elongate, concealed by scarious sheaths; fls spreading, cinnabar red, violet-red or violet; sep. to 1.5cm, obovate-lanceolate, acute to subobtuse, lateral sep. oblique; pet. smaller than sep., oblanceolate, acute or obtuse, oblique; lip to 6×8mm, vermilion, ovate-triangular, deeply 3-lobed, central callus large, faded yellow; column to 1cm, with 2 bidentate wings above. Colombia, Ecuador, Peru.

E.ceratistes Lindl. See *Encyclia ceratistes*.
E.chacaoense Rchb. f. See *Encyclia chacaoensis*.

E.chioneum Lindl. (*E.claesianum* Cogn.).
Stems to 65cm, erect or ascending, simple or usually branched, terete, slightly compressed towards apex. Lvs numerous, to 9×2cm, coriaceous, ovate-lanceolate to oblong-lanceolate, obtuse to acute and emarginate. Racemes terminal, to 8cm, arcuate to pendent, densely many-fld, usually subcapitate; fls often fleshy, fragrant, to 2cm diam., white, yellow or yellow-green; dorsal sep. to 10×7mm, elliptic, elliptic-oblong to elliptic-obovate, concave, lateral sep. oblique, acute; pet. to 8×4mm, oblong-spathulate, obtuse or rounded; lip to 9×11mm, 3-lobed, dolabriform to obliquely obovate, midlobe obovate-subquadrate or subquadrate, retuse and apiculate, disc with 2 basal calli and a longitudinal keel; column to 5mm. Colombia, Venezuela, Ecuador.

E.chondylobulbon Rich. & Gal. See *Encyclia chondylobulbon*.

E.ciliare L. (*E.viscidum* Lindl.).
Pseudobulbs tufted, oblong-compressed, to 16×2cm, unifoliate to trifoliate. Lvs to 28×8cm, oblong-ligulate to elliptic-oblong, coriaceous, glossy. Raceme to 30cm, erect, few- to several-fld; peduncle concealed by large, overlapping, purple-spotted sheaths; fls large, fragrant, white to green or pale yellow with white lip; sep. to 9×0.5cm, linear-lanceolate, acute or acuminate, reflexed; pet. to 8×0.5cm, elliptic-lanceolate, long-acuminate; lip adnate to basal half of column, to 5cm, deeply 3-lobed, lateral lobes semi-cordate, spreading and incurved, outer margin deeply lacerate-fimbriate, inner margin lunate, revolute, midlobe linear-filiform, rigid, acute, exceeding lateral lobes, disc 3-keeled; column to 2cm. Mexico to Panama, Venezuela to Bolivia, W Indies, Guyana, Brazil.

E.cilindraceum Lindl.
Fls small,produced in dense racemes,cream to pale lime green with a red-spotted white lip and a golden anther cap. Colombia, Ecuador.

E.cinnabarinum Salzm. ex Lindl.
Stems to 1.25m, cane-like, simple, leafy. Lvs to 11×3.5cm, alternately 2-ranked, oblong to elliptic-oblong, rounded to obtuse, fleshy-coriaceous. Raceme or panicle terminal, held clear of lvs, few- to many-fld; fls to 6cm diam., opening in succession over a period of several seasons, bright scarlet, crimson or orange-red; sep. spreading, to 2.5cm, oblong-oblanceolate, obtuse or acute, lateral sep. oblique; pet. spreading, subequal to sep., elliptic-lanceolate or elliptic-oblanceolate, obtuse; lip adnate to entire length of column, lamina to 13×18mm, 3-lobed, lateral lobes obliquely dolabriform, dentate, midlobe triangular-lanceolate, disc yellow spotted red; column to 13mm, slender. Mostly spring. Brazil. cf. *E.ibaguense.*

E.citrinum (La Ll. & Lex.) Rchb. f. See *Encyclia citrina*.
E.claesianum Cogn. See *E.chioneum*.
E.cochleatum L. See *Encyclia cochleata*.
E.concolor La Ll. & Lex. See *Encyclia concolor*.
E.confusum Rolfe. See *Encyclia baculus*.

E.conopseum R. Br. (*Amphiglottis conopsea* (R. Br.) Small). GREEN-FLY ORCHID.
Stems clumped, mat-forming, to 20cm, slender, compressed, unifoliate to trifoliate. Lvs to 9×1.5cm, rigid, narrowly oblong to linear-lanceolate, lustrous green, often tinged purple. Raceme to 16cm, terminal, lax, erect; fls to 2cm diam., fragrant, long-lived, grey-green, often tinged purple; dorsal sep. to 13×4mm, oblong-spathulate to oblanceolate, lateral sep. obliquely spathulate or oblong-obovate, margins involute; pet. to 12×2mm, linear-spathulate to narrow-oblanceolate, obtuse; lip to 6×8mm, cordate-reniform, 3-lobed, lateral lobes subrotund, midlobe narrower than lateral lobes, apex truncate, disc with 2 fleshy basal calli; column to 8mm. SE US.

E.coriifolium Lindl.
Stems to 25cm, clumped, strongly compressed, leafy toward apex. Lvs to 30×5cm, elliptic-oblong to linear-oblong, erect-spreading, rigid, coriaceous, dorsally carinate, apex obtuse, emarginate, base clasping. Raceme to 30cm, terminal, few- to many-fld; fls fleshy green or yellow-green, often tinged red or purple, subtended and enclosed by conspicuous, fleshy green, subulate bracts; dorsal sep. to 25×6mm, oblong-lanceolate or elliptic-lanceolate, acute, slightly concave, lateral sep. obliquely ovate or ovate-lanceolate, to 25×11mm, acute, often with a dentate keel at apex; pet. to 18×3mm, linear to narrow-oblanceolate, subacute; lip to 2×2.5cm, simple, cordate-reniform, cleft and apiculate, entire or erose, disc with a thick central keel; column to 1cm. Mexico to Panama, Venezuela, Ecuador, Brazil.

E.coronatum Ruiz & Pav.
Stems to 90×1cm, erect or suberect, subterete, leafy above, sheathed throughout by lf bases. Lvs closely 2-ranked, to 17×4cm, elliptic to lanceolate, fleshy-coriaceous, acute. Raceme to 40cm, terminal, pendent, many-fld; sep. and pet. cream to yellow-green, sometimes tinged brown, rose or violet at base, sep. to 20×9mm, lanceolate-spathulate, obtuse or acute, pet. to 18×7mm, ligulate-spathulate, obtuse or acute; lip 18×25mm, ivory tinted lime or grey-green, slightly undulate, lateral lobes large, suborbicular, midlobe bilobulate, rounded, lobules curved outwards; column to 14mm, white. C America, Northern S America, Trinidad.

E.corymbosum Ruiz & Pav. See *E.secundum.*

E.cristatum Ruiz & Pav. (*E.raniferum* Lindl.).
A plastic species, the variability manifest particularly in the shape of the lip and degree of fragrance. Stems numerous, stout, simple, leafy in upper reaches. Lvs to 25×5cm, erect to spreading, coriaceous, elliptic-lanceolate to elliptic-oblong. Infl. 1 to several racemes, simple, terminal, to 60cm, pendent, loosely many-fld; fls sometimes fragrant, long-pedicelled, fleshy; sep. and pet. yellow to pale green, spotted or streaked red-brown or purple, lip white; dorsal sep. elliptic-oblong to elliptic-lanceolate, subacute to obtuse, to 28×7mm, spreading, lateral sep. oblique, pet. to 25×5mm, linear-spathulate to narrow-oblanceolate, obtuse, spreading; lip to 15×17mm, adnate to column apex, obscurely 3-lobed, lateral lobes obliquely dolabriform, irregularly lacerate-fimbriate to dentate, midlobe separated from lateral lobes by slender claw, bilobulate at apex, lobules spreading, disc with 2 fleshy basal calli and a central keel; column to 1.5cm. C & S America, W Indies.

E.difforme Jacq. (*E.umbellatum* Sw.; *E.latilabrum* Lindl.).
Stems to 30cm, clumped, cane-like, flexuous, erect, or arching, concealed by persistent lf sheaths. Lvs to 11×4cm, ovate-elliptic to oblong-lanceolate, rounded to obtuse, amplexicaul, fleshy to coriaceous, light green. Infl. subumbellate to umbellate, terminal, short, 1- to many-fld; fls to 5cm diam., pale green, green-yellow or white; dorsal sep. lanceolate to oblong-obovate, to 30×8mm, lateral sep. elliptic to oblanceolate; pet. subequal to sep., slender, acute; lip to 2×3cm, transversely reniform, midlobe transversely oblong, entire to bilobed, truncate, disc with 2 small basal calli; column to 1cm, dilated in apical half. Florida, W Indies, Mexico to Brazil, Peru, Ecuador.

E.diguetii Ames. See *Encyclia tripunctata*.
E.diotum Lindl. See *Encyclia diota*.
E.dipus Lindl. See *E.nutans*.
E.discolor (Lindl.) Benth. See *Nanodes discolor*.

E.eburneum Rchb. f. (*E.leucocardium* Schltr.).
Stems to 60cm, slender, leafy in apical half. Lvs to 14×2.5cm, alternate, elliptic to lanceolate, acute or obtuse, lustrous deep green. Raceme terminal, few-fld; peduncle to 7.5cm, strongly fractiflex; fls to 7cm diam., borne in succession, fragrant, waxy; sep. and pet. white, ivory or yellow-green, dorsal sep. to 35×4mm, linear-lanceolate, lateral sep. similar, slightly oblique, pet. to 35×2mm, filiform; lip conspicuous, white, to 30×30mm, cordate-orbicular to subquadrate, often apiculate, disc with 2 basal calli. Autumn–winter. Panama.

E.endresii Rchb. f. See *Oerstedella endresii*.
E.falcatum Lindl. See *E.parkinsonianum*.
E.flavidum Lindl. See *E.leucochilum*.

E.floribundum HBK (*E.paniculatum* Ruiz & Pav.; *E.piliferum* Rchb. f.; *E.reflexum* Ames & Schweinf.).
Stems to 2.5m, simple, terete, slender to stout, erect or spreading. Lvs to 25×7cm, ovate-elliptic to linear-lanceolate, subcoriaceous, often tinged purple below. Raceme or panicle loose, terminal, usually much exceeding lvs, few- to many-fld; fls to 2.5cm diam., fragrant; sep. and pet. white-green to rose-purple, sep. fleshy, usually reflexed, to 15×4mm, elliptic to broadly oblanceolate, pet. to 15×2mm, filiform or oblong-spathulate, acute to obtuse; lip usually white, sometimes spotted red, lamina to 10×12mm, simple to 3-lobed, lateral lobes dolabriform to ovate-triangular, erose, midlobe short, usually bilobulate, lobules variable in shape, curved outwards, erose, disc with a 2-lobed callus at base, often with 1–3 longitudinal ridges; column to 7mm, dilated at apex. Mostly summer. Tropical Americas.

E.fragrans Sw. See *Encyclia fragrans*.

E.friederici-guilielmi (Lindl.) Rchb. f.
Stems 60–150cm, thick, cane-like, clumped. Lvs to 30×10cm, distichous, sheathing, obovate-oblong to elliptic, deep green. Raceme terminal, to 43cm, erect to pendent, densely many-fld; fls deep purple or light carmine red, column apex and callus pure white; dorsal sep. to 2.5cm, oblong-lanceolate or elliptic-lanceolate, lateral sep. oblique; pet. to 22mm, linear-oblanceolate; lip to 10×8mm, lateral lobes suborbicular, midlobe porrect, ligulate, acute, disc with 2 basal calli and central keel; column to 12mm. Peru.

E.fuscatum Sm. See *E.anceps*.

E.gastropodium Rchb.f.
Habit neat, tufted. Fls in a dense cluster, small, brilliant cerise with an orange mark on lip and a violet-black column; tepals rather broad, not expanding fully. Andes.

E.geminiflorum HBK (*E.cajamaracae* Schltr.).
Stems to 90cm, subpendent, much-branched; branches to 15cm, concealed by tubular lf sheaths. Lvs to 6×2cm, oblong-elliptic, obtuse, spreading, coriaceous. Infl. a short raceme, terminal, subumbellate, 2- or 3-fld; fls tough, yellow-green or maroon-green; dorsal sep. to 16×4mm, oblong-lanceolate, subacute or acuminate, revolute, lateral sep. oblique; pet. to 15×2mm, obliquely linear-lanceolate; lip to 12×10mm, broadly ovate, lateral lobes rounded or subquadrate, midlobe ovate-triangular, disc 2–3-keeled; column to 7mm, stout. Venezuela, Colombia, Ecuador, Peru.

E.ghiesbreghtianum Rich. & Gal. See *Encyclia ghiesbreghtiana*.
E.globosum Jacq. See *Jacquiniella globosa*.
E.gravidum Lindl. See *Encyclia gravida*.
E.guatemalense Klotzsch. See *Encyclia guatemalensis*.
E.guttatum Rich. & Gal. See *Encyclia maculosa*.
E.hanburyi Lindl. See *Encyclia hanburyi*.
E.hastatum Lindl. See *Encyclia hastata*.

E.ibaguense HBK (*E.radicans* auct. non Pav. ex Lindl.).
Stems to 2m, slender, scrambling, sheathed, elliptic in sec-

tion, branching and rooting freely at nodes, producing plantlets on older canes and infl. Lvs to 12×4cm, along stems, 2-ranked, semi-opposite to alternate, oblong to lanceolate, often tinted red in bright sun or coriaceous on older canes. Raceme terminal, subpyramidal, erect, to 70cm, simple or few-branched; peduncle enveloped by scarious, tubular sheaths; fls showy, often non-resupinate, variable in size and colour, orange-yellow to dark red or white-rose; sep. to 22×7mm, spreading, obovate to oblong-elliptic, acute to subobtuse, lateral sep. slightly oblique; pet. to 20×8mm, obliquely elliptic-lanceolate to elliptic-oblong, acute, entire or denticulate; lip to 15×17mm, suborbicular-cordate, deeply 3-lobed, cruciform, lateral lobes rounded to subquadrate, irregularly lacerate-dentate, midlobe separated from lateral lobes by broad claw, cuneate or oblong-cuneate, apex deeply bilobulate, lobules lacerate-dentate, disc usually yellow with 2 rounded, flattened calli at base and an erect central keel; column to 1.5cm. Mexico to Panama, Venezuela, Colombia, Peru, Guyana. cf. *E.imatophyllum*, *E.secundum*.

E.ibaguense var. *schomburgkii* (HBK) C. Schweinf. See *E.schomburgkii*.

E.ilense Dodson.
Fls large, pendulous, showy; tepals more or less equal, oblong-lanceolate, lime green tinted maroon; lip far larger than tepals, pure crystalline white, lunate, margins very deeply and finely fringed, the fringe standing erect in a tuft in the apical sinus. Ecuador.

E.imatophyllum Lindl. (*E.imetrophyllum* Paxt.; *E.palpigerum* Rchb. f.).
Differs from *E.ibaguense* and *E.secundum* in having a more obscurely 3-lobed lip. Stem erect, to 1m, slender or stout, slightly compressed. Lvs to 20×3.5cm, erect-spreading, oblong-ligulate to linear-lanceolate, coriaceous, light green. Raceme terminal, simple or branched, to 25cm, erect, densely many-fld; fls non-resupinate, rose to deep purple; pedicels to 3cm; sep. to 22×5mm, elliptic to oblong-lanceolate, acute, lateral sep. oblique; pet. to 2×1cm, obliquely elliptic, acute to acuminate; lip to 10×8mm, adnate to column, oblong, obscurely 3-lobed, lateral lobes shallow, subentire to fimbriate, midlobe transversely oblong to ovate, disc with 2 falcate, basal calli and a central keel extending to base of midlobe; column to 1cm. Mexico to Peru and Brazil, Trinidad. cf. *E.ibaguense*.

E.imetrophyllum Paxt. See *E.imatophyllum*.

E.incomptum Rchb.f.
New growths emerging from central node of previous year's stem, rooting freely. Fls in an arching raceme, very fleshy, glossy olive to lime green with a bronze tint especially on lip. C America.

E.incumbens Lindl. See *Encyclia aromatica*.
E.inversum Lindl. See *Encyclia bulbosa*.
E.kennedyi Fowlie & Withner. See *Encyclia kennedyi*.
E.kienastii Rchb. f. See *Encyclia kienastii*.
E.lamellatum Westc. ex Lindl. See *Dimerandra emarginata*.
E.lancifolium Pav. ex Lindl. See *Encyclia lancifolia*.

E.lanipes Lindl.
Differs from the related *E.purum* in having pubesc. pedicels and ovaries and yellow to bronze fls. Peru, Colombia, Bolivia.

E.latifolium (Lindl.) Garay & Sweet (*E.nocturnum* var. *latifolium* Lindl.).
Close to and often included in *E.nocturnum*. Stems to 50cm, compressed above, terete below, erect, 3- or 4-lvd. Lvs to 15×8cm, suborbicular to elliptic. Raceme terminal, 1-fld; fls pale yellow-green to yellow-brown; pedicel and ovary to 16cm; sep. to 6×1cm, linear-lanceolate, acuminate, margins slightly revolute; pet. to 55×7mm, ligulate-oblong, acuminate; lip white, to 5cm, adnate to column base, 3-lobed, lateral lobes narrowly ovate, acute, midlobe tinged yellow-green at

(a)

(b)

Epidendrum   (a) *E.ibaguense*   (b) *E.pseudepidendrum*

apex, larger than lateral lobes, linear-filiform, acute; column white. W Indies, Venezuela, Trinidad, Brazil.

E.latilabrum Lindl. See *E.difforme.*

E.laucheanum Rolfe ex Bonhof.
Stems to 22cm, simple, slender, erect. Lvs to 19×2cm, linear-lanceolate, spreading, coriaceous. Raceme to 50cm, terminal, arching or pendent, bearing to 100 fls; fls to 2.5cm diam., often fleshy; sep. and pet. pink-brown or purple to purple-green, sep. to 13×5mm, obovate to elliptic-oblong, concave, pet. to 11×1mm, obliquely linear to linear-spathulate, subacute to obtuse, reflexed; lip rigidly fleshy, yellow-green, lamina suborbicular, plicate, to 6×9mm, margins upcurved, often undulate, disc with central thickened keel; column to 6mm, stout. Guatemala, Honduras, Nicaragua, Costa Rica, Colombia.

E.leucocardium Schltr. See *E.eburneum.*

E.leucochilum Klotzsch (*E.flavidum* Lindl.; *E.spectatissimum* Rchb. f.).
Rhiz. thick, woody; stems numerous, clustered, slender, erect, to 80cm. Lvs to 25×7cm, 3–5 per cane, coriaceous, oblong to narrowly elliptic, obtuse, lustrous green above, pale dull green beneath. Infl. terminal, to 40cm, 3–15-fld; fls to 7.5cm diam.; sep. and pet. pale green, margins strongly recurved, sep. to 5×1cm, fleshy, linear-lanceolate to linear-oblanceolate, acute or acuminate, lateral sep. oblique, pet. to 50×5mm, similar to sep.; lip ivory-white, connate to column apex, free portion to 32×28mm, 3-lobed, lateral lobes dolabriform to suborbicular, midlobe lanceolate, disc with 2 basal calli and a central longitudinal keel; column white, to 24mm. Venezuela, Colombia.

E.lindleyanum (Batem. ex Lindl.) Rchb. f. See *Barkeria lindleyana.*
E.lineare Ruiz & Pav. See *Encyclia luteorosea.*
E.lividum Lindl. See *Encyclia livida.*

E.longipetalum A. Rich. & Galeotti non Lindl. & Paxt.
Fls produced over a long period on an elongate spike, bronze to olive green; sep. oblong-obovate; tepals very long and slender, deflexed far below lip, twisted; lip semi-orbicular, very obscurely 3-lobed. Mexico.

E.longipetalum Lindl. & Paxt. non A. Rich. & Galeotti. See *Encyclia alata.*
E.luteoroseum Rich. & Gal. See *Encyclia luteorosea.*
E.macrothyrsodes Rchb. f. See *E.sceptrum.*
E.maculosum Ames, Hubb. & Schweinf. See *Encyclia maculosa.*
E.mariae Ames. See *Encyclia mariae.*

E.marmoratum Rchb.f.
Stems pseudobulbous, stoutly cylindrical. Lvs leathery, broad. Infl. a tall, arching, crowded raceme; tepals white marbled blood red or maroon, bright green at base, sep. oblong-elliptic, pet. somewhat shorter, obovate; lip large, more or less triangular, emarginate with the margin recurved, white, strongly marked blood red with several prominent longitudinal ridges. Mexico.

E.medusae (Rchb. f.) Sieb. See *Nanodes medusae.*
E.meliosmum Rchb. f. See *Encyclia meliosma.*
E.michuacanum La Ll. & Lex. See *Encyclia michuacana.*
E.microbulbon Hook. See *Encyclia microbulbon.*
E.microphyllum Lindl. See *Lanium microphyllum.*
E.micropus Rchb. f. See *Encyclia tripunctata.*
E.mosenii Barb.-Rodr. See *E.strobiliferum.*
E.musciferum Lindl. See *E.anceps.*
E.nemorale Lindl. See *Encyclia adenocaula.*

E.nocturnum Jacq. (*E.tridens* Poepp. & Endl.).
A highly variable species. Stems to 1m, erect or suberect, slender or stout, simple, subterete at base, compressed above. Lvs 3–4 per stem, to 14×3cm, several to numerous, narrow-oblong to elliptic or ovate, fleshy to coriaceous, acute or obtuse, sometimes tinged maroon. Raceme terminal, short, sometimes branched, 1- to few-fld; fls large, showy, fragrant, to 6cm diam., slightly nodding; sep. and pet. white to yellow-green, often flushed pale amber with age, sep. to 90×8mm, linear-lanceolate, long-acuminate, recurved, lateral sep. slightly oblique, pet. to 80×3mm, linear to filiform, acuminate; lip white, adnate to column, deeply 3-lobed, lateral lobes to 4×1cm, obliquely ovate to ovate-lanceolate, obtuse to acuminate, entire or, rarely, dentate, midlobe to 55×3mm, long-acuminate, disc with 2 elongate keels between lateral lobes; column to 2.5cm, dilated in apical half. Tropical Americas.

E.nocturnum var. *latifolium* Lindl. See *E.latifolium.*

E.nutans Sw. (*E.dipus* Lindl.).
Stems to 60×1cm, erect to flexuous, simple, terete, leafy in apical half. Lvs to 28×6cm, coriaceous, oblong to oblong-lanceolate. Infl. drooping, terminal, to 50cm, many-fld, irregularly branched at base, emerging from 1–2 sheaths; fls 2–50 per raceme, to 2cm diam., fragrant; sep. and pet. soft green, sep. to 18×5mm, fleshy, oblong to oblanceolate, distinctly 5-nerved, obtuse or acute, lateral sep. acute, oblique, pet. shorter than sep., narrow-oblanceolate or spathulate; lip white tinted green, connate to column apex, free portion to 11×13mm, entire to erose, lateral lobes subrotund or subrhomboid, midlobe smaller than lateral lobes, bilobulate, disc with 2 basal calli and 3 longitudinal keels; column to 14mm. Venezuela, Brazil, Jamaica, Trinidad.

E.ochraceum Lindl. See *Encyclia ochracea.*

E.oerstedii Rchb. f. Related to and resembling *E.ciliare, E.nocturnum* and *E.parkinsonianum*; differs from the first in having entire, not ciliate, lateral lobes to lip, from the second by its stouter pseudobulbs and tougher lvs, and from the last in having an erect, not pendent habit. Costa Rica, Panama.
E.ottonis Rchb. f. See *Nidema ottonis.*

E.ovulum Lindl. See *Encyclia microbulbon.*
E.palpigerum Rchb. f. See *E.imatophyllum.*
E.paniculatum Ruiz & Pav. See *E.floribundum.*
E.panthera Rchb. f. See *Encyclia panthera.*
E.papyriferum Schltr. See *Encyclia panthera.*

E.paranthicum Rchb.f. (*Epidanthus paranthicus* (Rchb.f.) L.O.Williams).
Small, mat-forming with racemes of several minute creamy green and yellow fls. S America.

E.parkinsonianum Hook. (*E.falcatum* Lindl.; *E.aloifolium* Batem.).
Rhiz. thick, glossy, branching, sparse-rooting; stems terete, short, decurved, 1–2-lvd. Lvs to 50×5cm, lanceolate-falcate, fleshy, pendulous, clustered, lobster claw-like, deep green with paler spots to red-bronze in sun-baked conditions. Racemes short, terminal, pendent, 1–5-fld; fls to 15cm diam., showy, fragrant, long-lived; sep. and pet. white, pale yellow or yellow-green, becoming darker with age, often tinged mauve or purple-bronze below, sep. to 9×2cm, spreading, linear to linear-lanceolate, acute or acuminate, pet. to 8×1cm, spreading, linear-lanceolate, acuminate; lip to 8×4cm, white with a pale yellow-orange mark in throat, deeply 3-lobed, lateral lobes obtriangular, outer margins denticulate, midlobe linear, acuminate, to 55×4mm, disc with 2 flap-like keels; column to 3cm. Mostly summer–autumn. Mexico, Guatemala, Honduras, Costa Rica, Panama. The typical *E.parkinsonianum* has cool green tepals with a pure white lip. Plants with pink- or maroon-tinted fls with a yellow stain in the throat are often called *E.falcatum.*

E.patens Sw. non Hook.
Stems to 50cm, slender, clustered, arcuate to pendent. Lvs to 10cm, oblong to oblong-lanceolate, acute. Infl. to 13cm, pendent, few- to many-fld; fls to 3cm diam., fragrant, long-lived; sep. and pet. pale yellow or yellow-green usually fading to white, sep. to 1cm, oblong-lanceolate, acute, margins revolute, pet. to 1cm, oblanceolate to elliptic, margins revolute; lip cream-white, connate to column apex, 3-lobed, lateral lobes rounded, midlobe ovate, obtuse, sometimes bilobulate; column dilated toward apex. Mostly summer. W Indies, Brazil, Venezuela.

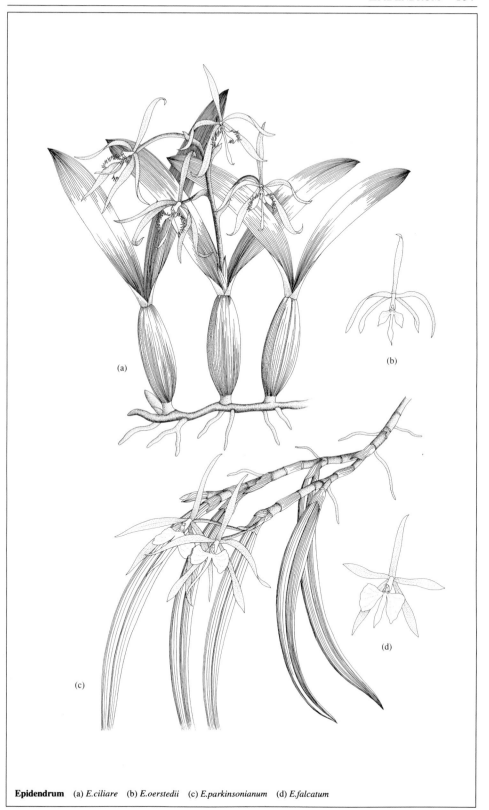

Epidendrum   (a) *E.ciliare*   (b) *E.oerstedii*   (c) *E.parkinsonianum*   (d) *E.falcatum*

E.pentotis Rchb. f. See *Encyclia baculus*.

E.peperomia Rchb.f.
Small, forming broad mats of creeping, bright green growth. Fls comparatively large, solitary or few together, but produced in great abundance; tepals slender, spreading, pale green; lip large, orbicular, glossy red-brown; column cool lime green with a cream anther cap. S America.

E.pfavii Rolfe.
Resembles *E.ibaguense* in habit. Fls long-lasting, brilliant cerise to magenta in long racemes; lip 3-lobed, the midlobe smaller and deeply cleft with 2 divergent lobules and a white marking at base. Costa Rica.

E.piliferum Rchb. f. See *E.floribundum*.
E.polybulbon Sw. See *Encyclia polybulbon*.
E.porpax Rchb. f. See *Nanodes mathewsii*.

E.porphyreum Lindl.
Canes slender. Raceme crowded, arching, several produced together, the whole appearing to be a single, branched infl.; fls pendulous, bright rosy purple with a white blotch on lip; tepals more or less equal, oblong-spathulate; lip basically oblong, large, 3-lobed with midlobe split into 2 divergent lobules, thus rather human in outline and suggestive of the lips of *Aceras* and *Orchis*. Ecuador.

E.prismatocarpum Rchb. f. See *Encyclia prismatocarpa*.

E.pseudepidendrum (Rchb. f.) Rchb. f. (*Pseudepidendrum spectabile* Rchb. f.).
Stems to 1m, robust, simple. Lvs 2-ranked in upper half of stem, to 20×4.5cm, suberect, linear-oblong or oblanceolate, coriaceous, deep green, keeled below. Raceme terminal, loose, to 15cm, semi-erect to arching; sep. and pet. lustrous apple green, sep. to 3×1cm, oblanceolate, acute to obtuse, pet. to 30×4mm, linear-oblanceolate, obtuse; lip bright orange or orange-red, to 17×22mm, subquadrate to suborbicular, undulate, retuse, finely fimbriate, disc with thickened yellow keels, sometimes crimson edged orange (`Auratum'); column apex thickened, orange-red. Summer–autumn. Costa Rica, Panama.

E.pugioniforme Reg.
Similar to *E.ciliare* in habit but with thinner lvs. Infl. a few-fld, pendent raceme; fls large with spreading, narrow, shiny olive tepals, an obovate-acuminate, green lip stained orange-red and a white column. Mexico.

E.purum Lindl. Stems elongate-fusiform, erect, to 50cm. Lvs to 22×1.5cm, in upper reaches of stem, linear or linear-lanceolate, obtuse, coriaceous, erect or suberect, light green. Panicle terminal, branches spreading, many-fld; fls to 2cm, campanulate, fragrant, white or green-white; sep. to 10×2mm, elliptic-linear or narrowly elliptic-lanceolate, acute or acuminate; pet. to 8×1mm, linear-filiform, acute; lip adnate to entire length of column, to 7×6mm, deeply 3-lobed, lateral lobes obliquely ovate or triangular, acute, midlobe ovate to spathulate, acute, porrect, disc with 2 calli at base, 3-keeled in front; column to 5mm, apex dilated. Venezuela to Bolivia.

E.pygmaeum Hook. See *Encyclia pygmaea*.
E.quadratum Klotzsch. See *Encyclia varicosa*.
E.radiatum Lindl. See *Encyclia radiata*.
E.radicans auct. non Pav. ex Lindl. See *E.ibaguense*.

E.ramosum Jacq.
Stems to 90cm, slender, simple to much-branched, often flexuous, concealed by lf sheaths. Lvs to 12×1.5cm, numerous, 2-ranked, linear to lanceolate or oblong-elliptic, obtuse and obliquely retuse at apex. Raceme terminal on branches, very short, few- to several-fld; peduncle slender, fractiflex; fls cream-white or pale green or yellow-green, sometimes tinged red, small; sep. to 13×3mm, linear-lanceolate to elliptic-oblong, lateral sep. slightly oblique; pet. to 13×2mm, linear to narrowly spathulate; lip claw adnate to column, lamina simple to obscurely trilobed, to 9×5mm, triangular ovate to broadly lanceolate, base cordate, disc with a longitudinal, bifurcate

callus at base; column short, stout. Mexico to Panama, W Indies to Venezuela, Brazil, Peru.

E.raniferum Lindl. See *E.cristatum*.
E.reflexum Ames & Schweinf. See *E.floribundum*.

E.rigidum Jacq.
Stems to 25cm, erect or ascending, simple, entirely concealed by lf sheaths. Lvs several, to 8.5×2.5cm, ligulate-oblong to elliptic-oblong, obtuse, coriaceous. Raceme terminal, to 15cm, erect or arching, sheathed; peduncle strongly compressed; fls loosely 2-ranked, minute, fleshy, green or yellow-green, sometimes concealed by bracts; sep. to 7×3mm, ovate-oblong or elliptic-oblong, subacute, lateral sep. oblique; pet. to 6×2mm, linear or oblanceolate-linear, obtuse; lip to 6×5mm, broadly ovate to suborbicular, obtuse, base cordate, often crenulate, disc with 2 small basal calli and a thickened median line; column to 4mm, stout, apex dentate. C & S America, W Indies.

E.sceptrum Lindl. (*E.macrothyrsodes* Rchb. f.; *E.sphenoglossum* Lehm. & Kränzl.).
Rhiz. creeping, rigid; pseudobulbs to 30cm, narrowly fusiform, compressed, slightly grooved, unifoliate to trifoliate. Lvs to 30×3cm, coriaceous, oblong or ligulate to lanceolate, apex bilobed. Infl. terminal, to 55cm, erect or arching, many-fld; sep. and pet. yellow or yellow-brown spotted dark purple, sep. to 20×4mm, oblong to lanceolate, acute or obtuse, pet. to 20×6mm, oblanceolate to obovate-spathulate, acute; lip white at base, strongly marked dark purple, to 14×14mm, rhomboid to subrotund, acute to apiculate, disc with 2 basal calli; column fleshy, pale yellow-brown. Venezuela, Colombia, Ecuador.

E.schlechterianum Ames. See *Nanodes discolor*.

E.schomburgkii Lindl. (*E.ibaguense* var. *schomburgkii* (HBK) C. Schweinf.; *E.splendens* Schltr.).
Stems to 75cm, sheaths often spotted purple. Lvs to 20×5cm, alternate, 2-ranked, oblong, obtuse, fleshy-coriaceous, rigid, spreading-horizontal. Raceme terminal, erect, much exceeding lvs, few- to many-fld; fls to 3.5cm, long-lived, rich vermilion-scarlet to bright orange; sep. and pet. to 2cm, linear-lanceolate; lip deeply 3-lobed, strongly carinate, lateral lobes broadly semi-ovate to falcate, incurved, lacerate, midlobe cuneate, apically bilobulate, dentate, apical margins usually upturned, disc with 2 yellow basal calli; column elongate, apex yellow, base dark red or purple. Mostly winter. Colombia, Venezuela, Guianas, Peru, Brazil.

E.schumannianum Schltr. See *Oerstedella schumanniana*.
E.schweinfurthianum Correll. See *Oerstedella schweinfurthiana*.

E.secundum Jacq. (*E.xanthinum* Lindl.; *E.corymbosum* Ruiz & Pav.).
Related to *E.ibaguense*, from which it can be distinguished by its 3-lobed callus and dependent lip. Stems to 1m, clumped, erect, terete, purple-brown to green-brown, loosely many-lvd. Lvs to 14×4cm, spreading, ovate-oblong to ovate-lanceolate, acute to obtuse, coriaceous. Infl. a raceme, terminal, simple or rarely branched, to 75cm, densely many-fld at apex; fls variable in colour, white to orange or rose-pink; sep. to 12×4mm, oblanceolate-oblong or elliptic-oblong, acute; pet. to 12×4mm, obovate-oblong to oblanceolate-oblong, subacute or obtuse; lip to 10×12mm, rotund-subreniform, deeply 3-lobed, lateral lobes rounded, dentate to lacerate, midlobe large, broadly cuneate, sharply dentate to lacerate; callus ovate-subquadrate, concave; column to 8mm, dilated in apical half. W Indies, Tropical S America. cf. *E.ibaguense*, *E.imatophyllum*.

E.selligerum Batem. ex Lindl. See *Encyclia selligera*.
E.skinneri Batem. ex Lindl. See *Barkeria skinneri*.

E.sophronitoides Lehm. & Kranzl.
Diminutive with tufted growths of 2-ranked leaves. Fls produced singly in succession, large in relation to the plant, bronze-pink with spreading, lanceolate tepals and a large,

slightly infolded, reniform lip; column tipped red-pink. Colombia, Ecuador.

E.spectabile (Batem. ex Lindl.) Rchb. f. See *Barkeria spectabilis.*
E.spectatissimum Rchb. f. See *E.leucochilum.*
E.sphenoglossum Lehm. & Kränzl. See *E.sceptrum.*
E.splendens Schltr. See *E.schomburgkii.*
E.spondiadum Rchb. f. See *Encyclia spondiada.*

E.stamfordianum Batem. (*E.basilare* Klotzsch).
Pseudobulbs to 25×2cm, fusiform, concealed by pale brown sheaths, usually bifoliate. Lvs to 24×6cm, linear-oblong to elliptic-oblong, obtuse, coriaceous. Raceme or panicle to 60cm carried basally on latest completed pseudobulb; peduncle green spotted purple; fls showy, fragrant; sep. and pet. pale yellow-green to pale bronze spotted or mottled red-brown or purple, sep. to 20×6mm, elliptic to ovate-lanceolate, acute, spreading, lateral sep. oblique, pet. to 19×3mm, linear to linear-oblanceolate, acute, crenulate-crisped; lip white, sometimes tinted or flushed rose, adnate to column, to 2×2.5cm, 3-lobed, lateral lobes obliquely oblong, rounded, recurved, midlobe separated from lateral lobes by slender claw, bilobulate, deeply emarginate, erose, disc with bilobed callus at base and central keel extending from base to middle of midlobe; column to 1cm, clavate, apex tinged red. Mexico to Panama, Venezuela, Colombia.

E.stenopetalum Hook. See *Dimerandra emarginata.*

E.strobiliferum Rchb. f. (*E.mosenii* Barb.-Rodr.).
Stems clustered, simple to much-branched, concealed by tubular, green-purple leaf-bearing sheaths. Lvs to 4×1cm, distichous, numerous, fleshy, spreading, elliptic to linear-lanceolate. Raceme terminal, to 3.5cm, few-fld; fls small, to 5mm, green to white, sometimes lined red, prominently nerved; dorsal sep. to 5×2mm, oblong-lanceolate or elliptic-lanceolate, acute to obtuse, lateral sep. obliquely ovate-oblong to oblong-lanceolate, acute; pet. narrower than sep., linear-oblanceolate, subacute to acute; lip to 4×3mm, entire, ovate-cordate to hastate, acute to acuminate, concave, disc with 2 minute, basal calli; column to 2mm, stout. C & S America (from Florida to Peru), W Indies.

E.tampense Lindl. See *Encyclia tampensis.*
E.tenuissimum Ames, Hubb. & Schweinf. See *Encyclia tenuissima.*
E.teretifolium Sw. See *Jacquiniella teretifolia.*
E.tesselatum Batem. ex Lindl. See *Encyclia livida.*
E.trachychilum Lindl. See *Encyclia ambigua.*
E.tridactylon Lindl. See *Amblostoma tridactylon.*
E.tridens Poepp. & Endl. See *E.nocturnum.*
E.tripunctatum Lindl. See *Encyclia tripunctata.*
E.trulla Rchb. f. See *Encyclia lancifolia.*
E.tuerckheimii (Schltr.) Ames, Hubb. & Schweinf. See *Encyclia tuerckheimii.*
E.umbellatum Sw. See *E.difforme.*
E.varicosum Batem. ex Lindl. See *Encyclia varicosa.*
E.variegatum Hook. See *Encyclia vespa.*
E.venosum Lindl. See *Encyclia venosa.*

E.veroscriptum Hagsater.
Close to *E.floribundum;* tepals lime or sap green; lip creamy white with a distinctive circle of burgundy spots around the ridged, sparsely spotted callus. Mexico.

E.verrucosum Sw. See *Oerstedella verrucosa.*

E.vesicatum Lindl.
Stems pendent, clothed with grey-green, broad, closely overlapping lvs, the uppermost few forming an involucral cup which subtends the short, congested spike of white-green fls. Brazil.

E.vespa Vell. See *Encyclia vespa.*
E.vinosum Schltr. See *E.catillus.*

E.violascens Ridl.
Stems erect, to 14cm, terete, simple or branched, many-lvd. Lvs to 20×3mm, coriaceous, rigid, oblong-lanceolate, acute, dark green above, puce below. Panicle terminal, to 20cm, few- to many-fld, erect, short-branched; peduncle maroon, filiform; bracts to 2mm, maroon; fls small; sep. and pet. red-purple, sep. fleshy, slightly concave, acute or obtuse, dorsal sep. to 5×2mm, oblanceolate, lateral sep. slightly broader, obovate or elliptic, oblique, adnate to column base, pet. membranous, to 4×0.5mm, linear to narrowly oblong, obtuse; lip light yellow-green, 3×4mm, transversely elliptic to rounded-subreniform, subtruncate, irregularly erose, disc 3-nerved, with 2 basal calli; column light green-yellow, erect, to 4mm. Venezuela, Brazil, Guyana.

E.virens Lindl. & Paxt. See *Encyclia belizensis.*
E.virgatum Lindl. See *Encyclia michuacana.*
E.viridipurpureum Hook. See *E.anceps.*
E.viscidum Lindl. See *E.ciliare.*
E.vitellinum Lindl. See *Encyclia vitellina.*
E.wallisii Rchb. f. See *Oerstedella wallisii.*
E.wendlandianum Kränzl. See *Encyclia venosa.*
E.xanthinum Lindl. See *E.secundum.*

E.xipheres Rchb. f. (*E.yucatanense* Schltr.).
Pseudobulbs to 3×1cm, clumped, ovoid, unifoliate. Lvs to 26×0.5cm, narrowly linear, conduplicate, subacute, coriaceous. Raceme or panicle to 36cm, loosely few-fld; fls small, spreading, long-lived; pedicellate ovaries densely echinate, to 1.5cm; sep. and pet. red-brown, usually edged and marked yellow or green-lavender, sep. to 14×3mm, elliptic-lanceolate, acute to acuminate, lateral sep. oblique, pet. to 14×1mm, linear-oblanceolate, acute to obtuse; lip dull yellow striped lavender, to 13×10mm, deeply 3-lobed, lateral lobes linear-spathulate, obtuse, midlobe subreniform to ovate-triangular, acute to subobtuse, undulate, disc with a fleshy callus and 3 keels; column to 7mm, fleshy. Spring–summer. Mexico, Guatemala, Honduras.

E.yucatanense Schltr. See *E.xipheres.*

E.grexes and cultivars.
E.Cardinal: tall, reed stem types with many lvs; terminal clusters of well-shaped orange red fls.
E.Lilac Queen: tall, reed-stem types with terminal clusters of lilac-mauve fls.
E.O'Brienianum: one of the first orchid hybrids made, very common in cultivation; reed-like stems with many lvs and terminal clusters of rosy crimson fls.
E.Orange Glow: tall, reed-stem types with many lvs and terminal clusters of bright orange-red fls with yellow lip.
E.Plastic Doll: enormous plants with reed-like stems, terminal cluster of green and yellow fls.
E.Swazi King: tall reed-stem types with many lvs and terminal clusters of orange-red fls.

Epigeneium Gagnep. (From Gk *epi*, upon, and *geneion*, chin, because of the position of the lateral sepals and petals in relation to the column foot.) About 35 species of epiphytes. Rhizomes long, creeping. Pseudobulbs usually remote, ovoid, conical or ellipsoid, often markedly 4-angled and tapering basally. Leaves 2, borne at apex, spreading, tough, oblong, obtuse or abruptly acute. Inflorescence terminal, racemose, semi-erect or arching; flowers 1–20, ivory, green-white or bronze suffused pink or purple and variously spotted and striped red or maroon, showy, fragrant, waxy; sepals and petals widely spreading, often in a vertical plane, narrow-oblong, long-acuminate, sometimes linear, twisted and recurved; lip broad, trilobed, motile; column short. SE Asia.

CULTIVATION   As for *Bulbophyllum*.

E.coelogyne (Rchb. f.) Summerh. (*Dendrobium coelogyne* Rchb. f.).
Pseudobulbs to 7cm, widely spaced on rhiz., narrow-ellipsoid, strongly tetragonal. Lvs to 15×5cm, glossy dark green, abruptly acute. Fls usually solitary, to 9cm diam., waxy, fragrant; sep. and pet. linear-lanceolate (lateral sep. wider than other seg.), twisted, recurved, yellow to deep yellow below, pale ochre above, spotted maroon; lip showy, midlobe fleshy, channelled, dark maroon to violet-black, lateral lobes erect, ivory marked purple. Burma, Thailand.

E.cymbidioides (Bl.) Summerh. (*Desmotrichum cymbidioides* Bl.).
Pseudobulbs to 4cm, clustered, oblong, squat, 4–5-angled, with thin basal sheaths. Lvs coriaceous, thick, obtuse or retuse, to 15cm. Infl. to 20cm; fls to 12, poorly scented, waxy, to 4cm diam.; sep. and pet. ligulate, cream to ochre; lip white to pale yellow, midlobe streaked purple at base with 3 calli, lateral lobes short, rounded. Java, Philippines.

E.lyonii (Ames) Summerh. (*Dendrobium lyonii* Ames).
Pseudobulbs to 6cm, remote obscurely angled with a sharp and distinct apical tooth remaining after fall of 2-year-old lvs. Lvs elliptic or oblong, to 15×4cm. Racemes to +15-fld; fls to 12cm diam.; sep. and pet. triangular, white to yellow, flushed garnet to maroon, tipped yellow or green; lip to 3cm, red-purple, midlobe triangular, lateral lobes basally dark red, spreading. Philippines.

E.triflorum (Bl.) Summerh. (*Desmotrichum triflorum* Bl.; *Dendrobium triflorum* (Bl.) Lindl.).
Pseudobulbs to 2cm, almost ovoid, bases dark brown. Lvs linear to linear-lanceolate, glossy dark green above, paler beneath, retuse, to 12×2cm. Raceme to 6cm; fls 2–6+; sep. and pet. yellow, equal, to 3cm; lip midlobe ovate-triangular, deep yellow, margins white, broad, basally dark brown, spotted red, lateral lobes triangular, white, interior dappled brown-red. Java.

Epipactis Zinn (*Helleborine* Mill.). (Gk name for this genus.) Some 24 species of temperate and tropical terrestrials. Rhizomes creeping or ascending; roots at nodes and buds, fibrous, fleshy. Stems solitary or many. Leaves lanceolate to ovate, 2-ranked or spiralling, usually plicate-ribbed. Spike lax or dense, erect or nodding, sometimes secund; bracts leafy; flowers pedicellate; petals and sepals spreading or incurved; lip spurless, constricted, basally cupped, apically spreading, ridged. Summer. N Temperate Zone, Tropical Africa, Thailand, Mexico.

CULTIVATION   See Introduction: Hardy Orchids.

E.atrorubens (Bernh.) Besser. BROAD-LEAVED HELLEBORINE.
Stems to 1m, glabrous or pubesc. Lvs 3–10, ovate to ovate-lanceolate, bract-like toward summit of stem. Spike 7–25cm, densely pubesc; sep. and pet. triangular, spreading, ruby red, sometimes amber; lip 5.5–6.5mm, with callus of 3 basal projections, apex cordate to reniform, edged deep green and spotted red, tip recurved. Late spring–late summer. Europe.

E.falcata Thunb. See *Cephalanthera falcata*.

E.gigantea Douglas ex Hook.
Stems to 90cm. Lvs 4–12, ovate to lanceolate. Spike to 15-fld, lax; lateral sep. ovate-lanceolate, bright green veined purple; pet. ovate, rose-pink ageing green; lip 14–18mm, base concave, red-verrucose, lateral lobes triangular, yellow, veined purple to brown, apical lobe orange-yellow tipped pink, 2-ridged, separated from lateral lobes by 2 pleats. Spring–summer. N America. . 'Serpentine Night': lvs and stem deep wine red.

E.helleborine (L.) Crantz.
Stems to 100cm, basally sheathed, pubesc. Lvs 5–15×2.5–10cm, 3–10, ovate to elliptic, spirally arranged, acuminate. Spike secund, 15–50-fld; sep. ovate, green tinted purple; pet. pale green to pink, elliptic to ovate; lip base concave, interior green, apex broadly ovate to cordate, cream-yellow, pink or purple, with 2 basal projections. Summer. Europe.

E.palustris (L.) Crantz. MARSH HELLEBORINE.
Rhiz. long, creeping. Stems to 50cm, pubesc.; basal sheaths tinted purple. Lvs oblong to oblong-lanceolate, spiralling. Spike lax, secund, 4–20-fld; floral bracts smaller toward

apex; sep. maroon to grey-green, interior red; pet. cream, flushed or lined garnet or maroon; lip undulate, veined pink to mauve within, spotted orange, apex ovate, cream or white with yellow stripe at base. Summer–early autumn. Europe.

E.purpurata Sm. VIOLET HELLEBORINE.
Rhiz. short. Stem 20–90cm, pubesc. Lvs 5–10, ovate-lanceolate to lanceolate, grey-green tinged purple. Spike 15–30cm, dense; fls nodding; sep. and pet. lanceolate, green below, white above, rarely tinted pink; lip base concave, exterior green, interior dappled violet, apex triangular, white with pink callus. Late summer–early autumn. NW & C Europe.

E.thunbergii A. Gray.
Rhiz. creeping. Stems erect, 30–70cm, flushed red-purple at base. Lvs 7–12cm, 5–10, sheathing stem at base, ovate-lanceolate, alternate, with prominent longitudinal veins. Fls golden-bronze; sep. to 1.5cm, ovate-lanceolate; pet. ovate, spotted maroon above; lip apex ovate. Summer. Japan, China, Korea.

E.veratrifolia Boiss. & Hohen. EASTERN MARSH HELLEBORINE; SCARCE MARSH HELLEBORINE.
Rhiz. creeping. Stems 20–150cm. Lvs 8–20, ovate-lanceolate to lanceolate, basally sheathing stem and reduced toward its summit. Spike lax, arching, with long floral bracts; fls nodding; pet. and sep. ovate, olive to buff, dappled deep red or purple-brown; lip base purple with brown basal projections, apex triangular, buff with a transverse red-brown stripe; spurless. Late spring–late summer. E Mediterranean, SW & E Asia, Somalia.

× **Epiphronitis** (*Epidendrum* × *Sophronitis*). Chiefly remarkable for one very attractive early hybrid which is still widely grown.

× **E. Veitchii**.
One of the earliest hybrids; small plants with upright stems bearing several leaves; infl. terminal with clusters of brilliant orange-red and yellow fls.

Eria Lindl. (From Gk *erion*, wool, referring to the woolly covering on the perianth.) Some 350 epiphytes or ter-restrials. Pseudobulbs slender, ellipsoid, ovoid or narrow-cylindric, often densely sheathed. Leaves 2 to many, folded when young, apical and basally or sheathing. Racemes terminal or axillary, lax, glabrous or pubescent; sepals almost equal, lateral sepals sometimes broader, fused along the column foot forming a small, spur-like or saccate projection; petals smaller; lip trilobed or entire, often with calli or longitudinal keels; column with 8 pollinia. Indopacific.

CULTIVATION   Grow *E.coronaria* in small pots of medium-density bark mix in part-shade and cool conditions. A short dry rest is required in winter; otherwise, water and feed plentifully. A well grown plant is a beautiful sight – neatly tufted growths topped by paired, leathery leaves and short racemes of white flowers, the lips combed with yellow and maroon. The other species favour intermediate conditions, again with dappled light and high humidity. The more slender the pseudobulbs, the more careful should be winter watering: do not allow excessive shrivelling. Where it can be accommodated, *E.javanica* is one of the most showy medium to large-sized orchids, best established on a long raft or at the foot of an epiphyte 'tree', where its stout rhizomes and robust foliage can spread freely. Propagate by division.

E.convallarioides Lindl. See *E.spicata*.

E.coronaria (Lindl.) Rchb. f. (*E.suavis* (Lindl.) Lindl.; *Trichosma suavis* Lindl.; *Trichosma coronaria* Lindl.).
Rhiz. very short. Pseudobulbs narrow-cylindric, stalk-like, to 14cm, pea-green becoming ash-grey and blackened with age. Lvs 2, terminal, alternate appearing opposite, to 14.5cm, broadly lanceolate, coriaceous to thinly fleshy, smooth, pale green, somewhat undulate with tips recurved. Infl. a short raceme, terminal on new growth, between lvs, semi-erect; fls to 7, to 2.5cm diam., waxy, slightly fragrant; sep. and pet. equal, oblong to triangular, subacute, forward-pointing and often concave above, sparkling white; lip trilobed, midlobe bright yellow, 5-ridged, lateral lobes erect, rounded, veined maroon to violet-black. Himalaya, Burma, Thailand, Malaysia.

E.dasyphylla Parish & Rchb. f. See *Trichotosia dasyphylla*.
E.ferox (Bl.) Bl. See *Trichotosia ferox*.

E.floribunda Lindl.
Pseudobulbs narrow-ellipsoid, stem-like, to 50cm. Lvs 2–5, borne apically, linear-lanceolate to elliptic, acute, soft, to 25cm. Infl. a crowded raceme, 1 to several from upper nodes of pseudobulb, arching, to 20cm; peduncle pubesc.; fls to 0.6cm diam., white, tinted pink; sep. obtuse, 3–5-veined; pet. ovate-oblong, lip midlobe flabellate, truncate, separated from lateral lobes by a ridge; column apex and stigma violet or maroon. Malaysia.

E.hyacinthoides (Bl.) Lindl.
Pseudobulbs clustered, oblong, basally sheathed, to 10cm. Lvs to 40×5cm, paired at apex of pseudobulb, narrow-lanceolate; petiole to 10cm+. Infl. erect, canescent, to 18cm; fls many, to 2cm diam., scented; tepals white, oblong, blunt; lip white, midlobe cordate, decurved, with 2 swellings at base and 2 pubesc. calli, lateral lobes narrow, erect, maroon or violet. Java.

E.javanica (Sw.) Bl. (*E.rugosa* Lindl.; *E.stellata* Lindl.).
Rhiz. slender, long. Pseudobulbs ovoid to laterally compressed pyriform, to 15×6.5cm. Lvs 2, to 30×8cm, lanceolate, narrowing to grooved stalk and sheathing base, erect, thick, dull green and obscurely grooved above, paler beneath with dark scurf when young. Infl. subterminal, erect, exceeding lvs, narrow-cylindric; peduncle pubesc., bracteate; fls numerous, to 4cm diam., star-like, on all sides of raceme; sep. and pet. sharply tapering, spreading, cream to white, sometimes flecked or lined maroon; lip midlobe long, abruptly acute, 3-ridged (central ridge yellow), lateral lobes short, erect. Summer. Across range.

E.meirax (King & Pantl. N.E. Br. See *Porpax meirax*.

E.ornata (Bl.) Lindl.
Pseudobulbs on a long rhiz., elliptic-oblong to lanceolate, to 11×5cm. Lvs usually 4, to 20cm, thick, olive green, elliptic, acute, narrowing to a stalk. Racemes to 45cm, ascending to arching, rusty tomentose; bracts ovate-lanceolate, orange or red-brown, to 8×2.5cm; fls 1–5cm diam.; sep. triangular-lanceolate, pale yellow-green, pubesc.; pet. lanceolate, exterior green-white streaked and dotted purple; lip white marked purple with crispate, dark violet margins. Java.

E.rigida Bl.
Pseudobulbs stem-like, to 1m+, curved, hanging. Lvs coriaceous, thick, dark green, narrow-lanceolate, to 14×1.25cm. Infl. many, lateral; bracts to 8×5mm, red-green; fls solitary, seldom opening fully, to 1.5cm diam., white; dorsal sep. to 1.5cm, hooded, lateral sep. recurved, tinted yellow below; pet. concave; lip white, midlobe to 3mm, apex deeply cleft, basal keels 3, central keel terminating in a tooth, lateral lobes erect, apically obtuse; column bears basal pad of callus covered in orange, clavate papillae. Borneo.

E.rosea Lindl.
Pseudobulbs ovoid or conic. Lvs linear-lanceolate to oblong, coriaceous, to 22×3cm; petiole to 5cm. Fls 3–4, rose or white suffused rose; dorsal sep. oblong-lanceolate, lateral sep. ovate-triangular, column foot projection triangular; pet. obovate, narrow, minutely crenate; lip midlobe oblong, margins minutely crenate and undulate, disc softly pubesc., lamellae undulate. China, Hong Kong.

E.rugosa Lindl. See *E.javanica*.

E.spicata (D. Don) Hand.-Mazz. (*E.convallarioides* Lindl.).
Pseudobulbs to 20cm, oblong or broadly ellipsoid, sheathed with old leaf bases. Lvs usually 4, apical, coriaceous, fleshy, lanceolate, acute, arched, to 20×5cm. Infl. to 15cm, arching, crowded for half length; flowering section narrow-ovate in outline; fls white to straw-coloured, glabrous or sparsely softly pubesc., lightly fragrant, seldom opening fully; sep. elliptic, broad, to 6×5mm, lateral sep. fused basally, forming an oblong projection at column base; pet. elliptic-ovate, lip obscurely trilobed, cuneate, triangular, papillose. Nepal, N India, Burma.

E.stellata Lindl. See *E.javanica*.
E.suavis (Lindl.) Lindl. See *E.coronaria*.
E.velutina Lodd. ex Lindl. See *Trichotosia velutina*.
E.vestita Lindl. See *Trichotosia vestita*.

Eria and Trichotosia   (a) *Eria javanica*   (b) *Eria coronaria*   (c) *Trichotosia vestita*

Eriochilus R. Br. (From Gk *erion*, wool, and *cheilos*, lip, referring to the pubescent disc on the lip.) 6 species of terrestrials. Tubers subterranean. Stems slender, pubescent or glabrous. Leaf basal, solitary, ovate-lanceolate. Peduncle slender; fls 1–6; dorsal sepal erect, lanceolate, lateral sepals clawed, deflexed or spreading; petals erect, shorter than or equalling sepals; lip apex sharply recurved, mid-lobe densely pubescent; column erect, winged or entire. Australia.

CULTIVATION   As for *Disa*, but with full sunlight and a short, dry winter rest.

E.cucullatus (Labill.) Rchb. f.
Stems to 25cm, slender. Lf to 3.5cm, ovate, acute. Fls emerging before lvs, pale to bright pink or white; dorsal sep. incurved, acute, linear to ovate-lanceolate, lateral sep. 11–17mm, spreading or deflexed, elliptic-lanceolate reduced to a slender claw; pet. linear to linear-spathulate; lip erect, concave, ovate-oblong, convex, pubesc., column wings lanceolate. Winter–mid-spring. Australia (except W Australia).

E.dilatatus Lindl.
Stems to 15cm, slender, glabrous or pubesc. Lf to 6cm, at or below mid-stem, sessile, ovate to ovate-lanceolate, sometimes reduced to a bract. Fls 1–13, white with red pet. tips and red-blotched lip; dorsal sep. oblong, constricted in basal half, lateral sep. 1.3–1.5cm, oblong-lanceolate, acute, becoming a slender claw; pet. equal dorsal sep., basally lanceolate, apically dilated; lip short, narrow, midlobe ovate-oblong, convex, recurved, pubesc. above. Early–mid summer. SW Australia.

Eriopsis Lindl. (Gk *opsis*, resemblance, and *Eria*.) 6 species of epiphytes. Rhizome short, clothed with papery grey bracts. Roots thick, dark grey-green. Pseudobulbs stoutly ovoid to pyriform, fissured, basally sheathed by leafy bracts. Leaves 2–3, borne apically, lanceolate to oblanceolate, acuminate, obscurely plicate, prominently veined beneath, basally conduplicate. Inflorescence racemose, borne basally, erect to arching; flowers pedicellate; sepals subequal, fleshy, lanceolate to broadly elliptic, the dorsal somewhat incurved and concave, the laterals spreading; petals narrower than sepals, spreading; lip obscurely obcordate, 3-lobed, lateral lobes erect to incurved, large, rounded, midlobe smaller than lateral lobes, orbicular to reniform, disc keeled or callused with crested lamellae; column elongate, arching. Tropical America.

CULTIVATION   As for *Cyrtopodium* but with protection from bright sunlight when in growth.

E.biloba Lindl. (*E.rutibulbon* Hook.; *E.schomburgkii* (Rchb. f.) Rchb. f.).
A variable species. Pseudobulbs to 45cm, narrowly cylindric to compressed-ovoid. Lvs to 40×8cm, rigidly fleshy or papery and flexible, dark green. Raceme to 1m, axis glabrous, green tinted maroon; fls many; sep. 12–25×8–10mm, ivory to tawny yellow flushed or edged oxblood, particularly beneath; pet. 12–25×6–8mm, usually more faintly coloured than sep.; lip 12–23×12–20mm, lateral lobes yellow to tan flushed and obscurely veined oxblood, midlobe cream spotted maroon. Costa Rica to Peru.

E.rutibulbon Hook. See *E.biloba*.
E.schomburgkii Rchb. f. See *E.biloba*.

Erycina Lindl. (From Erycina, the Aphrodite of Mount Eryx in Sicily.) 2 species of epiphytes allied to *Oncidium*. Mexico.

CULTIVATION   As for the smaller *Oncidium* spp.

E.diaphana (Rchb. f.) Schltr.
Closely resembles *E.echinata*, from which it can be distinguished by its lip, which is smaller (to 0.7cm), with slender, clavate, spreading lateral lobes and an obscurely quadrate, short, retuse midlobe.

E.echinata (HBK) Lindl. (*Erycina major* Schltr.; *Oncidium echinatum* HBK).
Rhiz. short, creeping to ascending. Pseudobulbs to 5cm, clustered, oval, stalked, sheathed at base, bronze-green. Lvs to 10cm, to 5 per bulb, narrow-oblong, acuminate, 2-ranked, sheathing, one terminal, articulate at base. Infl. to 15cm, racemose, arching, axillary, borne near base of pseudobulb, bracteate; fls to 2cm diam., to 10, borne loosely, cupped, yellow to green, lip golden yellow, column white, anth. cap red; sep. and pet. narrow-ovate, acuminate; tepals very small; lip to 1×0.8cm, proportionately very large, lateral lobes flabellate, rounded, somewhat incurved, central process waisted, midlobe distinctly orbicular to reniform, apiculate; ovary echinate.

E.major Schltr. See *E.echinata*.

Esmeralda Rchb. f. (Perhaps from Gk *smaragdus*, emerald, referring to the beauty of the flowers.) 2 species of scrambling, monopodial, epiphytes allied to *Vanda*. Leaves strap-shaped, folded when young. Racemes axillary; sepals and petals similar, spreading; lip mobile, midlobe ovate, basally saccate, longitudinal ridges 3–5, lateral lobes oblong, erect. Himalaya, SE Asia.

CULTIVATION   As for the warm-growing *Vanda* spp.

E.bella Rchb. f. See *E.clarkei*.

E.cathcartii (Lindl.) Rchb. f. (*Vanda cathcartii* Lindl.).
Stem to 2m, pendent. Lvs oblong, coriaceous, to 15×4cm. Infl. exceeding the lvs; fls 3–5, 4.5–8cm diam.; sep. and pet. ovate to broadly elliptic, white beneath, yellow closely and finely banded chocolate above; lip white, striped red, margins yellow, undulate, irregularly dentate. Spring–summer. E Himalaya.

E.clarkei Rchb. f. (*E.bella* Rchb. f.; *Vanda clarkei* (Rchb. f.) N.E. Br.).
Stem to 45cm, pendent; lvs oblong-lorate, coriaceous, to 16×4cm. Racemes 3–4 fld; fls to 7cm diam., fragrant; sep. and pet. yellow to ochre, banded brown; dorsal sep. oblong, to 3.5×1cm, lateral sep. oblong-falcate; pet. narrower, subfalcate; lip fleshy, white striped brown, base oblong, apex rounded, margin minutely serrate, calli ridged, lateral lobes erect, square, papillose. Autumn–winter. Nepal.

E.sanderiana (Rchb. f.) Rchb. f. See *Euanthe sanderiana*.

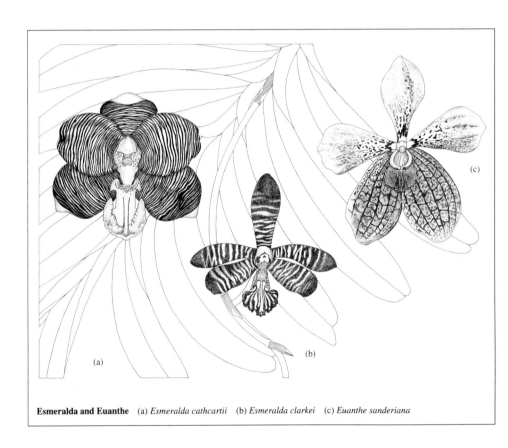

Esmeralda and Euanthe   (a) *Esmeralda cathcartii*   (b) *Esmeralda clarkei*   (c) *Euanthe sanderiana*

Euanthe Schltr. (From Gk *euanthes*, blooming, referring to the spectacular inflorescence.) 1 species, a monopodial, epiphyte. Stems tall, robust, clothed with leaf bases. Leaves to 40×5cm, ligulate, leathery, centrally grooved, recurved, alternate, in 2 ranks. Raceme ascending, axillary, 7–10-flowered; flowers 6–10cm diam., flat; sepals broadly ovate to suborbicular, dorsal sepal rose, tinged white, variably spotted blood red, lateral sepals tawny-yellow, net-veined or flushed brick-red to rose; petals similar to dorsal sepal, ovate-rhombic, dotted red; lip honey-coloured, streaked, veined or stained purple-red on midlobe, midlobe oblong, truncate, fleshy, spreading, apically recurved, basally saccate, disc with 3 ridges, lateral lobes round, erect, flanking column. Philippines.

CULTIVATION   As for *Vanda*.

E.sanderiana (Rchb. f.) Schltr. (*Esmeralda sanderiana* (Rchb. f.) Rchb. f.; *Vanda sanderiana* Rchb. f.).

Eulophia R. Br. ex Lindl. (From Gk *eulophos*, well-plumed, referring to the prominent crests on the lip of many species.) Over 250 species of terrestrials with pseudobulbs, tubers or fleshy roots. Leaves appearing with or after flowers, lanceolate to linear, sometimes plicate, sometimes fleshy. Inflorescence racemose, rarely paniculate, few- to many-flowered, arising beside leafy growth; flowers small or large, sometimes very showy; sepals and petals similar or dissimilar; lip almost always spurred, usually trilobed but sometimes entire, usually with crests or papillae inside; column long or short, with or without column foot; anther terminal, covered with an anther cap. Tropical and S Africa, Madagascar, W Indies, tropical America, southern US.

CULTIVATION   Cultivation as for evergreen, warm-growing *Calanthe* spp. except for those with succulent, aloe-like leaves. They require a sand/loam/bark mix (not bark and leafmould), full sunlight and a dry rest except when in growth.

E.alta (L.) Fawcett & Rendle.
Robust, 40–150cm; corm fleshy, 3–8cm. Lvs 4–6, to 100×3–10cm, linear-lanceolate, plicate, appearing with fls. Scape with several scarious sheaths; raceme laxly many-fld; fls green and dull purple-maroon; pedicel and ovary 20mm; bracts 20×4mm, linear; dorsal sep. 18×6mm, oblanceolate, acuminate, lateral sep. 23×7–8mm, obliquely oblanceolate, acuminate; pet. 13×7mm, obovate, obtuse; lip hinged to base of column foot, trilobed, 11–17mm long, 18–28mm wide when flattened, lateral lobes erect, midlobe broadly ovate or semi-orbicular, somewhat recurved, edge undulate, with 2 papillose crests; spur represented by rounded sac; column 14mm. W & C Africa, tropical America, Florida, W Indies.

E.congoensis Cogn. See *E.guineensis*.

E.cristata (Sw.) Steud.
Robust, to 1.5m, arising from chain of underground tubers. Lvs about 50×2–6cm, lanceolate, appearing after fls. Racemes 20–45cm, 13–40-fld; fls pink-lilac, lip purple; pedicel and ovary 2–3cm; bracts 1–2cm, lanceolate, acuminate; sep. 18–24mm, oblong, acute or obtuse, lateral sep. slightly longer than dorsal sep.; pet. similar but almost twice as wide; lip 13–24mm, trilobed, lateral lobes broadly rounded, midlobe elliptic-ovate, obtuse, with 2 semicircular, entire keels towards base and 5–7 broken keels in front; spur 3–4mm, conical with an acute, sometimes upturned apex. W & C Africa, Sudan, Ethiopia, Uganda.

E.cucullata (Sw.) Steud.
Robust, to 1m, arising from chain of underground tubers. Lvs 30–50×1cm, linear-lanceolate, ribbed, appearing after flowering. Scape with several scarious sheaths; raceme 10–20cm, laxly 2–10-fld; sep. green, tinged purple, pet. and lip pale to deep pink or purple, yellow or white in throat; pedicel and ovary 20mm; bracts 25mm, purple, lanceolate, acuminate; sep. 15–30×3–12mm, ovate, acuminate, reflexed; pet. 14–25×12–25mm, more or less orbicular, overlying column; lip 20–35×40mm, obscurely trilobed, lateral lobes broadly rounded, midlobe transversely oblong, truncate or slightly emarginate, with 2 teeth about 6mm long in throat; spur broadly saccate, 4–10mm; column arched, 10–20mm. Tropical Africa (widespread); Comoros Is.

E.euglossa (Rchb. f.) Rchb. f.
Pseudobulbs elongate, tapering, about 20cm. Lvs 20–30×1.5–6cm, lanceolate, fairly well developed at flower-ing time. Scape 40–200cm, with several sheaths; raceme 20–40cm, many-fld; fls pale green, lip white with pink or purple veins; pedicel and ovary 12mm; bracts 2.5–4cm, lanceolate, acuminate; sep. and pet. 12–14mm, oblong-lanceolate, acuminate; lip 12mm, trilobed, lateral lobes triangular, small, midlobe ovate, crenulate, with 2–3 keels; spur 6–8mm, clavate; column 6mm. W Africa, Zaire, Uganda.

E.gracilis Lindl.
Terrestrial, rarely epiphytic; pseudobulbous at base. Lvs 30–45×1–5cm, linear-lanceolate, acute, appearing with fls. Scape to 1m; raceme laxly many-fld; fls green; pedicel and ovary 12–18mm; bracts slightly shorter, lanceolate, acuminate; sep. 10–12mm, lanceolate, acute; pet. similar but smaller; lip 7–8mm, funnel-shaped, truncate, the front margin fimbriate, with a tooth-like callus near apex; spur 8mm, conical at base, constricted in middle, clavate at apex; column 4mm, stout. W Africa, Zaire, Angola.

E.guineensis Lindl. (*E.congoensis* Cogn.).
40–90cm; pseudobulbous at base. Lvs 10–45×4–10cm, obovate or elliptical, plicate, in a tuft at base of plant, appearing with fls. Scape with several sheaths; raceme 20–30cm, several- to many-fld; sep. and pet. green to chocolate or purple-green, lip pale to deep lilac or rose with magenta blotch in throat; pedicel and ovary arched, 20mm; bracts 8–10mm; sep. and pet. 20–30×4–6mm, linear-lanceolate, acute, curled back at tips; lip 20–40mm, trilobed near base, lateral lobes small, midlobe ovate, elliptic or obovate, more or less acute at apex; spur 10–30mm, slender, tapering from conical base; column 8mm long, 10mm wide. W Africa, Zaire, Uganda, Tanzania, Angola. var. *purpurata* Rchb. f. ex Kotschy (*E.quartiniana* A. Rich.). Differs from the typical variety (described above) as follows: lvs not developed, or only just starting to develop, at flowering time; midlobe of lip broadly obovate or suborbicular, rounded or emarginate at apex. var. *guineensis* occurs in forest and var. *purpurata* in savanna. W Africa, C Africa, Sudan, Ethiopia, E Africa to Zimbabwe.

E.horsfallii (Batem.) Summerh. (*E.porphyroglossa* Bolus; *Lissochilus giganteus* Welw.; *Lissochilus horsfallii* Bateman). Robust, up to 2m, with obscure pseudobulbs and thick, fleshy roots. Lvs in tuft at base, to 250×10cm, evergreen, petiolate, the lamina lanceolate, dark green, ribbed. Scape with a few sheathing lvs; raceme 30×11cm, many-fld; sep. shiny olive green, pet. pink, lip purple, lateral lobes green, veined purple;

Eulophia   (a) *E.streptopetala*   (b) *E.speciosa*   (c) *E.horsfallii*   (d) *E.guineensis*

pedicel and ovary 4cm; bracts 2cm, brown and withered at flowering time; sep. 25×10mm, erect, spathulate, acute; pet. 30×22mm, ovate, overlying column; lip 35mm, trilobed, lateral lobes erect, midlobe 20×13mm, with 3 fringed, cream lamellae down centre; spur 10mm; column 20mm, stout, arching; anth. cap purple. Tropical Africa (widespread).

E.lurida (Sw.) Lindl. See *Graphorkis lurida.*

E.macra Ridl.
60–120cm; pseudobulbs clustered, ovoid-conical, 3–5cm, irregularly ribbed. Lvs 3–4, well developed at flowering time, 40–60cm×3–7mm, narrowly linear. Scape with a few thin sheaths; panicle laxly many-fld; fls small, dull-coloured; pedicel 5mm, ovary 1mm; bracts 1–2mm; sep. 6×1mm, lanceolate, acute; pet. slightly shorter and wider; lip 8×5mm, entire, obovate, fimbriate in front, with several small crests in the throat; spur 3mm, somewhat club-shaped; column 1.5mm, apiculate; ovary 1mm. Madagascar.

E.paivaeana (Rchb. f.) Summerh. See *E.streptopetala.*

E.petersii (Rchb. f.) Rchb. f.
Robust, to 3m; pseudobulbs aerial, clustered, 3–30×1–8cm, ovoid or cylindrical, ribbed, yellow-green, 2–3-lvd towards apex. Lvs to 55×1–4.5cm, linear or linear-lanceolate, stiff, succulent, margins finely toothed. Scape with several sheaths, 2–4cm; panicle laxly many-fld; sep. and pet. apple green tinged with purple-brown, lip white with purple lamellae, lateral lobes green with purple veins; pedicel and ovary 4cm; sep. 20–30×5–6mm, linear or narrowly oblanceolate, erect, apex curled back; pet. 16–22×5–8mm, narrowly oblong, apex recurved; lip 16–30×8–17mm, trilobed, lateral lobes rounded, erect, midlobe 12–14mm wide, oblong, obtuse, margins undulate, with 3 lamellae turning to papillae near apex; spur 2–8mm, slightly incurved; column 10–13mm, with column foot less than 1mm long attached to base and lateral lobes of lip. Arabian peninsula; eastern Africa from Ethiopia to S Africa.

E.porphyroglossa (Rchb. f. Bol. See *E.horsfallii.*
E.pulchra (Thouars) Lindl. See *Oeceoclades pulchra.*
E.quartiniana A. Rich. See *E.guineensis* var. *purpurata.*
E.saundersiana Rchb. f. See *Oeceoclades saundersiana.*
E.scripta (Thouars) Lindl. See *Graphorkis scripta.*

E.speciosa (R. Br. ex Lindl.) Bol. (*Lissochilus speciosus* R. Br. ex Lindl.).
To 1.5m, arising from underground tubers. Lvs 2–3, fleshy, lanceolate, acute, appearing after flowering. Scape with 3 sheaths; raceme rather laxly several- to many-fld; sep. green, pet. and lip bright shiny yellow with 2–3 faint purple lines

radiating from mouth of spur; pedicel and ovary 20–25mm; bracts 9–10mm; sep. 7–10×3–5mm, reflexed, ovate, apiculate; pet. 16–20×16–22mm, spreading, suborbicular; lip 25×15–20mm, trilobed, lateral lobes erect, adnate to base of column for 3mm, midlobe oblong, obtuse, with 3–7 longitudinal ridges; spur 4–8mm, conical; column 7–10mm. Widespread in eastern Africa from Kenya to S Africa.

E.streptopetala Lindl. (*E.paivaeana* (Rchb. f.) Summerh.; *Lissochilus krebsii* Rchb. f.).
Robust, to 2m; pseudobulbs partly aerial, clustered, to 8×3cm, conical, ribbed, with several nodes, 5–6-lvd towards apex. Lvs 30–75×2–11cm, lanceolate, acute, pleated, partly developed at flowering time. Scape with a few sheathing lvs; raceme (rarely panicle) many-fld; sep. green, blotched with purple-brown, pet. bright yellow on outer surface, creamy yellow on inner, lip yellow, lateral lobes purple, spur red-purple; pedicel and ovary 20–25mm, arched so that fls face down; sep. 10–20×5–9mm, obovate, erect and spreading; pet. 10–20×10–20mm, suborbicular, lying parallel to column; lip 10–20×8–18mm, trilobed, lateral lobes erect, midlobe elliptic, convex, projecting forwards, with 3 longitudinal crests; spur 2–4mm, cylindrical, rounded at apex; column 5–9mm. Ethiopia, Kenya, Uganda, south to S Africa.

E.taitensis Cribb & Pfennig.
Pseudobulbs 10–18cm, to 3cm diam. at base, conical, set close together. Lvs 8–12, arising from nodes, arranged in fan, to 45×3cm, green, rigid, margin serrate. Raceme to 1m; bracts withered by flowering time; fls malodorous; sep. and pet. green-white with dark maroon marks, lip white to cream with purple veins; sep. and pet. oblong, sep. about 25×10mm, pet. 19×10mm; lip 22×20mm with 3 warty crests, obscurely trilobed, lateral lobes erect, midlobe undulate; spur 2mm. Kenya.

E.zeyheri Hook. f.
30–40cm, arising from chain of rather flattened underground tubers. Lvs to 55×5cm, lanceolate, acute, ribbed, just starting to develop at flowering time. Scape with a few sheaths; raceme short, densely many-fld; fls primrose yellow, midlobe of lip with orange blotch, lateral lobes with large purple blotch; pedicel and ovary 10–15mm; sep. 38–40×10mm, elliptic, acute; pet. similar, 35mm, all projecting forwards; lip 30×22mm, trilobed, with 2 keels running from base to junction of lobes, lateral lobes erect, rounded, midlobe 15mm wide, obovate, obtuse, the orange blotch covered with papillae; spur 4–5mm, horizontal, cylindrical; column 5mm. Nigeria, Zaire, eastern Africa from Sudan to S Africa.

Eulophiella Rolfe (Diminutive of *Eulophia*.) 3 species of robust epiphytes with long pseudobulbs. Leaves 3–6, plicate, articulated at apex of sheath. Inflorescence racemose, arising from base of mature pseudobulb; flowers large; lateral sepals adnate to column-foot; lip not spurred, trilobed, suborbicular, with crests or lamellae inside; column slender with channel on anterior face; rostellum trilobed, midlobe smaller than lateral lobes; pollinia sessile. Madagascar.

CULTIVATION As for *Chysis* but in warm conditions.

E.elizabethae Lind. & Rolfe.
Pseudobulbs 10–15×2.5cm, fusiform to oblong, 4–5-lvd. Lvs 45–60×3.5–5cm, narrowly lanceolate, acuminate. Raceme 35–45cm, arching, 12–15-fld; fls 3–4cm diam., white, sep. tinged with rose-pink outside, lip with a large yellow blotch; peduncle, bracts, ovary and pedicel vinous red; ovary and pedicel 2.5–3cm; sep. 20×11mm, elliptic, obtuse; pet. 17×13mm, elliptic-obovate; lip 14×13mm, trilobed, lateral lobes rounded, midlobe broadly obovate, slightly hairy at base with near the base a semicircular callus prolonged in front into 2 slightly divergent keels ending in teeth; column 7–10mm, foot 2mm.

E.peetersiana Kränzl. See *E.roempleriana*.

E.perrieri Schltr.
Similar to *E.elizabethae*, differing mainly in erect infl. with longer peduncle and smaller fls (2cm diam.). Fls white, tinged with red on outside, lip with a red spot at base of column and 2 yellow blotches, one at the base and one at the junction of the lobes; sep. 14×12mm, broadly ovate; pet. 13×10mm, obovate; lip 9×9mm, midlobe quadrate, the crests in the throat short, parallel and entire.

E.roempleriana (Rchb. f.) Schltr. (*E.peetersiana* Kränzl.).
Robust; rhiz. 15–60mm diam., elongated, bearing many wiry roots; pseudobulbs set 10–30mm apart, 8–30×2–4cm, narrowly ovoid, 4–8-lvd. Lvs 90–120×8–10cm, lanceolate, petiolate, erect or recurved. Raceme erect, to 120cm, 15–25-fld; fls pale to deep pink; ovary and pedicel 5–6cm, dull red; sep. and pet. 35–45mm, obovate-oblong, sep. slightly narrower than pet.; lip more or less orbicular, 40–45mm wide with 3 lamellae toward base, trilobed in apical half; side lobes erect, incurved; midlobe emarginate; column 2–2.5cm.

E. Rolfei (*E.elizabethae* × *E.roempleriana*.) Lvs several, lanceolate, acuminate. Raceme erect, to about 30-fld. Fls 6cm diam., intermediate between parents but resembling more *E.roempleriana*, pale to deep rose-pink, pale pink to almost white in centre, the lip with orange crests; sep. broadly ovate, obtuse; pet. broadly ovate, obtuse; lip projecting, trilobed, lateral lobes erect, midlobe obovate. Garden origin.

Eurychone Schltr. (From Gk *eurys*, broad, and *chone*, funnel.) 2 species of monopodial epiphytes. Stems short. Leaves several, set close together. Racemes axillary, pendent; flowers large, scented; sepals and petals free, similar; lip almost horizontal, broad, funnel-shaped, somewhat trilobed, narrowing into a spur; column short and stout; pollinia 2; caudicle and viscidium 1. Tropical Africa.

CULTIVATION As for *Aerangis*.

E.galeandrae (Rchb. f.) Schltr.
Stem short, 4–5-lvd. Lvs 7–17×1–3cm, narrowly cuneate, unequally bilobed at apex. Raceme to 15cm, 2–10-fld; fls white or pale pink with maroon-red streaks inside; tepals 14–18mm, linear-oblong, obtuse; lip 15–23mm, broadly funnel-shaped, obscurely trilobed; spur 8mm, club-shaped, apex reflexed; column stout, 4mm. Zaire, Gabon.

E.rothschildiana (O'Brien) Schltr. (*Angraecum rothschildianum* O'Brien).
Stem to 8cm; roots numerous. Lvs 6–20×1.5–7cm, broadly oblanceolate or oblong, unequally bilobed at apex, lobes sub-
acute. Racemes to 9cm, 2–12-fld; fls about 6cm diam., tepals white, usually tinged with pale green, lip white, green in centre, with chocolate-brown or purple blotch at base, spur green-brown or pink; sep. 20–25×5.5–7mm, elliptic, acute or apiculate; pet. slightly shorter and broader; lip 20–25mm long and wide, emarginate at apex, the edge undulate and erose; spur 15–25mm with a wide mouth, narrowed in middle and thickened and recurved towards apex; column 8–10mm. W Africa, Zaire, Uganda.

Flickingeria A.D. Hawkes. (For Edward A. Flickinger.) Some 70 species of epiphytes. Rhizome creeping or short, tufted with branched, erect aerial stems, each pseudobulb with a terminal leaf. Pseudobulbs and leaves diminish in size away from root system. Inflorescence bracteate, pseudo-terminal; flowers small, short-lived, produced singly in succession, or clustered, fragrant; lateral sepals fused to the column base; lip trilobed, midlobe apically fringed, folded or bilobed, keels 2–3, lateral lobes upward-pointing, almost enveloping column. Tropical Asia to Polynesia and Australasia.

CULTIVATION As for the warm-growing *Coelogyne* species.

F.comata (Bl.) A.D. Hawkes.
Stems to 1m. Pseudobulbs to 30mm, grooved, initially with brown papery bracts. Lvs elliptic to obovate, coriaceous, often arching. Fls to 25mm diam., cream often spotted purple; perianth seg. spreading; lip to 20mm, basal margins undulate-crispate, apically pubesc., midlobe tapering, blunt, lateral lobes irregularly dentate. NE Australia, New Guinea, Indonesia, Malaysia.

F.convexa (Bl.) A.D. Hawkes.
Stems slender, branching. Pseudobulbs spherical, glossy, remote. Lvs to 8cm, ovate, fleshy. Fls to 15mm diam., cream, lip yellow and red; perianth seg. spreading; sep. triangular, overlapping pet. base; lip to 10mm, forward-pointing, somewhat concave, midlobe apically bilobed, lateral lobes erect. NE Australia, Indonesia, Malaysia.

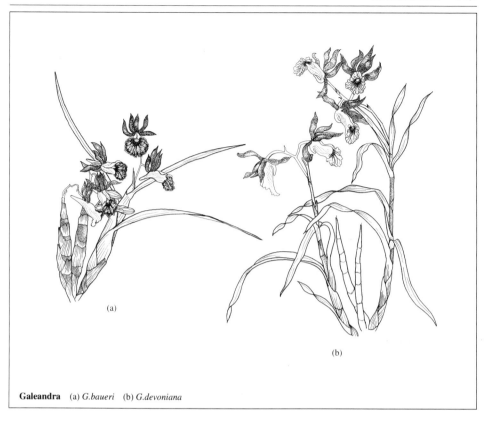

Galeandra   (a) *G.baueri*   (b) *G.devoniana*

Galeandra Lindl. (From Lat. *galea*, helmet, and Gk *andra*, stamens, describing the anther cap of some species.) About 26 species of terrestrials and epiphytes. Rhizomes short. Pseudobulbs erect, cane-like, narrow-fusiform to cylindric, or depressed-globose in terrestrial species, furrowed and clothed with coarse, grey sheaths. Leaves to 8, erect, plicate, narrow-lanceolate, grassy, slightly scarious, bright green, keeled, alternate in 2 ranks, bases sheathing stem and articulate, blades soon abscising. Inflorescence a few-flowered, terminal, nodding raceme, sometimes branched, bracteate; flowers often appearing suspended; sepals free, equal, spreading or forward-pointing, lanceolate; petals similar to sepals or shorter and wider, oblanceolate, reflexed, lip large, entire or obscurely 3-lobed, folded-tubular, adnate to base of column, spurred, the spur projecting behind insertion of perianth on ovary; column clavate, short, the foot sometimes pubescent. C & S America.

CULTIVATION   For the intermediate house, they bear clusters of spindle-shaped pseudobulbs clothed with grassy leaves and topped with slender nodding stalks hung with showy tubular flowers in shades of white, rose and chocolate. Pot in an open bark mix with additional moss and leafmould. Water and feed frequently during growth, shading from full sun. After flowering, reduce temperatures and water supplies and rest in bright sunlight. Propagate by division.

G.batemanii Rolfe. See *G.baueri.*

G.baueri Lindl. (*G.batemanii* Rolfe).
Pseudobulbs narrow-fusiform, to 30cm. Lvs to 20×2cm, linear-lanceolate. Sep. and pet. to 2×0.5cm, ochre to chocolate brown; lip to 5×3.5cm and rhombic if spread out, otherwise folded-tubular, margins crenate, forward-projecting or recurved, pale rose purple, base white or tan, spur to 2cm, slender, curved. Mexico to Panama and Surinam.

G.beyrichii Rchb. f. (*G.viridis* Burb. Rodr.).
Terrestrial. Rhiz. stout, scaly. Stems to 90cm, terete, slender above, pseudobulbous, swollen and buried at base, sheathed with reduced lvs. Raceme erect; fls numerous, to 4.5cm diam., pale green, lip green-white edged crimson and nerved lime green at base, tubular, pubesc. within. Florida, W Indies, Hispaniola, S America to Peru.

G.devoniana Lindl.
Pseudobulbs to 75cm, narrow-fusiform. Lvs to 20×1cm, linear-lanceolate. Sep. and pet. to 4.5×1cm, elliptic-lanceolate, somewhat falcate, olive green or pale brown stained or lined chocolate to oxblood; lip to 5×4.5cm, obcordate, obscurely 3-lobed if spread out, otherwise tubular, undulate, white veined rose or garnet in apical half, spur to 1.5cm, incurved, veined garnet or sulphur-green; column ivory. Guyana, Venezuela, Brazil.

G.viridis Barb. Rodr. See *G.beyrichii.*

Gastrochilus D. Don. (From Gk *gaster*, belly and *cheilos*, lip, referring to the saccate-swollen lip of the flower.) Some 20 species of monopodial, short-stemmed, epiphytes. Leaves few, coriaceous, alternate, 2-ranked, ligulate to oblong. Inflorescence an axillary raceme; sepals and petals similar, spreading; lip basally saccate, the sides fused to the column wings, midlobe forward-pointing, entire or fringed, pubescent. Himalaya, E Asia, Japan.

CULTIVATION   Epiphytes resembling small *Vanda* or *Trudelia* spp. but often with arched or wholly pendulous stems, broader leaves and rounded flowers in capitate racemes. They favour intermediate house conditions and should be planted in a loose mix of bark, dried FYM and coconut fibre in baskets, or attached to rafts. When growing most actively (as with all monopodial orchids, this can be readily judged by the fresh aerial root tips and leaf emergence), mist daily, plunge every second day and foliar-feed each fortnight: at this time, temperatures and humidity should be high and protection afforded from full sunlight. In the winter months, increase light and decrease humidity and water supplies, only misting occasionally on warm mornings.

G.acutifolius (Lindl.) O.Kuntze.
To 35cm. Lvs 6–10, oblong-lanceolate, fleshy, acute, to 15×3cm. Fls to 8, yellow or pale green, tinged and dotted dull brown, to 2cm diam.; sep. and pet. almost equal, oblong-lanceolate, fleshy, weakly reflexed; lip interior keeled, midlobe reniform, obscurely trilobed, papillose-pubesc., margins jagged, lateral lobes narrow, entire. N India to Thailand.

G.bellinus (Rchb. f.) O.Kuntze (*Saccolabium bellinum* Rchb. f.).
To 10cm. Lvs lorate, 10–20cm, coriaceous, semi-rigid. Infl. erect, stout; fls to 7, fragrant, thickly textured, to 4cm diam., yellow, blotched red to maroon; sep. and pet. obovate-oblong, fleshy, incurved and spreading; lip yellow, apex irregularly incised, callus papillose. Burma.

G.calceolaris (Buch.-Ham. ex Sm.) D. Don (*Aerides calceolaris* Buch.-Ham. ex Sm.).
Stem to 8cm, usually much shorter. Lvs narrow, linear-oblong, to 30×3cm. Infl. shorter than lvs; fls to 1.7cm diam., crowded, pale green to bronze, speckled red-brown, waxy, slightly fragrant, lip white spotted red-brown, spur yellow; dorsal sep. ovate-oblong, lateral sep. narrower, oblong, falcate; pet. equal to or shorter than sep., oblong-ovate; lip midlobe semicircular, margins fringed, callus pubesc., lateral lobes inconspicuous, erect. Himalaya, Indochina to Malaysia.

G.dasypogon (Sm.) O.Kuntze.
Stem pendent. Lvs 3–5, oblong, to 20×4cm. Fls crowded, to 2.5cm diam., bright yellow, spotted maroon; sep. and pet. oblong-lanceolate, subequal, spreading; lip midlobe semicircular, fleshy, margins with incisions tapering, pointed. Winter. India. See also *G.obliquus.*

G.lanceolatus Ridl. See *Scaphochlamys lanceolata.*
G.lancifolius Ridl. See *Scaphochlamys malaccana.*

G.obliquus (Lindl.) O.Kuntze.
Commonly confused with *G.dasypogon* and grown under that name. Tepals deep yellow; lip white edged purple-red and spotted purple-red within, midlobe broad, fringed, white blotched yellow and finely spotted red. India to Vietnam.

G.scaphochlamys Ridl. See *Scaphochlamys malaccana.*

Geodorum Jackson. (From Gk *geo*, earth, and *doron*, gift, referring to its terrestrial habit.) Some 16 species of terrestrials. Pseudobulbs subterranean. Leaves few, plicate, petiolate. Inflorescence lateral, dense, arching to pendulous at tip; flowers small, waxy, fragrant; sepals and petals similar, almost joined basally; lip sessile, erect, basally ventricose or saccate, apically fused with column foot. Indomalaya, W Pacific.

CULTIVATION   As for the evergreen, warm-growing *Calanthe* spp.

G.citrinum Jackson.
Lvs to 35cm, long-petioled. Scape to 30cm, 5–10-fld; fls green-yellow with red-purple longitudinal stripes on the lip apex; dorsal sep. 25mm; pet. to 10mm wide; lip carinate, marginally recurved, apically notched, disc with irregular central rows of wrinkles or papillae. Burma, Thailand, Malaysia.

G.densiflorum (Lam.) Schltr. (*G.purpureum* R. Br.).
Lvs to 30cm, 2–4, lanceolate to oblong-elliptic. Floral bracts linear-lanceolate, acuminate; sep. and pet. to 12mm, linear-oblong to oblanceolate-oblong, white, pink or purple; pet. broader, obtuse; lip white, striped purple, constricted centrally with 2 round apical lobes, disc basally callose, veined or warty at tip. Burma, Malaysia, Indonesia.

G.purpureum R. Br. See *G.densiflorum.*

Glossodia R. Br. (From Gk *glossa*, tongue, and *-oides*, like, referring to the tongue-shaped or strap-shaped calli at the lip base.) 2 species of terrestrials allied to *Caladenia*. Tubers small, ovoid, subterranean. Stems slender, unifoliate. Leaves emerging from scarious sheath, lying flat on ground, oblong to lanceolate. Inflorescence erect, 1- or 2-flowered; flowers blue to purple; sepals and petals subequal, spreading; lip short-unguiculate, simple, entire, bicallose at base; column erect, incurved, bialate, anther terminal, erect, bilocular, pollinia 4, lamellate, rostellum granular. E Australia.

CULTIVATION   As for *Caladenia*.

G.brunonis Endl. See *Elythranthera brunonis*.

G.major R. Br. Stems to 38cm. Lvs to 10×2cm, oblong or oblong-lanceolate, pubesc. Fls to 6.5cm diam.; tepals purple or mauve to white, to 2.5cm, lanceolate, acute to obtuse, often dotted purple, glandular-pubesc. above; lip to 1.2×0.5cm, ovate-lanceolate, anterior portion purple, glabrous, basal portion white, pubesc., calli large, linear, erect, purple.

G.minor R. Br. Resembles *G.major* except smaller. Lvs to 4cm, broadly lanceolate. Fls to 3cm diam.; tepals deep blue-violet, sometimes white, broadly lanceolate, obtuse, paler below; lip ovate, acute, base deep blue-violet, calli linear-clavate.

Gomesa R. Br. (For Dr Bernadino Antonio Gomes, Portuguese botanist and physician.) Some 20 species of epiphytes or lithophytes. Pseudobulbs short, usually somewhat compressed. Leaves 2–4 per pseudobulb, 1–2 borne apically, the others basally sheathing, elongate, petiolate. Inflorescence a basal raceme, axillary, arcuate or pendent, densely many-flowered, flowers small, fragrant, usually white, yellow or green; dorsal sepal and petals subsimilar, free, spreading, lateral sepals free or connate; lip articulated to column base, reflexed above, simple to trilobed, lateral lobes erect, enveloping column; midlobe spreading or reflexed, disc bicallose; column erect, subterete, apex usually winged, footless, pollinia 2, ovoid or subglobose, waxy, sulcate. Brazil.

CULTIVATION   Epiphytes for the cool or intermediate house. *G.crispa* is the most often encountered, a neat plant carrying full, arching racemes of lightly scented lime-green flowers. All require an open mix of fern fibre, medium-grade coarse bark and sphagnum. Water, feed and syringe freely when in growth and keep in buoyant, humid conditions in light shade. On completion of growths, move to a cooler, brighter place, watering only to prevent shrivelling of pseudobulbs. Propagate by division when repotting.

G.crispa (Lindl.) Klotzsch & Rchb. f.
Pseudobulbs to 10×2.5cm, oblong or oblong-conical, laterally compressed, clustered, often matt or slightly glaucous yellow-green, apically bifoliate. Lvs to 28×3.5cm, fairly thin-textured, ligulate or narrowly ligulate-lanceolate, acute or acuminate somewhat decurved, midrib prominent beneath. Infl. to 22cm, pendent; fls to 2cm across, fragrant, yellow, lime, olive or sea-green edged yellow, most parts strongly undulate; sep. to 10×2mm, usually free, oblong or oblong-ligulate, acute; pet. to 10×3mm, oblong or oblong-spathulate, subacute; lip to 8×4mm, simple, broadly oblong, obtuse, strongly recurved, disc bicarinate or bicristate, undulate-dentate sometimes very much paler or tinted rusty red; column to 5mm, subclavate. Brazil.

G.laxiflora (Lindl.) Klotzsch & Rchb. f. (*Odontoglossum laxiflorum* (Lindl.) Rchb. f.).
Similar to *G.crispa* except pseudobulbs smaller. Lvs acuminate. Infl. to 30cm; fls smaller; sep. and pet. not undulate, lateral sep. connate; lip ovate-oblong, disc prominently bicarinate. Brazil.

G.planifolia (Lindl.) Klotzsch & Rchb. f. (*Odontoglossum planifolium* (Lindl.) Rchb. f.).
Pseudobulbs to 8×2.5cm, oblong, apically bifoliate. Lvs to 20×3.5cm, fairly thick-textured, narrowly lanceolate, acute. Infl. to 25cm, arching, fls to 2cm across, yellow-green, highly

fragrant; dorsal sep. to 9×4mm, subspathulate, obtuse, lateral sep. to 9×6mm, oblong-ligulate, acute, connate, crispate; pet. to 9×4mm, oblong-spathulate, crispate; lip to 9×6mm, ovate, acute, concave, crispate-undulate, disc bicristate, undulate-denticulate with 2 oblong tubercles; column to 6mm, minutely biauriculate, subclavate. Brazil.

G.recurva R. Br. (*Odontoglossum recurvum* (R. Br.) Lindl.).
Pseudobulbs to 7×3.5cm, narrowly ovoid, compressed, apically bifoliate. Lvs to 30×3cm, subcoriaceous, linear-oblanceolate, acute. Infl. to 35cm, pendent; fls yellow-green, fragrant; sep. to 12×3mm, narrowly oblong-spathulate, acute, spreading, lateral sep. connate; pet. to 11×4mm, oblong-spathulate, apiculate or rounded; lip to 10×6mm, ovate, acute or obtuse, strongly recurved, disc prominently bicarinate; column to 5mm, fleshy, clavate, apex truncate. Brazil.

G.sessilis Barb. Rodr.
Pseudobulbs to 5×2.5cm, ovoid to oblong, compressed, apically bifoliate. Lvs to 20×2.5cm, thin-textured, narrowly lanceolate, acute or acuminate. Infl. to 35cm; fls to 1cm, short-stalked, yellow-green; sep. to 8×2mm, linear-ligulate, acute or acuminate, lateral sep. connate; pet. to 7×2mm, narrowly ligulate, acute or acuminate, undulate; lip to 6×3mm, ovate-oblong, acute, undulate, disc prominently bicristate, denticulate; column to 4mm, minutely biauriculate. Brazil.

Gongora Ruiz & Pav. (For Don Antonio Caballero y Gongora, Bishop of Cordoba, late 18th century.) Some 50 species of epiphytes, allied to *Stanhopea*. Rhizome short, creeping to elongate. Pseudobulbs ovoid, squat cylindric-pyriform, or ovoid-conical, stout, strongly ribbed or grooved with age, fleshy, enveloped by several fibrous overlapping bracts, apex 2–3-leaved. Leaves large, loosely plicate, conduplicate at base of blade narrowing to a grooved petiole. Inflorescence a long, arching or pendulous, basal raceme, loosely few- to many-flowered; flowers strongly scented, often dull-coloured and spotted, alternate or opposite in 2 close ranks along slender straight or flexuous axis, resembling a swan in outline or a hovering insect; pedicels slender, incurved, thus presenting lip facing downwards and into rachis; dorsal sepal usually adnate to column, erect-spreading; lateral sepals oblique, adnate to column foot, spreading or reflexed, wider than dorsal sepal; petals oblique, smaller than sepals, adnate to column, erect and spreading above; lip continuous with column foot, fleshy-waxy, narrow, complex, hypochile erect, corniculate or aristate, epichile variously gibbous-saccate to laterally compressed, apex bilobed, acute or acuminate; column slender, slightly arched, produced into a foot at base, wingless to broadly winged at apex, anther terminal, operculate, incumbent, unilocular or imperfectly bilocular, pollinia 2, waxy, ovoid to narrowly oblong. W Indies, Mexico to Peru & Brazil.

CULTIVATION   Superb orchids for the intermediate house; they produce long, chain-like racemes of gracefully held, insect-like blooms, often highly fragrant. Best grown in baskets or long-toms where the flowers can be shown to advantage. Cultivation as for the allied *Stanhopea*, but with rather more shade, moisture and higher temperatures when in growth.

G.armeniaca (Lindl. & Paxt.) Rchb. f. (*Acropera armeniaca* Lindl. & Paxt.; *Acropera cornuta* Klotzsch).
Pseudobulbs 3–4.5×1.75–2.5cm, ovoid, 2-lvd. Lvs 15–22×3–4.5cm, elliptic-lanceolate, acuminate. Infl. elongate, pendent, few to many-fld; fls to 5cm, inverted, waxy; sep. salmon-pink, yellow or orange, sometimes spotted purple-brown, dorsal sep. 1–1.8×0.75–1.2cm, broadly oblong to elliptic-oblong, acute, obtuse or apiculate, erect, concave, lateral sep. 1–1.7×1–1.4cm, obliquely ovate, acute, obtuse or apiculate, spreading or reflexed; pet. to 0.6×0.3cm, pale salmon-pink or orange, lanceolate, tips recurved; lip short-clawed, mesochile to 1.2cm, yellow, inflated, calceiform, obtuse, bearing an erect, linear-lanceolate projection; column to 1cm, subclavate above. Costa Rica, Panama, Nicaragua.

G.bufonia Lindl. See *G.quinquenervis*.

G.cassidea Rchb. f.
Pseudobulbs 4–6×2.75–4cm, ovoid-conical, slightly compressed, light green, 2-lvd. Lvs 20–36×4.5–6.5cm, lanceolate to elliptic-lanceolate, acuminate. Infl. to 30cm, pendulous, loosely few-fld; axis filiform, green-brown; fls green-brown to pink-brown; dorsal sep. 1.75–2.5×1.25–2cm, broadly elliptic to subrotund, cucullate, slightly narrower than lateral sep., broadly oblong to elliptic, obtuse to apiculate; pet. to 1.2×0.4cm, recurved, obliquely oblong-lanceolate, aristate; lip to 2.5×0.5cm; hypochile saccate, bilobulate, lobules erect, cuneate-obovate, subacute, epichile 0.9–1.3cm, basally gibbous, centre narrowly linear, apical lobules 2, linear-lanceolate; column to 1.5cm, mottled purple, broadly winged at apex. Guatemala, Honduras, Nicaragua.

G.galeata (Lindl.) Rchb. f. (*Acropera loddigesii* Lindl.).
Pseudobulbs to 3.5–4.5×1.75–2.5cm, clustered, ovoid, 1–2-lvd. Lvs 18–32×3.5–4.5cm, broadly lanceolate, acute. Infl. 15–28cm, arching to pendent, many-fld; peduncle purple; fls to 5cm, long-lived, yellow-brown to cream-green; sep. 2–2.5×1–1.2cm, ovate to ovate-oblong, concave, spreading, obtuse, reflexed; pet. to 0.6cm, oblong-falcate, apex bidentate; lip to 1.25×0.9cm, usually a brighter yellow or ochre than the tepals, hypochile large, recurved, epichile short, saccate; column to 1cm, yellow-green spotted purple, slightly bialate. Mexico.

G.jenischii hort. ex Rchb. f. See *G.quinquenervis*.
G.maculata Lindl. See *G.quinquenervis*.

G.quinquenervis Ruiz & Pav. (*G.bufonia* Lindl.; *G.jenischii* hort. ex Rchb. f.; *G.maculata* Lindl.; *G.tricolor* Rchb. f.).
Pseudobulbs 5.75–8×2.75–3.5cm, clustered, ovoid or ovoid-oblong to conical, bronze-green, 2-lvd. Lvs 38–60×8–15cm, lanceolate to elliptic-obovate, acute to acuminate, undulate, short-petiolate. Infl. to 90cm, pendent, many-fld; peduncle slender, tinged red-purple; fls to 5cm, inverted, thin-textured, except for lip, pale yellow, variously spotted, blotched and banded red or red-brown, dorsal sep. 2–2.3×1–1.2cm, elliptic to elliptic-lanceolate, acuminate, strongly revolute, lateral sep. to 3×1.8cm, obliquely ovate-lanceolate, acute to acuminate, reflexed, margins revolute; pet. to 1.2×0.2cm, lanceolate or linear-lanceolate, long-acuminate, recurved; lip to 2cm, laterally compressed, hypochile saccate, bearing 2 basal tubercles; epichile laterally compressed, basally gibbous, sulcate above, apex spur-like; column to 25mm, subclavate above. Mexico, C America, northern S America, Trinidad.

G.sanderiana Kränzl.
Pseudobulbs to 8–12cm, conical or pyriform-cylindrical, 2-lvd. Lvs 15–30×7.5–11cm, oblong to oblong-elliptic, acute. Infl. to 30cm, pendulous, few-fld; sep. yellow yellow-brown, dorsal sep. 2.75–4×1.25–3cm, ovate or ovate-elliptic, acute, concave, lateral sep. 3.75–4.5×3–4cm, broadly ovate, acute; pet. 4–5cm, white-yellow spotted rose, fleshy, linear; lip to 2.8×1.4cm, clawed; hypochile linear, expanded as 2 quadrate, erect lobes with a fleshy tubercle between, epichile thin, linear; column to 3.5cm, clavate, slightly winged. Peru.

G.scaphephorus Rchb. f. & Warsc.
Pseudobulbs 7.5–10cm, ovoid to subcylindrical. Lvs 30–55×7–10cm, broadly oblong or elliptic-oblong, acute. Infl. to 70cm, pendulous, loosely many-fld; fls yellow or yellow-white to red-brown, spotted dull dark; dorsal sep. 1–1.5×0.75–1cm, ovate-elliptic, acute, concave, lateral sep. 1.75–2×0.75–1cm, semiorbicular, acute, concave; pet. small, obliquely triangular, acute; lip to 2.5cm, hypochile to 1.5cm, strongly complanate, base with 2 erect, oblong lobules, epichile to 1cm, navicular or ovate, acuminate, base with an erect, quadrate keel; column to 1.5cm, apex winged. Peru.

G.tricolor Rchb. f. See *G.quinquenervis*.

Gongora   (a) *G.quinquenervis*   (b) *G.galeata*

Goodyera R. Br. (For John Goodyer (1592–1664), English botanist.) Some 40 species of evergreen or herbaceous, terrestrials, or, rarely, lithophytes or epiphytes. Rhizomes creeping, subterranean or on surface of soil. Leaves oblong to ovate, fleshy, minutely papillose above, often appearing velvety with coloured veins, arranged in basal rosette or a loose spiral on ascending stems; petioles clasping. Inflorescence a narrow-cylindric spike, erect, secund or spirally arranged; stalk often glandular-pubescent; sepals spreading or incurved and forming a hood; petals pointing forward to cover column; lip entire, saccate at base, interior pubescent. Spring–autumn. Temperate zones except Africa.

CULTIVATION Foliage orchids, they lack the great beauty of the related *Anoectochilus* and *Ludisia*, for which they compensate in hardiness and quiet charm. Of those listed here, *Gg.oblongifolia, pubescens, repens* and *tesselata* are hardy in climate zone 6 and may be established on leafy, acid soils in damp, sheltered woodland situations. The remaining species fare best in cool glasshouses, planted in pans filled with a mix rich in leafmould. Maintain shady, buoyant, humid conditions. Protect from slugs, snails, leaf scorch and overwet soils.

G.biflora (Lindl.) Hook. f.
Stem 5–7.5cm, sometimes decumbent, rooting nodally, tinted red. Lvs ovate, obtuse or subacute, green with white reticulate veins above, mauve-green beneath. Spike dense pubesc., 2–8-fld; bracts slender, 3-veined; fls white; lateral sep. spreading, dorsal sep. linear-lanceolate, recurved; pet. falcate, linear; lip blotched pink or yellow, margins undulate. Summer. Asia.

G.biflora var. *macrantha* (Maxim.) Hashim. See *G.macrantha*.
G.discolor Ker-Gawl. See *Ludisia discolor*.

G.foliosa (Lindl.) Benth.
Stem 15–30cm, slender. Lvs ovate-lanceolate, 3–5-veined. Spike glandular-pubesc., 5–7.5cm; fls pink often tinted orange; sep. 10–15mm, ovate-lanceolate; pet. oblong equalling dorsal sep.; lip with orange and white apical lobe. Summer. Asia.

G.grandis (Bl.) Bl.
Stem 50–100cm. Lvs 13–15cm, 6–8, ovate-oblong, alternate, pale green, undulate; petiole to 5cm. Spike 10–20cm; bracts, ovary and sep. glandular-pubesc.; fls purple; lateral sep. oblong, spreading; lip recurved. Summer. Australia, SE Asia, Japan.

G.hachijoensis Yatabe.
Stems 10–25cm, tinted red. Lvs to 6cm, green, oblong-ovate, veins white, reticulate, with a silver central flash. Spike dense; tepals incurved; sep. ovate-oblong, white stained brown-pink, single-veined; lip ovate, pale yellow. Autumn. Japan.

G.hispida Lindl.
Rhiz. creeping, then ascending to 15cm. Lvs remote, to 8cm, ovate-lanceolate apex acuminate, thin-textured, glabrous, slightly papillose, sometimes with a silvery central flash. Fls small, white, glandular in a glandular-hispid spike. India (Khasi Hills). Sikkim, Bhutan.

G.japonica Bl.
Stems to 35cm. Lvs oblong-ovate, flushed rose pink at first, later green tinted ginger to chocolate, midrib silver-striped. Spike lax; fls white, sep. ovate-lanceolate; pet. spathulate. Summer. China, Japan.

G.macrantha Maxim. (*G.biflora* var. *macrantha* (Maxim.) Hashim.; *G.picta* Boxall & Naves).
Stems 4–10cm. Lvs 2–4cm, ovate, acuminate, often undulate, deep red-green to copper, midrib silver. Fls 20–30mm, 1–3, pale red; dorsal sep. linear-oblong; pet. linear equalling sep.;

lip 17–20mm, lanceolate, recurved at tip; ovary pubesc. Summer. Japan, Korea.

G.oblongifolia Raf.
Stem to 45cm. Lvs 2–4×3–11cm, elliptic-oblong, dark blue-green with paler midrib and netted veins, sometimes undulate; petiole short. Spike to 30-fld, secund; bracts lanceolate; dorsal sep. pale green, lateral sep. ovate, oblique; pet. oblique, tapering, white with green midvein, forming hood with sep.; lip 4–7mm, straplike, rounded, recurved. Mid summer–early autumn. N America.

G.picta Boxall & Naves. See *G.macrantha*.

G.pubescens (Willd.) R. Br. RATTLESNAKE PLANTAIN.
Stem 40–50cm, pubesc. Lvs 3–8, ovate-oblong 3–9×2–4cm, blue-green, veins reticulate, silver-white above. Spike dense, cylindric, to 80-fld; fls white, bracts lanceolate; dorsal sep. and pet. forming hood each with a green midvein; lip pouch-like, apex recurved. Summer. N, C & E Europe.

G.repens (L.) Br. LESSER RATTLESNAKE PLANTAIN.
Rhiz. creeping. Lvs to 3cm, elliptic-ovate, dark lustrous green, sometimes obscurely net-veined silvery white. Spike secund; fls small, white, rounded. N America, N Eurasia. var. *ophioides*. WHITE-BLOTCHED RATTLESNAKE; NET LEAF, SQUIRREL EAR. Lvs distinctly veined silver-white. N America.

G.schlechtendaliana Rchb. f.
Stem 12–25cm. Lvs 2–4cm, in basal rosette, ovate-lanceolate pale blue-green with darker blotches. Spike secund; fls pale red, to 10; lateral sep. spreading, ciliate beneath, dorsal sep. forming hood with pet. Late summer. China, Korea, Taiwan, Japan.

G.tesselata Lodd.
Stems to 35cm, densely pubesc. Lvs 2–8×1–2.5cm, in basal rosette, ovate-lanceolate to elliptic-lanceolate, blue-green net-veined white; petiole short. Spike secund or cylindric; fls to 40, white; dorsal sep. oblong-lanceolate, concave; pet. spathulate, forming hood with dorsal sep.; lip 3–4mm, apex spreading. Summer. NE America.

G.velutina Maxim.
Stems to 20cm, purple-brown. Lvs 2–4cm, ovate, acuminate, velvety; dark green with white midrib above, maroon beneath. Fls pale red-brown; lateral sep. oblique, dorsal sep. and pet. forming hood; lip ovate. Autumn. Japan, S Korea, Taiwan.

Govenia Lindl. ex Lodd. (For James Robert Gowen (*d* 1862), secretary, Horticultural Society of London, 1845–50.) Some 30 species, terrestrials with buried, corm-like pseudobulbs, slender deciduous leaves and sheathed erect stems topped with racemes of hooded flowers. C & S America.

CULTIVATION   Plant in large pots filled with a very open, bark-based mix enriched with leafmould and dried farmyard manure. Maintain in light shade or dappled sunlight in the intermediate house, watering freely when in growth. Once the foliage falls away, severely limit water until plants are repotted at the commencement of new growth in spring.

G.liliacea (La Ll. & Lex.) Lindl.
Infl. to 60cm, to 18-fld.; tepals to 3cm, ovate-oblong, snow-white very finely banded pale rose within, pet. and dorsal sep.erect, forming a hood, lateral sep. porrect and somewhat falcate; lip strongly erect, smaller than tepals, flushed pink-brown below and spotted rusty brown toward the apex on its undersurface (the surface presented to the viewer). Mexico, Costa Rica.

Grammangis Rchb. f. (From Gk *gramma*, marking or letter, and *angos*, vessel, probably alluding to the markings on the flower.) 2 species of epiphytes resembling *Grammatophyllum*. Pseudobulbs lacking sheaths when mature, bearing 3–5 leaves at apex. Leaves flat, fleshy, articulated at apex of sheath, persisting on old pseudobulbs. Inflorescence racemose, arising from base of new pseudobulb; flowers large, perianth spreading; median sepal free, lateral sepals and petals joined at base, forming distinct mentum with column-foot; lip inserted at apex of column-foot, trilobed, without spur, with crests or calli inside; column thick, the foot with a deep hollow forming a nectary; pollinia sessile on the single viscidium. Madagascar.

CULTIVATION   Robust epiphytes for the intermediate house, carrying spectacular arching racemes of tiger-striped, hooded flowers. Plant in shallow, well crocked clay pots or baskets in an open, coarse bark mix with added dried FYM. Water and feed heavily when in growth, reduce watering to a minimum in winter. Position in light shade and high humidity, dropping temperature and humidity and increasing light when at rest. Propagate by division.

G.ellisii (Lindl.) Rchb. f.
50–60cm; pseudobulbs 8–20×4–6cm, 4-angled, 3–5-lvd at apex, those bearing the lvs fully developed by flowering time. Lvs 15–40×1.5–4cm, oblong, folded towards base, the apex oblique but not lobed. Raceme 15–20-fld, the fls set about 15mm apart; peduncle 25–35cm, stout, with several sheaths; fls yellow, with glossy mahogany-bronze to green-bronze markings, the lip striped red and yellow; pedicel and ovary 5cm; bracts large, to 5cm; dorsal sep. 40×20mm, obovate, undulate, lateral sep. similar but slightly narrower and acuminate; pet. similar but smaller; lip 18×18mm, obovate, trilobed above the middle, lateral lobes sickle-shaped, midlobe narrower and slightly longer, throat with a large, bifid callus and a central, prominent keel dividing at junction of lobes into 3 short crests flanked by 2 further toothed calli; column 10mm.

G.falcigera Rchb. f. See *Cymbidiella falcigera*.

G.fallax Schltr.
Habit and lvs similar to *G.ellisii* but flower-bearing pseudobulbs not fully developed until after flowering. Sep. yellow-green with violet-black apex, pet. white with dull red apex, lip white, dull red between calli; pedicel and ovary 25mm; bracts to 25mm; median sep. 22×12mm, obovate, acute and slightly hooded at apex, lateral sep. 25×15mm; pet. 20–21×12mm, obovate, rounded and slightly apiculate at apex; lip 16×15mm, trilobed, lateral lobes rounded, midlobe smaller than lateral lobes; basal callus entire, 1.5mm, median keel ending at junction of lobes in large, 3-crested callus dividing into 7 veins, the middle 3 continuing the crests of the calli; column 12mm.

G.pardalina Rchb. f. See *Cymbidiella pardalina*.

Grammatophyllum Bl. (From Gk *gramma*, letter, and *phyllon*, leaf, referring to the conspicuous markings of the sepals and petals.) Some 12 species of large epiphytes or terrestrials. Pseudobulbs short or elongate, stoutly cane-like, clustered, few to many-leaved. Leaves distichous, linear or ligulate, elongate, narrow. Inflorescence a basal raceme, elongate, erect or pendent, many-flowered; flowers often large, showy; sepals and petals similar, subequal, free, spreading; lip small, adnate to column base, erect, concave, lateral lobes embracing column, mid-lobe short, recurved-spreading, narrow or dilated; column erect, subterete, short, anther bilocular, pollinia 2, subglobose, viscidium crescent-shaped. SE Asia & Indonesia to New Guinea, Philippines, Polynesia.

CULTIVATION   The giants of the Orchidaceae, exceeded in height only by the slender twining stems of the saprophytic *Galeola*, they are seldom cultivated because of their considerable spread, but make magnificent specimens for the large intermediate to warm glasshouse or conservatory. Plant the cane-like pseudobulbs in baskets or beds of coarse bark mix with liberal additions of dried cow manure. Site in high humidity and dappled shade, mist and water frequently, allowing plants to dry between waterings. Well grown, plants will need support, the flower spikes especially.

G.scriptum (L.) Bl.
Pseudobulbs 50–200×3–6cm, long-ovoid to ellipsoid. Lvs to 55×7cm, coriaceous, linear-ligulate, dull green. Infl. to 125cm, erect to pendent, many-fld; fls to 4.5cm diam., usually rather cupped, waxy, variable in colour; sep. and pet. yellow-green, blotched dark brown, dorsal sep. arching over lip, concave, acute, undulate, lateral sep. falcate, pet. falcate, obtuse, undulate; lip deeply 3-lobed, lateral lobes white-yellow veined brown, erect, pubesc. below, midlobe yellow-white, centrally veined dark brown, pendent, callus yellow and white, slightly spotted and lined brown, sulcate; column white marked red-brown, arched. New Guinea, Philippines, Borneo, Celebes, Moluccas, Solomon Is.

G.speciosum Bl.
Pseudobulbs to 3m, subcylindrical, cane-like, erect to pendent, yellow with age. Lvs to 60×3cm, linear-ligulate, acute or obtuse, apex decurved. Infl. to 2m, erect, stout; fls to 12cm diam., long-lived, variable in colour; sep. and pet. to 5.5×3cm, yellow-green spotted and blotched dull orange-brown or dark red-brown, broadly oblong or elliptic-oblong, obtuse, slightly undulate, pet. somewhat falcate; lip to 3×2.5cm, white or white-yellow, striped yellow and red-brown, lateral lobes narrowly oblong, erect, obtuse, midlobe ovate, acute or obtuse, disc tricarinate, lined red; column to 2cm, pale green above, white spotted purple below, clavate. Malaya and Sumatra to Philippines.

Graphorkis Thouars. (From Gk *graphe*, writing, and *orchis*, orchid.) 5 species of epiphytes allied to *Eulophia*. Pseudobulbs well developed, leaves appearing after flowering. Inflorescence paniculate, laxly many-flowered; flowers mainly yellow-green, brown or purple; sepals and petals similar; lip trilobed, usually spurred. Tropical Africa, Madagascar, Mascarene Is., Comoros Is.

CULTIVATION   As for *Eulophia*.

G.lurida (Sw.) Kuntze (*Eulophia lurida* (Sw.) Lindl.).
Pseudobulbs 3–9×1–3cm, cylindrical, conical or ovoid, 4–6-lvd. Lvs to 40×3.5cm, lanceolate, acute or acuminate, appearing after flowering. Panicle 30–60cm; branches spreading, about 20cm long; sep. and pet. dull purple-brown, lip yellow; pedicel and ovary 6–18mm; sep. 5–6mm, oblong or spathulate, obtuse or apiculate; pet. similar but broader; lip 5×4mm, trilobed with 2 basal keels, lateral lobes obtuse or rounded, midlobe broadly obovate, somewhat emarginate or bifid at apex; spur 4mm, bent sharply forwards, cylindrical, somewhat bifid at apex; column 2–3mm with a hairy auricle on either side at base. W & C Africa, Uganda.

G.scripta (Thouars) Kuntze (*Eulophia scripta* (Thouars) Lindl.).
Pseudobulbs clustered, 3–14×1–4cm, ovoid-conical, the old ones leafless, covered with sheaths or sheath scars. Lvs 9–13, 8–11cm×8–14mm, grasslike, developing after fls. Panicle 22–65cm; peduncle 10–45cm; fls yellow marked with red; sep. and pet. 12–15×6–8mm, lip of similar length, trilobed, lateral lobes rounded, enfolding column, midlobe obovate, crenulate or emarginate; spur 3mm, straight; column 6–10mm. Madagascar, Mascarene Is., Comoros Is.

Grobya Lindl. (For Lord Grey of Groby (*d*1836), patron of British Horticulture.) Some 3 species of epiphytes. Rhizome short, branched. Pseudobulbs short, fleshy, usually ovoid. Leaves narrow, plicate, grass-like. Inflorescence a basal raceme, arching to pendent, basally sheathed; flowers large, short-pedicellate, yellow to green tinged and marked purple; dorsal sepal free, erect, forming a hood with petals, lateral sepals shortly connate, spreading or deflexed, far narrower than the dorsal sepal, inrolled, twisted and claw-like; petals erect to spreading; lip small, articulated with column foot, shortly unguiculate, erect, 3-lobed, lateral lobes erect, midlobe spreading, disc callose; column erect, subterete, biauriculate, with a short foot; pollinia 2, waxy, grooved. Brazil.

CULTIVATION   For the intermediate house, with cultural requirements similar to those of *Encyclia fragrans*.

G.amherstiae Lindl.
Pseudobulbs to 3.5cm, tufted, ovoid to subglobose, 4 to 6-lvd at apex. Lvs to 40×1.5cm, linear-lanceolate, rigid, subacute. Infl. to 15cm, arching, 1- to several-fld; tepals pale green to pale yellow tinged and spotted pale red-purple, lip pale yellow-white; dorsal sep. to 20×7mm, obovate-spathulate, lateral sep. oblong-lanceolate, twisted, margins incurved; pet. to 20×10mm, obliquely elliptic, obtuse; lip to 7×8mm, pale yellow, lateral lobes subrotund, curved upwards, midlobe transversely elliptic, 7-keeled, callus dull purple, bilamellate with a short median spur. E Brazil.

Grosourdya Rchb. f. (For Dr von Grosourdy, a 19th-century expert on the medicinal properties of S American plants.) Some 10 species of monopodial epiphytes. Sepals oblong-ligulate, apex broad, pointed; petals subequal, narrower; lip clawed, linear-subulate, elongate, abruptly expanded; midlobe 3-toothed, central tooth small, forward-pointing, keels 2, inflated, filamentous, curved forward, lateral lobes semicircular, spreading. Malaysia, Indonesia.

CULTIVATION   As for *Sarcochilus*.

G.muscosa (Rolfe) Garay (*Sarcochilus muscosus* Rolfe). Lvs linear-oblong, distichous. Infl. short; bracts oblong-ovate, subobtuse, apex recurved; fls few, dull yellow, sep. and pet. spotted red-brown at base, lip white, spotted and streaked purple near spur aperture, spur apex pale yellow; sep. elliptic-oblong, acute, lateral sep. fused to column foot; pet. elliptic-oblanceolate, subacute; lip mobile, attached to column foot, midlobe broad, ovate to triangular, subobtuse, lateral lobes broad, oblong, obtuse; basal sac oblong. Andaman Is., Thailand, Malaysia.

Gymnadenia R. Br. (From Gk *gymnos*, naked, and *aden*, gland: the pollinia are uncovered.) Some 10 species of herbaceous, terrestrial orchids. Tubers palmately lobed. Stem leafy. Spike cylindric, dense; lateral sepals spreading, oblong-ovate, decurved or patent, the dorsal forming a hood with petals; lip recurved, trilobed, lobes shallow; spur conspicuous. N America, temperate Eurasia.

CULTIVATION   See Introduction: Hardy Orchids. Both species are lime-loving.

G.conopsea (L.) R. Br. FRAGRANT ORCHID.
Tuber 3–6-lobed. Stems 15–65cm, glabrous; basal sheaths 2–3, brown. Lvs 4–8, linear-lanceolate, keeled beneath, light green, reduced toward summit of stem. Spike dense, 6–16cm; fls fragrant, pink, lilac or red, rarely white or purple; pet. and sep. 4–5mm; lip lobes equal; spur to 18mm, slender, decurved, exceeding ovary. Late spring–early summer. Europe.

G.odoratissima (L.) Rich. SHORT-SPURRED FRAGRANT ORCHID.
As *G.conopsea* except stem 15–30cm; lvs 4–6; pet. and sep. 2.5–3mm; lip midlobe exceeding lateral lobes; spur 4–5mm. Late spring–late summer. Europe, USSR.

Habenaria Willd. (From Lat. *habena*, strap, thong or rein, referring to the long, slender spur, petal and lip lobes of many species.) About 600 species of terrestrials, rarely epiphytes with tubers or fleshy roots. Leaves either 1–2, adpressed to the ground with sheath-like leaves on stem, or all along stem grading into bracts towards the top. Raceme terminal, 1- to many-flowered; flowers usually green and/or white, but sometimes yellow, orange, red or pink; sepals usually free, dorsal sepal often forming a hood with petals, lateral sepals spreading or reflexed; petals entire or bilobed; lip entire or trilobed, lateral lobes sometimes with fringed margins, spurred at base; spur long or short, often enlarged at apex; column long or short, stigmatic arms 2, from short and thick to long and slender. Tropics and subtropics.

CULTIVATION   As for *Disa*.

H.bonatea L. f. See *Bonatea speciosa*.

H.macrandra Lindl.
Terrestrial, 15–55cm; roots fleshy, cylindrical, woolly. Lvs in tuft at base of stem, with smaller lvs scattered along stem; basal lvs 3–7 with petiole to 7cm, blade to 24×6cm, lanceolate, acute, dark green. Raceme 4–20cm, laxly 2–11-fld; fls green and white, occasionally white; pedicel and ovary 20–35mm; sep. 15–30×3–5mm, lanceolate, acute, dorsal sep. erect, lateral sep. deflexed, oblique and slightly longer than dorsal sep.; pet. 16–36mm, erect, entire, narrowly linear; lip trilobed almost to base, midlobe 20–45mm, lateral lobes 30–55mm, all lobes filiform but midlobe slightly broader; spur 5–7.5cm, pendent, slightly curved, swollen towards apex; anth. 13–22mm. Tropical Africa (widespread).

H.macrantha A. Rich.
Terrestrial, 20–50cm with ovoid or ellipsoid woolly tubers 1–4cm long. Stem leafy; lvs 5–7, to 12×5cm, lanceolate, acute. Raceme to 12cm, rather laxly 2–9-fld; fls green or green and white; pedicel and ovary 23–30mm; sep. 20–25×7–10mm, lanceolate, acute, dorsal sep. erect, lateral sep. spreading or deflexed, oblique; pet. 20–25mm, entire, curved-lanceolate, papillose-hairy, adnate to dorsal sep.; lip 30–35mm, trilobed 9–15mm from base, midlobe 14–23×1–2mm, linear, obtuse, lateral lobes slightly longer, the outer edge divided into 6–10 narrow threads; spur 20–35mm, incurved, swollen at apex; stigmatic arms 10–17mm. Arabian Peninsula, Ethiopia, Uganda, Kenya.

H.procera (Sw.) Lindl.
Epiphytic, rarely terrestrial and growing in humus, to 60cm; tubers pubesc. Stem erect, leafy; lower lvs to 30×5.5cm, lanceolate or ovate, with sheathing bases. Raceme to 15cm, fairly densely to 35-fld; fls white, tepals green at the tips; sep. to 12×7mm, ovate; pet. similar, oblong; lip 15–30mm,

trilobed with undivided, oblong base, midlobe to 18×2mm, lateral lobes much longer and narrower, to 27mm; spur 7–8cm, swollen towards apex. W Africa, Zaire, Uganda.

H.pusilla Rchb. f. See *H.rhodocheila*.
H.radiata Thunb. See *Pecteilis radiata*.

H.rhodocheila Hance (*H.pusilla* Rchb. f.).
Terrestrial, 20–30cm. Lvs about 6, towards base of stem, to about 12×2cm, upper lvs grading into bracts, all lvs green or red-flushed with network of darker veins. Raceme about 10-fld; sep. and pet. green, lip yellow, orange or scarlet; dorsal sep. and pet. forming hood 9mm long, lateral sep. spreading or deflexed, twisted, 10mm; lip about 30×22mm, widening gradually from base, deeply trilobed, midlobe 15×12mm, obovate, bilobed at apex, the lobes rounded, lateral lobes about 10mm long and slightly less wide, with rounded edge; spur 5cm. S China and Indochina, south to Penang.

H.splendens Rendle.
Robust, terrestrial, 35–70cm; tubers ellipsoid or ovoid, 3–4cm. Stem leafy; lvs 6–12, the largest in the middle, to 20×6cm, ovate, acute, loosely funnel-shaped at base. Raceme to 22cm, fairly laxly 4–20-fld; sep. green, pet. and lip white; pedicel and ovary 25–35mm; dorsal sep. 23–30×12–13mm, erect, ovate, lateral sep. similar but spreading and 8–10mm wide; pet. 20–30×4–8mm, falcate, adnate to dorsal sep.; lip 25–40mm, trilobed to 7–13mm from base, the undivided part densely pubesc., midlobe 15–23×1mm, linear, lateral lobes 18–24mm, with 8–12 thread-like branches on outer margin towards apex; spur 25–50mm, pendent, S-shaped, slightly swollen at apex; stigmatic arms 16–20mm. Ethiopia, Uganda, Kenya, Tanzania, Malawi, Zambia.

H.susannae (L.) R. Br. See *Pecteilis susannae*.

Habenaria and Pecteilis (a) *Habenaria rhodocheila* (b) *Pecteilis susannae*

Hagsatera Gonzalez. (For Eric Hagsater, *b*1945, Mexican orchidologist.) 2 species, epiphytes related to *Epidendrum*, from which they differ in the short column with a concave rostellum, 8 pollinia and pronounced viscidium. The growth habit is also highly distinctive – the mature growths consist of a slender, erect stem terminating in a pseudobulbous swelling at whose base new stems arise, forming a tall, wand-like growth which tends to lack aerial roots. C America.

CULTIVATION   As for *Epidendrum*. These plants perform best if mounted on a raft or slab of fern fibre. Since the long stems rarely produce aerial roots, the basal root system should be kept moist and fresh and propagation by stem cuttings will usually fail.

H.brachycolumna (L.O.Williams) Gonzalez Tamayo.
To 1m tall. Fls to 4cm diam., 2–5 per terminal cluster; tepals oblong-lanceolate, olive to lime green; lip ovate-acuminate, the margins slightly inrolled and undulate, pale yellow-green strongly streaked and edged red-brown.

Haraella Kudo. (For Yoshe Hara.) 1 species, a dwarf, monopodial epiphyte with loose fans of tough, strap-shaped leaves seldom longer than 5cm. Flowers to 2cm diam., scented, produced singly or a few together on short racemes nestling in foliage; tepals yellow to yellow-green, obovate-elliptic, the sepals to twice the size of petals; lip translucent and crystalline off-white centrally blotched chestnut to maroon, to 2.5cm long, basically oblong, shallowly 3-lobed, lateral lobes rounded, midlobe subquadrate, deeply and finely fringed.Taiwan.

CULTIVATION   A dwarf epiphyte of great charm, producing disproportionately large flowers somewhat reminiscent of a Bee Orchid. The plants grow best mounted several together on a mossy bark slab or raft suspended in filtered light in intermediate conditions. Water and syringe throughout the year, taking precautions, however, against basal rots to which the small, tufted growths will quickly succumb in a cool, dull and overwet atmosphere.

H.retrocalla (Hayata) Kudo (*H.odorata* Kudo).

Hexadesmia Brongn. (From Gk *hex*, six, and *desmos*, band or fetter, referring to the six pollinia joined in 2 groups.) Some 15 species of epiphytes, allied to *Scaphyglottis*. Pseudobulbs clumped, slender fusiform, sometimes stalked, unifoliate to bifoliate. Inflorescence a raceme or fascicle, terminal, solitary to several-flowered; flowers small; sepals free, spreading, oblong to lanceolate, subequal, lateral sepals adnate to column foot forming a prominent mentum; petals similar to sepals; lip subarticulate with column foot, reflexed or recurved; column produced into a foot at base, clavate, erect or arcuate, anther terminal, operculate, incumbent, pollinia 6, waxy, unequal in size, laterally compressed. Tropical America.

CULTIVATION   As for *Encyclia fragrans*.

H.brachyphylla Rchb. f. See *H.fusiformis*.

H.crurigera (Batem. ex Lindl.) Lindl. (*Hexopia crurigera* Batem. ex Lindl.; *Scaphyglottis crurigera* (Batem. ex Lindl.) Ames & Correll).
Pseudobulbs fusiform-cylindrical, to 14cm, stalked, bifoliate. Lvs to 200×4mm, narrowly linear, erect-ascending, retuse. Raceme to 13cm, fractiflex; peduncle slender, flexuous, blue-green; fls white; sep. to 7×3mm, oblong-lanceolate to oblong-elliptic, acute or obtuse; pet. subequal to sep., linear-oblong to elliptic, oblique, acute to obtuse; lip to 10×5mm, oblong-cuneate or oblong-obovate, apex bilobed, lobules rounded, incurved; column to 6mm, clavate, slightly arcuate. Mexico, Guatemala, El Salvador, Costa Rica.

H.fasciculata Brongn. (*H.lindeniana* Rich. & Gal.; *Scaphyglottis lindeniana* (Rich. & Gal.) L.O. Williams).
Pseudobulbs to 30×2.5cm, ellipsoid or fusiform, stalked, bifoliate. Lvs to 25×5cm, linear-elliptic to lanceolate, acute or obtuse, coriaceous. Infl. a fascicle to 4cm, 2- to several-fld; fls red-green or yellow-green; sep. to 11×3mm, oblong-lanceolate to oblong-elliptic, acuminate, recurved, concave, lateral sep. oblique; pet. to 10×3mm, elliptic-lanceolate, acute to acuminate; lip to 11×6mm, oblanceolate to narrowly obovate, acute or truncate, apiculate; column to 8mm, slender. Mexico, Guatemala, Costa Rica, Panama.

H.fusiformis Griseb. (*H.brachyphylla* Rchb. f.; *Scaphyglottis fusiformis* (Griseb.) R.E. Schult.; *Scaphyglottis brachyphylla* (Rchb. f.) Schweinf.).
Pseudobulbs to 6×1cm, green, unifoliate. Lvs to 130×6mm, erect, subcoriaceous, linear to oblong, obtuse, apex minutely bilobed. Infl. 1- or 2-fld; sep. and pet. white, pale yellow or pale cream-green, faintly veined pink, sep. to 10×3mm, triangular-lanceolate to oblong-lanceolate, acute or acuminate, lateral sep. oblique, pet. to 8×3mm, elliptic-oblong to oblong-lanceolate, acute; lip to 8×5mm, white, simple, obovate-pandurate or spathulate, truncate or obtuse, thickened at base; column yellow-green, slender, subterete, clavate, to 5mm; anth. yellow. Costa Rica, Venezuela, Trinidad.

H.lindeniana A. Rich. & Gal. See *Scaphyglottis lindeniana*.

H.micrantha Lindl. (*Scaphyglottis micrantha* (Lindl.) Ames & Correll).
Pseudobulbs to 60×6mm, stipitate, usually bifoliate. Lvs to 120×6mm, slender, few- to many-fld borne on a slender peduncle; fls white to green-violet; sep. to 2×1.5mm, ovate, acute or apiculate, lateral sep. oblique; pet. to 2×1mm, obliquely elliptic or ovate, obtuse, apiculate; lip to 2×2.5mm, 3-lobed, lateral lobes obliquely subquadrate, rounded, erect, midlobe obliquely subquadrate to suborbicular, apiculate; column to 1.5mm, slender, arcuate. Guatemala, Panama, British Honduras.

H.reedii Rchb. f. See *H.sessilis*.

H.sessilis Rchb. f. (*H.reedii* Rchb. f.; *Scaphyglottis sessilis* (Rchb. f.) Foldats; *Scaphyglottis reedii* (Rchb. f.) Ames).
Pseudobulbs to 20cm, long-stalked, erect to pendent, dark brown, usually unifoliate. Lvs to 50cm, narrowly linear, apex minutely tridentate. Infl. a fascicle, to 8cm, 1- to several-fld, erect to pendent; fls pale green flushed brown; sep. fleshy, broadly ovate, to 3.5×3mm, acute, concave, lateral sep. oblique; pet. to 4×3mm, obovate-cuneate, acute or apiculate; lip to 7×5mm, pandurate-subquadrate, base geniculate; column to 3mm, pale green, anth. pale brown. Mexico, Venezuela, Colombia, Brazil.

Hexisea Lindl. (From Gk *hex*, six, and *isos*, equal, referring to the equal size of the six perianth segments.) 6 species of diminutive epiphytes. Rhizomes short. Pseudobulbs clustered, slender, furrowed-cylindric, developing apically and laterally, producing chains of stem-length with bracteate or leafy constrictions, often branching, overall appearance tufted, reed-like or shrubby. Leaves dark green, coriaceous, paired, opposite, apical or nodal, linear-lanceolate, sessile. Flowers small, in short-stalked terminal clusters, scarcely opening; sepals elliptic-lanceolate; petals oblanceolate, oblique; lip united to base of column, basally saccate, apex tongue-like. Throughout the year. C & N South America.

CULTIVATION As for cane-producing *Epidendrum* spp., except the smaller species resent prolonged drought.

H.bidentata Lindl.
Aggregate pseudobulbs to 45cm, each section to 6×1.25cm. Lvs to 9cm, usually smaller, slender, apically tridentate. Infl. to 4.75cm; fls to 6, to 1.5cm diam., sep. and pet. vermilion, cinnabar red or scarlet, lip ivory, yellow or dull maroon. Throughout genus range.

Himantoglossum Koch. (From Gk *himas*, strap, and *glossa*, tongue; referring to the length and shape of the lip midlobe.) Some 4 species of herbaceous terrestrials. Tubers 2, oblong-ovoid. Spike narrow-cylindric; sepals and petals forming a hood; lip trilobed, central lobe strap-like, deeply divided with divisions twisted, lateral lobes pendent, lanceolate to triangular, undulate. Late spring–mid summer. Europe, Mediterranean.

CULTIVATION See Introduction: Hardy Orchids.

H.caprinum (Bieb.) Spreng.
Tubers ellipsoid. Stems to 100cm, tinted purple-violet toward summit. Lvs ovate-lanceolate near base, becoming lanceolate. Spike to 45cm lax, 9–24-fld; bracts linear-lanceolate; fls bright purple; hood green-purple; pet. 2-veined; lip with minute projections and dark purple basal hairs, central lobe to 15mm, deeply divided, spur 4–6mm conical. E Europe.

H.hircinum (L.) Spreng. LIZARD ORCHID.
Stem 20–90cm, faintly spotted purple. Lvs 4–8, elliptic-oblong, basal lvs wither before flowering. Spike lax,

10–50cm, 15–80-fld; fls malodorous; exterior of hood green or grey-green, marked red, single-veined, interior striped and spotted red; lip 30–50mm, trilobed, spotted purple at base with reduced projections, central lobe 25–45mm, narrow, strap-like, spiral, unfurling as fl. opens, lateral lobes grey, purple to olive brown, rarely pink, spur conical, decurved. S Europe, Mediterranean.

H.longibracteatum (Bernh.) Schltr. See *Barlia robertiana*.

Holcoglossum Schltr. (From Gk *holkos*, furrow and *glossa*, tongue.) Some 4 species of monopodial epiphytes allied to and formerly included in *Vanda*. Leaves 6–10, terete, dark green, tapering. Inflorescence 1–5-flowered, axillary, slender, pendent; flowers white to pink-purple, spurred; petals and lateral sepals similar, margins undulate, dorsal sepal oblong to oblong-ovate, lateral sepals oblong; petals spathulate; lip trilobed, lateral lobes embracing column, deltate, toothed near tip, disc with parallel keels. SE Asia.

CULTIVATION As for *Papilionanthe teres*.

H.amesianum (Rchb. f.) Christenson (*Vanda amesiana* Rchb. f.).
Stem 30–50cm. Lvs to 20cm, subterete, tapering, sulcate, rigid. Fls to 4cm diam., fragrant, white, streaked or suffused pink; sep. and pet. ovate-oblong, pointed; lip midlobe undulate, ribbed, triangular, margins decurved, lateral lobes almost circular; column and spur white. SE Asia.

H.kimballianum (Rchb. f.) Garay (*Vanda kimballiana* Rchb. f.).
Stem to 30cm. Lvs to 22cm, terete, recurved. Fls to 5cm diam., 8–15; dorsal sep. and pet. oblong-obovate, white, often tinted violet, lateral sep. to 3.5cm, white, falcate, decurved; lip to 2.5cm, midlobe oval, basally keeled, with two shallow lobes and toothed margins, violet-red with darker veins, lateral lobes ovate-triangular, spotted yellow-red, recurved. Burma, China (Yunnan), Thailand.

Houlletia Brongn. (For M. Houllet, French horticulturist.) Some 10 species of epiphytes. Rhizome short. Pseudobulbs ovoid, fleshy, unifoliate. Leaves terminal, elliptic to lanceolate, plicate, petiolate, articulated. Racemes lateral, erect, arching or pendent, loosely 1 to several-flowered; peduncle stout, often flushed or spotted maroon; flowers large; sepals subequal, spreading, free; petals similar to sepals, narrower; lip continuous with column base, fleshy, spreading, hypochile narrow, with 2 narrow arched horns, epichile articulated, sometimes separated from basal portion by mesochile, simple or obscurely lobed, sometimes dentate-crenulate, ovate to ligulate, base truncate or auriculate; column erect or arcuate, clavate, sometimes with short foot, wingless, anther terminal, operculate, incumbent, pollinia 2, oblong. Tropical S America.

CULTIVATION As for *Stanhopea*.

H.boliviana Schltr. See *H.odoratissima*.

H.brocklehurstiana Lindl.
Pseudobulbs to 10cm, ovoid-oblong, clustered, furrowed with age. Lvs to 60cm, long-petiolate, elliptic to oblong-lanceolate, acute or acuminate. Infl. to 45cm, erect, loosely several-fld; fls to 7.5cm diam., fragrant; tepals dark red-brown marked deep purple or yellow, oblong, concave; lip yellow or yellow-white spotted purple-brown, shorter than pet., complex, hypochile oblong, with 2 lateral curved horns, epichile flushed purple-brown, triangular to tongue-shaped, recurved, lateral angles produced into short cusps; column yellow spotted red, clavate. Winter. Brazil.

H.landsbergii Lind. & Rchb. f. See *H.tigrina*.

H.odoratissima Lind. ex Lindl. & Paxt. (*H.picta* Lind. & Rchb. f.; *H.boliviana* Schltr.).
Pseudobulbs to 8×3cm, ovoid to pyriform, enveloped by grey sheaths. Lvs to 50×10cm, elliptic-lanceolate, acute or acuminate; petiole slender, to 20cm. Infl. to 85cm, basal, erect, several-fld; fls to 7.5cm diam., long-lived, fragrant; sep. to 4×2cm, chocolate-brown or deep maroon, edged pale brown, ovate to elliptic-oblong, obtuse, lateral sep. connate at base, concave; pet. to 3×1cm, linear-spathulate; lip to 2.5×2.5cm, white marked and striped red; hypochile subquadrate, with 2 lanceolate-falcate horns, epichile clawed, ovate-hastate, with triangular-lanceolate auricles at base; column pale brown marked red-maroon, slightly arcuate, to 2.5cm, slender. Autumn. Colombia, Venezuela, Peru, Bolivia, Brazil.

H.picta Lind. & Rchb. f. See *H.odoratissima*.

H.sanderi Rolfe.
Pseudobulbs to 7cm, ovoid-oblong, grooved. Lvs to 30×4.5cm, elliptic-lanceolate. Infl. to 30cm, basal, erect, loosely 2–4-fld; fls white-cream to bright yellow; sep. to 3.5×2.5cm, round-ovate, apiculate, concave; pet. shorter than sep., broadly obovate, acute; lip to 3cm, hypochile with 2 lateral lobes, obovate-spathulate to broadly obovate, with an obtuse tooth in front, mesochile fleshy, ovate-oblong, truncate, epichile oblong-subquadrate, truncate, denticulate at apex; column to 2cm, stout, arcuate, slightly clavate. Peru, Bolivia.

Huntleya Batem. ex Lindl. (For the Rev. J.T. Huntley (*fl.* 1837).) 10 species of epiphytes allied to *Bollea*. Rhizomes short, emerging from lower leaf axils with new growths and roots in older or particularly well-grown plants sometimes extending, becoming scandent. Pseudobulbs absent. Leaves 2-ranked, arranged in a regular fan, lanceolate to oblanceolate, conduplicate, glabrous, thin-textured to glossy subcoriaceous, basally overlapping. Inflorescence axillary, shorter than leaves; flowers solitary, large, fleshy, waxy, flat and widely spreading; sepals subequal, fleshy, spreading, lanceolate, ovate or rhombic, lateral sepals connate at base, inserted in column foot; petals similar to sepals; lip fleshy, short-clawed, articulated to apex of column foot, abruptly contracted at base, dilated above, basal callus transverse or semicircular, conspicuous, long-fimbriate or lacerate; column short, stout, arcuate, apex dilated, with a prominent foot, winged, forming a distinct hood over clinandrium, anther terminal, incumbent, operculate, pollinia 4, waxy, strongly compressed. C & S America.

CULTIVATION Handsome orchids for shaded, buoyant humid positions in the intermediate house. The habit, a neat fan of pale green, strap-shaped leaves, is unusual, as are the solitary, short-stemmed waxy flowers, star-shaped and often blotched and tessellated. Mount on rafts or pot in a loose bark mix. Water and mist frequently to encourage prolific aerial rooting but take care to avoid leaf scorch. Reduce water supplies when temperatures drop. A fortnightly dilute foliar feed in the summer months is recommended. Increase by detaching offsets.

H.burtii (Endress & Rchb. f.) Pfitzer (*H.meleagris* Lindl.; *Batemannia meleagris* (Lindl.) Rchb. f.).
Fls to 12cm diam., sporadically fragrant, waxy, long-lived; sep. to 6×2.5cm, cream to pale yellow, the surface with a raised pebbly or checkered texture and deepening to glossy chestnut-brown toward apex, elliptic-lanceolate to lanceolate, margins revolute or undulate; pet. to 3.5×2.5cm, similar in colour to sep., bearing a showy, lustrous, purple-brown blotch toward base, ovate to elliptic-lanceolate, acuminate, undulate; lip to 3×2.5cm, deep red-brown, base yellow to white, sometimes streaked purple, short-clawed, ovate-cordate, acute to acuminate, trilobulate, callus erect, semicircular with a crest of incurved, maroon hairs; column to 2cm, cream-green, wings suborbicular-triangular, anth. white. Summer–autumn. Costa Rica, Panama, Colombia, Brazil, Ecuador, Guyana.

H.cerina Lindl. See *Pescatorea cerina*.

H.citrina Rolfe.
Fls smaller than in other spp. (to 3.5cm diam.), with narrower tepals, pure lemon yellow, waxy, the incurved hairs of the lip callus often eyelash-like and dark purple, the underside of the column often streaked purple. Colombia, Ecuador.

H.heteroclita (Poepp. & Endl.) Garay. See *Chaubardia heteroclita*.

H.lucida (Rolfe) Rolfe.
Sep. and pet. to 4×1.5cm, purple-chestnut, white at base, with a green central band, broadly lanceolate to ovate-lanceolate, acute or acuminate, lateral sep. and pet. oblique, smaller than dorsal sep.; lip to 23×12mm, dark red, base and apex white, short-clawed, simple or obscurely 3-lobed, broadly lanceolate to ovate-lanceolate, lateral lobes small, rounded, callus with a semicircular, concave crest, lined brown; column to 14mm, white lined dark purple, anther cream. Venezuela.

H.meleagris Lindl. See *H.burtii.*

H.wallisii (Rchb. f.) Rolfe.
Close to *H.burtii* and sometimes treated as a subspecies or even synonym of that plant. Fls larger (12–20cm diam.), tepals broader and less undulate, deep rusty brown in their apical half to two-thirds and cream below overlaid with rich yellow, often with a few obscure islands of the brown coloration where it borders on the paler lower regions, pet. each with a bold red-maroon blotch at its base; lip very short-clawed, ovate-rhombic, white at base, rusty-brown above, callus hairs short, pale. Colombia, Ecuador. This species and *H.burtii* have been used in crosses with *Cochleanthes* to produce × *Huntleanthes.*

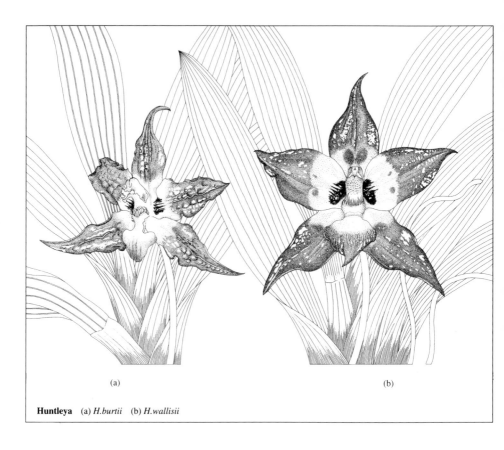

(a)   (b)

Huntleya   (a) *H.burtii*   (b) *H.wallisii*

Ionopsis HBK. (From Gk *ion*, violet, and *opsis*, appearance, referring to the resemblance of the flowers to violets in form and colour.) Ionopsidium Some 10 species of epiphytic or, rarely, terrestrials, allied to *Comparettia*. Habit compact, tufted. Rhizome slender, short or elongate. Pseudobulbs small or obsolete, with a solitary apical leaf or none. Leaves borne on rhizome, subcoriaceous or coriaceous, narrow, rigid, distichous, semi-terete or carinate below, overlapping at base. Inflorescence 1–3, a raceme or a delicately branching panicle, loosely few to many-flowered, erect, arching or pendulous; flowers showy; sepals subequal, erect or spreading, dorsal sepal free, lateral sepals connate at base, forming a short sac below lip; petals similar to dorsal sepal; lip large, showy, simple, short-clawed, adnate to column base, exceeding sepals and petals, disc bicallose; column short, erect, wingless, footless, anther terminal, incumbent, pollinia 2, waxy, obovate. Tropical and subtropical Americas.

CULTIVATION   As for the smaller *Oncidium* spp.

I.paniculata Lindl. See *I.utricularioides*.

I.satyrioides (Sw.) Rchb. f. (*I.teres* Lindl.; *I.testiculata* Lindl.).
Pseudobulbs usually reduced to obsolete. Lvs to 140×3mm, semi-terete, subulate, often tinged maroon. Infl. to 15cm, exceeding lvs; fls to 7mm, cream-white, often veined lilac; sep. to 7×2mm, oblong-lanceolate, acute; pet. slightly broader than sep., ovate-oblong, obtuse, slightly undulate; lip to 8×3mm, obovate, obtuse, undulate, disc with 2 basal, lamellate calli; column to 2mm. Spring–autumn. W Indies, Colombia, Venezuela, Trinidad, Demerara.

I.tenera Lindl. See *I.utricularioides*.
I.teres Lindl. See *I.satyrioides*.
I.testiculata Lindl. See *I.satyrioides*.

I.utricularioides (Sw.) Lindl. (*I.paniculata* Lindl.; *I.tenera* Lindl.).
Pseudobulbs to 3cm, ellipsoid, sometimes unifoliate at apex. Lvs to 17×2cm, linear to lanceolate or oblong-lanceolate, acute to obtuse, apiculate, coriaceous. Infl. to 75cm, a raceme or a panicle, loosely few- to many-fld; fls white to rose-purple or magenta, or pale pink veined deep rosy magenta; dorsal sep. to 6×3mm, oblong-lanceolate to elliptic-lanceolate, acute to obtuse, concave, lateral sep. similar, oblique, pet. to 7×3mm, ovate-elliptic or ovate-oblong, acute to obtuse, apiculate; lip to 16×8mm, flabellate-obcordate, bilobed, entire, undulate or crenulate, biauriculate at base, disc with 2 basal calli; column to 2mm. Winter–spring. Florida, W Indies, Mexico to Brazil, Peru.

Isabelia Barb.-Rodr. (For the Brazilian princess Isabel de Alcantara.) 1 species, an epiphyte. Rhizome short, creeping, sometimes branched. Pseudobulbs to 1cm, narrowly ovoid, clustered, enveloped by loose, fibrous bracts resembling a woven basket. Leaves to 6cm, 1 per pseudobulb, terminal, dark green, needle-like. Inflorescence short, terminal, 1- or 2-flowered; flowers to 1.2cm, waxy, long-lived; sepals white tinted rose-violet, subequal, spreading, obovate-oblong, lateral sepals connate at base forming small sac with lip; petals snow-white, narrow-oblong, obtuse; lip creamy white, broadly ovate, articulate with column base, simple, callose; column to 2mm, tipped violet or claret, fleshy, subterete, wingless. Brazil.

CULTIVATION Suitable for pans, bark slabs or rafts in humid, semi-shaded conditions in the intermediate house. Water throughout the year, decreasing supplies and allowing the medium to dry out between watering when at rest.

I.virginalis Barb.-Rodr.

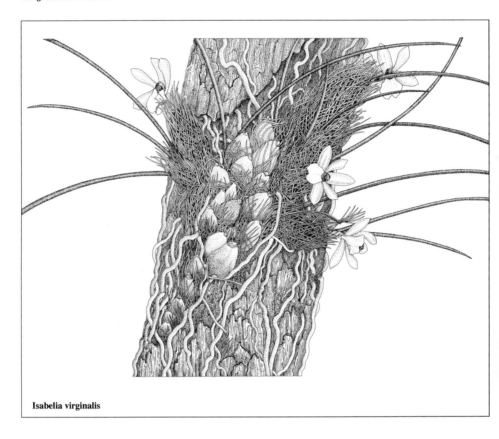

Isabelia virginalis

Isochilus R. Br. (From Gk *isos*, equal, and *cheilos*, lip, referring to the equal size of the lip to the other floral segments.) 2 species of epiphytes, lithophytes or terrestrials. Rhizome short, concealed by dark brown sheaths. Stems slender, erect. Leaves distichous, erect or spreading, joined to sheath, linear-lanceolate to oblong, acute, obtuse or retuse, coriaceous to subcoriaceous. Inflorescence a secund or distichous terminal raceme; flowers small, few or many; sepals more or less equal, free or connate to apex, swollen at base, apex acute or recurved, concave, dorsally keeled; petals similar to sepals, slender-clawed, oblique, not keeled; lip short-clawed, usually equalling petals, adnate to column base or column foot, simple or obscurely trilobed, linear to linear-lanceolate, acute to obtuse, sigmoid at base; column erect, subterete, wingless, apex dentate, pollinia 4, waxy, elongate, laterally compressed. Flowering throughout year. C America, northern S America, W Indies.

CULTIVATION As for *Jacquiniella*.

I.linearis (Jacq.) R. Br.
Lvs to 65×3mm, close-set, narrowly linear, apex obtuse, retuse. Infl. to 6cm; fls to 1cm, 1 to several, variable in colour, white, orange-yellow to bright rose-purple; sep. to 8×3mm, lateral sep. connate at base; pet. obovate to oblong-lanceolate; lip linear or linear-oblanceolate, usually deep rose-purple. Mexico to Brazil, W Indies.

I.lividus Lindl. See *Scaphyglottis livida*.

I.major Cham. & Schltr.
Lf sheaths spotted green, smooth. Infl. usually secund; fls numerous, crowded, large. Mexico to Panama, Jamaica.

I.prolifer R. Br. See *Scaphyglottis prolifera*.

Jacquiniella Schltr. (For Nicholas Joseph von Jacquin (1727–1817), Professor of Botany at Leiden.) Some 11 species of epiphytes, allied to *Isochilus*. Rhizome short. Stems tufted, slender, erect, fractiflex. Leaves fleshy, distichous, linear or linear-lanceolate, acute. Inflorescence apical, one- to several-fld; sepals free or shortly connate, subequal, fleshy, linear-oblong to elliptic-lanceolate, acute to obtuse; petals similar to sepals; lip free, short-clawed, adnate to column base, sometimes geniculate, apex simple or trilobed, column short, somewhat arcuate, with short foot, pollinia 4, waxy, ovoid, laterally compressed. Spring–summer. Tropical America.

CULTIVATION   Grow on rafts or in clay pots of very open bark mix with sphagnum, garden compost and charcoal. Site in a humid, semi-shaded, buoyant position in the cool to intermediate house. Water and syringe plentifully when in growth, reduce water and humidity and increase light during winter months.

J.globosa (Jacq.) Schltr. (*Epidendrum globosum* Jacq.).
Stem to 15cm. Lvs linear, obtuse to acute, deep green, sometimes marked purple. Fls small, usually solitary, olive-grown to green-yellow, not opening fully; sep. to 3×1.5mm, connate at base, elliptic, concave; pet. to 2×1mm, elliptic, acute; lip to 3×1.5mm, geniculate, saccate below middle, apex thickened; column to 1.5mm, pale yellow-green. Mexico to Brazil, W Indies.

J.teretifolia (Sw.) Britt. & Wils. (*Epidendrum teretifolium* Sw.).
Stem to 60cm, erect to ascending. Lvs to 50×2.5mm, subterete, grooved. Fls usually solitary, yellow-green, fleshy; sep. to 12×2mm, lanceolate, acute, lateral sep. oblique; pet. to 5×1.5mm, oblanceolate, obtuse; lip to 9×3mm, lateral lobes suborbicular, midlobe subterete, disc with 3 longitudinal keels; column to 5.5mm, white. W Indies, Mexico to Panama, Venezuela, Columbia.

Jumellea Schltr. (For Prof. Henri Jumelle (1866–1935), French botanist who worked on the flora of Madagascar.) Over 60 species of epiphytes or lithophytes. Stems long or short. Leaves usually distichous and strap-shaped, unequally and obtusely bilobed at apex. Flowers borne singly but often in great numbers, scented, white or green-white, fairly uniform throughout genus; dorsal sepal usually reflexed, lateral sepals fused at base below spur, lateral sepals and petals directed downwards; lip entire, narrowed at base, somewhat channelled, spurred; column expanded at base on anterior side into 2 arms joined on the inner side to the edge of the mouth of the spur and on the outer side to the lateral sepals and petals. Madagascar, Mascarene Is., Comoros Is., tropical and S Africa (2 species).

CULTIVATION   As for *Angraecum*.

J.comorensis (Rchb. f.) Schltr.
Stem to 30cm, somewhat flattened, pendent, branched, leafy. Lvs 3–7×1cm, linear-ligulate, dark green. Peduncle short, covered by 3 sheaths; pedicel and ovary 35–40mm; sep. 20–22×3–4mm, ligulate, obtuse; pet. of similar length but slightly narrowed toward base; lip 20×7mm, narrowly rhomboid; spur 9–11cm, filiform, tinged green toward apex. Comoros Is.

J.densefoliata Sengh.
Small, forming clumps; stem to 8cm; roots 1.5mm diam. Lvs 4–7×1cm, numerous, ligulate, leathery. Peduncle 1.5–2.5cm; pedicel and ovary 4–6cm; fls green-white with white lip; dorsal sep. 15×5mm, lateral sep. slightly larger; pet. 16×4mm; lip 10×10mm, narrow at base then suddenly expanded, narrowing again to an acuminate apex; spur 11–12cm. Madagascar.

J.filicornoides (De Wildeman) Schltr.
Stems 20–30cm, usually erect, forming large clumps. Lvs 7–8 pairs, 4.5–11×1–1.5cm, distichous, ligulate, dark green, held at an angle of 45° to stem. Fls glistening white, about 5cm diam., with strong, sweet, violet-like scent, turning apricot with age; pedicel and ovary 4cm, often sigmoid; sep. 22×4mm, lanceolate; pet. 20×2.5mm, narrowly lanceolate; lip 25×7mm, narrow from a narrow base, channelled; spur 2.5–3cm, slender. Tanzania to Mozambique and S Africa.

J.fragrans (Thouars) Schltr. (*Angraecum fragrans* Thouars).
Stems erect, flattened (6–10mm wide), covered at the base with transversely wrinkled sheaths, leafy toward apex. Lvs 4.5–11×1–1.5cm, linear-ligulate, thin-textured, vanilla-scented when dry. Peduncle 15mm, covered with 3 sheaths; pedicel and ovary 5–6cm; sep. and pet. 20mm, lanceolate, acute; lip 20mm, oblong-spathulate, acute; spur 3–3.5cm. Mascarene Is.

J.gracilipes Schltr.
Stem 5–7cm. Lvs 5–7, 8–40×0.5–2cm, stiff, ligulate, folded, dark green, forming fan at top of stem. Peduncle 2.5–5.5cm; pedicel and ovary 3.5–7cm; fls white, sep. and pet. turning apricot with age; sep. 22–23mm, stiff, linear-lanceolate, sub-

obtuse; pet. of similar length but narrower; lip 22–23×7–8mm, rhomboid-ovate, acuminate, the lower part channelled; spur 11–15cm, filiform; column 3.5–5mm. Madagascar.

J.major Schltr.
Large; stem 40–60cm long, over 1cm diam., pendent, covered with sheaths, with 11–17 lvs toward apex. Lvs to 45×7.5cm, ligulate, coriaceous, folded at base. Peduncle 6–7cm long; pedicel and ovary 9–10cm; fls white, fleshy; sep. 45–50×5–7mm, linear, acute; pet. slightly shorter and narrower; lip 35mm, narrow and channelled at base with a median keel 1mm high, then expanded into an acute, ovate-lanceolate blade 8–13mm wide; spur 6.5–7cm, first pendent, then horizontally recurved; column 5mm. Madagascar.

J.maxillarioides (Ridl.) Schltr. (*Angraecum maxillarioides* Ridl.).
Stem 8–20×2–3cm, covered with fibrous sheaths, forming large clumps. Lvs numerous, close-set, 20–25×4–5cm, ligulate, coriaceous. Infl. numerous; peduncle 1cm; pedicel and ovary 9cm; fls thick-textured, ivory, sometimes turning pink with age; sep. 36×9mm, lanceolate, obtuse; pet. slightly longer and narrower; lip 30–35×10mm, oblong, obtuse; spur 4cm, tapering to an obtuse apex from a wide mouth. Madagascar.

J.sagittata H. Perrier.
Short-stemmed, with fibrous sheaths at base. Lvs 5–6, 25–30×3–3.5cm, ligulate, obtuse, folded into a narrow base, with prominent dorsal vein. Infl. pendent, 2–3 arising below lvs; peduncle thin, 7–9cm with 4–5 sheaths at base; pedicel and ovary 7–7.5cm; fls white, scaly outside; dorsal sep. 30×8mm, lanceolate, acute, lateral sep. 40×6mm; pet. similar to dorsal sep.; lip 36–40×8–20mm, broadly lanceolate, acute, with a prominent keel on upper side; spur 5–6cm, pendent, slightly flattened toward mouth; column stout, 4×3mm. Madagascar.

J.spathulata Schltr.
Stem stout, to 30cm, covered with transversely wrinkled sheaths. Lvs 25–30×6mm, ligulate, thick-textured. Peduncle

short; pedicel and ovary 20mm; sep. lanceolate, acute; pet. lanceolate-spathulate, acute; lip ovate-spathulate, obtuse; spur 25mm, pendent, filiform; column stout. Madagascar.

J.teretifolia Schltr.
Stems short. Lvs 5–7, 10–20cm×2–3mm, cylindric, stiff, sub-obtuse. Infl. wiry, longer than lvs; peduncle 6–10cm with 3 sheaths in lower half; pedicel and ovary 4.5–5cm, very slender; sep. 35mm, linear-lanceolate, long-acuminate; pet. 30mm, linear, acuminate, slightly wider in middle; lip 30×7mm, narrowly clawed at base, then rhomboid and acuminate; spur about 13cm, filiform, pendent; column 4mm. Madagascar.

Kefersteinia Rchb. f. (For Herr Keferstein, *fl.* 1852, German orchid enthusiast.) Some 36 species of epiphytes allied to *Chondrorhyncha*. Rhizome short or absent. Pseudobulbs absent. Leaves equitant, subcoriaceous, articulated at base, linear-lanceolate to oblanceolate. Inflorescence erect to pendent, 1 to few-flowered; flowers thin-textured; sepals spreading, slightly concave, oblong-lanceolate to elliptic-ovate; petals slightly wider than sepals, otherwise similar, oblique; lip articulate to column-foot, entire to obscurely trilobed, base often saccate, apex recurved, finely dentate to fimbriate, callus basal, fleshy, simple to bilobed or bilamellate; column stout, subterete, with a distinct ventral keel, winged, with a short or inconspicuous foot forming a mentum; rostellum tripartite, anther terminal, operculate, incumbent, pollinia 4, waxy, laterally compressed. Costa Rica and Nicaragua to Brazil and Peru.

CULTIVATION See *Huntleya*.

K.costaricensis Schltr. (*Chondrorhyncha costaricensis* (Schltr.) P. Allen).
Lvs 12–18×1.5–2cm, lanceolate, acuminate, plicate. Infl. to 4cm, horizontal to arching or pendent, 1-fld; fls small, white or cream, often spotted rose to maroon, especially on the lip; sep. 0.8–1×0.4–0.5cm, elliptic-lanceolate, acute or apiculate; pet. 0.7–0.9×0.35–0.5cm, obliquely oblong, acute; lip to 1×0.8cm, entire, suborbicular, sometimes apiculate, callus erect, apex biscutellate; column to 0.7cm, erect, club-shaped at apex. Costa Rica, Panama.

K.gemma (Rchb. f.) Schltr.
Fls to 4cm diam.; tepals oblong-oblanceolate, truncate, cream finely flecked or spotted pink-red; lip narrow, flushed rosy mauve with a finely fimbriate margin. Colombia, Ecuador.

K.graminea (Lindl.) Rchb. f. (*Zygopetalum gramineum* Lindl.).
Lvs 18–36×1.75–2.5cm, narrowly lanceolate to linear-oblanceolate, acute or acuminate, sharply carinate beneath. Infl. to 7.5cm, several, suberect, 1 to 3-fld; fls to 4cm diam., pale green or yellow-green, spotted and marked maroon or red-maroon; sep. and pet. ovate-elliptic to oblong-lanceolate, acute, sep. to 2.3×1cm, pet. to 2×0.9cm; lip to 2.1×2.4cm, ovate to rotund, concave, emarginate, apex deflexed, erose-undulate, callus porrect, bilamellate, centre glandular-pubesc.; column to 1.4cm, erect, shallowly winged. Venezuela, Colombia, Ecuador.

K.lactea (Rchb. f.) Schltr. (*Zygopetalum lacteum* Rchb. f.; *Chondrorhyncha lactea* (Rchb. f.) L.O. Williams).
Lvs 8–12×1.25–2cm, oblong to elliptic-lanceolate, acute, obscurely plicate. Infl. to 2cm, erect or slightly arched; fls solitary, small, pure white, sometimes slightly spotted and streaked brown; sep. to 1×0.4cm, elliptic-lanceolate, subacute or obtuse; pet. similar to sep.; lip to 1×1cm, simple, suborbicular or cuneate-oblong, emarginate or apiculate, callus bifid, depressed; column to 0.6cm. Panama, Costa Rica, Mexico.

K.lojae Schltr. (*Chondrorhyncha lojae* (Schltr.) Schweinf.).
Lvs 15–20×1.25–2cm, oblanceolate to linear-oblanceolate, subacute. Infl. to 5cm, horizontal to ascending; fls solitary, thin textured, spreading, white, densely spotted red at centre; dorsal sep. to 1.4×0.6cm, oblong or oblong-lanceolate, acute; lateral sep. oblique, oblong-lanceolate, subacute, basally concave; pet. shorter than dorsal sep., subacute, slightly crenulate; lip to 1.3×1.2cm, short-clawed, ovate-rhombic, apex bilobed or retuse, erose-dentate, callus suborbicular-rhombic, bilobed. Peru, Ecuador.

K.mystacina Rchb. f.
Fls to 4cm diam.; tepals ovate-lanceolate, olive; lip yellow below, blade white, very deeply fimbriate. Panama, Colombia, Ecuador.

K.sanguinolenta Rchb. f. (*Zygopetalum sanguinolentum* (Rchb. f.) Rchb. f.).
Lvs 15–20×2–2.5cm, oblanceolate to linear-oblanceolate, acute, minutely apiculate. Infl. to 5cm; fls solitary, thin-textured, pale yellow to green, spotted purple or dark red; sep. 1–1.2×0.4–0.45cm, broadly lanceolate to oblong-ligulate, obtuse or subacute; pet. to 1×0.45cm, ovate-oblong to oblong-ligulate, obtuse or subacute; lip to 1cm, obovate to cuneate-flabellate, emarginate or rounded, strongly reflexed, basal margins denticulate, undulate, callus to 0.4cm, purple, ligulate, bidentate at apex; column to 0.9cm, wings fleshy, slightly pilose, white spotted purple. Venezuela, Ecuador.

K.tolimensis Schltr.
Lvs 18–25×2.5–3cm, broadly lanceolate, acute or acuminate. Infl. to 13cm, erect to pendent; fls solitary cream to yellow, spotted dark red-brown, maroon or violet, especially on lip; dorsal sep. 2–2.5×0.5–0.8cm, oblong-elliptic to ovate-elliptic, subacute to obtuse, lateral sep. to 2.7×0.8cm, lanceolate to oblong-lanceolate, subacute to obtuse; pet. to 2.2×1cm, ovate to ovate-elliptic, obtuse, undulate; lip to 2×2.3cm, suborbicular to subquadrate or transversely elliptic, entire or obscurely trilobed, emarginate to rounded, irregularly fimbriate-dentate, callus erect, bilamellate; column to 1.4cm, cream-brown marked maroon. Venezuela, Colombia, Ecuador.

Kegeliella Mansf. (Diminutive of the orchid genus name *Kegelia*, named for A.H.H. Kegel (1819–56), gardener under Van Houtte.) Some 3 species of epiphytes. Pseudobulbs ovoid, angulate, slightly compressed, 1–3-leaved at apex. Leaves ovate to broadly elliptic-lanceolate, acute, plicate, petiolate. Inflorescence a basal, pendent raceme, few- to many-flowered; flowers small; sepals subequal, free, spreading, exterior covered with glandular hairs; petals smaller than sepals, subsimilar; lip fleshy to membranous, unguiculate, trilobed, lateral lobes large, erect or spreading, oblique, midlobe small, sometimes concave; disc with an erect, fleshy callus; column elongate, slightly arched, footless, apex broadly alate, anther terminal, operculate, incumbent, unilocular, pollinia 2. Costa Rica, Panama, Jamaica, Trinidad, Surinam, Venezuela.

CULTIVATION   Warm to intermediate-growing. Plant on rafts or in baskets in an open medium; position in light shade with high humidity; water and syringe throughout the year.

K.houtteana (Rchb. f.) L.O. Williams (*Kegelia houtteana* Rchb. f.).
Pseudobulbs to 3.5×1.5cm, shiny light green, usually 3-lvd at apex. Lvs to 18×5cm, ovate to elliptic-lanceolate, green-brown above, maroon-brown beneath. Infl. to 10cm; peduncle densely black-glandular-pubesc.; tepals pale green or pale yellow blotched and banded red-brown, with red glandular hairs, column bright apple green; sep. to 15×4.5mm, lanceolate or elliptic-lanceolate, acute or acuminate, lateral sep. oblique; pet. to 13×2.5mm, lanceolate to elliptic-oblanceolate, acute or acuminate; lip to 11×9mm, 3-lobed, lateral lobes subdolabriform, midlobe subcordate to triangular or ovate, callus linguiform, bilobed, laterally compressed; column to 12mm. Jamaica, Panama, Trinidad, Colombia, Venezuela, Surinam.

Kingidium P. Hunt. (For Sir George King (1840–1909), who wrote *Orchids of the Sikkim-Himalaya* with R. Pantling (1852–1910).) Some 5 species of monopodial epiphytes. Inflorescence a panicle or raceme with many small flowers; dorsal sepal and petals free, similar, lateral sepals fused with the lip base forming a small projection, lip basally saccate, trilobed, midlobe wide, narrowing towards the base, lateral lobes erect, callus bilobed. India to W Malaya.

CULTIVATION   As for *Phalaenopsis*.

K.decumbens (Griff.) P. Hunt. See *K.deliciosum*.

K.deliciosum (Rchb. f.) Sweet (*K.decumbens* (Griff.) P. Hunt; *Phalaenopsis deliciosa* Rchb. f.; *Doritis wightii* (Rchb. f.) Benth. & Hook. f.).
Stem to 2.5cm. Lvs to 20cm, 3–6, oblong-lanceolate, undulate. Infl. to 15cm, branched; fls 1.5–2cm diam., many; tepals creamy white or yellow (*K.wightii*), lip marked pink-purple; dorsal sep. to 8.5mm; pet. oblong; lip basally saccate, midlobe with a bilobed appendage, lateral lobes erect, fleshy. SE Asia.

K.taeniale (Lindl.) P. Hunt (*Doritis taenialis* (Lindl.) Hook. f.).
Roots long, flat. Lvs to 10cm, 1–2, oblong-elliptic, narrow, pendent. Fls to 2cm diam., 6–8, pink-mauve; dorsal sep. oblong-lanceolate, lateral sep. elliptic; pet. ovate, shorter than lateral sep.; lip fused to column foot, basally spurred with 2 retrorse lateral lobes, midlobe oblong-spathulate, entire. India, Burma.

Koellensteinia Rchb. f. (For the Austrian Captain Kellner von Koellenstein.) Some 16 species of terrestrials or epiphytes, allied to *Zygopetalum*. Rhizome short. Stems short, usually pseudobulbous, unifoliate to trifoliate. Leaves linear-lanceolate to elliptic-oblong, mostly plicate, petiolate. Inflorescence a raceme or a panicle, lateral, erect or ascending, few- to many-flowered; flowers small; sepals and petals subsimilar, free, oblong to ovate, lateral sepals oblique; lip articulate to column foot, trilobed, lateral lobes erect or spreading, large, midlobe entire or bilobed, disc with erect callus; column short, often winged, with a conspicuous foot, anther terminal, incumbent, operculate, pollinia 2 or 4. S America.

CULTIVATION Grow in intermediate conditions in light shade and high humidity; plant in a free-draining, bark-based medium. Never allow to dry out completely for long periods.

K.brachystalix (Rchb. f.) Schltr. See *Otostylis brachystalix.*

K.graminea (Lindl.) Rchb. f.
Stems inconspicuous. Lvs to 26×1cm, narrowly linear to linear-lanceolate, *not* with impressed veins, acute. Infl. to 25cm, suberect, 1- to several-fld; fls to 2cm diam., white, cream or pale yellow, barred red-brown; sep. to 11×6mm, elliptic-ovate to oblong-ovate, acute, concave; pet. narrower than sep., oblong-lanceolate, subacute or obtuse; lip to 6mm, lateral lobes erect, ovate to ovate-oblong, obtuse to rounded, midlobe broadly reniform-flabellate, retuse to apiculate, callus fleshy, subquadrate, bilobed; column to 3mm, stout, winged. Spring. Colombia, Venezuela, Brazil, Guianas, Trinidad.

K.hyacinthoides Schltr.
Pseudobulbs to 10cm, cylindrical, apically unifoliate. Lvs to 35×8cm, erect, lanceolate to oblong-lanceolate, acute. Raceme to 30cm, erect, solitary, densely many-fld; fls light yellow or yellow-green; fls to 15×6mm, oblong-lanceolate to elliptic-lanceolate; pet. to 13×5mm, elliptic-oblong, apiculate; lip to 10×10mm, pandurate to trilobed, lateral lobes obliquely ovate to suborbicular, erect, midlobe rhombic to suborbicular or transversely elliptic, callus bilobed, erect, subconical-falcate; column to 5mm, wings involute, anth. pale yellow. Venezuela, Brazil.

K.ionoptera Lind. & Rchb. f. (*Aganisia ionoptera* (Nichols.) Lind. & Rchb. f.).
Pseudobulbs to 5cm, narrowly ovoid, unifoliate or bifoliate. Lvs to 25×3cm, narrowly elliptic-lanceolate. Raceme erect, several-fld; tepals yellow-white, marked or suffused violet, sep. to 14mm, ovate to oblong-elliptic, subacute, pet. similar to sep., smaller; lip to 10mm, white to yellow-white streaked or banded red-violet, sharply 3-lobed, lateral lobes erect, obliquely suborbicular to ovate, midlobe transversely oblong to reniform, retuse, callus fleshy, bilobed, retrorse; column short, winged. Peru, Ecuador.

K.kellneriana Rchb. f. (*Aganisia kellneriana* (Rchb. f.) Benth.).
Pseudobulbs to 30×6mm, clustered, subterete, unifoliate or bifoliate. Lvs to 70×4.5cm, linear-lanceolate. Raceme to 45cm, erect, few- to many-fld; fls to 2cm diam., fragrant; tepals pale green, sep. to 12×6mm, elliptic-lanceolate, acute, concave, fleshy, lateral sep. oblique, pet. to 11×4mm, ovate-oblong, concave; lip to 7×10mm, fleshy, white marked dark maroon-pink, short-clawed, lateral lobes erect, obliquely rhombic-triangular, obtuse, midlobe spreading, transversely oblong-reniform, slightly concave, callus erect, fleshy, bilobed, verrucose; column to 4mm, erect, subterete, green-white, anth. yellow-white. Mostly spring–early summer. Panama, Colombia, Venezuela, Brazil, Guyana.

K.tricolor (Lindl.) Rchb. f. (*Zygopetalum tricolor* Lindl.).
Resembles *K.kellneriana* except lvs smaller. Infl. loosely 8–15-fld; fls to 1.5cm diam., fragrant; tepals green-white, shorter and broader than *K.kellneriana*; lip white banded pale purple. Spring. Brazil, Guianas.

Lacaena Lindl. (One of the names of Helen of Troy, given to this genus on account of its beauty.) 2 species, epiphytes similar in habit to *Acineta* or *Lueddemannia*, from which they differ in the long, many-flowered, pendulous racemes of cupped, waxy flowers. These are characterized by the articulated, 3-lobed lip with a hairy callus, and by the two pollinia on a short stipe and round viscidium. Mexico to Panama.

CULTIVATION   As for *Acineta*.

L.bicolor Lindl. (*Lueddemannia sanderiana; Peristeria longiscapa*).
Infl. 30–40cm, strongly pendulous, to 15-fld; fls to 5cm diam., fragrant, fleshy, open-campanulate; tepals ovate-elliptic, scurfy beneath, yellow-green spotted, stained or streaked violet; lip 3-lobed, midlobe ovate, scarcely clawed, spotted rose-purple with a strong, dark purple-maroon blotch at its base, callus hairy, purple. Guatemala.

L.spectabilis (Klotzsch) Rchb.f. (*Nauenia spectabilis* Klotzsch).
Differs from *L.bicolor* in the slightly smaller fls with white to pink-white tepals and the lip spotted dull rose, lacking dark basal blotch, with narrowly and distinctly clawed, oblong to subquadrate midlobe and a single, glabrous callus. Mexico to Panama.

Laelia Lindl. (For Laelia, one of the Vestal Virgins.) About 70 species of epiphytes or lithophytes, rarely terrestrials, allied to *Cattleya* and *Encyclia*. Rhizome creeping, short or long; pseudobulbs elliptic, ovoid, conical, subglobose or cylindrical, with papery bracts at base. Leaves 1 to several, borne at apex of pseudobulb, leathery or fleshy, ovate to linear-lanceolate or ligulate, midrib often carinate below. Inflorescence on pseudobulb, emerging from a sheath, subsessile or pedunculate, usually racemose but sometimes paniculate or single-flowered; flowers showy, white, mauve, pink, scarlet, orange or yellow; sepals more or less equal, free, spreading; petals similar to sepals but usually longer or shorter and often wider; lip free or slightly joined to column, trilobed, lateral lobes folded up and enveloping column, usually larger than midlobe, disc smooth or lamellate; column usually long, sometimes winged, usually toothed at apex, anther terminal, operculate, pollinia 8, 4 in each anther cell, waxy, ovoid. C & S America, from W Indies south to Brazil.

CULTIVATION   A spectacular genus allied to *Cattleya* and involved in many hybrids with that genus. Suitable for the intermediate house, growing cases or sunny humid positions in the home. Very broadly, *Laelia* falls into four groups on the basis of vegetative characters; cultural requirements vary accordingly. In the first group, large and showy species such as *L.crispa*, *L.purpurata* and *L.tenebrosa* should be grown as for the unifoliate *Cattleya* spp. they superficially resemble. *Laelia anceps*, *L.autumnalis* and *L.gouldiana* are somewhat squatter plants with slender racemes of beautiful magenta flowers. Again, pot in a very open medium or mount on rafts, as for *Cattleya*; water, syringe and feed copiously when in growth; impose a dry rest from mid-autumn and a cooler, drier atmosphere to encourage the development of flowers in winter. This group will tolerate lower temperatures than most (winter min. 7°C/45°F) and will succeed in most situations provided they have maximum sunlight. In the third group, typified by *L.harpophylla*, habit tends to be rather willowy, with narrow leaves and slender, cane-like pseudobulbs: several of these species produce short racemes of flowers in vivid tones of flame, orange and yellow. They require a somewhat denser potting medium, high humidity and partial shade when in growth, and misting or infrequent watering when at rest to prevent shrivelling.

Semi-dwarf plants with rounded pseudobulbs and broader leaves, for example the orange-flowered *L.milleri* or the exceptionally showy magenta *L.speciosa*, again favour a denser medium, perhaps with additional rockwool or sphagnum and very small pots or baskets. Grow in full sunlight in intermediate conditions; water and feed freely when in growth and impose a cool dry rest otherwise, watering into prevent shrivelling and root death. *L.pumila*, a dwarf species with disproportionately large and extravagant blooms, is most closely allied to species in Group 1. Because of its size, however, it requires very careful cultivation in pans or half-pots of fern or coconut fibre, charcoal and sphagnum. Water and feed sparingly when in growth, maintaining high temperatures and humidity in a well ventilated position shaded from full sunlight; at other times, reduce temperatures and atmospheric humidity; admit full sunlight; maintain turgor by misting on warmer days (except when in flower). This species may grow continuously and is an excellent plant for growing cases.

Propagate by divisions of leaders with 2–3 backbulbs when repotting.

L.acuminata Lindl. See *L.rubescens*.

L.albida Lindl. (*L.discolor* A. Rich. & Gal.).
Resembling *L.autumnalis* but with smaller, paler fls. Pseudobulbs c5cm, ovoid, oblong or conical, 2-lvd. Lvs c15cm, linear to ligulate, leathery, dark green. Scape to 35cm, raceme 3–8-fld; fls scented, c5cm diam., white tinged pink, lip lined yellow; sep. 30×8mm, lanceolate, acute; pet. 25×12mm, narrowly elliptic, margins undulate; lip 20×16mm, oblong, lateral lobes obtuse, enclosing column, midlobe broadly ovate, reflexed, edge undulate. Winter. Mexico.

L.anceps Lindl.
Pseudobulbs 5–7cm, ovoid, obscurely 4-angled or laterally compressed, 1–2-lvd. Lvs to 15cm, fleshy, lanceolate, glossy green. Raceme erect, 50–70cm, 3–6-fld; fls fragrant, 8–10cm diam., rose-lilac or magenta, lip deep purple tinged with pink

and yellow in the throat, something wholly or largely white; sep. 50–60×15mm, lanceolate, acute; pet. 50–60×30mm, elliptic, acute; lip 45–50mm, funnel-shaped toward base, midlobe tongue-like, undulate. Winter. Mexico, Honduras. Many variants of this sp. have been described.

L.angereri Pabst.
Lithophytic, to 55cm with short rhiz.; pseudobulbs c20cm, cylindrical, somewhat thickened basally, 1-lvd. Lvs about 18×2cm, lanceolate. Peduncle erect, 20–25cm, rachis 10cm; raceme densely about 10-fld; fls brick-red, erect; ovary and pedicel 23mm; dorsal sep. 20×6mm, linear-elliptic, lateral sep. similar but slightly shorter and oblique; pet. 23×5.5mm, linear-elliptic; lip broadly elliptic in outline, lateral lobes semi-elliptic, apex rounded and slightly undulate, midlobe broadly elliptic with a short claw, disc 4-ridged, the 2 inner

ridges extending to the centre of the midlobe; column narrowly winged. Brazil.

L.autumnalis (La Ll. & Lex.) Lindl.
Pseudobulbs 6–15cm, flask- or pear-shaped, ribbed, 2–3-lvd. Lvs 10–15cm, fleshy, lanceolate, bright green. Raceme to 60cm, laxly 3–6-fld; fls scented, to 10cm diam., tepals rose-purple, lip rose-white with purple apex and yellow in centre; sep. to 50mm, lanceolate, acute; pet. rhomboid-elliptic, all with edges undulate; lip deeply trilobed with 2 crests in centre, lateral lobes ovate, obtuse, enclosing column, midlobe narrowly elliptic, deeply emarginate with an apiculus in the sinus. Autumn. Mexico.

L.autumnalis var. **furfuracea** (Lindl.) Rolfe. See *L.furfuracea*.

L.bahiensis Schltr.
To 45cm; rhiz. short; pseudobulbs 4–7cm×5–6mm, cylindrical, 1-lvd. Lvs 6–9×1.5–2cm, suberect, narrowly oblong, subacute, slightly fleshy. Raceme slender, erect, laxly 4–8-fld; peduncle to 30cm, rachis about 9cm; fls golden-yellow; pedicel and ovary 17–20mm; sep. 17mm, ligulate-oblong, obtuse, lateral sep. oblique; pet. similar to lateral sep. but slightly narrower; lip 15×10mm, ovate in outline, slightly clawed at base, the edges adnate to column, with 2 parallel ridges, trilobed in apical third, lateral lobes ovate-oblong, obtuse, midlobe obovate, apiculate, the edges slightly undulate; column 8mm, slightly curved. Brazil.

L.boothiana Rchb. f. See *L.lobata*.

L.bradei Pabst.
Small lithophyte; pseudobulbs 4×1cm, cylindrical. Lvs 3×1.5cm, elliptic, fleshy, the margins incurved. Infl. short; scape 5–6cm, raceme laxly few-fld; fls pale yellow; dorsal sep. 16×4mm, oblong, acute, lateral sep. slightly shorter and wider; pet. 16×4mm, falcate, acute; lip 11×9.5mm, lateral lobes 8×4mm, obtuse, midlobe 6–7×5mm, spathulate, with 2 ridges, the margins somewhat crisped; column 5mm. Brazil.

L.briegeri Blum.
Lithophytic; pseudobulbs pear-shaped. Racemes much taller than lvs; fls yellow; sep. lanceolate, acute, dorsal sep. 25×9mm, lateral sep. slightly shorter and broader; pet. similar to dorsal sep.; lip 17×16mm with 3–5 keels running from the base, the middle keel reaching the apex, deeply trilobed in apical half, midlobe 16×17mm, almost orbicular, lateral lobes erect. Brazil.

L.cinnabarina Lindl.
Lithophytic; pseudobulb 10–20cm, cylindrical, dark green, 1-rarely 2-lvd. Lvs 15–25cm, erect, linear-lanceolate, acute, rigid, fleshy. Raceme 25–50cm, 5–15-fld; fls about 5cm diam., deep orange-red, slender; tepals 22–28×4–5mm, linear, somewhat falcate, spreading; lip about 15mm, recurved, trilobed at about halfway, lateral lobes acute, midlobe very undulate on margin. Spring–early summer. Brazil. Fls easily mistaken for those of *L.harpophylla* or *L.milleri*: the former is a much more reedy plant with narrow lvs and short infl., the latter a squat, diminutive plant with obtuse – not acute – lateral lobes to lip.

L.crispa (Lindl.) Rchb. f.
Habit *Cattleya*-like. Pseudobulbs remotely spaced on rhiz., ovate-elliptic, laterally compressed, to 25cm, somewhat stalked at base. Lvs to 30cm, 1–2 per bulb, oblong-ligulate, obtuse, pale green. Raceme 4–7-fld, emerging from a tough sheath; fls very showy, 12cm diam., white, lip usually mainly purple with some yellow marks; sep. 7cm, lanceolate-spathulate; pet. wider, narrowly elliptic, undulate; lip lateral lobes enfolding column, midlobe oblong, acute, edge undulate. Autumn. Brazil.

L.crispata (Thunb.) Garay (*L.rupestris* Lindl.; *L.tereticaulis* Hoehne).
Lithophyte; pseudobulbs 4–10cm, oblong-cylindrical, 1-lvd. Lvs to 16×3cm, narrowly oblong, leathery, keeled below. Raceme to 26cm, 2–10-fld; fls to 4.5cm diam., pale pink, lip

white in throat, midlobe purple; tepals 20–22×8mm, broadly lanceolate, acute, the edges slightly undulate; lip 16×12mm, clawed at base, trilobed, lateral lobes erect, rounded, undulate, midlobe orbicular or ovate, reflexed, margin crisped. Brazil.

L.discolor A. Rich. & Gal. See *L.albida*.

L.endsfeldzii Pabst.
Lithophyte; pseudobulbs 12×1.5cm, conical, 1-lvd. Lvs oblong-lanceolate, transversely wrinkled on upper surface, midvein prominent below. Scape 30cm; raceme laxly several-fld; fls pale yellow, opening in succession; dorsal sep. 16×4mm, linear-oblong, obtuse, lateral sep. slightly shorter and wider; pet. 16×5mm, lanceolate, slightly curved; lip elliptic in outline, trilobed in upper third, lateral lobes semi-elliptic, rounded, midlobe orbicular, crisped, with 4 lamellae reaching the apex; column obscurely winged. Brazil.

L.esalqueana Blum. ex Pabst.
Lithophytic; pseudobulbs pyriform. Infl. barely exceeding lvs; fls yellow to orange; dorsal sep. 11×3.5mm, lateral sep. similar but slightly wider; pet. 12×4mm; lip 8×8mm, deeply trilobed in apical third, lateral lobes erect, midlobe 2.5×2.5mm, almost orbicular, with 3 longitudinal keels. Brazil.

L. × esperito-sanctensis Pabst. (*L.pumila × L.xanthina*.)
Fl. colour showing influence of both parents – golden and mauve; dorsal sep. 40×12mm, oblanceolate, lateral sep. similar but wider; pet. 40×22mm, ovate; lip 40×38mm, obscurely trilobed in apical quarter, all lobes rounded. Brazil.

L.fidelensis Pabst.
Epiphyte to 30cm; pseudobulbs about 4×3cm, ovoid, laterally compressed, 1-lvd. Lvs 10–12×3.5–4cm, oblong, obtuse, midvein impressed above and prominent below. Raceme 2-fld; fls rose-pink, disc usually pale yellow or white; sep. 45–55× 8.5–12mm, lanceolate, dorsal sep. slightly wider than lateral sep.; pet. 40–55×15–30mm, ovate or oblong, abruptly apiculate; lip 35–45×25–40mm, ovate, trilobed, lateral lobes minute, midlobe with apex rounded, slightly emarginate. Brazil.

L. × finckeniana O'Brien. (*L.anceps* var. *sanderiana × L.albida*.)
Believed to be a natural hybrid of the above species and intermediate in character between them. Pseudobulbs ovoid, 1-lvd. Fls white, the lip striped purple towards base, with a purple crescent-shaped mark on the midlobe and 3 yellow ridges at junction of lobes.

L.flava Lindl. (*L.fulva* Lindl.).
Lithophytic; pseudobulbs 3–4cm, narrowly ovoid, 1-lvd. Lvs 7–8cm, elliptic. Racemes 30–50cm, 3–10-fld; fls canary yellow, about 6cm diam.; tepals 20–30mm, lanceolate, falcate; lip narrow, recurved, trilobed, with 4–6 keels, lateral lobes obtuse, midlobe quadrate, edge undulate. Late spring. Brazil.

L.fulva Lindl. See *L.flava*.

L.furfuracea Lindl. (*L.autumnalis* var. *furfuracea* (Lindl.) Rolfe).
Closely allied to *L.autumnalis*. Pseudobulbs to 4cm, ovoid, slightly ribbed, 1-lvd. Lvs erect, to 10cm, lanceolate, acute, fleshy. Racemes to 35cm, 1–3-fld; fls to 12cm diam., sep. and pet. light purple, lip deep purple; sep. 50–60mm, lanceolate; pet. similar but wider, undulate; lip deeply trilobed, lateral lobes rounded, midlobe oblong or elliptic; ovary scurfy-glandular. Mexico.

L.ghillanyi Pabst.
Dwarf, lithophytic, about 15cm; pseudobulbs about 3×1cm, narrowly ovoid, 1–2-lvd. Lvs 4×2–2.5cm, elliptic, somewhat folded, obtuse, purple-green. Infl. 10cm; scape short, 5–6cm; raceme laxly 3-fld; fls pale to deep rose-violet or violet and white; sep. oblong, obtuse, dorsal sep. 18×7mm, lateral sep. slightly shorter and wider; pet. 18×9mm, elliptic; lip 12×14–15mm, trilobed, lateral lobes 10×6mm, midlobe 5mm wide, more or less orbicular, edge crisped, slightly emarginate, disc verrucose with 2 crests; column winged, 10mm. Brazil.

L.gloedeniana Hoehne.
Lithophytic with short, creeping rhiz.; pseudobulbs clustered, 7–10×2–3cm, almost cylindrical but tapered to apex, 1-lvd. Lvs 7–10×2.5–3.5cm, more or less erect, elliptic, fleshy. Infl. 20–40cm; raceme rather laxly about 8-fld; pedicel and ovary 25mm; fls yellow, lip veined red; tepals spreading, sep. oblong-lanceolate, dorsal sep. 24×6mm, obtuse, lateral sep. 22×5mm, slightly falcate, apex acute and reflexed, pet. 22×4mm, narrowly oblong; lip 15–16mm with 3 longitudinal ridges, ovate in outline, base truncate, trilobed at about halfway, lateral lobes acute, erect, midlobe reflexed, obovate, margin crisped; column 7mm. Brazil.

L.gloriosa (Rchb. f.) L.O. Williams. See *Schomburgkia fimbriata*.

L.gouldiana Rchb. f.
Similar to *L.autumnalis* but flowering slightly later, plants larger, fls with wider pet. Pseudobulbs to 8cm, fusiform. Lvs to 24×3cm, erect. Raceme 30–50cm, 2–6-fld; fls 8cm diam., rich purple; sep. lanceolate; pet. broadly ovate, undulate; lip 3-lobed, deep purple, paler in throat with 3-ridged golden callus, lateral lobes rounded or quadrate, striped within, midlobe spathulate. Mexico.

L.grandiflora Lindl. See *L.speciosa*.

L.grandis Lindl. & Paxt.
Pseudobulbs to 30cm, conical, 1–2-lvd. Lvs to 25cm, oblong. Raceme to 18cm, 2–5-fld; fls 10–18cm diam., sep. and pet. yellow-brown, lip white or off-white veined rose-purple; sep. to 8cm, lanceolate, acute; pet. wider and undulate; lip long-tubed, midlobe with serrate, wavy margin. Late spring–summer. Brazil.

L.harpophylla Rchb. f.
Epiphytic; pseudobulbs 15–30cm, clustered, slender, semiterete, 1–2-lvd, dark green flushed maroon. Lvs 15–20×3cm, linear-lanceolate, acute, thick-textured. Raceme shorter than lvs, 3–7-fld; fls 5–8cm diam., vermilion, lip with a paler margin and yellow in centre; tepals spreading, subequal, 40–45mm, narrowly lanceolate, acute; lip deeply trilobed, lateral lobes acute, midlobe linear-lanceolate, acute with 2 ridges in throat, margins crisped. Winter–spring. Brazil. cf. *L.cinnabarina, L.milleri.*

L.humboldtii (Rchb. f.) L.O. Williams. See *Schomburgkia humboldtii*.

L.itambana Pabst.
Dwarf lithophyte; pseudobulbs 2.5–3.5cm×6–8mm, narrowly cylindrical. Lvs 4.5×2.5cm, ovate, somewhat folded, fleshy. Raceme slightly exceeding lvs, 2-fld; fls erect, deep yellow; pedicel and ovary 4cm; dorsal sep. 25×10mm, narrowly elliptic, lateral sep. 20×12mm, narrowly ovate, slightly oblique; pet. 23×12mm, narrowly ovate, somewhat falcate, lip 15×15mm, orbicular, lateral lobes semicircular, midlobe round, edge crisped, disc with 2 smooth lamellae. Brazil.

L.jongheana Rchb. f.
Pseudobulbs 5cm, oblong, slightly compressed, 1-lvd. Lvs erect, 10–15cm, elliptic, obtuse. Infl. about 10cm, 1–2-fld; fls 12cm diam., rose-purple, sometimes pure white, lip yellow and white in throat; tepals spreading, sep. 50–60×14mm, lanceolate, acute; pet. 60–70×28mm, obovate, very slightly undulate; lip 55×30mm with about 7 ridges in throat, trilobed, lateral lobes triangular, forming a short tube, midlobe rounded, edge crisped; column about 3cm. Spring. Brazil.

L.liliputana Pabst.
Dwarf lithophyte to 6cm; pseudobulbs 8–15×8–10mm, tightly clustered, globose or oblong, dark purple. Lvs 10–15× 8–12mm, stiff, ovate, fleshy, somewhat folded, purple. Scape 1cm; infl. single-fld, fls rose-pink; ovary rose-violet, 2cm; dorsal sep. 14×4mm, linear-oblong, subacute, lateral sep. 12.5×4mm, narrowly falcate-triangular; pet. 15×3.5mm, falcate-lanceolate; lip almost orbicular, trilobed, lateral lobes oblong, almost equalling midlobe, midlobe 5×3.5mm, oblong, undulate, with 2 lamellae reaching apex, disc yellow with 4 lamellae. Brazil.

L.lobata (Lindl.) Veitch (*L.boothiana* Rchb. f.).
Pseudobulbs to 20cm, conical or fusiform, 1-lvd. Lvs to 20cm, lanceolate, coriaceous. Raceme to 40cm, 2–5-fld; fls about 13cm diam., rose-purple with darker veins, rarely pure white, lip with carmine-red markings; sep. 70mm, linear-lanceolate, acute, margins reflexed; pet. lanceolate, somewhat twisted and undulate; lip ovate, obscurely trilobed, lateral lobes erect forming a fairly long tube, midlobe with crisped edge and emarginate apex. Spring. Brazil.

L.longipes Rchb. f.
Pseudobulbs 6–8×2cm, narrowly oblong or conical, covered with white or pink membranous sheaths, 1-lvd. Lvs 7–15×2–3cm, elliptic-oblong, obtuse, fleshy, keeled below. Raceme far exceeds lvs, usually 2–4-fld but sometimes with more; fls to 5cm diam., sep. and pet. pale mauve-purple, rarely pure white, lip golden yellow or white with yellow throat; sep. 16–20×5mm, linear-oblong, obtuse; pet. similar but very slightly shorter; lip 12×10mm, trilobed, lateral lobes oblong, erect, margins recurved and undulate, midlobe ovate or oblong, obtuse, margin crisped-undulate; column very short. Brazil.

L.lucasiana Rolfe (*L.ostermayeri* Hoehne).
Lithophyte; pseudobulbs squat, pyriform, 1-lvd. Raceme few-fld, slightly longer than lvs; fls lilac to purple with a yellow lip (white forms also occur); dorsal sep. 20×7.5mm, oblong, apiculate, lateral sep. slightly wider; pet. 18×7.5mm; lip 15×15mm, deeply trilobed in apical half, lateral lobes erect, acute, midlobe orbicular, undulate. Brazil.

L.lundii Rchb. f. & Warm. (*L.regnellii* Barb. Rodr.).
Small, epiphytic; pseudobulbs 3–4×1–1.5cm, oblong, slightly compressed. Lvs 8–9×0.5cm, erect or spreading, fleshy, channelled above. Raceme arched, 2-fld, much shorter than lvs; fls white with rose-purple veins on lip; sep. 20–22×4–5mm, ligulate, acute, rather fleshy; pet. similar but slightly narrower; lip 20–23×11–12mm, narrowly elliptic-ovate, fleshy, deeply trilobed, lateral lobes erect, acute, midlobe reflexed, margin crisped and undulate, disc fleshy with 4 ridges; column 7–8mm. Brazil.

L.lyonsii (Lindl.) L.O. Williams. See *Schomburgkia lyonsii*.
L.majalis Lindl. See *L.speciosa*.

L.milleri Bl.
Diminutive lithophyte; pseudobulbs to 4cm, squat, flask-shaped, clustered, basally sheathed. Lvs to 6×3cm, rarely 2 per bulb, ovate-oblong, acute, keeled below, rigid, erect, dark green colouring purple in full sunlight. Raceme to 1m, few-fld; fls 6cm diam., orange-red, tinged with yellow in throat; tepals spreading, elliptic, acute, sep. 26–30×10–20mm, lateral sep. narrower than dorsal sep., pet. 30×18mm; lip 24×13mm, trilobed at about halfway, lateral lobes erect so that basal half is tubular, midlobe oblong, margin very undulate. Summer. Brazil. cf. *L.cinnabarina, L.harpophylla.*

L.monophylla (Griseb.) Hook. f. See *Neocogniauxia monophylla*.
L.ostermayeri Hoehne. See *L.lucasiana*.
L.peduncularis Lindl. See *L.rubescens*.

L.perrinii Lindl.
Epiphytic; pseudobulbs 15–25cm, ovoid, laterally compressed, 1-lvd. Lvs 15–25cm, dark green. Raceme 2–6-fld; fls showy, 12–14cm diam., flat, rose-pink or pure white, lip magenta with a yellow blotch in the throat; sep. to 70mm, lanceolate, acute; pet. wider, elliptic, acute; lip shorter than sep., lateral lobes small, midlobe reflexed, acute. Winter. Brazil.

L.pfisteri Pabst & Sengh.
Lithophytic; pseudobulbs 5–6cm, pear-shaped, 1-lvd. Lvs about 7×2.5cm, narrowly elliptic, somewhat conduplicate, leathery. Scape with several triangular sheaths; raceme densely 3–5-fld; fls purple, lip white in centre, edged dark purple; ovary 15–20mm; bracts 4–5mm; sep. 15–17×5mm, lanceolate, acute, dorsal sep. exceeds lateral sep.; pet. 17×4.5mm, narrowly lanceolate, slightly curved; lip 14×10–11mm, almost oblong with 4 longitudinal ridges,

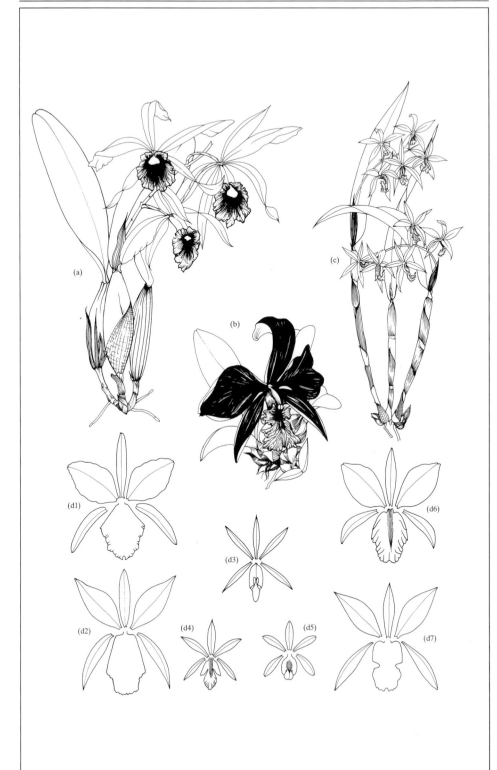

Laelia (a) *L.purpurata* (b) *L.speciosa* (c) *L.harpophylla* (d) Exploded flower outlines (i) *L.purpurata* (ii) *L.tenebrosa* (iii) *L.cinnabarina* (iv) *L.milleri* (v) *L.flava* (vi) *L.pumila* (vii) *L.autumnalis*

trilobed in apical third, lateral lobes rounded, midlobe 5.5mm diam., rounded, margin undulate. Brazil.

L.pumila (Hook.) Rchb. f.
Diminutive epiphyte; pseudobulbs 3–10cm, 1-lvd, slender, laterally compressed. Lvs to 10cm, oblong, obtuse. Infl. short, 1-fld; fls to 10cm diam., flat, slightly drooping, showy, spreading across lvs and pseudobulbs, rose-purple, rarely white, lip deep purple with yellow throat, sometimes edged and veined amethyst (*L.dayana* Rchb. f.); sep. 40–50×15–18mm, lanceolate, somewhat recurved; pet. similar but ovate, about 25mm wide; lip about 50×25mm, trilobed, lateral lobes erect, midlobe emarginate, margin undulate. Spring or autumn. Brazil.

L.purpurata Lindl.
Epiphytic, habit *Cattleya*-like: cf *L.crispa, L.tenebrosa.* Pseudobulbs to 50cm, spindle-shaped, somewhat laterally compressed, 1-lvd. Lvs 30–40×4–5cm, narrowly elliptic, leathery. Raceme to 30cm tall, 3–7-fld; fls fleshy, 15–20cm diam., tepals white tinged with pink, sometimes pure white, lip white at apex, purple towards base, yellow with purple veins in throat, rarely deep violet; tepals spreading, undulate with margins strongly revolute, particularly in basal portions, sep. 75–90×15mm, oblong-lanceolate, pet. similar but broader; lip 60–70mm, trilobed at about halfway, lateral lobes enfolding column so that base funnel-shaped, midlobe ovate to orbicular, 40mm diam., margin undulate. Spring–summer. Brazil.

L.regnellii Barb. Rodr. See *L.lundii.*

L.rubescens Lindl. (*L.acuminata* Lindl.; *L.peduncularis* Lindl.).
Epiphytic; pseudobulbs 3–6.5×2.5–3.5cm, orbicular, ovoid or oblong, compressed, glossy, 1–2-lvd. Lvs 5–20×2–4.5cm, oblong-elliptic, obtuse, rather fleshy. Scape to 75cm; raceme few- to several-fld; fls scented, very pale mauve to rose-purple, rarely white, lip with central purple or carmine blotch; pedicel and ovary 25–35mm; sep. 28–42×6–9mm, linear-lanceolate to oblanceolate, acute or obtuse; pet. 30–45×8–18mm, elliptic, acute, obtuse or apiculate; lip 22–35×20–22mm, trilobed at about halfway, lateral lobes short, midlobe more or less oblong, margins undulate, apex truncate or acute, disc with 2–3 central ridges; column 8–10mm. From Mexico through C America to Panama.

L.rupestris Lindl. See *L.crispata.*

L.sincorana Schltr.
Pseudobulbs 2–2.5cm, subglobose, somewhat laterally compressed, 1-lvd. Lvs 3.5–4.5×3–3.5cm, ovate or elliptic, apex rounded or slightly emarginate with a short apiculus, stiff, fleshy. Infl. about 6cm, 1–2-fld; fls showy, purple; sep. 45×15mm, oblong-ligulate, obtuse; pet. 45×30–35mm with 5 parallel ridges running from base to apex, lip trilobed in apical third, lateral lobes oblong, obtuse, midlobe subquadrate, deeply emarginate, margin undulate; column 20mm, apex slightly enlarged. Brazil.

L.speciosa (HBK) Schltr. (*L.grandiflora* Lindl.; *L.majalis* Lindl.).
Diminutive epiphyte; pseudobulbs to 6cm, ovoid-squat-pyriform, 1-lvd. Lvs to 15cm, oblong, subacute. Infl. to 15cm,

usually 1-fld, occasionally 2-fld; fls 12–18cm diam., tepals rose-lilac, rarely white, lip white spotted with deep lilac, margin pale lilac; sep. lanceolate, acute; pet. elliptic, undulate; lip lateral lobes small, obtuse, midlobe orbicular with 2 yellow ridges. Mexico.

L.superbiens Lindl. See *Schomburgkia superbiens.*

L.tenebrosa Rolfe.
Epiphytic, resembling *L.purpurata* in habit. Pseudobulbs conical to fusiform, to 30cm, 1-lvd. Lvs 20–30×6cm, oblong. Raceme to 30cm, about 4-fld; fls about 16cm diam.; tepals copper-bronze, lip rosy purple, darker in throat; tepals lanceolate, acute, undulate, sep. 75–80×14–16mm, pet. 75×20–25mm; lip 65–70×40–50mm with a short claw, trilobed in apical third, lateral lobes small, rounded, midlobe more or less truncate, edge crisped. Summer. Brazil.

L.tereticaulis Hoehne. See *L.crispata.*

L.thomsoniana (Rchb. f.) L.O. Williams.
Pseudobulbs 15–20cm, spindle-shaped, yellow-green. Panicle 1m or more, many-fld, the fls opening over a long period; fls to 7cm diam., creamy-white to yellow, lip dark purple; pet. linear-lanceolate, crisped in apical third; lip with undulate margin. Spring. Cuba, Cayman Is.

L.undulata (Lindl.) L.O. Williams. See *Schomburgkia undulata.*

L.virens Lindl. See *L.xanthina.*

L.weberbaueriana (Kränzl.) Schweinf. See *Schomburgkia weberbaueriana.*

L.xanthina Lindl. (*L.virens* Lindl.).
Pseudobulbs to 25×3cm, club-shaped, slightly ribbed, 1-lvd. Lvs to 30×6cm, ligulate, fleshy, blue-green. Raceme to 25cm, laxly 2–6-fld; fls to 8cm diam., sep. and pet. rich yellow, lip white, yellow in throat, streaked with crimson-purple; sep. 40×10–20mm, oblong, obtuse; pet. similar but slightly wider and more undulate, with margins rolled back; lip 30–35×25–30mm, fan-shaped, obscurely trilobed in basal half and forming a short tube, midlobe short, rounded, margin undulate; column 22mm. Spring–summer. Brazil.

L.grexes and cultivars (see also under × *Laeliocattleya*, × *Brassolaelia*, × *Brassolaeliocattleya*, × *Sophrolaeliocattleya* and × *Potinara*, intergeneric hybrids in which *Laelia* has been bred).
L.Amoena: compact plants with one leaf per pseudobulb; few purple fls on long infl.
L.Brazilian Gold: compact plants with one fleshy leaf per pseudobulb; clusters of golden yellow fls on tall infl.
L.Coronet: tall plants with one leaf per pseudobulb; clusters of small, bright orange fls on tall stems.
L.Gold Star: compact plants with one leaf per pseudobulb; fls in small clusters, deep gold.
L.Seagull: small plants with clusters of bright red fls on long infl.
L.Sparkling Ruby: small plants with brilliant red fls.

× **Laeliocattleya** (*Laelia* × *Cattleya*). A wide range of colourful hybrids between various members of these two genera and their hybrids. The plants are usually robust, upright, with one or two leaves at the apex of the pseudobulb. The inflorescence is terminal, with few to many flowers of various size. Always brightly coloured and conspicuous. Easily grown in bright light in intermediate conditions. A selection of some of the best grexes and cultivars is given below.

× *L.*Ann Follis `Lime Drop': small, strong plants; lovely pale green, starry fls, with spade shaped purple lip.

× *L.*Autumn Symphony: strong plants; fls wonderful iridescent hues of red and copper with wine red lip and white column.

× *L.*Belle of Celle: well=known hybrid with large, deep purple fls with full burgundy red lip and white column; several awarded clones.

× *L.*Blue Kahili: strong slender plants; fls in upright clusters, clear pale blue-lavender.

× *L.*Bonanza: large, strong plants; fls few but large and of excellent shape, deep lavender, with two golden eyes in the darker lip; many awarded clones.

× *L.*Cecile Simmons: strong plants; fls large, plum red with glistening texture.

× *L.*Chine 'Bouton d'Or': strong erect plants; large clusters of fls which are a vivid buttercup yellow with a broad red band across the apical part of the lip.

× *L.*Chit Chat: primary hybrid of great charm, very floriferous and quickly making large plants; small bright orange fls.

× *L.*Culminant 'La Tuilerie': strong large plants; beautiful pale lavender fls with dark lip; vigorous grower.

× *L.*Dorset Gold 'Orchidhurst': strong plants; fls large, bright golden yellow with dominant crimson lip and contrasting white column; many awards.

× *L.*Drumbeat 'Triumph': strong plants which are very floriferous; splendid deep lavender fls, lip velvety purple with 2 yellow patches near the base.

× *L.*Dusky Maid 'Christina': vigorous plants; fls outstanding, rich deep purple sep. and pet. with crimson velvet lip.

× *L.*Ecstasy: strong plants; fls stunning, pure white sep. and pet. contrast with brilliant purple lip; fragrant.

× *L.*Edgard Van Belle: early hybrid which is still in demand, vigorous plants with large infl; fls rich chinese yellow with brilliant deep red lip.

× *L.*Elegans: a primary hybrid, tall plants of slender habit; fls with creamy white sep. and pet., lip lavender or blue depending on the parental clones used; some clones are a beautiful pale 'blue'.

× *L.*Elizabeth Off 'Sparkling Burgundy': strong plants; fls in large clusters, rich sparkling burgundy.

× *L.*Fire Dance: compact plants; tall infl. bearing clusters of small, bright orange-red fls; several awarded clones.

× *L.*Gila Wilderness: strong growing compact plants; fls basically white but heavily coloured splash pet. types; 'Red Flare' has most purple-red colour on pet. and lip, 'Sunrise' is most peloric and 'Grandeur' is probably the finest.

× *L.*Gold Digger: strong plants of medium size; very floriferous, the fls yellow-orange, shiny, lip bright gold with a deep red flash in the throat.

× *L.*Golden Girl: tall plants with 2 lvs per pseudobulb; medium size, golden yellow fls in large clusters, long-lasting.

× *L.*Janice Matthews 'Ceylon': large plants with upright infl; fls rich chestnut coppery shade of reddish brown, very glossy, with fuchsia coloured lip.

× *L.*Jay Markell: strong plants, one of the finest semi-alba cattleyas; sep. and pet. clear crystal white, lip deep purple with two yellow eyes in the throat; several awarded clones.

× *L.*Lisa Ann: vigorous plants; strong dark reddish bronze fls in clusters, sep. orange, pet. magenta flushed with orange at the tip, lip deep magenta; several awarded clones.

× *L.*Mildred Rives: strong plants; very large fls, white sep. and pet., lip with deep magenta-purple mid lobe margined with a white frill; several awarded clones.

× *L.*Mini-Purple: one of the true mini-catts, a primary hybrid; lovely lavender-purple fls with darker lip.

× *L.*Mollie Tyler: large bifoliate plants with large clustered infl.; fls medium sized, brilliant lavender with dark magenta lip.

× *L.*Nippon: strong plants; large full fls with ruffled pet. and lip, white sep. and pet. faintly flushed pink, bright red purple lip with yellow throat; many awarded clones.

× *L.*Orange Sherbet 'Ripe Orange': tall plants with upright spikes; fls medium sized, frosty orange; other awarded clones.

× *L.*Orglade's Cheer: strong plants; large clusters of dark red shiny fls, beautiful cerise to purple lip.

× *L.*Prism Palette 'Mischief': strong compact plants; fls extraordinary splash pet. types, almost peloric, sep. cream, pet. basically pale pink with pink-purple tips, yellow centrally and a purple stripe on either side of the centre, lip frilly, purple in apical half, yellow at the base.

× *L.*Quadroon: tall plants; excellent flowers of medium lavender, lip brilliant red-purple.

× *L.*Roan Mountain: vigorous plants; fls 4–6 per pseudobulb; medium to large size, rich green sep. and pet., lip blood red with creamy white side lobes.

× *L.*Rojo: primary hybrid forming small upright plants; fls in dense clusters on tall infl., small, bright red, deep pink or scarlet; several awarded clones.

× *L.*Royal Emperor: medium sized plants; fls large, dark orange red with a yellow flash in the throat of the lip; several awarded clones.

× *L.*S.J. Bracey: one of the famous early yellows with red lip.

× *L.*Summerland Girl: tall plants with 2–3 leaves per pseudobulb; fls in large clusters, deep maroon red, very glossy, lip with white side lobes over the column, rich magenta mid lobe; several awarded clones.

× *L.*Teruko: primary hybrid which forms strong plants; fls rose lavender with darker centre on tall infl.

× *L.*Trick or Treat 'Orange Magic': tall plants with many clusters of fls soon making a specimen size; fls bright orange, glossy, with red dots on the narrow lip.

× *L.*Wine Festival: tall plants with 2–3 leaves per pseudobulb; large clusters of small fls, deep maroon red, very shiny, with magenta lip, spectacular; several awarded clones.

Laeliopsis Lindl. (From *Laelia* and Gk *opsis*, appearance, somewhat resembling the genus *Laelia*.) 2 species of epiphytes closely allied to *Broughtonia*. Rhizome short, creeping or ascending. Pseudobulbs clustered, ovoid to fusiform, unifoliate to trifoliate. Leaves fleshy, tips erose. Inflorescence terminal, a raceme or a panicle, few-to many-flowered; flowers showy; sepals and petals similar, free, spreading; lip entire or obscurely trilobed, narrowly obovate, tubular, enclosing column; column elongate, clavate, narrowly winged at apex, anther terminal, incumbent, operculate, pollinia 4. W Indies.

CULTIVATION   As for the smaller *Laelia* spp.

L.domingensis (Lindl.) Lindl. (*Broughtonia domingensis* (Lindl.) Rolfe).
Pseudobulbs to 6×5cm, clustered, somewhat laterally compressed, bifoliate or trifoliate. Lvs to 18×3cm, oblong, obtuse. Infl. to 104cm, slender, erect, usually a panicle; fls to 6cm diam., pink to lavender veined purple, short-lived; sep. to 33×6mm, linear-oblong; pet. to 30×12mm, broadly oblanceolate to obovate, acute; lip to 40×25mm, narrowly obovate, obscurely trilobed, lateral lobes forming tube, interior yellow, midlobe fringed, undulate, disc banded purple; column to 1.5cm, pink, slender, anth. pink. Mostly spring–summer. Hispaniola.

Lanium (Lindl.) Benth. (From Lat. *lana*, wool, referring to the pilose appearance of the flowers.) Some 6 species of epiphytes. Rhizome short or long-creeping, often branched. Secondary stems either pseudobulbous and apically bifoliate or narrowly cylindrical and multifoliate. Leaves rigid to fleshy, oblong to elliptic-ovate. Inflorescence a terminal raceme or a panicle, loosely few- to many-fld; flowers small, spreading; sepals linear-lanceolate to ovate-lanceolate, lateral sepals oblique, adnate to column base; petals similar to dorsal sepals, shorter; lip adnate to column to apex forming a short tube, lamina simple, concave, ovate or rhombic, acuminate; column dilated above, apex bidentate or biauriculate, anther terminal, operculate, incumbent, bilocular, pollinia 4, ovoid. Colombia, Venezuela, Guianas, Brazil, Peru.

CULTIVATION   As for *Epidendrum*.

L.avicula (Lindl.) Benth. (*Epidendrum aviculum* Lindl.).
Rhiz. stout, creeping. Secondary stems to 3cm, pseudobulbous. Lvs to 3×1.5cm, spreading, sessile, broadly elliptic to suborbicular, rounded or acute. Raceme to 16cm, several- to many-fld; peduncle densely tomentose; fls cream to yellow-brown or yellow-green, sometimes spotted red; sep. to 7mm, densely tomentose, lanceolate to oblong-lanceolate, acute or acuminate, lateral sep. oblique; pet. to 5mm, oblique, linear; lip lamina to 5×4mm, suborbicular to ovate-rhombic, acute to apiculate, base cuneate; column to 5mm, apex bidentate, dilated above. Brazil, Peru.

L.microphyllum (Lindl.) Benth. (*Epidendrum microphyllum* Lindl.).
Rhiz. elongate, creeping, branched; branches (stems) to 4cm, erect to ascending, multifoliate. Lvs to 3cm, distichous, linear-oblong, spreading, fleshy, acute. Raceme to 7cm, few- to several-fld; peduncle pilose, erect or suberect; fls yellow-brown flushed pink; sep. to 8×2mm, pilose, lanceolate or linear-lanceolate, carinate; pet. oblique, linear, shorter than sep., glabrous; lip lamina to 5×4mm, ovate, acuminate, glabrous, base rounded; column to 4mm, dilated above, obliquely bidentate below. Venezuela, Colombia, Ecuador, Peru,

Lankesterella Ames. (For Charles Lankester, English horticulturist active in Costa Rica this century.) 10 species, terrestrials and epiphytes similar to *Spiranthes* and *Goodyera*, mostly very dwarf with a basal leaf rosette, thinly fleshy roots and terminal racemes of small flowers.C & S America.

CULTIVATION   Rather undistinguished miniature orchids requiring shady, buoyant conditions in the intermediate house and year-round moisture. The species described here is epiphytic and bears a pendulous raceme: it fares best mounted on a pad of moss on a cork slab.

L.orotantha (Kränzlin) Garay.
Lvs to 5cm,obovate, shortly stalked. Infl. to 8cm, sharply pendulous; fls to 7, to 1.8cm diam. but never opening fully and usually remaining semi-closed and bud-like, each subtended by a bract, basically green, densely hairy, as is axis. Costa Rica to Peru.

Lemboglossum Halbinger. (From Gk *lembos*, boat or canoe, and *glossa*, tongue, referring to the boat-shaped lip.) Some 14 species of epiphytes formerly included in *Odontoglossum*. Rhizome short, creeping. Pseudobulbs clustered, rounded, laterally compressed, unifoliate to trifoliate at apex, subtended by 1–3 distichous, leaflike sheaths. Inflorescence a raceme or panicle, erect to pendent, few- to many-flowered; flowers large, showy; sepals subequal; petals subequal to sepals or wider; lip short-clawed, fused to column, lamina showy, variously shaped, callus fleshy, somewhat curved, lateral margins raised, central portion usually bidentate; column long, broad or slender, sometimes auriculate; pollinia 2, with laminar stipe. C America, Mexico. All species of *Lemboglossum* were transferred to *Rhynchostele* Rchb. f. in 1993 by Soto Arenas and Salazar.

CULTIVATION   Cool to intermediate conditions in light shade with humid, buoyant air and frequent watering when in growth, somewhat less so at other times. See also *Odontoglossum*.

L.bictoniense (Batem. ex Lindl.) Halbinger (*Odontoglossum bictoniense* (Batem.) Lindl.).
Pseudobulbs to 18×3.5cm. Lvs to 45×5.5cm, elliptic-oblong to lanceolate or linear, acute to acuminate, bright green or yellow-green, prominently nerved, conduplicate at base. Raceme or panicle to 80cm, erect, many-fld; fls to 5cm diam., often fragrant; tepals usually pale green or yellow-green banded or spotted red-brown, sep. to 2.5×1cm, elliptic-lanceolate to elliptic-oblanceolate, acute or acuminate, apex recurved, pet. smaller than sep., oblanceolate to linear-elliptic, oblique, obtuse to acute; lip to 2×2.5cm, subcordate, acute to rounded, crisped or crenulate, white to rose or magenta-tinted. Mexico, Guatemala, El Salvador. White, golden and lime-green self-coloured forms occur.

L.cervantesii (La Ll. & Lex.) Halbinger (*Odontoglossum cervantesii* La Ll. & Lex.; *Odontoglossum membranaceum* Lindl.).
Pseudobulbs to 6×3cm, ovoid, ancipitous. Lvs to 15×3cm, ovate-lanceolate to elliptic-oblong, acute to acuminate, slightly chartaceous. Raceme to 32cm, usually shorter, to 6-fld, covered with brown sheaths; fls fragrant; tepals white to rose irregularly banded brown-red in basal half, sep. to 3.5×1cm, narrowly ovate-oblong, pet. to 3×2cm, ovate-elliptic to suborbicular, abruptly acute or rounded; lip white to rose, striped purple at base, to 2.5×3cm, 3-lobed, lateral lobes erect, midlobe broadly cordate, irregularly dentate, callus yellow, 2-lobed; column white, to 1cm. Mexico, Guatemala.

L.cordatum (Lindl.) Halbinger (*Odontoglossum cordatum* Lindl.; *Odontoglossum hookeri* Lem.; *Odontoglossum lueddemanni* Reg.).
Pseudobulbs to 7.5×3.5cm. Lvs to 30×5cm, elliptic to lanceolate or oblong-ligulate, subacute, dark green, coriaceous. Raceme or panicle to 60cm, erect, many-fld; tepals yellow blotched and barred deep red-brown, sep. to 5×1cm, elliptic-lanceolate, acuminate, concave, keeled below, pet. to 3.5×1cm, ovate-lanceolate to elliptic-lanceolate, oblique, long-acuminate; lip to 2.5×2cm, usually white spotted red-brown, cordate, acuminate, margins involute at apex, slightly erose, callus 3-keeled. Mexico, Guatemala, Honduras, Costa Rica, Venezuela.

L.maculatum (La Ll. & Lex.) Halbinger (*Odontoglossum maculatum* La Ll. & Lex.).
Pseudobulbs to 9.5×3cm, ovoid. Lvs to 32×5.5cm, elliptic-lanceolate to elliptic-ligulate, acute to obtuse, fleshy. Infl. to 40cm, arcuate to pendent, sometimes branched, few- to many-fld; sep. chestnut-brown or pale yellow marked red-brown, sometimes barred green at base, to 4×1cm, lanceolate, acute or acuminate, keeled below; pet. yellow heavily spotted red-brown at base, to 3×1.5cm, elliptic-lanceolate, acute or acuminate; lip similar in colour to sep., to 2×2.5cm, cordate-reniform or cordate-triangular, subacute, dentate, crisped, callus yellow marked red, fleshy; column white. Mexico, Guatemala.

L.majale (Rchb. f.) Halbinger (*Odontoglossum majale* Rchb. f.; *Odontoglossum platycheilum* Weatherby).
Pseudobulbs to 7×2.5cm, ovoid, almost concealed by pale brown sheaths. Lvs to 30×3cm, linear-ligulate, subacute or obtuse, subcoriaceous, conduplicate at base. Raceme erect, to 14cm, 2–4-fld; tepals purple or rose, sep. to 3×1cm, narrowly oblong to lanceolate, acute, concave, keeled below, pet. smaller than sep., narrowly oblanceolate to elliptic-oblong, acute to subobtuse; lip rose blotched deep purple or carmine, to 3×3cm, ovate-subquadrate, retuse, recurved, callus bilobulate, dentate; column white, to 1.5cm, clavate. Guatemala.

L.rossii (Lindl.) Halbinger (*Odontoglossum rossii* Lindl.).
Pseudobulbs to 6×3.5cm, ovoid to ovoid-elliptic, wrinkled with age. Lvs to 14×2.75cm, elliptic to elliptic-lanceolate, acute or acuminate, subcoriaceous. Raceme to 20cm, usually far shorter, erect or arcuate, 1–4-fld; tepals white, pale yellow or pale pink, the sep. and lower portions of pet. mottled and spotted chocolate to rust, sep. to 4.5×1cm, oblong-elliptic to linear-lanceolate, acute or acuminate, slightly reflexed, pet. to 4×2cm, short-clawed, broadly elliptic to oblong-elliptic, acute or obtuse, crisped to undulate; lip to 3×3cm, broadly orbicular-subcordate, apex rounded or emarginate, undulate, callus deep yellow spotted red-brown; column rose-purple, to 2cm. Mexico, Guatemala, Honduras, Nicaragua.

L.stellatum (Lindl.) Halbinger (*Odontoglossum stellatum* Lindl.; *Odontoglossum erosum* Rich. & Gal.).
Pseudobulbs ovoid-ellipsoid to cylindrical, to 6×1.5cm. Lvs to 15×2.5cm, narrowly elliptic to oblanceolate or linear-ligulate, subobtuse to acuminate, narrowed and conduplicate at base. Raceme to 8.5cm, slender, 1–2-fld; tepals subsimilar, yellow-bronze barred brown, to 30×5mm, lanceolate to linear-lanceolate, acute to acuminate, sep. concave, keeled below, pet. sometimes yellow-white; lip white or pink marked mauve, to 2×2cm, ovate-triangular to suborbicular, obtuse to rounded, lacerate-dentate, callus extending onto base of blade as a short bifid plate; column to 12mm. Mexico, Guatemala, El Salvador.

L.uro-skinneri (Lindl.) Halbinger (*Odontoglossum uro-skinneri* Lindl.).
Resembles *L.bictoniense* except lvs lanceolate; tepals deep red to green, barred and mottled brown, to 3×1.5cm, pet. obliquely ovate-elliptic, lip to 3×3.5cm, pink, veined or spotted white. Guatemala, Honduras.

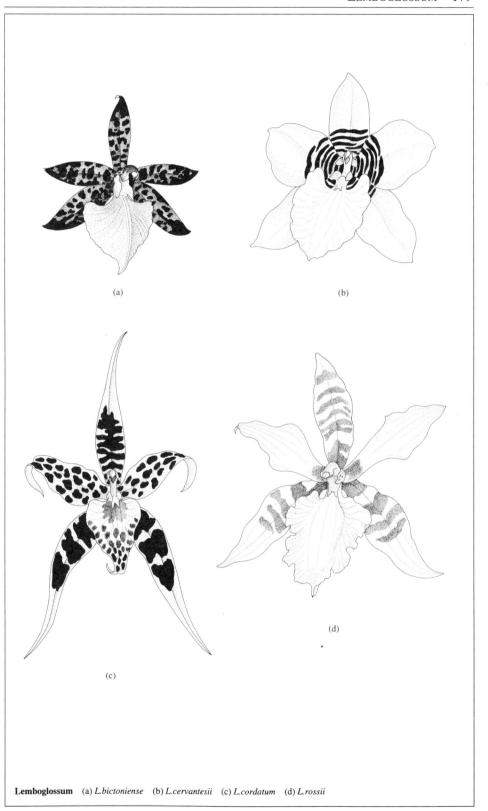

(a)

(b)

(c)

(d)

Lemboglossum   (a) *L.bictoniense*   (b) *L.cervantesii*   (c) *L.cordatum*   (d) *L.rossii*

Leochilus Knowles & Westc. (From Gk *leios*, smooth, and *cheilos*, lip, referring to the smooth lip of most species.) Some 15 species of epiphytes allied to *Oncidium*. Rhizome short. Pseudobulbs clustered, ovoid to ellipsoid, laterally compressed, enveloped by several leaf sheaths, apically unifoliate or bifoliate. Leaves ligulate to elliptic-lanceolate, coriaceous, short-petiolate. Inflorescence a raceme or a panicle, basal, base of pseudobulb, erect or arching, loosely few- to many-flowered; flowers small; sepals subequal, spreading, lateral sepals free or shortly connate; petals free, similar to sepals, slightly wider; lip adnate to column base, spreading, simple or obscurely trilobed, exceeding sepals, disc fleshy, callose; column short, erect, foot absent, biauriculate below stigma, apex truncate, rostellum elongate, anther terminal, incumbent, operculate, 1-celled, pollinia 2, waxy, globose. Mexico to Argentina, W Indies.

CULTIVATION   As for the cool-growing, pseudobulbous *Oncidium* spp.

L.carinatus (Lindl.) Knowles & Westc. (*Oncidium carinatum* Lindl.).
Pseudobulbs to 2.5×2cm, ovate to suborbicular, compressed, usually bifoliate. Lvs to 12×1.5cm, elliptic-lanceolate. Infl. to 15cm, erect to pendent, few- to many-fld; fls fragrant; sep. to 12×6mm, free, yellow-green flushed brown; pet. cream-yellow striped chestnut-brown; lip to 12×9mm, cream-yellow spotted brown near callus, ovate, concave, obtuse to retuse, disc with tuberculate callus, glabrous; column to 6mm, cream, anth. cream to yellow. Mostly summer. Mexico.

L.labiatus (Sw.) Kuntze (*Oncidium labiatum* (Sw.) Rchb. f.).
Pseudobulbs to 1.5×1.5cm, suborbicular, bright green, usually unifoliate. Lvs to 6.5×2cm, elliptic-lanceolate, tinged red-purple, sharply carinate below. Infl. to 23cm, erect to arching; fls fragrant; sep. to 8×5mm, yellow-green marked dark red-brown, lateral sep. connate to middle; pet. similar to sep., elliptic-oblong; lip yellow streaked red-brown, elliptic-oblong, base concave, disc with fleshy callus; column to 2mm, cream to pale brown, anth. cream to yellow. Mostly spring–summer. W Indies, Guatemala, Honduras, Panama, Trinidad, Costa Rica, Venezuela.

L.lieboldii Rchb. f. See *Papperitzia lieboldii*.
L.major Schltr. See *L.scriptus*.
L.mattogrossensis Cogn. See *Solenidium lunatum*.

L.oncidioides Knowles & Westc. (*Rodriguezia maculata* Lindl.; *Oncidium macrantherum* Hook.).
Pseudobulbs to 5×2.5cm, ovate to elliptic, compressed, unifoliate or bifoliate. Lvs to 17×3cm, oblong-lanceolate or elliptic-lanceolate, acute. Infl. to 16cm, arching to pendent, few- to many-fld; fls fragrant; sep. to 11×5mm, grey-green spotted and tinged dull red, lateral sep. connate to middle; pet. to 11×7mm, similar to sep.; lip to 12×9mm, grey-green with large red central blotch, obovate to elliptic, obtuse to retuse, disc with cup-shaped callus, pilose to shortly pubesc.; column to 5mm, pale green, anth. cream. Autumn–winter. Mexico to Guatemala, Honduras.

L.pulchellus (Reg.) Cogn. See *Oncidium waluewa*.

L.scriptus (Sw.) Rchb. f. (*L.major* Schltr.).
Pseudobulbs to 5×2.5cm, ovoid to suborbicular, compressed, unifoliate. Lvs to 15×3cm, elliptic-ligulate to elliptic-lanceolate, obtuse. Infl. to 25cm, erect to arching, 1- to several-fld; fls fragrant, pale yellow-green, marked or striped red-brown; sep. to 12×6mm, elliptic to lanceolate, lateral sep. free or shortly connate; pet. obovate to elliptic-lanceolate, subequal to sep.; lip to 14×9mm, obovate to obcordate, obtuse to retuse, callus cup-shaped, pilose to shortly pubesc.; column to 4mm, cream-green, anth. cream. Mostly autumn–winter. Mexico, Brazil, Guatemala to Panama, Cuba.

Lepanthes Sw. (From Gk *lepos*, scale, bark, and *anthos* flower, as the plant grows on the bark of trees.) Over 800 species of usually dwarf epiphytes or lithophytes. Rhizome short. Secondary stems tufted, erect or ascending, slender, generally bearing a single terminal leaf, enveloped by tubular sheaths. Leaves sessile or subsessile, coriaceous, sometimes papillose, appearing velvety and colourfully marked, ovate to suborbicular, apex tridentate. Inflorescence a raceme, axillary, small, solitary or fasciculate, 1- to many-flowered, usually lying flat on leaf surface; flowers small; sepals subequal, spreading, carinate, ovate to elliptic-lanceolate, lateral sepals variously connate; petals shorter than sepals, short-clawed, generally adnate to column; lip minute, 2- or 3-lobed, lateral lobes erect, acute, midlobe inconspicuous, adnate to column, column short, fleshy, footless, anther terminal, incumbent, operculate, 1-celled, pollinia 2, waxy, pyriform. Tropical America, W Indies.

CULTIVATION   As for *Pleurothallis*, but in somewhat cooler, shadier conditions. These plants, small and fragile, are often best grown in closed cases.

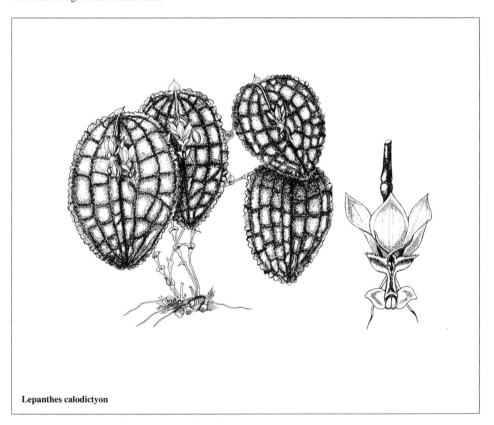

Lepanthes calodictyon

L.calodictyon Hook.
Secondary stems 2.5–5.25cm. Lvs to 4×2.5cm, elliptic, lime to emerald-green, appearing satiny, densely veined or patterned chocolate-brown to rusty red. Fls minute, yellow and red; sep. and pet. ciliate; lip red, spathulate. Ecuador, S Colombia.

L.chiriquensis Schltr. See *L.lindleyana*.

L.escobariana Garay.
Habit much as for *L.lindleyana*. Fls borne in succession on long, slender racemes, basically elliptic in outline, somewhat cupped, lacking tails, metallic yellow-bronze, the lower half with a broad vertical zone of brick red or scarlet; lip and petals white marked pink. Colombia.

L.exaltata Luer & Escobar.
Habit much as for *L.lindleyana*. Fls borne in succession on a long, slender raceme, relatively large; dorsal sep. obcordate, bronze, lateral sep. triangular, divergent, olive marked brick red; lip and pet. small, red. Colombia.

L.felis Luer & Escobar.
Habit small; lvs often tinted purple-bronze. Fls relatively large, cupped, supported on surface of leaf; dorsal sep. hooded, triangular, yellow lined purple-red, short-tailed, lateral sep. similar with short tails incurved; pet. small, very dark green, resembling eyes. Colombia.

L.gargantua. Rchb.f.
Far larger than other spp. described here. Stems to 30cm. Lvs large. Fls to 3cm diam., in congested racemes; sep. broad, yellow, lacking tails; pet. and lip small, peach to yellow. Colombia, Ecuador.

L.lindleyana Ørst. & Rchb. f. (*L.micrantha* Ames; *L.chiriquensis* Schltr.).
Secondary stems to 1cm, erect. Lvs 2.5–4.5×0.75–1.5cm, ovate to linear-lanceolate, acuminate. Infl. 1 to several, shorter than lvs, few-fld; fls to 1.5cm diam., produced in succession; sep. 2.5×1mm, yellow to tan, veins tinged red-brown, ovate-oblong to ovate-lanceolate, acute, minutely ciliate; pet. to 1×1.5mm, orange-yellow and scarlet, transversely elliptic or lanceolate, ciliate; lip to 1×2mm, maroon or dull red, papillate, transversely oblong-bilobed; column pink, to 1mm. Costa Rica, Panama, Colombia, Venezuela, Nicaragua.

L.micrantha Ames. See *L.lindleyana.*

L.pulchella (Sw.) Sw.
Secondary stems 0.5–1cm. Lvs 8–15×3–6mm, ovate, acute. Infl. to 2cm, 1 to several, few- to several-fld; fls minute; sep. 6–8×2–3mm, yellow with a median crimson line, ovate, long-acuminate, ciliate; pet. crimson, margins yellow, lobed, lobes subtriangular, ciliate; lip crimson, obscurely lobed, minutely ciliate; column to 1mm, crimson. Jamaica.

L.rotundifolia L.O. Williams.
Secondary stems short. Lvs 16–25×18–28mm, suborbicular to ovate-suborbicular. Infl. shorter than lvs, many-fld; fls minute, yellow and red; sep. to 3×2mm, suborbicular, acute or acuminate; pet. bilobed, lobes to 3.5×1mm, obliquely lanceolate, acute; lip to 1.5×2mm, bilobed. Panama.

L.secunda Barb.Rodr. See *Lepanthopsis floripectin.*

Lepanthopsis (Cogn.) Ames. (From the generic name *Lepanthes* and the Gk *opsis*, appearance, referring to the similarity of the genus of *Lepanthes.*) Some 40 species of diminutive epiphytes allied to *Lepanthes.* Rhizome slender, minute, creeping. Secondary stems tufted, slender, erect, enveloped by tubular sheaths, apically unifoliate. Leaves suborbicular to elliptic-oblong, acute to rounded, short-petiolate. Inflorescence raceme, axillary, solitary or clustered, few to many-flowered, often secund; flowers minute sepals subequal, lateral sepals deeply connate; petals thin, elliptic-oblong to orbicular; lip adnate to column base, sessile, simple; column minute, foot absent; anther terminal, opercular, incumbent, pollinia 2, waxy, pyriform. Tropical Americas.

CULTIVATION As for *Pleurothallis.*

L.astrophora (Rchb. f. ex Kränzl.) Garay (*Pleurothallis astrophora* Rchb. f. ex Kränzl.).
Secondary stems to 7×1cm, erect, terete. Lvs to 2.5×1cm, erect, coriaceous, elliptic to oblong-elliptic, obtuse. Infl. to 12cm, many-fld; peduncle filiform; fls star-like, bright rose-purple; sep. to 3×1.5mm, papillose, ovate, acute to obtuse, lateral sep. oblique; pet. to 2×1mm, papillose, obovate, acuminate to obtuse; lip to 2×1mm, fleshy, subquadrate, base obovate, subacuminate, papillose; column short, with a stigmatic wings, pale pink, anth. cream. Venezuela.

L.floripectin (Rchb. f.) Ames (*Pleurothallis floripectin* Rchb. f.; *Lepanthes secunda* Barb.Rodr.).
Secondary stems to 7cm. Lvs to 3.5×1.2cm, fleshy, suborbicular to elliptic-oblong, rounded. Infl. to 10cm, 1 to several, densely many-fld; peduncle filiform, erect, pink-green; fls in two close ranks resembling a comb, thin-textured, white to yellow-green, slightly tinged pink; sep. to 3mm, spreading, ovate, acute or obtuse; pet. minute, suborbicular-ovate, subacute; lip to 1×1mm, suborbicular to ovate, rounded at apex; column minute, dilated above, stigmas widely divergent, anth. white. Spring. Honduras, Costa Rica, Colombia, Venezuela, Brazil, Panama, Peru.

L.vinacea Schweinf.
Secondary stems to 5.5cm, erect-ascending, slender. Lvs fleshy, to 2×1cm, ovate to elliptic-oblong, obtuse. Infl. to 5cm, 1 to several, suberect, few to many-fld; peduncle filiform, pale green; fls bright purple, smooth-glandular; sep. to 3×1.5mm, ovate-lanceolate, subacute to obtuse, lateral sep. oblique; pet. to 1mm, ovate-elliptic to lanceolate, acute; lip to 1×1mm, fleshy suborbicular or orbicular, retuse; column minute, cream, anth. white. Venezuela. Ecuador.

Leptotes Lindl. (From Gk *leptotes*, delicacy, referring to the delicate appearance of many of the species.) Some 3 species of diminutive epiphytes. Rhizome creeping. Pseudobulbs stem-like small, thickened, cylindrical, apically unifoliate. Leaves fleshy, terete or subterete, erect. Inflorescence a terminal raceme, loosely 1- to few-flowered; peduncle short, slender, erect or arched; bracts inconspicuous; flowers spreading; sepals and petals subequal, subsimilar, free; lip adnate to column base, trilobed, lateral lobes distinctly short-unguiculate, clasping column, small, auriculate, midlobe larger than lateral lobes, reflexed, entire, disc smooth or with prominent midrib; column fleshy, short, erect, apex sometimes winged, anther terminal, pollinia 6, waxy. Brazil, Paraguay, Argentina.

CULTIVATION   Tufted orchids for the cool or intermediate house with small white and rose flowers. Cultivate as for small *Laelia* spp.

L.bicolor Lindl. (*Tetramicra bicolor* (Lindl.) Benth.).
Pseudobulbs to 30×8mm, fusiform-cylindrical, fleshy, erect or suberect. Lvs to 10×1cm, usually shorter, terete, acute, recurved to suberect, with a central groove above, lustrous dark green. Infl. shorter than lvs, 1- to several-fld; fls opening in succession, to 5cm diam., fragrant, sparkling white, the lip with a deep rose to purple, white-tipped midlobe; sep. to 22×5mm, linear-oblong to linear-lanceolate, acute; pet. to 22×3mm, linear-ligulate to linear-oblong, acute; lip to 20×7mm, fleshy, lateral lobes orbicular to subquadrate, midlobe narrowly ovate or oblong, apex narrowly acute; column to 5mm, purple or green, obscurely triquetrous. E Brazil, Paraguay.

L.tenuis Rchb. f.
Resembles *L.unicolor* except tepals yellow, lip white with a central violet blotch, midlobe transversely oblong or elliptic, obtuse or emarginate. Brazil.

L.unicolor Barb. Rodr.
Pseudobulbs to 1.5cm. Lvs to 55×8mm, erect to slightly curved, fleshy, subterete, acute, deeply grooved above. Infl. 1–2-fld, pendent; fls to 6cm diam., nodding, fragrant, white flushed shell pink to pale rose-lilac; sep. to 25×3mm, narrowly ligulate or linear-ligulate, acute; pet. to 25×2mm, subspathulate to linear-subspathulate, acute, somewhat fleshy, darker than sep.; lip to 2.5×1cm, fleshy, erect or recurved, lateral lobes minute, triangular, midlobe ovate to lanceolate, acuminate; column to 5mm, white-green, stout. Winter. Brazil.

Leucohyle Klotzsch. (From Gk *leukos*, white, and *hyle*, a wood.) Some 4 species of epiphytes allied to *Trichopilia*. Rhizome short, creeping. Pseudobulbs small or minute, erect, apically unifoliate. Leaves fleshy to subcoriaceous, suberect or arching, usually linear or narrow-lanceolate, basally sheathed. Racemes basal, from axils of sheaths, several-flowered; flowers mostly white, spotted crimson or purple on lip; sepals and petals similar, free, spreading, sometimes twisted; lip parallel to column, porrect, simple to trilobed, concave, base cuneate, enveloping column, callus 2-ridged; column erect, hooded over anther at apex, pollinia 2, pyriform, stipe oblong-linear. Tropical America from Panama to Peru.

CULTIVATION   As for *Trichopilia*.

L.subulata (Sw.) Schltr. (*Trichopilia subulata* (Sw.) Rchb. f.).
Pseudobulbs to 3×0.5cm, narrowly cylindrical or subcylindrical, clustered. Lvs to 25×1cm. Infl. to 15cm, pendent; fls to 4cm diam., slightly fragrant; sep. and pet. translucent white to pale yellow, lanceolate to linear-lanceolate, acute, slightly twisted; lip to 15×15mm, white spotted rose-purple, obscurely trilobed, suborbicular to obovate, emarginate to apiculate, deeply erose-lacerate; column to 9mm, erect, white, terete, anth. white. Panama, Trinidad, Peru, Venezuela, Colombia.

Liparis L.C. Rich. (From Gk *liparos*, fat, greasy or shining, referring to the shiny surface of the leaves of many species.) About 250 species of terrestrials and epiphytes, usually with pseudobulbs. Leaves 1 to several, thin-textured and plicate, or stiff, smooth and leathery. Raceme terminal, few- to many-flowered; flowers usually yellow-green or dull purple, usually fairly small; sepals and petals free, spreading or reflexed, lateral sepals sometimes adnate to each other; petals often linear; lip entire or bilobed, not spurred; column long, arched; pollinia 4, in 2 pairs. Pantropical and also temperate, with 1 species in GB.

CULTIVATION   The larger species from tropical and subtropical regions require shaded positions in the intermediate or warm house and a cultural regime similar to that of *Eria*. The remainder can be attempted in the alpine house or in sheltered, specially adapted corners of the bog or peat garden where they need painstaking establishment on living sphagnum combined with composted bark, soft water and a cool, humid atmosphere.

L.atropurpurea Lindl.
Terrestrial, to 30cm; pseudobulbs obscure. Lvs 3–4, 7.5–10cm with petiole 2–2.5cm, ovate or orbicular, asymmetrical at base. Raceme 10–20cm, laxly several-fld; fls dull purple; sep. linear, dorsal sep. 15mm, erect, lateral sep. slightly shorter, spreading; pet. about 15mm, narrowly linear, spreading; lip about 10×8mm, orbicular or obovate with 2 calli at base, fleshy, recurved, margin crenulate; column 8mm, slender, curved. Sri Lanka, S India.

L.bituberculata (Hook.) Lindl. See *L.nervosa*.

L.bowkeri Harv. (*L.neglecta* Schltr.).
Terrestrial or epiphytic, 12–30cm; pseudobulbs to 7cm, conic. Lvs 2–5, 6–12×3–6cm, lanceolate or ovate, plicate, light green. Raceme several-fld; fls yellow or yellow-green, turning buff-orange with age; sep. 6–11×1–4mm; pet. to 11mm, linear, deflexed; lip to 8×8mm, orbicular, with small bifid callus near base and metallic grey mid-line. Throughout much of tropical Africa; S Africa.

L.cespitosa (Lam.) Lindl.
Small, epiphytic, with ovoid pseudobulbs 1–2cm high set close together on a creeping rhiz. Lf 1, erect, coriaceous, light green, usually about 10×1cm, oblanceolate. Raceme to 15cm, densely many-fld; fls yellow or yellow-green, very small, non-resupinate; sep. 2–2.5mm, ovate, acute; pet. of similar length but narrower; lip 2.5×2mm, oblong, sometimes obscurely 4-lobed. Uganda, Tanzania, Malawi, Madagascar, Réunion, Sri Lanka and from NE India to Philippines, New Guinea, Solomon Is. and Fiji.

L.condylobulbon Rchb. f.
Epiphytic, forming dense clumps; pseudobulbs to 24×2cm, cylindrical but swollen at base. Lvs 2, to 20×2.5cm, narrowly lanceolate, thin-textured. Raceme to 22cm, fairly densely 15–35-fld; fls scented, cream to pale green, about 4mm diam.; sep. and pet. reflexed, sep. 2.5–3mm, dorsal sep. lanceolate, lateral sep. ovate, pet. 2–2.5mm, linear; lip erect at base then deflexed, 3×2mm, ovate, apex bifid, the edges toothed or ciliate. SE Asia, Polynesia, New Guinea, Australia.

L.cordifolia Hook. f.
Terrestrial; pseudobulbs to 4cm, ovoid, compressed, clustered. Lf 1, to 13×10cm, broadly ovate, cordate, acuminate. Infl. of similar length to lf; fls green, to 18mm diam.; sep. linear-lanceolate, acute; pet. linear, spreading; lip wedge-shaped, almost trilobed at apex, the margin denticulate. Sikkim.

L.elata Lindl. See *L.nervosa*.

L.elegans Lindl.
Terrestrial, with slender, creeping rhiz.; pseudobulbs set 1–2.5cm apart, 2–3cm long, ovoid, 2-lvd. Lvs 12–25×2–3cm, oblanceolate, narrowed at base to broad 2–6cm stalk. Raceme erect, 25–35cm, densely many-fld; sep. and pet. pale yellow-green, lip orange to salmon; pedicel and ovary 4mm; bracts 5mm; sep. 4×1.5mm, backward-curving; pet. 4×0.5mm, spreading; lip 4×1.5mm, erect at base then bent down sharply at about halfway, oblong, apex finely toothed and bifid. Sumatra to Philippines (not Java), Malaysia.

L.guineensis Lindl. See *L.nervosa*.

L.lacerata Ridl. Pseudobulbs 2–3cm, ovoid, 1-lvd. Lf to 18×4cm, lanceolate, narrowed to a stalk about 4cm long.

Raceme about 20cm, densely many-fld; fls white with an orange lip; pedicel and ovary 8mm; bracts 3mm; dorsal sep. 6×2mm, lateral sep. slightly shorter. pet. 6×1mm; lip 8mm, narrow at base then abruptly widening to 6.5mm at apex, erect at base then sharply bent down, apex deeply bilobed, lobes divergent, each with about 6 narrow 1.5mm teeth. Malaysia, Borneo, Sumatra.

L.latifolia (Bl.) Lindl.
Pseudobulbs about 8×3cm, conical, with large red-brown sheaths at base, flattened, 1-lvd. Lf to 33×7.5cm, lanceolate, channelled at base. Raceme erect, of similar length to lf, many-fld; fls yellow with orange-brown lip; pedicel and ovary 15mm; bracts 8–10mm; sep. 8×3mm, reflexed; pet. of similar length but 1mm wide; lip 10×9mm, basal half narrow, erect, apical half turned down, deeply bilobed, lobes rounded, finely toothed. Malaysia, Sumatra, Borneo, Java.

L.liliifolia (L.) Rich. ex Lindl.
Terrestrial, to 25cm; pseudobulbs 2×1cm, ovoid, covered with dry sheaths, 2-lvd. Lvs to 18×6cm, ovoid or elliptic, glossy green, keeled below. Raceme several- to many-fld; sep. pale green, pet. purple, lip translucent light purple with darker veins; pedicel and ovary 15mm; sep. 10×2mm, oblong-lanceolate, the edges rolled under; pet. to 10mm, filiform; lip 10×8mm, recurved, obovate, apiculate; column 4mm. Late spring–summer. N America, Sweden.

L.loeselii (L.) Rich. FEN ORCHID.
Terrestrial, to 25cm; pseudobulbs 10×5mm, ovoid, covered with dry sheaths, 2-lvd. Lvs to 20×6cm, oblong or elliptic, acute or obtuse, keeled below, glossy green. Raceme laxly few- to several-fld; fls dull yellow-green; sep. 5×1mm, narrowly oblong, edges recurved; pet. 5mm, filiform; lip 5×3mm, obovate or oblong, recurved at about halfway; column 3mm. Summer. Northern Europe; N America.

L.longipes Lindl. See *L.viridiflora*.
L.macrantha Rolfe. See *L.nigra*.
L.neglecta Schltr. See *L.bowkeri*.

L.nervosa (Thunb.) Lindl. (*L.bituberculata* (Hook.) Lindl.; *L.elata* Lindl.; *L.guineensis* Lindl.).
Terrestrial or lithophytic; pseudobulbs conical, to 4cm. Lvs 2–3, to 35×6cm, lanceolate, plicate, light green. Raceme densely many-fld; fls green or yellow-green, often with a maroon-purple lip; dorsal sep. about 6×2mm, oblong, reflexed, lateral sep. shorter, rolled up under lip; pet. to 6mm, linear, reflexed; lip 4×4mm, fleshy, recurved. Tropical Africa, tropical America, India to Japan and Philippines.

L.nigra Seidenf. (*L.macrantha* Rolfe).
Terrestrial, usually about 35cm but occasionally reaching 1m; pseudobulbs about 20×1cm, cylindrical, enclosed in sheaths. Lvs about 5, to 15×6cm, ovate, plicate. Raceme 25–35cm, fairly densely many-fld; scape winged, dark red-purple; fls deep red-purple, 15mm diam.; pedicel and ovary arched, 15mm, red-purple; dorsal sep. 18×3mm, linear, reflexed, lateral sep. 15×5mm, falcate, hidden under lip; pet. 17mm, filiform, reflexed; lip 14×14mm, bent down in middle, obovate, mucronate, the margin denticulate; column 7mm, red-purple. Taiwan.

L.nutans Ames.
Terrestrial; pseudobulbs to 3cm, pear-shaped, with distichous sheaths, 1-lvd. Lf 18–30×1.5–3cm, narrowly oblong-lanceo-

late, acute. Infl. shorter than lf; peduncle winged, much longer than rachis; rachis nodding, covered with distichous bracts, to 5cm, densely many-fld; fls brick red; sep. 7×3mm; pet. linear, 7×0.5mm; lip 8×8mm, fan-shaped, fleshy and somewhat channelled below column, with a basal callus; column 6mm. Philippines.

L.torta Hook. f.
Terrestrial; pseudobulbs about 2cm, conical, 1-lvd. Lf 14–15×2.5–3.5cm, lanceolate, coriaceous. Raceme of similar length to lf, laxly few- to many-fld; fls cadmium yellow; pedicel and ovary 17mm; sep. 10–12mm, linear-oblong, recurved; pet. 9–10mm, linear; lip 9–10×8–9mm, obovate, with bilobed basal callus, apex obscurely wavy; column winged. India.

L.tricallosa Rchb. f.
Pseudobulbs conical, about 12×2cm, 1-lvd. Lf to 18×5.4cm, ovate. Raceme to 45cm, scape and rachis purple; sep. pale

green, pet. purple, green towards base, lip pale green with purple-pink veins, becoming pink-tinged as fls age; dorsal sep. 20×2mm, lateral sep. slightly shorter; pet. 20mm, linear; lip about 18×18mm, broadly ovate, minutely toothed toward apex. Sumatra to Philippines.

L.viridiflora (Bl.) Lindl. (*L.longipes* Lindl.).
Epiphytic; pseudobulbs clustered, 1–9×1–2cm, ovoid or conical, 2–3-lvd. Lvs to 25×2.5cm, narrowly oblanceolate. Raceme pendent, 17–18cm, densely many-fld; fls green, very small; sep. 2–4×1–2mm, oblong; pet. 2–4mm, linear; lip 2–3×1.5–3mm, orbicular or ovate, recurved, fleshy; column arched, 2mm. Sri Lanka, India, Burma, Malaysia, China, Japan, Sumatra, Borneo, Philippines and Fiji.

Listera R. Br. (For Michael Lister (1638–1712), British zoologist, physician to Queen Anne.) Some 25 species of herbaceous terrestrials. Rhizomes short, roots slender. Stem erect. Leaves 2, rarely 1 or 3, sessile, almost opposite, sited just below stem centre. Raceme spike-like, slender, cylindrical; petals and sepals almost equal, patent or convergent; lip deeply divided from apex, sometimes with 2 basal lobes, central furrow produces nectar, spurless. Late spring–summer. Temperate Asia, N America, Europe.

CULTIVATION   Introduction: Hardy Orchids.

L.cordata (L.) R. Br. LESSER TWAYBLADE.
To 20cm. Stem glabrous then minutely pubesc. toward infl., bronze at base; basal sheaths 1–2. Lvs 1–3cm, ovate-deltate or triangular. Raceme to 6cm, lax, 4–12-fld; sep. to 2.5mm, olive-green to rust-coloured, narrow-elliptic, obtuse; pet. 3–4.5mm rusty-green; lip green flushed mauve, linear, with 2 small lateral lobes near base and apical lobe cleft, spreading. Europe, Asia, N America, Greenland.

L.ovata (L.) R. Br. TWAYBLADE.
Stem pubesc. toward infl. Lvs 20–60cm, ovate to broadly elliptic; basal sheaths 2–3, brown. Raceme 7–25cm, bracts ovate-lanceolate; fls green, rarely tinged red-brown; pet. and sep. incurved, forming lax hood; lip 7–15mm, strongly decurved, apically cleft, lateral lobes absent or greatly reduced. Europe to C Asia.

Listrostachys Rchb. f. (From Gk *listron*, spade, and *stachys*, ear of corn or spike.) 1 species, an epiphyte. Stems usually less than 6cm, rarely to 15cm, the lower part covered with overlapping leaf bases. Leaves 8–35×1–2cm, ligulate or linear-oblong, equally or unequally bilobed at apex, the lobes obtuse. Racemes erect or spreading, 10–25cm, densely many-flowered; flowers small, 2-ranked, white, sometimes with small red spots toward base and with red spur; pedicel and ovary 2mm; bracts very short; sepals and petals free, similar, sepals 2–3mm, ovate, petals similar but slightly shorter and narrower; lip entire, 2–3mm, obovate or more or less quadrate, apiculate, spurred, the mouth of the spur some distance from base of lip and column; spur 3.5–5mm, stout, dorsally compressed, clavate at apex; pollinia and stipites 2, viscidium 1. W Africa to Zaire.

CULTIVATION   As for *Angraecum*.

L.monteiroae Rchb. f. See *Cyrtorchis monteiroae*.

L.pertusa (Lindl.) Rchb. f. (*Angraecum pertusum* Lindl.).
(Described above.)

L.sedenii Rchb. f. Schltr. See *Cyrtorchis arcuata*.

Lockhartia Hook. (*Fernandezia* Lindl.). (For David Lockhart (*fl.*1827), Superintendent of the Trinidad Botanical Garden.) Some 30 species of epiphytes. Rhizome short. Pseudobulbs absent. Stems simple, elongate, erect or pendent, leafy. Leaves numerous, distichous, erect or spreading, bases overlapping, equitant. Inflorescence a raceme or a panicle, lateral or terminal, few- to many-flowered; flowers small, mostly yellow to white; sepals subequal, free, spreading or reflexed; petals usually larger than sepals, otherwise similar; lip entire to 3(–5)-lobed, lateral lobes linear to spathulate, incurved or recurved, midlobe lobulate, disc callose; column stout, short, footless, bialate or biauriculate, anther terminal, operculate, incumbent, pollinia 2, waxy. Tropical America.

CULTIVATION Epiphytes for bright, humid positions in the intermediate house, distinguished by their slender stems closely clothed with leaves and bright, *Oncidium*-like axillary flowers. Establish in an open bark mix with additional rockwool or sphagnum in small pans or baskets. Syringe regularly when in growth. Decrease water supplies a little over the winter months. Propagate by division.

L.acuta (Lindl.) Rchb. f. (*L.pallida* Rchb. f.; *Fernandezia acuta* Lindl.).
Lvs to 3×1cm, ovate-triangular, subacute or apiculate, coriaceous. Infl. to 9cm, paniculate, many-fld; peduncle filiform; fls to 1cm diam., white or pale yellow, sometimes marked pale brown; sep. to 4×3mm, ovate, obtuse, spreading; pet. to 5×3mm, elliptic-oblong, obtuse; lip to 6×4mm, yellow marked pale brown, lateral lobes linear, obtuse, midlobe subquadrate, obtuse, emarginate; callus 2-ridged, pilose, base tuberculate; column white, undulate, wings triangular. Panama, Trinidad, Venezuela, Colombia.

L.amoena Endress & Rchb. f.
Stems to 40×2.5cm, erect or pendent, laterally compressed. Lvs to 3.5×1cm, coriaceous, ovate-triangular, fleshy, subacute. Infl. to 3cm, a few-fld panicle; fls to 2cm; sep. and pet. bright yellow, sep. to 6×4mm, dorsal sep. ovate, obtuse, minutely apiculate, slightly reflexed, lateral sep. elliptic-lanceolate, subacute, strongly reflexed, pet. to 7×4mm, elliptic-oblong, obtuse, reflexed; lip to 10×8mm, bright yellow, slightly marked red-brown at base, complex, lateral lobes linear-ligulate, acute, incurved, midlobe subquadrate, truncate, undulate, 4-lobulate, basal lobules strongly reflexed, callus linear, slightly papillose; column with spreading wings. Costa Rica, Panama.

L.elegans Hook. (*Fernandezia elegans* (Hook.) Lodd.).
Stems to 30cm, erect to pendent, numerous. Lvs to 20×6mm, obliquely triangular, obtuse, subtruncate or retuse, coriaceous. Infl. usually an arching lateral raceme, 1- to many-fld; sep. and pet. pale yellow, sep. to 5×3mm, elliptic to ovate, apiculate, deeply concave, pet. to 5×3mm, obliquely ovate, obtuse to apiculate, slightly concave; lip to 6×5mm, yellow slightly marked purple-maroon, conspicuously 3-lobed, lateral lobes triangular, acute to obtuse, subentire, midlobe large, oblong-ligulate, rounded to emarginate, undulate, callus ligulate, obtuse or rounded, with 4 or 5 basal tubercles; column yellow, to 2mm, wings 2, subquadrate, denticulate. Colombia, Venezuela, Trinidad, Brazil.

L.longifolia (Lindl.) Schltr.
Stems to 35cm, pendent. Lvs to 40×1.8cm, obliquely and narrowly triangular. Fls to 1cm diam., usually solitary, primrose yellow with small red dots at base of lip. Venezuela to Bolivia.

L.lunifera (Lindl.) Rchb. f. (*Fernandezia lunifera* Lindl.).
Stems to 35cm, slender, erect. Lvs to 20×7mm, narrowly triangular-ligulate, subtruncate, subcoriaceous, rigid. Infl. usually terminal, a raceme, 1- to few-fld, erect to arching; fls long-stalked; sep. and pet. golden yellow, sep. to 6×5mm, broadly obovate to oblong, acute or rounded, reflexed, pet. to 5×3mm, oblong, obtuse or retuse; lip to 8×4mm, golden yellow finely spotted purple, spreading, sessile, lateral lobes to 4mm, linear, acute, erect, midlobe subquadrate, obscurely 4-lobulate, emarginate, callus verrucose; column to 2mm, yellow spotted purple, erect, wings 2, dentate. Brazil.

L.micrantha Rchb. f.
Stems to 40cm, erect to pendent. Lvs to 2×1cm, narrowly triangular, coriaceous, obliquely truncate or obtuse. Infl. a raceme or a panicle, subterminal, 1- to few-fld; fls small, yellow; sep. to 4×3mm, ovate to elliptic, concave, acute, apiculate; pet. to 4×2mm, ovate to elliptic-ovate, obtuse; lip to 5×5mm, lateral lobes basal, linear-oblong or linear-ligulate, acute or obtuse, spreading or reflexed, midlobe subrhombic to obovate, deeply retuse, callus slightly concave, sometimes cleft; column short, wings 2, triangular to subquadrate. Nicaragua to Surinam, Brazil.

L.oerstedii Rchb. f. (*Fernandezia robusta* Batem.; *L.robusta* (Batem.) Schltr.).
Stems to 45cm, erect. Lvs to 4cm, triangular, acute to obtuse, suberect. Infl. to 3.5cm, a pendent, axillary raceme, 1- to several-fld; fls to 2cm, bright yellow; sep. to 8×5mm, narrowly ovate to suborbicular, rounded, reflexed, concave; pet. to 9×5mm, broadly elliptic to subquadrate, truncate, reflexed; lip to 14×14mm, bright yellow spotted and barred dark red below, complex, 5-lobed, basal lobes elliptic, apex denticulate, undulate, central lobes ovate-triangular, erect, broadly obtuse, apical lobe bilobulate, undulate, callus to 7×4mm, light brown, quadrate, pilose, with 4 central papillose keels; column to 4mm, fleshy, wings 2, subquadrate, denticulate, spotted red. Mexico to Panama.

L.pallida Rchb. f. See *L.acuta*.

L.pittieri Schltr.
Stems to 20×4.5cm. Lvs to 3.5×1cm, narrowly triangular to linear-lanceolate, acute to acuminate. Infl. axillary, 1-fld; fls to 1.5cm diam., yellow to yellow-orange; sep. to 5×2mm, elliptic-lanceolate, minutely apiculate; pet. to 5×3mm, suborbicular to oblong-elliptic, acute to obtuse; lip to 8×6mm, oblong-subquadrate, deeply emarginate, entire to obscurely 3-lobed, disc with an ovate-oblong callus, orange, slightly papillose, apex thickened, with an erect, median spur. Costa Rica, Panama, British Honduras.

L.robusta (Batem.) Schltr. See *L.oerstedii*.

L.serra Rchb. f.
Similar to *L.oerstedii*, but fls to 2cm diam., yellow marked red-brown on lip; lip 3-lobed, lateral lobes oblong, incurved, midlobe broad. Ecuador.

Ludisia A. Rich. (Derivation of name obscure, possibly after the subject of an Ancient Greek elegy written by her widower.) 1 species, a terrestrial or lithophyte. Stems succulent, prostrate to ascending, segmented, terete, pink to brown with paler flecks, branching and rooting at nodes. Roots adhesive, ciliate. Leaves scattered along creeping stems or in a loose rosette on ascending (flowering) stems, subcordate to broad-elliptic, acute, to 9cm, fleshy, narrowed to a clasping petiole, velvety-papillose, bronze to black, typically with 5 longitudinal copper-red veins and broken venation between, underside pink to brown, glossy. Inflorescence a terminal, bracteate raceme to 15cm; axis pubescent, pink-green; flowers numerous, sparkling white, to 2cm diameter; dorsal sepals and petals forming a hood, lateral sepals reflexed; lip basally saccate, tip cleft and frilled, limb twisted; column glossy golden-yellow, diverging from lip; ovary twisted, pubescent. SE Asia, China, Indonesia.

CULTIVATION   Grown for its beautifully patterned, velvety leaves and slender spikes of white flowers. It is the largest and most robust of the jewel orchids (see *Anoectochilus* and *Macodes*) and, unlike its allies, will withstand almost any treatment provided some shade and temperatures over 10°C/50°F. Because of its attractive flowers and foliage and ease of propagation (sections of rhizome will root and sprout freely if buried, kept moist and given a little bottom heat), *Ludisia* is gaining popularity as a houseplant. Place the rhizomes, half-buried, in a mix of leafmould, coarse bark and charcoal in pans or half pots. Water freely, allowing a slight drying between each watering. Mist with soft water during warm weather. Ideally, maintain medium to high humidity, temperatures in excess of 15°C/60°F (if lower, reduce watering accordingly) and light to deep shade. Repot and divide after flowering, when the flowered growths will deteriorate.

L.discolor (Ker-Gawl.) A. Rich. (*Goodyera discolor* Ker-Gawl.; *Haemaria discolor* (Ker-Gawl.) Lindl.).
A highly variable species treated here as encompassing the several taxa named in *Haemaria* and recombined recently as species of *Ludisia*. These include *L.dawsoniana*, a large plant of particular vigour with chocolate brown leaves veined coppery red, and *L.otletae* with finely patterned narrow-lanceolate lvs and sparsely flowered spikes.

Lueddemannia Lind. & Rchb. f. (Named in honour of M.E. Lueddeman (*fl.* 1854), who cultivated orchids in Paris.) 2 species of epiphytes. Pseudobulbs clustered, ovoid to ovoid-oblong, usually apically bifoliate. Leaves rigid, erect, lanceolate to elliptic, plicate. Inflorescence from base of pseudobulbs, a lateral raceme, pendent, many-flowered; flowers often large, fleshy, rather spreading; sepals similar, free, ovate-elliptic to oblong-elliptic, lateral sepals oblique; petals smaller than sepals, oblanceolate to spathulate-elliptic; lip clawed, apex trilobed; lateral lobes erect, midlobe triangular; disc with an erect callus, crested or tuberculate; column clavate, arcuate, apex auriculate-alate, anther terminal, operculate, incumbent, unilocular, pollinia 2, compressed. Venezuela, Peru, Ecuador, Colombia.

CULTIVATION   As for *Stanhopea*.

L.pescatorei (Lindl.) Lind. & Rchb. f. (*L.triloba* Rolfe; *Cycnoches pescatorei* Lindl.).
Pseudobulbs to 13×7cm, slightly compressed, ovoid to ovoid-oblong, light yellow-brown. Lvs to 40×9cm, lanceolate to elliptic-lanceolate, acute. Infl. to 1m, strongly pendulous; fls crowded; peduncle light green spotted dark purple with scurfy dark hair; sep. to 27×14mm, ovate to ovate-elliptic, acute or obtuse, light red-brown finely spotted purple, interior bright red-maroon with pale brown margins; pet. to 23×9mm, spathulate-oblanceolate or oblanceolate, acute or subobtuse, bright golden-yellow, apical margins marked red; lip to 26×19mm, bright golden-yellow, fleshy, rigid, lateral lobes obliquely ovate-triangular, obtuse to subacute, midlobe minutely papillose, acute, disc central, with a warty callus, minutely papillose; column to 19mm, pale yellow-cream, apex winged, anth. pale yellow. Venezuela, Colombia, Ecuador, Peru.

L.triloba Rolfe. See *L.pescatorei*.

Luisia Gaudich. (For Dom Luis de Torres, Portuguese botanist.) Some 40 species of monopodial epiphytes. Stems slender, terete, branching near base, thus appearing clump-forming. Leaves alternate, remote, dark green, tinted maroon in optimum conditions, fleshy, slender, terete, attached to cylindric sheathing base. Inflorescences numerous, axillary, short, clustered; sepals and petals obovate, acute, forward-pointing; lip prominent, lobed, coloured, fused to column base. Tropical Asia to Polynesia.

CULTIVATION   As for *Papilionanthe*; the habit is, however, rather more compact than in that genus and the flowers (clustered, frog- or fly-like, green and mauve) altogether less showy. These are interesting and undemanding plants, best grown on blocks of fern fibre.

L.alpina Lindl. See *Trudelia alpina*.

L.megasepala Hayata.
Close in habit to *L.teretifolia*; fls larger, malodorous; tepals olive green, incurved; lip velvety, garnet-black. Taiwan.

L.psyche Rchb. f.
Lvs blunt, erect, to 15cm. Fls pale yellow-green, lip violet-brown, chequered white or yellow; sep. concave, obtuse, to 1.5cm; pet. linear to obovate, to 4cm; lip to 2.5cm, ovate-oblong, basally saccate with 2 lobe-like appendages. Burma, Laos.

L.teretifolia Gaudich.
Lvs tapering to a point, curving upwards, to 20cm. Fls yellow, green, or pale pink, lip base green and purple or yellow; dorsal sep. elliptic, lateral sep. lanceolate, exterior keeled, apical point fleshy; pet. linear-oblong; lip trilobed, cordate above, almost square below, basally inflated, midlobe cordate, undulate, lateral lobes elliptic, undulate at tips. India, SE Asia to N Caledonia.

Lycaste Lindl. (For Lykast, daughter of King Priam.) Some 45 species of epiphytes, terrestrials or lithophytes. Rhizomes short. Pseudobulbs to 14cm, usually ovoid, slightly laterally compressed. Leaves 1 to several, at apex of each pseudobulb and sheathing base, lasting 1–2 seasons, plicate, lanceolate, acuminate, bright lustrous green. Flowers appearing with or shortly before new growth, usually borne singly on 1–10 erect or spreading, sheathed stalks arising, from base of pseudobulb, large, fragrant; sepals erect to spreading, subequal, lanceolate to elliptic-lanceolate, obtuse or acuminate, connate at base with column-foot, forming a saccate mentum; petals similar to sepals, shorter, enclosing column; lip articulate with column-foot, trilobed, midlobe spreading to decurved, pubescent, entire to fimbriate or undulate, lateral lobes erect, disc often pubescent, callused; column long, semi-terete, arcuate, produced into foot at base; anther terminal, 1-celled, pollinia 4. Mexico, C America, W Indies, S America.

CULTIVATION   Robust plants for the cool or intermediate house. Squat pseudobulbs carry broad, ribbed leaves and a series of solitary waxen flowers from their bases, alongside new growth. With the exceptions of the smaller *Ll. aromatica, cruenta* and *deppei*, these plants are best maintained with 3–4 back bulbs at most and a vigorous lead. Pot in a mix of coarse bark, charcoal, sphagnum and leafmould, with a little dried FYM just prior to the end of the winter resting period. When in growth, water and feed freely and maintain in humid, buoyant conditions in light shade (avoid leaf scorch); aim to promote the largest and firmest possible pseudobulbs. Once growth is complete, reduce temperature and watering and increase light. Flowers and new growth tend to emerge simultaneously. In the three species mentioned above, flowers may well precede new shoots and water should be restricted until they are fully initiated.

L.aromatica (Graham ex Hook.) Lindl.
Pseudobulbs to 10×4.5cm, squat, dark green, obscurely ribbed. Lvs to 50×10cm, falling to leave 2 sharply-pointed remnants at apex of pseudobulb. Scapes to 17cm, fls to 8cm diam., bright yellow, sweetly scented; sep. to 4×2cm, green-yellow; pet. to 3.5×2cm, deep yellow; lip to 3cm, golden yellow, dotted orange, concave below, lateral lobes porrect, crenulate on front margin, midlobe square to rounded, constricted at base, margin undulate, disc pubesc., callus flap-like, truncate, broadly cuneate, extending over base of midlobe; column to 2.5cm. Spring. Mexico, Honduras, Guatemala.

L.barringtoniae (Sm.) Lindl.
Pseudobulbs ellipsoid, to 9×5cm. Lvs to 50×12cm. Infl. several; scapes to 12cm; bracts loose; fls to 7cm, pendent, waxy, long-lived, olive green; sep. to 4.5×1.5cm, dorsal sep. narrower; pet. similar; lip light buff-brown, to 4.5cm, long-clawed, lateral lobes at claw-apex narrowly falcate, midlobe blunt, marginally fimbriate, callus broad, deeply furrowed. Spring–summer. Cuba, Jamaica.

L.bradeorum Schltr.
Very close to *L.aromatica* and *L.cochleata*. Differs from the former in the broader sep. and smaller, less constricted midlobe of lip, from the latter in its richer orange-yellow sep. and smaller lip midlobe. Honduras, Costa Rica, Nicaragua.

L.brevispatha (Klotzsch) Lindl.
Pseudobulbs to 6.5×4cm, ellipsoid to ovoid. Lvs to 50×10cm. Scapes to 10cm, fls to 5cm diam.; sep. to 3×1.5cm, pale green, dotted pale rose; pet. to 2.5×1.5cm, white to rose; lip to 3cm, white, spotted rose to purple, somewhat concave below, lateral lobes incurved, forming tube; midlobe emarginate, disc slightly pubesc., callus short, flat, tongue-shaped. Costa Rica, Nicaragua, Panama, Guatemala.

L.campbellii C. Schweinf.
Fls small, produced before new growth, from bare pseudobulbs with spiny leaf remnants at apex; sep. green-yellow to apple-green, ovate-triangular, spreading; pet. broadly ovate, pale yellow, recurved; lip primrose yellow, more or less pandurate. Perlas Archipelago (off Pacific coast of Panama).

L.candida Lindl.
Very similar to *L.brevispatha*; differs in the narrower, far more concave lip which bears a grooved, linear, not a short, flat callus. Costa Rica.

L.ciliata (Ruiz & Pav.) Rchb. (*L.costata* (Lindl.) Lindl.; *L.fimbriata* (Poepp. & Endl.) Cogn.).
Pseudobulbs to 7cm, ovoid. Lvs to 25cm. Scapes numerous, to 10cm, fls to 10cm diam., not opening fully, nodding, waxy, deliciously fragrant, tepals green to ivory tinted green, lip cream, sometimes yellow, callus orange to yellow; sep. and

(a)   (b)

Lycaste   (a) *L.cruenta*   (b) *L.aromatica*

pet. narrow-oblong, falcate, obtuse, pet. parallel to sides of column; lip midlobe fimbriate to ciliate. Spring. Peru, Bolivia, Ecuador, Colombia.

L.cochleata Lindl. ex Paxt.
Similar to *L.aromatica*. Fls to 5cm diam.; sep. green-yellow, slightly pubesc. above at base; pet. deep orange; lip basally saccate, midlobe rounded at tip, fimbriate, callus slightly grooved, tip rounded. Spring. Guatemala, Mexico.

L.consobrina Rchb. f.
Close to *L.aromatica,* differing in the forward-pointing, broader tepals and the broad lip. Mexico, Guatemala..

L.costata (Lindl.) Lindl. See *L.ciliata.*

L.crinita Lindl.
Resembles *L.aromatica* except fls unscented; disc of lip pubesc.; pseudobulbs and lvs more robust; scapes longer. Spring–summer. Mexico, Guatemala.

L.crocea Lindl. See *L.fulvescens.*

L.cruenta (Lindl.) Lindl.
Pseudobulbs ovoid-oblong, to 10×5cm. Lvs to 45×15cm, elliptic-lanceolate to broadly elliptic. Scapes to 17cm, fls to 10cm diam., spicily scented; sep. to 5×2.5cm, yellow-green; pet. to 4×2.5cm, bright yellow to yellow-orange; lip yellow, dotted maroon, spotted crimson at base, saccate, white hairs in saccate portion, midlobe emarginate, pubesc., disc corrugated at base, with small, subquadrate, truncate callus. Spring. Mexico, Guatemala, Costa Rica, El Salvador.

L.denningiana Rchb. f. Pseudobulbs to 10×7cm. Lvs to 70×10cm. Scapes to 50cm×5mm, fls large, open; sep. fleshy, to 11×2.5cm, linear-falcate, light yellow-green; pet. to 5×2cm, green to cream, broadly falcate; lip bright orange, to 5×2.5cm, rigid, crispate, lateral lobes sharply recurved and folded back, midlobe rounded, sharply folded back, covering lateral lobes below lip and deeply grooved above; column cream, orange at base; anth. cream; pollinia yellow. Winter. Venezuela, Colombia, Ecuador.

L.deppei (Lodd.) Lindl.
Pseudobulbs and lvs similar to *L.aromatica* except more robust. Scapes to 17cm, fls to 9cm diam.; sep. to 6×2.5cm, pale green flecked or faintly lined oxblood to red; pet. to 4.5×2cm, white, flecked red at base; lip bright yellow with red dots, red lateral stripes at base, strongly veined, lateral lobes involute, midlobe strongly decurved, to 2cm, margins crenate, disc thickened in middle, callus small, rounded, sulcate. Spring–autumn. Mexico, Guatemala.

L.dowiana Endres & Rchb. f.
Resembles a smaller *L.macrophylla*; fls produced in abundance, sep. bronze to olive-green, forward-pointing then reflexed, pet. and lip creamy white, sometimes spotted rose, stained yellow below. Panama, Guatemala and further south.

L.fimbriata (Poepp. & Endl.) Cogn. See *L.ciliata.*

L.fulvescens Hook. (*L.crocea* Lindl.).
Allied to *L.longipetala*. Pseudobulbs to 10×5cm. Lvs to 80×8cm. Scapes to 25cm, fls nodding, to 10cm diam.; sep. and pet. yellow-green tinted bronze, sep. to 5.5×1.5cm, pet. shorter; lip to 2.5×1.5cm, lateral lobes small, orange-red, midlobe large with yellow, fimbriate margins, callus 2-lobed, front wider. Summer. Venezuela, Colombia.

L.gigantea Lindl. See *L.longipetala.*

L.lanipes Lindl.
A distinctive, green-fld species, it differs from *L.ciliata* in the very narrow, drooping, olive tepals, less closely toothed lip and 7-keeled callus; the fls are also heavily perfumed. Ecuador.

L.lasioglossa Rchb. f.
Pseudobulbs to 10×4cm, ovoid. Lvs to 55×12cm, strongly veined. Scapes slender, to 25cm, fls to 11cm diam.; sep. to 7×2cm, red-brown; pet. to 4×2cm, bright yellow; lip to 4×2cm, yellow flecked and striped purple, tubular below, midlobe densely pubesc., callus ovate-triangular, notched at apex; column densely pubesc. in middle. Spring–winter. Guatemala, Honduras.

L.leucantha (Klotzsch) Lindl. (*L.leucoflavescens* hort.).
Pseudobulbs ovoid, to 7.5×3.5cm. Lvs to 65×6cm. Fls to 10cm diam.; sep. brown-green to apple green, to 4.5×2cm; pet. yellow-white, to 4×2cm; lip to 3×2cm, conspicuously nerved, lateral lobes yellow, midlobe cream-white, pubesc., margin denticulate, callus rounded; column yellow-white. Costa Rica, Panama.

L.leucoflavescens hort. See *L.leucantha.*

L.locusta Rchb. f.
Similar in habit to *L.longipetala*, lvs smaller. Fls to 9cm; sep. and pet. sea-green, pet. smaller than sep.; lip dull green, margin white, midlobe large, oval, fimbriate; column slender, pubesc. Spring. Peru.

L.longipetala (Ruiz & Pav.) Garay (*L.gigantea* Lindl.).
Pseudobulbs to 15cm, oblong-ovoid, furrowed with age. Lvs to 80×9.5cm. Infl. robust; fls to 16cm diam.; sep. and pet. yellow-green, tinged brown, sep. to 8.5×3cm, pet. smaller; lip red-brown to violet-purple, lateral lobes short, midlobe oblong-ovate, margins denticulate or fimbriate. Summer. Ecuador, Peru, Colombia, Venezuela.

L.longiscapa Rolfe ex E. Cooper.
Differs from *L.denningiana* in the very long-stalked fls; tepals shorter, broader, bright apple green; lip smaller, rounded, burnt orange with a deep amber callus and a yellow margin. Ecuador.

L.macrobulbon (Hook.) Lindl.
Resembles *L.longipetala* except more robust, pseudobulbs larger. Fls to 6cm diam.; sep. green-yellow; pet. white-yellow, shorter than sep.; lip yellow, sparsely spotted brown at base, lateral lobes very short, blunt, midlobe large, oval. Spring–summer. Colombia.

L.macrophylla (Poepp. & Endl.) Lindl.
Pseudobulbs to 7×4cm, ovoid. Lvs to 50×9cm, strongly ribbed. Scapes to 14cm, fls nodding, to 9cm diam.; sep. olive-green, edged pink-brown, to 4×2cm; pet. white, spotted rose-pink, to 3.5×2cm, parallel to column; lip white, margins dotted rose, midlobe spreading, ciliate, callus concave, margin dotted pink; column white, dark purple to red at base; pollinia yellow. Spring–summer. Costa Rica, Panama, Colombia, Venezuela, Brazil, Peru, Bolivia.

L.powellii Schltr.
Pseudobulbs ellipsoid-ovoid, smooth to rigid, to 7×3.5cm. Lvs to 45×8cm. Scapes to 15cm; fls to 10cm diam.; sep. pale translucent green marked chestnut brown or wine-red, margins yellow, wide-spreading; pet. cream-yellow to white, dotted pink or wine-red, parallel to column, tips reflexed; lip white, dotted red, midlobe short, spreading, callus ligulate, obtuse, concave. Summer-autumn. Panama.

L.schilleriana Rchb. f.
Allied to *L.longipetala*. Fls to 12cm; sep. pale olive green; pet. white, dotted brown; lip yellow-white, lateral lobes small, midlobe white, flecked rose-pink, margin fringed. Spring. Columbia.

L.skinneri (Lindl.) Lindl. (*L.virginalis* (Scheidw.) Lind.).
Pseudobulbs ovoid, to 10×3.5cm. Lvs to 75×15cm. Scapes to 30cm, fls to 14cm diam.; sep. white to violet-rose, to 8×3.5cm; pet. red-violet, often marked deep rose-crimson, to 7.5×4cm; lip white to pale rose, flecked red-violet, to 5cm, lateral lobes pubesc., midlobe strongly decurved, disc pubesc. at centre, callus fleshy. Autumn–spring. Guatemala, Mexico, Honduras, El Salvador. The fl. colour of this widely cultivated species is highly variable; numerous colour forms have been named, ranging from white to shell-pink to burgundy.

L.suaveolens Summerh.
Fls large, spicily fragrant, arising from large, apically spined pseudobulbs just prior to completion of new growth; sep. lime green, lateral sep. lanceolate-falcate, spreading, dorsal sep. ovate-elliptic; pet. yellow-green, elliptic, acute; lip bright yel-

(a)

(b)

Lycaste   (a) *L.skinneri*   (b) *L.deppei*

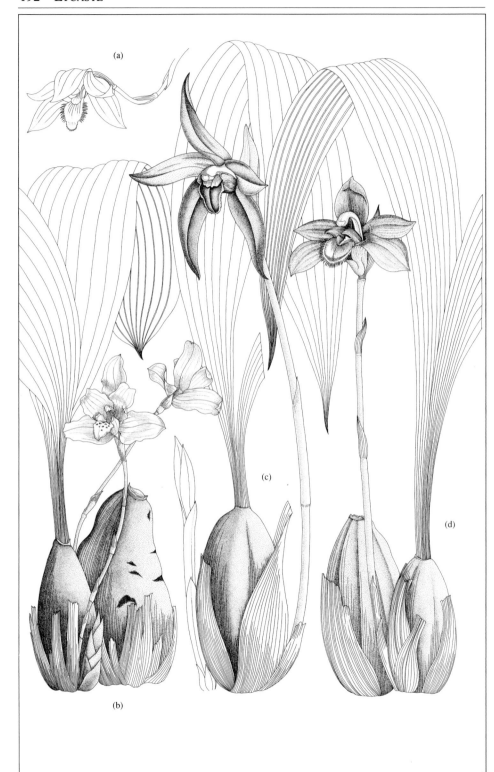

Lycaste (a) *L.barringtoniae* (b) *L.macrobulbon* (c) *L.longipetala* (d) *L.locusta*

low, basally concave, midlobe porrect, oblong, obscurely toothed below. El Salvador.

L.tricolor (Klotzsch) Rchb. f.
Pseudobulbs ovoid, to 8×3.5cm. Lvs to 35×7cm. Scapes to 11cm; bracts almost exceeding flower; sep. to 4×1cm, pale bronze-green, tinged rose-pink; pet. white to pale buff or pink, dotted rose; lip white dotted pink, lateral lobes involute, midlobe suborbicular to obovate, margins denticulate; callus small, obovate. Guatemala, Costa Rica, Panama.

L.trifoliata hort. ex Ross.
Plants small. Pseudobulbs narrow, not spined. Lvs thin, long-stalked. Fls short-stalked, nodding; tepals narrowly oblong, apple green, white below, forward-pointing; lip white, oblong, the margin densely fringed with long erect cilia. S America.

L.virginalis (Scheidw.) Lindl. See *L.skinneri*.

L.xytriophora. Lind. & Rchb. f. Allied to *L.longipetala*, lvs shorter. Scapes to 12.5cm, fls to 10cm diam.; sep. green-brown, to 4×2cm; pet. yellow-green, tips white, to 3×2cm; lip white tinted rose-pink on interior surface, to 3×1.5cm, midlobe marginally undulate, callus very small, yellow, dotted red; column to 3cm, pubesc. in anterior portion. Spring–summer. Costa Rica, Ecuador.

L.grexes and cultivars (see also under × *Angulocaste*).
L.Aquila: large plants with orange fls on tall stems; 'Detente' is a particularly fine clone.
L.Athena: plants with many fine dark pink fls.

L.Auburn: floriferous plants; fls in a wide range of colours, mostly whites pinks and reds, some orange and bicolors; there are numerous awarded clones of high quality.
L.Balliae: very floriferous plants; fls pink and pink-red; 'Superba' is a fine clone.
L.Brugensis: large plants; fls on erect stems, large, creamy yellow, yellow and orange shades with an orange lip.
L.Cassiopiea: compact plants; fls in attractive shades of peach-pink; several awarded clones.
L.Concentration: strong plants; fls bright yellow, long-lasting.
L.Guinevere: fls pale green on tall stems; flowering over a long season.
L.Hera: large plants and fls; apricot-yellow.
L.Imschootiana: large plants making fine specimens, very floriferous; fls cream or pale pink, freckled with fine red spots.
L.Jason: very floriferous plants; fls deep yellow-orange, often scented.
L.Koolena: well-shaped fls in shades of white, pink and red.
L.Libra: very free-flowering, up to 30 fls per bulb; fls orange-brown with darker orange spots.
L.Macama: well-shaped fls in pink and red shades.
L.Neptune: fls fine, pale green.
L.Pink Dream: very floriferous, somewhat cup-shaped fls in a fine deep pink.
L.Queen Elizabeth: fine, pale green to white fls.
L.Vulcan: fine shaped fls, variable, white, pink and red, the best a glowing orange-red.
L.Wyldfire: the best of the deep red-flowered hybrids.

Lyperanthus R. Br. (From Gk *lyperos*, mournful, and *anthos* flower, referring to the dark colour of the dried flowers of *L.nigricans*.) Some 8 species of glabrous herbaceous terrestrials. Leaf solitary, basal, lanceolate or ovate. Flowers in an erect, terminal raceme on bracteate stem; dorsal sepal incurved or erect; lateral sepals and petals lanceolate, spreading or erect; lip entire or trilobed, papillose, sometimes with raised longitudinal lines. Summer–autumn. Australia, New Zealand, New Caledonia.

CULTIVATION See *Caladenia*.

L.forrestii F. Muell.
To 23cm. Lvs 3, pale green, lower lf ovate-lanceolate, coriaceous, spreading, middle lf smaller, lanceolate, upper lf reduced, acute. Fls to 4, white, tinted pink, spotted and striped deep crimson; dorsal sep. erect, forming a hood, lateral sep. spreading; pet. lanceolate to falcate, 3-veined, sometimes spotted: all 2.5cm; lip obovate, lower half erect, upper recurved, margins crenulate, longitudinal venation prominent. W Australia.

L.nigricans R. Br. RED BEAK.
To 20cm. Lf to 9cm, ovate-cordate. Fls 2–8, white lined crimson; sep. and pet. to 3.5cm, tipped dark red-brown; dorsal sep. broadly lanceolate, incurved, lateral sep. linear, spreading or deflexed; pet. similar to lateral sep.; lip crimson-veined, tipped purple, ovate-lanceolate, sessile, trilobed, fringed or

minutely dentate, raised plate longitudinal. SE and central SW Australia.

L.serratus Lindl.
Similar to *L.suaveolens*, with strongly blue-pruinose, maroon tepals; readily identified by the white-pubesc. lip. W Australia.

L.suaveolens R. Br. BROWN BEAKS.
To 45cm. Lf to 20cm, linear-lanceolate, concave, margins incurved. Fls 2–8, sometimes fragrant, pruinose, dark red to brown; dorsal sep. to 2.3cm, forming a hood, lateral sep. and pet. equal, slightly exceeding dorsal sep., linear; lip trilobed, lateral lobes obtuse, midlobe ovate-oblong, recurved, glandular bordered with scale-like glands, grouped in threes. SE Australia, Tasmania.

× **Maclellanara** (*Brassia* × *Odontoglossum* × *Oncidium*). Trigeneric hybrids tolerant of intermediate growing conditions. Plants consist of a group of compressed pseudobulbs growing from a basal rhizome, each with one or two leaves at its apex and two or more leaf-like sheaths arising at its base. Inflorescences arise in the axils of these sheaths and may be simple or branched. Flowers with narrow sepals and petals, lip large, conspicuously marked with brown spots.

× *M.*Pagan Lovesong: very large fls on tall spikes; fls cream or yellow-green with large brown spots, lip larger than other sep. and pet. but similar coloration; many outstanding clones have received awards.

Macodes (Bl.) Lindl. (From Gk *mac(r)os*, long, an allusion to the elongated lip midlobe.) Some 10 species of evergreen terrestrials allied to *Anoectochilus* and *Ludisia* and closely resembling the latter except in its non-resupinate flowers. Summer. Malesia to Papuasia.

CULTIVATION   As for *Anoectochilus*.

M.petola (Bl.) Lindl.
Rhiz. fleshy, creeping, slender, rooting and branching at nodes. Lvs to 8, spiralling in a loose rosette, to 9×6cm, elliptic to ovate, acute, fleshy, papillose appearing velvety, bottle green with 5 longitudinal veins and many finer reticulate golden veins in obscure transverse bands above, purple-green beneath; petioles grooved, clasping at base. Infl. an erect, terminal spike to 20cm; fls small, white, lip rusty brown. Sumatra to Philippines. var. **argenteoreticulata** J.J. Sm. (*M.petola* var. *javanica* (Hook.f.) A.D. Hawkes). Lvs to 10cm, veins silver-green. Java.

M.sanderiana Rolfe (*Anoectochilus sanderianus* hort.).
Lvs to 7×4.5cm, broadly ovate to orbicular, emerald to deep bronze-green with 5 very conspicuous, golden or copper, shimmering, longitudinal veins and finer crowded reticulation of the same colour above, purple-green beneath. Fls brown-white, lip white. Papua New Guinea.

Macradenia R. Br. (From Gk *makros*, long, and *aden*, gland, referring to the long anther appendage.) Some 12 species of epiphytes. Pseudobulbs small, cylindrical, apically unifoliate, clothed at base with grey-white, scarious sheaths. Leaves fleshy to coriaceous. Inflorescence from base of pseudobulb, a raceme, loosely few to many-fld, erect to pendent; flowers small; sepals equal, free, slightly spreading; petals similar to sepals; lip erect, continuous with column base, 3-lobed, lateral lobes erect, clasping column, midlobe short, spreading; column footless, wingless, slightly grooved below, anther erect, pollinia 2, attached to viscid disc or gland by long membranaceous narrow stipe. Florida, W Indies, Mexico, S America.

CULTIVATION   Intermediate house orchids requiring sunny conditions and pot or basket culture in an open medium.

M.brassavolae Rchb. f.
Pseudobulbs to 4.5×1cm, curved, slightly compressed. Lvs to 18×3cm, oblong or oblong-lanceolate, acute or obtuse, subcoriaceous. Infl. to 25cm, pendent, few-to many-fld; peduncle dark maroon-red; fls showy, maroon sometimes striped white, margins yellow-green; sep. and pet. to 20×5mm, lanceolate to linear-lanceolate, acuminate, slightly spreading; lip to 19×8mm, fleshy, lateral lobes short, suborbicular-obovate, midlobe linear-lanceolate, recurved, acute, disc with a narrow central keel; column to 7mm, clavate, fleshy, apex with 2 subquadrate auricles, apical margin erose. Mexico, C America, Colombia, Venezuela, Ecuador.

M.lutescens R. Br.
Pseudobulbs to 5×1cm, slightly compressed. Lvs to 16×3cm, oblong-lanceolate, acute, coriaceous. Infl. to 17cm, pendent, loosely few-fld; fls white-yellow or dull yellow marked brown-purple; dorsal sep. to 12×6mm, broadly elliptic-oblong, acute, deeply concave, lateral sep. to 12×4mm, obliquely elliptic-lanceolate, acute, subfalcate; pet. to 11×3mm, oblong-elliptic, acute; lip to 10×7mm, lateral lobes obcordate to suborbicular, incurved, midlobe narrowly linear-lanceolate, reflexed, margins revolute, disc with 3 central keels; column to 8mm, clavate, apex irregularly dentate. Winter. Florida, W Indies, Venezuela, Colombia, Guyana, Surinam.

Malaxis Sol. ex Sw. (From Gk *malaxis*, softening, referring to the soft texture of the leaves of most species.) About 300 species of terrestrials, lithophytes or epiphytes. Rhizome tuberous, creeping. Leaves 1 to several, thin-textured, plicate, almost always deciduous. Raceme terminal, usually densely many-flowered; flowers usually small, non-resupinate, green, buff, dull orange or dull purple; sepals and petals free, spreading; lip larger than tepals, entire or lobed, margin often denticulate; column short, stigma ventral; anther terminal; pollinia 4, in 2 pairs. Cosmopolitan, mainly tropical Asia.

CULTIVATION   Largely terrestrial with plicate leaves and slender spikes of curious flowers. Some of the hardy species, for example *M.macrostachya*, *M.monophyllos*, *M.spicata* and *M.unifolia*, are sometimes grown for their flowers in the cool house or outside in zones 8–10, where their requirements are close to those of the hardier *Calanthe* species. *M.calophylla* described below is one of several species including *Mm. discolor, metallica* and *scottii* from SE Asia valued for their beautifully bronzed and purple-flushed foliage. These require warm, humid and shaded conditions (min. temperature 15°C/60°F), a substrate of composted bark, charcoal, leafmould and sphagnum, and careful watering throughout the year. They are suited to growing cases and are sometimes cultivated alongside *Anoectochilus, Lepanthes calodictyon*, and other fragile orchids noted for their foliage.

M.calophylla (Rchb. f.) Kuntze.
Terrestrial, with short, erect stem, usually 3-lvd. Lvs 7–12×4.5cm, ovate, acute, yellow-green with bronze central patch and transverse lines, edge often undulate. Peduncle 5–8cm; rachis to 15cm; raceme many-fld; fls small, pale pink or creamy yellow; dorsal sep. 3–4mm, lateral sep. 2.5×1mm; pet. 3.5mm, narrowly linear; lip about 3mm with long auricles, apex emarginate. Malaysia, Thailand.

M.ophioglossoides Muhlenb. ex Willd. See *M.unifolia*.

Masdevallia Ruiz & Pav. (For Jose Masdevall (*d*1801), Spanish botanist and physician.) Some 350 species of tufted evergreen, often diminutive epiphytes or lithophytes, lacking pseudobulbs; rhizome short-creeping. Secondary stems short, erect, apically unifoliate, thinly sheathed. Leaves fleshy, glabrous, coriaceous, dorsally carinate, erect or suberect, narrow-elliptic to obovate-spathulate, narrowed into a sulcate petiole at base, usually tridentate at apex. Inflorescence a terminal single or few-flowered raceme borne at junction of petiole and stem; peduncles erect, slender; flowers small or large, variously coloured, essentially triangular in outline due to showy, expanded sepals emerging from a papery bract; sepals showy, ovate to triangular, fused near base forming a narrow or cup-shaped tube, sometimes connate throughout, distal portions spreading, terminating in short to elongate tails, lateral sepals connate to base of lip forming a chin; petals much smaller than sepals, narrow, linear-oblong to subquadrate; lip small, articulated to column foot, sessile or short-clawed, often partially concealed within calyx; disc with or without calli; column short, erect to arching, apex entire or variously dentate, sometimes winged, foot short, anther operculate, unicellular, pollinia 2, pyriform, waxy. Mexico to Brazil and Bolivia. See also *Dracula, Dryadella, Scaphosepalum.*

CULTIVATION   Cool-growing tufted orchids of diminutive stature and exhibiting a remarkable range of colour and form in their (generally) tricorn-like flowers, from the vivid flames and magentas of *M.veitchiana* and *M.coccinea* to the long-tailed lilac *M.caudata* and small, sinister *M.rolfeana*. Pot in a mix of fine bark, charcoal and sphagnum in small, well crocked clays. Position in light shade in a buoyant, humid, cool environment – growth will deteriorate where temperatures exceed a day maximum of 25°C/75°F, night minimum 5°C/40°F. Although they should never be allowed to dry out, these plants are susceptible to damping off, and should therefore be watered carefully. An alternative, easily provided in a growing case is to bed the pots together in a tray of living sphagnum; this will encourage searching development of their wiry roots. Propagate by division, or raise from seeds.

M.abbreviata Rchb. f.
Densely caespitose. Lvs to 15×1.5cm, spathulate to oblong-oblanceolate, obtuse. Infl. to 18cm, slender, several-fld, erect or arcuate; fls small; sep. and pet. white spotted crimson; sepaline tube to 6mm, campanulate, dorsal sep. suborbicular-ovate or triangular-ovate, dentate, tail to 1.5cm, yellow, lateral sep. similar to dorsal sep., obliquely ovate; pet. spathulate-cuneate, retuse-apiculate, with anterior keel; lip to 5mm, pale yellow, oblong-pandurate, basal portion ovate, apical portion suborbicular or obscurely 3-lobed. Peru, Ecuador.

M.acrochordonia Rchb. f. See *M.trochilus*.

M.amabilis Rchb. f. & Warsc.
Lvs to 18×2.5cm, oblong to oblanceolate, obtuse, coriaceous, dark green. Infl. to 30cm, 1-fld; peduncle terete, slender; sepaline tube yellow-orange with crimson venation, to 2.5cm, narrowly campanulate-cylindrical, slightly curved, dorsal sep. free portion ovate to triangular, acuminate, orange-yellow or rose, with red venation, tails to 5cm, dull red, lateral sep. connate for half of length, ovate-triangular, orange-red tinged crimson, tails to 3.5cm; pet. to 6mm, narrowly oblong, apiculate, yellow streaked red; lip to 6mm, pandurate to oblong, apiculate, apex recurved and rounded, yellow-white. Peru.

M.amethystina Rchb. f. See *Porroglossum amethystinum.*
M.anchorifera Rchb. f. See *Scaphosepalum anchoriferum.*

M.angulata Rchb.f.
Plants large, robust, making dense clumps of tough lvs. Fls solitary, produced in abundance on short, arching or procumbent stalks, each to 5cm diam., sepaline cup deep, basally saccate, lateral sep. spreading, ovate, with tails to 3cm, dull golden yellow overlaid with fine, bright red spots and stripes, dorsal sep. narrower with a longer, erect tail, yellow with lines of fine red dots. Ecuador, Colombia.

M.angulifera Rchb.f.
Lvs fleshy, to 10cm. Fls solitary,on stalks equalling leaves, sepaline tube long, narrow, curving, red-yellow, sep. largely fused, spreading, triangular, lacking tails, forming a dull purple-red, triangular rim to tube. Colombia.

M.attenuata Rchb. f.
Lvs to 13×2cm, linear-oblanceolate, bright lustrous green. Infl. 1-fld, usually shorter than lvs; fls somewhat campanulate, waxy, green-white, to 2.5cm long; sepaline tube sometimes streaked red, interior pubesc., tails to 1.5cm, orange-yellow, lateral sep. connate for basal third; pet. white edged

green, oblong-lanceolate to subrhombic; lip to 5×2mm, white with brown apex, oblong-lanceolate to oblong-pandurate, with 2 longitudinal keels. Costa Rica, Panama.

M.auropurpurea Rchb. f. & Warsc.
Lvs to 12.5×2.5cm, oblong-oblanceolate, subacute or obtuse; petiole elongate. Infl. subequal to lvs, 1–3-fld; sepaline tube yellow tinged brown, to 1.5cm, dorsal sep. connate with lateral sep. for 1cm from base, free portion triangular, tail to 4cm, bright yellow, slender, lateral sep. deeply connate, free portion ovate-triangular, oblique, tail to 2.5cm, slender, bright yellow; pet. linear-oblong, acute or apiculate, with anterior keel; lip oblong-lanceolate, short-acuminate, base cordate, bicarinate, apex reflexed and papillose. Peru, Ecuador, Colombia, Bolivia.

M.ayabacana Luer
Resembles a larger, coarser *M.veitchiana* but with yellow-red fls with far longer and narrower sep. tails borne in succession on a stout stem. Ecuador, Peru.

M.barlaeana Rchb. f.
Stems very short, densely tufted. Lvs to 12.5×2.5cm, elliptic-oblanceolate or oblong, acute or obtuse. Infl. to 25cm, slender, erect, 1-fld; sepaline tube narrow, scarlet, campanulate-cylindric, slightly decurved, dorsal sep. to 4cm, red-orange with a median and marginal red lines, ovate-triangular to subquadrate, lateral sep. connate for two-thirds of length, bright carmine shaded scarlet, with 3 scarlet lines, elliptic-oblong, tails to 14mm, sometimes crossing each other; pet. minute, linear-oblong, minutely tridentate at apex, with longitudinal keel; lip white, with purple spot at apex, to 6mm, oblong-oblanceolate, longitudinally 2-keeled in centre, apex recurved. Peru.

M.bella Rchb. f. See *Dracula bella.*

M.bicolor Poepp. & Endl. (*M.herzogii* Schtr.).
A variable species to 10cm tall. Fls to 4cm diam., produced 2–3 together atop a triquetrous peduncle; sepaline tube deep, sep. fused to midway, lateral sep. broadly ovate, deep maroon to brown-black with yellow tails more or less equalling blades, dorsal sep. narrower, hooded, usually yellow, with a porrect tail. Venezuela to Bolivia.

M.biflora Reg. See *M.caloptera.*

M.bonplandii Rchb. f.
Lvs to 8×2cm, oblong-spathulate. Infl. to 20cm, erect, 1-fld; fls yellow-green; sepaline tube spotted brown-purple, to 2cm, sep. triangular to oblong-ligulate, acute, 2-keeled; pet. oblong, acute, slightly dilated toward middle, carinate; lip short-clawed; lamina oblong, apex broadly rounded, reflexed, papillose, bicarinate. Peru, Ecuador. Sometimes treated as a subspecies of *M.coriacea.*

M.brevis Rchb. f. See *Scaphosepalum breve.*
M.bruchmuelleri hort. See *M.coriacea.*

M.caesia Roezl.
A large and highly distinctive species with a pendulous growth habit, oblanceolate-ligulate, thickly glaucous lvs and solitary, pendulous fls 12cm across from tail to tail, these are a rich, semi-translucent amber with conspicous veins of a heavier texture, dotted purple-red on the exterior; the lip is large, verrucose and shiny purple-black. SW Colombia.

M.caloptera Rchb. f. (*M.biflora* Reg.).
Lvs to 8×2cm, ovate-oblong to lanceolate, rounded to obtuse, older lvs tinged red-brown. Infl. to 15cm, erect, 2–5-fld; fls small; sep. white streaked and spotted rust to crimson, tails yellow-orange, dorsal sep. round-triangular, hooded, keeled below, minutely dentate, tail slender, erect, to 1cm, lateral sep. ovate-oblong, recurved, tails to 1cm, decurved; pet. minute, white with a prominent anterior crimson keel, oblong-spathulate, apiculate, apical margins dentate; lip yellow streaked crimson, slightly larger than sep., oblong to obscurely 3-lobed, lateral lobes oblong, erect, midlobe orbicular-obovate, apiculate; column pale green marked crimson, to 4mm. Ecuador, Colombia, Peru.

M.calura Rchb. f.
Lvs to 10cm, broadly oblanceolate, coriaceous, blue-green. Infl. to 10cm, erect or arcuate, 1-fld; fls to 10.5cm across, deep burgundy with a black hue; sep. apices yellow, sepaline tube to 1.5cm, cylindrical, curved, dorsal sep. triangular, tails to 5cm, filiform, lateral sep. connate for 2cm, ovate-oblong, reflexed, slightly papillose above, tails with triangular sinus, filiform, parallel; pet. rich crimson, apex white, to 8mm, ovate, apex triangular; lip deep crimson, pandurate, base bilobulate, apex rounded and deflexed, bicarinate; column white. Costa Rica.

M.calyptrata Kränzl. See *M.corniculata.*

M.campyloglossa Rchb. f.
Fls solitary, carried on a slender, erect to procumbent stem; sep. lacking tails, green-white spotted purple along veins; lip relatively large, warty. Colombia, Ecuador, Peru.

M.candida Klotzsch & Karst. See *M.tovarensis.*

M.caudata Lindl. (*M.shuttleworthii* Rchb. f.)
Lvs to 8×3cm, obovate-spathulate, obtuse, pale green, thinly coriaceous. Infl. subequalling lvs, suberect; peduncle terete, slender, 1-fld; fls broad, slightly fragrant, to 15cm across, usually smaller; sepaline tube short, broad, fleshy, cup-like, dorsal sep. lime to buff, spotted and lined lilac, lamina to 2.5×2cm, obovate, concave, tails to 6.5cm, slender, yellow, lateral sep. buff flushed or spotted lilac or rose, free portion to 1.5×1.5cm, obliquely ovate, tails to 5cm, pale green, slender, deflexed; pet. white, concealed in tube, minute, linear-oblong, apex obliquely dentate; lip white spotted mauve-purple, oblong, apex reflexed; column to 7mm, white spotted mauve-purple on margins, foot arcuate. Colombia, Venezuela, Ecuador.

M.caudivolvula Kränzlin.
A distinctive species producing thickly textured, solitary fls in tones of pale green and cream with a faint purple-rose flush, the sepaline cup is short and virtually closed, the sep. tails are long, rigid, forward-pointing and spiral two to three times in a corkscrew fashion. Colombia.

M.chestertonii Rchb. f. See *Dracula chestertonii.*
M.chimaera Rchb. f. See *Dracula chimaera.*

M.chontalensis Rchb. f.
Habit small, tufted. Infl. erect, equalling or exceeding lvs; fls paired at apex, white with cream-yellow sep. tails; sepaline cup narrowly tubular, free portions of sep. short, tails equalling sepaline cup, forward-pointing. C America, Ecuador.

M.civilis Rchb. f.
Lvs to 25×1.5cm, linear or linear-oblong, subacute. Infl. to 8cm, mottled purple-black, 1-fld; fls fleshy, strongly scented, polished; sepaline tube to 2.5cm, cylindrical, gibbous below, yellow-green spotted purple, interior minutely papillose, sep. yellow-green, deep purple at base, to 4cm, ovate-triangular, tails short, yellow, recurved; pet. white with central purple stripe, small, spathulate, acute; lip mottled and spotted purple, to 1.5cm, oblong, obtuse, apex recurved and papillose, 2-keeled. Peru.

M.coccinea Lind. ex Lindl. (*M.lindenii* André; *M.harryana* Rchb. f.; *M.militaris* Rchb. f.).
Lvs erect, to 23×3cm, narrow-oblong to obovate-lanceolate, pale to deep glossy green. Infl. to 40cm, slender, suberect, 1-fld at apex; peduncle terete; fls large, showy, waxy, variable in colour; sep. deep crystalline magenta, crimson, scarlet, pale yellow or cream-white, sepaline tube to 2cm, campanulate-cylindric, slightly compressed, curved, sep. large, flattened, often longitudinally ridged, dorsal sep. to 8cm, narrowly triangular or linear, tail slender, erect or recurved, lateral sep. longer than dorsal sep., connate in basal third, ovate-attenuate, outer margin falcate, decurved with short tails; pet. to 1cm, usually off-white, translucent, linear, 2-lobed at apex with anterior, longitudinal keel; lip to 1cm, usually shorter, oblong, slightly pandurate above, bicarinate. Colombia, Peru.

Masdevallia   (a) *M.veitchiana*   (b) *M.tovarensis*   (c) *M.wageneriana*   (d) *M.schroederiana*

M.colibri hort. See *M.trochilus.*

M.coriacea Lindl. (*M.bruchmuelleri* hort.).
Lvs to 20×2cm, linear-oblanceolate, coriaceous, erect, deep green above, pale green and keeled below. Infl. to 20cm, pale green flecked purple, 1-fld; sepaline tube to 1.5cm, pale yellow spotted purple along veins, broadly cylindrical, dorsal sep. to 4cm, same colour as tube, ovate-triangular, with short, broad tail, lateral sep. to 3.5cm, yellow, oblong, acuminate; pet. to 1.5cm, white with central purple stripe, oblong to spathulate, obtuse; lip to 1.5cm, yellow-green with central purple stripe and marginal spots, oblong, pubesc. above, reflexed; column to 1cm, pale green, minutely dentate at apex. Colombia.

M.corniculata Rchb. f. (*M.inflata* Rchb. f.; *M.calyptrata* Kränzl.).
Lvs to 25×4cm, oblong-lanceolate. Infl. to 10cm, erect, 1-fld; bract large, pale green, keeled; fls to 8cm across, pale yellow marked or suffused red-brown; sepaline tube broadly cylindrical, curved, gibbous below, to 2cm, dorsal sep. free portion triangular, tail to 5cm, slender, lateral sep. connate for 3cm, oblong, reflexed, tail shorter than dorsal tail, recurved, slender; pet. white, tipped yellow, ligulate; lip yellow spotted purple, subpandurate, apex verrucose. Colombia.

M.cyathogastra Schltr. See *M.nidifica.*

M.davisii Rchb. f.
Lvs to 20×2cm, narrowly oblong-oblanceolate, apex subacute, bright lustrous green, coriaceous. Infl. to 25cm, erect, 1-fld; peduncle slender, terete; fls large, showy, fragrant, bright orange-yellow; sepaline tube narrowly campanulate-cylindric, to 17mm, with a prominent keel above, dorsal sep. ovate-triangular, tail slender, to 2.5cm, lateral sep. exceeding dorsal sep., connate for half of length, obliquely ovate-oblong, tail to 7mm; pet. small, concealed within tube, oblong, apex bilobed, apiculate, with anterior, longitudinal keel; lip smaller than pet., concealed within tube, oblong-pandurate, apex reflexed, apiculate. Peru.

M.dayana Rchb. f. See *Zootrophion dayanum.*

M.decumana Koniger.
Lvs broadly obovate, petiolate. Fls solitary, exceeding lvs, large, dull rose densely spotted and blotched purple-red, the spotting finer on the tan dorsal sep.; sepaline cup short and broad, dorsal sep. far smaller than laterals, triangular-ovate, hooded, with a long, erect tail, lateral sep. large,spreading, more or less free, elliptic-obovate, with slender, decurved tails equalling blades.N Peru, S Ecuador.

M.echidna Rchb. f. See *Porroglossum echidna.*
M.edwallii Cogn. See *Dryadella edwallii.*

M.elephanticeps Rchb. f. & Warscz.
Close to and possibly synonymous with *M.mooreana.* Fls very large and waxy, borne singly and near base of plant on short, reclining stalks; sep. basically yellow-green to lemon yellow with a broad, glossy, textured zone of red-brown to blood red occupying much of the blades of the lateral sep.; pet. white with a single maroon stripe; lip dark maroon. Colombia.

M.encephala Luer & Escobar.
Fls solitary, carried level with lvs, with a distinctive, globose, 'brain-like' sepaline cup which narrows to a very small opening from which the slender sep. tails diverge .Colombia.

M.ephippium Rchb. f. See *M.trochilus.*
M.erythrochaete Rchb. f. See *Dracula erythrochaete.*

M.floribunda Lindl. (*M.galeottiana* A. Rich. & Gal.; *M.myriostigma* Morr.).
Lvs to 12×2cm, oblong-oblanceolate, obtuse, dark lustrous green, coriaceous. Infl. usually exceeding lvs, numerous, erect to decumbent, 1-fld; fls to 4cm across; sep. pale yellow or buff-yellow spotted brown-crimson, sepaline tube to 1.5cm, cylindrical, dorsal sep. free portion to 1cm, ovate-triangular, tail to 12mm, slender, recurved, lateral sep. free por-

tion rotund to ovate, to 1.5cm, tail to 6mm, slender, recurved; pet. to 5×2mm, white, linear-oblong, apex dentate, with anterior keel; lip to 5×2cm, white with crimson-brown blotch at apex, linear-oblong to lanceolate-oblong, cordate at base, apex reflexed; column to 5mm, suberect. Mexico, Guatemala, Honduras, Costa Rica.

M.foetens Luer & Escobar.
Habit small. Lvs thick-textured. Fls solitary, short-stalked, malodorous; sepaline tube short, somewhat ventricose, yellow striped dull purple, sep.short, triangular, yellow marked purple, tails very long, yellow and strongly forward-pointing. Colombia.

M.galeottiana A. Rich. & Gal. See *M.floribunda.*
M.gibberosa Rchb. f. See *Scaphosepalum gibberosum.*
M.harryana Rchb. f. See *M.coccinea.*

M.herradurae Lehmann ex Kränzlin.
Habit small. Fls solitary, small, produced in abundance; sepaline cup short, rigid, spreading, purple-green, free portions of sep. short, triangular, tails long, relatively thick, purple, strongly divergent. Colombia.

M.herzogii Schltr. See *M.bicolor.*

M.ignea Rchb. f.
Lvs to 23×5cm, elliptic-lanceolate or oblong-lanceolate, coriaceous, dark green, suberect. Infl. to 40cm, erect, 1-fld; peduncle slender, terete; fls to 8cm across; sep. scarlet to orange, often tinged crimson, sepaline tube to 2cm, cylindrical, hooded, curved, dorsal sep. free portion to 1cm, triangular, tail to 4cm, slender, strongly deflexed, lateral sep. connate for 2.5cm, broadly falcate-ovate, acute, divergent, 3-nerved, margin reflexed, tails short; pet. white with purple median line, to 8mm, linear-oblong, acute, anterior margin keeled; lip stained orange-red at apex, fleshy, oblong, sulcate, margins crenate, apex recurved, apiculate; column white, lined purple, to 1cm, apex dentate. Colombia.

M.inflata Rchb. f. See *M.corniculata.*

M.infracta Lindl. (*M.longicaudata* Lem.).
Lvs to 14×2.5cm, lanceolate to oblong, subobtuse, erect, coriaceous, bright lustrous green. Infl. to 25cm, erect, 1–5-fld; peduncle triquetrous; fls produced in succession, yellow-white to ochre, white at base of tube, flushing orange to blood-red, campanulate, pendent; sepaline tube to 13mm, cupped, curved, dorsal sep. free portion to 5cm, ovate to triangular, tail to 4cm, filiform, lateral sep. free portion to 5cm, rotund-oblong, connate for 2cm, tails to 4cm, strongly divergent, filiform; pet. to 8mm, obliquely linear, apiculate, white to pale pink; lip to 1cm, linear or slightly pandurate, apex reflexed, apiculate, bicarinate, spotted red-brown at apex. Brazil, Peru.

M.ionocharis Rchb. f.
Stems short. Lvs to 12×1.5cm, narrowly elliptic-lanceolate, acute. Infl. 1-fld; peduncle to 10cm, slender, terete; fls to 1.5cm diam., excluding sep. tails; sepaline tube campanulate, to 13mm, yellow-white, sep. free portion green-white blotched rose-purple, triangular-ovate, keeled behind, tails to 2cm, slender, yellow; pet. minute, triangular-oblong, acute; lip minute, clawed, oblong-pandurate, purple, apex reflexed. Peru.

M.klabochorum Rchb. f. See *M.xanthina.*

M.laucheana Kränzl. ex Woolw.
Lvs to 12.5×2.5cm, obovate-oblanceolate, dark green; petiole short. Infl. shorter than lvs, erect, 1-fld, slender, pale green; fls to 1.8cm diam., excluding tails; sepaline tube campanulate, white flushed rose to mauve at base, free portions white to buff, ovate-triangular, tails to 2cm, rigid, incurved, orange. Costa Rica.

M.limax Luer.
Habit small, tufted. Lvs oblanceolate, glaucescent beneath. Fls yellow to pale orange, small, solitary, produced in abun-

dance on arching stems low among lvs, resembling *Arisarum* (Araceae) in shape – i.e., with a deep, wide sepaline tube, ventricose below, with ribbed walls and a strongly arching, hooded upper surface and apex, the aperture small, free portions of sep. very shallow, sep. tails slender, somewhat translucent, downward-pointing. SE Ecuador.

M.lindenii André. See *M.coccinea*.

M.livingstoneana Rchb.f. & Roezl.
Fls small, thick-textured, carried 1–2 per stem; sepaline cup short, free portions of sep. ovate -falcate, white with a strong red to maroon stain or streak at base, narrowing above to short, rather thick , fang-like tails, these olive with a purple-red tint. Panama. Unlike most other species listed here, *M.livingstoneana* favours a hot, humid atmosphere.

M.longicaudata Lem. See *M.infracta*.

M.ludibunda Rchb. f. (*M.estradae* Rchb. f.).
Lvs to 7.5×3cm, suberect, elliptic-spathulate, coriaceous, apex bifid. Infl. exceeding lvs, erect, 1-fld; peduncle slender, terete; fls to 7.5cm across, widely spreading; sepaline tube to 8mm, campanulate, dorsal sep. bright magenta with yellow base and margins, free portion obovate, concave, to 1.5cm, tails yellow, to 2.5cm, lateral sep. oblong, spreading, obtuse, white above, base magenta, margins recurved, tails yellow, slender, to 4cm; pet. white, linear-oblong, apiculate, anterior margin keeled to 8mm; lip white, oblong, sulcate at base, apiculate, to 8mm; column to 8mm, white spotted purple marginally, foot and apex purple, apex dentate. Colombia.

M.macrura Rchb. f.
Stems clustered, to 15cm. Lvs to 37×7cm, elliptic-oblong, obtuse, coriaceous, lustrous green. Infl. usually equalling lvs, erect, 1-fld; fls large, to 25cm across, fleshy; sep. red to dull brown-yellow, studded with many maroon warts, sepaline tube to 1.5cm, cylindrical or flattened, ribbed, dorsal sep. free portion to 15cm, lanceolate to narrowly triangular, acuminate, tail long, erect, yellow-green, lateral sep. to 12.5cm, ovate to oblong, connate for basal 4cm, tail long, strongly decurved; pet. to 1cm, pale yellow-brown, oblong-curved; lip to 8mm, yellow-brown spotted purple below, oblong, papillose, bicarinate, apex reflexed; column to 8mm, yellow, spotted crimson on foot. Colombia, Ecuador.

M.maculata Klotzsch & Karst.
Lvs to 18×3cm, linear-lanceolate, acute, coriaceous. Infl. to 25cm, several-fld; peduncle triquetrous; fls produced in succession, showy, spreading; sep. yellow or yellow-green, spotted and tinged red, sepaline tube to 16mm, flattened-cylindrical, orange-yellow above, red below, dorsal sep. free portion ovate-triangular, tail slender, to 7cm, lateral sep. connate to middle, ovate-oblong, tails tapering strongly, pale yellow, parallel or divergent; pet. small, oblong-ligulate, apiculate, white; lip to 1cm, oblong, papillose and dentate at apex, dull purple, apex recurved; column to 6mm. Venezuela, Peru, Colombia.

M.mejiana Garay.
Lvs to 12×1.5cm, usually erect, oblong-lanceolate, obtuse, subcoriaceous. Infl. to 10cm, ascending, 1–2-fld; fls to 7cm across, white flecked pink, tails yellow-orange; sepaline tube campanulate, free portions spreading, broadly ovate, or wholly fused forming a cup, tails fleshy, divergent. Colombia.

M.melanopus Rchb. f.
Lvs to 12.5×1.5cm, oblong-spathulate or oblanceolate, obtuse. Infl. numerous, to 25cm, slender, erect, loosely 3–8-fld; fls secund, to 2.5cm across; sep. and pet. white minutely spotted and flecked purple; sepaline tube shortly campanulate, to 6mm, gibbous below, sep. free portion triangular or suborbicular, concave, keeled behind, tails to 13mm, bright yellow, slender; pet. minute, spathulate-cuneate, retuse-apiculate, with anterior keel; lip to 4mm, white spotted purple, apex rounded into a yellow terminal

lobe, pandurate-oblong, anterior portion 2-keeled. Colombia, Ecuador, Peru.

M.militaris Rchb. f. See *M.coccinea*.

M.mooreana Rchb. f.
Lvs to 20×3cm, linear-oblong, coriaceous, dark green, spotted purple below. Infl. to 10cm, erect, stout, green spotted dull purple; fls horizontal, to 9cm across, fleshy, solitary; sepaline tube broadly cylindrical, slightly ventricose below, sep. long, tapering, forward-pointing, dorsal sep. yellow-white streaked purple at base, triangular, tail yellow, linear, to 5cm, lateral sep. crimson to purple, interior surface covered with many black-purple papillae, connate almost to middle, triangular, acute, tail yellow toward apex; pet. white with a central purple stripe, oblong, acute; lip black-purple, oblong, pubesc. above; column green-white, margins black-purple. Colombia, Venezuela.

M.mordax Rchb. f. See *Porroglossum mordax*.
M.muscosa Rchb. f. See *Porroglossum muscosum*.
M.myriostigma Morr. See *M.floribunda*.

M.nidifica Rchb. f. (*M.cyathogastra* Schltr.; *M.tenuicauda* Schltr.).
Stems short. Lvs to 5×7cm, spathulate or oblanceolate, acute to rounded, coriaceous. Infl. almost equalling lvs, 1-fld; peduncle filiform, dull green-crimson; fls small, variable in size and colour; sep. white, green-white or pale yellow, spotted and striped crimson, maroon to olive below, sepaline tube to 7mm, slightly inflated below, pubesc. within, dorsal sep. rotund to ovate-triangular, concave, pubesc. within, tails to 3cm, slender, crimson, lateral sep. ovate, tails similar to dorsal sep., yellow; pet. minute, cream with central purple streak, oblong, acute, keeled on anterior margin; lip to 4mm, yellow with 3 longitudinal purple lines, pandurate-oblong, acute to obtuse, curved; column to 4mm, pink marked crimson. Costa Rica, Peru, Ecuador, Colombia.

M.normanii hort. See *M.reichenbachiana*.

M.pachyantha Rchb. f.
Lvs to 20cm, oblanceolate, coriaceous, clustered, dark green. Infl. exceeding lvs, erect, 1-fld; fls large, to 12cm including tails; sepaline tube pale orange-yellow, broadly cylindrical, slightly curved, dorsal sep. pale yellow-green with brown-purple venation, triangular, keeled above, tail to 2.5cm, stout, erect, lateral sep. connate almost to middle, ovate-oblong, pale yellow-green heavily spotted rose-purple, tail bright yellow, shorter than dorsal tail; pet. white with brown-purple midline, ovate, acute; lip brown, dark brown-black toward apex, ligulate, apex reflexed; column green, margins purple-brown. Colombia.

M.pachyura Rchb.f.
Infl. racemose,exceeding lvs; fls 4–9 borne together, fleshy, white dusted and spotted with purple-red, tails bright yellow; sep. largely free, the dorsal broader than laterals, strongly hooded, laterals oblong-lanceolate, often revolute, tails usually shorter than sep., relatively thick. Ecuador.

M.pandurilabia Schweinf.
Lvs to 12×2.5cm, obovate, oblanceolate or elliptic, subacute to rounded, apex minutely tridentate; petiole to 5cm, slender. Infl. to 20cm, erect to arcuate, slender, 1-fld; fls small; sep. and pet. yellow-brown; sepaline tube to 5mm, interior pubesc., dorsal sep. suborbicular-ovate, tail slender, to 3.5cm, lateral sep. obliquely semiorbicular-ovate; tails similar to dorsal sep.; pet. minute, obliquely oblong-triangular, apex tridentate, base with a prominent lobule; lip to 4mm, ovate-pandurate, recurved, apiculate. Peru.

M.pelecaniceps Luer.
Highly distinctive species with solitary fls carried just above lvs on erect then nodding stalks; sep. dull yellow to olive green tinted and mottled maroon to blood red, sepaline cup very shallow, dorsal sep. virtually free, ovate-lanceolate, revolute, arching forwards and downwards, more or less equal to

Masdevallia (a) *M.caudata* (b) *M.trochilus* (c) *M.coccinea* (d) *M.elephanticeps*

laterals, lateral sep, connate on inner margins, forming a concave, broadly ovate-acute blade, outer margins revolute, tails
absent. Panama.

M.peristeria Rchb. f.
Lvs to 15×2.5cm, linear-lanceolate or oblong, coriaceous,
deep blue-green. Infl. to 7cm, 1-fld; peduncle terete, pale
green spotted crimson; fls to 12.5cm diam., fleshy, spreading;
sepaline tube to 2cm, broadly cylindric, gibbous below,
prominently ribbed, sep. yellow or yellow-green spotted crimson, reverse yellow-green, ovate-triangular, tails fleshy, to
3.5cm, triquetrous toward apex; pet. pale green-yellow, linear-oblong, acute, curved, minutely bidentate; lip to 1.5cm,
green-white with purple papillae, oblong-pandurate, base sulcate, rounded to truncate, papillose, apex reflexed; column
white-green, to 12mm, finely dentate. Spring–summer.
Colombia.

M.pinocchio Luer & Andreetta.
Lvs thick, fleshy. Peduncle triquetrous, exceeding lvs, bearing
several fls in succession over along period, often a few simultaneously in a congested raceme; sepaline cup shallow, dorsal
sep. exceeding laterals, narrowly triangular, standing erect
and tapering gradually to a long, thick tail, clear yellow-
green, lateral sep. broadly ovate, fused to two thirds on inner
margins, forming a broad, shield-shaped blade with a depression below insertion of lip, yellow-green with a strong, purple-red blush, tails short, downward-pointing; lip fleshy, dark
maroon, protruding, mobile. C Ecuador.

M.polysticta Rchb. f. non Hook. f.
Lvs to 15×2.5cm, subspathulate or oblanceolate, apex
rounded and minutely tridentate. Infl. to 25cm, pale green
spotted dull purple, loosely 3–9-fld; fls to 5cm diam., white or
pale lilac spotted dark red or purple; sepaline tube short, interior papillose, dorsal sep. free portion broadly ovate, cucullate, tail slender, to 2.5cm, lateral sep. narrowly oblong-lanceolate, oblique, with a yellow central line, margins reflexed
and slightly ciliate, tail slender, to 2.5cm; pet. minute, spathulate-cuneate, retuse, apiculate, with anterior keel; lip minute,
to 3mm, pandurate-oblong, keeled. Ecuador, Peru.

M.prodigiosa Koniger.
Fls large, orange, carried on short, more or less reclining
stalks; sepaline cup shallow, dorsal sep. very concave, tail
long, slender, reflexed, lateral sep. reflexed. N Peru.

M.pulvinaris Rchb. f. See *Scaphosepalum pulvinare.*

M.pumila Poepp. & Endl.
Lvs to 9×1cm, linear-oblanceolate or linear-spathulate, obtuse
or subacute, apex minutely tridentate, lustrous green. Infl. to
3.5cm, filiform, 1-fld; fls small, pure white; sepaline tube to
5mm, cylindrical, dorsal sep. small, triangular-lanceolate, to
3cm including fleshy tails, lateral sep. large; pet. to 5mm, linear-ligulate, obtuse, falcate; lip to 5mm, narrow-clawed,
ovate-oblong, apex rounded, base cordate. Peru, Venezuela.

M.punctata Rolfe. See *Scaphosepalum anchoriferum.*

M.racemosa Lindl.
Stems erect, at intervals of 3cm on rhiz. Lvs to 12.5×2cm,
elliptic-oblong, obtuse, suberect, coriaceous, lustrous or red-
green. Infl. to 35cm, erect or arcuate, slender, dull red-green,
4–15-fld; fls showy, to 6cm across; bright orange-scarlet
shaded crimson, sometimes almost yellow; sepaline tube to
1.5cm, cylindrical, narrow, dorsal sep. smaller than lateral
sep., free portion narrow ovate-triangular, acuminate,
reflexed, tail to 6mm, suberect, lateral sep. connate for basal
2.5cm, broadly obcordate, spreading, apiculate, with dark longitudinal veins; pet. pale yellow, to 8mm, short-clawed,
ovate; lip white, to 1cm, narrowly oblong, bicarinate; column
pale yellow above, pink below, to 1cm. Colombia.

M.reichenbachiana Endres (*M.normanii* hort.).
Lvs to 15×2.5cm, erect, oblanceolate-spathulate, acute, keeled
below, coriaceous, tridentate at apex. Infl. exceeding lvs,
slender, erect, 1–3-fld; peduncle terete, bright green; fls produced in succession, to 6cm across; sepaline tube white-yel-

low below, red-scarlet above, to 2.5cm, curved, funnel-
shaped, hooded or almost closed at apex by concave,
depressed dorsal sep., dorsal sep. sealing-wax red to pale yellow-white, lined red within, free portion to 12mm, triangular,
tail to 5cm, slender, recurved, yellow, lateral sep. yellow-
white, connate for half of length, ovate-triangular, decurved,
keeled behind, tails to 3.5cm, slender, yellow; pet. white, to
8mm, ovate-oblong, truncate, dentate; lip white, to 6mm,
oblong-pandurate, apex recurved; column white, to 8mm.
Spring–autumn. Costa Rica.

M.rolfeana Kränzl.
Resembles *M.reichenbachiana* except smaller. Infl. shorter
than lvs; fls to 5cm long, chocolate-brown to dark purple;
sepaline tube yellow at base, to 12mm; lip red. Spring–summer. Costa Rica.

M.rosea Lindl.
Lvs to 20×3cm, elliptic-lanceolate to obovate, acute, clustered, dark green. Infl. slightly exceeding lvs, slender, erect or
arcuate, 1-fld; sepaline tube to 2.5cm, compressed, scarlet and
vermilion, dorsal sep. to 5cm, slender, tail-like, red above,
yellow below, arching over broader, carmine, short, red-tailed
lateral sep.; pet. to 5mm, white, oblong; lip white, to 5mm,
oblong, shallowly pandurate, apex with many black papillae;
column white, curved. Spring–summer. Colombia, Ecuador.

M.rubiginosa Koniger.
Variable species. Lvs broadly obovate-spathulate. Fls solitary
on short stalks among or equalling lvs, basically tan covered
with minute rusty red papillae; sepaline cup broad and shallow, dorsal sep. smaller than laterals, rounded, reflexed, with
a slender tail, lateral sep. fused on inner margins , forming an
orbicular-reniform blade with short to medium tails descending directly from its lower margin; lip small, hinged. S
Ecuador, N Peru.

M.saltatrix Rchb. f.
Lvs fleshy. Fls solitary, not usually exceeding lvs, sepaline
tube long, slender, curving , sigmoid in outline with a ventricose lower surface, glossy red-brown, free portions of sep.
yellow spotted red, reduced to a shallow rim from which
diverge long, slender, yellow tails, these appear thrown back,
as if the whole flower were jumping forwards. Colombia.

M.schlimii Lind. ex Lindl.
Lvs to 20×5cm, obovate to elliptic, rounded or obtuse,
suberect. Infl. to 35cm, erect, to 8-fld; peduncle terete, light
green; fls nodding; sepaline tube short-cylindrical, ochre or
golden below, maroon within, dorsal sep. narrow-triangular,
long-tailed, golden-green, decurved and arching over larger
lateral sep., tail then becoming horizontal, to 4.8cm, lateral
sep. to 3cm, decurved, oblong-ovate, fused, forming a heart-
shaped shield covered with maroon papillae, tails to 4cm, yellow, slender, divergent; pet. white, to 6mm, falcate-oblong,
acute; lip white marked with short maroon transverse bars, to
6mm, linear-oblong to pandurate, acute, with 2 converging
ridges toward apex; column white, purple marginally, to
6mm. Spring. Colombia, Venezuela.

M.schmidt-mummii Luer & Escobar.
Infl. equalling lvs; fls solitary, large, white flecked and
streaked purple-rose, especially toward tips of sep., on tails
and on dorsal sep., lip rose-purple; dorsal sep broadly ovate-
triangular, deeply hooded with a long, slender tail falling over
and between lateral sep. and almost equalling peduncle in
length, lateral sep. more or less free, ovate-falcate, forward-
pointing, narrowing to slender tails which curve backwards
and cross each other. Colombia.

M.schroederiana Veitch.
Lvs to 15×2.5cm, oblanceolate. Infl. to 21cm, erect, 1-fld; fls
to 8cm across; sepaline tube short-campanulate, white, ribbed,
expanding as a flattened, bullate, oblong platform formed by
fusion of lateral sep., pearly white flushed ruby red in upper
portions and at dorsal sep., tails long, yellow, lateral tails held
horizontally, dorsal tail erect; pet. to 8mm, fleshy, clawed,
pale pink spotted rose-purple, oblong, obtuse, undulate; lip

Masdevallia   (a) *M.ignea*   (b) *M.schlimii*   (c) *M.melanopus*   (d) *M.macrura*

white-rose spotted rose-purple, to 1cm, pandurate-oblong, obtuse, apex recurved, bicarinate; column apex dentate. Winter–summer. Peru.

M.setacea Luer & Malo.
Fls large, solitary, on long, erect stalks, basically white to shell pink, sometimes with a rosy suffusion or lines, especially at prominent bases of lateral sep., tails creamy white or dull yellow-green; sepaline cup very shallow, sep. more or less free and equal, narrowly and bluntly oblong-obovate, quite remote from each other and in a roughly triangular configuration, far exceeded by the very long and slender tails. SE Ecuador, N Peru, Colombia. cf *M.xanthina.*

M.shuttleworthii Rchb. f. See *M.caudata.*
M.simula Rchb. f. See *Dryadella simula.*

M.stenorhynchos Kränzlin.
Fls borne several in succession in a congested raceme atop triquetrous peduncle, exceeding lvs, medium-sized and narrow, very generally resembling a large *Trisetella* in outline and colour; sepaline cup small and shallow, dorsal sep. yellow, forward-pointing, small, triangular with a long, slender, ascending, yellow tail, lateral sep. narrowly lanceolate-ovate, partly fused on inner margins, tapering finely to long, parallel and forward-pointing tails, blade yellow thickly overlaid with maroon spots and warts, tails yellow. Colombia.

M.strobelii Sweet & Garay.
Fls solitary, held just clear of lvs, comparatively large, bright orange with dense,sparkling white hairs within sepaline cup; sep. more or less equal, broad and rounded, largely fused in a deep cup, the free portions triangular-orbicular with long orange tails. SE Ecuador.

M.swertiifolia Rchb. f. See *Scaphosepalum swertiifolium.*
M.tenuicauda Schltr. See *M.nidifica.*

M.tovarensis Rchb. f. (*M.candida* Klotzsch & Karst.).
Stems short. Lvs to 14×2cm, erect, obovate to oblanceolate, obtuse, coriaceous, dark green. Infl. to 18cm, erect, 1–4-fld, flowering successively, often over several seasons; peduncle glabrous, triquetrous; fls to 3.5cm across, long-lived, pure crystalline white, tailed cream or jade; sepaline tube cylindrical, to 6mm, slightly gibbous below, dorsal sep. free portion to 40×6mm, filiform, tail erect, lateral sep. to 4×1cm, shaped like a lyre, connate for half of length, longitudinally ribbed, ovate-oblong, translucent, acuminate, tails short, pale yellow-green, often crossing over; pet. to 6×2mm, oblong, acute; lip to 6×2mm, oblong to spathulate, acute, recurved at apex with 2 central ridges; column purple with white base and apex, to 4mm, subterete, finely dentate. Venezuela.

M.triangularis Lindl.
Lvs to 15×3cm, obovate or elliptic oblong, obtuse, margins strongly recurved, coriaceous. Infl. to 15cm, erect, slender, 1-fld; fls broadly campanulate, spreading, to 12cm; sepaline tube broadly campanulate, sep. yellow-green heavily spotted purple-brown, free portion to 2cm, ovate-triangular, concave, keeled behind, tails to 4cm, purple, slender; pet. white to 6mm, oblong, tridentate at apex; lip white flecked purple, to 6×3mm, oblong, 3-lobed near apex, lateral lobes obscure, midlobe orbicular, reflexed, apex purple-haired; column to 5mm, white. Colombia, Venezuela.

M.triaristella Rchb. See *Trisetella triaristella.*

M.trochilus Lind. & André (*M.ephippium* Rchb. f.; *M.acrochordonia* Rchb. f.; *M.colibri* hort.).
Lvs to 18cm, narrowly elliptic-lanceolate, clustered, erect, lustrous green. Infl. to 30cm, erect, 1–3-fld; peduncle stout, triquetrous; fls produced in succession, to 20cm; sepaline tube yellow, short, cylindrical, dorsal sep. interior tawny yellow, exterior yellow stained chestnut-brown, concave, suborbicular, keeled, tail yellow, to 8cm, reflexed, lateral sep. forming

a chestnut-brown hemispherical cup, ribbed, tails similar to dorsal sep.; pet. white, linear-oblong, apex acute or tridentate; lip red-brown, clawed, oblong, apiculate, base auriculate, apex dentate; column white. Colombia, Ecuador.

M.tubulosa Lindl.
Lvs to 11×1.5cm, oblanceolate, obtuse, erect. Fls 1 per infl., 6–12cm, white to ivory; sep. narrow, forward-pointing, tubular. Colombia, Venezuela.

M.uniflora Ruiz & Pavon.
Infl. tall; fls solitary, bright pink to magenta fading to white or cream on tails and exterior; sepaline cup deep and broad, free portions of sep. ovate-triangular, broad, spreading, tipped with short , somewhat reflexed tails, the inner surface minutely papillose and sparkling. C Peru.

M.vampira Luer. See *Dracula vampira.*

M.veitchiana Rchb. f.
Lvs to 25×2.5cm, oblong to narrowly oblanceolate, subacute, pale green, erect. Infl. to 45cm, erect, 1-fld; fls variable, to 8cm across, showy; sep. interior shining vermilion covered with many iridescent purple papillae, exterior tawny yellow with dark venation, sepaline tube to 3cm, campanulate-cylindrical, dorsal sep. free portion to 3cm, triangular-ovate, margins often recurved, tail slender, to 3.5cm, lateral sep. larger than dorsal sep., broadly ovate or triangular, acuminate, connate for 3cm, tails short, often forward-pointing or overlapping; pet. to 1.5cm, oblong, acute, keeled, white; lip to 1.5cm, oblong to obscurely 3-lobed, apex papillose, reflexed, white; column short, semi-terete, white. Peru.

M.velifera Rchb. f.
Lvs to 20×2.5cm, lanceolate or linear-elliptic, obtuse, clustered, bright green. Infl. to 10cm, stout, 1-fld; fls to 7.5cm, malodorous; sepaline tube to 2cm, broadly cylindrical, gibbous below, dorsal sep. yellow-brown spotted red-brown, triangular, concave, tail to 5cm, stout, lateral sep. connate for 5cm, similar colour to dorsal sep. or shiny red-brown, oblanceolate-oblong, tail yellow, stout; pet. green-white or green-yellow, to 12mm, linear-oblong; lip dark purple, oblong-subquadrate, papillose; column yellow or yellow-green spotted red, curved, triquetrous. Colombia.

M.verrucosa Rchb. f. See *Scaphosepalum verrucosum.*

M.wageneriana Lind. ex Lindl.
Lvs to 5×1.5cm, elliptic to spathulate, suberect, coriaceous, lustrous dark green above. Infl. suberect to spreading, 1-fld; peduncle to 5cm, slender; fls to 6cm; sep. light green-yellow or cream, orange-yellow toward base, spotted and streaked violet, sepaline tube short, dorsal sep. free portion broadly ovate-oblong, to 1×1cm, concave on inner side, tails slender, to 5cm, sharply recurved, lateral sep. similar to dorsal sep., connate for more than half of length; pet. minute, narrowly oblong, truncate, bidentate at apex; lip clawed, rhomboidal, margin reflexed, dentate, pale yellow-green or white, spotted purple; column to 5mm, semi-terete, pale violet or white, spotted violet. Venezuela.

M.xanthina Rchb. f. (*M.klabochorum* Rchb. f.).
Lvs to 7.5×2cm, obovate-oblong, petiole short. Infl. erect; peduncle to 8cm, slender, terete, pale green, 1-fld; fls spreading; sepaline tube obscure, sep. bright yellow or cream with dark yellow venation, dorsal sep. obovate-oblong, cucullate, recurved at base, tails orange-yellow, erect, to 3.5cm, lateral sep. with purple spot at base, lanceolate, tails to 33mm, orange-yellow, slender; pet. white, to 4mm, oblong, anterior margin keeled; lip pale yellow slightly spotted crimson, fleshy, oblong; column white marked purple, tridentate at apex. Colombia, Ecuador.

M.xipheres Rchb. f. See *Porroglossum muscosum.*
M.zebrina Porsch. See *Dryadella zebrina.*

M.grexes and cultivars.

M.Angel Frost: robust plants with mid-green lvs; fls large, tangerine orange or red with white or purple hairs.

M.Angel Tang: small plants to 10cm; fls light orange with purple hairs.

M.Confetti: small plants which are profuse bloomers; fls fragrant, pale, with yellow tails and covered with bright pink dots.

M.Copper Angel: robust plants to 20cm; fls large and flat, coppery-orange.

M.Diana: small plants with fls more than 2.5cm diam., white overlaid with red stripes and with long yellow tails.

M.Doris: plants up to 15cm with fleshy lvs and usually 2 fls per infl.; fls orange, minutely spotted on the outside and with crimson stripes within and short red tails.

M.Falcata: tall plant, to 35cm; fls brilliant orange with red in the centre and with red tails.

M.Freckles: small plants to 7.5cm; fls pink or beige, heavily spotted with lavender or crimson, and with long curved tails.

M.Harlequin: small plants to 12.5cm; fls white, cream or pale pink, heavily striped with wine red or purple and short tails.

M.Heathii: vigorous plants to 25cm; fls orange or orange red and held well above the foliage.

M.Kimballiana: vigorous plants to 15cm; fls tubular at base, then opening widely, orange or yellow with self-coloured tails; easy to grow and flower.

M.Marguerite: lvs light green on plants to 12cm; fls well above the foliage, coppery orange and covered with short purple hairs, tails orange.

M.Measuresiana: robust plant to 15cm with long slender infl. bearing 1–2 white or pale pink fls.

M.Prince Charming: lvs fleshy, dark green, often purple beneath; fls often below the lvs, large and fleshy, orange striped with red and long red-hued tails.

M.Redwing: small plants to 12.5cm; fls on long slender infl., brilliant magenta.

M.Snowbird: strong plants to 12.5cm; fls large, held above the foliage, white with yellow tails.

Maxillaria Ruiz & Pav. (From Lat. *maxilla*, jaw, referring to the supposed resemblance of the column and lip to the jaws of an insect.) Over 600 species of epiphytes, occasionally lithophytes, rarely terrestrials, variable in size. Rhizome long or short, horizontal or ascending. Pseudobulbs large, small or almost absent, usually 1-leafed at apex and usually enclosed in sheaths, some of which may be leaf-bearing. Inflorescence always single-flowered; peduncles arising singly or in groups from base of pseudobulbs or axils of sheaths; flowers red, brown, yellow, white or mottled; sepals subequal, the lateral sepals joined at base to the column foot and forming a mentum with it; petals similar to sepals but usually smaller; lip attached to column foot, concave, entire or trilobed; column erect with a short foot, stout, anterior surface concave; anther terminal, with an operculum; pollinia 4, ovoid, attached to oblong stipe. Capsule erect, ovoid or obovoid. Tropical America from W Indies and Mexico to Brazil, with 1 species in Florida.

CULTIVATION   Cool or intermediate-growing, requiring an open bark mix, a brief winter rest, and light shade.

M.abelei Schltr. See *M.rufescens.*

M.acicularis Herb.
Pseudobulbs 1.5–2cm, clustered, ribbed, 2-lvd. Lvs to 7cm, acute, the midvein impressed above. Fls wine red, lip dark purple; sep. and pet. elongated, subacute; lip obscurely trilobed; column yellow. Brazil.

M.acutifolia Lindl. See *M.rufescens.*

M.alba Lindl.
Rhiz. ascending; pseudobulbs 4–5×2cm, ellipsoid, compressed, 1-lvd. Lvs to 30×1.5–2cm, ligulate, obtuse, slightly bilobed at apex, light green. Peduncles with several scarious bracts, arising in axils of sheaths on new growths; fls white; sep. 20×5–6mm, oblong-ligulate, acuminate; pet. 16–18× 4–5mm, oblong-elliptical, acute; lip 11–12×4.5–6mm, fleshy, obscurely trilobed with callus running from base to about middle, midlobe oblong-ovate, thickened at apex; column 8–9mm; ovary 2–3cm. Throughout most of tropical America.

M.amparoana Schltr. See *M.ringens.*
M.angustifolia Hook. See *M.variabilis.*

M.arachnites Rchb. f.
Epiphytic or lithophytic; pseudobulbs small, compressed, 1–3-lvd. Lvs 15–25×3cm, lanceolate, acute, light green. Infl. to 15cm; fls fragrant, sep. yellow-green, pet. white, lip golden yellow, all flushed with maroon; sep. 55–57×9mm, lanceolate, acuminate, margins recurved; pet. 45×13mm, lanceolate, acuminate, incurved, margins only slightly recurved; lip 17×10mm, trilobed towards apex, lateral lobes erect, midlobe truncate, all lobes with denticulate margin; column about 7mm. Venezuela, Colombia, Ecuador.

M.arbuscula Rchb. f.
Rhiz. slender, branched, with or without pseudobulbs. Lvs distichous, 2cm, linear-ligulate, unequally bilobed at apex. Peduncles axillary; fls somewhat globose, 1cm diam.; sep. and pet. white sometimes spotted with red, lip deep red; sep.

and pet. ligulate; lip ligulate with a slight constriction just before the enlarged and fleshy apex and a linear callus in the centre. Peru, Ecuador.

M.articulata Klotzsch. See *M.rufescens.*

M.aurea (Poepp. & Endl.) L.O. Williams.
Terrestrial; rhiz. creeping or ascending; pseudobulbs ovoid, set 6–10cm apart, with numerous basal sheaths, some leaf-bearing. Lvs 15–25×2–3cm, linear-elliptic. Infl. in clusters from axils of basal sheaths; fls yellow, the lip with brown marks; sep. 10–15mm, lanceolate-elliptic; pet. slightly smaller; lip recurved. Colombia.

M.boothii Lindl. See *Nidema boothii.*
M.bractescens Lindl. See *Xylobium bractescens.*
M.brevipedunculata Ames & Schweinf. See *M.nasuta.*

M.callichroma Rchb. f. (*M.setigera* var. *angustifolia* Klinge).
Pseudobulbs clustered, to 5×1.5cm, ovoid, compressed, dark brown, enclosed in long sheaths, 1-lvd. Lvs 30–45×4–5cm, with folded, petiolate base about 8cm. Infl. arising from base of pseudobulb; peduncle covered with loose sheaths, pale green with dark scales; fls yellow and white flushed with dark red; dorsal sep. to 55×8mm, lanceolate, mucronate, lateral sep. slightly shorter; pet. to 52×5mm, lanceolate, acute; lip to 24×14mm, trilobed in apical half, the base, lateral lobes and callus pubesc., lateral lobes erect, midlobe about 9×8mm, fleshy, ovate. Venezuela, Colombia.

M.camaridii Rchb. f. (*Camaridium ochroleucum* Lindl.; *M.lutescens* Scheidw.).
Rhiz. to 150cm, covered in grey sheaths, branched, pendent, straggling, the ends upturned; pseudobulbs to 8×2.5cm, ovoid, compressed, 1–2-lvd, set close together at base of plant, 5–12cm apart further up. Infl. arising from axils of sheathing lvs towards end of rhiz.; fls white, the lip yellow on midlobe, sometimes with transverse streaks of red-brown; dorsal sep. 26×7mm, oblong or oblanceolate, obtuse, lateral sep. slightly shorter and wider; pet. 24×6–7mm,

oblong; lip 13×13mm, trilobed, with toothed, glandular-hairy callus towards base, lateral lobes erect, midlobe truncate. C America, W Indies, Venezuela, Colombia, Brazil, Peru.

M.cobanensis Schltr.
Dwarf, epiphytic, 4–10cm; rhiz. short; pseudobulbs densely packed, 15–20×4–5mm, cylindrical but narrowing toward apex, slightly compressed, 1-lvd. Lvs erect or slightly spreading, 3.5–6×1–1.5cm, elliptic-ligulate, obtuse. Infl. short, arising at base of pseudobulb; fls dull pink-tan, veined with red-brown; sep. spreading, to 14mm, ligulate, apiculate, the lateral sep. oblique and forming short, obtuse mentum with column foot; pet. slightly shorter, ligulate-spathulate, obtuse, projecting forwards; lip 10×5.5mm, with longitudinal ridge from base to middle, concave, obovate, obscurely triloded, lateral lobes rounded, midlobe quadrate, slightly emarginate; column slender, 7mm, column foot 2.5mm; ovary 7mm. Summer. Mexico to Costa Rica.

M.coccinea (Jacq.) L.O. Williams ex Hodge.
Robust, to 50cm; rhiz. covered with overlapping, papery sheaths; pseudobulbs to 4cm, ovoid, compressed, 1-lvd. Lvs to 35×2.5cm, linear-oblong, acute or obtuse, folded at base. Infl. clustered; peduncles wiry, 6cm; fls bright rose-pink, carmine or vermilion; sep. to 12mm, spreading, fleshy, ovate-lanceolate, acuminate, concave; pet. to 8mm, ovate or ovate-lanceolate, acute or acuminate; lip to 8mm, fleshy, trilobed, lateral lobes erect, midlobe more or less ovate, recurved; column short. Capsule beaked. Greater & Lesser Antilles.

M.concava Lindl. See *Xylobium foveatum*.

M.consanguinea Klotzsch (*M.serotina* Hoehne).
Rhiz. creeping; pseudobulbs elongated, somewhat compressed, ribbed, 2-lvd. Lvs oblong-lanceolate, cuspidate, folded and narrowed toward base. Peduncles clustered, to 6cm; sep. yellow, margins red, pet. pale yellow, lip yellow-white with purple spots; sep. about 25×6mm, lanceolate, acute, spreading; pet. shorter and narrower, acuminate; lip 25×10mm, trilobed with a tongue-shaped callus between the lateral lobes, lateral lobes rounded, erect, midlobe ovate, obtuse, recurved; column arched. Brazil.

M.coriacea Barb. Rodr. See *M.desvauxiana*.

M.crassifolia (Lindl.) Rchb. f.
Rhiz. short and stout; pseudobulbs 1.5–3×0.5–1.5cm, oblong, compressed, 1-lvd at apex, covered with sheaths, some leaf-bearing. Lvs to 45×4cm, somewhat fleshy, linear to linear-oblong, obtuse or subacute, folded at base. Infl. 1–3 from lf axils; peduncle about 1cm with a scarious bract about half way; fls campanulate, fleshy, yellow to orange, usually with purple marks; pedicel and ovary 1–2cm; sep. 14–18×5–6mm, lanceolate, acute, concave; pet. 12–15×3–3.5mm, linear-oblanceolate, sometimes curved, the edge entire or denticulate; lip 13–15×6.5–8mm, elliptic, obscurely trilobed with longitudinal, hairy callus in basal half, margins entire or denticulate; column arched, 8–10mm. US (Florida), C America, W Indies, Venezuela, Brazil.

M.crassipes Kränzl.
Rhiz. creeping; pseudobulbs to 25×10mm, conical, set 1–1.5cm apart, 2-lvd at apex. Lvs to 9×1.5cm, lanceolate, acute, petiolate, fleshy-coriaceous. Infl. to 12cm; fls yellow edged with red, apex of lip purple, column tinged lilac; sep. 25×5mm, ovate-lanceolate, acuminate; pet. 18×3mm, ligulate-lanceolate, acute; lip 15×7–8mm, trilobed in apical half, lateral lobes erect, midlobe oblong, the edge undulate; column arched, 8mm. Brazil.

M.cucullata Lindl.
Pseudobulbs 4–5cm, elliptic, 1-lvd. Lvs to 20cm, ligulate, obtuse. Peduncle to 13cm, stiffly erect; fls dingy dark brown; sep. and pet. 25–28mm, lanceolate, acute; lip 23mm, trilobed, lateral lobes small. Mexico to Panama.

M.curtipes Hook.
Pseudobulbs clustered, 3.5–4×2cm, 1-lvd. Lvs about 15×2cm, broadly linear-lanceolate, acute. Infl. arising from base of pseudobulb; fls buff-yellow, underside of lip speckled with red; sep. and pet. 13–16×5mm, oblong, subacute; lip oblong in outline, obscurely trilobed with a shiny, purple-brown callus between the lobes, midlobe slightly reflexed; front of column shiny red-brown. Mexico to Honduras and El Salvador..

M.cyanea (Lindl.) Beer. See *Warreella cyanea*.
M.decolor Lindl. See *Xylobium palmifolium*.

M.densa Lindl. (*Ornithidium densum* (Lindl.) Rchb. f.)
Rhiz. ascending, covered with brown, scarious sheaths; pseudobulbs to 8cm, oblong, compressed, 1-lvd. Lvs to 40×5cm, linear to oblong-lanceolate, obscurely bilobed at apex. Peduncles clustered, axillary; fls variable in colour, green-white, yellow-green, white tinged with purple, dark maroon or red-brown; sep. about 10mm, linear-lanceolate, acuminate, keeled; pet. slightly smaller; lip obscurely trilobed, oblong, concave and clasping the column at base, apex channelled and recurved. Mexico, Guatemala, Honduras, Belize.

M.desvauxiana Rchb. f. (*M.coriacea* Barb. Rodr.; *M.petiolaris* A. Rich. ex Rchb. f.).
Epiphytic, occasionally lithophytic; rhiz. stout, creeping; pseudobulbs set close together, to 4×2.5cm, ovoid, somewhat compressed, 1-lvd. Lvs to 45×4.5cm, including folded, petiolate base to 10cm, blade elliptic, acute. Infl. arising from base of pseudobulb; peduncle 3cm, covered with overlapping, loose, tubular sheaths; fls fleshy, sep. dull apricot-yellow with maroon flush at base and apex, pet. maroon, the margins paler, lip mostly pink, deep maroon in centre, edge of midlobe almost white; sep. 25–35×13–18mm, ovate, apiculate; pet. to 30×18mm, obovate, rounded at apex; lip to 25mm, 20mm across lateral lobes, with smooth, longitudinal callus towards base, midlobe 8mm diam., the edge thin and undulate, the central part fleshy and verrucose. Guyana, French Guiana, Surinam, Venezuela, Brazil.

M.dichroma Rolfe. See *M.elegantula*.

M.discolor (Lodd.) Rchb. f.
Pseudobulbs clustered, to 7cm, ovoid, compressed, 1-lvd at apex. Lvs to 35×6cm, ligulate, unequally bilobed at apex. Peduncles 4–5cm, arising from base of pseudobulb; fls waxy, sep. and pet. apricot, variably spotted maroon, lip orange with deep maroon spots; sep. 22×7mm, lanceolate, acute, rather fleshy, the margins recurved; pet. 18×4mm, oblanceolate, acute; lip 13×7mm, obscurely trilobed, fleshy, with longitudinal, glandular-hairy callus running for most of its length. Guyana, French Guiana, Venezuela.

M.echinochila Kränzl.
Pseudobulbs clustered, 30–35×10mm, long-ovoid, 2-lvd at apex. Lvs to 10×0.5cm, linear, acute. Fls brown; sep. 20×5–6mm, oblong, acute, lateral sep. somewhat curved; pet. similar but slightly narrower; lip 15×8mm, entire, obovate, edge undulate. Brazil.

M.elegantula Rolfe (*M.dichroma* Rolfe).
Rhiz. stout, creeping; pseudobulbs to 6cm, narrowly ellipsoid, compressed, 1-lvd at apex, with several large, distichous, basal sheaths, the uppermost usually leaf-bearing. Lvs to 30×5.5cm, oblong-elliptic, acute, petiolate; petiole to 20cm. Peduncles to 25cm, almost covered with tubular sheaths; fls large, white tinged with purple-brown; sep. and pet. spreading, sep. 25–45×15mm, oblong, acute or subacute, lateral sep. slightly longer than dorsal sep., pet. slightly shorter and narrower than dorsal sep., obliquely lanceolate, acute or acuminate; lip 17×12mm, oval in outline, obscurely trilobed, apex obtuse, recurved; column about 1cm. Peru, Ecuador.

M.elongata Lindl. & Paxt. See *Xylobium elongatum*.

M.equitans (Schltr.) Garay (*Camaridium equitans* Schltr.; *M.mattogrossensis* Brade; *M.vandiformis* (Schltr.) C. Schweinf.).
Stems almost erect, clustered, to 30cm, leafy along length when young; when older, leafy at apex and the lower part covered in grey lf-bases. Lvs to 10cm×8mm, fleshy, bilaterally flattened, straight or recurved, with purple streak near edge of sheathing base. Peduncles covered with white sheaths, arising from lf axils; sep. and pet. cream, sep. flushed with pink, lip violet-purple with white apical margin; sep. 14–15×5–6mm, oblong, acute, spreading, rather fleshy; pet. 13×3mm, narrowly lanceolate, parallel to column; lip 14×6mm, fleshy, with median callus, obscurely trilobed, midlobe 4mm diam., apex recurved. Venezuela, Guyana, Brazil, Colombia, Peru.

M.ferdinandiana Barb. Rodr.
Rhiz. 10–25cm, creeping, branched; pseudobulbs well spaced, ovoid, compressed, 1-lvd at apex. Lvs 6–9cm× 6–8mm, linear-lanceolate, acute. Infl. 5–15mm; sep. and pet. green-white, spotted purple on outer surface, lip white with purple spots; sep. and pet. about 10×2.5–4mm, oblong, acute; lip erect, 10×8mm, broadly ovate in outline, obscurely trilobed, lateral lobes erect, midlobe suborbicular. Brazil.

M.fletcheriana Rolfe.
Pseudobulbs clustered, 3–5cm, oblong-ovoid, fairly compressed, 1-lvd at apex, with a pair of distichous, leaf-bearing sheaths. Lvs to 24×5.5cm, oblong or elliptic, petiolate; petiole 5–12cm. Peduncles 25–35cm, almost covered in loose sheaths; fls white or yellow with purple lines; sep. recurved or spreading, to 45×25mm, ovate, acute; pet. shorter and narrower, obliquely ovate-lanceolate, shortly acuminate, projecting forwards over column; lip to 50×30mm, obovate in outline, with oblong, fleshy callus above middle, obscurely trilobed, lateral lobes erect, midlobe suborbicular, recurved, undulate, trilobulate; column about 1.5cm, column foot 4cm. Peru.

M.foveata Lindl. See *Xylobium foveatum*.

M.friedrichsthalli Rchb. f.
Rhiz. erect or pendulous; pseudobulbs clustered, to 5cm, elliptic-oblong, slightly flattened, the upper pair of sheaths usually leaf-bearing. Lvs usually 2–3, 3–18cm, ligulate, obscurely bilobed at apex. Infl. 1 to several, about 3cm; fls variable in colour and size, often not opening wide, yellow-green to green-mauve; sep. to 30mm, linear-lanceolate, acute or acuminate; pet. similar but slightly smaller; lip entire, narrowly oblanceolate, thickened at apex. Mostly summer. Mexico and Belize to Panama and Colombia.

M.fuscata Klotzsch. See *M.picta*.

M.gracilis Lodd. (*M.punctata* Lodd.).
Pseudobulbs clustered, 20–25×10–13mm, ovoid, compressed, 2-lvd at apex. Lvs 10–20×1–1.5cm, linear-ligulate, acute. Infl. to 10cm; fls scented, yellow, sep. and pet. flushed with purple on outer edge, lip with purple marks; sep. 17–22×5–7mm, fleshy, narrowly lanceolate, acute; pet. 12–20×2–3mm, narrowly linear-lanceolate, acute; lip erect, 12–15×7–9mm, deeply trilobed in apical half, lateral lobes erect, midlobe oblong, edge undulate-denticulate. Brazil.

M.grandiflora (HBK) Lindl.
Pseudobulbs to 6cm, oblong-ovoid, compressed, 1-lvd at apex, when young surrounded by distichous, overlapping sheaths of which some are leaf-bearing. Lvs 11–28×5cm, elliptic to ligulate, acute, petiolate; petiole 3–10cm, laterally compressed. Peduncles 1–2, 12–25cm, with several loose, tubular sheaths; fls slightly nodding, milk-white, scented, fleshy, 10cm diam.; sep. spreading, dorsal sep. 35–45×20mm, ovate-oblong, acute, concave, lateral sep. slightly longer and wider forming conical mentum with column foot; pet. slightly shorter and narrower than dorsal sep., elliptic-lanceolate; lip parallel to column, recurved, 25×15mm, ovate in outline, obscurely trilobed, lateral lobes erect, apex fleshy; disc with 3

calli; column arched, 12–13mm. Summer. Ecuador, Peru, Colombia, Venezuela, Guyana.

M.heteroclita Poep..& Endl. See *Chaubardia heteroclita*.
M.heuchmannii Hook. See *M.variabilis*.
M.hirtilabia Lindl. See *M.parkeri*.
M.iridifolia Rchb. f. See *M.valenzuelana*.

M.juergensii Schltr.
Rhiz. with short, erect branches so that plant eventually forms a dense mound; pseudobulbs 1cm, ribbed. Lvs needle-like, 3–4cm. Fls 12mm diam., very dark red, almost black, the lip with wet-looking surface; sep. and pet. about 6mm, ovate, obtuse; lip tongue-like. Autumn–winter. Brazil.

M.jugosa Lindl. See *Pabstia jugosa*.

M.kautskyi Pabst.
Slender, tufted, epiphytic, with very short rhiz.; pseudobulbs 15×15mm, globose, wrinkled, 4-angled, 2-lvd. Lvs 17–25×4–5mm, narrowly linear, acute, midvein prominent below. Infl. very short, arising from base of pseudobulb; fls spreading or erect, yellow, lip spotted with dark purple towards apex; sep. 13–15×5mm, narrowly oblong, acute, lateral sep. slightly oblique; pet. linear, acute; lip 12×8.5mm, broadly elliptic in outline, shortly clawed at base, trilobed in apical quarter, lateral lobes small, rounded, midlobe 3×4mm, oblong; column 8mm, slender, curved; ovary 12mm. Brazil.

M.kegelii Rchb. f. See *M.parkeri*.
M.kreysigii Hoffsgg. See *M.picta*.
M.lactea Schltr. See *M.ringens*.
M.leontoglossa Rchb. f. See *Xylobium leontoglossum*.

M.lepidota Lindl. (*M.pertusa* Lindl.; *M.saxicola* Schltr.).
Epiphytic or terrestrial; pseudobulbs clustered, to 5×1.5cm, ovoid, covered with sheaths of which 1 may be leaf-bearing, 1-lvd at apex. Lvs linear-ligulate, to 35×2cm including folded petiolate base 2–4cm long. Peduncles arising from base of pseudobulb, to 12cm, red towards base, covered with loose, tubular sheaths; sep. and pet. yellow, marked with red at base, lip creamy yellow with maroon marks; sep. to 60×7mm, lanceolate, acuminate, dorsal sep. projecting forwards, lateral sep. spreading; pet. to 45×4mm, curved-lanceolate, acuminate, projecting forwards; lip 20×12mm, fleshy, with raised central callus bordered with hairs, obscurely trilobed, midlobe covered with yellow-green farina, apex dorsally keeled, mucronate. Venezuela, Colombia, Ecuador.

M.leucochila Hoffsgg. See *M.picta*.
M.lindeniana A. Rich. See *M.meleagris*.

M.linearis C. Schweinf.
Rhiz. erect, elongated, with very short branches, covered with overlapping, tubular, warty sheaths. Lvs in groups of 4–6, 13.5–40×0.5cm, narrowly linear, acuminate, the margins rolled back. Peduncles spreading, to 7cm, covered with tubular sheaths, arising in clusters from axils of leaf-bearing sheaths towards apex of stem and on branches; dorsal sep. 26×3.5mm, linear, acute, mucronate, lateral sep. slightly wider and curved; pet. like lateral sep. but smaller; lip parallel to column, recurved, 10mm, with longitudinal callus in basal two-thirds, trilobed near apex, lateral lobes erect, semi-elliptic, midlobe about 2mm, fleshy, narrowly triangular; column 5mm. Peru.

M.longifolia (Barb. Rodr.) Cogn. See *M.tarumaensis*.
M.loretoensis Schweinf. See *M.parkeri*.
M.lorifolia Rchb. f. See *M.parkeri*.

M.luteoalba Lindl.
Epiphytic or terrestrial; pseudobulbs clustered, ovoid, compressed, dark brown, covered with scarious sheaths, 1-lvd at apex. Lvs to 50×5cm, including folded, petiolate base, linear-ligulate, rigid, midvein prominent below. Peduncles to 12cm, covered with green sheaths spotted with brown; fls white and yellow, side lobes of lip with purple-brown veining; sep. 52×8mm, lanceolate, acute, margins recurved, lateral sep. somewhat curved; pet. 46×6mm, projecting forwards, lanceolate-falcate, margins recurved; lip 25×14mm, with longitudinal, pubesc. callus, thick-textured, lateral lobes small, mid-

Maxillaria   (a) *M.tenuifolia*   (b) *M.sanderiana*   (c) *M.valenzuelana*   (d) *M.picta*

lobe broadly ovate. Costa Rica, Panama, Venezuela, Colombia, Ecuador.

M.lutescens Scheidw. See *M.camaridii*.

M.macleei Batem. ex Lindl. See *M.uncata*.

M.macrura Rchb. f.
Pseudobulbs compressed, spherical, forming row on rhiz. Lvs ligulate, acuminate. Peduncles clustered; fls pink-tan, lip with red longitudinal streaks, to 12cm diam.; sep. and pet. linear-lanceolate, caudate; lip trilobed, shortly clawed at base, oblong in outline, with oblong callus between lobes. Mexico.

M.marginata Fenzl (*M.punktulata* Klotzsch; *M.tricolor* Lindl.).
Very similar to *M.picta*, differing mainly in rather smaller fls; sep. dull yellow with brown margin and tinged with brown towards apex; lip short, white, edged and irregularly spotted with brown, margin slightly undulate, lateral lobes short. Brazil.

M.mattogrossensis Brade. See *M.equitans*.

M.meleagris Lindl. (*M.lindeniana* A. Rich.; *M.punctostriata* Rchb. f.).
Rhiz. short; pseudobulbs clustered, 2–5.5×1–2cm, ellipsoid or ovoid, compressed, 1-lvd at apex. Lvs 15–40×0.5–2cm, linear, obtuse, coriaceous. Infl. to 8cm, arising from base of new growth; fls scented of coconut, variable in size and colour, buff-orange, buff-olive or flesh-coloured, marked with dark red, lip dark red; sep. 12–30×4–7mm, elliptic, acute, acuminate or obtuse; pet. similar but shorter and adnate to dorsal sep.; lip 7–16×4–8mm, trilobed towards base, recurved, with transverse ridge between the small, erect, lateral lobes, midlobe fleshy, ovate-orbicular to elliptic. Mexico, Guatemala, Panama.

M.monoceras Klotzsch. See *M.picta*.

M.mosenii Kränzl.
Rhiz. stout, 1cm diam.; pseudobulbs set obliquely, about 2cm apart, 4–4.5cm×3.5–5mm, 4- or 8-angled, enlarged at apex, glossy green-black, 2-lvd at apex, with large basal sheaths. Lvs 10–15cm×6–7mm, linear-lanceolate, long-acuminate, rigid. Peduncles solitary, of similar length to pseudobulbs, with large, almost transparent brown sheaths; fls yellow-brown, spotted with dull lilac inside; dorsal sep. 20×4mm, lanceolate, acute, concave, lateral sep. 20×5mm, oblong-lanceolate, forming short, obtuse mentum with column foot; pet. 15×4mm, obovate-oblong, obtuse; lip 17×6–7mm, almost entire. Brazil.

M.nana Hook. See *M.uncata*.

M.nasalis Rchb. f. See *M.nasuta*.

M.nasuta Rchb. f. (*M.nasalis* Rchb. f.; *M.oxysepala* Schltr.; *M.brevipedunculata* Ames & Schweinf.).
Pseudobulbs to 9×4cm, bilaterally flattened, clustered. Lvs to 60×4cm, linear, unequally bilobed at apex, glossy bright green. Peduncles about 8cm, arising at base of pseudobulbs; fls yellow-green flushed with maroon, lip mostly maroon or red, with yellow apex; sep. 32–37×7–8mm, lanceolate, acuminate, rather fleshy, margins somewhat recurved, apices stiff and keeled; pet. 25×6mm, oblanceolate, acute; lip 18×7mm, with a sticky, longitudinal callus towards base, obscurely trilobed, apex thick and keeled. Guatemala, Costa Rica, Venezuela, Colombia, Brazil.

M.nigrescens Lindl. (*M.rubrofusca* Klotzsch).
Pseudobulbs long-ovoid, compressed, the base covered with grey sheaths, 1-lvd. Lvs to 35×3.5cm, linear, rigid, folded and petiolate at base, the margins somewhat recurved. Peduncles to 14cm, covered with green sheaths marked with brown; sep. and pet. maroon-red, orange-maroon at apex, grading to yellow at base of sep., lip maroon-black; sep. 45–60×7–10mm, lanceolate, acute, dorsal sep. erect, lateral sep. spreading or reflexed; pet. 40–55×6mm, falcate-lanceolate, somewhat spreading; lip to 17×12mm with longitudinal callus at base, obscurely trilobed, apex fleshy. Venezuela, Colombia.

M.ochroleuca Lindl. var. **longipes** Sander.
Usually terrestrial, sometimes epiphytic; pseudobulbs clustered, to 8×4cm, ovoid, very compressed, ribbed, 1-lvd at apex and with 1–2 leaf-bearing sheaths at base. Lvs to

45×3cm, linear, keeled, unequally bilobed at apex. Peduncles arising in clusters from axils of sheathing lvs, to 16cm, with several sheaths; fls strongly scented, sep. and pet. white turning to yellow in apical half, lip white with orange midlobe; sep. 32×3.5mm, narrowly lanceolate, acute; pet. 29×2mm, narrowly lanceolate, acuminate; lip 11×6mm, with sparsely hairy callus in basal half, trilobed about halfway, lateral lobes erect, obtuse, sparsely hairy, midlobe fleshy, rough-textured, with scattered hairs below; ovary to 2cm. Venezuela, Brazil.

M.oxysepala Schltr. See *M.nasuta*.

M.pachyacron Schltr. See *M.reichenheimiana*.

M.pachyphylla Schltr.
Epiphytic; rhiz. pendent, usually curving up at tip, covered with brown sheaths; pseudobulbs set close together obliquely on rhiz., 25–35×7–9mm, cylindrical to conical, ribbed, 1-lvd. Lvs 10–15×1cm, spreading, oblanceolate, acute, thick-textured. Peduncles very short, about 15mm including ovary; fls pale yellow, lip yellow streaked with rose-pink near margin; sep. 18×10mm, ovate-oblong, acute, the lateral sep. oblique and forming blunt mentum with column foot; lip 17×17mm, with linear callus in basal third, trilobed, clawed at base, apex enlarged and obtuse, lateral lobes rounded; column 10mm, slightly curved, column foot 4mm. Brazil. var. **brunneo-fusca** Hoehne. Fls deep yellow-brown.

M.pallidiflora Hook. See *Xylobium pallidiflorum*.

M.palmifolia (Sw.) Lindl. See *Xylobium palmifolium*.

M.parkeri Hook. (*M.hirtilabia* Lindl.; *M.lorifolia* Rchb. f.; *M.kegelii* Rchb. f.; *M.loretoensis* Schweinf.).
Pseudobulbs clustered, 3.5×2–3cm, ovoid to subglobose, somewhat compressed, with large, spotted, grey-brown sheaths with incurved margins at base, 1-lvd at apex. Lvs with petiolate base about 5cm long, blade to 45×4cm, linear-ligulate, acute. Peduncles to 7cm, covered with sheaths; sep. yellow, pet. white with maroon veining towards base, lip orange-yellow, lateral lobes maroon-veined, midlobe margin white, column maroon with white apex; sep. 32–33×18–20mm, ovate, obtuse, rather fleshy, margins recurved, dorsal sep. erect, lateral sep. spreading; pet. 28×10mm, lanceolate, acute, projecting forwards; lip 23×16mm with a hairy longitudinal callus in basal half, trilobed about halfway, lateral lobes erect, obtuse, midlobe oblong-ovate, fleshy; column 10–12mm. Guyana, Surinam, Venezuela, Peru.

M.pendens Pabst.
Rhiz. to 2m, sometimes branched; pseudobulbs set well apart, to 6×4cm, ovoid, somewhat compressed, 1–2-lvd at apex and with 2 or more leaf-bearing sheaths with persistent bases at base of pseudobulb. Lvs to 25×5cm, lanceolate, acute, keeled. Peduncles to 5cm, arising in clusters from axils of sheathing lvs; ovary about 2cm; fls cream flushed with pink, sep. yellow at apex; sep. 16–21×4–5mm, lanceolate, acute; pet. 13–16×3–4mm, oblong, mucronate; lip difficult to flatten, 12×9mm, with basal callus with keeled veins radiating from it, trilobed about halfway, apex of midlobe deeply emarginate, erose. Guyana, Venezuela, Colombia, Brazil.

M.pertusa Lindl. See *M.lepidota*.

M.petiolaris A. Rich. ex Rchb. f. See *M.desvauxiana*.

M.picta Hook. (*M.fuscata* Klotzsch; *M.kreysigii* Hoffsgg.; *M.leucochila* Hoffsgg.; *M.monoceras* Klotzsch).
Pseudobulbs clustered or set a short distance apart, to 6cm, ovoid, compressed, ribbed, 1–2-lvd at apex. Lvs to 30cm, ligulate, acute. Peduncles clustered, 12–20cm; fls large, golden yellow inside, cream-yellow outside, cross-banded and flecked with purple-brown, lip yellow-white or cream spotted with red, column red-violet; sep. about 30mm, oblong, acute, curved forwards; pet. slightly shorter and narrower, parallel to column; midlobe tongue-shaped, deflexed, lateral lobes erect. Winter. Brazil.

M.plebeja Rchb. f.
Rhiz. ascending; pseudobulbs oblong, compressed. Lvs ligulate, acute, keeled below apex on outer surface, folded at base. Peduncles short; fls pale yellow, the lip darker, sep. and

pet. sparsely spotted with dark purple; sep. ovate, acute; pet. ligulate, acute; lip oblong in outline, obscurely trilobed in middle, with an oblong, waxy callus in basal half. Brazil.

M.porphyrostele Rchb. f.
Pseudobulbs clustered, to 4.5cm, broadly elliptic, 2-lvd. Lvs to 20×1.5cm, linear-ligulate, obtuse. Peduncles clustered, to 8cm; fls yellow, about 4cm diam.; sep. about 20mm, lanceolate, the tips incurved; pet. similar but shorter. Winter–spring. Brazil.

M.pubilabia Schltr. See *M.ringens.*
M.punctata Lodd. See *M.gracilis.*
M.punctostriata Rchb. f. See *M.meleagris.*
M.punctulata Klotzsch. See *M.marginata.*

M.reichenheimiana Rchb. f. (*M.pachyacron* Schltr.).
Pseudobulbs clustered, to 1.5cm, subglobose but fairly compressed, 1-lvd at apex and sometimes with a leaf-bearing sheath. Lvs to 4×2.5cm, elliptic, obtuse, apiculate, fleshy, blue-green mottled with grey, sometimes with white dots on upper side, slightly tinged with maroon on edge and underneath. Peduncles to 5cm, covered with brown sheaths; sep. orange, tinged with maroon, pet. yellow-orange, lip with yellow midlobe and callus, lateral lobes dark maroon; sep. and pet. lanceolate, acuminate, projecting forwards, sep. 32–35× 6mm, pet. 25×5mm; lip 15×8.5mm, with scattered glandular hairs and a longitudinal callus in basal half, trilobed in apical third, lateral lobes rounded, erect, midlobe fleshy, ovate, edge undulate; column about 5mm, apex fringed with glandular hairs. Trinidad, Costa Rica, Venezuela.

M.revoluta Klotzsch. See *M.variabilis.*

M.ringens Rchb. f. (*M.tuerckheimii* Schltr.; *M.rousseauae* Schltr.; *M.pubilabia* Schltr.; *M.amparoana* Schltr.; *M.lactea* Schltr.).
Pseudobulbs set close together, to 4×2.5cm, ellipsoid or ovoid, compressed, 1-lvd. Lvs to 54×5cm (usually smaller), elliptic-oblong, petiolate; petiole to 13cm. Peduncles to 18cm, covered with green sheaths spotted with maroon; sep. and pet. yellow-cream, tinged with orange-pink at apex, lip cream, underside of apex dark maroon; sep. 18–40×6–8mm, oblong, acute, spreading; pet. to 26×5.5mm, narrowly lanceolate, obtuse; lip 13–17×6–11mm, with a longitudinal callus with scattered white hairs in basal half, trilobed in apical third, lateral lobes rounded, erect, midlobe fleshy, truncate, edge undulate; column 6–7mm. Mexico to Panama; Venezuela to Peru.

M.rollissonii Lindl. See *Promenaea rollissonii.*
M.rousseauae Schltr. See *M.ringens.*
M.rubrofusca Klotzsch. See *M.nigrescens.*

M.rufescens Lindl. (*M.acutifolia* Lindl.; *M.rugosa* Scheidw.; *M.articulata* Klotzsch; *M.vanillodora* A. Rich. ex Rchb. f.; *M.abelei* Schltr.).
Very variable; rhiz. creeping; pseudobulbs usually clustered, 1.5–6cm, varying from small, subglobose, compressed to long-ovoid and 4-angled, sheaths sometimes caducous, sometimes persistent. Lvs 4–30×3–6cm, elliptic, oblong or ligulate, sometimes with petiole to 4cm. Fls variable in colour, from green-brown and cream to dull yellow or orange flushed with maroon, or maroon and white; sep. spreading, dorsal sep. 9–24×3–10mm, oblong, concave, lateral sep. similar but wider; pet. slightly shorter than dorsal sep., obliquely oblong or lanceolate; lip 8–20×6–12mm with longitudinal callus in basal half, trilobed about halfway, lateral lobes erect, midlobe truncate; column 7–16mm. Widespread in Tropical America.

M.rugosa Scheidw. See *M.rufescens.*

M.sanderiana Rchb. f.
Epiphytic or lithophytic; rhiz. short or long; pseudobulbs clustered, to 5cm, subglobose to ovoid, compressed, 1-lvd. Lvs to 40×5.5cm, narrowly oblong, acute or cuspidate, leathery, petiolate; petiole to 20cm. Peduncles basal and axillary, sometimes clustered, to 25cm, covered with tubular sheaths; fls large, fleshy, sep. and pet. white flecked with violet-purple, lip dull yellow with red markings, dark purple on outer

surface; dorsal sep. 60–75×20mm, oblong or oblong-lanceolate, lateral sep. wider and slightly longer, forming a conical mentum; pet. somewhat shorter; lip 30–35mm, ovate in outline, obscurely trilobed in basal half, lateral lobes erect, midlobe ovate to suborbicular, apex rounded and margin crisped; column about 15mm, the foot longer. Peru, Ecuador.

M.sanguinea Rolfe.
Rhiz. creeping, covered with overlapping sheaths; pseudobulbs 1–2.5cm, ellipsoid, slightly compressed. Lvs 25–40×0.4cm, narrowly linear, subacute. Peduncles short, about equalling pseudobulb; sep. red-brown, apices yellow, pet. pale yellow with red-brown spots, lip carmine-red or crimson-purple with black-purple crest; sep. 12–16×4–5mm, oblong, obtuse; pet. linear-oblong, obtuse; lip 12–14×6mm, almost entire, oblong, obtuse, with a shiny, linear callus; column 12mm, clavate. C America.

M.saxicola Schltr. See *M.lepidota.*

M.seidelii Pabst.
Dwarf epiphyte to 5cm; rhiz. ascending; pseudobulbs minute, erect, linear or linear-oblong, 2-lvd. Lvs 2.5–3cm×7–8mm, erect, awl-shaped with a groove above. Peduncles solitary, about same length as lvs, with 3 sheaths; fls white, erect; sep. 8–8.5×1.5mm, ligulate, acute, margins reflexed, lateral sep. oblique; pet. 7×1.5mm, ligulate, acute, somewhat oblique; lip 7mm, fleshy at base, lateral lobes obscure, densely puberulous, midlobe 2mm diam., narrowly obovate; column 3mm, club-shaped, curved, column foot 2mm. Brazil.

M.serotina Hoehne. See *M.consanguinea.*
M.setigera var. *angustifolia* Klinge. See *M.callichroma.*

M.sophronites (Rchb. f.) Garay.
Rhiz. long, creeping, covered in brown sheaths; pseudobulbs 1–1.5cm, subglobose when young, later slightly compressed, dull brown, 1-lvd, set 2–4cm apart on rhiz. Lvs to 2×1cm, elliptic, unequally bilobed at apex, fleshy, light glossy green. Sep. and pet. orange-red, lip midlobe yellow with cream edge, lateral lobes cream; fls rather cup-shaped; sep. 11–13×7mm, ovate, apiculate; pet. 8×5.5mm, ovate, apiculate; lip 7×7mm, not including basal claw, with smooth callus in basal half, trilobed toward base, lateral lobes erect, rounded, with erose margins, midlobe ovate, obtuse, glandular-tubercular with erose margin. Venezuela.

M.squalens (Lindl.) Hook. See *Xylobium variegatum.*
M.squamata Barb. Rodr. See *M.uncata.*
M.stapelioides Lindl. See *Promenaea stapelioides.*
M.stenobulbon Klotzsch. See *Xylobium pallidiflorum.*
M.stenostele Schltr. See *M.uncata.*

M.striata Rolfe.
Pseudobulbs clustered, 4.5–8cm, oblong to ovoid, fairly compressed, with several pairs of sheaths, some leaf-bearing, 1-lvd at apex. Lvs to 24×4–6cm, oblong to elliptical, leathery, petiolate; petiole to 10cm. Peduncles to 30cm, covered with tubular sheaths; fls large, green-yellow with purple-red stripes, lip white, lateral lobes veined with red-purple; dorsal sep. 45–70×12mm, oblong-lanceolate, acute, concave, lateral sep. of similar length but oblique and much wider at base and acuminate, forming conical mentum about 25mm long with column foot; pet. shorter and narrower than dorsal sep., obliquely lanceolate, acuminate, tips recurved; lip 35–40mm, with linear callus in basal half, obscurely trilobed near apex, lateral lobes erect, rounded, midlobe ovate-lanceolate, recurved, margins undulate; column 11mm, column foot about 20mm. Peru.

M.superba La Ll. & Lex. See *Govenia superba.*

M.tarumaensis Hoehne (*M.longifolia* (Barb. Rodr.) Cogn.).
Pseudobulbs to 3cm, somewhat compressed. Lvs to 50×2.5cm, ligulate, folded at base. Peduncle to 5cm; sep. and pet. yellow-brown, lip purple-red with longitudinal green stripe; sep. 14×6mm, oblong-elliptic, obtuse; pet. similar but narrower and acute; lip 13×7mm, obscurely trilobed, elliptic in outline, with raised, sticky callus. Brazil, Venezuela.

M.tenuifolia Lindl.
Rhiz. ascending; pseudobulbs about 2.5cm, ovoid, set 2.5–5cm apart. Lvs 20–35×1cm, linear, midvein impressed. Peduncles several, to 5cm; fls with a strong coconut scent, to 5cm diam., deep red mottled with yellow towards base of sep. and pet., lip mainly yellow, marked with dark red, column pale yellow, the front spotted with dark red; sep. spreading, 20–25mm, lanceolate or ovate, margins recurved; pet. shorter, projecting forwards; lip about 16×10mm, obscurely trilobed, midlobe tongue-shaped, deflexed. Spring–summer. Mexico to Honduras and Nicaragua.

M.tricolor Lindl. See *M.marginata*.

M.triloris E. Morr.
Pseudobulbs clustered, to 6×5cm, ovoid, compressed, with grey, scarious sheaths towards base, 1-lvd at apex. Lvs to 40×6cm, linear-ligulate, with dorsal keel. Fls fragrant, sep. and pet. yellow, white at base, with maroon patch on reverse, lip lateral lobes white with maroon veins, midlobe yellow with white margin; sep. 65–70×13–20mm, lanceolate or oblanceolate, spreading, stiff in texture, margins recurved; pet. 60×12mm, lanceolate, acute, projecting forwards; lip 28×16mm, stiff, with hairy longitudinal callus at base, trilobed at about halfway, lateral lobes erect, midlobe oblong, thickened, sparsely pubesc., reflexed, the edge undulate, usually with a minute, spur-like projection on the underside near the apex; column 12mm. Venezuela.

M.tuerckheimii Schltr. See *M.ringens*.

M.uncata Lindl. (*M.macleei* Batem. ex Lindl.; *M.nana* Hook.; *M.squamata* Barb. Rodr.; *M.stenostele* Schltr.).
Rhiz. to 80cm, pendent, covered with red-brown sheaths; pseudobulbs obscure, to 5mm, largely hidden by sheaths, set about 2cm apart, 1-lvd. Lvs to 8cm×3mm, stiff, linear, margins incurved. Peduncles arising among sheaths, to 1cm; fls green-cream, sometimes tinged with light maroon; sep. and pet. projecting forwards, sep. 11–14×3–5mm, ovate, apiculate, lateral sep. oblique, pet. to 9×4mm, obliquely ovate, apiculate; lip to 13×5mm, with smooth callus in middle, obscurely trilobed in apical half, midlobe slightly emarginate; column 11mm, including foot, with hook-like processes below apex. Mexico to Brazil and Peru.

M.valenzuelana (A. Rich.) Nash (*M.iridifolia* Rchb. f.).
Pendulous, lacking pseudobulbs. Lvs several, forming fan, to 18×1.5cm, fleshy, bilaterally flattened. Peduncles arising from lf axils, about 5cm; fls small, about 2.5cm diam.; sep. and pet. yellow-green, lip light brown with purple spots; sep. 11–14×5–6mm, ovate, acute or apiculate, rather fleshy, dorsal sep. erect, lateral sep. semi-spreading; pet. 9×3mm, oblong-

lanceolate, projecting forwards; lip 10×5mm, callus consisting of a line of white, glandular hairs broken into basal, median and apical strips, obscurely trilobed, fleshy. C America, W Indies, Venezuela, Colombia, Ecuador, Brazil.

M.vandiformis (Schltr.) C. Schweinf. See *M.equitans*.
M.vanillodora A. Rich. ex Rchb. f. See *M.rufescens*.

M.variabilis Lindl. (*M.angustifolia* Hook.; *M.heuchmannii* Hook.; *M.revoluta* Klotzsch).
Often terrestrial; rhiz. elongated, creeping or ascending; pseudobulbs set 3–6cm apart, 2–4cm high, cylindrical, flattened, 1-lvd at apex, with numerous basal sheaths, some leaf-bearing. Lvs 15–25cm, oblong-linear, leathery. Peduncles 2–3cm, in groups of 2–3; fls varying in colour from pale yellow to dark red; sep. spreading, elliptic-lanceolate; pet. similar but projecting; lip slightly shorter, tongue-shaped, reflexed, with dark red central callus. Throughout the year. Mexico to Panama.

M.variegata Ruiz & Pav. See *Xylobium variegatum*.

M.venusta Lindl.
Pseudobulbs 4–5cm high, ovate, somewhat flattened, 1-lvd. Lvs to 30cm, ligulate, acute. Peduncles to 15cm, covered in red-tinged sheaths; fls somewhat nodding, to 15cm diam., sep. and pet. milk-white, lip yellow with 2 red spots, margins of lateral lobes red; sep. to 75mm, lanceolate, acute, dorsal sep. concave, lateral sep. somewhat curved; pet. similar but slightly shorter; lip fleshy, trilobed, midlobe triangular, recurved. Winter–spring. Colombia.

M.villosa (Barb. Rodr.) Cogn.
Pseudobulbs clustered, to 8cm, cylindrical to oblong-ovoid, 1-lvd at apex, with several pairs of overlapping sheaths, the upper ones leaf-bearing. Lvs to 44×5cm, ligulate to oblong, leathery, petiolate; petiole to 9cm. Peduncles to 8cm, arising from base of pseudobulb, covered with loose, tubular sheaths; fls small, bell-shaped, yellow, yellow-brown or orange, lip sometimes white; sep. 15–20×8mm, ovate-oblong, acute, concave, lateral sep. oblique and forming a low mentum; pet. shorter and narrower than sep., lanceolate or oblanceolate; lip erect, parallel to column, somewhat recurved, 13–15×8mm, oblong-ovate in outline, obscurely trilobed above middle, lateral lobes erect; column to 10mm, column foot short. Peru, Brazil, Guyana.

M.vittariifolia L.O. Williams.
Pseudobulbs clustered, 5–6mm diam., subglobose. Lvs about 9cm, narrowly ligulate, arching. Fls 10cm diam., milk-white, lip with yellow lateral lobes and red midlobe. Summer–autumn. Costa Rica, Panama, Colombia.

Meiracyllium Rchb. f. (From Gk *meirakyllion*, little fellow or stripling, referring to the low creeping habit.) 2 species of epiphytes. Rhizomes creeping, sheathed. Stems short or absent, thickened, single-leaved. Leaf fleshy, coriaceous, broad, sessile. Inflorescence several-flowered, terminal, flowers large for the plant, sepals erect, spreading, similar, lateral sepals oblique, petals broader than sepals; lip fused to column foot, saccate or gibbous. C America.

CULTIVATION Grow in baskets or on rafts in semi-shaded, humid conditions in the intermediate house. Syringe frequently.

M.trinasutum Rchb. f.
Rhiz. terete, sheathed when young. Stems obscure. Lvs orbicular to elliptic, broad, sessile, obtuse or rounded, coriaceous to fleshy, 2.8–5×1.5–3.5cm. Infl. several-fld; bracts triangular, acute; fls red-purple; sep. oblong-elliptic, shortly acuminate or acute, margins reflexed; pet. elliptic, oblique, 0.7–1×0.3cm; lip ovate-cordate, fleshy, sessile, saccate-hooded, margins lobed at base. Mexico, Guatemala.

M.wendlandii Rchb.f.
Rhiz. stout. Stems ascending, curved, to 1cm. Lvs obovate, or oblong, obtuse or rounded, fleshy, coriaceous, to 5×2.3cm. Infl. single-fld; bracts ovate, acute; fls purple, base yellow; dorsal sep. oblong-elliptic, concave, acute, 1–1.7×0.4cm, lateral sep. oblong-lanceolate, margins minutely dentate; lip obovate or flabellate, concave, margins upturned, apex decurved, acuminate, 1–1.3×0.7cm. Mexico, Guatemala.

M.wettsteinii Porsch. See *Neolauchea pulchella*.

Mendoncella A.D. Hawkes. (For Luis Mendonca, editor of the orchid journal *Orquidea*.) Some 11 species of epiphytes allied to *Zygopetalum*. Rhizome short. Pseudobulbs ovoid to cylindrical, short, often clustered, base enveloped by several overlapping bracts and leaf sheaths, apex 1–2-leaved. Leaves lanceolate, petiolate, plicate, prominently veined. Inflorescence a basal raceme, erect or nodding, short to elongate, 1- to few-flowered; flowers often large; sepals subsimilar, free or slightly connate at base, spreading, lateral sepals oblique, articulated to column foot forming a short mentum; petals wider than sepals; lip articulated to column foot, trilobed, lateral lobes erect, often fimbriate, midlobe large, spreading, entire to fimbriate, apex recurved, disc with a fleshy, sulcate callus, dentate; column short, stout, curved, apex winged or auriculate, anther terminal, operculate, incumbent, subglobose, pollinia 4, waxy, pyriform, strongly compressed. Mexico to Guyana, Brazil, Peru.

CULTIVATION As for *Zygopetalum*.

M.burkei (Rchb. f.) Garay (*Zygopetalum burkei* Rchb. f.; *Zygopetalum prainianum* Rolfe; *Galeottia burkei* (Rchb. f.) Dressler & Christenson).
Pseudobulbs to 12×3cm, oblong-cylindrical. Lvs to 45×2cm, coriaceous, oblong-lanceolate or linear-elliptic, acute or acuminate, suberect. Infl. to 60cm, loosely few-fld; fls to 5cm diam., fragrant, waxy, long-lived; tepals to 3.5×1.5cm, pale brown, marked chestnut-brown, often edged green, the lip white marked violet on callus; sep. ovate-oblong to elliptic-lanceolate, acute or acuminate, pet. obliquely ovate-oblong to oblong, acute or apiculate; lip to 25×22mm, interior densely pubesc., clawed, obovate to obovate-suborbicular, undulate or denticulate, rounded and apiculate, apex recurved, callus semicircular, closely toothed; column to 15mm, clavate, biauriculate. Venezuela, Guianas, Brazil, Surinam.

M.grandiflora (A. Rich.) A.D. Hawkes (*Galeottia grandiflora* A. Rich.; *Batemania grandiflora* (A. Rich.) Rchb. f.; *Zygopetalum grandiflorum* (A. Rich.) Benth. & Hook. ex Hemsl.).
Pseudobulbs to 8×3cm, narrowly ovoid. Lvs to 50×7cm, lanceolate to elliptic-lanceolate, acute or acuminate. Infl. to 20cm, 2- to several-fld; fls to 8cm diam., showy, waxy, fragrant, long-lived, green or yellow-green, broadly striped red-brown, the lip white streaked red; sep. to 5×1.5cm, lanceolate, acuminate, apex recurved; pet. to 4.5×1.5cm, obliquely falcate, acuminate, apex recurved; lip to 3×2cm, erose, lateral lobes erect, obliquely ovate, basally carinate, midlobe obovate to ovate-rhombic, arcuate, slightly concave, apex strongly recurved, callus erect, lunate, denticulate; column to 3cm, white or pale yellow, streaked red, bialate, apex ciliate. Mexico, Guatemala, Costa Rica, Panama, Colombia, British Honduras.

M.jorisiana (Rolfe) A.D. Hawkes (*Galeottia jorisiana* (Rolfe) Schltr.; *Galeottia fimbriata* (Lind. & Rchb. f.) Dressler & Christenson; *Zygopetalum jorisianum* Rolfe).
Pseudobulbs to 10×2cm, ovoid-oblong. Lvs to 27×6cm, oblanceolate, acute. Infl. to 27cm, suberect, few-fld, pale green marked dark green or purple-green, the lip white, darkening to pale yellow at midlobes and marked purple on callus, fleshy-rigid; dorsal sep. to 30×12mm, oblong-lanceolate, acute or subobtuse, lateral sep. to 34×14mm, ovate-lanceolate, acute to acuminate; pet. to 26×10mm, obliquely oblong-lanceolate; lip to 20×19mm, fimbriate, elliptic to suborbicular-obovate, lateral lobes small, auriculate, midlobe large, elliptic-orbicular to subquadrate, apex rounded or truncate; callus large, carinate; column light yellow-green striped maroon, anth. white tinged pink. Venezuela, Brazil.

Mexicoa Garay. (For the country.) 1 species, a diminutive epiphyte, allied to and formerly included in *Oncidium*. Pseudobulbs to 4×2cm, ovoid to pyriform, apically unifoliate or bifoliate. Leaves to 15×1.5cm, equitant, thinly coriaceous, linear to linear-lanceolate, acute or subacute, arcuate. Inflorescence to 20cm, a basal raceme, seldom exceeding leaves; tepals white or yellow-tinged and veined rose, sometimes heavily so and appearing red-brown; sepals to 14×4mm, elliptic or narrowly oblanceolate, subacute; petals to 12×4mm, obliquely oblong-oblanceolate to obovate, subacute; lip to 17×11mm, bright yellow, ovate, deflexed, lateral lobes spreading, elliptic, midlobe to 12×7mm, cleft; callus yellow-orange, linear, bifid; column to 5mm, strongly incurved. Mexico.

CULTIVATION As for *Oncidium*.

M.ghiesbrechtiana (A. Rich. & Gal.) Garay (*Oncidium ghiesbrechtiana* A. Rich. & Gal.).

Micropera Lindl. (From Gk *mikros*, small, and *pera*, sac, referring to the saccate lip.) Some 15 species, epiphytes similar to *Aerides* and usually listed under the synonym *Camarotis* Lindl., they produce many small flowers in narrow, sometimes branching racemes; these are characterized by the long, twisted column and the strongly saccate lip. SE Asia, Polynesia, Australia.

CULTIVATION   As for *Vanda*.

M.obtusa (Lindl.) Tang & Wang.
Plants branching freely with age, forming dense mats of growth. Fls small; tepals oblong-elliptic, obtuse, white tinted pale rose; lip yellow, broadly and bluntly saccate. NE India to Thailand.

M.philippinensis (Lindl.) Garay.
Infl. usually branched, many-fld.; fls small,glossy ; tepals obovate, pale sap green; lip and column white tinted green, column with a slender, twisted, beak-like appendage. Philippines.

M.rostrata (Roxb.) Balakr. (*Camarotis purpurea*).
Larger than above spp. Fls produced in great abundance, deep rosy purple; tepals oblong-obovate; lip narrowly sacccate with a short, white mentum. NE India to Thailand.

Microterangis Schltr. ex Sengh. (From Gk *microteros*, smaller, and *angos*, vessel, referring to the spur on the tiny flowers.) 4 species of epiphytes. Short-stemmed, densely leafy. Leaves usually oblong or obovate, unequally and obtusely bilobed at apex. Racemes many-flowered; flowers small, 2–3mm diam., dull yellow, yellow-orange or red-brown; sepals and petals free, similar; lip entire or dentate at apex, spurred; spur of about the same length as the lip; column straight, very short; pollinia 2, with communal stipe and very small viscidium. Madagascar, Mascarene Is., Comoros Is.

CULTIVATION   As for *Aerangis*.

M.boutonii (Rchb. f.) Sengh. (*Angraecum boutonii* Rchb. f.; *Angraecopsis boutonii* (Rchb. f.) H. Perrier).
Stem short; roots slender, numerous. Lvs to 13×3cm, oblanceolate, unequally and obtusely bilobed at apex, 1 lobe often virtually absent. Raceme to 17cm, densely many-fld; peduncle very short, to 3cm; fls small, 2–3mm diam.; sep. and pet. ovate-triangular, pet. slightly shorter than sep.; lip tridentate at apex; spur filiform, of similar length to lip. Comoros Is.

M.hariotiana (Kränzl.) Sengh.
Stem 4–5cm, often less. Lvs 4–7, 5–15×1.5–4cm, obovate-oblong. Racemes numerous, pendent, sometimes 2–3 arising together; peduncle 1–4cm; rachis 10–20cm, densely many-

fld; fls red-brown; pedicel and ovary 2mm; sep. and pet. 1–2mm, ovate, obtuse; lip entire, subcordate at base, similar to tepals but slightly wider; spur 2mm, apex swollen. Comoros Is.

M.hildebrandtii (Rchb. f.) Sengh. (*Angraecum hildebrandtii* Rchb. f.).
Stem short; roots slender. Lvs ligulate, unequally and obtusely bilobed at apex. Raceme laxly many-fld; fls small, yellow-orange; sep. and pet. 2–3mm, ligulate, apex rounded; lip 2–3mm, oblong, acute; spur 2–3mm, filiform but swollen at apex. Comoros Is.

Microtis R. Br. (From Gk *mikros*, small, and *ous* ear.) Some 12 species of herbaceous terrestrials. Leaf solitary, elongate. Fls in dense spike; dorsal sepal incurved, erect, lateral sepals oblong or lanceolate; petals narrower than sepals, spreading, incurved; lip sessile, oblong, orbicular or ovate, disc with 2 basal calli, rarely 1 at apex. E Asia, Australia, New Zealand.

CULTIVATION   See Introduction: Hardy Orchids.

M.unifolia (Forst. f.) Rchb. f.
To 50cm. Lf rounded, elongate. Fls golden to pale green; dorsal sep. to 2mm, forming a hood, lateral sep. shorter, oblong, decurved or deflexed; pet. oblong, partly obscured by dorsal sep.; lip green, edged pale yellow, crenate, obtuse, calli 2, dark green. Late autumn–winter.

Miltonia Lindl. (For Lord Fitzwilliam Milton (1786–1857), landowner and orchidologist.) Some 20 species of epiphytes allied to *Odontoglossum*. Rhizome long and creeping or short. Pseudobulbs with 1 or 2 apical leaves, enveloped below by one to several pairs of distichous, often foliaceous sheaths. Leaves linear to elliptic-lanceolate or oblong, subcoriaceous, thin, glabrous, pale to dark green, sometimes fluorescent; petioles short or elongate. Inflorescence axillary, a raceme or rarely a panicle, erect or arching, loosely 1 to many-flowered; flowers small to large, showy, widely spreading; sepals subequal, free or lateral sepals shortly connate at base; petals similar to sepals or often wider; lip broadly spreading from column base, simple or pandurate, base sessile or shortly clawed; disc inconspicuous or lamellate at base; column short, footless, bi-alate or bi-auriculate at apex, bilobed or truncate; anther terminal, opercular, incumbent; pollinia 2, ovoid, waxy. Brazil, one species in Peru.

CULTIVATION   As for *Odontoglossum* .

M.candida Lindl.
Resembles *M.clowesii* except sep. and pet. oblong-obtuse; lip shorter than other seg., clasping column at base. Autumn. Brazil. Sometimes treated as *Anneliesia candida* (Lindl.) Brieger & Lueckel since 1983.

M.clowesii Lindl.
Allied to *M.candida* and *M.cuneata*. Pseudobulbs to 10cm, ovate-oblong, compressed. Lvs to 45×2.5cm, pale green, linear-ligulate, acute. Infl. a raceme, to 45cm, several-fld; fls to 8cm diam.; tepals yellow, heavily blotched and barred chestnut-brown; sep. to 4×1cm, lanceolate, acuminate, slightly undulate; pet. to 3.5×1cm, similar to sep.; lip white at tip, deep purple at base, to 4×2cm, flat, subpandurate, caudate; callus white or yellow with 5–7 keels of unequal length. Autumn. Brazil.

M.cuneata Lindl.
Similar to *M.clowesii*. Lvs dark green. Tepals chocolate-brown tipped and barred yellow-green; lip obovate, slightly undulate, white-cream; callus basal, 2-keeled, spotted rose-purple. Winter–spring. Brazil.

M.endresii (Rchb. f.) Nichols. See *Miltoniopsis warscewiczii*.

M.flavescens Lindl.
Rhiz. creeping. Pseudobulbs to 12×2.5cm, ovate-oblong, compressed. Lvs to 35×1.5cm, acute, apiculate, pale green. Infl. a raceme, to 10-fld; peduncle with distichous, pale brown sheaths; bracts to 6.5cm, straw-coloured, glume-like; fls fragrant, to 7.5cm diam., straw-yellow; tepals to 50×5mm, linear-oblong to linear-lanceolate, acute; lip to 2.5cm, yellow, spotted blood-red, ovate-oblong, acute, undulate, base pubesc., transversed by 4–6 radiating lines. Summer–autumn. Brazil.

M.moreliana Warn. See *M.spectabilis* var. *moreliana*.

M.phalaenopsis (Lind. & Rchb. f.) Nichols. See *Miltoniopsis phalaenopsis*.

M.regnellii Rchb. f.
Pseudobulbs to 9×1cm, ovate-oblong, compressed, amethyst, pale yellow-green. Lvs to 30×1.5cm, linear-ligulate, acute, bright green. Infl. a raceme, to 40cm, 3–5-fld; fls to 7.5cm diam.; tepals cream suffused rose to lilac or pale amethyst; sep. to 3×1cm, oblong-lanceolate, recurved at apex; pet. wider than sep. elliptic-oblong; lip to 3.5×3.5cm, pale rose streaked lilac or amethyst, margins white, rotund, obscurely trilobed; callus of several radiating yellow lines. Early autumn. Darker 'purple-blue' variants are sometimes described as 'Purpurea'.

M.roezlii (Rchb. f.) Nichols. See *Miltoniopsis roezlii*.

M.russelliana Lindl.
Pseudobulbs ovate-oblong, to 7.5cm, laterally compressed, clustered. Lvs to 25×2.5cm, linear-oblong to linear-lanceolate. Infl. a raceme, to 30cm, erect, several-fld; fls to 5cm diam.; tepals to 3cm, ovate-oblong, red-brown, margins green-yellow; lip oblong, concave, rose-lilac, apex white or pale yellow; disc purple, with 3 raised ridges. Winter–spring. Brazil.

M.schroederiana (Rchb. f.) Veitch.
Pseudobulbs to 5cm, ovoid-oblong. Lvs to 20cm, linear-oblong, acute. Infl. a raceme, erect, to 50cm, several-fld; fls fragrant, to 6cm diam.; tepals chestnut brown, marked and tipped pale yellow; sep. to 30×5mm, linear-lanceolate, acute, margins revolute; pet. similar to sep., to 25×5mm, inclined on either side of dorsal sep.; lip rose-purple at base, white above to 2.5×1.5cm, subpandurate, slightly convex; callus of 3 protuberances; column white, yellow dorsally, wings narrow. C America. Often treated as *Miltonioides confusa* (Garay) Brieger & Lueckel since 1983.

M.spectabilis Lindl.
Rhiz. stout, creeping. Pseudobulbs to 7×2.5cm, spaced at short intervals, strongly compressed, pale green-yellow, ovate-oblong. Lvs to 13×2cm, linear-ligulate, thin, apex rounded, pale yellow-green. Infl. to 25cm, erect, enclosed by imbricate, flattened sheaths; fls solitary, flat, to 10cm diam.; sep. to 4×1.5cm, white, often tinged rose at base, lanceolate-oblong; pet. similar to sep. with white patch at base, to 3.5×1.5cm; lip rose-violet, margins white or pale rose, to 5×4.5cm, obovate-orbicular; callus yellow with pink axial lines, 3-keeled, column white, pink-violet at apex; anther white; pollinia yellow. Autumn. Brazil. var. **bicolor** hort. Fls larger than species type; lip with large blotch of violet on upper half. var. **moreliana** (Warn.) Henfr. (*M.moreliana* Warn.). Fls deep plum-purple; lip streaked and shaded rose, deeply veined. This form more usually encountered in cultivation.

M.superba Schltr. See *Miltoniopsis warscewiczii*.
M.vexillaria (Rchb. f.) Nichols. See *Miltoniopsis vexillaria*.
M.warscewiczii Rchb. f. See *Oncidium fuscatum*.

M.grexes and cultivars (see also under × *Miltonidium*, *Miltoniopsis* and × *Odontonia*).
M.Anne Warne: yellow-green lvs and pseudobulbs; sep. and pet. shiny maroon red, raspberry red lip with darker veins; warm growing.
M.Bluntii: lvs and pseudobulbs yellow-green; fls lilac pink with a darker lip.

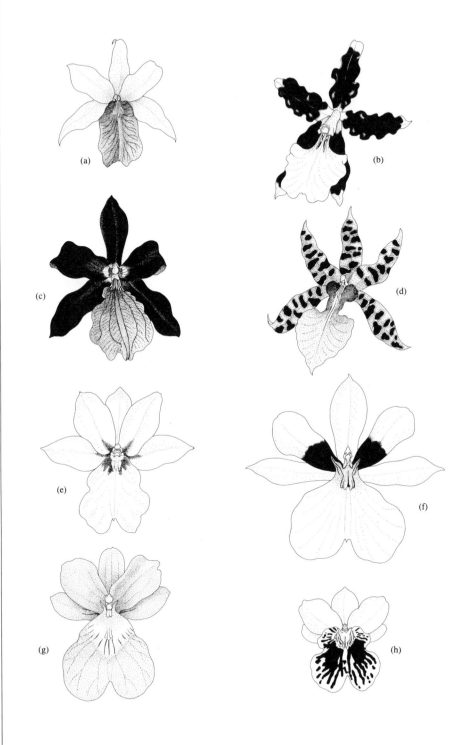

Miltonia and Miltoniopsis   (a) *Miltonia regnellii*   (b) *Miltonia cuneata*   (c) *Miltonia spectabilis* var. *moreliana*
(d) *Miltonia clowesii*   (e) *Miltoniopsis warscewiczii*   (f) *Miltoniopsis roezlii*   (g) *Miltoniopsis vexillaria*
(h) *Miltoniopsis phalaenopsis*

× **Miltonidium** (*Miltonia* × *Oncidium*). Intergeneric hybrids most of which will tolerate intermediate conditions. Plants consist of a group of compressed pseudobulbs growing from a basal rhizome, each with one or two leaves at its apex and two or more leaf-like sheaths arising at its base. Inflorescences arise in the axils of these sheaths and may be simple or branched. Flowers very varied in shape and often conspicuously marked in a variety of colours.

× *M.*Richard Peterson: erect branching sprays of many medium size fls; sep. and pet. yellow heavily dotted with brown, lip large, clear bright yellow with some brown spots around the crest.

Miltoniopsis Godef.-Leb. (*Miltonia* and Gk *opsis*, resemblance). PANSY ORCHID. 5 species of epiphytes or lithophytes closely allied to *Miltonia*. Rhizome short. Pseudobulbs clustered, unifoliate, subtended basally by many distichous, imbricate, foliaceous sheaths. Leaves narrowly linear to elliptic-lanceolate. Inflorescence a raceme, axillary, erect to arcuate, 1- to few-flowered; flowers large, showy, flattened; tepals spreading; petals reflexed near middle; lip large, flattened, basally auriculate, joined to column base by central keel; column short with dorsal keel, wingless, footless; anther incumbent, subglobose, pollinia 2, obpyriform; stigma orbicular to subquadrate; rostellum bifid, broadly triangular. Costa Rica, Panama, Venezuela, Ecuador, Colombia.

CULTIVATION See *Odontoglossum*.

M.phalaenopsis (Lind. & Rchb. f.) Garay & Dunsterv (*Miltonia phalaenopsis* (Lind. & Rchb. f.) Nichols.).
Pseudobulbs to 3.5cm, ovoid, strongly compressed, pale green-grey. Lvs to 22×0.5cm, pale green or glaucous, linear, acuminate. Racemes shorter than lvs, slender, 3–5-fld; fls to 6.5cm diam.; tepals pure white; sep. to 2×1cm, elliptic-oblong, acute; pet. wider than sep., elliptic, obtuse; lip to 2.5×3cm, white blotched and streaked purple-crimson or pale purple, 4-lobed, lateral lobes rounded, midlobe emarginate, flabellate; callus of 3 small, blunt teeth with yellow spot on either side. Late spring. Colombia.

M.roezlii (Rchb. f.) Godef.-Leb. (*Miltonia roezlii* (Rchb. f.) Nichols.).
Pseudobulbs to 6.5cm, ovoid-oblong, compressed. Lvs to 30×1.5cm, pale green with dark green longitudinal lines below, linear, acute. Racemes to 30cm, slender, 2–5-fld; fls to 10cm diam.; sep. to 5×2cm, white, ovate-oblong, acuminate; pet. similar, to 5×2.5cm, white blotched deep wine-purple at base; lip to 5×5.5cm, white, orange-yellow at base, widely obcordate, sinus apiculate, either side of base with corniculate auricle, 3 raised ridges on disc with 2 small dorsal teeth. Colombia.

M.vexillaria (Rchb. f.) Godef.-Leb. (*Miltonia vexillaria* (Rchb. f.) Nichols.).
To 30cm. Pseudobulbs to 6×2cm, oblong-ellipsoid, strongly compressed, grey-green. Lvs to 25×2.5cm, linear-oblong to linear-lanceolate, acute, pale green. Racemes to 30cm, lateral from base of pseudobulb, loosely 4–6-fld; fls large, to 10cm diam.; tepals rose-pink or white flushed rose-pink; sep. to 3×1.5cm, obovate-oblong, recurved above; pet. similar to sep., often slightly wider, margins white; lip much larger than sep., white or pale rose, deep rose on disc, suborbicular or reniform, with deep, triangular apical sinus, biauriculate at base; callus yellow, small, tridentate, bilobed at base; column short, wingless. Colombia, Ecuador.

M.warscewiczii (Rchb. f.) Garay & Dunsterv. (*Odontoglossum warscewiczii* Rchb. f.; *Miltonia endresii* (Rchb. f.) Nichols.; *Miltonia superba* Schltr.).
Pseudobulbs to 6cm, ovate-oblong, grey-green, compressed, distant on rhiz. Lvs to 30cm, linear-oblong or linear-lanceolate, acute, pale green. Racemes to 30cm, loosely 3–6-fld; fls to 7cm diam., cream-white, each seg. with a rose-purple blotch at base; sep. and pet. to 3×1.5cm, ovate-elliptic, acute; lip to 3.5×3.5cm, widely pandurate, dilated, with 2 small, rounded basal lobes, midlobe emarginate; callus yellow, with 3 short pubesc. ridges; column wings pale rose, narrow. Winter. Costa Rica.

*M.*grexes and cultivars (see also under *Miltonia*, × *Miltonidium* and × *Odontonia*).
*M.*Alexandre Dumas: pale green lvs; fls magnificent clear yellow with red-brick centre.
*M.*Anjou 'St Patrick': pale green lvs; fls deep crimson with some white stripes spreading from the centre.
*M.*Bleuana: one of the early primary hybrids; fls white, deep pink spots at the base of the pet. and orange mask on the lip.
*M.*Brutips: very floriferous grex; fls dark red with white border to all parts, mask on the lip darker red and bordered in white.
*M.*Charlesworthii 'Raphael': an early primary hybrid; fls white with deep spots at the base of the pet.; lip with a dark red mask; many other clones in pale colours but with the spots at the base of the pet.
*M.*Celle 'Wasserfal': pale green lvs; fls deep red-purple, lip streaked with lines and dots in white giving a waterfall-effect.
*M.*Derek Strauss: pale green lvs; fls very large, pastel shades including yellows and pinks; several awarded clones.
*M.*Edwige Sabourin 'Neige': pale green lvs; pure white fls, very large and prolific.
*M.*Emotion: pale green lvs; there are many clones of white, pink, lavender and various shades of pink-orange fls; 'Monique' has very large fls and 'Redbreast' is white with a brick red mask.
*M.*Eros 'Kensington': pale green lvs; rich red-purple fls with a white border.
*M.*Gascogne 'Vienne': pale green lvs; fls pink with a crimson mask outlined in white.
*M.*Gattonense: an old hybrid but still producing fine progeny; white fls with yellow mask on lip.
*M.*Hamburg: pale green lvs; fls with deep red sep. and pet. and a much paler lip, bordered in white and with a yellow and white mask.
*M.*Hannover 'Mont Millais': pale green lvs; fls bright red outlined in white, with yellow mask.
*M.*Hyeana: an early hybrid with well-shaped fls which are white with yellow mask.
*M.*Jean Sabourin 'Vulcain': pale green lvs; prolific bloomer with many deep burgundy-red fls with brown mask.
*M.*Jersey: pale green lvs; brilliant red fls.
*M.*Lambton Castle 'Cooksbridge': shapely fls in deep raspberry red, the small orange-red mask outlined in white.
*M.*Lyceana 'Stamperland': pale green lvs; fls prolific, white with large purple spots at base of the pet., yellow mask on lip.

*M.*Piccadilly 'Micheline': pale green lvs; fls deep rich red with mask outlined in white.

*M.*Robert Strauss Ardingly: white or creamy yellow fls with small red spots at the base of the pet. and orange-brown mask on the lip.

*M.*Saint Helier 'Trinity': lvs pale green; fls raspberry red with a very dark mask on the lip outlined in white.

*M.*Seine Diamant 'Medellin': pale green lvs; pure white fls with a faint touch of pink at the centre.

*M.*Storm 'La Tuilerie': pale green lvs; rich red fls with a yellow mask outlined in white.

*M.*Violet 'Tears': large fls with raspberry pink sep. and pet., lip white with pink border and large red mask which continues with spots and streaks across the lip.

× **Mokara** (*Arachnis* × *Ascocentrum* × *Vanda*). The introduction of *Ascocentrum* features to the *Aranda* crosses has produced a range of more compact Scorpion orchids of brilliant colours which are very popular as cut flowers in the Far East. Plants compact, upright, with long stems bearing alternate leaves in two rows. Inflorescences axillary, upright, with many brightly coloured flowers; sepals and petals fuller than the *Aranda* parents, lip small.

× *M.Khaw Phiak Suan:* dense infl. of many fls, bright yellow with few orange spots near the base, lip orange.

× M.Mak Chin On: tall plants with many upright spikes; fls intense imperial purple or cerise pink, very fine; many awarded clones.

× M.Panni: upright spikes of closely arrange fls; fls yellow with dense covering of red spots, lip brick-red.

× M.Walter Oumae: fls white, pink-mauve at the tips of the sep. and pet., covered with fine mauve spots, lip pink-mauve.

Mormodes Lindl. (From the Gk *mormo*, a hideous monster, and *-oides*, resembling, referring to the grotesque appearance of the flowers.) Some 70 species of epiphytes allied to *Catasetum*. Rhizome short. Pseudobulbs fleshy, cylindrical to fusiform, enveloped at base by several overlapping sheaths. Leaves distichous, sheathing base of pseudobulb and apical, plicate, elongate, articulated, usually thin-textured, persisting for one season. Inflorescence a lateral raceme, from nodes of pseudobulbs, erect to arching, loosely few to many-flowered; flowers showy, fleshy, often spreading, bisexual or unisexual; sepals and petals similar, free, spreading or reflexed, often narrow, lateral sepals oblique; lip very fleshy, adnate to column base, often reflexed, glabrous or pubesc., simple to 3-lobed; column stout, erect, obliquely twisted, wingless, footless, anther terminal, operculate, incumbent; pollinia 2 or 4, waxy, ovoid-oblong. C & S America.

CULTIVATION   See *Catasetum*.

M.aromaticum Lindl.
Pseudobulbs to 15×3cm, fusiform, compressed. Lvs to 60×6cm, lanceolate to linear-lanceolate, distinctly 3-nerved. Infl. to 32cm, ascending, many-fld; peduncle terete, to 6mm diam.; fls to 4cm diam., green-brown to purple-brown spotted dark purple, spicily fragrant; sep. to 32×15mm, fleshy, ovate-elliptic, acute; pet. to 16×18mm, darker than sep., elliptic-ovate, acute, finely dentate; lip to 25mm, fleshy, lateral lobes apiculate, midlobe triangular, acuminate, long-apiculate; column to 16mm. Mexico, El Salvador, Honduras.

M.atropurpureum Hook. See *M.hookeri*.

M.buccinator Lindl. (*Catasetum buccinator* (Lindl.) Lindl. ex Stein; *M.vernixium* Rchb. f.).
Pseudobulbs to 20×4cm, oblong-ellipsoid to ovoid, clustered, slightly compressed. Lvs to 40×6cm, oblong to narrowly lanceolate, acuminate. Infl. to 50cm, erect to arching, few to many-fld; fls to 6.5cm diam., the colour widely variable – green flushed pink with an ivory lip, bright lime green to pale yellow to deep wine red (*M.vernixium*), the lip lemon yellow, wholly deep yellow-orange (var. *aurantiacum* Rolfe), maroon with a somewhat paler lip, bronze with a rose-pink lip or wholly white; sep. to 3×1.5cm, linear to oblong-lanceolate, acute to acuminate, reflexed; pet. subequal to sep., obliquely linear to oblong-lanceolate, acute, slightly reflexed; lip to 3×3cm, strongly curved over column, slender-clawed, obovate or ovate-elliptic, apiculate, reflexed, apex truncate; column to 18mm, semiterete. Mostly late winter. Mexico, Guatemala, Panama, Colombia, Venezuela, Guyana.

M.colossus Rchb. f. (*M.macranthum* Lindl. & Paxt.; *M.wendlandii* Rchb. f.).
Pseudobulbs to 30×4.5cm, subcylindrical. Lvs to 30cm, ovate-elliptic. Infl. to 60cm, arcuate, densely many-fld; fls to 12cm diam., long-lived, fragrant, usually spreading, olive green to yellow tinted rose at base, the lip bronze to bright yellow with a few red spots at base; sep. to 50×8mm, linear-lanceolate, acuminate; pet. to 45×10mm, lanceolate, acuminate; lip to 5×2.5cm, short-clawed, simple, ovate-rhombic to ovate-elliptic, acute or acuminate, lateral margins strongly recurved; column to 17mm. Spring. Costa Rica, Panama.

M.histrio Lind. & Rchb. f. See *M.warscewiczii*.

M.hookeri Lem. (*M.atropurpureum* Hook.).
Pseudobulbs to 10cm, cylindrical to fusiform. Lvs linear-lanceolate, acuminate. Infl. short, erect, few-fld; fls to 4cm diam., fragrant, purple-red with fine purple spots (*M.atropurpureum*) to deep red-brown; sep. to 20×6mm, lanceolate, acuminate, strongly reflexed; pet. similar to sep. but somewhat shorter; lip to 16×16mm, obovate, truncate, apiculate, obscurely 3-lobed, lateral lobes strongly reflexed, pubesc. Winter. Costa Rica, Panama.

M.igneum Lindl. & Paxt.
Pseudobulbs to 35×5cm, cylindrical. Lvs lanceolate, acuminate, prominently veined. Infl. to 60cm, solitary or several produced in succession, arching, few to many-fld; fls to 5cm diam., fragrant, long-lived, variable in colour – yellow, olive-green or tan to red, often spotted red-brown, the lip white, yellow, olive, tan or brick red sometimes; sep. to 28×7mm, lanceolate, acuminate, sparsely spotted red, reflexed; pet. to 25×8mm, elliptic-lanceolate, acute, reflexed; lip very fleshy, clawed, subrotund, shortly apiculate, lateral margins reflexed. Spring. Costa Rica, Panama, Colombia.

M.macranthum Lindl. & Paxt. See *M.colossus*.

M.maculatum (Klotzsch) L.O. Williams (*Cyclosia maculata* Klotzsch; *M.pardinum*Batem.).
Pseudobulbs to 15cm, cylindrical to fusiform, clustered, several-lvd. Lvs to 38×3cm, linear-lanceolate, acuminate. Infl. to 40cm, arching to horizontal, densely many-fld; fld to 4cm, long-lived, fragrant, pale tawny-yellow spotted red-chocolate; sep. and pet. subsimilar, to 3.5×1cm, upcurved, ovate, acuminate; lip to 24×16mm, lateral lobes acuminate, midlobe large, acuminate; column to 18mm, semiterete. Autumn–early winter. Mexico. var. **unicolor** (Hook.) L.O. Williams (*M.pardinum* var. *unicolor* Hook.). Fls clear pale yellow.

M.pardinum Batem. See *M.maculatum*.
M.pardinum var. *unicolor* Hook. See *M.maculatum* var. *unicolor*.

M.rolfeanum Lind.
Pseudobulbs to 10cm, ovoid-fusiform to fusiform. Lvs to 38×5cm, lanceolate to elliptic-lanceolate, acuminate, pale green spotted dark green below. Infl. to 15cm, erect, loosely few-fld; fls to 10cm, pale green to golden-yellow marked red, the lip sometimes heavily stained dark red-brown within; sep. to 4.5cm, ovate to lanceolate, obtuse to acuminate; pet. subequal to sep., elliptic-oblong to obovate, obtuse or apiculate; lip subequal to sep., simple, obovate-oblong to elliptic, revolute, apex recurved, acute; column to 2.5cm, white tinged red, acuminate. Peru.

M.sinuatum Rchb.f. & Warscz.
Fls to 6cm diam.; tepals ovate-lanceolate, spreading, varying in colour from yellow to deep burgundy, overlaid in the finest forms with darker lines; lip distinctly 3-lobed, midlobe apiculate, lateral lobes rolled under, thus forming a funnel, sometimes hairy on upper (i.e. outer) surface, yellow to rose sometimes overlaid with dark purple-red lines. Guatemala, Costa Rica, Venezuela, Brazil, possibly Central America.

M.vernixium Rchb. f. See *M.buccinator*.

M.warscewiczii Klotzsch (*M.histrio* Lind. & Rchb. f.).
Pseudobulbs to 16×5cm, cylindrical to fusiform, slightly compressed. Lvs to 23×4.5cm, elliptic-lanceolate to linear-lanceolate, acuminate. Infl. to 50cm, slender, several-fld; fls polymorphic, very fleshy or thickened, particularly at apices, variable in colour – maroon, olive or yellow-green mottled maroon or striped and spotted rusty red, the lip maroon, green-white or yellow sparsely spotted purple or red-brown; sep. to 35×12mm, lanceolate to oblong-lanceolate, acute or acuminate, reflexed; pet. to 32×13mm, elliptic-lanceolate, acuminate, reflexed, undulate; lip to 32×13mm, pubesc., lateral lobes linear-oblanceolate, acute to subobtuse, twisted, midlobe linear to subtriangular, apex truncate or rounded, slightly reflexed; column to 27mm, arcuate, sulcate. Mexico, Guatemala, Honduras.

M.wendlandii Rchb. f. See *M.colossus*.

Mormolyca Fenzl. (From Gk *mormolyka*, hobgoblin, apparently referring to the bizarre profile of the flower and its sinister hue.) Some 6 species of epiphytes. Rhizome short, sometimes creeping. Pseudobulbs fleshy, subglobose to ellipsoid-cylindrical, apically unifoliate. Leaves large, coriaceous, erect, elliptic-oblong to ligulate, sessile or shortly-petiolate. Inflorescence basal, 1-flowered; peduncle slender; flowers fleshy; sepals similar, free, spreading, lateral sepals oblique; petals subsimilar to sepals but smaller; lip erect, 3-lobed, lateral lobes erect, small, midlobe large, ovate to subquadrate, decurved, disc callose; column arcuate, wings absent, footless; anther terminal, opercular, incumbent, pollinia 4, ovoid. C America, northern S America.

CULTIVATION   As for *Encyclia*.

M.gracilipes (Schltr.) Garay & Wirth.
Pseudobulbs to 3×1cm, ovoid-oblong to cylindrical, compressed. Lvs to 8×2cm, elliptic-oblong or ligulate, acute, sessile, light green, rugulose. Infl. to 23cm, usually exceeding lvs; sep. and pet. yellow-brown to orange-yellow or salmon pink; sep. to 34×13mm, lanceolate to ovate-lanceolate, apical margins involute, long-acuminate; pet. to 17×2mm, obliquely linear or linear-lanceolate, acute, base twisted; lip to 11×8mm, lime green to yellow-brown finely marked dark purple-brown, obovate or obovate-rhombic, abruptly acute, lateral lobes indented; column yellow, to 8mm, clavate, slender, arcuate. Venezuela, Colombia, Ecuador, Peru.

M.lineolata Fenzl. See *M.ringens*.

M.peruviana Schweinf.
Pseudobulbs to 2m, clustered, ellipsoid. Lvs to 14×1cm, ligulate or narrowly oblong, subacute, sessile. Infl. to 12cm, several, slender, erect; fls to 3cm diam., yellow; sep. to 20×5mm, oblong-lanceolate, mucronate; pet. to 19×4mm, linear-oblong, acute or apiculate; lip to 15×7mm, parallel to column, ovate-subquadrate, lateral lobes porrect, triangular-lanceolate, acuminate, midlobe subquadrate, truncate or rounded, callus ovate, concave, porrect, trilobulate; column to 13mm, slender, clavate. Peru.

M.ringens (Lindl.) Schltr. (*Trigonidium ringens* Lindl.; *M.lineolata* Fenzl).
Rhiz. slender, creeping. Pseudobulbs to 4×3cm, ellipsoid to subspherical, compressed. Lvs to 35×4cm, narrowly lanceolate to ligulate, acute to obtuse. Infl. to 35cm, usually equalling lvs; fls fleshy, yellow to lavender; sep. to 19×8mm, striped maroon-purple, elliptic-oblong, obtuse, lateral sep. forward-curving; pet. to 15×6mm, erect, elliptic-oblong, obtuse or rounded, convex; lip to 10×5mm, oblong-elliptic to ovate-elliptic, pilose, ciliolate, lavender to maroon edged yellow, 3-lobed, lateral lobes minute, acute to obtuse, midlobe suborbicular, decurved; callus fleshy, tridentate; column to 10mm, pilose. Mexico to Costa Rica.

Mystacidium Lindl. (From Gk *mystax*, moustache.) About 11 species of small monopodial epiphytes. Stem short; roots numerous. Leaves distichous, usually ligulate. Inflorescences racemose, axillary or arising from stem below leaves, few to several-flowered; flowers white, green or yellow-green; sepals and petals free, similar; lip entire or lobed at or near the base, spurred; column short and stout; rostellum trilobed; pollinia, stipites and viscidia 2. Tropical & S Africa.

CULTIVATION As for *Angraecum*.

M.brayboniae Summerh.
Stem very short; roots 3–4mm diam., grey-green with white streaks. Lvs 3–4, 2–5×1cm, elliptic, slightly bilobed at apex. Racemes 1–2, arising below lvs, 2.5–3.5cm, 5–8-fld; fls white, about 2cm diam., slightly cup-shaped; sep. and pet. 7–8×2mm, lanceolate, acute; lip trilobed toward base, 8mm long, 4mm wide across lobes, midlobe 3×2mm, ovate, obtuse; spur 19–21mm, tapering from a wide mouth. S Africa (E Transvaal).

M.capense (L. f.) Schltr. (*Angraecum capense* (L. f.) Lindl.; *M.filicorne* Lindl.).
Stem short; roots 3–5mm diam., grey-green with white streaks. Lvs 4–10, 8.5–13×1–1.5cm, ligulate, dark green, unequally and obtusely bilobed at apex. Racemes axillary or arising below lvs, 6–12-fld; fls white, 1.5–2.5cm diam.; sep. 8–12×2–3mm, lanceolate, acute; pet. slightly shorter and narrower; lip trilobed at base, 8–12×3mm, lanceolate, acute; spur 4–6cm, straight, slender, tapering. S Africa, Swaziland.

M.filicorne Lindl. See *M.capense*.

M.millari Bol.
Stem short; roots numerous, 4mm diam., grey with white streaks. Lvs 2–6, to 12×1.5cm, ligulate, unequally bilobed at apex, leathery, dark green with prominent reticulate venation, glabrous but with a rather velvety appearance particularly when young. Racemes pendent, arising below lvs, 2–5cm, fairly densely 7–10-fld, the fls somewhat drooping; fls white

with green anther-cap; 8–12mm diam.; pedicel and ovary 9–11mm; dorsal sep. 6–7×3mm, obovate, lateral sep. slightly longer, oblanceolate; pet. like dorsal sep.; lip 5–6mm, oblong-obovate, recurved at tip; spur 20mm, funnel-shaped in basal quarter, narrowing fairly abruptly to become slender. S Africa (Natal, Eastern Cape).

M.tanganyikense Summerh.
Dwarf; stem very short; roots 1mm diam. Lvs 3–4, to 5×1cm, oblanceolate, unequally and obtusely bilobed at apex, dark green with raised reticulate venation. Racemes arising at base of stem, to 6cm, laxly or densely several-fld; fls pale green or creamy white; pedicel and ovary 6–7mm; sep. and pet. spreading, lanceolate, acute; dorsal sep. 4×1mm, lateral sep. slightly longer and oblique; pet. slightly shorter; lip entire, similar to pet.; spur 10–20mm, tapering, slender, straight or slightly incurved. Tanzania, Malawi, Zambia, Zimbabwe.

M.venosum Harv. ex Rolfe.
Stem very short; roots numerous, 4–5mm diam., grey-green, streaked white. Lvs 3–4, to 6×1cm, ligulate, unequally bilobed at apex, sometimes with darker reticulate venation, usually deciduous in resting season. Racemes arising among roots at base of stem, 5–8.5cm, 4–7-fld; fls white, 17–20mm diam; sep. and pet. lanceolate, acuminate, recurved at tips; sep. 7–9×2–3mm; pet. 7×2mm; lip 9×2mm, lanceolate, with 2 small, rounded lobes at base; spur 3–4.5cm, slender, tapering. S Africa, Swaziland.

Nageliella L.O. Williams. (For Otto Nagel, who collected species in Mexico.) 2 species, epiphytes or terrestrials. Rhizome short-creeping. Pseudobulbs short, semiterete, clavate, striate, apex thickened, unifoliate. Leaves apical, semi-erect, fleshy, thickly coriaceous, subsessile, ovate-lanceolate to oblong-lanceolate, often flushed red-purple, mottled or spotted white and rugulose, tongue-like in appearance, sometimes with midrib obscurely impressed above and keeled below. Inflorescence terminal, a nodding to semi-erect raceme, panicle or subumbellate, few to many-flowered; branches short; flowers small, pink, magenta or red; sepals erect, connivent, dorsal sepal free, lateral sepals adnate to column foot forming a mentum; petals linear to lanceolate; lip adnate to column, basally swollen or saccate, simple to obscurely 3-lobed; column slender, arcuate, apex biauriculate, anther operculate, incumbent, pollinia 4, waxy. C America.

CULTIVATION   Small epiphytes for the cool and intermediate house, grown for their slender stems of magenta flowers and (*N.purpurea*) the attractively patterned, fleshy foliage. Pot in half pots or pans of medium- to fine-grade bark mix; position in light shade or, for better leaf colour, full sunlight; water freely throughout the growing season, very sparingly at cooler times of the year.

N.angustifolia (Booth ex Lindl.) Ames & Correll (*Hartwegia purpurea* var. *angustifolia* Booth ex Lindl.).
Pseudobulbs to 7cm, terete. Lvs to 10×2cm, erect, linear-lanceolate to oblong-lanceolate, acute to obtuse, marked dark red-brown. Infl. to 30cm; peduncle terete, filiform; fls produced in succession, nodding, bright magenta; dorsal sep. to 7×3mm, elliptic-oblong, subacute, lateral sep. obliquely ovate-elliptic, rounded to acute; pet. to 7×2mm, linear to linear-lanceolate, obtuse, finely denticulate; lip to 9mm, simple, basal portion geniculate, apical portion suborbicular, obscurely 3-lobed, deeply concave, retuse, crenate; column deep pink, slender. Guatemala.

N.purpurea (Lindl.) L.O. Williams (*Hartwegia purpurea* Lindl.).
Pseudobulbs slender, erect, to 8cm, strongly striate. Lvs to 12×3cm, lanceolate to ovate-lanceolate, often spotted brown-purple, subacuminate. Infl. to 50cm, erect; peduncle semiterete to compressed; fls red-purple; dorsal sep. to 9×4mm, elliptic, acute, lateral sep. to 10×2mm, ovate to oblong-lanceolate, acute to obtuse; pet. subequal to lateral sep., elliptic-lanceolate, acute to obtuse, minutely fimbriate; lip simple, to 11mm, apical portion deflexed, ovate-suborbicular, obtuse to acute, slightly concave, basal portion geniculate; column to 7mm, subterete, slender. Mexico, Guatemala, Honduras.

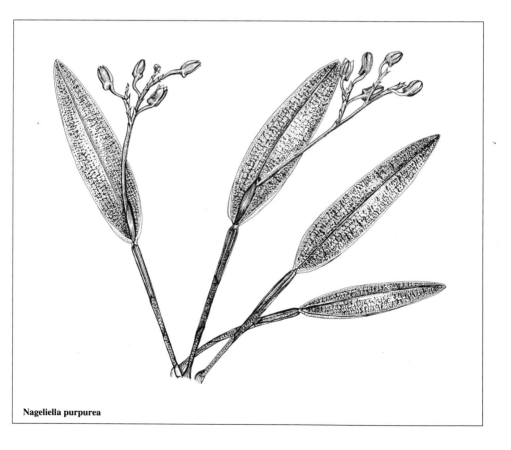

Nageliella purpurea

Nanodes Rchb. (From Gk *nanodes*, pygmy.) 3 species, diminutive epiphytes formerly included in *Epidendrum*. Stems tufted, cane-like, ascending to arching-pendulous, densely clothed in overlapping leaf sheaths. Leaves 2-ranked, near-opposite, glossy pale green, rather fleshy with conspicuous stem-encircling sheaths. Flowers solitary or paired, borne terminally, small, waxy, translucent with a simple lip. C & S America.

CULTIVATION As for *Epidendrum pseudepidendrum*.

N.discolor Lindl. (*Epidendrum discolor* (Lindl.) Benth.; *Epidendrum schlechterianum* Ames).
Stems 6.5–10cm, densely clustered, completely concealed by lf sheaths. Lvs 1.75–3×0.5–1cm, fleshy, recurved or spreading, elliptic to linear-oblong, obtuse, apiculate, dorsally carinate, light green. Fls to 1.5cm diam., usually paired, born terminally, translucent yellow-green or green-brown to pale pink-purple; dorsal sep. 1.2–1.8×0.3–0.4cm, lanceolate to oblanceolate, acute to acuminate, lateral sep. obliquely elliptic-lanceolate, acute or acuminate; pet. shorter than sep., narrowly elliptic to linear-lanceolate, acute, denticulate; lip 0.7–0.9×0.9–1.1cm, simple, reniform to ovate-suborbicular, apiculate, erose-ciliate, short-clawed; column to 6mm, slightly recurved. C & S America.

N.mathewsii Rolfe (*Neolehmannia porpax* (Rchb. f.) Garay & Dunsterville; *Epidendrum porpax* Rchb. f.).
Stems to 10cm. Lvs 1.5–2×0.7–0.9cm, fleshy, oblong, obtuse or retuse. Fls solitary, light purple-green; sep. 1–1.2×0.35–0.5cm, narrowly elliptic-lanceolate, acute; pet. 1–1.4×0.1cm, narrowly linear, obtuse; lip 0.75–1×1–1.8cm, fleshy, adnate to column, transversely oblong, decurved, callus fleshy, trilobulate. Mexico to Panama, Venezuela to Peru.

N.medusae Rchb. f. (*Epidendrum medusae* (Rchb. f.) Sieb).
Stems to 25cm, densely clustered, somewhat pendulous. Lvs 4–7×1.5–3cm, narrowly ovate-oblong, fleshy, apex bilobed, blue-green. Fls usually solitary, born terminally, to 8cm; sep. and pet. yellow-green tinged red-brown, 2.8–4.2×1–1.5cm, oblong or oblong-lanceolate, acute; lip 3–4.5×4–5.5cm, deep maroon, green at base, transversely oblong, emarginate, deeply lacerate-fimbriate; column to 13mm, fleshy. Ecuador.

Neobathiea Schltr. (For M. Henri Perrier de la Bâthie (1873–1958), a French botanist who worked mainly on Madagascan orchids.) 6 species of epiphytes. Stems usually short. Leaves ligulate, elliptic or oblanceolate. Raceme 1- to few-flowered; flowers white; sepals and petals free; lip trilobed, spurred, with the mouth of the spur immediately below the column, spur slender; column short, with 2 arms at the base tightly enclosing, and joined to, the sides of the mouth of the spur. Madagascar, Comoros Is.

CULTIVATION As for *Angraecum*.

N.filicornu Schltr.
To 6cm. Lvs 4–5, 4–5×1cm, narrowly elliptic. Flowers solitary, pure white; peduncle 2–2.5cm; pedicel and ovary 12mm; sep. 13×2.5mm, narrowly oblanceolate; pet. similar but slightly shorter and narrower; lip 20×10mm, trilobed at base, midlobe ovate-lanceolate, acute, lateral lobes subcordate; spur pendent, 14cm, becoming filiform from a funnel-shaped mouth; column 3.5mm, stout. Madagascar, Comoros Is.

N.perrieri (Schltr.) Schltr.
Small, almost stemless. Lvs 4–6, 3.5–7×1–2cm, oblong-spathulate, undulate. Fls 1–2, white; peduncle 6–12cm; pedicel and ovary 25mm; sep. 22mm, narrowly oblanceolate, acute; pet. similar but slightly smaller; lip trilobed at about halfway, 20mm×20mm, lateral lobes diverging, ovate, midlobe ovate, acute, twice as large as lateral lobes, the whole lip shaped like a spear-head; spur 7–10cm, filiform from a funnel-shaped mouth, curving forward, then pendent; column very short. Madagascar, Comoros Is.

Neobenthamia Rolfe. (From Gk *neos*, new, and for George Bentham (1800–1884), British botanist.) 1 species, a terrestrial or lithophyte. Roots fleshy. Stems clustered, branched, leafy, 90cm to 2m tall. Leaves linear-lanceolate, grass-like, distichous, to 28×2cm. Inflorescence terminal, racemose or paniculate, densely many-flowered; flowers white, the lip with a pubescent yellow centre edged with pink dots; sepals and petals spreading, similar, subequal, sepals 10–12mm, oblong-elliptic, petals 9–10mm, oblong-spathulate; lip entire, fleshy, 11×7mm, oblong-obovate, margin undulate; column short and thick, 2–3mm; anther-cap dull purple; pollinia in 2 pairs of 2. Tanzania.

CULTIVATION Intermediate to warm-growing orchids. Culture similar to that of *Sobralia*.

N.gracilis Rolfe.

Neocogniauxia Schltr. (From Gk *neos*, new, and for M.A. Cogniaux (1841–1916), Belgian botanist.) 2 species of epiphytes. Rhizome creeping. Secondary stems short, slender, terete, erect, enveloped by 1–3 tubular sheaths, apically unifoliate. Leaves coriaceous, erect or suberect, linear-oblong to linear-lanceolate. Inflorescence terminal, slender, surpassing leaves, erect to arching; fls solitary, showy, orange to scarlet; sepals and petals subequal, subsimilar, free, spreading; lip small, enveloping and parallel to column, simple to obscurely trilobed, often papillose; column short, subterete, 'arching, footless, clinandrium denticulate, pollinia 8, waxy, ovoid. Jamaica, Cuba, Haiti, Dominican Republic.

CULTIVATION   Epiphytes for bright airy positions in the cool house. Water and syringe very frequently; pot in a perfectly drained medium.

N.monophylla (Griseb.) Schltr. (*Trigonidium monophyllum* Griseb.; *Octadesmia monophylla* (Griseb.) Benth.; *Laelia monophylla* (Griseb.) Hook. f.).
Secondary stems to 9cm, enveloped by flecked sheaths. Lvs to 25×1cm, linear-oblong or linear-elliptic, obtuse, suberect. Infl. to 30cm, arching; bracts sheathing, spotted purple; fls to 5cm diam., showy, bright orange-scarlet; sep. to 22×8mm, elliptic-oblong or ovate-oblong, obtuse; pet. to 17×9mm, obovate-elliptic or elliptic-oblong, obtuse; lip to 9mm, ovate or obovate, apiculate, 3-lobed, midlobe cordate-semicircular, papillose, disc 3-ridged, with a sac-like growth on the central keel, papillose; column to 9mm, orange, auriculate, anth. purple. Autumn–winter. Jamaica.

Neofinetia Hu. (For Achille Finet (1862–1913), French botanist.) 1 species, a monopodial epiphyte, to 15cm. Stems short, branching basally, appearing tufted. Leaves to 10cm, alternate, in two ranks, basally overlapping and clothing stem, narrow-ligulate, falcate to recurved, tapering, fleshy, centrally grooved and folded above. Inflorescence axillary, a raceme, ascending; flowers to 10, white; sep. and pet. to 1cm spreading, linear-oblong to linear-lanceolate; lip to 10mm, obscurely 3-lobed, recurved, midlobe ligulate, lateral lobes erect, obtuse, spur very slender; column fleshy, winged. Japan, Korea.

CULTIVATION   Small and graceful epiphytes for humid, semi-shaded situations in the cool house. Pot in a fine bark mix and water throughout the year, allowing a slight drying between waterings.

N.falcata (Thunb.) Hu.
Variegated forms occur and are valued bonsai subjects.

Neogardneria Schltr. ex Garay. (From Gk *neos*, new and *Gardneria*, for George Gardner, an English plant collector.) Some 3 species of epiphytes. Pseudobulbs ovoid. Foliage lanceolate, plicate. Inflorescence lax; sepals and petals similar, free; lip subsessile, trilobed, midlobe narrow, abruptly deflexed, lateral lobes erect, callus fan-shaped, crested, irregularly furrowed. NE Tropical America.

CULTIVATION   Epiphytes for the intermediate house.

N.murrayana (Gardn.) Garay (*Zygopetalum murrayanum* Gardn.).
Pseudobulbs ovate, grooved to 7.5cm. Lvs lanceolate, membranous, acute, furrowed. Scapes shorter than lvs; fls pale yellow-green, lip white, lateral lobes streaked dark-purple; tepals ovate-lanceolate, acute, spreading, bases fused, subequal; lip trilobed, midlobe similar to lateral lobes, reflexed, lateral lobes oblong, erect, incurved, callus between lateral lobes crested, fleshy, recurved, furrowed. Brazil.

Neolauchea Kränzl. (From Gk *neos*, new, and for Herr Friedrich Wilhelm George Lauche (1827–1883), German dendrologist and gardener.) 1 species, an epiphyte. Rhizome elongate, creeping, branched. Pseudobulbs 1.8–2.5cm, borne at short intervals on rhizome, narrowly ovoid, enveloped by fibrous sheaths, 1-leaved at apex. Leaves 4–6cm, coriaceous, narrowly linear, subterete. Inflorescence to 5cm, terminal, slender, erect or arching, 1-flowered; flowers small, rose-red or lilac; dorsal sepal broadly ovate, apiculate, concave, lateral sepals shortly connate, adnate to column foot forming a sac-shaped mentum; petals larger than sepals, spreading, ovate-oblong; lip broadly ovate-oblong, concave, with 2 teeth near base; column short. S Brazil.

CULTIVATION   Epiphytes for the intermediate house.

N.pulchella Kränzl. (*Meiracyllium wettsteinii* Porsch).

Neomoorea Rolfe. (For F.W. Moore (1857–1950), orchid specialist and sometime Curator of Glasnevin Botanic Garden, Dublin.) 1 species, an epiphyte. Pseudobulbs ovoid, stout. Leaves 2, borne at apex of pseudobulbs, elliptic-lanceolate, plicate, acute or pungent. Inflorescence basal, erect or arched; flowers showy, waxy, fragrant; sepals free, spreading; petals similar, base narrower; lip deeply trilobed, mobile, attached to the column foot, midlobe lanceolate, concave, acuminate, basal crest shortly pedicellate, wings 2, lateral, spreading or erect, lateral lobes subreniform, spreading. Colombia, Panama.

CULTIVATION   A large and very showy orchid for lightly shaded, humid positions in the intermediate house. It demands a free-draining but fertile medium, copious water and feed when in growth and a short, dry rest once the pseudobulbs are mature – because of their size, the pseudobulbs may require two years to reach completion.

N.irrorata (Rolfe) Rolfe. See *N.wallisii.*

N.wallisii (Rchb. f.) Schltr. (*N.irrorata* (Rolfe) Rolfe; *Moorea irrorata* Rolfe).
Roots dimorphic: long, creeping and short, erect. Pseudobulbs ovoid, compressed, furrowed, 4–11×2.5–6cm. Lvs 45–75× 10–13cm. Infl. arched or erect, few- to 12-fld, 15–45cm; sep. and pet. red-brown to apricot, base white, lip pale yellow, banded and marked brown-purple, midlobe yellow, spotted red; sep. elliptic-lanceolate to elliptic-ovate, acute, concave, spreading, 2–2.8×1–1.8cm; pet. elliptic-obovate, acute; lip midlobe acuminate, callus crested.

Nephelaphyllum Bl. (From Gk *nephale*, cloud, and *phyllon*, leaf, referring to the hazy upper surface of the leaves.) Some 17 species of terrestrials. Rhizomes creeping, fleshy. Pseudobulbs 1-leaved, small, slender, or rudimentary. Leaves convolute, ovate-triangular to cordate, fleshy. Racemes erect; flowers non-resupinate; sepals and petals similar; lip trilobed or entire, interior ridged; spur short. Indonesia, Philippines, Hong Kong, India, China.

CULTIVATION   As for *Anoectochilus.*

N.pulchrum Bl.
Pseudobulbs subterete, dull purple, to 2.5cm, apex narrow. Lvs ovate to cordate, 6–10×4–6cm, thinly fleshy, glossy yellow-green above tinted bronze-pink with fine grey-green veins, strongly tinted purple-red beneath. Racemes dense, 3–5; fls fragrant; tepals pale green, exterior veined purple, lip white, base pale green and purple with yellow ridges; tepals sublinear, deflexed, to 1.5cm; lip elliptic, entire, ridges longitudinal, papillose; spur inflated, base constricted. Widespread, Malaysia to Indonesia.

Nervilia Comm. ex Gaudich. (From Lat. *nervus*, a vein, alluding to the prominently veined lvs of many species.) About 80 species of terrestrials arising from small, more or less globose tubers. Leaf broad, usually cordate, often pleated and lustrous, solitary, erect or prostrate, appearing after flowering. Inflorescence racemose, 1- to many-flowered; scape with 3–4 sheathing leaves, usually elongating after fertilization; flowers white, pink, dull purple, brown, green or yellow, sometimes fragrant; sepals and petals similar, lanceolate, spreading or projecting forwards; lip entire or trilobed, with or without a spur; column somewhat clavate; anther terminal; pollinia 2, granular. Arabia, mainland Africa, Madagascar, Mascarene Is., India, SE Asia to Japan, Pacific Is. and Australia.

CULTIVATION   Curious terrestrials for damp, shady positions in the warm house, valued for their pleated, heart-shaped leaves. Regime as for *Phaius* but with higher temperatures.

N.bicarinata (Bl.) Schltr. (*N.umbrosa* (Rchb. f.) Schltr.).
To 75cm; tubers globose, about 2.5cm diam. Lf lamina to 17×22cm, reniform, amplexicaule, cordate at base, dark green, pleated, on petiole 18–20cm long, sometimes just starting to appear at flowering time. Raceme laxly 4–12-fld, the fls pendent, thin-textured, green, lip creamy white, veined purple; sep. and pet. 20–30×4mm, ligulate-lanceolate, acute, projecting forwards; lip 28–30×20–24mm, obscurely triloved, with 2 fleshy ridges running from base to junction of lobes, midlobe ovate, acute, the apex recurved, lateral lobes erect; column 12–14mm, arched. Widespread in tropical Africa; Arabia.

N.kotschyi (Rchb. f.) Schltr.
10–28cm; tubers to 2cm diam., ovoid or ellipsoid, pubesc. Lf 3–12×4–13cm, prostrate or erect, thick-textured, broadly cordate or broadly ovate, acute, ribbed, the veins usually with a jagged keel on the upper surface. Raceme 2–7-fld, the fls horizontal or pendent, veined green-brown, lip white or pale yellow purple; sep. and pet. 14–20×2–3mm, linear-lanceolate,

acute, projecting forwards; lip 14–18×9–12mm, rather obscurely triloved at about half-way, lateral lobes triangular, acute, midlobe ovate, undulate, the front margin reflexed, pubesc. between 2 longitudinal, fleshy ridges; column arched, 7–9mm. Tropical Africa (widespread).

N.purpurata (Rchb. f. & Sonder) Schltr.
To 22cm. Lf erect, lamina to 10×4cm, ovate or elliptic, green above, purple beneath with prominent veins, borne on petiole to 15cm. Raceme 2–4-fld; fls horizontal or pendent, green or yellow-green, the lip veined with purple; sep. and pet. 18×22×4mm, linear-lanceolate, acute, projecting forwards; lip 18×13mm, obscurely triloved, pubesc. between 2 longitudinal fleshy ridges, midlobe triangular-ovate, obtuse, somewhat reflexed, lateral lobes erect, oblong; column 10mm, arched. Zaire, Zambia, Tanzania, Angola, S Africa.

N.umbrosa (Rchb. f.) Schltr. See *N.bicarinata*.

Nidema Britt. & Millsp. (Anagram of the related *Dinema*.) 2 species of epiphytes. Rhizome elongate, creeping, enveloped by papery bracts. Pseudobulbs fusiform to cylindrical, conspicuously stalked, apically unifoliate, usually widely spaced on rhizome. Leaves coriaceous, linear-ligulate to linear-lanceolate, articulated. Inflorescence a terminal raceme, few-flowered; flowers small; bracts conspicuous, acuminate, lanceolate; sepals free, subequal, usually linear to lanceolate; dorsal sepal erect, lateral sepals arched; petals subsimilar to sepals, oblique, smaller than sepals; lip articulated to column base, simple, acute or acuminate, sometimes papillose, disc with a grooved callus; column arching, with a short foot, wingless, anther terminal, operculate, incumbent, 4-celled, pollinia 4, waxy. Tropical America.

CULTIVATION   See *Epidendrum*.

N.boothii (Lindl.) Schltr. (*Maxillaria boothii* Lindl.; *Epidendrum boothii* (Lindl.) L.O. Williams).
Pseudobulbs to 6cm, cylindrical to narrowly ovoid, slightly compressed. Lvs to 25×1.5cm, linear-ligulate to narrowly lanceolate, acute or obtuse, lustrous bright green. Infl. to 15cm, loosely few-fld; fls white-green or ivory, fragrant; sep. to 20×4mm, linear-lanceolate to lanceolate, acute or acuminate, recurved; pet. to 15×4mm, elliptic-lanceolate to elliptic-ovate, acuminate, recurved; lip to 11×4mm, oblong-oblanceolate to linear-spathulate, subacute to rounded, serrulate, disc with 2 yellow, linear calli; column to 8mm. Mexico to Panama, W Indies, Northern S America.

N.ottonis (Rchb. f.) Britt. & Millsp. (*Epidendrum ottonis* Rchb. f.).
Pseudobulbs to 4cm, cylindrical to narrowly ellipsoid, slightly compressed. Lvs to 19×1cm, linear to linear-ligulate, acute or obtuse. Infl. to 11cm, erect, slender; fls white or cream, sometimes tinged yellow or green; sep. to 11×3mm, lanceolate or oblong-lanceolate, acuminate, concave; pet. to 7×2mm, lanceolate, elliptic-lanceolate or oblanceolate, acute or acuminate; lip to 7×2mm, fleshy, rigid, linear-oblong, apiculate, incurved, caniculate, disc 2-ridged; column to 4mm, pale cream or cream-green. W Indies, Panama, Colombia, Peru, Brazil, Nicaragua, Venezuela.

Nigritella Rich. (Diminutive of Lat. *nigritia*, blackness, referring to the flower colour.) 5 species, terrestrial herbs. Tubers 2, digitately lobed. Stems 5–30cm, angled, slender. Leaves linear to linear-lanceolate, channelled, minutely dentate, green. Spike 10–25cm, dense, conical becoming ovoid; flowers black-crimson, vanilla-scented; sepals and petals almost equal, lanceolate to triangular, spreading; lip subtriangular or ovate-lanceolate, entire, crenulate or triloved, spur short, saccate, obtuse. Summer. Scandinavia to Greece.

CULTIVATION   See Introduction: Hardy Orchids.

N.nigra (L.) Rchb. f. BLACK VANILLA ORCHID. Described above.

Notylia Lindl. (From Gk *notos*, back, and *tylos*, hump, referring to the recurved column apex.) Some 54 species of epiphytes with or without pseudobulbs. Rhizome short. Pseudobulbs small, compressed, clustered, basally sheathed by leaves, apically unifoliate. Leaves fleshy or coriaceous, distichous, imbricate or equitant. Inflorescence a lateral raceme or panicle, arching to pendent, few- to many-flowered; flowers small; sepals sub-similar, free or connate at base, narrow, erect or spreading; petals similar to sepals, smaller, oblique; lip sessile or clawed, entire or obscurely lobed, disc callose or carinate; column slender or stout, footless, wingless, erect, with a long erect rostellum, anther erect, oblong, pollinia 2, waxy, ovoid. Tropical C & S America.

CULTIVATION Grow in intermediate conditions in baskets or mounted on rafts; syringe and water throughout the year.

N.albida Klotzsch. See *N.barkeri*.

N.barkeri Lindl. (*N.bipartita* Rchb. f.; *N.albida* Klotzsch; *N.tridachne* Lindl. & Paxt.).
Pseudobulbs to 3×1cm, oblong to ellipsoid, compressed. Lvs to 20×4cm, coriaceous, broadly elliptic to ligulate, subacute to obtuse, pale green, apex obliquely tridenticulate. Raceme to 30cm, arching to pendent, many-fld; fls white to green-white, sometimes spotted yellow, faintly scented; sep. to 7×3mm, linear-lanceolate to elliptic-lanceolate, subacute to obtuse, concave, slightly inflexed, lateral sep. often connate forming a cleft synsepalum; pet. slightly shorter, narrower than sep.; lip to 6×2mm, short-clawed, ovate to narrowly triangular, subobtuse to acuminate, disc usually with a carinate callus; column to 3mm. Mexico to Panama.

N.bicolor Lindl.
Pseudobulbs to 10×5mm, ovoid, compressed. Lvs to 5×1cm, linear-lanceolate to elliptic-lanceolate, fleshy, acuminate. Raceme to 10cm, few- to many-fld; peduncle very slender, erect to pendent; sep. to 15×2mm, white, linear-lanceolate, spreading, lateral sep. connate at base, falcate; pet. to 13×2mm, white to purple-lavender spotted dull purple, obliquely lanceolate; lip to 9×2mm, white to purple-lavender, short-clawed, basal portion linear, apical portion dilated, erose, spreading, disc with a grooved callus, spotted dark purple; column to 5mm, erect, glabrous, anth. large. Summer. Mexico, Guatemala, Costa Rica.

N.bipartita Rchb. f. See *N.barkeri*.

N.bungerothii Rchb. f.
Pseudobulbs to 3×1cm, oblong, rugose. Lvs to 20×7cm, oblong, acute to obtuse, dark to olive green. Raceme to 45cm, pendent, densely many-fld; fls pale green to green-yellow; dorsal sep. to 8×2mm, lanceolate, curved, obtuse, lateral sep. to 7×3mm, connate, oblique, similar to dorsal sep.; pet. to 7×2mm, white marked yellow, linear-lanceolate, subacute; lip 6×2mm, white, short-clawed, ovate, base rounded or truncate, disc carinate; column to 3mm, pale green, terete, minutely pilose. Venezuela.

N.carnosiflora Schweinf.
Pseudobulbs to 1cm, compressed to subcylindrical, apex unifoliate. Lvs to 6.5×2cm, oblong-elliptic, cuneate beneath. Infl. a basal raceme, arcuate, several-fld; fls fleshy, spreading; dorsal sep. to 7×3mm, oblong, acute, concave; lateral sep. connate, oblong; pet. to 5×1mm, oblanceolate-oblong, acute; lip to 4×2mm, ovate-triangular, unguiculate; disc slightly puberulent; column to 3mm, stout. Peru.

N.mirabilis Schweinf.
Pseudobulbs reduced to absent. Lvs to 14×3mm, equitant, obliquely linear-oblong to linear-elliptic, acute to subobtuse, fleshy. Panicle to 3.5cm, 1- to few-fld; peduncle very slender; fls membranous, spreading, pale lilac and dark violet; dorsal sep. to 4×2mm, ovate-oblong to ovate-elliptic, concave, acute, lateral sep. free, obliquely lanceolate, acute; pet. resembling lateral sep.; lip to 4×2mm, long-clawed, simple, ovate or obovate, apiculate, base auriculate; column to 2mm, erect, slender, clavate. Venezuela, Peru.

N.multiflora Lindl. See *N.sagittifera*.

N.pentachne Rchb. f.
Pseudobulbs to 3×1cm, oblong to ovate-oblong, compressed. Lvs to 20×5cm, coriaceous, ligulate to oblong-lanceolate or elliptic, subacute to obtuse. Raceme to 35cm, pendent, slender, elongate, many-fld; sep. and pet. pale green to yellow, dorsal sep. to 10×3mm, lanceolate or oblanceolate, acute or acuminate, lateral sep. connate forming a synsepalum, bifid, acute or acuminate, recurved, pet. to 8×2mm, sometimes with a few orange spots, obliquely lanceolate, acute or acuminate lip to 6×3mm, white, long-clawed, dilated, to trulliform, acuminate, callus short, carinate; column to 5mm, slender, papillose. Panama, Colombia, Venezuela.

N.rhombilabia Schweinf.
Pseudobulbs to 20×6mm, narrowly cylindrical. Lvs to 14×2cm, linear to linear-oblong or elliptic-linear, acute to rounded, coriaceous, light green. Raceme to 25cm, many-fld, arching; fls pale yellow-green, fleshy; dorsal sep. to 8×3mm, deeply concave, oblong-lanceolate, acute, lateral sep. to 8×4mm, connate forming a synsepalum, oblong-elliptic, deeply concave; pet. to 8×2mm, linear to linear-oblanceolate, acute, falcate, reflexed-spreading; lip to 7×5mm, white, waxy, sessile, rhombic or ovate-rhombic, acute to acuminate, base rounded or cuneate, disc with a shallow longitudinal keel; column to 5mm, cream-white. Peru, Venezuela.

N.sagittifera (HBK) Link & Klotzsch (*N.multiflora* Lindl.).
Pseudobulbs to 15×6mm, inconspicuous, oblong. Lvs to 18×5cm, oblong or oblong-elliptic, obtuse, subcoriaceous, rigid, light green. Raceme to 30cm, arching, many-fld; fls clear green, the pet. with 2 round yellow spots; sep. to 7×3mm, membranous, deeply concave, linear-lanceolate, acute (lateral sep. connate forming a synsepalum), margins revolute; pet. to 6×2mm, linear-lanceolate, acute; lip white, to 5×2mm, fleshy, long-clawed, ovate-triangular, acute to acuminate, base truncate or cuneate; column to 3mm, pale green, apex geniculate. S America to Peru.

N.tridachne Lindl. & Paxt. See *N.barkeri*.

N.wullschlaegeliana Focke.
Pseudobulbs to 5×4mm, inconspicuous, ellipsoid to suborbicular. Lvs to 30×5mm, equitant, fleshy, obliquely oblong-lanceolate or elliptic-lanceolate, acute or subacute. Raceme to 5cm, subumbellate, basal, few-fld, arching; peduncle very slender; fls pale yellow-green or white marked purple, translucent, spreading; sep. to 7×2mm, lanceolate or linear-lanceolate, concave, acute, lateral sep. free; pet. to 6×2mm, obliquely linear-lanceolate, acuminate; lip to 6×1mm, short-clawed, oblong-linear at base to ovate-acuminate at apex, lateral margins irregularly toothed; column to 6mm, pale green, filiform, apex strongly recurved. S America to Peru.

N.yauaperyensis Barb. Rodr.
Pseudobulbs to 6×3mm, obliquely oblong. Lvs to 15×2cm, coriaceous, oblong to linear-oblong, obtuse. Raceme to 12cm, arching to pendent; fls white; dorsal sep. to 5×2mm, oblong or lanceolate to oblong-lanceolate, acute or subacute, lateral sep. linear to linear-lanceolate, basally connate, obtuse; pet. to 4×2mm, obliquely lanceolate to oblong-lanceolate, acute; lip to 4×2mm, fleshy, long-clawed, pubesc., ovate, obtuse, cordate at base, glabrous; column to 3mm, erect. Venezuela, Brazil.

Oberonia Lindl. (From Oberon, the fairy-king; an allusion to the quaint and variable forms of this plant.) Some 330 species of epiphytes, lacking pseudobulbs. Stems absent or very short, obscured by a laterally compressed fan of overlapping, fleshy leaf bases. Leaves flattened, equitant, carinate-conduplicate, oblong or linear, sword-shaped, acuminate. Inflorescence terminal, usually incurved, usually arched, flowers very small, crowded; sepals subequal, often reflexed; petals narrower, sometimes dentate; lip sessile from column base, usually trilobed, spreading, base concave, lateral lobes often enveloping the column. Old World Tropics. Z10.

CULTIVATION Curious epiphytes grown for their flattened fans of sword-shaped leaves and short, cat-tail-like racemes of green flowers. Because of their growth habit, cultivation in sphagnum-lined pouches of a fine bark mix attached to vertically suspended rafts is advised. All species require light shade and buoyant, humid, intermediate conditions. Water and syringe throughout the year except in cold weather.

O.brevifolia Lindl. See *O.disticha*.

O.disticha (Lam.) Schltr. (*O.brevifolia* Lindl.).
Lvs to 3.5×1cm. Spike slender, pendent, 4–5cm; fls bright ochre to orange-yellow; sep. ovate to triangular, broad; pet. linear; lip loosely enveloping column, base saccate, apex bilobed, margins serrate. E & W Africa.

O.iridifolia (Roxb.) Lindl.
Lvs 4–6, 5–25×1–2.5cm. Infl. dense, decurved, to 18cm; fls to 1mm diam., pale green or brown; sep. subequal ovate,

reflexed; lip orbicular, midlobe broad, rounded, bilobed, entire or erose, apex cleft, lateral lobes fringed. Himalaya, Burma, Philippines, Pacific. See Introduction for illustration.

O.kanburiensis Seidenf.
Lvs to 8.5×10cm. Infl. equalling or exceeding lvs. Bracts irregularly fringed; fls ochre to yellow, pet. pale yellow; sep. entire, to 1mm; pet. larger, ovate, coarsely fringed; lip to 1.3mm, lobes fringed, midlobe 1–2mm wide, bilobed. Thailand.

Octomeria R. Br. (From Gk *octo*, eight, and *meros*, a part, referring to the 8 pollinia which characterize the genus.) Some 150 species of epiphytes or terrestrials. Rhizome short or elongate, creeping. Secondary stems often tufted, elongate, erect, enveloped by several tubular sheaths, apically unifoliate. Leaves erect, fleshy to coriaceous, sessile or short-petiolate, elliptic-oblong or linear to terete. Inflorescence 1 to many, axillary, densely clustered to subcapitate, 1- to many-flowered; flowers often small; sepals subsimilar, free to shortly connate, spreading; petals shorter than sepals and usually similar to them in form; lip articulate to column base, shorter than petals, entire or obscurely 3-lobed, apex spreading or reflexed, disc with a shortly bilamellate callus; column short, subterete, incurved, with a short foot at base, wingless, anther terminal, operculate, incumbent, bilocular, pollinia 8, oblong-clavate. C & S America, W Indies.

CULTIVATION Intermediate-growing; suitable for baskets or mounting on rafts in brightly lit, humid conditions.

O.complanata Schweinf.
Secondary stems to 8.5cm, numerous, slender. Lvs to 4cm, subterete to triquetrous-subulate, slightly arching. Infl. several, 1-fld; fls to 17mm, pale golden-brown to dark maroon-red; dorsal sep. to 8×3mm, elliptic-lanceolate to oblong-lanceolate, concave, acute; lateral sep. to 9×2mm, shortly connate, narrowly oblong to oblong-lanceolate, subacute, carinate; pet. to 5.5×2mm, elliptic-lanceolate to oblong-lanceolate; lip to 3.5×2.5mm, ovate-oblong, lateral lobes small, narrowly lanceolate-triangular, edged red-maroon, incurved, midlobe ovate, disc bicarinate, keels basal, yellow, short; column to 2mm, slender, arched, white suffused red. Venezuela, Peru, Brazil.

O.diaphana Lindl.
Secondary stems to 8cm, erect, slender, subcylindrical. Lvs to 6×1.5cm, ovate to oblong-lanceolate, acute, fleshy, sessile, ascending to erect, convex. Infl. to 5mm, 1-fld; fls translucent white, unscented; sep. to 10mm, elliptic-lanceolate, acute or acuminate, concave, thin-textured; pet. to 10mm, linear-lanceolate, acute or acuminate; lip to 7mm, obscurely trilobed, yellow-white flecked red-maroon, ovate-oblong, base cuneate, dentate, slightly crisped, apex truncate, disc with 2 short lamellae. E Brazil.

O.erosilabia Schweinf.
Secondary stems to 19cm, subterete to tetragonal, 3–5-jointed. Lvs to 17×1cm, linear-elliptic or linear-oblong, acute or subacute, lustrous pale green, slightly recurved, subsessile or petiolate. Infl. numerous, subcapitate, 1- to few-fld; tepals pale cream-white to cream-yellow, subtranslucent, sep. to 7×2.5mm, lanceolate or oblong-lanceolate, acuminate, pet. to 6×1.5mm, similar to sep.; lip to 3×2mm, yellow with 2 small bright purple marks, ovate-oblong, lateral lobes auriculate, midlobe ovate or ovate-oblong, truncate, erose-dentate, disc with 2 fleshy keels; column to 2mm, cream-white, stout. Venezuela, Guyana.

O.gracilis Lodd. ex Lindl.
Secondary stems to 20cm, subterete, compressed above. Lvs to 20×2cm, linear-lanceolate. Fls to 2cm diam. in short 5-fld fascicles; tepals diaphanous, white, oblong-lanceolate; lip pale yellow, undulate. Brazil.

O.graminifolia (L.) R. Br.
Secondary stems to 5cm, remote, erect-ascending. Lvs to 11×1cm, narrowly linear-lanceolate to linear-oblong, erect, fleshy, sessile. Infl. 1- or 2-fld; fls pale yellow to yellow-green; sep. to 10×3mm, ovate or ovate-lanceolate, acuminate; lip to 6×3mm, fleshy, short-clawed, lateral lobes subquadrate to suborbicular, midlobe ovate, acute or acuminate, denticulate, disc with 2 oblique, fleshy, purple lamellae; column to 3mm, arched. Early winter. W Indies to Colombia & Brazil.

O.grandiflora Lindl.
Secondary stems to 20cm, terete or subterete, compressed above. Lvs to 20×1.5cm, coriaceous or subcoriaceous, linear-rhombic to linear-lanceolate, green-purple. Infl. 1- or 2-fld; fls to 2cm diam.; tepals translucent, white to straw-yellow, sep. to 13×3mm, narrowly elliptic-lanceolate, acute; lip to 8×6mm, yellow marked purple, short-clawed, lateral lobes erect, rounded, midlobe obovate to cuneate-flabellate, deeply emarginate, erose, disc bicarinate; column white marked red, short, stout, anth. white. Venezuela, Trinidad, Brazil, Surinam, Bolivia, Paraguay.

O.integrilabia Schweinf.
Secondary stems to 5cm. Lvs to 50×5mm, linear or linear-oblong to terete, acute, fleshy. Infl. 1- or 2-fld; fls rose to straw-yellow; sep. to 6×3mm, narrowly lanceolate to ovate-lanceolate, acute or shortly acuminate; pet. oblong-lanceolate to elliptic-lanceolate, acute or acuminate; lip to 3×3mm, simple or obscurely 3-lobed, ovate-elliptic or elliptic to suborbicular, emarginate, base cordate, disc with 2 central keels; column to 2mm, arched. Guyana, Venezuela.

O.nana Schweinf.
Secondary stems to 2.5cm. Lvs to 40×6mm, linear-lanceolate or linear-oblong, acute, fleshy-coriaceous, sessile, apex minutely denticulate. Infl. few-fld; fls produced in succession, thin-textured, pale translucent brown-yellow, the lip pale yellow; sep. to 4×2mm, elliptic-ovate, acute or subacute, concave; lip to 3×2mm, simple, elliptic to suborbicular, shortly acute or emarginate, base rounded-cuneate, disc with a short central callus; column to 1.5mm, cream. Venezuela.

O.oxycheila Barb. Rodr.
Secondary stems to 11×2cm, terete, erect to slightly arched. Lvs to 8×1.5cm, fleshy, lanceolate or oblong-lanceolate, erect-spreading, acute, sessile. Fls spreading to pendent, yellow-white, faintly scented; sep. to 5×1.5mm, fleshy, lanceolate or oblong-lanceolate, acute; pet. broadly ovate-rhombic, acute; lip to 4×2.5mm, ovate-oblong, narrowly clawed, lateral lobes small, erect, suborbicular, midlobe oblong-rectangular, apex tridentate, truncate, disc with 2 central calli, apex with a fleshy keel; column short. Brazil.

O.saundersiana Rchb. f.
Stems to 25cm. Lvs to 6cm, terete, subulate. Infl. fasciculate; fls yellow striped purple; sep. and pet. membranous, triangular, acute; lip 3-lobed, lateral lobes triangular, obtuse; midlobe oblong, acute; disc carinate; column incurved, clavate. Brazil.

O.steyermarkii Garay & Dunsterville.
Secondary stems to 5.5cm. Lvs to 5×1cm, lanceolate or narrowly lanceolate, acute, coriaceous, minutely tridenticulate. Infl. 1-fld; fls variable in colour, cream tinged pink, or pink to dark puce; dorsal sep. to 10mm, narrowly linear-lanceolate or lanceolate, apex produced into filiform tail, lateral sep. to 15mm; pet. to 8mm, lanceolate, with filiform tails; lip to 4×4mm, simple, broadly ovate to ovate-elliptic, disc with 2 central, lamellate calli; column to 2.5mm, dark purple, anth. yellow-cream. Venezuela.

O.surinamensis Focke.
Secondary stems to 10cm, numerous, base terete, apex compressed, 3- or 4-jointed. Lvs to 14×2cm, linear to oblong-elliptic, acute or obtuse, fleshy or subcoriaceous, pale dull green above, green to red-maroon below, usually petiolate. Infl. several, 1- to few-fld; fls yellow-white to pale yellow; sep. to 7×3.5mm, oblong-lanceolate to elliptic-lanceolate, acute or acuminate; pet. to 6.5×3mm, oblong-lanceolate, acuminate; lip to 4×4mm, lateral lobes small, broadly falcate-subovate, obtuse, midlobe obovate, denticulate, apex tridentate, disc with 2 short, dark maroon keels; column to 4mm, slender, arched, brown flushed pink-maroon, anth. pale yellow-brown. Peru, Brazil, Guianas, Venezuela, Colombia.

× **Odontioda** (*Odontoglossum* × *Cochlioda*). The earliest of the intergeneric crosses in the *Oncidium* alliance; the first hybrid was registered in 1904. Plants consist of a group of compressed pseudobulbs growing from a basal rhizome, each with one or two leaves at its apex and two or more leaf-like sheaths arising at its base. Inflorescences arise in the axils of these sheaths and may be simple or branched. Flowers very varied, many with rounded shape and wide sepals and petals, lip large or small depending on the ancestry; flowers of many colours often conspicuously marked in a variety of colours, the bright red of so many crosses inherited from the *Cochlioda* parent. Most of these hybrids are 'cool' growers though a few are tolerant of warmer conditions.

× *O.*Astmo 'Lyoth Zebra': very large and fine fls on a tall spike; sep. and pet. chestnut brown edged with yellow and with some white patches towards the centre, lip white apically, with some brown patches in the centre and a yellow crest at the base.

× *O.*Durham Castle 'Lyoth Supreme': very fine round fls, intense clear red.

× *O.*Durham Supreme 'Lyoth Galaxy': very fine round fls of large size; fls pale pink, heavily overlaid with wine red spots that coalesce, lip with broad red band and yellow around the basal crest.

× *O.*Eric Young: large white fls of excellent form, heavily marked with deep red.

× *O.*Golden Rialto 'St Helier': fls rather crowded on upright spikes; fls white with few large clear yellow spots on all sep. and pet. and centre of lip; the clone 'Lyoth Sunny' is a clear bright yellow, paler towards the centre, with two brown spots on the lip which is edged with white.

× *O.*Harrods Forever 'Lyoth Dresden': superb round fls of pastel pink with few brown-red spots, lip with a broad brown-red band across the centre and yellow basally.

× *O.*Heatonensis: primary hybrid made at the turn of the century; fls star shaped with elongated sep., pale pink with red spots, lip paler, white in the centre and with yellow in the throat.

× *O.*Ingmar: fine shaped fls of luminous orange red with lilac mauve tips to the sep. and pet., lip red basally with yellow crest, white flushed rose towards the apex.

× *O.*Joe's Drum: small to medium fls of fine shape, clear bright red.

× *O.*Keighleyensis: primary hybrid with small bright orange red fls of starry shape on short sprays.

× *O.*Lippestern: branching sprays bearing very round fls; sepals and petals a rich red-brown margined with white and with white tips, lip small but similar with yellow crest.

× *O.*Lynx: startling large fls; sep. and pet. with a yellow base and many large bright brown spots, lip white streaked and spotted with brown.

× *O.*Matanda: small to medium fls of intense cerise red, some spotting in darker red on the dorsal sep. and lip.

× *O.*Petit Port: very fine shaped fls of medium size; fls pale yellow-green, margined and striped with bright red, lip paler with fewer spots towards the base and cream flushed rose towards the tip.

× *O.*Red Rum: very fine fls in bright clear red.

× *O.*Saint Clement: very fine round fls of excellent substance; fls pink with dark red spots, lip paler with yellow crest; many fine awarded clones.

× *O.*Shelley: delightful fls of medium size, white flushed pink and with darker pin spots.

× *O.*Trixon: very fine fls in upright spikes; fls bright red with lilac tips to the sepals and lip, crest yellow; several awarded clones.

× **Odontobrassia** (*Brassia* × *Odontoglossum*). Intergeneric hybrids. Plants consist of a group of compressed pseudobulbs growing from a basal rhizome, each with one or two leaves at its apex and two or more leaf-like sheaths arising at its base. Inflorescences arise in the axils of these sheaths and may be simple or branched. Flowers mostly with long narrow sepals and petals, lip large or small depending on the ancestry, often contrasting with the sepals and petals. Tolerant of intermediate conditions.

× *O.*Gordon Dillon: upright spikes of attractive fls; fls with curved sep. and pet., yellow or cream overlaid with deep chocolate, lip oval, bright red.

× **Odontocidium** (*Odontoglossum* × *Oncidium*). Intergeneric hybrids. Plants consist of a group of compressed pseudobulbs growing from a basal rhizome, each with one or two leaves at its apex and two or more leaf-like sheaths arising at its base. Inflorescences arise in the axils of these sheaths and may be simple or branched. Flowers very varied, many with rounded shape but others have long narrow sepals and petals, lip large or small depending on the ancestry; flowers of many colours often conspicuously marked in a variety of colours. Most of these hybrids are 'cool' growers though a few are tolerant of warmer conditions.

× *O.*Crowborough `Spice Islands': branching spikes with many fls; fls golden yellow and orange with dark brown spits, lip large, white with yellow crest at the base.

× *O.*Jacobert: tall sprays of large fls often branching: fls rich coppery orange shades, some solid colours others patterned like odontoglossums, lip usually bright yellow or outlined in yellow; warm growing.

× *O.*Selsfield Gold: very large spikes bearing numerous fls; sep. and pet. bright yellow with brown blotches, lip primrose yellow, spotted with orange.

× *O.*Tiger Butter: large branching sprays bearing many small to medium fls; several awarded clones.

× *O.*Tigersun: tall sprays of large bright yellow fls but a tendency to fade with age; fls yellow throughout with chestnut brown spots on sep. and pet. and base of large yellow lip; several awarded clones.

Odontoglossum HBK. (From Gk *odontos*, tooth, and *glossa*, tongue, referring to the tooth-like processes of the lip.) Some 60 species of epiphytes or lithophytes. Rhizome short or creeping. Pseudobulbs variously compressed, usually ovoid or elliptic-oblong, 1–3-leaved at apex, enveloped at base by distichous, leaf-bearing sheaths. Leaves coriaceous or fleshy, variously shaped. Inflorescence basal, a raceme or a panicle, erect or arching, few- to many-flowered; bracts minute to conspicuous; flowers usually large and conspicuous, sometimes small; sepals subequal, spreading, free or lateral sepals basally connate; petals similar to sepals, often shorter; lip simple or 3-lobed, basal portion often claw-like and usually parallel with column, sometimes adnate to column, lateral lobes spreading or erect, midlobe deflexed, entire or emarginate, disc variously lamellate, cristate or callose, sometimes with radiate keels; column long, slender, footless, apex sometimes auriculate; anther terminal, operculate, incumbent, pollinia 2, waxy, entire or sulcate. S America.

CULTIVATION A genus of great horticultural importance, *Odontoglossum* has spawned countless hybrids, many of them intergeneric, and has, since the last century when vast sums changed hands for a single growth of *O.crispum*, enjoyed a popularity with orchid growers outdone only by that of *Cymbidium*. These plants are cool-growing and demand buoyant, freely ventilated and humid atmospheres in light shade. Their roots are slender: a correspondingly fine bark mix is advised, containing rockwool or sphagnum. Water and syringe freely when in growth, and impose drier cooler conditions when at rest. Never syringe in cold weather. The inflorescences of some will require training. Propagate by division.

Some of the most striking and widely grown species described originally as *Odontoglossum* (for example the showy Clown Orchid, *O.grande*, the eminently dependable *O.bictoniense*, the delicate white *O.convallarioides*, or nodding, rose *O.pendulum*, the diminutive *O.rossii* and *O.cervantesii*, with disproportionately large white flowers spotted chocolate and tinted rose) are now treated under segregate genera and can be located through the synonymy below. Their cultural requirements are largely the same as those described here, likewise the needs of many of the intergeneric hybrids, including ×*Wilsonara* and ×*Vuylstekeara*.

O.alexandrae Batem. See *O.crispum*.

O.angustatum Lindl. non Batem.).
Pseudobulbs cylindric to elliptic or ovoid, to 8cm, 1-lvd at apex, with 4 accessory lvs at base. Lvs to 42×4.5cm, oblanceolate or oblanceolate-oblong, sessile. Panicle short- or long-branched, usually exceeding lvs; sep. to 35×8mm, green, marked brown, linear-lanceolate, long-acuminate, undulate; pet. yellow, transversely barred brown, lanceolate to ovate-lanceolate, broader than sep., margins undulate; lip to 2.5×1cm, white, ovate to ovate-oblong or oblong, basal portion short-clawed, anterior portion barred brown, basal crest

closely and sharply toothed; column small, to 1.2cm, dilated at apex, wingless. Ecuador, Peru.

O.aureopurpureum Rchb. f.
Pseudobulbs to 6×4cm, oblong-ovoid, remote on tough rhiz., apically bifoliate. Lvs to 70×3cm, linear-oblong or oblong, acute or acuminate, coriaceous. Panicle much-branched, erect, to 160cm, many-fld; fls large, wide-spreading, golden-yellow marked and spotted purple, red or brown; sep. to 3.5×1cm, linear-lanceolate to ovate-lanceolate, long-acuminate, undulate-crisped, recurved, with long, fleshy claws; pet. shorter and broader than sep.; lip to 2.5×1cm, golden-yellow

with brown base and remainder spotted brown, fleshy, lance-olate, strongly recurved, margins crenate and undulate at base, disc with yellow basal callus of 2 fleshy keels; column yellow, to 1cm. Venezuela, Colombia, Ecuador, Peru.

O.bictoniense (Batem.) Lindl. See *Lemboglossum bictoniense.*

O.blandum Rchb. f.
Pseudobulbs to 3×2cm, ellipsoid, apically bifoliate. Lvs to 25×2.5cm, linear-lanceolate, acute or subacute. Fls showy, crowded near apex of 25cm, arching raceme, sep. and pet. white, heavily spotted maroon-crimson, to 25×3mm, lanceo-late, long-acuminate; lip to 23×10mm, white spotted purple, clawed, ovate, emarginate, acuminate, erose-dentate, callus yellow, 2-keeled, terminating in 2 slender, erect teeth, pubesc.; column with 3 or 4 apical cirri on each side. Venezuela to Peru.

O.brachypterum Rchb. f. See *Otoglossum brevifolium.*
O.brevifolium Lindl. See *Otoglossum brevifolium.*

O.cariniferum Rchb. f. (*O.hastilabium* var. *fuscatum* Hook.; *Oncidium cariniferum* (Rchb. f.) Beer). Pseudobulbs to 12×8cm, ovoid to elliptic-oblong, apically bifoliate. Lvs to 45×4cm, linear-ligulate, acute, coriaceous. Panicle to 1m, stout, erect or arcuate, many-fld, usually branched, branches spreading, fractiflex; fls to 5cm diam., fleshy, sep. and pet. deep chestnut-brown edged yellow, lanceolate, acute or acuminate, keeled on reverse; sep. to 25×5mm; pet. shorter than sep., sometimes incurved; lip white, pale yellow with age, long-clawed, to 1.5×2cm, reniform, apiculate, callus rose-mauve, consisting of 2 rhomboid, toothed keels; column white flushed purple, winged. Spring. Costa Rica, Panama, Venezuela.

O.cervantesii La Ll. & Lex. See *Lemboglossum cervantesii.*
O.chiriquense Rchb. f. See *Otoglossum chiriquense.*
O.cimiciferum Rchb. f. See *Oncidium cimiciferum.*

O.cirrhosum Lindl. (*Oncidium cirrhosum* (Lindl.) Beer).
Pseudobulbs to 8cm, oblong-ovoid, apically unifoliate. Lvs 30×3cm, linear-ligulate, acute. Raceme or panicle to 60cm, arching; sep. and pet. white variously blotched red-brown; sep. to 4×0.7cm, narrowly lanceolate, long-acuminate, termi-nating in a recurved point; pet. rhombic-lanceolate, long-acuminate, shorter and broader than sep.; lip to 3cm, white with red-brown blotches on midlobe, base yellow, 3-lobed, lateral lobes rounded, denticulate, erect to spreading, midlobe recurved, narrow-lanceolate, long-acuminate, disc with 2 horn-like keels; column to 1cm, with 2 hair-like auricles near apex. Spring. Ecuador, Peru, Colombia.

O.citrosmum Lindl. See *Cuitlauzina pendula.*

O.constrictum Lindl. (*O.sanderianum* Rchb. f.)
Pseudobulbs to 7.5cm, ovoid, ribbed, apically bifoliate. Lvs to 40×2cm, linear-lanceolate, acute. Raceme or lightly branched panicle to 60cm, arching, sep. and pet. yellow or pale olive blotched and banded red-brown, to 20×5mm, oblong-lanceo-late; lip to 2.5×1cm, white blotched pale red before callus, pandurate, apiculate, callus 2-keeled with erose margins; col-umn white. Autumn–winter. Venezuela, Colombia, Ecuador.

O.convallarioides (Schltr.) Ames & Correll. See *Osmoglossum convallarioides.*
O.cordatum Lindl. See *Lemboglossum cordatum.*
O.coronarium Lindl. See *Otoglossum coronarium.*
O.coronarium var. *chiriquense* (Rchb. f.) Veitch. See *Otoglossum chiriquense.*

O.crispum Lindl. (*O.alexandrae* Batem.).
Pseudobulbs to 7.5cm, ovoid, apically bifoliate. Lvs to 40×3cm, linear-lanceolate to linear-elliptic, acute. Raceme or (rarely) panicle, arching, to 50cm; fls to 8.5cm diam., very variable, showy usually sparkling white or pale rose, vari-ously spotted or blotched red or purple, sep. and pet. spread-ing, ovate-elliptic to oblong-elliptic, obtuse or acute to acumi-nate, undulate or finely and irregularly dentate; lip to 3×1.5cm, usually white or pink with a few red spots and a

yellow disc, short-clawed, oblong, acute, undulate, finely dentate, callus fleshy, 2-lobed at apex; column lightly arcuate, with 2 lacerate wings. Winter. Colombia.

O.cristatum Lindl. (*Oncidium cristatum* (Lindl.) Beer).
Pseudobulbs to 10cm, ovoid to oblong-ellipsoid, apically bifoliate. Lvs to 22×2cm, ligulate, acute. Raceme to 50cm, arching, sep. and pet. to 3×1cm, fleshy, cream-yellow with deep chestnut-brown blotches and markings, elliptic-lanceo-late or ovate-lanceolate, acuminate; lip white or cream-yellow with few brown spots, fimbriate-dentate, disc with a basal cal-lus of many long tooth-like projections; column to 1.5cm, arching, with 2 rounded, fimbriate wings above. Colombia, Ecuador, Peru.

O.crocidipterum Rchb. f. (*O.dormanianum* Rchb. f.)
Pseudobulbs to 6×3cm, ovoid to ellipsoid, often spotted pur-ple, usually apically bifoliate. Lvs to 25×4cm, oblong to lin-ear-lanceolate, acute. Raceme or short-branched panicle, ascending to arching; sep. and pet. white or pale yellow to yellow-brown spotted dark brown or chocolate-brown; sep. to 35×5mm, linear-lanceolate to lanceolate, acuminate; pet. to 30×7mm, linear-lanceolate to ovate-lanceolate, subacuminate; lip to 26×7mm, clear yellow blotched dark brown near callus, lanceolate, subacuminate, callus white, 2 parallel plates, papillose or pubesc.; column to 12mm, white, narrow-winged. Colombia, Venezuela. White-fld plants treated as ssp. *dorma-niarum* (Rchb. f.) Bockem.

O.dormanianum Rchb. f. See *O.crocidipterum* ssp. *dormani-anum.*

O.eduardii Rchb. f. (*Cyrtochilum eduardii* (Rchb. f.) Kranzl.)
Pseudobulbs to 10cm, ovoid-pyriform, apically bifoliate. Lvs to 25×3cm, ligulate, subcoriaceous. Panicle much-branched, suberect, far exceeding lvs; fls to 2.5cm, fragrant, sep. and pet. bright magenta or mauve-purple, oblong, undulate; lip similar to sep. and pet., short, tongue-shaped, with yellow cal-lus. Spring. Ecuador.

O.egertonii Lindl. See *Osmoglossum egertonii.*

O.epidendroides HBK (*Oncidium epidendroides* (HBK) Beer).
Pseudobulbs to 6cm, ovate-oblong, apically bifoliate. Lvs to 30×3cm, lanceolate to oblong-elliptic, acute. Panicle or raceme to 45cm, slightly arching; sep. and pet. bright yellow with 3–5 carmine spots; sep. to 35×7mm, lanceolate, acumi-nate, slightly undulate; pet. slightly wider than sep., sub-oblique; lip white spotted purple, shorter than sep., clawed, elliptic-oblong, sharply reflexed, margins crenate-undulate, callus linear-oblong, tridentate with 1–3 minute dentate calli on each side at base; column clavate, with 2 rounded auricles at apex. C America.

O.erosum Rich. & Gal. See *Lemboglossum stellatum.*
O.grande Lindl. See *Rossioglossum grande.*
O.grande var. *williamsianum* Rchb. f. See *Rossioglossum williamsianum.*

O.hallii Lindl. (*Oncidium hallii* (Lindl.) Beer).
Rhiz. short. Pseudobulbs to 10cm, ovoid or oblong-ovoid, apically unifoliate or bifoliate. Lvs to 30×4.5cm, elliptic-oblong or oblong-lanceolate, acute. Raceme (rarely a pan-icle) to 90cm, erect or arching; sep. and pet. pale yellow blotched chocolate-brown or purple-brown; sep. to 5.5×1cm, lanceolate or elliptic-lanceolate, long-acumi-nate; pet. ovate-lanceolate, shorter and broader than sep.; lip white blotched purple-brown, callus deep yellow, shortly clawed, lamina oblong, dentate to lacerate, basal portion crenulate, disc with large callus of several tooth-like keels; column to 2cm, arching, auricles divided into tooth-like processes or tendrils. Spring. Colombia, Ecuador, Peru.

O.harryanum Rchb. f.
Pseudobulbs to 8cm, ovoid-oblong, furrowed with age, api-cally bifoliate. Lvs to 44×4cm, oblong to oblong-elliptic, acute to obtuse, petiolate. Raceme to 1m, erect, 4–12-fld; fls variable; sep. to 4.5×2.5cm, buff to chestnut brown with vein-

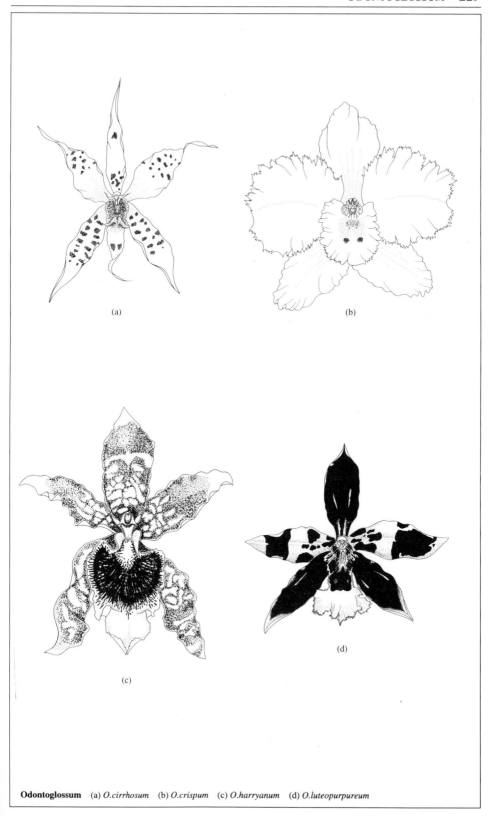

Odontoglossum (a) *O.cirrhosum* (b) *O.crispum* (c) *O.harryanum* (d) *O.luteopurpureum*

like streaks of yellow, elliptic-oblong, acute, undulate; pet. to 4×2cm, chestnut brown, white at base with broad, irregular lines of mauve-purple; lip 3-lobed, lateral lobes white striped purple, midlobe white to pale yellow disc with a prominent yellow, fimbriate callus; column to 1.5cm, with small, finely dentate auricles. Summer. Colombia, Peru.

O.hastilabium Lindl. See *Oncidium hastilabium*.
O.hastilabium var. *fuscatum* Hook. See *O.cariniferum*.

O. × hennisii Rolfe.
Pseudobulbs to 4cm, oblong-ovoid. Lvs to 15×2cm, linear-oblanceolate, acute. Infl. to 20cm, laxly 6-fld; sep. to 2.5cm, yellow spotted and blotched brown, lanceolate, acuminate, larger than similar pet.; lip to 2cm, spotted white and blotched red-brown, short-clawed, spreading, 3-lobed, lateral lobes dentate, rounded, midlobe narrow-ovate, long-acuminate; column to 1.5cm, clavate, yellow-white, apex dentate, acute. Peru, Ecuador. Natural hybrid.

O.hookeri Lem. See *Lemboglossum cordatum*.

O. × hunnewellianum Rolfe.
Pseudobulbs to 5cm, ovoid, apically bifoliate. Lvs to 30cm. Raceme to 40cm, branched, arching, loosely many-fld; fls to 5cm diam., fleshy, round, sep. and pet. yellow with large brown blotches, broadly lanceolate to ovate, acute; lip cream-white spotted red-brown, obovate-elliptic, margins crenulate to undulate, callus yellow, dentate; column wings entire. Autumn–spring. Colombia. Natural hybrid.

O.hystrix Batem. See *O.luteopurpureum*.
O.insleayi (Barker ex Lindl.) Lindl. See *Rossioglossum insleayi*.

O.kegeljanii Morr. (*O.polyxanthum* Rchb. f.).
Pseudobulbs to 8×3cm, pyriform, apically bifoliate. Lvs to 35×3cm, linear-lanceolate, mucronulate. Raceme to 40cm, arching, several-fld; sep. and pet. lemon-yellow blotched chestnut-brown, acute; sep. to 4.5×1.5cm, slightly longer than pet.; lip to 4×2.5cm, white blotched red-chestnut on apical lobe, narrowly clawed, oblong to suborbicular, crisped, callus consisting of 2 large, sharp, divergent teeth with some smaller teeth near base; column to 2.5cm, white blotched brown, anth. dark brown. Spring. Venezuela, Colombia, Ecuador, Peru.

O.krameri Rchb. f. See *Ticoglossum krameri*.
O.lawrenceanum hort. See *Rossioglossum insleayi*.
O.laxiflorum (Lindl.) Rchb. f. See *Gomesa laxiflora*.

O.lindenii Lindl.
Pseudobulbs to 6×5cm, ovoid, apically bifoliate. Lvs to 35×2cm, narrow-linear, erect, thin, margins revolute. Panicle short-branched, to 60cm, 5–7-fld; fls bright yellow; sep. to 2×1cm, short-clawed, lanceolate to oblanceolate, strongly undulate; pet. shorter, elliptic-spathulate, strongly undulate; lip to 1.5×1cm, ovate-lanceolate, callus prominent, fleshy, consisting of 2 erect plates clasping side of column with several long, toothed projections in front; column terete, yellow. Spring. Venezuela, Colombia, Ecuador.

O.lindleyanum Rchb. f.
Pseudobulbs to 7.5×3cm, ovoid to ovoid-oblong, apically bifoliate. Lvs to 30×2cm, linear-oblong to linear-lanceolate, acute. Raceme or panicle loosely several-fld, arching; fls fragrant, star-shaped, sep. and pet. to 30×5mm, yellow with central cinnamon-brown blotch and red-brown spots at base, linear-lanceolate, long-acuminate; lip to 3×1cm, red-brown tipped yellow, white at base spotted purple, lateral lobes small, midlobe linear-lanceolate, reflexed; column to 2cm, straight, with 2 narrow apical wings. Spring–summer. Colombia, Venezuela, Ecuador.

O.lucianianum Rchb. f.
Pseudobulbs to 4×2cm, pyriform, apically unifoliate or bifoliate. Lvs to 16×2.5cm, linear-oblanceolate, acute. Raceme to 40cm, erect; sep. and pet. to 18×8mm, yellow-brown spotted red-brown, lanceolate or narrowly ovate, subacute or acute; lip subequal to sep., yellow or yellow-white with

large chestnut-brown blotch in front of callus, triangular-lanceolate, basal portion subquadrate, callus white, pubesc., apex bilobulate; column to 7mm, wings linear-filiform. Venezuela.

O.lueddemannii Reg. See *Lemboglossum cordatum*.

O.luteopurpureum Lindl. (*O.hystrix* Batem.; *O.radiatum* Rchb. f.; *Oncidium luteopurpureum* (Lindl.) Beer).
Variable in size and colour. Pseudobulbs to 7×3cm, ovoid, apically bifoliate. Lvs to 60×2.5cm, oblanceolate or linear-lanceolate, acute, somewhat rigid. Raceme to 1m, suberect, loosely many-fld; sep. and pet. bright chestnut-brown tipped and marked yellow, ovate-lanceolate, acute or acuminate, undulate and, sometimes, fringed; sep. to 5×1.5cm; pet. to 4×1cm; lip to 3×2cm, yellow-white spotted brown, long-clawed, lateral lobes small, midlobe reniform, emarginate, fringed, callus golden-yellow, dentate; column wings dentate. Spring. Colombia.

O.maculatum La Ll. & Lex. See *Lemboglossum maculatum*.
O.majale Rchb. f. See *Lemboglossum majale*.
O.membranaceum Lindl. See *Lemboglossum cervantesii*.

O.naevium Lindl. (*Oncidium naevium* (Lindl.) Beer).
Pseudobulbs to 4×2.5cm, ovoid, grooved, apically bifoliate. Lvs to 35×2.5cm. Raceme arching; fls star-shaped, showy, to 6cm diam., sep. and pet. white blotched deep red-brown or red-purple, lanceolate, acuminate, margins undulate; lip white spotted red-brown, shorter than sep., linear-lanceolate, pubesc., disc yellow; column white, wings long-fimbriate, anth. white. Spring–summer. Venezuela, Colombia, Ecuador, Guianas.

O.nevadense Rchb. f.
Pseudobulbs to 10×5cm, ovoid, apically bifoliate. Lvs to 30cm, linear-lanceolate or ensiform, coriaceous. Raceme exceeding lvs, arching, to 15-fld; fls to 8.5cm diam., sep. and pet. similar, cinnamon edged yellow, sometimes longitudinally barred yellow at base, narrowly lanceolate or ovate-lanceolate, acuminate; lip shorter than sep., white barred chestnut-brown, triangular, acuminate, slightly recurved, deeply fimbriate or dentate, lateral lobes erect, parallel with column, semilunate, callus bilamellate; column to 6.5mm, white. Spring–summer. Colombia, Venezuela.

O.nobile Rchb. f. (*O.pescatorei* Lindl.).
Close to *O.crispum*. Pseudobulbs to 9cm, ovoid, speckled brown, apically bifoliate. Lvs to 20cm, ligulate, acute. Raceme or panicle to 60cm, usually branched, erect or arching, 10–100-fld; fls to 6cm diam., orbicular, lightly fragrant, sep. and pet. usually snow-white, sometimes tinged pale rose, ovate-elliptic or ovate-oblong, acute, margins undulate; lip white blotched purple-crimson at base, pandurate, undulate, midlobe cordate with an apical cusp, callus yellow. Spring. Colombia.

O.odoratum Lindl.
Pseudobulbs to 7.5cm, ovoid, apically bifoliate. Lvs to 30×4cm, lanceolate, acute. Raceme or panicle to 75cm; fls to 6.5cm diam., fragrant, pale to deep yellow dotted and blotched chocolate-brown; sep. to 35×7mm, ovate-lanceolate, acute or acuminate, apex reflexed; pet. to 30×6mm, lanceolate, long-acuminate, undulate; lip to 2.5×1cm, white at base, short-clawed, lateral lobes erect, rounded, lanceolate to oblong-elliptic, acuminate, striate at base, apical portion recurved, callus bidentate; column wings lanceolate, long-acuminate. Spring. Colombia, Venezuela.

O.oerstedii Rchb. f. See *Ticoglossum oerstedii*.
O.pendulum (La Ll. & Lex.) Batem. See *Cuitlauzina pendula*.
O.pescatorei Lindl. See *O.nobile*.
O.planifolium (Lindl.) Rchb. f. See *Gomesa planifolia*.
O.platycheilum Weatherby See *Lemboglossum majale*.
O.polyxanthum Rchb f. See *O.kegeljanii*.

O.praestans Rchb. f.
Pseudobulbs to 6cm, ovoid or pyriform-cylindrical, mottled purple-brown, apically bifoliate. Lvs to 23×1.5cm, linear-lanceolate or linear-oblong, acute, sessile or shortly

petiolate. Panicle or raceme to 30cm, few- to many-fld; fls large, spreading, yellow-green spotted cinnamon-brown or purple; sep. to 4×1cm, lanceolate or linear-lanceolate, acuminate; pet. shorter and slightly wider than dorsal sep., lanceolate or ovate-lanceolate, acuminate; lip to 2.5cm, simple, lanceolate, long-acuminate, apex slightly recurved, short-clawed, callus with 4 longitudinal keels, irregularly dentate; column to 1cm, wings porrect, decurved, lacerate. Peru.

O.pulchellum Batem. ex Lindl. See *Osmoglossum pulchellum*.
O.purum Rchb. f. See *O.wallisii*.
O.radiatum Rchb. f. See *O.luteopurpureum*.

O.ramosissimum Lindl.
Pseudobulbs to 12×5cm, ovoid to ovoid-oblong, apically, unifoliate. Lvs to 60×5cm, linear-lanceolate, acute. Panicle to 1.5m, erect, apex much-branched, densely many-fld; fls to 5cm diam., fragrant, sep. and pet. white spotted violet, undulate and reflexed, narrowly lanceolate, acuminate; lip to 18×7mm, white blotched violet at base, cordate or deltoid, acuminate, undulate, callus white, bilamellate, multidentate dorsally. Spring. Venezuela, Colombia, Ecuador.

O.ramulosum Lindl.
Pseudobulbs to 12×5cm, ovoid, usually pale brown, apically bifoliate. Lvs to 60×4cm, linear to linear-oblanceolate, acute, coriaceous. Panicle to 1m, erect or arching, short-branched, many-fld; sep. and pet. yellow, base marked deep brown; sep. to 15×6mm, acute to subobtuse, dorsal sep. obovate-oblong or spathulate, undulate, lateral sep. free, undulate; pet. to 12×6mm, spathulate to elliptic-obovate, acute to apiculate; lip to 10×5mm, yellow marked brown, sessile, ovate or ovate-oblong to elliptic-oblong, acute to obtuse, convex, callus yellow or pale yellow, 4–7-lobed; column brown, to 5mm. Colombia, Venezuela, Ecuador.

O.recurvum (R. Br.) Lindl. See *Gomesa recurva*.

O.retusum Lindl. (*Cyrtochilum retusum* (Lindl.) Kränzlin).
Pseudobulbs to 5cm, narrowly ellipsoid to ovoid, apically unifoliate. Lvs to 30×2cm, linear-lanceolate to elliptic-linear, obtuse to subacute. Panicle to 60cm, slender, short-branched, erect, loosely many-fld; sep. and pet. orange-red tinged yellow; sep. to 16×5mm, broadly oblanceolate to narrowly obovate, acute, concave, laterals oblique, dorsally carinate; pet. smaller than sep., narrowly oblong-obovate, acute; lip to 10×7mm, golden-yellow, sessile, oblong-subquadrate, recurved above, simple or slightly 3-lobed, retuse, disc with sulcate callus or 2 ridges to middle; column to 3mm, with prominent margin on each side. Ecuador, Peru, Colombia.

O.rigidum Lindl.
Pseudobulbs to 3.5cm, ovate or pyriform, apically unifoliate. Lvs to 15×1.5cm, linear-ligulate, acute, carinate. Panicle far exceeding lvs, loosely branched toward apex; sep. and pet. bright canary-yellow; dorsal sep. to 15×5mm, spreading, ovate-lanceolate, acuminate, concave, lateral sep. longer and narrower than dorsal sep.; pet. similar to dorsal sep., slightly wider; lip to 2×1cm, deep yellow, narrow-clawed, subquadrate, apex recurved, prominently apiculate, callus on claw, bilamellate, dentate in front; column clavate, wings irregularly lacerate. Peru, Ecuador.

O.rossii Lindl. See *Lemboglossum rossii*.
O.sanderianum Rchb. f. See *O.constrictum*.

O.schillerianum Rchb. f.
Pseudobulbs to 7×3.5cm, ovoid, apically unifoliate or bifoliate. Lvs to 30×3cm, thin, minutely apiculate. Raceme erect, surpassing lvs, several- to many-fld; fls fragrant, sep. and pet. yellow blotched brown or maroon, elliptic-lanceolate, acute to acuminate; sep. to 2.5×1cm; pet. slightly smaller, finely pubesc.; lip to 2×1cm, white at base, centre purple-brown tipped yellow, clawed, deflexed, lateral lobes small, erect, midlobe oblong, acute, undulate, pubesc., disc with 2 blunt calli; column green-cream. Winter–spring. Venezuela, Colombia.

O.spectatissimum Lindl. (*O.triumphans* Rchb. f.).
Pseudobulbs to 10×4cm, ovoid-ellipsoid, apically bifoliate. Lvs to 40×4cm, oblong-lanceolate, coriaceous, acute, petiolate. Raceme or panicle to 90cm, erect to arching, 5–12-fld; fls to 10cm diam., sep. and pet. golden-yellow variously spotted rich chestnut-brown; sep. to 5.5×1.5cm, oblong-lanceolate, acute or acuminate; pet. to 4.5×1.5cm, elliptic-lanceolate, acute, undulate; lip to 3.5×2cm, white apically blotched red-brown, short-clawed, oblong-ovate, long-apiculate, lacerate, crest bidentate; column to 3cm, arcuate, with finely toothed auricles. Spring. Colombia, Venezuela.

O.stellatum Lindl. See *Lemboglossum stellatum*.

O.tripudians Rchb. f.
Pseudobulbs to 10cm, oblong-ovoid or ellipsoid, apically bifoliate. Lvs to 25×2.5cm, bright green, oblong-lanceolate, acute or acuminate. Raceme arching, far exceeding lvs, sometimes branched, many-fld; sep. to 3.5cm, maroon-brown, yellow at base and tips, elliptic-lanceolate to elliptic-oblong, acuminate; pet. smaller than sep., golden-yellow blotched maroon-brown near base; lip to 2.5cm, white or cream blotched rose or purple-red, with short claw parallel to column, subquadrate to pandurate, dentate, disc white with 10-keeled calli, spotted purple-red; column to 1.5cm, arching, with 2 tridentate wings above. Colombia, Ecuador, Peru.

O.triumphans Rchb. f. See *O.spectatissimum*.
O.uro-skinneri Lindl. See *Lemboglossum uro-skinneri*.

O.wallisii Lind. & Rchb. f. (*O.purum* Rchb. f.).
Pseudobulbs to 9cm, ovoid, apically unifoliate. Lvs to 25×1.5cm, linear, acute or acuminate. Raceme or panicle arching, to 50cm or more; fls to 5cm diam., fleshy, sep. and pet. to 6.5×3.5cm, golden-yellow blotched cinnamon-brown, oblong-lanceolate, acute or apiculate; pet. with fewer markings and slightly smaller than sep.; lip white streaked rose-purple near apex, long-clawed, midlobe oblong-ovate or oblong-elliptic, tip sharply reflexed, fringed, callus linear, grooved, terminating in 2 teeth; column short, broadly winged. Colombia, Venezuela, Peru.

O.warscewiczii Rchb. f. See *Miltoniopsis warscewiczii*.
O.williamsianum Rchb. f. See *Rossioglossum williamsianum*.

O.grexes and cultivars (see also × *Odontioda*, × *Odontonia*, × *Odontocidium*, × *Colmanara*, × *Wilsonara*); many plants which have received awards are clones of the species *O.crispum*.

*O.*Aloretus 'Roke': very large fls, white with maroon blotches attractively arranged on the sep. and pet., brown markings on the lip.

*O.*Ardentissimum: early hybrid, mostly white with deep red markings.

*O.*Buttercrisp: lovely pale yellow fls with red markings on the white-bordered lip.

*O.*Costro: fls large, mauve-red.

*O.*Coupe Point 'Mont Millais': fls large with white pet., sep. flushed with rose, sep. and lip marked with brown.

*O.*Cristor: outstanding white fls.

*O.*Durham Pancho: fls large lemon yellow with deep gold markings on all parts.

*O.*Goldrausch: fls brilliant golden yellow with brown markings.

*O.*Grouville Bay 'Mont Millais': lovely white fls of good shape boldly marked with bright red.

*O.*Hambuhren Gold: fls rich golden with dark chestnut markings.

*O.*Incaspum: fls shapely white with spots and striped of dark red on all the parts.

*O.*Kopan: large branched spikes of yellow fls with mahogany spotting.

*O.*Lemon Drop: fls deep canary yellow with a few golden-brown markings on the lip.

*O.*Moselle: fls yellow with brown markings.

*O.*Nicky Strauss: fls well-shaped, white, heavily marked with red.

*O.*Pescalo: lovely whites of good shape, some with red markings.

*O.*Pumistor: fls large, white with red spots on the pet. and lip.

*O.*Rialto: lovely white with yellow markings.

*O.*Robesca: fls large, white with red markings.

*O.*Royal Occasion: lovely white with yellow markings on the lip.

*O.*Royal Wedding: lovely white with yellow markings.

*O.*Saint Brelade 'Jersey': a new line of breeding from *Lemboglossum rossii*, fls well shaped, deep red outline in white with a wide mottled margin on the lip.

*O.*Spendidum: small flowered white but very prolific on branching spikes.

*O.*Stonehurst Yellow: strong plants with large spikes of golden yellow fls marked with deeper yellow.

*O.*Stropheon: fls large of heavy texture, usually with white backgrounds heavily overlaid with deep purple-red; many clones have been awarded.

*O.*Tontor: outstanding white fls.

× **Odontonia** (*Odontoglossum × Miltonia*). Intergeneric hybrids of pastel colours with great charm. Plants consist of a group of compressed pseudobulbs growing from a basal rhizome, each with one or two leaves at its apex and two or more leaf-like sheaths arising at its base. Inflorescences arise in the axils of these sheaths and are usually simple. Flowers very varied, many with rounded shape but others with larger lip depending on the ancestry. Most of these hybrids are 'cool' growers though a few are tolerant of warmer conditions.

× *O.*Berlioz 'Lecoufle': large fls on tall infl; fls delicate mauve-pink on a white background with distinctive purple markings radiating from around the centre of the fl; several other clones have been awarded.

× *O.*Boussole 'Blanche': very floriferous hybrid often bearing two spikes at once; fls pure white with two very small maroon spots in the centre; long lasting.

× *O.*Debutante: semi-erect, branching sprays of medium-size fls; sep. and pet. are chocolate coloured with yellow tips, lip pure white; several awarded clones.

× *O.*Diane: unusual yellow fls in this generic cross; fls bright yellow with distinctive brown spots on the sep. and lip; several named clones, some awarded.

× *O.*Lulli 'Menuet': unusual white fls edged with mauve and with dark red spots towards the centre, lip large with a few orange dots in the throat.

× *O.*Molière: very large fls of splendid shape; fls white, sometimes flushed pink, margined with mauve and with purplish spots or lines on sep. and pet.; several awarded clones including 'Elite' and 'Lanni' which is almost pure white or very fine.

× *O.*Salam: vigorous plants with large fls; sep. and pet. deep peony purple-red, margined with white, lip broad and marked with a white border and yellow crest; several awarded plants including 'Fanion'.

× **Odontorettia** (*Odontoglossum × Comparettia*). Intergeneric hybrids with small plants. Pseudobulbs very small, usually with one apical leaf and two sheath like leaves at the base. Inflorescences long and slender, bearing relatively large, brightly coloured flowers. These hybrids require intermediate or warm conditions.

× *O.*Mandarine: small plants with upright sprays of brilliant orange fls.

× *O.*Violetta: small plants with upright sprays of pink and purple spotted fls.

Oeceoclades Lindl. (From Gk *oikeios*, private, and *klados*, branch.) About 30 species of terrestrials related to *Eulophia*. Pseudobulbs well developed, on woody rhizome, 1- to several-leaved at apex. Leaves usually stiff, leathery or fleshy, usually conduplicate, often variegated, petiolate, the petiole articulated above the pseudobulb. Inflorescence racemose or paniculate, arising from base of pseudobulb; flowers resupinate, thin-textured; sepals and petals almost similar, free, spreading; lip 3- or 4-lobed, usually spurred, often with a callus at the mouth of the spur; column short, erect; pollinia 2. Tropical & S Africa, Madagascar, Mascarene Is., Seychelles, Comoros Is., India to New Guinea, Polynesia and Australia, Florida, Caribbean, C & S America.

CULTIVATION A most attractive genus of intermediate to warm-growing terrestrial orchids. In addition to the erect spikes of bloom, several of these species bear beautifully mottled leaves, particularly those from Madagascar which show the characteristic colouring of smaller semi-xerophytes in this region – dull pink and brown/green banding and spotting (as can be found in , for example, *Aloe bakeri*). Pot in deep, heavily crocked clays containing a mixture of coarse bark, garden compost, leafmould, sharp sand and a little dried FYM. Maintain light shade (full sunlight for spp. with coloured leathery leaves); reduce water during the winter months, misting to prevent shrivelling.

O.angustifolia (Sengh.) Garay & P. Tayl.
Pseudobulbs 2×2cm, ovoid or pear-shaped, 1-lvd, occasionally 2-lvd, at apex. Lvs more or less erect, to 10cm×7mm, petiolate, linear, acute, dull green mottled with purple. Infl. erect, racemose or with a few branches, to 30cm, 5–15-fld; sep. green-white below, brown above, pet. white with green stripes, lip white, edge of midlobe ochre yellow, lateral lobes and disc spotted with red, spur green; sep. 8×3mm, oblanceolate or elliptic, acute; pet. 6×4.5mm, elliptic; lip 10–12×14–16mm, trilobed, lateral lobes erect, midlobe obo-

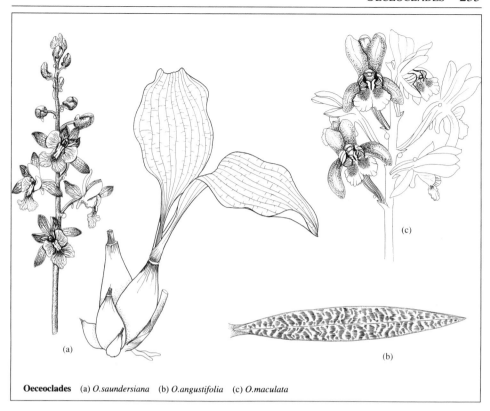

Oeceoclades (a) *O.saundersiana* (b) *O.angustifolia* (c) *O.maculata*

vate, bilobed; callus bilobed; spur globose or subglobose, slightly incurved, 3mm. Madagascar.

O.ecalcarata (Schltr.) Garay & P. Tayl. (*Eulophiopsis ecalcarata* Schltr.).

Pseudobulbs 4–6×1.5cm, ovoid or ellipsoid, set close together on rhiz., 4–5-lvd, the lvs fully developed at flowering time. Lvs 20–25cm×7–8mm, linear, acute, deciduous. Infl. racemose or paniculate with a long peduncle, laxly many-fld; sep. and pet. green dotted with red, lip golden yellow with red spots; pedicel and ovary 10mm; sep. 7–8mm, ovate, obtuse; pet. similar but slightly broader; lip 7mm, trilobed, lateral lobes erect, obtuse, midlobe like a transverse bow with sharp angles, rounded and apiculate in front; spur absent; column 4.5mm. Madagascar.

O.maculata (Lindl.) Lindl.

Pseudobulbs 2–4×1.5–2cm, obliquely conical, sometimes slightly ribbed, 1-lvd. Lvs 8–32×2–5.5cm, lanceolate, stiff, leathery, pale grey-green mottled with darker green, tapering to a short petiole. Raceme to 35cm, about 12-fld; sep. and pet. green-pink, lip white with 2 purple-pink blotches in throat and purple-veined lateral lobes; pedicel and ovary 12mm; sep. and pet. 9–10×3–4mm, lanceolate, pet. slightly wider, lateral sep. spreading and curving down; lip 9×8mm with 2 white, erect calli in throat, trilobed, lateral lobes rounded, erect, midlobe obovate, bilobed, lobes rounded; spur 4–5mm, bulbous at tip; column 3–4mm. Tropical Africa (widespread), Florida, Caribbean, C & S America.

O.pulchra (Thouars) Clements & Cribb (*Eulophia pulchra* (Thouars) Lindl.).

Robust, to 1m; pseudobulbs 12–16×1–1.5cm, spindle-shaped, surrounded with remains of fibrous sheaths, 2–3-lvd. Petiole 12–20cm; lf blade 20–70×3–6cm, lanceolate, fairly thin-tex-

tured. Raceme lax, to 1m; peduncle more than twice as long as rachis; fls yellow-green with small red-purple lines on pet. and lip, throat orange-yellow; pedicel and ovary 2–3cm; sep. 11×3mm, lanceolate, acute, lateral sep. curved and slightly narrower than dorsal sep.; pet. 9×4mm, oblong, acute; lip 6–7×12–15mm with a bifid callus 2mm long in the throat, trilobed, lobes obovate, lateral lobes obscure, midlobe deeply bilobed; spur short, globose, sometimes slightly bifid; column 4–5mm. Madagascar, Mascarene Is., Comoros Is., Asia and SE Asia to New Guinea, Polynesia and Australia.

O.roseovariegata (Sengh.) Garay & P. Tayl.

Pseudobulbs 2.5×2.5cm, ovoid, clustered, violet-brown, 2-lvd. Lvs prostrate, to 4×3.5cm, ovate, acuminate, margins undulate, dark purple-black mottled with pink. Infl. erect, racemose or slightly branched, to 55cm, laxly many-fld; sep. and pet. green flushed with purple outside, lip white, densely red-spotted, column yellow-green, anth. white; sep. 5–6×2mm, oblanceolate, obtuse, lateral sep. slightly curved; pet. 4–5×3mm, oblong-lanceolate, obtuse; lip 3.5–4×7–8mm, trilobed, lateral lobes erect, truncate, midlobe recurved, more or less quadrate, emarginate; spur 5mm, pendent, cylindrical. Madagascar.

O.saundersiana (Rchb. f.) Garay & P. Tayl. (*Eulophia saundersiana* Rchb. f.).

Pseudobulbs 6–20×1.5–2cm, conical or cylindrical, clustered, 1–3-lvd. Lf blade 10–22×4–8cm, glossy green, leathery, narrowing abruptly to a channelled petiole almost as long as blade. Raceme longer than lvs, 20–40-fld; fls yellow-green flushed with purple-brown and with purple-brown veins; sep. 10–20×5–6mm, oblanceolate; pet. 10–15×8mm, ovate; lip 15–20mm with 2 calli at base, 4-lobed, lobes rounded; spur 5–6mm, straight, cylindrical, obtuse. Tropical Africa (widespread).

Oeonia Lindl. (From Gk *oionos*, a bird of prey.) About 6 species of epiphytes, most with long, thin, branched stems. Racemes laxly few- to many-flowered; flowers green or white, the lip often spotted with red or rose pink; sepals and petals free; lip with 3–6 spreading lobes, enfolding column at base; anterior edge of anther toothed or bifid; pollinia 2. Madagascar, Mascarene Is.

CULTIVATION As for *Angraecum*, but with very frequent misting.

O.oncidiiflora Kränzl.
Stem to 80cm, pendent or ascending, sparsely branched, thin, bearing numerous roots and lvs. Roots 1.5–2.5mm diam., mostly aerial. Lvs 2–5×1–2.5cm, ovate-oblong or elliptic, clasping stem at base, bright green. Raceme to 15cm, laxly 2–7-fld; fls 25mm diam., green or yellow-green, lip white spotted with bright red in the throat; pedicel and ovary 15–20mm; sep. 10×4mm, obovate or oblong, obtuse; pet. similar but 2–3mm wide; lip 20–25×25mm, 4-lobed, the lower lobes 5×7mm, rounded, apical lobes 14–15mm wide, fan-shaped, throat scattered with small hairs; spur 7–20mm, tapering from a wide mouth then somewhat swollen at apex; column 2–3mm. Madagascar.

O.volucris (Thouars) Dur. & Schinz. Stems long, thin and branched, pendent or ascending. Lvs about 25×8mm, ovate or elliptic, spread along stem. Racemes 30–35cm, laxly few-fld; fls white; dorsal sep. 12–15×5–6mm, obovate-oblong, lateral sep. 24×8mm, oblanceolate; pet. 12–15×10–12mm, obovate; lip 25–30mm, papillose in throat, trilobed, lateral lobes small, inrolled, midlobe obovate, deeply emarginate or bilobed with a tooth between the lobes; spur 6mm, tapering gradually from mouth to apex; column very short. Range as for the genus.

Oeoniella Schltr. (Diminutive of *Oeonia*.) 2–3 species of epiphytes. Stems long and leafy. Racemes long or short, laxly few- to several-flowered; flowers mainly white; sepals and petals free; lip cone-shaped at base, surrounding the column, trilobed at apex; spur short; pollinia and stipites 2, viscidium 1. Madagascar, Mascarene Is., Seychelles.

CULTIVATION As for *Oeonia*.

O.polystachys (Thouars) Schltr.
Stem usually to 15cm, rarely to 60cm, branched, leafy; roots numerous, 2–3mm diam. Lvs 3–11×1.5–2cm, ligulate or oblong. Racemes arising from stem opposite lvs, erect, 15–25cm, 7–15-fld; fls white; pedicel and ovary 8mm; sep. 12–18×3mm, linear-lanceolate, acuminate, the lateral sep. longer than the dorsal; pet. 15–16mm, linear; lip 16–18mm, cone-shaped, trilobed at apex, lateral lobes broad, margin crenulate, midlobe linear, acuminate; spur 4mm, tapering to apex; column very short. Range as for the genus.

Oerstedella Rchb. f. (For Anders Sandoe Oersted (1816–72), Danish botanist.) Some 25 species of epiphytes or terrestrials allied to *Epidendrum*. Rhizome short. Stems clumped, cane-like, simple or branched, leafy, enveloped by numerous verrucose leaf-sheaths. Leaves numerous, distichous, coriaceous. Inflorescence a terminal (rarely axillary) raceme or a panicle, usually many-flowered; flowers showy; sepals broadly linear-lanceolate to oblong-lanceolate; petals subsimilar to sepals, oblique; lip clawed, adnate to column, 3-lobed, lateral lobes obtuse or acuminate, midlobe large, oblong to oblong-lanceolate, entire to crenulate, callus papillose; pollinia 4, waxy, viscidium absent. Tropical America.

CULTIVATION As for *Epidendrum pseudepidendrum*.

O.centradenia Rchb. f.
Differs from other species described here in its bright rose-magenta fls; tepals more or less equal, oblong-lanceolate; lip large, lateral lobes acutely triangular, divergent, midlobe far larger, deeply cleft, fishtail-like in shape, throat blotched white. Costa Rica, Panama.

O.endresii (Rchb. f.) Hagsater (*Epidendrum endresii* Rchb. f.; *Epidendrum adolphii* Schltr.).
Stems to 30cm, erect, tightly clustered, rigid, simple or branched. Lvs to 4.5×1.5cm, elliptic to oblong-lanceolate, obtuse. Raceme, to 15cm, erect, loosely few to several-fld; fls to 2.5cm diam., fragrant, opal-white tinged lavender to rose-purple; sep. to 11×5mm, elliptic to ovate-oblong, acute, pet. subequal to sep., oblanceolate to obovate-spathulate, obtuse; lip to 12×10mm, white blotched violet-purple, lateral lobes subtriangular, acute or obtuse, midlobe bilobulate, lobules spreading, callus submamillate; column subclavate, anth. purple-violet. Winter. Costa Rica, Panama.

O.schumanniana (Schltr.) Hagsater (*Epidendrum schumannianum* Schltr.).
Stems to 50cm, erect or bowed, clustered, leafy toward apex, covered with verrucose lf-sheaths. Lvs to 9×2.5cm, lustrous, lanceolate to elliptic-oblong, subacute or obtuse. Infl. to 60cm, erect, a raceme or a panicle, loosely many-fld; fls to 2.5cm diam., fragrant, long-lived, fleshy; sep. and pet. yellow spotted red-brown, sep. to 12×5mm, oblanceolate to ovate, acute or obtuse, pet. to 15×8mm, obovate or obovate-spathu-late, obtuse; lip to 15×12mm, dark lavender, lateral lobes oblong, obtuse, spreading, midlobe cuneate-obovate, bifid, entire to crenulate; disc with 2 submamillate basal calli. Costa Rica, Panama.

O.schweinfurthiana (Correll) Hagsater (*Epidendrum schweinfurthianum* Correll).
Stems slender, simple or branched toward apex. Lvs 11×2cm, elliptic-lanceolate, acute or obtuse. Raceme, to 10cm, few-fld; sep. and pet. brown, sep. to 12×7mm, elliptic to obovate-elliptic, obtuse, fleshy, pet. to 13×10mm, obovate-cuneate, rounded to truncate; lip to 15×18mm, deeply 3-lobed, lateral lobes bilobulate, lobules obcordate-ovate, midlobe deeply bilobulate, lobules obovate, crenulate, apex rounded, callus to 2mm, oblong, channelled, with 2 papillae; column to 6mm, apex bilobulate, lobules undulate-crenate. Guatemala.

O.verrucosa (Sw.) Hagsater (*Epidendrum verrucosum* Sw.).
Stems to 120×1cm, stout, reed-like. Lvs to 23×4cm, narrowly lanceolate to linear-lanceolate, acute, erect-ascending. Infl. to 40cm, usually a panicle, many-fld, erect; fls fragrant, long-lived, white to cream-yellow; sep. spreading, to 10×4mm, elliptic-oblong to elliptic-obovate, concave, subacute to obtuse; pet. to 10×3mm, oblanceolate to linear-spathulate, obtuse to subacute; lip to 12mm, deeply 3-lobed, lateral lobes obliquely oblong to elliptic-subquadrate, obtuse to truncate, apex crenulate, midlobe bilobulate, lobules cuneate to broadly subquadrate-flabellate, truncate, apex fimbriate, callus yel-

low, grooved, apex trilobulate; column to 5mm, clinandrium with 4 truncate lobes. Summer. C America, W Indies.

O.wallisii (Rchb. f.) Hagsater (*Epidendrum wallisii* Rchb. f.). Stems slender, to 70×1cm, erect, spotted purple. Lvs to 11×2.5cm, oblong-lanceolate, acute, curved to deflexed. Raceme arching to pendent, terminal or axillary, several-fld; fls to 4.5cm diam., fragrant, long-lived; sep. and pet. yellow to deep golden-yellow, spotted crimson, sep. to 25×11mm, spathulate, obtuse, pet. to 20×9mm, obovate, obtuse; lip to 25×28mm, white marked red-purple, cuneate-flabellate, 3-lobed, with radiating tuberculate lines; column to 6mm, stout. Autumn–early winter. Panama, Colombia. *O.pseudowallisii* differs only in the lip, which is striped rather than spotted or blotched red-purple.

× **Oncidioda** (*Cochlioda* × *Oncidium*). Intergeneric orchid hybrids requiring cool growing conditions. Plants consist of a group of compressed pseudobulbs growing from a basal rhizome, each with one or two leaves at its apex and two or more leaf-like sheaths arising at its base. Inflorescences arise in the axils of these sheaths and may be simple or branched. Flowers have narrow sepals and petals, lip large or small depending on the ancestry; flowers of many colours often conspicuously marked.

× *O.*Charlesworthii: branching sprays of small fls borne in profusion; fls bright red with pink and yellow lip.

Oncidium Sw. (From Gk *onkos*, mass, body, referring to the fleshy, warty calli on the lip of many species.) Some 450 species of epiphytes, lithophytes or terrestrials closely allied to *Odontoglossum, Brassia, Miltonia* and *Psychopsis*. Some authors now treat several *Oncidium* species as members of the genus *Cyrtochilum*. As the whole *Oncidium* complex is still undergoing revision, we have shown these names as synonyms. Rhizome short to long and creeping, enveloped at base by papery bracts. Pseudobulbs large and conspicuous to minute, variously shaped, subtended by distichous sheaths, 1–4-leaved. Leaves equitant, fleshy, coriaceous or soft, oblong-lanceolate to terete; in the softer-leaved species a basal pair of leaves often sheaths the pseudobulbs in its first season prior to abscising to leave the bulb apically bifoliate. Inflorescence a lateral raceme or panicle, often branching and elongated, erect, arching or pendent, loose or dense, few- to many-flowered; flowers variously coloured, often yellow or brown, large and showy to inconspicuous; sepals usually subequal, spreading or reflexed, free or with lateral sepals connate almost to apex; petals similar to dorsal sepal or larger; lip adnate to base of column, entire to 3-lobed, lateral lobes porrect, spreading or reflexed, small and auriculate to large, mid-lobe showy, spreading, emarginate or bifid, central portion usually with an isthmus – disc with cristate or tuberculate basal callus; column short, stout, footless, with a fleshy plate below stigma, with prominent, variously shaped wings or auricles on either side; anther terminal, incumbent, operculate, pollinia 2, waxy, deeply sulcate, affixed to a stipe. Subtropical & Tropical America.

CULTIVATION A large genus of cool and intermediate-growing orchids. They differ greatly in habit, but are easily recognized by their slender, branching sprays of small flowers in shades of yellow and brown. Some of the best-known species, for example *O.papilio*, are now included in separate genera (see synonymy). The smaller species with pronounced pseudobulbs and relatively soft growth require dappled sunlight and a humid, buoyant atmosphere in the cool house. Water and feed freely in the growing season, at other times only to prevent shrivelling. Pot in fine- to medium-grade bark-based mix in clay pans or baskets. The larger species with reduced pseudobulbs and massive, leathery, 'mule's ear' leaves should be mounted on bark or planted in baskets and afforded maximum light and humidity throughout the year. Their water requirement is not so great as that of the first group but they tend to favour a warmer and steamier situation. The inflorescences of species such as *O.cavendishianum* may attain two metres and require some training or, even, tying in to a trellis or the glasshouse framework. *O.pusillum*, a tiny plant with overlapping fleshy leaves and charming, large yellow flowers, needs to be treated as for the smaller *Laelia* species.

O.abortivum Rchb. f.
Pseudobulbs to 4×2.5cm, ellipsoid, clustered, strongly laterally compressed, unifoliate. Lvs to 16×2.5cm, oblong to oblong-lanceolate, acute, thin. Panicle to 30cm, many-fld, composed of fertile and abortive fls, branches 2-ranked; abortive fls consisting of linear seg., to 8mm, fertile fls 1–2, situated at branch apices, bright yellow banded dark purple-brown; dorsal sep. to 12×4mm, lanceolate to linear-lanceolate, acute, lateral sep. longer than dorsal sep.; pet. to 10×4mm, lanceolate to oblong-lanceolate, acute, oblique; lip bright yellow marked brown in centre, to 1.5×2mm, 3-lobed, lateral lobes subrotund, midlobe smaller than lateral lobes, triangular or ovate-triangular to lanceolate, acute, callus pale yellow, tubercles conical or cylindrical; column to 5mm, wings ligulate or deltoid, apical margins dentate. Venezuela.

O.acrobotryum Klotzsch. See *O.harrisonianum*.

O.altissimum (Jacq.) Sw. non Lindl.
Pseudobulbs to 10×5cm, ovoid-oblong, compressed, unifoliate or bifoliate. Lvs to 20×3cm, oblong or oblong-ligulate, acute. Panicle to 3m, short-branched toward apex, each branch 3–5-fld; fls to 3.5cm diam.; sep. and pet. yellow-green barred and blotched maroon, fleshy, narrow-lanceolate or oblanceolate, to 2×0.5cm, dorsally keeled, undulate; lip bright yellow, blotched maroon at base of midlobe, to 1×1cm, lateral lobes small, oblong, midlobe reniform, clawed, emarginate, callus with 10 tubercles; column to 5mm, slightly arching, with small, entire, rounded auricles. W Indies.

O.altissimum Lindl. See *O.baueri*.

O.ampliatum Lindl. (*O.bernoullianum* Kränzl.).
Pseudobulbs to 10×8cm, ovoid to suborbicular, tightly clustered on short rhiz., lustrous green spotted purple-brown, strongly compressed, unifoliate to trifoliate. Lvs to 40×10cm, elliptic-oblanceolate to ligulate, obtuse or broadly rounded, fleshy-coriaceous. Raceme or panicle to 60cm, few- to many-fld; fls to 2.5cm diam.; sep. bright to pale yellow spotted chocolate-brown, to 10×7mm, obovate-spathulate, concave, incurved; pet. to 10×9mm, yellow with a few brown spots, flat, suborbicular, basally clawed, rounded at apex; lip bright

yellow, paler below, to 2.5×3cm, deeply 3-lobed, lateral lobes small, subauriculate, midlobe broadly oblong or reniform, cleft or bilobed, callus pale cream marked yellow, fleshy, 3-lobed, midlobe trituberculate; column to 4mm, wings denticulate or lobulate. Guatemala to Peru, Venezuela, Trinidad.

O.ansiferum Rchb. f. (*O.delumbe* Lindl.; *O.lankesteri* Ames; *O.naranjense* Schltr.).
Pseudobulbs to 14×7cm, ovate-elliptic or elliptic-oblong, strongly compressed, unifoliate or bifoliate. Lvs to 45× 5.5cm, elliptic-oblong to elliptic-oblanceolate, subcoriaceous. Panicle to 1m, solitary or paired, much-branched; fls to 3cm diam.; sep. and pet. red-brown edged yellow, sep. to 17× 6mm, short-clawed, elliptic-oblong to lanceolate, spreading-reflexed, strongly undulate, pet. wider than sep., elliptic-oblong to elliptic-lanceolate, obtuse to subacute, strongly undulate; lip bright yellow with yellow-brown claw, to 18×13mm, pandurate, lateral lobes short, suborbicular, auriculate, midlobe broadly reniform to semi-orbicular to bilobulate with broadly triangular claw, callus yellow-white spotted pale brown, fleshy, obovate, 5-lobed, puberulent, ending in a central, porrect tooth; column to 6mm, stout, wings dolabriform, dentate-crenulate. Costa Rica, Guatemala, Panama, Nicaragua.

O.anthocrene Rchb. f. (*O.powellii* Schltr.).
Pseudobulbs to 15×5cm, ovoid-oblong, compressed, ridged, unifoliate or bifoliate. Lvs to 38×5cm, oblong-ligulate to oblong-lanceolate, obtuse or slightly retuse, coriaceous. Raceme rarely branching, to 1.2m, many-fld; fls to 6.5cm diam., waxy; sep. and pet. brown marked yellow, undulate, usually clawed; lip with central red-brown claw, pandurate, 3-lobed, lateral lobes small, yellow often spotted red-brown, midlobe bright yellow, cuspidate, bilobulate, callus yellow, toothed; column scarcely winged. Panama, Colombia.

O.ascendens Lindl.
Pseudobulbs to 2×1cm, ovoid, unifoliate or bifoliate. Lvs to 80×1cm, terete, lightly sulcate. Raceme to 50cm, simple or branched; fls small, yellow marked and stained red-brown; sep. spreading-reflexed, to 10×5mm, deeply concave, obovate; pet. resemble sep. in size, elliptic to subquadrate, apex rounded to truncate; lip yellow marked red near callus, larger than sep., lateral lobes obliquely oblong, small, erect, midlobe transversely elliptic to semi-orbicular, emarginate, callus erect, with suborbicular central keel flanked by several tubercles; column to 5mm, stout, wings narrow, falcate, incurved. C America, Mexico.

O.auriferum Rchb. f.
Pseudobulbs to 6×4cm, ovoid, clustered, compressed, unifoliate. Lvs to 25×2.5cm, linear, coriaceous. Panicle to 40cm, loosely many-fld, branches small, spreading; fls to 2.5cm diam.; sep. and pet. yellow with 2 or 3 pale brown bands, dorsal sep. to 10×4mm, elliptic or elliptic-oblong, obtuse, laterals ligulate to linear-ligulate, obtuse; lip golden-yellow with a blotch of pale red-brown either side of disc, to 15×20mm, pandurate, lateral lobes small, oblong, margins revolute, midlobe transversely oblong to reniform, apex cleft, margins wavy, separated from lateral lobes by broad claw, callus white, triangular, dentate; column wings broad, dolabriform, dentate. Venezuela, Colombia.

O.aurosum Rchb. f. See *O.excavatum*.

O.barbatum Lindl. (*O.ciliatum* Lindl.; *O.ciliatulum* Hoffsgg.; *O.fimbriatum* Hoffsgg.; *O.microglossum* Klotzsch).
Pseudobulbs to 6.5×3.5cm, ovate to ovate-oblong with well-defined central ridge, unifoliate. Lvs to 10×2.5cm, linear-lanceolate to ovate-oblong, acute or emarginate. Panicle to 50cm, short-branched, loosely few-fld; fls to 2.5cm diam., waxy; sep. and pet. yellow barred chestnut-brown, sep. to 1.4×0.5cm, clawed, ovate-lanceolate to elliptic-oblong, undulate, lateral sep. connate in basal half, pet. slightly shorter and broader than sep., clawed, obliquely oblong; lip to 1×2cm, bright yellow, spotted red on callus, lateral lobes equal midlobe, obovate, obtuse, midlobe obovate, emarginate to apiculate, callus orbicular, fimbriate, 5-toothed; column wings suborbicular to subquadrate. Brazil, Bolivia.

O.baueri Lindl. (*O.altissimum* Lindl. *O.hebraicum* Rchb. f.).
Rhiz. long-creeping. Pseudobulbs to 15×4cm, oblong-ovoid to cylindric, strongly compressed, usually bifoliate. Lvs to 78×6cm, ligulate to linear-oblong, acute to short-acuminate, slightly coriaceous. Panicle to 3m, much-branched, many-fld; fls to 3cm diam., waxy, long-lived; sep. and pet. green-yellow to bright yellow barred brown, sep. to 17×5mm, elliptic-lanceolate to obliquely linear-lanceolate, acute or short-acuminate, lateral sep. free, recurved at apex, pet. to 12×3mm, elliptic-lanceolate, acute with recurved apex; lip to 2×1cm, yellow with red-brown central blotch, pandurate to 3-lobed, lateral lobes small, midlobe transversely reniform, emarginate, broadly clawed, callus consisting of many teeth in 3 series, terminating in 3 subequal teeth; column to 6mm. Peru, Brazil, Bolivia, Ecuador.

O.bernoullianum Kränzl. See *O.ampliatum*.

O.bicallosum Lindl.
Resembles *O.cavendishianum* except infl. racemose, fls larger, yellow with green-brown suffusion, unspotted, lip lateral lobes smaller, callus bituberculate. Mexico, Guatemala, El Salvador.

O.bicolor Lindl.
Pseudobulbs to 7×3cm, ovoid, compressed, sharply ridged, unifoliate or bifoliate. Lvs to 18×6cm, oblong or oblong-elliptic, acute, base attenuate, coriaceous. Panicle to 1m, much-branched; fls numerous, small; sep. and pet. brown-yellow marked dark red-brown, dorsal sep. to 10×5mm, ovate to obovate, acute to rounded, concave, lateral sep. to 13×4mm, connate to middle or less, free portion oblong, acute, pet. to 12×6mm, narrowly obovate, acute to rounded, slightly undulate; lip bright yellow, to 2.5×3cm, pandurate, emarginate, callus white marked dark red-brown, pubesc., broadly triangular, tuberculate; column to 6mm. Venezuela, Brazil.

O.bicornutum Hook. See *O.pubes*.

O.bifolium Sims (*O.vexillarium* Rchb. f.; *O.celsium* A. Rich.).
Pseudobulbs to 9cm, ovoid or ovoid-oblong, clustered, grooved with age, bifoliate, rarely unifoliate. Lvs to 14×1.5cm, linear-ligulate, acute, subcoriaceous, often tinged bronze. Infl. simple, sometimes branched, to 35cm; fls 5–20, to 2.5cm diam.; sep. and pet. yellow marked red-brown, sep. ovate-elliptic, rounded, to 9×4mm, lateral sep. exceeding dorsal sep., pet. to 7×6mm, ovate, rounded or emarginate; lip rich golden-yellow, to 2×2.5cm, deflexed, lateral lobes small, triangular, midlobe large, short-clawed, reniform, strongly emarginate; callus yellow marked red-brown, tuberculate in front; column short, wing margins denticulate. Brazil, Uruguay, Argentina, Bolivia.

O.bifrons Lindl. See *O.warscewiczii*.

O.boothianum Rchb. f.
Pseudobulbs to 8cm, ellipsoid, strongly compressed, glossy green, unifoliate or bifoliate. Lvs to 30×9cm, ligulate, subacute, subcoriaceous. Panicle to 2m, arcuate to pendent, much-branched, many-fld; fls to 3cm diam.; sep. and pet. yellow marked red-brown, narrowly oblong, to 9×4mm; lip to 2×1cm, golden yellow marked red-brown, lateral lobes rounded, midlobe long-clawed, reniform, emarginate, larger than lateral lobes, callus white, verrucose, shortly pubesc. at base; column yellow, wings large, fringed. Venezuela.

O.brachyandrum Lindl. (*O.graminifolium* Lindl.).
Pseudobulbs to 8×4.5cm, ovoid to ellipsoid, clustered, compressed, often spotted purple, bifoliate or trifoliate. Lvs to 30×2cm, grassy, ligulate to linear-lanceolate. Raceme or panicle slender, elongated, few- to many-fld; sep. and pet. yellow or yellow-green mottled red-brown, sep. to 15×7mm, elliptic-oblong to elliptic-oblanceolate, acute to obtuse, concave, lateral sep. oblique, free or slightly connate, pet. smaller than sep., elliptic-oblanceolate to elliptic-oblong, rounded to subacute; lip yellow, to 2.5×2.5cm, broadly pandurate, emarginate, apical margin decurved, callus yellow marked red-

brown, linear, fleshy, 3-keeled; column to 7mm, yellow spotted brown at apex, wings small, auriculate. Mexico, Guatemala, Honduras.

O.bracteatum Rchb. f. & Warscz.
Pseudobulbs to 7.5×3.5cm, linear to ovoid-oblong, strongly compressed, bifoliate, rarely unifoliate. Lvs to 40×3cm, linear-ligulate, obtuse, coriaceous. Panicle to 120cm, short-branched, conspicuously bracteate; fls usually 3, to 2.5cm diam.; sep. and pet. bright yellow-green heavily blotched and spotted brown-purple, sep. to 15×5mm, free, undulate, lateral sep. linear, prominently keeled below, dorsal sep. oblong-lanceolate, acute, pet. to 14×4mm, linear-oblong, acute, undulate; lip bright to pale yellow with red-brown claw, to 13×15cm, obscurely 3-lobed, midlobe oblong, emarginate, disc fleshy, with erect, toothed callus; column to 6mm, narrowly winged. Costa Rica, Panama, Nicaragua, Colombia.

O.brenesii Schltr. See *O.obryzatum.*

O.brevilabrum Rolfe.
Pseudobulbs to 5.25cm, ovoid. Lvs to 32cm, linear. Panicles crowded; fls to 2cm diam., golden-yellow banded chocolate brown. S America.

O.bryolophotum Rchb. f. See *O.heteranthum.*

O.cabagrae Schltr. (*O.rechingerianum* Kränzl.).
Pseudobulbs to 11×3cm, ovoid-elliptic to sublinear, strongly compressed, spotted black-brown, usually bifoliate. Lvs to 25×3cm, linear-ligulate, acute, subcoriaceous. Panicle to 80cm, loosely many-fld; fls to 2.5cm diam., long-lived; sep. and pet. yellow, heavily blotched deep chestnut-brown, sep. to 12×6mm, clawed, elliptic-lanceolate, acute, apices recurved, lateral sep. keeled below, pet. broader than sep., elliptic-oblanceolate, undulate; lip bright yellow with red-brown claw, lateral lobes small, semi-orbicular, midlobe reniform, emarginate, callus white spotted brown, erect, fleshy, truncate, bidentate; column to 5mm, wings broad, bilobed, minutely dentate. Costa Rica, Panama.

O.caminiophorum Rchb. f.
Pseudobulbs to 4×3cm, suborbicular to narrowly ovoid, compressed, unifoliate. Lvs to 12cm, oblong or linear-oblong. Panicle to 50cm, branched from base, many-fld; fls to 2.5cm across; sep. bright yellow, brown in basal half, free, to 8×3mm, lanceolate to obovate-oblong, acute, lateral sep. reflexed at apex; pet. resembling sep. in colour but obovate-oblong, obtuse; lip bright yellow spotted red, with chestnut-brown band, to 1×1cm, pandurate, lateral lobes ovate, rounded, midlobe transversely elliptic to subrotund, apex cleft, separated from lateral lobes by narrow claw, callus subquadrate with 3 small teeth on each side at base; column wings small, truncate. Venezuela.

O.candidum Lindl. See *Palumbina candida.*

O.cardiochilum Lindl. (*O.ochmatochilum* Rchb. f.).
Pseudobulbs to 10×2.5cm, ovoid-cylindric, compressed, concealed by sheathing lf bases, bifoliate. Lvs to 75×6cm, linear-ligulate to narrowly oblanceolate, acute to acuminate, slightly conduplicate, subcoriaceous. Panicle to 2m, loosely many-branched, rachis distinctly fractiflex; fls to 2cm across, lilac-scented; sep. and pet. red-brown tipped and marked green-white, sep. free, lance-lanceolate to linear-elliptic, acute or acuminate and recurved at apex, to 20×5mm, lateral sep. oblique, dorsally strongly carinate, pet. shorter and wider than sep.; lip white tinged and spotted red-purple, to 17×15mm, broadly pandurate, 3-lobed, callus spotted brown, with several small tubercles on either side and a large terminal tubercle; column to 6mm, marked red-brown, wings reduced. Guatemala, Peru, Costa Rica, Panama, Colombia.

O.carinatum Lindl. See *Leochilus carinatus.*
O.cariniferum (Rchb. f.) Beer. See *Odontoglossum cariniferum.*

O.carthagenense (Jacq.) Sw. (*O.kymatoides* Kränzl.; *O.oerstedii* Rchb. f.).
Pseudobulbs absent or to 2.5cm, unifoliate, sheathed. Lvs to 50×7cm, broadly lanceolate to oblong-elliptic, acute or sub-acuminate, rigid and coriaceous, green spotted red-brown, keeled below toward base. Panicle to 2m, many-fld; fls to 2.5cm across, showy, pale yellow or white, variously blotched and spotted rose-purple; sep. to 1.5×1cm, clawed, rounded, undulate-crisped; pet. clawed, oblong to elliptic-oblong, obtuse, undulate-crisped; lip to 16×14mm, pandurate, 3-lobed, callus prominent, fleshy, erect, tuberculate; column to 4mm, fleshy, with large, bilobulate, lateral wings. Florida and W Indies, Mexico to Venezuela and Brazil.

O.cavendishianum Batem. (*O.pachyphyllum* Hook.).
Pseudobulbs to 2cm or absent, unifoliate. Lvs to 45×13cm, elliptic-oblong or broadly lanceolate, acute to subobtuse, usually yellow-green, flushed blood red in strong sunlight, thickly coriaceous, keeled below. Panicle to 2m on a stout erect scape, usually branched, many-fld; fls to 4cm diam., showy, fragrant, waxy; sep. and pet. yellow or green-yellow variously spotted and blotched red or brown, sep. to 1.5×1cm, obovate or suborbicular, obtuse or rounded, concave, undulate, dorsal sep. cochleate forming hood over column, pet. similar to sep., smaller, shortly clawed; lip deep yellow, larger than sep., deeply 3-lobed, undulate, callus white flecked red-brown, tubercled; column to 1cm, wings yellow spotted red, deflexed, falcate. Mexico, Honduras, Guatemala.

O.cebolleta (Jacq.) Sw. (*O.longifolium* Lindl.).
Pseudobulbs to 1.5×1.5cm, conical to subspherical, concealed by large white sheaths, unifoliate. Lvs to 40×2.5cm, subcylindric to terete, sulcate, erect or suberect, dull grey-green sometimes spotted purple, tapering to sharp apex. Raceme or panicle simple or short-branched, to 150cm, many-fld; peduncle green spotted dark purple; fls to 3.5cm diam.; sep. and pet. green-yellow marked deep red-brown, sep. to 1.5×1cm, obovate, obtuse, spreading-reflexed, undulate, pet. slightly smaller than sep., oblong, rounded to subacute, undulate; lip bright yellow spotted red-brown, to 2×2.5cm, deeply 3-lobed, lateral lobes large, obovate, entire to crenulate, midlobe reniform-flabellate, emarginate, callus spotted red-brown, a sharp projecting keel with several tubercles on either side; column to 5mm, wings small, spreading, subquadrate or bilobulate. Mexico and W Indies to Paraguay.

O.celsium A. Rich. See *O.bifolium.*
O.cerebriferum Rchb. f. See *O.ensatum.*

O.cheirophorum Rchb. f. (*O.dielsianum* Kränzl.). COLOMBIA BUTTERCUP.
Dwarf epiphyte. Pseudobulbs to 2.5×1.5cm, ovoid to suborbicular, tightly clustered, unifoliate. Lvs to 15×1.5cm, oblanceolate to linear-ligulate, subacute, thin. Panicle to 20cm, slender, densely many-fld; fls to 1.5cm diam., fragrant, bright yellow; dorsal sep. erect, short-clawed, to 5×3mm, deeply concave, obovate, minutely apiculate, lateral sep. to 6×3mm, obovate, recurved; pet. smaller than sep., short-clawed, rotund; lip larger than sep., lateral lobes erect, spreading, subquadrate to suborbicular, lower margin recurved, midlobe sessile, oblong to rotund, emarginate, margins upcurved, callus white, fleshy, with 3–5 apical teeth; column short, erect, wings obovate, porrect. Colombia, Panama, Costa Rica.

O.chrysomorphum Lindl.
Pseudobulbs to 5cm, ovoid, compressed, clustered, bifoliate or trifoliate. Lvs to 23cm, linear, subacute, slightly coriaceous. Panicle to 55cm, erect, branched from middle, densely fld, branches short, distichous, alternate, recurved; fls to 2cm across; sep. and pet. similar, golden yellow, to 10×2mm, oblong-lanceolate or spathulate, obtuse to acute or apiculate, reflexed, undulate; lip pale yellow, to 10×7mm, pandurate, 3-lobed, lateral lobes rounded, midlobe transversely elliptic to elliptic-reniform, clawed, obscurely 2-lobed, callus oblong, with 2 dorsal teeth and 2 teeth on each side; column wings obsolete. Colombia, Venezuela.

O.ciliatulum Hoffsgg. See *O.barbatum.*
O.ciliatum Lindl. See *O.barbatum.*

O.cimiciferum (Rchb. f.) Lindl. (*Odontoglossum cimiciferum* Rchb. f.; *O.flexuosum* Lindl. non Sims).
Pseudobulbs to 10×4cm, oblong-cylindrical, compressed, deeply grooved, unifoliate or bifoliate. Lvs to 65×5cm, linear-oblong to narrowly lanceolate, acute or acuminate. Panicle to 3m with many short branches; fls small, brown or green-yellow banded brown, reflexed, undulate; dorsal sep. to 12×4mm, spathulate to elliptic-lanceolate, acute, lateral sep. longer, obliquely oblong-oblanceolate, acute; pet. to 1×6mm, elliptic-obovate, acute; lip to 8×8mm, simple, ovate-triangular, subtruncate, convex, callus bright yellow, multilobulate; column to 4mm, wings obscure, broad, anth. brown, pollinia elongate, yellow. Venezuela, Colombia, Ecuador, Peru.

O.cirrhosum (Lindl.) Beer. See *Odontoglossum cirrhosum.*

O.citrinum Lindl.
Resembles *O.altissimum* vegetatively. Infl. simple or slightly branched, to 40cm, slender, several-fld; fls to 3.5cm diam.; sep. and pet. pale yellow or green-yellow faintly marked brown, to 12×3.5mm, spreading, ovate-oblong or ligulate, acute; lip clear yellow spotted and marked pale red-brown on callus, to 12×9mm, rounded-pandurate, 3-lobed, lateral lobes short, midlobe deeply emarginate, callus prominent, complex, bluntly dentate with short glandular hairs on central portion; column yellow blotched maroon, anth. pale yellow, unicellular. Trinidad, Venezuela, Colombia.

O.citrosmum (Lindl.) Beer. See *Cuitlauzina pendula.*

O.concolor Hook.
Pseudobulbs to 5×2.5cm, ovate-oblong, clustered, furrowed, usually bifoliate. Lvs to 15×2.5cm, ligulate-lanceolate, acute, subcoriaceous. Raceme to 30cm, pendent, loosely few- to many-fld; fls to 4cm diam., bright golden-yellow; sep. narrowly obovate-oblong, acute, to 2×1cm, concave, lateral sep. connate for half of length, longer and narrower than dorsal sep.; pet. elliptic-oblong, to 2×1cm, minutely apiculate, slightly undulate; lip to 3.5×3cm, prominently clawed, slightly convex, cuneate-orbicular, emarginate, callus bilamellate; column wings linear, tooth-like, spreading. Brazil.

O.confusum Rchb. f. See *O.ensatum.*
O.convolvulaceum Lindl. See *O.globuliferum.*

O.cornigerum Lindl.
Pseudobulbs to 10cm, subcylindrical, sulcate, compressed, unifoliate. Lvs to 15cm, fleshy, broadly ovate or elliptic-oblong, subacute, dark green. Panicle to 30cm; fls to 2cm diam., crowded in upper reaches of infl.; sep. and pet. bright yellow spotted and banded red-brown, dorsal sep. curved over column, concave, ovate, lateral sep. connate to middle or more, ovate-oblong, pet. clawed, obovate, obtuse, incurved; lip bright yellow, pandurate, lateral lobes narrow, horn-like, curved upwards and inwards, midlobe oblong-orbicular, crisped, callus corniculate, tubercled; column wings spreading, linear-triangular. Brazil.

O.corynephorum Lindl. See *O.volubile.*

O.crispum Lodd.
Pseudobulbs to 10×5cm, oblong or ovoid, clustered, compressed, wrinkled with age, dark brown, bifoliate or trifoliate. Lvs to 20×5cm, oblong-lanceolate, acute, subcoriaceous. Panicle to 110cm, erect to pendent, strongly branched, many-fld; peduncle glaucescent, often mottled dull crimson; fls to 10cm across, showy, all seg. strongly crisped-undulate; sep. and pet. chestnut-brown or copper-brown sometimes spotted yellow, sep. clawed, obovate-oblong, to 2.5×1.5cm, acute, lateral sep. connate towards base, pet. slightly wider than sep., short-clawed, ovate, rounded at apex; lip chestnut-brown or copper-red with yellow base and callus, short-clawed, deflexed, to 3×3cm, obscurely 3-lobed. Brazil.

O.crispum var. *forbesii* (Hook.) Burb. See *O.forbesii.*

O.crista-galli Rchb. f. (*O.iridifolium* Lindl.; *O.decipiens* Lindl.).
Diminutive epiphyte. Pseudobulbs to 1.5×1cm, ovoid, clustered, concealed by several leaflike bracts, terminated by an abortive lf, 1.5×1cm; leaflike bracts to 8×1cm, flat, thin, linear-ligulate to narrowly elliptic, acute. Infl. 1–4, slender, equalling lvs, filiform, 1- to few-fld; fls to 2cm diam.; sep. yellow-green, spreading, dorsal sep. to 6×4mm, elliptic-ovate or elliptic-lanceolate, slightly concave, acute or apiculate, keeled below, lateral sep. narrower than dorsal sep., obliquely elliptic-lanceolate, acute; pet. to 10×5mm, obliquely ovate-oblong, bright yellow barred red-brown; lip bright yellow marked red-brown on disc, complexly 3-lobed, lateral lobes spreading, obovate-spathulate, short-clawed, crispate, midlobe large, short-clawed, 4-lobed, apical lobules projecting, ovate to oblong, lateral lobules rounded, callus large, flat, lobulate with 1 or more papillae on each side; column to 4mm, wings fleshy, rounded to obliquely ovate. Mexico to Colombia, Peru, Ecuador.

O.cristatum (Lindl.) Beer. See *Odontoglossum cristatum.*

O.cryptocopis Rchb. f.
Pseudobulbs to 12cm, narrowly ovoid-conic, bifoliate. Lvs to 50×3cm, ligulate or linear-oblong, acute. Panicle to 2m, cascading, branches remote, short, few-fld; fls to 7.5cm across; sep. and pet. chestnut-brown edged golden-yellow, clawed, dorsal sep. to 2×2.5cm, short-clawed, broadly ovate, acute, apex recurved, margins undulate, lateral sep. long-clawed, exceeding dorsal sep., obliquely elliptic-ovate, acute or acuminate, apex recurved, pet. narrower than dorsal sep., ovate-lanceolate, obtuse, undulate-crisped, recurved, short-clawed; lip smaller than pet., chestnut-brown, pandurate-trilobed, lateral lobes small, triangular, reflexed, midlobe yellow, long-clawed, transversely oblong, retuse, central keel callused, papillose; column to 1cm, with 2 parallel, decurved horns in front, wings spreading, margins ciliate. Peru.

O.cucullatum Lindl.
Pseudobulbs to 5cm, ovoid to oblong, unifoliate or bifoliate. Lvs to 20×3.5cm, linear-ligulate or narrow-lanceolate, acute, dark green. Raceme or panicle slender, to 50cm, few- to many-fld; fls to 3.5cm diam.; sep. dark chestnut-brown or olive-green sometimes with yellow margin, to 12×6cm, ovate-oblong, concave, lateral sep. connate, bifid at apex; pet. similar to dorsal sep.; lip white to rose-purple spotted purple-crimson, to 2.5×3.5cm, basally 3-lobed, callus bright orange-yellow, with 5 tubercles; column short, stout, hooded. Colombia, Ecuador.

O.cucullatum var. *nubigenum* (Lindl.) Lindl. See *O.nubigenum.*
O.cucullatum var. *phalaenopsis* (Lind. & Rchb. f.) Veitch. See *O.phalaenopsis.*

O.dasystyle Rchb. f.
Pseudobulbs to 5cm, oval, clustered, compressed, furrowed with age, unifoliate or usually bifoliate. Lvs to 15×2.5cm, narrowly lanceolate, subacute, bright green, keeled. Raceme or panicle to 40cm, sparsely branched, several-fld; peduncle slender; fls to 4cm diam.; sep. and pet. subequal, pale yellow blotched purple-brown, to 1.5cm, ovate-lanceolate, lateral sep. connate to middle; lip pale yellow, short-clawed, undulate, midlobe broadly reniform, large, callus dark purple, cordate, 2-lobed; column wings quadrate-orbicular, anth. beaked. Brazil.

O.decipiens Lindl. See *O.crista-galli.*

O.deltoideum Lindl.
Pseudobulbs to 7.5cm, ovoid, compressed, bifoliate or trifoliate. Lvs to 25×3cm, linear or oblong-lanceolate, acute, subcoriaceous. Panicle to 80cm, branches spreading, loosely many-fld; fls to 2.5cm diam., pale golden-yellow, sometimes spotted red; sep. to 12×6mm, spathulate to oblong-oblanceolate, acute or obtuse, clawed, apex recurved; pet. shorter and wider than sep., ovate-spathulate, subacute to rounded, apex recurved, undulate; lip shorter and wider than sep., simple,

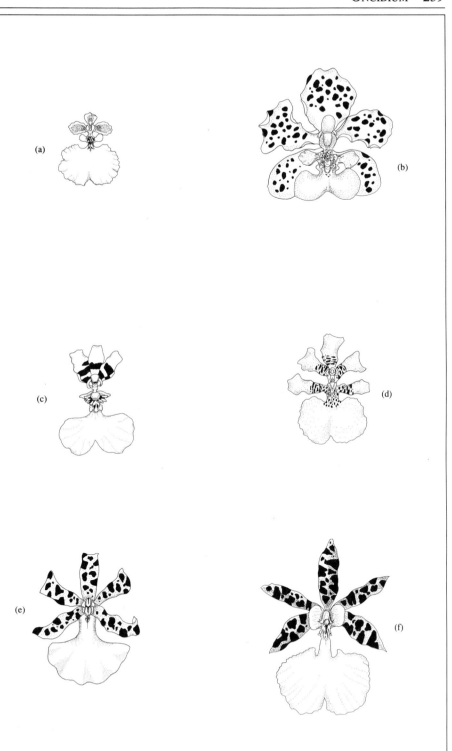

Oncidium   (a) *O.bifolium*   (b) *O.cavendishianum*   (c) *O.flexuosum*   (d) *O.globuliferum*   (e) *O.splendidum*
(f) *O.tigrinum*

cordate-reniform, subacute or apiculate, callus pale yellow surrounded by red band, toothed and verrucose; column to 6mm, wings broadly semi-ovate, entire to minutely dentate. Peru.

O.delumbe Lindl. See *O.ansiferum*.
O.diadema Lindl. See *O.serratum*.
O.dielsianum Kränzl. See *O.cheirophorum*.
O.digitatum Lindl. See *O.leucochilum*.

O.divaricatum Lindl.
Pseudobulbs to 4cm, subspherical, strongly compressed, yellow-green, unifoliate. Lvs to 30×8cm, oblong, coriaceous, obtuse. Panicle to 2m, much-branched, many-fld; peduncle dull purple; fls to 2.5cm; sep. and pet. yellow blotched chestnut-brown, sep. to 12×6mm, spathulate, pet. larger than sep., short-clawed, oblong, obtuse; lip yellow spotted chestnut-brown, to 1.5×1.5cm, lateral lobes large, rotund, midlobe small, transversely oblong, emarginate, undulate, callus 4-lobed, cushion-like; column glabrous, wings rounded. Brazil.

O.echinatum HBK. See *Erycina echinata*.
O.egertonii (Lindl.) Beer. See *Osmoglossum egertonii*.

O.ensatum Lindl. (*O.cerebriferum* Rchb. f.; *O.confusum* Rchb. f.).
Pseudobulbs to 10×5cm, ovoid or ellipsoid, pale blue-green, slightly compressed, bifoliate. Lvs to 100×3cm, yellow-green, linear-lanceolate, long-acuminate, subcoriaceous, carinate below. Panicle to 2m, many-fld; fls to 3cm diam.; sep. and pet. clear yellow or yellow marked olive-brown, spreading-reflexed, undulate, short-clawed, sep. to 15×5mm, oblanceolate, acute; lip bright yellow, broadly pandurate, to 18×13mm, lateral lobes small, obtuse or auriculate, margins recurved, midlobe separated from lateral lobes by broad claw, transversely subreniform to suborbicular-cordate, emarginate, callus white, prominent, fleshy; column short, wings broad, crenulate. British Honduras to Panama.

O.epidendroides (HBK) Beer. See *Odontoglossum epidendroides*.

O.excavatum Lindl. (*O.aurosum* Rchb. f.).
Pseudobulbs to 18cm, ovoid-oblong, slightly compressed, clustered, lustrous green, unifoliate or bifoliate. Lvs to 50×4cm, linear to linear-ligulate. Panicle to 1.5m, stout, many-fld; fls to 3.5cm diam.; sep. and pet. golden yellow, spotted and barred red-brown basally, strongly undulate, dorsal sep. to 1.5×1cm, obovate-oblong or oblanceolate, acute, lateral sep. narrower, oblong-oblanceolate, acute, pet. larger than sep., obovate-oblong, apex retuse; lip to 2×2cm, lateral lobes small, rounded, red-brown, midlobe short-clawed, transversely oblong, emarginate, yellow, red towards base, callus consisting of 5 lines of tubercles with a decurrent plate on either side; column to 5mm, wings oblong, porrect, slightly notched. Ecuador, Peru.

O.falcipetalum Lindl. (*Cyrtochilum falcipetalum* (Lindl.) Kränzl.).
Pseudobulbs to 15×5cm, oval or ovoid-oblong, unifoliate or bifoliate. Lvs to 60×5.5cm, oblanceolate to lanceolate-ligulate. Panicle to 6m, short-branched, flexuous; fls to 7cm diam.; sep. russet-brown edged yellow, to 3×2.5cm, clawed, strongly undulate, dorsal sep. rounded, lateral sep. ovate, sub-acute; pet. yellow blotched chestnut-brown, smaller than sep., ovate-lanceolate, acute, strongly undulate; lip green-brown or purple-brown with yellow base and shiny brown sides, to 12×5mm, linear, lateral lobes triangular, reflexed, midlobe lanceolate to oblong-obovate, acute, callus bright yellow, fleshy, tubercled and ridged; column yellow-brown, spotted yellow-brown near base, to 1cm, wings small, horn-like. Venezuela, Colombia, Ecuador, Peru.

O.fimbriatum Hoffsgg. See *O.barbatum*.

O.flexuosum Sims (*O.haematochrysum* Rchb. f.; *O.haematoxanthum* Rchb. f.).
Pseudobulbs to 9×3cm, often remote, ovoid-oblong, strongly compressed, often yellow-green, bifoliate or rarely unifoliate.

Lvs to 22×3cm, oblong-ligulate or linear-lanceolate, acute, subcoriaceous, bright green. Panicle to 1m, usually many-fld; fls to 2cm diam.; sep. and pet. bright yellow blotched and barred red-brown, dorsal sep. to 4×2mm, obovate-oblong, obtuse, concave, lateral sep. similar, base connate, apex bifid, pet. similar to dorsal sep., slightly larger; lip bright yellow marked red-brown on callus, to 13×15mm, clawed, lateral lobes auriculate, midlobe broadly reniform, emarginate, callus cushion-like, with 3 denticulate lobes in front; column wings subquadrate, curved forward. Brazil, Argentina, Paraguay, Uruguay.

O.flexuosum Lindl. non Sims. See *O.cimiciferum*.

O.forbesii Hook. (*O.crispum* var. *forbesii* (Hook.) Burb.).
Resembles *O.crispum* except infl. simple, sep. and pet. rich chestnut-brown with yellow-marbled margins, column wings entire, spotted red. Brazil.

O.fulgens Schltr. See *O.obryzatum*.

O.fuscatum Rchb.f. (*Miltonia warscewiczii* Rchb. f.).
Rhiz. abbreviated. Pseudobulbs to 12.5×2.5cm, oblong-cylindric, strongly compressed, dark green. Lvs to 33×3.5cm, linear-oblong, acute or obtuse, bright green. Infl. a panicle or rarely a raceme, to 54cm, suberect to arcuate, exceeding lvs, often loosely branched, many-fld; fls widely spreading; tepals cinnamon, white or yellow at apex, to 2.5×1.5cm, oblong-spathulate, margins undulate; lip to 3×2.5cm, rose-purple, tinged yellow and red-brown, margins white, ovate-suborbicular or suborbicular-obovate, deeply bilobed at apex; disc with 2 small yellow teeth; column short, stout, wings rounded. Peru, Colombia, Costa Rica.

O.galeottianum Drapiez. See *Cuitlauzina pendula*.

O.gardneri Lindl.
Resembles *O.crispum* except sep. and pet. brown striped yellow marginally, oblanceolate, lip with very small lateral lobes, midlobe yellow spotted red-brown marginally, brown at base, column wings entire. Brazil.

O.ghiesbrechtiana A. Rich. & Gal. See *Mexicoa ghiesbrechtiana*.

O.globuliferum HBK (*O.wercklei* Schltr.; *O.scansor* Rchb. f.; *O.convolvulaceum* Lindl.).
Rhiz. to 5m, slender, flexuous. Pseudobulbs remote, to 2.5×2cm, suborbicular to elliptic, unifoliate. Lvs to 6×2cm, elliptic-oblong, coriaceous. Infl. to 9cm, 1-fld; fls to 3.5cm; sep. and pet. basally spotted red or red-brown, dorsal sep. to 16×7mm, elliptic-oblong, acute, undulate, lateral sep. similar, obliquely lanceolate to oblong, short-clawed, pet. wider than sep., short-clawed, elliptic-oblong, subacute, undulate; lip to 3×4cm, bright yellow marked red-brown on claw and callus, lateral lobes small, midlobe large, spreading, deeply bilobed, undulate, callus small, triangular, tubercled; column wings spreading, green-yellow. Colombia, Venezuela, Costa Rica, Panama.

O.graminifolium Lindl. See *O.brachyandrum*.
O.guttatum (L.) Rchb. f. See *O.luridum*.

O.haematochilum Lindl.
Vegetatively similar to *O.lanceanum*. Panicle to 60cm, many-fld; fls to 5cm diam., long-lived, fragrant; sep. and pet. yellow-green blotched rich cinnamon, clawed, to 2.5cm, dorsal sep. suborbicular, lateral sep. free, oblong, pet. obovate-oblong, undulate; lip bright crimson, margin yellow spotted red, broadly clawed, base biauriculate, lamina transversely oblong, emarginate, callus bright crimson, 5-parted, verrucose, central portion a raised subtriangular plate; column wings rose-purple, reniform, recurved. Colombia, Trinidad.

O.haematochrysum Rchb. f. See *O.flexuosum*.
O.haematoxanthum Rchb. f. See *O.flexuosum*.
O.hallii (Lindl.) Beer. See *Odontoglossum hallii*.

O.harrisonianum Lindl. (*O.acrobotryum* Klotzsch).
Pseudobulbs to 2.5×2cm, subspherical, compressed, unifoliate. Lvs to 15×3cm, rigid, fleshy, linear-oblong, acute,

recurved, grey-green. Panicle to 30cm, many-fld; fls to 1.5cm diam.; sep. and pet. golden-yellow blotched red or red-brown, dorsal sep. obovate, subacute, to 10×5mm, concave, recurved, lateral sep. spathulate, slightly wider than dorsal sep., pet. similar to lateral sep., smaller; lip golden-yellow, larger than sep., spreading-deflexed, 3-lobed, lateral lobes small, faintly striped chocolate-brown, subquadrate, midlobe clawed, transversely oblong or reniform, emarginate, callus 5-lobed; column short, fleshy, wings falcate. Brazil.

O.hastatum Lindl.
Pseudobulbs to 11×6cm, ovoid-conical, compressed, bifoliate. Lvs to 43×3cm, linear to lanceolate, acute or acuminate. Panicle to 1.5m, loosely branched, branches suberect, 6- or more fld; fls to 4cm diam.; sep. and pet. yellow-green or yellow, heavily spotted and barred deep maroon, sep. to 24×7mm, narrowly lanceolate, acuminate, undulate, pet. shorter than sep., lanceolate, acuminate; lip to 2×1.5cm, lateral lobes white, rotund-subquadrate or oblong, midlobe tinged and blotched rose-purple, short-clawed, ovate-elliptic, acuminate, callus white lined rose-purple, 4-lobed, lateral lobes short; column wings incurved, subquadrate-rounded. Mexico.

O.hastilabium (Lindl.) Garay & Dunsterv. (*Odontoglossum hastilabium* Lindl.).
Pseudobulbs to 6×4cm, ovoid, compressed, unifoliate or bifoliate. Lvs to 35×4cm, oblong-lanceolate, obtuse or mucronate, pale green. Panicle to 80cm, many-fld; fls to 7.5cm diam., opening in succession, fragrant, long-lived; sep. and pet. pale cream-yellow or pale green, banded chocolate-brown, sep. to 4×1cm, linear-lanceolate, long-acuminate, keeled below, pet. smaller than sep.; lip white with rose-purple base, to 3.5×2cm, triangular, lateral lobes small, porrect, falcate, midlobe narrowly clawed, cordate or suborbicular, acute or apiculate, callus 3-keeled, median keel trilobulate at front; column lavender, bright yellow at base, narrowly winged. Venezuela, Colombia, Peru.

O.hebraicum Rchb. f. See *O.baueri*.

O.heteranthum Poepp. & Endl. (*O.bryolophotum* Rchb. f.; *O.ionops* Cogn. & Rolfe; *O.megalous* Schltr.).
Pseudobulbs to 5×3cm, ovoid or ellipsoid, slightly compressed, clustered, light green, bifoliate, rarely unifoliate. Lvs to 20×3.5cm, narrowly linear to elliptic-lanceolate, acute or acuminate, subcoriaceous, keeled below. Panicle to 1m, erect to pendent, branches short, with 1–3 fertile fls toward apex, lower fls abortive; sterile fls broadly spreading, seg. linear to oblanceolate, lip usually entirely aborted; fertile fls to 1cm diam.; sep. and pet. pale yellow-green marked red-brown, sep. to 10×3mm, free, elliptic-lanceolate to ligulate, obtuse to subacute, often undulate, pet. wider than sep., obovate-oblong, obtuse to subacute; lip bright yellow slightly marked red-brown, to 1.5×1.5cm, broadly pandurate, lateral lobes broadly triangular, margins recurved, midlobe sessile to shortly clawed, transversely reniform, deeply bilobed, callus white marked brown, toothed and crested; column to 4mm, erect, wings transversely oblong, often recurved. Costa Rica, Panama, Venezuela, Colombia, Ecuador, Peru, Bolivia.

O.hians Lindl. (*O.leucostomum* Hoffsgg.; *O.quadricorne* Klotzsch.).
Pseudobulbs to 1.5cm, ovoid-subrotund, compressed, unifoliate. Lvs to 7×1cm, ovate to linear-oblong, acute to subobtuse, coriaceous. Infl. simple or slightly branched, to 25cm, very slender, few-fld; fls to 1cm diam., wide-spreading, ochre; sep. to 5×3mm, obovate, rounded; pet. broadly oblong, smaller than sep.; lip larger than sep., yellow with some red-brown spots, obovate-subquadrate, sessile, retuse, callus white, large, with 4 red-spotted, fleshy, finger-like lobes; column to 2mm, white, broadly winged. Brazil.

O.holochrysum Rchb. f. See *O.onustum*.

O.hookeri Rolfe.
Pseudobulbs to 6×1.5cm, narrowly conical, clustered, ridged, bifoliate. Lvs to 20×1.5cm, linear-ligulate or oblanceolate,

apex rounded. Panicle to 45cm, many-fld; fls to 1cm diam.; sep. and pet. yellow flushed orange-brown, to 5×1mm, oblong, acute, reflexed; lip yellow marked orange or pale chestnut at base, to 6×5mm, lateral lobes linear-oblong, spreading, midlobe clawed, broadly obovate-cuneate, callus with 5 flattened lobes; column to 2mm, wingless. Brazil.

O.hyphaematicum Rchb. f.
Pseudobulbs to 10cm, oblong, clustered, compressed, unifoliate. Lvs to 30cm, oblong-lanceolate or ligulate, subacute, subcoriaceous. Panicle much-branched, to 1.5m, loosely many-fld; fls to 3.5cm diam., stained red below; sep. and pet. red-brown blotched deep red-brown, tipped yellow, ovate-lanceolate to oblong-lanceolate, acute, strongly undulate; lip canary-yellow, pale yellow below flushed and spotted crimson, broadly clawed, reniform, lateral lobes subreniform, midlobe reniform, emarginate, callus 5-keeled; column pale yellow, wings hatchet-shaped. Ecuador.

O.incurvum Barker ex Lindl.
Pseudobulbs to 10×3cm, ovoid, ribbed, compressed, bifoliate or trifoliate. Lvs to 40×2cm, linear-ligulate, acute, dark green. Panicle to 2m, branches numerous, distichous, many-fld, arcuate; fls to 2.5cm diam., fragrant; sep. and pet. white streaked and blotched lilac and rose-pink, undulate, dorsal sep. to 12×3mm, linear-oblanceolate, acute, lateral sep. longer than dorsal sep., curved, pet. to 14×3mm, linear-lanceolate, subacute; lip rose-pink blotched white, to 1.5×1cm, pandurate, lateral lobes small, suborbicular to oblong, midlobe clawed, suborbicular, apiculate, callus yellow marked brown, 5-toothed; column to 7mm, white, bidentate, wings tinged pink. Mexico.

O.insculptum (Rchb. f.) Rchb. f.
Pseudobulbs to 12.5×5cm, ovoid, compressed, clustered, bifoliate. Lvs to 45cm, ensiform to narrowly linear, acute to acuminate. Panicle loosely branched in upper half, pale green-brown, flexuous, branches short, few-fld; fls to 3.5cm diam., polished, dark cinnamon; sep. and pet. edged yellow-white, clawed, crisped-undulate, to 1.5cm, dorsal sep. suborbicular, lateral sep. ovate-oblong, pet. broadly ovate; lip narrowly oblong, reflexed, concave, lateral lobes small, apex blue-grey, callus triangular, prominent, dentate towards front; column narrowly winged. Ecuador.

O.insleayi (Barker & Lindl.) Lindl. See *Rossioglossum insleayi*.

O.ionops Cogn. & Rolfe. See *O.heteranthum*.

O.iridifolium Lindl. See *O.crista-galli*.

O.isthmii Schltr.
Pseudobulbs to 12×4cm, narrowly ovoid to linear-oblong, compressed, longitudinally ridged, usually bifoliate. Lvs to 45×3cm, linear-lanceolate, acute, suberect, subcoriaceous. Panicle to 1m, many-fld; fls to 2.5cm diam., yellow marked copper-brown; sep. free, clawed, dorsal sep. to 12×5mm, oblanceolate, undulate, shorter than lateral sep., obliquely oblong, acute, undulate; pet. to 12×5mm, oblong-oblanceolate, subacute, undulate; lip spreading-deflexed, pandurate, lateral lobes auriculate, suborbicular, midlobe narrowly clawed, transversely reniform, emarginate, callus fleshy, brown, 7-lobed; column to 4mm, wings prominent. Costa Rica, Panama.

O.janeirense Rchb. f. See *O.longipes*.

O.jonesianum Rchb. f.
Pseudobulbs to 1×1cm, ovoid, unifoliate. Lvs to 40×1.5cm, terete, pendent, grooved, fleshy. Raceme to 50cm, usually pendent, to 15-fld; fls to 7.5cm diam., showy, long-lived; sep. and pet. yellow-white spotted chestnut-brown, ovate-oblong, to 2.5×1cm, rounded, spreading, undulate; lip to 2×1cm, clawed, lateral lobes yellow-orange, auriculate, spreading, midlobe white spotted crimson, transversely oblong, emarginate, undulate, callus fleshy, lobed and tubercled; column white spotted red, to 7mm, wings oblong. Brazil, Paraguay, Uruguay.

O.kienastianum Rchb. f. (*O.trilingue* Sander).
Pseudobulbs to 8cm, oblong-ovoid, bifoliate. Lvs to 50×2.5cm or more, oblong-oblanceolate, acute or acuminate. Panicle long-scandent, short-branched above, few-fld; fls large; sep. and pet. rich chocolate-brown edged pale yellow, undulate, dorsal sep. to 1.5×1cm, short-clawed, ovate-triangular, acute, lateral sep. exceeds dorsal sep., long-clawed, oblong-cuneate, acute, pet. similar to dorsal sep., apex reflexed; lip to 15×12mm, lateral lobes yellow spotted brown, small, midlobe brown, ovate-triangular, undulate to crisped, recurved above, callus yellow, 3-keeled, lateral keels with 3 lamellae on each side; column wings minute, curved. Peru, Colombia.

O.kramerianum Rchb. f. See *Psychopsis krameriana.*
O.kymatoides Kränzl. See *O.carthagenense.*
O.labiatum (Sw.) Rchb. f. See *Leochilus labiatus.*
O.lacerum Lindl. See *O.stipitatum.*

O.lanceanum Lindl.
Pseudobulbs reduced or absent. Lvs to 50×10cm, elliptic-oblong to lanceolate-oblong, acute, thickly coriaceous, dark green spotted maroon. Panicle to 30cm, few- to many-fld; fls to 6cm diam., fragrant, long-lived, waxy; sep. and pet. yellow or green-yellow, heavily spotted purple-brown or chocolate-brown, sep. to 3.5×2cm, short-clawed, elliptic-oblong, obtuse, undulate, shorter than lateral sep., pet. slightly narrower than sep., obovate-spathulate, obtuse; lip pale purple, base deep rose-purple, larger than sep., lateral lobes small, basal, triangular-oblong, midlobe broadly clawed, spathulate, callus deep rose-purple, 3-lobed; column to 7mm, pale yellow-green below, dark purple above. Colombia, Venezuela, Brazil, Trinidad, Guianas.

O.lankesteri Ames. See *O.ansiferum.*

O.leopoldianum (Kränzl.) Rolfe.
Rhiz. long-creeping. Pseudobulbs to 2.5cm, ovoid-oblong to ovoid-cylindrical, unifoliate or bifoliate. Lvs to 16×2cm, oblanceolate, acute. Panicle to 2.5m, scandent, many-branched; fls to 4cm diam., spreading; sep. and pet. white with purple central portion, sep. short-clawed, to 2.5×1cm, broadly elliptic, obtuse, pet. smaller than sep., subsessile, elliptic-ovate, subacute; lip purple-violet, smaller than pet., deltoid, slightly 3-lobed, callus yellow; column yellow. Peru.

O.leucochilum Batem. ex Lindl. (*O.digitatum* Lindl.).
Pseudobulbs to 13×6cm, ovoid, compressed, furrowed with age, unifoliate or bifoliate. Lvs to 60×4.5cm, dull green, ligulate, acute or obtuse, coriaceous. Panicle to 3m, strongly branched, many-fld; fls to 3.5cm diam.; sep. and pet. bright green to white-green blotched and barred deep red-brown or green-brown, to 2.5×1cm, elliptic-oblong to oblanceolate, acute to obtuse, slightly undulate; lip white tinged pink or yellow, to 2.5×2.5cm, pandurate, lateral lobes small, ovate to oblong, obtuse, margins reflexed, midlobe narrowly clawed, transversely oblong or reniform, emarginate, margins undulate, callus tinged purple, oblong, terminating in 5–9 slender teeth, 3 apical teeth recurved; column to 8mm, fleshy, wings rose-pink to rose-magenta. Mexico, Honduras, Guatemala.

O.leucostomum Hoffsgg. See *O.hians.*

O.lietzii Reg.
Pseudobulbs conical or subfusiform, to 12×2cm, lustrous green, unifoliate or bifoliate. Lvs to 20×5cm, ligulate or elliptic-oblong, acute, recurved. Raceme or panicle to 70cm, arching; peduncle purple spotted white; fls to 3.5cm diam.; sep. and pet. yellow or green-yellow barred bright red-brown, dorsal sep. to 15×8mm, spathulate, obtuse, concave, lateral sep. connate to near apex, shorter than dorsal sep., emarginate, pet. to 16×9mm, spathulate, obtuse, incurved; lip to 1×1cm, slightly convex, lateral lobes incurved, narrowly oblong, yellow with few chocolate-brown spots, margins recurved, midlobe chocolate-brown, callus pale orange-brown, large, verrucose-tuberculate; column to 5mm, pubesc. Brazil.

O.limminghei E. Morr. ex Lindl. See *Psychopsis limminghei.*

O.longicornu Mutel (*O.unicorne* Lindl.; *O.monoceras* Hook.).
Pseudobulbs to 7×2cm, oblong-conical, clustered, slightly compressed, unifoliate or bifoliate. Lvs to 20×3cm, oblong to oblong-lanceolate, acute. Panicle to 45cm, branches elongate, slender, 2-ranked; fls to 2cm across; sep. pale green or red-brown, dorsal sep. to 6×3mm, elliptic-oblong, acute, concave, lateral sep. to 6×2mm, connate to middle, oblong; pet. red-brown, tipped yellow, subequal to sep., oblong, reflexed, undulate; lip to 11×8mm, apical half yellow, basal half red, lateral lobes oblong, margins recurved, midlobe flabellate, emarginate, callus red, a long, incurved horn; column yellow-green, to 5mm, subclavate, slightly incurved, wings absent. Brazil.

O.longifolium Lindl. See *O.cebolleta.*

O.longipes Lindl. & Paxt. (*O.janeirense* Rchb. f.).
Pseudobulbs to 2.5cm, ovoid-pyriform, clear green, 2–4-foliate, remotely or erratically spaced along a slender creeping rhiz. Lvs to 15×2cm, linear-lanceolate or oblong, soft, pale green, basally conduplicate. Raceme to 15cm, erect, loosely 2–6-fld; fls to 3.5cm diam., usually smaller, long-lived; sep. and pet. yellow-brown or pale red-brown spotted and streaked yellow, yellow-tipped, sep. to 16×4mm, oblong to spathulate, acute, undulate, apex reflexed, lateral sep. connate at base, pet. similar to sep., shorter and broader, obtuse; lip rich deep yellow, lateral lobes oblong-rounded with pale red-brown claw, margins undulate, midlobe reniform or transversely oblong, emarginate, callus white-spotted with 2 very prominent teeth in front; column wings narrow, inconspicuous. Brazil.

O.loxense Lindl. (*Cyrtochilum loxense* (Lindl.) Kränzl.).
Pseudobulbs to 12.5×4cm, ovoid to pyriform, slightly compressed, furrowed, unifoliate. Lvs to 40×5cm, narrowly lanceolate or ligulate, acute or acuminate. Panicle to 1.8m, vine-like, several-fld; fls to 7.5cm diam., borne at irregular intervals, fleshy; sep. cinnamon-brown barred bright or pale yellow, to 2.5×1cm, clawed, ovate-oblong, subacute, undulate; pet. wider than sep., obtuse; lip to 2×2.5cm, bright orange, pale yellow-orange on disc, lateral lobes reduced to minute auricles, midlobe spathulate, callus crimson-spotted, consisting of 4 shallow plates behind and a central, fringed plate with many bristles on each side; column wings obscure. Ecuador, Peru.

O.lucasianum Rolfe.
Pseudobulbs to 5cm, ovoid, slightly compressed, bifoliate. Lvs to 20cm, linear-lanceolate, acute. Panicle to 1m, arcuate, few- to many-fld; fls to 3cm diam., golden-yellow; dorsal sep. to 17×8mm, obovate-oblong, undulate, lateral sep. similar to dorsal sep., free or connate in basal half; pet. wider than sep., short-clawed, broadly oblong; lip pandurate-trilobed, to 2×2cm, lateral lobes small, midlobe suborbicular-reniform, cordate, basally bilobulate, callus 5-lamellate, verrucose; column short, wings semi-ovate, erose. Peru.

O.lunatum Lindl. See *Solenidium lunatum.*

O.luridum Lindl. (*O.guttatum* (L.) Rchb. f.).
Pseudobulbs to 1.5cm. Lvs solitary, borne from stout rhiz., to 85×15cm, oval to elliptic-oblong, acute to obtuse, coriaceous, light green spotted pale purple-brown. Panicle to 1.5m, short-branched; fls to 4cm diam.; sep. and pet. usually yellow-brown or red-brown variously marked and spotted yellow, sep. to 2×1cm, clawed, spathulate to obovate or suborbicular, strongly undulate, pet. shorter than sep. and somewhat oblong, otherwise similar; lip equals pet., broadly pandurate, lateral lobes small, revolute, midlobe rounded, short-clawed, entire or crenulate, emarginate, callus white or yellow spotted purple, composed of 5 fleshy, tuberculate lobules; column to 5mm, white, wings pale pink. Florida, W Indies and Mexico and Guyana and Peru.

O.luteopurpureum (Lindl.) Beer. See *Odontoglossum luteopurpureum.*
O.macrantherum Hook. See *Leochilus oncidioides.*

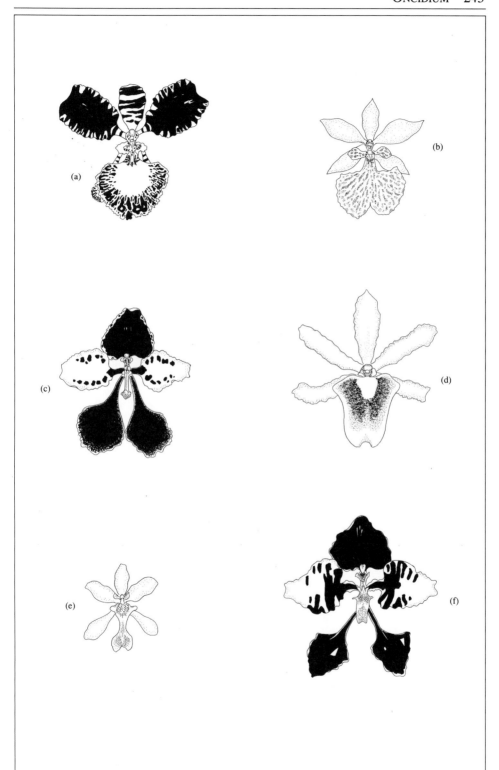

Oncidium   (a) *O.crispum*   (b) *O.cucullatum*   (c) *O.falcipetalum*   (d) *O.fuscatum*   (e) *O.ornithorhynchum*
(f) *O.superbiens*

O.macranthum Lindl. (*Cyrtochilum macranthum* (Lindl.) Kränzl.).
Pseudobulbs to 15cm, ovoid to oblong-conical, bifoliate. Lvs to 55×5cm, oblong to linear-oblanceolate, acute. Panicle to 3m, short-branched, lax or twining, each branch 2–5-fld; fls to 10cm diam., long-lived, showy; sep. dull yellow-brown, to 4.5×3cm, clawed, strongly undulate, oblong-suborbicular; pet. golden-yellow, to 3.5×3cm, suborbicular-ovate, short-clawed, strongly undulate-crisped; lip smaller than sep. and pet., obscurely 3-lobed, white bordered with violet-purple, triangular, callus white, 6-toothed; column to 1cm, wings brown-purple, flabellate, bilobed or retuse. Ecuador, Peru, Colombia.

O.maculatum Lindl.
Pseudobulbs to 10×4cm, ovoid, clustered, strongly compressed, bifoliate. Lvs to 25×5cm, linear-ligulate to oblong-elliptic, coriaceous. Raceme or panicle to 1m, erect, many-fld; fls to 5cm diam., fragrant; sep. and pet. similar, bronze to yellow blotched dark chestnut-brown, to 3×1cm, oblong-elliptic to elliptic-lanceolate, obtuse to acuminate, apex often reflexed, spreading; lip to 3×2cm, white marked red-brown, obscurely 3-lobed, midlobe ovate-oblong, truncate, apiculate, undulate, callus 4-keeled, slightly puberulent. Mexico, Guatemala, Honduras.

O.marshallianum Rchb. f.
Pseudobulbs to 15×4cm, ovoid-oblong, clustered, slightly compressed, furrowed with age, bright green, bifoliate. Lvs to 30×4cm, bright green, ligulate-lanceolate, acute, subcoriaceous. Panicle to 1.8m, many-fld; fls to 5.5cm diam., variable; sep. to 2×1cm, dull yellow, barred pale red-brown, obovate-oblong, rounded, concave, lateral sep. longer and narrower than dorsal sep., connate in basal third, almost concealed by lip; pet. to 2.5×2cm, canary-yellow spotted pale red-brown towards centre or base, broadly obovate-oblong, emarginate, undulate; lip to 4×4cm, clawed, lateral lobes bright yellow spotted red, small, midlobe large, broadly subreniform, emarginate, bright yellow, claw and callus spotted red-orange; column to 7mm, wings oblong-subquadrate, entire. Brazil.

O.massangei Morr. See *O.sphacelatum.*
O.megalous Schltr. See *O.heteranthum.*

O.meirax Rchb. f.
Pseudobulbs to 2.5×1.5cm, ovoid to ovoid-oblong, compressed, unifoliate. Lvs to 7.5×1.5cm, lanceolate or oblong-lanceolate to linear-lanceolate, acute or obtuse, base attenuate and conduplicate. Raceme or panicle to 25cm; peduncle compressed at apex, basal portion triquetrous; sep. and pet. yellow unevenly flushed maroon, linear or linear-oblanceolate to oblanceolate-spathulate, dorsal sep. to 9×3mm, lateral sep. to 11×3mm, free, oblique; lip yellow tipped maroon, simple, to 9×7mm, ovate to ovate-triangular, acute, base cordate, callus a raised plate, tubercled; column to 5mm, wings absent. Colombia, Venezuela, Ecuador, Peru.

O.microchilum Batem. & Lindl. (*Cyrtochilum microchilum* (Lindl.) Cribb).
Pseudobulbs to 3.5×3cm, ovoid or spherical, compressed, unifoliate. Lvs to 30×6.5cm, elliptic or elliptic-oblong, acute, coriaceous, olive, keeled below. Panicle to 1.5m, erect, much-branched, few- to many-fld; fls to 2.5cm diam., long-lived; sep. pale brown marked yellow, short-clawed, suborbicular to elliptic-oblong, to 1.5×1cm, concave, keeled below; pet. chestnut-brown or purple-brown barred and edged yellow, smaller than sep., oblanceolate, obtuse, undulate, incurved; lip smaller than pet., broadly triangular, lateral lobes white flecked maroon-purple, suborbicular, revolute, midlobe white with a purple spot, obscure, apiculate, sharply decurved, callus central, tubercled, yellow spotted purple above, purple below; column to 6mm, deep red, slightly pubesc., wings white, curved. Guatemala, Mexico.

O.microglossum Klotzsch. See *O.barbatum.*
O.monoceras Hook. See *O.longicornu.*
O.naevium (Lindl.) Beer. See *Odontoglossum naevium.*

O.nanum Lindl. (*O.patulum* Schltr.).
Pseudobulbs to 1.5×1cm, unifoliate. Lvs to 20×4cm, dull green with liver red spots, elliptic to elliptic-oblanceolate, acute. Panicle to 25cm, short-branched, few- to many-fld; fls to 1.5cm diam.; sep. and pet. ochre spotted rust, to 10×5mm, spathulate to obovate, obtuse, cucullate-concave; lip bright yellow, transversely oblong, larger than sep., lateral lobes marked red-brown, small, semi-orbicular, revolute, midlobe large, transversely oblong or reniform, emarginate, callus honey-brown, tuberculate, with 2 perpendicular ridges; column ochre flushed maroon, to 4mm. Venezuela, Peru, Brazil, Guianas.

O.naranjense Schltr. See *O.ansiferum.*

O.nigratum Lindl. & Paxt.
Pseudobulbs to 12×6cm, ovoid to ovoid-oblong, strongly compressed and furrowed, pale brown or yellow-green, bifoliate. Lvs to 35×6cm, linear to narrow-lanceolate, coriaceous. Panicle to 1.8m, arcuate, lightly to much-branched, many-fld, branches to 60cm; sep. and pet. white or cream heavily banded and marked deep red-chocolate, undulate, sep. free, to 20×4mm, lanceolate, acute, lateral sep. oblique, pet. to 15×5mm, similar to sep.; lip yellow-brown or clear yellow, marked purple-brown, to 13×10mm, ovate, apex recurved, conspicuously to obscurely 3-lobed, callus yellow spotted red, erect, multituberculate, basal tubercles arranged in 2 transverse series; column to 5mm, curved, wings semi-rotund or triangular, white. Venezuela, Colombia, Guyana.

O.nodosum E. Morr. See *Psychopsis krameriana.*

O.nubigenum Lindl. (*O.cucullatum* var. *nubigenum* (Lindl.) Lindl.).
Resembles *O.cucullatum* except smaller, fls smaller, lip white with violet spot in front of callus. Ecuador, Peru, Colombia.

O.oblongatum Lindl.
Pseudobulbs to 10×3.5cm, ovoid to ellipsoid, compressed, bifoliate. Lvs to 45×2.5cm, ligulate to linear-lanceolate, conduplicate, subcoriaceous. Panicle to 1.4m, erect, short-branched, many-fld; fls to 3cm diam., bright yellow spotted red-brown at base of seg.; sep. to 15×5mm, elliptic-oblanceolate, acute to subobtuse; pet. wider than sep., obliquely elliptic-oblanceolate, rounded, slightly undulate; lip to 2.5×1.5cm, pandurate, lateral lobes small, triangular, reflexed, midlobe with short, narrow claw, subreniform, deeply retuse, slightly undulate, callus fleshy, 4-lobed below, with 3 teeth at apex; column to 7mm, stout, wings auriculate, rounded. Mexico, Guatemala.

O.obryzatoides Kränzl. See *O.obryzatum.*

O.obryzatum Rchb. f. (*O.obryzatoides* Kränzl.; *O.fulgens* Schltr.; *O.brenesii* Schltr.).
Pseudobulbs to 10×4cm, ovoid, elliptic-oblong or suborbicular, compressed, ridged, glossy, unifoliate. Lvs to 45×4cm, linear-elliptic to linear-oblong, subacute. Panicle to 1m, many-fld; fls variable, to 3.5×2.5cm, yellow marked chocolate-brown; sep. to 15×5mm, obovate-spathulate, truncate or obtuse, clawed; pet. wider than sep.; lip larger than sep. and pet., pandurate, lateral lobes small, narrowly short-clawed, midlobe dilated, reniform, with a deep central sinus, callus white or yellow sparsely spotted chocolate-brown, surrounded by red-brown blotch, consisting of a number of toothed lobes; column to 4mm, wings prominent, porrect, erose. Colombia, Venezuela, Peru, Ecuador, Panama, Costa Rica.

O.ochmatochilum Rchb. f. See *O.cardiochilum.*
O.oerstedii Rchb. f. See *O.carthagenense.*

O.onustum Lindl. (*O.holochrysum* Rchb. f.).
Pseudobulbs to 4cm, ovoid to oblong, compressed, unifoliate or bifoliate. Lvs to 12.5×2cm, linear-oblong or oblong, acute. Raceme or panicle to 40cm, often secund; fls to 2.5cm across, deep golden-yellow; sep. to 8×6mm, ovate to elliptic, cucullate, lateral sep. apiculate; pet. twice as large as sep., rotund, undulate; lip exceeds pet., rounded, deeply 3-lobed, lateral lobes small, spreading, midlobe round, callus 3-lobed, lateral

lamellae cochleate, large; column to 2mm, wings crescent-shaped, obtuse. Panama, Colombia, Ecuador, Peru.

O.ornithorhynchum HBK.
Pseudobulbs to 6×3cm, ovoid to pyriform, smooth, semilucent pale grey-green, compressed, usually bifoliate. Lvs to 35×3cm, linear-lanceolate to ligulate, acute, pale or grey-green, soft. Panicle to 50cm, strongly arching, many-fld; fls to 2.5cm, fragrant, showy en masse; sep. and pet. white, pink or lilac, short-clawed, to 11×6mm, narrow-oblong to elliptic; lip darker than sep. and pet., pandurate, lateral lobes small, recurved, midlobe clawed, obovate, emarginate, upper margins recurved, callus golden-yellow or deep orange, consisting of 5 toothed lamellae with 2 horn-like tubercles in front; column to 5mm, wings broadly triangular, erose, anth. strongly beaked. Mexico, Guatemala, Costa Rica, El Salvador.

O.pachyphyllum Hook. See *O.cavendishianum*.

O.panamense Schltr.
Pseudobulbs to 16×6cm, ovoid-oblong, ridged, compressed, bifoliate. Lvs to 75×4cm, linear-lanceolate, acute, subcoriaceous; petioles elongate. Panicle to 3.5m, erect to pendent or scandent, many-fld; fls to 2.5cm diam.; sep. and pet. yellow blotched and barred olive to brown, slightly undulate, sep. short-clawed, to 13×5mm, elliptic-ovate, acute, pet. similar to sep., tips recurved; lip to 1.5×1.5cm, yellow blotched red-brown to yellow-brown below callus, obscurely 3-lobed, rounded, cleft, emarginate, callus white, erect, 4-keeled, tridentate at apex; column to 5mm, wings prominent, usually serrate. Panama.

O.papilio Lindl. See *Psychopsis papilio*.
O.papilio var. *kramerianum* (Rchb. f.) Lindl. See *Psychopsis krameriana*.
O.patulum Schltr. See *O.nanum*.
O.pelicanum Lindl. See *O.reflexum*.

O.phalaenopsis Lind. & Rchb. f. (*O.cucullatum* var. *phalaenopsis* (Lind. & Rchb. f.) Veitch).
Allied to *O.cucullatum*. Lvs narrow. Raceme to 25cm, slender, few-fld; fls to 3cm across; sep. and pet. white, barred and spotted dark purple; lip white tinted rose-purple, spotted purple around callus, midlobe reniform. Ecuador.

O.phymatochilum Lindl.
To 60cm. Pseudobulbs to 12.5×2.5cm, ovoid-oblong, often purple-brown, slightly compressed, unifoliate. Lvs to 35×7.5cm, elliptic to oblanceolate, acute to acuminate, coriaceous. Panicle to 60cm, pendent, loosely many-fld; fls to 5cm diam., showy; sep. to 35×3mm, pale yellow marked red-brown, sometimes white spotted red-orange, delicate, narrow, spreading-reflexed, undulate, keeled below; pet. shorter than sep. and broader; lip to 18×11mm, white spotted red-orange on callus, pandurate, lateral lobes auriculate, spreading-reflexed, undulate, midlobe clawed, ovate-cordate, apiculate, undulate, callus fleshy, triangular with a basal dentate flap on each side, 3-tubercled at apex; column to 5mm, slender, wings broad, dentate, white spotted red. Mexico, Guatemala, Brazil.

O.powellii Schltr. See *O.anthocrene*.

O.pubes Lindl. (*O.bicornutum* Hook.).
Pseudobulbs to 7×1.5cm, subcylindrical, slightly compressed, clustered, unifoliate or bifoliate. Lvs to 12×3cm, lustrous dark green above, narrowly oblong-lanceolate, acute, subcoriaceous. Panicle to 60cm, branches alternately 2-ranked; fls to 2.5cm diam.; sep. and pet. usually chestnut to brick red banded and spotted yellow, dorsal sep. and pet. to 12×8mm, obovate or obovate-oblong, subtruncate, lateral sep. connate almost to apex, linear-ligulate, smaller than pet., recurved, subacute; lip red-brown edged yellow, slightly shorter than sep., lateral lobes small, linear, reflexed, midlobe large, suborbicular, emarginate, recurved, callus pubesc., tuberculate, dentate in front; column white, to 4mm, wings subfalcate, with villous hairs around stigma. Brazil, Paraguay.

O.pulchellum Hook. See *Tolumnia pulchella*.

O.pulvinatum Lindl.
Pseudobulbs to 5cm diam., suborbicular-oblong, compressed, unifoliate. Lvs to 30×8cm, oblong, acute, fleshy, erect, yellow-green. Panicle to 3m, flexuous, many-fld, loosely branched, branches often further branched; fls to 2.5cm diam.; sep. and pet. yellow with red-brown or red-orange base, sep. to 13×6mm, ovate-spathulate, subacute to obtuse, undulate, dorsal sep. bent forward, concave, pet. similar to sep., obtuse-truncate; lip pale yellow spotted red or red-orange, wider than sep., lateral lobes suborbicular, fimbriate-undulate, midlobe subreniform, emarginate, callus white spotted red, cushion-like, papillose; column to 4mm, clavate, wings rounded. Brazil.

O.pumilum Lindl.
Pseudobulbs small or absent, unifoliate. Lvs arising from creeping rhiz., oblong to ligulate, acute, to 12×3.5cm, coriaceous. Panicle to 15cm, short-branched, densely many-fld; fls to 1cm diam., slightly campanulate; sep. and pet. somewhat incurved, straw-yellow spotted red-brown, obovate-oblong, obtuse; lip pale yellow marked red either side of callus, larger than sep. and pet., lateral lobes largest, ovate-oblong, midlobe subquadrate, curved forwards, callus 2-ridged; column oblong, acute, decurved. Brazil, Paraguay.

O.pusillum (L.) Rchb. f. (*Psygmorchis pusilla* (L.) Dodson & Dressler).
Diminutive epiphyte to 7cm. Lvs to 6×1cm, fleshy, narrow-oblong or elliptic, broad at base, apex sharply acuminate, equitant, conduplicate, the bases overlapping to form a flattened fan, through which wiry roots sometimes emerge. Infl. to 6cm, axillary; fls 1–4, to 2.7×1.5cm, yellow marked rusty-red. C & S America, W Indies.

O.pyramidale Lindl.
Pseudobulbs to 7cm, ovoid to cylindrical, compressed, unifoliate to trifoliate. Lvs to 20×3cm, oblanceolate to elliptic-oblong, acute or acuminate. Panicle to 50cm, erect to pendent, loosely many-fld, branches short, often compound; fls to 2.5cm diam., fragrant, canary-yellow, often spotted red; sep. and pet. reflexed, dorsal sep. to 7×3mm, oblanceolate-oblong, obtuse, lateral sep. slightly longer than dorsal sep., free, linear-oblanceolate, acute, pet. wider than dorsal sep., ovate-oblong, acute or apiculate; lip to 12×12mm, sessile, pandurate, lateral lobes small, rounded, reflexed, midlobe clawed, reniform or obovate-reniform, bilobulate in front, callus tubercled; column to 3mm, sigmoid, wings bilobed, divergent. Peru, Ecuador, Colombia.

O.quadricorne Klotzsch. See *O.hians*.
O.quadripetalum Sw. See *Tolumnia tetrapetala.*.
O.racemosum (Lindl.) Rchb. f. See *Solenidium racemosum*.

O.raniferum Lindl.
Pseudobulbs to 6.5×2cm, ovoid to oblong, bifoliate. Lvs to 17×1.5cm, linear to narrow-oblanceolate, thin. Panicle to 35cm, erect, branches to 11cm, spreading; fls to 1.5cm across; sep. and pet. pale or bright yellow spotted red-brown, sep. minute, oblong-elliptic, pet. similar to sep., smaller; lip yellow, to 4×3mm, lateral lobes small, linear-oblong, spreading, midlobe obcordate, partially crenulate, callus red-brown, large, obscurely 2-lobed; column short, erect, narrow-winged. E Brazil.

O.rechingerianum Kränzl. See *O.cabagrae*.

O.reflexum Lindl. (*O.pelicanum* Lindl.; *O.suave* Lindl.).
Pseudobulbs to 8×5cm, ovoid to broadly ellipsoid, compressed, unifoliate or bifoliate. Lvs to 35×4cm, linear-lanceolate, acute, chartaceous. Panicle to 75cm, slender, straggling, loosely branched; fls to 4cm diam.; sep. and pet. pale yellow-green speckled dull red-brown, spreading, strongly reflexed, undulate, sep. elliptic-oblanceolate or linear-oblong, to 15×5mm, pet. linear-oblong, acute, slightly larger than sep.; lip to 2×2.5cm, bright yellow spotted red at base, pandurate, lateral lobes small, suborbicular, strongly revolute, midlobe clawed, transversely oblong, apically cleft, callus keeled with *c*8 tubercles; column to 5mm, stout. Mexico, Guatemala.

O.rigbyanum Paxt. See *O.sarcodes*.

O.robustissimum Rchb. f.
Pseudobulbs short, broadly elliptic, compressed, unifoliate. Lvs to 40cm, ovate-elliptic or oblong, fleshy, keeled below, olive-green. Panicle to 2m, branches to 15cm, numerous, spreading; fls to 2.5cm diam.; sep. and pet. tipped yellow, red-brown at base, to 1.2×0.4cm, sep. cuneate-oblong or cuneate-obovate, apex rounded, pet. subequal to sep., oblong-oblanceolate, obtuse or truncate; lip yellow spotted or striped cinnamon, to 1×1cm, lateral lobes rounded, serrate, midlobe flabellate, emarginate, callus pulvinate, pilose. Brazil.

O.sanderae Rolfe.
Pseudobulbs to 6cm, ovoid, slightly compressed, unifoliate. Lvs to 45×8cm, elliptic to oblong, acute to rounded. Infl. to 80cm; fls produced in succession, large, showy, spreading; dorsal sep. red-brown, to 10×1cm, linear-oblanceolate, acute, lateral sep. to 7×2cm, yellow marked red, oblong-lanceolate, acute, decurved, undulate; pet. similar to dorsal sep., smaller; lip to 4×3.5cm, pale yellow, lateral lobes semi-orbicular, undulate-crisped, pale yellow spotted red-brown, midlobe clawed, suborbicular, undulate-crisped, pale yellow spotted red-brown near margin, callus 5-lobed; column to 1cm, wings with gland-tipped cilia. Peru

O.sarcodes Lindl. (*O.rigbyanum* Paxt.).
Pseudobulbs to 14×3cm, subfusiform, clustered, slightly compressed, dark green, bifoliate, rarely trifoliate. Lvs to 25×5cm, oblong, acute or obtuse, coriaceous, glossy green. Panicle to 1.8m, short-branched above; fls to 5cm diam., long-lived; sep. and pet. glossy, deep chestnut-brown edged yellow, dorsal sep. to 15×13mm, obcordate to obovate, concave, lateral sep. smaller, obovate-oblong, keeled below, slightly undulate, pet. larger than sep., obovate, obtuse, undulate; lip bright yellow spotted red-brown at base, to 2×2cm, lateral lobes small, oblong or suborbicular, margins reflexed, midlobe transversely elliptic, emarginate, undulate, callus an oblong lobed plate with a central tooth at each side. Brazil.

O.scansor Rchb. f. See *O.globuliferum*.

O.schillerianum Rchb. f.
Pseudobulbs to 5cm, ovoid-oblong, distant on rhiz., bifoliate. Lvs to 15×3cm, oblong. Panicle to 1.2m, scandent, loosely branched, branches short, often compound, few-fld; fls small, yellow-green barred brown; sep. to 15×5mm, oblong to oblanceolate, acute or apiculate; pet. wider than dorsal sep., acute or obtuse, undulate; lip to 2×2cm, pandurate to 3-lobed, lateral lobes semi-triangular or semi-ovate, short-clawed, midlobe large, cordate-reniform, retuse, callus multituberculate, tipped with 3 prominent tubercles; column dilated towards base, wings broadly dolabriform, dentate. Peru, Brazil.

O.serratum Lindl. (*O.diadema* Lindl.).
Pseudobulbs to 12cm, oblong-ovoid, compressed, bifoliate. Lvs to 55×4cm, narrowly linear-oblanceolate, acute. Panicle to 4m, loosely branched above, twining, many-fld; fls to 7.5cm diam., wide-spreading; sep. long-clawed, bright chestnut-brown edged yellow, dorsal sep. to 2.5×3.5cm, suborbicular, crisped-undulate, serrate, lateral sep. exceeds dorsal sep., ovate-oblong, obtuse, deflexed, margins strongly undulate and serrate; pet. chestnut-brown tipped bright yellow, smaller than sep., short-clawed, ovate-oblong, obtuse, strongly crisped and fimbriate; lip purple-brown with white margin and callus, to 1.5×1cm, hastate, callus consisting of a central plate with 2 acute teeth in front and a notched plate on each side; column to 8mm, wings narrowly cuneate, dentate at apex. Ecuador, Peru.

O.sessile Lindl. ex Paxt.
Pseudobulbs to 10×4cm, ovoid-oblong, compressed, bifoliate. Lvs to 38×3cm, linear to narrow-oblong, subacute to acute. Panicle to 60cm, branched above middle, erect, branches short, spreading; fls to 3.5cm diam., spreading, canary-yellow centrally spotted red-brown; sep. free, oblong-elliptic to oblong-obovate, to 17×5mm, obtuse, slightly undulate; pet.

shorter and wider than sep.; lip to 2×2.5cm, sessile, pandurate-trilobed, callus 3-lobed, anterior portion bilamellate; column short, dilated near base, wings broad, dentate, truncate. Venezuela, Colombia, Peru.

O.sphacelatum Lindl. (*O.massangei* Morr.).
Pseudobulbs to 15×5cm, ovoid-ellipsoid, compressed, sharp-edged, bifoliate or trifoliate. Lvs to 100×3.5cm, linear-ligulate or linear-lanceolate, acute, subcoriaceous. Panicle to 1.5m, short-branched; fls to 3cm diam.; sep. and pet. bright yellow blotched and spotted red-brown, often short-clawed, elliptic to obovate, acute and reflexed at apex, undulate; lip golden-yellow marked red-brown in front of callus, to 18×17mm, pandurate, lateral lobes small, rounded, midlobe transversely oblong, undulate, emarginate, callus fleshy, trilobed and toothed, white or yellow spotted orange-brown; column white spotted crimson on margins, to 6mm, subclavate, wings edged brown, oblong, with erose-crenate margins. Mexico to El Salvador.

O.sphegiferum Lindl.
Pseudobulbs to 4cm diam., broadly oval to subrotund, clustered, strongly compressed, unifoliate. Lvs to 20×4cm, elliptic-oblong, acute, pale green. Panicle to 1.2m, many-fld; fls to 2.5cm diam., bright orange, each seg. stained red-brown at base; sep. clawed, ovate; pet. clawed, oblong, apiculate; lip subpandurate, lateral lobes suborbicular, dentate, midlobe transversely oblong, emarginate, pale orange to bright orange, callus cushion-like, oblong, slightly papillose; column narrow-winged. Brazil.

O.spilopterum Lindl.
Pseudobulbs to 4×2.5cm, clustered, ovoid-compressed, becoming deeply sulcate, apex bifoliate. Lvs to 20×2.5cm, subcoriaceous, linear-lanceolate, acute. Infl. to 40cm, erect to pendent, simple, loosely several-fld; fls pendent; sep. and pet. violet-brown marked yellow-green; dorsal sep. to 10×5mm, ovate-oblong, acute, lateral sep. to 14×4mm, oblong, acute, basally connate; pet. to 10×6mm, ovate-subquadrate, base shortly unguiculate; lip to 2.5×3cm, sulphur-yellow, basally 3-lobed, lateral lobes oblong, auriculate, midlobe reniform, emarginate, crisped-undulate; callus violet-purple, fleshy, densely tuberculate; column fleshy, wings quadrate. Brazil, Paraguay.

O.splendidum A. Rich. ex Duchartre.
Pseudobulbs to 5×4.5cm, rotund, compressed, dull brown-green or purple-green, unifoliate. Lvs to 30×4.5cm, elliptic-oblong, subcoriaceous, V-shaped in cross section, often tinged purple. Panicle to 1m, erect, many-fld; peduncle glaucous; fls to 6cm diam., showy, long-lived; sep. and pet. bright yellow blotched and spotted rich red-brown, sep. to 2.5×1cm, elliptic-lanceolate, slightly apiculate, undulate, reflexed at apex, pet. to 3×1cm, elliptic-oblong, obtuse, reflexed at apex; lip golden-yellow, spreading, pandurate, to 4×2cm, lateral lobes small, rounded, tinged lavender, midlobe short-clawed, subreniform, emarginate, undulate, callus 3-lamellate; column to 1cm, wings rounded, concave. Guatemala, Honduras.

O.stelligerum Rchb. f.
Pseudobulbs to 8×3.5cm, ovoid-ellipsoid, compressed, bifoliate. Lvs to 16×3.5cm, elliptic-oblong, subacute, coriaceous. Panicle to 80cm, several-branched; fls large, stellate; sep. and pet. yellow spotted brown, to 2.5×1cm, spreading, oblong-ligulate or elliptic-lanceolate, subacuminate; lip yellow-white with dark yellow callus, to 2×1.5cm, pandurate, lateral lobes narrowly clawed, short, spreading-reflexed, obliquely semi-orbicular, midlobe cordate to suborbicular, shortly and abruptly cuspidate, undulate, callus keeled; column to 1cm, stout, wings subquadrate-rounded. Mexico, Guatemala.

O.stenotis Rchb. f.
Pseudobulbs to 14×4cm, linear-oblong, compressed, unifoliate or bifoliate. Lvs to 60×5cm, cuneate-oblong to linear-oblong, obtuse to subacute, subcoriaceous. Panicle to 1.5m, short-branched, usually densely many-fld; fls to 3cm diam.; sep. and pet. yellow blotched and barred red-brown, spreading, undulate, with recurved apices, sep. to 20×8mm, dorsal

sep. oblong-lanceolate, apiculate, lateral sep. lanceolate to linear-lanceolate, acute, pet. to 16×6mm, lanceolate, acute; lip to 2×1.8cm, bright yellow with brown claw, pandurate, lateral lobes short-clawed, subquadrate to suborbicular, midlobe transversely subreniform, dilated, emarginate and bilobulate, callus erect, fleshy, multidenticulate; column to 7mm with 2 parallel, fleshy lobules below stigma. Costa Rica, Panama, Nicaragua.

O.stipitatum Lindl. (*O.lacerum* Lindl.).
Pseudobulbs to 1×1cm, broadly truncate at apex, unifoliate. Lvs to 70×1cm, cylindrical, becoming pendent with age, acuminate, sulcate. Panicle slender, equalling lvs, pendent, many-fld; fls to 2cm diam.; sep. and pet. yellow marked or tinged red-brown, sep. subequal, to 7×4mm, spreading, short-clawed, dorsal sep. obovate-spathulate, obtuse, concave, lateral sep. obliquely obovate, acute, pet. to 8×3cm, elliptic-oblong, obtuse, undulate; lip bright yellow, to 2×2cm, pandurate, lateral lobes falcate, obliquely obtuse, midlobe narrowly clawed, transversely semi-orbicular to oblong, abruptly dilated, bilobulate, undulate, callus an elevated, rounded-transverse plate, terminating in an erect, rounded tubercle; column to 2.5mm, narrow-winged. Panama, Nicaragua, Honduras.

O.stramineum Lindl.
Pseudobulbs inconspicuous, unifoliate. Lvs to 20×4cm, oblong-lanceolate, obtuse or subacute, suberect, coriaceous, rigid; petiole short, stout. Panicle stout, exceeding lvs, short-branched; fls to 2cm diam.; sep. and pet. white or straw-coloured, sep. to 8×6mm, subrotund, widely spreading, emarginate, concave, lateral sep. speckled red, pet. narrower than sep., short-clawed, oblong-suborbicular; lip white or straw-coloured, speckled red, wider than sep., short-clawed, lateral lobes spreading, oblong, obtuse, slightly incurved, midlobe reniform, broadly clawed, emarginate, callus of several, plate-like keels; column white, wings marked purple, broad. Mexico.

O.suave Lindl. See *O.reflexum.*

O.superbiens Rchb. f. (*Cyrtochilum superbiens* (Rchb. f.) Kränzl.).
Pseudobulbs to 10×3.5cm, elongate-ovoid, compressed, unifoliate or bifoliate. Lvs to 60×6cm, oblong-ligulate or linear-oblanceolate, acute, subcoriaceous. Panicle to 4m, twining, irregularly branched, branches to 15cm, few-fld; fls to 8cm diam.; sep. red-brown tipped yellow, to 3.5×2.5cm, clawed, undulate, rounded at apex, dorsal sep. suborbicular to ovate, base subcordate, lateral sep. longer than dorsal sep., briefly fused at base; pet. smaller than dorsal sep., ovate-oblong, yellow banded brown toward base, undulate, apex reflexed; lip purple or maroon, shorter than pet., short-clawed, perpendicular to column, oblong, auriculate, recurved, callus yellow, fleshy, with a central ridge and a prominent acute tubercle on each auricle; column to 1cm, wings small, falcate, either side of stigma. Colombia, Venezuela, Peru.

O.superfluum Rchb. f. See *Capanemia superflua.*

O.teres Ames & Schweinf.
Vegetatively similar to *O.stipitatum.* Panicle to 45cm, many-fld; fls to 1.5cm across; sep. and pet. yellow, heavily spotted red-brown, sep. free, to 6×4mm, short-clawed, suborbicular, concave, pet. subequal to sep., obovate-oblong, undulate; lip bright yellow, spotted red-brown below, to 8×8mm, pandurate, lateral lobes small, ligulate or oblong-spathulate, acute to obtuse, separated from midlobe by short claw, midlobe dilated, transversely reniform, obscurely bilobulate, callus yellow spotted red-brown, prominent, fleshy, tuberculate; column to 3mm, wings acute, incurved. Panama.

O.tetrapetalum (Jacq.) Willd. See *Tolumnia tetrapetala.*

O.tigratum Rchb. f. & Warsc.
Pseudobulbs to 10×4cm, variable in shape, dull green, compressed, bifoliate. Lvs to 20×3.5cm, dull green. Panicle to 40cm, short-branched, branches loosely several-fld, fractiflex; fls to 2.5cm diam., showy; sep. and pet. spreading or reflexed, deep yellow marked brown or crimson, dorsal sep. to 9×3cm,

cuneate-oblong, apiculate, lateral sep. slightly longer than dorsal sep., oblique, pet. shorter and wider than sep., flabellate, rounded and often apiculate; lip to 12×8mm, bright yellow banded brown basally with white callus, short-clawed, pandurate, lateral lobes auriculate, midlobe cordate-reniform, retuse, callus verrucose, apex with variable projection flanked by 2 teeth; column yellow tinged purple at apex, recurved, clavate below, wings yellow marked red-brown, broad, cleft. Venezuela, Colombia, Peru.

O.tigrinum La Ll. & Lex. (*O.unguiculatum* Lindl.).
Pseudobulbs to 10×6cm, subglobose, compressed, bifoliate or trifoliate. Lvs to 45×2.5cm, narrowly oblong, acute, coriaceous, bright green. Panicle to 90cm, stout, usually erect, loosely branched, many-fld; fls to 7.5cm diam., violet-scented, long-lived; sep. and pet. bright yellow heavily blotched deep brown, similar, narrowly oblong, acute, reflexed at apex, undulate, sep. to 2.5×1cm, pet. shorter; lip bright yellow, to 3.5×4cm, with narrow claw, often tinged brown, spreading, lateral lobes small, rounded, midlobe transversely broad-oblong, emarginate, callus 3-keeled, terminating in 3 blunt teeth; column wings oblong, entire. Mexico.

O.tricolor Hook. See *Tolumnia tetrapetala.*
O.trilingue Sander. See *O.kienastianum.*

O.triquetrum (Sw.) R. Br.
Pseudobulbs absent. Lvs 4 or more, triquetrous, to 15×1.5cm, linear-ligulate, acute, sulcate. Raceme to 20cm, slender, simple or slightly branched above, 5–15-fld; fls to 1.5cm diam., long-lived; sep. and pet. white-green spotted dark purple or rose, margins white, deeply tinged and spotted crimson, sep. broadly lanceolate, acute, lateral sep. connate, bifid at apex, slightly concave, to 10×4mm, pet. broader than sep., triangular-ovate, apiculate, clawed, undulate; lip usually white spotted and streaked purple or red-purple, to 1.5×1cm, lateral lobes small, rounded, midlobe large, cordate-ovate, apiculate, callus orange-yellow, small, subglobose; column to 4mm, wings triangular-oblong, acute at apex, outer margin crenulate. Jamaica.

O.uaipanese Schnee. See *O.nigratum.*
O.unguiculatum Lindl. See *O.tigrinum.*
O.unicorne Lindl. See *O.longicornu.*

O.varicosum Lindl.
Pseudobulbs to 12cm, ovate-oblong, compressed, clustered, often ribbed, bifoliate or trifoliate. Lvs to 25cm, rigid, ligulate, acute, dark green. Panicle to 1.5m, loosely branched, usually pendent, many-fld; fls to 3cm diam.; sep. and pet. yellow-green spotted and barred pale red-brown, sep. to 7mm, obovate, concave, lateral sep. connate for half of length, pet. narrowly oblong, undulate-crisped; lip bright yellow, much larger than sep., spreading, lateral lobes small, suborbicular, slightly crenate in front, midlobe to 4×5.5cm, transversely reniform, 2–4-lobed, callus fleshy, multidentate; column wings oblong. Brazil.

O.variegatum (Sw.) Sw. See *Tolumnia variegata.*
O.vexillarium Rchb. f. See *O.bifolium.*

O.volubile (Poepp. & Endl.) Cogn. (*O.corynephorum* Lindl.).
Pseudobulbs to 5cm, narrowly oblong-cylindrical, clustered, slightly compressed, bifoliate. Lvs to 45×4cm, linear-oblanceolate, acute or acuminate. Panicle to 7m, scandent, branches loose, short, simple, few-fld; fls to 5cm diam., spreading; sep. light violet-purple or cinnamon-brown, free, to 2.5×1.5cm, long-clawed, dorsal sep. ovate-suborbicular, obtuse, lateral sep. oblique; pet. pale cinnamon or pale violet, white above middle, shorter than sep., short-clawed, obliquely ovate, acute; lip deep maroon, base yellow or white, to 1.5×1.5cm, pandurate-obovate, sessile, callus small, 3-toothed, tubercled; column to 5mm, clavate, wings absent. Peru.

O.volvox Rchb. f.
Pseudobulbs to 7×5cm, ovoid or oblong-pyriform, clustered, slightly compressed, furrowed, bifoliate. Lvs to 36×3cm, linear to oblong or narrow-lanceolate, obtuse, coriaceous. Panicle to 5m, loosely branched; fls to 2.5cm diam.; sep. and pet. yellow

or yellow-brown, spotted and marked red-brown, sep. to 17×6mm, free, oblong, narrow-elliptic or oblong-lanceolate, acute to acuminate, undulate, pet. similar to sep., slightly undulate; lip to 18×16mm, bright yellow marked dark brown, pandurate-trilobed, lateral lobes small, subtriangular, midlobe transversely elliptic or reniform, emarginate or bilobulate, short-clawed, callus composed of 4 toothed plates; column to 7mm, yellow, wings dolabriform, entire or crenulate. Venezuela

O.waluewa Rolfe (*Waluewa pulchella* Reg.; *Leochilus pulchellus* (Reg.) Cogn.).
Pseudobulbs to 7×1.5cm, oblong-cylindrical, grooved, slightly compressed, unifoliate. Lvs to 9×1cm, lanceolate, acute, petiolate, subcoriaceous. Infl. pendent, to 10cm, slender, densely fld above; fls 6–20, to 2cm diam.; sep. green-white or cream, strongly concave, dorsal sep. to 10×4mm, oblong-spathulate, curved over column, lateral sep. shorter and wider than dorsal sep., connate almost to apex; pet. white to green-white barred purple, wider than sep., obovate, obtuse; lip similar in colour to pet., to 8×6mm, narrow at base, rhomboid, deeply 3-lobed above, lateral lobes rounded, reflexed, midlobe reniform, cleft, callus purple, linear, tubercles forming the image of an insect; column wings narrowly linear, curved forwards. Brazil, Paraguay.

O.warscewiczii Rchb. f. (*O.bifrons* Lindl.).
Pseudobulbs to 8×3cm, ovoid, compressed, unifoliate or bifoliate. Lvs to 30×3.5cm, cuneate-ligulate, subcoriaceous; petiole conduplicate. Raceme to 50cm, to 15-fld; fls to 3cm diam., golden-yellow; bracts conspicuous, papery, spathaceous; dorsal sep. to 12×6mm, oblong, obtuse, slightly undulate, lateral sep. connate almost to apex, obovate, bifid, keeled below, to 15×10mm; pet. similar to dorsal sep., larger; lip to 2×2cm, pandurate, lateral lobes small, auriculate, midlobe suborbicular to oblong at base, apex bilobed, callus fleshy, narrow, terminating in 5 short, divergent teeth; column to 1cm, apex dilated, wings narrow. Costa Rica, Panama.

O.wentworthianum Batem. ex Lindl.
Pseudobulbs to 10×4.5cm, ovoid-ellipsoid, dark green mottled brown, compressed, bifoliate. Lvs to 35×3cm, ligulate, acute, subcoriaceous. Panicle to 1.5m, pendent, short-branched, many-fld; fls to 3cm diam.; sep. and pet. deep yellow blotched red-brown, spreading-reflexed, undulate, sep. to 2×1cm, elliptic or elliptic-obovate, rounded to acute, pet. shorter than sep., obliquely ovate-elliptic, rounded to subtruncate; lip to 2.5×2.5cm, transversely oblong, deflexed, lateral lobes pale yellow, small, rounded, curved forward, crenate, midlobe pale yellow blotched red-brown, obcordate to obreniform, emarginate, undulate, callus fleshy, spotted red-brown, triangular, with 3 teeth flanked by ridges; column to 7mm, wings triangular, crenulate, often spotted red-brown. Mexico, Guatemala.

O.wercklei Schltr. See *O.globuliferum*.

O.xanthodon Rchb. f.
Pseudobulbs to 12cm, ovoid to ellipsoid, compressed, unifoliate. Lvs to 60×6cm, oblanceolate, acute or acuminate. Panicle

to 2.7m, slender, climbing, loosely many-branched, branches slender, few-fld; fls to 5cm diam.; sep. and pet. deep brown edged yellow, wide-spreading, recurved, undulate, sep. to 2×2cm, ovate-oblong, acute, clawed, lateral sep. longer than dorsal sep., pet. similar to but smaller than dorsal sep.; lip smaller than pet., rich chocolate brown with yellow callus, pandurate-trilobed, basal portion subquadrate with reflexed lateral lobes, midlobe spathulate, recurved, acute, callus 1-keeled, tuberculate; column adnate to base of lip, wings minute. Ecuador, Colombia.

O.zebrinum (Rchb. f.) Rchb. f.
Pseudobulbs remotely spaced on rhiz., ovoid, slightly compressed, smooth, bifoliate. Lvs to 50×5cm, ligulate or elliptic-lanceolate, acute or acuminate. Panicle to 4m, much-branched, branches few- to several-fld; fls to 3.5cm diam.; sep. and pet. white barred red to violet, sep. to 2×1cm, elliptic-lanceolate or oblanceolate, acute or acuminate, undulate-crisped, pet. smaller than sep., obliquely oblong-ovate, acuminate, undulate-crisped; lip white, yellow-green at base, smaller than pet., triangular-lanceolate, spreading from base then strongly reflexed, callus yellow, often marked red, 3-lobed above with a central, apically dentate keel; column to 6mm, wings minute, lanceolate, anth. yellow-brown marked pink or maroon-brown. Venezuela.

O.grexes and cultivars (see also × *Odontocidium*, × *Maclellanara* and × *Wilsonara*).
*O.*Boissiense: large golden yellow blooms marked with chestnut.
*O.*Ella 'Flambeau': the best of the varicosum type; fls bright lemon yellow with chestnut callus.
*O.*Fantasy 'Orchidglade': equitant; stunning colours rich green-yellow overlaid with maroon-red.
*O.*Fire Opal: equitant, rich pink shades over creamy white, sep. and pet. darker than lip; rich chestnut callus and shield on lip contrasts with white column.
*O.*Goldiana: thin leaved type; long branching sprays of small golden fls.
*O.*Green Gold: mule ear type; large fls clear green covered with brown spots contrasting with bright yellow lip, long-lasting.
*O.*Guinea Gold: thin leaved type; long branching sprays of bright golden fls.
*O.*Gypsy Beauty: white and burgundy red with raspberry lip apex.
*O.*Hawaiian Adventure: mule ear type; large sprays of rich brown and yellow fls.
*O.*Red Belt: equitant; lovely red fls on branching sprays.
*O.*Spanish Beauty: equitant; branching sprays of red fls, lip white spotted with red.
*O.*Sultamyre: superb example of the varicosum type of breeding; large yellow fls; many clones of which the best are 'Louis d'Or' and 'Thérèse'.
*O.*William Thurston: equitant, long branching sprays; fls in a wide range of colours in yellow, beige and dark brown.

Ophrys L. (From Gk *ophrys*, referring to a plant with two leaves.) Some 30 species of terrestrial herbs. Tubers 2–3, smooth, fleshy, globose or ovoid. Leaves in a loose basal rosette and on flowering stems. Spike erect, clothed with, ultimately, bract-like leaves; sepals 3, glabrous, green-yellow to rose or white, spreading or reflexed, oblong or ovate; petals 2, usually narrower than sepals; lip flat, concave or convex, entire to trilobed, velvety above often with glabrous, shiny, mirror-like patch (speculum), sometimes with swelling below and apical appendage, spurless. Europe, N Africa, W Asia. Pollination is by pseudo-copulation: male insects are attracted by the highly-specialized mimicry of the flowers and a scent resembling female pheremones. Tubers used for salep in E Europe, Middle East.

CULTIVATION   See Introduction: Hardy Orchids.

O.apifera Huds. BEE ORCHID.
Stems to 50cm. Basal lvs ovate to lanceolate, acute. Spike lax, 2–11-fld; sep. 8–15mm, oblong-ovate, spreading or deflexed, green or purple-violet, rarely white, with green longitudinal veins; pet. green or purple, triangular to linear-lanceolate or oblong, slightly revolute; lip 10–13mm, trilobed, central lobe broadly ovate, convex, margins dark red-brown, sometimes ochre or bicolour, recurved, velvety, appendage deflexed, yellow, sometimes absent, lateral lobes to 3mm, triangular-ovate, villous, speculum red-brown with yellow apical spots and margins. Mid spring–mid summer. W & C Europe.

O.arachnites (L.) Reichard. See *O.holoserica*.

O.araneola Rchb. (*O.litigiosa* Camus; *O.sphegodes* ssp. *litigiosa* (Camus) Bech.)
To 45cm. Lvs 5–9, ovate-lanceolate. Bracts exceed ovary; fls 6–10; sep. 6–10mm, green, revolute; pet. 4–8mm, green single-veined; lip 5–8mm, obscurely trilobed, pale to dark brown or olive green, entire, velvety, speculum blue, glabrous, loosely H-shaped. Spring–early summer. S & SC Europe..

O.bertolonii Moretti.
To 35cm. Leaves 5–7, ovate-lanceolate to lanceolate, acute. Spike 3–8-fld; sep. 8–10mm, deep pink-lilac, basally tinted green; pet. 4–6mm, linear-lanceolate, lilac; lip 10–13mm, entire or trilobed, concave, deep purple-black, velvety, speculum blue-violet, paler at edges; apical appendage yellow, margins glabrous. Late spring. S & C Europe.

O.bombyliflora Link.
Stems to 25cm. Basal lvs 4–6, oblong-lanceolate. Spike lax, 5–14-fld; sep. 9–12mm, green, ovate, obtuse, lateral sep. spreading or deflexed; pet. 3–4mm, triangular, purple at base, green at apex, velvety; lip to 10mm, trilobed, lobes deflexed appearing globose-inflated at tips, dark brown, velvety, speculum blue-violet with paler margin. Late spring–early summer. Mediterranean.

O.ciliata Biv. (*O.speculum* Link; *O.vernixia* sensu lato).
To 50cm. Basal lvs 3–5, oblong-lanceolate. Fls 2–15; sep. 6–8mm, oblong, green to purple-brown, forming hood; pet. purple-brown, lanceolate, one-third to half sep. length; lip to 13mm, trilobed, round or linear, margins revolute, brown to brown-purple, villous, speculum almost covering lobes, glabrous iridescent blue bordered yellow. Late spring–early summer. Mediterranean, N Africa.

O.fuciflora (F.W. Schmidt) Moench. See *O.holoserica*.

O.fusca Link.
Stems to 40cm. Basal lvs 4–6, oblong-lanceolate to ovate. Spike lax, 1–10-fld; sep. 9–11mm, oblong or ovate, dorsal slightly incurved forming loose hood, lateral sep. spreading, green to yellow-green, rarely pink; pet. linear to linear-oblong, two-thirds sep. length, green, yellow or light brown; lip 10–15mm trilobed, flat or convex, lateral lobes oblong-ovate (sometimes obscure), central lobe reniform, ovate, notched or bilobed, maroon, velvety above, speculum 2-segmented, iridescent blue, violet or brown, margin sometimes white or yellow. Mid–late spring. Mediterranean, SW Romania.

O.fusca ssp. *iricolor* (Desf.) K. Richt. See *O.iricolor*.

O.holoserica (Burm. f.) Greuter (*O.arachnites* (L.) Reichard; *O.fuciflora* (F.W. Schmidt) Moench). LATE SPIDER ORCHID.
Stems to 55cm. Basal lvs 3–7, ovate-oblong. Spike lax, 6–14-fld; bracts exceeding ovary; sep. 9–13mm, ovate-oblong, dorsal slightly incurved, bright pink to magenta or white with green mid-vein; pet. triangular, rarely linear-lanceolate, half sep. length, pink to rose-purple, velvety; lip 9–16mm, ovate to obovate, entire, rarely incised or trilobed, dark brown to dark maroon or ochre, velvety, sometimes edged yellow, central projections minute, appendage upcurved, often 3-toothed. Late spring–mid summer. Europe, Mediterranean, USSR.

O.insectifera L. (*O.muscifera* Huds.). FLY ORCHID.
Stems to 50cm, slender. Lvs 7–9, linear-lanceolate, along ascending stem. Spike lax, 2–14-fld; bracts exceeding ovary; sep. 6–8mm, oblong-ovate, slightly concave, spreading, dorsal incurved; pet. 4–6mm, linear, revolute, violet-black, velvety; lip 9–10mm, trilobed, central lobe emarginate, flat or concave, ovate, violet-black or purple, paler at tip, sometimes with yellow margin, lateral lobes spreading, speculum reniform or rectangular, pale blue or violet. Late spring–summer. Europe inc. Scandinavia.

O.iricolor Desf. (*O.fusca* ssp. *iricolor* (Desf.) K. Richt.).
To 30cm. Basal lvs 3–4, ovate to ovate-lanceolate. Spike 1–4-fld; sep. to 12mm, oblong to ovate, yellow-green; pet. to 9mm, ligulate, olive or bronze, sometimes with small projections; lip to 25mm, trilobed, slightly convex, margins recurved, lateral lobes deep maroon, velvety, brown, glabrous beneath, speculum iridescent metallic blue. Late winter–late spring. Mediterranean.

O.litigiosa Camus. See *O.araneola*.

O.lutea Cav. YELLOW BEE ORCHID.
To 40cm. Basal lvs 3–5, ovate or ovate-lanceolate, acute. Spike lax, 1–7-fld; bracts exceeding ovary; sep. 9–10mm, green, ovate to oblong-ovate, dorsal sep. incurved; pet. linear-oblong, obtuse, yellow-green, one-third to half sep. length; lip 12–18mm, oblong, dark brown to purple-black with a flat, yellow border to 3mm deep, lateral lobes ovate, midlobe reniform, emarginate to spreading-emarginate, speculum entire or bilobed, iridescent metallic grey-blue. Late winter–late spring. Mediterranean.

O.muscifera Huds. See *O.insectifera*.

O.scolopax Cav. WOODCOCK ORCHID.
To 45cm. Basal lvs 5–6, lanceolate to oblong-lanceolate. Spike 3–10-fld; sep. 8–12mm, oblong to ovate, pink to mauve; pet. lanceolate to triangular, pink or red, one-fifth to half sep. length; lip 8–12mm, midlobe ovate, brown to black-purple, velvety, margins recurved, glabrous, lateral lobes triangular, dark brown with basal projections, speculum circular or loosely X-shaped, blue or violet, edged yellow or white, spotted dark brown. Early–late spring. S Europe.

O.speculum Link. See *O.ciliata*.

O.sphegodes Mill. EARLY SPIDER ORCHID.
Stems 10–45cm. Basal lvs 5–9, ovate-lanceolate. Spike to 10-fld, lax; sep. 6–12mm, oblong-ovate to lanceolate, dorsal sep. narrowest, green, rarely white or purple; pet. half sep. length, oblong-triangular to lanceolate, green to purple-green or brown-red, 1–3-veined, often undulate; lip ovate, rich

Ophrys (a) *O.ciliata* (a1) ssp. *lusitanica* (b) *O.lutea* (b1) ssp. *melena* (b2) ssp. *murbeckii* (c) *O.fusca* (c1) ssp. *omegaifera* (c2) *O.iricolor* (c3) *O.fusca* ssp. *durieui* (d) *O.sphegodes* (d1) ssp. *planimaculata* (d2) ssp. *aesculapii* (d3) *O.araneola* (d4) *O.sphegodes* ssp. *provincialis* (d5) ssp. *atrata* (d6) ssp. *mammosa* (d7) ssp. *spruneri* (e) *O.ferum-equinum* (f) *O.bertolonii* (g) *O.argolica* (h) *O.reinholdii* (h1) ssp. *straussii* (i) *O.cretica* (j) *O.scolopax* (j1) ssp. *apiformis* (j2) ssp. *cornuta* (j3) ssp. *heldreichii* (k) *O.carmeli* (l) *O.holoserica* (l1) ssp. *maxima* (l2) ssp. *candica* (l3) ssp. *oxyrrhynchos* (l4) ssp. *exaltata* (m) *O.arachnitiformis* (3 forms) (n) *O.apifera* (o) *O.tenthredinifera* (p) *O.bombyliflora* (q) *O.insectifera*

maroon-chocolate brown, velvety, margins patent or deflexed, speculum H-shaped, maroon or deep indigo, often bordered yellow. Spring. Europe.

O.sphegodes ssp. *litigiosa* (Camus) Bech. See *O.araneola*.

O.tenthredinifera Willd. SAWFLY ORCHID.
To 45cm. Basal lvs 3–9, ovate to lanceolate. Spike lax, 3–8-fld; sep. 6–14×10mm, ovate, concave, lilac to pale rose, often veined green; pet. triangular, one-third to half sep. length,

rose purple to pink, velvety, obtuse; lip 8–14mm, entire or obscurely trilobed, obovate or oblong with basal swelling, brown-purple, velvety, margin hirsute, yellow to green, pale brown or maroon, speculum small, grey-blue bordered yellow or white, bilobed, sometimes spotted brown. Late spring–early summer. Mediterranean..

O.vernixia Brot. sensu lato. See *O.ciliata.*

× **Opsistylis** (*Vandopsis* × *Rhynchostylis*). These intergeneric crosses can be large or small plants depending on which *Vandopsis* species is used as the parent. Stems upright, leaves alternate, in 2 rows, narrowly channelled. Inflorescences axillary, on upright spikes, flowers round with flat sepals and petals and a small lip, usually very intensely coloured. The plants need bright light, high humidity and warm temperatures to grow and flower well. They grow extremely well out of doors in the humid tropics but are less easy in the glasshouse. The large plants in which *Vandopsis gigantea* is a parent soon become unwieldy, while those bred from *Vandopsis parishii* are much smaller and have very desirable flowers.

× *O*.Kultana: spreading or upright infl. of many well-spaced fls; fls basically ochre-yellow overlaid with coalescing spots of deep wine red, white surrounding the mauve column, lip bright mauve-purple.

× *O*.Lanna Thai: small plants; upright spikes of small fls, intense burgundy red with white centre surrounding the column.

Orchis L. (From the Gk *orchis*, testicle, referring to the tuberoids of some species.) Some 35 species of herbaceous terrestrials. Tubers entire, globose to elliptic, 2–3. Leaves linear-lanceolate to oblong-ovate, basal or almost basal, often spotted with spathe-like leaves sheathing emerging spike. Inflorescence an erect, crowded terminal raceme; flowers purple, red, yellow, or white; bracts membranous; petals and sepals equal, or petals sometimes smaller, incurved, forming a hood, or lateral sepals sometimes spreading; lip entire or trilobed, central lobe entire or divided, papillose or glabrous above; spur slender or saccate; ovary cylindric, twisted. Spring–summer. Temperate N Hemisphere.

CULTIVATION   See Introduction: Hardy Orchids.

O.aristata Fisch. ex Lindl. See *Dactylorhiza aristata*.

O.collina Banks & Sol. (*O.saccata* Ten.).
Tubers ovoid. Stems 10–40cm, erect. Basal lvs 2–4, sometimes spotted, oblong-ovate to oblong-ligulate. Infl. cylindric or oblong, 2–15 fld; dorsal sep. 10–12mm, incurved, ovate-oblong, forming hood with pet., lateral sep. spreading or erect; pet. oblong-lanceolate, dark olive green to red; lip to 10mm, ovate to obovate, undulate, green-pink often blotched white; spur conical, short, decurved. Late winter–mid spring. Mediterranean.

O.comperiana Steven. See *Comperia comperiana*.

O.coriophora L. BUG ORCHID.
Tubers ellipsoid. Stems 15–60cm. Basal lvs 4–10, linear to linear-lanceolate. Infl. oblong or cylindric, dense; bracts lanceolate equalling or exceeding ovary; pet. and sep. to 10mm, ovate-lanceolate, forming a violet-brown hood; lip trilobed, incurved, dark purple-red to purple-green, basally paler, sometimes spotted dark purple, lateral lobes denticulate, slightly shorter than central lobe of lip; spur conical, decurved, apically incurved. Mid- spring–early summer. SC & E Europe. ssp. *fragrans* (Pollini) Sudre. As *O.coriophora* but central lobe exceeds laterals, spur equals or exceeds lip, fls paler, fragrant, bracts white.

O.coriophora ssp. *sancta* (L.) Hayek. See *O.sancta*.
O.elata Poir. See *Dactylorhiza elata*.
O.iberica Willd. See *Dactylorhiza iberica*.
O.incarnata Soó. See *Dactylorhiza incarnata*.

O.italica Poir. (*O.longicurris* Link).
Tubers ellipsoid. Stems 20–45cm, erect. Lvs 5–10, oblong-lanceolate, margins undulate, sometimes spotted dark purple-brown. Infl. dense, conical, becoming ovoid or globose, upper

fls opening first; sep. and pet. to 10mm, ovate-lanceolate, incurved, forming hood, lilac-rose beneath, sometimes striped red; lip pink, trilobed, to 16mm, rose-white above, often spotted purple, central lobe divided, lobules, 2, linear-elongate, lateral lobes linear, red or magenta towards tip; spur cylindric, decurved. Summer. Mediterranean.

O.lactea Poir.
As *O.tridentata* except stem to 20cm, lvs oblong-lanceolate, infl. dense, sep. spreading, veined green below, basally flushed green; lip linear-oblong to square, central lobe apically finely dentate, white, spots purple, sometimes forming a continuous line. Summer. Mediterranean.

O.laxiflora Lam.
Tubers ellipsoid or globose. Stem to 120cm, usually shorter, erect. Lvs 3–8, lanceolate or linear, patent. Infl. lax, ovoid or cylindric, 6–20-fld; bracts 3–7-veined, lanceolate, tinted red-purple; sep. rose pink, lilac or red, oblong, spreading, lateral sep. deflexed, dorsal sep. almost erect; pet. oblong, incurved, forming hood; lip trilobed, centre sometimes white, lateral lobes oblong, reflexed, midlobe reduced or absent; spur cylindric, horizontal or vertical. Spring–early summer. Western Continental Europe, Mediterranean, Channel Is.

O.laxiflora ssp. *palustris* (Jacq.) Bonnier & Layens. See *O.palustris*.

O.longicornu Poir.
Tubers subglobose. Stem 10–35cm. Lvs 6–8 in a basal rosette, oblong-lanceolate. Infl. dense, oblong, lax; bracts lanceolate, veined, tinged green or red; sep. to 6mm (pet. smaller), oblong, incurved, forming hood, white to pale pink or maroon; lip shallowly trilobed, midlobe white, spotted purple, lateral lobes larger than central lobe, recurved, deep purple-violet to pink or red; spur cylindric, patent or

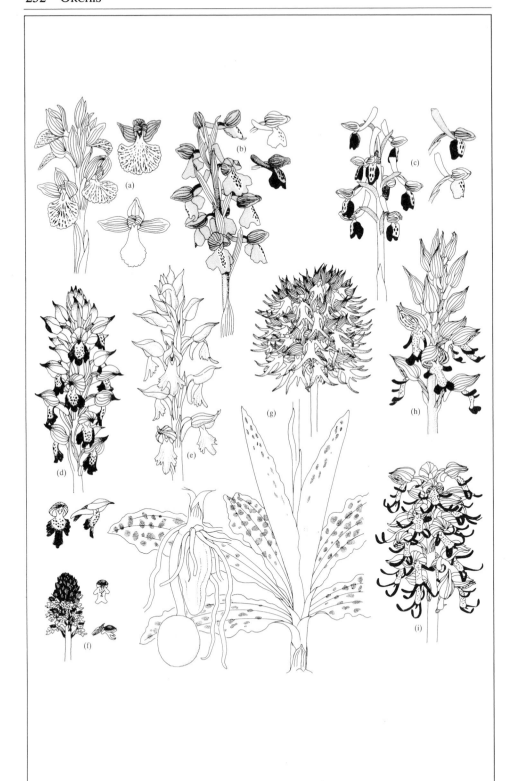

Orchis (a) *O.papilionacea* and variants (b) *O.morio* and variants (c) *O.longicornu* and variants (d) *O.coriophora* and (beneath) ssp. *fragrans* (e) *O.sancta* (f) *O.ustulata* (g) *O.italica* (h) *O.militaris* (i) *O.simia*

upcurved, to 1.6cm. Late winter–mid spring. W Mediterranean.

O.longicurris Link. See *O.italica*.

O.maculata L. See *Dactylorhiza maculata*.

O.maderensis Summerh. See *Dactylorhiza foliosa*.

O.mascula L. EARLY PURPLE ORCHID.
Tubers ellipsoid. Stems 20–60cm, erect. Lvs 3–5 in lower half of stem, becoming sheaths above, oblanceolate to linear-lanceolate, glossy, often spotted dark purple. Infl. dense, cylindric or ovoid, 6–20-fld; bracts lanceolate, tinted purple, 1–3-veined; fls purple; sep. 6–8mm, oblong-lanceolate or ovate, lateral sep. spreading or reflexed, dorsal sep. and pet. forming hood; lip 8–15mm, trilobed, white, centrally spotted purple or crimson, lateral lobes slightly deflexed or flat, midlobe apically notched, 1–1.5 times length of laterals; spur horizontal or vertical. Mid spring–mid summer. Europe.

O.militaris L. MILITARY ORCHID.
Stems 20–45cm, erect. Basal lvs 3–5, oblong-lanceolate to ovate. Infl. dense, conical, becoming cylindric as fls open; bracts ovate-lanceolate, tinted purple; sep. and pet. to 15mm, ovate-lanceolate, forming white to grey-pink hood, veined purple above; lip to 15mm, trilobed, white to dark purple (central lobe lighter), spotted red, lateral lobes linear, falcate, midlobe narrow, becoming triangular, apically bilobed, lobes oblong or ovate, with short dentations between; spur cylindric, decurved. Mid-spring–midsummer. Europe, Mediterranean, USSR.

O.morio L. GREEN-WINGED ORCHID.
Stems 5–50cm. Basal lvs 5–9, oblong-lanceolate to oblong-ovate, becoming sheaths on stem. Infl. pyramidal or oblong, apical fls opening last; bracts lanceolate, veined; sep. and pet. typically green-white lined purple-red, oblong-ovate, forming hood (sep. larger); lip to 10mm, rosy pink to purple, trilobed, recurved, midlobe apically notched, truncate, sometimes dark-spotted, lateral lobes smaller, veined, tinged green; spur cylindric, patent, horizontal or upcurved, equal or exceeding lip. Spring–midsummer. Europe, Mediterranean. Colour variants occur with white, cream, yellow and purple fls.

O.pallens L.
Stem 15–40cm. Lvs 4–6, oblong or oblong-ovate, becoming sheaths. Infl. dense, ovoid or oblong; fls yellow; bracts single-veined, olive green; sep. 7–9mm, lateral sep. deflexed, ovate-oblong, dorsal sep. erect, forming hood with dorsal pet.; lip trilobed, lateral lobes orbicular, midlobe truncate, slightly emarginate; spur patent, horizontal to ascending. Mid-spring–early summer. C & SE Europe.

O.palustris Jacq.
Stems 80–100cm. Lvs 4–6, linear to linear-lanceolate, keeled. Infl. cylindric, slightly lax; fls purple or pink; lateral sep. oblong, erect, patent; lip to 10mm, flabellate-cuneate, trilobed, midlobe equal or exceeding rounded-rectangular lateral lobes, centre white, dotted purple (rarely entire, dark purple); spur tapering or parallel, ascending. Mid-spring–midsummer. N Europe, USSR.

O.papilionacea L. BUTTERFLY ORCHID.
Stems 15–40cm, angular, erect. Basal lvs lanceolate to linear-lanceolate, erect. Infl. lax, ovoid, 2–8-fld (rarely cylindric, dense); bracts tinted red, lanceolate, 3–4-veined; fls purple, rarely red or brown; sep. and pet. to 18mm, forming a lax hood, deep red or purple, prominently veined; lip 12–25mm, entire, cuneate or fan-shaped, remotely dentate, rose to red, dark-spotted or longitudinally striped, or absent; spur cylindric, descending. Spring–early summer. Mediter-ranean.

O.praetermissa Druce. See *Dactylorhiza praetermissa*.

O.provincialis Lam. & DC. PROVENCE ORCHID.
Tubers ovoid. Stem 15–35cm. Lvs 2–5, oblong-lanceolate or lanceolate, dark-spotted or plain. Infl. lax to dense, cylindric, 7–20-fld; bracts lanceolate, 1–3-veined; fls pale yellow or white, lip deeper, centre orange-yellow, spotted maroon; sep. 9–11mm, ovate-oblong, lateral sep. spreading, deflexed, mid-

dle erect; pet. smaller; lip round-ovate, trilobed, lateral lobes ovate to round, midlobe smaller, truncate, rounded; spur cylindric, patent. Mid spring–early summer. S Europe. ssp. *pauciflora* (Ten.) Camus. As *O.provincialis* except with lvs sparsely spotted or unspotted, fls 3–7, spike lax, ovary exceeds bracts, lip 13–15mm, trilobed, lateral lobes recurved, midlobe incised. Mid spring–early summer. EC Mediter-ranean.

O.purpurea Huds. LADY ORCHID.
Tubers ellipsoid. Stem 30–80cm. Lvs 3–6, oblong to oblong-ovate, glossy. Infl. dense, cylindric, many-fld; bracts ovate-lanceolate; sep. 12–14mm, forming hood with pet., brown-purple or pink beneath, sometimes spotted purple, rarely pale green with white lip; lip to 15mm, trilobed, lateral lobes linear, midlobe obcordate or triangular, often with small dentation, pale rose or white, spotted purple; spur decurved. Mid-spring–midsummer. Europe, Mediterranean.

O.purpurella T. & T.A. Stephenson. See *Dactylorhiza purpurella*.

O.quadripunctata Ten.
Tubers ovoid. Stems straight or flexuous, slender, 10–40cm. Lvs 2–4, linear to oblong-lanceolate, usually spotted purple. Spike lax, ovoid or cylindric, to 20-fld; bracts lanceolate, 1–3-veined; fls pink to violet, red or white; dorsal sep. 3–5mm, ovate, lateral sep. spreading, dorsal sep. recurved, erect, forming a lax hood with pet., to 5mm; lip orbicular, trilobed or entire, lateral lobes 4–7mm, oblong-ovate, midlobe oblong, basal blotch white with 2–6 purple spots. Late spring–early summer. Mediterranean.

O.saccata Ten. See *O.collina*.

O.saccifera Brongn. See *Dactylorhiza saccifera*.

O.sambucina L. See *Dactylorhiza sambucina*.

O.sancta L. (*O.coriophora* ssp. *sancta* (L.) Hayek).
As *O.coriophora* except lvs 6–12, oblong-lanceolate to linear, persisting longer than in other ssp. Lower bracts 3–5-veined, fls pink to lilac-red; median sep. 9–12mm, elongate, patent, apically ascending; lip flat, incurved, lateral lobes rhombic, 3–4-dentate, midlobe entire; spur narrowing apically, incurved. Mid spring. E Mediterranean.

O.sesquipedaliensis Willd. See *Dactylorhiza elata*.

O.simia Lam. MONKEY ORCHID.
Tubers ovoid. Stems 20–45cm. Lvs 3–5, oblong-lanceolate to ovate. Infl. dense, broadly cylindric to ovoid, lower fls open last; bracts one-fifth to half ovary length, ovate-lanceolate; sep. and pet. to 10mm, ovate-lanceolate, to 10cm, forming hood, pale pink to red beneath, often streaked red, interior spotted or veined red; lip trilobed, to 20mm, white to rose pink, dotted purple, lateral lobes linear, slender, obtuse, midlobe deeply divided, lobules 2, linear, slender, magenta toward apex; spur decurved, cylindric. Early spring–early summer. Europe.

O.traunsteineri Rchb. See *Dactylorhiza traunsteineri*.

O.tridentata Scop. TOOTHED ORCHID.
Tubers ellipsoid. Stems 15–45cm, erect. Lvs 3–4, oblong to ovate-lanceolate, largely basal, a few sheathlike higher on stem. Infl. conical to ovoid, fls white to rose-pink to violet, lip spotted maroon; bracts lanceolate, single-veined; sep. and pet. ovate-oblong (sep. tapering, acuminate), forming veined hood; lip length exceeds width, trilobed, lateral lobes incurved, falcate, truncate, dentate, midlobe triangular, twice length of laterals, bilobed or notched, lobules minutely dentate; spur cylindric, decurved. Mid spring–early summer. C & S Europe.

O.ustulata L. BURNT ORCHID.
Stems erect, 12–35cm. Lvs 2–3, oblong Infl. dense, ovoid, becoming cylindric; fls scented, buds dark purple; bracts single-veined, ovate to lanceolate; sep. and pet. 3–3.5mm, forming hood, brown-purple beneath, pink above; lip 4–8mm, trilobed, lateral lobes spreading, oblong, midlobe bilobed or entire, white to pale pink, spotted red; spur cylindric, decurved. Mid spring–late summer. Europe, USSR.

Orchis (×1) (a) *O. lactea* (b) *O.tridentata* and (below) ssp. *commutata* (c) *O. purpurea* (d) *O. collina* (e) *O. mascula* (f) *O. pallens* (g) *O. provincialis* and (right) ssp. *pauciflora* (h) *O. quadripunctata* (i) *O. anatolica* (j) *O. laxiflora* and (right) ssp. *palustris*

Ornithocephalus Hook. (From Gk *ornis*, bird, and *kephale*, head, referring to the apex of the column, which resembles a bird's bill.) Some 50 species of epiphytes. Rhizome short, concealed by overlapping leaf sheaths. Pseudobulbs absent. Leaves jointed to leaf sheaths, distichous, overlapping, fleshy to subcoriaceous, arranged in a fan. Inflorescence a raceme, lateral, few- to many-flowered; flowers small; sepals subequal, free, spreading or reflexed, concave; petals larger than sepals, concave, short-unguiculate; lip entire or trilobed, sessile or subsessile; disc with a basal fleshy callus; column short, wingless, footless, anther terminal, incumbent, operculate, pollinia 4, waxy, borne on a slender stipe, rostellum long, slender, beak-shaped. Tropical America.

CULTIVATION   As for *Oberonia* but with bright light and a slight winter rest.

O.bicornis Lindl.
Lvs to 7×12cm, lanceolate to oblong-lanceolate, acute or apiculate, rigid, erect-spreading. Infl. seldom exceeding lvs, few- to many-fld; peduncle slender, flexuous, densely lanuginose; fls small, to 5mm diam., white-green or white-yellow; sep. to 3×2mm, suborbicular, spreading, apiculate, hispid below; pet. subequal to sep., suborbicular-flabellate, oblique, base cuneate, erose; lip to 7mm, lateral lobes inconspicuous, linear-spathulate, recurved, midlobe linear-oblong or oblong, acute to rounded, dorsally carinate; column to 5mm, slender. Guatemala, Honduras, Panama, Costa Rica.

O.bonplandii Rchb. f.
Lvs to 20×6mm, fleshy, lanceolate or oblong-lanceolate, acute, deep green. Infl. to 4cm, few-fld; peduncle minutely denticulate; sep. to 3×2mm, pale green, elliptic to elliptic-ovate, apiculate, lateral sep. oblique; pet. slightly larger than sep., pale green, flabellate to ovate-flabellate, truncate or rounded; lip to 5×2mm, white, margins, yellow-green toward base, entire, narrowly oblong, acute, disc with 2 large, yellow-green, fleshy, alate calli; column to 2mm, yellow-green, rostellum to 4mm. Venezuela, Colombia.

O.gladiatus Hook. (*O.inflexus* Lindl.).
Lvs to 60×7mm, oblanceolate to oblong, acute to acuminate. Infl. to 7cm, suberect to arching, loosely few to several-fld; peduncle glabrous, narrowly winged; fls small, pale cream-green or white marked green; sep. to 4×2.5mm, elliptic-oblong to suborbicular, deeply concave, margins slightly erose, slightly recurved; pet. to 4×4mm, cuneate-obovate or flabellate, rounded or truncate, slightly erose; lip to 7×3mm, entire, linear-oblong, acute to rounded, base cordate-triangular, callus large, suborbicular-ovate; column to 1mm, cream-green, anth. cream-

green, base yellow-green. Mexico, C America, Grenada, Tobago, Trinidad to Brazil, Peru, Bolivia.

O.grandiflorus Lindl.
Lvs to 15cm, few, narrowly oblong, obtuse. Infl. surpassing lvs, arcuate, densely many-fld.; fls to 18mm diam.; sep. and pet. white, with bright green basal spot, concave; lateral sep. smaller, reflexed; lip saccate, strongly carinate beneath; callus horse shoe-shaped, green; column white. Brazil.

O.inflexus Lindl. See *O.gladiatus*.

O.iridifolius Rchb. f.
Lvs to 85×6mm, fleshy, linear-ensiform, acute or acuminate. Infl. to 8cm, spreading, loosely many-fld; peduncle slender, fractiflex, winged; fls small, white; sep. to 3×2mm, elliptic to suborbicular, spreading, ciliate; pet. to 4×5mm, broadly flabellate, base cuneate, apex rounded, ciliate; lip to 5.5×6mm, spreading, lateral lobes fleshy, suborbicular to subquadrate, apex rounded, midlobe ovate, suborbicular, concave; column to 3mm, fleshy. Mexico, Guatemala.

O.myrticola Lindl.
Lvs to 25×1cm, narrowly linear-lanceolate to ligulate-lanceolate, falcate, acute or acuminate. Infl. to 8cm, ascending, arching, densely many-fld; peduncle glandular-pubesc.; fls small, lemon-scented, exterior glandular-pubesc., white and green; sep. to 4×2mm, ovate, rounded, dentate; pet. to 4.5×4.5mm, almost transparent, suborbicular, entire to undulate-crisped; lip to 5×2.5mm, entire, reflexed, ligulate-oblong, acute, base cordate, disc with 5 fleshy calli, papillose; column to 2mm, erect. Brazil, Bolivia.

O.navicularis Barb. Rodr. See *Zygostates lunata*.
O.planifolius Rchb. f. See *Dipteranthus planifolius*.

Ornithophora Barb. Rodr. (From Gk *ornis*, bird, and *phoros*, bearing, referring to the birdlike appearance of the column seen from one side.) 2 species of dwarf epiphytes. Pseudobulbs sited along slender rhizomes, compressed ovoid-pyriform, glossy, apex 2-leaved; sheaths 1–2, leafy. Leaves linear-lanceolate, channelled, acute, suberect. Inflorescence basal, erect, lax, racemose; tepals oblong-lanceolate, reflexed to spreading, free; lip clawed, lamina transversely semicircular with acute, erect, lateral lobes, callus on claw fleshy, trilobed, at lip base with 4 fan-shaped ridges; column arcuate. Brazil.

CULTIVATION   Dwarf epiphytes for the cool or intermediate house, they form large colonies of small pseudobulbs and grass-like foliage. The flowers, equally small, are delicate, pale and charming seen *en masse*. To accommodate the spreading habit, establish on rafts or slabs of fern or palm fibre suspended vertically in a bright, airy place. Spray over at least once daily except at coolest times of the year.

O.radicans (Lind. & Rchb. f.) Garay & Pabst (*Sigmatostalix radicans* Lind. & Rchb. f.).
Pseudobulbs oblong-ligulate, compressed, basal sheaths distichous, leaf-bearing, apex 2-leaved. Lvs linear-ligulate, grassy, apex acute, 10–18×0.2–0.4cm. Infl. 7–15cm; fls white-green or green-yellow, lip white, callus yellow, column maroon, anth.

cap yellow; dorsal sep. oblong-spathulate, narrow, acute, 4×1mm, reflexed, lateral sep. ovate-falcate, narrow; pet. oblong-spathulate, apex rounded to subtruncate; lip trilobed, claw narrow, margin weakly undulate, midlobe saggitate to semi-round, apex notched, lateral lobes basal, long, acuminate, narrow; disc base crested.

Osmoglossum Schltr. (From Gk *osme*, odour, and *glossa*, tongue or lip, referring to the sweet fragrance of the type species.) 7 species of epiphytes, formerly included in *Odontoglossum*. Rhizome short; roots clay-white. Pseudobulbs clustered, ovoid to elliptic-ovoid, enveloped by several distichous, overlapping leafy sheaths, apex usually bifoliate. Leaves erect to spreading, linear-ligulate, acute, coriaceous, base conduplicate. Raceme produced from axil of last basal leaf; peduncle compressed; bracts triangular-lanceolate, scarious, acute to acuminate; flowers usually small, fleshy, white, often tinged purple; sepals free, usually concave; lip sessile, porrect to sharply curved, entire, subequal to sepals and petals, fused to column foot, callus fleshy, 3-keeled; column short, winged, stigma transversely reniform; anther incumbent, galeate, usually white, pollinia 2, obpyriform. Mexico, Guatemala, El Salvador, Honduras, Costa Rica.

CULTIVATION   As for *Odontoglossum*.

O.anceps Schltr. See *O.egertonii*.

O.convallarioides Schltr. (*Odontoglossum convallarioides* (Schltr.) Ames & Correll).
Pseudobulbs to 8.5×3cm, ovoid to ovoid-elliptic. Lvs to 40×1cm, linear-ligulate. Infl. to 40cm, erect, few-fld; fls to 1.5cm diam., fragrant, white, sometimes tinged pink or lavender; sep. to 10×7mm, elliptic to oblong-elliptic, acute to subacute, concave; pet. wider than sep., suborbicular to obovate, obtuse or minutely apiculate; lip to 10×8mm, often spotted purple-red, obovate, apex subacute to obtuse, concave, callus yellow-orange, to 3.5×3.5cm, consisting of 3 fleshy ridges, lateral ridges terminating in a triangular tooth, middle ridge narrowly triangular; column to 4mm, apex obscurely 3-lobed, lobes entire. Spring. Mexico, Guatemala, Honduras, Costa Rica.

O.egertonii (Lindl.) Schltr. (*O.anceps* Schltr.; *Odontoglossum egertonii* Lindl.; *Oncidium egertonii* (Lindl.) Beer).
Pseudobulbs to 10×3cm, ovoid or elliptic-oblong, usually glossy yellow-green. Lvs to 50×1.5cm, thin, narrowly linear-ligulate. Infl. erect, to 40cm, 5–10-fld; fls to 2cm diam., white marked lilac; dorsal sep. to 15×6mm, ovate-oblong to elliptic-oblong, acute to subobtuse, lateral sep. connate almost to apex, broadly elliptic, apex bifid; pet. subequal to sep.,

oblique, ovate to broadly elliptic, concave, margin crisped; lip to 12×9cm, oblong-subquadrate or oblong-elliptic, apiculate, concave, apex sometimes reflexed; callus to 5×5mm, yellow spotted brown, quadrate, with 3 fleshy ridges, lateral ridges terminating in a triangular tooth, middle ridge narrowly triangular; column to 4mm, 3-lobed, lobes lacerate-dentate. Usually spring. Mexico, Guatemala, Honduras, Costa Rica.

O.pulchellum (Batem. ex Lindl.) Schltr. (*Odontoglossum pulchellum* Batem. ex Lindl.). LILY OF THE VALLEY ORCHID.
Pseudobulbs to 10×3.5cm, ovoid to ovoid-elliptic, furrowed. Lvs to 35×1.5cm, linear-ligulate. Infl. to 50cm, erect or slightly pendent, loosely 3–10-fld; fls to 3cm diam., fragrant, long-lived; sep. and pet. white above, tinted rose below; dorsal sep. to 2×1.5cm, obovate to elliptic, concave, apiculate, lateral sep. to 2×1cm, connate at base, oblique, broadly elliptic, apiculate; pet. to 2×1.5cm, suborbicular to obovate, subobtuse, apiculate, concave, margin often crisped; lip to 2×1cm, white, pointing upwards in flower, abruptly decurved at apex of callus, pandurate, apex recurved, margins crisped; callus to 7×5mm, yellow spotted red, with 3 fleshy ridges, oblong-quadrate, middle ridge narrowly triangular; column to 5mm, white, apex 3-lobed, lobes sharply dentate. Autumn–winter. Mexico, Guatemala, El Salvador.

Otochilus Lindl. (From Gk *ous*, ear, and *cheilos*, lip; referring to the small ear-like appendages at the base of the lip.) Some 4–6 species of epiphytes or lithophytes. Pseudobulbs arising near or from apex of previous season's pseudobulb, thus chain-like in habit, cylindric to tetragonal, and winged, apically bifoliate. Leaves linear to narrow-elliptic or ligulate, falling in second season. Inflorescence terminal, bracteate, slender; petals and sepals almost equal, narrow, free, spreading; lip sessile, basally saccate, midlobe entire, lateral lobes erect; column slender. Himalaya to SE Asia.

CULTIVATION   As for *Bulbophyllum*, although the chain-like habit may necessitate some support or culture on long rafts.

O.fuscus Lindl.
Lvs to 12cm. Infl. to 10cm, a pendent spike or raceme; fls to 1.25cm diam.; sep. linear, spreading, white or pale pink; pet. similar, narrower; lip basally concave, midlobe linear, narrowing basally; column brown.

Otoglossum (Schltr.) Garay & Dunsterv. (From Gk *ous*, ear, and *glossa*, tongue, referring to the auriculate lateral lobes of the lip.) Some 8 species of epiphytes; rhizomes thick, creeping. Pseudobulbs 1- or 2-leaved at apex and basally clothed by 1–2 leaf-bearing sheaths, well spaced on rhizome. Leaves fleshy. Raceme erect, large, long-stalked; flowers showy; sepals and petals subsimilar, spreading, obovate; lip pandurate, deflexed, basally replicate, adnate to foot of column; column small, base decurved, forming a blunt mentum with the ovary, apex cucullate, auriculate, stigma subquadrate to orbicular, anther operculate, incumbent, pollinia 2, fixed to a small viscidium by a subquadrate stipe. C & S America.

CULTIVATION   As for *Odontoglossum*.

O.brevifolium (Lindl.) Garay & Dunsterv. (*Odontoglossum brevifolium* Lindl.).
Pseudobulbs ovoid to ovoid-cylindrical, to 11cm, compressed, apically unifoliate with 1–2 leaf-bearing sheaths at base. Lvs to 30×9cm, ovate to elliptic-oblong, coriaceous, petiolate. Infl. to 60cm, erect, rarely pendent, stout, few- to many-fld; fls to 5cm diam.; sep. and pet. rich chestnut brown, margins and bases yellow blotched chestnut, dorsal sep. to 3×2cm, obovate or obovate-oblong, obtuse or retuse, undulate, lateral sep. oblique, obovate-oblong, undulate, pet. to 3×2cm, obovate or elliptic-oblong, obtuse or retuse, undulate; lip bright golden yellow with central brown band, to 2.5cm, lateral lobes small, erect, semi-ovate or semi-triangular, apex rounded, midlobe cuneate to obovate, apex bilobed or retuse, disc with fleshy keel with a transverse frontal callus and a fleshy callus at base of each lateral lobe; column to 8mm, bialate, wings trilobed, dentate. Spring. Colombia, Ecuador, Peru.

O.chiriquense (Rchb. f.) Garay & Dunsterv. (*Odontoglossum chiriquense* Rchb. f.; *Odontoglossum coronarium* var. *chiriquense* (Rchb. f.) Veitch.).
Pseudobulbs to 11×6cm, unifoliate with 1–2 leaf-bearing basal sheaths, ovoid-oblong, compressed, often dull purple. Lvs to 30×9cm, elliptic-oblong, obtuse or retuse, coriaceous; petiole short. Infl. to 45cm, stout, erect, many-fld; fls to 7.5cm diam.; sep. and pet. bright yellow spotted and blotched rich chestnut brown, sep. free, to 3×2cm, widely spreading, obovate to elliptic-oblong, obtuse, strongly undulate, lateral sep. small, erect, auriculate, pet. subequal to sep.; lip to 2.5cm, subpandurate, 3-lobed, midlobe spreading or reflexed, obovate, obtuse or emarginate, disc tuberculate; column to 1cm, stout. Usually spring. Costa Rica, Panama, Colombia, Peru.

O.coronarium (Lindl.) Garay & Dunsterville (*Odontoglossum coronarium* Lindl.).
Similar to *O.chiriquense* with narrower lvs and infl. to 1m tall; fls 7–11, to 6cm diam.; tepals obovate-orbicular, undulate-crispate, glossy ochre massively overlaid with chestnut to brick-red blotches; lip shorter than tepals, midlobe clawed, flabellate, primrose yellow. Colombia, Ecuador.

Otostylis Schltr. (From Gk *ous*, ear, and *stylos*, style.) Some 3 species of terrestrials allied to *Zygopetalum*. Pseudobulbs small, with several distichous, overlapping sheaths, apex 1- to several-leaved. Leaves narrowly lanceolate to narrowly elliptic. Inflorescence a lateral raceme, loosely to densely few to many-flowered; peduncle stout, slightly compressed; sepals and petals subsimilar, free, oblong to ovate-elliptic; lip often clawed, simple or trilobed, lateral lobes small, triangular or auriculate, midlobe large, ovate to obovate, disc with a raised callus, semicircular to reniform, dentate or undulate; column short, often with a short foot, wings 2, usually subquadrate or auriculate, clinandrium sometimes lobulate, anther terminal, operculate, incumbent, pollinia 4, compressed. Colombia, Venezuela, Trinidad, Guyanas to Brazil.

CULTIVATION   As for *Odontoglossum*.

O.brachystalix (Rchb. f.) Schltr. (*Zygopetalum brachystalix* Rchb. f.; *Aganisia brachystalix* (Rchb. f.) Rolfe; *Koellensteinia brachystalix* (Rchb. f.) Schltr.).
Pseudobulbs to 2cm, ovoid. Lvs to 70×5cm, linear-lanceolate, acute, plicate, apex recurved, strongly nerved. Infl. to 90cm, many-fld; sep. and pet. white, sep. to 18×12mm, ovate-elliptic to elliptic-lanceolate, acute to obtuse, lateral sep. oblique, pet. to 17×10mm, ovate or obovate, obtuse; lip white, to 12×12mm, lateral lobes erect, triangular, midlobe suborbicular or ovate to obovate, obtuse, callus pale yellow, irregularly dentate; column to 7mm, white marked purple at base, wings ovate to rectangular. Colombia, Venezuela, Trinidad, Guyana.

O.lepida (Lind. & Rchb. f.) Schltr. (*Aganisia lepida* Lind. & Rchb. f.).
Pseudobulbs to 6×1cm, fusiform to ovoid-fusiform, clustered. Lvs to 65×6cm, linear-lanceolate to linear-oblanceolate, acute or acuminate, plicate. Infl. to 70cm, several to many-fld; sep. and pet. white tipped pale rose, sep. to 20×10mm, elliptic-lanceolate to elliptic-oblong, acute, lateral sep. oblique, pet. similar to sep., oblique; lip to 18mm, white, simple, ovate-suborbicular, rounded or truncate, base cuneate, callus yellow, consisting of a W-shaped transverse ridge, dentate, crenulate; column to 8mm, white, wings subquadrate. Venezuela, Brazil, British Guyana.

Pabstia Garay (Colax Lindl.). (Named in honour of Dr. Guido Pabst, author of numerous articles on Brazilian orchids.) Some 5 species of epiphytes allied to *Zygopetalum*. Pseudobulbs ovoid-cylindrical, with 2 leaves at apex and basally sheathed by leafy bracts. Leaves lanceolate, distichous, plicate. Inflorescence equalling leaves, few-flowered; flowers large, showy; sepals free, subequal; petals subsimilar to sepals, often with distinct coloration; lip shorter than sepals and petals, simple to trilobed, clawed, disc with a fleshy, basal, grooved callus; column curved, stout, dorsally pubesc., anther terminal, operculate, incumbent, pollinia 4, globose or subglobose, stipe obovate-oblong. Brazil.

CULTIVATION   As for *Coelia*.

P.jugosa (Lindl.) Garay (*Maxillaria jugosa* Lindl.; *Colax jugosus* (Lindl.) Lindl.).
Pseudobulbs 5.5–7×1.75–3cm, elongate-ovoid, clustered, compressed. Lvs 15–25×4.5–5cm, subcoriaceous, short-acuminate, dark lustrous green. Infl. 12–20cm, erect or arching 1-to few-fld; fls 5.5–7.5cm diam., fleshy, fragrant, long-lived; sep. to 3–3.25×1.5–1.7cm, white or cream, oblong or obovate-oblong, obtuse, spreading; pet. to 2.8×1.6cm, white or green-white, heavily blotched, spotted or broken-banded dark chocolate, maroon or rose-purple, narrowly obovate-oblong, obtuse or rounded, erect-spreading; lip to 2.5×1.3cm, white or cream, streaked and blotched violet-purple or rose purple, fleshy, deeply 3-lobed, lateral lobes small, erect, rounded, midlobe semicircular, rounded, disc 4-ridged, puberulent; column to 1.3cm, white spotted purple above. Summer. Brazil.

Palumbina Rchb.f. (Lat. *palumbina*, belonging to pigeons – the flower resembles a dove with outspread wings). 1 species, an epiphyte. Pseudobulbs elliptic, narrow, compressed, sheathed, to 4.5×1.5–2cm. Leaves 1 per bulb, borne apically, linear-lanceolate, acute to acuminate, subcoriaceous. Inflorescence lateral, few-flowered; peduncle dark purple, slender; flowers white, petal base dotted violet, callus yellow, spotted red; dorsal sepal erect, elliptic to oblong-elliptic, broad, round to obtuse, to 1×0.5cm, lateral sepals fused; petals obovate, rounded or weakly notched, to 1×0.8cm; lip ovate-elliptic, sessile, obtuse to rounded, convex, callus warty; column fused to the lip, apex winged. Guatemala.

CULTIVATION   As for the smaller *Oncidium* species.

P.candida (Lindl.) Rchb.f. (*Oncidium candidum* Lindl.).

Panisea Lindl. (From Gk *pas*, all, and *isos*, equal; referring to the uniformity of the flower segments.) Some 9 species of terrestrials. Pseudobulbs small, clustered, each with 1–2, narrow-lanceolate to oblong-lanceolate, plicate leaves. Inflorescence a lateral raceme with few flowers and membranous bracts; sepals and petals subequal, lateral sepals basally saccate; lip fused to column base, claw sigmoid. NE India, SE Asia. .

CULTIVATION   As for *Coelogyne*.

P.uniflora (Lindl.) Lindl.
Pseudobulbs to 15mm, oblong, basally sheathed, bifoliate. Lvs 5–10cm, linear to linear-lanceolate, acuminate. Scape erect, usually shorter than pseudobulbs; fls solitary, yellow-brown; sep. and pet. to 20mm, oblong-lanceolate; lip trilobed, keeled, with 2 central ridges, margins undulate, midlobe ovate, entire, with 4 elongated dark brown spots, lateral lobes narrow, acute, longer. N India. .

Paphinia Lindl. (Named after *Paphia*, the Cypriot name for Aphrodite.) Some 5 species of epiphytes. Pseudobulbs small, ovoid to ovoid-oblong with several 2-ranked, overlapping sheaths, unifoliate to trifoliate. Leaves usually large, plicate, membranaceous, acute, lanceolate, prominently nerved. Inflorescence a basal raceme, short, erect to pendent, 1- to several-flowered, flowers large, showy; sepals subsimilar, lateral sepals articulated to column foot forming a short mentum; petals similar to sepals, smaller; lip articulate to column foot, smaller than tepals, unguiculate, trilobed, lateral lobes erect, falcate, oblong to ovate, midlobe obliquely triangular to sagittate, disc callose or variably crested with glandular hairs; column clavate, curved, with a short basal foot, apex often auriculate, anther terminal, operculate, incumbent, unilocular, pollinia 4, obovate or oblong, stipe elongate. Northern S America, Guatemala.

CULTIVATION   As for *Stanhopea* but with no dry rest.

P.cristata (Lindl.) Lindl.
Pseudobulbs to 5×2.5cm, becoming grooved, slightly compressed, light green. Lvs to 25×4.5cm, elliptic-lanceolate to linear-lanceolate, acute to acuminate, light green. Infl. to 15cm, pendent; sep. and pet. to 6×2cm, white to yellow, heavily striped red or red-brown, linear-lanceolate to elliptic-lanceolate, acute to acuminate, concave; lip to 2×1.6cm, dark chocolate-purple with a white claw, fleshy, deeply 3-lobed, lateral lobes linear-falcate, acute, margins white, midlobe ovate-hastate to subsagitatte, acute or obtuse, cristate-fimbriate, disc with a fleshy white, laciniate callus; column to 3cm, yellow-green marked red-maroon at base, foot to 1cm, wings obliquely triangular. Venezuela, Colombia, Trinidad, Guyanas, Surinam.

P.lindeniana Rchb. f.
Pseudobulbs to 6.5×2.5cm. Lvs to 27×7cm, elliptic-oblong, acute to acuminate, petiole slender, terete. Infl. to 10cm, pendent, few to several-fld; sep. and pet. white variably marked dark red-purple, sep. to 5×2cm, fleshy, lanceolate, acuminate, concave; lateral sep. smaller than dorsal sep., apex reflexed, pet. to 4.5×1.5cm, similar to sep.; lip to 2.5×1.5cm, white, shaded dark red-purple at base, fleshy, slightly concave, lateral lobes obliquely ovate, acute, apically dentate, midlobe semi-hastate, densely fimbriate-papillose, disc with an elevated crest bearing numerous white fusiform hairs; column to 2.5cm, cream-green spotted light red at base, with a short fleshy foot. Venezuela, Brazil, Colombia, Peru, Guyana.

Paphiopedilum Pfitz. (From Gk Paphos, an Aegean island with a temple to Aphrodite, and *pedilon*, slipper, describing the saccate lip formed by the third petal of each flower.) VENUS' SLIPPER. About 60 species of sympodial terrestrials, occasionally epiphytes or lithophytes. Roots thick, often ciliate, spreading from the base of each new growth and supporting the fans of leaves which cover an abbreviated stem. Pseudobulbs absent. Leaves 2 to several, leathery, conduplicate, oblong, ligulate or elliptic, lasting more than one year, plain green or mottled with light or dark markings, in some species purple beneath. Flowers waxy, carried one to several on a slender terminal stalk; dorsal sepal large, erect, lateral sepals fused to form a synsepalum; petals horizontal or pendent; lip strongly saccate, forming a pouch; column short, bearing a fleshy staminode (a modified sterile stamen) at its apex, behind which the stigmatic surface is borne on a short stalk between 2 fertile anthers bearing the 2 pollinia; ovary inferior, 1-celled. Fruit a capsule, splits lengthwise when ripe; seeds fusiform or ellipsoid, wind-dispersed. SE Asia, India, Indonesia, SW China, New Guinea, Philippines, Solomon Is. A few natural hybrids occur within this horticulturally important genus and the past 120 years have seen artificial hybridization proceeding at a considerable pace; the trend towards breeding larger and rounder flowers with overlapping segments of heavier substance has recently shown a return to further use of primary and near primary crosses. The first artificial hybrid, registered by Veitch in 1869, was *P.×harrisianum*, a cross between *P.barbatum* and *P.villosum*, resulting in long-lasting, dark, glossy flowers. A few further notable examples are *P.×arthurianum* (*P.fairrieanum* × *P.spicerianum*), *P.×leeanum* (*P.insigne* × *P.spicerianum*), *P.×maudiae* (*P.callosum* × *P.lawrenceanum*) in both coloured and albino forms. Divisions of these and many other early hybrids are still in cultivation.

Many of the species described below were originally combined in *Cypripedium*; these synonyms, long-defunct, have not been recorded here.

CULTIVATION   A heated glasshouse or conservatory is desirable though plants can be grown satisfactorily under artificial lights in an indoor structure or on a windowsill providing certain needs are met. Relative humidity should be high, between 65–75% at all times. Shade from direct sunlight is essential on sunny days; light requirement 5000–10,000 lux. The temperature needed is 15–18°C/60–65°F night-minimum with a day lift of at least 5°C/9°F; species from cooler locations (e.g. *P.hirsutissimum, P.insigne, P.fairrieanum, P.spicerianum, P.venustum*) will tolerate a night-minimum of 7°C/45°F. With the exception of *P.venustum*, it can generally be assumed that other mottled-leaved species require warmer conditions, as do plain-leaved species with multiple-flowered inflorescences. A preferred day-maximum of 28°C/82°F should be aimed at, achieved by the use of shading and fans and by increasing moisture in the air around the plants rather than opening vents to allow escape of the humidity so vital to the well-being of these orchids.

Water throughout the year, aiming to drench the medium, which should be perfectly porous, once it begins to dry out. Plants should not be allowed to dry out completely, but waterlogged conditions are disastrous. Although foliar feeding and overhead misting are beneficial in optimum conditions, never allow water to stand on foliage or to settle for long periods in the centre of growths, as this encourages botrytis and is likely to result in the loss of flower buds and entire leads.

Compost can be composed of a variety of mixtures using conifer-bark, perlag, perlite and charcoal with possible additions of sphagnum moss and/or coir; 4 grams of dolomite lime should be added to each litre of mix. *P.bellatulum* benefits from the addition of broken chalk to the crocks. When plants are in active growth fertilizer should be applied; in winter, when growth is slow, pot feeding should be at intervals of 3–4 weeks, increasing to fortnightly in the warmer, longer days of summer.

Fertilizer can be applied at shorter intervals if foliar feeding is practised. A fertilizer made specifically for orchids is preferable but a half-strength solution of any balanced fertilizer can be used, bearing in mind that high nitrogen content after flowering will aid new growth, followed by high potash to encourage optimum flower development. Annual repotting is desirable as plants deteriorate rapidly when breakdown of compost impairs its free-draining qualities.

A number of rots and moulds can develop and spread fast if the affected part is not removed immediately. Insect pests can often be removed by hand as soon as these are noticed; aphids will sometimes infest the flowers and a lookout should be kept for ants which carry them into the glasshouse. Mealy bugs and scale insects occasionally attack the leaves and stems and mice can be a real problem, biting into flower buds to eat the immature pollens. An appropriate insecticide may be applied, paying scrupulous attention to the manufacturer's instructions.

Vegetative propagation is effected by division of plants, though this should be approached with caution as some species are notoriously shy-flowerers until multiple growths are achieved.

P.acmodontum Schoser ex M.W. Wood.
Closely allied to *P.argus* but differs in its smaller fls. Lvs oblong, elliptic, tessellated pale and dark green above, to 18×4cm. Infl. erect, 1-fld, to 25cm; bract ovate, to 3cm; dorsal sep. 4cm×31mm, white or pink, veined dark purple or purple-green; synsepalum 32×15mm, white tinged purple, veined purple and green; pet. spreading, 43×14mm, sparsely ciliate, green beneath, purple above, veined and spotted dark purple in basal half; lip deeply saccate, 10×23mm, bronze or olive green with darker veins; staminode ovate, 10×9mm. Spring. Philippines (Visayan Sea, Negros).

P.adductum Asher.
Closely related to *P.rothschildianum* but recognized by its decurved pet. and abbreviated staminode. Lvs about 6, to 26×4.2cm, oblong-ligulate to slightly lanceolate, dark green, margin hyaline. Infl. 2–3-fld, arching, to 29cm, pubesc.; bracts 4cm×13mm, green veined maroon; fls glabrous; sep. pale green-yellow or white, veined maroon; dorsal sep. arching, ovate, 6.5×3cm; synsepalum ovate, 6.5×3cm; pet. arcuate-dependent, linear-tapering, to 15cm×9mm; lip porrect, to 47×21mm, grooved on back; staminode rectangular, not covering stigma. Winter. Philippines.

P.appletonianum (Gower) Rolfe.
Lvs 6–8, narrowly elliptic to oblong-elliptic, to 25×4cm, obscurely tessellated pale and darker green with purple marking on lower base. Infl. 1–2-fld, to 48cm; bract green, lanceolate, to 2cm; fls 6–10cm across; sep. pale green, veined green, dorsal sep. ovate, cordate at base, apiculate above, 4.4×2.4cm, basal margins recurved; synsepalum elliptic-lanceolate, to 3×1.5cm; pet. spathulate, to 5.8×1.8cm, half-twisted in apical half, green, striped darker with maroon-black spots in basal half, purple above; lip 3–5cm, ochre to pale purple, veined darker; staminode transversely elliptic, to 1cm. Winter–spring. Philippines.

P.argus (Rchb. f.) Stein.
Lvs 3–5, narrowly elliptic, mottled pale and dark green above, purple at base beneath. Infl. 1-fld, to 45cm, purple or green, mottled purple, shortly pubesc.; bract elliptic, to 4.5cm×1.8cm; fls 6.5cm across; dorsal sep. to 4.5×3.5cm, white veined green, spotted purple toward base; synsepalum to 4.4×2cm, white veined green; pet. recurved, ligulate, to 6.5cm×1.8cm, white veined green, purple at apex, heavily spotted maroon, maroon hairs on margin long at base, shorter toward apex; lip green flushed pink, veined green, to 4.5×2.5cm; staminode lunate, to 0.9×1.1cm, pale brown-green, veined green. Spring. Philippines (Luzon).

P.armeniacum S.C. Chen & Liu.
Closely allied to *P.delenatii* but differs in growth habit, fl. colour and size of lip. Growths to 15cm apart on rhiz. Lvs 5–7, oblong, to 12cm×2.3cm, marbled dark and light blue-green above, densely spotted purple beneath, margins minutely serrulate. Infl. 1-fld, to 26cm, green spotted purple, brown-pubesc.; bract about 1.5cm, green spotted purple, brown-pubesc.; fls large, bright golden yellow; dorsal sep. ovate, to 5×2.5cm, pubesc. near base; synsepalum ovate, to 3.5×2cm; pet. ovate, rounded, to 5×3.5cm, ciliate, pubesc. at

base; lip inflated, thin-textured, to 5×4cm, margins incurved, white pubesc. and dotted purple inside at base; staminode large, convex, cordate, acute, to 2×2cm. Spring–summer. China (Yunnan).

P.barbatum (Lindl.) Pfitz.
Very closely allied to *P.callosum*. Terrestrial or lithophytic. Lvs about 5, narrowly oblong-elliptic to elliptic, to 1.5×4cm, base sparsely ciliate, mottled pale and dark green above, pale green beneath. Infl. 1–2-fld, erect, to 36cm; bract ovate, to 2.5×1.5cm, green, pubesc.; fls about 8cm diam.; dorsal sep. ovate, to 5×5.5cm, white, green at base, veined purple; synsepalum narrowly ovate, to 3.5×1.5cm, pale yellow-green, veined green, flushed purple; pet. pale green beneath, purple above, veined darker, upper margin spotted dark maroon, deflexed, to 6×1.5cm, ciliate; lip to 4.5×2.5cm, incurved lateral lobes warty; staminode lunate, to 1×1cm, pale green, veined darker. Spring–summer. Peninsular Malaysia and Penang Is.

P.barbigerum Tang & Wang.
This relatively little known species related to *P.insigne* and *P.gratrixianum* differs in its small plant bearing small flowers, narrow leaves and differently shaped staminode. Lvs 4–6, suberect, linear, to 19×1.3cm, green. Infl. 1-fld, erect, about 16cm; bract elliptic, to 2cm; fls about 6cm diam.; dorsal sep. subcircular, up to 3.2×3cm, white with green base; synsepalum elliptic, to 3.5×1.5cm; pet. oblong-ligulate to ligulate-spathulate, to 3.4×0.9cm, fawn margined cream, base ciliate, margin undulate and sparsely ciliate; lip to 3×1.5cm, tan-brown, outer surface glabrous; staminode transversely elliptic, 0.6×0.8cm, pubesc., bearing a central boss. China (Guizhou, Yunnan).

P.bellatulum (Rchb. f.) Stein.
Calcicolous in limestone crevices with roots in a layer of leaf-mould and moss. Lvs 4–5, oblong-elliptic, to 14×5cm, dark green mottled pale green above, spotted purple below. Infl. 1-fld, rarely 2-fld, to 4.5cm; bract to 27×25mm, pubesc., pale green, spotted purple; fls round, 5.5–8cm diam., white or cream, heavily spotted maroon; dorsal sep. concave, to 3.5×4cm; synsepalum deeply concave, to 22×27mm; pet. somewhat concave, to 6×4.5cm; lip narrowly ovoid, to 4×2cm, margins strongly incurved; staminode 11×9mm. Summer. W Burma, Thailand.

P.bougainvilleanum Fowlie.
Most closely allied to *P.violascens* but differs in having longer, more strongly tessellated lvs and greener fls with smaller lips. Lvs 6–7, narrowly elliptic, to 22×4.2cm, pale green, tessellated darker. Infl. 1-fld, to 23cm; bract elliptic, 2.6cm, pale green; fls about 5cm across; sep. white, veined green, outer surface purple-pubesc., pet. white, veined green, apical margins flushed purple; lip and staminode green, veined darker; dorsal sep. ovate, to 3.8×4cm; synsepalum concave, ovate, to 2.7×1.7cm; pet. falcate, narrowly elliptic, to 5×2cm; lip to 5×2.6cm, narrowing to apex; staminode lunate, minutely pubesc., to 11×14mm. Autumn. Papua New Guinea.

P.bullenianum (Rchb. f.) Pfitz.
Closely allied to *P.appletonianum* and *P.hookerae*. Lvs 6–8, to 14×5.5cm, tessellated dark and light green above, some-

Paphiopedilum   (a) *P.bellatulum*   (b) *P.concolor*   (c) *P.godefroyae*   (d) *P.delenatii*   (e) *P.armeniacum*

times flushed purple beneath. Infl. erect, 1-fld, to 25cm, pubesc.; bract 15–21mm, ciliate; fls to 9.5cm across; dorsal sep. usually concave, to 3×2cm, outer surface shortly pubesc., white, veined green, often marked purple at base; synsepalum lanceolate, to 2.5×1.5cm, white, veined green; pet. spathulate, to 5×1.5cm, ciliate, green at base, purple above, margins spotted maroon-black; lip to 4cm, emarginate at apex, ochre-green; staminode to 9×8mm, deeply incised at apex. Winter. Borneo, Sumatra, Peninsular Malaysia. var. *celebesense* (Fowlie & Birk) Cribb. Differs by having fewer spots on petal margins and lack of prominent emarginate apex to the lip.

P.callosum (Rchb. f.) Stein.
Very closely allied to *P.barbatum*. Lvs 3–5, narrowly elliptic, to 20×4.5cm, ciliate at base, tessellated pale and dark above, lower surface sometimes purple at base. Infl. 1-fld, rarely 2-fld, to 40cm; bract ovate to elliptic, to 28×20mm, green, sometimes marked purple, ciliate; fls 8–11cm across; sep. white flushed purple in lower half, veined purple and green, dorsal sep. broadly ovate, to 5.5×6cm, margins ciliate, recurved; synsepalum concave, to 3×2.5cm; pet. sometimes reflexed, sub-sigmoid, rounded at apex, to 6.5×2cm, white to yellow-green, apical third purple, maroon-spotted on upper margin and sometimes basal half; lip to 4.5×2.5cm, incurved lateral lobes warty, green, flushed maroon; staminode lunate, 11×7mm. Summer. Thailand, Cambodia, Laos. var. *sublaeve* (Rchb. f.) Cribb. Fls smaller than typical species; dorsal sep. smaller; pet. shorter, broader, less sigmoid, borne at 45° from horizontal, warty on upper margin. Peninsular Thailand, NW Malaysia.

P.charlesworthii (Rolfe) Pfitz.
Related to *P.spicerianum* and *P.druryi*, but differs in its pure white staminode and large, distinctively coloured and shaped dorsal sep. Lvs oblong-elliptic or linear-oblong, to 15cm×28mm, green above, spotted purple near base beneath. Infl. 1-fld, 8–15cm, pale green, pubesc.; bract obovate, to 32×20mm, pale green, spotted maroon, ciliate; fls to 8cm across; dorsal sep. transversely elliptic to circular, to 5.5× 6.5cm, spreading or reflexed, outer surface finely pubesc., pink, veined darker; synsepalum elliptic, to 4cm×28mm, pale yellow, flecked and veined purple, finely pubesc. on outer surface; pet. horizontal, slightly incurved, ligulate-spathulate, to 4.5×1.5cm, slightly ciliate toward apex; lip wide-mouthed, to 43×27mm, pink-brown, veined darker, hairy within; staminode obovate, to 10×10mm, glabrous, white with central raised yellow boss. Autumn. Burma (Shan States only).

P.ciliolare (Rchb. f.) Stein.
Resembles *P.superbiens* but differs in the shape of the staminode and shorter lip. Lvs 4–6, oblong-elliptic to elliptic-oblanceolate, to 1.5×5cm, sparsely ciliate at base, mottled pale and darker green above, tinged purple at base beneath. Infl. 1-fld, erect, 20–32cm, purple, shortly pubesc.; bract ovate-lanceolate, 2–3cm, pubesc., ciliate; fls 7–9cm across; sep. white at base, pale purple and green above, veined purple, dorsal sep. ovate, to 5.5×5cm, ciliate; synsepalum elliptic-ovate, to 32×22mm; pet. slightly falcate, oblanceolate, to 7×2cm, ciliate, upper margins warty, white, spotted and veined dark purple; lip to 6×3.5cm, incurved lateral lobes warted, dark brown-purple; staminode transversely reniform, 3-lobed at apex, narrowly incised at base, to 14×7mm. Summer. Philippines.

P.concolor (Lindl.) Pfitz.
Terrestrial or lithophytic on limestone hills often in dense shade. Lvs 4–6, oblong to elliptic-oblong, to 14×4cm, tessellated dark and pale green on outer surface, finely spotted purple beneath. Infl. 1–2-fld, rarely 3-fld, to 8cm, finely white-pubesc., purple or green spotted purple; bracts ovate, to 15×16mm, pubesc., green, spotted purple; fls to 7cm diam., yellow, rarely ivory or white, finely spotted all over with purple; dorsal sep. broadly ovate, to 35×33mm; synsepalum concave, elliptic to ovate, to 3×3cm; pet. elliptic, rounded at apex, to 4.5×2.5cm; lip ellipsoidal, fleshy, margins incurved, to 38×15mm; staminode shortly trullate to subtriangular,

minutely ciliate, to 13×12mm. Summer–autumn. SE Burma, SW China (Yunnan), Thailand, Indochina.

P.curtisii (Rchb. f.) Stein. See *P.superbiens*.

P.dayanum (Lindl.) Stein.
Lvs oblong-lanceolate, to 21×5cm, tessellated dark and light yellow-green or blue-green, margins near apex minutely serrate. Infl. 1-fld, to 25cm, maroon, purple-pubesc.; bract lanceolate, to 2.5cm, pale green, pubesc.; fls to 14.5cm across; sep. white veined green, dorsal sep. ovate, to 5×2cm, ciliate; synsepalum ovate, to 5×2cm; pet. oblanceolate-spathulate, to 8×1.5cm, purple-pink, purple-ciliate; lip deep maroon, 5×2cm, apical margin ciliate, lateral lobes incurved, warted; staminode green, veined darker, transversely elliptic, reniform, 6×13mm. Summer. Borneo (Sabah only).

P.delenatii Guill.
Closely related to *P.armeniacum* and *P.micranthum*. Lvs 6–7, elliptic to oblong-elliptic, to 11×4cm, margins ciliate at base, mottled dark and pale green above, spotted purple below. Infl. 1-fld but commonly 2-fld, to 22cm, purple, white-hirsute; bract elliptic to ovate, to 15×10mm, green spotted purple, shortly pubesc.; fls to 8cm diam., pale pink with red and yellow markings on staminode, pubesc. within and without; dorsal sep. ovate, to 3.5×2.5cm; synsepalum similar, 3×2.9cm; pet. broadly elliptic, rounded at apex, 4.3×5cm; lip ellipsoidal to subglobose, 4×3cm, margins incurved, minutely pubesc.; staminode somewhat convex, ovate, to 17×16mm, ciliate. Spring. Vietnam.

P.druryi (Bedd.) Stein.
Stems short on a creeping rhiz. Lvs 5–7, suberect or spreading, narrowly oblong, to 20×3cm, coriaceous, light green with darker veins. Infl. 1-fld, erect, to 25cm; bract ovate, 12mm, green, purple-pubesc.; fls green-yellow or chartreuse, a central maroon-brown streak on dorsal sep. and pet., lip honey-yellow; dorsal sep. curved forward over lip, elliptic, to 4×3cm, pubesc., shortly ciliate on margins; synsepalum ovate, to 3.5×2.5cm, pubesc.; pet. incurved-porrect, narrowly oblong, slightly drooping, often dilated toward apex, to 43×18mm, pubesc., margins undulate and reflexed; lip slightly compressed, to 4.5×1.5cm; column short; staminode obcordate, 10–12mm long and wide with a small raised boss below centre. Summer. S India; perhaps extinct in the wild.

P.emersonii Koopowitz & Cribb.
Allied to *P.delenatii* and the Chinese *P.armeniacum*, *P.malipoense* and *P.micranthum*. Lvs about 4, coriaceous, ligulate, to 23cm×37mm, green, lower surface slightly keeled. Infl. erect, to 11.5cm, 1-or possibly 2-fld, subtended by a white, papery, basal, sterile sheath; bract elliptic, conduplicate, 28×22mm, white, papery; fls 8.5–9.5cm across, subcampanulate, sep. white, campanulate, thick-textured, pet. white, flushed pink at base, lip creamy, rim flushed pink, spotted purple within, yellowing with age; staminode bright yellow marked with red; dorsal sep. elliptic-ovate, hooded over lip, margins recurved, 4.5cm×32mm, surfaces pubesc., outer side keeled; synsepalum elliptic subcircular, 3.5×3.5cm, both surfaces pubesc., outer side keeled; pet. broadly elliptic to subcircular, incurved, to 4.5×4.5cm, pubesc., villous at base; lip subporrect, 3.5×3cm, flared at base, apical margin incurved, grooved along veins; column short; staminode convex, trullate, 20×10mm; stigma spathulate, shortly papillose; anth. 2, with dry pollen. Spring. China (probably Guizhou).

P.exul (Ridl.) Rolfe.
Closely allied to *P.insigne* and *P.gratrixianum*. Terrestrial or lithophytic. Lvs 4–5, suberect, linear, to 35×3cm, yellow-green. Infl. 1-fld, to 18cm, slender, green, pubesc.; bract narrowly elliptic to elliptic, 44×24mm, green to yellow-green; fls about 6.5cm across; dorsal sep. ovate-elliptic, 4.5×3cm, outer surface pubesc., mainly white, centre yellow with raised maroon spots; synsepalum oblong-elliptic, 4.5×2.5cm, pale yellow-green, veined darker; pet. incurved, subhorizontal,

Paphiopedilum (a) *P.glaucophyllum* (b) *P.victoria-mariae* (c) *P.victoria-regina* (d) *P.insigne* (e) *P.villosum* (f) *P.hirsutissimum*

narrowly oblong, 5cm×17mm, ciliate, pubesc. at base, margins undulate, glossy, buff-yellow, veined darker; lip 3.5cm×19mm, glossy, buff, veined darker; staminode obovate, 8×9mm. Summer. Peninsular Thailand.

P.fairrieanum (Lindl.) Stein.
Lvs 4–8, linear-ligulate, to 28×3cm, margins serrulate toward apex, mid to dark green, faintly mottled above, paler beneath. Infl. 1-fld, rarely 2-fld, to 45cm, green; bract elliptic, 14×8mm, white, purple-pubesc.; fls showy, sep. white, veined green and purple, somewhat purple suffusion on dorsal sep., pet. similar; dorsal sep. elliptic, to 8×7cm, ciliate, apical margins recurved, lateral margins undulate; synsepalum ovate, 3.5×2.5cm; pet. S-shaped, 5×1.5cm, ciliate, margins undulate; lip deep, outcurved at apex, 4cm×25mm, olive to yellow-green, veined darker; staminode elliptic, 9×7mm, yellow, centre veined green and purple. Autumn. Sikkim, Bhutan, NE India.

P.glanduliferum (Bl.) Stein (*P.praestans* (Rchb. f.). Pfitz.).

Terrestrial, rarely epiphytic. Lvs 4–6, linear-oblong, to 40×5.5cm, basal margins sparsely ciliate, green, glabrous. Infl. 2–5-fld, to 50cm, purple to green-brown, shortly pubesc.; bract ovate, to 4.5cm, glabrous, pale yellow-green striped purple; fls to 16cm across, sep. and pet. yellow veined maroon, pet. margins maroon-warted on base, lip yellow, veined and flushed purple; dorsal sep. ovate to 5.5×3cm; synsepalum similar, to 5.5×3cm; pet. deflexed, linear-tapering, to 10×1cm, apical parts papillose, basal margins sparsely ciliate, usually twisted; lip subporrect, to 5.5×2cm, lateral lobes incurved; staminode convex, oblong to subquadrate, 17×12mm, sides hirsute. Summer. W New Guinea and adjacent islands.

P.glaucophyllum J.J. Sm.
Closely allied to *P.victoria-regina*; differs in its glaucous foliage; dorsal sep. lacking maroon stripes on veins; deflexed, long-ciliate white petals spotted purple, and obtuse staminode. Lvs 4–6, narrowly oblong-elliptic, to 28.5cm×53mm, glaucous, scarcely mottled when young, basal margins ciliate. Infl. to 20- or more-fld, green, mottled purple, pubesc.; rachis with internodes to 5cm; bracts elliptic, to 18mm, green, ciliate; fls in succession, never more than 2 open at a time, to 8.5cm across; dorsal sep. ovate to broad, to 33×32mm, shortly ciliate, outer surface pubesc., white or cream, centre yellow-green, veins flushed maroon; synsepalum ovate, to 32×18mm; pet. deflexed at 10–20° below horizontal, linear, to 5cm×9mm, apical half twisted, long-ciliate, pubesc. at base, white, spotted purple; lip to 4×2cm, pubesc. at base, pink-purple, finely spotted darker, margins pale yellow; staminode ovate, 15×9mm, green, apical half flushed purple. Summer. E Java. var. *moquetteanum* J.J. Sm. Differs from species type in its usually longer broader lvs, to 55×10cm, longer scape, few larger fls to 10cm across; dorsal sep. narrower, longer, yellow finely speckled purple. SW Java.

P.godefroyae (Godef.-Leb.) Stein.
Terrestrial or lithophytic. Lvs 4–6, oblong-elliptic, to 14cm×29mm, basal margins sparsely ciliate, tessellated dark and pale green above, usually spotted purple beneath. Infl. 1–2-fld, erect, to 8cm, purple, very shortly pubesc.; bract conduplicate, ovate, to 1.5cm, purple, shortly pubesc., fls about 5cm across, white or ivory-white, all seg. usually spotted purple; dorsal sep. concave, broadly ovate, to 33×37mm; synsepalum ovate, to 3×3cm; pet. oblong-elliptic, rounded, to 5.5×3cm, margins often undulate; lip ellipsoidal, to 3.5×1.5cm, margins strongly incurved; staminode transversely elliptic, to 9×11mm, apical margin 1–3-toothed, pubesc., ciliate. Summer. Peninsular Thailand, adjacent islands.

P.gratrixianum (Mast.) Guill.
Related to *P.villosum*; differs in its smaller and differently marked flowers. Lvs 4–7, suberect, linear, to 30×2.3cm, green, spotted purple near base beneath. Infl. 1-fld, to 25cm; bract narrowly oblong-lanceolate to obovate, to 4.5×1.5cm,

green, spotted purple, glabrous; fls 7–8cm across; dorsal sep. ovate to obovate, to 5.2×4.6cm, white above, pale green below, purple-hairy; synsepalum ovate-elliptic, to 5×2.5cm, pale green, outer surface purple-pubesc.; pet. spathulate, to 5.2×2.5cm, glossy, yellow, flushed and veined purple-brown, minutely ciliate, reflexed side margins; lip to 4.2×2.8cm, tapering to apex, yellow flushed brown; staminode obcordate, 11×11mm, yellow, basal half purple-hairy, pustular with a central knob. Winter. Laos, possibly Vietnam.

P.haynaldianum (Rchb. f.) Stein.
Closely allied to *P.lowii*; differs in its villous peduncle; longer and narrower, heavily spotted dorsal sep., more tapering lip, and narrower staminode, simple excised at its apex. Terrestrial, lithophytic, or rarely epiphytic. Lvs 6–7, linear-ligulate, to 45×5cm. Infl. arching, 3–4-fld, to 51cm, purple, white-villous; bracts oblong-lanceolate, to 4.5cm; fls to 12.5cm across; dorsal sep. obovate-elliptic, apex cucullate, to 6×2.5cm, basal margin recurved, creamy white, sides flushed purple, centre green or yellow with basal half spotted maroon; synsepalum elliptic, 4.5×2.5cm, pale green, spotted maroon at base; pet. arcuate, spathulate, half-twisted, to 8cm×14mm, ciliolate, green or yellow, basal half spotted maroon, purple above; lip to 4.5cm×23mm, ochre-green, veined darker, purple-pubesc. within; staminode obovate, 12×8mm, apex incised, a short protuberance at base. Spring. Philippines (Luzon & Negros).

P.hirsutissimum (Lindl. ex Hook.) Stein.
Terrestrial or epiphytic. Lvs 5–6, linear-ligulate, to 45×2cm, green, spotted purple beneath. Infl. 1-fld, to 25cm, densely long-haired, subtended by 11cm sheath at base; bract elliptic, to 28mm, pubesc.; fls to 14cm across, sep. pale yellow to pale green with glossy dark brown suffusion almost to margins, pet. pale yellow, lower half spotted purple-brown, apical half flushed rose-purple; dorsal sep. ovate-elliptic, 4.5×4cm, margins undulate, ciliate; synsepalum similar, 36×22mm; pet. horizontal to deflexed, spathulate, 7cm×22mm, half-twisted toward apex, basal margins strongly undulate, pubesc., ciliate; lip 4.5×2cm; staminode subquadrate, convex, 10×8mm, pale yellow, spotted purple toward base, glossy dark brown toward middle. Spring–summer. NE India (Assam, Manipur, Lushai, Naga Hills). var. *esquirolei* (Schltr.) Cribb. Differs in its slightly larger fls, pet. to 8cm and shorter pubescence on peduncle and ovary. SW China (Yunnan and Guizhou) to N Thailand.

P.hookerae (Rchb. f.) Stein. Lvs 5–6, oblong-elliptic, 23×5cm, boldly tessellated dark and light green above. Infl. 1-fld, to 50cm, purple, white-pubesc.; bract lanceolate, 30×14mm, pale brown, pubesc.; fls about 8cm across; dorsal sep. ovate, 4cm×29mm, basal margins reflexed, cream, centre flushed green; synsepalum elliptic, to 3×1.5cm, pale yellow; pet. deflexed, half-twisted in middle, spathulate, 5.5cm×22mm, ciliate, pale green, basal two-thirds spotted brown, apical third and margins purple; lip 42×17mm, brown, lateral lobes warted, apical margin ciliate, slightly reflexed; staminode circular, 10×10mm, apically excised, lateral lobes incurved-falcate at apex. Summer. Borneo (Sarawak and W Kalimantan). var. *volonteanum* (Sander ex Rolfe) Kerch. Differs in its narrower lvs, spotted purple below, pet. broader and more obtuse, lip slightly constricted below the horizontal mouth. Borneo (Sabah only).

P.insigne (Wallich ex Lindl.) Pfitz.
Very variable in fl. size and colour. Lvs 5–6, ligulate, to 32×3cm, green, spotted purple at base beneath. Infl. 1-fld, to 25cm, green, very shortly purple-pubesc.; bract elliptic or oblong-elliptic, to 5cm, glabrous, spotted purple at base; fls 7–10cm across; dorsal sep. ovate-elliptic to obovate-elliptic, 6.4×4cm, apical margins incurved, pale green, inner surface with raised maroon spots, margin white; synsepalum elliptic, 5×2.5cm, pale green, spotted brown; pet. slightly incurved, spathulate, 63×18mm, upper margin undulate in basal two-thirds, yellow-brown, veined red-brown; lip 5×3cm, yellow,

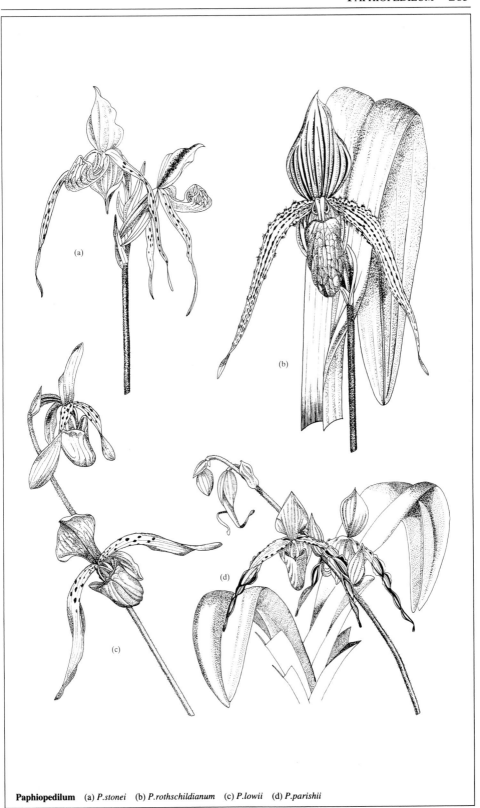

Paphiopedilum   (a) *P.stonei*   (b) *P.rothschildianum*   (c) *P.lowii*   (d) *P.parishii*

marked purple-brown; staminode obovate, 10mm, yellow with purple hairs on surface, raised boss in centre. Autumn–winter. NE India (Meghalaya, Khasia Hills), E Nepal.

P.javanicum (Reinw. ex Lindl.) Pfitz.
Allied to *P.dayanum* but differs in its smaller, differently coloured flowers, reniform staminode lacking lateral teeth at apex, shorter dorsal sep., and shorter spotted pet. with margins only shortly ciliate. Lvs 4–5, narrowly elliptic, 23×4cm, pale green, veined and mottled darker. Infl. 1-fld, to 36cm, purple, shortly white-pubesc.; bract elliptic, to 25×14mm, pale green, lightly spotted purple, margins and midvein ciliate; fls to 9.5mm across; dorsal sep. ovate to elliptic, to 38×29mm, shortly ciliate, outer surface pubesc., pale green, veined darker, margin white-pink; synsepalum lanceolate, 26×13mm, outer surface pubesc., pale green; pet. usually deflexed at about 45° to horizontal, narrowly oblong, to 48×14mm, pale green, apical quarter pink-purple, basally spotted maroon; lip 4×2cm, outer surface shortly pubesc., lateral lobes verrucose, green, veined darker, often flushed brown; staminode reniform, 8×10mm, surface pubesc. Spring–summer. Java, Bali, Flores, possibly Sumatra. var. *virens* (Rchb. f.) Pfitz. Differs in pet. possibly less spotted. Lower slopes of Mount Kinabalu; Crocker Range in Sabah.

P.kolopakingii Fowlie.
Allied to *P.stonei* but differs in having many more, smaller fls. Terrestrial or lithophytic. Lvs 8–10, suberect, ligulate, to 60×8cm, green. Infl. to 14-fld, arching, to 70cm; bracts elliptic-lanceolate, to 5×1.5cm, green-ochre striped purple; fls to 10cm across; sep. white veined dark red-brown, pet. green, veined red, lip ochre, veined darker, staminode yellow; dorsal sep. ovate, 6.5×3.5cm, finely pubesc.; synsepalum ovate, 47×26mm, 2-keeled on back; pet. falcate, linear-tapering, to 7×8cm, minutely pubesc.; lip grooved behind, apex sharp, to 6cm×28mm; staminode convex, subquadrate, 15×10mm, sides pubesc. Borneo, central Kalimantan only.

P.lawrenceanum (Rchb. f.) Pfitz.
Closely related to *P.callosum* and *P.barbatum*; differs in having boldly tessellated lvs, very large dorsal sep., spreading pet. with upper and lower margins warted and differently shaped staminode. Lvs 5–6, elliptic to narrowly elliptic, to 19×6.5cm, dark green mottled yellow-green above, pale green beneath. Infl. 1-fld, to 31cm, pubesc., maroon; bract ovate, green, veined maroon; fls. to 11.5cm across; dorsal sep. broadly ovate-subcircular, to 62×62mm, lateral margins slightly reflexed, white, veined maroon above, green, below; synsepalum narrowly lanceolate, to 4×1.4cm, white flushed green, veined maroon; pet. at right angles to dorsal sep., ligulate, about 6cm×11mm, green with purple apex, margins purple-ciliate and maroon-warted; lip 65×32mm, lateral lobes incurved and maroon-warted, green overlaid dull maroon, spotted maroon within; staminode lunate, to 11×14mm, green veined darker, margin purple. Summer. Borneo (Sarawak and Sabah).

P.lowii (Lindl.) Stein.
Epiphytic or rarely lithophytic. Closely allied to *P.haynaldianum* but differs in lacking spotting on its more ovate-elliptic dorsal sep., narrower pet. with more, smaller spotting basally, shorter broader lip and broader staminode, 3-toothed at its apex. Lvs 4–6, linear-ligulate, to 40×5cm, green. Infl. erect to arching, 3–7-fld, to 50cm, green mottled purple, shortly pubesc.; bracts elliptic, to 4.5×2cm, yellow, marked purple, pubesc.; fls to 14cm across; dorsal sep. elliptic-ovate, to 5.5cm×32mm, margins undulate and ciliate, pale green, basal half mottled purple, basal margins recurved; synsepalum elliptic, to 4cm, outer surface 2-keeled, pale green; pet. spathulate, often once-twisted in middle, to 9×2cm, ciliate, pale yellow, apical third purple, basal two-thirds spotted maroon; lip to 40×27mm, dull ochre brown; staminode obovate, apically 3-toothed, with a long erect hook at base, 10×7mm, pale ochre to brown-

green. Spring–summer. Peninsular Malaysia, Sumatra, Java, Borneo, Sulawesi.

P.malipoense S.C. Chen & Tsi.
Allied to *P.armeniacum* but differs in fl. colour and its distinctive bicoloured staminode. Terrestrial on rocks in mixed montane forest. Growths occur on a more or less creeping, elongated rhiz. Lvs 7–8, leathery, oblong or narrowly elliptic, to 20×4cm, dark green, lower surface keeled and marked with purple. Infl. to 30cm, 1-fld; bract about 1.5cm; fls about 9cm across, sep. and pet. green with purple stripes and spots; dorsal sep. elliptic-lanceolate, to 45×22mm, 5-nerved, inner surface sparsely pubesc., villous without; synsepalum ovate-lanceolate, 7-nerved, 38×24mm; pet. obovate, about 40×34mm, villous at base, ciliolate, 9-veined, inner surface pubesc.; lip pale grey spotted purple within, deeply saccate, horizontal, 4.5cm, subglobose, margins inrolled, base villous within, outside finely pubesc.; staminode convex, broadly ovate-oblong, to 14×13mm, surface bearing 4 raised bosses in apical half. Spring. China (SE Yunnan).

P.mastersianum (Rchb. f.) Stein.
Lvs 4–6, to 30cm×43mm, oblong-elliptic, upper surface faintly tessellated dark and pale green. Infl. 1-fld, to 30cm, maroon, densely hairy; bract ovate-elliptic, green, ciliate, 29×20mm; fls to 9.5cm across; dorsal sep. broadly ovate, to 37×43mm, outer surface pubesc., cream with green centre; synsepalum ovate, to 29×20mm, green-yellow; pet. slightly reflexed, oblong-spathulate, to 5.5×2cm, very shortly ciliate, glossy, tinged green, spotted dark maroon near base, apical half flushed brown; lip to 52×30mm, pale rosy-brown spotted pale brown on lateral lobes; staminode lunate, to 11×10mm, base divided, apical margin excised, lateral lobes of apical margin incurved-falcate, pale green and brown. Summer. Moluccas (Ambon, Buru).

P.micranthum Tang & Wang.
Most closely related to *P.malipoense* but differs in fl. colour and its distinctive staminode. Growths clustered. Lvs 4–5, oblong-elliptic, to 15×2cm, upper surface mottled dark and pale green, spotted purple beneath. Infl. erect, 1-fld, to 20cm, purple, villous; fls large, thin-textured, sep. and pet. pale yellow, flushed pink above, veined red-purple; dorsal sep. ovate, to 2.5×3cm, outer surface villous; synsepalum elliptic, to 24×11mm; pet. elliptic-subcircular with rounded apex, to 33×34mm, ciliate, inner surface white-pubesc.; lip deeply inflated, elliptic-ovate, to 65×47mm, rose-pink, paler near base, spotted purple within; staminode convex, conduplicate longitudinally, circular to elliptic, 10×12.5mm, white flushed pink at base, yellow above, spotted red. Spring. SW China (Yunnan).

P.niveum (Rchb. f.) Stein.
Closely related to *P.concolor* (though nowhere overlapping in distribution) but differs in its taller infl., smaller fls, white in colour usually lightly spotted with purple, smaller ellipsoid lip and transversely elliptic staminode. Growths often clustered. Lvs 4–5, ligulate to narrowly elliptic, to 19×3.5cm, mottled very dark and pale green above, heavily dotted purple beneath, basal margins ciliate; infl. 1–2-fld, to 25cm, purple, shortly but densely white-pubesc.; bracts conduplicate, broadly ovate, to 14×12mm, white to pale green, spotted purple; fls about 6m diam., white, often dotted purple near base of seg. and front of lip, pubesc. on outside and base of pet. within, staminode yellow-centred; dorsal sep. very broadly ovate, to 3×5cm; synsepalum concave, ovate, to 28×22mm; pet. elliptic, rounded, to 39×26mm, margins shortly ciliate; lip ovoid to ellipsoidal, to 3×1.7cm, margins incurved; staminode broader than long, transversely elliptic, 1–3-toothed at apex, to 9×12mm. Summer. N Malaysia and S Thailand.

P.papuanum (Ridl.) Ridl.
Allied to *P.mastersianum* but differs in its smaller fls, dorsal sep. smaller with purple veins, pet. shorter and narrower, broader staminode and ovary with shorter hairs. Lvs 4–6, oblong to oblong-elliptic, to 22×4.2cm, tessellated

dark and light green, veined dark green. Infl. 1-fld, to 28cm; bract ovate, to 1.5cm, pubesc.; fls to 9cm across; dorsal sep. ovate, to 25×26mm, ciliate, pubesc., outside, white with centre tinged yellow or green, veined purple; synsepalum elliptic-lanceolate, to 18×13mm; pet. oblong-lanceolate, to 42×17mm, ciliolate, dull maroon, basal half spotted black; lip to 3.7×1.4cm, dull crimson or brown-maroon; staminode 5×6mm, transversely lunate, notched above with short blunt apical teeth. Spring–summer. Highland New Guinea.

P.parishii (Rchb. f.) Stein.
Allied to *P.lowii* and *P.haynaldianum* but differs in its tapering green and black pet. with black warts on the margins and by its differently shaped staminode. Epiphytic or sometimes lithophytic. Lvs 5–8, ligulate, to 45×7.5cm, green. Infl. arching to suberect, to 50cm, to 9-fld; bracts large, conduplicate, broadly elliptic, to 4×3.5cm, margins undulate; fls to 13cm; sep. cream to green, veined darker, dorsal sep. elliptic, to 4.5×3cm, incurved on basal margins, recurved on apical margins; synsepalum ovate, to 4×2.9cm, margins recurved, outer surface 2-keeled; pet. decurved-pendent, linear-tapering, to 10.5×1.1cm, apical half spirally twisted, ciliate, basal margins undulate, green, spotted dark maroon below, margins and apical half dark maroon, maroon spots on lower basal margin; lip tapering to narrow apex, to 4.5×2cm, green, yellow-green or flushed purple; staminode obcordate, to 14×9mm, cream veined dark green. Summer. E & NE Burma, Thailand, SW China. var. *dianthum* (Tang & Wang) Cribb & Tang. Differs in having slightly larger fls, less spotted pet., papillose floral axis and bracts, glabrous, ovary and larger lip. SW China only.

P.philippinense (Rchb. f.) Stein.
Most closely allied to *P.randsii* and *P.sanderianum*; differs from the former in its longer tapering pet. and smaller narrower lip, and from the latter in its erect habit, much shorter pet., shorter dorsal sep., small blunt lip and smaller stamin-. ode. Terrestrial or lithophytic. Lvs to 9, ligulate, leathery, to 50×5cm. Infl. erect, 2–4-fld, to 50cm; bracts elliptic, pubesc., to 5×2cm; fls variable in size; sep. white, dorsal sep. ovate, to 5×2.5cm, striped maroon; synsepalum similar, to 5.5×3cm; pet. linear, tapering to apex, to 13cm×6mm, ciliate, white or yellow at base, maroon above, dark maroon warts on margin in basal half; lip small, rather ovoid, 3.8×1.4cm, white; staminode convex, yellow, veined green, purple-pubesc. on sides. Summer. Philippines and islands off N Borneo coast; on limestone, sea level to *c*500m. var. *roebelenii* (Veitch) Cribb differs in its larger fls with longer pet. to 13cm. Philippines (Luzon only).

P.praestans (Rchb. f.) Pfitz. See *P.glanduliferum*.

P.primulinum M.W. Wood & Tayl.
Lvs 4–7, narrowly oblong-elliptic, to 17×3.8cm, green, apex and lower margins ciliate. Infl. many-fld, opening in succession, lengthening to 35cm or more; bracts elliptic, 1.7cm, green; fls 6–7cm across, pale yellow with yellow-green sep.; dorsal sep. ovate, to 2.6×2.6cm, ciliate, pubesc. on reverse surface; synsepalum ovate, to 2.6×1.4cm; pet. linear-tapering, spreading; twisted in apical half, ciliate, 15° to horizontal, to 3.2×0.8cm; lip to 3.5×1.9cm, bulbous toward base; staminode oblong-ovate, to 8×7mm. Summer. N Sumatra. var. *purpurascens* (M.W. Wood) Cribb. Differs in having fls flushed purple.

P.purpuratum (Lindl.) Stein.
Lvs 3–8, elliptic to oblong-elliptic, to 17×4.2cm, pale green below, tessellated light and darker green above, shortly ciliate toward base of margins. Infl. erect, 1-fld, to 20cm, slender, purple, purple-pubesc.; bracts narrowly ovate-elliptic; fls to 8cm across; dorsal sep. ovate-cordate, 3.5×3.6cm, white, veined purple-maroon; synsepalum lanceolate, to 2.7×1.5cm, green, veined darker; pet. more or less horizontal, narrowly elliptic to oblong, to 4.6×1.3mm, margin ciliate, glossy maroon, green-white near base, lower two-thirds spotted black-maroon; lip to 4×2cm, incurved, lateral lobes verru-

cose, brown-maroon; staminode lunate, to 8×11mm, pubesc. with acute apical teeth, pale ochre-purple, veined darker. Autumn. Hong Kong, adjacent parts of Guangdong Province of China, and Hainan Is.

P.randsii Fowlie.
Very closely allied to *P.philippinense* but differs in its thick fleshy lvs with yellowish border and shorter linear pet., not twisted and tapering only toward their apex. Growths clustered. Lvs 5–6, oblong, leathery, green, to 35×6cm. Infl. 3–5-fld, to 40cm, purple, densely hairy; bracts ovate, to 3×2cm, pubesc.; fls white, sep. and pet. veined maroon; dorsal sep. ovate, 4.2×2.2cm; synsepalum ovate, 3.2×2cm; pet. deflexed, arcuate, linear, 4.5×0.6cm; lip rounded and grooved at apex, 3.2×1.5cm, green-yellow; staminode convex, subquadrate, truncate, 5×4mm, pubesc. on sides, yellow. Summer. Philippines (Mindanao only).

P.rothschildianum (Rchb. f.) Stein.
Closest allies are *P.glanduliferum* and *P.adductum* but differs from them in its longer petals at an acute angle to the horizontal and a distinctive staminode. Terrestrial or lithophytic, often in large clumps. Lvs several, linear, to narrowly oblanceolate, to 60×5cm, sparsely ciliate at base, green; infl. 2–4-fld, erect, to 45cm, purple, shortly pubesc.; bracts ovate-elliptic, to 5.5cm, ciliate and hairy on midvein, pale green or yellow, striped purple; fls very large, to 30cm diam.; dorsal sep. ovate, to 6.6×4.1cm, ivory-white or yellow veined maroon; synsepalum similar but smaller, about 5.7×3.3cm; pet. to 12.4×1.4cm, narrowly tapering to rounded apex, yellow or ivory-white marked maroon; lip subporrect, grooved on back, about 5.7×2.2cm, golden, heavily suffused purple; staminode linear, bifid at apex, geniculate, to 16×5mm, margins and base densely glandular-pubesc., pale yellow-green. Spring–summer. Borneo.

P.sanderianum (Rchb. f.) Stein.
Lithophytic on vertical SE-facing limestone cliffs. Lvs 4–5, arcuate-pendent, linear, to 45×5.3cm, shiny, green. Infl. horizontal or slightly ascending, 2–5-fld; bracts elliptic-lanceolate, to 5cm, red-brown, margins and midvein ciliate. Fls about 7cm across, to 95cm; sep. yellow striped maroon; dorsal sep lanceolate, slightly concave, to 6.5×2.5cm; synsepalum similar, 2-keeled, to 6×2cm; pet. ribbon-like, pendent, undulate, twisted, tapering to apex, to 90×0.9cm, off-white to yellow, spotted maroon, maroon warts on basal margins, basal half ciliate, apex minutely pubesc.; lip subporrect, pointed at apex, to 5×2.5cm, lateral lobes incurved; staminode convex, oblong, to 13×11mm, basal and side margins pubesc. Winter. Borneo (Sarawak).

P.spicerianum (Rchb. f. ex Mast. & T. Moore) Pfitz.
Terrestrial or lithophytic. Lvs 4–5, spreading to pendent, narrowly oblong-elliptic to ligulate, to 30×6cm, basal margins undulate, glossy dark green, spotted purple toward base beneath. Infl. 1-, rarely 2-fld, to 35cm; bract elliptic, to 3cm; fls to 7cm across; dorsal sep. curving forward, obovate to transversely elliptic, to 4.2×5cm, sides recurved, both surfaces pubesc., white with central maroon vein and green-tinged base; synsepalum ovate, to 3.5×2.2cm, off-white; pet. falcate, linear-tapering, to 3.9×1.3cm, upper margin undulate, ciliate toward apex only, yellow-green with central brown-purple vein, flecking on other veins; lip to 4.3×3cm, glossy, pale green, flushed brown with darker veins; staminode obovate or transversely elliptic-obcordate, glabrous, 10×6mm. Winter. NE India, NW Burma.

P.stonei (Hook.) Stein.
Allied to *P.kolopakingii* but differs in its larger, more boldly marked fls. Lvs about 5, ligulate, to 70×4.5cm, green. Infl. 2–4-fld, to 70cm; bracts to 5.5×2.2cm; fls to 12cm across; sep. white, lined dark maroon, dorsal sep. ovate, to 5.7×4.4cm; synsepalum elliptic-ovate, to 5×3.4cm; pet. linear-tapering, dependent, to 15×0.75cm, sometimes twisted in apical half, yellow, lined and spotted maroon, sometimes flushed maroon in apical half; lip forward-pointing, grooved

Paphiopedilum (a) *P.spicerianum* (b) *P.fairrieanum* (c) *P.appletonianum* (d) *P.argus* (e) *P.lawrenceanum*
(f) *P.mastersianum* (g) *P.*Maudiae (h) *P.callosum*

on back, to 5.7×2.8cm, pale yellow, strongly flushed pink and veined darker; staminode convex, subcircular, 14×11mm, coarsely hairy margined, yellow. Summer. Borneo (Sarawak only). var. *platytaenium* (Rchb. f.) Stein. Differs in having broader pet., to 2cm wide.

P.sukhakulii Schoser & Sengh.
Allied to *P.wardii* but differs in having greener fls, broader horizontal pet. marked with bold spots, shorter and broader sep., a longer staminode and lvs without purple spotting on their reverse. Roots thick, pubesc. Lvs 3–4, oblong-elliptic, 13×4.5cm, tessellated dark and yellow-green above. Infl. 1-fld; bracts 20×9mm, green; fls about 12cm across; sep. white veined green, spotted purple at base, outer surface pubesc., dorsal sep. concave, to 4×3cm, ciliate; synsepalum lanceolate, 3.4×1.6cm; pet. subhorizontal, to 6.2×2cm, green heavily spotted maroon, margins ciliate; lip saccate, 5×2.3cm, green, veined and flushed maroon, lateral lobes warty; staminode pubesc., 8×11mm, lower margin tridentate with lateral teeth incurved. Autumn. NE Thailand only.

P.superbiens (Rchb. f.) Stein. (*P.curtisii* (Rchb. f.) Stein).
Lvs 4–5, elliptic to oblong-elliptic, to 24×5cm, tessellated dark and light green above, flushed purple at base beneath. Infl. 1-fld to 23cm, purple; bracts elliptic-lanceolate, to 3cm; fls to 8cm across; sep. white veined green and purple, marked green or purple-green at centre, pet. white, spotted maroon-purple, sometimes flushed purple, raised spots on upper margin and in basal half, lip dark maroon; dorsal sep. ovate, to 5.8×5.3cm, ciliate; synsepalum ovate, to 4×1.9cm; pet. somewhat recurved-falcate, to 7.5×1.9cm, ciliate, half-twisted in apical half; lip large, to 6.5×3cm, lateral lobes warted; staminode transversely reniform, to 12×20mm, apex bluntly 3-toothed. Summer. N & C Sumatra.

P.tonsum (Rchb. f.) Stein.
Variable in fl. size, pet. and staminode shape and pet. spotting. Lvs about 6, oblong-elliptic, to 20×4.5cm, veined green, upper surface mottled darker green. Infl. 1-fld, erect, to 35cm; bract elliptic-ovate, to 24×1.2cm; fls to 14cm across; sep. white, veined and tinged yellow-green, pet. olive to yellow-green, veined darker, black-warted on inner surface, lip olive-brown, flushed pink, veined darker; dorsal sep. obovate, about 4.5×4cm; synsepalum ovate, about 3.5×1.5cm; pet. slightly drooping, about 6.5×2cm; lip saccate, 5.5×3.3cm; staminode subreniform, dentate on lower margin, to 11×14mm. Autumn–winter. N & C Sumatra.

P.urbanianum Fowlie.
Related to *P.javanicum* and *P.argus*, differing from the former in its pet. markings, larger flat dorsal sep., brown-red lip and staminode; differs from the latter in its narrow, ciliate pet. and shape of staminode. Lvs 4–5, narrowly or oblong-elliptic, to 20×4cm, tessellated dark and light green above, basal margins ciliate. Infl. erect, 1-fld, rarely 2-fld, to 25cm; bract ovate, to 3×2cm, green veined maroon, pubesc.; fls to 10.5cm across; dorsal sep. ovate to broadly ovate, to 3.6×4.2cm, white veined green; synsepalum concave, ovate, to 3.1×1.9cm, green veined darker; pet. slightly narrowed, oblanceolate, to 6×1.8cm, white lined green, basal two-thirds spotted maroon, apical half purple; lip to 4.5×3cm, dull purple, lateral lobes marked maroon, ciliate on apical margin; staminode subcircular to almost hexagonal, to 10×10mm, yellow-green lined green. Spring. Philippines.

P.venustum (Wallich) Pfitz. ex Stein.
Somewhat variable but recognized by its dark sea- or slate-green tessellated lvs, veined lip and recurved pet. with raised maroon spots. Lvs 4–5, elliptic to oblong-elliptic, to 25×5.5cm, surface dull to almost rough, ciliate near base, tessellated dark green and grey green above, densely spotted purple beneath. Infl. 1-fld (rarely 2-fld), to 23cm; bract elliptic-lanceolate, to 2.5cm; fls 8–9cm across, sep. white veined green, pet. white veined with green, warted maroon-black, flushed purple in apical half; dorsal sep. ovate, to 3.8×2.8cm, outer surface hirsute; synsepalum similar, to 3cm; pet.

oblanceolate, recurved, ciliate, to 5.4×1.4cm; lip to 4.3×3.2cm, yellow tinged purple and veined green, lateral lobes verrucose; staminode reniform, to 9×11mm, minutely pubesc. with short, blunt, lateral apical teeth. Winter. NE India, E Nepal, Sikkim, Bhutan.

P.victoria-mariae (Sander ex Mast.) Rolfe.
Allied to *P.victoria-regina* but differs in certain floral characteristics. Lvs oblong-ligulate, ciliate near base, to 30×6.5cm, green mottled darker, flushed purple at base beneath. Infl. to 1m+, many-fld in succession showing 2 or 3 at a time; bracts elliptic-oblong, ciliate, green, to 3cm; fls 8–9cm across; dorsal sep. broadly ovate to obovate, to 2.9×3cm, ciliate, outer surface long-pubesc., pale yellow with centre bright green; synsepalum ovate, to 2.8×1.7cm, ciliate, outer surface long-pubesc.; pet. linear, horizontal-reflexed, to 4×1.1cm, shortly ciliate, twisted in apical half, green flushed brown to red-purple; lip tapers to apex, to 4×2.5cm, purple, margined yellow or green, lateral lobes finely spotted; staminode curved in apical half, to 10×7mm. Spring. S & CW Sumatra.

P.victoria-regina (Sander) M.W. Wood.
Lvs 4–6, narrowly oblong-elliptic, margins ciliate at base, to 28×6cm, green, flushed purple beneath. Infl. to 60cm, arching, rachis flexuous; bracts elliptic, ciliate, to 3.5×2.8cm, green; fls to 32 in succession, showing 1–2 at a time; dorsal sep. subcircular-elliptic, to 3×3cm, yellow-green or white, lower half flushed green or yellow, veined dark purple, margins undulate, outer surface long-pubesc.; synsepalum elliptic, to 3×2.1cm, yellow-green, veined purple; pet. horizontal, ligulate, slightly recurved, to 4×0.8cm, yellow or pale yellow, spotted and streaked dark maroon, twice twisted, ciliate; lip to 4.1×2.1cm, pink with white rim, bulbously inflated, lateral lobes broadly rounded at apex; staminode convex, to 9×7.5mm, green, heavily flushed dark maroon, basal half pubesc. Autumn. Sumatra.

P.villosum (Lindl.) Stein.
This widespread and variable species is allied to *P.insigne* and *P.gratrixianum* but differs from both in having a shorter fl. stem, larger bract, larger fls with broader pet., longer lip and a villous ovary. Lvs 4–5, linear-ligulate, to 42×4cm, green, margins ciliate at base, spotted at base beneath. Infl. suberect to arching, 1-fld, to 24cm, densely hairy; bracts elliptic, to 6.5×3.8cm, glabrous, green, spotted maroon; fls to 11.5cm across; dorsal sep. obovate, to 6.5×3.5cm, basal margins reflexed, green, margined white, glossy maroon areas in centre; synsepalum ovate, adpressed to ovary, to 3.5×2.6cm, pale green; pet. incurved, obovate-spathulate, to 7×3cm, glossy, ciliate, red-brown with central maroon stripe; lip tapering to apex, to 6×3.8cm, ochre, flushed pink or red; staminode obcordate-obovate, about 16×14mm, verrucose, hirsute, a glossy knob in centre. Winter–spring. NE India, Burma, Thailand. var. *boxallii* (Rchb. f.) Pfitz. Differs in fl. colour with seg. narrower at base, dorsal sep. heavily spotted and purple marking on the lip.

P.violascens Schltr.
Variable in lf and fl. size and shape of staminode. Terrestrial or, rarely, epiphytic. Lvs 4–6, elliptic to oblong-elliptic, to 22×4cm, grey-green, mottled darker above. Infl. 1-fld, to 30cm; bracts elliptic-lanceolate to elliptic-ovate, to 2.4cm, pubesc., ciliate; fls to 7.5cm, across; dorsal sep. broadly ovate, to 4.3×3cm, outer surface pubesc., white veined green; synsepalum ovate, to 2.6×1.6cm, pubesc. on outer surface, green veined darker; pet. deflexed 45°, obliquely oblong, to 4.4×1.8cm, minutely ciliate, white or green-white, apical three-quarters heavily flushed purple; lip to 5×2cm, deeply saccate, margin ciliate, green to ochre; staminode semicircular, to 7.5×14mm, green with purple pubescence. Spring. New Guinea and adjacent islands near coast.

P.wardii Summerh.
Allied to *P.sukhakulii* but differs in shape and colour of fls and in having dark green marbled lvs resembling those of

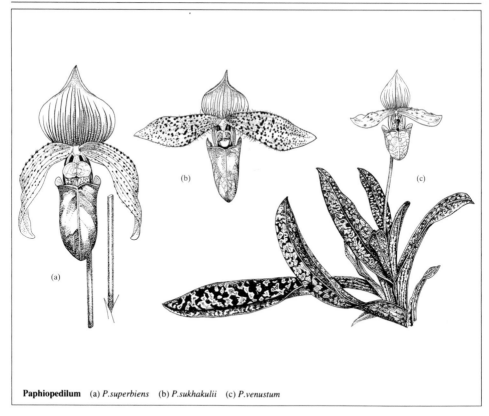

Paphiopedilum   (a) *P.superbiens*   (b) *P.sukhakulii*   (c) *P.venustum*

P.venustum. Lvs 3–5, oblong-lanceolate, to 17cm, dark blue-green mottled paler above, mottled purple beneath. Infl. 1-fld, to 20cm; bracts lanceolate, ciliate, green flushed purple, 2–3cm; fls 8.5–10cm across; dorsal sep. ovate, to 5×3cm, outer surface pubesc., white veined green; synsepalum lanceolate, to 4.5×2.2cm; pet. oblong-lanceolate to oblong, to 6.5×1.7cm, spreading, somewhat pendulous to about 30° from horizontal, green-white flushed brown-purple, spotted dark maroon all over; lip to 5×2cm, lateral lobes warty, green-tinged or ochre, finely spotted brown; staminode lunate, to 10×14mm, finely pubesc., pale green veined darker. Winter. N Burma, SW China.

P.wentworthianum Schoser.
Related to *P.violascens* and *P.bougainvilleanum* but differs in its glossier more spreading pet., undulate on their upper margin. Lvs about 5, narrowly oblong to elliptic-oblong, to 25×4.5cm, tessellated light and dark green, shortly pubesc. Infl. 1-fld, to 35cm tall; bract elliptic-ovate, to 2.4cm; fls about 8cm across; dorsal sep. concave, broadly ovate, to 3.2×3.5cm, cream veined green with green centre; synsepalum ovate, to 2.5×2.6cm; pet. oblong-elliptic, spreading, about 20° below horizontal, to 4.5×2.5cm, glossy purple above, merging to brown and green toward base, ciliate, upper margin undulate; lip to 4.5×2.2cm, yellow-green flushed brown; staminode lunate, to 10×12mm, shortly pubesc., green. Spring. Bougainville and Guadalcanal.

P.grexes and cultivars.
*P.*A. de Lairesse: robust plants with beautiful mottled lvs; fls several on each stem, creamy yellow with maroon red striping.
*P.*Aladin: foliage medium green, somewhat mottled in some clones; fls strawberry pink.
*P.*Albion: dark green mottled lvs on small plants; fls white with bright green staminode.

*P.*Alma Gevaert: beautifully mottled lvs; fls lime green and white on tall stems, dorsal sep. striped.
*P.*Amanda 'Joyance': mid-green lvs; fls deep red.
*P.*Angela: grey-green-mottled lvs on small plants; fls white or pale pink spotted with pink-red.
*P.*Astarte: plain green lvs; fls pale yellow, fading to cream or white.
*P.*Berenice: strong plants with mid-green lvs; fls several on each tall stem, yellow-green with rose-pink pet. and brown-lined lip.
*P.*Betty Bracey 'Springtime': mid-green lvs; fls large, round, rich yellow-green with wide white border on dorsal sep.
*P.*Bingleyense: mid-green lvs; fls on tall stems, deep red.
*P.*Black Diamond: foliage very dark green and grey, attractively mottled; fls small, pale strawberry pink.
*P.*British Bulldog: medium green lvs; fls green-brown with heavily spotted white dorsal sep.
*P.*Caddiana: mid-green lvs; fls small but rich lime green.
*P.*Carat Gold: strong plants with mid-green lvs; fls round, golden yellow-green with white border on dorsal sep.
*P.*Cardinal Mercier: small plants with mid-green lvs; fls small but deep red.
*P.*Charles Sladden: small plants with densely mottled lvs; fls on short stems, rosy red with darker stripes.
*P.*Chianti 'Chilton': strong plants with mid-green lvs; fls large, round, golden yellow-green.
*P.*Christopher: strong plants with mid-green lvs; fls singly on tall stems, yellow-green with white border on dorsal, few spots.
*P.*Clair de Lune 'Edgard van Belle': the best of the 'Maudiae' types: large plants with distinctively mottled foliage; fls large on tall stems, lime green and white.
*P.*Cymatodes 'Beechense': large plants with beautifully mottled lvs; fls large, cream with wine red stripes and spots, the pet. with warts along the margin, lip brown.

*P.*Danaqueen: medium green lvs; fls rich chestnut brown with spotted dorsal sep.

*P.*Darling: attractively mottled dark green lvs; fls large on tall stems, attractive deep pink. Several fine clones have been awarded.

*P.*Delaina: attractively mottled, dark green lvs; several pink fls, usually borne consecutively.

*P.*Delophyllum: attractively mottled dark green lvs; several deep pink fls are borne consecutively.

*P.*Delrosi: attractively mottled foliage; very attractive fls on tall stems, deep pink with deeper pink striping.

*P.*Demura: small plants with mottled lvs; fls deep raspberry pink with white, heavily spotted dorsal sep.

*P.*Deperle: attractively mottled dark green lvs; fls cream or white. Some tetraploid clones with larger fls have been awarded.

*P.*Diana Broughton: plants with mid-green lvs; fls rather small, on tall stems, yellow-green with white margin to dorsal sep.

*P.*Dusty Miller: mid-green lvs on robust plants; white fls slightly freckled on dorsal sep., of fine form on tall stems.

*P.*Emerald: beautiful mottled foliage; attractive lime green and white fls.

*P.*Ernest Read: like an improved *P.callosum*; mottled foliage; fls on tall stems with large dorsal sep. shadow striped wine red and green on cream.

*P.*F.C. Puddle: mid-green lvs; white or pale lemon fls with few freckles on dorsal sep.

*P.*Faire-Maud: small plants with mottled lvs; fls small on tall slender stems, rich wine red with striped dorsal sep.

*P.*Frau Ida Brandt: robust plants with beautiful mottled lvs; fls large, several on each stem, white or cream and densely striped in wine red.

*P.*Freckles: robust plants with mid-green lvs; fls white or pale pink, well covered with rosy-red freckles.

*P.*Gorse: mid-green lvs; large round fls, rich yellow-green.

*P.*Goultenianum: similar to the above but fls wine red and white instead of green and white.

*P.*Goultenianaum 'Album': strong plants with beautifully mottled lvs; fls lime green and white with striped dorsal sep. and down-swept warted pet.

*P.*Gowerianum: strong plants with mottled foliage; fls lime-green and white or wine red and white, dorsal sep. boldly striped.

*P.*Harrisianum: strong plants with mottled lvs; red-brown glossy fls with striped dorsal on strong stems. The first *Paphiopedilum* hybrid made and flowered in 1869.

*P.*Hellas 'Westonbirt': well-known plant with mid-green lvs; fls lovely bright brown/golden with wide white margin on dorsal sep.

*P.*Henriette 'Fujiwara': mid-green lvs; several fls on tall slender stems, white and lime green resembling the *P.haynaldianum* parent but lacking spots.

*P.*Holdenii: attractive mottled foliage; fls lime green and white with striped dorsal sep.

*P.*Kay Rinaman 'Val': famous cross with mid-green lvs; large round fls, green-gold with white border on dorsal sep.

*P.*King of Sweden: famous cross with mid-green lvs; fls large, oval, lime green on tall stems.

*P.*Lawrebel 'Boynton': a beautiful primary hybrid with distinctive mottled lvs and large rosy fls with darker red stripes.

*P.*Leeanum: primary hybrid with light green lvs; fls small, yellow-brown dorsal edged white, with some small spots.

*P.*Leyburnense: lvs mid-green; fls deep strawberry pink with white staminode.

*P.*Madame Martinet: attractively mottled dark green lvs; very pretty pink fls on tall stems.

*P.*Makuli: attractive mottled foliage; fls small and distinctive, lime green and white or wine red and white, some forms very dark red with near black warts on pet.

*P.*Makuli 'Cat's Eyes': attractive mottled foliage; fls small and distinctive, lime green and white.

*P.*Maudiae: one of the best-known slipper orchids with attractive mottled lvs; fls distinctive, lime green and white with striped dorsal sep. Many slipper orchids similar to this in colour and shape are known as Maudiae types. Named clones include 'Magnificum' and 'The Queen'.

*P.*Maudiae 'Coloratum': attractive mottled lvs; fls on strong upright stems, large, wine red and white with striped dorsal sep. and green-brown lip.

*P.*Meadowsweet 'Purity': mid-green lvs; fls white or cream tinged with yellow.

*P.*Miller's Daughter: most famous of the white hybrid slipper orchids; lvs mid-green; fls white, good shape on tall stems; some clones slightly freckled.

*P.*Muriel Hollington: mid-green lvs; fls on tall stems, yellow or beige with few spots.

*P.*Nettie McMay: strong plants with attractive mottled foliage; fls on tall stems, large, wine red and white with large striped dorsal sep. and wart on pet.

*P.*Noche: lvs mid- to dark green; fls on short stems, deep wine red.

*P.*Olivia: a beautiful primary hybrid with dark mottled lvs; fls opening green and fading to a beautiful shell pink.

*P.*Onyx: attractively mottled lvs; fls green and white on tall stems.

*P.*Orchilla 'Chilton': famous red fls with narrow white margin to dorsal sep.

*P.*Paeony 'Regency': famous breeder; strong plants with medium green lvs; fls large, red and brown with white margin to dorsal sep.

*P.*Papa Rohl: an unusual primary hybrid with mottled lvs; fls green with a striped dorsal sep. and long, spotted pet.

*P.*Peter Black 'Emerald': strong plants with medium green lvs; fls green-brown with white, heavily spotted dorsal sep.

*P.*Primcolor: small plants with dark green lvs; fls clear yellow, several opening consecutively.

*P.*Psyche: primary hybrid; small plants with mottled lvs and white fls.

*P.*Red Maude: attractively mottled lvs; fls wine red with white margin to dorsal sep., pet. warted.

*P.*Redstart: medium green lvs; well-known wine-red fls.

*P.*Rosy Dawn: lvs mid-green, fls white, beige or pale pink with pink-red spots.

*P.*Royalet: medium green lvs; fls deep wine red, some with narrow white margin to dorsal sep.

*P.*Sheila Hanes 'Sweet Afton': mid-green lvs; lime green fls with white margin on dorsal sep.

*P.*Shillianum: large robust plants with mid-green lvs faintly mottled; several fls, cream base colour but heavily overlaid with stripes and spots in wine red.

*P.*Shireen: large robust plants with mid-green lvs; fls on tall stems, borne consecutively, dorsal sep. yellow and lip pink, pet. spirally twisted and hairy on the margins.

*P.*Silvara: lvs mid-green; fls on tall stems opening yellow green and fading to a glistening white.

*P.*Sir Redvers Buller: medium green, faintly mottled lvs; fls small but strong red-brown with lines of fine spots on white dorsal sep.

*P.*Small World: medium green lvs; rich chestnut brown to red with white dorsal, heavily spotted.

*P.*Song of Mississippi: strong robust plants with attractively mottled foliage; fls on tall strong stems, several appearing consecutively, dorsal sep. striped, lip pink, pet. twisted and spotted with darker colour.

*P.*St Alban: attractive mottled lvs in grey-green; fls small but deep wine red, early flowering.

*P.*St Swithin: large robust plants with mid-green lvs; fls large, several simultaneously, yellow-brown with dorsal and ventral sep. conspicuously striped in brown, lip large, brown.

*P.*Startler 'Glace': medium green lvs; fls on tall stems, deep wine red.

*P.*Sunset 'Alpha': medium green lvs; fls rich dark red.

*P.*Susan Tucker: robust plants with mid-green lvs; fls white on strong stems.

*P.*Swanilda: robust plants with mid-green lvs; fls white on strong stems.

*P.*Toby Strauss: mid-green lvs; very large fls, green or yellow and white, some with beige tones, clones variable.

*P.*Tommie Hanes 'Althea': well-known cross with mid-green lvs; fls lime green and white, fading to yellow.

*P.*Transvaal: large robust plants with dark green lvs; fls borne consecutively, yellow-pink with striped dorsal sep. and twisted pet.

*P.*Vanda M. Pearman: attractively mottled grey and dark green lvs; very pretty pink and white fls on short stems, sometimes scented.

*P.*Vintage Harvest 'Vinho Verde': strong growing plants with mid-green lvs; fls very large, round, medium green with white margin on dorsal sep.

*P.*Vintner's Treasure: foliage attractively mottled and flushed with purple beneath; fls on tall stems, wine red but very dark almost black in some clones.

*P.*Vodoo Magic: foliage attractively mottled; fls very dark wine red.

*P.*Whitemoor 'Norriton': large robust plants with mid-green lvs; fls white.

*P.*Wiertzianum: large robust plants with beautifully mottled lvs; fls several simultaneously, large, creamy base colour heavily overlaid with dark wine red stripes and spots.

*P.*Winston Churchill: strong plants with medium green foliage; large fls on strong stems, rich chestnut brown with heavily spotted white dorsal sep.

*P.*Yerba Buena: well-known cross with mid-green lvs; fls on strong stems, medium green and white.

Papilionanthe Schltr. (From Lat. *papilio*, moth and Gk *anthos*, flower.) Some 11 species of monopodial epiphytes or terrestrials. Stems slender, terete, erect or scrambling, often branching and rooting at nodes. Leaves in 2 ranks, alternate, terete, narrowly tapering, pungent or obtuse, obscurely grooved above, basally sheathing. Inflorescence usually a short, axillary raceme or panicle; sepals obovate, obtuse, weakly undulate, lateral sepals clawed; petals suborbicular, spreading, margins more undulate than in lateral sepals; lip trilobed, minutely pubescent, base saccate, midlobe bifid, broad, cuneate, lateral lobes large, often erect; spur saccate, conical. Himalaya to Malaysia.

CULTIVATION Vigorous scrambling epiphytes. *P.teres* and *P.hookeriana*, formerly included in *Vanda*, require sunny positions in the intermediate or warm house in baskets or beds of open bark mix. Syringe and water freely throughout the year. The former especially is an important garden plant and cut flower in the tropics and subtropics, notably in Singapore and Hawaii. Its hybrid offspring are listed under *Vanda*. *P.vandarum*, from cool hilly districts, requires lower temperatures (min. 7°C/45°F) and drier conditions in winter. Its stems are more slender than in the other two species listed here, a deep green and decked with short racemes of lace-like flowers. It is one of the most beautiful orchids for basket cultivation in the cool house. Propagate all by stem cuttings or division.

P.hookeriana (Rchb. f.) Schltr. (*Vanda hookeriana* Rchb. f.).
Stems scrambling, to 2.2m. Lvs 7–10×0.3cm. Infl. to 30cm; fls 2–12; dorsal sep. and pet. white or pale mauve, chequered deep mauve, faintly spotted, lateral sep. nearly white, lip deep purple, midlobe pale mauve marked purple; dorsal sep. obovate-oblong, obtuse, erect, undulate, crisped, to 2×1.5cm, lateral sep. spreading; pet. elliptic to orbicular, undulate, base twisted to reflexed; lip midlobe reniform to flabellate, to 3×4cm, weakly trilobed, lateral lobes triangular-falcate to oblong; spur short, to 0.2mm. Malaysia, China, Borneo, Vietnam.

P.teres (Roxb.) Schltr. (*Vanda teres* (Roxb.) Lindl.).
Stems to 1.75m but branching to form scrambling mats. Lvs erect and incurved, to 20×0.4cm. Infl. produced in continuous succession, 15–30cm; fls 3–6 per raceme, 5–10cm diam.; sep. and pet. white or ivory deepening to rose or magenta, lip buff to golden, banded or dotted blood-red or mauve; sep. ovate to subrhombic, undulate, obtuse, spreading, to 4×3cm; pet. orbicular, undulate, base twisted, to 4.5×4cm; lip midlobe fla-bellate to obcordate, deeply cleft, lateral lobes enveloping column; spur to 2.5cm, funnel-shaped. Thailand, Burma, Himalaya..

P.vandarum (Rchb. f.) Garay (*Aerides vandarum* Rchb. f.).
Stems to 2m, slender, terete, branching tangentially, sprawling, dark green, freely producing flattened grey roots and cascading or forming densely tangled clumps. Lvs to 10cm, borne at 45° to stem, slender, tapering, pungent, dark green often flushed purple. Infl. to 8cm, seldom branching, bearing flowers over several seasons; fls to 5 per infl., nocturnally fragrant, to 5cm diam., crystalline white, often tinted opal or basally flushed lilac to pink; sep. to 3.5×1.75cm, obovate, basally clawed, reflexed, undulate to crispate; pet. broader, more undulate, strongly reflexed and twisted; lip midlobe clawed, broadly obcordate, apically ruffed and deflexed, claw 3-ridged, lateral lobes falcate, erect, acuminate, apically denticulate with secondary, toothed lobe toward sinus of lateral and midlobes; spur cylindric, to 2cm. India, Burma.

Papilionanthe (a) *P.teres* (b) *P.hookeriana* (c) *P.vandarum*

Papperitzia Rchb. f. (For William Papperitz, friend of Heinrich Reichenbach.) 1 species, an epiphyte. Rhizome short, creeping. Pseudobulbs to 1cm, clustered, ancipitous, apex 1-leaved. Leaves to 7cm, linear, acuminate, coriaceous, glabrous, articulated. Inflorescence a basal raceme, erect to pendent, few- to several-flowered; fls to 1.5cm, green, yellow-pubesc.; dorsal sepal free, hood-like, subcaudate, conical-spurred, lateral sepals connate, navicular, subcaudate; petals free, similar to dorsal sepal; lip adnate to column base, fleshy, funnel-shaped at base forming a saccate pouch, pubescent within, callus trilobulate, slightly enveloping column; column short, apex alate-auriculate, footless, rostellum elongate, anther terminal, operculate, incumbent, pollinia 2, ceraceous. Mexico.

CULTIVATION   As for *Encyclia*.

P.lieboldii (Rchb. f.) Rchb. f. (*Leochilus lieboldii* Rchb. f.).

Paraphalaenopsis A.D. Hawkes. (From Gk *para*, beside, and *Phalaenopsis*.) Some 4 species of monopodial epiphytes resembling *Phalaenopsis* except in their cylindrical, caniculate leaves. Borneo.

CULTIVATION   As for *Phalaenopsis*.

P.denevei (Sm.) A.D. Hawkes (*Phalaenopsis denevei* Sm.).
Lvs 3–6, fleshy, to 70×1cm. Infl. axillary to 13-fld, bracts triangular; tepals spreading, green-yellow to yellow-brown, lip white, spotted crimson; dorsal sep. ovate-elliptic to narrow-elliptic, to 2.5×1cm, lateral sep. ovate-elliptic, to 3×1.5cm; pet. ovate-lanceolate, basally cuneate, apically falcate, to 2.5×1cm; lip midlobe linear-spathulate, papillose, callus wrinkled, minutely toothed, lateral lobes oblong to triangular, falcate, to 1×5cm. W Borneo.

P.labukensis (P.S. Shim) A. Lamb & C.L. Chan.
Lvs to 1.6cm. Sep. and pet. raspberry pink, dotted and edged yellow, lip yellow, spotted purple, axe-shaped toward apex. Borneo.

P.laycockii (M.R. Henderson) A.D. Hawkes.
Fls to 5, to 1m. Infl. dense, to 15-fld; bracts ovate, to 1cm; fls magenta to lilac, lip blotched yellow and brown; dorsal sep. lanceolate-elliptic, narrow, to 4×1.5cm, lateral sep. ovate-lanceolate, oblique, to 4.5×1.5cm; pet. subfalcate, lanceolate, basally fleshy, cuneate, to 4×1.5cm; lip midlobe forward pointing, linear-spathulate, apical lobes triangular, disc pale yellow, striped brown, lateral lobes linear-oblong, erect, apex truncate to rounded; column white. SC Borneo.

P.serpentilingua (Sm.) A.D. Hawkes.
Lvs to 30cm. Infl. to 7-fld; fls scented, sep. and pet. white above, lip lemon yellow, banded purple; dorsal sep. elliptic to obovate-elliptic, to 1.5×1cm, lateral sep. elliptic to obovate-elliptic, to 2×1cm; pet. rhombic-lanceolate, basally fleshy, cuneate; lip midlobe recurved, linear, tip bifid, callus toothed, lateral lobes linear, falcate, to 1cm. W Borneo.

Pecteilis Raf. (From Lat. *pecten*, comb, referring to the form of the lip lateral lobes.) Some 4 species of herbaceous terrestrials. Stems erect. Leaves linear to ovate, cauline or, basal rosulate. Inflorescence erect; flowers few, white or white and yellow; sepals similar, spreading, free; petals narrower; lip trilobed, midlobe entire, lateral lobes fringed, spreading; spur slender. Tropical Asia.

CULTIVATION   Beautiful terrestrials for the cool and intermediate house. The most commonly grown is *P.susannae* with a strikingly fringed lip. Cultural requirements as for *Disa*.

P.radiata (Thunb.) Raf. (*Habenaria radiata* Thunb.).
Stem to 45cm, erect, terete. Lvs 3–7, linear-lanceolate, acuminate, 2–10×0.3–0.7cm. Infl. terminal; bracts lanceolate, acuminate, to 1cm; fls 1–3; sep. ovate-lanceolate, acuminate, to 1×0.5cm, green; pet. white, ovate, subacute, margins white, jagged, minutely toothed; lip white, trilobed, to 2×3cm, midlobe linear-ligulate, acute, lateral lobes obovate, spreading, back and side margins deeply and irregularly divided; spur decurved, green. Japan, Korea.

P.sagarikii Seidenf.
Stem to 25cm. Lvs 2–3, ovate, 10–12×6–9cm, glossy, apex obtuse or rounded, in a basal rosette. Infl. erect, scape 2–4-sheathed; fls few, white or cream, fragrant; dorsal sep. ovate, acute, erect, to 2.5×1.5cm, lateral sep. lanceolate, acute, suberect, spreading; pet. similar, smaller; lip weakly decurved, convex, sometimes bright yellow, base obscurely trilobed, apex subobovate, rounded or obtuse, to 2–5×2cm, lateral lobes obscure, rounded; spur filiform, weakly incurved, 3–5cm. Thailand.

P.susannae (L.) Raf. (*Habenaria susannae* (L.) R. Br.).
Stem to 1–20m, leafy. Lvs elliptic, to 12×5cm, concave, sessile. Raceme to 20cm; fls 4–6, white to green-white, fragrant; dorsal sep. subcircular, to 3cm diam., lateral sep. spreading linear, to 3.5×2.5cm, margins reflexed; pet. linear, falcate, to 1.5cm; lip trilobed, midlobe linear-spathulate, entire, to 3cm, lateral lobes deeply fringed; spur strongly decurved. China, Burma, Malaya.

Peristeria Hook. (From the Gk *peristera*, a dove, referring to the dove-like appearance of the column.) Some 11 species of epiphytes or terrestrials allied to *Acineta*, from which it can be distinguished by the articulated lip. Rhizome short. Pseudobulbs fleshy, oblong-ovoid to subconical, dull green, 1- to several-leaved. Leaves often elongate, plicate, conspicuously petiolate. Inflorescence a basal raceme, erect to pendent, short or elongate; peduncle stout, terete; flowers numerous, opening in succession, showy, thickly fleshy, cupped, subglobose, highly fragrant; sepals subequal, suborbicular, dorsal sepal free; lateral sepals united at base; petals similar to sepals, smaller; lip fleshy, hypochile articulate or continuous with column base, concave, 3-lobed, lateral lobes erect, spreading, clasping column epichile rounded, simple, articulated to hypochile, disc often callose; column short, stout, footless, erect to slightly arcuate, apex often bialate or biauriculate, anther terminal, operculate, incumbent, bilocular, pollinia 2, waxy, pyriform or oblong. Panama to Colombia, Venezuela, Guyanas, Brazil, Peru.

CULTIVATION   As for *Stanhopea* but in intermediate to warm conditions with water throughout the year.

P.aspersa Rolfe.
Epiphytic or terrestrial. Pseudobulbs to 11×6cm. Lvs to 75×12cm, 1–4 per pseudobulb, elliptic-lanceolate. Infl. to 15cm, arching, densely several-fld; fls to 3cm diam., heavily scented; sep. and pet. red-yellow or orange-yellow spotted red-maroon, sep. to 3.5×3.5cm, concave, elliptic, obtuse, lateral sep. wider than dorsal sep.; pet. to 2.8×1.8cm, elliptic-lanceolate, concave, obtuse; lip orange spotted dark maroon, clawed, hypochile to 2×1.7cm, continuous with column foot, 3-lobed, lateral lobes elliptic to subrhombic, separated by 2 elevated calli, midlobe elliptic-oblong, epichile to 17mm, elliptic-oblong, slightly recurved, with an apical V-shaped callus; column to 15mm, usually biauriculate. Venezuela, Brazil, Colombia.

P.barkeri Batem. See *Acineta barkeri*.

P.elata Hook.
Terrestrial. Pseudobulbs to 12×8cm. Lvs to 100×12cm, 3–5 per pseudobulb, broadly lanceolate or oblanceolate, acuminate, clear green. Infl. to 130cm, erect, many-fld; fls waxy, very strongly scented, white; sep. to 3×2.5cm, broadly concave, ovate to suborbicular, acute to obtuse; pet. to 25×18mm, elliptic-obovate, obtuse; lip to 3cm, hypochile continuous with column base, 3-lobed, lateral lobes white spotted red-rose, obovate to elliptic-obovate, separated by a transverse, oblong callus, midlobe ovate to elliptic, concave, epichile white, subquadrate, retuse, with a central, fleshy, sulcate callus; column to 11mm, white, subconic. Costa Rica, Panama, Venezuela, Colombia.

P.pendula Hook.
Epiphytic. Pseudobulbs to 15×5cm. Lvs to 80×12cm, 2–4 per bulb, elliptic-lanceolate to oblong-lanceolate, acute to acuminate. Infl. to 20cm, several-fld, pendulous; fls pale green or yellow-green, tinged and spotted red-purple; sep. to 3.5×2.5cm, ovate-subrotund to ovate-elliptic, obtuse; pet. slightly smaller than sep., ovate-elliptic; lip enclosed by lateral sep., hypochile to 2.5cm, 3-lobed, lateral lobes erect, elliptic to subquadrate, separated by a lunate callus, midlobe oblong, epichile ovate-rhombic or ligulate, recurved, obtuse, with a large, sulcate, V-shaped callus; column to 15mm, wings 2, porrect, oblong, obtuse. Venezuela, Peru, Brazil, Guyanas, Surinam.

Pescatorea Rchb. f. (For V. Pescatore of Château Celle St. Cloud near Paris, orchid collector.) Some 15 species of epiphytes allied to *Huntleya* and *Bollea*. Rhizome short. Pseudobulbs absent. Leaves distichous, arranged in a fan, thin-textured, membranaceous to subcoriaceous, conduplicate. Fls. showy, solitary, on short, slender, erect or arching stalks; sepals fleshy, concave, dorsal sepal free, lateral sepals shortly connate; petals subsimilar to sepals, narrower; lip fleshy, articulated with column foot, base contracted into a ligulate claw, continuous with column foot, trilobed, lateral lobes small, midlobe rounded, convex or ventricose, revolute, disc with a prominent, fleshy, semicircular, pluricarinate callus; column stout, erect, subterete, pilose, base produced into a short foot, anther terminal, operculate, incumbent, bilocular, pollinia 4, waxy. Costa Rica to Colombia.

CULTIVATION   As for *Huntleya*.

P.bella Rchb. f.
Resembles *P.cerina* except fls larger, to 9cm diam.; tepals white-violet or pale violet, tips striped deep purple-violet; lip yellow-white, apex blotched purple-violet, hooded, callus large, marked purple, pluricarinate; column purple, base blotched yellow-white, spotted purple. Colombia.

P.cerina (Lindl.) Rchb. f. (*Huntleya cerina* Lindl.; *Zygopetalum cerinum* (Lindl.) Rchb. f.).
Lvs to 60×5cm, erect or arching, elliptic-lanceolate to linear-lanceolate, acute or acuminate. Infl. to 10cm, erect to horizontal; fls to 7.5cm diam., highly fragrant; sep. creamy white or pale lemon yellow, blotched yellow-green at base of lateral sep., dorsal sep. to 32×18mm, obovate to elliptic-linear, obtuse, lateral sep. to 35×20mm, elliptic-lanceolate, obtuse; pet. creamy white, similar to dorsal sep.; lip to 30×25mm, yellow, lateral lobes subfalcate, callus large, often marked red-brown; column to 15mm, white, anth. violet. Costa Rica, Panama.

P.dayana Rchb. f.
Lvs to 60×5cm, oblong-oblanceolate, acuminate. Infl. to 11cm; fls to 7.5cm diam., highly fragrant, long-lived; tepals milk-white, often tipped rose-purple; sep. to 45×25mm, oblong-obovate, obtuse; pet. smaller, suborbicular-rhomboid; lip to 30×23mm, white flushed purple-violet, ovate or elliptic to oblong, convex, retuse, callus purple-violet, large, lunate, several keeled; column white, anth. purple. Colombia. .

P.lehmannii Rchb. f.
Lvs to 45×1.5cm, linear-lorate, acute. Infl. to 15cm, often horizontal; fls to 8.5cm diam., waxy, fragrant, long-lived; sep. and pet. white, densely marked red-purple, oblong-cuneate, slightly concave, acute; lip dark purple, front portion oblong, retuse, revolute, with numerous, long, purple papillae, callus with many chestnut-brown keels. Colombia, Ecuador.

Phaius Lour. (*Phajus*) (From Gk *phaios*, grey, referring to the flowers which darken with age or damage.) Some 50 species of terrestrials. Stems with or without pseudobulbs, sometimes cylindric and rather cane-like. Leaves few, large, plicate. Inflorescence an axillary, erect raceme; flowers showy; sepals and petals similar, spreading; lip entire or lobed, sessile, erect, fused to the column; base spurred or inflated. Indomalaya, S China, Tropical Australia.

CULTIVATION Striking terrestrials for shaded, humid positions in the intermediate or warm greenhouse. The most commonly grown is *P.tankervilleae* with broad leaves overtopped by erect racemes of topaz to chocolate and rose-pink flowers. *P.flavus* is valued for its yellow-spotted leaves. Plant in beds or pot in well-crocked clay long-toms in a mix of bark, leafmould, charcoal, garden compost and a little dried FYM. Water throughout the year, allowing a slight drying between applications and avoiding wetting of foliage. Repot every third year and increase by division.

P.australis F. Muell.
Pseudobulbs ovoid, clustered, 4–7-leaved, to 7×7cm. Lvs lanceolate, plicate, dark green, to 125×10cm. Infl. to 2m; fls 4–10, to 10cm diam., maroon, veined yellow above, white below; sep. elliptic, acuminate; pet. oblong-ovate, to 6cm; lip midlobe crisped, lateral lobes entire, enveloping the column and callus plate, from lip base to apex; spur to 10mm, narrow. Australia.

P.callosus (Bl.) Lindl.
Pseudobulbs 6–12cm. Lvs elliptic to oblong-lanceolate, acuminate 60–110×16–26cm; petiole to 40cm. Sep. and pet. yellow-brown above, red-brown beneath, lip long-pubesc., white often golden yellow, blotched violet or yellow, streaked red-brown, spur yellow; sep. and pet. oblong, obtuse, to 5cm; lip trilobed, crenate, plicate, midlobe rectangular, forward-pointing, lateral lobes round; spur conic. Malaysia.

P.flavus (Bl.) Lindl. (*P.maculatus* Lindl.).
Pseudobulbs ovoid-cylindric, to 10–15×5–6cm. Lvs elliptic-lanceolate, acuminate, spotted pale yellow, 40–48×10–11cm. Infl. 30–45cm; fls 6–8cm diam., yellow, rarely white, lip streaked brown, spur white; sep. oblong, to 4cm; pet. similar, smaller; lip remotely trilobed, rhombic-orbicular, interior hirsute, midlobe trapezoid, lateral lobes rounded; spur conic. India, Malaysia, Java.

P.francoisii (Schltr.) Summerh. (*Gastrorchis francoisii* Schltr.).
Similar to *P.humblotii* except lip laterals yellow, dotted red, apical point of midlobe deeper red, tepals narrower. Madagascar.

P.grandifolius Lour. See *P.tankervilleae*.

P.humblotii Rchb. f.
45–80cm. Pseudobulbs spheric. Lvs elliptic-lanceolate, plicate, acute, 25–40×6–10cm. Infl. 60–90cm; fls 7–10, rose, blotched white and red, lip midlobe deeper; sep. ovate, 3–3.5×2cm; pet. similar, smaller; lip to 3×3cm, trilobed, base hirsute, lateral lobes rounded, erect, apex teeth 2, yellow. Madagascar.

P.maculatus Lindl. See *P.flavus*.

P.mishmensis (Lindl.) Rchb. f. (*P.roseus* Rolfe).
To 140cm, usually shorter. Pseudobulbs obscure. Stems fleshy, sheathed below, leafy above. Lvs 6–8, elliptic-lanceo-late to oblong-ovate, plicate, 15–30×8–12.5cm. Infl. lax, to 30cm; fls erect, 5–6cm diam., pale rose, purple-brown or dark red, lip pink or white, speckled purple; sep. linear-oblong, erect, spreading concave, to 3.5×1cm; pet. linear-oblanceo-late, narrow, acute, to 3×0.6cm; lip cuneate at base, midlobe subquadrate or oblong, entire, notched, lateral lobes rounded, embracing column, disc ridge central, pubesc.; spur conical, arched, narrow, to 1.5cm. India, Burma, Thailand to Philippines.

P.roseus Rolfe. See *P.mishmensis*.

P.tankervilleae (Banks) Bl. (*P.grandifolius* Lour.; *P.wallichii* Hook. f.).
60–200cm. Pseudobulbs ovoid-conic, 2.5–6cm. Lvs elliptic-lanceolate, acuminate, 30–100×20cm; petiole 15–25cm. Infl. erect; fls 10–20, 10–12.5cm diam.; white, green or rose beneath, red yellow-brown, or white above, edged gold, lip interior pink to burgundy, base yellow, exterior white, mid-lobe red-orange or white and pink; sep. and pet. lanceolate or oblanceolate, spreading, acuminate; lip tubular becoming triloobed, ovate-lanceolate, acuminate, acute or truncate, apex crisped, recurved; spur slender, apex forked. Himalaya to Australia.

P.tetragonus Rchb. f.
Stems to 30cm+, 4-angled, subalate. Lvs ovate-lanceolate, plicate, long-acuminate. Infl. lax; fls large, 8–10, maroon, tinted green above, green below, lip orange-red, streaked yel-low; sep. and pet. similar oblong, acute; lip midlobe crisped, apex broad-pointed, central lamellae, 3, lateral lobes embrac-ing column. Mauritius, Sri Lanka.

P.tuberculosus (Thouars) Bl.
Rhiz. short, ascending. Pseudobulbs along rhiz., small, obscured by lf sheaths, 5–6-leaved. Lvs lanceolate, narrow, plicate, 30–60×2–3cm; petiole long, sheathing. Infl. 40–65cm; fls white, lip midlobe white, margins spotted lilac or violet, lateral lobes yellow, dotted red, disc and callus yel-low; sep. elliptic-lanceolate, 3.2–4.4cm; pet. similar, slightly smaller, to 2.4cm; lip spreading, obscurely trilobed, midlobe deflexed, spreading, undulate, lateral lobes semi-orbicular, glabrous, erect, spreading; disc base glandular-pubesc., ridges 3, warty. Madagascar.

P.wallichii Hook. f. See *P.tankervilleae*.

Phaius   (a) *P.tankervilleae*   (b) *P.flavus*

Phalaenopsis Bl. (From Gk *phalaina*, moth and *opsis*, appearance.) MOTH ORCHID. About 50 species of monopodial epiphytes. Stems short, usually simple, composed of overlapping leaf bases, freely producing adventitious roots. Leaves 2–6, distichous, alternate, broad-obovate or oval, often drooping, glabrous, glossy or coarsely papillose, dark green flushed purple or mottled grey, green and silver, midvein sometimes sunken, base conduplicate with a distinct abscission line above short, fleshy sheath. Inflorescence axillary, appearing basal, erect to arching, a simple or branched raceme; flowers one to many; sepals almost equal, free, spreading, elliptic to broadly spathulate, usually smaller than petals; lip 3-lobed, fused to column foot or at right angles, midlobe fleshy with complex basal calli, apex often lobed, the lobes terminating in horn-like projections or filaments, highly coloured, lateral lobes erect. Asia, Australasia.

CULTIVATION Epiphytes for the intermediate or warm greenhouse, growing cases (especially *P.cornu-cervi* and *P.violacea*) and warm, shaded and humid positions in the home. Grown for their beautiful moth-like flowers matched, in some species, by superbly marked foliage (*P.schilleriana* and *P.stuartiana*). Many grexes are now offered. Grow in pots, baskets or on rafts. The medium should consist of coarse bark, perlag and charcoal. Rooting is freely adventitious and should be encouraged by frequent mistings (periodically with a dilute feed), but never when temperatures are below 18°C/65°F, at which point rots will be encouraged by an accumulation of moisture in the vulnerable growth axis. A humid, buoyant atmosphere is essential, as is shade. Drench pots throughout the year whenever the medium begins to dry out. Propagate by meristem culture or by plantlets sometimes produced on old inflorescences. Easily raised from seed.

P.amabilis (L.) Bl. (*P.grandiflora* Lindl.).
Lvs to 5, elliptic, to obovate, coriaceous or fleshy, glossy green above, to 50×10cm. Infl. arching, to 1m; fls to 10cm diam., fragrant, sep. and pet. white, often pink below, sep. elliptic-ovate, to 4×2.5cm, pet. larger, almost circular; lip white, base red, margins yellow, midlobe cruciform, side projections triangular, with 2 yellow-tipped appendages, callus almost square, yellow, dotted red, ridges 2, lateral lobes oblanceolate. E Indies, Australia.

P.amboinensis J.J. Sm.
Lvs to 4, elliptic to oblong-elliptic or oblanceolate, to 25×10cm. Infl. 1 or several, arching; fls few, cream to orange-yellow, striped cinnamon; dorsal sep. elliptic to ovate-elliptic, lateral sep. broadly ovate or ovate-elliptic, keeled near apex; pet. ovate or rhombic-ovate; lip clawed, midlobe ovate or oblong-ovate, central keel margins serrate, apex merging with spherical callus, lateral lobes oblong-ligulate, apex falcate. Indonesia.

P.aphrodite Rchb. f.
Resembles *P.amabilis* except in fls to 7cm diam.; lip midlobe subtriangular, not cruciform, callus with deeper red markings. Philippines to Taiwan.

P.cochlearis Holtt.
Lvs 2–4, oblong-ovate to oblong-elliptic, prominently veined above, to 20×10cm. Infl. branched, to 50cm; fls few, white to pale green or yellow, sep. and pet. with 2 light to orange-brown basal stripes, dorsal sep. narrow to lanceolate-elliptic, to 20×10mm, somewhat revolute, lateral sep. ovate, pet. narrow-elliptic or lanceolate-elliptic; lip fleshy, midlobe primrose, striped red to orange-brown, orbicular, apex rounded or notched, disc ridged, central calli lamellate, lateral lobes oblong-linear, centrally grooved. Sarawak.

P.corningiana Rchb. f.
As *P.sumatrana* except fls few, to 5cm diam.; sep. and pet. pale yellow, apex vertically or horizontally barred mahogany red to crimson, dorsal sep. obovate to oblanceolate, lateral sep. ovate, apex channelled, pet. lanceolate; lip midlobe and column base deep magenta to carmine, midlobe elliptic-oblong, narrow, convex, central keel apex callused, pubesc., callus forked, orange-yellow, lateral lobes oblong-ligulate. Borneo, Sarawak.

P.cornu-cervi (Breda) Bl. & Rchb. f.
Lvs oblong to ligulate, apex often shallowly bilobed, to 25×4cm, olive green. Infl. to 40cm, branching, floral axis flattened, broad with 2 rows of alternate bracts; fls waxy yellow to yellow-green; sep. marked red-brown, blotches stripes and spots cinnamon, apices keeled, dorsal sep. obovate-elliptic, margins weakly recurved, lateral sep. elliptic to elliptic-lanceolate; pet. lanceolate; lip fleshy, white, midlobe anchor-shaped, projections hooked, lateral lobes almost square, red-brown or striped cinnamon. SE Asia.

P.delicosa Rchb. f. See *Kingidium delicosum*.
P.denevei Sm. See *Paraphalaenopsis denevei*.

P.equestris (Schauer) Rchb. f.
Lvs to 5, oblong, apex channelled, base tapering, to 20×6.5cm, somewhat coriaceous, dark green above, often flushed rose-purple beneath. Infl. 1 to many, arched, simple or branched, to 30cm; fls to 4cm diam.; sep. and pet. rose or white suffused rose, sep. oblong-elliptic, margins slightly recurved, pet. elliptic; lip deep pink to purple, midlobe ovate, concave, apex fleshy, callus 6–8-sided, peltate, yellow, spotted red, lateral lobes oblong, marked yellow. Philippines, Taiwan.

P.fasciata Rchb. f.
Stem short. Lvs elliptic to obovate, to 20cm. Infl. erect or arched; fls fleshy, waxy, pale to deep yellow, to 4cm diam., sep. and pet. striped or banded red-brown to cinnamon; dorsal sep. elliptic, lateral sep. ovate-elliptic; pet. similar, oblique; lip midlobe oblong-ovate, convex, apex magenta, base orange-yellow, central keels terminal, callus ovate, orange, central disc orange, papillose, projecting appendage forked, lateral lobes ligulate, dotted orange. Philippines.

P.fimbriata J.J. Sm.
Lvs oblong-elliptic, arched 15–25cm. Infl. to 30cm, pendent; fls many, opening simultaneously, white to cream, basal bars magenta; sep. and pet. ovate-elliptic, to 2cm; lip midlobe ovate, convex, fleshy, fringed, upcurved, central keel dentate, terminal callus white-pubesc., callus at lateral lobe junction with 3 plates, lateral lobes oblong, convex. Java, Sumatra.

P.gigantea J.J. Sm.
Lvs 5–6, oblong-ovate, pendent, coriaceous, glossy, to 50×20cm. Infl. to 40cm; fls scented, cream to dull yellow, sep. and pet. blotched and lined maroon to dark purple, sep. spreading, elliptic, base fused to the column foot, pet. elliptic; lip fleshy, white, striped, or lined magenta, midlobe ovate, apical callus ovoid, bidentate, lateral lobes triangular, centrally callused. Borneo, Sabah.

P.grandiflora Lindl. See *P.amabilis*.

P.hieroglyphica (Rchb. f.) H. Sweet (*P.lueddemanniana* var. *hieroglyphica* (Rchb. f.) Veitch).
Lvs broadly ligulate, coriaceous, to 30×10cm. Infl. pendent or arched; sep. and pet. white lined red-purple, apex tinted green, ovate-elliptic, apex keeled; lip to 2cm, midlobe truncate, apex jagged, central keel pubesc., fleshy, terminal callus ovoid, lateral lobes oblong, apex notched, callus between lateral lobes papillose, appendages 2, forked. Philippines.

P.×intermedia Lindl. (*P.aphrodite × P.equestris*.)
Lvs elliptic, fleshy, arched, green above, purple beneath, to 30×8cm. Fls white to deep rose; dorsal sep. elliptic, lateral sep. ovate, to 4cm; pet. elliptic; lip midlobe obovate, apex tapering, bidentate, central callus almost square, lateral lobes obovate. Philippines.

Phalaenopsis   (a) *P.stuartiana*   (b) *P.schilleriana*   (c) *P.aphrodite*   (d) *P.amabilis*

P.× leucorrhoda Rchb. f. (*P.aphrodite × P.schilleriana.*)
Lvs green above, spotted silver-grey, purple beneath. Infl. arching, pendent, to 70cm. Fl. variable, pure white to deep rose, margins rose; sep. elliptic to ovate; pet. reniform to circular; lip white, dotted or lined yellow and purple (rarely entirely purple), midlobe variable, apex tapering, filamentous or anchor-shaped, appendages 2, callus irregularly dentate, deep yellow, rarely paler, spotted deep red, lateral lobes spathulate. Philippines.

P.lindenii Loher.
Lvs oblong-lanceolate, dappled silver-white, to 25×4cm. Infl. dense, fls tinged white, dotted rose at centre; dorsal sep. oblong-elliptic, lateral sep. oblong-ovate; pet. elliptic-rhombic; lip to 1.5cm, midlobe circular, centrally concave, tipped purple-pink, lined rose, apex pointed, central callus 6–8-sided, lateral lobes obovate to ligulate, white, basally dotted red or orange, with 3 purple lines at apex. Philippines.

P.lobbii (Rchb. f.) H. Sweet.
Lvs broad, elliptic, to 13×5cm. Sep. and pet. cream, dorsal sep. oblong-elliptic, lateral sep. ovate, pet. obovate, to 8×5mm; lip with 2 vertical red-brown stripes, fused to column foot, midlobe mobile, triangular, apex rounded, basal plate margins irregular, minutely dentate, central callus fil. 4. India, Himalaya.

P.lueddemanniana Rchb. f. Lvs oblong-elliptic, arched, spreading or pendent, dull olive green, to 30×10cm, usually shorter. Infl. erect or pendent, to 30cm, branched or simple, flexuous, becoming horizontal; fls to 6cm diam.; sep. and pet. white, laterally or horizontally striped brown-purple, dorsal sep. elliptic to oblong-elliptic, lateral sep. ovate-elliptic, to 3cm, pet. smaller; lip to 2.5cm, carmine, base yellow, midlobe oblong to ovate, apical callus white, pubesc., papillose at lobe junction, projection bifid, lateral lobes oblong. Philippines.

P.lueddemanniana var. *hieroglyphica* (Rchb. f.) Veitch. See *P.hieroglyphica*. *P.lueddemanniana* var. *purpurea* (Rchb. f.) Veitch. See *P.pulchra*.

P.maculata Rchb. f.
Lvs 2–3, oblong-ligulate, to 20×4cm. Infl. arched, simple; fls few; sep. and pet. white or pale rose, banded purple, dorsal sep. oblong-elliptic, lateral sep. ovate-elliptic, shorter than sep.; lip white, midlobe oblong, convex, base keeled, apex purple, callused, central callus appendage bifid, lateral lobes oblong, apex notched. Borneo, Sulawesi.

P.mannii Rchb. f.
Lvs 4–5, oblong, to 40×7cm. Infl. pendent, usually simple; fls fragrant, to 4.25cm, many, opening in succession; sep. and pet. green or yellow, blotched cinnamon, sep. ovate-lanceolate, apex keeled beneath, pet. lanceolate, margins revolute, to 2cm; lip to 10mm, white and purple, midlobe anchor-shaped, callus often hirsute, basally continuing into midlobe, forming a central, semicircular callus, lateral lobes almost square, toothed, papillose. Himalaya, Vietnam.

P.mariae Warner & Williams.
Lvs fleshy, ligulate, to 30×7cm. Infl. pendent, branched or simple; fls to 5cm diam.; sep. and pet. oblong-elliptic, white or cream, horizontally striped and blotched brown-red, base rarely spotted purple; lip pale mauve to purple, midlobe expanded, apex dentate, central keel and apical callus pubesc., central callus projections several, bifid, lateral lobes broadly ligulate, apices toothed. Philippines.

P.micholitzii Rolfe.
Lvs obovate, arching to pendent, to 16×6cm. Infl. arching; fls successional, white to pale green; dorsal sep. elliptic, lateral sep. ovate; pet. ovate-elliptic, to 3×2cm; lip fleshy, midlobe rhombic, central patch villous, apical swelling tapering to a basal keel, central callus bifid, lateral lobes falcate, calli orange-yellow. Philippines.

P.pallens (Lindl.) Rchb. f.
Lvs elliptic to obovate, fleshy, pendent, to 20cm. Infl. arching

or erect; fls solitary or few, to 5cm diam., sep. and pet. pale lemon to yellow-green, horizontal lines and dashes brown, oblong-elliptic, to 2cm; lip to 2cm, midlobe white, ovate, narrow, apex margins dilated, dentate, base keeled, apical callus pubesc., callus appendages at lobe junction 2, bifid, lateral lobes oblong, yellow. Philippines.

P.parishii Rchb. f.
Lvs elliptic to obovate, fleshy, arching or pendent, to 12×5cm, dark green. Infl. erect or arching, to 15cm; fls open simultaneously; sep. and pet. white, sep. elliptic to circular, dorsal sep. to 8mm, lateral sep. to 10mm, pet. elliptic to obovate; lip to 1.5cm, midlobe purple, triangular, callus semicircular, margins fringed, central disc projections bristle-like, lateral lobes vestigial, triangular, white or yellow, spotted brown or purple. Himalaya, Vietnam.

P.pulcherrima (Lindl.) J.J. Sm. See *Doritis pulcherrima*.

P.pulchra (Rchb. f.) H. Sweet (*P.lueddemanniana* var. *purpurea* (Rchb. f.) Veitch).
Lvs oblong-elliptic, arched, fleshy, to 15×5cm. Fls few, deep magenta-purple, with faint stripes or bars; dorsal sep. erect, elliptic, lateral sep. ovate; pet. elliptic or ovate-elliptic; lip midlobe ovate to flabellate, keel irregularly dentate, disc papillose, apex callused, midlobe callus fleshy, bifid, lateral lobes oblong-linear, erect. Philippines.

P.reichenbachiana Rchb. f. & Sander.
Lvs elliptic to obovate, to 35×7cm. Infl. erect or arched, to 45cm; fls to 4cm diam.; sep. and pet. green-white to yellow, barred red-brown and cinnamon, dorsal sep. elliptic or elliptic-ovate, lateral sep. ovate to ovate-lanceolate, pet. ovate to ovate-elliptic; lip base orange-yellow, midlobe ovate, angular, tipped magenta and pale violet, apex margins with minute irregular dentations, callus yellow, bifid, lateral lobes white, oblong-linear to circular, becoming papillose. Philippines.

P.sanderiana Rchb. f.
Lvs 1–3, elliptic or oblong-elliptic, dark green above, marked silver-grey beneath. Infl. to 80cm, axis purple, branched or simple; fls to 7.5cm diam., colour and marking variable, sep. and pet. ovate-elliptic, pink, dappled white, or wholly white; lip to 3cm, midlobe triangular, white or yellow, striped purple or brown, apex with 2 filiform projections, callus horseshoe-shaped, yellow or white, spotted red, brown, or purple, lateral lobes ovate, white, spotted pink. Philippines.

P.schilleriana Rchb. f.
Lvs elliptic, dark green, mottled silver-grey above, purple beneath, to 45×11cm. Infl. branching, pendent; fls to 250+, fragrant, white to pink, mauve and rose-purple; sep. and pet. edged white, dorsal sep. elliptic to 3.5cm, lateral sep. similar, ovate, basally spotted carmine-purple, pet. rhombic, undulate; lip midlobe circular, white to magenta, appendages 2, anchor-shaped, central callus base truncate, lateral lobes elliptic, spreading, basally yellow, dotted red-brown. Philippines.

P.speciosa Rchb. f.
Lvs elliptic, arched or recurved, to 20×8cm. Infl. arched or pendent, to 30cm; fls fleshy; sep. and pet. oblong-elliptic, white-rose, blotched purple, pet. bases striped white; lip midlobe ovate, white, marked purple, central keel serrate, apical callus pubesc., central callus appendage bifid, lateral lobes triangular, yellow at base, tips white. Nicobar Is.

P.stuartiana Rchb. f.
Lvs fewer, narrower and shorter than in *P.schilleriana*, elliptic-oblong, green blotched grey above, purple beneath, to 35×8cm. Infl. branched, pendent, to 60cm; fls to 6cm diam., fragrant; sep. white, lateral sep. elliptic to ovate-elliptic, yellow, dotted red-brown at base; pet. almost square to circular, lacking yellow base; lip to 2.5cm, almost circular, apex anchor-shaped, callus spotted orange, almost square, apical projections on lateral lobes similar to lateral sep. in colour, obovate, basal appendages white, horn-like. Philippines.

P.sumatrana Korth. & Rchb. f.
Lvs oblong to obovate, to 30×11cm. Infl. erect or slightly

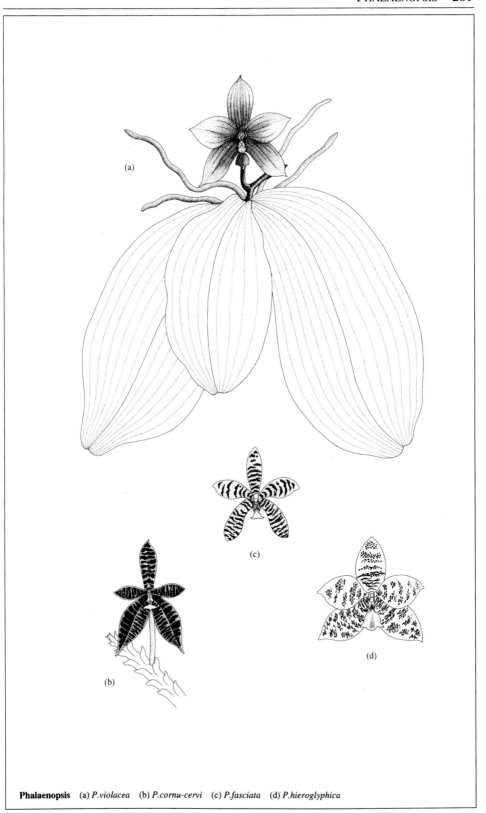

Phalaenopsis   (a) *P.violacea*   (b) *P.cornu-cervi*   (c) *P.fasciata*   (d) *P.hieroglyphica*

arched, rarely branched, to 30cm; fls to 5cm diam.; sep. and pet. oblong-lanceolate, white to pale yellow, banded cinnamon; lip midlobe oblong-elliptic, white, with red or purple stripes flanking a central keel, apex hirsute, callus of several forked plates, lateral lobes linear-oblong, cream, often spotted orange, margin brown or yellow, apices bidentate. Malaysia, Sumatra, Borneo, Java.

P.violacea Witte.

Habit diminutive. Lvs elliptic to obovate, to 25×12cm, glossy light green. Infl. ascending or arched, thick, jointed, to 12.5cm; fls few (usually only one opening at the time), to 4.5cm diam.; sep. and pet. broadly elliptic, sharply acute, obscurely keeled beneath, often slightly incurved, amethyst fading to white or lime green at apex; lip midlobe oblong, convex, apiculate, with central keel, violet tipped with white pubescence, central crest yellow, forked toward midlobe, lateral lobes short, erect, oblong, yellow; column white or amethyst. Flower colour variable; good forms are of the deepest mauve and often fragrant. Sumatra, Borneo, Malaysia.

*P.*grexes and cultivars.

*P.*Abendrot: large plants with dark green lvs and tall spikes; fls deep pink, up to 10cm diam.

*P.*Allegria: large plants with arching and branching sprays of nearly pure white fls.

*P.*Barbara Moler: compact plants with long, branching fl. spikes; fls star-shaped, 5–7.5cm diam., white heavily overlaid with pink spots and solid pink near the centre; some forms are yellow-green with light brown blotches, lip purple and orange.

*P.*Cabrillo Star 'Santa Cruz': strong growing plants with long arching spikes; fls of good shape, 10–10.5cm diam., white, generously dotted with magenta freckles, lip very dark magenta.

*P.*Capitola 'Moonlight': large robust plants with very strong arching spikes of many fls; fls white, 10–10.5cm diam.

*P.*Caribbean Sunset: compact plants; fls star-shaped, yellow, striped and spotted with chestnut.

*P.*Carmen Coll: compact plants; strong spikes of deep pink fls, darker in the centre, lip brilliant orange and petunia purple.

*P.*Cassandra: small but compact and strong plants; fls white with spotted sep., miniature.

*P.*Cast Iron Monarch 'The King': very large plants with tall arching sprays; a famous hexaploid clone with large white fls to 12.5cm diam.

*P.*Doris: one of the first of the large white-fld hybrids, large plants with long arching sprays; also a few pale pink clones.

*P.*Elise de Valec 'Boissy': strong plants with branching spikes; fls good shape, white or cream, heavily overlaid with red spots, lip outlined with yellow.

*P.*Esme Hennessy: compact plants; well-shaped white fls, red lip.

*P.*Gladys Read 'Snow Queen': large robust plants with arching sprays of many fls; fls pure white; 10–12.5cm diam.

*P.*Golden Amboin: strong growing plants with tall spikes; fls star-shaped, primrose yellow, evenly dusted with fine chestnut freckles, lip orange red, 7.5–9cm diam.

*P.*Golden Emperor: compact plants with few-fld sprays of lemon yellow fls, orange lip.

*P.*Golden Sands: medium-sized plants with branching spikes; fls lemon yellow with dense covering of fine light brown spots, orange at the lip base.

*P.*Gorey 'Trinity': strong plants with tall spikes; fls large and good shape, deep yellow which does not fade, white towards the centre and with darker yellow on the lip.

*P.*Hennessy: compact plants with branching fl. spikes blooming throughout the year; fls well-shaped, 7.5–11cm diam., white to light pink with red or pink stripes, lip purple and orange.

*P.*Henriette Lecoufle 'Boule de Neige': very large plants with branching sprays of exquisite, large, pure white fls.

*P.*Hilo Lip: robust plants with dark green lvs and tall spikes; fls various shades of pink with contrasting white lip, up to 7.5cm diam.

*P.*Joey: small plants; fls green-yellow barred with light brown, lip lilac, orange at the base.

*P.*Line Renaud 'Casino de Paris': robust plants with tall arching spikes; fls white or pale pink with deep red purple lip, good shape.

*P.*Lippeglut: large plants with dark green lvs and tall arching spikes; fls deep pink with darker lip of excellent shape and size. Lipperose, Lippstadt and Lippexauber are rather similar.

*P.*Little Mary: compact but strong plants with large arching and branching sprays; 3.8cm diam., excellent shape, deep pink with dark magenta lip, long-lasting.

*P.*Lundy 'Mont Millais': robust plants with tall arching spikes; fls of good shape, creamy yellow with pink stripes, lip deeper yellow and rose pink.

*P.*Mistinguett: large robust plants with tall spikes; fls 7.5–10cm diam., deep pink throughout and finely dotted with a deeper pink especially on the lip.

*P.*Nero Wolfe: strong plants; fls pink, striped with darker pink, lip red.

*P.*Ondinette: compact plants, branching sprays; fls round, large petals, deep pink with white lip.

*P.*Opaline: large plants with dark green lvs and robust fl. spikes; very large white fls of excellent shape and substance.

*P.*Orchid World: compact plants; fls bright yellow, spotted darker yellow but paler in centre, lip orange at base

*P.*Orglade's Clever Face: strong compact plants with short spikes, often branching; fls strong yellow background with heavy chestnut striping, orange red lip.

*P.*Orglade's Lemon Dew: vigorous, compact plants with branching spikes; fls pale lemon yellow, white towards the centre and with darker yellow on lip, very floriferous.

*P.*Party Dress: compact plants with large branching sprays of many fls, small, up to 5cm diam., round and pink.

*P.*Party Poppers: small but strong plants with branching sprays; fls variable, miniature whites, pastel pinks and stripes.

*P.*Pink Leopard: compact plants with large sprays; fls of good shape, white, heavily freckled with red, lip marked with chestnut.

*P.*Redfan: large robust plants with tall spikes; fls *c*7.5cm diam., white with ruby red lip.

*P.*Sierra Gold 'Suzanne': compact plants; lovely golden yellow fls with white lip.

*P.*Sophie Hausermann: small plants with few, rich brick-red fls.

*P.*Sourire: large plants with attractive silvery mottled lvs; fls pale to deep pink, good shape, 7.5–10cm diam.

*P.*Temple Cloud: large plants with long arching spikes; fls 10–14cm diam., pure white and heavy textured, long-lasting.

*P.*Zauberrose: large, robust plants with tall arching spikes; fls deep pink with very large pet., lip darker, excellent shape and size.

*P.*Zuma Chorus: compact plants with branching spikes; fls white striped magenta, lip attractively marked in orange and bright rose pink, column pink.

Pholidota Lindl. (From Gk *pholis*, scale and *ous*, ear; the bracts are scaly and ear-like.) RATTLESNAKE ORCHID. 29 species of epiphytes or terrestrials. Rhizomes creeping. Pseudobulbs clustered or remote, cylindric or conical, smooth or ribbed, often becoming laterally compressed and 4-sided with age, basally sheathed. Leaves solitary or paired, apical, linear, obovate or elliptic, acute, glabrous, obscurely plicate, stalked. Inflorescence racemose, from centre of new shoots, erect then sharply decurved and pendulous, spiralling or flexuous; bracts conspicuous overlapping, closely 2-ranked, concave, papery, subtending each flower; flowers numerous, small, white to brown; dorsal sepal ovate to elliptic, broad, coriaceous, few-veined, lateral sepals ovate to ovate-oblong, often basally grooved, or with prominent midrib; petals ovate or obovate to linear, few- or many-nerved, flat to concave; lip sigmoid to straight, basally saccate, lateral margins erect, often forming lobes, apex bilobed or entire often with keels and calli. Indomalaya, W Pacific.

CULTIVATION   Intriguing epiphytes for the intermediate house. The wand-like, spiralling racemes are clothed in slightly inflated bracts, resembling a rattlesnake's tail.

P.articulata Lindl. (*P.khasiyana* Rchb. f.).
Pseudobulbs slender or swollen, wrinkled, to 15cm, borne at apex of previous year's pseudobulb. Lvs ovate to linear-lanceolate, to 20×5cm, venation prominent. Infl. to 6.5cm; bracts brown, to 1cm, falling as fls open; fls to 65, fragrant; sep. and pet. cream, green-white to pink, tips rarely darker, lip similar, keels buff, central constriction green-yellow to yellow-brown. India, China, Burma, Thailand to Celebes.

P.chinensis Lindl.
Pseudobulbs ovoid, wrinkled, to 11cm. Lvs to 20cm, ovate-oblong to linear-lanceolate. Infl. axis strongly flexuous, to 30cm; fls to 35, green-white to white, lip cream-white, column pale buff, tinged pink; dorsal sep. to 1×1cm, ovate to elliptic, obtuse to acute, 5–9 veined, midrib prominent, lateral sep. ovate to ovate-oblong, apical point often broad, midrib with a rounded to flattened keel; pet. ovate-lanceolate to linear-lanceolate, midrib sometimes swollen; lip basal lobes erect, rounded, basal nerves keeled, apically recurved to reflexed, entire, tip obtuse to acute, sometimes with swollen venation or minutely papillose. Burma, China.

P.convallariae (Rchb. f.) Hook. f.
Pseudobulbs slender to swollen, wrinkled when dry, to 7cm. Lvs linear-lanceolate, to 21×2.5cm, midrib prominent beneath. Infl. axis flexuous, to 10cm; fls 3–28; dorsal sep. to 10×5mm, ovate to ovate-oblong, midrib prominent, lateral sep. similar, midrib often prominently keeled; pet. to 7×5mm, ovate, venation sometimes branched; lip to 6.5mm, base deeply concave, lateral margins rounded, basal depression shallow, basally fused, apical lobes semi-elliptic, overlapping, keels 3–5, prominent. India, Burma.

P.imbricata (Roxb.) Lindl.
Pseudobulbs clustered, cylindric, swollen, longitudinally wrinkled or sunken, appearing translucent olive green, to 10cm. Lvs ovate-oblong to linear-lanceolate to 50×10cm, coriaceous, underside light green, often tinted red, venation prominent. Infl. to 15cm, spiralling; bracts papery, light brown, imbricate, persistent, concealing fls; fls to 130, white to cream, tinted yellow to pink; dorsal sep. ovate, forming a hood to 7×5mm, lateral sep. ovate-oblong, to 8×5mm; pet. falcate, apex truncate or rounded; lip basally concave, with 1–2 orange spots, lateral lobes erect, triangular to semi-orbicular, central nerves forming orange to yellow, wing-like keels, apex bilobed, lobes semi-elliptic, tip rounded, acute. Vietnam, Solomon Is., Australia to Fiji.

P.khasiyana Rchb. f. See *P.articulata*.

Phragmipedium Rolfe. (From Gk *phragma*, partition, and *pedilon*, slipper, referring to the trilocular ovary and the slipper-shaped lip.) LADY-SLIPPER. Some 20 species of terrestrials, lithophytes or epiphytes. Stems short, clustered, clothed with leaves; roots fibrous. Leaves distichous, overlapping in fans, coriaceous, sulcate, conduplicate, usually ligulate, arching. Inflorescence a raceme or panicle, terminal, erect, usually several-flowered; peduncle usually terete, pubescent, sheathed; ovary shortly pedicellate, trilocular; flowers large, showy, short-lived; dorsal sepal free, slightly concave, lateral sepals fused as a synsepalum; petals free, spreading or pendent, similar to sepals or long-caudate; lip sessile, inflated, slipper-shaped, margins involute; column short, stout; fertile stamens 2, laterally adnate, anther 2-celled; staminode peltate-scutate, triangular, rhombic or rounded; pollen granular. C & S America. Formerly included variously in *Cypripedium*, *Paphiopedilum*, and *Selenipedium*.

CULTIVATION   As for warm-growing *Paphiopedilum* spp.

P.Ainsworthii (*P.longifolium* × *P.Sedenii*).
Strong-growing plants; fls produced consecutively, white and pale pink, larger than in *P.Sedenii*.

P.besseae Dodson & J. Kuhn.
Fls to 6cm diam.; dorsal sep. ovate-lanceolate, pet. oblong-elliptic, larger, all bright scarlet; lip strongly pouched, fiery red to golden yellow or peach. Colombia, NE Peru.

P.boissierianum (Rchb. f.) Rolfe.
Lvs 6–8, to 80×5cm, acute. Raceme subequal to lvs, erect, loosely 3–15-fld; tepals bronze or olive green veined dark green, edged white or brown, dorsal sep. to 6×1.5cm, lanceolate or oblong-lanceolate, acuminate, undulate-crisped; synsepalum to 6×3cm, ovate-oblong, pet. to 10cm, widely spreading, linear-lanceolate, twisted, undulate-crisped; lip unguiculate, pendent, obovate-saccate, brown in front, lateral lobes strongly incurved, heavily spotted green-brown; staminode transversely elliptic-reniform. Ecuador, Peru.

P.caricinum (Lindl. & Paxt.) Rolfe.
Terrestrial. Lvs 3–7, rigid, suberect, to 50×1.5cm, narrowly linear. Raceme or panicle to 40cm, several-fld; fls borne in succession; tepals bronze to olive edged purple-green, dorsal sep. to 2.5×1.5cm, ovate-lanceolate to lanceolate, acute to obtuse, undulate, synsepalum broadly ovate-oblong, acute, to 2.5×1.5cm, pet. to 8×4mm, linear-lanceolate, acute, pendent, twisted, undulate; lip yellow-green, to 3.5cm, lateral lobes spotted dark green and purple, strongly incurved. Peru, Bolivia, Brazil.

P.caudatum (Lindl.) Rolfe (*P.warscewiczianum* (Rchb. f.) Schltr.).
Lvs 5–9, to 60×6cm. Raceme to 80cm, 2–4-fld; fls largest of the genus, to 125cm across; sep. white to yellow-green with dark green venation, dorsal sep. to 15×3cm, lanceolate, acute, arched over lip, strongly undulate to spiralled, synsepalum to 10×4.5cm, lanceolate to ovate-lanceolate, long-acuminate, strongly undulate; pet. purple-brown to green-brown, to

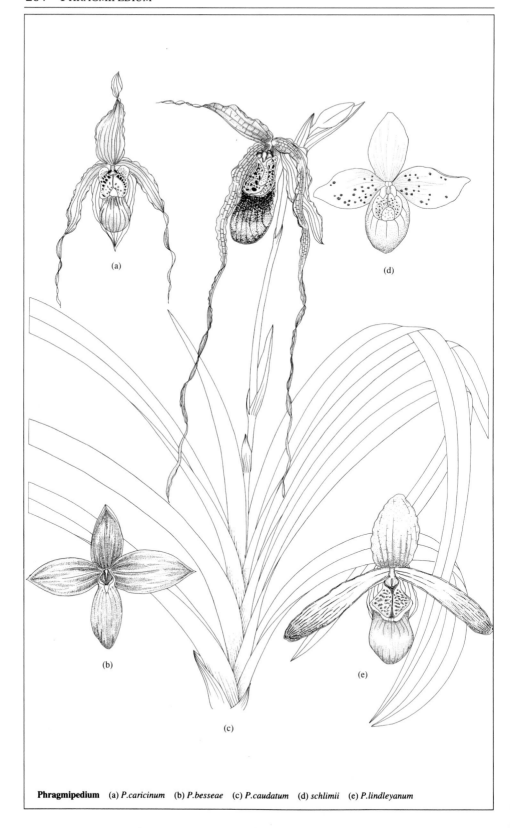

Phragmipedium   (a) *P.caricinum*   (b) *P.besseae*   (c) *P.caudatum*   (d) *schlimii*   (e) *P.lindleyanum*

60×1cm, linear-lanceolate, pendulous, spiralling; lip yellow near base, apex tinted pink or maroon, veined green, to 7×2cm, calceolate, 3-lobed, lateral lobes strongly incurved, spotted green. Mexico to Peru, Venezuela, Colombia, Ecuador.

P.Dominianum (*P.caricinum × P.caudatum*).
Stem erect. Lvs linear-elongate. Infl. 3-fld; fls yellow-green, tinged with copper-brown; lip deep red-brown in front, with sharper reticulations, yellow-green behind, mouth incurved, yellow spotted dark purple.

P.Grande (*P.longifolium × P.caudatum*). Very large plants; tall infl. with several large fls simultaneously, green-brown with very long pet.

P.hartwegii (Rchb. f.) L.O. Williams.
Lvs to 60cm. Raceme to 90cm, loosely several-fld, with several basal, red-brown sheaths; fls green-yellow; dorsal sep. to 5×2cm, ovate-oblong, attenuate above, undulate, synsepalum ovate-elliptic, to 5×4cm, undulate; pet. to 9cm, linear-ligulate or linear-lanceolate, pendent, twisted, slightly undulate-crisped; lip unguiculate, slightly slipper-shaped, lateral lobes retuse, subquadrate. Ecuador, Peru.

P.klotzscheanum (Rchb. f.) Rolfe.
Lvs to 35×1cm. Raceme to 60cm, erect, 2–3-fld; fls opening singly; sep. pink-brown veined maroon, dorsal sep. to 3×1cm, lanceolate, subacute, synsepalum to 3×2cm, ovate, obtuse; pet. pale brown veined green or maroon, to 5×1cm, pendent, linear, obtuse, twisted; lip to 3×1.5cm, slipper-shaped, lateral lobes strongly incurved, minutely pubesc., yellow spotted brown, midlobe white. Venezuela, Guyana.

P.lindenii (Lindl.) Dressler & N. Williams (*Cypripedium caudatum* var. *lindenii* (Lindl.) Veitch).
Resembles *P.caudatum* except lip simple, unpouched, similar to pet., wider at base. Colombia, Peru, Ecuador.

P.lindleyanum (Schomb. ex Lindl.) Rolfe.
Lvs 4–7, to 50×6cm. Raceme or lightly branched panicle to 1m, 3–7-fld; sep. pale green or yellow-green, veined red-brown, pubesc. below, dorsal sep. to 3.5×2cm, elliptic, obtuse, concave, synsepalum to 3×2.5cm, elliptic, obtuse; pet. yellow-green at base, white-green toward apex, margins and veins flushed purple toward apex, to 5.5×1cm, linear-oblong, apex rounded, undulate; lip pale yellow-green with yellow-brown venation, to

3×1.5cm, 3-lobed, lateral lobes spotted light purple, incurved, midlobe inflated, margins incurved. Venezuela, Guyana.

P.longifolium (Warsc. & Rchb. f.) Rolfe.
Lvs to 60×4cm. Infl. to 40cm, several-fld, erect; fls produced singly, long-lived; dorsal sep. pale yellow-green, veined dark green or rose, edged white, to 6×2cm, lanceolate, acute, erect or curved forward, sometimes undulate, synsepalum to 6×4cm, pale yellow-green, veined dark green, ovate, acute; pet. pale yellow-green, margins rose-purple, to 12×1cm, spreading, linear or linear-lanceolate, twisted; lip yellow-green, to 6×1.5cm, slipper-shaped, 3-lobed, margins strongly incurved and spotted pale rose to magenta. Costa Rica, Panama, Colombia, Ecuador.

P.Nitidissimum (*P.caudatum × P.*Conchiferum).
Large plants with several fls simultaneously; fls yellow-green with pink margins and brown lip.

P.pearcei (Rchb.f.) Rauh. & Senghas.
Infl. to 30cm; fls to 7cm diam., sep. and pet. green, lined maroon, pet. pendulous, undulate, twisted, ribbon-like; lip bowl-like, glossy olive veined darker green, rim strongly revolute, white dotted maroon. Ecuador, Peru.

P.sargentianum (Rolfe) Rolfe.
Lvs to 50×6cm. Raceme or panicle to 40cm, 2–4-fld; tepals green or yellow-green veined purple-green, dorsal sep. to 3×1.5cm, ovate-elliptic, acute, concave, ciliate, synsepalum to 3×2cm, ciliate, pet. to 6×1.5cm, oblong-ligulate, acute, spreading, slightly twisted, ciliate, margins tinged purple; lip yellow or yellow-green veined purple, slipper-shaped, lateral lobes spotted purple, with 2 small, white tubercles on inner margin. Brazil.

P.schlimii (Lind. & Rchb. f.) Rolfe. Lvs to 35×3cm. Raceme or panicle to 50cm, 5–10-fld; tepals white flushed rose-pink, dorsal sep. to 2×1cm, ovate-oblong, obtuse, concave, synsepalum broader than dorsal sep., pet. slightly longer than sep., spreading, spotted pink at base, elliptic; lip rose-pink, inflated, ellipsoid, lateral lobes incurved, streaked white and rose-carmine. Colombia.

P.Sedenii (Rchb. f.) Pfitz. (*P.longifolium × P.schlimii.*) Sep. ivory white, flushed pale rose, exterior rose-pink; pet. white, margins tinged rose-pink, twisted; lip rose-pink, lobes white spotted rose; staminode white, slightly dotted pink.

P.warscewiczianum (Rchb. f.) Schltr. See *P.caudatum*.

Platanthera L.C. Rich. (From Gk *platys*, wide, and Lat. *anthera*, anther.) Some 100 species of terrestrial herbs. Tubers 2, ovoid to ellipsoid, tapering. Stem erect. Basal leaves 1–3, ovate, reduced to sheaths on stem. Spike cylindric; flowers green or white; dorsal sepal and petals incurved, forming a hood, lateral sepals spreading, recurved; lip linear-oblong to lanceolate, entire or, rarely, 3-lobed; spur cylindric, long. Summer. Temperate N and S hemisphere.

CULTIVATION   See Introduction: Hardy Orchids.

P.bifolia (L.) Rich. LESSER BUTTERFLY ORCHID.
To 50cm. Basal lvs almost opposite, oblong-lanceolate, broadly elliptic or obovate. Spike to 20cm; bracts equal ovary; fls fragrant, white, tinted green; lateral sep. lanceolate, spreading, recurved; lip 8–12mm, decurved, white, rarely lime-green, spur to 40mm, slender, almost horizontal, exceeding ovary. Late spring–summer. Mediterranean, USSR.

P.blephariglottis (Willd.) Lindl.
To 50cm, erect, leafy. Basal lvs 2–4, elliptic to lanceolate. Spike 15–25-fld; fls white; sep. oblong-ovate, lateral sep. reflexed; pet. oblong, finely dentate or entire; lip ovate, fringed, spur to 20mm. Mid–late summer. N America.

P.chlorantha (Custer) Rchb. (*P.montana* Rchb. f.). GREATER BUTTERFLY ORCHID.
As *P.bifolia* except spike lax, lateral sep. ovate-lanceolate; fls earlier, larger, darker green, less fragrant, spur 18–40mm, apex slightly dilated. Late spring–summer. Europe, Mediterranean. .

P.ciliaris (L.) Lindl.
To 100cm. Basal lvs 5–30×1–5cm, 2–4, lanceolate, ridged.

Spike 30–60-fld; fls orange; bracts lanceolate; sep. ovate, lateral sep. spreading; pet. linear, fringed at apex; lip to 25mm, oblong, fimbriate, spur 25–35mm. Mid summer–early autumn. Eastern N America..

P.grandiflora (Bigelow) Lindl.
Stem to 120cm, erect, glabrous. Lvs elliptic to lanceolate, basally sheathing stem. Spike to 25cm, 30–60-fld; sep. elliptic, lateral sep. spreading; pet. oblong, margins finely dentate; lip to 25mm, narrowing toward base, fimbriate, spur to 25mm, slender. Summer. Eastern N America.

P.integra (Nutt.) Gray.
Stem to 60cm, leafy, erect. Basal lvs lanceolate. Spike cylindric, dense; fls golden-yellow; dorsal sep. obovate, concave, lateral sep. orbicular, obtuse; lip oblong, rounded, finely denticulate, spur to 6mm, slender. Summer. C and eastern N America.

P.japonica (Thunb.) Lindl.
To 60cm. Basal lvs oblong, sheathing stem. Fls golden to lime-green; sep. oblong-lanceolate, spreading, dorsal sep. smaller forming hood with pet.; lip ligulate, spur to 15mm downward-pointing. Summer. SW and eastern N America.

P.montana Rchb. f. See *P.chlorantha*.

P.nivea (Nutt.) Luer.
To 60cm. Lvs lanceolate, sheathing stem below, bract-like on stems. Spike cylindric; fls white; dorsal sep. ovate, lateral sep. oblong, falcate, upper edge obscurely lobed near base; pet. oblong, falcate, basally dilated; lip linear-elliptic, recurved from centre, spur 15mm, almost horizontal. Summer–early autumn. Southwest & N eastern America.

P.orbiculata (Pursh) Lindl.
To 60cm. Basal lvs 2, almost opposite, elliptic-oblong to orbicular, fleshy. Spike lax; fls green-white; sep. ovate to ovate-lanceolate, reflexed, dorsal sep. orbicular, erect; pet. ovate to ovate-lanceolate, reflexed; lip to 24mm, linear-oblong, pendent, slightly recurved, spur to 50mm, slender, cylindric. Summer–early autumn. Northern N America.

P.psycodes (L.) Lindl.
To 90cm. Lvs elliptic to lanceolate, sheathing base of stem, reduced toward apex. Spike 8–12cm; fls purple; bracts lanceolate, sometimes edged purple; dorsal sep. elliptic, concave, lateral sep. elliptic-ovate, spreading; pet. obovate, denticulate; lip 3-lobed, fimbriate, spur 12–18mm slender. Eastern N America.

Platystele Schltr. (From Gk *platys*, broad, and *stele*, column, referring to the short, broad column characteristic of the genus.) Some 12 species of small epiphytes, closely allied to *Pleurothallis*. Rhizome short; secondary stems small, tufted, apically unifoliate. Leaves conduplicate at base forming a conspicuous petiole. Inflorescence a raceme or a fascicle, terminal or lateral, slender, short or elongate, usually many-flowered; flowers small, opening in succession, pedicellate; sepals similar, subequal, somewhat spreading, lateral sepals shortly connate; petals subsimilar to sepals; lip minute, fleshy, simple, ovate to suborbicular, disc with an inconspicuous or prominent callus; column short, broad, apex dilated, anther terminal, operculate, incumbent, unilocular, pollinia 2, waxy, obpyriform. C & S America.

CULTIVATION   As for *Pleurothallis*.

P.compacta (Ames) Ames (*Stelis compacta* Ames; *Pleurothallis compacta* (Ames) Ames & Schweinf.).
Secondary stems inconspicuous, concealed by white scarious sheaths. Lvs to 55×35mm, linear-oblanceolate, obtuse, apex minutely tridentate, coriaceous. Infl. to 10cm, densely many-fld; fls minute, yellow-green, usually spotted purple; sep. to 3×1mm, elliptic-oblong, subacute or rounded, lateral sep. almost free, oblique; pet. to 3×1.5mm, obliquely oblong-elliptic to oblanceolate, rounded; lip to 1mm, ovate-cordate or ovate-suborbicular, acute or acuminate. Mexico, Guatemala, Honduras, Costa Rica, Panama.

P.johnstonii (Ames) Garay *(Pleurothallis johnstonii* Ames).
Secondary stems to 2mm. Lvs to 6×4mm, oblong-lanceolate to oblong-elliptic, rounded, apex minutely tridentate. Infl. to 22mm, 1- to few-fld, erect or arching; fls minute, cream-white; sep. narrowly lanceolate or ovate-lanceolate, attenuate-acuminate; lateral sep. smaller than dorsal sep., free; pet. similar to dorsal sep., oblique; lip to 1mm, ovate, acute, papillose; disc with an elevated, transverse callus, emarginate. Venezuela.

P.misera (Lindl.) Garay (*Pleurothallis misera* Lindl.; *Humboldtia misera* (Lindl.) Kuntze).
Secondary stems to 20mm. Lvs to 60×10mm, oblanceolate or oblong-spathulate, acute or subobtuse. Infl. to 17cm, filiform, few to many-fld; fls small, tan or green suffused purple; sep. to 3mm, ovate, acute; pet. to 3mm, ovate-lanceolate, acuminate; lip to 2mm, velvety, ovate-oblong or ovate-lanceolate, acute or acuminate; column minute, anth. white. Peru.

P.ornata Garay (*Pleurothallis ornata* (Garay) Foldats).
Secondary stems to 5mm. Lvs to 22×3mm, light green, ovate-spathulate or oblanceolate, rounded or obtuse, apex minutely tridentate. Infl. usually shorter than lvs, erect or ascending, densely many-fld; fls minute, purple; sep. to 1mm, ovate or ovate-elliptic, acute or obtuse; pet. oblong-oblanceolate, acute; lip dark purple, ovate, acute or acuminate, concave, finely glandular; column to 0.5mm, pale purple. Venezuela.

P.ovalifolia (Focke) Garay & Dunsterv. (*Stelis ovalifolia* Focke; *Pleurothallis ovalifolia* (Focke) Rchb. f.).
Secondary stems small or absent. Lvs to 8×4mm, elliptic to obovate, somewhat fleshy, acute or apiculate. Infl. to 15mm, erect or ascending, 1 to few-fld; fls minute, pale cream or pale yellow; sep. to 2×1mm, membranaceous, elliptic to ovate, acute or obtuse, shortly connate; pet. smaller than sep., oblong-oblanceolate, subacute; lip subequal to pet., ovate-triangular to ovate-lanceolate, acute or acuminate. W Indies, Trinidad, Venezuela, Surinam, Guyana, Brazil.

P.stenostachya (Rchb. f.) Garay (*Pleurothallis stenostachya* Rchb. f.; *Humboldtia stenostachya* (Rchb. f.) Kuntze).
Secondary stems to 3.5cm, enclosed within several tubular, white sheaths. Lvs to 35×5mm, suberect-spreading, coriaceous, obovate to linear-spathulate, obtuse. Infl. to 1.5cm, axillary, few to several-fld; fls minute; tepals yellow-green or yellow-brown, acute; sep. to 1.5×1mm, elliptic, acute; pet. similar; lip dark maroon edged white, fleshy, elliptic, densely papillose; column dark maroon, anth. white. Mexico to Panama, Venezuela, Colombia, Ecuador.

Plectorrhiza Dockr. (From Gk *plektos*, twisted, and *rhiza*, root.) 3 species of epiphytes. Roots tangled. Stems long, wiry. Leaves persistent, many, central veins prominent. Inflorescence a raceme; flowers small, fragrant; sepals and petals almost equal; lip attached to column base, trilobed, saccate, lateral lobes small, midlobe small, hollow or fleshy, spur horizontal or at right angles to column, pubescent projection near opening. Australia, Lord Howe Is.

CULTIVATION   Epiphytes for brightly lit positions in the intermediate house.

P.tridentata (Lind.) Dockr. TANGLE ORCHID.
To 30cm. Roots from internodes, tangled. Lvs to 10cm, 4–20, linear-oblong, falcate, acute. Racemes to 12cm, lax, 3–15-fld; fls fragrant, green, sometimes marked red-brown; dorsal sep. forms a hood; lip shorter than sep., trilobed, appendage hirsute, spur to 3cm, narrow, white with pale green basal blotch. Late summer–mid winter. E Australia.

Plectrelminthus Raf. (From Gk *plektron*, spur, and *helmins*, worm.) 1 species, an epiphyte. Roots stout, arising from base of stem. Stem short, leafy. Leaves numerous, 10–35×1.5–3.5cm, ligulate, unequally bilobed at apex, light yellow-green. Racemes arising from axils of lower leaves, pendent, to 60cm, rachis flexuous, 4–12-fld; flowers scented, fleshy, pale green, usually tinged with bronze, lip ivory-white, tipped green; ovary and pedicel twisted so that the lip lies parallel to the rachis: in a pendent inflorescence it therefore points upwards; sepals 3.5–5cm, lanceolate, acute, petals slightly shorter, lower edges of lateral sepals project backwards behind spur and are joined at base; lip 6cm including a basal claw 12–15mm long and an acuminate tip around 15mm long, the intermediate part fan-shaped, the edge undulate; basal claw with 2 projections meeting in middle and forming a V-shape; spur 17–25cm, cylindric, coiled; column large; anther-cap with beak-like projection. W Africa, from French Guinea to Zaire.

CULTIVATION   As for *Angraecum*.

P.caudatus (Lindl.) Summerh. (*Angraecum caudatum* Lindl.).

Pleione D. Don. (For Pleione, mother of the Pleiades.) INDIAN CROCUS. Some 16 species of dwarf, deciduous epiphytes or terrestrials. Pseudobulbs clustered, usually only 2 seasons' growth persisting, ovoid to conic, globose, ellipsoid or pyriform. Leaves emerging rolled, among bracts, thin-textured, erect to arched, plicate, petioles short. Inflorescence solitary, terminal in emerging growth, bracteate; flowers 1–2, slender-stalked, occasionally fragrant, white, pink to magenta, rarely yellow; sepals and petals free, spreading, lanceolate; lip marked brown, yellow or red, rolled-tubular, entire to obscurely trilobed, sometimes fused to column base, apical margins irregularly toothed, laciniate or fimbriate, callus forming few or many hirsute lines or lamellae on upper surface. India to Taiwan, Thailand.

CULTIVATION   These small and beautiful orchids will thrive in the alpine and cold greenhouse. *P.formosana* has been grown successfully outdoors in Zone 7, in pockets of perfectly drained peaty soil on the rockery and given minimal winter protection. They require annual repotting at the end of a cool dry rest, preferably several pseudobulbs to a pan in a fairly dense bark-based medium rich in leafmould. Commence watering to promote flower, then leaf development. Following flowering in spring, keep moist and well fed in bright airy conditions to ensure full leaf and pseudobulb formation. As the leaves wither, reduce water and temperatures.

P.aurita Cribb & Pfennig.
Pseudobulbs conical, to 4.5cm. Lf solitary. Infl. erect, to 16cm; fl. solitary, pale pink to rose or purple, paler at base; bract pale pink, venation darker; dorsal sep. elliptic to oblong-elliptic to 4cm, concave, incurved, lateral sep. elliptic, to 4.5cm; pet. ligulate or spathulate, rounded or obtuse, to 4.5cm, sharply reflexed, like a hare's ears; lip to 4cm, obscurely trilobed at apex, undulate, margins irregularly toothed, callus 5-ridged, orange-yellow, pubesc. China (Yunnan).

P.bulbocodioides (Franch.) Rolfe (*P.pogonioides* (Rolfe) Rolfe).
Pseudobulbs pyramidal or conical, to 3cm. Lf solitary, elliptic-lanceolate, narrow, to 14cm+, acute. Infl. erect, to 20cm; fl. solitary, pink to rose-purple or magenta, lip marked dark purple; dorsal sep. oblanceolate to 4.5cm, lateral sep. narrow, elliptic, to 4.4cm; pet. oblanceolate, to 5cm; lip obovate, obscurely trilobed, to 4.5cm, apical margins irregular, notched, callus lamellae 4–5, irregularly toothed. China.

P.formosana Hay. (*P.pricei* Rolfe).
Pseudobulbs globose to ovoid, often slightly flattened, to 3cm, green to dull dark purple. Lf solitary, elliptic to oblanceolate, to 25×5cm. Infl. to 25cm; fls 1–2, white, lilac or magenta, lip white, typically stained or marked yellow; dorsal sep. elliptic-oblanceolate, narrow, to 6cm, acute, lateral sep. elliptic, narrow, oblique, subacute; pet. linear to oblanceolate; lip entire or trilobed, tip notched, apical margin undulate, fimbriate, lamellae 2–5, entire or jagged. E China, Taiwan.

P.forrestii Schltr.
Pseudobulbs narrow-ovoid or conical, to 3×1.5cm, dark green flushed purple at base, old pseudobulbs with a collar-like lf base at the apex. Lf solitary, elliptic-lanceolate, to 15×4cm. Infl. precedes lf; fl. solitary, pale golden yellow or white, lip spotted brown or crimson; sep. oblanceolate, lateral sep. oblique, to 40×10mm; pet. oblanceolate, falcate; lip elliptic-obovate, fimbriate, apex notched, lamellae 5–7, entire. China, N Burma.

P.hookeriana (Lindl.) Williams.
Pseudobulbs ovoid or conical, to 3×1.5cm, purple or green,

Pleione (a) *P.maculata* (b) *P.formosana* (c) *P.yunnanensis*

often in clusters and stoloniferous. Lf solitary, elliptic-lanceolate to oblanceolate, to 20×4.5cm; petiole to 4cm. Infl. to 15cm, appearing with the lf; fl. solitary; sep. and pet. lilac-pink to rose, sometimes dotted pale violet, rarely white, lip white, dotted yellow-brown or purple, lamellae and disc yellow, dorsal sep. oblanceolate or oblong-lanceolate, lateral sep. lanceolate, falcate, pet. oblanceolate, spreading; lip cordate, obscurely trilobed, apex notched, margin fringed, callus lamellae 7, barbed. C Nepal to S China.

P.humilis (Sm.) D. Don.
Pseudobulbs olive green, pyriform, to 6×2cm. Lf solitary, oblanceolate, to elliptic, to 2.5×3.5cm, acute. Infl. emerging before lf; fls 1–2, nodding or spreading, white, lip spotted and streaked bronze or blood red, central zone pale yellow; dorsal sep. linear-oblanceolate, almost acute, to 5cm, lateral sep. oblanceolate, oblique, to 5.5×9cm; pet. linear to oblanceolate, oblique, almost acute; lip oblong-elliptic, base saccate, apex notched, obscurely trilobed, apical margins jagged, lamellae 5–7, barbed, lateral lobes incurved, erect. Burma, NE India.

P.× lagenaria Lindl. (P.maculata × P.praecox.)
Pseudobulbs squat-ellipsoid, to 25×25mm. Lvs 1–2, oblanceolate, acute, to 32×5cm. Fls. 1–2 per pseudobulb, almost erect, spreading; pet. and sep. pink to rose-purple, lip white, central patch yellow, margins blotched purple, sep. linear-lanceolate, to 5×1cm, acute, pet. linear, acute; lip obscurely trilobed, to 4×3cm, midlobe almost rectangular, toothed, lateral lobes erect, callus of 5 longitudinal, papillose lines along centre, extending to apex. Asia, SW China.

P.limprichtii Schltr.
Pseudobulbs conical to ovoid, pale to deep green or purple, to 4×2.5cm. Lf solitary, lanceolate, appearing after fls, to 1.5×0.5cm. Fls 1–2, rose-pink to magenta, lip paler, spotted ochre or crimson, lamellae white; dorsal sep. elliptic, to 3.5×1cm, lateral sep. narrow-elliptic, acute; pet. oblanceolate, falcate, acute; lip almost orbicular, apex obscurely trilobed, to 4×3.5cm, apical margins deeply and irregularly laciniate, callus lamellae 4, minutely toothed or jagged. SW China, N Burma.

P.maculata (Lindl.) Lindl.
Pseudobulbs turbinate, beaked, covered in the netted, fibrous remnants of sheaths. Lvs 2, elliptic-lanceolate to oblanceolate, acute, to 25×3.5cm. Fls erect, fragrant, cream, rarely streaked pink, lip white, central blotch yellow, apical margins blotched purple, lamellae white; dorsal sep. oblong-lanceolate, lateral sep. lanceolate, falcate, to 4×1cm; lip oblong, obscurely trilobed, midlobe notched, margin undulate, jagged, callus extending to apex, comprising 5–7 papillose lines. India, Bhutan, Burma, SW China, Thailand.

P.pogonioides (Rolfe) Rolfe. See P.bulbocodioides.

P.praecox (Sm.) D. Don.
Pseudobulbs turbinate, beaked, green, dappled or spotted red-brown or purple. Lvs usually 2, elliptic-lanceolate, acuminate, to 2.5×1cm; petiole to 6cm. Infl. appearing at lf fall, to 13cm; fls. 1–2, white to rose-purple, lamellae yellow; sep. oblong-lanceolate, 7×1cm; pet. linear-lanceolate, falcate, to 7cm; lip midlobe cleft, toothed or deeply and irregularly fringed, callus forming 3–5 papillose lines. Indochina, Burma.

P.pricei Rolfe. See P.formosana.

P.speciosa Ames & Schltr.
Pseudobulbs ovoid to conical, to 3×1.5cm. Lf elliptic-lanceolate, to 15cm+, partially developed at flowering. Infl. to 22cm; fls 1–2, bright magenta, lip blotched peach, lamellae yellow; dorsal sep. elliptic, narrow, acute, lateral sep. narrow, elliptic, oblique, to 7cm; pet. oblanceolate, falcate; lip almost rhombic to obovate, appearing whole and truncate, apical margins minutely toothed, callus comprising 2–4 minutely toothed keels. China.

P.yunnanensis (Rolfe) Rolfe.
Pseudobulbs squat, conical, to 2×1.5cm. Lf lanceolate to elliptic, narrow-acuminate; petiole to 5.5cm. Infl. erect, appearing before lvs; fls 1–2, pale lavender to rose pink, rarely white; lip flecked red or purple; dorsal sep. oblong-oblanceolate, obtuse, to 4×1cm; pet. oblanceolate, obtuse; lip obscurely trilobed, midlobe subrectangular, undulate, lacerate, callus 5-ridged, entire, lateral lobes erect or incurved. N Burma, China.

P.grexes and cultivars.
P.Alishan: pseudobulbs large and dark; fls 2 per stem, pale to dark pink with variable lip markings; 'Sparrowhawk', 'Goldfinch' and 'Merlin' are the best clones.

P.Barcema: pseudobulbs flattened and wrinkled, green; fls January (cross between autumn- and spring-flowering species), mid-lavender-pink with frilled lip.

P.Brigadoon: large purple-hued pseudobulbs: fls 2 per stem, pale mauve shading to violet, lip marked with red and yellow. 'Stonechat' and 'Woodcock' are good cvs.

P.Eiger: pseudobulbs large, green; fls 2 per stem in January and February, mostly white shaded with pink.

P.El Pico: pseudobulbs rather flat, dark green; fls late, pale mauve pink to dark rosy purple. 'Goldcrest', 'Kestrel' and 'Pheasant' are the best clones.

P.Erebus: pseudobulbs variable from squat to pyriform; fls pale violet purple, lip white spotted with dark red and with yellow lamellae. 'Redshank' and 'Willow Warbler' are good clones.

P.Fuego: pseudobulbs small, dark green; flowers prolifically, rather variable.

P.Hekla: pseudobulbs tall, pyriform, dark green to purple; fls elegant, petunia purple with a frilled lip. 'Partridge' is a particularly fine dark clone.

P.Irazu: pseudobulbs rather small, dark green: fls mallow purple or strawberry purple with a white lip. 'Mallard' is a particularly dark form.

P.Shantung: pseudobulbs very large, green to dark purple; fls deep yellow or white flushed with pink. The best-known and most vigorous clone is 'Muriel Harberd' and is the largest apricot-coloured cv.; 'Fieldfare' has large pale yellow fls.

P.Stromboli: pseudobulbs large, rather flat, dark green to purple-black; fls on tall stems, mostly dark red-pink. 'Fireball' is one of the most intensely coloured of all Pleione cultivars.

P.Tongariro: pseudobulbs green; fls 2 per stem, long-lasting, various shades of imperial purple, the lip marked with red and yellow. 'Jackdaw' has the darkest fls.

P.Versailles: the first hybrid Pleione raised; fls 2 per stem, very pale mauve-pink to deep rose pink. The clone 'Bucklebury' is particularly fine and very floriferous.

Pleurothallis R. Br. (From Gk *pleuron*, rib, and *thallos*, stem, referring to the rib-like stems of many species.) More than 1000 species of epiphytes or lithophytes allied to *Restrepia*, *Stelis* and *Masdevallia*. Rhizome short or protracted, creeping. Secondary stems not pseudobulbous, small to elongate, usually tufted, erect, thinly sheathed, usually unifoliate. Leaves terminal, coriaceous to fleshy, often flushed purple-red with age, sessile or petiolate, erect to spreading, often basally sulcate or conduplicate, linear-lanceolate to ovate, sagittate or spathulate. Inflorescence a raceme, terminal or, rarely, lateral, 1- to many-flowered, short to elongate; flowers small, sometimes secund, subtended by inconspicuous bracts; sepals subequal, erect or spreading, dorsal sepal free or briefly connate with lateral sepals, lateral sepals slightly to entirely connate, concave or gibbous at base; petals smaller than sepals, sometimes clavate at apex; lip usually shorter than petals, entire or 3-lobed, usually unguiculate; column shorter than or equal to lip, often alate, footless or with short foot, anther terminal, operculate, incumbent, 1- or 2-celled, pollinia 2, waxy, ovoid or pyriform, lacking a stipe. Tropical America. Many of the larger species described here will be considerably smaller in cultivation.

CULTIVATION Small tufted plants suited to growing cases or buoyant, shady conditions in the cool to intermediate house. Pot tightly in pans containing a fine-grade bark-based orchid mix. Keep moist at all times and syringe during warm weather. Propagate by division.

P.acrisepala Ames & Schweinf. See *P.brighamii*.

P.amethystina Ames. See *P.segoviensis*.

P.angustisegmenta Schweinf. See *Barbosella cucullata*.

P.araguensis Ames. See *P.secunda*.

P.astrophora Rchb. f. ex Kränzl. See *Lepanthopsis astrophora*.

P.atropurpurea (Lindl.) Lindl. See *Zootrophion atropurpureum*.

P.barbarselloides Schltr. See *P.brighamii*.

P.brighamii S. Wats. (*P.barboselloides* Schltr.; *P.periodica* Ames; *P.acrisepala* Ames & Schweinf.).
Secondary stems to 6mm. Lvs to 9×1cm, oblanceolate to elliptic-oblong, obtuse or acute, coriaceous, bright lustrous green. Infl. to 10cm, 1- to several-fld, filiform; fls yellow striped red-brown or with green and brown markings; dorsal sep. to 3×3mm, elliptic to oblong-lanceolate, acute to acuminate, lateral sep. connate to middle or more, oblong to ovate-oblong, obtuse; pet. to 4×2mm, obovate or spathulate, acute or acuminate; lip to 4×2mm, oblong-ligulate, obtuse, ciliate, with an auriculate lateral lobe at each side near base, disc with 2 intramarginal keels, base fleshy. Guatemala and British Honduras to Panama.

P.calerae Schltr. See *P.immersa*.

P.cardiostola Rchb. f.
Secondary stems to 20cm. Lvs to 14×4cm, fleshy-coriaceous, lanceolate to narrowly ovate, acuminate, light green; petiole to 18cm, terete. Fls usually solitary, successive, brown or pale green-brown, to 3cm diam., interior downy; pedicel to 1cm; dorsal sep. to 1.5×1cm, broadly ovate, obtuse or acute, 7-nerved, lateral sep. fused, fleshy, broadly ovate or cordate; pet. to 9×3mm, fleshy, lanceolate to oblanceolate; lip to 3×4mm, fleshy, ovate to subrhombic, light green-yellow, with central depression; column fleshy, white, to 2mm. Venezuela, Colombia, Ecuador.

P.cerea Ames. See *P.octomerioides*.

P.ciliaris (Lindl.) L.O. Williams. See *Trichosalpinx ciliaris*.

P.ciliata Knowles & Westc. See *P.lanceana*.

P.compacta (Ames) Ames & Schweinf. See *Platystele compacta*.

P.dura Lindl. See *Trichosalpinx dura*.

P.endotrachys Rchb. f. (*P.platyrachis* (Rolfe) Rolfe; *P.pfavii* Rchb. f.; *Kraenzlinella platyrachis* (Rolfe) Rolfe).
Secondary stems to 2cm, stout. Lvs to 20×3cm, oblanceolate-ligulate, acute to obtuse, fleshy, apex minutely tridentate, petiolate. Infl. to 35cm, erect, few- to many-fld; fls fleshy, opening in succession; sep. bright red or orange-red, white toward base, spreading, inner surfaces verrucose except at bases, dorsal sep. to 20×6mm, ovate-lanceolate, subacute, cucullate, lateral sep. to 20×4mm, connate below middle, lanceolate, acute; pet. bright red, to 5×1mm, ligulate, rounded, verruculose; lip to 6×2mm, fleshy, curved, callused at margins; column dilated, alate, foot short. Mexico to Panama, Colombia, Venezuela.

P.floripectin Rchb. f. See *Lepanthopsis floripectin*.

P.fulgens Rchb. f.
Secondary stems minute. Lvs to 8.5×2cm, elliptic to obovate-spathulate, attenuate. Infl. a few-fld fascicle; peduncle subequal to lvs; fls bright cinnabar-red; dorsal sep. to 9×4mm, ovate-lanceolate, acuminate, lateral sep. to 12×3mm, connate to middle, gibbous at base; pet. to 4×2mm, lanceolate, acute; lip to 5×3mm, elliptic, obtuse, lateral lobes small, erect, with 2 calli near middle. Costa Rica, Panama.

P.gelida Lindl.
Secondary stems to 35cm, unifoliate; sheaths to 8cm, brown. Lvs to 25×7cm, ovate-elliptic to oblong-elliptic, subacute to obtuse, coriaceous. Infl. 1- to several-fld, to 30cm, erect; fls secund, pale yellow to green-yellow, downy above; dorsal sep. to 8×3mm, oblong-lanceolate to oblong-elliptic, strongly concave, lateral sep. connate almost to middle, to 7×3mm, narrowly oblong to elliptic; pet. to 4×2mm, oblong to spathulate, obtuse or truncate, often emarginate; lip to 3×1mm, oblong-cuneate, rounded or truncate, with 2 lamellate calli near middle; column to 2mm. Florida, Mexico to Panama, W Indies, S America.

P.ghiesbreghtiana Rich. & Gal. See *P.quadrifida*.

P.glomerata Ames. See *P.ruscifolia*.

P.grobyi Batem. ex Lindl. (*P.picta* Lindl.; *P.marginata* Lindl.).
Secondary stems to 1cm. Lvs to 7×1cm, obovate, spathulate or oblanceolate, purple-green below, coriaceous, short-petiolate. Infl. to 15cm, loosely few- to several-fld; fls small, membranous, green, white or yellow-orange, marked red-purple; dorsal sep. to 10×3mm, ovate to ovate-lanceolate, acute to acuminate, concave, lateral sep. connate, forming a bidentate lamina to 12×3mm; pet. to 3×1mm, obliquely obovate to lanceolate, acute or obtuse; lip to 3×1mm, oblong, rounded or obtuse, canaliculate; column to 3mm, clavate, alate, apex tridentate. Mexico and W Indies to Peru and Brazil.

P.immersa Lind. & Rchb. f. (*P.krameriana* Rchb. f.; *P.lasiosepala* Schltr.; *P.calerae* Schltr.).
Secondary stems to 7cm, stout, enveloped by 2 brown tubular sheaths. Lvs to 19×4cm, coriaceous, oblong-oblanceolate, lustrous bright green, apex obtuse and retuse. Infl. to 40cm, erect, loosely many-fld; peduncle slightly compressed; fls usually pendent, yellow-green or purple-brown with dark venation; dorsal sep. to 14×4mm, elliptic-lanceolate, acute, dorsally keeled below middle, densely pubesc. above, lateral sep. connate almost to apex, to 13×7mm, elliptic-oblong; pet. to 4×3mm, obovate-spathulate; lip to 5×2mm, triangular-hastate, arcuate-decurved, disc 3-nerved, with an intramarginal linear callus on each side; column to 4mm with short foot, slender, arcuate, apex trilobed, wings irregularly dentate. Mexico, Guatemala, Honduras, Costa Rica, Venezuela, Colombia, Panama.

P.intermedia Schltr. See *P.loranthophylla*.

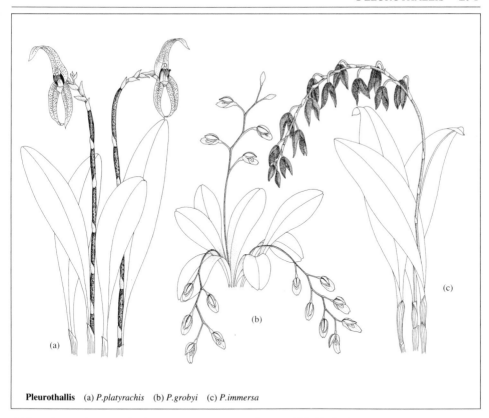

Pleurothallis   (a) *P.platyrachis*   (b) *P.grobyi*   (c) *P.immersa*

P.johnstonii Ames. See *Platystele johnstonii*.
P.krameriana Rchb. f. See *P.immersa*.

P.lanceana Lodd. (*P.ciliata* Knowles & Westc.; *P.plumosa* Lindl.).
Stems short, unifoliate. Lvs to 9×3cm, erect to pendent, elliptic-oblong, obtuse, fleshy. Infl. 1–3, produced in succession, exceeding lvs, many-fld; fls small; dorsal sep. yellow flecked purple-crimson, to 10×2mm, linear, acute, apex swollen, lateral sep. yellow, connate almost to apex, to 10×5mm, linear-lanceolate, acute, concave, pubesc.; pet. golden-yellow tinged pink, to 3mm, ovate, lacerate, acuminate; lip yellow-brown spotted maroon, to 3×2mm, fleshy, elliptic, rounded, papillose; column to 2mm, dark maroon, apex yellow, arcuate, alate. Guatemala, Costa Rica, Trinidad, tropical S America.

P.lasiosepala Schltr. See *P.immersa*.
P.lindenii Lindl. See *P.secunda*.
P.longissima Lindl. See *P.quadrifida*.

P.loranthophylla Rchb. f. (*Rhynchopera punctata* Karst.; *P.punctata* (Karst.) Schltr.; *P.intermedia* Schltr.).
Stems to 10cm, erect. Lvs to 10×3.5cm, suberect, coriaceous, elliptic-oblong, apex tridentate, lustrous bright green; petiole to 7cm, terete, glabrous. Infl. 1 to few racemes, loosely several-fld; fls light brown tinged maroon, variously spotted maroon; dorsal sep. to 11×2mm, lanceolate, acute, lateral sep. entirely connate, to 10×4mm, slightly bifid; pet. to 8×2mm, lanceolate, apex attenuate; lip to 6×3mm, ovate, acute; column short, pale brown-green, terete, curved. Venezuela, Colombia, Ecuador, Peru, Bolivia.

P.marginata Lindl. See *P.grobyi*.
P.mathewsii Lindl. See *P.phalangifera*.
P.megachlamys Schltr. See *P.tuerckheimii*.
P.miersii Lindl. See *Barbrodria miersii*.
P.misera Lindl. See *Platystele misera*.
P.octomeriae Schltr. See *P.octomerioides*.

P.octomerioides Lindl. (*P.octomeriae* Schltr.; *P.cerea* Ames).
Secondary stems to 15cm, borne at frequent intervals on creeping rhiz. Lvs to 12×2cm, narrowly elliptic to oblong-lanceolate. Fls borne in clusters, fleshy, small; sep. pale yellow, to 7×2mm, spreading, narrowly obovate, obtuse, lateral sep. shortly connate, slightly oblique; pet. pale yellow, slightly smaller than sep., narrowly elliptic-oblong, acute or subacute; lip to 3×1mm, fleshy, oblong, papillose; column to 2mm, alate, apex dentate, with minute foot; anth. red or yellow. Mexico to Panama.

P.ophiocephala Lindl. See *Restrepiella ophiocephala*.
P.ornata (Garay) Foldats. See *Platystele ornata*.
P.ospinae R.E. Schult. See *Restrepia antennifera*.
P.ovalifolia (Focke) Rchb. f. See *Platystele ovalifolia*.
P.pauciflora Schltr. See *P.pruinosa*.
P.periodica Ames. See *P.brighamii*.
P.pfavii Rchb. f. See *P.endotrachys*.

P.phalangifera (Presl) Rchb. f. (*P.mathewsii* Lindl.).
Secondary stems to 34cm. Lvs to 17×8cm, erect, sessile, ovate to ovate-elliptic. Infl. 1 to 30cm, loosely few- to many-fld; fls large, spreading, yellow-green to purple; dorsal sep. to 40×7mm, base lanceolate, long-attenuate above, lateral sep. connate to apex, lanceolate, long-acuminate; pet. to 35×3mm, linear-lanceolate, caudate, erose; lip to 5×3mm, deflexed in middle, 3-lobed, lateral lobes erect, orbicular, midlobe oblong, apiculate; column to 4mm, dilated above, foot short. Venezuela and Colombia to Peru.

P.picta Lindl. See *P.grobyi*.
P.pittieri Schltr. See *P.velaticaulis*.
P.platyrachis (Rolfe) Rolfe. See *P.endotrachys*.
P.plumosa Lindl. See *P.lanceana*.

P.prolifera Herb. ex Lindl.
Secondary stems to 20cm. Lvs to 8×4cm, fleshy-coriaceous, ovate to ovate-lanceolate. Infl. shorter than lvs, few- to many-

fld; fls small, deep purple or red-brown; sep. to 9×3mm, oblong or oblong-lanceolate to triangular-lanceolate, acute, 3-nerved, lateral sep. connate in basal half; pet. to 5×1mm, oblanceolate to spathulate, acuminate to acute, pale purple, dentate; lip to 5×2.5mm, elliptic to ovate, obtuse or rounded, base fimbriate, apex denticulate, papillose within; column to 3mm, papillose. Venezuela, Brazil.

P.pruinosa Lindl. (*P.pauciflora* Schltr.).
Secondary stems to 8cm. Lvs to 5×1cm, coriaceous or subcoriaceous, elliptic-oblong or lanceolate. Infl. 1–3, few-fld, usually exceeding lvs; fls pale yellow or white-green; dorsal sep. to 4×2mm, lanceolate to ovate-lanceolate, concave, 1–3-nerved, lateral sep. entirely connate, to 4×3mm, ovate to suborbicular, concave, 2- or 4-nerved; pet. minute, slender, 1-nerved; lip to 2×1mm, fleshy, triangular-lanceolate to ovate, acute or acuminate, disc obscurely 3-keeled; column to 1mm, stout. Honduras, Costa Rica, Panama, Venezuela, Colombia, Ecuador, Peru, Guianas, W Indies.

P.puberula Klotzsch. See *Restrepiella ophiocephala*.
P.punctata (Karst.) Schltr. See *P.loranthophylla*.

P.quadrifida (La Ll. & Lex.) Lindl. (*P.longissima* Lindl.; *P.ghiesbreghtiana* Rich. & Gal.).
Secondary stems to 17cm, usually shorter. Lvs to 16×3cm, oblanceolate to elliptic-oblong, obtuse, glossy grey-green. Infl. to 40cm, many-fld; fls fragrant, pendent, yellow or pale yellow-green; dorsal sep. to 10×4mm, ovate-oblong to elliptic-lanceolate, subacute, concave, lateral sep. almost entirely connate, elliptic-oblong to ovate, cucullate, subacute; pet. to 10×4mm, short-clawed, narrow-ovate to elliptic-lanceolate; lip to 6×3mm, basal portion fleshy, orbicular, crenulate, apical portion ovate; column to 4mm, slender, apex dentate. Mexico to Panama, W Indies, Venezuela, Colombia.

P.ruscifolia (Jacq.) R. Br. (*P.glomerata* Ames).
Secondary stems to 40cm, slender, rigid. Lvs to 20×6cm, elliptic-oblong to lanceolate, coriaceous, short-stalked. Fls clustered, slightly fragrant, to 2cm, pale green to pale yellow; dorsal sep. to 10×3mm, ovate-lanceolate, concave near base, lateral sep. connate to apex, to 10×3mm, lanceolate; pet. to 8×1mm, slender; lip to 2×1.5mm, fleshy, ovate to subquadrate, acute, disc 3-nerved; column to 2mm, with a prominent foot. W Indies, Guatemala, Costa Rica, Panama, northern S America.

P.secunda Poepp. & Endl. (*P.lindenii* Lindl.; *P.araguensis* Ames).
Secondary stems to 40cm. Lvs to 30×6cm, erect, elliptic or oblong, sessile or shortly petiolate, bright green above, glaucous green below. Infl. to 20cm, pendent, few-fld; sep. translucent yellow-green, dorsal sep. to 15×6mm, ovate-oblong to lanceolate, lateral sep. entirely connate, to 15×12mm, suborbicular-ovate, acuminate, concave, striped purple; pet. red or yellow, to 15×3mm, lanceolate or elliptic, acuminate, porrect; lip yellow, minute, suborbicular-ovate; column white-yellow, minute. Venezuela, Colombia, Ecuador, Peru.

P.segoviensis Rchb. f. (*P.amethystina* Ames).
Secondary stems densely caespitose, to 6cm. Lvs to 13×1.5cm, oblanceolate to ligulate, retuse. Infl. to 17cm, few- to several-fld, slender-stalked; fls variable in colour, yellow-green blotched brown to dark red-purple; dorsal sep. shortly connate with lateral sep., to 11×4mm, lanceolate to oblong-lanceolate, acute or acuminate, interior pilose to glabrous,

margins slightly revolute, lateral sep. connate almost to apex, narrowly elliptic, apex bidentate, interior pilose to glabrous; pet. to 4×2mm, obliquely oblong, glabrous; lip to 4×2mm, lateral lobes basal, erect, oblong to lanceolate-falcate, midlobe oblong, obtuse or rounded, disc 2-ridged; column to 3mm, curved, foot short. Mexico to Panama.

P.sertularioides (Sw.) Spreng.
Rhiz. slender, creeping. Secondary stems to 5mm. Lvs to 40×4mm, linear-oblanceolate to linear-spathulate, obtuse. Infl. filiform, usually shorter than lvs, 1- or 2-fld; fls straw-yellow; sep. to 5×1mm, lanceolate, acute or acuminate, lateral sep. shortly connate, slightly gibbous; pet. to 4×1mm, linear-lanceolate, acuminate, 1-nerved; lip to 3×1mm, fleshy, sessile, linear-lanceolate, obtuse, minutely auricled; column to 2mm, with short foot, apex slightly trilobulate. Mexico, Guatemala, Honduras, Nicaragua.

P.stenopetala Lodd. ex Lindl.
Secondary stems to 14cm. Lvs to 10×3cm, elliptic-oblong or oblanceolate, obtuse; petiole to 2cm. Infl. to 27cm, many-fld; fls yellow-white or green-white; sep. to 2cm, narrow-lanceolate or linear, acute, interior pubesc., lateral sep. free, oblique at base; pet. to 6mm, obliquely oblong, rounded, apiculate, with a fleshy mid-nerve; lip to 6mm, ovate to rhombic, recurved, base cuneate, anterior portion papillose; column to 5mm, clavate, alate, wing triangular, concave. Brazil.

P.stenostachya Rchb. f. See *Platystele stenostachya*.
P.stigmatoglossa Rchb.f. See *Restrepiella stigmatoglossa*.

P.tribuloides (Sw.) Lindl.
Secondary stems to 1cm. Lvs to 7×1.5cm, obovate to oblanceolate, retuse, subcoriaceous. Infl. a fascicle of 1–3 fls; peduncle to 1cm; fls minute, to 8mm, brick-red or dark maroon; sep. to 8×4mm, papillose, dorsal sep. oblong-lanceolate or oblanceolate, acute, concave below middle, lateral sep. often entirely connate, oblong or oblong-lanceolate, acute, cucullate; pet. to 3×1mm, obliquely oblong-oblanceolate, acute, fleshy; lip to 3×2mm, linear or oblong-lanceolate, bidentate below middle, ciliate, disc fleshy; column to 3mm, alate above. C America, W Indies.

P.tuerckheimii Schltr. (*P.megachlamys* Schltr.).
Secondary stems to 35cm. Lvs to 25×7cm, elliptic to oval or lanceolate, obtuse, coriaceous. Infl. to 35cm, erect, solitary, loosely many-fld; fls large, purple-maroon and white or cream, papillose-puberulent; dorsal sep. to 25×6mm, lanceolate, acuminate, cucullate, lateral sep. connate almost to apex, to 25×9mm, elliptic to oblong-lanceolate; pet. white, to 8×4mm, ovate to oblong-obovate, apex rounded and cucullate; lip to 10×3mm, linear-lanceolate, reflexed, base auriculate, callus 2-keeled, papillose; column to 4mm, apex 4-toothed. Mexico to Panama.

P.velaticaulis Rchb. f. (*P.pittieri* Schltr.).
Secondary stems to 30cm. Lvs to 22×9cm, oblanceolate-ligulate, petiolate. Racemes shorter than lvs, many-fld; fls fragrant, pale green or yellow-green; dorsal sep. to 6×2mm, ovate or oblong-lanceolate, subacute, 3-nerved, lateral sep. to 5×2mm, almost free, lanceolate, acute, 3-nerved; pet. to 3mm, oblong to oblong-lanceolate, obtuse, 1-nerved; lip to 2mm, ovate-oblong, obtuse, 3-lobed, lateral lobes fleshy, auriculate; column to 1mm. Costa Rica, Panama, W Indies, Venezuela to Peru.

P.verrucosa (Rchb. f.) Rchb. f. See *Scaphosepalum verrucosum*.

Podangis Schltr. (From Gk *pous*, foot, and *angos*, vessel.) 1 species, an epiphyte. Stem 2–3cm, rarely to 11cm, 3–4-leaved at apex. Leaves 4–16cm×5–12mm, fleshy, bilaterally flattened. Inflorescence a raceme, shorter than leaves, densely-flowered, subcapitate; flowers glistening, translucent white; anthers green; pedicel and ovary 8–12mm; sepals and petals free, 3.5–5mm, broadly elliptic, obtuse; lip 6mm, more or less orbicular, entire, crenulate; spur 11–14mm, wide-mouthed, constricted in middle, swollen and often bifid at apex; column stout, 1.5mm; pollinia and stipites 2. Tropical Africa.

CULTIVATION   As for *Angraecum*.

P.dactyloceras (Rchb. f.) Schltr.

Pogonia Juss. (From Gk *pogon*, beard, referring to the bearded or fringed crest of the lip typical of the genus.) 3 species of herbaceous terrestrials. Roots fibrous, slender. Tubers globose, usually producing a single leaf. Inflorescence 1 to 3-flowered; flowers terminal; sepals subequal, free or slightly ringent, usually erect; petals similar to sepals, held over lip, shorter and wider than sepals; lip sessile or clawed, erect, simple or 3-lobed, inrolled round column, smooth or lammellate, bearded or fringed; column free, elongate, subterete, wingless, footless, clinandrium denticulate, anther terminal, operculate, incumbent, pollinia 2, granular. Widely distributed, mostly temperate Asia and N America.

CULTIVATION   Hardy orchids suitable for bog gardens, streamsides and damp acid pockets in the rock garden. See Introduction: Hardy Orchids.

P.divaricata (L.) R. Br. See *Cleistes divaricata*.

P.ophioglossoides (L.) Juss. (*Arethusa ophioglossoides* L.). Roots fleshy, pubesc. Stems to 40cm, slender, terete, green or brown-green. Lvs to 12×3cm, ovate to elliptic or ovate-lanceolate, obtuse to subacute. Fls rose to white, fragrant; dorsal sep. to 23×6mm, elliptic-oblong to linear-oblong, subobtuse, lateral sep. to 27×6mm, linear-oblong to linear-lanceolate, acute to obtuse; pet. to 25×11mm, obovate-elliptic to oblong-elliptic, rounded; lip to 25×10mm, narrowly oblong-spathulate, apex lacerate-dentate, disc bearded, with short, fleshy, yellow-white bristles; column to 10mm. US.

P.rosea (Lindl.) Rchb. f. See *Cleistes rosea*.

Polycycnis Rchb. f. (From Gk *polys*, many, and *kyknos*, swan, in allusion to the resemblance of the flowers to swans.) Some 14 species of epiphytes closely allied to *Cycnoches*. Rhizome short. Pseudobulbs short, ovoid to subcylindrical, bases enveloped by coriaceous, leafy sheathing bracts, 1–3-leaved at apex. Leaves large, plicate, conduplicate, petiolate. Inflorescence a basal raceme, erect to pendent, few- to many-flowered; flowers showy, pedicellate; sepals free, subequal, spreading or reflexed, carinate; petals subsimilar to sepals, sometimes with an elongate, stalked base; lip usually with a trilobed hypochile, adnate to column base, lateral lobes erect or spreading, apex usually pubesc., epichile inserted on the under-surface of hypochile, simple or obscurely 3-lobed, subcordate to obovate-lanceolate, acute or acuminate, disc often with a pubesc. callus; column elongate, terete, slender, arched, apex dilated, footless, sometimes winged, anther terminal, operculate, incumbent, unilocular, pollinia 2, waxy, cylindrical, with a prominent stipe. Panama and Costa Rica to Colombia, Guyana and Peru.

CULTIVATION   As for *Catasetum*.

P.barbata (Lindl.) Rchb. f. (*Cycnoches barbatum* Lindl.). Pseudobulbs to 4.5×2.5cm, clustered, ovoid, grooved. Lvs to 40×10cm, elliptic-lanceolate, acute or acuminate. Infl. to 32cm, usually pendent, loosely many-fld; fls thin-textured, short-lived, pale, clear yellow spotted red, the lip white spotted red or purple; pedicel elongate, pubesc.; sep. to 25×8mm, lanceolate, acuminate, concave; pet. to 24×3mm, narrowly oblanceolate; lip with hypochile to 9mm, lateral lobes auriculate, erect, epichile obscurely 3-lobed, ovate, acuminate, lateral lobes subauriculate, disc with a densely long-pubesc. callus; column to 22mm. Costa Rica, Panama, Colombia, Venezuela, Brazil.

P.muscifera (Lindl. & Paxt.) Rchb. f. (*Cycnoches muscifera* Lindl. & Paxt.). Pseudobulbs to 6cm, subcylindrical. Lvs to 37×12cm, elliptic, acute; petiole to 11cm. Infl. to 60cm, erect to arching; peduncle pubesc.; fls small, thin-textured, olive green to pale brown marked light maroon, the lip light brown-green spotted maroon; sep. to 20×5mm, oblong-lanceolate or linear-lanceolate, acute, slightly concave; pet. to 22×3mm, linear or linear-oblanceolate, slightly sigmoid, acute; lip to 20mm, hypochile with 2 basal, linear-falcate horns, lateral lobes erect, obliquely lanceolate, acuminate, epichile simple or obscurely 3-lobed, ovate-hastate, acute or acuminate, disc with a fleshy, subelliptic, long-pubesc. keel; column to 2cm, winged at apex. Panama, Venezuela, Colombia, Ecuador, Peru, Bolivia.

P.ornata Garay. Pseudobulbs with 2–3 lvs at apex, these not distinctly stalked. Infl. strongly pendulous; fls to 2.5cm diam.; tepals pale brick red to buff spotted red-brown; lip very narrow, brown-pink, Venezuela, Ecuador.

P.vittata (Lindl.) Rchb. f. (*Houlletia vittata* Lindl.). Pseudobulbs to 7cm, lustrous pale green-brown, ovoid-subconical to subcylindrical. Lvs to 54×15cm, elliptic to oblong-lanceolate, acute; petiole to 9cm. Infl. to 20cm, erect or suberect, loosely many-fld; fls to 5cm diam., spreading, white or cream, densely striped deep red-maroon or chocolate; sep. to 30×5mm, lanceolate to linear-lanceolate, acute to acuminate, concave; pet. to 25×5mm, obliquely lanceolate or elliptic-lanceolate, acuminate; lip to 18mm, fleshy, hypochile clawed, 3-lobed, with a small, linear, pubesc. horn at base, fleshy keel separating lateral lobes, lateral lobes small, porrect, ovate-oblong, obtuse, epichile rhombic or ovate-rhombic, acute or rounded, glabrous, disc with a longitudinal, sulcate callus; column to 1.5cm. Colombia, Venezuela, Guianas, Brazil, Peru.

Polystachya Hook. (From Gk *polys*, many, and *stachys*, spike.) About 150 species of epiphytes, occasionally lithophytes or terrestrials. Stems usually pseudobulbous at base, clustered on a woody rhizome, the pseudobulbs 1- to several-noded, bearing 1 to several leaves. Inflorescence terminal on pseudobulb, racemose, paniculate or more or less spicate, 1- to many-flowered. Flowers non-resupinate, usually not opening wide, often pubescent on outside, white, green, brown, yellow, orange, pink or purple, rarely red; lateral sepals oblique, forming mentum with column foot; lip entire or trilobed, with or without a callus, often fleshy and recurved; column short and stout with more or less elongated foot; pollinia 2, stipes 1. Africa, Madagascar, east to Philippines, Indonesia and New Guinea, S US, Caribbean, C & S America.

CULTIVATION   Epiphytes usually of compact habit and small stature, suitable for pans, baskets and rafts in brightly lit, humid, intermediate conditions. A brief dry rest should be imposed in winter.

P.adansoniae Rchb. f.
Epiphytic, occasionally lithophytic, 10–30cm. Pseudobulbs 2.5–9×1cm, oblong, conical or cylindrical, ribbed, green or yellow-green, 2–3-lvd at apex. Lvs to 20×1.5cm, linear or ligulate, slightly lobed at apex. Spike 5–12cm, densely many-fld; fls yellow-green or almost white, anth. and tip of lip purple or brown; bract 4–8mm, hair-like; median sep. 3.5×1.5mm, ovate, acuminate, lateral sep. 4–5.5×2.5–3mm, obliquely ovate, acuminate; mentum narrow, 7mm high; pet. 2×1mm, linear-oblong; lip to 4×3mm, trilobed in apical half, recurved, with fleshy, pubesc. callus between lobes, lateral lobes rounded, midlobe lanceolate, acuminate; column 1.5mm; ovary 3–5mm. Widespread, Tropical Africa.

P.affinis Lindl. (*P.bracteosa* Lindl.).
Epiphytic, erect or pendent, to 50cm. Pseudobulbs almost orbicular but dorso-ventrally flattened, 1–5cm wide, 2–3-lvd. Lvs 9–28×2.5–6cm, including 5–14cm petiole; lamina oblanceolate or oblong. Infl. racemose or paniculate, erect or pendent, to 40cm, laxly many-fld; peduncle covered with overlapping scarious sheaths; fls fragrant, white or yellow with red-brown markings, outside pubesc.; sep. 6.5–8×3–6mm, median sep. lanceolate, lateral sep. obliquely triangular-ovate, forming mentum 4.5–6mm high; pet. 5.5–6.5×1.5–2mm, oblanceolate, truncate; lip 6.5–7.5× 4.5–5.5mm, recurved, obscurely trilobed, lateral lobes erect, midlobe 2–3×2.5–3.5mm, ovate to suborbicular, subacute or rounded; disc with fleshy, puberulent ridge; column 1mm. W Africa, Central African Republic, Zaire, Uganda, Angola.

P.bella Summerh.
Epiphytic, 15–20cm. Pseudobulbs to 4×2cm, oval, compressed, 1–2-lvd. Lvs 5–16×2–3cm, elliptic or ligulate, leathery, petiolate. Infl. racemose or paniculate, erect, pubesc., to 25cm, fairly densely many-fld; fls yellow or golden yellow, the lip with deep orange central streak; pedicel and ovary arched, 9–10mm; median sep. 12–14×3–3.5mm, lateral sep. 15–17×5–5.5mm, obliquely lanceolate, acute; pet. 8–11×1.5mm, linear-oblanceolate; lip 9.5–11.5×5–5.5mm, obscurely trilobed, lateral lobes erect, 1mm, midlobe 4.5–5×2.5mm, triangular-lanceolate, acuminate, fleshy, recurved, with low callus at base; column 2.5–3.5mm. Kenya.

P.bracteosa Lindl. See *P.affinis*.
P.buchananii Rolfe. See *P.concreta*.

P.campyloglossa Rolfe.
Dwarf, epiphytic, to 12cm. Pseudobulbs 1–2×0.5–1cm, ovoid or globose, 2–3-lvd. Lvs 5–10×1–2cm, oblanceolate or linear, minutely bilobed at apex, dark green sometimes edged with purple. Raceme slightly longer than lvs, 2–6-fld; peduncle pubesc.; sep. and pet. buff, green, yellow-green or yellow, lip white, lateral lobes purple-veined; pedicel and ovary 5mm, pubesc.; median sep. 8–13×4–7mm, ovate, acute, lateral sep. to 14×10mm, obliquely triangular, acute, forming mentum 6.5–9.5mm high; pet. 6.5–9.5×2–3mm, oblanceolate; lip 8–11×6–9.5mm, trilobed, recurved, with pubesc. disc and conical callus at junction of lobes, lateral lobes erect, rounded, pubesc., midlobe 4–5×2–5mm, ovate, fleshy, glabrous; column 3mm, stout. E Africa, Malawi.

P.concreta (Jacq.) Garay & Sweet (*P.buchananii* Rolfe; *P.flavescens* (Lindl.) J.J. Sm.; *P.luteola* (Sw.) Hook.; *P.rufinula* Rchb. f.; *P.tessellata* Lindl.).
Large, epiphytic, sometimes lithophytic, rarely terrestrial. Pseudobulbs 1–5×1cm, ovoid or conical, sometimes ribbed, 3–5-lvd. Lvs to 30×5.5cm, oblanceolate or elliptic, minutely bilobed at apex, dark green, sometimes purple-tinged. Panicle to 50cm, many-fld; peduncle covered with scarious sheaths; fls rather fleshy, small, yellow, pale green, pink or dull red-purple with white or cream lip; pedicel and ovary 6mm; median sep. 2–3×2–2.5mm, ovate, acute, lateral sep. 3–5.5×3–3.5mm, obliquely ovate, apiculate, forming mentum 3–4mm high; pet. 2–3.5×1mm, oblanceolate; lip 3.5–5×2.5–4mm, trilobed about halfway, recurved, with fleshy longitudinal callus running from base to junction of lobes, lateral lobes 1mm, triangular or oblong, midlobe 1.5–2.5×2–3mm, suborbicular; column 1–2mm, foot to 3mm. Widespread in tropical Africa; Florida, C & S America.

P.cultrata Lindl. See *P.cultriformis*.

P.cultriformis (Thouars) Spreng. (*P.cultrata* Lindl.; *P.gerrardii* Harv.).
Epiphytic or lithophytic, to 25cm. Pseudobulbs 2–18cm, 2–12mm wide at base, conical or cylindrical, clustered on rhiz., 1-lvd. Lf 3–36×1–5.5cm, elliptic, acute or obtuse, auriculate at base, articulated 2–6mm above apex of pseudobulb. Infl. racemose or paniculate, to 30cm, several- to many-fld; fls white, green, yellow, pink or purple; pedicel and ovary 6mm; bracts 4–5mm; median sep. 4–8×2–4.5mm, ovate, apiculate, lateral sep. 5–8×3–6mm, obliquely triangular, apiculate, mentum to 7mm; pet. 3.5–7.5×1–2.5mm, linear to spathulate; lip 4–8×3–6mm, recurved, trilobed in apical half, with fleshy yellow central callus, lateral lobes rounded, midlobe 1.5–4.5×1.5–3.5mm, oblong, apiculate; column 0.5–3.5mm. Widespread in tropical Africa; S Africa, Madagascar, Mascarene Is., Seychelles.

P.dendrobiiflora Rchb. f. (*P.tayloriana* Rendle).
Epiphytic on *Xerophyta* spp., lithophytic or terrestrial. Pseudobulbs 1.5–5×0.5–1cm, conical, ribbed, clustered, 5–10-lvd. Lvs 8–25×0.5–1.5cm, linear, grass-like, deciduous. Infl. paniculate, borne on old pseudobulbs when plants leafless, to 80cm; peduncle covered with brown, scarious sheaths; branches few to many; fls in clusters of 1–3, well spaced out, opening over a long period, opening wide, pale to deep lilac-pink or white, lip sometimes with red or lilac spots; pedicel and ovary 10–12mm; dorsal sep. 6.5–12×3–4mm, oblong, obtuse, lateral sep. similar but oblique, mentum conical, 3–5mm high; pet. 6–12×2.5–4.5mm, oblong, rounded; lip 7–11×4–5.5mm, entire, with yellow, slightly pubesc. longitudinal callus toward base, ovate-oblong, recurved, rounded at apex, the edge often undulate; column 2.5–4mm, winged; anth. cap deep lilac. Burundi, Kenya, Tanzania, Malawi, Zambia, Zimbabwe, Mozambique, Angola.

P.flavescens (Lindl.) J.J. Sm. See *P.concreta*.

P.foliosa (Hook. f.) Rchb. f. (*P.stenophylla* Schltr.).
Erect epiphyte to 45cm. Pseudobulbs to 2cm, ovoid. Lvs 2–5, to 20×3cm, narrowly elliptic, obtuse. Peduncle covered with scarious sheaths; panicle with several branches, rather laxly many-fld; fls fleshy, green or yellow-green; median sep. 3×2mm, ovate, acute, lateral sep. 4×2.5mm, obliquely trian-

gular, acuminate; pet. to 2.5mm long, less than 1mm wide, linear or narrowly oblanceolate; lip to 4×3mm, trilobed, with farinose disc and ovoid callus, midlobe oblong, apex recurved, emarginate, lateral lobes triangular-falcate, acute; column to 1mm, column foot less than 1mm. Tropical C & S America, Grenada.

P.galeata (Sw.) Rchb. f.
Epiphytic, to 40cm. Pseudobulbs 6–14cm×2–5mm, cylindrical, clustered, 1-lvd. Lf 8–27×1–3.5cm, oblanceolate or ligulate, acute or obtuse, coriaceous, articulated 1–5mm above apex of pseudobulb. Raceme shorter than lf, pubesc., to 6-fld; fls white, green, yellow-green, yellow or pink, with some purple spots; dorsal sep. 7–14×3–7mm, ovate, apiculate, pubesc., lateral sep. 10–22×6–18mm, obliquely triangular, pubesc., with recurved apiculus, mentum 13–22mm high; pet. 4.5–11×1–3.5mm, spreading, linear or spathulate; lip 10–21.5×4–14mm, fleshy, trilobed, recurved, lateral lobes erect, midlobe 3–7×2–8mm, pubesc. in centre, quadrate to orbicular, apiculate, the apiculus reflexed; column 1–3mm. W Africa, Zaire, Angola.

P.gerrardii Harv. See *P.cultriformis*.

P.goetzeana Kränzl.
Erect or pendent epiphyte. Pseudobulbs 5–15×5–7mm, obliquely conical, 3–4-lvd. Lvs 8–22cm×4–8mm, linear, grass-like, usually deciduous. Raceme erect, shorter than lvs, 3–5-fld; peduncle covered with scarious sheaths; sep. lime green or yellow-green, purple-veined, pet. and lip white, the lip with yellow central line; pedicel and ovary 6mm, arched, pubesc.; dorsal sep. 9–14×3.5–5.5mm, lanceolate, lateral sep. 13–15×7–9mm, obliquely triangular, acute, mentum 5–8mm high, broadly conical; lip 11–15×9–10mm, recurved, pubesc., trilobed at about the middle, with a yellow, pubesc. keel running from the base to junction of lobes, lateral lobes erect, rounded, midlobe 5.5–8×6–9mm, subquadrate, apiculate, the edge undulate; column 4–5mm. Tanzania, Malawi.

P.kermesina Kränzl.
Epiphyte, to 11cm. Pseudobulbs to 2cm×1–1.5mm, arising from middle of previous growth, 2-lvd. Lvs 2–4cm×1.5–2.5mm, linear, acute. Raceme shorter than lvs, 1–3-fld; fls rather fleshy, orange or scarlet, opening almost flat, with sep. and pet. recurved near apex; dorsal sep. 4×4mm, ovate or orbicular, obtuse, lateral sep. 5×6.5mm, obliquely ovate-orbicular, obtuse, forming mentum 3mm high; pet. 4×1.5mm, oblong; lip 8–9×4mm, fleshy, with long, hairy claw, obscurely trilobed, lateral lobes rounded, midlobe 3.5×3.5mm, orbicular, with a tooth-like callus at junction of lobes; column 1mm. Zaire, Uganda.

P.lawrenceana Kränzl.
Lithophytic, forming clumps. Pseudobulbs 2.5–5.5×1–1.5cm, conic-elliptic, glossy green with 2–3 nodes, 3–4-lvd. Lvs to 15×2cm, lax, ligulate, slightly bilobed at apex. Raceme to 16cm, laxly 6–8-fld; peduncle pubesc.; fls fleshy, pubesc. on outside; sep. and pet. yellow-green flushed with maroon, lip bright pink, occasionally pale pink, with white callus; dorsal sep. 9×4.5mm, ovate, acute, lateral sep. 11×6.5mm, obliquely ovate-triangular, acuminate, forming subconical, incurved mentum 5.5mm high; pet. 8×2.5mm, oblanceolate, obtuse; lip 9×8mm, recurved, trilobed, lateral lobes erect, oblong, midlobe 7×6mm, broadly ovate, obtuse, with central groove and smooth, fleshy callus; column 2mm. Malawi.

P.leonensis Rchb. f.
Pseudobulbs subglobose, 1cm diam., set closely on rhiz., 3–6-lvd. Lvs 7–20×1–2.5cm, lanceolate, acuminate. Raceme to 20cm, laxly several-fld; sep. and pet. pale green, usually flushed with purple-brown, lip white, lateral lobes tinged purple; median sep. 3–4mm, ovate, obtuse, lateral sep. 4–5mm, obliquely triangular, obtuse, forming narrow, cylindrical mentum 5–6mm high; pet. 4mm, oblong, obtuse; lip 6mm, trilobed, lateral lobes triangular-oblong, obtuse, midlobe ovate, obtuse; disc pubesc.; column 2mm, stout. W Africa.

P.luteola (Sw.) Hook. See *P.concreta*.

P.melliodora Cribb.
Epiphytic, forming large clumps; pseudobulbs about 3×2cm, oblong, bilaterally flattened, 1-lvd. Lf 15×3cm, erect, narrowly oblong-elliptic, rounded at apex. Raceme to 10cm, to 8-fld; fls honey-scented, waxy, white, the lip purple-edged with yellow callus, anth. cap pink; median sep. 12×7mm, ovate, acuminate, lateral sep. 15×10mm, obliquely triangular, acuminate, with wide median keel on outside, mentum 8mm high, conical, bilobed at apex; pet. 11×4.5mm, oblong, acute; lip 11×9mm, recurved, obscurely trilobed; column 4mm long. Tanzania.

P.minuta (Aubl.) Frappier ex Cordm. See *P.concreta*.

P.modesta Rchb. f.
Small epiphyte, rarely lithophyte. Pseudobulbs 8–25×3–15mm, conic or ovoid, yellow or purple, clustered on rhiz., 3–5-lvd. Lvs to 8×1.5mm, lanceolate, edged purple. Infl. racemose or with a few short branches, densely several- to many-fld; fls glabrous, fleshy, pale yellow tinged with purple, lip usually darker yellow; pedicel and ovary 3–4mm; bracts 2–3mm, triangular, acute; median sep. 3×2mm, ovate, acute, lateral sep. 5×3mm, obliquely triangular, forming rounded mentum 3mm high; pet. 3×1mm, oblanceolate; lip 4×3mm, trilobed, recurved, with no callus but with a pubesc. cushion, lateral lobes erect, 1mm, rounded or acute, midlobe 1–2mm, suborbicular, bullate, obtuse or emarginate; column 1.5mm. Resembling *P.concreta* and sometimes considered conspecific, but differing mainly in lack of callus and much smaller size. Widespread, tropical Africa.

P.mystacidioides De Wildeman.
Creeping or pendent epiphyte with dimorphic stems; pseudobulbs either narrowly cylindrical and stem-like with many distichous lvs, or swollen with 1 terminal lf, in either case arising some distance above base of previous growth. Lvs fleshy, bilaterally compressed, 2–15cm×5–10mm. Infl. single-fld; fls relatively large, white with red or purple marks, or pale brown; sep. 8–9mm, pubesc.; lip 10–11×5–6mm, trilobed, lateral lobes small, midlobe oblong, slightly emarginate. Ivory Coast, Cameroun, Zaire.

P.odorata Lindl.
Epiphytic, rarely lithophytic, 20–40cm. Pseudobulbs 2–4.5×0.5–1.5cm, almost globose to narrowly conical, 4–8-lvd. Lvs 13–26×3–4cm, oblanceolate to elliptic, minutely bilobed at apex. Panicle 10–30cm, including peduncle to 15cm; branches 6–15, many-fld; fls scented, pubesc. outside, white, pale green or dull red-brown; sep. flushed with red or purple, lip white, midlobe pink-tinged, callus yellow; median sep. 5×2.5–3mm, ovate, acuminate, lateral sep. 8–9×4–5.5mm, obliquely ovate, apiculate, forming mentum 4–5.5mm high; pet. 4.5–5×1–1.5mm, oblanceolate; lip 7–8×5–7.5mm, recurved, trilobed about halfway, lateral lobes erect, 4×2.5mm, midlobe 2.5–3×3.5mm, suborbicular, emarginate, the edge crenulate; callus fleshy, 2×1mm, lying between lateral lobes; column 2–2.5mm. W Africa, Zaire, Uganda, Tanzania, Angola.

P.ottoniana Rchb. f.
Dwarf epiphyte. Pseudobulbs 10–20×8–12mm, obliquely conical, in chains or clustered. Lvs 2–3, 7–12cm×6–9mm, linear or linear-lanceolate. Raceme erect, 1–6-fld; fls white tinged with pink or lilac, lip with yellow central stripe; pedicel and ovary 10mm; median sep. 10–11×2–3mm, lanceolate, acute, lateral sep. 12–14×7mm, obliquely lanceolate; pet. 10×2mm, oblanceolate; lip obscurely trilobed in basal half, 10–11mm, reflexed toward apex; column 5mm, slender; anth. cap violet. S Africa, Swaziland.

P.paniculata (Sw.) Rolfe.
Erect epiphyte, 22–40cm. Pseudobulbs 5–18cm×13–22mm, cylindric, clustered, with 3–4 nodes, 3–4-lvd. Lvs 10–30×2–3.5cm, distichous, ligulate, unequally bilobed at apex. Panicle to 21cm, many-fld; peduncle glabrous, 5–13cm; fls small, orange or vermilion, the lip marked with darker red; median sep. 3×1mm, lanceolate, acute, lateral sep.

3–4×1.5–2mm, obliquely lanceolate, acute, forming conical mentum to 1.5mm high; pet. 2.5–3×0.5mm, oblanceolate; lip 2.5–3×1.5–2mm, entire, ovate or elliptic; column 1mm. W Africa to Zaire.

P.pubescens (Lindl.) Rchb. f.
Epiphytic or lithophytic. Pseudobulbs conical, 2–3-lvd. Lvs 6–7×1.5–2cm, broadly lanceolate or elliptic. Raceme erect, several- to many-fld; peduncle and rachis pubesc.; fls opening fairly widely, golden yellow, lateral sep. and lip with red lines; pedicel and ovary 10–15mm; median sep. 10–12×4mm, lanceolate, acute, lateral sep. obliquely ovate, 14×7mm; pet. 11–12×4mm, oblanceolate; lip 9–12mm, trilobed about halfway, lateral lobes 1–2mm, covered with white, silky hairs, midlobe 5–6mm; column very short. S Africa, Swaziland.

P.rufinula Rchb. f. See *P.concreta*.
P.stenophylla Schltr. See *P.foliosa*.
P.tayloriana Rendle. See *P.dendrobiiflora*.
P.tessellata Lindl. See *P.concreta*.

P.villosa Rolfe.
Epiphytic, rarely lithophytic. Pseudobulbs to 4×1.5cm, oblong or conical, sometimes slightly bilaterally flattened, ribbed, yellow-green with 2–3 nodes, 3–4-lvd. Lvs to 18×3cm, oblanceolate or ligulate, rounded or minutely bilobed at apex. Raceme 15–20cm, including pubesc., 10–13cm peduncle, densely many-fld; fls densely hairy on outside, primrose-scented, pale green, white or cream, the lip white with purple spots on side lobes and at base of midlobe; pedicel and ovary 9–10mm; bracts to 15×7mm, broadly ovate, acuminate; median sep. 7–10×3–4mm, ovate, acute, lateral sep. 9–13×4–7mm, obliquely lanceolate, acuminate, slightly keeled on outside, mentum 4mm high, rounded; pet. 6–7×1.5–2mm, oblanceolate, acute; lip 5–8×3–4mm, rather fleshy, recurved, trilobed, with glabrous yellow callus at junction of lobes, lateral lobes erect, rounded, midlobe 2.5×2.5mm, bullate, ovate, acute or acuminate; column 1.5mm. Tanzania, Zambia, Malawi.

P.virginea Summerh.
Epiphytic. Pseudobulbs 5–11cm, cylindrical or conical,

loosely clustered on short, creeping rhiz., 1-lvd. Lf 12–26×1–3cm, lanceolate, obtuse, articulated 1mm above apex of pseudobulb. Raceme 4–9cm, shorter than lf, to 10-fld, the fls opening in succession; fls white, scented; median sep. 8.5–12×4.5–7.5mm, ovate, apiculate, lateral sep. 8.5–12×4.5–9.5mm, obliquely triangular, forming conical mentum 9–10mm high; pet. 8–13×3–4.5mm, elliptic to ovate; lip 11.5–15.5×8–11mm, recurved, trilobed, with central fleshy callus, lateral lobes erect, rounded, midlobe 4–6×4–6.5mm, triangular to subquadrate, apiculate; column 1–3mm. Zaire, Burundi, Rwanda, Uganda.

P.vulcanica Kränzl.
Epiphytic or lithophytic. Pseudobulbs 1–9cm×5–15mm, narrowly cylindrical, tightly clustered on short, creeping rhiz., 1-lvd. Lf 2.5–11cm×1–4mm, linear, articulated 3–4mm above apex of pseudobulb. Raceme 2–9cm, shorter than lf, to 5-fld, the fls borne in succession; sep. creamy white flushed with rose-pink, pet. and lip wine red or purple; median sep. 3–6.5×1.5–3.5mm, ovate, apiculate, lateral sep. 4–8×3.5–9mm, obliquely triangular, apiculate, forming conical mentum 7–8mm high; pet. 3–6×1–2.5mm, spathulate, obtuse; lip 5–10×4–7mm, fleshy, recurved, trilobed, with or without a somewhat pubesc., fleshy callus in middle, lateral lobes erect, midlobe 1–4×1.5–6mm, suborbicular, apiculate; column 1–2mm; anth. cap rose-purple. Zaire, Uganda.

P.zambesiaca Rolfe.
Small, epiphytic, often lithophytic. Pseudobulbs 1–2×1cm, ovoid, slightly bilaterally flattened, often wrinkled, forming clumps or chains, 2–3-lvd. Lvs 3–8×1–1.5cm, lanceolate or oblanceolate, pale glaucous green, often purple-edged. Raceme 5–7.5cm, usually shorter than lvs, pubesc., 3–20-fld; fls pubesc. on outside, yellow or yellow-green, lip white or pale yellow, purple-veined on lateral lobes; pedicel and ovary 6–9mm; bracts 4–6mm, white tinged green, ovate, acuminate; median sep. 8–10×3.5–4.5mm, ovate, acute, lateral sep. 9–12×4–6mm, obliquely triangular, acuminate, keeled on outside; pet. 6–7×1.5–2mm, oblanceolate; lip 6–7×4–5mm, fleshy, recurved, with brown, pubesc. callus at base, lateral lobes erect, rounded, midlobe bullate, ovate, acute; column 1.5mm. Tanzania, Malawi, Zambia.

Pomatocalpa Breda. (From Gk *pomatos*, flask or cup, and *kalpe*, pitcher, referring to the lip shape.) Some 60 species of monopodial epiphytes. Stems short or long, rarely climbing. Leaves oblong or lorate. Racemes nodal, erect or decurved, often branched, dense; flowers many, small; sepals and petals free, spreading, almost equal; lip trilobed, base fused to column foot, midlobe forward-pointing or recurved, fleshy, ovate-triangular or semi-orbicular, lateral lobes triangular, broad, posterior margin fused to column foot; spur round, saccate, a ligulate projection from the back wall often extends to the mouth. China, Malaysia, Australia, Polynesia.

CULTIVATION   As for *Aerangis*.

P.latifolia (Lindl.) J.J. Sm.
Stems 5–30cm, stout. Lvs oblong, glossy, coriaceous, often yellow-green, to 20×4cm. Infl. erect, 15–40cm; sep. and pet. green-yellow, speckled or edged maroon; dorsal sep. to 0.5×0.2cm, concave, lateral sep. shorter; pet. to 0.5×0.2cm; lip yellow, midlobe ovate-triangular, lamellae on interior wall crenate, truncate, white, weakly suffused violet, interior of lateral lobes spotted red; spur yellow-green, speckled brown. Malaya, Sumatra, Java.

P.siamensis (Rolfe ex Downie) Summerh. (*Cleisostoma siamensis* Rolfe ex Downie).
Stems to 35cm, leafy. Lvs linear-oblong, to 17×2cm. Infl. branched, 40–50cm; fls minutely pubesc; dorsal sep. ovate, obtuse, apex notched, exterior minutely pubesc., lateral sep. fleshy, ovate, acute, to 0.4–0.2cm; pet. spathulate, apex irreg-ular, slightly oblique, to 0.4–0.2cm; lip trilobed, to 0.4cm, midlobe cordate, base broad, lateral lobes truncate; spur stout, cylindric, fleshy; callus oblong, erect, irregularly truncate, thick near aperture, with 2 backward-pointing lamellae. Thailand.

P.spicata Breda.
Stem short, stout. Lvs oblong-lorate, coriaceous, undulate, to 28×2cm. Infl. dense, simple or branched, decurved, to 15cm; fls pale yellow, sep. and pet. blotched maroon, spur lamellae violet, tipped white; sep. and pet. ovate-oblong, obtuse, to 0.5cm, lateral sep. incurved, obovate, pet. narrow at base, lip midlobe ovate-triangular, obtuse, spur interior with dentate, 2-ridged lamellae on dorsal surface. India to Vietnam, Philippines.

Ponerorchis Rchb. f. (From Gk *poneros*, worthless, and *orchis*.) Some 24 species of terrestrials. China, Japan.

CULTIVATION   As for the hardier *Calanthe* spp.

P.graminifolia Rchb. f.
Roots tuberous, ovoid. Stems slender, 8–15cm. Lvs linear, to 12×0.8cm, acute to acuminate, arching. Racemes secund; fls few, rose-purple; sep. oblong, obtuse, 1-nerved, lateral sep. oblique; pet. ovate, oblique, erect, forming a hood with the dorsal sep.; lip ascending, deeply trilobed, lobes ovate; spur to 2cm. China, Japan.

Porpax Lindl. (From Lat. *porpax*, shield-handle, a reference to the shape of the leaves.) Some 10 species of minute epiphytes. Pseudobulbs turbinate or spherical, flattened, clustered along rhizomes. Leaves 2, sessile. Flowers 1–3, at apex of pseudobulb; sepals forming a tube with the small, free petals, dorsal sepal forming a hood, lateral sepals basally oblique, fused to the column foot. Tropical Asia.

CULTIVATION   As for *Polystachya*.

P.meirax King & Pantl. (*Eria meirax* (King & Pantl.) N.E. Br.).
Pseudobulbs turbinate, to 10mm diam., dry sheaths reticulate. Lvs 2, elliptic-oblong, to 2.5cm, emerging after fls. Fls solitary, dull brown; bract erect, concave; sep. fused, tubular, bilobed, lobes ovate; pet. shorter than tube, oblong-lanceolate; lip ovate-orbicular, notched, midlobe oblong, apex tapering, entire, lateral lobes rounded. Autumn. Sikkim.

Porroglossum Schltr. (From the Gk *porro*, forward, and *glossa*, tongue, referring to the porrect lip.) Some 30 species of epiphytes or terrestrials closely allied to *Masdevallia*. Rhizome short to elongate. Pseudobulbs absent. Secondary stems erect or ascending, stout to slender, shorter than leaves, enveloped by 2 or 3 overlapping sheaths, bearing a single apical leaf. Leaves erect, fleshy or coriaceous, elliptic to obovate, sometimes tinged purple, smooth to verrucose. Inflorescence a lateral raceme, few to several-flowered, erect; flowers produced in succession often resupinate; sepals fleshy to membranaceous, fused at base forming a campanulate tube, glabrous or pubesc., apices contracted into short to elongate tails; petals smaller than sepals, linear or oblong, obtuse or rounded; lip adnate to apex of column-foot, fleshy, obtriangular or obovate, glabrous to pubesc., with a long linear claw curved around apex of column-foot, callus basal, longitudinal or transverse; column short, erect, semiterete, usually broadly winged, foot elongate, porrect, with a free apex, pollinia 2, obliquely pyriform. Venezuela, Colombia, Ecuador, Peru to Bolivia.

CULTIVATION   As for *Masdevallia*.

P.amethystinum (Rchb. f.) Garay (*Masdevallia amethystina* Rchb. f.; *Scaphosepalum amethystinum* (Rchb. f.) Schltr.). Secondary stems to 15mm, erect, slender. Lvs to 100×14mm, narrowly obovate, acute, long-petiolate. Infl. to 25cm, few-fld; peduncle filiform, glabrous; sep. bright rose, dorsal sep. to 5×7mm, transversely obovate, acuminate, apex reflexed, tail to 2mm, lateral sep. to 9×7mm, obliquely oblong, obtuse, tails to 14mm, orange, slender; pet. to 4×2mm, translucent, ovate, rounded; lip to 4×4mm, white tinged and spotted dark purple, cuneate, broadly obtuse, base deflexed; column to 2mm, stout, foot to 5mm. Ecuador.

P.echidna (Rchb. f.) Garay (*Masdevallia echidna* Rchb. f.; *Scaphosepalum echidna* (Rchb. f.) Schltr.). Secondary stems to 7cm, erect, stout. Lvs to 14×1.5cm, elliptic-oblong to narrowly obovate, verrucose, petiolate, acute, dull green tinged purple. Infl. to 20cm, few-fld; peduncle downy; sep. brown or green with brown venation, exterior slightly verrucose, dorsal sep. to 7×6mm, obovate or triangular-oblong, obtuse, tail to 25mm, erect to reflexed, lateral sep. to 8×8mm, broadly oblong or triangular-oblong, obtuse, tails to 25mm, slender, reflexed; pet. to 4×1.5mm, translucent brown, linear-oblong, rounded; lip to 8×4mm, light brown flecked red, or dark brown, obovate-spathulate, obtuse, apex ciliate, disc with a cushion-like longitudinal callus; column to 3mm, stout, foot to 8mm. Colombia.

P.meridionale Ortiz. Secondary stems to 1cm, slender. Lvs to 4.5cm, green mottled purple below, elliptic, obtuse to subacute, verrucose, long-petiolate. Infl. to 10cm; peduncle slender, glabrous; sep. clear pale purple spotted purple, dorsal sep. to 7×5mm, ovate, subacute, exterior subverrucose, tail to 9mm, erect, lateral sep. to 7×6mm, transversely ovate, obtuse, tails to 8mm, orange-brown; pet. translucent, to 4×1mm, ovate-oblong, rounded; lip to 4×4mm, purple, cuneate-obtriangular, truncate, pubesc., apiculate, disc with a transverse basal callus; column to 2.5mm, stout, foot to 4mm. Peru.

P.mordax (Rchb. f.) Sweet (*Masdevallia mordax* Rchb. f.; *Lothiania mordax* (Rchb. f.) Kränzl.). Secondary stems to 2cm, slender, erect, dark brown-black. Lvs to 8cm, narrowly elliptic to narrowly obovate, subacute, subverrucose, long-petiolate. Infl. to 15cm; peduncle glabrous, slender; sep. pale green tinged purple, erose, subverrucose, dorsal sep. to 20×8mm, ovate, obtuse, concave, tail absent, lateral sep. to 18×4mm, obliquely ovate, obtuse; pet. to 5×2mm, translucent, ovate, rounded; lip to 5×5mm, pale green, cuneate-obtriangular, obtuse, ciliate, disc with a deep purple, longitudinal callus; column to 2.5mm, stout, foot to 5mm. Colombia.

P.muscosum (Rchb. f.) Schltr. (*Masdevallia muscosa* Rchb. f.; *P.xipheres* (Rchb. f.) Garay; *Masdevallia xipheres* Rchb. f.; *Scaphosepalum xipheres* (Rchb. f.) Schltr.). Secondary stems to 4cm, slender, erect. Lvs to 15×2cm, green tinged purple, elliptic to narrowly ovate, acute or obtuse, peti-

olate or subpetiolate. Infl. to 26cm, few-fld; peduncle slender, erect, densely green-white-pubesc.; sep. light brown to brown or green, exterior glabrous to subverrucose, dorsal sep. to 8×6mm, obovate, subacute to obtuse, tail to 30mm, slender, erect or reflexed, lateral sep. to 10×6mm, obliquely ovate, acute to obtuse, tails to 30mm, slender; pet. to 5×1.5mm, clear yellow-white to brown, ovate-oblong, rounded; lip to 5.5×4mm, white tinged rose or purple, cuneate to obovate-spathulate, obtuse, apex ciliate, disc with a low, longitudinal callus; column to 2.5mm, stout, foot to 6mm. Colombia, Ecuador, Venezuela.

P.olivaceum Sweet. Secondary stems to 1.5cm, slender, erect. Lvs to 10×1.5cm, narrowly elliptic, acute, slender-petiolate, subverrucose to prominently verrucose. Infl. to 27cm, several-fld; peduncle slender, erect; sep. light brown to light yellow-brown, veined dark brown, dorsal sep. to 5×6mm, obovate, obtuse, tail to 3mm, slender, reflexed, lateral sep. to 4×7mm, obliquely oblong, broadly obtuse, tails to 13mm, slender; pet. to 5×2mm, clear pale yellow or pale brown, ovate-oblong, rounded; lip to 5×4mm, yellow, distal portion purple, short-pubesc., obtuse, apex ciliate, disc with a raised, longitudinal callus, rounded; column to 2mm, stout, foot to 5mm. Ecuador, Colombia.

P.portillae Luer & Andreetta. Secondary stems to 1.5cm, erect, slender, dark brown-black. Lvs to 6×1.5cm, elliptic, obtuse; petiole elongate, slender, dark-brown-black. Infl. to 11cm, few-fld; peduncle erect, slender, glabrous, fls non-resupinate; sep. yellow tinged rose-pink, minutely spotted purple, dorsal sep. to 7×6mm, obtuse, concave, tail to 5mm, reflexed, lateral sep. to 6×8mm, transversely oblong, obtuse, tails to 7mm, reflexed; pet. to 5×1mm, rose-pink, ovate-oblong; lip to 5×5mm, rose flecked purple, obtriangular, truncate, apex ciliate, obscurely 3-lobed, disc with a low basal callus; column to 2.5mm, stout, foot to 4mm. Ecuador.

P.rodrigoi Sweet. Secondary stems to 0.5cm, slender, erect. Lvs to 4.5cm, elliptic, obtuse to subacute, petiolate. Infl. to 7cm; peduncle slender, glabrous; sep. purple, dorsal sep. to 5×6mm, transversely ovate, obtuse, concave, tail to 1.5mm, recurved, slender, lateral sep. to 4×5mm, obliquely ovate, obtuse, tails to 5mm, light yellow; pet. to 3×1.5mm, clear red-purple, ovate-oblong, rounded; lip to 3×3mm, white tinged rose-pink, cuneate, obtuse, retrorse, apiculate, disc with a low basal callus; column to 2mm, stout, red-purple, foot to 3mm. Colombia.

P.xipheres (Rchb. f.) Garay. See *P.muscosum*.

× **Potinara** (*Brassavola* × *Cattleya* × *Laelia* × *Sophronitis*). Quadrigeneric hybrids made from species and hybrids of these genera and named after a french orchid grower, Monsieur Potin. The plants are mostly smaller and more compact in growth than the brassolaeliocattleyas, cattleyas and laeliocattleyas and have smaller flowers than those hybrids. The best red and orange colours, as well as some very fine yellows, are found in this group of intergeneric hybrids. A selection of the finest is listed below.

× *P*.Alyce: strong plants; fls large, excellent shape, solid red with darker red lip.

× *P*.Amangi: vigorous plants of medium size; fls true crimson red of excellent shape; several awarded clones.

× *P*.Carrousel 'Crimson Triumph': strong plants; fls clear burgundy red with full red lip, fine form, one of the best of the early red cattleyas.

× *P*.Fortune Peak: typical cattleya-type plant of medium size; fls pale green-pink with brilliant raspberry red lip with yellow flash in the centre.

× *P*.Fortune Teller: strong plants, sometimes tall; rich shades of orange and yellow orange, sometimes veined red, with darker orange lip; many fine awarded clones.

× *P*.Gordon Siu 'Red Radiance': compact plants; striking red fls of excellent form; one of the best of the large flowered red cattleyas.

× *P*.Sao Paulo: strong plants, one of the best semi-yellows; fine large blooms with yellow sep. and pet. contrasting with rich purple lip.

× *P*.Tapestry Peak: strong plants; fls lovely pink with deep purple and yellow in the throat of the ruffled lip, excellent shape; several awarded clones.

× *P*.Twenty Four Carat: small plants with fls of excellent shape; fls bright golden yellow throughout.

Prasophyllum R. Br. (From Gk *prason*, leek, and *phyllon*, leaf.) Some 70 species of terrestrials. Leaf sheathed, solitary, terete, sometimes bract-like. Flowers in a slender-stalked spike or raceme, non-resupinate, green, white or purple, sometimes fragrant; dorsal sepal lanceolate, erect, recurved or forming a hood, lateral sep. free or partially fused; lip sessile or attached to a projection at the column base, lanceolate oblong or ovate, fimbriate, entire or denticulate, base concave, apex recurved, callus broad or reduced to a central ridge. Winter–summer. Australia, New Zealand.

CULTIVATION   Terrestrial orchids for the alpine or cool house.

P.australe R. Br.
To 75cm. Fls sessile, white tinted green or brown; dorsal sep. to 8mm, ovate-lanceolate, recurved or erect, concave, lateral sep. fused, or free; pet. centrally striped red-brown, smaller than lateral sep., yellow-green; lip white, basally convex, undulate, callus abruptly terminating in two mounds. Australia.

P.despectans Hook. f. SHARP MIDGE ORCHID.
To 40cm. Lvs reduced to narrow sheaths. Raceme dense, pyramidal; fls small, to 45, pale yellow-green, brown or purple; dorsal sep. to 2mm, ovate, concave, acuminate, lateral sep. 2.5–4.5mm, lanceolate-falcate, cylindric, basally fused; pet. to 3mm, ovate-lanceolate, acute; lip to 3.5mm, mobile, lanceolate, recurved, callus raised, minutely serrate or entire. SE Australia, Tasmania.

P.elatum R.Br.
To 1.5m. Fls many, highly fragrant; tepals yellow-green to purple-black, typically olive with darker veins; lip white, flabellate, undulate, veined green; column red, anth. cap yellow. Australia.

P.rufum R. Br. RED MIDGE ORCHID.
To 40cm. Lvs reduced to narrow sheaths. Spike dense 2–6cm, fls few to many, green or red-brown to dark maroon, rarely grey-green and red; dorsal sep. to 3mm, broad-ovate, hooded, lateral sep. diverging, exceeding dorsal sep., often gland-tipped; pet. lanceolate to triangular; lip obovate, crenate, deep purple, denticulate at tip; callus raised, dark. SE Australia.

Promenaea Lindl. (For Promeneia, the prophetess of Dodona mentioned by Herodotus.) Some 15 species of diminutive epiphytes. Rhizome short. Pseudobulbs small, clustered, fleshy, ovoid to circular, laterally compressed, bearing to 5 leaves, 1–3 at apex, the others basally sheathing. Leaves ovate-lanceolate, short-petioled or sheathing, sometimes conspicuously veined, plicate or undulate, olive to sea-green, obscurely conduplicate. Inflorescence axillary, from base of pseudobulb, shorter or equalling leaves, horizontal to pendent, 1–2-flowered; flowers often showy, fleshy, pure primrose yellow to cream spotted and streaked maroon; sepals and petals subsimilar, free; lateral sepals adnate to column foot forming a short mentum; lip articulated to apex of column foot, trilobed, lateral lobes enveloping column, narrow, erect, midlobe spreading, disc with a lobed or tuberculate callus; column produced into a short foot at base, fleshy, subterete, wingless, anther terminal, operculate, incumbent, pollinia 4, waxy, obovoid, compressed. Brazil.

CULTIVATION For the cool or intermediate house. Grow in pans of a fine-grade bark mix in semi-shade. Water carefully throughout the year.

P.citrina D. Don. See *P.xanthina*.

P.rollissonii (Lindl.) Lindl. (*Maxillaria rollissonii* Lindl.).
Pseudobulbs to 2.5cm. Lvs to 9×2.5cm, thin-textured, oblong to lanceolate, acute or acuminate. Infl. to 6cm; sep. and pet. pale yellow, recurved: sep. to 22×8mm, ovate-oblong, acuminate, concave; pet. to 18×10mm, ovate-spathulate, acuminate, concave; lip shorter than lateral sep., yellow spotted red-purple, lateral lobes small, oblong-subfalcate, acute or obtuse, denticulate-undulate, midlobe ovate or obovate, short-acuminate, disc with a transverse callus; column to 8mm, clear yellow-green, subclavate. Brazil.

P.stapelioides (Lindl.) Lindl. (*Maxillaria stapelioides* Lindl.).
Pseudobulbs to 2.5cm. Lvs 3–10×0.75–2.5cm, ovate-lanceolate to oblong-ligulate, grey-green, papillose. Infl. to 5cm; fls to 5cm diam.; sep. and pet. cream to buff with broken, concentric bands of maroon, ovate, acute, spreading; lip dark purple, lateral lobes paler than midlobe, linear-falcate, midlobe ovate-oblong or ovate-suborbicular; column pale yellow-green. Brazil.

P.xanthina (Lindl.) Lindl. (*Maxillaria xanthina* Lindl.; *P.citrina* D. Don).
Pseudobulbs to 2×1.5cm. Lvs 2.5–7×0.75–1.5cm, ovate-lanceolate to oblong, acute, grey-green. Infl. 2.5–10cm horizontal to nodding; fls to 5cm diam., strongly fragrant, long-lived; sep. and pet. primrose yellow, sep. to 20×10mm, ovate-lanceolate to oblong-lanceolate, acute, pet. subequal to sep., narrowly ovate, acute; lip to 15×12mm, bright yellow, lateral lobes slightly spotted brick red, oblong-subfalcate, obtuse, midlobe obovate or obovate-suborbicular, obtuse or rounded, apex denticulate, disc with a fleshy 3-lobed crest; column to 17mm, arcuate, clavate, spotted red. Brazil.

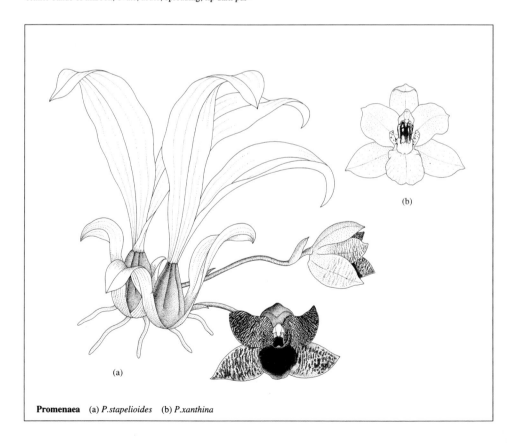

(b)

(a)

Promenaea   (a) *P.stapelioides*   (b) *P.xanthina*

Psychopsis Raf. BUTTERFLY ORCHID. (From Gk *psyche*, butterfly, and *opsis*, appearance referring to the flower shape.) 5 species of epiphytes closely allied to and formerly included in *Oncidium*. Rhizome short. Pseudobulbs clustered, orbicular to subquadrate, strongly laterally compressed, wrinkled, basally enveloped by thin overlapping sheaths, unifoliate. Leaves oblong-elliptic, acute, erect, rigidly coriaceous, often dotted or mottled oxblood, conduplicate; petiole short. Inflorescence a raceme, erect to arcuate, born from base of pseudobulb, covered by sheathing bracts at the nodes; flowers showy, pedicellate, produced successively over several seasons a year; dorsal sepal free, erect, spathulate, acute, narrow, revolute and undulate, lateral sepals ovate-oblong, obtuse, subfalcate, crispate, crenate to undulate; petals similar to dorsal sepal; lip pandurate, 3-lobed, lateral lobes orbicular, midlobe large, transversely subquadrate, spreading, disc prominent, fleshy, with various numbers of calli; column long, erect, biauriculate with antennae-like processes from upper portion of auricles; anther terminal, operculate; pollinia 2, waxy, pyriform. C & S America.

CULTIVATION   A genus of spectacular orchids, *Psychopsis* bears exceptionally large tiger-striped blooms a few at a time in slow succession on stems arising from often sickly-appearing, fleshy, dull green and liver-red plants. Provide full sunlight and high summer temperatures (30–40°C/85–105°F). Pot tightly in the most open mixture of equal parts coarse bark and charcoal, surrounding the lead base with fresh sphagnum at first to promote rooting. Alternatively, mount on rafts or cork slabs. Suspend plants in a dry, airy position, water freely during the short growing period and give a weak foliar feed every third week. Once pseudobulbs are completed, withhold water, providing only a heavy misting every second day (minimum winter temperature 65°F). Do not remove flower spikes, which may continue to produce flowers even though they appear spent.

P.krameriana (Rchb. f.) H. Jones (*Oncidium kramerianum* Rchb. f.; *Oncidium nodosum* E. Morr.; *Oncidium papilio* var. *kramerianum* (Rchb. f.) Lindl.).
Pseudobulbs to 3cm diam., tightly clustered, dull purple-brown, strongly compressed. Lvs to 16×6cm, elliptic-oblong, acute, deep green mottled purple above, spotted dull maroon beneath. Infl. erect, to 1m; peduncle terete, nodes prominent; fls produced singly in succession, to 12cm diam., showy; sep. deep red-brown with golden yellow margins or bands; dorsal sep. to 5×1cm, linear-spathulate, acute, erect, strongly undulate, lateral sep. to 7×1cm, red-brown blotched yellow, obliquely ovate-elliptic, falcate, subacute, margins undulate-crisped; pet. similar to dorsal sep.; lip deep red-brown, to 4.5×4cm, subpandurate, 3-lobed, lateral lobes suborbicular, dorsal margin erose, midlobe far larger than laterals, with a central yellow blotch, reniform to transversely oblong, apex cleft, base short-clawed, margins undulate-crisped, callus prominent, deep bronze-purple, obscurely 3-lobed at front, 2-lobed at base; column to 1cm, green, with 2 prominent lateral wings above, each terminating in small, black glands. Costa Rica, Panama, Ecuador, Peru, Colombia.

P.limminghei (E. Morr. ex Lindl.) E. Luckel & G.J. Braem (*Oncidium limminghei* E. Morr. ex Lindl.).
Pseudobulbs to 2×1.5cm, spaced at 1–2cm intervals on rhiz., ovate-elliptic, prostrate. Lvs to 3.5×3.5cm, elliptic to ovate-elliptic, pale green-brown mottled maroon. Infl. erect, 2–3-fld; peduncle slender, to 10cm; fls to 3.5cm diam.; dorsal sep. dull red-brown, to 1.5×1cm, ovate-spathulate, obtuse to acute, lat-

eral sep. smaller than dorsal sep.; pet. bright red-brown barred with pale yellow-brown, slightly larger than sep., ovate-oblong, truncate; lip cream-yellow spotted orange-brown, to 2.5×2.5cm, 3-lobed, lateral lobes large, oblong, recurved, midlobe larger than lateral lobes, triangular, clawed, bilobulate; 3-ridged; column erect, wings fimbriate. Brazil, Venezuela. Sometimes referred to the monotypic genus *Psychopsiella* since 1982.

P.papilio (Lindl.) H. Jones (*Oncidium papilio* Lindl.; *P.picta* Raf.).
Pseudobulbs to 5cm. Lvs to 25×7cm, ovate to elliptic-oblong, deep olive green mottled red-brown. Infl. to 120cm, erect or suberect, simple or branched, 1 or 2 fls opening at once; peduncle strongly compressed, dilated above, green spotted oxblood or maroon; fls to 15cm diam.; dorsal sep. and pet. purple-brown mottled yellow-green, to 10×0.5cm, linear-oblanceolate, acute, erect, slightly dilated near apex, margins slightly undulate, lateral sep. bright chestnut red barred or blotched deep yellow, oblong-lanceolate, acuminate, to 5×2cm, falcate, decurved, margins strongly undulate; lip to 4×3.5cm, 3-lobed, lateral lobes small, semi-orbicular, yellow spotted orange-brown, midlobe distinctly clawed, broadly suborbicular, apex emarginate, golden yellow bordered or heavily mottled red-brown at margins, strongly undulate-crisped, disc with a fleshy callus of 3 erect ridges, pale yellow or white spotted red-brown; column to 1cm, erect, wings oblong, fimbriate, ending at tip in capitate, fleshy teeth. Trinidad, Venezuela, Colombia, Ecuador, Peru.

P.picta Raf. See *P.papilio*.

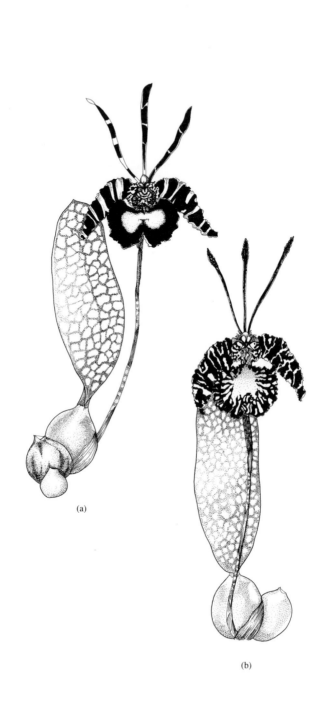

(a)

(b)

Psychopsis   (a) *P.krameriana*   (b) *P.papilio*

Pterostylis R. Br. (From Gk *pteron*, wing, and *stylos*, column or style, referring to the wings on the upper column.) GREENHOOD. Some 60 species of terrestrial herbs. Tubers subterranean, fibrous. Leaves in a basal rosette or reduced to bracts on stem. Flowers green, often striped or tinted purple, brown or red; dorsal sepal incurved, arched, the petals pressed against it, forming a hood, concealing the column, lateral sepals deflexed or erect, fused into a lower lip; lip with a mobile claw and often a basal appendage. Australia, New Zealand, W Pacific.

CULTIVATION   Terrestrials for the alpine house. See Introduction: Hardy Orchids.

P.acuminata R. Br.
To 25cm. Lvs 4–8, ovate to oblong, obtuse or acute, keeled, petiolate, 2–5cm; stem bracts 2. Fl. solitary, pale green, marked white; pet. and dorsal sep. tipped pink, dorsal sep. erect, becoming horizontal, acuminate, lateral sep. fused, spreading apically forming sinus, lobes constricted, tips filiform, extending to 1cm above the hood; pet. narrowing basally, abruptly tapering; lip sharply deflexed, narrow-ovate, acuminate, basal appendage penicillate. Mid-spring–early summer. E Australia, New Caledonia, New Guinea.

P.australis Hook. f. See *P.banksii*.

P.banksii Hook. (*P.australis* Hook. f.).
To 35cm, stems basally sheathed. Lvs 4–6, to 20cm, linear, sessile, cauline, keeled beneath, pale green. Fls pale green, stripes darker, pet. and sep. tipped orange-pink, lip with a single red ridge above, margins green, tip exserted from hood, appendage arching, tubular, apically pubesc. Autumn–winter. New Zealand.

P.baptistii Fitzg.
To 40cm. Lvs 4–8, oblong to ovate, conspicuously net-veined, 3–6cm; stem bracts 2. Fls solitary, to 6cm, pale green, marked dark green and white, dorsal sep. and pet. tipped pink; dorsal sep. erect, sharply curved at mid point, lateral sep. fused to dorsal, forming an apical sinus, filiform tips erect or recurved, extending to 15mm above the hood; lip 13–20mm, obovate, narrowing to a decurved apex. Mid summer–mid autumn. C & SE Australia.

P.coccinea Fitzg. SCARLET GREENHOOD.
To 22cm. Lvs ovate to oblong-elliptic, lanceolate, stem lvs 3–5. Fls 1–2, green to green hued scarlet, hood sharply incurved; dorsal sep. with a filiform tip, to 15mm, lateral sep. embracing hood, tips free, to 4.5cm, erect or incurved above hood; lip red-brown, to 10mm, clawed, oblong, 2-toothed or notched, keeled centrally, appendage penicillate, slender. Mid winter–mid spring. NE Australia.

P.concinna R. Br.
To 30cm. Lvs 4–6, ovate to oblong, petiolate, undulate or entire. Fls 1–2; perianth striped dark green, tips tinged brown; hood erect, incurved, dorsal sep. with filiform tip to 3mm, lateral sep. enveloping hood, projecting vertically, tips to 20mm, sometimes clavate; lip to 10mm, dark brown, notched. SE Australia.

P.cucullata R. Br.
To 15cm. Lvs oblong to elliptic, sessile, to 10cm, often scattered along the stem. Fl. solitary, red-brown, often green and white at base, incurved; dorsal sep. slightly exceeding pet., lateral sep. loosely embracing hood, apical fil. to 10mm; lip oblong, brown, apically curved, blunt. Summer–autumn. C & SE Australia.

P.curta R. Br.
To 30cm. Lvs ovate or oblong, sometimes irregularly undulate, to 10cm, petiolate, in a low rosette. Fl. solitary, to 4.5cm, white, striped green, tinted brown and green, hood erect, becoming incurved, lateral sep. embracing hood, free apical fil. to 12mm; lip to 20mm, centrally ridged, apically twisted; brown. Summer–autumn. C & SE Australia.

P.nutans R. Br. PARROT'S BEAK ORCHID.
To 30cm. Lvs 3–6, ovate to oblong, undulate, in a basal rosette. Fls 1–2, translucent, striped green, sometimes tipped red, hood arched; lateral sep. basally deflexed, loosely embracing hood, fimbriate, apical fil. exceeding hood; lip sharply recurved, to 15mm, green, central ridge red-brown, densely fringed, exserted. Spring–autumn. E Australia, New Zealand.

P.pedunculata R. Br. MAROONHOOD.
To 25cm. Lvs 4–6, ovate to oblong, sometimes undulate, obtuse, veins prominent. Fls 1–2, green and white, tipped dark red-brown; hood erect, basally incurved, loosely embraced by lateral sep., free apical fil. to 30mm, sinus narrow; lip to 5mm, ovate, dark red-brown. Summer–autumn. E Australia.

Rangaeris (Schltr.) Summerh. (A near anagram of *Aerangis*.) About 6 species of monopodial epiphytes or lithophytes. Stems long or short; roots stout. Leaves ligulate, conduplicate. Inflorescences racemose; flowers mostly white, often scented, particularly in the evening; sepals and petals free, subsimilar; lip entire or trilobed, spurred; column short or long; pollinia and stipites 2, viscidium 1 or 2; rostellum bifid or trifid. Tropical & S Africa.

CULTIVATION As for *Angraecum*.

R.amaniensis (Kränzl.) Summerh.
Stem 20–30cm; roots numerous, 8–9mm diam. Lvs 12–16, distichous, to 11×2cm, ligulate, obtusely bilobed at apex. Racemes arching or pendent, to 22cm, densely to 12-fld, rachis subflexuous; fls sweetly scented, especially at night, white, sometimes tinged green, spur apricot; sep. and pet. lanceolate, acuminate, spreading, the tips slightly recurved; sep. 11–13×1.5–2mm; pet. similar but slightly narrower; lip 13mm, obscurely lobed in basal half; spur 14mm, pendent, slender. Ethiopia, Rift Valley, Zimbabwe.

R.brachyceras (Summerh.) Summerh. See *Cribbia brachyceras*.

R.muscicola (Rchb. f.) Summerh.
Stem short; roots stout, 4–5mm diam. Lvs 7–8, forming a fan, to 18×2cm, ligulate, folded, straight or slightly recurved, dark green, thick-textured, unequally bilobed at apex. Racemes usually 2, from axils of lower lvs, to 11cm, 10–12-fld, the fls in 2 rows; fls white, turning apricot with age, sweet-scented; pedicel and ovary 25mm; bracts black, sheathing; sep. 8–9×4mm, dorsal sep. ovate, erect, lateral sep. slightly longer and deflexed; pet. 8×3mm, lanceolate, slightly reflexed; lip 9×7mm, entire, broadly ovate or subquadrate, apiculate; spur 8–9cm, slender, pendent, straight or slightly curved; column 3×2mm. Tropical Africa (widespread), S Africa.

R.rhipsalisocia (Rchb. f.) Summerh.
Stem erect; roots stout. Lvs several, forming a fan, fleshy, bilaterally flattened and equitant, 7–8×0.5–1cm, linear, acute. Racemes 5–8cm, to 10-fld; fls secund, fls scented at night, white or cream, spur tinged green; pedicel and ovary 2–3mm, ovary densely hairy; bracts 5–7mm, broadly ovate; sep. and pet. 8–9mm, lanceolate, acute, pet. slightly shorter than sep.; lip of similar length, ovate, acute; spur 7–14mm, hooked at apex; column short and stout. W Africa, Zaire, Angola.

× **Renanopsis** (*Renanthera* × *Vandopsis*). Intergeneric hybrid which has been made several times in Singapore and produced some outstanding flowers on giant plants. The tall or very tall plants bear alternative leaves in two rows throughout their length of several metres. Inflorescences axillary, long and branched with large flowers of very heavy substance; flowers bold red with darker spotting.

× *R.*Lena Rowland: famous early hybrid of enormous size and producing quantities of splendid fls; fls thick and heavy, vivid red with darker spotting; many clones have been awarded throughout the world.

× **Renantanda** (*Renanthera* × *Vanda*). This intergeneric hybrid is a favourite in the Far East and many crosses have been made. The progeny make tall plants with upright stems, the alternate leaves in two rows, leaves narrowly channelled. The inflorescences are axillary, on upright spikes, sometimes branching. The flowers are star-shaped with rounded sepals and petals and a small lip, usually very brightly coloured. They are long-lasting on the plant and as cut flowers. The plants need bright light, high humidity and warm temperatures to grow and flower well. They grow extremely well out of doors in the humid tropics but are less easy in the glasshouse.

× *R.*Ammani: tall plants with upright spikes; fls large, pale orange freckled with red, lip bright red.

× *R.*Azimah: strong, branched infl. with many well shaped fls; fls flat, heavy textured, opening orange then turning yellow, lip canary yellow with red sides lobes.

× *R.*Lily Aow 'Dream City': tall plants with upright, branching spikes of many large fls; fls deep pink with maroon tessellation, lip bright cerise pink with gold striations on the base and side lobes.

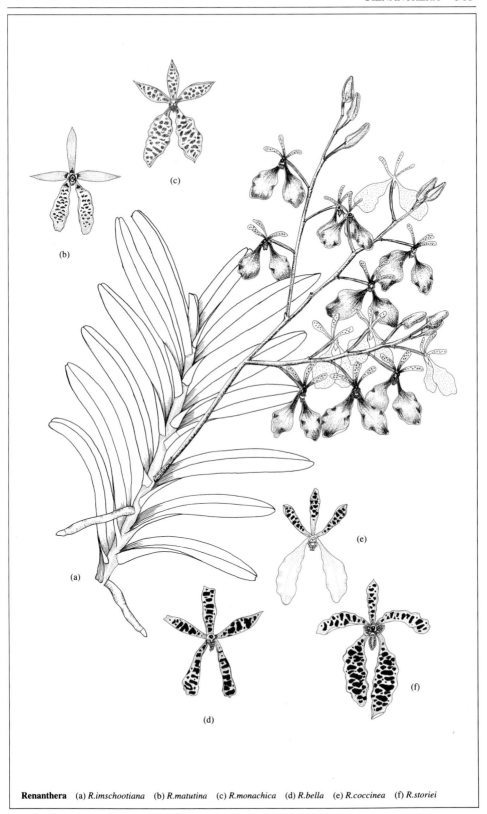

Renanthera   (a) *R.imschootiana*   (b) *R.matutina*   (c) *R.monachica*   (d) *R.bella*   (e) *R.coccinea*   (f) *R.storiei*

Renanthera Lour. (From Lat. *renes*, kidneys, and *anthera*, anther, referring to the kidney-shaped pollinia.) Some 15 species of robust, monopodial epiphytes. Leaves usually oblong-ligulate, conduplicate, coriaceous, 2-ranked, alternate, apex unequally bilobed. Racemes dense, sometimes branching; flowers many, yellow, red and orange; dorsal sepal and petals similar, spreading, lateral sepals almost parallel, larger; lip smaller than the other segments, trilobed, base saccate or spurred, midlobe reflexed, ligulate, callus lamellate, lateral lobes erect. Indomalaya Philippines, New Guinea.

CULTIVATION   See *Vanda*.

R.angustifolia Hook. f. See *R.matutina*.

R.annamensis Rolfe.
To 30cm. Lvs oblong, spreading, distichous, coriaceous. Racemes to 25cm; spur and base of sep. and pet. yellow, spotted crimson, lip lobes and pet. apex deep crimson; dorsal sep. narrow-oblong, obtuse, concave, to 1.5cm, lateral sep. spathulate, concave, obtuse, to 1.8cm; pet. oblong, narrow, similar to lateral sep.; lip midlobe cordate to orbicular, obtuse, calli at base 5, fleshy, lateral lobes triangular, erect, fleshy; sac oblong, obtuse. Vietnam.

R.bella J.J. Wood.
To 75cm. Lvs to 13×1cm. Peduncle 17–28cm. Infl. almost horizontal; fls yellow-cream to pink or crimson, blotched dark crimson, yellow to apricot at centre, lip yellow, densely blotched dark red and maroon; dorsal sep. elliptic, narrow, erect, undulate, acute, base cuneate, margins revolute, undulate; pet. narrow-elliptic, weakly undulate and hooded; lip midlobe oblong, reflexed, to 0.2cm, callus oblong, lateral lobes oblong, rounded, clasping the column; spur conic, obtuse. Malaysia.

R.coccinea Lour.
To 45cm. Lvs linear-oblong, 9–12×2–3cm. Dorsal sep. pale pink, speckled bright red or cinnabar red, speckled orange-yellow, lateral sep. bright red, lip pale yellow at base, midlobe deep red-purple, lateral lobes edged and streaked red; dorsal sep. lanceolate-spathulate, narrow at base, channelled, lateral sep. ovate-oblong; claw linear, weakly undulate, interior margins crisped; pet. narrow, spathulate; lip midlobe ovate, base rounded, lateral lobes rounded. SE Asia.

R.elongata (Bl.) Lindl.
Lvs lorate, emarginate, 6–13cm. Racemes erect to pendent, often branched; peduncle 15–20cm. Fls dull red or yellow, blotched red, lip red, calli yellow; dorsal sep. lanceolate-spathulate, base channelled, obtuse to rounded, apical margins recurved, lateral sep. free, ovate, elongate, margins undulate; lip midlobe oblong-spathulate, obtuse, lateral lobes broadly triangular; spur to 0.3cm. Java.

R.imschootiana Rolfe.
Stem scrambling, becoming elongated, woody and bare with age. Lvs fleshy, to 10×2.5cm. Fls 3–4cm diam.; sep. red or orange, base yellow, pet. yellow, spotted red, lip and column

red; dorsal sep. linear to oblanceolate, to 2.5×0.5cm, lateral sep. oblong, clawed, lower margins weakly undulate, weakly papillose above; pet. similar to dorsal sep. but slightly shorter; lip midlobe elliptic, concave, pendent or spreading, callus base tubular, lateral lobes lanceolate, base auriculate; spur to 0.4cm. India, Burma, Indochina.

R.matutina (Bl.) Lindl. (*R.angustifolia* Hook. f.; *R.micrantha* Bl.).
To 90cm. Lvs narrowly cylindric to lorate, fleshy, sulcate above, 12–16cm. Infl. erect, branching horizontally, 60–90cm; fls 2.5–5cm diam., crimson or vermilion, spotted scarlet, lip white and orange-yellow, spotted red, midlobe red-brown; sep. and pet. similar, spreading, arching, narrow-oblong or clavate, tip truncate or obtuse, revolute; lip to 0.7×0.8cm, midlobe ligulate, revolute, lateral lobes short, revolute; spur cylindric, obtuse, weakly recurved. Thailand to Sumatra.

R.micrantha Bl. See *R.matutina*.

R.monachica Ames.
Resembling *R.matutina* in habit except shorter and stouter. Infl. axillary, simple, to 18.5cm; fls some 2.5cm diam., yellow, spotted red; dorsal sep. lanceolate, narrow-acute, to 1.5cm, lateral sep. lanceolate; pet. subfalcate, acuminate; lip minute, fleshy, base saccate, cylindric, to 0.15cm, midlobe oblong, rounded, to 2.5cm, lateral lobes triangular to acute. Philippines.

R.storiei Rchb. f. To 30cm. Lvs broadly oblong, distichous, 10–20cm+. Infl. paniculate, horizontal; peduncle woody; fls 4–7.5cm diam., dorsal sep. and pet. orange, mottled deep red, lateral sep. rose-purple, spotted crimson, lip red, lobes white, striped red, midlobe base and callus white; dorsal sep. oblanceolate, narrow, to 3cm, lateral sep. oblong, undulate, clawed; pet. cuneate-ligulate, obtuse, margins undulate to crisped; lip midlobe ligulate, obtuse, forward-pointing, lamellae 2, quadrate at aperture, lateral lobes triangular, acute; spur conical. Philippines.

R.grexes.
R.Brookie Chandler: very large plants bearing long sprays of bright red fls.

× **Renanthopsis** (*Renanthera* × *Phalaenopsis*). Rather few crosses have been made to produce this hybrid genus as the plants have proved difficult to grow and flower. The stems are upright with the alternate leaves in two rows, leaves narrowly channelled. The inflorescences are axillary, on upright spikes, often branched. The flowers are star shaped with rounded sepals and petals and a small lip. The plants need bright light, high humidity and warm temperatures to grow and flower well. They grow extremely well out of doors in the humid tropics but are less easy in the glasshouse.

× R.Mildred Jameson: branching spikes of golden or beige fls with many fine chestnut spots; many awarded clones.

Restrepia HBK. (For José E. Restrepo, a Colombian who explored the Antioquian Andes of Colombia.) Some 30 species of typically diminutive epiphytes, allied to *Pleurothallis*. Rhizome short, pseudobulbs absent. Secondary stems tufted, slender, compressed, enveloped by papery bracts, each bearing a single terminal leaf. Leaves fleshy or coriaceous, suberect, obscurely conduplicate, jointed to stem. Inflorescence terminal, usually shorter than leaves, 1-several-flowered sometimes remontant; flowers small to large often lying on or held barely clear of leaf surface, variously coloured cream, yellow-green, buff and ox-blood, tinted, speckled or striped shades of red and purple; dorsal sepal free, erect, narrow, apex slightly swollen, lateral sepals connate usually forming a boat-like synsepalum, broad, bifid, base cucullate, apex recurved; petals similar to dorsal sepal, smaller; lip smaller than sepals, articulate to column base, simple to trilobed, bidentate or bilobulate at apex, lateral lobes erect, midlobe narrow, ligulate; column slender, elongate, arcuate, wingless, anther terminal, operculate, incumbent, pollinia 4, waxy, pyriform. Mexico to Argentina.

CULTIVATION   As for *Pleurothallis*.

R.antennifera HBK.
Secondary stems to 15cm, erect or ascending; sheathing bracts to 4cm, spotted purple. Lvs to 9×4cm, fleshy-coriaceous, ovate, elliptic-ovate to ovate-suborbicular, subacute to obtuse or rounded. Infl. to 10cm, slender; fls large for genus, translucent; sep. pale yellow striped maroon-purple, tails tinged green; dorsal sep. to 40×4mm, concave, linear-lanceolate, tail-like, lateral sep. to 40×15mm, far broader than dorsal, connate forming a synsepalum, narrowly elliptic, bidentate; pet. to 23×2mm, porrect, similar to dorsal sep.; lip to 15×5mm, pale brown spotted maroon, 3-lobed at base, lateral lobes falcate, setose, midlobe oblong-pandurate, papillose; column to 7mm, cream-brown at apex, white below, slightly arcuate, clavate. Venezuela, Colombia, Ecuador.

R.cucullata Lindl. See *Barbosella cucullata*.

R.elegans Karst. (*R.punctulata* Lindl.).
Secondary stems 2–6cm, erect, clustered; sheathing bracts white, tubular, acute. Lvs 2.5–6×1.25–4cm, coriaceous, elliptic or ovate-elliptic, subobtuse, minutely tridentate. Infl. 1.75–4cm, slender, erect-ascending; dorsal sep. to 25×3mm, white lined maroon, apex maroon, erect, lanceolate, long-attenuate, lateral sep. to 24×9mm, orange-brown marked maroon, oblong-elliptic, synsepalum base saccate; pet. similar to dorsal sep., smaller; lip to 11×5mm, pale brown marked maroon, apex emarginate, base 3-lobed, lateral lobes erect, falcate, acuminate, midlobe oblong-oblanceolate, glandular-granulose; column to 5mm. Venezuela.

R.guttulata Lindl. (*R.maculata* Lindl.; *R.pardina* Lem.; *R.leopardina* hort.).
Secondary stems 5.5×11cm, erect, terete; sheathing bracts to 3.5cm, tubular. Lvs 4–8×1.25–3cm, coriaceous, lanceolate or ovate-lanceolate, subacute. Infl. to 7cm, slender; fls 1.75–5cm; dorsal sep. to 25×3mm, white, veined and tipped rose-purple, lanceolate to long-attenuate at apex, lateral sep. to 25×10mm, light orange-brown spotted dark maroon, forming an ovate-

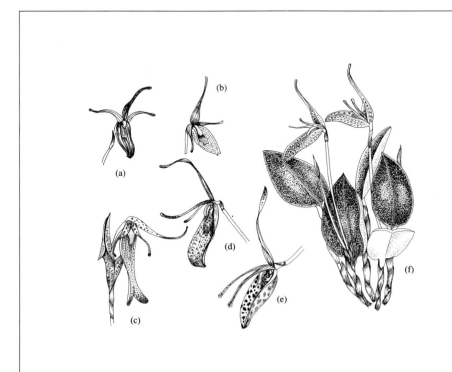

Restrepia   (a) *R.hemsleyana*   (b) *R.elegans*   (c) *R.chocoënsis*   (d) *R.antennifera*   (e) *R.pelyx*   (f) *R.guttulata*

lanceolate synsepalum; pet. to 13×1mm, similar to dorsal sep.; lip to 10×4mm, light brown spotted rose, fleshy, apex verrucose, 3-lobed, lateral lobes aristate, midlobe oblong-pandurate or elliptic-pandurate, truncate; column to 5mm, pale cream with a basal maroon spot. Venezuela, Colombia, Ecuador.

R.lansbergii Rchb. f. & Wagner.
Secondary stems to 6.5cm, usually shorter, erect or arcuate. Lvs 3.25–6×1–2.5cm, rigid, oblong to elliptic, strongly recurved, obtuse, tridentate, light green to dark green, often flushed purple-red. Infl. slightly surpassing lvs, slender; dorsal sep. to 30×3mm, apex purple-maroon, base white lined dark maroon-purple, lanceolate, apex clavate, finely papillate, lateral sep. to 30×10mm, forming an obovate, bidentate synsepalum,

cream-white spotted dark maroon, obovate, bidentate; pet. to 19×1mm, similar to dorsal sep.; lip to 9×2mm, pale yellow-brown spotted dark maroon-purple, sometimes suffused maroon, finely erose-crenulate, lateral lobes falcate, midlobe linear-ligulate, retuse; column to 5mm, yellow-cream flushed rose, anth. white. Venezuela.

R.leopardina hort. See **R.guttulata**.
R.maculata Lindl. See **R.guttulata**.
R.miersii (Lindl.) Rchb. f. See **Barbrodria miersii**.
R.pardina Lem. See **R.guttulata**.
R.punctulata Lindl. See **R.elegans**.
R.ophiocephala Rchb. f. See **Pleurothallis ophiocephala**.

Restrepiella Garay & Dunsterv. (Diminutive form of *Restrepia*, an allied genus.) 1 species, an epiphyte allied to *Pleurothallis*. Pseudobulbs absent. Secondary stems tufted, slender, basally enveloped by tubular sheaths, apically unifoliate. Leaves thickly coriaceous, erect, sessile or shortly petiolate, obscurely conduplicate. Inflorescence short, solitary, fasciculate, born from leaf-base, i.e. at apex of secondary stems, 1- or many-flowered; flowers small; sepals velutinous, dorsal sepal free, lateral sepals free or briefly connate; petals velutinous, smaller than sepals, carinate; lip articulated to column foot, arcuate, simple to obscurely 3-lobed, disc with a carinate, longitudinal callus; column erect or arcuate, short, stout, with a distinct basal foot, anther terminal, operculate, incumbent, pollinia 4, waxy. Costa Rica and Venezuela to Peru.

CULTIVATION As for *Pleurothallis*.

R.ophiocephala (Lindl.) Garay & Dunsterv. (*Pleurothallis ophiocephala* Lindl.; *Pleurothallis puberula* Klotzsch; *Pleurothallis stigmatoglossa* Rchb. f.).
Secondary stems to 20cm. Lvs to 20×4cm, oblong to lanceolate, acute to obtuse; petiole sulcate. Fls solitary, dull yellow or yellow-white blotched purple, fleshy, interior papillose-pubesc.; sep. elliptic-oblong to ligulate-oblong, obtuse or rounded, dorsal sep. to 2.8×0.8cm, lateral sep. to 2.5×0.4cm; pet. to 0.8×0.3cm, elliptic-oblong to obovate-oblong, rounded, margins white-fimbriate; lip to 0.3×0.2cm, fleshy, recurved, elliptic-oblong, obtuse; column to 0.2cm, short, stout, apex tridentate, winged. Mexico, Guatemala, El Salvador, Costa Rica.

Rhinerrhiza Rupp. (From Gk *rhine*, file and *rhiza*, root, referring to the rasp-like nature of the roots.) 2 species of short-stemmed monopodial epiphytes. Roots dark, rough, papillose. Stems flat, sheathed with old leaf bases. Leaves oblong, rigid, coriaceous. Inflorescence racemose, axillary, pendent; flowers ephemeral; sepals and petals equal, almost filiform; lip mobile, attached to the column base, trilobed, lateral lobes oblong, with a dentate callus arising from the bases and a larger central callus, spur frontal, pouch-like. NE & SW Australia.

CULTIVATION As for *Vanda*.

R.divitiflora (Muell. ex Benth.) Rupp (*Sarcochilus divitiflorus* F. Muell. ex Benth.). RASPY ROOT.
Stems 6–8cm, erect or pendent. Lvs 5–15cm, 3–6, oblong, margins slightly undulate, shallow-grooved above. Infl. 6–30cm, 1–8, fl. buds dormant for several months, opening suddenly and dying within 48 hours; fls pale orange, dotted and blotched red; sep. and pet. 30–50×2mm, narrow-linear, tapering, filiform; lip to 4mm, white, clawed, midlobe subtriangular, white-saccate, lateral lobes suboblong, spur to 1mm, forward-pointing. Midsummer–mid-autumn. NSW, Queensland.

R.moorei (Rchb. f.) M. Clements, B. Wallace & D. Jones.
Stems to 12cm. Lvs 3–8, oblong, tinged pink or mauve. Fls to 15mm diam., fragrant, 10–50, tawny yellow, dotted and blotched brown; pet. and sep. spathulate, concave, narrowing at base; lip fleshy, white or yellow, midlobe minute, lateral lobes to 5mm, crescent-shaped, erect, incurved, callus fleshy, spur to 3mm, conical. NE Australia.

Rhyncholaelia Schltr. (Gk *rhynchos*, snout, and *Laelia*, the name of a closely allied genus.) 2 species of robust epiphytes or lithophytes formerly included in *Brassavola*, from which they differ in their habit, resembling unifoliate *Cattleya* spp., and large pale flowers with very showy lips. Mexico, C America.

CULTIVATION   As for the unifoliate *Cattleya* spp. but with maximum sunlight at all times.

R.digbyana (Lindl.) Schltr. (*Brassavola digbyana* Lindl.).
Epiphytic. Rhiz. thick, creeping. Pseudobulbs to 15cm, clavate, ridged, sheathed with papery grey-white bracts, compressed, unifoliate, clustered. Lvs to 20×5.5cm, erect, rigidly coriaceous, oblong-elliptic, obtuse, powdery grey-green. Infl. to 13cm, 1-fld; fls to 17.5cm diam., strongly scented, long-lived; sep. and pet. pale yellow-green; sep. to 10×2.5cm, ligulate-oblong to elliptic-lanceolate, obtuse; pet. to 9×3cm, obliquely elliptic-lanceolate, obtuse; lip to 7.5×8cm, white to cream-white, tinged green, emarginate, obscurely 3-lobed, lateral lobes small, erect, enveloping column forming a tube, midlobe deeply and heavily lacerate-fimbriate; disc lamellate; column to 3.5cm, semiterete. Mexico, Belize.

R.glauca (Lindl.) Schltr. (*Brassavola glauca* Lindl.).
Epiphytic or terrestrial. Rhiz. stout, creeping. Pseudobulbs to

9cm, oblong-fusiform, compressed, unifoliate, clothed in thin sheaths. Lvs to 12×3.5cm, erect, thickly coriaceous, elliptic-oblong, obtuse, leaden green, somewhat glaucous. Infl. to 10cm, erect; fls to 12.5cm diam., fragrant, long-lived; sep. and pet. white, olive-green or very pale lavender; sep. to 6.5×1.5cm, linear-elliptic to oblong-lanceolate, subobtuse or subacuminate; pet. linear or oblong-oblanceolate, oblique, obtuse to subacute, slightly undulate; lip rounded, to 5.5×4cm, white to yellow-cream, with a rose-pink or purple mark at base, throat sometimes striped red-purple, very obscurely 3-lobed, lateral lobes enveloping column at base forming a tube, midlobe transversely oblong-subquadrate, margin basically entire, slightly undulate; column to 1cm, stout, clavate, clinandrium dentate. Mexico, Guatemala, Honduras.

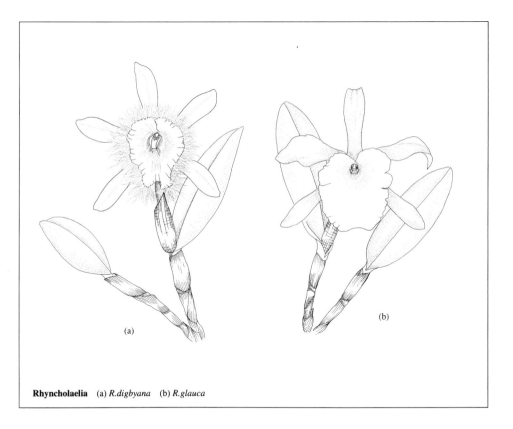

Rhyncholaelia   (a) *R.digbyana*   (b) *R.glauca*

Rhynchostylis Bl. (From Gk *rhynchos*, beak and *stylos*, column, referring to the beaked column.) FOXTAIL ORCHID. 3 species of monopodial epiphytes. Leaves alternate, basally overlapping, sessile, coriaceous, linear to linear-oblong. Inflorescence axillary, a dense cylindrical raceme; flowers white, marked pink, mauve or purple; sepals and petals spreading, obtuse, lateral sepals fused to column foot, the petals narrower, smaller; lip entire or trilobed, basally saccate or with a deflexed spur, pubescent, apically ovate, concave, acute. Tropical Asia.

CULTIVATION As for *Vanda*.

R.coelestis (Rchb. f.) Rchb. f.
Stems thick, to 20cm. Lvs to 20cm, ligulate, fleshy. Infl. erect; fls to 2cm diam., waxy; sep. and pet. ovate-oblong, obtuse, white, apically blotched indigo; lip obovate-oblong, white tipped mauve or indigo, spur saccate. Thailand.

R.gigantea (Lindl.) Ridl.
Stems to 20cm. Lvs to 35cm, linear, thick, channelled. Infl. 20–35cm, 2–4 per plant, pendulous; fls fragrant, white, spotted violet to dark purple; lip to 3cm diam., white, terminal lobes bright purple; sep. elliptic-oblong, rounded or obtuse;

pet. similar; lip apically trilobed, triangular, fleshy, disc with 2 pubesc. ridges descending into the short, inflated, retrorse spur. Burma, Indochina, Thailand. Fls pure white in var. *petotiana*.

R.retusa (L.) Bl.
Stems 10–20cm. Lvs to 45cm, linear, oblong, channelled, blunt. Raceme to 30cm; fls fragrant, white, spotted purple; dorsal sep. oblong, lateral sep. ovate, obtuse; pet. narrower, oblong, basally saccate, pubesc., rounded, concave. Tropical Asia.

× **Rhynchovanda** (*Rhynchostylis* × *Vanda*). Very attractive hybrids with long flower spikes, especially those bred from *R.coelestis* and the amethyst tetraploid form of *R.gigantea*. Stems upright. Leaves alternate in two rows, narrowly channelled. Inflorescences are axillary, on upright spikes; flowers round, usually in shades of blue, with a small lip. They are long-lasting on the plant and as cut flowers. The plants need bright light, high humidity and warm temperatures to grow and flower well. They grow extremely well out of doors in the humid tropics but are less easy in the glasshouse.

× *R.*Sagarik Wine: one of the earliest hybrids and still one of the best; fls deep-purple mauve to blue; many awarded clones.
× *R.*Blue Angel: compact plants that are very free flowering; upright spikes of small, dainty blue fls.
× *R.*Wok Yoke Sim: upright spikes of deep blue fls.

Robiquetia Gaudich. (Named for Pierre Robiquet, French scientist.) Some 40 species of monopodial epiphytes. Leaves distichous, elliptic or oblong, narrow. Inflorescence axillary, pendent, racemose; fls small, many; sepals and petals free, dorsal sepal hooded; lip trilobed, midlobe linear or tapering, concave, fleshy, often with a basal ridge, lateral lobes small with variable fleshy thickenings; spur almost cylindric. Indomalaya to Fiji.

CULTIVATION As for *Vanda*.

R.bertholdii (Rchb. f.) Schltr. (*Saccolabium bertholdii* Rchb. f.).
Stems fleshy, to 15cm. Lvs to 25cm, oblong, alternate, apex unequally bilobed. Infl. to 20cm; fls white, pink or dark pink, apical margins green; sep. oblong; pet. ovate; lip triangular; spur apex dark pink, swollen. Vanuatu, Solomon Is., Fiji.

R.mooreana (Rolfe) J.J. Sm. (*Saccolabium mooreanum* Rolfe).
Lvs to 15cm, oblong, coriaceous, margins recurved, mottled beneath. Infl. oblong or ovoid; fls dense, green-white to rose purple; sep. oblong, concave; pet. ovate-oblong; lip midlobe

fleshy, navicular, lateral lobes rounded, erect. New Guinea, Solomon Is.

R.spathulata (Bl.) J.J. Sm. (*Cleisostoma spathulata* Bl.).
Stems pendent, to 50cm+. Lvs to 20×5cm. Infl. pendent, to 25cm; fls dense to 1cm diam., sep. and pet. burnt sienna, edged bronze-yellow with similar central line, lip ochre; sep. and pet. obtuse, apically thickened above; lip midlobe triangular, lateral lobes triangular, sited at the spur aperture; spur apically compressed. Java, Malaysia.

Rodriguezia Ruiz & Pav. (For the Spanish botanist Don Manuel Rodriguez.) Some 35 species of epiphytes. Rhizome short or elongate. Pseudobulbs small, ovoid or elliptic-oblong, laterally compressed, enveloped by conspicuous, 3–6 overlapping leaf-sheaths, apex unifoliate or bifoliate. Leaves rigidly coriaceous and somewhat fleshy, often with a rather grainy texture and rough margins, narrowly ligulate to elliptic-lanceolate, distichous, acute or obtuse obscurely conduplicate with midvein sunken above, carinate beneath. Inflorescence a basal raceme, erect or deflexed, few to many-flowered; flowers often showy, white or yellow to magenta or scarlet, often crystalline-textured; dorsal sepal free, spreading, concave, lateral sepals connate, often geniculate or gibbous; petals similar to dorsal sepal, oblique; lip unguiculate, adnate to column-base, simple, obovate or ovoid to spathulate, produced into short spur at base, disc carinate or cristate; column short or elongate, erect, clavate, slender, subcylindrical, footless, biauriculate at apex, anther terminal, operculate, incumbent, unilocular, pollinia 2, waxy, ovoid or subglobose. Tropical America.

CULTIVATION Compact plants for the intermediate house. The most commonly grown species are *R.candida* with snow-white flowers and *R.lanceolata* with crimson or ruby red flowers of a remarkable sparkling quality. Pot in shallow clay pans in a fine to medium-grade bark mix with additional sphagnum or rockwool. The roots are fine and easily broken and plants as a whole tend to damp off rather easily. Water throughout the year, allowing a slight drying between applications and feeding and misting freely when in growth. Position in bright filtered light in the cooler and drier end of the house. Propagate by division. Susceptible to scale insect.

R.batemannii Poepp. & Endl.
Pseudobulbs to 5×2.5cm, elliptic to oblong, strongly compressed, apex unifoliate. Lvs to 35×4cm, strongly coriaceous, linear to oblong, acute to shortly acuminate. Infl. to 25cm, ascending or pendent, loosely few to many-fld; fls fragrant, thin-textured, white, white marked yellow or pale lilac spotted lilac; dorsal sep. to 35×12mm, ligulate or lanceolate to oblong-elliptic, acute, lateral sep. to 50×12mm, largely connate, forming a synsepalum, deeply concave, oblong-lanceolate; pet. to 35×13mm, obovate-oblong or ligulate, acute; lip to 48×25mm, obovate-cuneate, emarginate, disc bicarinate; column to 2cm, often pubesc., auricles oblong-lanceolate, obtuse. Peru, Venezuela, Brazil.

R.candida Batem. ex Lindl.
Pseudobulbs to 5×3cm, elliptic or ovate-elliptic in outline, clustered, strongly compressed, apex unifoliate. Lvs to 15×4.5cm, usually shorter, oblong to oblong-lanceolate, acute or subacute. Infl. to 30cm, arcuate to pendent, few-fld; fls large, showy, fragrant, white; dorsal sep. to 30×15mm, narrowly obovate to oblong-obovate, lateral sep. connate forming a synsepalum, oblanceolate, deeply concave, bifid; pet. to 33×17mm, erect, obliquely obovate, emarginate, truncate; lip to 54×27mm, narrowly obovate, emarginate, bilobulate, margins involute, callus yellow, fleshy, basal, elevated; column to 25mm, white, terete. Venezuela, Brazil, Guyana.

R.compacta Schltr.
Pseudobulbs to 2.5×1.5cm, elliptic-oblong, apex unifoliate. Lvs to 14×2.5cm, ligulate to oblong-ligulate, obtuse, coriaceous. Infl. to 4.5cm, slender, deflexed, few-fld; fls to 5cm, fragrant; tepals pale yellow or green-yellow, dorsal sep. to 2.5cm, narrowly oblong, obtuse, lateral sep. to 26mm, largely connate, forming a synsepalum, base geniculate, apex bifid, pet. to 2.5cm, oblong, obtuse; lip to 2.5×1cm, yellow, obovate-spathulate, deeply emarginate, base produced into a short spur; column minutely pubesc. at base. Nicaragua, Costa Rica, Panama.

R.decora (Lem.) Rchb. f.
Pseudobulbs to 2.5cm, ovoid, apex unifoliate. Lvs to 15×2.5cm, rigidly coriaceous, oblong or linear-oblong, acute. Infl. to 40cm, usually shorter, erect or slightly arching, loosely few to many-fld; fls to 3.5cm, slightly fragrant; tepals white or yellow-white, spotted or mottled dark red-purple; dorsal sep. to 12×4mm, elliptic-oblong, acute, lateral sep. to 15mm, narrowly oblong, apiculate; pet. to 14×6mm, elliptic-oblong, shortly acuminate; lip to 28×14mm, white, broadly clawed, orbicular, apex bilobed, base narrow, callus 5-keeled, keels spotted red, basal spur to 2mm; column terete, horns purple. Autumn–winter. Brazil.

R.granadensis (Lindl.) Rchb. f.
Pseudobulbs to 3cm, ovoid, usually wholly concealed by lf-sheaths, apex unifoliate. Lvs to 15cm, lanceolate, acute, coriaceous. Infl. to 15cm, pendent, loosely several-fld; fls to 3cm diam., white, lip marked yellow; dorsal sep. and pet. similar

to 2.5cm, ovate or lanceolate, acute; lateral sep. to 2.5cm, connate forming a navicular synsepalum; lip to 3.5cm, ovate or obovate, emarginate, base narrow, tubular, basal spur to 2cm, callus yellow; column to 3cm. Colombia.

R.lanceolata Ruiz & Pav. (*R.secunda* HBK).
Pseudobulbs to 4×2.5cm, elliptic-oblong to ovate-oblong, strongly laterally compressed, mostly concealed by lf-sheaths, apex unifoliate. Lvs to 25×3.5cm, linear-oblong to elliptic-oblong, subacute or obliquely emarginate. Infl. 8–40cm, erect or ascending, loosely to densely many-fld; fls small, pink to rose-red of a sparkling quality; dorsal sep. to 14×8mm, ovate to ovate-oblong, subacute, apiculate; lateral sep. to 16×10mm, connate forming a synsepalum, gibbous at base; pet. to 14×8mm, ovate or obovate to elliptic, concave, acute or apiculate; lip to 18×9mm, obovate-oblong, undulate, deeply emarginate; callus fleshy, conspicuously bicarinate sometimes paler or white; column to 6mm, apex bidentate, base finely pubesc. Panama, Colombia, Venezuela, Peru, Brazil, Trinidad, Guyana, Surinam.

R.lindenii Cogn. See *R.pubescens*.
R.lindmanii Kränzl. See *Solenidium lunatum*.

R.maculata (Lindl.) Rchb. f.
Pseudobulbs to 2.5cm, ovoid to ovoid-oblong, apex unifoliate. Lvs to 15×1.5cm, linear-lanceolate, acute, coriaceous. Infl. 6–15cm, arching to pendent, loosely several-fld; fls to 3cm, fragrant; tepals yellow spotted cinnamon, sep. to 14×6mm, thin-textured, ovate-oblong, acute, lateral sep. connate, gibbous, pet. similar to dorsal sep.; lip to 25×10mm, yellow-brown blotched dark brown, base white, long-clawed, obovate-cordate, deeply cleft, apex bilobed, base narrow, disc tricarinate; column to 8mm. Brazil.

R.maculata Lindl. See *Leochilus oncidioides*.

R.pubescens (Lindl.) Rchb. f. (*R.lindenii* Cogn.).
Pseudobulbs to 3.5×1.5cm, oblong, apex unifoliate. Lvs to 13×2cm, coriaceous, oblong-ligulate, acute. Infl. 5–15cm, arching to pendent, loosely several to many-fld; fls to 3.5cm diam., fragrant, pure white; sep. to 15×5mm, oblong-lanceolate, acute or acuminate; pet. to 14×5mm, ovate-lanceolate to lanceolate-spathulate, acute, minutely apiculate; lip to 17×10mm, long-clawed, subcordate to obovate-cordate to subdeltoid, deeply emarginate, bilobed, undulate, disc yellow, with several keels; column to 8mm, densely pubesc. Brazil.

R.secunda HBK. See *R.lanceolata*.

R.venusta (Lindl.) Rchb. f.
Pseudobulbs to 3×1.5cm, narrowly ovoid to ovoid-oblong, apex unifoliate. Lvs to 15×2.5cm, linear-lanceolate, acute, coriaceous, dark green. Infl. 8–17cm, arching, loosely few-fld; fls to 3.5cm, strongly fragrant, white; sep. to 15×9mm, obovate, acute, lateral sep. connate, gibbous; pet. to 17×7mm, obovate-oblong, acute; lip to 22×14mm, long-clawed, obovate-obcordate to triangular-obcordate, deeply emarginate, undulate, base narrow, disc yellow, fleshy, bicarinate; column to 9mm. Brazil, Peru.

Rodrigueziella Kuntze. (For Dr Joao Barbosa Rodriques, Brazilian botanist.) 1 species, an epiphyte allied to *Gomesa*. Pseudobulbs small, clustered, ovoid or ovoid-oblong, compressed, ancipitous, apex usually bifoliate. Leaves to 15×1.5cm, linear-lanceolate, acuminate. Inflorescence more or less equalling leaves, secund, suberect or arching, many-flowered; flowers to 3cm; pendent, small, fragrant, sepals and petals similar, green-yellow to green-brown, erect, narrowly lanceolate; lip complex, apical portion brown, basal portion white or yellow-white, ovate-oblong to pandurate, projecting between lateral sepals, disc with 2 basal, pubescent calli, yellow; column short. Brazil.

CULTIVATION As for *Gomesa*.

R.gomesioides (Barb. Rodr.) O. Kuntze (*Gomesa theodorea* Cogn.; *Hellerorchis gomezoides* (Barb. Rodr.) A.D. Hawkes; *Theodorea gomesioides* Barb. Rodr.).

Rossioglossum (Schltr.) Garay & Kenn. (For J. Ross, who collected orchids in Mexico in the 1830s.) Some 6 species of epiphytes closely allied to *Odontoglossum* but distinguished by the free (not partly adnate) lip perpendicular to the column with auriculate basal lobes and specialized callus. Rhizome short; roots brown-white, thick. Growth somewhat glaucous at first. Pseudobulbs clustered, ovoid, laterally compressed, furrowed with age, subtended by several scarious sheaths, usually bifoliate. Leaves broadly elliptic to lanceolate, acute to obtuse, narrowing to short conduplicate petioles, often grey-brown scaly below when young. Raceme lateral, erect or bowed, usually few-flowered; bracts linear to oblong; flowers showy, large, usually yellow marked with brown; sepals and petals subequal or with petals wider; lip free, short-clawed, often pandurate or 3-lobed, deflexed, lateral lobes small, auriculate, midlobe large, callus prominent, fleshy or protuberant lobes; column slightly arcuate, with semi-orbicular auricles on either side of stigma, canaliculate or produced into a plate below stigma; anther incumbent, pollinia 2, yellow, pyriform. Mostly autumn–winter. Mexico to Panama.

CULTIVATION Extremely showy orchids formerly included in *Odontoglossum* and much in demand for cool to intermediate-growing collections or cultivation as a potplant in the home; *R.grande* with great chestnut-banded flowers and a comic face-like callus is the well-known Clown Orchid. Pot every two years in a relatively dense medium (failures have been common in recent years because of the rise of bark-dominated mixtures) containing some leafmould, sphagnum and dolomitic limestone; place in a cool, well ventilated and brightly lit situation, avoiding sunscorch and wetting of the rather fleshy foliage. Water and feed copiously when in growth to provide the plumpest possible pseudobulbs. On their completion, withhold water except to prevent excessive

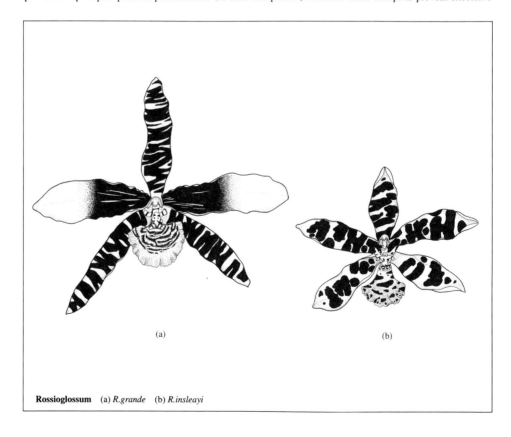

(a)   (b)

Rossioglossum   (a) *R.grande*   (b) *R.insleayi*

shrivelling. Flower spikes will develop in late summer and autumn, blooming in winter. Repot and recommence watering on first appearance of new growth. Propagate by division on repotting.

R.grande (Lindl.) Garay & Kenn. (*Odontoglossum grande* Lindl.). CLOWN ORCHID.
Pseudobulbs 5–10×3.5–6cm, orbicular to ovoid, glaucescent, clustered, faces convex, compressed to sharp narrow lateral margins. Lvs to 40×6.5cm, elliptic to lanceolate, acute, sage green, coriaceous, glabrous. Raceme 14–30cm, 2–8-fld; fls to 15cm diam., wide-spreading, long-lived, waxy, the patches of red-brown coloration glossy; sep. to 8.5×2cm, yellow, transversely barred and flecked rust to chestnut brown, lanceolate, acute to acuminate and recurved at apex, margins undulate; pet. to 8×3cm, yellow, basal half solidly deep red-brown with yellow tips and margins, oblanceolate to oblong, obtuse to acute, margins undulate; lip cream-white or cream-yellow, flecked or banded red-brown, without claw, to 4.5cm, pandurate, obscurely 3-lobed, lateral lobes rounded, revolute, midlobe suborbicular to quadrate, ruffed, callus yellow, quadrate, conspicuously bicorniculate, the protuberances eye-like, winged brick red; column to 1.5cm, minutely pubesc., with 2 oblong or rounded auricles. Late autumn–winter. Guatemala, Mexico.

R.insleayi (Barker ex Lindl.) Garay & Kenn. (*Oncidium insleayi* Barker ex Lindl.; *Odontoglossum insleayi* (Barker ex Lindl.) Lindl.).
Fls readily distinguished from *R.grande* by its revolute tepals and, therefore, slender mien, and the broken banding on its petals – *R.grande* is solidly chestnut in the basal half of the petals. Pseudobulbs to 10cm, bifoliate or trifoliate. Lvs to 12.5cm, elliptic-oblong, similar to *R.grande*. Raceme to 30cm,

erect, 5–10-fld; fls to 10cm diam.; tepals yellow or yellow-green, broken-banded chestnut-red, elliptic-oblong, obtuse, wide-spreading, margins strongly recurved; lip bright yellow spotted red-cinnamon near margins, orbicular-reniform, 3-lobed, lateral lobes upcurved, midlobe narrowly clawed, spathulate, undulate; column short with 2 red, subulate horns. Mostly autumn. Mexico.

R.powellii Schltr. See *R.schlieperianum*.

R.schlieperianum (Rchb. f.) Garay & Kenn. (*R.powellii* Schltr.; *R.warscewiczii* Bridges ex Stein).
Vegetatively similar to *R.grande*. Raceme robust, to 25cm, erect, 2–8-fld; fls to 10cm diam.; tepals pale yellow to bronze, blotched and barred yellow-ochre to rust, sep. ovate-lanceolate, subacute, margins incurved, pet. oblong-elliptic; lip similar colour to sep., pandurate, obscurely 3-lobed, lateral lobes erect, rounded, midlobe oblong-spathulate, obtuse to retuse, margins recurved, callus bright yellow marked red, with short central keel; column short with incurved, filamentous horns at apex. Autumn. Costa Rica, Panama.

R.warscewiczii Bridges ex Stein. See *R.schlieperianum*.

R.williamsianum (Rchb. f.) Garay & Kenn. (*Odontoglossum williamsianum* Rchb. f.; *Odontoglossum grande* var. *williamsianum* Rchb. f.).
Resembles closely *R.grande* except infl. longer, fls smaller, with little red-brown blotching, pet. shorter, broader, broadly rounded, column wings uncinate. Spring. Costa Rica, Guatemala, Honduras, Mexico.

Sarcochilus R. Br. (From Gk *sarx*, flesh, and *cheilos*, lip; referring to the fleshy lip of the flower.) Some 15 species of diminutive monopodial epiphytes and lithophytes. Stem short, often branching at base, becoming tufted, sheathed with old leaf bases. Leaves obovate to linear-falcate, somewhat fleshy with sunken midveins. Flowers in axillary racemes; sepals and petals, almost equal, lateral sepals fused completely or partially to the column base; lip stalked, mobile, trilobed, saccate, with short, poorly developed spur, central lobe small, fleshy, attached to the spur near its aperture, disc with grooved calli. Papuasia, Australia, Polynesia, SE Asia.

CULTIVATION Exceptionally compact and attractive plants producing clumped, short stems of clean foliage and arching racemes of colourful flowers. Their cultural requirements are much the same as those of *Phalaenopsis* or *Vanda*, but their stature allows for greater flexibility both in their use and display and in the manipulation of their environment. Excellent plants for windowsill and growing cases.

S.australis (Lindl.) Rchb. f. (*S.barklyanus* F. Muell.).
Stem to 2cm. Lvs 2–7cm, to 15, usually fewer, linear to falcate, slightly twisted, coriaceous. Racemes pendulous; fls fragrant, 2–15; sep. and pet. pale yellow-green to brown, dorsal sep. ovate to lanceolate, narrow, suberect, lateral sep. 8–15mm, lanceolate, decurved and incurved, pet. linear to lanceolate, almost erect; lip white tinted yellow, midlobe erect, ovate to obovate, calli prominent, lateral lobes half length of dorsal sep. with fine red or white lines, spur decurved. Mid autumn–mid winter. E Australia, Tasmania.

S.barklyanus F. Muell. See *S.australis*.

S.ceciliae F. Muell.
Stems 2–12cm, erect. Lvs to 10cm, linear to lanceolate, often marked brown. Infl. erect, narrow, exceeding lvs; fls pink to purple, 6–15; dorsal sep. narrow, obovate, lateral sep. 8–12mm, ovate not contracted at base (cf *S.roseus*); lip to 2mm, midlobe downy, lateral lobes oblong-falcate, ciliate, spur obtuse, disc with golden yellow calli, almost fused to lateral lobes. Late autumn–mid winter. NSW, Queensland.

S.divitiflorus F. Muell. ex Benth. See *Rhinerrhiza divitiflora*.

S.falcatus R. Br. ORANGE BLOSSOM ORCHID.
Stems to 8cm, semi-pendulous. Lvs to 10cm, 3–8, oblong-falcate, base conspicuously sheathed and to some degree auricled, fleshy, olive green. Racemes loose, arching, borne below lvs; fls to 12, fragrant, white, sep. striped purple below; sep. and pet. ovate, narrowing basally; lip 4–6mm; midlobe erect, narrow, fleshy, yellow, lateral lobes oblong, orange spotted or banded garnet; spur thin, fleshy, grooved with narrow central calli near apex and on lateral walls. Mid summer–mid autumn. E Australia, NSW, Victoria, Queensland.

S.fitzgeraldii F. Muell. RAVINE ORCHID.
Stems to 60cm. Lvs to 14cm, 4–8, linear to narrow-oblong, falcate, fleshy, slightly twisted. Racemes to 20cm, numerous; fls 4–15, white or pink, blotched cerise or crimson at centre, sometimes extending to the apices; lip less than half sep. length, midlobe triangular, fleshy, yellow or orange, lateral lobes subfalcate, central callus narrow, spur, blunt, fleshy, forward-pointing.

Mid–late autumn. NSW, Queensland.

S.Fitzhart (*S.fitzgeraldii* × *S.hartmannii*).
Vigorous artificial hybrid. Stems shorter than in *S.fitzgeraldii* and densely tufted. Lvs to 10cm, subcoriaceous, pale green, narrow-lanceolate to falcate. Racemes to 15cm, ascending; fls to 3cm diam., white centrally spotted pink or maroon. Winter–spring. Garden origin.

S.hartmannii F. Muell.
Stems to 50cm. Lvs to 20cm 4–10, linear to narrow oblong, falcate. Raceme dense; fls to 3cm diam., 5–25; sep. and pet. white, basally spotted maroon, ovate, narrowing basally; lip minute, thick, waxy, midlobe conical, lateral lobes to 2mm embracing the column, striped garnet within, callus fleshy, ridged, base of column spotted or wholly red. Autumn. NSW, Queensland.

S.hillii (F. Muell.) F. Muell. (*S.minutiflos* Bail.).
Stems to 5cm. Lvs to 10cm, 2–10, linear, channelled, fleshy, spotted. Infl. narrow, seldom exceeding lvs; fls 2–10, pale pink or white, fragrant; sep. ovate-oblong or ovate wider than pet.; lip 3–4mm, midlobe sub-erect, interior white-pubesc., lateral lobes erect or incurved, interior striped purple, spur narrowly conical, decurved, fleshy, calli and disc yellow or orange, lateral calli pronounced. Late autumn–mid winter. NSW, Queensland.

S.minutiflos Bail. See *S.hillii*.
S.muscosus Rolfe. See *Grosourdya muscosa*.

S.olivaceus Lindl.
Stems to 8cm, semi-pendulous. Lvs to 15cm, 2–8, oblong, rarely falcate, dark green, sometimes tinted purple, margins often undulate, thinner and darker than in *S.falcatus*. Fls 2–12, olive to golden green; sep. and pet. equal, linear-oblong; lip clawed, white marked maroon; midlobe oblong, lateral lobes oblong-falcate, callus fleshy, spur blunt, fleshy. Mid summer–early autumn. NSW, Queensland.

S.roseus (Clemesha) Clemesha.
Resembles *S.ceciliae* except lvs shorter with fewer markings, fls thicker, bright rose pink, lateral sep. basally contracted, lip with glabrous lateral lobes, margins entire. Late autumn–mid winter. NE Australia.

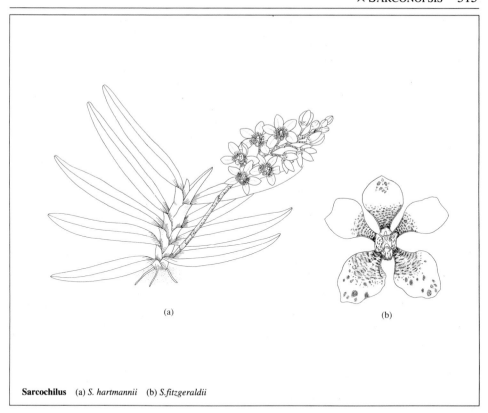

Sarcochilus   (a) *S. hartmannii*   (b) *S.fitzgeraldii*

× **Sarconopsis** (*Sarcochilus* × *Phalaenopsis*). A small hybrid genus of rather fleshy flowers in which the *Phalaenopsis* parent has greatly increased the size of the flowers and the *Sarcochilus* parent has made the plants easier to grow than *Phalaenopsis* in cooler temperatures. The stems are short, upright with the alternate leaves in two rows, leaves wide and fleshy. The inflorescences are axillary, on upright spikes, sometimes branching. The flowers are rounded, in pastel colours. They are long-lasting on the plant and as cut flowers. The plants need shady conditions, high humidity and intermediate temperatures to grow and flower well.

× *S.*Macquarie Lilac: vigorous plants with branching spikes; fls white flushed pink or lilac.

× *S.*Macquarie Sunset: small plants with large fls, fls pale pink with deep raspberry pink flush at the base of the sep. and pet., lip white margined with red.

Satyrium Sw. (From Gk *satyrion*, ancient Gk name for an orchid.) Over 100 species of terrestrials. Tubers globose, ovoid or ellipsoid. Foliage leaves at or toward base of flowering stem, or on separate sterile shoot; rest of flowering stem with sheath-like leaves. Spike terminal, few- to many-fld; bracts often large, reflexed; flowers white, green, yellow, orange, red, pink or lilac; sepals joined at base to petals and lip; petals similar but usually narrower; lip forming hood with wide or narrow mouth; the apex sometimes reflexed, and bearing 2 spurs, long or short, slender or blunt, 2 extra vestigial spurs occasionally present, rarely spurs absent; column erect, incurved, held inside lip; pollinia 2. Mainland Africa, particularly S Africa; Madagascar (5 species), Asia (2 species).

CULTIVATION   As for *Disa*, but a slightly more open mixture and in intermediate conditions.

S.bicorne (L.) Thunb.
Slender, 15–60cm. Lvs 2, adpressed to ground, 3–18cm, broadly ovate to orbicular; stem with several sheathing lvs. Spike densely few- to many-fld; fls dull yellow or green-yellow, tinged with purple-brown, fragrant; ovary 8–14mm; bracts about twice that length, reflexed; sep. 6–9mm, fused to pet. and lip for about one-third of their length; pet. slightly shorter; lip 6–9mm, forming hood with mouth facing down; spurs 10–22mm, slender, parallel to ovary and stem. S Africa (Cape Province).

S.carneum (Ait.) R. Br.
Robust, to 80cm. Lvs 2, adpressed to ground, 8–23cm, broadly ovate to orbicular; stem with several sheathing lvs, the lowest 2 sometimes partly spreading. Spike densely several- to many-fld; fls fleshy, pale to deep rose pink, lip darker than sep. and pet.; ovary 11–18mm; bracts about twice as long, spreading or reflexed; sep. and pet. 13–18mm, free almost to base, lanceolate-oblong, the tips rolled back; lip 15mm, wide-mouthed with reflexed apical flap 2mm long; spurs 18–25mm, slender, parallel to ovary and stem. S Africa (SW Cape).

S.ciliatum Lindl. See *S.nepalense.*

S.coriifolium Sw.
Robust, 20–75cm. Lvs 2–4, 3–15cm, elliptic or ovate, suberect or spreading, thick-textured, purple-spotted below; stem with several sheathing lvs. Spike densely several- to many-fld; fls nodding or held horizontally, bright orange or yellow, tinged with red; ovary 10–14mm; bracts 2–3× as long, reflexed; sep. and pet. 7–13mm, fused in basal third, oblong, the pet. narrower than the sep.; lip 10–13mm with reflexed apical flap 2mm long and dorsal keel 1mm high, very hooded, the mouth facing the ground; spurs 9–12mm, slender, parallel to ovary. S Africa (Cape Province).

S.erectum Lindl.
Robust, 10–50cm. Lvs 2, adpressed to ground, 4–15cm, ovate to orbicular, fleshy; stem with several sheathing lvs, the lower ones partly spreading. Spike densely several- to many-fld; fls pale to deep pink with darker marks and sweet, pungent scent; ovary 6–14mm; bracts 2–3× as long, reflexed; sep. and pet. 10–15mm, obovate-oblong, obtuse, joined for one-third of their length to each other and lip, then deflexed or spreading; lip 10–15mm, wide-mouthed, with partly reflexed apical flap 3–4mm long and with dorsal keel; spurs 5–11mm, tapering from a fairly wide mouth. S Africa (Cape Province).

S.macrophyllum Lindl.
Slender or robust, to 1m. Lvs 2–3, near base of stem but not adpressed to ground, 5–30cm, ovate or lanceolate, spreading, light green; stem with several sheathing lvs. Spike fairly densely many-fld; fls pale to deep pink; ovary 8–13mm; bracts 2–4× as long, reflexed; sep. and pet. 7–14mm, fused to each other and lip for over half their length, then spreading; lip 10–12mm with short apical flap, wide-mouthed; spurs 13–26mm, slender, tapering, parallel to ovary and stem. S & C Tropical Africa, S Africa, Swaziland.

S.membranaceum Sw.
Slender or robust, to 50cm. Lvs 2, adpressed to ground, 2–12cm, broadly ovate, obtuse; stem with several sheathing lvs, usually dry and membranous by flowering time. Spike laxly or densely few- to many-fld; fls pale to deep pink, rarely almost white; ovary 9–18mm; bracts 1–2× as long, reflexed, usually dry and membranous by flowering time; sep. and pet. 9–11mm, oblong, the lip and pet. with serrate edge, fused for about one-quarter of their length; lip 9–11mm, wide-mouthed, with apical flap 3mm long, serrate, reflexed; spurs 20–30mm, standing away from ovary and stem. S Africa (Cape Province).

S.nepalense D. Don (*S.ciliatum* Lindl.).
Robust, 50–75cm. Lvs in basal rosette. Spike 2.5–15cm, densely many-fld; fls bright pink, 10–13mm diam. Summer. Pakistan to SW China. Plants formerly known as *S.ciliatum*, from Nepal and Tibet, have ciliate sep. and pet., but these are now usually included in *S.nepalense.*

S.odorum Sonder.
Robust, to 50cm with leafy stem. Lvs 2–6, the largest 4–24cm long, spreading, ovate, fleshy. Spike rather laxly to fairly densely few- to many-fld; fls pale green or yellow-green tinged with purple-brown, with strong, sweet pungent scent; ovary 9–13mm; bracts 1–3× as long, reflexed; sep. 4–8mm, oblong, deflexed; pet. just over half as long; lip 8–10mm, wide-mouthed, with apical flap 2mm long; spurs 13–18mm, slender, arched, occasionally with small extra spurs to 3mm. S Africa (Cape Province).

S.pumilum Thunb.
Very small, tufted, producing clumps of rounded lvs barely breaking the soil surface. Fls comparatively large on short spikes, hooded, green overlaid with blood-red to maroon mottling. S Africa (Cape Province).

Scaphosepalum Pfitz. (From Gk *skaphe*, bowl, and *sepalum*, referring to the concave form of the sepals.) Some 30 species of diminutive epiphytes lithophytes allied to *Masdevallia* and *Pleurothallis*. Rhizome short, tufted or elongate, creeping. Pseudobulbs absent. Secondary stems short, erect or ascending, slender to stout, concealed by scarious sheaths, unifoliate. Leaves elliptic to oblong-spathulate, erect or arching, subfleshy to coriaceous, contracted toward base into a short, grooved petiole. Inflorescence secund or distichous, a raceme, erect to pendent, few- to many-flowered; flowers usually somewhat cupped, small, opening in succession; sepals narrow, spreading, thickened, dorsal sepals mostly free, tailed, the lateral sepals largely united forming a concave synsepalum, their apices contracted into tails, with 2 fleshy distal calli; petals inconspicuous; lip small, simple or obscurely 3-lobed, delicately articulate to column foot, disc usually with 2 toothed crests; column incurved, base produced into a short foot, apex broadly winged, margins denticulate, anther terminal, operculate, incumbent, pollinia 2, waxy, obovate, laterally compressed. Tropical Americas.

CULTIVATION As for *Masdevallia*.

S.amethystinum (Rchb. f.) Schltr. See *Porroglossum amethystinum*.

S.anchoriferum (Rchb. f.) Rolfe (*Masdevallia anchorifera* Rchb. f.; *S.punctatum* (Rolfe) Rolfe; *Masdevallia punctata* Rolfe).
Epiphytic. Secondary stems to 3cm. Lvs to 20×2.5cm, elliptic, acute. Infl. to 20cm, ascending to pendent, several-fld; dorsal sep. to 15×6mm, ovate, acute, margins revolute, lateral sep. to 12×12mm, elliptic, callus to 7×6mm, triangular, densely pubesc., yellow or yellow-orange spotted red-purple, tails to 5mm, slender, recurved; pet. to 5×3mm, ovate, acute; lip to 5×2.5mm, yellow or orange tinged or spotted red-purple, oblong-subpandurate, apex serrulate; column to 5mm, green tinged red, slender. Costa Rica, Panama.

S.antenniferum Rolfe (*S.reversum* Kränzl.).
Epiphytic or terrestrial. Secondary stems to 5cm. Lvs to 27×7cm, erect, elliptic, subacute. Infl. to 60cm, loosely to densely many-fld, erect; peduncle stout, verrucose; tepals dull green to yellow-green, marked and tinged purple, dorsal sep. to 18×7mm, ovate-linear, apiculate, revolute, glandular within, lateral sep. to 15×10mm, ovate, truncate to obtuse, apical calli to 7×3mm, broadly lunate, tails to 12mm, slender, decurved, verrucose, pet. to 7×3mm, obliquely ovate, acute; lip to 5×3mm, green spotted purple, subpandurate, apex rounded, denticulate; column to 6mm, green tinged purple. Colombia, Ecuador, Peru.·

S.breve (Rchb. f.) Rolfe (*Masdevallia brevis* Rchb. f.).
Epiphytic. Secondary stems to 3cm. Lvs to 14×2cm, narrowly elliptic, acute. Infl. to 25cm, loosely several to many-fld, flexuous; peduncle filiform, ascending to horizontal, verrucose; sep. and pet. yellow to yellow-green marked purple, dorsal sep. to 18×4mm, ovate, acute, margins revolute, lateral sep. to 12×7mm, oblong, obtuse, callus to 6×4mm, ovate, yellow to orange marked red, tails to 13mm, slender, deflexed, straight; pet. to 4×2mm, elliptic, obtuse, shortly apiculate; lip to 4×2mm, yellow to green tinged or marked purple, subpandurate, apex serrulate; column to 5mm, green marked red-maroon. Venezuela, Colombia, Ecuador, Guyana, Bolivia.

S.clavellatum Luer.
Epiphytic. Secondary stems to 1.5cm. Lvs to 11×1.5cm, narrowly elliptic, acute. Infl. to 20cm, several-fld, erect to pendent; sep. yellow-brown or orange to red, dorsal sep. to 13×3mm, narrowly oblong-pandurate, obtuse, lateral sep. to 10×6mm, ovate, acute, callus slightly recurved, callus to 5×1mm, ovoid; pet. to 3×2mm, clear yellow veined red, obliquely ovate, acute; lip red to yellow, subequal to pet., oblong, apex rounded, finely denticulate; column to 3mm, red. Panama, Costa Rica, Ecuador.

S.echidna (Rchb. f.) Schltr. See *Porroglossum echidna*.
S.elasmotopus Schltr. See *S.microdactylum*.

S.gibberosum (Rchb. f.) Rolfe (*Masdevallia gibberosa* Rchb. f.).
Epiphytic. Secondary stems to 4cm. Lvs to 19×8cm, erect, narrowly elliptic, acute. Infl. to 50cm, loosely many-fld;

peduncle erect to ascending, slender, verrucose; sep. and pet. light green to green-white, tinged and spotted purple, dorsal sep. to 57×4mm, ovate, acute, tail dark purple, lateral sep. to 10×10mm, ovate, callus to 13×3mm, narrowly falcate-triangular, fleshy, white spotted purple, tails to 25mm, white, slender, strongly divergent, straight; pet. to 3×2mm, ovate-oblong, acute; lip to 3×2mm, light-green to purple tinged red-brown, obscurely 3-lobed, lateral lobes small, rounded, midlobe oblong, subpandurate; column to 3.5mm, green spotted purple, slender. Colombia.

S.microdactylum Rolfe (*S.elasmotopus* Schltr.).
Epiphytic or terrestrial. Secondary stems to 2cm. Lvs to 18×3cm, narrowly elliptic to oblanceolate, acute or obtuse. Infl. to 15cm, slender, distichous; sep. and pet. light yellow or yellow-green tinged and spotted red to brown, dorsal sep. to 8×3cm, fleshy, oblong, obtuse, lateral sep. to 9×6mm, oblong to broadly elliptic, bifid, strongly carinate, callus to 3×1mm, ovoid; pet. to 3×2mm, ovate or elliptic, acute; lip to 3×1.5mm, light yellow marked red, lingulate to pandurate-oblong; column yellow deeply tinged red-purple, to 3mm. Mexico, Guatemala, Honduras, Costa Rica, Panama, Colombia.

S.ochthodes (Rchb. f.) Pfitz. See *S.verrucosum*.

S.ovulare Luer.
Epiphytic. Secondary stems to 6mm. Lvs to 40×7mm, erect, elliptic, acute. Infl. to 40mm, subdensely few-fld, pendent; sep. purple or yellow marked purple, dorsal sep. to 3×5mm, ovate, acute, largely connate to lateral sep., lateral sep. to 5×6mm, ovate, acute, callus obliquely triangular; pet. to 2×1mm, rose marked purple, obliquely oblong, obtuse; lip to 2.5×1mm, purple, oblong, serrulate; column to 2.5mm, rose, slender. Ecuador.

S.pulvinare (Rchb. f.) Rolfe (*Masdevallia pulvinaris* Rchb. f.; *S.rolfeanum* Kränzl.).
Epiphytic or terrestrial. Secondary stems to 7cm. Lvs to 28×6cm, erect, elliptic, acute. Infl. to 60cm, many-fld; peduncle erect, densely verrucose; sep. and pet. green tinged or spotted red-purple, dorsal sep. to 15×5mm, basal portion ovate, apical portion narrowly linear, revolute, slightly pubesc., lateral sep. to 15×9mm, ovate, acute, minutely pubesc., callus to 8×2mm, narrowly elliptic, yellow-grey, tails to 6mm, green, slender, verrucose; pet. to 5×3mm, obliquely ovate, acute; lip to 5×2.5mm, green spotted purple, subpandurate, apex rounded, slightly dentate; column to 5mm, green, slender. Colombia.

S.punctatum (Rolfe) Rolfe. See *S.anchoriferum*.

S.rapax Luer.
Epiphytic. Secondary stems to 9mm. Lvs to 35×10mm, erect, elliptic, subacute. Infl. to 40mm, few-fld, ascending to pendent; sep. purple spotted deep purple, dorsal sep. to 9×3mm, ovate-triangular, apiculate, revolute, serrulate, lateral sep. to 7×6mm, ovate, minutely ciliate, obtuse, callus to 3.5×1.5mm, fleshy, oblong, tails to 4mm, slender, slightly decurved; pet. to 2.5×1.5mm, white marked purple, obliquely ovate, obtuse;

lip to 3×2mm, purple, obscurely 3-lobed, lateral lobes oblong, midlobe oblong, serrulate; column to 3mm, green spotted purple, slender. Ecuador.

S.reversum Kränzl. See *S.antenniferum*.
S.rolfeanum Kränzl. See *S.pulvinare*.

S.swertiifolium (Rchb. f.) Rolfe (*Masdevallia swertiifolia* Rchb. f.).
Epiphytic. Secondary stems to 2.5cm. Lvs to 21×4cm, elliptic, acute, obscurely plicate. Infl. to 15cm; peduncle filiform, ascending to horizontal; sep. and pet. white to pale yellow marked and spotted red to brown, dorsal sep. to 14×5mm, basal portion ovate-triangular, apical portion linear, revolute, lateral sep. to 11×12mm, elliptic, callus to 8×5mm, rose and purple, transversely lunate, tails to 40mm, slender; pet. to 3×3mm, ovate, obtuse; lip to 4×3mm, white to pale yellow tinged purple, obscurely 3-lobed, lateral lobes small, rounded, midlobe subpandurate, reflexed; column to 4mm, white and purple. Colombia, Ecuador.

S.verrucosum (Rchb. f.) Pfitz. (*Masdevallia verrucosa* Rchb. f.; *Pleurothallis verrucosa* (Rchb. f.) Rchb. f.; *S.ochthodes* (Rchb. f.) Pfitz.).
Epiphytic or terrestrial. Secondary stems to 3.5cm. Lvs to 13×2.5cm, obovate, elliptic or spathulate-oblong. Infl. to 50cm, erect, slender, many-fld; peduncle densely verrucose; fls appearing inflated, basically yellow; sep. yellow to green tinged or spotted red-brown, dorsal sep. to 8×4mm, fleshy lanceolate, revolute, narrowly obtuse, lateral sep. to 7×6mm, elliptic, obtuse, callus to 3×2mm, ovoid, tails to 1.5mm, recurved; pet. to 4×2mm, yellow-green finely striped brown, oblong-ligulate, acute; lip to 4×2mm, white tinged rose-purple, pandurate, apex rounded, serrate; column to 4mm, green tinged purple, slender. Colombia.

S.xipheres (Rchb. f.) Schltr. See *Porroglossum muscosum*.

Scaphyglottis Poepp. & Endl. (From Gk *skaphe*, boat, and *glotta*, tongue, referring to the concave lip.) Some 30 species of epiphytes or lithophytes. Stems simple, branched or clustered, straggling, linear to slender-fusiform where pseudobulbous, apically unifoliate to multifoliate. Leaves narrow, fleshy-coriaceous, spreading. Inflorescence terminal or axillary, a raceme or fascicle; flowers small; sepals subequal, erect or spreading, ovate to oblong; lateral sepals strongly oblique, adnate to column foot forming a short mentum; petals similar to sepals, smaller; lip articulate with column foot, entire to 3-lobed, reflexed or geniculate; column short, sometimes alate or auriculate, produced into a foot at base, anther terminal, operculate, incumbent, pollinia 4 or 6, waxy. Tropical America.

CULTIVATION Intermediate-growing epiphytes for sunny positions in an open bark-based mix. Water moderately throughout the year.

S.amethystina (Rchb. f.) Schltr. (*Ponera amethystina* Rchb. f.).
Stems simple or branching, pseudobulbous, to 12×1cm, stipitate, bifoliate. Lvs to 12×1cm, linear to oblong, apex obliquely bilobed. Terminal fascicles few to many-fld; fls white to violet; sep. to 8×3mm, elliptic-oblong to oblanceolate, acute, concave; pet. to 6×1mm, linear-oblong to oblanceolate, acute, falcate; lip cuneate-flabellate, 9×5mm, lateral lobes, ovate-oblong, obtuse, midlobe subquadrate, retuse or truncate, undulate; column to 7mm, clavate, apex biauriculate. Guatemala, Costa Rica, Panama, Colombia, Venezuela.

S.brachyphylla (Rchb. f.) Schweinf. See *Hexadesmia fusiformis*.
S.crurigera (Batem. ex Lindl.) Ames & Correll. See *Hexadesmia crurigera*.
S.fusiformis (Griseb.) R.E. Schult. See *Hexadesmia fusiformis*.

S.lindeniana (A. Rich. & Gal.) L.O. Williams (*Hexadesmia lindeniana* A. Rich. & Gal.).
Pseudobulbs stem-like, to 30×2.5cm, narrow fusiform, compressed, bifoliate. Lvs to 25×4.5cm, elliptic-oblong to elliptic-lanceolate or linear, obtuse, retuse. Terminal fascicle to 4cm, fls several, yellow-green to red-green often veined purple; sep. to 11×4mm, elliptic to oblong-lanceolate, acute to subobtuse, concave; pet. to 10×3mm, linear-lanceolate to elliptic-ovate, acute to acuminate, falcate, slightly undulate; lip to 11×6mm, pandurate to oblong-cuneate, acute or truncate, retuse, finely erose; column to 8mm, slender, bialate, with a prominent posterior tooth. Mexico to Panama.

S.lindeniana (Rich. & Gal.) L.O. Williams. See *Hexadesmia fasciculata*.

S.livida (Lindl.) Schltr. (*Isochilus lividus* Lindl.). Stems densely fasciculate-branched, pseudobulbous, narrowly fusiform-cylindrical, to 120×5mm, stipitate, bifoliate. Lvs to 200×5mm, erect, linear, apex bilobulate. Fls to several per fascicle, green to pale yellow-green striped purple; dorsal sep. to 5×2mm, elliptic-oblong, acute, concave, lateral sep. to 4×2mm, obliquely ovate-triangular, acute to obtuse, concave; pet. to 4×1mm, linear, apex acute, recurved, entire to slightly crenate; lip to 3×3mm, subquadrate to ovate-quadrate, truncate, emarginate, base cordate; column to 12mm, with short foot, apex bialate. Mexico, Guatemala, Honduras.

S.micrantha (Lindl.) Ames & Correll. See *Hexadesmia micrantha*.

S.prolifera (R. Br.) Cogn. (*Isochilus prolifer* R. Br.; *Ponera prolifera* (R. Br.) Rchb. f.).
Stems fasciculate-branching, erect or ascending, to 20cm, fusiform-cylindrical, shortly stipitate, slightly compressed, bifoliate. Lvs to 40×5mm, spreading, linear-ligulate, pale green, obtuse or emarginate. Fls fasciculate, spreading, white to yellow; sep. to 5×1mm, erect, narrowly oblong-spathulate, revolute, acute; pet. subequal to sep., narrowly linear-subspathulate, obtuse; lip to 5×2mm, entire, oblong, fleshy, long-attenuate below, rounded, retuse; column to 4mm, cream, slender, erect, anther white to pale brown, strongly compressed. Brazil, Venezuela, Guyana, Surinam.

S.reedii (Rchb. f.) Ames. See *Hexadesmia sessilis*.
S.sessilis (Rchb. f.) Foldats. See *Hexadesmia sessilis*.

S.violacea (Lindl.) Lindl. (*Cladobium violaceum* Lindl.; *Ponera violacea* (Lindl.) Rchb. f.).
Stems to 15cm, slender, branched, cylindrical or fusiform-cylindrical, striate, bifoliate. Lvs to 17×1cm, linear-oblong or linear-lanceolate, obtuse, apex bilobulate. Fls solitary or in very sparse fascicles, minute, rose to purple-violet; sep. broadly oblong or oblong-lanceolate, to 4×2mm, acute, decurved; lip to 3×2mm, fleshy, chanelled, recurved, oblong-obovate, to elliptic-obovate, obtuse to rounded or slightly retuse; column to 2mm, stout, clavate, arcuate, alate. Venezuela, Guyana, Brazil, Peru.

Schoenorchis Bl. (From Gr. *schoinos*, reed or rush, and *orchis*, referring to the rush-like leaves.) Some 25 species of monopodial epiphytes. Stems erect or pendent, short, sometimes branching, rooting at base. Leaves narrow, terete, linear or linear-lanceolate. Inflorescence simple or branched, erect or horizontal; petals and sepals similar, free; lip trilobed, midlobe straight, fleshy, laterally compressed, lateral lobes erect, clasping column, obtuse; spur cylindric or elliptic, often decurved, sometimes callused near aperture. Indomalaya to China, Fiji, Australia.

CULTIVATION   See *Vanda*.

S.densiflora Schltr. See *S.micrantha.*

S.gemmata (Lindl.) J.J. Sm. (*Saccolabium gemmata* Lindl.). Stem 15–30cm. Lvs linear, subterete, curved, 6.5–12.5× 0.5cm. Infl. branched; fls purple, pet. interior and lip apex white; sep. linear-obovate, partly fused; pet. obtuse, falcate; lip concave, fleshy, terminating in a blunt cylindric spur with 2 calli at its aperture, midlobe round-ovate, entire, concave. N India, Nepal.

S.micrantha Bl. (*S.densiflora* Schltr.). Stems densely branched, slender, tufted, rooting at base, to 15cm. Lvs fleshy, arched, to 3.5×0.2cm. Infl. horizontal, to 5cm; fls white, becoming yellow; sep. to 2mm, oblong, obtuse; pet. similar; lip midlobe fleshy, acute, interior callused, exterior keeled, lateral lobes erect; spur elliptic, forward-pointing, callused near aperture. Vietnam, Malaysia, Java to Fiji, New Guinea, Australia.

Schomburgkia Lindl. (Named in honour of the German botanist Sir Robert Schomburgk.) Some 12 species of epiphytes or lithophytes. Rhizome short or elongate. Pseudobulbs fusiform to cylindric, sometimes short-stalked and laterally compressed, resembling *Laelia* spp. (i.e. *S.superbiens*) or thickly cylindrical and ribbed, the interior hollow and colonized by ants (e.g. *S.tibicinis*), clothed in thin, papery sheaths. Leaves 2–4, spreading, borne at or near apex of pseudobulbs, mostly oblong to oblong-lanceolate, rigidly coriaceous. Inflorescence terminal, a raceme or a panicle, elongate, erect, many-flowered; flowers often large, showy, pedicellate; sepals subequal, free, spreading, undulate; petals similar to sepals but broader; lip articulated with column base, 3-lobed, lateral lobes erect, sometimes loosely clasping column, midlobe spreading, recurved, undulate, disc with a carinate callus; column porrect, anther terminal, incumbent, operculate, pollinia 8, waxy. Tropical America, W Indies.

CULTIVATION   As for the larger *Laelia* spp.

S.crispa auct. non Lindl. See *S.fimbriata.*

S.fimbriata (Vell.) Hoehne (*Laelia gloriosa* (Rchb. f.) L.O. Williams; *S.gloriosa* Rchb. f.; *S.crispa* auct.). Pseudobulbs to 30×5cm, clavate, slightly compressed and furrowed toward apex. Lvs to 32×6cm, 2–3 per bulb, narrowly oblong, obtuse. Raceme, to 75cm, 8–15-fld; fls large, showy; sep. and pet. to 40×12mm, light yellow-brown tinged purple, veined claret to dark brown, narrowly oblong, obtuse or apiculate; lip to 20×18mm, white edged pale yellow-brown to pink edged pink-brown, lateral lobes narrowly elliptic, midlobe yellow-brown to pink-brown, ovate-elliptic, obtuse, with 3 central keels; column to 18mm, white, apex yellow and pink. Venezuela, Guyana, Surinam.

S.gloriosa Rchb. f. See *S.fimbriata.*

S.humboldtii (Rchb. f.) Rchb. f. (*Laelia humboldtii* (Rchb. f.) L.O. Williams). Pseudobulbs to 25×7cm, narrowly ovoid-conical or pyriform. Lvs to 20×7cm, 2–3 per bulb, oblong to elliptic to elliptic-ovate, acute to obtuse. Infl. to 120cm, usually a raceme, few-to many-fld; sep. and pet. rose-violet, sep. to 4×1cm, elliptic-lanceolate to oblong-lanceolate, acute, lateral sep. oblique, pet. to 3.5×1.5cm, elliptic-lanceolate to oblong-lanceolate or spathulate, obtuse to rounded; lip to 4×4cm, white veined violet, lateral lobes auriculate to obliquely triangular, midlobe suborbicular to subquadrate, emarginate or rounded, disc yellow, with a 5- to 7-keeled callus, jagged-toothed toward apex; column white marked rose, to 21mm. Venezuela.

S.lyonsii Lindl. (*Laelia lyonsii* (Lindl.) L.O. Williams). Pseudobulbs to 35×3cm, narrowly fusiform, compressed, bifoliate. Lvs to 30×6cm, oblong. Raceme to 1m; sep. and pet. white spotted purple, sep. to 23×10mm, ovate-oblong, obtuse, shortly apiculate, lateral sep. slightly falcate, pet. slightly larger than sep., apex rounded; lip to 16×12mm, similar in colour to tepals but edged, yellow, ovate, obtuse; column to 10mm, curved. Autumn. Jamaica.

S.rosea Lind. ex Lindl. Pseudobulbs to 15cm, fusiform, bifoliate. Lvs to 25×6cm, elliptic-oblong, rounded. Raceme to 55cm, densely few- to many-fld;

sep. and pet. dark purple-violet, sep. to 21×6mm, oblong-lanceolate to elliptic-lanceolate, acute, pet. oblong, acute or acuminate; lip to 17×12mm, rose, ovate, 3-lobed, lateral lobes subovate, midlobe suborbicular, apex rounded, disc yellow, keeled; column to 10mm, apex erose-denticulate. Venezuela, Colombia.

S.splendida Schltr. Close to *S.rosea* in general appearance; infl. bracts to 8cm, tinted pink; fls to 10cm diam.; tepals glossy deep purple-red, narrow, strongly undulate; lip magenta with shallow, not reflexed lateral lobes, an oblong-ovate, undulate midlobe, a thinly lined dusky pink callus and a white anth. cap. SW Colombia, NW Ecuador.

S.superbiens (Lindl.) Rolfe (*Laelia superbiens* Lindl.; *Cattleya superbiens* (Lindl.) Beer). Pseudobulbs to 30×4cm, fusiform to ellipsoid, compressed, furrowed, widely spaced on a tough, vigorous rhizome. Lvs to 30×6.5cm, 1–2 per bulb, oblong to linear-lanceolate, acute to obtuse. Raceme to 80cm, many-fld; fls large, showy, to 13cm diam., mauve-purple marked yellow; sep. to 7×1.5cm, linear-oblong to oblong-lanceolate, acute to obtuse; pet. to 4.5×2cm, narrowly oblong-oblanceolate, acute to rounded; lip to 5.5×3.5cm, lateral lobes short, midlobe obovate to obcordate, emarginate, undulate-crisped, disc yellow, with 5 or 6 crisped keels; column to 3cm, dull purple, arcuate, clavate. Mexico, Guatemala, Honduras.

S.tibicinis (Batem.) Batem. Pseudobulbs to 55×4cm, stoutly cylindric, hollow, strongly ribbed. Lvs to 35×7cm usually shorter, 2–3 per bulb oblong or elliptic-oblong, obtuse to rounded. Infl. a raceme or a panicle, elongate, many-fld; fls large, maroon to bright purple-magenta; sep. to 50×17mm, elliptic-oblong to elliptic-oblanceolate, subacute to rounded, undulate; pet. subequal to sep., linear-spathulate to oblanceolate, subacute to rounded, undulate-crisped; lip to 4×4cm, yellow-white to purple, lateral lobes large, suborbicular to subobovate, apex rounded, midlobe small, suborbicular-obcordate, retuse, subentire to crisped, disk 5- to 7-keeled; column to 23mm, clavate, arcuate, alate, apex tridentate. Mexico, C America to Panama.

S.undulata Lindl. (*Laelia undulata* (Lindl.) L.O. Williams). Pseudobulbs to 25×5cm, fusiform, grooved. Lvs to 30×5cm, 2, rarely 3 per pseudobulb, oblong to oblong-ligulate. Raceme to 150cm, many-fld; sep. and pet. to 3.5×1.5cm, deep maroon, oblong to narrowly elliptic, rounded, strongly undulate, twisted; lip to 27×20mm, bright rose-purple marked white, lateral lobes rounded, midlobe oblong, shortly apiculate, apex decurved, disc with 3–5 white keels; column to 16mm, stout. Early spring. Trinidad, Venezuela, Colombia.

S.weberbaueriana Kränzl. (*Laelia weberbaueriana* (Kränzl.) Schweinf.). Pseudobulbs to 37cm, cylindric, grooved. Lvs to 26×6cm, 2–3 per pseudobulb, oblong or elliptic-oblong, obtuse. Raceme to 75cm, densely several to many-fld; sep. and pet. yellow-brown streaked dark brown, sep. to 3cm, oblong, acute or apiculate, undulate, pet. similar, shorter, obtuse or truncate; lip to 20×13mm, white, arching, broadly obovate, obscurely 3-lobed, slightly retuse, apiculate, disc with 4 or 5 undulate keels; column to 13mm, arcuate, broadly alate. Peru.

Scuticaria Lindl. (From Lat. *scutica*, lash, referring to the drooping whip-like leaves.) 5 species of epiphytes or lithophytes. Rhizome short, simple or branched, enveloped by several, overlapping sheaths. Pseudobulbs very small, terete, apically unifoliate. Leaves elongate, fleshy, usually pendent, terete or subterete, sulcate above. Inflorescence lateral, 1- to few-flowered; flowers often large, showy; sepals subsimilar, free, erect to spreading, lateral sepals adnate to column foot forming a mentum; petals similar to dorsal sepal; lip adnate to apex of column foot, concave, sessile, 3-lobed, lateral lobes erect, midlobe smaller, rounded or emarginate; column erect, subterete, with a small basal foot, wingless, anther terminal, operculate, incumbent, unilocular or bilocular, pollinia 4, waxy, ovoid, stipe inconspicuous. Brazil, Guyana, Venezuela, Colombia.

CULTIVATION   As for the larger *Oncidium* spp. Mount on vertically suspended rafts.

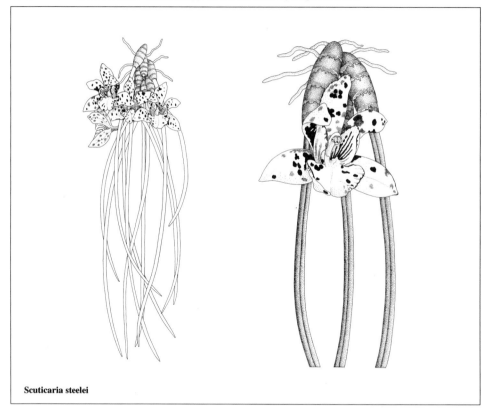

Scuticaria steelei

S.hadwenii (Lindl.) Hook.
Lvs to 45×1cm, deflexed, terete, acute, dark green. Infl. to 5cm, arching or pendent, 1- or 2-fld; fls to 7.5cm diam., fragrant, waxy, long-lived, yellow blotched chestnut-brown, the lip white or pale yellow, blotched and spotted bright red or chocolate; sep. to 4.5×1.5cm, oblong, acute, spreading; pet. similar to sep.; lip to 3.5×3cm, suborbicular to obovate, concave, interior pilose, callus oblong, dorsally tridentate, gibbous; column to 15mm, flushed red, slightly pilose. Spring–autumn. Brazil, Guianas.

S.steelei (Hook.) Lindl.
Lvs to 145×1cm, pendent, terete. Infl. to 4cm, 1–3-fld, pendent; fls to 7.5cm diam., fragrant, long-lived, waxy, yellow or pale green-yellow, irregularly marked maroon-brown or red, the lip pale green-white or pale yellow striped chestnut or rusty red; dorsal sep. to 5×1.5cm, elliptic-oblong to obovate, acute, convex, lateral sep. to 4×2cm, obliquely elliptic or oblong-elliptic, subacute, convex; pet. to 4.5×1.5cm, obliquely oblong or lanceolate, subacute; lip to 4×4.5cm, concave, finely pilose, apically 3-lobed, lateral lobes erect-incurved, somewhat rounded, midlobe transversely oblong to obovate, emarginate, callus transverse, 5-dentate, finely pilose; column to 22mm, semi-terete, yellow-white marked pink-purple. Colombia, Venezuela, Brazil, Guianas, Surinam.

Sedirea Garay & H. Sweet. (An anagram of the generic name *Aerides*.) 1 species, a monopodial epiphyte. Stem short, to 8-leaved. Roots fleshy, nodal. Leaves 5–7cm, leathery, strap-like, linear-oblong, keeled, bases clothing stem. Raceme to 15cm axillary; fls fragrant; sepals and petals to 13mm, spreading, oblong, obtuse, green to white, lateral sepals fused to column foot, basally striped maroon or brown; lip 3-lobed, midlobe obovate-spathulate, concave, basally inflated, white, callus ridged dark violet, spotted paler rose, lateral lobes shorter, spur conical, tapering to tip. Japan, Korea, Ryukyu Is.

CULTIVATION See *Neofinetia*.

S.japonica (Lind. & Rchb. f.) Garay & H. Sweet (*Aerides japonica* Lind. & Rchb. f.).

Seidenfadenia Garay. (For Gunnar Seidenfaden (1908–).) 1 species, a monopodial epiphyte, resembling *Aerides* but the crest-shaped rostellum projects across the anther. Stem short. Leaves to 60cm, dense, narrow, linear, acuminate, centrally channelled above, dull green. Racemes erect, dense, to 26cm; flowers 1.2 to 2cm diameter; sepals and petals white, almost equal, oblong, spreading; lip rosy purple, obtuse, flat, with 2 filamentous basal projections, spur laterally compressed, obtuse. Burma and Thailand.

CULTIVATION As for *Aerides*.

S.mitrata (Rchb. f.) Garay (*Aerides mitrata* Rchb. f.).

Selenipedium Rchb. f. (From Gk *selene*, moon, and *pedilon*, sandal, referring to the crescent-shaped rim of the lip.) 5 species of terrestrial slipper orchids. Stems to 5m, slender, reed-like. Leaves alternate, widely spaced on stems, usually lanceolate, chartaceous, prominently plicate, sheathing stems at base. Inflorescence a terminal bracteate spike; flowers to 10; dorsal sepal free, lateral sepals fused in synsepalum; petals free, narrower than dorsal sepal; lip prominent, inflated, slipper-like; ovaries short-pedicelled, slender, pubescent. Tropical America. It is unlikely that true *Selenipedium* spp. are present in collections today. Most species of *Phragmipedium* have at times been included in *Selenipedium* and may still be labelled as such in cultivation; see *Phragmipedium*.

CULTIVATION As for *Sobralia* but with heavy shade and temperatures some 5°C/9°F higher.

S.chica Rchb. f.
Infl. pubesc.; fls red-green to dull orange-brown; dorsal sep. ovate, acute; pet. drooping, lanceolate; lip strongly inflated, like *Cypripedium* spp.

Serapias L. (From the Gk name for Apis (Serapis), the sacred bull of Memphis.) TONGUE ORCHID. Some 10 species of terrestrial herbs. Tubers 2–5, entire, globose. Leaves lanceolate, erect, shiny. Spike lax or dense, clothed with bracts equal to or exceeding flowers; petals and sepals forming a deep, forward-pointing hood, conspicuously veined; lip trilobed, spurless, narrowing basally, apical lobe abruptly recurved, tongue-like, protruding from hood, usually pubescent above. Azores to Mediterranean.

CULTIVATION See Introduction: Hardy Orchids.

S.azorica Schltr. See *S.cordigera*.

S.cordigera L. (*S.azorica* Schltr.).
Tubers 2–3, ovoid to globose, one sessile, the others attached to stolons. Stems 15–50cm. Lvs to 15×1.5cm lanceolate, 5–8. Spike dense, 5–15-fld; bracts tinted dull purple, veins maroon; hood to 2.5cm, ash-grey to purple, pet. to 2.5cm, rounded basally, undulate, minutely toothed, black-purple; lip almost 3× length of other seg., dark purple with 2 ridges, lateral lobes red or purple, partly hidden by hood, midlobe cordate, pubesc., pale to deep yellow, sometimes orange. Mid spring–early summer. Mediterranean.

S.lingua L.
To 30cm. Spike 2–8-fld; bracts violet, sometimes green, equalling fls. Sep. and pet. light pink or purple, to 2cm, with red or purple parallel venation; lip yellow, violet-pink to magenta or white with purple-black ridges, apical portion to 2×0.8cm, lanceolate to ovate. Late spring–summer. Mediterranean.

S.neglecta de Notaris.
To 30cm. Tubers 2, ovoid. Lvs 4–10, ovate to linear-lanceolate. Spike 2–8-fld; bracts green, tinted purple with maroon veins; sep. and pet. ovate-lanceolate, lilac; lip cordate, ×3 longer than other seg., pubesc., lateral lobes partly obscured by hood, red or purple, margins purple-back, midlobe deep yellow, rarely orange, with 2 dark maroon, parallel basal ridges. Late spring–early summer. W & C Mediterranean.

Sievekingia Rchb. f. (For C. Sieveking, Mayor of Hamburg.) Some 15 species of epiphytes. Rhizome short. Pseudobulbs ovoid-conical to subcylindrical, furrowed, enveloped at base by papery bracts, apically 1–2-leaved. Leaves mostly lanceolate or elliptic-lanceolate, acute or acuminate, plicate, coriaceous, petiolate. Inflorescence a basal raceme, erect to strongly pendent, few- to many-flowered; flowers thin-textured; sepals subsimilar, free, concave, spreading, lateral sepals oblique; petals subequal to sepals, narrower, entire to deeply and finely fimbriate; lip connate to column base, usually sessile, concave, simple or trilobed, often fimbriate, disc callose, dentate or lamellate; column stout, arched, apex usually winged, pollinia 2, concave. Costa Rica to Guyana, Colombia to Ecuador, Peru and Bolivia.

CULTIVATION As for *Stanhopea*, but water throughout the year.

S.dunstervilleorum Foldats. See *S.jenmanii*.

S.jenmanii Rchb. f. (*S.dunstervilleorum* Foldats). Pseudobulbs to 3×2cm, ovoid, slightly compressed, yellow-green, 1-lvd at apex. Lvs to 22×5cm, oblong or narrowly lanceolate, acute or acuminate, pale to dark green. Infl. short, deflexed, few-fld; fls fleshy; sep. to 20×8mm, white to pale yellow, elliptic to oblong-elliptic, acute to subacute; pet. to 19×5mm, pale orange-yellow, linear-oblong or oblong-lanceolate, acute; lip to 16×20mm, orange-yellow, concave, 3-lobed, lateral lobes erect, obtuse, falcate, midlobe ligulate, subacute or obtuse, apiculate, smaller than lateral lobes, disc with a cleft callus produced into 3 serrate-dentate keels; column to 16mm, pale yellow, apex orange, erect, clavate. Venezuela, Guyana.

S.reichenbachiana Rolfe (*Gorgoglossum reichenbachianum* F.C. Lehm.). Pseudobulbs to 2cm, ovoid, clustered. Lvs usually 2, to 15cm, narrowly elliptic, acuminate; petiole usually spotted dull red.

Infl. to 10cm, 5-fld, sharply pendent; fls to 5cm diam.; pet. and lobes of lip highly fimbriate with long yellow fil.; sep. ivory to yellow-green; pet. ivory-green flushed orange-yellow; lip yellow spotted purple on disc, with orange-yellow keels; column orange-yellow. Colombia.

S.suavis Rchb. f. Pseudobulbs to 3×1.5cm, ovoid, clustered, 1-lvd at apex. Lvs to 25×3cm, lanceolate to elliptic-lanceolate, acute or acuminate. Infl. short, pendulous, few- to several-fld; fls to 2.5cm diam.; pet. and lip entire, not fimbriate; sep. to 17×8mm, pale lemon-yellow, spreading, elliptic-lanceolate, acute, concave; pet. to 15×6mm, orange, lanceolate, acute; lip to 11×10mm, orange spotted dark red-purple, ovate or obovate-rhombic, acute, lateral lobes erect, spreading, disc distinctly or obscurely 3-ridged, central keel cleft; column to 8mm, green, slightly curved, wings broad, orange. Mostly summer. Nicaragua, Costa Rica, Panama, Colombia.

Sigmatostalix Rchb. f. (From Gk *sigma*, S-shaped, and *stalix*, stake, referring to the sigmoid appearance of the slender column.) Some 35 species of epiphytes. Rhizome short, creeping. Pseudobulbs small, often clustered, ancipitous, compressed, bases enveloped by several distichous, overlapping, leaf sheaths, apically unifoliate or bifoliate. Leaves coriaceous or subcoriaceous, narrow. Inflorescence a lateral raceme borne from base of pseudobulb, few- to many-flowered, usually surpassing leaves; peduncle slender, erect or arching; flowers small, thin-textured; sepals and petals similar, subequal, free or shortly connate, spreading or reflexed; lip subsessile or long-clawed, simple to trilobed, slightly reflexed, disc with a fleshy, basal callus; column elongate, slender, erect, terete, apex slightly dilated, anther terminal, operculate, incumbent, unilocular, pollinia 2, waxy, stipe linear-triangular. Mexico and C America to Brazil, Peru, Bolivia and Argentina.

CULTIVATION Cultivation as for *Odontoglossum* in the cool or intermediate house, but they will usually succeed best if mounted on rafts or cork slabs.

S.amazonica Schltr. Pseudobulbs to 4cm, ellipsoid to ovoid, clustered, apically unifoliate. Lvs to 15×1.5cm, linear to oblong-elliptic, acute or subacute, subpetiolate. Infl. often surpassing lvs, erect or spreading, loosely few-fld; fls spreading, to 1.5cm; sep. green-yellow, to 7×2mm, oblong-lanceolate, acute, lateral sep. oblique; pet. yellow-green barred brown, similar to sep.; lip to 7×6mm, rich yellow, simple, obovate-cuneate, apex rounded, base narrow, disc with a large, elliptic-ligulate callus; column to 7mm. Peru, Brazil, Surinam.

S.graminea (Poepp. & Endl.) Rchb. f. (*Specklinia graminea* Poepp. & Endl.). Pseudobulbs to 12mm, ellipsoid-cylindrical to oblong-cylindrical, apically unifoliate. Lvs to 50×2mm, narrowly linear, subacute, arching to recurved. Infl. to 6cm, erect to spreading, loosely few-fld; fls pale yellow spotted or striped purple to red; sep. to 2.5×1mm, concave, elliptic-lanceolate or oblong, acute; pet. subequal to sep., obliquely ovate, acute; lip to 3×3mm, unguiculate, ovate-subquadrate, retuse, base truncate, callus suborbicular, centrally carinate; column to 1.5mm, clavate, apex winged, rostellum triangular. Peru.

S.guatemalensis Schltr. Pseudobulbs to 4×2cm, elliptic-oblong or ovoid, clustered, apically unifoliate. Lvs to 13×1.5cm, ligulate to elliptic to lanceolate, acute or subacuminate, subcoriaceous, erect-spreading. Infl. to 34cm, erect or suberect, loosely several-fld; fls to 1.5cm diam., pale green to yellow, often marked brown,

the lip deep yellow, heavily marked red-brown; sep. to 9×2.5mm, ligulate-lanceolate, acute, reflexed; pet. subequal to sep., obliquely lanceolate, acute; lip to 6×5mm, fleshy-unguiculate, simple to obscurely 3-lobed, ovate-suborbicular, spreading or slightly convex, base auriculate-sagittate, apex truncate or apiculate, callus small, suberect; column to 7mm, yellow spotted red-brown, clavate. Mexico to Panama.

S.hymenantha Schltr. Pseudobulbs to 3.5×2cm, elliptic-oblong or ovoid, apically unifoliate. Lvs to 14×1cm, subcoriaceous, linear-ligulate, acute. Infl. to 14cm, erect; fls minute, pale brown or green marked tan; tepals to 2mm, oblong, acute, often reflexed; lip to 1.5×2mm, subsessile, simple to obscurely 3-lobed, spreading or slightly convex, ovate-elliptic, obtuse, callus bilobulate, transversely subreniform; column to 1.5mm. Costa Rica, Panama.

S.peruviana Rolfe. Pseudobulbs to 15mm, ovoid or ovoid-cylindrical, apically unifoliate. Lvs to 50×4mm, narrowly linear or linear-oblong, subobtuse or bifid. Infl. equalling lvs, loosely few-fld; fls spreading, pale yellow, often striped dark purple; sep. to 3.5×1.5mm, oblong or oblong-lanceolate, acute or subacute, apex recurved; pet. subequal to sep., oblong-lanceolate, acute, base with a conical tooth; lip to 4×5mm, subsessile, subreniform or orbicular-reniform, anterior margin rounded, undulate, disc with a large, lobulate callus; column to 2.5mm, clavate, apex auriculate. Peru.

S.radicans Lind. & Rchb. f. See *Ornithophora radicans*.

Smitinandia Holtt. (For Tem Smitinand, Thai botanist.) 1 species, a monopodial epiphyte to 20cm. Leaves to 10×1.5cm, 5–8, oblong, narrow, along stems. Inflorescence to 7cm, racemose; flowers to 1cm diam., saccate-spurred; sepals and petals to 3mm, subequal, ovate, obtuse, pale pink or sparkling white suffused lilac, sometimes spotted purple; lip mobile, 3-lobed, purple, midlobe ligulate with a transverse basal ridge, fleshy, lateral lobes smaller, rounded, forward-pointing; spur parallel with ovary. SE Asia.

CULTIVATION   See *Vanda*.

S.micrantha (Lindl.) Holtt. (*Saccolabium micranthum* Lindl.; *Cleisostoma micranthum* (Lind.) King & Pantl.).

Sobralia Ruiz & Pav. (For the Spanish botanist Dr Francisco Sobral, *fl.* 1790.) About 100 species of terrestrials or, less commonly, epiphytes. Rhizomes short. Secondary stems usually leafy, simple or rarely branched, reed- or cane-like, slender, clumped, short to elongate, erect or bowed. Leaves alternate, 2-ranked, tough, plicate-ribbed, usually lanceolate, basally sheathing or clasping. Inflorescence usually a short, bracteate, terminal raceme, sometimes longer and lateral; flowers produced in succession, large, showy, *Cattleya*-like, often short-lived; sepals subequal, free or basally connate; petals similar to sepals, usually somewhat wider and undulate; lip adnate to column at base, entire or obscurely trilobed, margins involute, enveloping column, appearing funnelform with a spreading, crisped limb, disc with a smooth, lamellate or crested callus; column elongate, stout, footless, narrowly winged, apex trilobed, anther terminal, operculate, incumbent, pollinia 8. Tropical C & S America.

CULTIVATION   Showy terrestrials for the intermediate or warm house, they produce short-lived, showy, *Cattleya*-like blooms in succession on closely clumped, reed-like stems. Pot in well drained tubs or beds containing a coarse bark mix with portions of leafmould, garden compost and dried FYM. Afford full sunlight or, when in bloom, light shade. Water and feed freely when in growth (which is often continuous), at other times keep just moist. These orchids are best left undisturbed, except for the removal of exhausted canes. Large specimens have excellent potential as landscaping plants both under glass and outdoors in tropical and subtropical regions. Propagate by division after flowering.

S.candida (Poepp. & Endl.) Rchb. f.
Stems to 90cm, clustered. Lvs few to several, to 22×3cm, lanceolate, long-acuminate. Infl. terminal, arcuate, 1-fld; fls white or cream-white; sep. to 30×6mm, lanceolate, acute; pet. similar; lip narrow, to 3×1.5cm, white to pale pink, obscurely 3-lobed above; column to 2cm, apex alate. Peru, Venezuela, Bolivia.

S.cattleya Rchb. f.
Stems to 2m, tough, erect, the outer stems sometimes bending with weight of blooms, older stems often becoming thickened and bulbous at base. Lvs to 30×7cm, narrowly elliptic-lanceolate or ovate-lanceolate, acuminate glossy dark green, strongly ribbed. Infl. several, shorter than lvs, few- to several-fld; fls large, showy, to 7.5cm diam., fragrant; sep. to 5.5×1.5cm, oblong-elliptic to oblong-ligulate, white or cream, margins rose-pink or maroon-pink, subacute; pet. to 4.5×1.5cm, maroon-pink marked white, ovate to oblong-oblanceolate, obtuse, undulate; lip to 4.5×5cm, maroon-purple, base and margins white, obscurely 3-lobed, lateral lobes erect, midlobe oblong, emarginate, undulate, disc yellow, 3-keeled, apex fimbriate; column to 2.5cm, white, clavate. Venezuela, Colombia.

S.chlorantha Hook. See *S.macrophylla*.

S.decora Batem. (*S.sessilis* Hook. non Lindl.).
Stems to 75cm; lf sheaths black-warty or scurfy. Lvs to 22×7cm, lanceolate to oblong-lanceolate, long-acuminate. Infl. short, 1- or 2-fld; fls to 10cm diam., fragrant, short-lived; sep. and pet. white or white-lavender, sep. to 5×1.5cm, linear-oblong, apiculate, recurved, pet. to 4×1cm, elliptic-oblong, acute; lip to 3.5×4.5cm, rose-purple or lavender, tubular, base cucullate, apex rounded, apiculate, undulate, disc streaked yellow and brown, with numerous minute lamellae; column to 2.5cm, white, clavate. Spring–summer. Mexico, Honduras, Guatemala, Nicaragua, Costa Rica.

S.dichotoma Ruiz & Pav. (*S.mandonii* Rchb. f.).
Stems to 3m, robust, simple or sparsely branched. Lvs to 35×9cm, oblong-lanceolate to ovate-lanceolate, long-acuminate. Infl. lateral, spreading or arching, sometimes branching, loosely few- to many-fld; fls to 10cm diam., fragrant, fleshy, exterior white, interior red to violet-red or rose; sep. to

6×1.5cm, elliptic-oblong to oblanceolate-oblong, acute, apiculate; pet. slightly wider than sep., oblong-oblanceolate to oblong-spathulate, undulate; lip to 6×6cm, ovate-subquadrate, simple to obscurely 3-lobed, lateral lobes suborbicular, midlobe cleft, undulate-crisped, disc with several longitudinal keels, central keels incised at apex; column to 3cm, clavate. Colombia, Venezuela, Bolivia, Peru.

S.fragrans Lindl.
Stems to 45cm, erect or ascending, 2-edged, sparsely leaved toward apex only. Lvs to 25×5cm, lanceolate to oblong-lance-olate, acute to acuminate, smooth, somewhat fleshy. Infl. to 16cm, 1- or 2-fld; fls to 7.5cm diam., fragrant, ephemeral; sep. to 4×1cm, dull purple-green or ivory, linear to oblong-lanceolate, acute; pet. subequal to sep., pale yellow, lanceolate to linear-oblanceolate, acute to obtuse; lip to 3.5×2cm, bright yellow, obovate to elliptic-obovate, basal margins strongly involute, apex deeply fimbriate, disc deep yellow with to 9 jagged keels; column white, to 2cm, clavate. Spring. Guatemala to Panama, Colombia.

S.leucoxantha Rchb. f. (*S.powellii* Schltr.).
Resembles *S.micrantha* except fls smaller, sepals and petals white, lip to 7×5cm, white marked yellow to orange in centre, column large, to 5cm. Summer–early autumn. Costa Rica, Panama, Colombia.

S.liliastrum Lindl.
Stems to 3m. Lvs to 25×4cm, narrowly lanceolate, long-acuminate, striate. Fls to 10cm diam., produced in succession on a flexuous axis amid spathe-like bracts, fleshy, fragrant, short-lived, white veined or tinged yellow or rose; sep. to 7×1.5cm, oblong-lanceolate, acute; pet. to 7×2.5cm, oblance-olate to obovate, acute to rounded, undulate; lip to 6.5×5.5cm, infundibular, emarginate, undulate-crisped, disc yellow; column to 5cm, erect or slightly arcuate, clavate, white marked yellow. Summer–early autumn. Venezuela, Colombia, Brazil, Guianas.

S.lindleyana Rchb. f.
Stems to 60cm. Lvs to 13×5cm, ovate-lanceolate to elliptic-lanceolate, acuminate. Infl. 1-fld; fls to 10cm diam., fragrant, short-lived, fleshy; sep. and pet. white, fading yellow-topaz, sep. to 5×1cm, elliptic-oblong to elliptic-lanceolate, acute,

Sobralia violacea

pet. to 4.5×1.5cm, elliptic to elliptic-oblong; lip to 5×4cm, white spotted red, obovate or cuneate-flabellate, obscurely 3-lobed, lobes rounded, dentate-lacerate, disc with a tricorniculate callus, pubesc.; column to 2cm, biauriculate. Mostly summer. Costa Rica, Panama.

S.macrantha Lindl.
Stems to 2m. Lvs to 30×8cm, narrowly to broadly lanceolate, spreading, long-acuminate, glossy pale to midgreen, somewhat scabrous, strongly ribbed. Fls to 25cm diam., produced in succession, fleshy, short-lived, fragrant; sep. and pet. rose-purple, sep. to 10×3cm, linear-oblong, acute, recurved, pet. to 9×4cm, oblong-obovate, rounded, undulate; lip to 11×7cm, rose-purple, white at base, centre tinged yellow, basal portion forming a compressed tube, apical portion rotund, bilobulate, crisped to undulate; column to 4cm, clavate. Spring–autumn. Mexico to Costa Rica. The species most commonly encountered in cult. Many cvs have been recorded, most now probably lost. These include white, deep magenta, crimson, large-fld and dwarf-growing variants.

S.macrophylla Rchb. f. (S.chlorantha Hook.).
Stems to 1.2m. Lvs to 21×8cm, elliptic-oblong to elliptic-ovate, acute or acuminate, lustrous bright green. Infl. 1- or 2-fld; fls opening in succession, fleshy, short-lived, fragrant, pale yellow-green; sep. to 7×1.5cm, forming a partial tube, lanceolate, acute, recurved; pet. subequal to sep., oblong-oblanceolate to oblong-ligulate, acute, recurved; lip to 8×4cm, obovate-spathulate, rounded, recurved, disc golden-yellow, with minute central keels; column to 5cm, white, subterete. Costa Rica, Venezuela, Panama, Colombia, Brazil.

S.mandonii Rchb. f. See S.dichotoma.

S.powellii Schltr. See S.leucoxantha.

S.rosea Poepp. & Endl.
Differs from S.ruckeri in fls produced only one at a time, basically pale shell or flesh pink, the lip very large and frilly, edged with broken lines of magenta with a golden throat overlaid with radiating lines of orange-red. Colombia, Bolivia.

S.rosea hort. non Poepp. & Endl. See S.ruckeri.

S.ruckeri Lind. ex Lindl. (S.rosea hort. non Poepp. & Endl.).
Stems to 2m, robust, erect. Lvs to 38×9cm, coriaceous, lanceolate to oblong-lanceolate, acuminate. Infl. to 25cm, erect, bearing 4 open fls at any time on an elongated, flexuous rachis; fls opening in succession, fleshy, fragrant, long-lived, pale rose-lilac to rose-purple; sep. to 11×2.5cm, free or shortly connate, oblanceolate to oblong-oblanceolate, acute; pet. to 11×3.5cm, ligulate to elliptic-oblong, acute; lip to 11×5.4cm, margins deep rose-purple, centre yellow-white, infundibular, enveloping column, truncate to emarginate, apically dentate-lacerate, disc glabrous to pubesc., lamellate; column to 5cm, white, slightly curved. Summer–early autumn. Venezuela, Colombia, Ecuador, Peru.

S.sessilis Lindl. non Hook.
Stems to 1.2m. Lvs to 30×10cm, broadly oblong-lanceolate, acuminate, erect, bases and sheaths dark short-pubesc., this extending onto stems. Infl. several-fld; fls produced in succession, to 10cm diam., fleshy, fragrant, short-lived, white to dark rose; sep. to 5.5×2cm, lanceolate to oblong-lanceolate, spreading, slightly reflexed; pet. to 5×2cm, oblanceolate to oblong-ligulate, oblique; lip to 5×3.5cm, infundibular, tinted yellow at base, apical portion erose-denticulate, recurved, disc with 2 longitudinal erect lamellae at base; column to 2.5cm, clavate, curved, with 2 ventral lamellae. Autumn. Brazil, Venezuela, Guianas.

S.sessilis Hook. non Lindl. See S.decora.

S.suaveolens Rchb. f.
Close in habit to S.decora but stems to 45cm, glabrous. Lvs to 20×5cm, lanceolate to oblong-lanceolate, apex minutely tridentate. Infl usually 2- or 3-fld; fls to 6cm diam., waxy, fragrant, yellow-cream; sep. to 30×5mm, ligulate to linear-lanceolate, acute or acuminate; pet. subsimilar to sep., oblique, acute; lip to 25×15mm, elliptic to obovate, apex fimbriate-lacerate, obscurely 3-lobed, midlobe suborbicular, disc apically fimbriate-lacerate, pale brown, with several yellow keels; column to 12mm, curved. Summer. Venezuela, Panama.

S.violacea Lind. ex Lindl.
Stems to 1.2m. Lvs to 27×7cm, ovate-lanceolate to oblong-lanceolate, long-acuminate, strongly plicate, sheaths somewhat coarse or warty. Infl. several-fld; fls opening in succession, to 13cm diam., fleshy, fragrant, short-lived; sep. to 7.5×2cm, usually dark rose-purple, oblong to oblong-oblanceolate, shortly acuminate; pet. paler than sep., often a delicate shade of violet, otherwise similar, to sep.; lip to 7.5×5cm, deep yellow-orange toward base, margins deep rose-purple, infundibular, slightly crisped, disc with several narrow, transverse keels; column to 4cm, clavate. Mostly summer. Colombia, Venezuela, Peru, Bolivia. A variant is sometimes offered with white fls and a rich orange-yellow disc.

S.warscewiczii Rchb. f.
Stems robust, compact, eventually becoming warty. Lvs to 18×6cm, broadly oblong to ovate-elliptic, acute or acuminate, rigid, coriaceous. Infl. 1-fld; fls bright purple; sep. to 5×2cm, broadly oblanceolate, acute; pet. to 5×3cm, obovate-cuneate, acute; lip to 5×3cm, flabellate, emarginate, apically undulate-crisped, disc with 2 lamellae at base, slightly verrucose; column to 3cm. Panama.

S.xantholeuca Rchb. f.
Stems 1–2m. Lvs to 17m, lanceolate, long-acuminate, plicate, somewhat deflexed, sheaths dull grey-green spotted red-brown. Fls solitary, produced in succession, short-lived, showy, nodding; sep. and pet. to 10cm, narrow-lanceolate, ivory to lemon yellow, the pet. often somewhat shorter than sep.; lip tubular strongly crisped, deep yellow flushed and streaked dark orange-yellow in the throat. C America. 'Albescens': fls pale primrose. 'Nana': to 75cm. 'Superba': fls rich ivory, lip marked orange to burnt siena in throat. 'Wigan's Var.': sep. and pet. ivory tinted primrose, lip ivory flushed yellow; fls tinted rose at first.

Solenangis Schltr. (From Gk *solen*, pipe or tube, and *angos*, vessel.) 5 species of epiphytes or lithophytes. Stems elongated, often scandent; roots numerous. Leaves lanceolate, ligulate or terete, or absent. Racemes axillary; flowers small, white, pink-white, green or yellow-green; sepals and petals free, subsimilar; lip entire or obscurely trilobed, spurred; pollinia 2, stipes and viscidium 1. Tropical Africa, Comoros Is., Madagascar.

CULTIVATION See *Angraecum*.

S.clavata (Schltr.) Schltr.
Stem elongated, scandent. Lvs 1.5–5×0.5–1.5cm, broadly lanceolate, ovate or elliptical, obscurely bilobed at tip. Racemes 5–15mm, many-fld; fls white, or tepals green and lip white; pedicel and ovary 5mm; sep. and pet. 1.5–2mm, ovate-oblong, obtuse, concave, keeled on outside; lip very small, trilobed, lateral lobes rounded, midlobe triangular, minute; spur 5–7mm, stout, club-shaped; column 1mm. W Africa.

S.scandens (Schltr.) Schltr.
Stems long, scandent; roots numerous, about 1mm diam. Lvs 3–9×1–2.5cm, elliptic-lanceolate. Racemes 2–9cm, several-fld; fls white, green-white or yellow-green, sometimes tinged pink; pedicel and ovary 10mm; sep. and pet. 5–7mm, ovate; lip 5–6mm, entire, ovate, concave; spur 20–25mm, tapering to become slender from a funnel-shaped mouth but with the apex inflated. W Africa, Zaire.

S.wakefieldii (Rolfe) Cribb & Joyce Stewart (*Tridactyle wakefieldii* Rolfe; *Angraecum wakefieldii* Rolfe).
Stem scandent, to 1m, slender, with many roots. Lvs 1.5–3×0.5–1.5cm, lanceolate, acutely bilobed at apex, set 1–2.5cm apart on stem. Infl. 4–6cm, laxly 4–6-fld; fls white; pedicel and ovary 1–2cm; dorsal sep. 3×1.5mm, oblong, lateral sep. 4–4.5×1.5mm, oblong-lanceolate; pet. 3.5×1.5mm, lanceolate or oblanceolate; lip 10mm, trilobed, midlobe 3.5×1mm, lateral lobes spreading, 4.5–5×0.5mm, the apices slightly recurved; spur 6–7cm, narrowing to become filiform from a mouth 2mm wide; column 1mm. Kenya, Zanzibar.

Solenidium Lindl. (From Gk *solenidion*, small canal, referring to the apparently channelled claw of the lip.) Some 2 species of epiphytes. Rhizome short. Pseudobulbs clustered, compressed, grooved, apically bifoliate. Leaves thin. Inflorescence a lateral raceme, erect or ascending, few- to many-flowered; tepals subequal, free or connate at base, spreading; lip adnate to column foot, unguiculate, sometimes with a pair of small basal lobes; disc callose; column erect to arcuate, with a short foot, apex conspicuously winged, anther terminal, operculate, incumbent, unilocular, pollinia 2, ovoid, stipe narrow, viscidium prominent. Northern S America.

CULTIVATION See *Rodriguezia*.

S.lunatum (Lindl.) Kränzl. (*Oncidium lunatum* Lindl.; *Rodriguezia lindmanii* Kränzl.; *Leochilus mattogrossensis* Cogn.).
Pseudobulbs to 3.5×2cm, ellipsoid-ovoid, strongly compressed. Lvs to 13×2cm, erect, coriaceous, oblong or oblong-lanceolate, acute to obtuse. Infl. to 25cm, erect or ascending, few- to many-fld; peduncle light green, slightly compressed; fls to 2cm diam.; sep. and pet. light yellow-brown marked red-brown, slightly fleshy, sep. to 10×5mm, obovate to obovate-oblanceolate, retuse to subacute; lip to 10×9mm, white spotted brown reniform, ciliate, with a narrow claw bearing small auriculate lobes at base, disc 2-crested; column to 6mm, white marked red-brown, basal portion pubesc., anth. brown. Venezuela, Guyana, Brazil.

S.racemosum Lindl. (*Oncidium racemosum* (Lindl.) Rchb. f.).
Pseudobulbs to 6×2.5cm, ovoid to cylindrical, compressed, usually lustrous light brown. Lvs to 30×2cm, linear or linear-lanceolate, acute or acuminate. Infl. to 35cm, erect or suberect, loosely many-fld; fls to 2.5cm diam., long-lived, yellow blotched and barred chestnut brown; sep. and pet. to 14×6mm, obovate to ovate-oblong, truncate or emarginate; lip to 14×5mm, entire, broadly cuneate, lamina broadly ovate or obovate, obtuse, callus white, bilobulate, oblong, pubesc.; column to 5mm, stout, green-brown or brown, apex dentate. Winter. Colombia, Venezuela.

× **Sophrocattleya** (*Sophronitis* × *Cattleya*). Intergeneric hybrids which mostly form very small plants with well shaped, small flowers of intense colours.

× *S*.Beaufort: one of the true mini-cattleyas; fls varied in this cross, pure yellow, orange and almost red, usually with a bright yellow lip; several awarded clones.

× *S*.Doris 'Pamela': small compact plants; fls of beautiful proportions, a superb flaming orange red.

× **Sophrolaelia** (*Sophronitis* × *Laelia*). Intergeneric hybrids with small, mostly rather slender plants and brightly coloured flowers.

× *S*.Cheerio 'Clarissa': one of the true mini-cattleyas; very small plants with clusters of small, bright lavender-pink fls of good shape.

× *S*.Gratrixiae: early hybrid, small plants; fls small, brilliant fiery red.

× *S*.Orpetii: red miniature plants; fls nicely shaped pink or dark pink, often with yellow in the throat.

× *S*.Psyche: an early hybrid with intense clear red fls.

× **Sophrolaeliocattleya** (*Sophronitis* × *Laelia* × *Cattleya*). Trigeneric hybrids of species and hybrids of these genera. The plants are usually smaller than those of other cattleya hybrids and easier to grow in cooler conditions. The flowers are mostly intense, glowing colours of various shades of red.

× *S*.Anzac 'Doris' and 'Orchidhurst': fine clones of one of the most vibrant early red hybrids, lip dark and velvety.

× *S*.Bellicent: compact plants, easy to grow; medium size, red-lavender fls with slightly darker veining on sep. and pet., much darker coloured shapely lip; several awarded clones.

× *S*.Brandywine 'Pamela Martin': strong, compact plants; fls stunning, glowing red, with deeper red lip.

× *S*.Dixie Jewels 'Suzuki': small compact plants; stunning solid red fls of excellent form and substance, glistening texture; superb.

× *S*.Estelle Jewel 'Mojave': compact small plants; fls superb red-magenta, prolific.

× *S*.Falcon 'Westonbirt': and 'Alexanderi': small plants; fls lovely bright red with glowing golden yellow in the throat.

× *S*.Hazel Boyd: small compact plants often described as mini-catts; brilliant fls of excellent shape in a wide range of copper, apricot and red tones; many awarded clones.

× *S*.Hong Kong: small to medium size plants; fls rich reddish bronze to lavender, lip deep lavender to red.

× *S*.Jewel Box 'Dark Waters': a stunning winter-flowering plant of compact shape which is an important parent of many red crosses; fls brilliant crimson red.

× *S*.Jewel Box 'Scheherezade': compact plants that can be grown to specimen size; fls rich glowing red in clusters.

× *S*.Lindores 'Orchidglade': small plants; brilliant rosy-red fls with rich crimson lip and clear yellow throat.

× *S*.Little Hazel: a true mini-catt; fls small, shiny, bright red or orange red with excellent shape.

× *S*.Madge Fordyce: small compact plants; fls small and neat, beautiful bright scarlet red; the clone 'Red Orb' has won many awards.

× *S*.Marion Fitch 'La Tuilerie': strong plants that flower twice a year; fls in large clusters, rich red.

× *S*.Mine Gold: miniature plants with tall infl.; fls bright golden yellow with a red flash along the centre of sep. and pet., deep velvety red lip.

× *S*.Naomi Girl: compact plants; superb fls of medium size in a wide range of sunset colours.

× *S*.Naomi Kerns 'Fireball': strong but small plants; fls a lovely coppery red with rich red lip.

× *S*.Natalie Canipelli 'Moonshot': large bifoliate plants bearing many fls in upright clusters; fls cerise red of intense colour.

× *S*.Orglade's Early Harvest: one of the true mini-catts; plants small and compact; small fls of excellent shape, bright daffodil yellow.

× *S*.Paprika 'Black Magic': small but strong plants; fls bright red; the clone 'Tahiti' has orange red sep. and pet. and a red lip; the clone 'Golden Delight' is bright yellow orange with a darker orange lip.

× *S*.Petite's Wink: true miniatures; clusters of small yellow fls, some with red markings or patches in the lip.

× *S*.Pink Doll: one of the true mini-catts; fls large for the plant, brilliant shades of pink, lavender and red; several awarded clones.

× *S*.Precious Stones 'True Beauty': truly miniature plants which are free-flowering and easy to grow; fls bright red with purple-red lip, small but excellent shape.

× *S*.Pumpkin Festival: strong compact plants; gorgeous rich red fls of fine form, lip enhanced by well defined crescent of golden yellow below the column.

× *S*.Rajah's Ruby: strong, compact plants; large heads of brilliant, glowing red fls.

× *S*.Rosemary Clooney 'Nanae': strong plants bearing impressive heads of many fls; sep. and pet. rich golden yellow, lip bright burgundy red with gold venation in the throat.

× *S*.Tangerine Jewel: strong, compact plants: fls in clusters, bright orange red, good shape.

× *S*.Tropic Flare 'Magic Fire': strong but small plants; fls small to medium size, rich scarlet red sep. and pet., deep red lip.

× *S*.Vallezac: small plants; fls fine deep red of large size and good substance.

× *S*.Wendy's Valentine: compact plants of medium size; fls excellent shape, brilliant crimson red with yellow flash at base of lip.

Sophronitella Schltr. (From Gk *sophron*, chaste or modest, referring to its inconspicuous habit.) 1 species, an epiphyte. Pseudobulbs oblong spindle-shaped or narrow-ovoid, 1.5–3×0.3–0.8cm, densely clustered, basal nodes 1–2; apical leaf solitary. Leaf linear, coriaceous, folded along the axis, abruptly acute, 4–7×0.3–0.5cm. Inflorescence erect; 1–2-flowered; flowers purple-violet, fleshy; sepals oblong-lanceolate, acute, 2×0.3–0.4cm; petals oblong, acute; lip fused to the column foot, obovate, narrow, entire, abruptly acute, basal callus pouched. E Brazil.

CULTIVATION   See *Sophronitis*.

S.violacea (Lindl.) Schltr. (*Sophronitis violacea* Lindl.).

Sophronitis Lindl. (From Gk *sophron*, modest, referring to the small flowers of the type species.) Some 9 species of diminutive epiphytes or lithophytes. Rhizome creeping. Pseudobulbs clustered on rhizome, small, apically unifoliate. Leaves fleshy or coriaceous, erect or spreading. Inflorescence a short, apical raceme, 1- to many-flowered; flowers showy, usually bright red, violet or scarlet, often marked yellow on lip; sepals subequal, free, flat, spreading; petals wider than sepals; lip smaller than petals, shortly adnate to column or sessile, simple to trilobed, lateral lobes clasping column; column short, stout, winged, anther terminal, operculate, incumbent, pollinia 8, in pairs. E Brazil, Paraguay.

CULTIVATION   Exquisite dwarf orchids with disproportionately large carmine or scarlet flowers for well ventilated situations in light shade in the cool house, or growing case. Pot in small clay pans in a fine bark mix with added sphagnum moss, charcoal and sterilized leafmould. Alternatively, attach to rafts or cork slabs. Water throughout the year, allowing a slight drying between each application; mist freely growing plants in warm weather. Propagate by careful division – these plants are slow to bulk up and should be encouraged to form 'large' colonies. Susceptible to overwatering and, equally, to rapid desiccation.

A parent of many intergeneric hybrids involving *Cattleya, Laelia* and *Rhyncholaelia* (*Brassavola*), imparting a dwarf habit, strong shades of red, carmine and cinnabar, broad petals and a neat, tight lip.

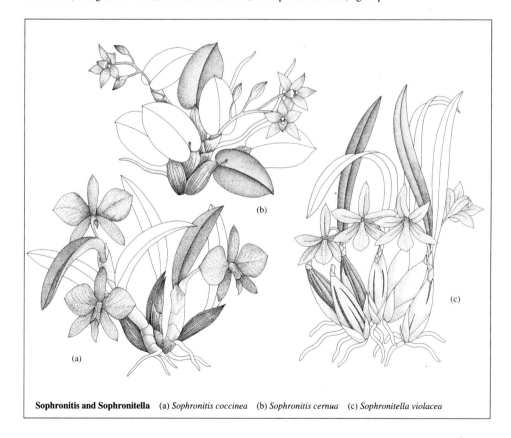

Sophronitis and Sophronitella   (a) *Sophronitis coccinea*   (b) *Sophronitis cernua*   (c) *Sophronitella violacea*

S.cernua Lindl. (*S.modesta* Lindl.).
Pseudobulbs to 2×1cm, ovoid or subcylindrical, tightly clustered. Lvs to 2.5×2cm, broadly ovate-oblong to ovate-elliptic, obtuse, coriaceous, lustrous dark grey-green above, flushed purple-red below. Infl. to 5cm, erect or spreading, few-fld; fls to 3cm diam.; fleshy, deep cinnabar-red, the lip a deeper tone fading to white or orange-yellow at base; sep. to 12×5mm, elliptic or ovate-oblong, acute; pet. to 12×6mm, ovate or ovate-rhombic, obtuse; lip to 10×7mm, simple, ovate or ovate-triangular, acute or acuminate, disc cristate; column to 5mm, erect, apex tridenticulate. Autumn–winter. E Brazil.

S.coccinea (Lindl.) Rchb. f. (*S.grandiflora* Lindl.; *S.militaris* Rchb. f.).
Pseudobulbs to 40×6mm, fusiform or ovoid-cylindrical, clustered, erect or ascending. Lvs to 6×2.5cm, narrowly ovate to elliptic-oblong, fleshy to coriaceous, erect to spreading, lustrous dark green sometimes flushed purple, acute or obtuse, short-petiolate or sessile. Infl. to 6cm, suberect, usually 1-fld; fls to 7.5cm diam., fleshy, usually vivid scarlet, the lip marked yellow at base although white and magenta-fld forms occur; sep. to 22×10mm, broadly oblong or elliptic-oblong, obtuse; pet. to 30×30mm, ovate-orbicular to rhombic, obtuse; lip to 20×22mm, trilobed, lateral lobes erect, triangular-orbicular, obtuse, midlobe oblong or oblong-triangular, concave, obtuse or acute; column to 9mm, white, apex often bilobed. Autumn–winter. E Brazil.

S.grandiflora Lindl. See *S.coccinea*.
S.modesta Lindl. See *S.cernua*.
S.militaris Rchb. f. See *S.coccinea*.
S.violacea Lindl. See *Sophronitella violacea*.

Spathoglottis Bl. (From Gk *spathe*, broad blade, and *glotta*, tongue, an allusion to the form of the lip.) Some 40 species of fibrous-rooted, terrestrials with broad, conical to ovoid, sheathed pseudobulbs. Leaves lanceolate, plicate, basally sheathing. Inflorescence raceme arising from basal leaf axils, lateral; flowers many; sepals and petals spreading, erect, sepals narrower than petals; lip midlobe lanceolate to spathulate, bilobed below, with depressed pubescent callus and small dentations at the base. Asia to Australia.

CULTIVATION As for *Phaius*.

S.aurea Lindl.
Pseudobulbs ovoid, to 2.5cm, 2–4-leaved. Lvs narrow-lanceolate, to 100×5cm. Infl. to 60cm+, 4–10 fld; fls to 7cm diam., golden, callus, lip midlobe base and lateral lobes spotted crimson; sep. and pet. elliptic to ovate, shallow-concave; lip midlobe lanceolate, at base with 2 triangular teeth or lobes, callus teeth 2, triangular, lateral lobes oblong, erect. Summer. Malaysia.

S.ixioides (D. Don) Lindl.
Pseudobulbs globose to ovoid. Lvs apical, 2–3, linear, to 20cm. Infl. erect, slender, lax; fls yellow, minutely pubesc.; sep. and pet. elliptic to oblong, spreading, almost equal; lip oblong, basally concave or almost saccate, midlobe obcordate, the disc between the lateral lobes with 2 elongate calli divided by a ridge, lateral lobes bifid, conical. India.

S.lilacina Griff. See *S.plicata*.

S.petri Rchb. f.
Lvs to 45cm, lanceolate. Infl. to 60cm, apex purple, racemes dense; fls 9–12, to 4cm diam.; pet. and sep. lilac, sep. ligulate, pet. elliptic, acute; lip cuneate, dilated, apex trilobed, midlobe short, almost acute, callus furrowed, between lateral lobes 2 lines of yellow to ochre hairs, lateral lobes ligulate, purple, disc white. Vanuatu, New Caledonia.

S.plicata Bl. (*S.lilacina* Griff.).
Pseudobulb short, leafy. Lvs linear-lanceolate, to 120×7cm; petiole to 15cm. Infl. to 1m, axis minutely pubesc. fls purple, rose or lilac; dorsal sep. elliptic to 0.6cm, lateral sep. similar, falcate; pet. elliptic-ovate; lip midlobe clawed, cuneate, callus on the midlobe claw, cordate, yellow, sparsely villous, lateral lobes basal, oblong-obovate; column winged. India, SE Asia to Philippines.

S.pubescens Lindl.
Lvs linear, to 30×2cm. Scape pubesc., to 45cm; fls to 2.5cm diam., dull yellow, lip basally violet; lip saccate, midlobe cuneate or obcordate with 2 tubercles at base, callus 3-ridged, lateral lobes oblong, broad. Autumn–winter. India, Burma, China.

S.tomentosa Lindl.
Lvs lanceolate, to 60×2.5cm. Infl. to 35cm, axis densely velutinous; fls to 4.5 diam., deep pink to mauve, white or yellow, centre dappled red; lateral sep. elliptic-oblong, to 2.5×1.5cm; pet. ovate, spreading; lip midlobe slender, apex reniform, lateral lobes oblong, cuneate. Philippines.

S.trivalvis Wallich. See *Acriopsis javanica*.

S.grexes.
*S.*Kewensis: fls rich deep purple.
*S.*Penang Beauty: fls clear pale yellow.

Spiranthes L.C. Rich. (From Gk *speira*, spiral, and *anthos*, flower, an allusion to the spiral inflorescence.) Some 50 species of terrestrials or, rarely, epiphytes lacking pseudobulbs. Roots clustered, fleshy to tuberous. Stem concealed by leaf sheaths. Leaves in a basal rosette and a few reduced, clothing stems, sometimes absent. Inflorescence a terminal raceme borne on an erect stem, loosely or densely few- to many-flowered; flowers small to large, usually arranged spirally; sepals free, dorsal sepal narrow, usually erect, lateral sepals erect or spreading; petals narrow, often adherent to dorsal sepal; lip sessile or clawed, simple to 3-lobed, concave or gibbous, usually adnate to column; column terete, footless or with a distinct foot, clinandrium often continued into rostellum, anther dorsal, sessile or stipitate, pollinia 2. Cosmopolitan.

CULTIVATION As for *Disa* for tropical and subtropical spp.; for the hardy *Ss.cernua, gracilis, romanzoffiana, sinensis, spiralis*, see Introduction: Hardy Orchids.

S.cernua (L.) Rich. (*Gyrostachys cernua* (L.) Kuntze; *Ibidium cernuum* (L.) House).
Lvs to 25cm, linear to linear-lanceolate, acute to acuminate. Infl. to 60cm, erect, downy, densely fld, conspicuously spiralling; fls to 1cm, fragrant, white; dorsal sep. to 11×3mm, oblong-lanceolate, acute or subacute, lateral sep. to 11×2mm, lanceolate, acute or subacute, pet. to 11×3mm, linear or linear-lanceolate, subacute; lip to 10×6mm, ovate-oblong, recurved, apex dilated, erose-crispate; disc with a prominent, basal, pubesc. callus; column to 5mm. E Canada to S Florida and Texas; naturalized W Europe.

S.cinnabarina (La Ll. & Lex.) Hemsl. (*Neottia cinnabarina* La Ll. & Lex.; *Gyrostachys cinnabarina* (La Ll. & Lex.) Kuntze).
Lvs to 23×3cm, linear-lanceolate to oblanceolate, subobtuse to shortly acuminate. Infl. to 90cm, erect, downy, densely many-fld toward summit; fls to 2.5cm, tubular, yellow-orange to golden-scarlet; sep. and pet. minutely papillose, tips recurved, sep. to 25×32mm, lanceolate, acute or acuminate, pet. to 22×25mm, falcate, linear-lanceolate, acuminate; lip to 25×6mm, elliptic-lanceolate to obovate-lanceolate, long-acuminate; disc with 2 basal, longitudinal calli; column to 10mm. Texas, Mexico, Guatemala.

S.gracilis (Bigelow) Beck (*Neottia gracilis* Bigelow; *Gyrostachys gracilis* (Bigelow) Kuntze; *Ibidium gracilis* (Bigelow) House).
Lvs to 6.5×2.5cm, broadly ovate to ovate-lanceolate. Infl. to 65cm, sometimes downy toward apex, loosely or densely-fld; fls to 1cm, faintly scented; sep. and pet. to 5.5mm, white, dorsal sep. oblong-elliptic to oblong-lanceolate, acute to obtuse, lateral sep. lanceolate, acute to acuminate, pet. linear, obtuse or subacute; lip to 6×2.5cm, white with a central green stripe, oblong-elliptic to oblong-quadrate, crenulate to erose; disc with short, erect basal calli; column to 3mm. Nova Scotia to Manitoba, Minnesota and Iowa to Texas and Florida.

S.lanceolata (Aubl.) Léon. See *Stenorrhynchos lanceolatum*.

S.romanzoffiana Cham.
Lvs to 30cm, linear-oblong to -lanceolate. Infl. to 50cm, 12–35-fld; fls in 3 spiralling ranks; tepals to 1.2cm, lanceolate, forward-pointing forming a tube, the tips erect, green-white to cream; lip small, white, decurved at apex. N America.

S.sinensis (Pers.) Ames.
Readily distinguished from other spp. listed here by the sparkling rose-magenta tepals to 0.5cm and the pure white undulate-crispate lip. Russia, Asia, Australasia.

S.speciosa (Gmel.) A. Rich. See *Stenorrhynchos speciosum*.

S.spiralis (L.) Chevall. LADY'S TRESSES.
Roots clustered, tuberous. Lvs to 2.5cm, ovate, acute, glossy dark green, appearing after fls, in lateral spreading rosettes. Infl. to 10cm, slender, stalk downy; fls to 5mm diam., fragrant, sparkling snow-white except for lime-green venation in lip, numerous, strongly spirally arranged, sheathed by cucullate, cuspidate bracts; sep. and pet. projected forward, hooding channelled and crenate lip. Europe.

S.tortilis (Sw.) Rich. (*Neottia tortilis* Sw.; *Ibidium tortile* (Sw.) House).
Lvs to 30cm, narrowly linear. Infl. to 75cm, erect, densely fld; fls to 1cm, often scented; white; sep. to 6×2mm, dorsal sep. oblong-elliptic to oblong-lanceolate, subacute, lateral sep. lanceolate, acute to acuminate; lip to 6×3mm, ovate to subquadrate, strongly recurved, apical margin undulate-crenulate; disc white marked green or yellow-green, with mammillate calli. S US to W Indies, Guatemala.

S.vernalis Engelm. & Gray.
Lvs to 30×1cm, narrowly lanceolate to linear, acuminate. Infl. to 85cm, very downy toward apex, densely fld; fls to 1.5cm, usually scented, yellow or white, sometimes green; sep. to 10×3mm, lanceolate to oblong-lanceolate, acute to obtuse, lateral sep. lanceolate, acute, pet. to 9×2mm, linear to linear-elliptic, obtuse; lip to 8×6mm, fleshy, recurved, broadly ovate to ovate-rhombic, apex slightly undulate; calli incurved, pubesc. Florida to Texas, Mexico, Guatemala.

Stanhopea Frost ex Hook. (For the Earl of Stanhope, President of the London Medico-Botanical Society 1829–37.) Some 55 species of epiphytes, lithophytes or (rarely) terrestrials allied to *Coryanthes* and *Gongora*. Rhizomes short. Pseudobulbs to 7cm, fleshy, apically unifoliate, rarely bifoliate, ovoid to pyriform, sulcate. Leaves to 50×15cm, elliptic to oblong-lanceolate, large, obscurely plicately veined, coriaceous or subcoriaceous, contracted at base forming a petiole. Inflorescence a raceme, from base of pseudobulb, strongly pendent, short, loosely few-flowered; bracts large, chartaceous, imbricate, concealing ovaries; flowers short-lived, large, showy, fragrant, fleshy; sepals oblong to ovate-oblong, free or with lateral sepals connate at base, spreading-reflexed or recurved, undulate lateral sepals wider; petals similar, narrower and thinner than sepals; lip thickly fleshy, complex, adnate to or connate with base of column; hypochile subglobose or calceiform, concave; mesochile (when present) short, entire or divided, usually with 2 narrow, falcate, fleshy horns; epichile articulated to mesochile, entire or 3-lobed, variously shaped; column elongate, erect or arcuate, clavate, wingless to prominently winged above; anther terminal, operculate, incumbent, 1-celled, pollinia 2, waxy, elongate. C & S America (Mexico to Brazil).

CULTIVATION   Epiphytes for the cool or intermediate house. Among the most spectacular of all orchids, they produce thrusting, pendulous racemes of massive waxy flowers. The blooms are intricately structured, with a complex lip and strongly reflexed tepals, resembling giant moths or even, in one species, a sheep's skull; they are deliciously scented and, in well established plants, produced in abundance. These qualities, combined with their great ease of culture, should offset the fact that *Stanhopea* flowers seldom last longer than two days, having developed and opened with startling, often visible rapidity.

Establish in wooden baskets lined with sphagnum and filled with a coarse bark mix with added leafmould and dried manure. Inflorescences tend to bury themselves and wither where pots are used; baskets will permit the racemes to escape, usually through their bases. Water and syringe freely when in growth and suspend in a humid airy place in bright, filtered light. Apply a weak foliar feed every second week when in full growth. Once the new pseudobulbs are fully developed, reduce water and temperature and remove all shading. Until the emergence of new growths and roots, water only to prevent excessive shrivelling. Propagate by division. Red spider mite may be a problem on resting or neglected plants.

S.anfracta Rolfe.
Fls to 6cm diam., 7 to 13 per raceme; tepals ovate, fleshy, not reflexed but outspread and downward-pointing, rich apricot to orange; lip orange with a dark amber eye spot on either side of hypochile, hypochile bent at midpoint, mesochile with thick horns, epichile reflexed and thickened above; column translucent white. E Andes from Ecuador to Bolivia.

S.annulata Mansf.
Fls to 4cm diam., two on a short, thickly sheathed raceme; tepals ovate-falcate, cream, pale primrose or orange-yellow, sep. far larger than pet., the laterals strongly reflexed, rather ear-like, pet. sharply folded back at midpoint; lip pale yellow to orange, hypochile with two pale red basal spots and girdled with a thickened ring,   mesochile lacking horns, epichile short. Colombia, Ecuador.

S.aurea Lodd. ex Lindl. See *S.wardii*.

S.candida Barb. Rodr. (*S.randii* Rolfe).
Raceme lateral, short, 2–4-fld; peduncle to 6cm; fls pure white to ivory vanilla-scented; sep. to 5×2cm, concave; pet. to 4×1.5cm; lip pure white, variously tinted and spotted rose-purple, to 3.5cm, divided; hypochile ovate, concave, sides bidentate, marginal horns close to base; mesochile apically truncate or retuse, lacking horns; epichile slightly convex, acuminate, triangular; column arcuate, wings rounded, to 4.5cm, pale cream; anth. yellow-cream. Venezuela, Colombia, Peru, Brazil.

S.cirrhata Klotzsch.
Fls to 6cm diam., two on a thickly sheathed raceme; tepals apricot to pale golden orange, lateral sep. large, ovate-orbicular, reflexed, pet. smaller, narrower, folded sharply back; lip apricot with saccate hypochile, mesochile with short, thick, dark purple-red horns. Nicaragua to Panama.

S.convoluta Rolfe. See *S.tricornis*.

S.costaricensis Rchb.f.
Fls to 9cm diam., 5–7 per rac.; tepals spreading to reflexed, ivory to dull yellow spotted red-brown, lateral sep. broadly ovate, larger than the narrow pet. and dorsal sep.; lip white to cream densely spotted red-brown, hypochile with two dark eyes at base and two swollen projections beneath, mesochile with distinct, terete horns, epichile broad and long. Guatemala

to Panama.

S.eburnea Lindl. (*S.grandiflora* (Lodd.) Lindl. non HBK).
Raceme, 2–4-fld; peduncle pale green to white; fls to 15×12cm, waxy, ivory-white variously dotted purple; sep. to 7×4cm, thin, slightly revolute; pet. to 7×2.5cm, recurved margins dotted purple; lip to 7cm; hypochile long, bicorniculate at base, interior lightly pubesc., slightly tinged orange-brown, exterior tinged pale pink; mesochile hornless; epichile small, subacute, laterally bidentate; column slender, to 7.5cm, apically bialate, green-white. Summer. Brazil, Guyana, Venezuela, Trinidad, Colombia.

S.ecornuta Lem.
Fls to 6cm diam., two per raceme; tepals pure to creamy white with pale red dots scattered at their bases, lateral sep. large, rounded and somewhat concave above, appearing to billow, pet. smaller; lip squat, yolk-yellow, hypochile enlarged and strongly saccate, dotted red, mesochile lacking horns, epichile short, with protuberances. Guatemala to Panama.

S.florida Rchb.f.
Fls to 8cm diam., 5–8 per raceme; tepals yellow-orange to dirty pink-tinted cream, finely spotted with red-brown, ovate-lanceolate, somewhat revolute and undulate; lip buff to pale pink flecked red-brown, hypochile with two dark red-brown eyes at base, elongate, rather flat, mesochile with pronounced, terete horns, epichile broad. Colombia to Peru.

S.grandiflora Lindl. non HBK. See *S.eburnea*.

S.jenischiana Kramer ex Rchb. f.
Raceme pendent, loosely 4–5-fld; bracts to 8×4.5cm, white; peduncle white, subterete, to 15cm; tepals reflexed, orange-yellow dotted and marked dark maroon, tinged maroon at base; sep. to 7×4cm; pet. to 5.5×2cm, biauriculate at base; lip complex; hypochile interior orange-yellow, tinged dark purple-brown, exterior orange-brown, almost white apically with deep purple blotch on each side; mesochile and epichile waxy, spotted white, epichile tinged deep purple-brown at base; column white spotted purple. Panama, Venezuela, Colombia, Ecuador.

S.marshii Rchb. f. See *S.saccata*.

S.martiana Batem. ex Lindl.
Fls to 8cm diam, 2–3 per raceme; tepals spreading, oblong-

Stanhopea (a) *S.tigrina* (b) *S.eburnea*

elliptic, rather blunt, white spotted and blotched dark chocolate brown to maroon, especially near base; lip white with
large dark brown eyes at base of hypochile (these sometimes
coalescing), hypochile short, concave, mesochile with long,
flattened horns tapering to bristle-like tips, epichile narrow, 3-
lobed above. W Mexico. Superficially not unlike *Embreea
rodigasiana*.

S.oculata (Lodd.) Lindl.
Infl. to 25cm, pendent, several-fld; fls white or yellow, spotted red-purple; sep. to 7×5cm, ovate, acute or obtuse, concave; pet. to 5.5×2cm, oblong-lanceolate, acute, undulate; lip
to 6.5cm, with 2 large basal spots, fleshy; hypochile to
3.5×1.5cm,, concave; mesochile to 3cm, with 2 porrect
horns; epichile to 3×3cm, ovate-elliptic, acute; column to
6cm, arcuate, apically winged. Mexico, Guatemala,
Honduras, Belize.

S.pulla Rchb. f.
Raceme short, usually 2-fld; bracts large; fls small, to 7cm
diam., apricot yellow; sep. reflexed, dorsal sep. narrower;
pet. bright yellow, smaller than sep; lip simple, waxy, light
brown with red-brown markings; hypochile connate to column base, base widely inflated, broadly concave ventrally,
red-brown elongate keel on inner disc, apex terminating in a
fleshy, short, subcordate protuberance connivent with
hypochile-apex; column wingless. Summer. Costa Rica,
Panama.

S.radiosa Lem. See *S.saccata*.
S.randii Rolfe. See *S.candida*.

S.ruckeri Lindl.
Fls to 8cm diam., 4–7 per raceme; tepals yellow-orange to
creamy white densely blotched red-black; lip white blotched
red-black with a pair of red-black eyes at base of elongate
hypochile, mesochile with terete horns, epichile broad.
Mexico to Nicaragua.

S.saccata Batem. (*S.marshii* Rchb. f.; *S.radiosa* Lem.).
Raceme 2–3-fld; peduncle to 25cm; bracts to 5cm, spotted; fls
scented of orange or cinnamon, green-yellow to cream, regularly flecked brown and purple; sep. to 6.5×4.3cm, dorsal sep.
smaller; pet. to 5×2.5cm, margins undulate; lip waxy;
hypochile deeply saccate, orange marked red, terminating in a
pair of slender horns and a conduplicate, 3-lobed lamina;
mesochile laterally bicorniculate, horns to 3×1cm, slightly
incurved, falcate, flat; epichile ovate, yellow-white, interior
flecked red, conduplicate, 3-lobed, midlobe shortest; column
to 4.5cm, slender, arcuate below, bialate. Mexico, Guatemala,
El Salvador.

S.tigrina Batem. ex Lindl.
Raceme to 15cm, 2–4-fld; fls large, to 20cm diam., deep yel-

low massively barred or blotched purple-brown, strongly fragrant; sep. to 8×5cm, reflexed; pet. to 7.5×1.5cm, reflexed,
margins undulate; lip to 7.5cm; hypochile golden-yellow,
each side dotted brown-purple, rounded, semiglobose, radiating toothed lamellae within cavity; mesochile bicorniculate,
ivory-white, spotted purple on lateral horns; epichile
equalling horns, ivory, variously spotted purple, ovate, apex
tridentate; column broad, to 8cm long, broadly alate.
Summer–autumn. Mexico to Brazil.

S.tricornis Lindl. (*S.convoluta* Rolfe).
Raceme short, 2 or more-fld; fls large, to 12cm diam., white
to cream; sep. to 6.5×3.6cm, dorsal sep. reflexed over ovary,
lateral sep. spreading; pet. smaller, connivent over column,
orange-tipped or tinged pink; lip to 4cm, yellow, interior
orange; hypochile to 2cm, subglobose, exterior with white
longitudinal lines, interior dotted purple; mesochile scarcely
distinct, orange, 2 incurved lateral horns, small porrect horn
at base; epichile oblong, apex slightly trilobed, to 2×1cm; column to 4cm, arcuate, broadly bialate. Peru, Colombia,
Ecuador.

S.venusta Lindl. See *S.wardii*.

S.wardii Lodd. ex Lindl. (*S.aurea* Lodd. ex Lindl.; *S.venusta*
Lindl.).
Raceme lateral, to 10-fld; bracts large, scarious, thin; fls over-
poweringly scented of spice or chocolate, to 14cm diam.,
green-white to pale yellow or peach, variously dotted red-purple, orange-yellow at base; sep. to 5.5×3.5cm, concave, margins recurved; pet. to 5×1.5cm, recurved, margins undulate;
lip fleshy; hypochile orange each side with large purple-
brown spot, saccate, thickened and sulcate above; mesochile
cream to pale yellow-green, short with 2 erect, arcuate,
acuminate horns to 3cm; epichile joined to mesochile apex,
fleshy, broad ovate, acute, sulcate, margins revolute, to
2.5×3cm; column pale green, arcuate, broadly winged above,
to 4cm. Venezuela to Peru, Mexico to Panama.

S.warscewicziana Klotzsch.
Raceme to 25cm, loosely several-fld; fls strongly and
muskily scented, large, waxy, green-white to cream-yellow
spotted maroon or purple; sep. to 6.5×4.5cm, erect-spreading, dorsal sep. concave, lateral sep. reflexed; pet. to
5.5×2.5cm, reflexed, undulate; lip to 5.5×3cm, deep apricot-
yellow at base with maroon blotch on each side, cream-
white above; hypochile short, saccate, ventrally bidentate,
sulcate above; mesochile with 2 prominent, incurved,
acuminate horns, to 3.5cm; epichile suborbicular-elliptic,
acute to reflexed; column to 5cm, arcuate, broadly bialate
above to near middle. Mexico, Guatemala, Brazil,
Honduras.

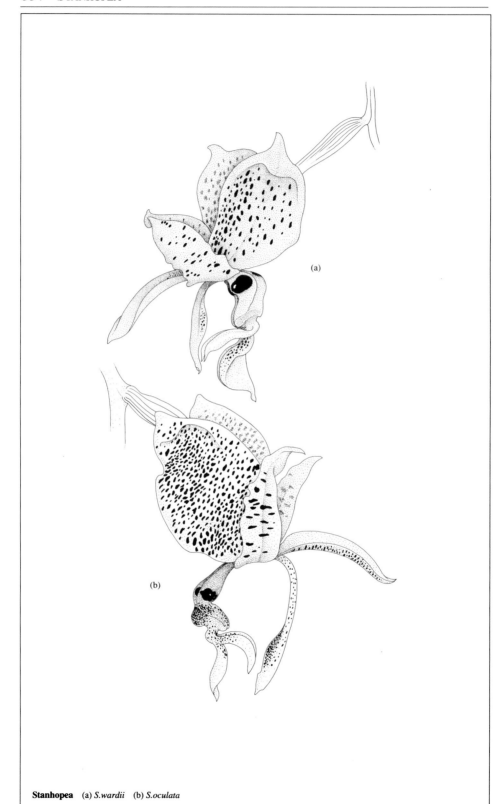

Stanhopea   (a) *S.wardii*   (b) *S.oculata*

Stelis Sw. (From Gk *stelis*, classical name for mistletoe, perhaps similar in habit to these non-parasitic epiphytes.) Over 500 species of small, caespitose epiphytes or lithophytes. Rhizome horizontal, creeping; secondary stems erect, loosely sheathed, unifoliate, lacking pseudobulbs. Leaves fleshy or coriaceous, oval to linear, subsessile or petiolate, suberect. Inflorescence a raceme, long, slender, usually axillary, secund or distichous; flowers small or minute, numerous; sepals subequal or with dorsal sepal longest, variously connate, usually spreading; petals much smaller, broad with thickened apical margins, often including column and lip; lip subsessile, almost equal to petals, simple to trilobed, fleshy; column short, thickened above, footless, apex usually trilobed; anther terminal, operculate, pollinia 2, waxy. Brazil and Peru to W Indies and Mexico.

CULTIVATION   As for *Pleurothallis*.

S.allenii L.O. Williams.
To 40cm; secondary stems to 15cm. Lvs to 19×7cm, coriaceous, elliptic to ovate-elliptic, acute or obtuse. Raceme to 30cm, bearing 1 to several fls to base, with cucullate sheaths to 2.5cm; bracts infundibuliform, to 2cm; fls largest of genus, near-black; sep. to 15×9mm, dorsal sep. cucullate, lateral sep. connate to their apices, basally gibbous and cucullate; pet. to 1×1.5mm, apex deeply thickened; lip smaller than pet., truncate, apex with transverse callus. Panama.

S.aprica Lindl. (*S.miersii* Lindl.; *S.hymenantha* Schltr.; *S.herzogii* Schltr.).
Secondary stem to 10cm, terete. Lvs to 8×1cm, erect, linear-oblanceolate or linear-elliptic, obtuse, apex obliquely tridentate. Raceme solitary, to 15cm, few to many-fld; bracts to 11cm, tubular-cucullate, acute or obtuse; fls minute, spreading, secund, lightly pendent, green-white to green-yellow; sep. to 1.5×1mm, glabrous, connate below, indistinctly 3-nerved, shallowly concave; pet. smaller than sep. cuneate-obovate, thickened above, concave; lip yellow-green, exceeding pet., subquadrate-obovate, sharply apiculate, concave; disc with fleshy bilobed callus near base; column small, cream-green. Summer. Mexico to Panama.

S.argentata Lindl. (*S.huebneri* Schltr.; *S.heylindiana* Focke; *S.endresii* Rchb. f.).
Secondary stems short, to 5.5cm, slender. Lvs to 10×2.5cm, oblanceolate or elliptic-ligulate, apex obtuse to rounded, subsessile, coriaceous, clear green above, dull pale green beneath. Raceme to 20cm, loosely many-fld, suberect; peduncle glabrous, terete, pale green often tinged maroon; bracts minute, infundibular, pale green; fls to 8mm diam., pale pink to red-purple or red-green; sep. to 5.5×5mm, subequal, spreading, broadly orbicular-rhombic, covered with crystalline exudations giving the whole a sparkling and rather soft appearance; pet. to 1.5×0.8mm, transversely cuneate-subquadrate, thickened at truncate apex, with white crystalline flecks; lip similar to pet. but shorter, fleshy, brown, transversely oblong, truncate in front with short, erect apicule; column pale brown; anther cream lightly spotted pale pink-maroon, pollinia cream. Mexico to Panama, Brazil and Mexico.

S.barbata Rolfe (*S.microchila* Schltr.; *S.costaricensis* Schltr.; *S.cinerea* Schltr.; *S.bryophila* Schltr.).
To 15cm, glabrous; secondary stems to 1.5cm. Lvs to 50×8mm, linear-oblanceolate to narrowly spathulate, acute or obtuse, 3-cusped at apex. Raceme densely-fld, filiform; fls small, ochrous green or red-brown, spreading; sep. to 1.5×2.5mm, connate at base, interior purple-pubesc.; pet. to 0.75×1mm, 3-nerved, marked red-purple, apical margin thickened, truncate; lip small, fleshy, oblong, obtuse, with 2 incurved longitudinal calli or lobes; column short, thick. Guatemala, Costa Rica, Panama.

S.bidentata Schltr.
To 15cm, glabrous; secondary stems to 4cm, erect. Lvs to 80×7mm, narrowly oblanceolate to linear, erect, apically bi- or tridentate. Raceme loosely few-fld, to 11cm, erect, filiform; bracts to 3mm, scarious; fls to 7mm diam., purple or white tinged green, purple or red-brown; sep. to 2×2mm, 3-nerved, concave; pet. to 1×1mm, concave, cuneate; lip fleshy, triangular-ovate, obtuse, apically bidentate, with transverse

callus near base, apex and dorsal surface deeply concave. Summer. Mexico, Guatemala, Honduras.

S.bryophila Schltr. See *S.barbata*.

S.ciliaris Lindl.
To 30cm, glabrous; secondary stems to 3cm, stout. Lvs to 15×3cm, broadly oblong to linear, obtuse, apex tridentate or retuse. Raceme exceeding lvs, many-fld; bracts red, to 2mm; fls small, deep purple; sep. to 4×2.5mm, ovate, 3-nerved, ciliate; pet. to 1×1.5mm, ovate-rhomboid, thickened along central vein and above; lip ovate, fleshy, subtruncate or obtuse, recurved at apex; disc with callus on either side at base; column blotched purple, short. Winter. Mexico, Guatemala, Honduras, Costa Rica.

S.cinerea Schltr. See *S.barbata*.
S.compacta Ames. See *Platystele compacta*.
S.costaricensis Schltr. See *S.barbata*.

S.cresenticola Schltr. (*S.isthmii* Schltr.; *S.praemorsa* Schltr.).
To 20cm; secondary stems to 2cm, slender, clustered. Lvs to 9×1cm, coriaceous, oblanceolate, acute or obtuse. Raceme to 18cm, densely many-fld, suberect to arcuate; bracts minute, infundibuliform; fls green to yellow-green; sep. subequal, to 1.5×1.5mm, 1-nerved, interior papillose; pet. smaller than sep., flabellate, slightly thickened and broadly rounded at apex; lip narrower than pet., rhombic-ovate, transversed by fleshy callus, apex incurved. Costa Rica, Panama.

S.drosophila Barb. Rodr. See *S.dusenii*.

S.dusenii Garay (*S.drosophila* Barb. Rodr.; *S.intermedia* Poepp. & Endl.).
To 15cm; secondary stems to 4cm, densely fasciculate. Lvs to 90×8mm, variably fleshy, linear-lanceolate to linear-elliptic, obtuse, mid-nerve slightly sulcate. Raceme to 10cm, many-fld, erect to arcuate; bracts pale green; fls minute, pale yellow often tinged green; sep. to 1.5×1.5mm, subequal, acute, 3-nerved, concave, ventral surface muricate; pet. to 0.5×0.5mm, apex fleshy, truncate or slightly emarginate; lip similar to pet. with transverse callus in middle; column yellow-cream; anther cream, pollinia yellow. Venezuela, Guyana, Brazil, Peru, Bolivia.

S.endresii Rchb. f. See *S.argentata*.

S.fragrans Schltr. (*S.osmalantha* Barb. Rodr.).
To 12cm. Rhiz. short; secondary stems to 3cm, slender. Lvs to 6×1cm, oblanceolate-ligulate, subacute. Raceme erect, exceeding lvs, 8–15-fld; fls grey tinged rose; sep. to 5mm, ovate-rhombic, interior and margins slightly ciliate; pet. minute, reniform, subtruncate, glabrous; lip minute, hemispherical, obtuse; column short, truncate. Brazil.

S.fraterna Lindl. See *S.inaequisepala*.
S.herzogii Schltr. See *S.aprica*.
S.heylindiana Focke. See *S.argentata*.
S.huebneri Schltr. See *S.argentata*.
S.hymenantha Schltr. See *S.aprica*.

S.inaequisepala Hoehne & Schltr. (*S.parahybunensis* Barb. Rodr.; *S.fraterna* Lindl.).
Secondary stems to 8cm. Lvs to 14×2.5cm, light green, subcoriaceous, oblong to elliptic-oblong, lightly recurved, apex rounded; petiole terete, to 9cm. Raceme to 20cm, slender, many-fld; fls small; sep. to 3×2.5mm, fleshy, brown tinged

dark maroon, strongly recurved, lateral sep. smaller, concave, connate at base; pet. minute, fleshy, deep maroon-purple; lip almost equal to pet., very fleshy, semiorbicular, ventrally truncate; column maroon-pink; anther pink, pollinia yellow. Venezuela, Guyana, Brazil.

S.intermedia Poepp. & Endl. See *S.dusenii.*
S.isthmii Schltr. See *S.cresenticola.*
S.microchila Schltr. See *S.barbata.*
S.miersii Lindl. See *S.aprica.*

S.ophioglossoides (Jacq.) Sw.
Secondary stems to 7cm, erect or ascending. Lvs to 14×1.5cm, elliptic-oblong to linear-oblong, subcoriaceous, tridentate at apex. Raceme to 20cm, slender, densely many-fld; fls minute, yellow-green tinged purple; sep. to 3×3mm, ovate-deltoid, concave, connate up to middle; pet. minute, obovate-triangular; lip minute; fleshy, apex rounded or sub-truncate. Early autumn. W Indies, Brazil.

S.osmalantha Barb. Rodr. See *S.fragrans.*
S.ovalifolia Focke. See *Platystele ovalifolia.*
S.parahybunensis Barb. Rodr. See *S.inaequisepala.*
S.praemorsa Schtr. See *S.cresenticola.*

S.purpurascens A. Rich. & Gal. (*S.purpusii* Schltr.).
To 43cm, stout, glabrous; secondary stems to 19cm, erect or ascending, clustered. Lvs to 20×4cm, linear-oblanceolate to oblong-lanceolate, apex obtuse and refuse, usually sessile. Raceme to 33cm, 1 or 2, loosely many-fld; bracts to 5mm, clasping rachis; fls red-brown or purple to purple-green, to 1cm diam., spreading; sep. to 4×4mm, 3–6-nerved, connate up to middle; pet. to 1mm, apical margin thickened, often verrucose; lip fleshy, to 1×1mm, rounded to subreniform, apex round to obtuse; disk with transverse, fleshy ridge below; column short. Winter. Mexico, Guatemala, Honduras, El Salvador, Costa Rica.

Stenia Lindl. (From the Gk *stenos*, narrow, referring to the slender pollinia which characterize the genus.) Some 8 species of epiphytes. Rhizome short. Pseudobulbs absent. Leaves strap-shaped, with overlapping bases forming a fan. Inflorescence from the axils of leaf-sheaths, basal, short, recurved, 1-flowered; flowers large, showy; sepals and petals subsimilar, free, spreading, lateral sepals adnate to column foot; lip fleshy, continuous with column foot, concave to saccate and slipper-shaped, simple to 3-lobed, lateral lobes small, entire, disc with a transverse crest or lamellae, cristate; column erect, elongate, semiterete, stout, produced into a short foot, anther terminal, operculate, incumbent, bilocular, pollinia 4, linear-cylindrical. Central & Northern S America.

CULTIVATION As for *Huntleya.*

S.calceolaris (Garay) Dodson & Bennett.
Close to *S.guttata*, fls to 2.5cm diam., pale lime green, sep. lightly and sparsely spotted rusty brown, pet. more densely spotted, lip shoe-shaped, green-white spotted red-brown. Ecuador, Peru.

S.guttata Rchb. f.
Lvs to 13×3.5cm, elliptic to obovate-oblong, acute. Infl. short; fls thin-textured, bright yellow-green to straw-yellow, spotted dark purple or brown; dorsal sep. to 26×8mm, ovate-oblong, subacute, lateral sep. to 26×10mm, obliquely ovate-lanceolate; pet. similar to dorsal sep.; lip obscurely 3-lobed, deeply saccate, lateral lobes inconspicuous, semiorbicular, midlobe ovate-triangular with a 7-toothed, transverse crest; column obscurely ridged at sides. Peru.

S.pallida Lindl.
Lvs to 15×4cm, rigid, lightly recurved, obovate-oblong to elliptic-oblong. Infl. to 6cm, erect or arching; sep. and pet. cream to pale yellow-green, thin-textured, translucent, sep. to 35×17mm, concave, subacute or shortly acuminate, dorsal sep. oblong or obovate-oblong, lateral sep. elliptic-ovate to oblong-lanceolate, exceeding dorsal sep.; pet. to 35×15mm, ovate to oblong-lanceolate, acute; lip to 3.2×1.5cm, cup-like, white to pale yellow-green, obscurely 3-lobed, lateral lobes erect, rounded, spotted maroon, mid-lobe subtriangular, acute or obtuse, disc with a transverse, central callus, dentate; column to 1.3cm, erect, pale green, white-pubesc., foot to 5mm. British Guyana, Venezuela, Trinidad, Brazil, Peru.

Stenoglottis Lindl. (From Gk *stenos*, narrow, and *glotta*, tongue; the lip is narrow.) 4 species of terrestrials, lithophytes or epiphytes. Roots fleshy, tuberous. Leaves few to many, in a basal rosette. Raceme erect, laxly or densely flowered, the peduncle with scattered bract-like leaves. Flowers white, pink or lilac-mauve with darker spots; sepals free or shortly joined to base of column; petals lying forwards over column; lip longer than sepals and petals, 3- or 5-lobed, spurred or unspurred; column short and broad. Tropical & S Africa.

CULTIVATION As for *Disa*, although *S.longifolia* is extremely resilient and will grow in any damp, loamy medium given bright light and a slight winter rest (when it may lose its leaves). It may even seed itself.

S.fimbriata Lindl.
Terrestrial, lithophytic or epiphytic at a low level, erect, 10–40cm, roots long, tuberous. Lvs 6–10, spreading, 2.5–5×0.5–1.5cm, lanceolate or oblong, acute, undulate, green spotted dark purple-brown. Raceme subsecund, few- to many-fld; fls rose-lilac with purple spots on lip and sometimes also on sep. and pet.; sep. 3–8×2–5mm, spreading, ovate, obtuse; pet. 3–6×2–4mm, overlying column, oblong-obovate, apical margin sometimes fimbriate; lip 6–15mm, trilobed at about half-way, midlobe longer and narrower than lateral lobes, all lobes acute; spur absent; column less than 1mm; staminodes small, falcate, smooth. S Africa (E Cape, Transkei, Natal, Transvaal), Swaziland. Possibly conspecific with *S.zambesiaca*.

S.longifolia Hook. f.
Terrestrial of lithophytic, erect, 30–100cm. Roots long and tuberous. Lvs few to many, 9–24×1–4cm, lanceolate-oblong, acute, slightly undulate, sometimes finely spotted purple-brown, especially on stem. Raceme crowded; fls pale rose-lilac heavily spotted purple, the lip particularly; sep. 7–10mm, ovate or oblong, obtuse; pet. 4–6mm, ovate, acute, overlying column; lip 12–16mm, 5-lobed in apical third, all lobes acute, midlobe longer than lateral lobes; spur absent; column 1–2mm; staminodes large, apex swollen and tuberculate. South Africa (Natal and Transvaal).

S.woodii Schltr.
Terrestrial or lithophytic, 10–20cm; roots tuberous. Lvs 5–20, 5–15×1–3cm, lanceolate-elliptic or ovate-lanceolate, acute, often glaucous green, not undulate. Raceme subsecund, few- to many-fld; fls white, pale pink or rose-crimson, lip usually with some purple spots; sep. 4–6mm, ovate, obtuse; pet. 3–5mm, lying over column, ovate; lip 10–14mm, trilobed in apical half, midlobe narrow, acute, lateral lobes much wider and truncate; spur 1.5–3mm, straight or slightly curved; column less than 2mm; staminodes erect, clavate, obscurely lobed at apex. South Africa (Natal and Transkei) and Zimbabwe.

S.zambesiaca Rolfe.
Epiphytic or lithophytic, 10–35cm tall with woolly, ellipsoid, tuberous roots. Lvs 6–12, 4–12×1–2cm, ligulate-lanceolate or oblanceolate, acute, undulate, sometimes spotted with dark brown. Raceme erect, subsecund, fairly laxly few to many-fld; fls pink or lilac, the lip with purple spots or streaks; sep. 3–6mm, dorsal sep. narrowly elliptic, lateral sep. slightly longer and wider; pet. 5–6×3–4mm, lying over column; lip 5–12mm, trilobed in apical third, lateral lobes with truncate apex, midlobe acute, narrower than lateral lobes and usually slightly longer; spur absent; column 1–2mm; staminodes club-shaped, tuberculate at apex. Tanzania, Malawi, Zimbabwe, Mozambique, South Africa (Transvaal).

Stenorrhynchos Rich. (From Gk *stenos*, narrow, and *rhynchos*, snout, referring to the slender rostellum typical of the genus.) Some 60 species of terrestrials. Rhizome short. Pseudobulbs absent, roots fibrous. Stems usually leafy. Leaves basal, membranaceous, sessile or petiolate, often in a low rosette, conduplicate. Inflorescence a terminal raceme, erect, few to many-flowered, with large, membranous bracts; flowers small to large, often showy; sepals free, subsimilar, dorsal sepal erect, concave, forming a hood with petals, lateral sepals oblique, erect or spreading, concave at base forming a saccate mentum; petals free at base, apex connate; lip adnate to column foot, basally saccate; enveloping column, entire to trilobed, disc often pubesc.; column short, with a distinct foot, terete, rostellum narrow, bidentate, anther dorsal, narrow, pollinia 4, granular, linear-clavate. C & S America. The gender of this genus is sometimes given as masculine. As published, however, the name has a Greek, not Latin, termination, *-os*, not *-us*. The Greek *rhynchos* is neuter and that is taken here to be the gender of the genus name.

CULTIVATION As for *Phaius*.

S.lanceolatum (Aubl.) Rich. (*Limodorum lanceolatum* Aubl.; *Spiranthes lanceolata* (Aubl.) Léon).
Lvs to 40×5cm, produced after flowering, oblong-lanceolate to elliptic-oblong, acute or obtuse, petiolate. Infl. to 23cm, many-fld; peduncle light green, finely white-pubesc.; fls showy, suberect, white or green-white to orange-red or crimson; sep. to 3×0.7cm, narrowly to broadly lanceolate, subacute to acuminate, exterior glandular-pilose; pet. to 2×0.6cm, oblong-lanceolate to lanceolate, acute or acuminate, falcate; lip to 2.5×1cm, sessile, simple to obscurely 3-lobed, obovate-lanceolate to rhombic-lanceolate, acuminate or acute, centrally saccate; callus bicarinate, linear, pubesc.; column 1cm. Tropical America.

S.speciosum (Gmel.) Rich. (*Spiranthes speciosa* (Gmel.) A. Rich.).
Lvs to 25×6cm, ovate-orbicular to elliptic-oblong or oblanceolate, acute or acuminate, sessile or petiolate, dark green often spotted or lined silver. Infl. held clear or leaves, densely few to many-fld; peduncle coral pink to bright red, glabrous or pale-hirsute; fls bright orange-red to fleshy pink; sep. to 2×0.6cm, lanceolate or elliptic-lanceolate, acute or acuminate, involute, apex recurved; pet. to 2×0.5cm, obliquely lanceolate to oblanceolate, acute or acuminate; lip to 2×1cm, sessile, triangular-lanceolate or rhombic-lanceolate, acute to apiculate, obscurely 3-lobed, lateral lobes rounded, midlobe oblong, involute; disc with 2 basal, fleshy calli, pubesc.; column to 7mm, densely pilose. Mexico to northern S America, W Indies.

× **Stewartara** (*Ada* × *Cochlioda* × *Odontoglossum*). A recent trigeneric hybrid which does best in cool growing conditions. Plants consist of a group of compressed pseudobulbs growing from a basal rhizome, each with one or two leaves at its apex and two or more leaf-like sheaths arising at its base. Inflorescences arise in the axils of these sheaths. Flowers have long narrow sepals and petals and large lip.

× *S.Joyce:* long elegant sprays of slender fls in shades of ginger-brown and orange, modest size.

Summerhayesia Cribb. (For V.S. Summerhayes (1892–1974), who worked for many years at Kew on African orchids.) 2 species of epiphytes. Stems short with roots arising from base. Leaves fleshy, distichous, folded. Racemes few to many-flowered, arising from leaf axils; flowers creamy white to pale yellow, fleshy; sepals and petals similar, lateral sepals connate at base enclosing spur; lip entire, concave, spurred, spur slender, cylindric; column short, stout; pollinia 2, deeply cleft, stipites short, viscidium slipper-shaped. Tropical Africa.

CULTIVATION   See *Angraecum*.

S.laurentii (De Wildeman) Cribb.
Stem short. Lvs 10–22cm×6–9mm, linear or narrowly ligulate, fleshy, bilobed at apex, the lobes rounded. Raceme 13–40cm, many-fld; fls yellow-white or cream; sep. and pet. 7–8mm, elliptic, rounded at apex; lip ovate, of similar length; spur 6–7.5cm, pendent, straight. Liberia, Ghana, Ivory Coast, Zaire.

S.zambesiaca Cribb.
Stem 2–3cm. Lvs 3–7, suberect or recurved, to 15×1–1.5cm, linear-ligulate, fleshy, folded, unequally and obtusely bilobed at apex. Racemes 1–2, to 15cm, 4–5 (rarely to 13)-fld; fls secund, non-resupinate, fleshy, creamy yellow, the outside of the sep., ovary and base of spur sparsely covered with short, rusty hairs; sep. and pet. 11–14mm, ovate; lip 11–12mm, ovate, acute, very concave; spur 16–20cm, pendent, straight, slender; column 3mm. Zambia, Malawi, Zimbabwe, Mozambique.

Sunipia Lindl. (Apparently from a vernacular name in Nepal.) Some 20 species of epiphytes with creeping rhizomes. Pseudobulbs bearing a single coriaceous leaf at apex. Inflorescence racemose, lateral; sepals almost equal, lateral sepals fused; petals spreading; lip entire, broad, tongue-shaped, midlobe oblong, concave, margins recurved; column short and wide. India, SE Asia to Taiwan.

CULTIVATION   As for *Bulbophyllum*.

S.cirrhata (Lindl.) P.F. Hunt (*S.paleacea* (Lindl.) P.F. Hunt; *Ione paleacea* Lindl.; *Ione cirrhata* Lindl.; *Bulbophyllum paleaceum* (Lindl.) Hook. f.).
Pseudobulbs 25–38cm, ovoid, smooth. Lvs linear-oblong, centrally grooved. Fls 4–6, pendent; sep. pale green, striped red, dorsal sep. lanceolate, arched, lateral sep. fused, 2-toothed, projecting under the lip; pet. rounded, spreading, pale yellow-green; lip red-brown, cuneate; disc with 2 basal keels, terminating in an oblong callus. Autumn. India.

S.paleacea (Lindl.) P.F. Hunt. See *S.cirrhata*.

Symphyglossum Schltr. (From Gk *symphyes*, grown together, and *glossa*, tongue, referring to the lip which is adnate to the column.) Some 6 species of epiphytes. Pseudobulbs ovoid, enveloped by several distichous leaf sheaths, 1–2-leaved at apex. Leaves linear, erect or suberect. Inflorescence a terminal raceme or a panicle, arching to pendent, loosely many-flowered; flowers usually showy; sepals oblong or oblanceolate, dorsal sepal free; lateral sepals basally connate; petals adnate to column near base, wider than sepals; lip simple, unguiculate, reflexed above, callus basally bicarinate or tricarinate; column subterete, apex slightly dilated, anther terminal, operculate, incumbent, rostellum suberect, bidenticulate, pollinia 2, pyriform, stipe linear-ligulate. Venezuela, Colombia, Ecuador, Peru.

CULTIVATION   As for the smaller *Oncidium* spp.

S.sanguineum (Rchb. f.) Schltr. (*Mesospinidium cochliodum* Rchb. f.; *Cochlioda sanguinea* (Rchb. f.) Benth.).
Pseudobulbs to 5cm, clustered, slightly compressed, pale green, sometimes mottled brown. Lvs to 22×1.5cm, linear, acute or obtuse. Infl. to 50cm; fls to 2.5cm diam., rose-red, the lip rose-pink fading to white at base; sep. to 11×5mm, narrowly elliptic or ovate-lanceolate, subacute; pet. to 11×4mm, elliptic-oblong, apiculate; lip to 1cm, ovate to subtriangular, callus bicarinate, keels oblong to triangular; column terete. Autumn–spring. Ecuador.

Taeniophyllum Bl. (From Gk *tainia*, fillets, bands, and *phyllon*, leaf.) Some 100 species of epiphytes apparently lacking stems or, indeed, any vegetative parts and appearing as a mass of flattened, pale, adhesive roots. Roots flattened, spreading. Rhizome very short. Pseudobulbs absent. Stems few, minute, prostrate or ascending, few-leaved or scaly. Leaves minute, scarcely recognizable, linear or scale-like. Inflorescence a lateral raceme, few-flowered; flowers minute, often non-resupinate, short-pedicellate; sepals and petals subequal, subsimilar, free or shortly connate; lip spurred or saccate, simple to trilobed, midlobe fleshy; column short, 2-winged, rostellum short or elongate, anther bilocular, pollinia 4. Mostly New Guinea.

CULTIVATION Apparently stemless and leafless orchids grown as curiosities for their massed, photosynthesizing roots, established (with some difficulty) on pads of sphagnum and leafmould strapped to heavily textured bark and suspended in shady, humid, warm conditions (min. 18°C/65°F). Mist daily.

T.filiforme J.J. Sm. (*T.macrorhizum* Ridl.).
Roots elongate, to 1.5m, subcylindrical, slender. Infl. to 6.5cm, slender, with distichous, overlapping bracts; fls produced in succession, short-lived, minute, pale yellow; lip larger than sep.

and pet., spurred, obscurely 3-lobed, concave, spur saccate, acute. Malay Peninsula, Sumatra, Java, Celebes.

T.macrorhizum Ridl. See *T.filiforme*.

Tainia Bl. (From Gk *tainia*, fillet, referring to the long, narrow leaf and petiole, or the keels on the lip.) Some 40 species of terrestrials or epiphytes. Pseudobulbs sheathed. Leaf solitary, apical, fleshy, petiolate, plicate. Inflorescence erect, borne basally, usually racemose; sepals and petals similar, spreading, lateral sepals often fused to the column foot, forming a small spur; lip trilobed or entire, keeled, with a saccate base or small spur. Indomalaya, China.

CULTIVATION As for *Phaius*.

T.hookeriana King & Pantl.
Terrestrial. Pseudobulbs to 8×6cm, ovoid, grey-green. Lf to 50cm, lanceolate to elliptic-lanceolate, acute, petiole slender, to 27cm. Infl. to 90cm, lax, 10–25-fld; fls yellow-green, striped bronze to brown, lip white tinted yellow, spotted red around the keels, midlobe flushed rose, spur brown; sep. and pet. to 2.5cm, lanceolate; lip basally triangular, apex trilobed, midlobe elliptic, lateral lobes almost erect, rounded, spur 3–4mm, disc with 3 keels. India, N Thailand.

T.speciosa Bl.
Pseudobulbs to 6cm, glossy, rectangular. Lf to 20cm, ovate-lanceolate; petiole to 22cm. Infl. to 45cm; fls 4–6, pale green to green-white, narrowly striped purple; sep. and pet. long-acuminate, pet. smaller, lateral sep. spreading; lip to 2.2cm, entire, fused to column foot, tip revolute, central keel downy. Malaysia, Java, Borneo.

Telipogon HBK. (From Gk *telos*, extremity, and *pogon*, beard, referring to the hairy apex of the column.) Some 110 species of epiphytes or terrestrials. Rhizome creeping or decumbent. Pseudobulbs absent. Secondary stems slender, short to elongate, seldom exceeding 80cm, erect or rambling, branched, sometimes, enveloped by leaf sheaths. Leaves subcoriaceous or fleshy, few to numerous, basal, 2-ranked, narrow, conduplicate, basally sheathing and overlapping. Inflorescence terminal, a raceme, erect or suberect, often elongate, 1- to several-flowered; flowers showy; bracts small, inconspicuous; sepals subequal, small, free, concave, carinate; petals larger than sepals, spreading or slightly concave, usually reticulated, often prominently veined; lip similar to petals, sessile, usually simple, dorsally carinate, sometimes basally papillose, disc with a conspicuous basal callus; column short, stout, footless, occasionally alate, long-setose, anther dorsal, erect, bilocular, pollinia 4, waxy, in pairs on a long, linear stipe. Costa Rica, Northern S America.

CULTIVATION This genus contains several slender-stemmed plants of high montane mist forests remarkable for their large tricorne flowers, often with intricate markings and of a rather sinister beauty. They grow with some difficulty in conditions suitable for *Masdevallia*, but demand consistently cool temperatures and a very buoyant, humid atmosphere with light shade and frequent misting.

T.andicola Rchb. f.
Lvs to 10×1.5cm, oblanceolate, acute. Infl. to 10cm, several-fld; peduncle basally triquetrous, apically bialate; sep. to 14×5mm, pale green, lanceolate to ovate-lanceolate, acute, lateral sep. oblique; pet. to 15×14mm, pale green, veined dark green, obovate to suborbicular, apiculate, minutely pilose; lip to 15×17mm, white-green to pale green, veined dark green, transversely broadly elliptic to subobovate, apex rounded, apiculate, base densely pilose, callus red-maroon, pubesc.; column to 5mm, setose, base mauve, apex yellow. Venezuela, Colombia, Ecuador.

T.biolleyi Schltr. See *T.bruchmuelleri*.

T.bruchmuelleri Rchb. f. (*T.biolleyi* Schltr.).
Lvs to 6×1.5cm, fleshy, light green, oblong to lanceolate, apiculate. Infl. to 10cm, erect, 1- to few-fld; peduncle light green, sharply alate; sep. to 20×6mm, bright yellow-green, narrowly elliptic-lanceolate to lanceolate, acute, lateral sep. oblique; pet. to 22×11mm, light yellow-green, flushed pink-maroon at base, elliptic to obovate-oblanceolate, acute or shortly acuminate, clawed; lip to 19×20mm, light yellow-green, narrowly elliptic to suborbicular, apiculate, callus maroon, broadly ovate, pubesc.; column to 5mm, brown-maroon, pubesc. Nicaragua to Colombia and Venezuela.

T.croesus Rchb. f.

Lvs to 7.5×1cm, subcoriaceous, oblanceolate, acute. Infl. to 11cm, few-fld; peduncle alate-triquetrous; fls produced in succession, to 5cm diam.; sep. to 25×9mm, pale yellow or green-white, some pale pink venation, ovate-lanceolate to triangular-lanceolate, acuminate, lateral sep. oblique; pet. to 22×25mm, apically white to bright yellow, base pink, suborbicular, apiculate; lip to 30×40mm, similar colour to pet., transversely subelliptic, apiculate, callus densely pubesc.; column to 10mm, maroon, glabrous. Venezuela, Colombia.

T.dendriticus Rchb. f.

Lvs to 20×3mm, subcoriaceous, linear-lanceolate, acute. Infl. to 6cm, 1- or 2-fld; fls to 2.5cm diam., pale yellow-green veined brown; sep. to 10×3mm, narrowly triangular, acuminate; pet. to 12×12mm, broadly rhombic; lip to 15×19mm, transversely ovate-rhombic, obtuse, minutely apiculate, disc finely pilose; column densely long-setose. Panama, Colombia.

T.gnomus Schltr.

Lvs to 10×2cm, oblanceolate to elliptic-oblong, acute, apiculate. Infl. to 17cm, 1- to several-fld; peduncle narrowly winged toward apex; fls thin-textured, spreading, pale yellow veined red-brown or purple; sep. to 23×7mm, lanceolate or oblong-lanceolate, acute or acuminate, lateral sep. oblique; pet. to 27×24mm, suborbicular-rhombic to obovate-rhombic; lip to 26×32mm, transversely ovate-oblong, apex rounded, apiculate; column short, densely setose. Peru.

T.klotzscheanus Rchb. f.

Lvs to 3.5×1.5cm, fleshy-subcoriaceous, elliptic-oblong to elliptic-ovate, acute or acuminate, often grey-green. Infl. to 23cm, few-fld; peduncle terete, flexuous; fls pale green, veined purple or dark green; sep. to 20×6mm, lanceolate, acute or acuminate; pet. to 28×18mm, ovate, acute or acuminate; lip to 27×28mm, ovate to suborbicular, acute or acuminate, callus purple; column to 5mm, maroon-pink, pubesc., erect. Colombia, Venezuela.

T.nervosus (L.) Druce.

Lvs to 2×1cm, fleshy, spreading, elliptic, acute, rugose above, revolute. Infl. to 25cm, erect, loosely several-fld; sep. to 10×5mm, pale green, ovate, acuminate; pet. to 14×12mm, yellow-green or cream-brown, strongly veined brown or purple, broadly ovate-elliptic, acute or apiculate; lip to 14×17mm, similar colour to pet., transversely elliptic or broadly ovate, apiculate, callus elevated, fleshy, pubesc.; column fleshy, purple-maroon, sparsely pilose or pubesc. Venezuela, Colombia, Ecuador.

T.papilio Rchb. f. & Warsc.

Lvs to 60×17mm, oblong-oblanceolate or oblanceolate, apiculate. Infl. to 17cm, erect, 1- to several-fld; peduncle subterete to narrowly winged; fls thin-textured, spreading, yellow or orange-yellow, veined red; sep. to 18×7mm, narrowly triangular to ovate-lanceolate, acuminate, concave, dorsally keeled, lateral sep. oblique; pet. to 19×18mm, obliquely obovate-rhombic, acute; lip to 19×25mm, transversely ovate-suborbicular, apex rounded, minutely apiculate, base setose; column long-pubesc. Peru.

T.pulcher Rchb. f.

Similar to *T.nervosus*, but with fewer fls, each to 5cm diam., the pet. and lip broader, cream with distinct red-brown veins, lip strongly stained red-brown at base, column densely hairy. Colombia, Ecuador.

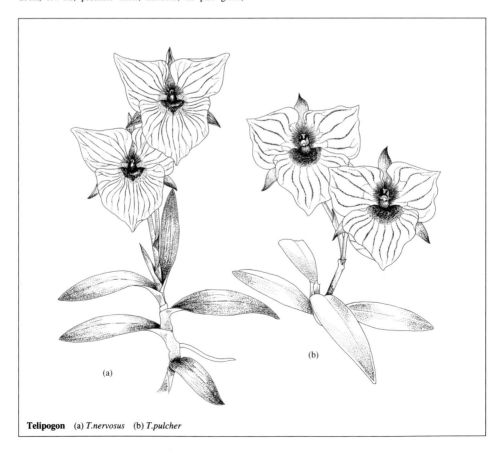

(a)

(b)

Telipogon (a) *T.nervosus* (b) *T.pulcher*

T.radiatus Rchb. f.
Lvs to 6×1cm, ligulate to elliptic-lanceolate, acute, subcoriaceous. Infl. to 9cm, erect, few-fld; fls to 3.5cm diam., golden-yellow, striped rich brown; sep. to 15×5mm, narrowly triangular or triangular-ligulate, acuminate; pet. to 25×21mm, broadly ovate-rhombic, acute; lip to 20×27mm, sessile, transversely ovate-rhombic to broadly obovate, obtuse; callus short, rounded, densely pilose; column to 5mm, densely setose. Peru, Colombia, Panama.

Tetramicra Lindl. (From Gk *tetra*, four, and *mikros*, small, referring to the four small divisions of the anther.) Some 10 species of epiphytes or terrestrials. Rhizome elongate, scrambling, often branched. Pseudobulbs very small or absent. Secondary stems short, remote, slightly thickened, leafy. Leaves fleshy, short, subterete, equitant. Inflorescence a terminal raceme, elongate, slender, rigid, with papery sheaths, loosely flowered; flowers small, showy, stalked; sepals similar, free, spreading; petals somewhat narrower than sepals; lip adnate to column base, larger than tepals, parallel to column, trilobed, lateral lobes prominent on a short claw, spreading, midlobe broad, entire; column forming a gibbous nectary at base, erect, winged, clinandrium tridentate, anther terminal, operculate, incumbent, convex, imperfectly 4-celled, pollinia 8, waxy. W Indies, Florida. Z10.

CULTIVATION   As for the smaller *Encyclia* species.

T.bicolor (Lindl.) Benth. See *Leptotes bicolor*.

T.canaliculata (Aubl.) Urban (*T.elegans* (Hamilt.) Cogn.; *Cyrtopodium elegans* Hamilt.).
Secondary stems to 2cm, erect, 1–4-lvd. Lvs to 18×1cm, narrowly cylindrical, usually recurved, canaliculate above. Infl. to 60cm, erect; fls opening in succession, to 5cm diam., long-lived, slightly fragrant, green tinged red, the lip bright rose, often striped violet; sep. to 10mm, oblong-lanceolate, acute or obtuse; pet. to 10mm, lanceolate to oblanceolate or subspathulate; lip to 15mm, deeply 3-lobed, lateral lobes elliptic, rounded, midlobe obovate, rounded or emarginate. Late spring–early summer. Florida, Greater Antilles.

T.elegans (Hamilt.) Cogn. See *T.canaliculata*.

T.eulophiae Rchb.f.
Differs from the above in fls to 1.5cm diam.; tepals grey-red; lip 3-lobed, rosy-purple, lateral lobes auriculate. Cuba.

Teuscheria Garay. (For Heinrich Teuscher (1891–1984), German botanist.) Some 7 species of epiphytes. Rhizome short or elongate, enveloped by overlapping sheaths. Pseudobulbs distant or clustered, small, ovoid or pyriform, enveloped by several leaf sheaths, 1-leaved at apex. Leaves oblong to linear-lanceolate, attenuate, petiolate. Inflorescence from base of pseudobulb, erect to pendent, 1-flowered; flowers large; sepals fleshy, erect or ascending, dorsal sepal free, lateral sepals adnate to column foot forming a short mentum; petals sub-similar to sepals; lip adnate to column foot, subequal to sepals, trilobed, apical portion enveloping column, base with a retrorse appendage; column erect, with a prominent foot, wingless, rostellum triangular, pollinia 4, cartilaginous. Mexico, C America, Venezuela, Ecuador, Colombia.

CULTIVATION   As for *Bifrenaria*.

T.wageneri (Rchb. f.) Garay (*Bifrenaria wageneri* Rchb. f.; *Stenocoryne wageneri* (Rchb. f.) Kränzl.; *T.venezuelana* Garay).
Rhiz. short. Pseudobulbs to 2.5cm, ovoid-pyriform. Lvs to 35×2.5cm, linear-oblong or linear-lanceolate, acute or acuminate, erect or suberect; petiole to 15cm. Infl. to 10cm, pendent; peduncle dark maroon-purple, to 7.5cm, sheaths brown-purple; fls short-lived, bronze tinged light maroon, the lip white flushed pink at margins; sep. elliptic, obtuse or subacute, concave, dorsal sep. to 19×7mm, lateral sep. to 25×8mm, oblique; pet. to 18×5mm, obliquely oblanceolate, subacute; lip to 23×18mm, cuneate-flabellate, irregularly dentate-crenulate, 3-lobed, lateral lobes suborbicular, midlobe 2.5×7mm, semiorbicular, disc basal, with an elevated, longitudinal callus, golden-farinose; column to 7mm. Venezuela.

T.venezuelana Garay. See *T.wageneri*.

Thelymitra Forst. & Forst. f. (From Gk *thelys*, female, and *mitra*, cap, hat or turban, referring to the hooded column of many species.) Some 45 species of herbaceous terrestrials. Tubers subterranean. Leaf glabrous, rarely pubescent, solitary, ovate-lanceolate or terete. Raceme terminal, tall, erect; flowers blue, pink, yellow or red, single or many; sepals and petals similar; column erect, prominent wings united in front basally, extending above the anther, forming a hood (often bilobed) with entire, fringed or pubescent appendage. Australia, Malaysia, New Caledonia, New Zealand.

CULTIVATION   Terrestrial orchids for acid mixes in bright filtered light in the cool house.

T.carnea R. Br.
Stem to 35cm, slender, red tinted, flexuous. Lf to 15cm, linear, terete or channelled, basally tinged red. Stem bracts 2, sheathing. Fls 1–4, bright salmon pink or cream (sep. darker); sep. and pet. oblong or ovate-elliptic; column pale green or pink, apex yellow, wings erect, slender, smooth. E & SW Western Australia.

T.crinita Lindl.
Stem to 75cm. Fls to 10, to 4cm diam., bright blue, dorsal surface of column covered with black and yellow calli. W Australia.

T.ixioides Sw.
Stems to 60cm. Lf linear to lanceolate, channelled. Fls white, blue, pink, mauve or violet, dorsal sep. and lateral sep. often spotted dark blue; column hood trilobed, edged yellow with clavate glands forming dorsal crest. NZ, New Caledonia, temperate Australia.

T.nuda R. Br.
Stem to 1m. Fls many, crowded, lilac-blue, to 4cm diam., fragrant. E Australia.

T.pauciflora R. Br.
Stems to 50cm. Lf narrow, linear to lanceolate, channelled

above, fleshy. Fls 1–2cm diam., 1–15, pale to bright blue, rarely pink or white; lip smaller than other seg.; column to 5mm, white or blue, arms erect (often oblique), apically white, mauve or pink-pubesc. E & SW Western Australia, NZ.

T.venosa R. Br.
Stems to 75cm. Lf to 30cm, narrow linear, channelled. Fls to 6, blue, rarely pink or white, venation distinct; sep. exceeding pet.; lip broadly ovate, irregularly undulate; column erect, wings white, blunt, spirally inrolled. SE Australia.

Thrixspermum Lour. (From Gk *thrix*, hair, and *sperma*, seed, referring to the long thin seeds.) Some 100 species of monopodial epiphytes. Roots nodal, adventitious. Stems short, dense or long, scandent. Leaves coriaceous, strap-shaped, alternate along stem. Inflorescence axillary, racemose, often several from one node; flowers alternate in 2 rows or scattered, short-lived but blooming in long succession, flowering often triggered by a drop in temperature; perianth segments similar, narrow; lip fused to the column foot, midlobe variable, fleshy, lateral lobes almost erect, saccate containing a callus. Indomalaya to Taiwan and W Pacific.

CULTIVATION   As for *Angraecum*.

T.arachnites (Bb.) Rchb. f. See *T.centipeda*.

T.amplexicaule (Bl.) Rchb. f. (*T.lilacinum* Rchb. f.).
Stems climbing, pale yellow-green, often spotted purple, to 2m. Lvs ovate, basally cordate and clasping, olive green, to 6.5×4cm. Scape 10–25cm, closely and conspicuously bracteate; fls white or pale lilac; pet. and sep. spreading, ovate, obtuse, to 1.6cm, pet. smaller; lip midlobe white, fleshy, blunt, callus yellow, basal patch orange-red-pubesc., lateral lobes crescent-shaped, forward-pointing. Sumatra to Philippines.

T.calceolus (Lindl.) Rchb. f.
Stems creeping or hanging, flattened, internodes to 2cm. Lvs oblong, fleshy, twisted at base, tip obtuse, cleft. Infl. to 3cm, 1–3 per node; bracts overlapping; fls few, white, fragrant, fleshy; sep. acute, to 2.5cm; pet. smaller; lip to 1.5cm, tip

orange-yellow, lateral lobes white, midlobe fleshy, obtuse, lateral lobes erect, narrow, forward-pointing, sac rounded, callus white in front of sac, below it an orange, yellow-spotted patch. Sumatra, Borneo, Malaysia.

T.centipeda Lour. (*T.arachnites* (Bl.) Rchb. f.; *Dendrocolla arachnites* Bl.).
Stems to over 15cm. Lvs fleshy, linear to ligulate, obtuse, spotted purple when young, to 12×1.75cm. Infl. to 10cm with closely overlapping, flattened bracts in upper half; fls to 7.5cm across, lime green to pale yellow, lip white, basally spotted rusty orange; sep. and pet. both narrow-lanceolate, finely tapering with pendulous tips; lip to 1.5cm diam., midlobe fleshy, folded, lateral lobes obtuse, falcate, sac spotted mauve within, sparsely pubesc. Malaysia, Burma.

T.lilacinum Rchb. f. See *T.amplexicaule*.

Thunia Rchb. f. (For Franz, Graf von Thun (1786–1873).) Some 6 species of terrestrials. Pseudobulbs clustered, terete, cane-like, with spent leaf bases forming papery sheaths. Leaves 2-ranked, alternate on pseudobulbs, lasting 1–2 years, sessile, oblong-lanceolate, acute. Inflorescence a short terminal raceme or cluster, lax, bracteate; flowers fragrant, generally resembling the more showy *Cattleya* spp., crystalline white or magenta; sepals and petals similar, lanceolate; lip showy, bell-shaped or tubular, frilled and expanded apically, enclosing column. Himalaya to Burma.

CULTIVATION   Pot canes annually in a mix of turfy loam, leafmould, bark and dried FYM. Position in a brightly lit, well ventilated location in the cool or intermediate house away from direct sunlight, draughts and dripping water or straying mist. Water and feed copiously when in growth. After flowering, dry canes entirely (foliage is usually lost) and remove to a cool dry place in full sunlight. Increase by division, stem cuttings placed on warm sphagnum or perlite, or by plantlets developing on badly grown plants (i.e. too much heat and water, too little rest).

T.alba (Lindl.) Rchb. f. (*T.marshalliana* Rchb. f.).
Stems to 1m, erect, tufted. Lvs 10–15cm, elliptic-lanceolate, sessile, tapering toward tip, thinly fleshy, glaucous. Infl. to 30cm, nodding; bracts ovate-oblong; fls 4–6, white, often not opening fully; sep. 6–7cm, narrow-oblong, acute, almost equal, free; pet. similar; lip orange or yellow, striped purple, oblong, tubular to funnelform, dilating toward apex, margins undulate or crispate, spur short, horizontal. India, Burma, China.

T.bensoniae Hook. f.
Stems to 45cm; basal sheaths leafy, subcircular, reflexed. Lvs linear-lanceolate, sheathing. Fls 5–7cm diam., very fragrant;

sep. and pet. white tinted or flushed lilac to magenta or wine red, especially toward their tips, linear-lanceolate, spreading, equal; lip trilobed, midlobe deep lilac to mauve-red, oblong, ruffled, lateral lobes short, obtuse, toothed, spur horizontal, notched, short, disc yellow, crested. NE India.

T.marshalliana Rchb. f. See *T.alba*.

T.pulchra Rchb. f.
Lvs fleshy, lanceolate. Fls pure white, throat pale cinnabar red; lip entire, margins irregular, partly revolute, crests yellow and brown, spur vestigial or absent. Burma, Vietnam.

Thunia alba

Ticoglossum Rodriguez ex Halbinger. (From the native name *tico* and Lat. *glossum*, tongue.) 2 species of epiphytes, formerly included in *Odontoglossum*. Rhizomes short. Pseudobulbs ovoid to discoid, compressed, ancipitous, with several leafy basal sheaths, apically unifoliate. Leaves elliptic-lanceolate, acute, petiolate. Raceme from axils of basal bracts, subequal to leaves, few-flowered; bracts ovate, acute; ovaries pedicellate, terete; flowers showy, white or rose; sepals sessile, ovate to elliptic, apiculate; petals broadly short-clawed, subequal to sepals; lip short-clawed, variously shaped, callus fleshy, yellow spotted red, posterior portion with many trichomes; column short, with 2 small bodies at sides of stigma, wings absent; anther incumbent, pollinia 2, conical to reniform. Costa Rica.

CULTIVATION   See *Odontoglossum*.

T.krameri (Rchb. f.) Rodriguez & Halbinger (*Odontoglossum krameri* Rchb. f.).
Pseudobulbs to 5×4cm, subrotund or ovoid, pale green or blue-green. Lvs to 25×4cm, coriaceous, dull green. Infl. to 25cm, porrect or pendent, often several per growth, loosely 2–3-fld; bracts to 1cm; fls to 4.5cm diam., glossy, long-lived, tepals rosy violet, lilac or ivory-white with a lilac suffusion; sep. to 2×1cm, elliptic-ligulate to elliptic-oblong, acute; pet. smaller than sep., ligulate or oblanceolate, apex rounded; lip to 2×1.5cm, subreniform, violet or rose-violet, marked and spotted purple, with white and red-brown bands in front of basal callus, clawed, emarginate, callus yellow spotted red or purple, bilamellate on claw. Costa Rica. var. **album** (Rodriguez) Halbinger. Fls ivory-white; callus yellow.

T.oerstedii (Rchb. f.) Rodriguez ex Halbinger (*Odontoglossum oerstedii* Rchb. f.).
To 20cm. Pseudobulbs 5×2.5cm, ovoid, slightly compressed, dark green. Lvs to 12.5×3cm, erect, coriaceous. Infl. to 17cm, erect, slender, 2–5-fld; bracts to 12mm; fls to 4cm diam., fragrant, waxy, long-lived, tepals white; sep. to 2×1cm, spreading, narrowly elliptic-oblong, obtuse to subacute; pet. wider than sep., obovate-oblong to elliptic-oblong, obtuse; lip white with golden-yellow base, to 2.5×2.5cm, obscurely 3-lobed, lateral lobes small, auriculate, midlobe suborbicular, emarginate, callus white spotted orange, subquadrate, bicarinate, erect; column to 7mm. Spring. Costa Rica.

Tolumnia Raf. (named probably for *Tolumnius* a Rutulian mentioned by Vergil.) 21 species, small epiphytes and lithophytes often starting life as terrestrials. Traditionally treated as the 'Equitant' or 'Variegata' Oncidiums. They differ from *Oncidium* in lacking pseudobulbs, in their tufted, sometimes stoloniferous, habit, and their fleshy, conduplicate to triquetrous or terete leaves, 2-ranked in a loose fan. The flowers are disproportionately large and carried in fine racemes and panicles; sepals smaller than petals, the laterals more or less united and held behind lip; petals large; lip far larger than tepals, usually strongly 4-lobed with a prominent basal callus; column with pronounced, sometimes petal-like wings. Florida, Caribbean. In addition to those listed here, several other beautiful species may become more readily available in cultivation. See Guido Braem (1995) in *American Orchid Society Bulletin* vol. 64.2.

CULTIVATION   Plant in very small, shallow clay pots in an extremely open bark mix, or establish in baskets, or on rafts, bark slabs or twigs. Suspend in a bright position in the warm glasshouse; maintain high humidity; water and syringe frequently but avoid stagnant rooting conditions and water lodged in growths. Propagate by division or stolons of well established plants.

T.calochila (Cogn.) Braem.
Lvs terete. Fls to 2cm diam.; tepals yellow-green, dorsal sep. ovate-lanceolate; pet. ovate; lip bright yellow with small lateral lobes and large, cordate, deeply and finely fringed midlobe. Hispaniola.

T.guttata auct. See *T.tetrapetala*.

T.pulchella (Hook) Raf. (*Oncidium pulchellum* Hook.).
Lvs to 20×1.5cm, equitant, flattened laterally or triquetrous, linear-ligulate, keeled. Raceme or panicle to 50cm, erect or arcuate, many-fld; fls to 2.5cm diam., variable in size and colour, usually white, tinged pink or lilac-rose, sometimes solid bright magenta; sep. to 10×4mm, ovate, oblong or spathulate, cuneate, concave, lateral sep. concealed by lip, connate almost to apex, tip cleft; pet. wider than sep., obovate, apex rounded or apiculate, undulate; lip to 2.5×3cm, subquadrate, lobes 4, large, rounded, callus white marked yellow, 3-lobed; column to 2mm, wings triangular-oblong or falcate. Jamaica, Guianas, Cuba, Hispaniola.

T.tetrapetala (Jacq.) Braem (*Oncidium quadripetalum* Sw.; *Oncidium tetrapetalum* (Jacq.) Willd.; *Oncidium tricolor* Hook.).
Lvs in tufts of 4 or more, to 20×0.5cm, triquetrous, sharp-edged, linear-ligulate, sulcate. Raceme sometimes branched, exceeding lvs, erect, usually dark purple, many-fld; fls to 2.5cm diam., variable in colour; sep. and pet. usually chestnut to rusty red barred and marked yellow or purple-rose, sep. to 8×3mm, spathulate, acute, keeled, lateral sep. largely connate, pet. wider than sep., broadly elliptic, broadly clawed, acute, undulate; lip white or pink blotched red to fore of callus, to 13×16mm, broadly clawed, lateral lobes small, obovate-oblong, midlobe transversely reniform, broadly emarginate, callus of 7 tubercles; column to 4mm, wings falcate, pale rose spotted yellow. W Indies. Sometimes treated as *Tolumnia guttata*.

T.variegata (Sw.) Braem (*Oncidium variegatum* (Sw.) Sw.).
VARIEGATED ONCIDIUM.
Lvs 4–6, distichous, lanceolate, acute, recurved, conduplicate, serrulate, dark green, to 15×1.5cm. Raceme or panicle to 45cm, slender; fls to 2cm diam., long-lived, white to pink richly stained brown or crimson-purple; dorsal sep. to 9×3mm, short-clawed, concave, broadly spathulate, subacute, lateral sep. larger than dorsal sep., oblanceolate to narrow-spathulate, connate almost to apex; pet. wider than sep., short-clawed, obovate to suborbicular, obtuse, sometimes emarginate, crenulate-undulate; lip to 1.5×2cm, pandurate, lateral lobes obovate to suborbicular, reflexed, erose-dentate, midlobe broadly oblong or reniform, deeply emarginate, crenulate, callus white-yellow, tuberculate; column to 3mm, wings broad, toothed. Florida, W Indies.

Trias Lindl. (From Gk *trias*, triad, alluding to the arrangement of the floral envelopes.) Some 10 species of epiphytes, allied to *Bulbophyllum*. Rhizomes creeping; pseudobulbs almost spherical. Leaves fleshy, solitary. Fls solitary; sepals almost equal, fleshy, spreading, lateral sepals fused to column foot; petals oblong or linear, small; lip fleshy, mobile, narrow, spreading toward the apex. SE Asia.

CULTIVATION   As for *Bulbophyllum*.

T.picta (Parish. & Rchb. f.) Hemsl.
Pseudobulbs 1.4–1.5cm diam., ovoid. Lvs 5.5–7.5cm, coriaceous, solitary, lanceolate, tapering to a slender point. Infl. borne basally, short, slender; fls to 2cm across; sep. ovate to triangular, yellow to yellow-green, spotted red, spreading, recurved, lateral sep. oblique, fleshy, fused to column foot; pet. broadly ovate, emarginate; lip small, oblong, obtuse, narrowing to a short stalk, attached to column foot, maroon or olive, spotted red, convex above, rough to papillose. Burma, Thailand.

Trichocentrum Poepp. & Endl. (From Gk *thrix*, hair, and *kentron*, spur, referring to the long slender spur in the flowers of some species.) Some 30 species of epiphytes. Rhizome short. Pseudobulbs clustered, very small or obsolete, fleshy, apically unifoliate, rarely bifoliate. Leaves fleshy to coriaceous. Inflorescence lateral, basal, short-stalked, 1- to few-flowered; flowers comparatively large, spreading; sepals similar, free; petals subequal to sepals; lip fleshy, suberect, basally adnate to column, simple to obscurely 3-lobed or pandurate, produced at base into a slender or sac-like spur, disc with a fleshy crested callus; column short, stout, footless, prominently winged, anther terminal, operculate, incumbent, papillose, pollinia 2, waxy. Tropical America.

CULTIVATION   Charming small epiphytes for the intermediate house. They fare best mounted on rafts or slabs of palm or fern fibre and suspended in dappled sunlight. Plunge daily when in growth; mist at other times except when in flower.

T.albococcineum Lind.
Lvs to 9×4cm, fleshy, elliptic or oblong-lanceolate, acute, sometimes spotted red. Infl. to 7.5cm, slender, usually horizontal, 1- to few-fld; fls produced in succession, long-lived; sep. and pet. variable in colour, usually yellow-brown above, yellow-green below, dorsal sep. to 2×1cm, obovate-oblong, acute, lateral sep. oblique, elliptic-oblong, subacute, pet. to 18×8mm, oblong-oblanceolate, acute; lip to 25×22mm, pale or deep purple, base blotched dark purple, clawed, subquadrate-pandurate, base subcordate, spur to 12mm, curved, conical; column to 5mm, wings triangular-lanceolate, porrect, decurved. Mostly summer–autumn. Ecuador, Peru, Brazil.

T.candidum Lindl.
Lvs to 7×2cm, fleshy, rigid, elliptic to ovate-elliptic, obtuse. Infl. to 2cm, 1–3-fld; fls produced in succession; sep. and pet. white marked yellow, sep. to 13×5mm, narrowly elliptic to elliptic-oblanceolate, subacute, apex recurved, pet. to 12×5mm, elliptic-obovate, subacute, apex recurved; lip to 18×9mm, white marked yellow, pink-purple near base, elliptic-obovate, slightly recurved, undulate, retuse, spur gibboussaccate, disc bicarinate, fleshy; column to 5mm, apex pubesc., wings to 3×2mm, oblong-subquadrate, subacute to rounded. Mexico, Guatemala.

T.capistratum Rchb. f. (*T.panamense* Rolfe).
Lvs to 10×2.5cm, fleshy, elliptic-lanceolate to oblong-lanceolate, dark green flushed purple. Fls solitary in succession, fleshy, short-lived; sep. and pet. to 12×4mm, pale yellow-green, lime green or pink-maroon, fleshy, waxy, oblanceolate to oblong-lanceolate; lip to 17×7mm, white blotched pink-purple at base, elliptic to ovate-elliptic, emarginate, concave, acute to rounded, spur to 4mm, extended into 4 or 5 short lobes, themselves resembling short spurs; column to 5mm, wings obliquely ovate-falcate, obtuse. Summer–autumn. Panama, Costa Rica, Venezuela, Colombia.

T.panamense Rolfe. See *T.capistratum*.

T.pulchrum Poepp. & Endl.
Lvs to 10×2.5cm, fleshy, rigid, linear-oblong or oblong-elliptic, subacute. Infl. to 4.5cm, horizontal or pendent, 1- or 2-fld; fls white spotted red-purple; sep. and pet. spreading, concave, fleshy, rigid, dorsal sep. to 20×14mm, ovate-elliptic, acute, lateral sep. to 20×12mm, elliptic-oblanceolate or ellipticovate, pet. subequal to sep., elliptic or ovate-elliptic; lip to 30×18mm, fleshy, sessile, obovate to elliptic, emarginate, slightly crenulate, reflexed, spur to 5cm, disc with 2 yellow keels, finely ciliate; column to 6mm, yellow-brown spotted red, wings short, erect, subquadrate, irregularly dentate-ciliate. Colombia, Venezuela, Ecuador, Peru.

T.tigrinum Lind. & Rchb. f.
Lvs to 12×3cm, elliptic-oblong, erect to spreading, coriaceous, obtuse, deep green usually spotted liver red. Infl. to 15cm, suberect to pendent, 1- or 2-fld; fls to 6cm, showy; sep. and pet. yellow-green spotted and irregularly banded maroonbrown, sep. to 36×12mm, narrowly elliptic-oblong, acute, slightly recurved, pet. to 38×5mm, narrowly oblong-oblanceolate, acute, slightly recurved; lip white, blotched rose-red towards base, to 45×45mm, broadly ovate, apex bilobulate, disc with 5 yellow keels; column to 8mm, wings lacerate. Spring–early summer. Ecuador, Peru.

Trichoceros HBK. (From Gk *thrix*, hair, and *keras*, horn, referring to the two hairy processes of the column which resemble antennae.) Some 6 species of small epiphytes or terrestrials. Rhizome elongate, creeping to ascending, branching, enveloped by leaf-sheaths. Pseudobulbs small, approximate to distant, enveloped by distichous, imbricating leaf-sheaths, apex unifoliate. Leaves small, fleshy or thinly coriaceous, unjointed. Inflorescence 1 or 2, from base of pseudobulb, a raceme, usually surpassing leaves, loosely few to several-flowered; flowers sinister, insect-like, hairy, small, spreading; sepals free, spreading, subequal; petals subsimilar to sepals; lip often borne uppermost, usually trilobed, lateral lobes erect or spreading, often retrorse, midlobe large, usually ovate; column short, stout, wingless, footless, clinandrium with conspicuous dark cilia, resembling antennae, anther terminal, bilocular, pollinia 4. Colombia, Ecuador, Peru, Bolivia, Venezuela.

CULTIVATION   Dwarf creeping orchids with bizarre fly-like flowers on slender stalks. Establish on rafts of fern fibre or wood with a moss/leafmould pad. Suspend vertically in shady, buoyant conditions in the cool or intermediate house, misting over early each day and drenching in warm weather. Flowering is often remontant. Increase by severing the slender scrambling rhizomes.

T.antennifer (H.&B.) HBK (*T.parviflorus* HBK). FLY ORCHID. Fls to 2cm diam.; dorsal sep. and pet. similar, ovate-rhombic, grey-green spotted and striped dark red-brown, lateral sep. somewhat longer and paler; lip larger than pet., pale green-white densely spotted maroon to chestnut, midlobe ovate, tongue-like, lateral lobes narrow and outspread, like 2 arms; column glossy red-brown with dense purple-black bristles on dorsal surfaces. Ecuador to Bolivia.

T.muralis Lindl. Fls to 2cm diam.; sep. ovate, yellow-green with blotchy red-brown stripes, pet. similar in colour but larger and more rounded; lip deep red-brown, lobes large, rounded; column with rusty red bristles. Ecuador.

T.parviflorus HBK. See *T.antennifer*.

Trichoglottis Bl. (From Gk *thrix*, hair, and *glotta*, tongue, referring to the hirsute lip.) Some 60 species of monopodial epiphytes. Stems frequently branched, climbing or pendent. Leaves often 2-ranked and overlapping, oblong to elliptic, narrow. Inflorescence short, axillary; flowers large; lateral sepals fused to the column foot; lip fleshy, partly pubescent, base saccate or spurred, containing a ligulate projection, often hairy, midlobe simple or trilobed, lateral lobes erect; column projections papillose or hirsute. Indo-Malaya to Taiwan, Polynesia.

CULTIVATION   As for *Phalaenopsis*.

T.brachiata Ames. Stems erect, 30–60cm. Lvs oblong to oblong-elliptic, rigid, 3–8×2.5–4cm. Fls axillary, solitary, to 4.5cm diam., sep. and pet. dark purple-brown, spreading, lip white to deep rosy purple, crested white; dorsal sep. to 2×1.5cm, lateral sep. similar, ovate to ovate-lanceolate, to 2.5×1.5; pet. lanceolate to oblong-elliptic, to 2×0.7cm; lip 5-lobed, fused to column base, saccate or strongly concave below. Philippines.

T.luzonensis Ames. Stems to 6cm, flattened, stout. Lvs ligulate, coriaceous, apex unequally bilobed, to 20×3.2cm. Infl. paniculate; fls ivory-yellow, spotted red-brown, fleshy, to 3.2cm diam.; dorsal sep. and pet. spathulate, obtuse, to 2cm, lateral sep. similar,

clawed, to 1.6×0.7cm; lip trilobed, saccate, hirsute, midlobe oblong, rigid, fleshy, stiffly pubesc., disc papillose, lateral lobes triangular, erect, wide, minutely pubesc., spur round, hirsute, to 2mm. Philippines.

T.philippinensis Lindl. Stems to 90cm, erect, branched, leafy. Lvs oblong to oblong-ovate, to 6×3cm. Fls axillary, to 3cm diam., fragrant; tepals brown-green to yellow-brown or yellow, marked brown; dorsal sep. oblong, to 1.5×0.6cm, lateral sep. lanceolate; pet. linear-spathulate, to 1.6×0.5cm; lip white, fused to column foot, cruciform, midlobe laterally compressed, lateral lobes narrow, triangular. Philippines.

Trichopilia Lindl. (From Gk *thrix*, hair, and *pilion*, a cap, the like of which conceals the anther.) Some 30 species of epiphytes. Rhizome short, creeping. Pseudobulbs small, laterally compressed, clustered, cylindrical to ovoid, basally sheathed, apically unifoliate. Leaves oblong to ovate-lanceolate, tapering at base, fleshy or coriaceous, suberect, conduplicate. Inflorescence lateral, basal, short or elongate, arching or pendent, several often borne on one pseudobulb, 1- to several-flowered; flowers large, showy, spreading; sepals and petals narrow, sometimes strongly twisted-spiralling or undulate, the petals similar to dorsal sepal, i.e. broader than lateral sepals; lip adnate to column base, simple to trilobed, inrolled and funnel-shaped, opening to a wavy-margined limb, disc smooth, callose or carinate; column slender, clavate, erect, clinandrium fimbriate, entire to trilobed, anther operculate, incumbent, terminal, unilocular, pollinia 2, waxy, pyriform. Tropical C & S America.

CULTIVATION   Intermediate-growing, of compact habit, valued for their solitary flowers with striking, twisted tepals. Pot in pans or baskets in a medium-grade bark mix. Position in good light and high humidity. Impose a short, dry winter rest.

T.candida Lind. ex Lindl. See *T.fragrans*.

T.coccinea Warsc. ex Lindl. See *T.marginata*.

T.fragrans (Lindl.) Rchb. f. (*T.candida* Lind. ex Lindl.; *T.wagneri* (Rchb. f.) Rchb. f.).
Pseudobulbs to 13×3cm, oblong to ovoid, slightly compressed. Lvs to 30×7cm, oblong-ligulate to oblong-lanceolate, acute or acuminate, erect or suberect. Infl. to 30cm, a raceme, pendent, few-fld; fls to 12cm diam., fragrant, long-lived; sep. and pet. to 4×0.8cm, white or light green, narrowly linear-lanceolate, acute to acuminate slightly reflexed, undulate; lip to 3×2.5cm, white with a central golden-yellow blotch, short-clawed, lamina elliptic to subquadrate, emarginate, basal margins enveloping column, apical portion spreading, erose-undulate, disc with a narrow basal keel; column to 2cm, white, alate at apex. Winter. W Indies, Venezuela, Colombia, Ecuador, Peru, Bolivia.

T.galeottiana A. Rich.
Resembles *T.tortilis* except infl. numerous, 1-fld, short, pendent; fls to 12.5cm diam., long-lived; sep. and pet. yellow to olive-brown, edged pale green, lanceolate, acute; lip striped and barred purple-crimson, throat pale yellow, midlobe obreniform, margins white, disc deep yellow, sometimes spotted red-brown. Late Summer-autumn. Mexico.

T.kienastiana Rchb. f. See *T.suavis*.

T.laxa (Lindl.) Rchb. f.
Pseudobulbs to 12cm, ovoid to ellipsoid, strongly compressed. Lvs to 40×5cm, coriaceous, linear-oblong to oblong-elliptic, subacute. Infl. to 30cm, a raceme, erect to pendent, loosely few- to several-fld; fls to 7cm diam., fragrant, waxy; sep. and pet. to 3.6×0.5cm, dull rose tinted or striped green or buff, narrowly linear-elliptic to linear-lanceolate, acute or acuminate; lip to 2.6×0.4cm, white to white-green, basal portion tubular-involute, subquadrate to obovate above, recurved, emarginate, base short-clawed; disc with basal longitudinal keels; column to 1.3cm, white to pale green, slender. Autumn-early winter. Venezuela, Colombia Peru.

T.leucoxantha L.O. Williams.
Pseudobulbs to 4.5×3.5cm, oblong-elliptic to suborbicular. Lvs to 20×6cm, subcoriaceous, elliptic-lanceolate, acute. Infl. to 7cm, arching to pendent, 1 to few-fld; fls to 7.5cm diam., fragrant, with blotched yellow at lip base; sep. to 3.5×1cm, lanceolate to oblanceolate, acute; pet. slightly shorter than sep., oblong-elliptic, subobtuse, minutely apiculate; lip to 3.5×3.5cm, campanulate, 3-lobed, lateral lobes rounded, undulate, midlobe spreading-reflexed, emarginate, undulate, disc with a conspicuous median keel; column to 1.8cm, slender, terete, clinandrium fimbriate. Summer. Panama.

T.maculata Rchb. f. (*T.powellii* Schltr.).
Pseudobulbs to 6×2.5cm, ellipsoid-oblong, strongly ancipitous, enveloped by densely purple-spotted sheaths. Lvs to 14×3cm, elliptic-lanceolate to oblong-lanceolate, acute to subobtuse, subcoriaceous, dull green. Infl. to 6cm, usually solitary, slender, arching to pendent, 1, rarely 2-fld; fls to 6cm diam., fragrant, somewhat waxy; sep. and pet., pale yellow to olive, linear to linear-lanceolate, acuminate usually strongly twisted; sep. to 4×0.5cm, pet. to 3.5×0.6cm; lip to 4×2cm, white, throat yellow finely striped red, apex spreading-deflexed, 3-lobed, lateral lobes broadly rounded, undulate, midlobe transversely elliptic, emarginate, disc with a short, inconspicuous, median keel; column to 17mm, white, slender, subclavellate, apex 3-lobulate, minutely denticulate. Mostly winter. Guatemala, Panama.

T.marginata Henfr. ex Moore (*T.coccinea* Warsc. ex Lindl.).
Pseudobulbs to 14×2.5cm, linear, strongly compressed. Lvs to 30×5cm, lanceolate to elliptic-lanceolate, coriaceous, acute. Infl. short, arching to pendent, few-fld; fls to 10cm diam., fragrant; sep. and pet. fleshy pink to red with paler, strongly undulate margins, sep. to 6×1cm, narrowly lanceolate to oblanceolate, acute, spreading, pet. to 5.5×1.2cm, oblanceolate, acute, spreading; lip to 8×5cm, white, deep red-rose within, tubular, 3-lobed, lateral lobes inrolled forming a tube, midlobe deeply cleft, undulate, disc obscurely keeled; column terete, forming an obscurely 3-lobed hood over anther. Guatemala to Colombia.

T.oicophylax Rchb. f.
Pseudobulbs to 6×2cm, ovate to ovate-oblong, strongly compressed, pale yellow-green. Lvs to 12×3cm, subcoriaceous, light green, oblong-lanceolate, acute. Infl. to 16cm, arching to pendent, 1- to few-fld; sep. to 5×0.7cm, translucent pale green, linear-lanceolate, acute; pet. similar to sep., slightly wider; lip to 5×4cm, white, pale yellow at base, undulate, lateral lobes suborbicular inrolled, midlobe obcordate, emarginate; disc tricarinate; column to 2cm, pale green to white, anther white. Venezuela, Colombia.

T.powellii Schltr. See *T.maculata*.

T.suavis Lindl. & Paxt. (*T.kienastiana* Rchb. f.).
Pseudobulbs to 8×6cm, oblong-obcordate or oblong-ovoid to suborbicular, fleshy, usually dull grey-green. Lvs to 40×8cm, elliptic-lanceolate to elliptic-oblong, acute, subcoriaceous. Infl. short, arcuate to pendent, few-fld; fls to 10cm diam., delicately fragrant, variable in colour; sep. and pet. to 5.5×1cm, white or cream-white, sometimes spotted pale violet-rose or red, spreading, lanceolate, acute, usually undulate not twisted; lip to 6.5×5cm, white or cream-white, often densely spotted pale violet-rose or spotted and lined yellow on disc (*T.kienastiana*), throat yellow or yellow-orange, undulate-crisped, reflexed, lateral lobes rounded inrolled-tubular, midlobe retuse or emarginate, disc with a prominent, erect, median keel; column elongate, slender, apex 4-lobulate, fimbriate. Mostly spring. Costa Rica, Panama, Colombia.

T.subulata (Sw.) Rchb. f. See *Leucohyle subulata*.

T.tortilis Lindl.
Pseudobulbs to 12×2cm, narrowly ovoid to cylindrical, enveloped by brown-spotted sheaths. Lvs to 22×5cm, elliptic-lanceolate to elliptic-oblanceolate, acute to acuminate, coriaceous, lustrous pale green above, often paler with short-lived brown scurf below. Infl. 4–10cm, usually solitary, arching to pendent, slender, 1–2-fld; fls to 15cm diam., fragrant, waxy; sep. and pet. to 8×1cm, subsimilar, off-white tinted pale

lavender to fleshy purple-brown or yellow-grey with livid blotches, margins much paler, linear, acute or acuminate, strongly twisted; lip to 6.5×4.5cm, white to pale yellow, throat yellow spotted brown or crimson, inrolled-tubular, apex spreading-deflexed, lateral lobes rounded, semiovate, midlobe transversely elliptic-subrotund, emarginate, crisped, undulate; column to 2cm, white-green, slender, subclavellate, apex 3-lobulate, fimbriate. Winter. Mexico, Guatemala, Honduras, El Salvador.

T.turrialbae Rchb. f.
Pseudobulbs to 10×2cm, linear, strongly ancipitous. Lvs to 20×5cm, elliptic-lanceolate, acute, subcoriaceous. Infl. short, arcuate to pendent, 1- to few-fld; fls to 7.5cm diam., fragrant; sep. and pet. to 3×0.8cm, white or clear yellow, lanceolate to ovate-lanceolate, acuminate, lateral sep. connate; lip to 4×3cm, white to yellow, trumpet-shaped, throat lined or spotted orange-brown, obscurely 3-lobed, lateral lobes reflexed, undulate, midlobe rounded, retuse, disc with an elongate median keel; column subterete, elongate, apex 3-lobulate, minutely denticulate. Summer. Costa Rica, Panama.

T.wagneri (Rchb. f.) Rchb. f. See *T.fragrans*.

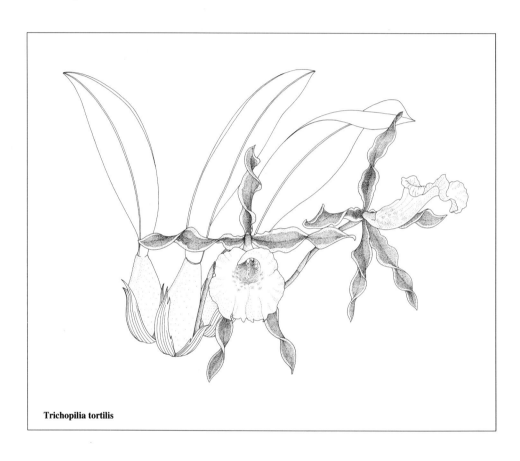

Trichopilia tortilis

Trichosalpinx Luer. (From Gk *thrix*, hair, and *salpinx*, trumpet referring to the trumpet-shaped sheaths of the secondary stems, which have ciliate margins.) About 100 species of tufted or sprawling epiphytes. Rhizome short. Pseudobulbs absent. Secondary stems erect, slender, simple, enveloped by overlapping, tubular sheaths, margins ciliate, apically unifoliate. Leaves thick to fleshy, elliptic or ovate to orbicular, articulate, conduplicate. Inflorescence a terminal raceme; flowers small, resupinate; dorsal sepal free, lateral sepals free to entirely connate; petals smaller than sepals, entire to fimbriate; lip articulated to column foot, equaling petals or smaller, simple to trilobed, often fimbriate; column elongate, with a distinct foot, winged, anther terminal, operculate, incumbent, pollinia 2, waxy, clavate. C & S America.

CULTIVATION   As for *Pleurothallis*.

T.ciliaris (Lindl.) Luer (*Pleurothallis ciliaris* (Lindl.) L.O. Williams).
Secondary stems to 9cm; sheaths to 1cm, ovate to ovate-lanceolate. Lvs to 6.5×1.5cm, linear-lanceolate, elliptic-oblong or elliptic, acute or subobtuse, green-purple. Infl. several, to 2.5cm, few-fld; fls purple-red, sometimes yellow-green; dorsal sep. to 4×2mm, elliptic-oblong or ovate-oblong, concave, acute, ciliate, lateral sep. connate, to 3×3mm, suborbicular-oblong, recurved above, ciliate; pet. minute, oblong or ovate-oblong, obtuse, ciliate; lip to 2×1mm, simple, oblong-spathulate or obovate-oblong, apex rounded, base biauriculate, ciliate, disc with a linear, forked callus; column to 2mm, slender, arcuate, apex tridentate. Mexico to Costa Rica.

T.dura (Lindl.) Luer (*Pleurothallis dura* Lindl.).
Lvs to 20×6mm, ovate to elliptic-oblong, acute or obtuse, subcoriaceous, short-petiolate. Infl. usually solitary, to 8cm, many-fld; fls to 6mm; dorsal sep. to 4mm, ovate-lanceolate, acuminate, deeply concave, lateral sep. free, shorter than dorsal sep., subsimilar; pet. to 2mm, oblong-oblanceolate, obtuse; lip subequal to pet., oblong to ovate-oblong, apex rounded, sulcate or bicarinate, base biauriculate; column to 2mm, wings lateral, obtuse, falcate. Peru, Ecuador.

Trichotosia Bl. (From Gk *trichos*, hairy, describing the hairy stems of plants of this genus.) Some 50 species of epiphytes allied to *Eria*. Rhizome creeping. Pseudobulbs stem-like, erect or pendulous, often pubescent. Leaves paired or several clothing pseudobulb, linear to lanceolate with conspicuous sheaths, rusty-pubescent throughout. Inflorescence a nodal raceme, piercing leaf sheath, arching or pendulous; sepals red-hirsute beneath, green, cream or pale pink above; lip entire or weakly trilobed, keels absent or pubescent, often papillose. India, Malaysia, Thailand to SW Pacific Is.

CULTIVATION   As for *Eria*.

T.dasyphylla (Parish & Rchb. f.) Kränzl. (*Eria dasyphylla* Parish & Rchb. f.).
Lvs elliptic to obovate, fleshy, subacute to 8cm. Infl. to 5cm; fls green-yellow, disc on lip with 2 maroon patches; dorsal sep. small, lateral sep. triangular, acute, basally saccate, appearing short-spurred; pet. broad-oblong; lip obovate, cuneate, midlobe broad, veins prominent, lateral lobes minute. India, Nepal, Vietnam, Thailand.

T.ferox Bl. (*Eria ferox* (Bl.) Bl.).
Stem stout, to 1.85m, hirsute. Lvs lanceolate, to 10cm. Infl. to 10cm; fls 8–15, remote, lip white or pale yellow, edged red; sep. ovate, red-pubesc., obtuse, basal projection to 0.8mm; pet. subspathulate; lip variable, midlobe broad-crenate, disc 3-ridged, warty, pubesc., lateral lobes undulate, erect. Malaysia, Thailand, Borneo.

T.velutina (Lodd. ex Lindl.) Kränzl. (*Eria velutina* Lodd. ex Lindl.).
Stems to 40cm, softly villous. Lvs to 75cm, coriaceous, oblong-lanceolate, downy beneath. Infl. to 2cm; bracts 2; fls green-white or cream to pale pink, lip white-yellow, base often marked purple; sep. ovate to lanceolate; pet. linear, obtuse; lip midlobe short, keels 2, lateral, merging at base, bifid, lateral lobes rounded. Burma, Malaysia, Vietnam, Borneo.

T.vestita (Lindl.) Kränzl. (*Eria vestita* Lindl.).
Stems tufted, ascending, stout, leafy, 15–25cm. Lvs lanceolate, acute, recurved, spreading, hirsute, 13–18cm. Racemes to 15.5cm, flexuous; fls sessile, sep. orange-red, curved, pet. and lip white. Malaysia.

Tridactyle Schltr. (From Gk *tri-*, triple, and *daktylos*, finger, referring to the lip which is usually trilobed.) About 36 species of epiphytes and lithophytes. Stems often elongated; roots stout, sometimes verrucose. Leaves distichous, usually ligulate and coriaceous. Inflorescence racemose, few- to many-flowered, the flowers set in 2 rows facing the same way; flowers yellow-green, straw-orange, yellow, green-white or white; sepals and petals subsimilar; lip usually trilobed, spurred, often with auricles at the mouth of the spur. Tropical & S Africa.

CULTIVATION   As for *Angraecum*.

T.anthomaniaca (Rchb. f.) Summerh.
Stems long, pendent, often branched, leafy for most of their length; roots numerous, 2–3mm diam., verrucose. Lvs 4.5–7.5×1–1.5cm, oblong, bilobed at apex, slightly succulent, olive green. Racemes arising opposite lf axils, about 1cm, densely 3–4-fld; fls straw-coloured, all perianth parts spreading; pedicel and ovary 4mm, papillose; sep. 5×1.5–2mm, lanceolate, acute, the lateral sep. somewhat falcate; pet. 5×1mm; lip 5×2mm, more or less entire, rhomboid, margin ciliolate; spur 10mm, slender, parallel to ovary; column short and stout, anther-cap brown. Tropical Africa (widespread).

T.bicaudata (Lindl.) Schltr.
Stems 30–50cm, usually erect but sometimes pendent, woody toward base, covered with remains of old leaf bases, leafy toward apex; roots to 8mm diam., light grey, very slightly verrucose. Lvs variable in size and texture, usually about 15×1.5cm, ligulate, slightly folded, unequally and obtusely bilobed at apex. Racemes to 10cm, borne along stem, 18–20-fld; fls 9–10mm diam., yellow or green-yellow; dorsal sep. 4×1.5mm, oblong, lateral sep. 5×2.5mm, somewhat falcate, tips reflexed; pet. 4×1mm, narrowly lanceolate; lip 5–6mm, trilobed about halfway, with triangular, acute, 1mm auricles at base, midlobe 2mm, narrowly triangular, lateral lobes 3mm, linear, tips fimbriate; spur 1.5–2mm, straight; column 1mm. Tropical Africa (widespread), S Africa.

T.citrina Cribb.
Stem short, to 6cm, erect; roots stout. Lvs 3–4, forming a fan, 7–14×1–1.5cm, stiff, suberect, folded, slightly glaucous green, unequally bilobed at apex. Racemes 1–2 arising from base of stem, arching, 9–10cm, fairly densely to 10-fld; fls creamy yellow or green-yellow, 25mm from tip of dorsal sep. to apex of lip; pedicel and ovary 6mm; bracts very small; dorsal sep. 10×2.5mm, erect, lanceolate, acute, lateral sep. slightly wider, deflexed, the tips reflexed; pet. similar to lateral sep.; lip 15mm, trilobed in apical third, midlobe 5×1mm, lanceolate, acute, lateral lobes shorter, slightly truncate at tip; spur 4–5cm, slender, tapering, pendent; column 5mm. Tanzania, Malawi, Zambia.

T.gentilii (De Wildeman) Schltr.
Stems long, woody, branched, becoming pendent; roots around 3mm diam., arising from base and lower part of stem. Lvs 5–6, ligulate, to 10×1.5cm, rather fleshy. Racemes arising below lvs, about 6cm, 7–12-fld; fls pale green, scented in the evening; dorsal sep. 8×2mm, lanceolate, acute, tip reflexed, lateral sep. slightly longer and wider, curving back; pet. slightly longer and narrower than dorsal sep.; lip 15–18mm, trilobed at about halfway, midlobe 5mm, lateral lobes 8–10mm, fimbriate; auricles 1–2mm, acute; spur 5–8cm; column 4–5mm; anther-cap orange-brown. Ghana, Nigeria, Cameroun, Zaire, Uganda, Zambia, S Africa (Natal).

T.tricuspis (Bol.) Schltr.
Stems usually short and erect, but can be long and pendent; roots stout, 5mm diam., numerous, often forming tangled mass. Lvs borne toward top of stem, 7–13×1.5–2cm, ligulate, dark green, slightly folded, unequally and obtusely bilobed at apex. Racemes 6–15cm, arising toward base of stem, densely several- to many-fld; pedicel and ovary 3mm; dorsal sep. 7×1mm, lanceolate, acute, the tips often recurved; pet. similar, 6×1mm; lip 8mm, trilobed in apical third, midlobe 3mm, triangular-lanceolate, acute, lateral lobes 2–2.5mm, usually upward-curving, the apices truncate or slightly fimbriate; spur 15mm, slender, straight, parallel to ovary; column 2mm. Tropical Africa (widespread).

T.tridactylites (Rolfe) Schltr. (*Angraecum tridactylites* Rolfe.)
Stems to 60cm, erect or pendent, the lower part woody, covered with old leaf bases. Lvs to 8, 16–18×1.5–2cm, distichous, ligulate, glossy green, unequally and obtusely bilobed at apex. Racemes arising along stem below lvs, 4–5cm, 8–10-fld; fls pale straw-orange or green-cream, scented, 8–10mm diam.; dorsal sep. 6×2mm, lanceolate, acute, lateral sep. similar but oblique and slightly wider; pet. 5×1mm, lanceolate, acute; lip 5mm, trilobed about halfway, midlobe 2mm, triangular, lateral lobes 3mm, filiform toward tips; spur 9–10mm, horizontal; column 1.5mm. Tropical Africa (widespread).

T.tridentata (Harv.) Schltr.
Stems woody, to 40cm, erect or pendent, sometimes branched; roots arising at base, 4mm diam. Lvs to 10 on apical half of stem, 7–10cm×2–4mm, terete, usually with a groove along upper surface, dull olive-green. Racemes borne on bare part of stem and among lower lvs, 15–20mm, densely 4–8-fld; fls dull straw-orange, column and anther-cap slightly darker, about 6mm diam., all parts spreading; pedicel and ovary 2.5–3mm; bracts less than 1mm; dorsal sep. 3–3.5×1.5mm, ovate, acute, lateral sep. similar but slightly shorter and broader; pet. 3×1mm, lanceolate, acute; lip 4×1mm, trilobed toward apex, midlobe 1–1.5mm, triangular, lateral lobes varying from slightly longer to slightly shorter than midlobe, becoming filiform; spur 6–9mm, slender, parallel to ovary; column 1mm, stout. Tropical Africa (widespread), S Africa.

T.wakefieldii Rolfe. See *Solenangis wakefieldii*.

Trigonidium Lindl. (From the Gk *trigonon*, a triangle and *eidos*, resemblance, referring to the triangular form of the floral parts.) Some 15 species of epiphytes or lithophytes. Rhizome short or elongate. Pseudobulbs variously shaped, slightly compressed, sulcate, 1- to 5-leaved, usually 2-leaved at apex. Leaves coriaceous or subcoriaceous, conduplicate, elongate. Scapes ascending from base of pseudobulbs and from axils of cataphylls of rhizome, slender, short or elongate, 1-flowered; flowers large; sepals often united at base forming a triquetrous, turbinate tube, free portions spreading or reflexed; petals smaller than sepals; lip smaller than petals, trilobed, lateral lobes erect parallel to column, midlobe fleshy, spreading-recurved; disc with a fleshy central callus; column short, subterete, wingless, sometimes with a short foot, anther terminal, operculate, incumbent, unilocular, pollinia 4, waxy. Mexico to Brazil & Peru.

CULTIVATION   As for *Maxillaria*.

T.acuminatum Batem. ex Lindl. (*T.tenue* Lodd. ex Lindl.).
Epiphytic. Pseudobulbs to 4cm, cylindrical to ovoid or ellipsoid, rugose, apically 1–2-lvd. Lvs to 27×1.5cm, erect, linear or linear-oblanceolate, acute, erect. Infl. to 18cm, erect; fls straw-coloured to green-brown, interior striped and veined deep brown, sometimes wholly purple-brown; sep. to 28×10mm, lanceolate or oblanceolate to ovate-lanceolate, long-acuminate, abruptly recurved; pet. to 12×3mm, oblong-ligulate to oblong-obovate, acute to obtuse; lip to 8×4.5mm, concave, deeply 3-lobed, lateral lobes erect, oblong to triangular, subacute to rounded, midlobe ovate to obovate, rounded, disc with a linear-clavate callus; column to 5mm, white, erect. Venezuela, Colombia, Peru, Surinam, Brazil, Guyana.

T.brachyglossum (A. Rich. & Gal.) Schltr. See *T.egertonianum*.

T.egertonianum Batem. ex Lindl. (*T.brachyglossum* (A. Rich. & Gal.) Schltr.).
Epiphytic. Pseudobulbs to 9×4cm, ellipsoid to ovoid, 2-lvd at apex. Lvs to 60×3cm, suberect, linear or linear-lanceolate, obtuse to acute, subcoriaceous. Infl. to 30cm, 1 to several, erect; fls to 3.5cm, tubular-campanulate, long-lived; sep. and pet. yellow-green to pink-tan flecked and veined brown, dorsal sep. to 4.5×2cm, elliptic-oblanceolate to obovate-spathulate, acute to obtuse, spreading, lateral sep. to 4×1.5cm, obliquely oblong to obovate-oblanceolate, acute to rounded, strongly recurved; pet. to 22×6mm, lanceolate to oblong-lanceolate, acute to obtuse; lip to 10×4mm, yellow-tan or pink-tan with brown venation, 3-lobed, lateral lobes elliptic-oblanceolate, obtuse, apex often crenulate, midlobe broadly ovate, acute, recurved, verrucose, disc with a linear-clavate callus; column to 7mm, yellow-cream marked purple, erect. Mostly spring. Mexico to Panama and Colombia.

T.lankesteri Ames.
Pseudobulbs to 8×3cm, ovoid, apex 3–5-lvd. Lvs to 27×4cm, oblong-lanceolate, subcoriaceous, acute, slender-petiolate. Infl. to 16cm, usually solitary; fls to 5cm; sep. to 5×2cm, light green-brown to cinnamon-brown, elliptic-oblanceolate, acute, strongly reflexed; pet. to 2.5×1cm, green-brown, sometimes spotted purple, broadly oblanceolate, apiculate, spreading; lip to 15×5mm, white spotted brown, 3-lobed, lateral lobes triangular, acute, midlobe ovate, obtuse, recurved, densely verrucose below, disc with a ligulate callus; column to 1cm, arcuate, footless. Spring–summer. Costa Rica, Panama.

T.monophyllum Griseb. See *Neocogniauxia monophylla*.

T.obtusum Lindl.
Epiphytic. Pseudobulbs to 6×4cm, ovoid to oblong, suberect, apex 1–2-lvd. Lvs to 35×6cm, suberect, subcoriaceous, linear-lanceolate tooblanceolate, acute. Infl. to 15cm, usually solitary, erect; fls large; sep. to 4.2×1.2cm, yellow-green shaded pale maroon or pale brown veined light maroon, lanceolate or oblong-lanceolate, acute to obtuse, subcoriaceous; pet. to 2.2×1.7cm, membranaceous, oblanceolate or obovate-oblong, acute to obtuse, white veined rose or purple; lip to 1×0.5cm, ovate to elliptic, white marked red-maroon, lateral lobes oblong, acute to obtuse, margins red, midlobe yellow, ovate, rounded, dorsally tuberculate, disc with a basal, ligulate callus; column to 8mm, white, erect, subterete. Venezuela, Guyanas, Colombia, Bolivia, Brazil.

T.ringens Lindl. See *Mormolyca ringens*.
T.tenue Lodd. ex Lindl. See *T.acuminatum*.

Trisetella Luer. (From the Lat. *tri-*, three, and *seta*, bristle, referring to the hair-like tails of the sepals.) Some 20 species of diminutive tufted epiphytes, lacking pseudobulbs allied to *Masdevallia*. Secondary stems short, erect or ascending, unifoliate, concealed by 2 or 3 thin, overlapping sheaths. Leaves fleshy to coriaceous, erect, narrow, articulated, duplicate, linear to elliptic, sessile or petiolate. Racemes solitary or clustered, arising from junction of secondary stem and leaf, few-flowered, erect; peduncle slender, smooth or verrucose; bracts 1 per flower, tubular-thin, somewhat sheathing; flowers opening in succession, small; sepals thin-textured, smooth to finely pubesc., dorsal sepal small, mostly fused to lateral sepals forming a sepaline cup, apex contracted forming a tail, lateral sepals large, their inner margins almost entirely united forming a typically oblong synsepalum, concave, apices contracted into slender tails; petals small, very thin-textured, ovate-oblong to elliptic; lip simple to trilobed, ovate-oblong to subpandurate, disc with 2 longitudinal calli, smooth to verrucose; column terete or subterete, with a narrow foot, articulated to lip base, clinandrium erose, anther hooded, operculate, terminal, incumbent, pollinia 2, waxy, obovoid to pyriform. Tropical C & S America.

CULTIVATION   As for *Masdevallia*.

T.triaristella (Rchb. f.) Luer. (*Masdevallia triaristella* Rchb. f.) A dwarf plant, seldom exceeding 8cm. Fls solitary or (rarely) paired, buff stained chocolate or dark maroon; lateral sep. fused into an oblong-carinate blade with 2.5cm green divergent trails, dorsal sep. short, hooded, long-tailed. This species differs from *T.triglochin* in warted peduncle and larger fls with longer sepaline tails. Costa Rica, Panama, Colombia, Ecuador.

T.tridactylites (Rchb. f.) Luer. See *T.triglochin*.

T.triglochin (Rchb. f.) Luer (*Masdevallia triglochin* Rchb. f.; *T.tridactylites* (Rchb. f.) Luer).
Secondary stems to 6mm. Lvs to 70×4mm, dark green, sometimes tinged and mottled purple beneath, narrowly elliptic to linear, acute. Infl. densely few-fld to 9cm; bracts to 4mm; dorsal sep. to 6×6mm, yellow to red-brown or purple, ovate, obtuse, finely erose, concave, tail to 15mm, yellow, erect, synsepalum to 21×11mm, orange-brown to red-brown or purple, oblong, acute to obtuse, tails to 12mm, slender; pet. to 4×2mm, clear yellow, tinged purple, oblong to ovate-oblong, truncate, minutely erose; lip to 4×2mm, purple, ovate-oblong, obtuse to rounded; column to 4mm, yellow tinged red or purple. Ecuador, Panama, Costa Rica, Peru, Venezuela, Colombia, Bolivia.

Trudelia Garay. (For N. Trudel, Swiss horticulturalist.) 6 species of monopodial epiphytes. Stems to 20cm, slender, clothed with overlapping bases of 2-ranked leaves. Leaves strap-shaped, conduplicate, to 15cm, apically bidentate, denticulate. Inflorescence few-flowered, shorter than leaves; flowers showy, fleshy, resupinate, green; sepals and petals opening partially; lip attached to the column base, basally saccate, margins thickened, fleshy above, longitudinally ridged; column erect, foot absent. India, Thailand.

CULTIVATION   Cool-house epiphytes, potting and watering regimes as for *Vanda*.

T.alpina (Lindl.) Garay (*Vanda alpina* (Lindl.) Lindl.; *Luisia alpina* Lindl.).
Lvs broad, linear, apex unequally bilobed, to 16×1.5cm. Fls to 2.5cm diam., sep. and pet. green-yellow, lip yellow streaked maroon or purple, lateral lobes purple; sep. incurved, narrow, dorsal sep. obovate-spathulate, to 1.3×0.5cm, lateral sep. obovate-falcate; pet. oblong-elliptic, narrow, incurved, to 1.2cm; lip trilobed, spurless, fleshy, midlobe ovate, concave, basally cordate, apical projections 2, horn-like, lateral lobes rounded, concave, erect. India, Himalaya.

T.cristata (Lindl.) Sengh. (*Vanda cristata* Lindl.).
Lvs ligulate, coriaceous, keeled, recurved, apex tridentate, truncate, to 12×5×1.8cm. Infl. equal or shorter than lvs; fls 4–5cm diam.; sep. and pet. olive, lime green or dull yellow, lip white or gold, striped purple on frilled crests; sep. spathulate-oblong, incurved, narrow to 2.5cm; pet. linear-oblong, narrow, incurved; lip trilobed, oblong, to 2×1.5cm, midlobe almost pandurate, 5–7-ridged, apex bilobed, lateral lobes erect, triangular, margins undulate; spur conical. Himalayas, Bangladesh.

T.griffithii (Lindl.) Garay (*Vanda griffithii* Lindl.).
Lvs channelled, recurved, apex trilobed. Sep. and pet. yellow-brown above, chequered, lip lilac, basally blotched deep yellow; sep. linear-oblong, recurved; pet. acuminate; lip ovate, furrowed, elongate, base concave, irregularly divided, midlobe ligulate, emarginate. Bhutan.

T.pumila (Hook. f.) Sengh. (*Vanda pumila* Hook. f.).
Lvs ligulate, curved, apex tridentate, unequal to 20×2cm. Infl. axillary, erect, to 3 fld; fls 5–6.2cm, fragrant, sep. and pet. yellow or cream, lip paler, streaked purple; sep. oblanceolate, narrow, to 3×0.8cm; pet. linear, narrow; lip to 2.5cm, midlobe ovate, broad, concave, lateral lobes triangular, erect, acute; spur almost conical. India, Bhutan, Thailand.

Vanda Jones (Sanskrit name for *Vanda tessellata*.) Some 35 species of monopodial epiphytes. Leaves flat, ligulate, alternate, in 2 opposite ranks, midvein keeled beneath. Inflorescence an axillary raceme; flowers often large, many; sepals and petals free, often distinctly clawed, spreading; lip fused to the column base; midlobe forward-pointing, often keeled, lateral lobes erect; spur conical to oblong, sometimes incurved. Himalaya to Malaysia.

CULTIVATION Showy epiphytes; some, for example *V.coerulea*, the famous 'Blue Orchid', hail from Northern India, flower in autumn and winter and are suitable for the cool house or conservatory; others flower in spring and summer and favour the warm greenhouse or growing case, as befits their origins in Southeast Asia. Most, however will adapt readily to the intermediate house, particularly the Indonesian *V.tricolor* (red to chestnut-spotted with a mauve lip); the deliciously scented *V.denisoniana* (ivory flecked rust) and *V.tessellata* (cream overlaid in faint bronze-green with a blue lip). These plants are rigidly monopodial, producing long, tough stems clothed with closely 2-ranked leaves. The leaf bases are pierced by the emerging racemes and stout aerial roots. Pot in baskets or orchid pots with perfect drainage and containing the coarsest bark-based mix. Rooting into the substrate serves largely to anchor the plant: a healthy growth of aerial roots is essential, even if they require frequent misting or to be guided to the potting mixture to maintain active green root tips. Older specimens may have bare stem bases, in which case cut away the lower portion of stem altogether, replanting only the healthy, leafy, rooting summit; this keeps plants within bounds and promotes vigorous root production. In summer provide light shade in warm, humid conditions and water and mist frequently, applying a dilute foliar feed when in full growth. During the winter, reduce temperatures and humidity, admitting maximum light and ventilating where possible.

Several of the most important *Vanda* species have now been reassigned to other genera – for example *V.(Papilionanthe) teres*, a sun-loving, slender-stemmed scrambler with large blooms in bright colours much favoured for floral decoration in Polynesia and South East Asia and the progenitor of many grexes and cultivars (retained here under *Vanda* for ease of reference). *Vanda (Trudelia) alpina* is a charming, green-flowered dwarf able to withstand lower temperatures than most of its allies. By contrast, *V.(Euanthe) sanderiana* is a robust plant for the most steamy recesses of the warm house; its massive, rounded blooms are beautifully patterned.

V.alpina (Lindl.) Lindl. See *Trudelia alpina*.
V.amesiana Rchb. f. See *Holcoglossum amesianum*.

V.bensonii Batem.
Lvs lorate, coriaceous, 18–25cm. Racemes erect, stout, to 45cm; fls 10–15, to 5cm diam., white beneath, yellow-green above, dotted and veined red-brown, lip pink or rose-purple; sep. and pet. obovate, obtuse; lip base oblong, expanding, becoming reniform, lateral lobes oblong-falcate; disc 5-ridged, auricles at base small. Burma, Thailand.

V.brunnea Rchb. f.
Lvs ligulate, narrow, apex notched. Fls olive above, lip pale yellow-white; sep. and pet. oblong, cuneate, obtuse; lip midlobe ligulate, bilobed, lateral lobes semicircular. India, Burma.

V.cathcartii Lindl. See *Esmeralda cathcartii*.
V.clarkei (Rchb. f.) N.E. Br. See *Esmeralda clarkei*.

V.coerulea Griff. ex Lindl.
Stems stout, 75–150cm. Lvs pale green, coriaceous, 8–25cm, apex toothed and truncate. Infl. erect or suberect, 20–60cm; fls 7–10cm diam., pale to deep lilac-blue, obscurely chequered, lip darker; dorsal sep. spathulate-obovate, clawed, broad, lateral sep. similar, larger, to 5.5×2.5cm; pet. obovate, claw twisted; lip midlobe linear-oblong, 2-ridged, fused, apex bi-tuberculate. India, Burma, Thailand.

V.coerulescens Griff.
Stem to 10cm, terete. Lvs 12.5–20cm. Infl. suberect to pendent, to 50cm+; fls many, 2.5–3.5cm diam., pale lilac, pale blue or white, lip deeper; sep. and pet. obovate-spathulate; lip midlobe obovate, apex notched, margins above reflexed, with 2 thickened ridges, lateral lobes oblong. Burma, Thailand.

V.cristata Lindl. See *Trudelia cristata*.

V.dearei Rchb. f.
Lvs recurved, 40–45×4.5cm. Racemes pendent; fls 3–5, lemon yellow or cream, veined brown, fragrant; sep. and pet. elliptic, obtuse, reflexed, undulate; lip midlobe subrectangular, lateral lobes ovate, oblique. Sunda Is.

V.denisoniana Bens. & Rchb. f. (including var. *hebraica* Rchb. f.).
Lvs to 30×2cm, lorate to ligulate, recurved. Racemes to

15cm, arching; fls 5–6, to 5cm diam., lime green, to ivory, often mottled or spotted ginger, strongly vanilla-scented, lip base marked cinnamon to orange; dorsal sep. oblong-spathulate, lateral sep. ovate, oblique, broader; pet. spathulate; lip base bilobed, expanding terminal lobes diverging, callus 5-ridged. Burma, Thailand.

V.gigantea Lindl. See *Vandopsis gigantea*.
V.griffithii Lindl. See *Trudelia griffithii*.

V.helvola Bl.
Racemes erect, shorter than lvs, 3–5-fld; fls 4–5cm diam., yellow to burgundy, shading to purple; sep. and pet. spathulate, undulate, pointed, reflexed, lateral sep. fused under lip; lip midlobe triangular-hastate, base saccate, calli opposite column, centre convex, apex truncate, deflexed, flat, ridged, lateral lobes incurved, quadrangular. Java.

V.hookeriana Rchb. f. See *Papilionanthe hookeriana*.

V.insignis Bl.
Stem suberect. Lvs linear-ligulate, 22.5–30×2.5cm. Infl. pendent, shorter than lvs; fls 5–5.5cm diam., tawny-yellow, spotted chocolate-brown above, yellow-white beneath, lip midlobe white, limb rose-purple; sep. spathulate, fleshy; pet. similar, narrower; lip subobovate, midlobe pandurate, suddenly expanding to a half-moon-shaped limb; lateral lobes short-auriculate. Moluccas.

V.kimballiana Rchb. f. See *Holcoglossum kimballianum*.

V.lamellata Lindl.
To 15cm. Lvs narrow, recurved, 30–42cm. Infl. erect or suberect; fls many, 2.5–5cm diam., pale yellow, blotched chestnut, lip lateral lobes white; sep. and pet. spathulate or oblong, obtuse, lateral sep. broader than dorsal, falcate; lip midlobe oblong-retuse, longitudinal ridges 2, tubercles near apex 2, lateral lobes erect, auriculate. Philippines, N Borneo.

V.lilacina Teijsm. & Binnend.
To 15cm. Lvs 4–8, oblong, arched. Infl. erect; fls lilac, rarely mottled purple, lip base white; sep. and pet. obovate-oblong, obtuse; lip midlobe erect, weakly trilobed, apex round, spur curved. Thailand, Burma, Laos to China.

V.limbata Bl.
Stems to 90cm+. Lvs linear, recurved, 15–20cm. Infl. 15–20cm, erect; fls 10–12, cinnamon, blotched and chequered

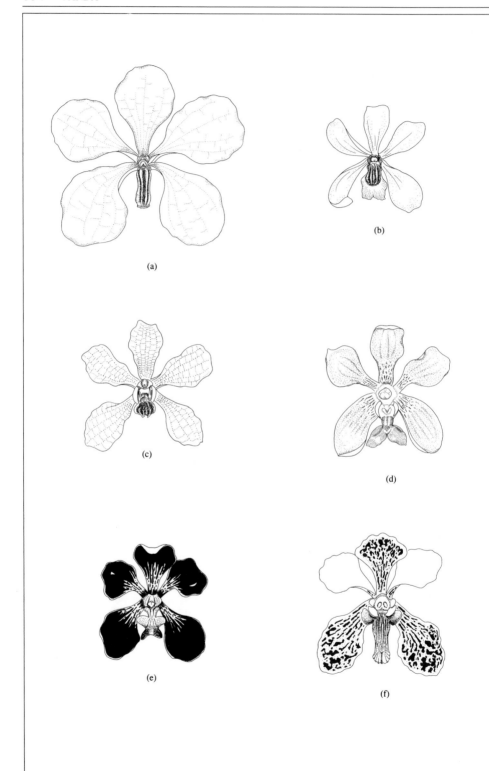

Vanda   (a) *V.coerulea*   (b) *V.coerulescens*   (c) *V.tessellata*   (d) *V.denisoniana*   (e) *V.merrillii*   (f) *V.tricolor*

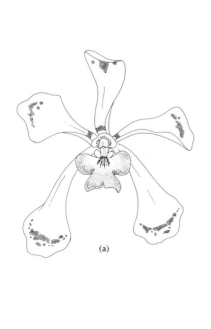

(a)

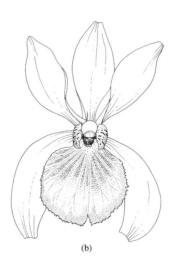

(b)

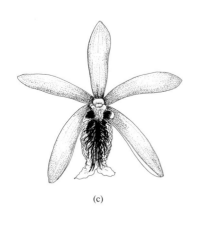

(c)

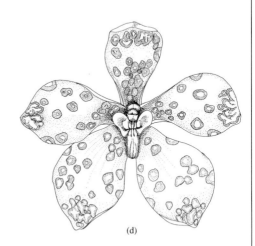

(d)

Vanda and allies   (a) *Vanda luzonica*   (b) *Holcoglossum kimballianum*   (c) *Trudelia cristata*   (d) *Vandopsis gigantea*

dark red-brown, edged yellow, tinged lilac above, lip rose-lilac, edged white; sep. and pet. spathulate, subequal, similar; lip midlobe quadrate to subpandurate, angles rounded, apex truncate, disc 5–7-ridged, margins deflexed, lateral lobes small, rounded. Java.

V.lowii Lindl. See *Dimorphorchis lowii*.

V.luzonica Loher.
To 30cm. Lvs narrow-oblong, coriaceous, 15–35cm. Infl. erect, to 20cm+; bracts orbicular-ovate; fls to 5cm diam., white, base line narrow, transverse, purple, scattered dots few, violet to crimson-purple, lip violet-purple or amethyst; sep. and pet. obovate, obtuse, spreading to 2.5cm; lip base saccate, midlobe pandurate to oblong, convex, obtuse, lateral lobes erect, auriculate. Philippines.

V.merrillii Ames & Quis.
To 1.5m. Lvs linear-oblong, recurved, 25–32×2–3.5cm. Infl. axillary, lax; fls 7–11, 3–3.5cm, fleshy, waxy, glossy, fragrant, yellow suffused carmine or red, lip midlobe yellow blotched red, lateral lobes white, dotted purple; sep. and pet. obovate, base narrow; lip midlobe pandurate, apex retuse, convex, minutely bilobed, lateral lobes subquadrate, erect, incurved. Philippines.

V.pumila Hook. f. See *Trudelia pumila*.

V.roeblingiana Rolfe.
To 70cm. Lvs linear-oblong, oblique, truncate, 20–30×3–4cm. Fls to 5cm diam., yellow, longitudinally striped red-brown, lip midlobe yellow; sep. and pet. ovate-oblong, obtuse; lip midlobe hastate, pubesc., minutely dentate, apex dilated, lateral lobes subquadrate, erect. Philippines.

V.roxburghii R. Br. See *V.tessellata*.
V.sanderiana Rchb. f. See *Euanthe sanderiana*.

V.spathulata Spreng.
To 60cm. Lvs lorate, 5–10×1.5–3cm. Infl. 30–45cm, pseudoterminal; terminal; fls few, to 3cm diam., golden yellow; sep. and pet. oblong-spathulate, flat; lip midlobe suborbicular, obscurely trilobed, lateral lobes obovate, broad, small. India, Sri Lanka.

V.suavis Rchb. f. See *V.tricolor* var. *suavis*.
V.teres (Roxb.) Lindl. See *Papilionanthe teres*.

V.tessellata (Roxb.) D. Don (*V.roxburghii* R. Br.).
To 60cm. Lvs linear-lorate, conduplicate, strongly decurved-arching, 15–20cm. Infl. suberect, 15–25cm, 6–10-fld; fls 4–5cm diam., tepals yellow-green or very pale blue, chequered brown, edged white, lip violet to blue, edged white; sep. and pet. ovate to elliptic-oblong, clawed, undulate; lip to 2×1.2cm, midlobe pandurate, convex, apex truncate, bilobed, lateral lobes lanceolate, acute. India, Burma to Malaysia.

V.tricolor Lindl.
To 100cm. Lvs ligulate, curved, overlapping, 37–45cm. Infl. spreading or ascending, 7–+10-fld; fls fragrant, 5–7.5cm

diam., variable in colour, usually pale yellow, densely dotted bright red-brown, white beneath, lip bright magenta-purple above, white streaked red-brown beneath, spur white; sep. and pet. ovate-oblong to orbicular-obovate, clawed, undulate, fleshy, 2–3cm, pet. base twisted; lip midlobe subpandurate, apex deeply notched, 3-ridged above, convex, lateral lobes almost quadrate, incurved. Java, Laos. var. *suavis* (Rchb. f.) Lindl. (*V.suavis* Rchb. f.). As *V.tricolor* except racemes often longer, denser; fls white, dots few, red-purple; lip purple.

V.undulata Lindl.
To 40cm. Lvs narrow-oblong, flat 7–10×2cm. Infl. stout, 15–20cm; fls few, 3–4cm diam., white suffused pink, tips green, lip yellow-green, striped pink; sep. and pet. reflexed, margin undulate; lip midlobe concave, lateral lobes erect, embracing column; disc 2-keeled. Himalaya.

V.grexes and cultivars.
V.Deva: large plants with strap lvs; fls large and flat, deep violet-pink with very dark markings on sep.; many clones.
V.Diana: tall plants with terete lvs; fls white with some yellow inside base of lip.
V.Fuchs Sunrise: tall plants with brilliant yellow-green fls.
V.Jennie Hashimoto: tall plants with semi-terete lvs; fls pink with orange-red tessellation on sep.; very floriferous in summer.
V.Josephine Van Brero: tall plants with semi-terete lvs; fls pink with yellow-orange tinge.
V.Kasem's Delight: compact plants with strap lvs; fls large, flat, clustered, deep blue-pink, often very dark, with near black markings, many clones.
V.Mem. Madame Pranerm: tall plants with strap lvs; fls clear golden yellow overlaid with orange brown, fine shape.
V.Miss Joaquim: tall plants with terete lvs; fls pale lavender pink with large darker rose lip.
V.Nellie Morley: tall plants with semi-terete lvs; fls deep pink with darker freckles, deep violet lip, usually in spring and autumn.
V.Onomea: large plants with strap lvs; fls pink or lilac with red-mauve markings.
V.Patricia Low: tall plants with terete lvs; fls well spaced, creamy pink with red and yellow lip.
V.Roman Empress: tall plants with strap lvs; striking flowers with lilac pet. and lime green sep., fine shape.
V.Rose Davis: compact plants with strap lvs; fls deep blue-lilac with chequered markings in darker colour in summer.
V.Rothschildiana: compact plants with strap lvs; large fls deep lavender blue with darker chequered markings, close together, mid-winter.
V.Tan Chay Yan: tall plants with terete lvs; fls well spaced, deep peachy pink with brick red lip; very floriferous.
V.Thonglor: compact plants with strap lvs; fls clustered, deep rose pink with dark red shading and markings on sep.

Vandopsis Pfitz. (From *Vanda* and Gk *opsis*, appearance.) 8 species of monopodial epiphytes or terrestrials. Leaves coriaceous. Racemes erect, drooping or pendent; flowers fleshy, few to many; sepals and petals similar, oblong-ovate to spathulate, free, base narrow; lip base concave, apically upcurved, tip incurved, sometimes spurred, midlobe laterally compressed, calli few to many, lateral lobes erect. SE Asia to Malaysia.

CULTIVATION   As for *Vanda*.

V.gigantea (Lindl.) Pfitz. (*Vanda gigantea* Lindl.).
To 75cm. Lvs recurved, strap-shaped, fleshy, to 60×7cm. Infl. pendent, to 40cm; fls to 7cm diam., yellow, blotched red; sep. more densely blotched and smaller than pet., violet beneath; lip linear-oblong, apically incurved, longitudinal ribs white, the midrib prominent, extending to the tip, callus conical, bilobed. Burma.

V.lissochiloides (Gaudich.) Pfitz.
To 150cm, often woody at base. Lvs to 60×5cm, recurved, pointed, coriaceous. Infl. erect, to 120cm; fls to 20cm diam., yellow above, speckled violet, violet-red beneath; sep. and pet. oblong-obovate, obtuse, pet. shorter, narrower than sep.; lip basal seg. rounded, forward-pointing, crested, central rib prominent, flanking ribs less so. E Malaysia.

Vanilla Mill. (From Spanish *vainilla*, a diminutive of *vaina*, a pod or sheath.) About 100 species of scandent epiphytes; roots adventitious, arising at nodes, aerial or clinging, rooting in soil where they touch the ground. Stems succulent, cylindrical, jointed, climbing or trailing, green or brown, after channelled. Leaves present or absent, fleshy, sessile or shortly petiolate, borne single at nodes. Racemes or panicles usually axillary, occasionally terminal, few to many-flowered; flowers large, white, yellow or green, the lip sometimes marked with purple or yellow; sepals and petals free, similar; lip usually larger, adnate to column at base and forming a funnel; column long, curved. Capsules cylindrical, dehiscent; seeds relatively large. Tropics and subtropics of Old and New World.

CULTIVATION   The scrambling, vine-like habit of this intermediate to warm-growing genus is highly unusual within Orchidaceae, as is the great non-ornamental value of *V.planifolia*, the vanilla orchid, grown for its pods on support shrubs and trees throughout the tropics. All produce trusses of large, waxy, highly fragrant flowers, usually in shades of white, green, cream and topaz: the rope-like growth of some (notably the near-leafless species) is also curiously attractive. Stem cuttings with growing tips should be taken cleanly at a node or constriction and allowed to dry before insertion in damp perlite in a heated case (temperature circa 27°C/80°F). Once the thick, adhesive roots have developed (not to be confused with the smaller, largely inactive 'hook' roots found in several species), the young plants should be moved on to well drained pots of a coarse bark mix with added leafmould and sphagnum moss. Syringe and water freely; maintain high temperatures and light shade. As the stems grow and begin to clamber, furnish support by tying in to a cork slab, moss pole or moss-covered trellis. Leafy species, particularly *V.planifolia*, demand high temperatures and good water supplies throughout the year. The thick-stemmed 'leafless' species will tolerate cooler, drier conditions and bright light once established. In optimum conditions, the stems may become bare and wither at the base, leaving the vines wholly epiphytic and free to clamber through their supports or form large knots: in such cases, regular misting and foliar feeding are essential. Principally affected by scale insect.

V.anaromatica Griseb. See *V.inodora*.
V.articulata Northr. See *V.barbellata*.

V.barbellata Rchb. f. (*V.articulata* Northr.).
Stems 1cm diam., terete, branching, succulent, of indefinite length. Lvs to 4cm, lanceolate, short-lived. Racemes axillary, to 12-fld; fls yellow-green or buff, lip white, purple towards apex; sep. 40–48×12–15mm, elliptic; pet. 40×16mm, elliptic, keeled; lip to 33mm long, 42mm wide when flattened, funnel-shaped, the edge undulate, with disc of white hairs, becoming yellow papillae near apex; column to 3cm. Capsule to 10×1cm, pendent, cylindrical. Summer. S Florida, Cuba, W Indies.

V.fragrans (Salisb.) Ames. See *V.planifolia*.
V.grandiflora Lindl. See *V.pompona*.

V.humblotii Rchb. f.
Stems 1–1.5cm diam., green-brown, of indefinite length. Lvs vestigial, scale-like. Panicles to 30cm, axillary, 12–20-fld; fls bright yellow, lip with chestnut-brown patch in throat; sep. 6–7×2cm, lanceolate; pet. somewhat longer and broader; lip 6cm, funnel-shaped, the edge undulate, with short brown papillae and rosy red hairs over 1 cm long in throat. Comoros Is.

V.imperialis Kränzl.
Stems green, succulent, very long. Lvs to 28×12cm, subsessile, succulent, elliptic. Racemes to 15cm, densely several- to many-fld; bracts imbricate, 1–3cm; fls yellow or cream, lip blotched with rose-pink or purple; sep. and pet. 6–8cm, lanceolate or oblanceolate; lip 5–7cm forming a tube narrow at the base, much expanded above with lacerate scales in the centre and long hairs toward apex, apex undulate and reflexed; column 4cm, joined to lip for most of its length. Ivory Coast, Ghana,

Cameroun, Congo, Zaire, Uganda, Tanzania.

V.inodora Schiede (*V.anaromatica* Griseb.).
Stem to 8mm diam., green, terete, succulent. Lvs to 25×12cm, broadly ovate, apiculate, yellow-green. Racemes axillary, 5–6-fld; fls yellow-green, lip white with yellow crest; sep. 5.5×2cm, oblong-lanceolate, thick-textured; pet. similar but narrower; lip to 5cm long, 3cm white when flattened, funnel-shaped, the edge undulate, with fleshy crest in centre; column 2.5cm. Spring–autumn. Florida, C America, W Indies, NE South America.

V.phaeantha Rchb. f.
Stem to 8mm diam., green, terete, of indefinite length. Lvs 10–12×3.5cm, oblong, fleshy. Racemes axillary, several-fld; fls short-lived, pale green, the lip white striped with yellow; sep. and pet. 9×1.5cm, oblanceolate; lip adnate to column, tubular, narrow at base, expanded above, undulate and reflexed at apex; disc composed of papillae; column 6.5cm. Capsule 10×1cm, pendent, cylindrical. Late spring–summer. Florida, W Indies.

V.phalaenopsis Rchb. f. ex Van Houtte (*V.roscheri* Rchb. f.).
Stems 10–20mm diam., succulent, of indefinite length. Lvs vestigial, brown, to 3cm. Raceme to 30cm, many-fld; fls white flushed with pink, salmon, coral-pink or yellow in the throat, sweet-scented; sep. to 8×2.5cm, lanceolate-oblong, apiculate; pet. similar but wider; lip to 8×4.5cm, funnel-shaped, with 4 rows of laciniate crests and digitate lamellae toward the base; column to 2.5cm long. Capsule to 17.5cm×7.5mm. Seychelles, Kenya, Tanzania, Mozambique, S Africa (Natal).

V.planifolia G. Jackson (*V.fragrans* (Salisb.) Ames). VANILLA.
Stems 1cm diam., green, terete, of indefinite length. Lvs 15×5cm, oblong, fleshy. Racemes axillary, densely several-fld;

Vanilla (a) *V.planifolia* (b) *V.phalaenopsis*

fls pale yellow-green, the lip with yellow hairs; sep. and pet. 5–6×1cm, oblanceolate; lip 4×3cm, tubular, adnate to column margin fringed, curled back; column 3.5cm. Capsule 15–25cm, pendent, cylindrical. Spring. Florida, W Indies, C & S America. 'Variegata': stems and lvs striped yellow to cream.

V.polylepis Summerh.
Stems to 8m long, 1–1.5cm diam., succulent, bright green. Lvs to 24×6.5cm, fleshy, lanceolate to ovate. Racemes to 20-fld, with 1–3 fls opening at a time; fls white or green-white, the lip yellow in throat and usually maroon-purple towards apex; sep. to 6×2cm, oblanceolate, fleshy; pet. similar but slightly wider and less fleshy, with exterior keel terminating in a point about 2mm long; lip to 6×2.5cm, adnate to column for 3cm at base, funnel-shaped, the edge undulate; disc with up to 12 rows of branched scales 2mm long, the basal 3cm of lip papillose; col-

umn to 4.5cm. Capsule to 15×1.5cm. Zaire, Kenya, Zambia, Malawi, Zimbabwe, Angola.

V.pompona Schiede (*V.grandiflora* Lindl.).
Scandent, rooting at nodes. Lvs to 25×10cm, fleshy, ovate to oblong; petiole to 2cm. Raceme to 10cm; fls green-yellow with orange-yellow marks on lip; pedicel and ovary to 5cm; bracts to 1.5cm, ovate; sep. and pet. to 8×1cm, spreading, fleshy, narrowly oblanceolate, acute or subobtuse with dorsal keel; lip to 8×4cm, adnate to column at base, more or less tubular, apex undulate, bilobed or emarginate; disc with warty veins and dentate lamellae. Capsule to 15cm, aromatic. C America, tropical S America, Trinidad; naturalized Lesser Antilles.

V.roscheri Rchb. f. See *V.phalaenopsis*.

× **Vascostylis** (*Ascocentrum* × *Rhynchostylis* × *Vanda*). These trigeneric hybrids are mostly made by crossing *Ascocenda* hybrids with species of *Rhynchostylis*. The stems are upright with the alternate leaves in two rows, leaves narrowly channelled. The inflorescences are axillary, on upright spikes, sometimes branching. The flowers are rounded with flat sepals and petals and a small lip, usually very brightly coloured, often in shades of blue and violet. The plants need bright light, high humidity and warm temperatures to grow and flower well. They grow extremely well out of doors in the humid tropics but are less easy in the glasshouse.

× *V.*Precious: upright spikes of large rich blue fls.
× *V.*Susan 'Hansley': upright spikes of deep blue fls with white column and base of lip.

× **Vuylstekeara** (*Cochlioda* × *Miltonia* × *Odontoglossum*). A trigeneric hybrid usually made from *Odontioda* × *Miltonia* crosses. Plants consist of a group of compressed pseudobulbs growing from a basal rhizome, each with one or two leaves at its apex and two or more leaf-like sheaths arising at its base. Inflorescences arise in the axils of these sheaths and may be simple or branched. Flowers with well shaped sepals and petals, lip large, often conspicuously marked in a variety of colours. Most of these hybrids are 'cool' growers though a few are tolerant of warmer conditions.

× *V.*Cambria 'Plush': tall spikes with large fls; sep. and pet. rich vivid crimson, lip white, heavily speckled with crimson, with a crimson base around the yellow crest; the clone 'Lensing's Favourite' is a yellow form which arose in meristem propagation.
× *V.*Edna 'Stamperland': medium size fls of intense colours on tall spikes; sep. and pet. scarlet, lip rosy red.
× *V.*Frederica 'Perfection': well shaped fls with white background and distinctive purple spots in the middle of sep. and pet. and lip, crest yellow.

× *V.*Jersey: richly coloured fls with very little white between the dark wine red spots of the sep. and pet., lip large, similar to sep. and pet. but with magenta border and yellow crest.
× *V.*Rutilant 'Colombia': sturdy plants with fine sprays of bright red fls with a yellow crest.

Warmingia Rchb. f. (For Prof. Eugenius Warming (1841–1924), who discovered the type species.) Some 2 species of epiphytes. Pseudobulbs short, unifoliate. Leaves coriaceous, oblong or narrowly oblong. Inflorescence near base of pseudobulb, an axillary raceme, pendent, loosely to densely few-flowered; flowers small, white; sepals subequal, free; petals similar, denticulate; lip sessile, continuous with column base, spreading, distinctly 3-lobed, lateral lobes short, divergent, denticulate, midlobe elongate, disc bicallose, sulcate; column short, free, erect, subterete, wingless, footless, apex curved, anther terminal, operculate, incumbent, unilocular or imperfectly bilocular, pollinia 2, waxy, subglobose, stipe triangular. Brazil.

CULTIVATION Intermediate-growing orchids requiring a medium-gauge bark mix, a short, semi-dry winter rest, and dappled sunlight.

W.eugenii Rchb. f.
Pseudobulbs to 2×0.4cm, cylindrical or conical to oblong, compressed. Lvs to 10×2.5cm, narrowly elliptic-oblong or subspathulate, obtuse or subacute, short-petiolate. Infl. to 12cm, many-fld, robust; fls translucent white; sep. to 1.5×0.3cm, narrowly lanceolate, acute or acuminate; pet. to 1.4×0.4cm, ligulate-lanceolate, denticulate-fimbriate, long-acuminate; lip to 1.1×0.6cm, 3-lobed toward base, lateral lobes rounded, irregularly lacerate-dentate, midlobe linear-lanceolate or oblanceolate, acuminate, obscurely serrate, callus yellow, basal; column to 3mm, subcylindrical, apex bilobed. E Brazil.

Warrea Lindl. (For the English plant collector Frederick Warre.) 7 species of terrestrials. Rhizome short. Pseudobulbs cylindrical to ovoid or ellipsoid, short, enveloped by several leaf sheaths. Leaves few, distichous, plicate, articulated, conduplicate at base. Inflorescence a raceme, lateral, from base of pseudobulbs, erect, few- to many-flowered; flowers often large, showy; sepals subequal, concave, dorsal sepal free, lateral sepals connate to column foot, oblique; petals subsimilar to sepals, slightly smaller; lip adnate to column foot, concave, simple to obscurely trilobed, lateral lobes erect, clasping column, midlobe rounded or bilobulate, disc fleshy, carinate or crested; column stout, clavate, wingless, often elongate, semiterete, with a short foot, anther terminal, operculate, incumbent, bilocular, pollinia 4, waxy, subglobose. C America and Northern S America.

CULTIVATION As for *Phaius*.

W.costaricensis Schltr.
Pseudobulbs often poorly developed, cylindrical. Lvs to 60×7.5cm, lanceolate, acute or acuminate, prominently veined, short-petiolate. Infl. equalling or surpassing lvs; fls to 6.5cm diam., red-bronze, the lip pale copper with darker markings; sep. to 3.5×1.5cm, concave, ovate-oblong, obtuse; pet. to 3×1.5cm, obliquely obovate, obtuse; lip to 3×3cm, entire, suborbicular, callus to 1.5cm, basal, narrow; column to 2.5cm, slender, arched. Summer. Costa Rica, Panama.

W.cyanea Lindl. See *Warreella cyanea*.
W.tricolor Lindl. See *W.warreana*.

W.warreana (Lodd. ex Lindl.) Schweinf. (*W.tricolor* Lindl.; *Aganisia tricolor* (Lindl.) Bois).
Pseudobulbs to 12×2.5cm, ovoid, conical or ellipsoid. Lvs to 60×10cm, oblong-lanceolate to elliptic-lanceolate, acuminate. Infl. to 100cm, stout, loosely several- to many-fld; fls fleshy, nodding, yellow-brown to white, the lip ivory, edged white with a purple blotch; sep. to 3.5×2.5cm, ovate or ovate-elliptic, acute to obtuse, apiculate; pet. similar to dorsal sep., slightly smaller; lip to 3.5×3.5cm, simple or subsimple, suborbicular to obovate-rhombic, slightly emarginate, subcrenulate, disc fleshy, 3-ridged; column to 2.5cm, curved, subclavate. Colombia, Venezuela, Brazil, Peru.

Warreella Schltr. (Diminutive of *Warrea*.) 2 species, epiphytes or terrestrials allied to *Warrea*. Pseudobulbs to 5×1.7cm, ovoid, smooth, olive green to yellow-brown, concealed by leaf sheaths. Leaves to 40×4.5cm, lanceolate-acuminate, conduplicate, usually equitant. Raceme to 60cm, solitary, basal, emerging from axils of leaf sheaths, many-flowered; peduncle flushed red-maroon; sepals to 1.6×0.7cm, white flushed pale pink, elliptic to elliptic-oblong, obtuse; petals similar to sepals but smaller and narrower, oblique; lip to 1.4×1cm, white flushed rose to purple, simple, obovate to elliptic, truncate to emarginate, undulate, disc 3–5-ridged, white; column to 0.7cm, white, curved, anther white. Colombia, Venezuela.

CULTIVATION As for *Phaius*.

W.cyanea (Lindl.) Schltr. (*Warrea cyanea* Lindl.; *Maxillaria cyanea* (Lindl.) Beer).
Described above.

× **Wilsonara** (*Cochlioda* × *Odontoglossum* × *Oncidium*). One of the earliest of the trigeneric hybrids, usually crosses between *Odontioda* and *Oncidium* or *Odontocidium*. Plants consist of a group of compressed pseudobulbs growing from a basal rhizome, each with one or two leaves at its apex and two or more leaf-like sheaths arising at its base. Inflorescences arise in the axils of these sheaths and may be simple or branched. Flowers very varied, usually with rounded shape, of many colours often conspicuously marked in a variety of colours. Most of these hybrids are 'cool' growers though a few are tolerant of warmer conditions.

× *W.*Gold Moselle: large branching sprays of brightly coloured fls of small to medium size; fls bright yellow, heavily overlaid with small red-brown spots that coalesce, lip large, less heavily spotted with brown-red.

× *W.*Tiger Talk: tall branching sprays with many small to medium fls; sep. and pet. deep chestnut brown tipped with cream, lip golden yellow with cream apex.

× *W.*Widecombe Fair: enormous branching sprays of small white fls heavily marked with deep mauve spots.

Xylobium Lindl. (From the Gk *xylon*, wood, and *bios*, life, referring to epiphytic habit of the species.) Some 30 species of epiphytes or terrestrials allied to *Maxillaria*. Rhizome short. Pseudobulbs short to elongate, strongly furrowed, apically unifoliate to trifoliate. Leaves large, plicate, short to long-petiolate. Inflorescence from base of pseudobulb, a raceme, erect or arching, short or elongate, few to many-flowered; flowers rarely showy, short-pedicellate; sepals subequal, erect, spreading, dorsal sepal free, lateral sepals connate to column foot forming a short mentum; petals similar to dorsal sepal, smaller; lip loosely hinged to column foot, sessile, entire to conspicuously 3-lobed, lateral lobes erect, clasping column, midlobe short, spreading, often papillose, disc fleshy, callose; column short, erect, slightly arcuate, subterete, sulcate, with a prominent foot, anther terminal, incumbent, operculate, unilocular, pollinia 4, waxy, ovoid. Tropical America.

CULTIVATION Intermediate-growing orchids requiring an open bark potting mix, bright, humid conditions and a slight winter rest.

X.bractescens (Lindl.) Kränzl. (*Maxillaria bractescens* Lindl.). Pseudobulbs to 3cm, oblong-conical to ovoid-conical. Lvs to 30×6cm, 1 at apex of pseudobulb, oblong-elliptic, acute. Infl. to 45cm, arching, loosely several-fld; fls large; sep. and pet. dull yellow or green-yellow, dorsal sep. to 20×5mm, oblong-lanceolate, acute, margins revolute, lateral sep. subequal, triangular-lanceolate, falcate; pet. to 17×4mm, oblong-lanceolate; lip to 18mm, red-brown, apex recurved, lateral lobes ovate-triangular, recurved, midlobe large, ovate, callus oblong; column short, stout. Ecuador, Peru.

X.elongatum (Lindl. & Paxt.) Hemsl. (*Maxillaria elongata* Lindl. & Paxt.). Pseudobulbs to 27×1.5cm, cylindrical, clustered, bifoliate. Lvs to 40×10cm, elliptic to oblong-lanceolate, acute or acuminate, long- or short-petiolate. Infl. to 30cm, several- to many-fld; fls large, fleshy, white to pale yellow, often marked brown or purple; sep. to 25×6mm, lanceolate to oblong-lanceolate, acute or acuminate, lateral sep. oblique, falcate; pet. to 18×5mm, obliquely oblong-lanceolate, acuminate, involute; lip to 20×9mm, lateral lobes rounded, erose, midlobe ovate-oblong, obtuse, fleshy, margins upcurved, with numerous red-purple papillae, callus 3–5-keeled, densely papillose or tuberculate; column to 13mm, stout, arcuate, compressed. Mexico, Guatemala, Costa Rica, Panama.

X.foveatum (Lindl.) Nichols. (*Maxillaria foveata* Lindl.; *Maxillaria concava* Lindl.). Pseudobulbs to 10×4cm, ovoid to oblong-conical, often clustered, bifoliate or trifoliate. Lvs to 45×7cm, elliptic to oblanceolate, acute or acuminate. Infl. to 30cm, suberect to arching, subdensely many-fld; fls white to yellow; sep. to 15×5mm, elliptic-oblong to oblong-lanceolate, acute, lateral sep. falcate; pet. to 10×4mm, oblique, lanceolate to elliptic-lanceolate, obtuse; lip white, sometimes striped red, lateral lobes upcurved, rounded or truncate, midlobe suborbicular, retuse or truncate, fleshy, callus 3- to 5-keeled; column to 10mm, stout. Mexico, Guatemala to Panama, northern S America.

X.gracile Schltr. See *X.leontoglossum*.

X.leontoglossum (Rchb. f.) Benth. ex Rolfe (*Maxillaria leontoglossa* Rchb. f.; *X.gracile* Schltr.). Pseudobulbs to 9cm, ovoid-fusiform, clustered, unifoliate. Lvs to 90×11cm, suberect, elliptic-lanceolate, acute, long-petiolate. Infl. erect to arching, stout, densely few- to many-fld; fls cream to golden-yellow spotted pale red, sometimes tinged maroon; sep. to 27×12mm, oblong-lanceolate, acute;

pet. to 25×7mm, oblong-oblanceolate, acute; lip white to pale yellow, to 20×11mm, lateral lobes narrow, erose, midlobe suborbicular, fleshy, apex rounded, with numerous pink papillae, callus oblong; column white, short. Colombia, Peru, Ecuador, Venezuela.

X.pallidiflorum (Hook.) Nichols. (*Maxillaria pallidiflora* Hook.; *Maxillaria stenobulbon* Klotzsch). Pseudobulbs to 18×1cm, narrowly cylindrical or stem-like, unifoliate. Lvs to 41×8.5cm, elliptic to oblong-elliptic, acute or acuminate. Infl. to 18.5cm, erect to arching, loosely few to several-fld; fls white to yellow-green or pale green; sep. to 18×6mm, oblong-lanceolate, acute, lateral sep.; pet. to 12×4mm, similar to dorsal sep.; lip to 14×7mm, white to yellow-orange, ovate to elliptic-oblong, cuneate below, apical portion obscurely lobed, midlobe with numerous white papillae, callus tricarinate; column to 10mm, green-white, stout. W Indies, Venezuela to Peru.

X.palmifolium (Sw.) Fawcett (*Maxillaria decolor* Lindl.; *Maxillaria palmifolia* (Sw.) Lindl.). Pseudobulbs to 7.5cm, ovoid-cylindrical, unifoliate, compressed. Lvs to 42×8cm, broadly lanceolate to oblong-lanceolate, acuminate. Infl. to 10cm, loosely few to many-fld; fls fragrant; sep. and pet. white to yellow-white, dorsal sep. to 18×5mm, ovate-oblong, acute, lateral sep. to 22×9mm, triangular-lanceolate, oblique, pet. to 14×3mm, linear-oblong, acuminate; lip white, entire or obscurely 3-lobed, to 16×9mm, obovate-oblong, apex fleshy, retuse, verrucose, margins incurved, crisped, disc with 5 thickened calli; column to 14mm. W Indies.

X.squalens (Lindl.) Lindl. See *X.variegatum*.

X.variegatum (Ruiz & Pav.) Garay & Dunsterv. (*Maxillaria variegata* Ruiz & Pav.; *X.squalens* (Lindl.) Lindl.; *Maxillaria squalens* (Lindl.) Hook.). Pseudobulbs to 8×4.5cm, ovoid to pyriform, dark purple-brown with age, bifoliate or trifoliate. Lvs to 70×10cm, oblong-lanceolate to oblong-elliptic, acute, petiolate. Infl. to 20cm, densely many-fld; sep. and pet. pale yellow-white to flesh-colour, sep. to 26×9mm, oblong-lanceolate to ovate-lanceolate, acute, lateral sep. falcate, oblique, pet. to 20×5mm, obliquely lanceolate or ovate-lanceolate, acute; lip to 19×11mm, flesh-colour, flushed maroon, apex dark maroon-violet, slightly arcuate, lateral lobes semi-obovate, apex rounded, erose, midlobe oblong to suborbicular, densely verrucose, callus central, oblong, tricarinate; column to 5mm, stout. Costa Rica, Venezuela, Colombia, Ecuador, Peru, Bolivia, Brazil.

Ypsilopus Summerh. (From Gk *ypsilon*, the letter Y, and *pous*, foot, referring to the Y-shaped stipites.) About 4 species of epiphytes; stems short. Leaves linear. Racemes arising from leaf axils; flowers white or green; sepals and petals free, spreading, petals slightly shorter and narrower than sepals; lip rhomboid-lanceolate, spurred; column short; pollinia 2, stipites divided into 2 in upper half, the apices somewhat enlarged; viscidium 1. Kenya, Tanzania, Malawi, Zambia, Zimbabwe.

CULTIVATION As for *Aerangis*.

Y.erectus (Cribb) Cribb & Joyce Stewart.
Stem 2–3cm; erect, covered with old lf bases; roots smooth, grey, 3–4mm diam. Lvs 4–5 forming fan, 6–15×0.5–1cm, linear, folded, sometimes slightly recurved. Racemes 1–2 arising from base of plant, arched, to 12cm, 3–12-fld; fls white, scented; pedicel and ovary 15mm; sep. 8×3mm, lanceolate, acute, margins recurved, dorsal sep. erect, lateral sep. deflexed; pet. 7×2mm, reflexed, lanceolate, acuminate; lip entire, 7×3mm, rhombic; spur 5–6cm, very slender, slightly incurved, turning green towards tip; column 1.5mm; anth. cap brown. Tanzania, Malawi, Zambia, Zimbabwe, S Africa (Natal).

Y.longifolius (Kränzl.) Summerh.
Pendent; stem to 4cm. Lvs several, 5–23cm×1.5–4mm, narrowly linear, acute. Racemes pendent, 3–8cm, 2–9-fld; fls 15mm diam., white, turning green toward tips of seg.; pedicel

and ovary 9–12mm, scabrid; sep. ovate-lanceolate, acute, dorsal sep. 6–7.5×2.5–4mm, lateral sep. 6–9×2–3mm, rather oblique; pet. 5.5–6.5×2–3mm, lanceolate, acuminate; lip 6.5–7.5×2–3.5mm, slightly recurved, ovate or rhombic, obscurely trilobed in middle, apex fleshy, acute; spur 3.5–4cm, pendent, slender; column 1.5–2.5mm. Kenya, Tanzania.

Y.viridiflorus Cribb & Joyce Stewart.
Pendent; stem to 3cm. Lvs iris-like, 4–25cm×2–5mm, linear, acuminate, bilaterally flattened. Infl. 2–6cm, usually 1-fld, sometimes 2-fld; peduncle wiry, to 5cm; fls green-white or pale yellow-green, outside scabrid; pedicel and ovary 5–7mm; sep. 7–9×1.5–2mm, lanceolate, acute, lateral sep. somewhat oblique; pet. 6–8×1.5–2mm, linear-lanceolate, acuminate; lip entire, 7–8×2mm, lanceolate, acuminate, deflexed; spur 15–18mm, pendent, slender; column 1mm. Tanzania.

Zeuxine Lindl. (From Gk *zeuxis*, yoking, referring to the partial union of the lip and column.) Some 70 species of terrestrials lacking pseudobulbs. Stem creeping and ascending, glabrous. Leaves alternate or loosely spiralling to rosulate at stem summit, often membranaceous, sessile or petiolate. Inflorescence terminal, few- to many-flowered; flowers small, not opening well; sepals subequal, dorsal sepal forming a hood with petals, concave, lateral sepals free; lip sessile, base often saccate, centre contracted, apex dilated; column short, anther dorsal, bilocular, pollinia 2, pyriform. Tropical Africa to Tropical Asia and Fiji Is.

CULTIVATION As for *Anoectochilus*, but most (except *Zz. regia* and *violascens* here) will tolerate cool to intermediate temperatures.

Z.goodyeroides Lindl. (*Monochilus galeatus* Lindl.).
Lvs to 5×2cm, ovate, acute, deep velvety green, often flushed purple below, midvein white-green. Infl. loosely few-fld; fls to 6mm diam., interior white, exterior red; dorsal sep. ovate, acute, lateral sep. lanceolate; pet. falcate, obtuse; lip saccate, midlobe small. Himalaya.

Z.regia (Lindl.) Trimen (*Monochilus regius* Lindl.).
Stem leafy at base, few-lvd. Lvs to 6.5×1.5cm, deep velvety green, midvein white-green. Infl. loosely few-fld; fls to 6mm diam.; sep. and pet. green; lip complex, snow-white. S India, Ceylon.

Z.strateumatica (L.) Schltr.
Stem often tinged purple, several-lvd. Lvs to 7cm, sessile,

narrowly linear, often flushed purple. Infl. to 5cm, densely fld; fls to 1cm diam.; sep. and pet. white, green-white or pink, sep. to 4mm, dorsal sep. ovate, concave, lateral sep. lanceolate, pet. oblong, obtuse; lip bright yellow to yellow-green, saccate, midlobe subquadrate, entire or bifid. Afghanistan to S China, SE Asia to Malay Peninsula, naturalized Florida.

Z.violascens Ridl.
Stem to 20cm, leafy at base. Lvs to 2.5×1cm, stalked, dark purple-green, midvein paler. Infl. to 10cm, slender, few-fld; peduncle pilose; fls to 12mm diam., white or rose-pink; lip with a small yellow blotch. Sumatra, Borneo, Malay Peninsula.

Zootrophion Luer. (From Gk for menagerie, an allusion to the resemblance of the flowers to the heads of various animals.) Some 12 species of epiphytes allied to *Masdevallia* and *Pleurothallis*. Rhizome short. Pseudobulbs absent. Secondary stems short, tufted, enveloped by scarious sheaths, each bearing a single, terminal leaf. Leaves subcoriaceous or coriaceous, duplicate, articulated. Flowers solitary, often small, born below articulation of leaf; dorsal sepal concave, connate to lateral sepals at base and apex, forward-pointing like a skull or a set of mandibles; petals smaller than sepals, acute; lip articulated to column foot, trilobed, lateral lobes erect, acute; disc with a thick basal callus; column erect, subterete, winged, anther terminal, operculate, unilocular, pollinia 2, waxy. Tropical S America.

CULTIVATION As for *Masdevallia*.

Z.atropurpureum (Lindl.) Luer (*Specklinia atropurpurea* Lindl.; *Pleurothallis atropurpurea* (Lindl.) Lindl.; *Cryptophoranthus atropurpureus* (Lindl.) Rolfe).
Stems to 50cm. Lvs to 9×3cm, coriaceous, elliptic-obovate, subobtuse, short-petiolate. Fl. deep crimson; sep. to 15×5mm; pet. to 4×2mm, oblong, truncate; lip to 4×1mm, hastate, lateral lobes folded in front, base minutely biauriculate; column to 2mm, erect. Jamaica, Panama, Colombia, Ecuador, Peru.

Z.dayanum (Rchb. f.) Luer (*Masdevallia dayana* Rchb. f.; *Cryptophoranthus dayanus* (Rchb. f.) Rolfe).
Stems to 11cm. Lvs to 10×5.5cm, erect, ovate to elliptic, subobtuse, apiculate, short-petiolate. Fl. pendent, yellow or golden-yellow, marked dark red-purple; sep. to 4cm, elliptic-oblong, lateral sep. smaller, oblique, pet. minute, obliquely ovate-subquadrate; lip to 6mm, clawed, lateral lobes small, midlobe triangular-hastate, acute; column short, arcuate. Peru, Colombia.

Zygopetalum Hook. (From Gk *zygon*, yoke, and *petalon*, petal, referring to the fusing of sepals and petals with the base of the column.) Some 20 species of epiphytes or terrestrials. Rhizome short. Pseudobulbs short, stout, fleshy, basally enveloped by long-sheathed leaves, apex 2- to several-leaved, stems sometimes leafy and cane-like, not pseudobulbous. Leaves distichous, elongate, often glossy, thin-textured, shallowly plicate or strongly ribbed, especially on articulate sheath of basal leaves. Inflorescence a raceme from base of pseudobulb, short or elongate, erect or arching, 1- to many-flowered; flowers small to large, showy, spreading, waxy, white, yellow or green banded or mottled maroon to magenta, lip far paler, often white suffused rose to violet, sometimes fragrant; sepals and petals subsimilar, free or shortly connate, lateral sepals adnate to column foot forming a short mentum; lip articulated to column foot, sessile, deeply or obscurely trilobed, lateral lobes often small, spreading or erect, midlobe broadly spreading, disc basal, with a prominent, polymorphic callus, entire, lobed or dentate, often transverse; column short, stout, subterete, incurved, base produced into a short foot, apex sometimes 2-winged, anther terminal. Operculate, incumbent, bilocular, pollinia 4, waxy, obovoid. Mexico to Peru & Brazil.

CULTIVATION   For the cool and intermediate house, producing erect racemes of fleshy, often highly fragrant blooms in shades of green, brown and violet. General requirements as for *Odontoglossum*.

Z.aromaticum Rchb. f. See *Z.wendlandii*.

Z.brachypetalum Lindl.
Pseudobulbs to 5cm, ovoid-oblong, apex bifoliate or trifoliate. Lvs to 60cm, lanceolate-ensiform. Infl. surpassing lvs, erect, several-fld; fls to 3.5cm, waxy, fragrant, long-lived; tepals green mottled brown or purple-brown, sep. to 3×1cm, oblong, acute or acuminate; pet. to 2.5×1cm, linear-ligulate, acute, convex; lip to 3×2.5cm, white, streaked red-violet or blue-violet, obovate, base cuneate, retuse or emarginate, undulate; column to 12mm, bright green, clavate. Brazil.

Z.brachystalix Rchb. f. See *Otostylis brachystalix*.
Z.burkei Rchb. f. See *Mendoncella burkei*.
Z.cerinum (Lindl.) Rchb. f. See *Pescatorea cerina*.
Z.cochleare Lindl. See *Cochleanthes flabelliformis*.

Z.crinitum Lodd. (*Z.mackayi* var. *crinitum* (Lodd.) Lindl.; *Z.pubescens* Hoffsgg.)
Pseudobulbs to 7×4cm, elongate-ovoid, slightly grooved, lustrous dark green. Lvs to 40×5cm, lanceolate or linear-lanceolate, acute or acuminate, lustrous green. Infl. to 50cm, erect-spreading, few to several-fld; fls 6.25–9cm, diam., strongly fragrant, long-lived, waxy; tepals grey-green or yellow-green, streaked and spotted chestnut-brown, sep. 27.5–50× 7.5–15mm, fleshy, oblong to obovate-oblong, acute; pet. slightly narrower than lateral sep., oblong, acute; lip to 50×38mm, white veined red or purple, veins densely pubesc., obscurely 3-lobed, lateral lobes small, auriculate, midlobe obovate, rounded, slightly emarginate, undulate-crenulate, callus small, yellow, incurved, deeply sulcate to centre; column to 20mm, white or yellow lined red, apex narrowly 2-winged, basally villous. E Brazil.

Z.gramineum Lindl. See *Kefersteinia graminea*.

Z.graminifolium Rolfe.
Pseudobulbs to 5cm, distant on rhiz., apex usually bifoliate or trifoliate. Lvs to 40×1.5cm, narrowly linear-lanceolate, grass-like. Infl. equalling lvs, densely several to many-fld; fls to 5.5cm diam.; tepals green, densely marked and blotched grey-maroon or black-brown; sep. to 25×7mm, oblong-spathulate, acute, concave; pet. similar to sep.; convex; lip violet-blue streaked white, to 23×20mm, subsessile, broadly obovate or obcordate, subtruncate, emarginate, slightly undulate, glabrous, callus sulcate; column to 15mm, clavate, glabrous. Brazil.

Z.grandiflorum (A. Rich.) Benth. & Hook. ex Hemsl. See *Mendoncella grandiflora*.

Z.intermedium Lindl. (*Z.mackayi* Paxt. non Hook.).
Pseudobulbs to 8×5cm, ovoid-conical, 3- to 5-leaved. Lvs to 50×6cm, ligulate to elliptic-lanceolate, acute or acuminate, lustrous bright green. Infl. to 40cm, suberect, few-fld; fls to 7.5cm diam., waxy, scented strongly of hyacinths, long-lived; tepals green or yellow-green, blotched red-brown or crimson, oblong-lanceolate; lip to 35×30mm, white with numerous radiating purple-violet lines, broadly obovate to flabellate,

basally 3-lobed, lateral lobes small, auriculate, midlobe obovate to obcordate, emarginate, undulate, callus horseshoe-shaped, sulcate; column to 13mm, pilose. Peru, Bolivia, Brazil.

Z.jorisianum Rolfe. See *Mendoncella jorisiana*.
Z.lacteum Rchb. f. See *Kefersteinia lactea*.
Z.lindeniae Rolfe. See *Zygosepalum lindeniae*.

Z.mackayi Hook.
Closely resembles *Z.intermedium* except infl. to 70cm; tepals often incurved, pet. smaller than sep.; lip broadly fan-shaped or subquadrate, glabrous; column glabrous. Brazil.

Z.mackayi Paxt. non Hook. nec (Lodd.) Lindl. See *Zygopetalum intermedium*.
Z.mackayi var. *crinitum* (Lodd.) Lindl. non Hook. nec Paxt. See *Z.crinitum*.

Z.maxillare Lodd.
Pseudobulbs to 7.5cm, ovoid-oblong, apex bifoliate or trifoliate. Lvs to 35×2.5cm, conspicuously veined, narrowly lanceolate, subacuminate. Infl. to 35cm, erect or arching, several-fld; fls to 6cm, waxy, fragrant, long-lived; tepals light green blotched and barred bronze-brown; sep. to 25×10mm, oblong, acute or acuminate; pet. to 22×8mm, oblong-lanceolate, acuminate; lip violet-blue or purple-blue, 3-lobed, lateral lobes narrowly oblong, erect, midlobe subrotund-obovate, emarginate, convex, undulate, callus violet-purple, semilunate, fleshy, grooved; column to 11mm, subclavate, glabrous. Brazil, Paraguay.

Z.mosenianum Barb. Rodr.
Stems to 150cm, scandent, leafy, clothed with sheathing lf-bases. Lvs to 25×3.5cm, articulated to lf-bases, deciduous, arching, linear-lanceolate, acuminate. Infl. to 40cm, few to several-fld; fls to 5cm diam., waxy, fragrant; tepals pale green blotched purple-brown, sep. fleshy, to 25×10mm, ovate-lanceolate, acute, pet. to 23×8mm, ligulate-lanceolate, acute; lip to 26×20mm, white, with radiating violet lines, fleshy, obovate, emarginate, base truncate, undulate, disc fleshy, semicircular, with violet hairs; column to 13mm, subclavate. Brazil.

Z.murrayanum Gardn. See *Neogardneria murrayana*.
Z.prainianum Rolfe. See *Mendoncella burkei*.
Z.pubescens Hoffsgg. See *Z.crinitum*.
Z.rostratum Hook. See *Zygosepalum labiosum*.
Z.sanguinolentum (Rchb. f.) Rchb. f. See *Kefersteinia sanguinolenta*.
Z.tatei Ames & Schweinf. See *Zygosepalum tatei*.
Z.tricolor Lindl. See *Koellensteinia tricolor*.

Z.wendlandii Rchb. f. (*Warscewiczella wendlandii* (Rchb. f.) Schltr.; *Z.aromaticum* Rchb. f.; *Chondrorhyncha aromatica* (Rchb. f.) P. Allen).
Lvs to 30×2.5cm, linear-ligulate to elliptic-lanceolate, acute or acuminate. Infl. to 9cm, 1-fld; fls large; tepals pale green or yellow-green, dorsal sep. to 30×8mm, elliptic-lanceolate, acuminate, lateral sep. to 32×10mm, lanceolate, acuminate,

Zygopetalum   (a) *Z.intermedium*   (b) *Z.crinitum*   (c) *Z.maxillare*

pet. to 30×6mm, lanceolate, acuminate, spreading; lip to 25×17mm, lavender or violet, margins white, subpandurate, obscurely 3-lobed, apex reflexed, undulate, callus lunate to rhombic, sulcate, violet; column white, narrowly bialate. Costa Rica, Panama.

Zygosepalum Rchb. f. (From Gk *zygon*, yoke, and Lat. *sepalum*, sepal.) Some 6 species of epiphytes. Rhizome ascending, simple or branched. Pseudobulbs often remote, enveloped by several, distichous, overlapping, leafy sheaths when young, 1–4-leaved at apex. Leaves plicate, linear-lanceolate to lanceolate. Inflorescence lateral, 1- to few-flowered; peduncle sheathed; flowers large, showy; sepals similar, free, lateral sepals adnate to column foot; petals subsimilar to sepals; lip conspicuous, adnate to apex of column foot forming a short mentum, basally dilated, simple to trilobed, ovate to suborbicular-obovate, disc with a basal, lunate callus; column semiterete, with a basal foot, apex winged, clinandrium fimbriate-dentate, anther rostrate, operculate, incumbent, pollinia 4, obovoid. Venezuela, Colombia, Peru, Brazil, Guianas.

CULTIVATION See *Zygopetalum*.

Z.labiosum (L.C. Rich.) Garay (*Zygopetalum rostratum* Hook.; *Z.rostratum* (Hook.) Rchb. f.).
Pseudobulbs to 6.5×3.5cm, ovoid-oblong, suberect, compressed. Lvs to 25×5cm, oblong-lanceolate to lanceolate, acuminate, suberect, apex recurved. Infl. to 20cm, usually 1-fld; peduncle recurved or ascending; fls to 5cm diam., green to yellow, suffused maroon at centre, the lip white striped violet at base, reflexed; sep. to 6×1.5cm, thin-textured, lanceolate, acuminate, concave; pet. shorter than sep., linear-lanceolate, acuminate, concave; lip to 5.5×5cm, short-unguiculate, obscurely 3-lobed, reflexed or ascending, ovate to suborbicular-ovate, acute to apiculate, callus violet, finely denticulate; column to 2.5cm, erect, white, suffused violet, erect. Colombia, Venezuela, Guianas, Brazil.

Z.lindeniae (Rolfe) Garay & Dunsterv. (*Zygopetalum lindeniae* Rolfe; *Menadenium lindeniae* (Rolfe) Cogn.).
Pseudobulbs to 6×3cm, ovoid to ovoid-elliptic, compressed. Lvs to 25×3cm, subcoriaceous, lanceolate, acute to acuminate. Infl. to 20cm, arching to pendent, fls white to rose, the lip white veined and edged rose-purple, linear-lanceolate, acuminate, concave; sep. to 60×10mm; pet. to 60×8mm; lip to 4.5cm, membranaceous, ovate, acute or acuminate, short-unguiculate, concave, callus fleshy, elevated; column to 2.5cm, rose, erect, wings subspathulate-obovate. Venezuela, Peru, Brazil.

Z.rostratum (Hook.) Rchb. f. See *Z.labiosum*.

Z.tatei (Ames & Schweinf.) Garay & Dunsterv. (*Zygopetalum tatei* Ames & Schweinf.).
Pseudobulbs to 6×1.5cm, cylindrical, compressed, grooved. Lvs to 16×2.5cm, subcoriaceous, oblong to oblanceolate, acute, often revolute. Infl. to 50cm, erect, few-fld, fls green or yellow-green to dull lavender-brown, marked dark brown, the lip white flushed pink-violet at base; sep. to 27×10mm, lanceolate to ovate-lanceolate, acute or acuminate; pet. to 27×8mm, oblong to oblong-lanceolate, acute, apiculate; lip to 25×25mm, apical portion ovate-rhombic to reniform, acute or rounded, slightly undulate, basal portion with a fleshy, elevated callus; column to 12mm, wings ovate to triangular, fleshy. Venezuela, Guyana, Brazil.

Zygostates Lindl. (From Gk *zygostates*, balance or scales; the two processes resemble a balance.) Some 4 species of dwarf epiphytes. Leaves fleshy to coriaceous, compressed, equitant, forming a fan, articulate, attached to thickened sheaths scarcely distinguished as pseudobulbs. Inflorescence an axillary raceme; flowers small; sepals subequal, free, spreading or reflexed; petals similar to sepals, broader; lip continuous with column base, simple, concave, spreading, with a fleshy, basal appendage; column subterete, arcuate, wingless, rostellum elongate, anther terminal, operculate, incumbent, unilocular, pollinia 4, ovoid. Brazil.

CULTIVATION As for *Oberonia*.

Z.alleniana Kränzl.
Lvs to 30×2mm, fleshy, linear, acuminate. Infl. to 4cm, erect, few-fld; fls minute, pellucid; sep. to 3mm, obovate-spathulate, rounded, reflexed; pet. to 4mm, clawed, spathulate, serrulate; lip to 4mm, navicular, acute, entire. Brazil.

Z.grandiflora (Lindl.) Cogn. See *Dipteranthus grandiflorus*.

Z.lunata Lindl. (*Ornithocephalus navicularis* Barb. Rodr.).
Lvs to 7×2cm, oblong-spathulate, obtuse. Infl. to 15cm, erect or arching, many-fld; fls minute; sep. to 4×2mm, white or yellow stained green, concave, ovate, acute, white-green; pet. to 4×5mm, lunate, serrate, green-yellow; lip to 5×3mm, white, concave, ovate, obtuse, fimbriate-serrulate, basal appendage subquadrate, yellow. Brazil.

Names no longer in use

Acropera Lindl.
   A.armeniaca Lindl. & Paxt. See *Gongora armeniaca.*
   A.cornuta Klotzsch. See *Gongora armeniaca.*
   A.loddigesii Lindl. See *Gongora galatea.*

Bothriochilus Lem.
   B.bellus Lem. See *Coelia bella.*
   B.densiflorus (Rolfe) Ames & Correll. See *Coelia densiflora.*
   B.guatemalensis (Rchb. f.) L.O. Williams. See *Coelia guatemalensis.*
   B.macrostachyus (Lindl.) L.O. Williams. See *Coelia macrostachya.*

Camarotis Lindl. See *Micropera.*

Cirrhopetalum Lindl.
   C.antenniferum Lindl. See *Bulbophyllum antenniferum.*
   C.biflorum (Teijsm. & Binnen.) J.J. Sm. See *Bulbophyllum biflorum.*
   C.cumingii Lindl. See *Bulbophyllum cumingii.*
   C.collettii Hemsl. See *Bulbophyllum wendlandianum.*
   C.fascinator Rolfe. See *Bulbophyllum putidum.*
   C.gracillimum Rolfe. See *Bulbophyllum gracillimum.*
   C.graveolens Bail. See *Bulbophyllum graveolens.*
   C.guttulatum Hook. f. See *Bulbophyllum guttulatum.*
   C.leopardinum Teisjm. & Binnend. See *Bulbophyllum binnendijkii.*
   C.longiflorum (Thouars) Schltr. See *Bulbophyllum longiflorum.*
   C.longissimum Ridl. See *Bulbophyllum longissimum.*
   C.maculosum Lindl. See *Bulbophyllum umbellatum.*
   C.mastersianum Rolfe. See *Bulbophyllum mastersianum.*
   C.medusae Lindl. See *Bulbophyllum medusae.*
   C.ornatissimum Rchb. See *Bulbophyllum ornatissimum.*
   C.picturatum Lodd. See *Bulbophyllum picturatum.*
   C.putidum Teijsm. & Binnend. See *Bulbophyllum putidum.*
   C.refractum Zoll. & Moritz. See *Bulbophyllum refractum.*
   C.robustum Rolfe. See *Bulbophyllum graveolens.*
   C.rothchildianum O'Brien. See *Bulbophyllum rothschildianum.*
   C.roxburghii Lindl. See *Bulbophyllum roxburghii.*
   C.umbellatum hort. non (Forst. f.) Hook. & Arn. See *Bulbophyllum umbellatum.*
   C.umbellatum (Forst. f.) Hook. & Arn. See *Bulbophyllum longiflorum.*

   C.vaginatum Lind. See *Bulbophyllum vaginatum.*
   C.wallichii Lindl. See *Bulbophyllum retusiusculum.*

Colax Lindl.
   C.jugosus (Lindl.) Lindl. See *Pabstia jugosa.*

Corysanthes R. Br.
   C.cheesmanii Hook. f. ex T. Kirk. See *Corybas aconitiflorus.*
   C.pruinosa R. Cunn. See *Corybas pruinosus.*
   C.bicalcarata R. Br. See *Corybas aconitiflorus.*

Cryptophoranthus Barb. Rodr.
   C.atropurpureus (Lindl.) Rolfe. See *Zootrophion atropurpureum.*
   C.dayanus (Rchb. f.) Rolfe. See *Zootrophion dayanum.*

Cyclosia Klotzsch. See *Mormodes.*

Cyperorchis Bl.
   C.elegans (Bl.) Lindl. See *Cymbidium elegans.*
   C.mastersii (Lindl.) Benth. See *Cymbidium mastersii.*

Cyrtidium Schltr.
   C.rhomboglossum Lehm. & Kränzl. See *Cyrtidiorchis rhomboglossum.*

Cyrtochilum Kunth.
   C.eduardii (Rchb. f.) Kränzl. See *Odontoglossum eduardii.*
   C.falcipetalum (Lindl.) Kränzl. See *Oncidium falcipetalum.*
   C.loxense (Lindl.) Kränzl. See *Oncidium loxense.*
   C.maculatum Lindl. See *Oncidium maculatum.*
   C.microchilum (Lindl.) Cribb. See *Oncidium microchilum.*
   C.retusum (Lindl.) Kränzl. See *Odontoglossum retusum.*
   C.superbiens (Rchb. f.) Kränzl. See *Oncidium superbiens.*

Diacrium Benth.
   D.amazonicum Schltr. See *Caularthron bicornutum.*
   D.bicornutum (Hook.) Benth. See *Caularthron bicornutum.*
   D.bigibberosum Hemsl. See *Caularthron bilamellatum.*
   D.bilamellatum (Rchb. f.) Hemsl. See *Caularthron bilamellatum.*
   D.indivisum Broadway. See *Caularthron bilamellatum.*
   D.venezuelanum Schltr. See *Caularthron bilamellatum.*

Dinema Lindl.
   D.polybulbon (Sw.) Lindl. See *Encyclia polybulbon.*

Drakaea Lindl.
D.irritabilis (F. Muell.) Rchb. f. See *Arthrochilus irritabilis*.

Evelyna Poepp. & Endl. See *Elleanthus*.

Galeottia Nees.
G.burkei (Rchb. f.) Dressler & Christenson. See *Mendoncella burkei*.
G.fimbriata (Linden & Rchb. f.) Dressler & Christenson. See *Mendoncella jorisiana*.
G.grandiflora A. Rich. See *Mendoncella grandiflora*.
G.jorisiana (Rolfe) Schltr. See *Mendoncella jorisiana*.

Gastrorchis Thouars. See *Phaius*.

Haemaria Lindl.
H.discolor (Ker-Gawl.) Lindl. See *Ludisia discolor*.

Hartwegia Lindl.
H.purpurea Lindl. See *Nageliella purpurea*.
H.purpurea var. *angustifolia* Booth ex Lindl. See *Nageliella angustifolia*.

Humboldtia Vahl.
H.misera (Lindl.) Kuntze. See *Platystele misera*.
H.stenostachya (Rchb. f.) Kuntze. See *Platystele stenostachya*.

Kraenzlinella Kuntze. See *Pleurothallis*.

Lissochilus R. Br.
L.giganteus Welw. See *Eulophia horsfallii*.
L.horsfallii Batem. See *Eulophia horsfallii*.
L.krebsii Rchb. f. See *Eulophia streptopetala*.
L.speciosus R. Br. ex Lindl. See *Eulophia speciosa*.

Lothiania Kränzl. See *Porroglossum*.

Lothoniania Kränzl. See *Porroglossum*.

Macroplectrum Pfitz.
M.sesquipedale (Thouars) Pfitz. See *Angraecum sesquipedale*.

Mesospinidium Rchb.
M.cochliodum Rchb. f. See *Symphyglossum sanguineum*.

Monachanthus Lindl. See *Catasetum*.

Myanthus Lindl. See *Catasetum*.

Myrmecophila Rolfe
M.tibicinis (Bateman ex Lindl.) Rolfe. See *Schomburgkia tibicinis*.

Neolehmannia Kränzl.
N.porpax (Rchb. f.) Garay & Dunsterville. See *Nanodes mathewsii*.

Ornithidium Salisb.
O.densum (Lindl.) Rchb. f. See *Maxillaria densa*.

Pseudepidendrum Rchb. f.
P.spectabile Rchb. f. See *Epidendrum pseudepidendrum*.

Psygmorchis Dodson & Dressler.
P.pusilla (L.) Dodson & Dressler. See *Oncidium pusillum*.

Quekettia Lindl.
Q.micromera (Barb. Rodr.) Cogn. See *Capanemia micromera*.

Rhynchopera Klotzsch. See *Pleurothallis*.

Rhynchostele Rchb. f. See *Lemboglossum*.

Saccolabium Bl.
S.bellinum Rchb. f. See *Gastrochilus bellinus*.
S.bertholdii Rchb. f. See *Robiquetia bertholdii*.
S.calopterum Rchb. f. See *Ascoglossum calopterum*.
S.curvifolium Lindl. See *Ascocentrum curvifolium*.
S.gemmata Lindl. See *Schoenorchis gemmata*.
S.micranthum Lindl. See *Smitinandia micrantha*.
S.mooreanum Rolfe. See *Robiquetia mooreana*.

Sarcanthus Lindl.
S.pallidus Lindl. See *Cleisostoma racemiferum*.

Spiculaea Lindl.
S.irritabilis (F. Muell.) Schltr. See *Arthrochilus irritabilis*.

Stenocoryne Lindl.
S.wageneri (Rchb. f.) Kränzl. See *Teuscheria wageneri*.

Theodorea Barb. Rodr.
T.gomesioides Barb. Rodr. See *Rodrigueziella gomesioides*.

Trichosma Lindl.
T.coronaria Lindl. See *Eria coronaria*.
T.suavis Lindl. See *Eria coronaria*.

Waluewa Reg.
W.pulchella Reg. See *Oncidium waluewa*.

Warscewiczella Benth. & Hook.
W.flabelliformis (Sw.) Cogn. See *Cochleanthes flabelliformis*.
W.marginata Rchb. f. See *Cochleanthes marginata*.
W.wendlandii (Rchb. f.) Schltr. See *Zygopetalum wendlandii*.

Zosterostylis Bl.
Z.arachnites Bl. See *Cryptostylis arachnites*.

Index of Popular Names

Orchid Hybrid Abbreviations

What follows is a list of all hybrid genera included in this Manual, together with the names of natural genera that have been recorded as parents of hybrids. The list is based on the International Orchid Commission's *Handbook on Orchid Nomenclature and Registration* (4th edn, 1993).

Apart from names lost to synonymy like *Gastrophaius* (*Gastrorchis* × *Phaius*) and fictions like *Selenopanthes* (*Selenipedium* × *Lepanthes*), the *Handbook* lists some 627 recorded hybrid genera, whether artificially made or arising in nature. Of these, only a small proportion is described in the *Manual of Orchids*, but they include all widely grown hybrid genera.

The International Registration Authority for Orchid Hybrids (IRAOH) uses a standard abbreviation for the name of each hybrid genus registered and for the name of each natural genus giving rise to a registered grex. In the list below, these abbreviations appear in the right-hand column. Some short names are retained in full for registration (e.g. *Ada, Aranda, Disa, Diuris, Orchis*). The abbreviations are reproduced here not only because they are of importance in hybrid registration, but also because they appear in the nursery trade and in orchid literature.

Genera known to have given rise to natural hybrids only and never, therefore, to have appeared in registration are also listed but are signified by having no entry in the right-hand column (e.g. *Aceras, Barlia, Sobralia*).

In a few genera the IRAOH urges the use of *horticulturally recommended names* for the purpose of hybrid registration. These genus names may be no longer botanically acceptable for the entities to which they refer. In recent years, few orchid growers or popular works, for example, have placed *Encyclia* in *Epidendrum*, *Rhyncholaelia* in *Brassavola*, or *Papilionanthe* in *Vanda*. In each case the former name has been generally accepted as a sensible 'splitting' from the latter. Meanwhile, *Cirrhopetalum* tends to be included in *Bulbophyllum* nowadays but still exists as a horticulturally recommended name and as such has even spawned 'intergeneric' hybrids with *Bulbophyllum*, viz. *Cirrhophyllum* (*Crphm.*). Similarly, names that are legitimate or have botanical priority may be rejected in favour of horticulturally recommended names that are faulty or of more recent vintage but which happen to have an established history in registration; for example, the IRAOH prefers *Haemaria* to *Ludisia*.

The IRAOH retains these 'wrong' names because they circumvent the problem of having to recognize that long-established and recorded lineages are more mixed and unstable than is strictly necessary for the purpose of clear, useful and consistent registration. × *Brassocattleya*, for example, still represents all hybrids between *Brassavola sensu stricto* and *Cattleya*, and between *Rhyncholaelia* and *Cattleya*. To enforce this, the IRAOH does not recognize the genus *Rhyncholaelia* as distinct from *Brassavola* for the purpose of registration. The alternative (if botanically more credible) would be the renaming of all hybrids made between *Rhyncholaelia* and *Cattleya* together with any trigeneric crosses (*Brassavola* × *Rhyncholaelia* × *Cattleya*) and the creation of a vast new synonymy – which no one needs.

In the list below, the horticulturally recommended name (HR) is given on the right-hand side of any 'equals' sign, as they arise. The name accepted by botanists and by the Editors of this Manual appears on the left. Of course, this is not to say that all genera (or all of *one* genus) with a recommended name are no longer botanically acceptable. *Brassavola* and *Vanda*, for example, are 'good' genera containing numerous species apart from those referred to *Rhyncholaelia* and *Papilionanthe*.

Abbreviations

Acacallis	= *Aganisia* (HR)	*Cattleya*	*C.*
Acampe	*Acp.*	*Cattleyopsis*	*Ctps.*
Aceras		× *Cattleytonia*	*Ctna.*
Acineta	*Acn.*	*Caularthron*	= *Diacrium* (HR)
Ada	*Ada*	*Cephalanthera*	
Aerangis	*Aergs.*	*Chiloschista*	*Chsch.*
Aeranthes	*Aerth.*	*Chondrorhyncha*	*Chdrh.*
Aerides	*Aer.*	× *Christieara*	*Chtra.*
Aganisia	*Agn.*	*Chysis*	*Chy.*
× *Alexanderara*	*Alxra.*	*Cischweinfia*	*Cisch.*
× *Aliceara*	*Alcra.*	*Cleisostoma*	*Cleis.*
Amblostoma	*Amb.*	*Clowesia*	= *Catasetum* (HR)
Amesiella	= *Angraecum* (HR)	*Cochleanthes*	*Cnths.*
Anacamptis		*Cochlioda*	*Cda.*
Angraecum	*Angcm.*	*Coeloglossum*	
Anguloa	*Ang.*	*Coelogyne*	*Coel.*
× *Angulocaste*	*Angcst.*	*Comparettia*	*Comp.*
Anoectochilus	*Anct.*	*Constantia*	*Const.*
Arachnis	*Arach.*	*Coryanthes*	*Crths.*
× *Aranda*	*Aranda*	*Cryptopus*	*Crypt.*
Arethusa	*Aret.*	*Cycnoches*	*Cyc.*
× *Ascocenda*	*Ascda.*	*Cymbidiella*	*Cymla.*
Ascocentrum	*Asctm.*	*Cymbidium*	*Cym.*
× *Ascofinetia*	*Ascf.*	*Cynorkis*	*Cyn.*
Ascoglossum	*Ascgm.*	*Cypripedium*	*Cyp.*
× *Asconopsis*	*Ascps.*	*Cyrtopodium*	*Cyrt.*
Aspasia	*Asp.*	*Cyrtorchis*	*Cyrtcs.*
Barkeria	*Bark.*	*Dactylorhiza*	*Dact.*
Barlia		*Dendrobium*	*Den.*
Batemannia	*Btmna.*	× *Dialaelia*	*Dial.*
Bifrenaria	*Bif.*	*Diaphananthe*	*Dpthe.*
Bletia	*Bletia*	*Diplocaulobium*	
Bletilla	*Ble.*	*Disa*	*Disa*
Bollea	*Bol.*	*Diuris*	*Diuris*
Brassavola	*B.*	*Domingoa*	*Dga.*
Brassia	*Brs.*	× *Doritaenopsis*	*Dtps.*
× *Brassocattleya*	*Bc.*	*Doritis*	*Dor.*
× *Brassoepiden-*		*Dracula*	*Drac.*
drum	*Bepi.*		
× *Brassolaelio-*		*Embreea*	*Emb.*
cattleya	*Blc.*	*Encyclia*	= *Epidendrum* (HR)
Bromheadia		× *Epicattleya*	*Epc.*
Broughtonia	*Bro.*	*Epidendrum*	*Epi.*
Bulbophyllum	*Bulb.*	*Epipactis*	*Epcts.*
		× *Epiphronitis*	*Ephs.*
Caladenia	*Calda.*	*Erycina*	*Ercn.*
Calanthe	*Cal.*	*Esmeralda*	= *Arachnis* (HR)
Calopogon	*Cpg.*	*Euanthe*	= *Vanda* (HR)
Catasetum	*Ctsm.*	*Eulophia*	*Eupha.*

Eulophiella	*Eul.*		*Nigritella*	
Eurychone	*Echn.*		*Notylia*	*Ntl.*
Flickingeria	*Flkga.*		× *Odontioda*	*Oda.*
			× *Odontobrassia*	*Odbrs.*
Galeandra	*Gal.*		× *Odontocidium*	*Odcdm.*
Gastrochilus	*Gchls.*		*Odontoglossum*	*Odm.*
Gomesa	*Gom.*		× *Odontonia*	*Odtna.*
Gongora	*Gga.*		× *Odontorettia*	*Odrta.*
Goodyera			*Oeoniella*	*Oenla.*
Grammato-			*Oerstedella*	= *Epidendrum* (HR)
phyllum	*Gram.*		× *Oncidioda*	*Oncda.*
Graphorkis	*Grks.*		*Oncidium*	*Onc.*
Gymnadenia			*Ophrys*	
			× *Opsistylis*	*Opst.*
Habenaria	*Hab.*		*Orchis*	*Orchis*
Hexadesmia	*Hex.*		*Ornithophora*	*Orpha.*
Hexisea	*Hxsa.*		*Osmoglossum*	= *Odontoglossum* (HR)
Himantoglossum			*Otoglossum*	= *Odontoglossum* (HR)
Holcoglossum	= *Neofinetia* (HR)		*Otostylis*	*Otst.*
Huntleya	*Hya.*			
			Pabstia	*Pab.*
Ionopsis	*Inps.*		*Paphiopedilum*	*Paph.*
			Papilionanthe	= *Vanda* (HR)
Jumellea	*Jma.*		*Paraphalaenopsis*	= *Phalaenopsis* (HR)
			Pecteilis	= *Habenaria* (HR)
Kefersteinia	*Kefst.*		*Pescatorea*	*Pes.*
Kingidium	= *Kingiella* [*King.*] (HR)		*Phaius*	*Phaius*
			Phalaenopsis	*Phal.*
Laelia	*L.*		*Phragmipedium*	*Phrag.*
× *Laeliocattleya*	*Lc.*		*Platanthera*	
Laeliopsis	*Lps.*		*Plectorrhiza*	*Plrhz.*
Leochilus	*Lchs.*		*Plectrelminthus*	*Plmth.*
Lepanthes	*Lths.*		*Pleione*	*Pln.*
Leptotes	*Lpt.*		*Pleurothallis*	*Pths.*
Lockhartia	*Lhta.*		*Polycycnis*	*Pcn.*
Ludisia	= *Haemaria* [*Haem.*] (HR)		*Polystachya*	*Pol.*
Luisia	*Lsa.*		*Pomatocalpa*	*Pmcpa.*
Lycaste	*Lyc.*		× *Potinara*	*Pot.*
			Promenaea	*Prom.*
× *Maclellanara*	*Mclna.*		*Psychopsis*	= *Oncidium* (HR)
Macodes	*Mac.*		*Pterostylis*	*Ptst.*
Macradenia	*Mcdn.*			
Masdevallia	*Masc.*		*Rangaeris*	
Maxillaria	*Max.*		× *Renanopsis*	*Rnps.*
Meiracyllium			× *Renantanda*	*Rntda.*
Mendoncella	*Mdcla.*		*Renanthera*	*Ren.*
Mexicoa	= *Oncidium* (HR)		× *Renanthopsis*	*Rnthps.*
Micropera	*Micr.*		*Restrepia*	*Rstp.*
Miltonia	*Milt.*		*Rhinerrhiza*	*Rhin.*
× *Miltonidium*	*Mtdm.*		*Rhyncholaelia*	= *Brassavola* (HR)
Miltoniopsis	= *Miltonia* (HR)		*Rhynchostylis*	*Rhy.*
× *Mokara*	*Mkra.*		× *Rhynchovanda*	*Rhv.*
Mormodes	*Morm.*		*Robiquetia*	*Rbq.*
Mormolyca	*Mlca.*		*Rodriguezia*	*Rdza.*
Mystacidium	*Mycdm.*		*Rodrigueziella*	*Rdzlla.*
			Rossioglossum	= *Odontoglossum* (HR)
Nageliella	*Ngl.*			
Neobathiea	*Nbth.*		*Sarcochilus*	*Sarco.*
Neofinetia	*Neof.*		× *Sarconopsis*	*Srnps.*
Neogardneria	*Ngda.*			

Satyrium	*Satm.*	*Tetramicra*	*Ttma.*
Scaphyglottis	*Scgl.*	*Thelymitra*	*Thel.*
Schomburgkia	*Schom.*	*Thunia*	*Thu.*
Sedirea	= *Aerides* (HR)	*Trichocentrum*	*Trctm.*
Seidenfadenia	= *Aerides* (HR)	*Trichoglottis*	*Trgl.*
Selenipedium	= *Phragmipedium* (HR)	*Trichopilia*	*Trpla.*
Serapias	*Srps.*	*Tridactyle*	
Sigmatostalix	*Sgmx.*	*Trigonidium*	*Trgdm.*
Sobralia			
× *Sophrocattleya*	*Sc.*	*Vanda*	*V.*
× *Sophrolaelia*	*Sl.*	*Vandopsis*	*Vdps.*
× *Sophrolaelio-*		× *Vascostylis*	*Vasco.*
cattleya	*Slc.*	× *Vuylstekeara*	*Vuyl.*
Sophronitella	= *Sophronitis* (HR)		
Sophronitis	*Soph.*	*Warrea*	*Wra.*
Spathoglottis	*Spa.*	× *Wilsonara*	*Wils.*
Stanhopea	*Stan.*		
Stenia	*Stenia*	*Xylobium*	*Xyl.*
× *Stewartara*	*Stwt.*		
Symphyglossum	= *Cochlioda* (HR)	*Zygopetalum*	*Z.*
		Zygosepalum	*Zspm.*

Bibliography

All published in London unless otherwise specified

Encyclopaedic Surveys

Bateman, J. 1867. *A Second Century of Orchidaceous Plants*. Reeve & Co.

Bechtel, H., Cribb, P. & Launert, E. 1992. *Manual of Cultivated Orchid Species*. 3rd edn, Blandford Press.

Bentham, G. & Hooker, J.D. 1883. Orchideae. In *Genera Plantarum* 3, L. Reeve & Co.

Cullen, J. (ed.) 1992. *The Orchid Book*. Cambridge University Press.

Dietrich, H. 1980. *Bibliographia Orchidacearum*.

Hawkes, A.D. 1965. *Encyclopaedia of Cultivated Orchids*. Faber & Faber.

Hooker, W.J. 1849. *A Century of Orchidaceous Plants*. Reeve, Bentham & Reeve.

Linden, J. 1860. *Pescatorea*. Gand.

—— 1885–1901. *Lindenia*. Gand.

Lindley, J. 1838–42. *Sertum Orchidacearum*.

—— 1830–1840. *Genera and Species of Orchidaceous Plants*. Ridgways.

—— 1852–9. *Folia Orchidacea*. J. Matthews.

Pridgeon, A. (ed.) 1992. *The Illustrated Encyclopedia of Orchids*. Headline.

Reichenbach, H.G. (Reichenbach filius) 1854–1900. *Xenia Orchidacea*. A. Brockhaus, Leipzig.

—— 1864. Orchides. In Walpers, *Annales Botanices* 6.

Sander, F. 1888–94. *Reichenbachia*. St. Albans.

—— 1901. *Sander's Orchid Guide*. St. Albans.

Schlechter, R., 1914. *Die Orchideen*; 2nd edn, ed. E. Miethe (1927); 3rd edn, ed. F.G. Brieger, R. Maatsch & K. Senghas, appearing in parts and continuing (1972–present).

Sheehan, T. & Sheehan, M. 1994. *Illustrated Survey of Orchid Genera*. Timber Press, Portland, Oregon, and Cambridge University Press.

Veitch, J. & Sons. 1887–94. *A Manual of Cultivated Orchidaceous Plants*. 2 vols, repr. 1963, A. Asher & Co., Amsterdam.

Horticultural Guides
(see also Bechtel et al., Cullen, Hawkes, Pridgeon, Sander, Veitch above)

Baker, M.L. & Baker, C.O. 1991. *Orchid Species Culture: Pescatorea–Pleione*. Timber Press, Portland, Oregon.

Bechtel, H. 1969. *Orchideen in Heim*. Landbuch Verlag, Hannover.

Black, P.M. 1980. *The Complete Book of Orchid Growing*. Ward Lock.

Bristow, A. 1985. *Orchids: a Wisley Handbook*. Cassell/Royal Horticultural Society.

Ferguson, B. (ed.) 1988. *All About Growing Orchids*. Ortho Books, San Ramon, California.

Hartmann, W.I. 1971. *Introduction to the Cultivation of Orchids*.

Hunt, P.F. 1978. *The Country Life Book of Orchids*. Country Life.

James, I.D. 1988. *The Orchid Grower's Handbook*. Blandford Press.

McQueen J. & McQueen B. 1992. *Miniature Orchids*. Timber Press, Portland, Oregon.

Northen, R.T. 1990. *Home Orchid Growing*. 4th edn, Prentice Hall, New York.

Pridgeon, A.M. (ed.) 1988. *Handbook on Orchid Culture*. American Orchid Society, West Palm Beach, Florida.

—— (ed.) 1990. *Handbook on Orchid Pests and Diseases*. American Orchid Society, West Palm Beach, Florida.

Rentoul, J.N. 1980–1989. *Growing Orchids* (series). Lothian, Melbourne.

Richter, W. 1969. *Orchideen*.

Rittershausen, B. & Rittershausen, W. 1980. *Orchids as Indoor Plants*. Blandford Press.

—— 1985. *Orchid Growing Illustrated*. Blandford Press.

Sander, D. 1979. *Orchids and their Cultivation*. 9th edn, Blandford Press.

Stewart, J. 1988. *Orchids – A Kew Gardening Guide*. Royal Botanic Gardens, Kew, in association with Collingridge.

Williams, B.A., et al. 1980. *Orchids for Everyone*.

Williams, B.S. 1897. *The Orchid Grower's Manual,* 7th edn; repr. 1982.

Hardy orchids

Bailes, C. 1994. Havens for Orchids. *The Garden* 119 (ix): 425–7.

Cribb, P. 1987. Orchids hardy in the British Isles. *Plantsman* 8: 196–228.

—— & Bailes, C. 1989. *Hardy Orchids: Orchids for the Garden and Frost-free Greenhouse.* Christopher Helm.

Conservation

Arp, G.K. 1977. The conservation of tropical orchids in the temperate zone greenhouse. *American Orchid Society Bulletin* 46: 809–12.

Dunsterville, G.C.K. 1975. A letter to Orchid Conservationists. *American Orchid Society Bulletin* 44: 883–5.

Hagsater, E. 1976. Can there be a different view of orchids and their conservation? *American Orchid Society Bulletin* 45: 18–21.

Hunt, P.F. 1968. Conservation of Orchids. *Orchid Review* 76: 320–27.

Light, M.H.S. 1990. Doing your part for conservation. *American Orchid Society Bulletin* 59: 786–93, 897–903, 1014–22.

Pritchard, H.W. (ed.) 1989. *Modern Methods in Orchid Conservation.* Cambridge University Press.

Thompson, P.A. 1980. *Orchids from Seed.* Royal Botanic Gardens, Kew.

Illustration

Bauer, F. & Lindley, J. 1830–1838. *Illustrations of Orchidaceous Plants.* J. Ridgway & Sons.

Cogniaux, A. & Goossens, A. 1896. *Dictionaire Iconographique des Orchidées.* 17 vols, Brussels.

Sprunger, S. (ed.) 1986. *Orchids from Curtis's Botanical Magazine.* Eugen Ulmer, Stuttgart (English edn, Cambridge University Press, 1986).

Schuster, C. 1974. Orchidacearum Iconum Index. *Feddes Repertorium,* Beihefte 60.

Stewart, J. & Stearn, W.T. 1993. *The Orchid Paintings of Franz Bauer.* Timber Press, Portland, Oregon.

Warner, R. 1862–78. *Select Orchidaceous Plants.* Lovell Reeve & Co.

—— & Williams, B.S. 1882–97. *The Orchid Album.* B.S. Williams.

Biology and Systematics

Allen, P.H. 1959. Orchid hosts in the tropics. *American Orchid Society Bulletin* 28: 243–4.

Arditti, J. (ed.) 1977. *Orchid Biology: Reviews and Perspectives,* I. Cornell University Press, Ithaca, New York.

—— (ed.) 1982. *Orchid Biology: Reviews and Perspectives,* II. Cornell University Press, Ithaca, New York.

—— (ed.) 1984. *Orchid Biology: Reviews and Perspectives,* III. Cornell University Press, Ithaca, New York.

—— (ed.) 1987. *Orchid Biology: Reviews and Perspectives,* IV. Cornell University Press, Ithaca, New York.

—— (ed.) 1990. *Orchid Biology: Reviews and Perspectives,* V. Timber Press, Portland, Oregon.

Burgeff, H. 1959. Mycorrhiza of Orchids. In Withner (1959).

Darwin, C. 1862. *On the Various Contrivances By Which British and Foreign Orchids are Fertilised By Insects.* John Murray.

Dodson, C.H. 1962. The importance of pollination in the evolution of the orchids of tropical America. *American Orchid Society Bulletin* 31: 525–34, 641–9, 731–5.

—— 1966. Studies in orchid pollination – *Cypripedium, Phragmipedium* and allied genera. *American Orchid Society Bulletin* 35: 125–8.

Dodson, C.H., Dressler, R.L., Hills, H.G., Adams, R.M. and Williams, N.H. 1969. Biologically active compounds in orchid fragrances. *Science* 164: 1234–49.

Dressler, R.L. 1961. The structure of the orchid flower. *Missouri Botanical Garden Bulletin* 49: 60–69.

—— 1968. Observations on orchids and euglossine bees in Panama and Costa Rica. *Revista de Biología Tropical* 15: 143–83.

—— 1969. Pollination by euglossine bees. *Evolution* 22: 202–10.

—— 1971. Dark pollinia in hummingbird-pollinated orchids, or do hummingbirds suffer from strabismus? *American Naturalist* 105: 80–83.

—— 1974. Classification of the orchid family. *Proceedings of the Seventh World Orchid Conference,* 534–7.

—— 1976. The use of pollinia in orchid systematics. *First Symposium on Scientific Aspects of Orchids* (Detroit), 1–15.

—— 1979. The subfamilies of Orchidaceae. *Selbyana* 5: 197–206.

—— 1981. *The Orchids: Natural History and Classification.* Harvard University Press, Cambridge, Massachusetts. 2nd edn, 1990.

—— 1986. Recent advances in orchid phylogeny. *Lindleyana* 1: 5–20.

—— 1990a. The Neottieae in orchid classification. *Lindleyana* 5: 102–109.

—— 1990b. The Spiranthoideae: grade or subfamily? *Lindleyana* 5: 110–116.

—— 1993. *Phylogeny and Classification of the Orchid Family.* Dioscorides Press, Portland, Oregon.

Garay, L. 1960. On the origin of the Orchidaceae. *Botanical Museum Leaflets of Harvard University* 19(3): 57–96.

—— 1972. On the origin of the Orchidaceae, 2. *Journal of the Arnold Arboretum* 52: 202–15.

Hills, H.G., Williams, N.H. and Dodson, C.H. 1968. Identification of some orchid fragrance components. *American Orchid Society Bulletin* 37: 967–71.

Holman, R.T. & Heimermann, W.H. 1973. Identification of the components of orchid fragrance by gas chromatography – mass spectrometry. *American Orchid Society Bulletin* 38: 578–84.

International Orchid Commission. 1993. *Handbook of Orchid Nomenclature and Registration*, 4th edn.

Johansson, D.R. 1975. Ecology of epiphytic orchids in West African rain forests. *American Orchid Society Bulletin* 44: 125–36.

—— 1977. Epiphytic orchids as parasites of their host trees. *American Orchid Society Bulletin* 46: 703–7.

Jones, D.L. 1974. The pollination of *Acianthus caudatus* . *Victorian Naturalist* 91: 272–4.

—— 1975. The pollination of *Microtis parviflora* . *Annals of Botany* 39: 585–9.

Jones, D.L. & Gray, B. 1974. The pollination of *Calochilus holtzei*. *American Orchid Society Bulletin* 43: 604–6.

—— 1976a. The pollination of *Bulbophyllum longiflorum*. *American Orchid Society Bulletin* 45: 15–17.

—— 1976b. The pollination of *Dendrobium lichenastrum*. *American Orchid Society Bulletin* 45: 981–3.

—— 1977. The pollination of *Dendrobium ruppianum*. *American Orchid Society Bulletin* 46: 54–7.

Jones, K. 1967. The chromosomes of orchids. Pt 2: Vandeae. *Kew Bulletin* 21: 151–6.

—— 1974. Cytology and the study of orchids. In *The Orchids: Scientific Studies*, ed. C. L. Withner. John Wiley and Sons, New York.

Jones, K. & Daker, M.G. 1968. The chromosomes of orchids. Pt 3: Catasetinae. *Kew Bulletin* 22: 421–7.

Knudson, L. 1922. Non-symbiotic germination of orchid seeds. *Botanical Gazette* 73: 1–25.

Madison, M. 1977. Vascular epiphytes: their systematic occurrence and salient features. *Selbyana* 2: 1–13.

Mulay, B.N., Deshpande, B.D. and Williams, H.B. 1958. Study of velamen in some epiphytic and terrestrial orchids. *Journal of the Indian Botanical Society* 37: 123–7.

Mulay, B.N. & Panikar, T.K.B. 1956. Origin, development and structure of velamen in the roots of some species of terrestrial orchids. *Proceedings of the Rajasthan Academy of Science* 6: 31–48.

Neales, T.F. & Hew, C.S. 1975. Two types of carbon fixation in tropical orchids. *Planta* (Berlin) 123: 303–6.

Newton, G.D.& Williams, N.H. 1978. Pollen morphology of the Cypripedioideae and Apostasioideae. *Selbyana* 2: 169–82.

Northen, R.T. 1952. Pollen-shooting mechanism of *Catasetum*. *American Orchid Society Bulletin* 21: 859–62.

—— 1970. The mysterious movements of pollinaria. *Orchid Digest* 34: 87–8.

—— 1971. The remarkable thrift of *Spiculaea ciliata*. *American Orchid Society Bulletin* 40: 898–9.

—— 1972. *Pterostylis* and its sensitive gnat trap. *American Orchid Society Bulletin* 41: 801–6.

Nuernbergk, E.L. 1963. On the carbon dioxide metabolism of orchids and its ecological aspect. *Proceedings of the Fourth World Orchid Conference*, 158–69.

Ogura, T. 1953. Anatomy and morphology of the subterranean organs in some Orchidaceae. *Journal of the Faculty of Science of the University of Tokyo: Botany* 6: 135–57.

Pridgeon, A.M. 1987. The velamen and exodermis of orchid roots. In Arditti (1987), 139–92.

Pijl, L. Van Der & Dodson, C.H. 1966. *Orchid Flowers: Their Pollination and Evolution*. University of Miami Press, Coral Gables, Florida.

Rayner, E. 1977. Orchids as medicine. *South African Orchid Journal* 8(4): 120.

Reinikka, M.A. 1995. *A History of the Orchid*. Revised edn, Timber Press, Portland, Oregon.

Rolfe, R.A. 1902–12. The evolution of the Orchidaceae. *Orchid Review* 17–20.

Rosso, S.W. 1966. The vegetative anatomy of the Cypripedioideae. *Journal of the Linnean Society: (Botany)* 59: 309–41.

Ruinen, J. 1953. Epiphytosis: a second view on epiphytism. *Annales Bogoriensis* 1: 101–57.

Sanford, W.N. 1974. Ecology of orchids. In Withner (1974).

Schlechter, F. 1926. Das System der Orchidaceen. *Notizblatt des Botanischen gartens und Museums Berlin* 9: 563–91.

Schultes, R.E. & Pease, A.S. 1963. *Generic Names of Orchids: their Origin and Meaning*. Academic Press, New York.

Schweinfurth, C. 1959. Classification of orchids. In Withner (1959).

Stewart, J. (ed.) 1992. *Orchids at Kew*. HMSO, London.

Stoutamire, W. 1974. Terrestrial orchid seedlings. In Withner (1974), 101–28.

Warcup, J.H. 1975. Factors affecting symbiotic germination of orchid seed. In *Endomycorrhiza*, ed. F.E. Sanders, B. Moss and P. B. Tinker. Academic Press.

Williams, N.H. 1975. Stomatal development in *Ludisia discolor*: mesoperigenous subsidiary cells in the monocotyledons. *Taxon* 24: 281–8.

Williams, N.H. & Broome, C.R. 1976. Scanning electron microscope studies of orchid pollen. *American Orchid Society Bulletin* 45: 699–707.

—— 1972. Selective attraction of male euglossine bees to orchid floral fragrances and its importance in long distance pollen flow. *Evolution* 26: 84–95.

Withner, C. (ed.) 1959. *The Orchids: A Scientific Survey*. Ronald Press, New York.

—— (ed.) 1974. *The Orchids: Scientific Studies*. John Wiley, New York.

Hybrids
(see also International Orchid Commission (1993) under *Biology and Systematics* above)

Koopowitz & Hasegawa (1989). See under *Paphiopedilum* below.

Moir, W.W.G. 1974. Intergenerics in the Oncidiinae. *Orchid Review* 82: 156–60.

—— 1975a. Intergenerics of the Lesser Laeliinae. *Florida Orchidist* 18: 61–4.

—— 1975b. The wasted efforts in breeding. *Orchid Review* 83: 298–302.

—— 1978. Surprises in breeding orchids. *Orchid Review* 86: 161–4.

—— 1987. Breeding the *Oncidium* sect. *Oncidium* (erroneously the Equitant-Variegata Oncidiums). *Orchid Digest* 42: 85–91.

Rolfe, R.A. & Hurst, C. 1909. *Orchid Stud Book*. F. Leslie & Co.

Sander's List of Orchid Hybrids. First published in 1905, supplements published by the Royal Horticultural Society (see *Orchid hybrid and cultivar nomenclature* in the Introduction to this Manual).

Journals

The American Orchid Society Bulletin, 1932 and continuing (American).

Australian Orchid Review, 1936 and continuing (Australian).

Orchidata, 1965 and continuing (American).

Orquidea, 1938 and continuing (Mexican).

Orchid Digest, 1937 and continuing (American).

Die Orchidee, 1949 and continuing (German).

Orchideeën, 1934 and continuing (Dutch).

Orchid Journal, 1952–5 (American).

The Orchadian, 1963 and continuing (Australian).

The Orchid Review, 1893 and continuing (British).

Orchis, 1906–20 (German).

Orquideologia 1966 and continuing (S American).

Philippine Orchid Review 1948–59 (Philippine).

South African Orchid Journal, 1970 and continuing (South African).

REGIONAL TREATMENTS

Europe (including Mediterranean region and Near East)

Allan, B., Woods, P., Clarke, S. 1993. *Wild Orchids of Scotland*. HMSO, Edinburgh.

Buttler, K.P. 1991. *Field Guide to Orchids of Britain and Europe*. Crowood Press, Swindon.

Camus, E.G. 1908. *Monographie des Orchidées*. Lechevalier, Paris.

Danesch, O. & E. 1962. *Orchideen Europas*. Hallwag, Bern.

—— 1969. *Orchideen Europas: Sudeuropa*. Hallwag, Bern.

Davies, P. & J., & Huxley, A. 1983. *Wild Orchids of Britain and Europe*. Chatto & Windus, Hogarth Press.

Delforge, P. 1995. *Collins Photo Guide: Orchids of Britain and Europe*. Harper/Collins, London.

Delforge, P. & Tyteca, D. 1984. *Guide des Orchidées d'Europe*. Duculot, Paris.

Duperrex, A. 1961. *Orchids of Europe*. Blandford Press.

Godfery, M.J. 1933. *British Orchidaceae*. Cambridge University Press.

Keller, G. & Schlechter, R. 1925–43. Monographie und Iconographie der Orchideen Europas und des Mittelmeergebietes, 1–45. *Feddes Repertorium*, Sonderbeiheft A., Berlin.

Landwehr, J. 1977. *Orchideën van Europa*. Natuurmonumenten, Netherlands.

Nelson, E. & Fischer, H. 1931. *Die Orchideen Deutschlands und der angrenzenden Gebiete*. Frisch, Berlin.

Reichenbach, H.G. 1851. Orchideae. In *Flora Germanica Recensitae*, Hofmeister, Leipzig.

Renz, J. 1978. Orchidaceae. In Rechinger, K.H., *Flora Iranica*, 126, Akad. Druck- und Verlagsanstalt, Graz.

Summerhayes, V.S. 1968. *Wild Orchids of Britain*, 2nd edn. Collins.

Sundermann, H. 1975. *Europäische und mediterrane Orchideen*. 2. Aufl. Brücke, Hannover.

Africa

Ball, J.S. 1978. *Southern African Epiphytic Orchids*. Conservation Press, Johannesburg.

Bolus, H. 1918. *The Orchids of the Cape Peninsula*. 2nd edn, ed. H.M.L. Bolus and A.M. Greene, Darter Brothers and Co., Cape Town.

—— 1893–1913. *Orchids of South Africa*. W. Wesley & Son.

Compton, R.H. 1976. The flora of Swaziland. *Journal of South African Botany*, supp. vol. 11.

Cribb, P.J. 1977. New orchids from South Central Africa. *Kew Bulletin* 32: 137–87.

—— 1979. New or little-known orchids from East Africa. *Kew Bulletin* 34: 321–40.

—— 1989. *Orchidaceae* (part 3). *Flora of Tropical East Africa*. A.A. Balkema, Rotterdam.

—— & Stewart, J. 1985. Additions to the orchid flora of Tropical Africa. *Kew Bulletin* 40 (2).

Harrison, E.R. 1972. *Epiphytic Orchids of Southern Africa*. Natal Branch of the Wildlife Protection and Conservation Society of South Africa, Durban, South Africa. Washington Press, Seattle and London.

Jacot Guillarmod, A. 1972. *Flora of Lesotho*. J. Cramer, Lehre.

Kränzlin, F. 1898. *Orchidacearum Genera et Species*. I. Mayer & Müller, Berlin.

La Croix, I.F., La Croix, E.A.S. and La Croix, T.M. 1991. *Orchids of Malawi*. Balkema, Rotterdam.

Morris, B. 1970. *The Epiphytic Orchids of Malawi*. The Society of Malawi, Blantyre.

Nihoul, E., Schelpe, E.A. & Hunt, P.F. 1969. A provisional checklist of the orchids in the Congo-Kinshasa. *American Orchid Society Bulletin* 38: 578–84.

Piers, F. 1968. *Orchids of East Africa*. J. Cramer, Lehre.

Rolfe, R.A. 1897. Orchidaceae. *Flora of Tropical Africa*, 7. Reeve & Co.

—— 1913. Orchidaceae. *Flora Capensis*. Reeve & Co.

Sanford, W.W. and Adanlawo, I. 1973. Velamen and exodermis characters of West African epiphytic orchids in relation to taxonomic grouping and habitat tolerance. *Botanical Journal of the Linnean Society* 66: 307–21.

Schelpe, E.A. 1966. *An Introduction to the South African Orchids*. Purnell and Sons, Cape Town.

—— 1970. Fire-induced flowering among indigenous South African orchids. *South African Orchid Journal* 1(2): 21–2.

—— 1976. The early history of South African orchidology. *South African Orchid Journal* 7: 77–80.

See also Schelpe (1971) under *Disa* below.

Schlechter, R. 1915. Orchidaceae Stolzianae. In A. Engler, *Botanische Jahrbücher*.

—— 1918. Versuch einer naturlichen Neuordnung der afrikanischen angraekoiden Orchidaceen. *Bot. Centralblatt*, 36 (2).

—— 1924. Contributions to South African Orchidology. *Annals of the Transvaal Museum* 10.

Segerback, L.B. 1983. *Orchids of Nigeria*. A.A. Balkema, Rotterdam.

Solch, A. 1972. Orchidaceae. In *Prodromus einer Flora von Sudwestafrika*, J. Cramer, Lehre.

Stewart, J. 1973. A second checklist of the orchids of Kenya. *American Orchid Society Bulletin*, 42: 525–531.

—— 1974. Orchidaceae. In A. Agnew, *Upland Kenya Wild Flowers*, Oxford University Press.

—— 1976. The Vandaceous group in Africa and Madagascar. *Proceedings of the 8th World Orchid Conference* (1975): 239–48.

—— and Campbell, B. 1970. *Orchids of Tropical Africa*. W.H. Allen.

—— & Hennessy E.F. 1981.*Orchids of Africa*. Macmillan.

—— and Linder, H., Schelpe, E. & Hall, A. 1982. *Wild Orchids of South Africa*. Macmillan, Johannesburg.

—— 1994. Orchidaceae. In Agnew, A.D.Q., and S. Agnew, *Upland Kenya Wild Flowers*, 2nd edition. East African Natural History Society, Nairobi.

Summerhayes, V.S. 1936. African Orchids VIII. *Kew Bulletin* 221–33.

—— 1937. African Orchids IX. *Kew Bulletin* 457–66.

—— 1938. African Orchids X. *Kew Bulletin* 141–53.

—— 1942. African Orchids XII. *Botanical Museum Leaflets, Harvard University*, 10: 257–99.

—— 1948. African Orchids XVIII. *Kew Bulletin* 3: 277–302.

—— 1949. African Orchids XIX. *Kew Bulletin* 4: 427–43.

—— 1957. African Orchids XXIV. *Kew Bulletin* 12: 107–26.

—— 1958. African Orchids XXVI. *Kew Bulletin* 13: 257–81.

—— 1960. African Orchids XXVII. *Kew Bulletin* 14: 126–57.

—— 1966. African Orchids XXX. *Kew Bulletin* 20: 165–99.

—— 1968a Orchidaceae. In F.N. Hepper (ed.), *Flora of West Tropical Africa*, 2nd edn. Crown Agents for Overseas Governments and Administrations, London, 3(1): 180–276.

—— 1968b. Orchidaceae (Part 1). In E. Milne-Redhead and R. M. Polhill (eds), *Flora of Tropical East Africa*, Crown Agents for Overseas Governments and Administrations, London.

Williamson, G. 1977. *The Orchids of South Central Africa*. J. M. Dent.

Madagascar and neighbouring islands

Perrier de la Bâthie, H. 1939–41. *Flore de Madagascar, Orchidacées*. Tananarive.

Richard, A. 1828. *Orchidées des Iles de France et Bourbon*. Paris.

Schlechter, R. 1913. *Orchidaceae de Madagascar – Orchidaceae Perrierianae Madagascarienses*.

Thouars, A. du Petit. 1913. *Orchidées des Iles Australes de l'Afrique*. Paris.

See also Hillerman & Holst (1986) under *Angraecum* below.

North America

See also Ames (1922) under *Pogonia* below.

Case, F. 1987. *Orchids of the Western Great Lakes Region*. Cranbrook Institute of Science, Bloomfield Hills, Michigan.

Correll, D.S. 1950. *Native Orchids of North America*. Stanford University Press, California.

Luer, C. 1972. *The Native Orchids of Florida*. New York Botanical Garden, New York.

—— 1975. *The Native Orchids of The United States and Canada (excluding Florida)*. New York Botanical Garden, New York.

Sheviak, C.J. 1974. An introduction to the ecology of the Illinois Orchidaceae. *Illinois State Museum Science Papers* 14: 1–89.

Stoutamire, W.P. 1964. Seeds and seedlings of native orchids. *Michigan Botanist* 3: 107–19.

—— 1971. Pollination in temperate American orchids. *Proceedings of the Sixth World Orchid Conference*, 233–43.

Thien, L.B. & Marcks, B.G. 1972. The floral biology of *Arethusa bulbosa, Calopogon tuberosus* and *Pogonia ophioglossoides. Canadian Journal of Botany* 50: 2319–25.

Central and South America (including West Indies)

Acuna Gate, J. 1938. Catalogo descriptivo de las orquideas Cubanas. *Estacion Experimental Agronomica*, Havana, Boletin 60.

Adams, C.D. 1972. Orchidaceae. In *Flowering Plants of Jamaica*. University of the West Indies, Mona, Jamaica. .

Ames, O. & Correll, D.S. 1952–3. Orchids of Guatemala. *Fieldiana* (Bot.) 26: 1–727. Reprinted Dover (1985) as *Orchids of Guatemala and Belize*.

Arosemana, A.G., Estrada, R.G., De Jurado, C. & Konanz, M.M. 1988. *Orquideas de la Costa Del Ecuador.*

Bateman, J. 1837–43. *The Orchidaceae of Mexico and Guatemala.*

Cogniaux, A. 1893–1906. Orchidaceae. In Martius, *Flora Brasiliensis*, Leipzig.

—— 1909–10. Orchidaceae. In Urban, *Symbolae Antillanae*, 6.

Correa, M.N. 1970. Orchidaceae. In *Flora Patagonica* 8.

Dodson, C.H. & Bennett, D.E. 1989. Orchids of Peru. *Icones Plantarum Tropicarum*, series II (1, 2). Missouri Botanical Garden, St Louis, Missouri.

—— & Marmaol, P. 1989. Orchids of Ecuador. *Icones Plantarum Tropicarum*, series I (5, 6). Missouri Botanical Garden, St Louis, Missouri.

—— & Vasquez, R. 1989. Orchids of Bolivia. *Icones Plantarum Tropicarum*, series I (3, 4). Missouri Botanical Garden, St Louis, Missouri.

Dunsterville, G. & Garay, L. 1959–76. *Venezuelan Orchids Illustrated.* 6 vols, André Deutsch.

—— 1979. *Orchids of Venezuela: An Illustrated Field Guide.* Botanical Museum, Harvard University, Cambridge, Massachusetts.

Escobar, R. (ed.) 1990. *Native Colombian Orchids.* Editorial Colina, Medellin.

Fawcett, W. & Rendle, A.B. 1910. Orchidaceae. In *Flora of Jamaica*, vol. 1, British Museum.

Foldats, E. 1969–70. Orchidaceae. In *Flora de Venezuela*, 15, Instituto Botanico, Caracas.

Garay, L. & Sweet, H. 1974. Orchidaceae. In *Flora of the Lesser Antilles*, Arnold Arboretum, Harvard University, Jamaica Plain, Massachusetts.

—— 1978. Orchidaceae, pt. 1. In *Flora of Ecuador.*

Gumprecht, R. 1975. Orchideen in Chile. *Die Orchidee* 26: 127–32.

Hagsater, E. & Salazar, G. 1990. Orchids of Mexico. *Icones Orchidacearum*, fasc. I. Asociación Mexicana de Orquideologia, Mexico City.

Hamer, F. 1974. *Las Orquídeas de El Salvador.* 2 vols, Ministerio de Educacion, San Salvador.

—— 1983–4. Orchids of Nicaragua. *Icones Plantarum Tropicarum*, Missouri Botanical Garden, St Louis, Missouri.

Hoehne, F. C. 1940–53. *Flora Brasilica – Orchidaceas.* São Paulo.

—— 1949. *Iconografia de Orchidaceas do Brasil.* São Paulo.

León, Bro. 1946. Orquídeas. In *Flora de Cuba*, vol. 1, Contribuciones Ocasionales del Museo de Historia Natural del Colegio de La Salle.

McQueen, J. & McQueen, B. 1993. *Orchids of Brazil.* Timber Press, Portland, Oregon.

McVaugh, R. 1985. *Orchidaceae in Flora Novo-Galiciana: A Descriptive Account of the Vascular Plants of Western Mexico*, vol. 16. University of Michigan Press, Ann Arbor.

Ortiz Valdivieso, P. 1976. *Orquídeas de Colombia.* Bogotá: Colciencias.

Pabst, G. & Dungs, F. 1975–7. *Orchidaceae Brasilienses.* 2 vols, Kurt Schmersow, Hildesheim.

Rodrigues, J. Barbosa. 1877. *Genera et Species Orchidearum Novarum.* Fleiuss, Rio de Janeiro.

Schlechter, R. 1919–29. Mehrere längere Artikel über südamerikanische Arten und Gattungen. *Feddes Repertorium.*

—— & Hoehne, F.C. 1921–2. Contribuicoes ao Conhecimento das Orquidáceas do Brasil. *Anexos das Memorias do Instituto de Butantan*; also in *Archivos de Botanico do Estado de São Paulo.*

—— 1922–3. Beitrage zur Orchideenkunde von Zentralamerika. *Feddes Repertorium* Beihefte XVII: 4–95; XIX: 3–307.

Schultes, R.E. 1960. *Native Orchids of Trinidad.* Pergamon Press.

Schweinfurth, C. 1958–61. Orchids of Peru. *Fieldiana.*

Williams, L. 1939. *Las Orquídeas del Noroeste Argentino (Lilloa)* 4.

—— 1956. An enumeration of the Orchidaceae of Central America, British Honduras and Panama. *Ceiba* 5: 1–256.

—— 1951. Orchidaceae of Mexico. *Ceiba* 2: 1–321.

—— & Allen, P. 1980. *Orchids of Panama.* Reprinted with checklist by R.L. Dressler, Missouri Botanical Garden, St Louis, Missouri.

Zimmermann, W. 1934. Orchidaceae Novae Brasilienses. *Bibliotheca Botanica* 109.

Asia (including Philippines)

Ames, O. 1909. Notes on Philippine Orchids. *Philippine Journal of Science*, 4.

—— & Schweinfurth, C. 1920. The Orchids of Mount Kinabalu, British North Borneo. *Orchidaceae* 6. Merrymount Press, Boston.

—— 1925. Enumeration of Philippine Apostasiaceae and Orchidaceae. In *Enumeration of Philippine Flowering Plants*, Manila.

—— & Quisumbing, E. 1931–6. New or noteworthy Philippine Orchids, 1–6. *Philippine Journal of Science*, 44–59.

Backer, C.A. 1952. Beknopte Flora van Java. *Orchidaceae* 1–3. Rijksherbarium, Leiden.

Banerji, M.L. & Pradhan, P. 1984. *The Orchids of Nepal Himalaya*. J. Cramer, Vaduz.

Bose, T.K. & Bhattacharjee, S.K. 1980. *Orchids of India*. Nayo Prokash, Calcutta.

Comber, J. 1990. *Orchids of Java*. Royal Botanic Gardens, Kew.

Duthie, J.F. 1906. Orchids of the North-Western Himalaya. *Annals of the Royal Botanic Garden, Calcutta*, 9.

Gagnepain, F. & Guillaumin, A. 1932. *Orchidacées. Flore Générale de L'Indo-Chine*, 2. Masson, Paris.

Garay, L. & Sweet, H. 1974. *Orchids of the Southern Ryukyu Islands*. Botanical Museum, Harvard University, Cambridge, Massachusetts.

Grant, B. 1895. *The Orchids of Burma*. Rangoon.

Holttum, R.E. 1964. *Flora of Malaya*, vol. I. *Orchids of Malaya*, 3rd edn, Government Printing Office, Singapore.

Hooker, J.D. 1890. *Orchideae in Flora of British India* 5, Reeve & Co.

—— 1895. A Century of Indian orchids. *Annals of the Royal Botanic Garden, Calcutta*, 5.

Hu, S.Y. 1971. The Orchidaceae in China. *Quarterly Journal Taiwan Museum*.

—— 1977. *The Genera of Orchidaceae in Hong Kong*. Chinese University Press, Hong Kong.

Isaac-Williams, M. 1988. *An Introduction to the Orchids of Asia*. Angus & Robertson, Auckland.

King, G. & Pantling, R. 1898. The orchids of the Sikkim-Himalaya. *Annals of the Royal Botanic Garden, Calcutta*, 8.

Kränzlin, F. 1931. Orchidacearum Sibiriae Enumeratio. *Feddes Repertorium*, Beihefte 65.

Lin, T.-P. 1975. *Native Orchids of Taiwan*. Taipei.

Maekawa, F. 1971. *The Wild Orchids of Japan in colour*. Seibundo Shinkosha, Tokyo.

Pradhan, U.C. 1976–9. *Indian Orchids: Guide to Identification and Culture*. Kalimpong.

Santapau, H. & Kapadia, A. 1966. *The orchids of Bombay*.

Schlechter, R. 1919. Orchideologiae Sino-Japonicae Prodromus. *Feddes Repertorium*, Beihefte 4.

—— 1934. Blütenanalysen neuer Orchideen, IV. *Indische und malesische Orchideen*. Feddes Repertorium, Beheifte 74.

Seidenfaden, G. 1975. *Contribution to a Revision of the Orchid Flora of Cambodia, Laos and Vietnam, 1. A Preliminary Enumeration*. Fredensborg, Denmark.

—— 1975–. *Orchid Genera in Thailand*. Dansk Botanisk Arkiv.

—— & Smitinand, T. 1958–65. *The Orchids of Thailand: A Preliminary List*. The Siam Society, Bangkok.

—— & Wood, J.J. 1992. *The Orchids of Peninsular Malaysia and Singapore*. Olsen & Olsen, Fredensborg.

Smith, J.J. 1903. *Icones Bogorienses – Orchidées*. E.J. Brill, Leiden.

—— 1905. *Die Orchideen von Ambon*. Landsdrukkerij, Batavia.

—— 1905. *Die Orchideen von Java in Flora von Buitenzorg*, 6.

—— 1905–24. Die Orchideen von Java, 1–8. *Bulletin du Departement de l'Agriculture aux Indes Néerlandaises*.

—— 1928. Orchidaceae Buruenses. *Bulletin de Jardin Botanique de Buitenzorg*, 9.

—— 1928. Orchidaceae Seranenses. *Bulletin de Jardin Botanique de Buitenzorg*, 10.

—— 1930–38. Icones Orchidacearum Malayensium, 1–2. *Bulletin de Jardin Botanique de Buitenzorg*.

—— 1931. On a collection of Orchidaceae from Central Borneo. *Bulletin de Jardin Botanique de Buitenzorg* 11.

—— 1933. Enumeration of the Orchidaceae of Sumatra and Neighbouring Islands. *Feddes Repertorium* 32.

Teo, C. 1985. *Native Orchids of Peninsula Malaysia*. Times Books International, Singapore.

Valmayor, H. 1984. *Orchidiana Philippiana*. Samhwa Printing Co., S. Korea.

Pacific (including New Guinea)

Guillaumin, A. 1948. Orchidacées. In *Flore analytique et synoptique de la Nouvelle-Calédonie*, Paris.

Hallé, N. 1977. Orchidacées. *Flore de la Nouvelle-Calédonie et Dépendances*, 8, Musée National d'Histoire Naturelle, Paris.

Hunt, P.F. 1969. Orchids of the Solomon Islands. *Philosophical Transactions of the Royal Society of London*, 255.

Kränzlin, F. 1929. Neu-Caledonische Orchideen. *Vierteljahresschrift der Naturforschenden Gesellschaft*, Zürich, 74.

Lewis, B. & Cribb, P. 1989. *Orchids of Vanuatu*. Royal Botanic Gardens, Kew.

—— 1991. *Orchids of the Solomon Islands and Bougainville*. Royal Botanic Gardens, Kew.

Millar, A. 1978. *Orchids of Papua New Guinea*. Australian National University Press, Canberra.

Parham, J.W. 1972. Orchidaceae. In *Plants of the Fiji Islands*, Suva, Fiji.

Schlechter, R. 1982. *The Orchidaceae of German New Guinea.* English translation, Australian Orchid Foundation, Melbourne. (Originally published 1914–28 as Die Orchidaceen von Deutsch-Neuguinea, *Feddes Repertorium,* Beihefte 1 & 21.)

Seemann, B. 1865–73. Orchideae. In *Flora Vitiensis,* Reeve & Co.

Smith, J.J. 1909–34. Die Orchideen von Niederländisch-Neu-Guinea. In *Résultats de l'expedition scientifique Néerlandaise à la Nouvelle Guinée,* E. J. Brill, Leiden.

Van Bodegom, J. 1973. *Enige Orchideeen van West Nieuw Guinea.* Enschede, Nederland.

Van Royen, P. 1980. *The Orchids of the High Montains of New Guinea.* J. Cramer, Vaduz.

Australia

Clements, M.A. 1989. Catalogue of Australian Orchidaceae. *Australian Orchid Research* 1: 1–160.

Dockrill, A.W. 1967. *Australasian Sarcanthinae.* The Australian Native Orchid Society, Sydney.

—— 1969. *Australian Indigenous Orchids, I. The Epiphytes; the Tropical Terrestrial Species.* Halstead Press, Sydney.

Firth, M.J. 1965. *Native Orchids of Tasmania.* C.L. Richmond, Devonport, Tasmania.

Fitzgerald, R.D. 1875–1894. *Australian Orchids.* Sydney.

Jones, D.L. 1988. *Native Orchids of Australia.* Reed Books, Frenchs Forest, New South Wales.

Nicholls, W.H. 1969. *Orchids of Australia.* T. Nelson, Melbourne.

Richards, H., Wooton, R. & Datodi, R. 1988. *Cultivation Of Australian Native Orchids,* 2nd edn.

Stoutamire, W.P., 1975. Pseudocopulation in Australian orchids. *American Orchid Society Bulletin* 44: 226–33.

New Zealand

Johns, J. & Molloy, B. 1983. *Native Orchids of New Zealand.* A.H. & A.W. Reed, Wellington.

Moore, L.B. & Edgar, E. 1970. Orchidaceae. In *Flora of New Zealand,* vol. 2, Wellington, New Zealand.

GENERA

Acampe
Seidenfaden, G. 1988. *Opera Botanica* 95.

Acanthephippium
Seidenfaden, G. 1986. *Opera Botanica* 89.

Aceras
See Nelson 1968 under *Serapias.*

Acineta
Schlechter, R. 1947. Die Gattung *Acineta. Orchis* 11: 21–47.

Acriopsis
de Vogel, E. 1986. *Orchid Monographs* 1.

Aerangis
Stewart, J. 1979. A revision of the African species of *Aerangis. Kew Bulletin* 34: 239–319.

—— 1986. Stars of the islands: a new look at the genus *Aerangis* in Madagascar and the Comoro Islands. *American Orchid Society Bulletin* 55: 792–802, 903–9, 1008–15, 1117–25.

Aerides
Seidenfaden, G. 1973. Contributions to the orchid flora of Thailand V. *Botanisk Tidsskrift* 68: 68–80.

Wood, J. & Kennedy, G.C. 1977. Some showy members of the genus *Aerides. Orchid Digest* 41: 205–8.

Aerides
Seidenfaden, G. 1988. *Opera Botanica* 95.

Senghas. 1988. In Brieger, *Die Orchideen,* 3rd edn, 20. See Schlechter under *Encyclopaedic Surveys* for full citation.

Angraecum
Garay, L., 1973. Systematics of the genus *Angraecum. Kew Bulletin* 28: 495–516.

Hillerman, F.E. & Holst, A.W. 1986. *An Introduction to the Cultivated Angraecoid Orchids of Madagascar.* Timber Press, Portland Oregon.

See also Schlechter (1918) under *Africa* above.

Anoectochilus
Seidenfaden, G. 1978. *Dansk Botanisk Arkiv* 32 (2).

Arachnis
Seidenfaden, G. 1988. *Opera Botanica* 95.

See also Tan under *Dimorphorchis.*

Arpophyllum
Garay, L. 1974. Synopsis of the genus *Arpophyllum. Orquidea* (Mexico) 4: 16–19.

Arthrochilus
Blaxell, D.F. 1972. *Arthrochilus* and related genera in Australasia. *Contributions from the New South Wales National Herbarium* 4: 275–83.

Arundina
Seidenfaden, G. 1986. *Opera Botanica* 89.
Senghas, K. 1984. In Brieger, *Die Orchideen*: 837.

Ascocentrum
Seidenfaden, G. 1988. *Opera Botanica* 95.

Ascoglossum
Brieger. 1988. *Die Orchideen*, 3rd edn.

Aspasia
Williams, N.H., 1974. The taxonomy of *Aspasia. Brittonia* 26: 333–46.

Barkeria
Halbinger, F. 1973. The genus *Barkeria. American Orchid Society Bulletin* 42: 620–26.

Barlia
See Nelson (1968) under *Serapias*.

Bletia
Dressler, R.L. 1968. Notes on *Bletia. Brittonia* 20: 182–90.

Bletilla
Tan, K.W. 1969. The systematic status of the genus *Bletilla. Brittonia* 21: 202–214.

Bothriochilus
Pridgeon, A.M. 1978. Una revisión de los Géneros *Coelia* y *Bothriochilus. Orquídea* (Mexico) 7: 57–94.
Williams, L.O. 1940. The orchid genera *Coelia* and *Bothriochilus. Botanical Museum Leaflets, Harvard University* 8: 145–8.

Brassavola
Jones, H.G. Nomenclature revision of the genus *Brassavola* of the Orchidaceae. *Annalen des Naturhistorischen Museums in Wien* 79: 9–22.

Brassia
Kooser, R.G. & Kennedy, G.C. 1979. The genus *Brassia. Orchid Digest* 43: 164–72.

Bromheadia
Seidenfaden, G. 1983. *Opera Botanica* 72.

Broughtonia
Withner, C. 1995. *The Cattleyas and their Relatives.* Vol. 5, *The Bahamian and Carribean Species.* Timber Press, Portland, Oregon.

Bulbophyllum
Rentoul, J.N. 1977. Australian bulbophyllums. *Orchid Review* 85: 261–2.
Seidenfaden, G. 1973. Notes on *Cirrhopetalum* Lindl. *Dansk Botanisk Arkiv* 29(1): 1–260.
—— 1979. Orchid genera in Thailand VIII: *Bulbophyllum. Dansk Botanisk Arkiv* 33(3).
Vermeulen, J.J. 1987. *A taxonomic revision of Continental African Bulbophyllinae.* Orchid Monographs, vol. 2. E.J. Brill, Leiden.
—— 1991. *Orchids of Borneo.* Vol. 2, *Bulbophyllum.* Bentham-Moxon Trust, Royal Botanic Gardens, Kew.

Calanthe
Seidenfaden, G. 1975. Orchid genera in Thailand I: *Calanthe. Dansk Botanisk Arkiv* 29(2).

Catasetum
Dodson, C.H. 1975. *Selbyana* 1: 130–38 .
Gregg, K.B. 1975. The effect of light intensity on sex expression in species of *Cycnoches* and *Catasetum. Selbyana* 1: 101–13.
Mansfeld, R. 1932. Die Gattung *Catasetum. Feddes Repertorium* 30: 257–75 (1933), 31: 99–125.

Cattleya
Braem, G.J. 1983. *Cattleya.* Brucke Verlag, Hildesheim.
Fowlie, J.A. 1977. *Brazilian bifoliate Cattleyas and their colour varieties.*
Withner, C. 1948. The genus *Cattleya. American Orchid Society Bulletin* 17: 296–306, 363–9.
—— 1988. *The Cattleyas and Their Relatives.* Vol. 1: *The Cattleyas.* Timber Press, Portland, Oregon.

Cattleyopsis
See Withner (1995) under *Broughtonia*.

Cleisostoma
Garay, L., 1972. On the systematics of the monopodial orchids I. *Botanical Museum Leaflets, Harvard University* 23: 168–76.
Seidenfaden, G. 1975. Orchid genera in Thailand II: *Cleisostoma. Dansk Botanisk Arkiv* 29(3): 1–80.

Coelia
See under *Bothriochilus*.

Coelogyne
Das, S. 1976. Flowering calendar of Coelogynes. *Orchid Review* 84: 210–11.
Seidenfaden, G. 1975. Orchid genera in Thailand III, *Coelogyne*. *Dansk Botanisk Arkiv* 29(4).

Corymborkis
Rasmussen, F.N. 1977. The genus *Corymborkis*: taxonomic revision. *Botanisk Tidsskrift* 71: 161–92.

Coryanthes
Kennedy, G. 1978. Some members of the genus *Coryanthes*. *Orchid Digest* 42: 31–7.

Corybas
Van Royen, P. 1983. The genus *Corybas*. J. Cramer, Vaduz.

Cryptostylis
Cady, L. 1967. The genus *Cryptostylis* in Australia. *Australian Plants* 4: 75–7, 91.

Cycnoches
Allen, P.H., 1952. The swan orchids: a revision of the genus *Cycnoches*. *Orchid Journal* 1: 173–84, 225–30, 349–54, 397–403.
See also Gregg (1975) under *Catasetum*.

Cymbidium
Du Puy, D. & Cribb, P. 1988. *The Genus Cymbidium*. Christopher Helm.
Hunt, P.F. 1970. Notes on the Asiatic orchids V. *Kew Bulletin* 24: 75–99.
Pradhan, G. M., 1976. The *Cyperorchis* species of northern India. *Orchid Digest* 40: 115–17.

Cypripedium
Cash, C. 1991. *The Slipper Orchids*. Timber Press, Portland, Oregon.
Franchet, A. 1894. Les *Cypripedium* de l'Asie Orientale. *Journal de Botanique* 8: 225–33, 249–56, 265–71.
Holman, R.T. 1976. Cultivation of *Cypripedium calceolus* and *Cypripedium reginae*. *American Orchid Society Bulletin* 45: 415–22.
Stoutamire, W.P. 1967. Flower biology of the Lady's-slippers. *Michigan Botanist* 6: 159–75.
Whitlow, C. E. 1977. Growing temperate Cypripediums in containers. *American Orchid Society Bulletin* 46.

Dactylorhiza
Nelson, E. 1976. *Monographie und Ikonographie der Orchidaceen-Gattung Dactylorhiza*. Speich, Zurich.
Senghas, K. & Sundermann, H. 1968. Probleme der Orchideengattung *Dactylorhiza*. *Die Orchidee*, Sonderheft.

Dendrobium
Baker, M. & Baker, C. 1995. *Orchid Species Culture – Dendrobiums*. Timber Press, Portland, Oregon.
Cribb, P. 1983. A Revision of *Dendrobium* Section *Latouria*. *Kew Bulletin* 38: 229–306
—— 1986. The 'Antelope' Dendrobiums. *Kew Bulletin* 41: 615–92.
Kränzlin, F., 1910. *Das Pflanzenreich* 45: 25–313.
Reeve, T.M. & Woods, P.J.B. 1989. A revision of *Dendrobium* section *Oxyglossum*. Notes R.B.G. *Edinburgh* 46: 161–305.
Schelpe, S. and Stewart, J. 1990. *Dendrobiums: an introduction to the species in cultivation*. Orchid Sundries, Gillingham.
Seidenfaden, G. 1985. *Opera Botanica* 83.
Upton, W.T. 1989. *Dendrobium Orchids of Australia*. Timber Press, Portland, Oregon.

Dimorphorchis
Soon, P.S. 1980. Notes on Sabah orchids, part I. *Orchid Digest* 44: 193–5.
Tan, K. 1975 & 1976. Taxonomy of *Arachnis, Armodorum, Esmeralda* and *Dimorphorchis*. *Selbyana* 1: 1–15 & 365–73.
See also Senghas in Brieger (1988) under *Ascoglossum*.

Disa
Johnson, K.C. 1967. *Disa uniflora* – a method of cultivation and its hybridisation with *D.racemosa*. *Journal of the Botanical Society of South Africa*. 53: 19–26.
Lindquist, B. 1965. The raising of *Disa uniflora* seedlings in Gothenburg. *American Orchid Society Bulletin* 34: 317–19.
Schelpe, E.A. 1968. *Disa* hybrids. *Journal of the Botanical Society of South Africa* 54: 34–35.
—— 1971. The genus *Disa* and allied genera in South Africa. *Proceedings of the Sixth World Orchid Conference*, 157–9.

Doritis
See Seidenfaden (1988) under *Ascocentrum*.

Dracula
Hawley, R.M. 1977. *Masdevallia chimaera* and the marvellous monsters. *American Orchid Society Bulletin* 46: 600–609.
Luer, C.A., 1978. *Dracula*, a new genus in the Pleurothallidinae (Orchidaceae). *Selbyana* 2: 190–98.
—— & Escobar, R. 1988–. *Thesaurus Dracularum*. Missouri Botanical Garden, St Louis, Missouri.
Kennedy, G. 1979. The genus *Dracula*. *Orchid Digest* 43: 31–8.

Encyclia
Dressler, R.L. & Pollard, G.E. 1976. *The genus Encyclia in Mexico.* Asociación Mexicana de Orquideologia, Mexico City.
Withner, C. 1995. See under *Broughtonia.*

Epidendrum
Ames, O., Hubbard, F.T. & Schweinfurth, C. 1936. *The genus Epidendrum in the United States and Middle America.*

Epigeneium
Summerhays, V.S. 1957. Notes on Asiatic orchids II. *Kew Bulletin* 259–68.
Seidenfaden, G. 1980. Orchid genera in Thailand IX. *Dansk Botanisk Arkiv* 34: 68–82.

Epipactis
Senghas, K. & Sunderman, H. 1970. Probleme der Orchideengattung *Epipactis. Die Orchidee*, Sonderheft.

Eria
Seidenfaden, G. 1982. Orchid genera in Thailand X. *Opera Botanica* 62: 1–157.

Esmeralda
See Seidenfaden (1988) under *Ascocentrum*

Eulophia
Hall, A.V. 1965. Studies of the South African Species of *Eulophia. Journal of South African Botany*, suppl. vol. V.
Summerhayes, V.S. & Hall, A.V. 1962. The type species and conservation of the name *Eulophia* R. Br. ex Lindl. *Taxon* 11: 201–3.

Eulophiella
Bosser, J. & Morat, P. 1969. Contribution a l'étude des Orchidaceae de Madagascar IX: Les Genres *Grammangis* et *Eulophiella. Adansonia* 9: 299–309.
Kennedy, G.C. 1972. The genus *Eulophiella. Orchid Digest* 36: 120–22.

Galeandra
Rolfe, R.H., 1892. Galeandras. *Gardeners' Chronicle* 12(2): 430–31.
Teuscher, H. 1975. Die Gattung *Galeandra. Die Orchidee* 26: 1–5.

Gastrochilus
See Seidenfaden (1988) under *Ascocentrum.*

Geodorum
Seidenfaden, G. 1983. *Opera Botanica* 72.

Goodyera
Ackerman, J.D. 1975. Reproductive biology of *Goodyera oblongifolia . Madroño* 20: 191–8.
Christian, P. 1975. *Quarterly Bulletin of the Alpine Garden Society* 43: 322–4.
Kallunki, J.A. 1976. Population studies in *Goodyera* with emphasis on the hybrid origin of *G. tesselata. Brittonia* 28: 53–75.

Habenaria
Ames, O. 1910. The genus *Habenaria* in North America. *Orchidaceae* 4: 1–288.

Hexisea
Dressler, R.L. 1974. The genus *Hexisea. Orquidea* (Mexico) 4: 197–200.

Holcoglossum
See Seidenfaden (1988) under *Ascocentrum.*

Kingidium
See Seidenfaden (1988) under *Ascocentrum.*

Lacaena
Jenny, R. 1979. Die Gattung *Lacaena. Die Orchidee* 30: 55–61.

Laelia
Jones, H.G. 1976. Review of sectional division in the genus *Laelia* of the Orchidaceae. *Botanischer Jahrbucher* 97: 309–16.
Withner, C. 1990. *The Cattleyas and Their Relatives*, vol. 2, *Laelias.* Timber Press, Portland, Oregon.

Laeliopsis
See Withner (1995) under *Broughtonia.*

Liparis
Seidenfaden, G. 1976. Orchid genera in Thailand IV. *Dansk Botanisk Arkiv* 31: 1–105.

Lockhartia
Teuscher, H. 1974. The genus *Lockhartia. American Orchid Society Bulletin* 43: 399–405.

Ludisia
Seidenfaden, G. 1978. *Dansk Botanisk Arkiv* 32 (2).

Luisia

Seidenfaden, G. 1971a. *Dansk Botanisk Arkiv* 27 (4).

—— 1971b. Note on the genus *Luisia*. *Dansk Botanisk Arkiv* 27(4): 1–101.

—— 1988. In *Opera Botanica* 95.

Lycaste

Aoyama, M. & Karasawa, K. 1988. Karyomorphological studies on *Lycaste*. *Bulletin of the Hiroshima Botanical Garden* 10: 7–45.

Fowlie, J.A. 1970. *The genus Lycaste*. Day Printing Corp., Pomona (California).

Oakeley, H. 1991. Various papers in *American Orchid Society Bulletin* 60.

—— 1993. *Lycaste species: the Essential Guide*. Dr H.F. Oakley National Collection *Lycaste*, Beckenham, Kent, England.

Malaxis

Cribb, P. 1978. A synopsis of *Malaxis* in Africa. *Kew Bulletin* 32 : 737–41.

Masdevallia

Braas, L., 1978. The genus *Masdevallia*. *Orchid Review* 86: 30–43.

Luer, C.A. 1983. *Thesaurus Masdevalliarum*. Helga Koniger, Munich.

Kränzlin, F. 1925. *Masdevallia*. *Feddes Repertorium* Beihefte 34.

Woolward, F.H. 1890–96. *The genus Masdevallia*. Republished 1978, Lyne & Son.

Meiracyllium

Dressler, R.L. 1960. The relationships of *Meiracyllium*. *Brittonia* 12: 222–5.

Mormodes

Allen, P.H. 1959. *Mormodes lineatum*: a species in transition. *American Orchid Society Bulletin* 28: 411–14.

Pabst, G.F.J. 1978. An illustrated key to the species of the genus *Mormodes*. *Selbyana* 2: 149–55.

Nephelaphyllum

Seidenfaden, G. 1986. *Opera Botanica* 89.

Oberonia

Seidenfaden, G. 1968. The genus *Oberonia* in mainland Asia. *Dansk Botanisk Arkiv* 25(3): 1–125.

Seidenfaden, G. 1978. In *Dansk Botanisk Arkiv* 33(1).

Odontoglossum

Bateman, J. 1874. *A Monograph of Odontoglossum*. Reeve & Co.

Bockemuhl, L. 1989. *Odontoglossum: A Monograph and Iconograph*. Kurt Schmersow, Hildesheim.

Escobar, R., 1976. El genero *Odontoglossum*. *Orquideologia* 11: 21–57, 119–60. 257–302.

Halbinger, F. 1982. *Odontoglossum* y generos Afines en Mexico y Centroamerica. *Orquidea* 8: 155–282.

Oeceoclades

Garay, L.A. & Taylor, P. 1976. The genus *Oeceoclades*. *Botanical Museum Leaflets, Harvard University* 24: 249–74.

Summerhayes, V.S. 1957. The genus *Eulophidium*. *Bulletin du Jardin Botanique de l'Etat* (Bruxelles) 27: 391–403.

Oncidium

Garay, L.A. 1970. *A reappraisal of the genus Oncidium*. *Taxon* 19: 443–67.

—— & Stacy, J.E. 1974. *Synopsis of the genus Oncidium*. *Bradea* 1(40): 393–424.

Kränzlin, F. 1922. In *Das Pflanzenreich* 80: 25–290.

See also Moir under *Hybrids* above.

Ophrys

Danesch, E. & Danesch, O. 1972. *Orchideen Europas, Ophrys-Hybriden*. Hallwag, Bern.

Nelson, E. 1962. *Gestaltwandel und Abbildung erörtert am Beispiel der Orchidaceen Europas und der Mittelmeerländer mit einer Monographie und Ikonographie der Gattung Ophrys*.

Stebbins, G.L. & Ferlan, L. 1956. Population variability, hybridization, and introgression in some species of *Ophrys*. *Evolution* 10: 32–46.

Orchis

Senghas, K. & Sunderman, H. 1972. Probleme der Orchideengattung *Orchis*. *Die Orchidee*, Sonderheft.

Paphinia

Jenny, R. 1978. Die Gattung *Paphinia*. *Die Orchidee* 29: 207–15.

Paphiopedilum

Asher, J.R. 1980. A checklist for the genus *Paphiopedilum*. *Orchid Digest* 44: 175–84, 213–28; (1981) 45: 15–26, 57–65.

Bennett, K.S. 1985. *The Tropical Asiatic Slipper Orchids: Genus Paphiopedilum*. Angus & Robertson, North Ryde, New South Wales.

Birk, L.A. 1983. *The Paphiopedilum Grower's Manual*. Pisang Press, Santa Barbara, California.

Cash, C. 1991. See under *Cypripedium*.

Cribb, P. 1987. *The Genus Paphiopedilum*. Royal Botanic Gardens, Kew.

Graham, R. & Roy, R., 1982. *Slipper Orchids*. Croom Helm.
Koopowitz, H. & Hasegawa, N. 1989. *Novelty Slipper Orchids: Breeding and Cultivating Paphiopedilum Hybrids*. Angus & Robertson, North Ryde, New South Wales.

Papilionanthe
Garay, L.A. 1974. On the systematics of the monopodial orchids. 2. Key to *Papilionanthe*. *Botanical Museum Leaflets, Harvard University*, 23 (10): 369–75.
See also Seidenfaden (1988) under *Ascocentrum.*

Paraphalaenopsis
See Sweet (1980) under *Phalaenopsis.*

Pecteilis
Seidenfaden, G. 1977. In *Dansk Botanisk Arkiv* 31 (3).

Pescatorea
Baker, M. & C. 1991. See under *Horticultural Guides* above.
Fowlie, J.A. 1968. A key and annotated checklist to the genus *Pescatorea*. *Orchid Digest* 32: 86–91.

Phaius
Baker, M. & C. 1991. See under *Horticultural Guides* above.
Seidenfaden, G. 1986. *Opera Botanica* 89.

Phalaenopsis
Baker, M. & C. 1991. See under *Horticultural Guides* above.
Sweet, H.R. 1968–9. A revision of the genus *Phalaenopsis*. *American Orchid Society Bulletin* 37: 867–77, 1089–1104; 38: 33–42, 225–39, 321–36, 505–519, 681–94, 888–901.
Sweet, H.R. 1980. *The Genus Phalaenopsis*. Orchid Digest Inc., Pomona, California.

Pholidota
Baker, M. & C. 1991. See under *Horticultural Guides* above.
Seidenfaden, G. 1986. *Opera Botanica* 89.
de Vogel. 1989. *Orchid Monographs* 3.

Phragmipedium
Baker, M. & C. 1991. See under *Horticultural Guides* above
Cash, C. 1991. See under *Cypripedium.*
Garay, L.A. 1979. The genus *Phragmipedium*. *Orchid Digest* 43: 133–48.

Pleione
Baker, M. & C. 1991. See under *Horticultural Guides* above.
Butterfield, J. & Bailes, C. (1986). Recent advances in *Pleione* breeding. *Orchid Review* 94.
Cribb, P. & Butterfield, I. 1988. *The Genus Pleione*. Timber Press, Portland, Oregon.
Hunt, P.F. & Vosa, C.G. 1971. The cytology and taxonomy of the genus *Pleione*. *Kew Bulletin* 25: 423–32.
Hunt, P.F. & Butterfield, I. 1979. The genus *Pleione*. *Plantsman* 1(2): 112–23.
Wimber, D. & Cribb, P. 1981. A cytological study of the species and hybrids in the genus *Pleione*. *Plantsman* 3: 178–88.

Pleurothallis
Luer, C.A. 1986–1989. *Icones Pleurothallidinarum* I–VI. Missouri Botanical Garden, St. Louis, Missouri.

Pogonia
Ames, O. 1922. A discussion of *Pogonia* and its allies in the northern United States. *Orchidaceae* 7: 3–44.
See also Thien and Marcks (1972) under North America above.

Polystachya
Podzorski, A. & Cribb, P. 1979. A revision of *Polystachya* sect. *Cultriformes*. *Kew Bulletin* 34: 147–86.

Porroglossum
Sweet, H.R., 1972. The genus *Porroglossum*. *American Orchid Society Bulletin* 41: 513–24.

Pterostylis
Cady, L. 1969. An illustrated check-list of the genus *Pterostylis*. *Australian Plants* 5: 60–74.

Renanthera
See Seidenfaden (1988) under *Ascocentrum.*

Rhynchostylis
See Seidenfaden (1988) under *Ascocentrum.*

Satyrium
Duckitt, F. 1977. Satyriums and their culture. *South African Orchid Journal*, 8: 121–5.

Schomburgkia
Withner, C. 1993. *The Cattleyas and Their Relatives*. Vol. 3, *Schomburgkia, Sophronitis and Other South American Genera*. Timber Press, Portland, Oregon.

Serapias
Christian, P. 1975. The Genus *Serapias*. *Alpine Garden Society Bulletin* 43:189–98.

Nelson, E. 1968. Monographie und Ikonographie der Orchidaceen-Gattungen *Serapias, Aceras, Loroglossum, Barlia*. E. Nelson, Chernex-Montreux.

Sigmatostalix
Kränzlin, F. 1922. In *Das Pflanzenreich* 80: 301–12.

Sophronitis
Burns, W.T. 1961. *Sophronitis* hybridizing. *Orchid Digest* 25: 5–15.
See also Withner (1993) under *Schomburgkia*.

Stanhopea
Dodson, C.H. & Frymire, G.F. 1961. Preliminary studies in the genus *Stanhopea*. *Annals of the Missouri Botanical Garden* 48: 137–72.
Dodson, C.H., 1975. Clarification of some nomenclature in *Stanhopea*. *Selbyana* 1: 46–55.

Tainia
Seidenfaden, G. 1986. *Opera Botanica* 89.

Tetramicra
See Withner (1995) under *Broughtonia*.

Thunia
See Seidenfaden (1986) under *Tainia*.

Tolumnia
Braem, G.J. 1995. *Tolumnia* in the Caribbean Islands. *American Orchid Society Bulletin* 64: 2.

Trichoglottis
See Seidenfaden (1988) under *Ascocentrum*.
See Senghas in Brieger (1988) under *Aerides*.

Trichotosia
Seidenfaden, G. 1982. *Opera Botanica* 62.

Trudelia
See Senghas in Brieger (1988) under *Aerides*.

Vanda
Grove, D. 1995. *Vandas, Ascocendas and their hybrids with other genera*. Timber Press, Portland, Oregon.
See also Tanaka and Kamemoto (1961) under *Hybrids*, Seidenfaden (1988) under *Ascocentrum*, and Senghas in Brieger (1988) under *Aerides*.

Vandopsis
See Seidenfaden (1988) under *Ascocentrum*.

Zygopetalum
Garay, L.A. 1973. El Complejo *Zygopetalum*. *Orquideología* 8: 15–34.